WELCOME TO THE PACIFIC NORTHWEST

With its rugged coast, commanding peaks, forested islands, and cool cities, the Pacific Northwest strikes an ideal balance between outdoorsy and cosmopolitan. In Seattle, Portland, and Vancouver, farm-to-table restaurants, sophisticated hotels, and cutting-edge galleries await. Beyond the cities, the wineries of Oregon's Willamette Valley, cute towns of Washington's San Juan Islands, and national parks from Crater Lake to Olympic beg to be explored. Whether your ideal trip involves hiking a trail or window-shopping, the Pacific Northwest delivers.

TOP REASONS TO GO

★ **Hip Cities:** Quirky Portland, eclectic Seattle, and gorgeous Vancouver entice.

★ **Coastal Fun:** Beaches, whale sightings, tidal pools, headland walks.

★ **Mountains:** Mt. Rainier, Mt. Hood, Mt. Olympus, and Mt. St. Helens inspire awe.

★ **Craft Beverages:** Wineries, microbreweries, artisan coffee, and boutique distilleries.

★ **Seafood:** Fresh local crab, razor clams, sea scallops, oysters, and salmon.

★ **Scenic Drives:** On the Oregon Coast, in the Cascade Range, through evergreen forests.

Fodor's PACIFIC NORTHWEST

Publisher: Amanda D'Acierno, *Senior Vice President*

Editorial: Arabella Bowen, *Editor in Chief*; Linda Cabasin, *Editorial Director*

Design: Tina Malaney, *Associate Art Director*; Chie Ushio, *Senior Designer*; Ann McBride, *Production Designer*

Photography: Jennifer Arnow, *Senior Photo Editor*; Mary Robnett, *Photo Researcher*

Production: Linda Schmidt, *Managing Editor*; Evangelos Vasilakis, *Associate Managing Editor*; Angela L. McLean, *Senior Production Manager*

Maps: Rebecca Baer, *Senior Map Editor*; Mark Stroud (Moon Street Cartography), David Lindroth, *Cartographers*

Sales: Jacqueline Lebow, *Sales Director*

Marketing & Publicity: Heather Dalton, *Marketing Director*; Katherine Punia, *Publicity Director*

Business & Operations: Susan Livingston, *Vice President, Strategic Business Planning*; Sue Daulton, *Vice President, Operations*

Fodors.com: Megan Bell, *Executive Director, Revenue & Business Development*; Yasmin Marinaro, *Senior Director, Marketing & Partnerships*

Copyright © 2015 by Fodor's Travel, a division of Random House LLC

Writers: Shelley Arenas, Kimberly Bowker, Andrew Collins, Chloë Ernst, Carolyn B. Heller, Adriana Janovich, Sue Kernaghan, Chris McBeath, Rob Phillips, Dave Sandage, AnnaMaria Stephens, Christine Vovakes

Editor: Amanda Sadlowski

Editorial Contributors: Caroline Trefler (*Portland and Vancouver editor*), Doug Stallings (*Victoria editor*), Stephen Brewer, Jacinta O'Halloran

Production Editor: Carolyn Roth

20th Edition

ISBN 978-1-101-87812-5

ISSN 1098–6774

All details in this book are based on information supplied to us at press time. Always confirm information when it matters, especially if you're making a detour to visit a specific place. Fodor's expressly disclaims any liability, loss, or risk, personal or otherwise, that is incurred as a consequence of the use of any of the contents of this book.

SPECIAL SALES

This book is available at special discounts for bulk purchases for sales promotions or premiums. For more information, e-mail specialmarkets@penguinrandomhouse.com

PRINTED IN THE UNITED STATES OF AMERICA

10 9 8 7 6 5 4 3 2 1

CONTENTS

MAPS

ABOUT THIS GUIDE

Fodor's Recommendations

Everything in this guide is worth doing—we don't cover what isn't—but exceptional sights, hotels, and restaurants are recognized with additional accolades. **Fodor's Choice★** indicates our top recommendations; and **Best Bets** call attention to notable hotels and restaurants in various categories. Care to nominate a new place? Visit Fodors.com/contact-us.

Trip Costs

We list prices wherever possible to help you budget well. Hotel and restaurant price categories from **$** to **$$$$** are noted alongside each recommendation. For hotels, we include the lowest cost of a standard double room in high season. For restaurants, we cite the average price of a main course at dinner or, if dinner isn't served, at lunch. For attractions, we always list adult admission fees; discounts are usually available for children, students, and senior citizens.

Hotels

Our local writers vet every hotel to recommend the best overnights in each price category, from budget to expensive. Unless otherwise specified, you can expect private bath, phone, and TV in your room. For expanded hotel reviews, facilities, and deals, visit Fodors.com.

Top Picks	Hotels & Restaurants
★ Fodor's Choice	🏨 Hotel
	⇨ Number of rooms
Listings	🍴 Meal plans
✉ Address	✕ Restaurant
✉ Branch address	⚜ Reservations
☎ Telephone	👔 Dress code
🖷 Fax	🚫 No credit cards
🌐 Website	$ Price
✉ E-mail	
🎫 Admission fee	**Other**
⊙ Open/closed times	⇨ See also
Ⓜ Subway	☞ Take note
✛ Directions or Map coordinates	🏌 Golf facilities

Restaurants

Unless we state otherwise, restaurants are open for lunch and dinner daily. We mention dress code only when there's a specific requirement and reservations only when they're essential or not accepted. To make restaurant reservations, visit Fodors.com.

Credit Cards

The hotels and restaurants in this guide typically accept credit cards. If not, we'll say so.

EUGENE FODOR

Hungarian-born Eugene Fodor (1905–91) began his travel career as an interpreter on a French cruise ship. The experience inspired him to write *On the Continent* (1936), the first guidebook to receive annual updates and discuss a country's way of life as well as its sights. Fodor later joined the U.S. Army and worked for the OSS in World War II. After the war, he kept up his intelligence work while expanding his guidebook series. During the Cold War, many guides were written by fellow agents who understood the value of insider information. Today's guides continue Fodor's legacy by providing travelers with timely coverage, insider tips, and cultural context.

EXPERIENCE THE PACIFIC NORTHWEST

WHAT'S WHERE

Numbers refer to chapters

2 Portland. With its pedestrian-friendly Downtown and great public transit, Portland is easy to explore. The city has become a magnet for fans of artisanal food, beer, wine, and spirits, and its leafy parks and miles of bike lanes make it a prime spot for outdoors enthusiasts.

3 The Oregon Coast. Oregon's roughly 300 miles of rugged shoreline are every bit as scenic as the more crowded and famous California coast. Oregon Dunes National Recreation Area, the Oregon Coast Aquarium, Cannon Beach, and the Columbia River Maritime Museum are key highlights.

4 The Willamette Valley and Wine Country. Just beyond the Portland city limits and extending south for 120 miles to Eugene, the Willamette Valley is synonymous with exceptional wine-making.

5 The Columbia River Gorge and Mt. Hood. Less than an hour east of Portland, the Columbia Gorge extends for about 160 miles along the Oregon-Washington border. Sailboarding, kitesurfing, hiking, and white-water rafting abound. Just 35 miles south of Hood River, iconic Mt. Hood is renowned for hiking and skiing.

6 Central Oregon. The swatch of Oregon immediately east of the Cascade Range takes in a varied landscape, with the outdoorsy city of Bend as the regional hub. Make time for the funky mountain town of Sisters and the world-famous rock climbing of Smith Rock State Park.

7 Crater Lake National Park. The 21-square-mile sapphire-blue expanse is the nation's deepest lake and a scenic wonder. You can drive the loop road around the lake, hike, or take a guided boat tour.

8 Southern Oregon. Artsy Ashland and Old West–looking Jacksonville have sophisticated restaurants, shops, and wineries. Nearby, Oregon Caves National Monument is a fascinating natural attraction while the Klamath Falls region has some of the best birding and wildlife-viewing in the state.

9 Seattle. As the Pacific Northwest's hub of arts and culture, this world-class and picturesque city has a vibrant mix of swanky restaurants and cocktail bars, first-rate coffee shops and brewpubs, and trendy boutique hotels, alongside pedestrian-friendly neighborhoods loaded with indie retail and dining.

WHAT'S
WHERE

10 Washington Cascade Mountains and Valleys. Right outside Seattle, you can tour the waterfront and museums of underrated Tacoma and bike past tulip fields in the Skagit Valley. The state capital, Olympia, is a good jumping-off point for exploring the towns near Mt. Rainier and Mount St. Helens National Volcanic Monument.

11 The San Juan Islands. This relaxing and stunningly beautiful archipelago is prime whale-watching and kayaking territory.

12 Olympic National Park. Centered on Mt. Olympus and framed on three sides by water, this 922,651-acre park covers much of Washington's forest-clad Olympic Peninsula.

13 Olympic Peninsula and Washington Coast. Wilderness envelops most of the Olympic Peninsula, with the Olympic Mountains at its core. Rugged terrain and few roads limit interior accessibility, but U.S. Highway 101 offers breathtaking forest, ocean, and mountain vistas.

14 North Cascades National Park. This 505,000-acre expanse of mountain wilderness is part of an area with more than half of the glaciers in America.

15 North Central Washington. Along the beautiful North Cascades Highway, you'll encounter spectacular scenery and logging towns such as Sedro Wooley and Marblemount, as well as Winthrop.

16 Mount Rainier National Park. The fifth-highest mountain in the Lower 48, Mt. Rainier is massive and unforgettable.

17 Washington Wine Country. This fertile valley east of the Cascades has long been known for apple and cherry orchards, and in recent years as a highly prized wine-making area—including the vineyards around Yakima, Zillah, Prosser, and Benton City.

18 Spokane and Eastern Washington. Characterized by rolling, dry, treeless hills and anchored by the state's second-largest city, Spokane, this area takes in the vast Columbia River valley and an eclectic mix of cities and towns, including wine-centric Walla Walla.

19 Vancouver and Victoria. Cosmopolitan Vancouver is a glorious city with tall fir trees, rock spires, the ocean at your doorstep, and a vibrant atmosphere. Victoria, with its stately Victorian houses and walkable Downtown and waterfront, is a stunner.

THE PACIFIC NORTHWEST PLANNER

Fast Facts	Border Crossing into Canada

Fast Facts

Currency and Exchange. The units of currency in Canada are the Canadian dollar (C$) and the cent, in almost the same denominations as U.S. currency. A good way to be sure you're getting the best exchange rate is by using your credit card or ATM/debit card. The issuing bank will convert your bill at the current rate. An increasing number of credit card companies offer cards that don't charge exchange fees—if you travel abroad often, it's worth applying for one of these.

Packing. It's all about layers here. The weather can morph from cold and overcast to warm and sunny and back again in the course of a few hours, especially in spring and early fall.

Taxes. Oregon has no sales tax, although many cities and counties levy a tax on lodging and services. Room taxes, for example, vary from 6% to 10.4%. The state retail sales tax in Washington is 6.5%, but there are also local taxes that can raise the total tax to 11.5%, depending on the goods or service and the municipality; Seattle's retail sales tax is 9.5%. A Goods and Services Tax (GST) of 5% applies on virtually every transaction in Canada except for the purchase of basic groceries.

Border Crossing into Canada

Air and Ferry Travel. You are required to present a passport to enter or reenter the United States. To enter Canada by air you must present a valid passport or an Air NEXUS card; by land or sea you need to present one of the following: 1) passport, 2) a trusted-traveler program card (i.e., Global Entry, NEXUS, SENTRI, or FAST card, 3) a U.S. Passport Card, or 4) an Enhanced Driver's License (issued only in the states of Michigan, New York, Vermont, and Washington).

Car Travel. You will need one of the aforementioned documents (*see above*) to cross the border by car. In addition, drivers must carry owner registration and proof of insurance coverage, which is compulsory in Canada. The Canadian Non-Resident Inter-Provincial Motor Vehicle Liability Insurance Card, available from any U.S. insurance company, is accepted as evidence of financial responsibility in Canada. If you are driving a car that is not registered in your name, carry a letter from the owner that authorizes your use of the vehicle.

The main entry point into British Columbia from the United States by car is on Interstate 5 at Blaine, Washington, 48 km (30 miles) south of Vancouver. Three highways enter British Columbia from the east: Highway 1, or the Trans-Canada Highway; Highway 3, or the Crowsnest Highway; and Highway 16, the Yellowhead Highway, which runs from the Rocky Mountains to Prince Rupert.

Border-crossing procedures are usually quick and simple, although the wait can be trying on weekends and during busy holiday periods. Every British Columbia border crossing is open 24 hours (except the one at Aldergrove, which is open from 8 am to midnight). The Interstate 5 border crossing at Blaine, Washington (also known as the Douglas, or Peace Arch, border crossing), is one of the busiest border crossings between the United States and Canada. Listen to local radio traffic reports for information about wait times.

U.S. Passport Information U.S. Department of State ☎ *877/487–2778* ⊕ *www.travel.state.gov.*

Getting Around

Car Travel. You'll need a car to get around all but the major cities of the Pacific Northwest. Although a car will also grant you more freedom to explore the outer areas of Portland, Seattle, Vancouver, and Victoria, these four cities have adequate public transportation and taxi fleets—although cabs tend to be expensive. In most other towns in the region, even if bus or train service exists between two points, you'll likely need a car to get around once you arrive.

Interstate 5 is the major north–south conduit in the U.S. part of the region, offering a straight shot at high speeds—when there aren't traffic snarls, of course (these are especially common along the 75-mile stretch from northern Seattle to Olympia)—from Oregon's southern border all the way up to the Canadian border. Seattle and Portland are both along Interstate 5, and Vancouver is about 30 miles across the border from where it ends. This makes driving between the major hubs an easy option, though it's also possible to travel between them by train or bus. Except for the beautiful lower half of Oregon, below Eugene, Interstate 5 is pleasant and green but not especially dramatic as far as scenery goes, at least compared with the rest of the region as a whole.

U.S. 101, on the other hand, is one of the main attractions of the region. It starts in Washington, west of Olympia, makes a very wide loop around Olympic National Park, then heads south through Oregon, hugging the coast almost the whole way down. Most of the road is incredibly scenic, but this is not a very quick way to traverse either state. Make sure you want to commit to the coastal drive, which can be windy and slowgoing in some parts, before getting on the 101—it takes some time to work your way over from Interstate 5, so jumping back and forth between the two isn't very practical.

The Cascade Range cuts through the middle of Washington and Oregon, which means that east–west journeys often meander over mountain passes and can be either beautiful and relaxing (summer) or beautiful and treacherous (at times, in winter). Interstate 90 is the main east–west artery in Washington, connecting Seattle with Spokane, but Highway 20, which passes through North Cascades National Park, is more scenic. Interstate 84 is Oregon's major east–west artery; not far east of Portland it enters the stunningly picturesque Columbia River Gorge.

⇨ *See also Car Travel in Travel Smart for driving times to various regions from Seattle and Portland.*

When to Go

Hotels in the major tourist destinations often book up early in summer, so it's important to make reservations well in advance. Spring and fall are also excellent times to visit, although rain is more prevalent then. Prices for accommodations, transportation, and tours can be lower and crowds smaller during the off-season in the most popular destinations. In winter, snow is uncommon in the lowland areas but abundant in the nearby mountains, where ski resorts abound and chains and snow tires are often required for driving.

CLIMATE

Average daytime summer highs are in the 70s, but occasional hot spells do produce temperatures as high as 100°F in Portland and Seattle; winter temperatures are generally in the 40s, but this depends heavily on elevation—in the mountains temperatures can drop much lower. Rainfall varies greatly from one locale to another. In the coastal mountains, for example, 160 inches of rain falls annually, creating temperate rain forests. In much of the rest of the area, near-desert conditions prevail, with rainfall as low as 6 inches per year. Seattle and Portland average only around 36 inches of rainfall a year—less than New York, Chicago, or Miami. However, from October through March a light rain is present during portions of nearly every day.

OREGON
TOP ATTRACTIONS

Cannon Beach

(A) The nearest town on the dramatically rocky, windswept Oregon Coast from Portland also happens to be one of the most idyllic communities in the coastal Northwest. This town, anchored by 235-foot-tall Haystack Rock, is rife with beachside hiking trails, fine art galleries, and cafés specializing in organic coffee, Oregon wines, and fresh-caught seafood. Nearby Oswald West and Ecola state parks have some of the most stunning beaches and hiking trails in the state.

Columbia River Gorge

(B) The 110-mile section of the breathtaking Columbia River provides some of the Pacific Northwest's most spectacular vistas. Towering cliffs on both the Washington and Oregon sides of the river form a dramatic backdrop, and meandering highways line both banks. Water and wind sports abound, and a growing wine-making, craft-brewing, and culinary scene has flourished in recent years.

Columbia River Maritime Museum, Astoria

(C) At this dazzling, contemporary facility in the steadily gentrifying town of Astoria, where the northern Oregon Coast meets the Columbia River, you can tour a fully operational U.S. Coast Guard lightship, and check out engaging exhibits on local shipwrecks, marine life, and how the mighty Columbia has driven the economic and cultural development of the Pacific Northwest.

Crater Lake National Park

(D) The deepest lake in the United States is also the clearest, a fact readily grasped as soon as you behold this searing-blue body of water. It's closed much of the year due to snow, but in summer this 21-square-mile lake is southern Oregon's foremost attraction—the nearly century-old Crater Lake Lodge, perched on the southern shore, makes a memorable overnight and dinner venue.

High Desert Museum, Bend

(E) Evocative and intricate walk-through dioramas and an indoor-outdoor zoo with creatures great and tiny convey the high desert's past and present in a delightfully airy and family-friendly space just south of Bend.

Mt. Hood

(F) Just 60 miles east of Portland, the state's highest mountain is the only place in the Lower 48 where you can ski year-round. There are five different facilities, Timberline Lodge Ski Area being the most scenic.

Oregon Sand Dunes

(G) The 41 miles of rolling bluffs that make up Oregon Dunes National Recreation Area bring out the kid in visitors of all ages—there's something inherently happy about frolicking amid these massive mountains of sand, some of them climbing nearly 500 feet higher than the surf. Here you can hike, ride horseback, and race on a dune buggy, and there's great boating and fishing (plus several excellent seafood restaurants) in the nearby town of Florence.

Powell's Bookstore, Portland

(H) The Downtown Portland legend is the world's largest bookstore carrying both new and used titles, and with its coffee-house, late hours, and endless aisles of reading, it's also a prime spot for literary-minded people-watching.

Willamette Valley Wine Country

(I) Within easy day-tripping of Portland, this swath of fertile, hilly countryside is home to more than 200 wineries and has earned a reputation as one of the finest producers of Pinot Noir in the world—some say the best outside Burgundy. Winemakers in these parts also produce first-rate Pinot Gris and Chardonnay.

WASHINGTON TOP ATTRACTIONS

Hurricane Ridge, Olympic National Park

(A) Of the dozens of stunning panoramas within Olympic National Park, this 5,200-foot-high bluff offers the most memorable views—it takes in the vast Olympic mountain range as well as the Strait of Juan de Fuca and, beyond that, Vancouver Island. In summer, rangers lead tours through the wildflower- and wildlife-rich terrain.

Johnston Observatory, Mt. St. Helens

(B) Named for a brave volcanologist who perished in the terrifying 1980 eruption of Mt. St. Helens, this visitor center and observatory affords mind-blowing views of the hulking—often steaming—lava dome that lies deep within the mountain's crater. You reach this spot by driving the scenic Spirit Lake Highway.

LeMay–America's Car Museum, Tacoma

(C) Downtown Tacoma is home to several superb cultural sights, including the International Museum of Glass, Washington State History Museum, and Foss Waterway Seaport, but the massive vintage car collection at the LeMay, which occupies a sleek new building on the south edge of downtown, is arguably the city's star attraction. It ranks among the world's most impressive automobile museums.

Long Beach Peninsula

(D) Just two hours by car from Portland and three from Seattle, this 28-mile-long barrier peninsula rises from the mouth of the Columbia River north along the state's southwestern coast, providing visitors with rolling stretches of sand dunes, family-friendly amusements, and endless opportunities to view wildlife, from migrating birds to black bears.

Mount Rainier National Park

(E) Don't be intimidated by the formidable reputation of Mt. Rainier's 14,411-foot summit. It's true that only highly experienced hikers with guides should attempt this climb, but the national park that surrounds this snowcapped peak has plenty of terrain accessible to everyone, including 240 miles of well-maintained trails. The Skyline Trail makes for a moderately challenging 5-mile loop along alpine ridges and wildflower-strewn meadows—it's one of the best Mt. Rainier hikes if you have only one day to explore the mountain.

Orcas Island, San Juan Islands

(F) Of the three main islands in this laid-back, friendly, and beautiful archipelago that sits snug between Bellingham and Vancouver Island, Orcas has the best balance of scenery, seclusion, and diversions. It's home to 2,409-foot Mt. Constitution and surrounding Moran State Park, several picturesque harbors popular for fishing and kayaking, and a sophisticated mix of country inns and farm-to-table restaurants.

Pike Place Market, Seattle

(G) The Pacific Northwest abounds with stellar farmers' markets, but Downtown Seattle's creaky and colorful Pike Place is the mother of them all, established in 1907 and still thriving (despite a near brush with the wrecking ball during the 1960s).

Seattle Center and the Space Needle

(H) Almost every trip includes a stop at Seattle Center, which was built for the 1962 World's Fair and is home to the Space Needle, museums, and performance halls. Most of the city's major events are held here, but even on quiet weekends there's still something for everyone: Pacific Science Center and Children's Museum, Experience Music Project (EMP), and the Chihuly Garden and Glass exhibit.

VANCOUVER AND VICTORIA TOP ATTRACTIONS

The Bill Reid Gallery, Vancouver

(A) If First Nations heritage is your thing, be sure to visit this repository of regional art, one of the best of its kind in North America. It is as much a showcase for new artists as it is a showcase of Bill Reid's work, most famous of which is the statue *The Spirit of Haida Gwaii, The Jade Canoe*, on display at the Vancouver International Airport.

Capilano Suspension Bridge, Vancouver

(B) It's just a 20-minute drive across Burrard Inlet from Downtown Vancouver to reach the surprisingly momentous North Shore mountains, home to Grouse Mountain and its aerial tramway, and the famed Capilano Suspension Bridge, a 450-foot cedar-plank swing bridge that crosses 230 feet above the frothy Capilano River.

Dr. Sun Yat-Sen Chinese Garden, Vancouver

(C) "Life is not measured by the number of breaths we take," according to the old saying, "but by the places and moments that take our breath away." That sentiment sums up this elegant Downtown destination. It's the first authentic Ming Dynasty–style garden outside of China to incorporate symbolism and design elements from centuries-old Chinese gardens.

Granville Island, Vancouver

(D) Take the foot-passenger ferry across the inlet from Downtown, and bring your appetite. This small island houses an extremely popular indoor market, a marina, theaters, restaurants, coffee shops, parks, and dozens of crafts shops and artist studios. Wander the stalls in the market, then grab a bench outside to get your fill of delicacies and the view.

Museum of Anthropology, Vancouver

(E) The city's most spectacular museum displays art from the Pacific Northwest and around the world—dramatic totem poles and canoes; exquisite carvings of gold, silver, and argillite; and masks, tools, and textiles from many cultures.

Stanley Park, Vancouver

(F) An afternoon in this gorgeous 1,000-acre wilderness, just blocks from Downtown Vancouver, can include beaches, the ocean, the harbor, Douglas fir and cedar forests, First Nations sculptures, and a view of the North Shore Mountains. Walk, bike, picnic, or just take the trolley tour around the perimeter, but don't miss it.

Butchart Gardens, Victoria

(G) Just 20 minutes from downtown Victoria, the 55-acre Butchart Gardens was planted in a limestone quarry in 1904. Highlights include the Japanese and Italian gardens, as well as the proliferation of roses and 700 other varieties of flowers. On summer nights you can enjoy a fireworks display.

Inner Harbour, Victoria

(H) The lovely capital of British Columbia has a remarkably intimate and pedestrian-friendly Downtown that wraps around the harbor. Street entertainers and crafts vendors—and lots of people—come out to stroll the waterfront walkway in summer.

Royal British Columbia Museum, Victoria

(I) At this superb museum, you can learn about the culture and human history of British Columbia, dating back several thousand years to the earliest First Peoples inhabitants. Other exhibits touch on natural history, European settlement, and maritime heritage.

TOP EXPERIENCES

Shopping at the Portland Saturday Market and Portland Farmers' Market, Portland, OR

The expansive outdoor Saturday market is actually open Saturday and Sunday (from March through Christmas). At the attractive market grounds you'll find every imaginable creation: offbeat patio sculptures, jewelry made from recycled wares, and stylish yet practical housewares to name a few. A 15-minute walk south on Saturday mornings and early afternoons, the unrelated Portland Farmers' Market at PSU campus, on the verdant Park Blocks, is one of the nation's most acclaimed foodie gatherings—several vendors sell delish breakfast and lunch fare.

Skiing Mt. Hood, OR

Just 60 miles east of Portland, the state's highest mountain is the only place in the Lower 48 where you can ski year-round (although trails are limited in summer). There are three different facilities on this mammoth, snowcapped mountain. Timberline Lodge Ski Area is the one that remains open year-round, and its runs pass beside the venerable 1930s Timberline Lodge. Nearby Mt. Hood Skibowl has less interesting terrain but the most night-skiing acreage in the country. Around the north side of the mountain, you'll find the most challenging, extensive, and interesting terrain at Mt. Hood Meadows Ski Resort, which offers some 2,000 acres of winter snowboarding and ski fun.

White-Water Rafting on the Rogue River, Grants Pass, OR

Of the many excellent places for white-water rafting in Oregon, the Rogue River offers some of the most thrilling rides. Several outfitters offer trips along this frothy, 215-mile river in the southwestern part of the state, from half-day adventures well suited to beginners to multiday trips that include camping or overnights in local lodges.

Picnicking at Silver Falls State Park, OR

The lush Silver Falls State Park, about 25 miles east of Salem, is so impressive that serious campaigns to admit it to the National Park System have taken place recently. In the meantime, it's something of a secret treasure. The 8,700-acre swath of sky-scraping old-growth Douglas firs climbs into the foothills of the Cascade Range, where rain and melting snow supply the torrent that roars through 14 different waterfalls, several of them more than 100 feet tall.

Driving through the Columbia Gorge, OR/WA

The roughly 110-mile section of the mighty Columbia River that extends from just east of Portland to Goldendale, Washington, provides some of the most stunning scenery in the Pacific Northwest. Towering cliffs on both the Washington and Oregon sides of the river form a dramatic backdrop, and meandering highways line both banks (on the Washington side, Highway 14 is slower but offers better views). There's much to see and do in the Gorge: visit the 620-foot-high Multnomah Falls; stroll among the sophisticated restaurants, shops, and wineries in charming Hood River; or try your luck at sailboarding, a sport well suited to the river's high winds.

Attending the Oregon Shakespeare Festival in Ashland, OR

Sunny, hilly, and attractive Ashland is a charming small city in its own right, with a bustling downtown popping with notable restaurants specializing in farm-to-table cuisine and wines from nearby vineyards. But the Oregon Shakespeare Festival, which presents world-class plays (from Shakespeare to classics to contemporary), on three different stages from mid-February to early November, really put this town on the map. Try to see a play in the largest venue, the Elizabethan, which replicates London's famed Fortune Theatre.

Coffeehouse-Crawling in Seattle, WA

Sure, for kicks, it's worth stopping by the original branch of Starbucks, which is across the street from Pike Place Market. But as arguably the nation's coffeehouse capital, Seattle has far more interesting java joints to consider. Especially fertile (coffee) grounds for coffeehouse-hopping include the Capitol Hill, Queen Anne, Ballard, and Fremont neighborhoods—try Espresso Vivace and Victrola Coffee Roasters for stellar espresso.

Biking around Lopez Island, WA

Whether you're an ardent cyclist or an occasional weekender, Lopez Island offers some of the best biking terrain in the West. This laid-back, gently undulating island that's part of Washington's fabled San Juan archipelago is ringed by a beautiful main road and dedicated bike paths. As you cycle past lavender fields, blackberry bushes, horse farms, and occasional patches of woodland, you'll encounter little automobile traffic. There are a few bike-rental shops, and the Lopez Island Soda Fountain is a fine spot for refreshments.

The Laser-Light Show at Grand Coulee Dam, WA

You truly get a sense of the awesome magnitude of the Columbia River when you view some of the enormous hydroelectric facilities set along this meandering Northwest river. The Grand Coulee Dam, built in 1932, ranks among the world's biggest concrete structures, and towers over the landscape. On summer evenings, grab a seat and watch the nightly laser-light show projected across the dam. This is a favorite family activity in this otherwise relatively remote part of northeastern Washington.

Wine Tasting in Walla Walla, WA

Although you'll find super wine-making in several parts of the region, including Oregon's Willamette Valley and Washington's nearby Yakima and Columbia valleys, the dapper college town of Walla Walla has evolved into the Northwest's best overall wine-country hub. The handsomely revived historic downtown abounds with smart boutiques, lively cafés and restaurants, and several prominent tasting rooms. And throughout the surrounding vineyard-studded hills you'll find elegant inns and some of the most critically acclaimed, if still somewhat underrated, wineries in the country.

Riding the Ferry to Victoria, BC

This is a perfectly simple way to admire the region's coastal scenery, from the mountains in Olympic National Park to the meandering shorelines of the San Juan Islands (if you're coming from Port Angeles or Anacortes, Washington) and Gulf islands (if you're coming from mainland British Columbia). Numerous ferries of many sizes ply the waters around Victoria and Vancouver Island, and the trip is best enjoyed on an open deck, while devouring a cup of clam chowder.

FLAVORS OF THE PACIFIC NORTHWEST

Pacific Northwest cuisine highlights regional seafood, locally grown produce, and locally raised meats, often prepared in styles that borrow Pan-Asian, French, and Italian influences. All of the region's major and even many smaller cities have top-rated, nationally renowned dining spots, as well as funky, inexpensive little eateries that also pride themselves on serving seasonal and often organic ingredients.

Seafood

The Northwest's dining scene is forever eclectic because of the combined abundance of fresh seafood and the imaginative ways it's cooked. Many restaurants, such as the Portland-based chain McCormick & Schmick's, print menus daily and feature a "fresh list" with more than 30 types of seafood represented, most of which are caught from local waters. And since Dungeness crab, salmon, tuna, sole, oysters, spotted prawns, scallops, and swordfish are all within pole's reach, chefs take serious and artful pleasure in discovering ways to fry, grill, bake, stir-fry, sear, poach, barbecue, and sauté the latest catch in new, inventive ways.

Block + Tackle/Roe, Portland, OR. On the city's hip Division Street restaurant row, Block + Tackle has become a go-to for creatively prepared seafood classics, while at the intimate, reservations-only Roe—located in the discreet back section of the restaurant—you can sample a seven-course meal of artfully prepared fish and shellfish.

Matt's in the Market, Seattle, WA. Right next to Seattle's prime source of fresh fish, Pike Place Market, Matt's serves a must-try oyster po'boy and Penn Cove mussels with chorizo or Dungeness crab bisque, and pan-roasted fillets of wild salmon and lingcod served with light vinaigrettes.

Blue Water Café, Vancouver, BC. Ask the staff to recommend wine pairings from the BC-focused list, and enjoy exquisitely prepared seafood, which may include overlooked varieties such as mackerel, sardines, and herring.

Locavore Movement

Pacific Northwest chefs are fanatical, in a delicious way, about sustainability, presenting dishes with ingredients raised, grown, or foraged within about 100 miles. Northwest chefs are so determined to maintain an unwavering connection to the land that many hire professional foragers, or on occasion can be found tromping off into the woods themselves. Bounties of morels, chanterelles, and bolete mushrooms (fall), stinging nettles and fiddlehead ferns (spring), and huckleberries and blackberries (summer) now grace the menus of many restaurants. From both Portland and Seattle, farmland immediately surrounds urban boundaries; therefore, daily deliveries of asparagus, eggplant, pears, cherries, and other fruits and vegetables is achievable, along with locally raised game from area ranches and farms.

Higgins, Portland, OR. One of Portland's longtime culinary stars, chef Greg Higgins relies heavily on herbs and produce from nearby farms in such standout dishes as warm beets, asparagus, and artichokes; and venison terrine with dried sour cherries and roasted-garlic mustard.

Imperial, Portland, OR. Talented chef Vitaly Paley produces incomparably fresh and complex fare utilizing strictly seasonal and regional ingredients, from local rabbit and duck to peaches and wild mushrooms.

Lark, Seattle, WA. Naturally raised veal sweetbreads come with a sunchoke purée, and spring nettles are stuffed into spinach ravioli at Lark, where the small menu names every local farm that contributes to its dishes.

Sitka & Spruce, Seattle, WA. Wild greens and edible flowers always show up in salads or as garnishes alongside fresh seafood or free-range chicken from Vashon Island farms at chef Matt Dillon's tiny temple to the Northwest.

The Herbfarm, Woodinville, WA. Every year the Herbfarm honors mushroom season with the Mycologist's Dream menu, which sees the fungi go into everything from ravioli to flan. The rest of the year, blackberries may mingle with rose geranium in ice cream, or caviar may be accompanied by a jelly flavored with wild ginger and local rhizomes.

Wineries

Thanks to a mild climate with soil, air, water, and temperature conditions comparable to regions of France, the Northwest is recognized for producing prime varieties of wine. In charming, rural settings, some just outside the cities, petite to larger vineyards offer behind-the-scenes tours where sampling the merchandise is encouraged. The Northwest is also a notable region for its production of organic and biodynamic wines. In keeping with the sustainable food and farm movement, vineyards are developing fertilization, production, harvesting, and fermentation techniques that produce flavorful, eco-friendly varieties that set the standard in the wine world.

Artisanal Cocktails

Thanks to the growing number of craft distilleries that have sprung up in the Northwest, with the bulk of them in Portland (Clear Creek eau de vie, Aviation gin, New Deal vodka), bars and restaurants in Oregon and Washington have begun turning their attention to producing creative, artisanal cocktails, often using local and seasonal ingredients, including fresh juices and herbs garnered from farmers' markets. Bourbon and gin lovers never had it so good, as these drinks seem to be at the base of most creations; for the rest, there are plenty of obscure lavender-infused liqueurs to choose from. Classic drinks are also much appreciated. In Seattle, several bartenders are single-handedly restoring the dignity of the martini, the Manhattan, and the French 75.

Expatriate, Portland, OR. Northeast Portland's cozy Asian-inspired boîte has become renowned for inspired drinks—try the Infante, with Pueblo Viejo Blanco tequila, fresh lime, orgeat, local honey, and nutmeg—and delectable snacks.

Teardrop Lounge, Portland, OR. The expansive cocktail list here changes seasonally and emphasizes interesting mixers, such as basil-lemon soda, marionberry–pink peppercorn honey, and jalapeño syrup.

Spur Gastropub, Seattle, WA. This lively and trendy Belltown gastropub turns out artful, colorful cocktails, including the refreshing Empress, made with Jamaican rum, fresh grapefruit juice, and St. Germain liqueur.

Zig Zag, Seattle, WA. Zig Zag pours the best martinis in Seattle, along with more exotic fare like the Trident (cynar, aquavit, dry sherry, and peach bitters) and inventive, improvised cocktails.

PORTLAND WITH KIDS

Many of Oregon's best kids-oriented attractions and activities are in greater Portland. Just getting around the Rose City—via streetcars and light-rail trains on city streets and kayaks, excursion cruises, and jet boats on the Willamette River—is fun. For listings of family-oriented concerts, performances by the Oregon Children's Theatre, and the like, check the free *Willamette Weekly* newspaper.

Museums and Attractions

On the east bank of the Willamette River, the **Oregon Museum of Science and Industry** (OMSI) is a leading interactive museum, with touch-friendly exhibits, an Omnimax theater, the state's biggest planetarium, and a 240-foot submarine moored just outside in the river. Along Portland's leafy Park Blocks, both the **Oregon History Museum** and the **Portland Art Museum** have exhibits and programming geared toward kids.

In Old Town, kids enjoy walking amid the ornate pagodas and dramatic foliage of the **Lan Su Chinese Garden.** This is a good spot for a weekend morning, followed by a visit to the **Portland Saturday Market,** where food stalls and musicians keep younger kids entertained, and the cool jewelry, toys, and gifts handcrafted by local artisans appeal to teens. Steps from the market is the **Oregon Maritime Museum,** set within a vintage stern-wheeler docked on the river. And just up Burnside Street from the market, **Powell's City of Books** contains enormous sections of kids' and young adults' literature.

Parks

Portland is dotted with densely wooded parks—many of the larger ones have ball fields, playgrounds, and picnic areas. The most famous urban oasis in the city, **Forest Park** (along with adjoining **Washington Park**) offers a wealth of engaging activities. You can ride the MAX light rail right to the park's main hub of culture, a complex comprising the **Oregon Zoo, Portland Children's Museum,** and **World Forestry Discovery Center Museum.** Ride the narrow-gauge railroad from the zoo for 2 miles to reach the **International Rose Test Garden** and **Japanese Garden.** From here it's an easy downhill stroll to **Northwest 23rd and 21st avenues'** pizza parlors, ice-cream shops, and bakeries.

Outdoor Adventures

Tour boats ply the **Willamette River,** and a couple of marinas near OMSI rent **kayaks** and conduct **drag-boat races** out on the water. There are also several shops in town that rent **bikes** for use on the city's many miles of dedicated bike lanes and trails. There's outstanding **white-water rafting** just southeast of Portland, along the Clackamas River. On your way toward the Clackamas, check out **North Clackamas Aquatic Park** and **Oaks Amusement Park,** which have rides and wave pools galore.

Nearby **Mt. Hood** has camping, hiking, and biking all summer, and three of the most family-friendly ski resorts in the Northwest—**Timberline** is especially popular for younger and less experienced boarders and skiers. From summer through fall, the pick-your-own berry farms and pumpkin patches on **Sauvie Island** make for an engaging afternoon getaway—for an all-day outing, continue up U.S. 30 all the way to **Astoria,** at the mouth of the Columbia River, to visit the **Columbia River Maritime Museum** and **Fort Stevens State Park,** where kids love to scamper about the remains of an early-20th-century shipwreck.

SEATTLE WITH KIDS

Seattle is great for kids. After all, a place where floatplanes take off a few feet from houseboats, and where harbor seals might be spotted on a routine ferry ride, doesn't have to try too hard to feel like a wonderland. And if the rain falls, there are plenty of great museums to keep the kids occupied. A lot of child-centric sights are easily reached via public transportation, and the piers and the aquarium can be explored on foot from most Downtown hotels. A few spots (Woodland Park Zoo, the Ballard Locks, and Discovery Park) are easier to visit by car.

Museums

Several museums cater specifically to kids, and many are conveniently clustered at the Seattle Center. The Center's winning trio is the **Pacific Science Center**, which has interactive exhibits and IMAX theaters; the **Children's Museum**, which has exhibits on Washington State and foreign cultures plus plenty of interactive art spaces; and, of course, the **Space Needle**. For older, hipper siblings there's a skate park; the Vera Project, a teen music and art space; and the **EMP Museum**, which features exhibits on pop culture and music history.

Downtown there are miles of waterfront to explore along the piers. The **Seattle Aquarium** is here and has touch pools and otters—what more could a kid want?

Parks and Outdoor Attractions

Discovery Park has an interpretive center, a Native American cultural center, easy forest trails, and accessible beaches. **Alki Beach** in West Seattle is lively and fun; a wide paved path is the perfect surface for wheels of all kinds—you can rent bikes and scooters, or take to the water on rented paddleboats and kayaks. **Volunteer Park** has wide lawns and shallow pools made for splashing toddlers.

The **Woodland Park Zoo** has 300 different species of animals, from jaguars to mountain goats, cheap parking, and an adjacent playground; stroller rentals are available. Watching an astonishing variety of boats navigate the ship canal at the **Ballard Locks** will entertain visitors of any age.

Hotels

Downtown, the **Hotel Monaco** offers a happy medium between sophisticated and family-friendly. The colorful, eccentric decor will appeal to kids but remind adults that they're in a boutique property. Fun amenities abound, like optional goldfish in the rooms, and toys in the lobby. Surprisingly, one of the city's most high-end historic properties, the **Fairmont Olympic**, is also quite kid-friendly. The hotel's decor is a little fussy, but the grand staircases in the lobby will awe most little ones, and there's a great indoor pool area. In addition, the hotel offers babysitting, a kids' room-service menu, and toys and board games.

GREAT ITINERARIES

WASHINGTON AND OREGON

Northwest Coast and Cities, 10 days

The hip and urbane cities of Seattle and Portland bookend this itinerary, with the verdant Olympic Peninsula, rugged Oregon Coast, and undulating Willamette Valley Wine Country at the heart, giving you the best of the city and the country in one trip.

Days 1 and 2: Seattle

Start in **Seattle,** where you can spend a couple of nights exploring this picturesque and dynamic city's highlights. Most of the must-see attractions—**Pike Place Market, Seattle Art Museum,** the **Seattle Aquarium**—are steps from Downtown hotels, and it's only a short walk or monorail ride to reach the **Seattle Center,** with its iconic **Space Needle** and such family-friendly draws as the **Pacific Science Center, Children's Museum,** and **EMP Museum.** You could cram several of these attractions into one busy day, but it's better to break them up over two days. Or spend your second day exploring some of the city's lively neighborhoods, including Capitol Hill, with its scenic **Volunteer Park,** and Ballard, where you can check out the **Lake Washington Ship Canal** and **Hiram M. Chittenden Locks** park.

Day 3: Bainbridge Island and Port Townsend
(2 hours by car ferry and car from Seattle)

Take the 35-minute car ferry from Seattle across Puget Sound to laid-back and beautiful **Bainbridge Island,** stopping for lunch and browsing the shops in the village of Winslow and touring **Bloedel Reserve.** Continue on Highways 305, 3, and 104, stopping in the cute Scandinavian town of **Poulsbo,** and continuing to the northeastern corner of the Olympic Peninsula, where the charming towns of **Port Townsend** and **Port Angeles** make good overnight bases and have several fine dinner options.

Days 4 and 5: Olympic National Park
(1 hour by car from Port Townsend, 15 minutes by car from Port Angeles)

The next morning, launch into a full day at **Olympic National Park.** Explore the **Hoh Rain Forest** and **Hurricane Ridge** (the nearest section to Port Angeles) before heading back to Port Angeles or Port Townsend for the evening. Start Day 5 with a drive west on U.S. 101 to **Forks** and on to **La Push** via Highway 110, a total of about 45 miles. Here, an hour-long lunchtime stroll to **Second** or **Third Beach** will offer a taste of the wild Pacific coastline. Back on U.S. 101, head south to **Lake Quinault,** which is about 100 miles from Lake Crescent. Check into the **Lake Quinault Lodge,** then drive up the river 6 miles to one of the rain-forest trails through the lush Quinault Valley.

Days 6 and 7: The Oregon Coast
(3 hours from Lake Quinault to Astoria)

Leave Lake Quinault early on Day 6 for the scenic drive south on U.S. 101. Here the road winds through coastal spruce forests, periodically rising on headlands to offer Pacific Ocean panoramas. Spend your first night in the up-and-coming town of **Astoria,** just across the Columbia River from Washington. The next day, after visiting Astoria's excellent **Columbia Maritime Museum,** continue south on U.S. 101, where small coastal resort towns like **Cannon Beach** and **Manzanita** beckon with cafés, shops, and spectacular beach parks. Be sure to walk out to the gorgeous beach at **Oswald West State Park** in Manzanita. Take a detour onto the **Three Capes Loop,** a stunning 35-mile byway off U.S. 101. Stop in **Newport** (on the loop), 130 miles south of Astoria, for your second night on the coast—this bustling town has several good restaurants and is home to the **Oregon Coast Aquarium.**

Day 8: Eugene and the Willamette Valley

(2½ hours by car from Newport to Eugene or 4 hours by car stopping at Oregon Dunes)

From Newport, continue south along the coast on U.S. 101 for 50 miles, stopping in the charming village of **Florence** for lunch. Then head south another 20 miles to briefly get a look at the soaring mountains of sand that make up **Oregon Dunes National Recreation Area,** before backtracking back to Florence and cutting inland on Highway 126 about 60 miles to the artsy, friendly college town of **Eugene,** which is at the southern end of the Willamette Valley wine region. Eugene has plenty of overnight options, or you could continue north 90 miles on Interstate 5 to spend the night in the heart of the wine country at **Newberg,** where you'll find dozens of wineries, several fine restaurants, and a few upscale inns and hotels.

Days 9 and 10: Portland

(1 hour 45 minutes by car from Eugene, 40 minutes by car from Newberg)

On Day 9, visit some of the Willamette Valley's wineries, and then, from either Eugene or Newberg, continue into the hip, outdoorsy, and food-driven city of **Portland.** Be sure to visit the several attractions found at green and beautiful **Washington Park,** the chic shops and restaurants of the **Pearl District,** and the **Portland Art Museum,** situated along Downtown's dapper Park Blocks. Like Seattle, the Rose City is renowned for its quirky, inviting

neighborhoods, which abound with locavore-minded restaurants, artisanal-coffee roasters, swanky cocktail lounges, and smart boutiques—**Hawthorne, Division Street, Mississippi,** and **Alberta** are among the best areas for exploring. From Portland, it's a straight three-hour drive back up to Seattle; if you have an extra day, consider a detour east into the magnificent **Columbia River Gorge.** En route to Seattle, you could also easily detour to **Mt. St. Helens, Mt. Rainier,** and the surprisingly vibrant and engaging city of **Tacoma.**

GREAT ITINERARIES

OREGON

Best of Oregon, 10 days

With 10 days, you can get a taste of Oregon's largest city, eco-conscious Portland, while also getting a nice sense of the state's geographical diversity—the mountainous and sweeping coast, gorgeous Crater Lake, the rugged Cascade Mountains, and the eastern high-desert regions.

Days 1 and 2: Portland

Start by spending a couple of days in Portland, where you can tour the museums and attractions that make up **Washington Park**, as well as the **Lan Su Chinese Garden** in Old Town, and the excellent museums and cultural institutions along Downtown's leafy **Park Blocks**. This city of vibrant, distinctive neighborhoods offers plenty of great urban exploring, with Nob Hill, Hawthorne, and the Mississippi Avenue Arts District among the best areas for shopping, café-hopping, and people-watching. If you have a little extra time, consider spending a couple of hours just south of the city in the **Willamette Valley Wine Country**—it's an easy jaunt from Portland.

Days 3 and 4: Oregon Coast

(1½ hours by car from Portland to Cannon Beach)

Leave Portland early on Day 3 for the drive west about 100 miles on U.S. 30 to the small city of **Astoria**, which has several excellent spots for lunch and the **Columbia River Maritime Museum**. Pick the main scenic highway down the Oregon Coast, U.S. 101, and continue south, stopping at **Fort Stevens State Park** and the **Fort Clatsop National Memorial**. End the day in charming **Cannon Beach** (26 miles south of Astoria), which has a wealth of oceanfront hotels and inns, many with views of one

of the region's seminal features, 235-foot-tall **Haystack Rock**. Be sure to check out the stunning beach scenery at nearby **Ecola State Park** and **Oswald West State Park**.

The following morning, continue south down U.S. 101. In **Tillamook** (famous for its cheese), take a detour onto the **Three Capes Loop,** a stunning 35-mile byway. Stop in small and scenic **Pacific City** (at the south end of the loop) for lunch. Once you're back on U.S. 101, continue south to **Newport**, spending some time at the excellent **Oregon Coast Aquarium** as well as Oregon State University's fascinating **Hatfield Marine Science Center**. Your final stop is the charming village of **Florence**, 160 miles (four to six hours) from Cannon Beach.

Day 5: Eugene

(2½ hours by car from Florence to Eugene with detour at Oregon Dunes)

Spend the morning driving 20 miles south of Florence along U.S. 101 to scamper about the sandy bluffs at **Oregon Dunes National Recreation Area** near Reedsport. Then backtrack to Florence for lunch in Old Town before taking Highway 126 east for 60 miles to the attractive college city of **Eugene**, staying at one of the charming inns or bed-and-breakfasts near the leafy campus of the University of Oregon. Take a walk to the summit of **Skinner Butte**, which affords fine views of the city, and plan to have dinner at one of the top-notch restaurants at the **5th Street Public Market**. Budget some additional time in Eugene the following morning to visit two excellent University of Oregon museums, the **Jordan Schnitzer Museum of Art** and the **Oregon Museum of Natural History**.

Days 6 and 7: Crater Lake and Ashland

(3 hours by car from Eugene to Crater Lake National Park or Prospect)

From Eugene, take Interstate 5 south for 75 miles to Roseburg, and then head east along Highway 138 (the Umpqua River Scenic Byway), which twists and turns over the Cascade Range for 85 miles to the northern entrance of **Crater Lake National Park.** Once inside the park, you can continue along Rim Drive for another half hour for excellent views of the lake. Overnight in the park or in nearby **Prospect.**

The following morning, take the lake boat tour to **Wizard Island** and hike through the surrounding forest. In the afternoon, head southwest on Highway 62 to Interstate 5, and then on to **Ashland,** 95 miles (about two hours) from Crater Lake. Plan to stay the night in one of Ashland's many superb bed-and-breakfasts. Have dinner and attend one of the **Oregon Shakespeare Festival** productions (mid-February through early November).

Days 8 and 9: Bend
(3½ hours by car from Ashland)

Get an early start out of Ashland, driving east along scenic Highway 140, which skirts picturesque **Upper Klamath Lake,** and then north on U.S. 97, stopping if you have time at **Collier Memorial State Park,** to reach the outdoorsy resort town of **Bend.** Here you can spend two nights checking out the parks, mountain hikes, microbreweries, and restaurants of the state's largest city east of the Cascades. Be sure to visit the outstanding **High Desert Museum,** the **Old Mill District,** and **Mt. Bachelor Ski Area.**

Day 10: Hood River
(3 hours by car from Bend)

From Bend, continue north up U.S. 97, and then northwest up U.S. 26 to **Mt. Hood,** 105 miles total. Have lunch at the historic **Timberline Lodge,** admiring the stunning views south down the Cascade

Range. Pick up Highway 35 and drive around the east side of Mt. Hood and then north 40 miles up to the dapper town of **Hood River,** in the heart of the picturesque Columbia Gorge. Spend the night at one of the attractive inns, and try one of this town's stellar restaurants for dinner. From here it's just a 60-mile drive west along a scenic stretch of Interstate 84 to reach Portland.

GREAT ITINERARIES

WASHINGTON

Best of Washington, 10 days

It's hard to say which is more alluring for Washington visitors: the island and sculpted bays of Puget Sound, the volcanic peaks of the Cascade Range, or the lively neighborhoods and first-rate attractions, locavore-minded restaurants, and trendy music clubs of Seattle. Here's a tour that reveals all of the state's charms.

Days 1 and 2: Seattle

Begin with two days of touring this world-class hub of acclaimed arts, culture, and dining, visiting Downtown's must-see sites, including **Pike Place Market**, the **Seattle Art Museum**, and—a bit north—the **Seattle Center** (and its iconic **Space Needle**). Set aside at least a half day to investigate some of the city's liveliest neighborhoods, including **Capitol Hill**, with its indie shops, hipster bars, and diverting cafés, and similarly inviting **Ballard** and **Fremont**. If you have extra time, consider a quick day trip to up-and-coming **Tacoma**, with its several excellent museums (including the **LeMay Car Museum** and **International Museum of Glass**), and the wine-tasting hub of **Woodinville**.

Days 3 and 4: Olympic National Park
(3 hours by car ferry and car from Seattle, via Bainbridge Island)

Get an early start from Seattle on Day 3, taking the ferry from Downtown across Puget Sound to scenic **Bainbridge Island** for lunch and shopping in the village of **Winslow**, and perhaps a quick tour of **Bloedel Reserve**, before continuing the drive to historic **Port Angeles**, which you can use as an overnight base for exploring **Olympic National Park**.

Hurricane Ridge is the park's nearest section, but on Day 4, depending on how ambitious you are, you could drive west to the **Hoh Rain Forest** section of the park, as well as the coastal areas out at **La Push**, and possibly all the way down to **Lake Quinault** (125 miles from Port Angeles). Try to visit at least one of the rain forests, where you can hike amid huge stands of Douglas firs and Sitka spruces.

Day 5: Whidbey Island
(1½ hours by car and car ferry from Port Angeles)

Drive from Port Angeles to the Victorian-era town of **Port Townsend**, a good stop for lunch and a look at the **Northwest Maritime Center**, and then catch the ferry to **Whidbey Island**, where there are plenty of sophisticated shops, galleries, restaurants, and inns in the laid-back, friendly hamlets of **Langley**, **Greenbank**, and **Coupeville** (where you disembark the ferry). Nature lovers shouldn't miss **Ebey's Landing National Historic Reserve**. To be closer to where you're headed on Day 6, you might consider staying just north of Whidbey on **Fidalgo Island**, which is home to **Anacortes**, where ferries leave for the San Juan Islands.

Days 6 and 7: The Northern Cascades
(2½ hours by car from Whidbey Island to North Cascades National Park)

Leave the Puget Sound region, perhaps stopping in the picturesque Skagit Valley towns of **La Conner** and **Mount Vernon** for lunch, and head for Washington's stunning, skyscraping Cascades Range, passing through the old logging town of **Sedro-Woolley** and making your way up the dramatic **North Cascades Highway** (Highway 20) into **North Cascades National Park**. You could stay in the park at **Skagit River Resort** or a bit farther east in **Winthrop**.

On Day 7, turn south and follow the upper Columbia River down into **Chelan**

(2½ hours from North Cascades), the base area for exploring fjordlike, 55-mile-long **Lake Chelan**, the state's deepest lake, which you can explore by boat or even floatplane. Stay in Chelan, up at the north end of the lake at **Stehekin** (go by floatplane to save time), or a bit farther south and west in the endearingly cute, if kitschy, Bavarian-style town of **Leavenworth**, with its gingerbread architecture and cozy German restaurants.

Day 8: Walla Walla
(4 hours by car from Chelan)

From the Lake Chelan area, it's a long but pleasant 200-mile drive southeast, much of it along the mighty Columbia River, to reach what's developed into the most impressive of the Pacific Northwest's wine-producing areas, **Walla Walla**. This once-sleepy college and farming town has blossomed with stylish restaurants and shops in recent years, and you'll find dozens of tasting rooms, both in town and in the surrounding countryside.

Day 9: Yakima Valley
(2½ hours from Walla Walla)

The great wine touring continues as you return west from Walla Walla through the **Tri-Cities** communities of Pasco, Kennewick, and Richland, following Interstate 82 to **Yakima**. Good stops for visiting

wineries include **Richland, Benton City, Prosser,** and **Zillah.** Yakima itself is a good overnight stop.

Day 10: Mount Rainier National Park
(2½ hours from Yakima)

On the morning of Day 10, take U.S. 12 west from Yakima 102 miles to Ohana-pecosh, the southern entrance to **Mount Rainier National Park.** When you arrive, take the 31-mile, two-hour drive on Sunrise Road, which reveals the "back" (northeast) side of Rainier. A room at the **Paradise Inn** is your base for the night. On the following day, energetic hikers could tackle one of the four- to six-hour trails that lead up among the park's many peaks. Or, if it's your last day of traveling, try one of the shorter ranger-led walks through wildflower meadows. It's about a two-hour drive back to Seattle.

Alternatives

You really need a couple of days to enjoy one of Washington's loveliest areas, the **San Juan Islands,** ideally spending a night on two of the three main islands. If you're unable to add two days, you could easily make time by cutting out the Walla Walla–Yakima portion.

GREAT ITINERARIES

VANCOUVER AND VICTORIA

British Columbia's Top Cities, 7 days

Easily reached from Washington via a combination of ferry and roads, Vancouver and Victoria are a pair of gems. The former is a fast-growing, contemporary city—Canada's third largest—with a mix of enchanting outdoor activities and world-class cultural and culinary diversions. Much smaller, Victoria is surprisingly relaxed and compact for a provincial capital—it's renowned for its colorful gardens, well-groomed bike paths, and picturesque Inner Harbour.

Days 1 through 4: Vancouver

Start with two or three days in Vancouver itself. You'll want to dedicate a full day to touring 1,000-acre **Stanley Park**, with its 9-km (5½-mile) seawall for walking, cycling, and skating; and the **Vancouver Aquarium Marine Science Center**, a family favorite. From the park, you're at the edge of Vancouver's bustling **West End**, which is rife with interesting shopping and breezy cafés. Continue up the city's main retail drag, **Robson Street**, to reach some of Vancouver's top museums, including the **Vancouver Art Gallery** and the **Bill Reid Gallery of Northwest Coast Art**.

On additional days in Vancouver, explore the Victorian-era **Gaslamp Quarter** and adjacent **Chinatown**, home to the very interesting **Dr. Sun Yat-Sen Classical Chinese Garden**. Stroll over to hip and exciting **Yaletown**, a trendy warren of dining and shopping, and catch the Aquabus across False Creek to **Granville Island**, a former industrial wasteland that's become arguably—with Stanley Park—Vancouver's premier attraction. Here you can eat and shop your way through 50,000-square-foot **Granville Island Public Market**, taking a seat outside and admiring the yachts and sailboats plying False Creek. It's also well worth detouring from the Downtown area to stroll through the charming **Kitsilano** neighborhood, near Granville Island, a gentrified patch of dining and shopping with a lovely beach park affording fine views of the city skyline. On this side of town, you're within easy driving or busing distance to a pair of top attractions, the **Museum of Anthropology** on the campus of University of British Columbia, and **Queen Elizabeth Park**, the highest point in the city.

On your final day in Vancouver, explore the mountains and parks of the **North Shore**, hiking across **Capilano Suspension Bridge** and through the adjoining rain forest, and taking the aerial tram to the top of **Grouse Mountain.** You could visit these attractions before catching the ferry from Horseshoe Bay across the Georgia Strait to Nanaimo, and then making the two-hour drive south to Victoria. Or if you're headed to Victoria directly from Downtown Vancouver, you could instead drive south from Vancouver to Tsawwassen, and catch a ferry to Swartz Bay, from which it's a 30-minute drive south to Victoria.

Days 5 through 7: Victoria

(4 hours from Vancouver via Horseshoe Bay–Nanaimo ferry, 3 hours via Tsawwassen–Swartz Bay ferry)

British Columbia's compact, verdant, and welcoming capital city, Victoria, is compact enough to explore mostly on foot, although with a car you can more easily reach some of the city's interesting outlying attractions, as well as the wineries of the Saanich Peninsula. Give yourself a couple of days to see the top sites, including the artful architecture of Chinatown;

1

the **Emily Carr House,** dedicated to one of the nation's most celebrated artists; and the fascinating **Royal British Columbia Museum,** where you could easily spend a few hours. Plan to have high tea at the regal **Fairmont Empress** hotel, which overlooks the city's picturesque **Inner Harbour.**

This is a great area for biking, with older residential areas like **Oak Bay, Rockland,** and **Fairfield** popular for touring on foot or on two wheels—highlights include **Abkhazi Garden** and **Craigdarroch Castle.**

Set aside a full day for a side trip outside of Victoria proper to the **Saanich Peninsula,** with its wineries, bike paths, and perhaps the most impressive attraction in the entire region, 55-acre **Butchart Gardens.**

Alternatives

En route from Vancouver to Victoria, many travelers tack on a couple of days in the nearby **Gulf Islands,** which are just off Vancouver Island and bear a strong resemblance in scenery and personality to the **San Juan Islands.**

OUTDOOR ADVENTURES

HIKING

In the Pacific Northwest, hiking is potentially a year-round sport, though only experts should attempt hiking in the snowy higher elevations in winter. One of the greatest aspects of this region is the diverse terrain, from high alpine scrambles that require stamina to flowered meadows that invite a relaxed pace to stunning coastal areas that offer a mix of level and precipitous terrain.

Of course, many of the best trails in the region are in national parks (Crater Lake, Olympic, Mt. Rainier, and North Cascades among them). We've focused on trails elsewhere in the region, including some spectacular hidden gems.

Best Hikes

Forest Park, Portland, OR. You can easily walk to the network of more than 80 miles of densely forested trails, many leading to spectacular vistas, from Downtown hotels, making this 5,000-acre urban wilderness one of the most accessible in the country. A good place to start is Washington Park, with its Japanese Garden and International Rose Test Garden.

Oswald West State Park, Manzanita, OR. The trails at this state park just south of popular Cannon Beach, lead to sweeping headlands, to a sheltered beach popular for surfing, and to the top of Neahkahnie Mountain, from which you have a view of more than 20 miles of coastline.

Smith Rock State Park, Redmond, OR. Although world-famous for rock climbing, this maze of soaring rock formations has a number of trails well suited to casual hikers; the 3-mile Smith Rocks Loop hike is a favorite.

Table Rock, Central Point, OR. Comprising a pair of monolithic rocky peaks outside Medford, Table Rock makes a great quick and relaxing scramble—from the top, you're treated to wonderful views of the Cascades.

Wallowa Mountains, Enterprise, OR. This range of granite peaks in eastern Oregon, near Hells Canyon, is rife with crystalline alpine lakes and meadows, rushing rivers, and thickly forested valleys that fall between mountain ridges. Trails lead from both Enterprise and La Grande.

Beacon Rock State Park, North Bonneville, WA. Although Multnomah Falls, on the Oregon side of the Columbia Gorge, provides access to plenty of cool trails, the hiking at this park across the river provides bigger wows and fewer crowds. Scaling the 848-foot rock for which the park is named is fun and easy, but you can also access longer and more challenging day hikes to Hamilton Mountain and Table Mountain.

Cape Disappointment State Park, Ilwaco, WA. One of the top spots on the Washington coast for a beach hike, Cape Disappointment is at the mouth of the Columbia River and also contains exhibits documenting Lewis and Clark's journey, which ended here.

Moran State Park, Orcas Island, WA. Explore the 14 hiking trails at Moran State Park, which contains the largest mountain in the San Juan Islands, for exhilarating views of the islands, the Cascades, the Olympics, and Vancouver Island.

Snow Lake, Snoqualmie, WA. Relative proximity to Seattle makes this 8-mile trail into the dramatic Alpine Lakes Wilderness a bit crowded on weekends, but don't let that deter you—this hike is one of the state's true stunners.

BEACHES

Unless you're a truly hardy soul, or you've brought your wet suit, taking a trip to the beach in the Pacific Northwest probably won't involve much swimming—water temperatures in these parts rarely exceed 55°F, even in late summer. However, residents of this part of the world love going to the coast. The mountainous coastline in Oregon—which frequently inspires comparisons with everywhere from Big Sur to New Zealand—is home to rugged, curvy, smooth-as-glass beaches ideal for tide pooling, strolling, and surfing. And you'll find similarly spectacular scenery as you continue into Washington, along the Long Beach Peninsula, up around the coast of Olympic National Park, and in the many islands of Puget Sound. Across the border, both Victoria and Vancouver have lovely, graceful beaches set against gorgeous mountain backdrops. Throughout the region, from spring through fall, there's a good chance of spotting whales swimming and diving just offshore (and plenty of tour boats offer cruises that afford better views).

Best Beaches

Cannon Beach, OR. The nearest coastal town to Portland also contains some of the state's most breathtaking beaches, including a stretch that fringes downtown. The 235-foot-tall Haystack Rock rises monumentally above the beach, and on the north side of town, Ecola State Park is a long stretch of rocky headlands punctuated by secluded beaches.

Cape Kiwanda State Natural Area, Pacific City, OR. Yet another formation called Haystack Rock, this one soaring to 340 feet, defines the coast at this dramatic stretch of beach that's part of Oregon's famed Three Capes Loop scenic drive. Massive waves pound the wide beach here, which has dozens of tidal pools at low tide.

Cape Perpetua Scenic Area, Yachats, OR. This 2,700-acre oceanfront wilderness on the central coast of Oregon is home to an 800-foot-high coastal lookout point, steep and easy hiking trails (including one through a fern-filled rain forest), an educational nature center, and a rocky but beautiful beach.

Oregon Dunes National Recreation Area, Reedsport, OR. Smooth, wind-sculpted dunes—some rising as high as 500 feet—are the highlight of this recreation area near Florence, the largest expanse of coastal sand dunes on the continent.

Port Orford, OR. The westernmost town in the continental United States, this artsy small town along the southern coast is home to several great little beaches, including Battle Rock Wayside Park, which is just steps from downtown, and Garrison Beach State Wayside, a long stretch of sand extending north from Port Orford headland.

Alki Point and Beach, Seattle, WA. The quintessential sunning, beachcombing, and kite-flying stretch of sand, this West Seattle park encompasses 2½ miles of beachfront and is steps from several restaurants.

Second and Third Beaches, Olympic National Park, WA. These national park beaches are ideal for tide pooling, kayaking, surfing, and watching gray whales frolic offshore in spring and fall.

Kitsilano Beach, Vancouver, BC. A lovely urban beach in the quiet and charming Kitsilano neighborhood, the shore here has plenty of diversions (tennis, a huge pool) and gorgeous views of the city skyline and North Shore Mountains in the distance.

BIKING

From the cities to the coastal and mountain highways, the Pacific Northwest is ideal for—and hugely popular with—biking enthusiasts. You'll find rental shops as well as a handful of bike-tour operators in Portland, Seattle, Vancouver, and Victoria, and in all of these cities as well as a number of smaller towns, dedicated bike lanes and separate multiuse trails (for bikes, runners, and pedestrians) proliferate. And although bikes aren't permitted on many hiking trails, including many of those in national parks, roads in parks and many other scenic regions have wide shoulders and are well suited to cycling adventures.

Best Biking Routes

Columbia Historic Highway, OR. Just 17 miles east of Portland, this narrow, rolling highway climbs through the spectacular Columbia Gorge, past Multnomah Falls, and by the Vista House at Crown Point, a dramatic scenic overlook.

Portland and Sauvie Island, OR. Among America's most bike-crazy cities, Portland has miles of dedicated bike lanes and plenty of rental shops. In town, biking is a great way to explore leafy East Side neighborhoods like Hawthorne, Mississippi, and Alberta, which all abound with hip shops and cafés. Nearby are the rural and relatively flat roads of Sauvie Island, with its bounty of pick-your-own berry farms.

U.S. 97, near Bend, OR. The 40 miles or so north from Lava Butte through Bend and on up to Smith Rock State Park have awesome high-desert scenery and receive plenty of sunshine year-round.

Burke-Gilman Trail, Seattle, WA. Extending along an abandoned rail line through Seattle, including part of the lively Ballard community, this multiuse trail draws plenty of bikers year-round. The city itself has many miles of bike lanes and paths.

Highway 20, North Cascades National Park, WA. You'll want to be in pretty good shape before tackling the hilly and spectacular North Cascades Highway, but few roads in the state offer more mesmerizing scenery.

Lopez Island, San Juan Islands, WA. All the islands in Puget Sound, including Whidbey and Bainbridge to the south, are massively popular with cyclists, but rural Lopez Island—with its gently rolling terrain and very little auto traffic—is especially well suited to two-wheel traffic.

Mount Vernon and La Conner, WA. Biking around these two picturesque Skagit County communities is popular year-round, but this activity is especially fun in spring, when Tulip Country Bike Tours arranges trips through the region's glorious tulip fields.

Lochside Regional Trail, Victoria, BC. A fun way to get from the ferry terminal at Swartz Bay to Downtown Victoria, and to access a number of wineries, this 29-km (18-mile) level route is along a former rail track.

Lower Seymour Valley Conservation Reserve, Vancouver, BC. Easily reached from Downtown Vancouver, the reserve in the soaring North Shore Mountains comprises some 25 km (15½ miles) of trails through leafy rain forests, plus an easier, paved, 10-km (6-mile) track.

Seaside Route, Vancouver, BC. The 32-km (20-mile) Seaside Route, which curves around the seawall through False Creek and Stanley Park and then south into Kitsilano, is particularly dramatic.

WHALE-WATCHING
IN THE PACIFIC NORTHWEST

The thrill of seeing whales in the wild is, for many, one of the most enduring memories of a trip to the Pacific Northwest. In this part of the world, you'll generally spot two species—gray whales and killer "orca" whales.

About 20,000 grays migrate up the West Coast in spring and back down again in early winter (a smaller group of gray whales live off the Oregon coast all summer). From late spring through early autumn about 80 orcas inhabit Washington's Puget Sound and BC's Georgia Strait. Although far fewer in number, the orcas live in pods and travel in predictable patterns; therefore chances are high that you will see a pod on any given trip. Some operators claim sighting rates of 90 percent; others offer guaranteed sightings, meaning that you can repeat the tour free of charge until you spot a whale.

COMMON PACIFIC NORTHWEST SPECIES

0   20   40   60   80   100 (ft)

Killer (orca) whale. The killer whale is actually a member of the dolphin family. These white-breasted whales with shiny black dorsal fins live in family-like pods with complex social hierarchies.

Minke whale. The smallest of the great whales, minkes generally feed near the coast and are often spotted around the San Juan Islands and off the coast of Victoria.

Humpback whale. The humpback can leap entirely from the water (known as a full breach). Comparable to gray whales in size, humpbacks are seen most often during spring and fall migrations.

Gray whale. This magnificent creature—noted for its double blowhole—migrates annually between Mexico and the Arctic, making it by far the most common species sighted along the Oregon and Washington coast.

Sperm whale. The only toothed (rather than baleen) great whale, this prodigious animal is observed infrequently because it generally inhabits very deep waters.

Blue whale. Considered the largest animal ever to have lived, the blue whale can weigh up to 200 tons and primarily dwells several miles off-coast, but sightings do occur throughout the Northwest. The whales can blow up to 30 feet in the air.

TAKING A TOUR

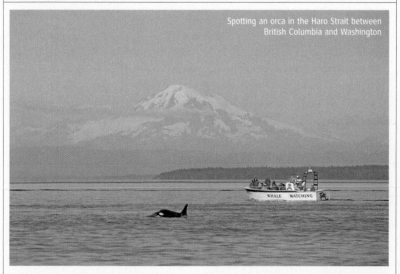
Spotting an orca in the Haro Strait between British Columbia and Washington

CHOOSING YOUR BOAT

The type of boat you choose does not affect how close you can get to the whales. For the safety of whales and humans, government regulations require boats to stay at least 100 meters (328 feet) from the pods, though closer encounters are possible if whales approach a boat when its engine is off.

Motor Launches. These cruisers carry from 30 to more than 80 passengers. They are comfortable, with washrooms, protection from the elements, and even snack-and-drink concessions. They can be either glass-enclosed or open-air.

Zodiacs. Open inflatable boats, Zodiacs carry about 12 passengers. They are smaller and more agile than cruisers and offer both an exciting ride bouncing over the waves and an eye-level view of the whales. Passengers are supplied with warm, waterproof survival suits. Note: Zodiac tours are not recommended for people with back or neck problems, pregnant women, or small children.

Most companies have naturalists on board as guides, as well as hydrophones that, if you get close enough, allow you to listen to the whales singing and vocalizing. Although the focus is on whales, you also have a good chance of spotting marine birds, Dall's porpoises, dolphins, seals, and sea lions, as well as other marine life. And, naturally, there's the scenery of forested islands, distant mountains, and craggy coastline.

MOTION SICKNESS

Seasickness isn't usually a problem in the sheltered waters of Puget Sound and the Georgia Strait, but seas can get choppy off the Washington and Oregon coasts. If you're not a good sailor, it's wise to wear a seasickness band or take anti-nausea medication. Ginger candy often works, too.

THE OREGON AND WASHINGTON COAST

A full breach in open waters is a thrilling sight

WHEN TO GO

Mid-December through mid-January is the best time for viewing the southbound migration, with April through mid-June the peak period for the northbound return (when whales swim closer to shore). Throughout summer, several hundred gray whales remain in Oregon waters, often feeding within close view of land. Mornings are often the best time for viewing, as it's more commonly overcast at this time, which means less glare and calmer seas. Try to watch for vapor or water expelled from whales' spouts on the horizon.

WHAT IT COSTS

Trips are generally 2 hours and prices for adults range from about $25 to $40.

RECOMMENDED OUTFITTERS

Depoe Bay, with its sheltered, deepwater harbor, is Oregon's whale-watching capital, and here you'll find several outfitters.

Dockside Charters (☎ 800/733–8915 ⊕ www. docksidedepoebay.com) and **Tradewind Charters** (☎ 800/445–8730 ⊕ www. tradewindscharters.com) have excellent reputations. Green-oriented **Eco Tours of Oregon** (☎ 888/868–7733, ⊕ www.ecotours-of-oregon. com) offers full day tours that depart from Portland hotels and include a stop along the coast at Siletz Bay, a 75-minute charter boat tour, lunch, and stops at state parks near Newport and Lincoln City.

Along the Washington coast, several of the fishing-charter companies in Westport offer seasonal whale-watching cruises, including **Deep Sea Charters** (☎ 800/562–0151 ⊕ www.deepseacharters.net) and **Ocean Sportfishing Charters** (☎ 800/562–0105, ⊕ www.oceansportfishing. com).

BEST VIEWING FROM SHORE

Washington: On Long Beach Peninsula, the North Head Lighthouse at the mouth of the Columbia River, makes an excellent perch for whale sightings. Westport, farther up the coast at the mouth of Grays Harbor, is another great spot.

Oregon Coast: You can spot gray whales all summer long and especially during the spring migration—excellent locales include Neahkanie Mountain Overlook near Manzanita, Cape Lookout State Park, the Whale Watching Center in Depoe Bay, Cape Perpetua Interpretive Center in Yachats, and Cape Blanco Lighthouse near Port Orford.

PUGET SOUND AND GEORGIA STRAIT

Killer whales in the Puget Sound

WHEN TO GO

Prime time for viewing the three pods of orcas that inhabit this region's waterways is March through September. Less commonly, you may see minke, gray, and humpback whales around the same time.

WHAT IT COSTS

Trips in the San Juan waters are from 3 to 6 hours and prices range from $60 to $120 per adult. Trips in Canada are generally 4 to 6 hours and prices range from $125 to $175 per adult.

RECOMMENDED OUTFITTERS

Many tours depart from Friday Harbor on San Juan Island, among them **Eclipse Charters** (☎ 360/376–6566 ⊕ www.orcasislandwhales. com), **San Juan Excursions** (☎ 800/809–4253 ⊕ www. watchwhales.com), and **Western Prince Cruises** (☎ 800/757–6722 ⊕ www.

orcawhalewatch.com). **San Juan Cruises** (☎ 800/443–4552 ⊕ www.whales.com) offers both day- and overnight whale-watching cruises between Bellingham and Victoria.

One rather fortuitous approach to whale-watching is simply to ride one of the **Washington State Ferries** (☎ 888/808–7977 ⊕ www. wsdot.wa.gov/ferries) out of Anacortes through the San Juans. During the summer killer-whale season, naturalists work on the ferries and talk about the whales and other wildlife.

In Canada, **Wild Whales Vancouver** (☎ 604/699–2011 ⊕ www.whalesvancouver.com) departs from Granville Island on both glass-domed and open-air vessels. **Vancouver Whale Watch** (☎ 604/274–9565 ⊕ www.vancouverwhale-

watch.com) is another first-rate company.

Victoria has an even greater number of whale-watching outfitters. **Great Pacific Adventures** (☎ 877/733–6722 ⊕ www.greatpacificadventures.com), **Springtide Whale Tours** (☎ 800/470–3474 ⊕ www.victoriawhalewatching.com) and **Prince of Whales** (☎ 888/383–4884 ⊕ www.princeofwhales.com) use boats equipped with hydrophones. The latter also offers trips on a 74-passenger cruiser.

BEST VIEWING FROM SHORE

A prime spot for viewing orcas is Lime Kiln State Park, on the west side of San Juan Island. On the Canadian side, you can sometimes see whales right off Oak Bay in Victoria.

CRUISES

Alaska Cruises

During the Alaska cruise season (May–September), Seattle and Vancouver are among North America's busiest ports of embarkation. Ships debarking from these ports proceed directly to Alaska, with one exception: those leaving from Seattle usually make one stop in Victoria or, occasionally, Prince Rupert, BC. Additionally, many of the cruise lines that sail in Alaska (Carnival, Celebrity, Holland America, Norwegian, Princess, Regent Seven Seas, Royal Caribbean, Seabourn, and Silversea are the biggies) stop in Astoria, on the northern Oregon Coast, during their seasonal repositioning cruises, when they move ships between Alaska and California, the Mexican Riviera, or even the Caribbean via the Panama Canal. These cruises typically take place in April or May and then again in October, usually starting or ending in Vancouver or Seattle, and sometimes calling in Victoria; additionally, Norwegian Cruise Line often calls on the BC port of Nanaimo during these repositioning cruises. **Cruise Lines International Association** (⊕ *www.cruising. org*) is a good starting point if you don't have a specific carrier in mind.

Pacific Northwest Cruises

From early April through early November, a few cruise lines with smaller ships offer excursions focused specifically on the Pacific Northwest, usually around the San Juan Islands and Puget Sound (leaving from Seattle), or along the Columbia and Snake rivers (leaving from Portland or Clarkston, WA). **Un-Cruise Adventures** (formerly America Safari Cruises) offers seven-day trips exploring Puget Sound, the Olympic Peninsula, the San Juan Islands, the Gulf Islands, Victoria, and other parts of Vancouver Island; and seven-day excursions (some of them wine themed) along the Columbia and Snake rivers, calling at Richland, Clarkston–Hells Canyon, Walla Walla, The Dalles, Hood River, Bonneville Dam, Portland, and Astoria.

American Cruise Lines runs seven-day excursions along the Columbia and Snake rivers, departing either from Portland or Clarkston (WA), on a Victorian-style stern-wheeler, the *Queen of the West*. The same company offers seven-day Puget Sound cruises out of Seattle that stop at Anacortes, Port Townsend, Poulsbo, Port Angeles, Victoria, BC, and the San Juan Islands. **Bluewater Adventures** provides a number of tours along the coast of British Columbia, with a particular focus on the Gulf Islands and northern Vancouver Island.

Cruise Line Contacts

American Cruise Lines ☎ *800/460–4518* ⊕ *www.americancruiselines.com.*

Bluewater Adventures ☎ *888/877–1770* ⊕ *www.bluewateradventures.ca.*

Un-Cruise Adventures ☎ *888/862–8881* ⊕ *www.un-cruise.com.*

PORTLAND

WELCOME TO PORTLAND

TOP REASONS TO GO

★ **Appreciate the parks:**
Head to Washington Park's Japanese Garden and International Rose Test Garden; stroll along the Willamette in Tom McCall Riverfront Park, or ramble amid the evergreens atop Mt. Tabor.

★ **View works of art:**
Take part in either the First Thursday Pearl District or Last Thursday Alberta Street art walks if you can. Galleries stay open late, often with receptions and openings.

★ **Float on:** Gaze at Portland's gorgeous skyline in the afternoon light, while gently gliding down the Willamette River aboard the *Portland Spirit.*

★ **Sample the liquid assets:** Visit a few of the dozens of superb local producers of craft spirits and beer, artisanal coffee and tea, and fine wine.

★ **Eat locally:** Plenty of visitors to Portland build their entire daily itineraries around eating; food trucks, cafés, and restaurants showcase the city's farm-to-table, locavore ethic.

1 Downtown. At the center of it all, Portland's Downtown boasts the Portland Art Museum, Pioneer Courthouse Square, and the Portland Farmers' Market along with notable restaurants.

2 Old Town/China-town. This is the area for Asian-inspired public art and the Lan Su Chinese Garden. It's also home to the Portland Saturday Market, North America's largest open-air handicraft market.

3 Pearl District. Bordering Old Town to the northwest is Portland's trendy and posh

2

and bars draw a younger but still sophisticated crowd.

5 Forest Park. Forest Park is the largest forested area within city limits in the nation. Trailheads are easily accessible from Nob Hill.

6 North. The "fifth quadrant," North Portland sits on the peninsula formed by the joining of the Willamette River and the Columbia River. Part working-class, part trendy, North Mississippi Avenue and North Williams Street are hip dining and drinking destinations.

7 Northeast. Containing the Rose Garden basketball arena, the Lloyd Center Mall, the Alberta Arts District, and some of the city's poorest and most affluent neighborhoods, Portland's Northeast quadrant is diverse.

8 Southeast. The vibrant pockets of foodie-approved restaurants make the Southeast a Portland cultural must-see. This neighborhood is also kid-friendly with the OMSI science museum and Mount Tabor Park.

9 West Hills and Southwest. This neighborhood is home to Washington Park, which contains the Hoyt Arboretum, International Rose Test Garden, Japanese Garden, and Portland Children's Museum.

GETTING ORIENTED

Geographically speaking, Portland is relatively easy to navigate. The city's 200-foot-long blocks are highly walkable, and mapped out into quadrants. The Willamette River divides east and west and Burnside Street separates north from south. "Northwest" refers to the area north of Burnside and west of the river; "Southwest" refers to the area south of Burnside and west of the river; "Northeast" refers to the area north of Burnside and east of the river; "Southeast" refers to the area south of Burnside and east of the river. As you travel around the Portland metropolitan area, keep in mind that named east and west streets intersect numbered avenues, run north to south, and begin at each side of the river. For instance, Southwest 12th Avenue is 12 blocks west of the Willamette. Most of Downtown's streets are one-way.

neighborhood teaming with upscale restaurants, bars, and shopping, along with pricey condos and artists' lofts. Don't leave Portland without visiting Powell's City of Books here.

4 Nob Hill. From funky to fabulous, this neighborhood's exciting shopping, restaurants,

LLOYD DISTRICT

Memorial Coliseum

Rose Garden Arena

N.E. Holladay St.

Oregon Convention Center

7

TO AIRPORT

N.E. Lloyd Blvd.

N.E. Everett St.

Burnside Bridge

E. Burnside St.

S.W. Ankeny St.

S.E. Ash St.

Tom McCall Waterfront Park

S.E. Belmont St.

BUCKMAN DISTRICT

S.E. Main St.

Morrison Bridge

S.E. Madison St.

Hawthorne Bridge

S.E. Hawthorne Blvd.

S.E. Clay St.

S.E. Market St.

TO HAWTHORNE DISTRICT

EAST OF WILLAMETTE RIVER

Updated by Andrew Collins

What distinguishes Portland, Oregon, from the rest of America's cityscapes? Or from the rest of the world's urban destinations for that matter? In a Northwest nutshell: everything. For some, it's the wealth of cultural offerings and never-ending culinary choices; for others, it's Portland's proximity to the ocean and mountains, or simply the beauty of having all these attributes in one place.

Strolling through Downtown or within one of Portland's numerous neighborhoods, there's an unmistakable vibrancy to this city—one that is encouraged by clean air, infinite trees, and a blend of historic and modern architecture. Portland's various nicknames—Rose City, Bridgetown, Beervana, Brewtopia—tell its story in a nutshell.

Rich cultural offerings, prime historic and modern architecture, endless recreational activities, and a friendly feel make Portland alluring for just about everyone. But it seems that Portland's food scene is one of its biggest attractions these days. It's true that Portland's filled with amazing restaurants—though it's not necessarily the recipes that are causing all the commotion. Rather, it's the "locavore" movement—using ingredients that are raised, grown, or foraged within a reasonable distance—that's got diners and chefs excited. Often, diners experience savory fish, fowl, or pasta dishes made with seasonal fruit and vegetable accompaniments that have just been plucked from the vine or ground.

PORTLAND PLANNER

WHEN TO GO

Portland's mild climate is best from June through September. Hotels are often filled in July and August, so it's important to book reservations in advance. Spring and fall are also excellent times to visit. The weather usually remains quite good, and the prices for accommodations, transportation, and tours can be lower (and the crowds much smaller) in the most popular destinations. In winter, snow is uncommon in the city but abundant in the nearby mountains, making the region a skier's dream.

Average daytime summer highs are in the 70s; winter temperatures are generally in the 40s. Rainfall varies greatly from one locale to another. In the coastal mountains, for example, 160 inches of rain fall annually, creating temperate rain forests. Portland has an average of only 36 inches of rainfall a year—less than New York, Chicago, or Miami. In winter, however, the rain may never seem to end. More than 75% of Portland's annual precipitation occurs from October through March.

GETTING HERE AND AROUND

AIR TRAVEL

It takes about five hours to fly nonstop to Portland from New York, four hours from Chicago and Atlanta, and 2½ hours from Los Angeles. Flying to Seattle takes just under an hour, and flying to Vancouver takes just over an hour.

Portland International Airport (PDX) is an efficient, modern airport with service to most major national and a handful of international destinations. It's a relatively uncrowded facility, and both check-in and security lines tend to proceed quickly. It's also easily accessible from Downtown Portland, both by car and public transit.

Portland International Airport *(PDX).* This is the city's—and the region's— major airport. You'll find a pretty good selection of local restaurants and shops inside the terminal. ✉ *7000 N.E. Airport Way, Portland* ☎ *877/739–4636* ⊕ *www.pdx.com.*

GROUND TRANSPORTATION

Taking the MAX, Portland's light rail train, to and from Portland International Airport is straightforward. The Red Line MAX stops right at the terminal, and the approximately 35- to 45-minute ride to Downtown costs $2.50. Trains run daily from early morning until around midnight—MAX won't be available to some very late-arriving passengers, but it generally runs early enough to catch even the first flights of the day out of Portland, which typically depart around 6 am. You purchase your ticket before boarding at one of the vending machines located in the terminal and at every MAX stop; tickets are also good on TriMet buses and the Portland Streetcar, and transfers within two hours of the time of purchase are free.

Contacts TriMet/MAX ☎ *503/238–7433* ⊕ *www.trimet.org.*

CAR TRAVEL

Portland is a fairly easy city to navigate by car, and if you're planning to explore neighboring regions—such as the coast, Willamette Wine Country, and Columbia Gorge—it's best to do so by car, as public transportation options to these areas, especially the coast, is limited. That said, parking Downtown can get expensive and a car isn't necessary for getting around the city itself. One practical strategy is going without a car during the days you plan to spend in the city center, and then renting a car just for those days when you're venturing outside of the city or exploring some of the East Side neighborhoods, which have ample free parking. Most major rental agencies have Downtown offices, and renting Downtown can save you plenty of money, as you avoid paying the hefty taxes and surcharges that airport agencies charge.

Portland is easily reached via the West Coast's major interstate highway, Interstate 5, which connects Portland to Seattle (which is a three hours' drive north) and Eugene (a little over two hours' drive south). Interstate 84 begins in Downtown Portland and runs east into the Columbia Gorge and eventually to Idaho. U.S. 26 is the main route to the Oregon Coast west from Downtown, and to Mt. Hood going east. Bypass freeways are Interstate 205, which links Interstate 5 and Interstate 84 before crossing the Columbia River north into Washington, and Interstate 405, which arcs around western Downtown. Most city-center streets are one way, and some Downtown streets—including 5th and 6th avenues—are limited primarily to bus and MAX traffic (with just one lane for cars, and limited turns).

PARKING Compared with other major U.S. cities, Portland has ample parking, even Downtown, both metered and in garages. The most affordable and accessible option is to park in one of several city-owned "Smart Park" lots. Rates start at $1.60 per hour (short-term parking, four hours or less) to $5 per hour (long-term parking, weekdays 5 am–6 pm), with a $15 daily maximum; weekends and evenings have lower rates. The best part about Smart Park is that hundreds of participating merchants validate tickets, covering the first two hours of parking when you spend at least $25 in their establishments.

There are numerous privately owned lots around the city as well; fees for these vary and can be quite pricey, and Downtown hotels also charge significantly (as much as $30 to $40 nightly).

Downtown street parking is metered only, and enforcement is vigilant. You can use cash or a credit card to pay ($1.60 per hour) at machines located on each block; display your receipt on the inside of your curbside window. Metered spaces are mostly available for one to three hours, with a few longer-term spaces available on certain streets.

Outside of the Downtown core, you'll find plenty of free street parking, although time limits (usually an hour to three hours) are enforced in some busier, commercial parts of town. You can find a number of streets with unmetered parking relatively close to Downtown, by heading west of the Pearl District and north of Burnside Street, in Nob Hill and environs. On the east side of the river, unmetered parking is the norm.

TAXI TRAVEL

Taxi fare is $2.50 at flag drop plus $2.60 per mile; each additional passenger is charged $1. Cabs sometimes cruise Downtown streets, but it's far more reliable to phone for one. The major companies are Broadway Cab, New Rose City Cab, Portland Taxi Company, and Radio Cab. The trip between Downtown Portland and the airport takes about 30 minutes by taxi, and the fare averages $35–$40.

Taxi Contacts Broadway Cab ☎ 503/333-3333 ⊕ www.broadwaycab. com **New Rose City Cab** ☎ 503/282-7707 ⊕ www.newrosecitycabco.biz **Portland Taxi Company** ☎ 503/256-5400 ⊕ www.portlandtaxi.net. **Radio Cab** ☎ 503/227-1212 ⊕ www.radiocab.net.

TRIMET/MAX TRAVEL

TriMet operates an extensive system of buses, streetcars, and light-rail trains. The Central City streetcar line runs from Nob Hill through the Pearl District, Downtown, and Portland State University campus to South Waterfront. From the Pearl District, the Central Loop streetcar line crosses the Willamette River to the East Side, stopping at the Oregon Convention Center and continuing south to the Oregon Museum of Science and Industry (OMSI). Eventually, the streetcar will cross back to the West Side from just south of OMSI to South Waterfront via the new Tilikum Crossing transit-pedestrian bridge, which is expected to open in September 2015. At first, the bridge will be open only to buses and MAX light rail, but eventual plans call for the streetcar to use the bridge, too.

Metropolitan Area Express, which everybody simply calls MAX, links the eastern and western Portland suburbs with Downtown, Washington Park and the Oregon Zoo, the Lloyd Center district, the Convention Center, and the Rose Quarter. Once the new Tilikum Crossing Bridge opens in fall 2015, an extension of Downtown's MAX Green line will bring service to Southeast Division Street, Sellwood, and the suburbs south of the city. From Downtown, trains operate daily from about 5 am–1 am, with a fare of $2.50 for up to two hours of travel (transfers to other MAX trains, buses, and streetcars are free within this time period), and $5 for an unlimited all-day ticket, which is also good system-wide. A seven-day visitor pass is also available for $26. The ticket for riding without a fare is stiff.

Upon boarding TriMet buses, the driver will hand you a transfer ticket that's good for up to two hours, on all buses, MAX trains, and streetcars. Be sure to hold onto it whether you're transferring or not; it also serves as proof that you have paid your fare. The most central bus routes operate every 10 to 15 minutes throughout the day. Bikes are allowed in designated areas of MAX trains, and there are bike racks on the front of all buses that everyone is free to use.

Contacts TriMet/MAX ⊠ *Ticket Office at Pioneer Courthouse Square, 701 S.W. 6th Ave., Downtown* ☎ *503/238–7433* ⊕ *www.trimet.org.*

TOURS

BIKE TOURS

Portland is famously bike-friendly, with miles of dedicated bike lanes and numerous rental shops *(see the Sports and the Outdoors chapter for more details)*. There are also a couple of great companies that offer guided rides around the city, covering everything from eating and brewpub-hopping to checking out local parks and historic neighborhoods.

Cycle Portland Bike Tours and Rentals. Trust your guide at Cycle Portland to know Portland's popular and lesser-known spots. Tour themes include Essential Portland, Taste of Portland, Breweries by Bike, and several others. A well-stocked bike shop is on-site and serves beer on tap. Bike and helmet are included with tours. ⊠ *117 N.W. 2nd Ave., Old Town/Chinatown* ☎ *503/902–5035, 844/739–2453* ⊕ *www. portlandbicycletours.com* ⧉ *From $40.*

FAMILY **Pedal Bike Tours.** This reliable company takes riders into the heart of the city and out to the beauty that surrounds it, from the Columbia Gorge to the Willamette wine country. If one of the many tours offered here doesn't meet your criteria, custom tours are available, too. Bikes and helmets are included with each tour. ⊠ *133 S.W. 2nd Ave., Downtown* ☎ *503/243–2453* ⊕ *www.pedalbiketours.com* ⬚ *From $49.*

BOAT TOURS

Portland Spirit River Cruises. Two major rivers lined with pleasant scenery make Portland Spirit River Cruises an engaging tour option. There are brunch, lunch, and dinner cruises, as well as those centered on themes like holidays, tea parties, or live music. Some cruises have a sightseeing option that doesn't include the meal and are less expensive. The company also offers high-speed Explorer Cruises from June through September, which take in about 120 miles of sights along both the Willamette and Columbia rivers; these depart and return to Downtown Portland. Additionally, departing from the town of Cascade Locks (a one-hour drive east of Portland), the stern-wheeler *Columbia Gorge* cruises the Columbia Gorge. ⊠ *Foot of S.W. Salmon St., at Tom McCall Waterfront Park, Downtown* ☎ *503/224–3900, 800/224–3901* ⊕ *www.portlandspirit.com* ⬚ *From $28.*

WALKING TOURS

Walk the Portland beat with guides who share their personal Portland knowledge, including history, food, brews, arts, and sights.

Food Carts Portland. Get to know the city's famed food-cart scene by tagging along with Brett Burmeister, a true expert on the subject. This 90-minute tour is not just a great way to sample bites from some favorite carts, but also an opportunity to learn more about the culture behind the carts. The tour starts at a predetermined Downtown food cart. ✍ *tours@foodcartsportland.com* ⊕ *www.foodcartsportland.com/tours* ⬚ *From $37.50.*

Portland Walking Tours. A slew of tours are offered by this well-established company, but it's the Beyond Bizarre tour that generates the most buzz. Ghost-hunter wannabes and paranormal junkies make this a popular tour that often sells out during the peak season. If it's unavailable, there's also the Underground Portland tour, which highlights the sinister history of Portland, along with a few other options, including tours that focus on the local food scene. Departure points vary depending on the tour. ☎ *503/774–4522* ⊕ *www.portlandwalkingtours.com* ⬚ *From $20.*

VISITOR INFORMATION

Travel Portland Information Center ⊠ *Pioneer Courthouse Square, 701 S.W. 6th Ave., Downtown* ☎ *503/275–8355, 877/678–5263* ⊕ *www.travelportland.com* ⊙ *May–Oct., weekdays 8:30–5:30, Sat. 10–4, Sun. 10–2; Nov.–Apr., weekdays 8:30–5:30, Sat. 10–4.*

EXPLORING

One of the greatest things about Portland is that there's so much to explore. This city rightfully boasts that there's something for everyone. What makes discovering Portland's treasures even more enticing is that its attractions, transportation options, and events are all relatively accessible and affordable.

DOWNTOWN

Portland has one of the most attractive, inviting Downtown centers in the United States. It's clean, compact, and filled with parks, plazas, and fountains. Architecture fans find plenty to admire in its mix of old and new. Whereas many urban U.S. business districts clear out at night and on weekends, Portland's Downtown is decidedly mixed-use, with plenty of residential and commercial buildings, and an appealing mix of hotels, shops, museums, restaurants, and bars. You can easily walk from one end of Downtown to the other, and the city's superb public transportation system—which includes MAX light rail, buses, and the streetcar—makes it easy to get here from other parts of the city. A day pass is recommended.

TOP ATTRACTIONS

FAMILY

Fodor'sChoice

★

Governor Tom McCall Waterfront Park. Named for a former governor revered for his statewide land-use planning initiatives, this park stretches north along the Willamette River for about a mile from near the historic Hawthorne Bridge to Steel Bridge. Broad and grassy, Waterfront Park affords a fine ground-level view of Downtown Portland's bridges and skyline. Once an expressway, it's now the site for many annual celebrations, among them the Rose Festival, classical and blues concerts, Gay Pride, Cinco de Mayo, and the Oregon Brewers Festival. The arching jets of water at the **Salmon Street Fountain** change configuration every few hours, and are a favorite cooling-off spot during the dog days of summer. ■ TIP➔ Both the Hawthorne Bridge and Steel Bridge offer dedicated pedestrian lanes, allowing joggers, cyclists, and strollers to make a full loop along both banks of the river, via Vera Katz Eastside Esplanade. ⊠ *S. W. Naito Pkwy. (Front Ave.), from south of Steel Bridge to south of Hawthorne Bridge, Downtown* ⊕ *www. portlandoregon.gov/parks.*

Oregon History Museum. Impressive eight-story-high trompe l'oeil murals of Lewis and Clark and the Oregon Trail invite history lovers into this Downtown museum that is operated by the Oregon Historical Society and relates the state's story from prehistoric times to the present. A pair of 9,000-year-old sagebrush sandals, a covered wagon, and an early chainsaw are displayed in "Oregon My Oregon," a permanent exhibit that provides a comprehensive overview of the state's past. Other spaces host large traveling exhibits and changing regional shows. The center's research library is open to the public Tuesday through Saturday; its bookstore is a good source for maps and publications on Pacific Northwest history. ⊠ *1200 S.W. Park Ave., Downtown* ☎ *503/222–1741* ⊕ *www.ohs.org* ☝ *$11* ☉ *Mon.–Sat. 10–5, Sun. noon–5.*

Downtown

← TO JELD-WEN FIELD

S.W. Pine St.

S.W. Oak St.

S.W. Washington St.

S.W. Alder St.

S.W. Stark St.

MAX LIGHT RAIL

S.W. 12th Ave.

S.W. 11th Ave.

S.W. 10th Ave.

S.W. 9th Ave.

S.W. Park Ave.

6th Ave.

Transit Mall

5th Ave.

Transit Mall

S.W. 4th Ave.

S.W. 3rd Ave.

S.W. 2nd Ave.

MAX LIGHT RAIL

❷

S.W. Morrison St.

S.W. Yamhill St.

S.W. Taylor St.

CENTRAL CITY STREETCAR

S.W. Main St.

BUS

S.W. Salmon St.

First ◆ Congregationalist Church

❸

❹

S.W. 3rd Ave.

S.W. Main St.

S.W. 1st Ave.

S.W. Natlo Pkwy. (Front Ave.)

GOVERNOR TOM McCALL WATERFRONT PARK

❺

South Park Blocks

S.W. Broadway

S.W. 6th Ave.

S.W. 5th Ave.

S.W. 4th Ave.

S.W. Madison St.

S.W. Jefferson St.

Hawthorne Bridge

26

26

❻

S.W. 2nd Ave.

S.W. Columbia St.

S.W. Clay St.

❼

S.W. Market St.

S.W. Mill St.

Willamette River

Harrison St.

KEY

- ⊶ Max Light Rail
- ←- Streetcar
- ········ Bus
- 🚲 Bike only

0 ————— 1/4 mile

0 ————— 1/4 kilometer

Pioneer Square, Downtown

Pioneer Courthouse Square. Often billed as the living room, public heart, and commercial soul of Downtown, Pioneer Square is not entirely square, but rather an amphitheater-like brick piazza. Special seasonal, charitable, and festival-oriented events often take place in this premier people-watching venue, although over the years, as other parts of Downtown (the Park Blocks, the Pearl District) have become more trendy, the square has lost a bit of its prominence. Directly across the street is one of Downtown Portland's most familiar landmarks, the classically sedate **Pioneer Courthouse**, built in 1869, it's the oldest public building in the Pacific Northwest. A couple of blocks east of the square, you'll find **Pioneer Place Mall**, an upscale retail center that spans four city blocks. ⊠ *701 S.W. 6th Ave., Downtown* ⊕ *www.thesquarepdx.org*

Fodor's Choice
★
Portland Art Museum. The treasures at the Pacific Northwest's oldest arts facility span 35 centuries of Asian, European, and American art—it's an impressive collection for a midsize city. A high point is the Center for Native American Art, with regional and contemporary art from more than 200 tribes. The **Jubitz Center for Modern and Contemporary Art** contains six floors devoted entirely to modern art, including a small but superb photography gallery, with the changing selection chosen from more than 400 pieces in the museum's permanent collection. The film center presents the annual Portland International Film Festival in February and the Northwest Filmmakers' Festival in early November. Also, take a moment to linger in the peaceful outdoor sculpture garden. Kids under 17 are admitted free. ⊠ *1219 S.W. Park Ave., Downtown* ☎ *503/226–2811, 503/221–1156 film schedule* ⊕ *www.*

portlandartmuseum.org ✉ *$15* ⊙ *Tues., Wed., and Sat. 10–5, Thurs. and Fri. 10–8, Sun. noon–5.*

Fodor'sChoice
★ **Portland Farmers' Market.** On Saturday from mid-March through mid-December, local farmers, bakers, chefs, and entertainers converge at the South Park Blocks near the PSU campus for Oregon's largest open-air farmers' market—it's one of the most impressive in the country. It's a great place to sample the regional bounty and to witness the local-food obsession that's revolutionized Portland's culinary scene. There's plenty of food you can eat on the spot, plus nonperishable local items (wine, hazelnuts, chocolates, vinegars) you can take home with you. There's a smaller Wednesday market, May through November, on a different section of the Park blocks (between Southwest Salmon and Southwest Main). On Monday, June through August, the market is held at Pioneer Courthouse Square, and at other times the Portland Farmers' Market is held in different locations around town (check the website for details). ✉ *South Park Blocks at S.W. Park Ave. and Montgomery St., Downtown* ☎ *503/241–0032* ⊕ *www.portlandfarmersmarket.org* ⊙ *Mid-Mar.–mid-Dec., Sat. 8:30–2; May–Oct., Mon. and Wed. 10–2.*

West End. A formerly rough-around-the-edges section of Downtown, sandwiched between the Pioneer Square area and the swanky Pearl District, this triangular patch of vintage buildings—interspersed with a handful of contemporary ones—has evolved since the early 2000s into one of the city's most vibrant and eclectic hubs of retail, nightlife, and dining. Hip boutique hotels like the Ace, McMenamins Crystal, and Sentinel rank among the city's trendiest addresses. Along Stark Street, formerly the heart of Portland's LGBT scene, there are still a couple of gay bars, but now you'll also find noteworthy restaurants and lounges. ✉ *S.W. 13th to S.W. 9th Aves., between W. Burnside St. and S.W. Alder St., Downtown* ⊕ *www.wepdx.com.*

WORTH NOTING

Portland State University. The only public university in the city takes advantage of Downtown's South Park Blocks to provide trees and greenery for its 29,500 students. The attractive, compact, but steadily growing campus, between Market Street and Interstate 405, spreads west from the Park Blocks to 12th Avenue and east to 5th Avenue. Seven schools offer undergraduate, master's, and doctoral degrees. Close to the Portland Art Museum and Oregon History Museum at the Oregon Historical Society, PSU doesn't have any major attractions of its own, but the campus blends almost imperceptibly with a pretty part of Downtown, and it's the site—along the leafy South Park Blocks—of the city's largest farmers' market on Saturday mornings. ✉ *Park Ave. and Market St., Downtown* ☎ *503/725–3000* ⊕ *www.pdx.edu.*

OLD TOWN/CHINATOWN

The Skidmore Old Town National Historic District, commonly called Old Town/Chinatown, is where Portland was born. The 20-square-block section, bounded by Oak Street to the south and Hoyt Street to the north, includes buildings of varying ages and architectural designs. Before it was renovated, this was skid row. Vestiges of it remain in parts of Chinatown; older buildings are gradually being remodeled, and lately the immediate area has experienced a small surge in development. Portland doesn't have a gay district per se—the scene permeates just about every neighborhood of this extremely LGBT-welcoming city. But you will find many of Portland's gay nightspots in Old Town (and a few others close by in Downtown's West End). MAX serves the area with a stop at the Old Town/Chinatown station.

Fodor's Choice
★
Lan Su Chinese Garden. In a twist on the Joni Mitchell song, the city of Portland and private donors took down a parking lot and unpaved paradise when they created this wonderland near the Pearl District and Old Town/Chinatown. It's the largest Suzhou-style garden outside China, with a large lake, bridged and covered walkways, koi- and water lily–filled ponds, rocks, bamboo, statues, waterfalls, and courtyards. A team of 60 artisans and designers from China literally left no stone unturned—500 tons of stone were brought here from Suzhou—in their efforts to give the windows, roof tiles, gateways, including a "moongate," and other architectural aspects of the garden some specific meaning or purpose. Also on the premises are a gift shop and a two-story teahouse, operated by Portland's esteemed Tao of Tea company, overlooking the lake and garden. ⊠ *239 N.W. Everett St., Old Town/Chinatown* ☎ *503/228–8131* ⊕ *www.lansugarden.org* ☜ *$9.50* ☼ *mid-Oct.–mid-Apr., daily 10–5; mid-Apr.–mid-Oct., daily 10–6.*

FAMILY
Oregon Maritime Museum. Local model makers created most of this museum's models of ships that once plied the Columbia River. Contained within the stern-wheeler steamship *Portland*, this small museum provides an excellent overview of Oregon's maritime history with artifacts and memorabilia. The Children's Room has nautical items that can be touched and operated. The *Portland* was the last steam-powered stern-wheel tugboat operating in the United States, and volunteer-guided tours include the pilothouse and engine room. ⊠ *Portland steamship, end of S.W. Pine St., in Tom McCall Waterfront Park, Old Town/Chinatown* ☎ *503/224–7724* ⊕ *www.oregonmaritimemuseum.org* ☜ *$7* ☼ *Wed., Fri., and Sat. 11–4.*

FAMILY
Fodor's Choice
★
Portland Saturday Market. On weekends from March to Christmas, the west side of the Burnside Bridge and the Skidmore Fountain area hosts North America's largest ongoing open-air handicraft market. If you're looking for jewelry, yard art, housewares, and decorative goods made from every material under the sun, then there's an amazing collection of works by talented artisans on display here. Entertainers and food booths add to the festive feel (although be careful not to mistake this market for the food-centric PSU Portland Farmers' Market, which also takes place on Saturday, on the other side of Downtown). If taking the MAX train to the market, get off at the Skidmore Fountain stop. ⊠ *2 S.W. Naito Pkwy. at foot of S.W. Ankeny, in Tom McCall Waterfront Park, Old Town/Chinatown* ☎ *503/222–6072* ⊕ *www.portlandsaturdaymarket.com* ☼ *Mar.–Dec., Sat. 10–5, Sun. 11–4:30.*

Pearl District and Nob Hill

NOB HILL

PEARL DISTRICT

Vivace Coffee

Tanner Springs Park

Amtrak

TO BROADWAY BRIDGE

PGE Park

0   1/4 mile

0   1/4 kilometer

KEY

– ← – Sreetcar

Quimby St., Nob Hill ☎ *503/224–3483* ⊕ *www.bullrundistillery.com/* ⊙ *Wed.–Sun. noon–6.*

Fodor'sChoice ★   **Clear Creek Distillery.** A pioneer in what has become an internationally acclaimed local distillery scene, this producer of high-quality spirits is tucked down a quiet street in an industrial area just north of Nob Hill. Just ring the bell and someone will unlock the wrought-iron gate and let you into a cozy tasting room where you can sample Clear Creek's world-famous Oregon apple and pear brandies, distinctive Douglas Fir Eau de Vie, and other liqueurs and grappas. ■**TIP→ If the peaty, highly prized McCarthy's Oregon Single Malt Whiskey is available, grab a bottle—they sell out fast.** ⊠ *2389 N.W. Wilson St., Nob Hill* ☎ *503/248–9470* ⊕ *www.clearcreekdistillery.com* ⊙ *Mon.–Sat. 9–5.*

FOREST PARK

One of the largest city parks in the country, Forest Park stretches eight miles along the hills overlooking the Willamette River west of Downtown. More than 70 miles of trails through forests of Douglas fir, hemlock, and cedar (including a few patches of old growth) offer numerous options for those looking to log some miles or spend some time outside.

Fodor's Choice ★ **Forest Park.** One of the nation's largest urban wildernesses (5,170 acres), this city-owned, car-free park has more than 50 species of birds and mammals and more than 80 miles of trails through forests of Douglas fir, hemlock, and cedar. Running the length of the park is the 30-mile Wildwood Trail, which extends into adjoining Washington Park (and is a handy point for accessing Forest Park), starting at the Vietnam Veteran's Memorial in Hoyt Arboretum. You can access a number of spur trails from the Wildwood Trail, including the 11-mile Leif Erikson Drive, which picks up from the end of Northwest Thurman Street and is a popular route for jogging and mountain biking. ■TIP→ **You can find information and maps at the Forest Park Conservancy office and website.** ⊠ *Forest Park Conservancy, 1505 N.W. 23rd Ave., West Hills* ☎ *503/223–5449* ⊕ *www.forestparkconservancy.org* ⊘ *Daily 5 am–10 pm*

NORTH

Long dismissed as the city's "fifth quadrant," North Portland has come into its own in recent years, as the comparatively low cost of real estate has made it popular with young entrepreneurs, students, and other urban pioneers. Marked by a 31-foot-tall roadside statue of the strapping lumberman Paul Bunyan (on the National Register of Historic Places), the neighborhood occupies the peninsula formed by the confluence of the Willamette River (to the west) and the Columbia River (to the north). In the working-class, portside neighborhood of St. Johns, old-school barbershops and hardware stores sit alongside a steadily growing mix of hipster-favored shops, restaurants, and cafés. Farther south (and closer to Downtown), North Mississippi and North Williams avenues, which are about 10 short blocks apart, have become home to some of the hottest food, drink, and music venues in the city.

Fodor's Choice ★ **North Mississippi Avenue.** One of North Portland's strips of indie retailers, the liveliest section of North Mississippi Avenue stretches for several blocks and includes a mix of old storefronts and sleek new buildings that house cafés, collectives, shops, music venues, and an excellent food-cart pod, Mississippi Marketplace. Bioswale planter boxes, found-object fences, and café tables built from old doors are some of the innovations you'll see along this eclectic thoroughfare. At the southern end of the strip, stop by the ReBuilding Center, an outlet for recycled building supplies that has cob (clay-and-straw) trees and benches built into the facade. About a 10-minute walk east and running parallel to North Mississippi, the bike-friendly North Williams corridor is an even newer thoroughfare of almost entirely new, eco-friendly buildings rife with trendy restaurants, nightspots, and boutiques. To get here on MAX light rail, get off at the Albina/Mississippi station. ⊠ *N. Mississippi Ave. between N. Fremont and N. Skidmore Sts., Boise, North.*

NORTHEAST

Containing the Rose Garden basketball arena, the Oregon Convention Center, Lloyd Center Mall, the Alberta Arts District, and some of the city's poorest and most affluent neighborhoods, Portland's Northeast

Northeast and Southeast

N. E. Killingsworth St.

N. E. Alberta St.

TO AIRPORT →

N. E. Prescott St.

N. E. Fremont St.

N. E. Knott St.

N. E. Russell St.

99E

N. E. Broadway

Weidler St.

Lloyd Center

HOLLYWOOD

Halsey St.

TO I-205 →

Memorial Coliseum

Rose Garden Arena

Oregon Convention Center

30 84

N.E. Glisan St.

E. Burnside St.

S. E. Stark St.

S. E. Belmont St.

S. E. Yamill St.

N. Mississippi Ave.

Martin Luther King Jr. Blvd.

N. E. 33rd Ave.

N. E. 42nd Ave.

N. E. Cully Blvd.

N. E. 57th Ave.

N. E. Sandy Blvd.

S. E. Madison St.

S. E. Hawthorne Blvd.

Mt. Tabor Park

N.W. Naito Pkwy. (Front Ave.)

M. L. King Jr. Blvd.

Grand Ave.

S. E. 20th Ave.

S. E. 28th Ave.

S. E. 30th Ave.

S. E. 60th Ave.

S. E. Division St.

S. E. Powell Blvd.

26

S. E. 50th Ave.

1 miles

1 kilometers

26

99E

S-W. Naito Pkwy. (Front Ave.)

S.-W. Macadam Ave.

Ross Island

43

Willamette River

Oaks Bottom Wildlife Refuge

S. E. Milwaukee Ave.

S. E. Mcloughlin Blvd.

S. E. Holgate Blvd.

Eastmoreland General Hospital

Reed College

S. E. Woodstock Blvd.

S. E. 72nd Ave.

S. E. 82nd Ave.

Lents Park

S. E. Bybee Blvd.

EASTMORELAND

S. E. 13th Ave.

S. E. 52nd Ave.

205

S. E. Tacoma St.

quadrant is diverse to say the least. Still the epicenter of the city's relatively small—compared with other U.S. cities the size of Portland—African American community, the inner parts of Northeast have slowly gentrified over the last half century. In the Irvington, Laurelhurst, and Alameda neighborhoods, you'll find some of the largest, most historic homes in town.

Lined with many excellent—and generally quite affordable—restaurants, bars, galleries, and boutiques, Alberta Street has become one of the city's trendiest neighborhoods. It also hosts a bustling street art fair the last Thursday of every month during summer (primarily between 12th and 31st avenues). Nearer to Downtown, the Lloyd Center—both the name of a rather prosaic shopping mall and the surrounding neighborhood (containing the Oregon Convention Center and Rose Garden) is an unfortunately drab example of late-20th-century urban renewal. The area serves a purpose, as it's home to the bulk of the East Side's hotels, but it lacks the historic charm and indie spirit of other neighborhoods on this side of the river.

EXPLORING

East Burnside and 28th Avenue. A roughly T-shaped dining and retail district that's less defined but no less popular and impressive than some of the East Side's other culinary and shopping hot spots (like N.E. Alberta and Division Streets), this diverse neighborhood comprises a slew of mostly food-related ventures along East Burnside Street from about 22nd to 28th avenues. Then, where Burnside meets 28th Avenue, you'll find several blocks of first-rate eateries as well as a handful of boutiques in either direction, heading north up to about Glisan Street and south down to about Stark Street. The neighborhood isn't close to any light-rail stops, but you can get here easily from Downtown via Bus 20, and street parking is free and abundant. ⊠ *E. Burnside St. from 22nd to 28th Aves., and 28th Ave. from N.E. Glisan to S.E. Stark Sts., Kerns, Northeast.*

The Grotto. Owned by the Catholic Church, the National Sanctuary of Our Sorrowful Mother, as it's officially known, displays more than 100 statues and shrines in 62 acres of woods. The grotto was carved into the base of a 110-foot cliff, and has a replica of Michelangelo's *Pietà*. The real treat is found after ascending the cliff face via elevator, as you enter a wonderland of gardens, sculptures, and shrines, and a glass-walled cathedral with an awe-inspiring view of the Columbia River and the Cascades. There's a dazzling Festival of Lights at Christmastime (late November and December), with 500,000 lights and more than 150 holiday concerts in the 600-seat chapel. Daily masses are held here, too. ■ TIP→ **Hours can vary seasonally so call ahead if visiting late in the day.** ⊠ *8840 N.E. Skidmore St. Main entrance: N.E. Sandy Blvd. at N.E. 85th Ave., Northeast* 🕾 *503/254–7371* ⊕ *www.thegrotto.org* 🎟 *Plaza level free; elevator to upper level $4.50* ⊙ *Daily 9–sunset.*

■ NEED A
BREAK?

Pix Patisserie. In a handsome café and bar with a small patio along East Burnside Street, Pix is famous for its sweet treats, including passion-fruit macarons and dark-chocolate truffles. The adjoining Bar Vivant serves authentic Spanish tapas and has one of the most impressive selections

of champagne in the country. ⊠ *2225 E. Burnside St., Kerns, Northeast*
☎ *971/271-7166* ⊕ *www.pixpatisserie.com.*

Fodor'sChoice   **Northeast Alberta Street.** Few of Portland's several hipster-favored East
★   Side neighborhoods have developed as quickly and as interestingly as
Northeast Alberta Street, aka Northeast Alberta, aka the Alberta Arts
District, which has morphed from a downcast area into a funky strip of
hippie-driven counterculture into a considerably more eclectic stretch
of both indie arts spaces and downright sophisticated bistros and galleries. Extending a little more than a mile, Northeast Alberta offers
plenty of one-of-a-kind dining and shopping; you'll find virtually no
national chains along here. The area is also home to some of the best
people-watching in Portland, especially during the Last Thursday (of the
month) art walks, held May–September from 6 pm until 9:30 pm. The
Alberta Street Fair in August showcases the neighborhood's offerings
with arts-and-crafts displays and street performances. ■TIP➜ **Northeast Alberta is about a mile from the smaller but similarly intriguing
North Mississippi and North Williams corridors; fans of indie dining
and shopping could easily spend a full day strolling or biking among
both areas.** ⊠*N.E. Alberta St. between N.E. Martin Luther King Jr.
Blvd. and N.E. 30th Ave., Alberta Arts District, Northeast* ⊕*www.
albertamainst.org.*

SOUTHEAST

Bounded on the west by the Willamette River and on the north by Burnside Avenue, the city's Southeast quadrant comprises several of Portland's
hottest and hippest neighborhoods. Packed with shade trees, Craftsman-
style houses, and backyard chicken coops, this neighborhood is industrial close in (the river to 7th)—an increasingly trendy food and retail
district known as the Central Eastside, which has also lately blossomed
with top-quality artisanal distilleries and urban wineries—and middle- to
upper-middle-class residential farther out (8th to 82nd). You'll encounter vibrant pockets of foodie-driven restaurants—as well as bars, coffeehouses, markets, food-cart pods, and boutiques—along east–west
running Division, Hawthorne, Belmont, Stark, and Burnside streets,
making Southeast a Portland cultural must-see. Other Southeast highlights include the Eastbank Esplanade on the Willamette River (which
connects with Downtown via several historic bridges), the kid-focused
science museum Oregon Museum of Science and Industry (OMSI), and
the beautiful park at Mt. Tabor, an inactive volcanic cinder cone.

TOP ATTRACTIONS

Fodor'sChoice   **Division Street.** Back in the early 1970s, Division Street (or "Southeast
★   Division," as many locals call it) was earmarked for condemnation as
part of a proposed—and thankfully never built—freeway that would
have connected Downtown to Mt. Hood. For many years, this street
sat forlornly, just a long stretch of modest buildings and empty lots.
These days, Southeast Division—no longer threatened with condemnation—is one of the hottest restaurant rows in the city, perhaps even the
Western United States, and sleek three- and four-story contemporary
condos and apartments are popping up like dandelions. Bus 4 crosses

the Hawthorne Bridge from Downtown and continues along Division Street; there's also plenty of free street parking in the neighborhood. ⊠ *S.E. Division St. from 30th to 39th Aves., Southeast.*

Fodor'sChoice ★ **Hawthorne District.** Stretching from the foot of Mt. Tabor to Southeast 12th Avenue, with some blocks far livelier than others, this eclectic commercial thoroughfare was at the forefront of Portland's hippie and LGBT scenes in the '60s and '70s. As the rest of Portland's East Side has become more urbane and popular among hipsters, young families, students, and the so-called creative class over the years, Hawthorne has retained an arty, homegrown flavor. An influx of trendy eateries and shops opening alongside the still-colorful and decidedly low-frills thrift shops and old-school taverns and cafés make for a hodgepodge of styles and personalities—you could easily spend an afternoon popping in and out of boutiques, and then stay for happy hour at a local nightspot or even later for dinner. ■ TIP➔ **Bus 14 runs from Downtown along the length of Hawthorne, and there's plenty of free street parking, too.** ⊠ *S.E. Hawthorne Blvd., between S.E. 12th and S.E. 50th Aves., Buckman, Southeast* ⊕ *www.thinkhawthorne.com.*

Fodor'sChoice ★ **House Spirits Distillery.** One of the stalwarts of Distillery Row—a group of seven craft spirits producers mostly clustered together in the Central Eastside—this highly respected outfit opened in 2004, moved into a spacious 14,000-square-foot facility in fall 2014, and has earned international acclaim for its Aviation American Gin and Krogstad Festlig Aquavit. Other favorites include Westward Oregon Straight Malt Whiskey made with locally sourced barley, and—apt in java-loving Portland—coffee liqueur produced using pot-distilled rum and the city's fine Stumptown Coffee beans. In the cozy tasting room, you can also browse a fine selection of barware, books, and other booze-related gifts. Tours are offered Saturdays at 1 and 3 pm. ■ TIP➔ **Check out the Distillery Row website (⊕ www.distilleryrowpdx.com), where you can view a map of other nearby distilleries and order a Distillery Row Passport, which costs $20 but includes a $5 gift card, complimentary tastings and tours, and discounts at a number of restaurants, hotels, and shops around the city.** ⊠ *68 S.E. Stark St., Southeast* ☏ *503/235–3174* ⊕ *www.housespirits.com* ☾ *Sun.–Wed. noon–5, Fri.–Sat. noon–6.*

FAMILY
Fodor'sChoice ★ **Mt. Tabor Park.** A playground on top of a volcano cinder cone? Yup, that's here. The cinders, or glassy rock fragments, unearthed in the park's construction, were used to surface the respite's roads; the ones leading to the top are closed to cars, but popular with cyclists. They're also popular with cruisers—each August there's an old-fashioned soapbox derby. Picnic tables and tennis, basketball, and volleyball courts make Mt. Tabor Park a popular spot for outdoor recreation, but plenty of quiet, shaded trails and wide-open grassy lawns with panoramic views of the Downtown skyline appeal to sunbathers, hikers, and nature lovers. The whole park is closed to cars every Wednesday. ■ TIP➔ **Just down the hill on the west side of Mt. Tabor, you'll find the lively cafés and restaurants of the hip Hawthorne District.** ⊠ *S.E. 60th Ave. and S.E. Salmon St., Mt. Tabor, Southeast* ⊕ *www.portlandoregon.gov/parks* ☾ *Daily dawn–dusk.*

FAMILY

Fodor's Choice

★

Oregon Museum of Science and Industry (*OMSI*). Hundreds of engaging exhibits draw families to this outstanding interactive science museum, which also has an Omnimax theater and the Northwest's largest planetarium. The many permanent and touring exhibits are loaded with enough hands-on play for kids to fill a whole day exploring robotics, ecology, rockets, animation, and outer space. Moored in the Willamette River as part of the museum is a 240-foot submarine, the USS *Blueback,* which can be toured for an extra charge. OMSI also offers some very cool event programming for adults, including the hugely popular monthly OMSI After Dark nights, where "science nerds" can enjoy food, drink, and science fun, and the twice-monthly OMSI Science Pub nights, where local and national experts lecture on a wide range of topics at theater-pubs in Portland. ■TIP➔ **OMSI's excellent restaurant, Theory, open for lunch, offers great views of the Willamette River and Downtown skyline.** ⊠ *1945 S.E. Water Ave., Central East Side, Southeast* ☎ *503/797–4000, 800/955–6674* ⊕ *www.omsi.edu* ✉ *Museum $13, planetarium $7.50, Omnimax $8.50, submarine $6.75; combined ticket $23* ⊙ *Mid-June–early Sept., daily 9:30–7; early Sept.–mid-June, daily 9:30–5:30.*

Fodor's Choice

★

SE Wine Collective. Opened in 2012 along Division Street's white-hot restaurant row, this growing collective houses nine small wineries and has quickly become the city's leading incubator for *vino* entrepreneurs. The spacious facility includes a large, light-filled tasting bar with glass roll-up doors (offering a peek at the vinification process) and a main wall and bench seating made from old wine barrels. The tasting bar is also a wine bar, so you can sample the artisanal wines produced on-site, or order a flight, glass, or bottle (to go or to enjoy on-site) as well as tasty small plates from an extensive menu. Although Oregon is chiefly known for Pinot Noir, Pinot Gris, and Chardonnay, the wineries at the collective produce a richly varied assortment of varietals, including a heady Syrah from Helioterra, a supple Viognier from Jackalope Wine Cellars, and a peppery Cabernet Franc from Willful Wines. ■TIP➔ **Here, and at several other wineries in the city, you can by a PDX Urban Wineries Passport for $20; it comes with a $5 gift card, free tastings, and discounts at a number of local eateries and other businesses.** ⊠ *2425 S.E. 35th Pl., Richmond, Southeast* ☎ *503/208–2061* ⊕ *www.sewinecollective.com* ⊙ *Mon. and Wed.–Fri. 4 pm–10 pm, Sat. 1 pm–10 pm, Sun. 1 pm–8 pm.*

WORTH NOTING

Central Eastside. This expansive 681-acre tract of mostly industrial and commercial buildings was largely ignored by all but local workers until shops, galleries, and restaurants began opening in some of the neighborhood's handsome, high-ceilinged buildings beginning in the '90s. These days, it's a legitimately hot neighborhood for shopping and coffeehouse-hopping by day, and dining and clubbing at night. Businesses of particular note in these parts include urban-chic coffeehouses (Water Avenue, Coava), breweries (Base Camp Brewing, Cascade Brewing Barrel House, Commons Brewery), shops and galleries, and restaurants (ClarkLewis, Le Pigeon, Biwa, Bunk Sandwiches). In the past few years, a number of acclaimed craft distilleries and urban wineries have joined the mix, including House Spirits and New Deal Distillery among the former, and Clay Pigeon and Coopers Hall among the latter. This is a large neighborhood, and some streets are a bit desolate (though still quite safe), but you can reach it via the East Side Streetcar, and walking from Downtown across the Hawthorne or Burnside bridges. If you're coming by car, street parking is relatively easy to find. ⊠ *Willamette River to S.E. 12th Avenue from Burnside to Division Sts., Southeast* ⊕ *www.ceic.cc.*

Laurelhurst Park. Completed in 1914 by Emanuel Mische, who trained with the iconic Olmsted Brothers landscaping design firm, resplendent Laurelhurst Park's hundred-year-old trees and winding, elegant paths are evocative of another time, and may trigger an urge to don a parasol. Listed on the National Register of Historic Places, Laurelhurst offers plentiful trails, playgrounds, tennis courts, soccer fields, horseshoe pits, an off-leash area for dogs, a serene pond with ducks, and many sunny and shady picnic areas. Take a stroll around the large spring-fed pond and keep an eye out for blue heron, the city's official bird. On the south side of this 31-acre park is one of the busiest basketball courts in town. Though the park is always beautiful, it is especially so in fall. The trendy dining and café culture of East Burnside and 28th and Belmont Street are within walking distance. ⊠ *S.E. 39th Ave. and S.E. Stark St., Laurelhurst, Southeast* ⊕ *www.portlandoregon.gov/parks.*

WEST HILLS AND SOUTHWEST

Forming a natural western border of Downtown and Nob Hill, the West Hills extend as a high (up to around 1,000 feet in elevation) ridgeline from Southwest to Northwest Portland. Part of this lofty neighborhood is residential, containing some of the largest and finest homes in the city, many of them with knockout views of the Downtown skyline and Mt. St. Helens and Mt. Hood in the distance. Technically, Downtown Portland is in the city's Southwest quadrant, as are most of the attractions included in the aforementioned West Hills section of town. But when locals mention Southwest, they're generally referring to the area south and southwest of Downtown, a mostly middle- to upper-middle-class residential district with a few commercial pockets. The most interesting section is the RiverPlace and, a bit farther south, South Waterfront development along the Willamette River. A formerly industrial tract, this area has been rapidly developed since the early 2000s into a contemporary mixed-use neighborhood of both mid- and high-rise glass-and-steel condos, office buildings, a huge expansion of prestigious Oregon Health and Science University, and a growing but still limited number of restaurants, hotels, and shops. RiverPlace begins just south of Hawthorne Bridge and is easily accessed from Tom McCall Waterfront Park—there's a pretty pedestrian promenade along the river, with a handful of sidewalk cafés and boutiques.

TOP ATTRACTIONS

Hoyt Arboretum. Twelve miles of trails, which connect with others in Washington Park and Forest Park, wind through the arboretum, which has more than 1,400 species of plants and one of the nation's largest collections of coniferous trees; pick up trail maps at the visitor center.

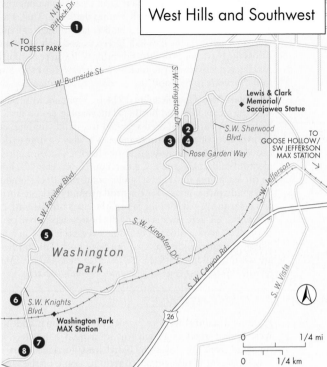

West Hills and Southwest

Guided 90-minute tours ($3 suggested donation) are offered most Saturdays at noon from May through September. Also here are the Winter Garden and a memorial to veterans of the Vietnam War. The visitor center is a half mile from the Washington Park MAX station. ✉ *4000 S.W. Fairview Blvd., Arlington Heights, West Hills* 🕾 *503/865-8733* ⊕ *www.hoytarboretum.org* ✉ *Free* ⊙ *Arboretum daily 5 am–10 pm; visitor center weekdays 9–4, weekends 11–3.*

Fodor's Choice **International Rose Test Garden.** Despite the name, these grounds are not an
★ experimental greenhouse laboratory, but rather three terraced gardens, set on 4½ acres, where more than 10,000 bushes and some 550 varieties of roses grow. The flowers, many of them new varieties, are at their peak in June, July, September, and October. From the gardens you can take in highly photogenic views of the Downtown skyline and, on fine days, the Fuji-shaped slopes of Mt. Hood, 50 miles to the east. Summer concerts take place in the garden's amphitheater. It's a pretty but hilly 30- to 40-minute walk from Downtown, or you can get here via MAX light rail (either to Washington Park or Kings Hill/S.W. Salmon Street stations); then transfer to Bus No. 63 (no weekend service) or Washington Park shuttle (late May–early September only). ✉ *400 S.W. Kingston Ave., Arlington Heights, West Hills* 🕾 *503/227-7033* ⊕ *www. rosegardenstore.org* ✉ *Free* ⊙ *Daily 7:30 am–9 pm.*

Portland Rose Festival parade

Fodor's Choice ★   **Japanese Garden.** One of the most authentic Japanese gardens outside Japan, this serene landscape unfolds over 5½ acres of Washington Park, just a short stroll up the hill from the International Rose Test Garden. This serene spot, designed by a Japanese landscape master, represents five separate garden styles: Strolling Pond Garden, Tea Garden, Natural Garden, Sand and Stone Garden, and Flat Garden. The Tea House was built in Japan and reconstructed here. The east side of the Pavilion has a majestic view of Portland and Mt. Hood. Take MAX light rail to Washington Park station, and transfer to Bus No. 63 (no weekend service) or the Washington Park Shuttle (May–Aug. only). ■ TIP➔ **The public tours are given by knowledgeable volunteers. Check for tour times at the admission gate.** ✉ 611 S.W. Kingston Ave., Arlington Heights, West Hills ☎ 503/223–1321 ⊕ www.japanesegarden.com ⬛ $9.50 ☉ Oct.–Mar., Mon. noon–4, Tues.–Sun. 10–4; Apr.–Sept., Mon. noon–7, Tues.–Sun. 10–7.

FAMILY   **Oregon Zoo.** This beautiful animal park in the West Hills, famous for its Asian elephants, is undergoing a two-decade-long series of major improvements and expansions to make the zoo more sustainable and provide more stimulating spaces, education and conservation opportunities, as well as improved guest amenities and event spaces. Major draws include an African Savanna with rhinos, hippos, zebras, and giraffes. Steller Cove, a state-of-the-art aquatic exhibit, has Steller sea lions and a family of sea otters. Take the MAX light rail to the Washington Park station. ✉ 4001 S.W. Canyon Rd., Arlington Heights, West Hills ☎ 503/226–1561 ⊕ www.oregonzoo.org ⬛ $11.50 ☉ Late May–Aug., *daily 9–6; Mar.–mid-May and Sept.–Dec., daily 9–4; Jan. and Feb., daily 10–4.*

WORTH NOTING

Oregon Holocaust Memorial. This memorial to those who perished during the Holocaust bears the names of surviving families who live in Oregon and southwest Washington. A bronzed baby shoe, a doll, broken spectacles, and other strewn possessions await notice on the cobbled courtyard. Soil and ash from six Nazi concentration camps is interred beneath the black granite wall. The memorial is operated by the nearby Oregon Jewish Museum and Center for Holocaust Education, on the edge of Nob Hill at 1953 N.W. Kearney Street, and hosts rotating history and art exhibits, films, concerts, and lectures. ⊠ *S.W. Wright Ave. and S.W. Park Pl., Arlington Heights, West Hills* ☎ *503/226–3600* ⊕ *www.ojmche.org* ✉ *Free* ☉ *Daily dawn–dusk.*

Pittock Mansion. Henry Pittock, the founder and publisher of the *Oregonian* newspaper, built this 22-room, castlelike mansion, which combines French Renaissance and Victorian styles. The opulent manor, built in 1914, is filled with art and antiques. The 46-acre grounds, north of Washington Park and 1,000 feet above the city, have superb views of the skyline, rivers, and the Cascade Range, including Mt. Hood and Mt. St. Helens. The mansion is a half-mile uphill trek from the nearest bus stop. The mansion is also a highly popular destination among hikers using Forest Park's and Washington Park's well-utilized Wildwood Trail. ⊠ *3229 N.W. Pittock Dr., Hillside, West Hills* ☎ *503/823–3623* ⊕ *www.pittockmansion.com* ✉ *$9.50* ☉ *July and Aug., daily 10–5; Sept.–Dec. and Feb.–June, daily 11–4.*

FAMILY **Portland Children's Museum.** Colorful sights and sounds offer a feast of sensations for kids of all ages where hands-on play is the order of the day. Visit nationally touring exhibits, catch a story time, a sing-along, or a puppet show in the Play It Again theater, create sculptures in the clay studio, splash hands in the waterworks display, or make a creation from junk in the Garage. The museum shares the same parking lot as the zoo and can also be reached via the MAX light rail Washington Park stop. ⊠ *4015 S.W. Canyon Rd., Arlington Heights, West Hills, Portland* ☎ *503/223–6500* ⊕ *www.portlandcm.org* ✉ *$10* ☉ *Mar.–Aug., daily 9–5; Sept.–Feb., Tues.–Sun. 9–5.*

FAMILY **World Forestry Center Discovery Museum.** This handsomely designed, contemporary museum across from the zoo contains interactive and multimedia exhibits about forest sustainability. A white-water raft ride, smokejumper training simulator, and Timberjack tree harvester all provide different perspectives on Pacific Northwest forests. On the second floor the forests of the world are explored in various travel settings. A canopy lift ride hoists visitors to the 50-foot ceiling to look at a Douglas fir. ⊠ *4033 S.W. Canyon Rd., Arlington Heights, West Hills, Portland* ☎ *503/228–1367* ⊕ *www.worldforestry.org* ✉ *$9* ☉ *Daily 10–5.*

WHERE TO EAT

These days, rising-star chefs and the foodies who adore them are flocking to Portland. In this playground of sustainability and creativity, many of the city's hottest restaurants change menus weekly—sometimes even daily—depending upon the ingredients they have delivered to their door that morning from local farms. The combination of fertile soils, temperate weather, and nearby waters contributes to a year-round bountiful harvest (be it lettuces or hazelnuts, mushrooms or salmon) that is within any chef's reach.

And these chefs are not shy about putting new twists on old favorites. Restaurants like Le Pigeon, Beast, Ox, Ned Ludd, Natural Selection, and Aviary have all taken culinary risks by presenting imaginatively executed, often globally inspired fare while utilizing sustainable ingredients. There's a strong willingness in and around Portland for chefs to explore their creative boundaries.

Menus frequently extend across nations and continents. First-time visitors to Portland always seem to be impressed by the culinary scene's international diversity, especially when it comes to Asian and Mediterranean fare, but you'll also find outstanding examples of Peruvian, Russian, regional Mexican, and dozens of other ethnic restaurants. Of course, seafood is prevalent, with chefs regularly taking advantage of the availability of fresh salmon, albacore, halibut, crab, oysters, and mussels from the rivers and the Pacific Ocean.

Most of the city's longtime favorites are concentrated in Nob Hill, the Pearl District, and Downtown. But many of the city's most exciting food scenes are on the East Side, along Alberta Street, Mississippi Avenue, Williams Avenue, Fremont Street, Martin Luther King Jr. Boulevard, Burnside Street, 28th Avenue, Belmont Street, Hawthorne Boulevard, and Division Street, and tucked away in many neighborhoods in between. Serious food enthusiasts will definitely want to make some trips to some of these vibrant, if out-of-the-way neighborhoods.

HOURS, PRICES, AND DRESS

Compared to many other major cities, Portland restaurants aren't open quite as late, and it's unusual to see many diners after 11 pm even on weekends, though there are a handful of restaurants and popular bars that do serve late, albeit often with limited bar menus.

One aspect to Portland's dining scene that many locals and out-of-towners find appealing is how reasonably priced top-notch restaurants are. Particularly welcome in Portland is happy hour, when both inventive cocktails as well as small plates of food can be a good value; you can easily put together a fine early—or in some cases late-night—dinner by grazing from the happy-hour menu at a restaurant that also has a bar scene.

In Portland, many diners dress casually for even higher-end establishments—a proclivity that's refreshing to some and annoying to others. In any case, jeans are acceptable almost everywhere.

In alphabetical order by neighborhood. Use the coordinate (✛ B2) at the end of each listing to locate a site on the corresponding map.

WHAT IT COSTS IN U.S. DOLLARS				
	$	$$	$$$	$$$$
At Dinner	Under $16	$16–$22	$23–$30	Over $30

Restaurant prices are the average cost of a main course at dinner, or if dinner is not served, at lunch.

DOWNTOWN

$
BAKERY
FAMILY
Fodor'sChoice
★

✕**Blue Star Donuts.** The lines outside much-hyped competitor Voodoo Doughnut are longer, but that doesn't mean you should bypass a chance to sample the creative confections at this handsome, light-filled doughnut shop on the street level of a glassy condo tower in the West End. Part of Micah Camden's nouvelle–fast-food empire (that includes Little Big Burger, Boxer Ramen, and Son of a Biscuit), Blue Star opens at 7 or 8 each morning and remains open until that day's fresh-baked stock of delicious doughnuts is sold out. Flavors change regularly, but often include blueberry-bourbon-basil, bacon-maple, and Valrhona chocolate crunch with a Boston-cream-style filling. Stumptown coffee is served, too. If you have time for just one Portland doughnut shop, choose this one; if possible, though, try them both. Additional locations can be found in Hawthorne and North Mississippi. ⑤ *Average main: $4* ✉ *1237 S.W. Washington St., West End, Downtown* ☎ *503/265–8410* ⊕ *www.bluestardonuts.com* ⑤ *Average main: $4* ✉ *3753 N. Mississippi Ave., Mississippi, Downtown* ☎ *503/265–8410* ⊕ *www.bluestardonuts. com* ⑤ *Average main: $4* ✉ *3549 S.E. Hawthorne Blvd., Hawthorne, Southeast* ☎ *503/477–9635* ⊕ *www.bluestardonuts.com* ✛ *D4.*

$$$
PACIFIC
NORTHWEST
Fodor'sChoice
★

✕**Clyde Common.** Gourmands from all walks of life—politicians, rock stars, socialites, and hipsters—eat and drink at this bustling bistro and bar in the Ace Hotel. Long, communal tables dominate the space, which means you never know who you'll end up sitting next to. With wood-and-canvas decor, expansive front windows, and an open kitchen, the restaurant has a warm, airy feel, although it can get loud. The seasonally driven menu showcases the region's bounty; you might start with quail stuffed with maple-bourbon sausage, before tucking into a plate of black-truffle tagliatelle pasta with chicken-heart ragout, *chicharrons*, pears, and egg yolk. The cocktail list is one of the best in the city; try the barrel-aged Negroni made with Beefeater gin, Cinzano sweet vermouth, Campari, and orange peel, or the bartender's daily punch. Weekend brunch is memorable and there are great happy-hour deals, too. ⑤ *Average main: $27* ✉ *Ace Hotel, 1014 S.W. Stark St., West End* ☎ *503/228–3333* ⊕ *www.clydecommon.com* ✛ *D4.*

$$$
ASIAN FUSION

✕**Departure Restaurant + Lounge.** This swanky rooftop restaurant and lounge on the top floor of The Nines hotel looks fresh out of L.A.—a look and feel that is, indeed, a departure from Portland's usual no-fuss vibe. The retro-chic interior has an extravagant, space-age, airport-lounge feel, and the outdoor patio—furnished with low, white couches and bright-orange tables and chairs—offers panoramic views of the Downtown skyline. It's not just about the view here at this see-and-be-seen

BEST BETS FOR PORTLAND DINING

Fodor's writers and editors have selected their favorite restaurants by price, cuisine, and experience in the lists below. In the first column, Fodor's Choice properties represent the "best of the best" in every price category. You can also search by neighborhood for excellent eats—just peruse our reviews on the following pages.

Fodor'sChoice ★

Andina, $$$, p. 80
Apizza Scholls, $, p. 86
Ava Gene's, $$$, p. 86
Block + Tackle, $$, p. 87
Blue Star Donuts, $, p. 72
Broder, $, p. 88
Castagna Restaurant, $$$$, p. 88
Clyde Common, $$$, p. 72
Country Cat, $$, p. 88
Higgins, $$$, p. 75
Imperial, $$$, p. 75
Interurban, $, p. 82
Irving Street Kitchen, $$$, p. 80
Kachka, $$, p. 89
Langbaan, $$$$, p. 89
Lardo, $, p. 90
Laurelhurst Market, $$$, p. 90
Lauretta Jean's, $, p. 90
Le Pigeon, $$$, p. 91
Natural Selection, $$$$, p. 83

Ned Ludd, $$$, p. 83
Olympic Provisions, $$, p. 91
Ox Restaurant, $$$$, p. 83
PaaDee, $, p. 91
Pazzo Ristorante, $$$, p. 76
Pok Pok, $, p. 92
Ración, $$$, p. 77
Roe, $$$$, p. 92
Salt & Straw Ice Cream, $, p. 81
Screen Door, $$, p. 84
Tamale Boy, $, p. 85
Toro Bravo, $$, p. 86
Trifecta Tavern, $$, p. 92

By Price

$

Apizza Scholls, p. 86
Bollywood Theater, p. 87
Broder, p. 88
Interurban, p. 82
Ken's Artisan Pizza, p. 89
Lardo, p. 90

Lauretta Jean's, p. 90
Mi Mero Mole, p. 77
Pine State Biscuits, p. 84
Pok Pok, p. 92
Salt & Straw Ice Cream, p. 81
Tamale Boy, p. 85

$$

Aviary, p. 82
Block + Tackle, p. 87
Country Cat, p. 88
Kachka, p. 89
Olympic Provisions, p. 91
Toro Bravo, p. 86

$$$

Andina, p. 80
Clarklewis, p. 88
Clyde Common, p. 72
Grüner, p. 75
Higgins, p. 75
Imperial, p. 75
Le Pigeon, p. 91
Meriwether's Restaurant, p. 81
Pazzo Ristorante, p. 76
Ración, p. 77

$$$$

Beast, p. 82
Castagna Restaurant, p. 88
Langbaan, p. 89
Natural Selection, p. 83
Ox Restaurant, p. 83
Roe, p. 92

By Cuisine

ASIAN

Aviary, $$, p. 82
Bamboo Sushi, $$, p. 86
Bollywood Theater, $, p. 87
Departure, $$$, p. 72
Langbaan, $$$$, p. 89
PaaDee, $, p. 91
Pok Pok, $, p. 92
Smallwares, $$, p. 85

BRUNCH

Broder, $, p. 88
Country Cat, $$, p. 88
Irving Street Kitchen, $$$, p. 80
Meriwether's Restaurant, $$$, p. 81
Pine State Biscuits, $, p. 84
Screen Door, $$, p 84
Tasty n Alder, $$$, p. 77
Tin Shed Garden Cafe, $, p. 85
Veritable Quandary, $$$, p. 77

Portland's Food Carts

Throughout Portland at any given mealtime, around 600 food carts are dishing up steaming plates of everything from Korean tacos to shawarma to artisanal cupcakes. While food carts have seen a rise in popularity throughout the country, the culture is especially strong in Portland.

Brightly colored and mostly stationary, the carts tend to cluster in former parking lots in pods ranging from three to nearly 60 establishments, oftentimes ringing a cluster of picnic tables or a covered awning.

With plate prices averaging $6 to $9, cart fare provides a quick, inexpensive, and delicious alternative to traditional sit-down restaurants if you don't mind sitting outside. Cart dining is also an easy way to sample Portland's many ethnic food offerings.

For up-to-date information on hours and locations, check out the extensive local blog **Food Carts Portland** (⊕ www.foodcartsportland.com), the corresponding FoodCartsPDX iPhone and Droid apps FoodCartsPDX, and the Twitter thread @pdxfoodcarts.com.

TOP PODS

Downtown, S.W. 9th (and 10th) and Alder: Covering more than an entire city block, this Downtown pod, home to nearly 60 carts, is the largest in the city. The spot is lively during the workweek but slower on the weekends. We recommend the signature Thai chicken dish at **Nong's Khao Man Gai**; battered fish-and-chips at **The Frying Scotsman**; kielbasa and other Polish classics at **EuroDish**; the porchetta-and-arugula sandwich at the **People's Pig Wood-Fired Grill**; and kalua pig at the Hawaiian cart **808 Grinds**.

Downtown, S.W. 3rd and Washington: This pod has an international bent, with some of the city's oldest Mexican carts on-site, plus Egyptian, Greek, Indonesian, Lebanese, and Vietnamese establishments. We recommend the spicy Southwest mac and cheese and pulled-pork sliders at **I Heart This Cart**; falafel or chicken shawarma at **El Masry Egyptian** cart; and vegan cheesesteak at **DC Vegetarian.**

Southeast, Tidbit Food Farm and Garden (S.E. Division and 28th): Southeast Portlanders were saddened to see the Good Food Here (on Belmont) and Cartopia (on Hawthorne) carts close in 2014 to make way for new construction projects, but this new, beautifully designed cart colony with a large central dining area and a fire pit has given cart hounds a reason to rejoice. Try the Heartbreak Hotel hot dog topped with bacon, cheddar, ketchup, and a fried egg at **Timber's DogHouse PDX**; the blistered-crust wood-fired pizzas (the one with fennel sausage is killer) at **Pyro Pizza**; and the stick-to-your-ribs braised tri-tip plate, with roasted red peppers and onions, followed by a slice of pineapple upside-down cake, at **Love Belizean.** You can also grab a pint of local IPA or porter to accompany your meal at Scout Beer Garden.

late-night lounge. The seafood-focused Pan-Asian dishes, which include big-eye tuna *poke* (salad), crispy squid with spicy miso, scallop skewers with asparagus, and wok-fried chili prawns with candied walnuts, are served in small portions and are consistently excellent, thanks to charismatic chef Gregory Gourdet's dedication to quality and creativity. ⑤ *Average main: $25* ✉ *Nines Hotel, 525 S.W. Morrison St., Downtown* ☎ *503/802–5370* ⊕ *www.departureportland.com* ⊗ *No lunch* ✛ *D4.*

$$$
MODERN
EUROPEAN

✕ **Grüner.** Grüner means "greener" in German, and this sleek West End restaurant with angular furniture and blond-wood tables and chairs focuses strongly on seasonal Northwest produce and modern interpretations of recipes culled from throughout verdant Germany's Alps, forests, and river valleys. Start, perhaps, with the Swabian *maultaschen,* a hearty ravioli in a fragrant beef broth filled with beef, pork, spinach, and onion. Then consider traditional *choucroute garnie* with housemade meats, or quark spaetzle served with Black Forest ham, leeks, zucchini, hen-of-the-woods mushrooms, and crème fraîche. Available only at Grüner's bar, the burger topped with smoked bacon, fontina, pickled red onions, aioli, and house-made ketchup is one of the best in town. Be sure to check out the terrific wine list with its emphasis on German, Austrian, and northern Italian wines; Grüner Veltliner is well represented, of course. Sister establishment Kask, next door, is a hip and cozy craft-cocktail lounge featuring simpler bar snacks. ⑤ *Average main: $25* ✉ *527 S.W. 12th Ave., West End, Downtown* ☎ *503/241–7163* ⊕ *www. grunerpdx.com* ⊗ *Closed Sun. No lunch Sat.* ✛ *D4.*

$$$
PACIFIC
NORTHWEST
Fodor'sChoice
★

✕ **Higgins.** One of Portland's original farm-to-table restaurants, this classic eatery, opened in 1994 by renowned namesake chef Greg Higgins, has built its menu—and its reputation—on its dedication to local, seasonal, organic ingredients. Higgins' dishes display the diverse bounty of the Pacific Northwest, incorporating ingredients like heirloom tomatoes, forest mushrooms, mountain huckleberries, Pacific oysters, Oregon Dungeness crab, and locally raised pork. A reasonably priced bistro menu is available in the adjoining bar, where comfortable leather booths and tables provide an alternative to the formal, white-tableclothed main dining room. Don't miss the house-made charcuterie plate with Higgins pickles or the tender duck confit entrée. ⑤ *Average main: $28* ✉ *1239 S.W. Broadway, Downtown* ☎ *503/222–9070* ⊕ *higginsportland.com* ⊗ *No lunch weekends* ✛ *D5.*

$$$
PACIFIC
NORTHWEST
Fodor'sChoice
★

✕ **Imperial.** Tall concrete pillars, exposed brick and ductwork, soft overhead lighting, and rustic wood tables and floors create an industrial-chic vibe at acclaimed chef Vitaly Paley's buzzy restaurant inside the hip Hotel Lucia. Open for breakfast, lunch, and dinner, and serving up exemplary contemporary Pacific Northwest fare from a wood-fired grill and rotisserie in the open kitchen, Paley draws inspiration—and ingredients—from the surrounding area. Menu highlights include Dungeness crab omelet, duck meatballs, grilled king salmon with corn purée and chanterelles, and a mixed grill of Oregon lamb (T-bone, leg, shoulder, and merguez sausage). Imperial has one of the best Downtown happy hours, and a stellar cocktail program to match; try the Konami Code with cognac, vermouth, Becherovka liqueur, framboise, and orange bitters. Paley also operates the hip and casual Portland Penny Diner, also inside the Lucia. $\boxed{S}$ *Average main: $25* ⊠ *Hotel Lucia, 410 S.W. Broadway, Downtown* ☎ *503/228–7222* ⊕ *www.imperialpdx.com* ✛ *D4.*

$ ✕ **Kenny & Zuke's Delicatessen.** The reputation of this Jewish deli beside
DELI the hip Ace Hotel is based largely on its much-revered pastrami. Cured
FAMILY for seven days, then smoked for 10 hours and steamed for three, the
rich and flavorful meat is best tasted on a rye bread sandwich or, if
your appetite is heartier, the warm, sauerkraut-packed Reuben. Kenny
& Zuke's makes its own pickles and produces its own bagels, proofing the dough for 36 hours before hand-forming the circles then boiling and baking them in small batches. The open and airy Downtown
space serves omelets, Benedicts, biscuits, and breakfast sandwiches all
day (it's open until 8 or 9, depending on the day), along with a wide
selection of soups, salads, and meaty sandwiches. The Thurman Street
location, in a no-frills space furnished with picnic tables, specializes in
the bagels, and the North Williams location, which bills itself as a deli-
bar, stays open late serving food and cocktails. $\boxed{S}$ *Average main: $14*
⊠ *1038 S.W. Stark St., West End, Downtown* ☎ *503/222–3354* ⊕ *www.*
kennyandzukes.com $\boxed{S}$ *Average main: $14* ⊠ *3901 N. Williams Ave.,*
Boise, North ☎ *503/287–0782* ⊕ *www.kennyandzukes.com* $\boxed{S}$ *Average main: $14* ⊠ *2376 N.W. Thurman St., Nob Hill* ☎ *503/954–1737*
⊕ *www.kennyandzukes.com* ⊙ *No dinner* ✛ *D4.*

$$$ ✕ **Little Bird Bistro.** Celeb-chef Gabriel Rucker of Le Pigeon fame opened
BISTRO this lively Downtown sister restaurant which has gained a following
for its deliciously curated charcuterie board and a certain notoriety for
its decadent $32 burger, which is topped with a large serving of seared
foie gras (it's available sans foie for $12). This classic but casual bistro
is highly popular with the business-lunch set, but open until midnight
(with a limited but still extensive menu after 10), it also pulls pretheater
diners and postdrinks noshers. Other notable dishes include a classic
cassoulet of duck leg and pork belly, smoked-salmon belly with Brussels sprouts and porcini butter, and crispy rabbit with bacon, caramelized apples, turnips, and mustard. There are a couple of prix-fixe
options, too, and a commendable dessert list that includes a knockout
passion-fruit pudding cake with coconut-Graham crumble, huckleberries, passion-fruit curd, and mint. $\boxed{S}$ *Average main: $26* ⊠ *219 S.W. 6th*
Ave., Downtown ☎ *503/688–5952* ⊕ *www.littlebirdbistro.com* ⊙ *No*
lunch weekends ✛ *E4.*

$$$ ✕ **Pazzo Ristorante.** The aromas of roasted garlic and wood smoke greet
ITALIAN patrons of the bustling, street-level dining room of the Hotel Vintage
Fodor'sChoice Plaza. The unprepossessing decor of dark wood and terra cotta and
★ the menu of deceptively simple contemporary Italian cuisine belie the
fact that Pazzo serves some of the most beautifully prepared, flavorful
food in Downtown: consider the thinly pounded beef carpaccio with
pickled shimeji mushrooms and edible chrysanthemums, and ravioli
filled with fennel and topped with Dungeness crab and a chive-butter
sauce. All the baked goods are made in the adjacent Pazzoria Bakery &
Cafe. Breakfast is served daily. $\boxed{S}$ *Average main: $26* ⊠ *Hotel Vintage*
Plaza, 627 S.W. Washington St., Downtown ☎ *503/228–1515* ⊕ *www.*
pazzo.com ✛ *E4.*

2

$$$ ✕ **Ración.** In the same shiny West End condo tower that's home to the
TAPAS   Downtown branches of Blue Star Donuts and Lardo, this sleek space
Fodor's Choice   specializing in gorgeously complex and playful modern Spanish small
★   plates presents a true feast for the senses. Most of the seating is around
a polished-wood L-shape counter that faces the open kitchen—a great
spot for mingling with fellow diners and watching chef Anthony Cafiero
work his molecular magic. Specialties from the small menu include Ser-
rano ham with walnut purée, dandelion greens, and mushroom caramel,
and an egg poached sous vide with Brussels sprouts, oyster cream, and
smoked oil. The best approach here, especially if it's a special occasion,
is ordering the five-course $55 chef's tasting menu. The cocktails here are
every bit as interesting as the food, using such cockeyed ingredients as Ser-
rano ham–infused gin and ginger-habanero syrup. $ *Average main: $25*
✉ *1205 S.W. Washington St., West End, Downtown* ☎ *971/276–8008*
⊕ *www.racionpdx.com* ☉ *Closed Sun. and Mon. No lunch* ✣ *D4.*

$$$ ✕ **Tasty n Alder.** The first Downtown venture of celebrated Portland
ECLECTIC   chef John Gorham, this all-day brunch and evening dinner spot serves
some of the most interesting food in the city. Designed for sharing, the
tapas-style menu draws on global influences and delivers bold, delicious
flavors. Try the *patatas bravas*, potatoes served with fried egg on top
and aioli on the side, and the Korean fried chicken (yes, for breakfast),
served with rice, house kimchi, and eggs cooked two ways (pickled and
over-easy). At dinnertime, Tasty n Alder turns up the class, offering a
selection of top-notch steaks from family-run ranches, along with well-
crafted original cocktails. The atmosphere is modern, clean, and inviting. $ *Average main: $24* ✉ *580 S.W. 12th Ave., West End, Downtown*
☎ *503/621–9251* ⊕ *www.tastyntasty.com* ✣ *D4.*

$$$ ✕ **Veritable Quandary.** As trendy eateries have come and gone in Down-
AMERICAN   town Portland over the years, this long-standing local favorite has con-
tinued to excel as both a charming weekend brunch option and a lively,
see-and-be-seen dinner spot. The beautiful outdoor patio overlooking
the Hawthorne Bridge is an oasis of roses, fuchsias, and hanging bego-
nia baskets. The menu emphasizes fresh, flavorful produce and seafood,
and the 200-plus-wine list is one of the best in town. The convivial
bar, with its deep wooden booths, is a laid-back spot for drinks and
lighter fare, including outstanding beef and veggie burgers. $ *Average
main: $27* ✉ *1220 S.W. 1st Ave., Downtown* ☎ *503/227–7342* ⊕ *www.
veritablequandary.com* ✣ *E5.*

OLD TOWN/CHINATOWN

$ ✕ **Mi Mero Mole.** Graffiti and murals decorate one concrete wall of this
MEXICAN   colorful Old Town–Chinatown eatery dedicated to Mexico City–style
street food, proof that superb ethnic food still exists in the Chinatown
neighborhood (even if none of it, at the moment, is Chinese). This is
some of the most flavorful, authentic Mexican food in town. You pick
as many items as you'd like from the list of perfectly seasoned fill-
ings, including pork *mole verde* with tomatillo and green chili, smoked
tongue with potatoes and cactus in salsa verde, and butternut squash
cooked in a rich chocolate mole sauce. Then choose your format for
eating these delicacies: a combo platter, quesadillas, burritos, tacos,

and so on. There's an extensive list of fine tequilas and mezcals, plus several handcrafted margaritas. There's a smaller, original branch on Division Street in Southeast. [$] *Average main: $10* ✉ *32 N.W. 5th Ave., Old Town/Chinatown* ☎ *971/266–8575* ⊕ *www.mmmtacospdx.com* ⊗ *Closed Sun.* [$] *Average main: $10* ✉ *5026 S.E. Division St., Clinton, Old Town/Chinatown* ☎ *503/232–8226* ⊕ *www.mmmtacospdx.com* ⊗ *Closed Mon. No lunch Tues.–Thurs.* ⊹ *E4.*

$ ✕ **Voodoo Doughnut.** The long lines outside this Old Town 24/7 doughnut
BAKERY   shop, marked by its distinctive pink-neon sign, attest to the fact that this irreverent bakery is almost as famous a Portland landmark as Powell's Books. The aforementioned sign depicts one of the shop's biggest sellers, a raspberry-jelly-topped chocolate voodoo-doll doughnut, but all the creations here, some of them witty, some ribald, bring smiles to the faces of customers—even those who have waited 30 minutes in the rain. The Loop (covered in Fruit Loops cereal), Grape Ape (vanilla frosting, grape dust, and lavender sprinkles), and Dirty Snowballs (marshmallow topping, dipped in coconut, with peanut butter center) are other faves. The location, sandwiched between an adult theater and a beer garden in a slightly seedy section of Old Town, makes this a not-quite-appropriate venue for very young kids—plus some of the more amusing doughnuts are adult themed. ■TIP➔ A second location in Northeast tends to be a bit less crowded. [$] *Average main: $4* ✉ *22 S.W. 3rd Ave., Old Town/ Chinatown* ☎ *503/241–4704* ⊕ *www.voodoodoughnut.com* ▭ *No credit cards* [$] *Average main: $4* ✉ *1501 N.E. Davis St., Old Town/ Chinatown* ☎ *503/235–2666* ⊕ *www.voodoodoughnut.com* ⊹ *E4.*

PEARL DISTRICT

$$$ ✕ **Andina.** This popular upscale Pearl District restaurant offers an inven-
PERUVIAN   tive menu—a combination of traditional Peruvian and contemporary
Fodor's Choice   "Novoandina" cuisines—served in a large but nook-filled space. The
★   extensive seafood offerings include four kinds of ceviche, grilled octopus, and pan-seared scallops with white and black quinoa. There are also entrées with chicken, duck, beef, and lamb. A late-night bar offers sangria, small plates, and cocktails. Don't miss the traditional Peruvian pisco sour, a lemon and pisco liqueur cocktail topped with a froth of egg whites and bitters. There's live music most evenings. [$] *Average main: $27* ✉ *1314 N.W. Glisan St., Pearl District* ☎ *503/228–9535* ⊕ *www. andinarestaurant.com* ⊹ *C3.*

$$$ ✕ **Irving Street Kitchen.** You might come to this hip Pearl District res-
MODERN   taurant set inside a gorgeously transformed warehouse building just
AMERICAN   because you heard about the rich butterscotch pudding with roasted-
Fodor's Choice   banana caramel and peanut butter bonbons (it's available to go, sold
★   in its own adorable canning jar); but chances are, once you see the exposed-brick-and-wood-beam walls, striking Edison bulb chandeliers, inviting central bar, and patio seats on a converted loading dock, you'll want to stay. And you'll be glad you did. The well-executed contemporary American dinner and brunch fare includes duck-fat-poached halibut with baby artichokes and sour-pickle aioli and a smoked-brisket-and-fried-egg sandwich with pepper pickles and cheesy Cajun fries which reflect chef Sarah Schafer's creative, if rather decadent, hand

in the kitchen. Wines by the glass are dispensed from state-of-the-art taps, ensuring freshness. $ *Average main: $26* ⊠ *701 N.W. 13th Ave., Pearl District* ☎ *503/343–9440* ⊕ *www.irvingstreetkitchen.com* ⊗ *No lunch weekdays* ✢ *C3.*

$$
MEDITERRANEAN
⨉**Mediterranean Exploration Company.** The latest venture by cookbook author and celeb-chef John Gorham, this tribute to Mediterranean cuisine occupies a handsome former warehouse on historic 13th Avenue in the Pearl. MEC (for short) is an energy-filled, open space with a mix of communal and individual tables—it's surprisingly affordable considering the quality and portions, particularly if you opt for the $40 tasting menu. Food is served family style, and highlights include house-made *labneh* (strained yogurt) with olive oil and fried cauliflower; Lebanese lamb tartare kibbeh; Nazareth kebabs with beef and lamb; and *chreime,* a traditional Jewish fish stew from Tripoli. There are plenty of veggie options, too. Save room for cardamom ice cream, over which your server ladles robust Turkish coffee. Many drinks from the cocktail menu also touch on the region, such as the Casablanca, with three types of rum, lime, date sugar, and rose water. $ *Average main: $22* ⊠ *333 N.W. 13th Ave., Pearl District* ☎ *503/222–0906* ⊕ *www. mediterraneanexplorationcompany.com* ⊗ *No lunch* ✢ *D3.*

$
BAKERY
⨉**Pearl Bakery.** Known for its excellent pastries and fresh baked breads (which are served at many top restaurants around town), this superb café was the first of the city's true artisan bakeries. It offers light breakfasts and delicious sandwiches (the tomato-basil-mozzarella on a puffy *pistolet* roll is particularly good) for lunch. The cakes, cookies, and croissants are among the best in the city. $ *Average main: $7* ⊠ *102 N.W. 9th Ave., Pearl District* ☎ *503/827–0910* ⊕ *www.pearlbakery. com* ⊗ *No dinner* ✢ *C3.*

NOB HILL

$$$
PACIFIC
NORTHWEST
⨉**Meriwether's Restaurant.** The 5-acre Skyline Farm just 12 miles away grows all the produce for this high-end, yet quaint and unpretentious restaurant on the edge of the north end of the Northwest 23rd shopping district. A lush covered and heated garden patio allow diners to eat alfresco even during cooler months. The farm-to-table offerings include the Skyline Farm beet salad with spiced coconut, feta, and almonds and Dungeness crab risotto. The dessert menu features tasty seasonal treats like pumpkin pots de creme. The weekend brunch, where the omelets, scrambles, and Benedicts are made with farm-fresh eggs, is wildly popular—and for good reason. $ *Average main: $26* ⊠ *2601 N.W. Vaughn St., Nob Hill* ☎ *503/228–1250* ⊕ *www.meriwethersnw.com* ✢ *A1.*

$
CAFÉ
FAMILY
Fodor'sChoice
★
⨉**Salt & Straw Ice Cream.** In 2011, cousins Kim and Tyler Malek started a business with a small pushcart and a humble idea—to create unique ice-cream flavors with quality, local ingredients. Today, Salt & Straw Ice Cream has grown into three brick-and-mortar ice-cream parlors around town, with lines out the door at each location, and it is recognized as one of the best ice-cream makers in the nation. Seasonal, local ingredients drive the flavors here, and constant experimentation keeps ice-cream lovers coming back. Ongoing favorites include almond brittle with salted ganache, pear and blue cheese, and honey-balsamic strawberry

with black pepper, but each month five special concoctions are featured. Locally produced Woodblock chocolate bars and house-made salted-caramel sauce are among the toppings. The location in Nob Hill is handiest if you're staying at a Downtown hotel, but the original on Alberta and newest branch on S.E. Division Street are just as popular; expect a long line, but take heart in knowing that the patient staff works fast, even while encouraging patrons to sample the wildly imaginative flavors. $ *Average main: $5* ✉ *838 N.W. 23rd Ave., Nob Hill* ☎ *971/271–8168* ⊕ *www.saltandstraw.com* $ *Average main: $5* ✉ *3345 S.E. Division St., Richmond, Southeast* ☎ *503/208–2054* ⊕ *www.saltandstraw.com* $ *Average main: $5* ✉ *2035 N.E. Alberta St., Alberta District, Nob Hill* ☎ *503/208–3867* ⊕ *www.saltandstraw.com* ✛ *A2.*

NORTH

$ ✕ **Interurban.** A laid-back North Mississippi gastropub with an L-shape
MODERN   indoor bar and a bi-level back patio with lush landscaping and a shaded
AMERICAN   pergola, Interurban is both a convivial drinkery and a fine spot for
Fodor's Choice   affordable, well-crafted American fare served from midafternoon until
★   2:30 (hours are earlier on weekends, with brunch kicking off at 10 am).
The kitchen creates consistently good and creative food, with starters like venison tartare with house-made potato chips and whiskey-infused chicken-liver mousse with bacon and foie gras. More substantial but still bargain-priced items include a rotisserie lamb sandwich with local Mama Lil's hot peppers, *fromage blanc,* and Dijon aioli, and brined and roasted game hen cooked on a rotisserie. A big part of Interurban's success is the extensive selection of cocktails and microbrews. $ *Average main: $13* ✉ *4057 N. Mississippi Ave., North Mississippi, North* ☎ *503/284–6669* ⊕ *www.interurbanpdx.com* ◷ *No lunch weekdays* ✛ *F1.*

NORTHEAST

$$ ✕ **Aviary.** Eschewing many culinary conventions, this visionary Alberta
ASIAN FUSION   Street eatery serves up innovative dishes that sometimes push boundaries but consistently succeed in flavor and execution. The simple menu of small plates (order two to three per person) is influenced by Asian flavors and uses European cooking techniques, combining unusual ingredients that offer pleasing contrasts in flavor and texture. For example, the charred octopus, cooked to the perfect tenderness, is served with scallion pancakes and a salad of papaya, beans, and cashews. The signature dish, a mini wok containing crispy pig ears over mildly sweet coconut rice, is served with Chinese sausage, avocado, mint, and cilantro. The dining room is warm yet simple with white walls and concrete floors—a nice contrast to the boldness of the plates. The helpful waitstaff is available to guide and explain, easing adventurous eaters outside their comfort zones, where the payoff is big. $ *Average main: $18* ✉ *1733 N.E. Alberta St., Alberta District, Northeast* ☎ *503/287–2400* ⊕ *aviarypdx.com* ◷ *Closed Sun. No lunch* ✛ *H1.*

$$$$ ✕ **Beast.** This meat-centric examplar of Portland's cutting-edge culinary
PACIFIC   scene occupies a nondescript red building with subtle signage. Chef-
NORTHWEST   owner Naomi Pomeroy, who also operates the trendy Expatriate bar

across the street, has appeared on TV's *Top Chef Masters* and garnered countless accolades. Inside her surprisingly casual restaurant, the seating is communal, at two large tables that seat 8 and 16. The six-course prix-fixe dinner (and four-course brunch on Sunday) changes weekly, depending on the meat at the market—substitutions are declined, so vegetarians won't find Beast a good fit. Most dishes are prepared right before your eyes in the open kitchen: there might be chicken and duck-liver mousse, wine- and truffle-braised beef, foie-gras bon bons, or steak tartare with quail-egg toast. There are two seatings per night at 6 and 8:45; view the week's menu online starting Tuesday afternoon. $ *Average main: $75* ✉ *5425 N.E. 30th Ave., Concordia, Northeast* ☎ *503/841–6968* ⊕ *www.beastpdx.com* ⌖ *Reservations essential* ⊘ *Closed Mon. and Tues.* ✛ *H1.*

$$$$
VEGETARIAN
Fodor'sChoice
★

✕ **Natural Selection.** With a full two hours of table time from the start of your reservation, this modern-rustic European-style café encourages you to slow down and savor your meal—and there's so much to savor. A small vegetarian restaurant with cocoa-colored walls and exposed-filament Edison bulbs over each table, Natural Selection serves a four-course, fixed-price menu (available with or without wine pairings) whose brilliance rests in the pure and natural flavors of its ingredients. Assembled in new combinations—tomato-almond soup with fennel, parsnip, and watercress, for example, or chard gnocchi with winter squash, apple, basil, and balsamic vinegar—the ingredients, which change by season, send your taste buds on lovely explorations with each bite. $ *Average main: $45* ✉ *3033 N.E. Alberta St., Concordia, Northeast* ☎ *503/288–5883* ⊕ *www.naturalselectionpdx.com* ⊘ *Closed Sun.–Tues.* ✛ *H1.*

$$$
PACIFIC
NORTHWEST
Fodor'sChoice
★

✕ **Ned Ludd.** Named for the founder of the Luddites, the group that resisted the technological advances of the Industrial Revolution, this Northwest-inspired kitchen prepares its food the most low-tech way possible: in a wood-burning brick oven, over an open flame. Sourcing most of its ingredients locally (or carefully, if they come from afar), Ned Ludd's menu varies completely depending on the season and weather. The whole roasted trout, a delicious constant on the menu, has a crisp, charred exterior and a moist, flavorful interior and comes with charred leeks and carrot-and-fennel salad. Consider the house-made pickle plate and any one of the salads or roasted vegetable dishes to accompany the meal. Fitting the simple, from-the-earth theme, the decor incorporates salvaged wood, dried flowers, and small succulent plants under glass domes. On Monday nights, the kitchen is turned over to two talented staff members—line cook Nicholas Ford and server Brandon Gomez—for pizza night, served up with Oregon microbrews and a healthy dose of old-school rap. ■TIP➔ **If you visit on a Monday, order the always-changing special pie for a taste of both what's in season and in play with chef Ford.** $ *Average main: $23* ✉ *3925 N.E. Martin Luther King Blvd., King, Northeast* ⊕ *www.nedluddpdx.com* ⊘ *No lunch* ✛ *G1.*

$$$$
ARGENTINE
Fodor'sChoice
★

✕ **Ox Restaurant.** Specializing in "Argentine-inspired Portland food," Ox is all about prime cuts of meat prepared well. In a dimly lit dining room with hardwood floors, exposed brick walls, and a bar against the front window, the flannel-shirt-and-white-apron clad waitstaff serves beef, lamb, pork, and fish dishes cooked over flames in a large, hand-cranked grill. The *asado Argentino,* a platter of short ribs, chorizo, *morcilla* (blood sausage), and skirt steak with a few sides, is an ideal choice for two. Or try the grass-fed Uruguayan rib eye for one, which is a better choice than the skirt steak. The vegetable-based sides provide cool complements to the rich asados: try the chopped endive salad with pear, Gruyère, arugula, pecans, and Dijon vinaigrette, or the buttered beet salad with sweet onion, blue cheese, and walnuts. Save room for the chef's dessert specialty, a vanilla bean *tres leches* cake accompanied by banana pudding, dulce de leche, and a traditional *alfajor* cookie. ⑤ *Average main: $34* ⊠ *2225 N.E. Martin Luther King Blvd., Eliot, Northeast* ☎ *503/284–3366* ⊕ *oxpdx.com* ☾ *Closed Mon. No lunch* ✛ *G1.*

$

SOUTHERN

✕ **Pine State Biscuits.** Loosen your belt a notch or two before venturing inside this down-home Southern restaurant that's especially beloved for its over-the-top breakfast biscuit fare. Pat yourself on the back, or belly, if you can polish off the Reggie Deluxe (a fluffy house-baked biscuit topped with fried chicken, bacon, cheese, an egg, and sage gravy), a masterful mélange of calorie-laden ingredients. Other gut-busting favorites include the steak-club biscuit sandwich, shrimp and grits, and andouille corn dog featuring locally made Otto's sausage. Pine State began at the Saturday Portland Farmers' Market and continues to excel there. The Alberta location, which has both counter and booth seating, keeps the longest hours, serving hungry bar goers into the wee hours. A sleek branch on S.E. Division opened in summer 2014. ⑤ *Average main: $7* ⊠ *2204 N.E. Alberta St., Alberta District, Northeast* ☎ *503/477–6605* ⊕ *www.pinestatebiscuits.com* ☾ *No dinner Mon.–Wed. $7* ⊠ *1100 S.E. Division St., Central East Side, Southeast* ☎ *503/236–3346* ⊕ *www.pinestatebiscuits.com* ✛ *H1.*

$

BARBECUE

✕ **Podnah's Pit BBQ.** Firing up the smoker at 5 every morning, the pit crew at Podnah's spends the day slow cooking some of the best Texas- and Carolina-style barbecue in the Northwest. Melt-in-your-mouth, oak-smoked brisket, ribs, pulled pork, chicken, and lamb are all served up in a sassy vinegar-based sauce. Some sides, like the delicious green-chili mac and cheese, rotate on and off the menu, but the collard greens, barbecue baked beans, and the iceberg wedge, topped with blue cheese and a punchy Thousand Island dressing, are excellent mainstays. Delicious Southwestern and Tex-Mex fare is served at breakfast on weekend mornings. ⑤ *Average main: $15* ⊠ *1625 N.E. Killingsworth St., Vernon, Northeast* ☎ *503/281–3700* ⊕ *podnahspit.com* ✛ *H1.*

$$

SOUTHERN

Fodor'sChoice

★

✕ **Screen Door.** The line that forms outside this Southern cooking restaurant at brunch and dinner is as epic as the food itself. But think of the wait that precedes the meal—which you can spice up with cocktails from the bar—as a chance to ramp up your appetite and fully anticipate the experience to come. A large, packed dining room with canned pickles and peppers along the walls, this Portland hot spot does justice to authentic Southern cooking. Try the fried chicken plate—two moist pieces of meat in crisp and peppery buttermilk batter, accompanied by creamy mashed potatoes and collard greens cooked in bacon fat—or the Screen Door plate with your choice of four sides (consider the mac and cheese, creamy grits, and most any of the salads on the rotating seasonal menu). ⑤ *Average main: $16* ⊠ *2337 E. Burnside St., Kerns,*

Northeast ☎ *503/542–0880* ⊕ *www.screendoorrestaurant.com* ⊗ *No lunch weekdays* ✛ *H3.*

$$
ASIAN FUSION

✕ **Smallwares.** Chef-owner Johanna Ware happily admits to taking creative liberties in the kitchen of her colorful, contemporary bistro in Northeast Portland's somewhat under-the-radar Beaumont neighborhood, describing her restaurant concept as "small plates of inauthentic Asian cuisine meant to be shared." The name of the place, as well as the drinks-centric Barwares lounge in back, is a play on her last name, and the intimate space decorated in a bold black, red, and white color scheme provides the perfect, vibrant milieu for sampling such creatively flavorful treats as rice cakes topped with sea urchin, turmeric chutney, and poppy seed; hanger steak with red miso, chanterelles, balsamic vinegar, and *hijiki* seaweed; and fried kale with candied bacon, fish sauce, and mint. A short menu is served in Barwares until 1 am, and there's an extensive selection of sakes and Asian-inspired cocktails. $ *Average main: $20* ⊠ *4605 N.E. Fremont St., Beaumont, Northeast* ☎ *971/229–0995* ⊕ *www.smallwarespdx.com* ⊗ *No lunch* ✛ *H1.*

$
MEXICAN
Fodor's Choice
★

✕ **Tamale Boy.** Chef Abel Hernandez hails from Veracruz by way of Mexico City, and while he's adept at preparing tamales—both the Oaxacan style wrapped in banana leaves and the more conventional style wrapped in corn husks (try the version filled with roasted pasilla peppers, onions, corn kernels, and *queso fresco*), he also turns out fabulous ceviche and *alambre de camarones* (adobe shrimp with bacon and Oaxacan cheese over flat corn tortillas). Be sure to start with an order of table-side guacamole, and the El Diablo margarita with roasted-habanero-infused tequila and mango purée. Order at the counter in the simple dining room that's brightened with a colorful mural by L.A.-based artist Steven Lopez. When the weather cooperates, take your seat in the expansive side patio. $ *Average main: $7* ⊠ *1764 N.E. Dekum St., Woodlawn, Northeast* ☎ *503/206–8022* ⊕ *www.tamaleboy.com* ⊗ *Closed Mon.* ✛ *G1.*

$
CAFÉ
FAMILY

✕ **Tin Shed Garden Cafe.** Sided in metal, this busy restaurant on Alberta Street is known for its hearty breakfasts—namely, its biscuits and gravy, shredded-potato cakes, egg and tofu scrambles, and breakfast burritos; in fact, it's so well-known that there can be a long wait for a table for breakfast on weekends. The lunch and dinner menus have creative choices as well, like a creamy artichoke sandwich and a mac and cheese of the day. There's a kid's menu containing simple scrambles, sandwiches, and noodles (in the $2–$4 range). Dogs are allowed on the comfortable outdoor patio; there's even a dog menu with a variety of free-range meat dishes (in the $6–$7 range). With a large stone fireplace and chimney, the covered, comfortable outdoor area doubles as a beer garden on warm spring and summer evenings, and the adjacent garden rounds off the property with a peaceful sitting area. $ *Average main: $12* ⊠ *1438 N.E. Alberta St., Alberta District, Northeast* ☎ *503/288–6966* ⊕ *www.tinshedgardencafe.com* ⚠ *Reservations not accepted* ✛ *H1.*

$$ **✕ Toro Bravo.** The success of this wildly popular and impressively authen-
TAPAS tic Spanish tapas bar has spawned a popular cookbook and helped spur
Fodor'sChoice chef-owner John Gorham to create something of a restaurant empire
★ in Portland: he operates three other superb eateries around town. This
bustling spot with closely spaced tables and a lively vibe caters heavily
to groups, as the small-plates format is perfect for sharing. Best bets
include marinated sheep's cheese with rose-petal harissa and mint, grid-
dled bacon-wrapped dates with honey, Basque-style pipérade with a duck
egg and grilled bread, duck-liver-mousse terrine with morel mushrooms
and mustard, and oxtail croquettes topped with chili mayo. There's a
long dessert list that includes a richly delicious olive-oil cake topped
with apple-caramel sauce. If you're feeling indecisive, order the "chef's
choice for the table," which at $40 is a good value for a remarkable vari-
ety of dishes. ⑤ *Average main: $20* ✉ *120 N.E. Russell St., Northeast*
☎ *503/281–4464* ⊕ *www.torobravopdx.com* ⊗ *No lunch* ✛ *G1.*

SOUTHEAST

$$$ **✕ Ava Gene's.** Stumptown Coffee founder Duane Sorenson has steadily
ITALIAN shifted from cafés to full-service restaurants in recent years, having scored
Fodor'sChoice considerable acclaim with his Northwest hunter-gatherer–inspired restau-
★ rant Woodsman Tavern and, in 2013, the fantastic rustic Italian eatery
Ava Gene's, which ranks among the top tables in town both in popularity
and quality. Capsule-shape lamps dangle from the vaulted ceiling of this
buzzy dining room with two long rows of banquette seating and several
more closely spaced tables. Chef Joshua McFadden draws on regional,
home-style recipes from throughout Italy, but focuses on local produce.
You could make an impressive feast of three or four *giardini* (gardens)
sides, such as pumpkin with brown butter, currants, and pecans. Satisfy-
ingly hearty mains include spaghetti with artichokes, *bottarga* (cured fish
roe), and lemon, and the tender culotte steak with radishes and anchovy
butter. The cocktail and wine programs are also top-notch. Next door,
Sorenson's Roman Candle Baking Co. produces delicious wood-baked
Roman-style flatbread pizzas, artisanal breads, and light brunch and
lunch fare. ⑤ *Average main: $27* ✉ *3377 S.E. Division St., Richmond,*
Southeast ☎ *971/229–0571* ⊕ *www.avagenes.com* ⊗ *No lunch* ✛ *G6.*

$ **✕ Apizza Scholls.** The pies at Apizza Scholls, lauded by Anthony Bour-
PIZZA dain, Rachael Ray, and most any pizza lover who visits, deserve the
Fodor'sChoice first-class reputation they enjoy. The greatness of the pies rests not
★ in innovation or complexity, but in the simple quality of the ingredients. The dough is made by hand in small batches and baked to
crispy-outside, tender-inside perfection. The toppings—including basil,
pecorino romano, and house-cured bacon—are fresh and delicious and
served no more than three per pie. While the decor is rather plain and
you'll likely have to wait for a table (reservations are recommended),
you'll forget all once you take your first bite and start basking in
the glory of some of the best pizza in the city. ⑤ *Average main: $13*
✉ *4741 S.E. Hawthorne Blvd., Hawthorne, Southeast* ☎ *503/233–1286*
⊕ *www.apizzascholls.com* ⊗ *No lunch* ✛ *G6.*

$$ **✕ Bamboo Sushi.** The best sushi spot in Portland is also the most envi-
SUSHI ronmentally sustainable, sourcing its fish conscientiously from fishing

2

operations that follow guidelines set by the Monterey Bay Aquarium and Blue Ocean Institute. Try the black cod with smoked soy and roasted garlic glaze or the house-smoked wild ivory salmon *nigiri*. Or, opt for a couple of the signature rolls, like the Lucky 13, an albacore tuna, cucumber, and avocado roll topped with red crab, scallops, *yuzu tobiko* (flying fish roe), and cilantro, or the vegetarian Green Machine, with tempura fried asparagus and green onion topped with avocado and cilantro sweet chili aioli. The sleek, modern interior gives the place a polished, classy feel, and although no item is priced over $20, a meal of several small plates can quickly become spendy. Sidewalk tables allow you to bask in the sunshine while enjoying your meal. There's a second location on 23rd Avenue in Nob Hill, and the owners opened Bamboo Izakaya, with a focus on tasty and sophisticated Japanese bar fare, in Alberta in fall 2014. ⑤ *Average main: $18 ⊠ 310 S.E. 28th Ave., Kerns, Southeast* ☎ *503/232–5255* ⊕ *www.bamboosushi.com* ⊙ *No lunch* ⑤ *Average main: $18 ⊠ 1409 N.E. Alberta St., Alberta District, Southeast* ☎ *503/889–0336* ⊕ *www.bambooizakaya.com* ⊙ *No lunch.* ⑤ *Average main: $18 ⊠ 836 N.W. 23rd Ave., Nob Hill* ☎ *971/229– 1925* ⊕ *bamboosushi.com* ⊙ *No lunch.* ✛ *H4.*

$$
SEAFOOD
Fodor's Choice
★

✕ **Block + Tackle.** This airy, high-ceiling space on trendy Division Street showcases the inventive techniques and dedication to freshness of chef Trent Pierce, who also operates a stellar reservations-only prix-fixe restaurant, Roe, in a small space reached through Block + Tackle's dining room. Offering a conventional à la carte approach, this scene-y seafood spot has a large central communal table, several tables to one side, a long bar, and a large chalkboard menu listing the day's specials and local oysters. Try Dungeness crab Louie with deviled egg and avocado, or the grilled-mackerel sandwich with honey mustard, caraway butter, pickles, and capers. The small-plates portions are designed for sharing. ⑤ *Average main: $22 ⊠ 3113 S.E. Division St., Southeast* ☎ *503/236–0205* ⊕ *www. blockandtacklepdx.com* ⊙ *Closed Mon. and Tues. No lunch* ✛ *H6.*

$
INDIAN

✕ **Bollywood Theater.** Set beneath a soaring beamed ceiling, and with a welcoming mix of worn wooden seating, kitschy decor, bright fabrics, and intoxicating smells, this lively restaurant along Division Street's hoppin' restaurant row specializes in Indian street food and reflects chef-owner Troy MacLarty's colorful, delicious, authentic vision of India as experienced on several trips. Order at the counter, and your food will be brought to you—there's a mix of two-tops and communal tables, with additional seating on a spacious patio. Nosh on *vada pav* (spicy potato dumplings with chutney), *gobi* Manchurian (Indo-Chinese fried cauli-flower with lemon, curry leaves, and sweet-and-sour sauce), and beets roasted in coconut milk, before moving on to one of the larger plates, such as Goan-style shrimp served with a full complement of chutneys, paratha bread, and dal. There's even a market to one side of the open-plan dining room selling spices, curries, and other edibles and gifts from India.The original location in the Alberta Arts District is cute but small, and often crowded. ⑤ *Average main: $12 ⊠ 3010 S.E. Division St., Richmond, Southeast* ☎ *503/477–6699* ⊕ *www.bollywoodtheaterpdx. com* ⑤ *Average main: $12 ⊠ 2039 N.E. Alberta St., Alberta District, Northeast* ☎ *971/200–4711* ⊕ *www.bollywoodtheaterpdx.com* ✛ *H6.*

$
SCANDINAVIAN
Fodor's Choice
★
✕ **Broder.** This delightful neighborhood café—one of the most outstanding brunch spots in town—serves fresh and delicious Scandinavian food with fun-to-pronounce names like *friterade applen* (apple fritter) and *aebleskivers* (Danish pancakes). All the food—the hashes, the baked egg scrambles, the Swedish breakfast boards—is delicious. The Swedish meatballs and egg, shrimp, and chicken salads are also excellent midday choices. The light and narrow space, decorated with rustic modern furniture and accented with white tile and mirrors, has a laid-back and friendly vibe. Though you'll likely have to wait for a table at breakfast, the café serves complimentary coffee and borrows seating from adjacent sister restaurant, Savoy, which opens later in the day. Owner Peter Bro opened a second location, Broder Nord, in North Portland in 2014; that branch also has dinner service. $ *Average main: $11* ✉ *2508 S.E. Clinton St., Hosford-Abernethy, Southeast* ☎ *503/736–3333* ⊕ *www.broderpdx.com* ⊗ *No dinner* $ *Average main: $11* ✉ *2240 N. Interstate Ave., Eliot, North* ☎ *503/282–5555* ⊕ *www.broderpdx.com* ⊗ *No lunch Sun.–Tues.* ✛ *H6.*

$$$$
PACIFIC
NORTHWEST
Fodor's Choice
★
✕ **Castagna Restaurant.** Enjoy artful Pacific Northwest cuisine—like grilled halibut, kohlrabi, and mussels, or summer beans, chanterelles, wilted sorrel, and roasted-duck jus—at this tranquil Hawthorne restaurant. Dinner options from chef Justin Woodward's monthly changing menu include either a classic three-course prix fixe for $75 or a lavish 10-course tasting menu that runs $125; opt for the superb wine pairings for an additional $40 or $60 (with the tasting menu). Next door is the more casual Cafe Castagna, a bistro and bar open nightly, serving simple but still superb burgers, pastas, salads, seafood grills, and other less expensive fare. $ *Average main: $75* ✉ *1752 S.E. Hawthorne Blvd., Hawthorne, Southeast* ☎ *503/231–7373* ⊕ *www.castagnarestaurant.com* ⊗ *Restaurant: Closed Sun.–Tues. No lunch. Cafe: No lunch* ✛ *H6.*

$$$
PACIFIC
NORTHWEST
✕ **Clarklewis.** Located in a former warehouse between the Willamette River and the train tracks in the industrial Central East Side, this upscale restaurant serves up inventive, farm-fresh, modern American cuisine and has an excellent happy hour. The daily changing menu features entrées like fire-grilled lamb with harissa, ratatouille, raisin-and-pinenut gremolata, and a balsamic glaze, and agnolotti pasta with shishito peppers, Dungeness crab, and mascarpone. If you're feeling indecisive or adventurous, let the chef bring you a four-course prix-fixe ($55) meal, which is served family style and spans the menu. The glass-paned garage doors that run along the front wall let in natural light and refreshing breezes when open in summer. $ *Average main: $23* ✉ *1001 S.E. Water Ave., Central East Side, Southeast* ☎ *503/235–2294* ⊕ *www.clarklewispdx.com* ⊗ *Closed Sun. No lunch Sat.* ✛ *F5.*

$$
SOUTHERN
Fodor's Choice
★
✕ **Country Cat.** Pork lovers rejoice: you've found hog heaven. House-cured, slow-cooked country ham and bacon and samplers of pork shoulders, head, and belly await you at this neighborhood craft eatery run by James Beard–nominated chef and in-house butcher Adam Sappington. The menu emphasizes Southern dishes with a Northwest twist, such a fish fry with beer-battered Pacific rockfish, hickory-smoked duck leg with chanterelles and pickled plums, and skillet fried chicken. This is one of the tastiest brunch experiences in town—standouts include

2

pumpkin pancakes with roasted apples and salted-caramel butter, and eggs Benedict with smoked steelhead over a sweet-cream biscuit. There's also a bar here where the Bloody Mary comes garnished with beef jerky, pickled vegetables, and a giant olive. ⑤ *Average main: $18* ✉ *7937 S.E. Stark St., Montavilla, Southeast* ☎ *503/408–1414* ⊕ *www. thecountrycat.net* ✛ *H4.*

$ ✕**Ken's Artisan Pizza.** Doug-fir beams, old wine barrels, and hungry PIZZA crowds surround the glowing, beehive-shaped wood oven in the open-kitchen of this thin-crust pizza joint. Ken Forkish, also of Ken's Artisan Bakery and Trifecta Tavern, uses fresh, organic ingredients for the dough, sauces, and toppings of his pies. Fans rave about the margherita with arugula, the handpressed fennel sausage with onion, and the soppressata with basil. While the roasted vegetable plate and Caeser salad are delicious and the wine selection is solid, pizza is the real star. Be prepared for a wait. ⑤ *Average main: $14* ✉ *304 S.E. 28th Ave., Kerns, Southeast* ☎ *503/517–9951* ⊕ *www.kensartisan.com* ✍ *Reservations not accepted* ⊘ *No lunch* ✛ *H4.*

$$ ✕**Kachka.** In a city with a sizable population of Russian immigrants, RUSSIAN the success of this new Central East Side establishment decorated to Fodor'sChoice resemble a *dasha* is hardly surprising, although it's really the devotion ★ of the city's foodies that resulted in Kachka's white-hot popularity; reservations are a good idea here. If you are expecting heavy cuisine, you'll be surprised by the wonderfully creative and often quite light fare, including plenty of shareable small plates, like crispy beef tongue with sweet onion sauce, orange, and pomegranate; panfried sour-cherry *vareniki* (Ukranian dumplings), and—of course—caviar with blini and all the usual accompaniments. Another crowd-pleaser on the menu is the classic chicken Kiev, prepared the old-fashioned way, oozing with butter. And, yes, there's an extensive vodka selection, plus several Russian beers (the wines are mostly from Oregon and France, but there are some notable Slovenian and Hungarian selections). ⑤ *Average main: $19* ✉ *720 S.E. Grand Ave., Central East Side, Southeast* ☎ *503/235–0059* ⊕ *www.kachkapdx.com* ⊘ *No lunch* ✛ *G5.*

$$$$ ✕**Langbaan.** Guests reach this tiny, wood-paneled, 24-seat gem with THAI an open kitchen by walking through the adjoining PaaDee restaurant Fodor'sChoice and pushing open a faux bookshelf that's actually a door. Of course, ★ you won't even get this far unless you've called ahead to reserve a table: this very special prix-fixe restaurant, serving the most interesting and consistently delicious Asian food in Portland, is only open Thursday–Saturday, with a 6 pm seating each night and an additional 8:30 seating Friday and Saturday. Owner Earl Ninsom and chef Rassamee Ruaysuntia present a weekly changing 10-course, $65 tasting menu that often features exquisite recipes and even some ingredients you'll rarely find outside Thailand. Expect boldly flavorful fare like lobster with fish-sauce-cured pork, mint, shallots, tropical *lambutan* fruit, peanuts, and coconut; or roast duck breast with monkey apple, heart of palm, cherry tomatoes, and a fragrant red curry. There's a $30 wine-pairing option, too—a great deal, all in all, considering the caliber of food and service. ⑤ *Average main: $65* ✉ *6 S.E. 28th Ave., Southeast* ☎ *971/344–2564* ⊕ *www.langbaanpdx.com* ✍ *Reservations essential* ⊘ *Closed Sun.–Wed. No lunch* ✛ *H4.*

$

AMERICAN

Fodor'sChoice

★

Lardo. One of several spots around Portland that has become known for advancing the art of sandwich making, Lardo offers a steady roster of about a dozen wonderfully inventive variations, plus one or two weekly specials, along with no-less-impressive sides like maple carrots, escarole Caesar salads, and "dirty fries" topped with pork scraps, marinated peppers, fried herbs, and Parmesan. Sandwiches of particular note include the tender Korean-style braised pork shoulder with kimchi, chili mayo, cilantro, and lime, and grilled mortadella with provolone, marinated peppers, and mustard aioli. Wash it all down with a drink from the terrific craft-beer and cocktail selection. ■TIP→ **The Hawthorne branch is especially inviting for its large, covered, outdoor seating area, which it shares with the dessert-themed food cart, Hungry Heart Cupcakes.** $ *Average main: $10* ✉ *1212 S.E. Hawthorne Blvd., Southeast* ☎ *503/234–7786* ⊕ *www.lardosandwiches.com* $ *Average main: $10* ✉ *4090 N. Williams Ave., Boise, North* ☎ *503/841–5373* ⊕ *www.lardosandwiches.com* $ *Average main: $10* ✉ *1205 S.W. Washington St., West End, Downtown* ☎ *503/241–2490* ⊕ *www.lardosandwiches.com* ✢ *H6.*

$$$

PACIFIC

NORTHWEST

Fodor'sChoice

★

Laurelhurst Market. With an artisanal butcher shop anchoring the right side of the building, Laurelhurst Market offers some of the best meaty fare in Portland. Case in point: the Wagyu brisket smoked for 12 hours and marinated in Ozark barbecue sauce, and the beef short ribs braised with red wine and prunes. Despite the meat-centric focus, Laurelhurst delivers when it comes to veggies, too: the reasonably priced seasonal salads and sides can serve as interesting, flavorful complements to the meaty main courses or, mixed and matched, as meals themselves. The candlelit dining room is comfortable and sophisticated and the stainless steel kitchen along the back wall underneath the beef cuts diagram illustrates what this place is all about: the preparation and serving of outstanding meat. The butcher shop sells fantastic sandwiches at lunchtime; you can take your purchase to go or eat at one of the restaurant tables, though there's no waitstaff on duty. $ *Average main: $27* ✉ *3155 E. Burnside St., Laurelhurst, Southeast* ☎ *503/206–3097* ⊕ *www.laurelhurstmarket.com* ✢ *H4.*

$

CAFÉ

Fodor'sChoice

★

Lauretta Jean's. Kate McMillen and Noah Cable's pie-focused operation began as a stall at Portland's Saturday farmers' market at PSU and now comprises a couple of charming, homey, brick-and-mortar cafés, with the most atmospheric along Division Street in Southeast. While it's the delicious pies—with feathery-light crusts and delicious fillings like tart cherry, salted pecan, and chocolate-banana cream—that have made Lauretta Jean's a foodie icon in Portland, these cheerful eateries also serve exceptional brunch fare, including the LJ Classic, a fluffy biscuit topped with an over-easy egg, Jack cheese, bacon, and strawberry jam. In the evening, it's a popular spot for desserts and coffee, or even cocktails—the Peppermint Fancy with housemade schnapps and marshmallows along with hot cocoa pairs nicely with the sea-salt brownie. $ *Average main: $6* ✉ *3402 S.E. Division St., Richmond, Southeast* ☎ *503/235–3119* ⊕ *www.laurettajean.com* ☾ *No dinner* $ *Average main: $6* ✉ *600 S.W. Pine St., Southeast* ☎ *503/224–9236* ⊕ *www.laurettajean.com* ☾ *Closed weekends. No dinner* ✢ *H6.*

$$$
FRENCH
Fodor's Choice
★

✕**Le Pigeon.** Specializing in adventurous Northwest-influenced French dishes of extraordinary quality, this cozy and unassuming restaurant consistently ranks among the city's most acclaimed dining venues. The menu changes regularly but often features items like beef-cheek bourguignon, chicken and oxtail with semolina gnocchi, and seared foie gras with chestnut, raisins, bacon, and cinnamon toast (especially exceptional). And, yes, pigeon is served, too. Everything is prepared with balance, nuance, and attention to detail. Less adventurous eaters might opt for the burger, delicious in its own right, and there's always a vegetarian option as well. With exposed brick, mismatched antique china, communal tables, and a counter overlooking the open kitchen that allows diners to interact with the chefs, the atmosphere at this 42-seat restaurant is trendy yet casual. While not required, reservations are a good idea, especially on weekends. James Beard–winning chef Gabriel Rucker also operates an excellent sister restaurant in Downtown, Little Bird Bistro. ⑤ *Average main: $26* ✉ *738 E. Burnside St., Central East Side, Southeast* ☎ *503/546–8796* ⊕ *www.lepigeon.com* ⊙ *No lunch* ⑤ *Average main: $26* ✉ *219 S.W. 6th Ave., Downtown* ☎ *503/688–5952* ⊕ *littlebirdbistro.com* ⊙ *No lunch weekends* ✛ *H4.*

$$
MODERN
AMERICAN
Fodor's Choice
★

✕**Olympic Provisions.** Salumist Elias Cairo made a name for himself throughout the country with his artisanal charcuterie, such as smoked chorizo, pepper-coated capicola, and pork-pistachio pâté, which is sold in fine grocery stores nationally as well as at numerous Portland farmers' markets and gourmet shops. Now Cairo, alongside chef Alex Yoder, is gaining recognition for a pair of stellar, meat-centric restaurants—Olympic Provisions Northwest and Olympic Provisions Southeast—in which you can order platters of charcuterie and cheeses along with more eclectic seasonal American fare. Consider the starter of olive-oil-poached albacore with corona beans, and main dishes that include braised short ribs, roasted French garlic sausage with white beans and tarragon mustard, and roasted chicken thighs with eggplant caponata and garlic-yogurt sauce. The original Central East Side location is in a smartly designed warehouse space and features a glowing "Meat" sign which quite simply says it all. The Northwest branch is in an airy storefront space on the northern edge of the Pearl District. Both spots are popular for brunch and happy hour, and carry extensive cocktail and wine lists. ⑤ *Average main: $22* ✉ *107 S.E. Washington St., Central East Side, Southeast* ☎ *503/954–3663* ⊕ *www.olympicprovisions.com* ⊙ *No dinner Mon.* ⑤ *Average main: $22* ✉ *1632 N.W. Thurman St., Southeast* ☎ *503/894–8136* ⊕ *www.olympicprovisions.com* ⊙ *No dinner Mon.* ✛ *G5.*

$
THAI
Fodor's Choice
★

✕**PaaDee.** Hiding in the shadow of adjoining, attention-hogging, reservations-only sister restaurant Langbaan, PaaDee serves some of the freshest, most flavorful Thai food in town, and at remarkably fair prices given the complexity of the cooking, the warmth of the staff, and the attractiveness of the dining room, which is on the ground floor of a contemporary condo building at the restaurant-blessed intersection of 28th and Burnside. The kitchen here specializes in traditional Thai comfort fare: grilled squid skewers with chili-lime sauce; wild-caught prawns with lemongrass, scallions, ground rice, and a spicy lime dressing; and sautéed pork belly with basil, chili, green beans, and a fried egg rank among the most popular dishes. The bar pours some interesting cocktails and well-chosen local wines and beers, too. $ *Average main: $14* ✉ *6 S.E. 28th Ave., Kerns, Southeast* ☎ *503/360–1453* ⊕ *www. paadeepdx.com* ✛ *H4.*

$

ASIAN

Fodor'sChoice

★

✕ **Pok Pok.** Andy Ricker, the owner of one of Portland's most talked-about restaurants, regularly travels to Southeast Asia to research street food and home-style recipes to include on the menu of this always-hopping spot. Ike's Vietnamese chicken wings, deep-fried in caramelized fish sauce and garlic, are legendary. Other favorites include the namesake green papaya salad and the charcoal-roasted game hen. The menu is designed for sharing, and some dishes are quite fiery—discuss your preferences with the knowledgeable staff before ordering. Diners have the option of sitting outside under tents, or in the funky, cavelike interior. Across the street, sister space Whiskey Soda Lounge is both a Pok Pok waiting area and restaurant in its own right, with a full bar and a limited Pok Pok menu. The Pok Pok mini empire includes Pok Pok Noi in the funky Alberta District and Sen Yai noodle house, a few blocks east of the original Pok Pok on Division. $ *Average main: $14* ✉ *3226 S.E. Division St., Richmond, Southeast* ☎ *503/232–1387* ⊕ *www.pokpokpdx.com* ✛ *H6.*

$$$$

SEAFOOD

Fodor'sChoice

★

✕ **Roe.** With its unmarked entrance in the back of lively restaurant Block + Tackle, and just a handful of tables and a few counter seats overlooking the open kitchen, this intimate spot feels a little under the radar—but it isn't. Roe is regularly lauded by the national restaurant press, and with good reason. The menu changes often and always features a mix of raw and cooked fare, perhaps silver-snapper ceviche with corn, tomato "caviar," smoked-citrus *nuoc mam*, and edamame mousse; and butter-poached blue prawns with buttered-popcorn emulsion and piquillo and padron peppers. Chef Trent Pierce runs both Block + Tackle and Roe, but saves his most complex, inventive creations for Roe, which is open just four nights a week and offers either four- or seven-course prix-fixe menus ($75 or $115 per person), with different wine- and beverage-pairing options available for an additional charge. $ *Average main: $75* ✉ *3113 S.E. Division St., Southeast* ☎ *503/232–1566* ⊕ *www.roepdx. rest* ⌖ *Reservations essential* ⊘ *Closed Sun.–Tues. No lunch* ✛ *H6.*

$$

MODERN AMERICAN

Fodor'sChoice

★

✕ **Trifecta Tavern.** Baker extraordinaire Ken Forkish (of Ken's Artisan Bakery and Artisan Pizza fame) opened this extremely well-received tavern in 2014 inside a converted garage in the industrial Central East Side. The menu still reflects the owner's devotion to wood-fired ovens—there's even a Negroni cocktail infused with charred maple wood on the menu—but you'll also discover an exhaustive selection of snacks and larger plates that have never met with an open flame, such as the compressed-watermelon salad with sheep's milk vinaigrette and spiced almonds. You could make a meal of several bar snacks (Oregon bay shrimp rolls, deviled eggs), or dive into more substantial fare like pork shank with miso broth, or the 18-ounce "Big-Ass Steak," served with wood-fired marrow bones. The airy dining room, with red-leather booths and glass garage-door windows, is festive, if a bit loud. $ *Average main: $20* ✉ *726 S.E. 6th Ave., Central East Side, Southeast* ☎ *503/841–6675* ⊕ *www.trifectapdx.com* ⊘ *No lunch* ✛ *G5.*

WHERE TO STAY

Portland has an unusually rich variety of distinctive, design-driven boutique hotels, historic properties, and charming B&Bs, and while you'll find the usual mix of budget-oriented, midrange, and upscale chains here, if you'd rather avoid cookie-cutter brand-name properties, you're in the right city.

Although you won't find ultraluxury brands like Four Seasons or W Hotels, the vast majority of Downtown properties are high-end, with the rates to prove it, especially during the week when conventions are in town, and during the summer high season, when many properties command at least double what they can during the slower, wetter winter months.

A B&B might make a better option than a larger hotel if you're looking for a more personal and authentic Portland experience. Most of Portland's smaller accommodations are in lively neighborhoods abundant with distinctive shopping and dining, and most often, an inn will offer unique guest rooms, deluxe home-cooked breakfasts, and friendly and knowledgeable innkeepers.

HOTEL PRICES

Although rates have risen considerably in Portland in recent years as the city's popularity has soared, rates even at upscale Downtown hotels are usually a notch or two lower than what you'd pay in other West Coast cities, such as Seattle and San Francisco. In summer, when the city is abuzz with festivals and festival goers, it can be difficult to find a room in Downtown for under $300 nightly. Most of the time, however, even the more luxurious hotels will run you under $250 per night, and there are a lot of options around $175 or less. Outside Downtown, but still within city limits, it is much easier to find rooms in midrange chains and B&Bs for a little over $100 nightly, and at a handful of reliable budget properties around town (we've included several in this chapter), for under $100 nightly.

If you don't mind a dull but pleasant suburban location, the surrounding towns of Beaverton, Lake Oswego, Gresham, and Vancouver, Washington, abound with chain hotels with rates typically 25% to 50% lower than what you'd pay in Portland, and nearly always with free parking. *Hotel reviews have been shortened. For full information, visit Fodors.com.*

WHAT IT COSTS IN U.S. DOLLARS			
$	**$$**	**$$$**	**$$$$**
Hotels	Under $110	$110–$175	$176–$250	Over $250

Hotel prices are the lowest cost of a standard double room in high season.

In alphabetical order by neighborhood. Use the coordinate (✢ B2) at the end of each listing to locate a site on the corresponding map.

DOWNTOWN

$$ **Ace Hotel.** The quintessential Portland hipster hotel, the Ace is sand-
HOTEL   wiched between Stumptown Coffee and Clyde Common restaurant,
Fodor's Choice   a block from Powell's Books and the Pearl District, and right in the
★   heart of Downtown's ever-trendy West End neighborhood. **Pros:** prime
Downtown location; unique design and artwork in each room; free city
bicycles available for guests. **Cons:** water pressure can be weak; some
shared baths. $ *Rooms from: $155* ⊠ *1022 S.W. Stark St., Downtown*
☎ *503/228–2277* ⊕ *www.acehotel.com* ☞ *78 rooms* ⦿ *No meals* ✛ *D4.*

$$$ **Benson Hotel.** Portland's venerable grande dame may now be over-
HOTEL   shadowed by several other upscale properties in town in terms of lux-
ury, especially given the steep rates, but the Benson has hosted most
every president since it opened in 1913. **Pros:** historic building; beautiful
lobby; excellent location; excellent service. **Cons:** rooms and hallways
are a bit dark; many bathrooms are quite small. $ *Rooms from: $249*
⊠ *309 S.W. Broadway, Downtown* ☎ *503/228–2000, 800/716–6199*
⊕ *www.bensonhotel.com* ☞ *230 rooms, 57 suites* ⦿ *No meals* ✛ *D4.*

$$$ **Courtyard by Marriott–Portland City Center.** More boutique feeling than
HOTEL   typical Courtyards, this LEED-certified hotel has individual check-in
kiosks in its lobby rather than one big reception desk, and the spacious,
tasteful rooms showcase local art and photography. **Pros:** environmen-
tal consciousness; in the heart of Downtown; good on-site restaurant.
Cons: only some rooms have tubs; rates are not much lower than some
significantly fancier competitors. $ *Rooms from: $179* ⊠ *550 S.W. Oak
St., Downtown* ☎ *503/505–5000* ⊕ *www.marriott.com* ☞ *253 rooms,
3 suites* ⦿ *No meals* ✛ *E4.*

$$$ **Embassy Suites Portland–Downtown.** The grand lobby of the former
HOTEL   Multnomah Hotel, built in 1912, offers an extravagant welcome to
FAMILY   this all-suites hotel located close to both the riverfront and Old Town.
Pros: central location; atmospheric old building; breakfast and evening drinks and snacks included. **Cons:** surrounding blocks can feel
a bit seedy (though still quite safe) at night; no in-and-out privileges
in $27 self-park garage across the street. $ *Rooms from: $189* ⊠ *319
S.W. Pine St., Downtown* ☎ *503/279–9000, 800/643–7892* ⊕ *www.
embassyportland.com* ☞ *276 suites* ⦿ *Breakfast* ✛ *E4.*

$$$$ **Heathman Hotel.** From the teak-paneled lobby to the marble fireplaces
HOTEL   to the rosewood elevators with Warhol prints at each landing, this
Fodor's Choice   wonderfully atmospheric, art-filled 1927 hotel exudes refinement. **Pros:**
★   superior service; central location adjoining Portland Center for the Performing Arts, and a block from Portland Art Museum; outstanding art
collection. **Cons:** some rooms are small; expensive parking. $ *Rooms
from: $269* ⊠ *1001 S.W. Broadway, Downtown* ☎ *503/241–4100,
800/551–0011* ⊕ *portland.heathmanhotel.com* ☞ *110 rooms, 40 suites*
⦿ *No meals* ✛ *D5.*

$$$ **Hotel deLuxe.** This retro-glam 1912 boutique hotel with its original
HOTEL   chandeliers, gilded ceilings, black-and-white photography (arranged
Fodor's Choice   by movie themes), heavy drapes, and hip cocktail lounge evokes Hol-
★   lywood's golden age, but with welcome modern touches like flat-screen
TVs, free Wi-Fi, and iPod docks. **Pros:** fun and artistic vibe; friendly
and helpful staff; nice touches like pillow menu, preprogrammed iPods,

BEST BETS FOR PORTLAND LODGING

Fodor's offers a selective listing of fine lodging experiences in every price range, from the city's best budget beds to its most sophisticated luxury hotels. Here we've compiled our top recommendations by price and experience. The very best properties—in other words, those that provide a particularly remarkable experience in their price range—are designated in the listings with the Fodor's Choice logo.

spiritual book library, and classic movies. **Cons:** standard rooms are a bit compact; location is less central than competitors. $ *Rooms from: $189 ✉ 729 S.W. 15th Ave., Downtown ☎ 503/219–2094, 866/986–8085 ⊕ www.hoteldeluxeportland.com ➫ 97 rooms, 33 suites* ☉No meals ✛ C4.

$$$ 🔲 **Hotel Lucia.** Black-and-white celebrity photos from Pulitzer Prize–win-
HOTEL ner and native Oregonian David Hume Kennerly, comfy leather chairs, and stylish low-slung furniture adorn the rooms of this nine-story, 1909 European-style boutique hotel in the heart of Downtown. **Pros:** prime location; luxurious amenities; two outstanding restaurants. **Cons:** lim-ited shelf and storage space in the small bathrooms; steep rates during busy times. $ *Rooms from: $229 ✉ 400 S.W. Broadway, Downtown ☎ 503/225–1717, 866/986–8086 ⊕ www.hotellucia.com ➫ 127 rooms, 33 suites* ☉No meals ✛ D4.

$$$ 🔲 **Hotel Modera.** Decorated with local artwork, sleek, contemporary
HOTEL furnishings, and wood-and-marble accents, this boutique property is both upscale and accessible, and offers a location convenient to the Southwest Park Blocks and Portland State University. **Pros:** friendly staff; nice courtyard; great bar-restaurant; individually bagged ice in hand-carved chests in every hall. **Cons:** rooms on the small side; no on-site gym; a 10- to 15-minute walk from West End and Pearl Dis-trict dining and nightlife. $ *Rooms from: $209 ✉ 515 S.W. Clay St., Downtown ☎ 503/484–1084, 877/484–1084 ⊕ www.hotelmodera.com ➫ 167 rooms, 7 suites* ☉No meals ✛ D6.

$$$$ 🔲 **Hotel Monaco.** This artsy Downtown Portland outpost of the
HOTEL Kimpton-operated Monaco boutique-hotel brand offers eclectic tex-
Fodor's Choice tiles and patterns, bright spaces and bold colors, quirky amenities like
★ complimentary companion goldfish for your room, and the overall sense that staying here is a lot of fun. **Pros:** sumptuous interior; interesting decor; impeccable service; well-equipped fitness center; excellent on-site restaurant and bar. **Cons:** design style may not suit all; pricey. $ *Rooms from: $289 ✉ 506 S.W. Washington St., Downtown ☎ 503/222–0001, 888/207–2201 ⊕ www.portland-monaco.com ➫ 86 rooms, 135 suites* ☉No meals ✛ E4.

$$$ 🔲 **Hotel Rose.** This recently renovated and rebranded boutique property
HOTEL overlooking the Willamette River affords stellar views of the water, easy access to the waterfront park and the events that take place there (Rose Festival, Blues Festival, Gay Pride, and so on), and—as part of the Pineapple Hospitality chain—a pineapple-cupcake welcome at recep-tion. **Pros:** central location on the riverfront; typically lower rates than many comparable Downtown hotels; complimentary bike rentals; easy access to the MAX. **Cons:** rooms not facing the river have dull views; no on-site fitness facility. $ *Rooms from: $219 ✉ 50 S.W. Morrison St., Downtown ☎ 503/221–0711, 866/866–7977 ⊕ www.hotelfifty.com ➫ 140 rooms, 1 suite* ☉No meals ✛ E5.

$$$ 🔲 **Hotel Vintage Plaza.** This historic landmark takes its theme from Ore-
HOTEL gon vineyards, with rooms named after local wineries, complimentary wine served every evening, and an extensive collection of Oregon vin-tages displayed in the tasting room. **Pros:** terrific on-site Italian restau-rant, Pazzo; friendly staff; several distinctive and romantic specialty

suites. **Cons:** pricey parking; some street noise on the lower levels on the Washington Street side. $ *Rooms from: $249* ✉ *422 S.W. Broadway, Downtown* ☎ *503/228–1212, 800/263–2305* ⊕ *www.vintageplaza.com* ➥ *96 rooms, 21 suites* ❑ *No meals* ✛ *D4.*

$$$
HOTEL
Mark Spencer Hotel. This family-owned hotel, with a prime location in the hip West End near Powell's Books and the Pearl District, is one of the better values in town, with most of its warmly decorated rooms containing well-equipped kitchenettes. **Pros:** commitment to the arts; afternoon tea and cookies and evening local wine tasting; most rooms have kitchenettes. **Cons:** some rooms are small and dark; street noise can be a problem. $ *Rooms from: $219* ✉ *409 S.W. 11th Ave., Downtown* ☎ *503/224–3293, 800/548–3934* ⊕ *www.markspencer.com* ➥ *36 rooms, 66 suites* ❑ *Breakfast* ✛ *D4.*

$
HOTEL
McMenamins Crystal Hotel. Travelers who appreciate good music and good beer—especially together—love this West End branch of the McMenamin brothers' unorthodox empire, which is home to three bars and a restaurant and is affiliated with the Crystal Ballroom concert venue a block away. **Pros:** historic building with eccentric, rock-star vibe and decor; lots of bars and dining both on-site and on surrounding blocks; shared-bath rooms are extremely affordable. **Cons:** quirky vibe isn't for everyone; shared bath down the hall in most rooms; no TVs. $ *Rooms from: $105* ✉ *303 S.W. 12th Ave., Downtown* ☎ *503/972– 2670, 855/205–3930* ⊕ *www.mcmenamins.com/crystalhotel* ➥ *51 rooms, 9 with bath* ❑ *No meals* ✛ *C4.*

$$$$
HOTEL
Fodor's Choice
★
The Nines. On the top nine floors of a former landmark department store, this swanky hotel, part of the Starwood Luxury Collection, has the city's poshest accommodations, with luxe decor, great views, and two see-and-be-seen restaurants. **Pros:** stunning views; swanky vibe and cool design; two scene-y restaurants. **Cons:** rooms facing the atrium and overlooking the bar and restaurant can be noisy; expensive valet-only parking. $ *Rooms from: $329* ✉ *525 S.W. Morrison St., Downtown* ☎ *503/222–9996, 877/229–9995* ⊕ *www.thenines.com* ➥ *318 rooms, 13 suites* ❑ *No meals* ✛ *D4.*

$$$
HOTEL
The Paramount Hotel. This pale-stone, 15-story hotel overlooking Director Park is a few blocks from Pioneer Square, the Arlene Schnitzer Concert Hall, the Portland Art Museum, the MAX, and the streetcar. **Pros:** central location; beautiful granite bathrooms; excellent bar and restaurant off lobby. **Cons:** small fitness facility; parking is expensive. $ *Rooms from: $219* ✉ *808 S.W. Taylor St., Downtown* ☎ *503/223–9900* ⊕ *www.portlandparamount.com* ➥ *152 rooms, 2 suites* ❑ *No meals* ✛ *D5.*

$$$$
HOTEL
RiverPlace Hotel. With textured wall coverings, pillows made of Pendleton wool, and a color palette of slate blue, mustard yellow, and a variety of browns, this Kimpton-operated boutique hotel on the banks of the Willamette River captures the look and feel of the Pacific Northwest. **Pros:** stellar views and park-side riverfront location; rooms are spacious and airy; some suites have wood-burning fireplaces. **Cons:** location on south edge of Downtown is a bit of a walk from bars, restaurants, and shopping. $ *Rooms from: $309* ✉ *1510 S.W. Harbor Way, Downtown* ☎ *503/228–3233, 888/869–3108* ⊕ *www.riverplacehotel.com* ➥ *39 rooms, 45 suites* ❑ *No meals* ✛ *E6.*

$$$
HOTEL
Fodor'sChoice
★

▦ **Sentinel Hotel.** Formerly known as the Governor Hotel, the grand Sentinel Hotel underwent a $6 million renovation and rebranding in 2014 to take it from historic to hip-historic; all guest rooms and public spaces in the landmark, early-20th-century buildings were brought up-to-date, and the hotel now reflects a very Portland vibe, with locally sourced textiles, furnishings, and goods. **Pros:** indie style meets luxury; central location; spacious, well-designed rooms; well-equipped gym. **Cons:** pricey valet parking. ⑤ *Rooms from: $199* ⊠ *614 S.W. 10th Ave., Downtown* ☎ *503/224–3400, 888/246–5631* ⊕ *www.sentinelhotel.com* ⤳ *76 rooms, 24 suites* †⦿| *No meals* ✢ *D4.*

$$$
HOTEL

▦ **The Westin Portland.** This pale-stone, upscale hotel combines luxury with convenience, with Pioneer Square and the MAX just two blocks away, and West End and Pearl District dining within a 10-minute walk. **Pros:** prime Downtown location (a stone's throw from one of the city's largest, most established food-cart pods); handsome rooms; plush bedding. **Cons:** pricey overnight parking; attractive but not especially distinctive rooms. ⑤ *Rooms from: $209* ⊠ *750 S.W. Alder St., Downtown* ☎ *503/294–9000, 888/625–5144* ⊕ *www.westinportland.com* ⤳ *189 rooms, 16 suites* †⦿| *No meals* ✢ *D4.*

PEARL DISTRICT

$$$
HOTEL
Fodor'sChoice
★

▦ **Residence Inn–Pearl District.** Opened in spring 2014, this sleek, six-floor, all-suites hotel is the trendy Pearl District's first hotel. **Pros:** new, modern design both inside and out; best location for proximity to Pearl District businesses; in-room kitchens; many rooms can sleep four to six guests. **Cons:** a little far from Downtown attractions; parking costs $32 nightly. ⑤ *Rooms from: $179* ⊠ *1150 N.W. 9th Ave., Pearl District* ☎ *503/220–1339, 888/236–2427* ⊕ *www.marriott.com* ⤳ *224 suites* †⦿| *Breakfast* ✢ *D2.*

NOB HILL

$$
B&B/INN

▦ **Heron Haus.** In a stately, ivy-covered mansion built in 1904, this bright and lovely Tudor Revival home sets you on a lush, fern-covered hillside within walking distance of Forest Park, overlooking the trendy Nob Hill shopping and dining area, and just a 10-minute walk to the streetcar. **Pros:** serene environment; discerning owners have great local knowledge; off-street parking. **Cons:** the residential neighborhood is a bit inconvenient to the Downtown core; no tubs in bathrooms. ⑤ *Rooms from: $175* ⊠ *2545 N.W. Westover Rd., Nob Hill* ☎ *503/274–1846* ⊕ *www.heronhaus.com* ⤳ *6 rooms* †⦿| *Breakfast* ✢ *A2.*

$$$
HOTEL
FAMILY
Fodor'sChoice
★

▦ **Inn @ Northrup Station.** Bright colors, bold patterns, and retro designs characterize this Nob Hill hotel containing luxurious suites with full kitchens or kitchenettes. **Pros:** roomy suites have kitchens and feel like home; steps from Nob Hill shopping, dining, and the streetcar; free parking. **Cons:** the bold color scheme isn't for everyone; a 15-minute walk, or slightly shorter streetcar ride, from Downtown core; in demand so it can be hard to get a reservation. ⑤ *Rooms from: $199* ⊠ *2025 N.W. Northrup St., Nob Hill* ☎ *503/224–0543, 800/224–1180* ⊕ *www.northrupstation.com* ⤳ *70 suites* †⦿| *Breakfast* ✢ *B2.*

$$ 🏨 **Silver Cloud Inn–Portland.** The sole Portland branch of a small, Seattle-
HOTEL area, midprice hotel chain is just a block from the lively upper end of
N.W. 23rd Avenue and a great alternative to the bustle Downtown.
Pros: free parking; close to Nob Hill boutiques and dining as well as
Forest Park hiking trails; easy access to bus and streetcar. **Cons:** gym
but no pool; not especially close to Downtown; front rooms face a
busy street. $ *Rooms from: $159* ✉ *2426 N.W. Vaughn St., Nob Hill*
☎ *503/242–2400, 800/205–6939* ⊕ *www.silvercloud.com* ➾ *75 rooms,
6 suites* ⊚ *Breakfast* ✛ *A1.*

NORTH

$$ 🏨 **Caravan–The Tiny House Hotel.** In keeping with the artsy, idiosyncratic
B&B/INN vibe of the surrounding Alberta Arts District, this cluster of itty-bitty
custom-built houses-on-wheels offers visitors the chance to experience
Portland's unabashed quirky side. **Pros:** a quirky, only-in-Portland experience; in the heart of Alberta's hip retail-dining district; all units have
kitchenettes. **Cons:** these houses really are tiny; 15-minute drive or
35-minute bus ride from Downtown; often books up weeks in advance
(especially weekends). $ *Rooms from: $125* ✉ *5009 N.E. 11th Ave.,
Alberta Arts District, North* ☎ *503/288–5225* ⊕ *www.tinyhousehotel.
com* ➾ *6 cottages* ⊚ *No meals* ✛ *G1.*

$ 🏨 **Viking Motel.** When this clean, family-run, midcentury motel opened
HOTEL in the late 1970s, it served the nearby shipyard; today, this eco-friendly
Fodor'sChoice property is arguably Portland's best bargain lodging, catering to savvy
★ visitors who take the nearby MAX to Downtown Portland. **Pros:** rock-
bottom rates (and free parking and Wi-Fi); friendly owners who take
great pride in the property's upkeep; just off Interstate 5 and a block from
MAX light-rail station. **Cons:** North Portland neighborhood is 15-minute
drive north of Downtown; few frills. $ *Rooms from: $65* ✉ *6701 N.
Interstate Ave., Arbor Lodge, North* ☎ *503/285–4896, 800/308–5097*
⊕ *www.vikingmotelportland.com* ➾ *26 rooms* ⊚ *No meals* ✛ *E1.*

NORTHEAST

$$ 🏨 **DoubleTree by Hilton–Portland.** This bustling, business hotel maintains
HOTEL a steady customer base in meetings and special events, so you will
find all the usual business-friendly perks and luxuries, and—as a lei-
sure traveler—the best rates on weekends. **Pros:** convenient location
for light rail, conventions, and concerts and Trail Blazers basketball
games; nice views from upper floors. **Cons:** pool is outdoors; hotel
can be crowded with conventioneers; surrounding Lloyd District has
chain shops and movie theaters but lacks charm. $ *Rooms from: $149*
✉ *1000 N.E. Multnomah St., Lloyd District, Northeast* ☎ *503/281–
6111, 800/222–8733* ⊕ *www.doubletree.com* ➾ *458 rooms, 18 suites*
⊚ *No meals* ✛ *H2.*

$ 🏨 **Everett Street Guesthouse.** Innkeeper Terry Rusinow proudly assures
B&B/INN guests who stay in her 1907 Craftsman-style bed-and-breakfast that
they won't encounter any "frilly curtains, teddy bears, or potpourri"—
indeed, the two cozy rooms and adjacent cottage are tastefully appointed
with well-chosen artwork and crafts. **Pros:** affordable; simple, tasteful

rooms; short walk from the terrific restaurants and bars of 28th and Burnside. **Cons:** with so few rooms and great rates, it can book up fast; 10-minute drive or 20-minute bus ride from Downtown. $ *Rooms from: $90* ✉ *2306 N.E. Everett St., Kerns, Northeast* ☎ *503/230–0211* ⊕ *www.everettstreetguesthouse.com* ⇨ *2 rooms with shared bath, 1 cottage* ⦿| *Breakfast* ✛ *H3.*

$$
B&B/INN
Fodor'sChoice
★

🖭 **Lion and the Rose Victorian B&B.** Oak and mahogany floors, original light fixtures, and a coffered dining-room ceiling set a tone of formal elegance in this 1906 mansion, while the wonderfully friendly, accommodating, and knowledgeable innkeepers—Dusty and Steve—make sure that you feel perfectly at home. **Pros:** gorgeous house; top-notch service; home-cooked meals. **Cons:** young children not allowed in main house; nearest commercial neighborhood, the Lloyd District, is pretty bland. $ *Rooms from: $155* ✉ *1810 N.E. 15th Ave., Irvington, Northeast* ☎ *503/287–9245, 800/955–1647* ⊕ *www.lionrose.com* ⇨ *7 rooms, 1 apartment* ⦿| *Breakfast* ✛ *H1.*

$$
HOTEL
FAMILY
Fodor'sChoice
★

🖭 **McMenamins Kennedy School.** In a renovated elementary school on the edge of a trendy Northeast Portland neighborhood, Oregon's famously creative McMenamin brothers hoteliers have created a quirky and fantastical multiuse facility with rooms that feature original schoolhouse touches like chalkboards and cloakrooms and literature-inspired themes, a movie theater, a restaurant, a warm outdoor soaking pool, a brewery, and several small bars. **Pros:** funky and authentic Portland experience; room rates include movies and use of year-round soaking pool; free parking; close to trendy Alberta Arts District. **Cons:** rooms have showers but no tubs; no TVs in rooms; 20-minute drive or 40-minute bus ride from Downtown. $ *Rooms from: $139* ✉ *5736 N.E. 33rd Ave., Concordia, Northeast* ☎ *503/249–3983* ⊕ *www.kennedyschool.com* ⇨ *57 rooms* ⦿| *No meals* ✛ *G1.*

$$
B&B/INN

🖭 **Portland's White House Bed and Breakfast.** Hardwood floors with Oriental rugs, chandeliers, antiques, and fountains create a warm and romantic mood at this lavish 1910 Greek Revival mansion in the historic Irvington District. **Pros:** over-the-top romantic; excellent service; a short drive or bus ride to several hip East Side restaurant and retail districts. **Cons:** in residential neighborhood a few miles from Downtown; nearest commercial neighborhood is the rather bland Lloyd District. $ *Rooms from: $135* ✉ *1914 N.E. 22nd Ave., Irvington, Northeast* ☎ *503/287–7131, 800/272–7131* ⊕ *www.portlandswhitehouse.com* ⇨ *8 suites* ⦿| *Breakfast* ✛ *H1.*

AIRPORT

The airport is about a 20- to 25-minute drive away from Downtown Portland, and as expected you can find a number of chain properties here, all offering much lower rates than comparable Downtown hotels.

$$
HOTEL

🖭 **Aloft Portland Airport at Cascade Station.** High-end vibrant design, sophisticated amenities, and close proximity to the Cascade Station MAX station make the first Aloft in Oregon a standout amid the generally mediocre hotels near the airport. **Pros:** lots of high-tech amenities; welcoming social areas; stylish, spacious rooms. **Cons:** airport location; no sit-down restaurant; no complimentary breakfast. $ *Rooms from: $159* ✉ *9920 N.E. Cascades Pkwy., Airport, Northeast*

🖂 *503/200–5678* ⊕ *www.aloftportlandairport.com* ⬌ *136 rooms*
🍽 *No meals* ✛ *H1.*

$$ 🛏 **Embassy Suites Portland Airport.** Suites in this eight-story atrium hotel,
HOTEL within view of the airport, come with separate bedrooms, living areas
with sleeper sofas, and flat-screen TVs. **Pros:** spacious suites; full break-
fast and happy-hour cocktails included; walking distance from Cascade
Station chain shops and restaurants. **Cons:** airport location; parking is
$10. ⑤ *Rooms from: $149* ✉ *7900 N.E. 82nd Ave., Airport, Northeast*
🖂 *503/460–3000* ⊕ *www.portlandairport.embassysuites.com* ⬌ *251
suites* 🍽 *Breakfast* ✛ *H1.*

SOUTHEAST

$$ 🛏 **Evermore Guesthouse.** Just a block from the trendy dining along South-
B&B/INN east Portland's hip Division Street, this beautifully restored, 1909 Arts
Fodor'sChoice and Crafts–style mansion contains spacious, light-filled rooms, some
★ with private balconies, claw-foot soaking tubs, and good-size sitting
areas; one detached suite has a full kitchen, and a cozy and romantic
third-floor room has skylights and pitched ceilings. **Pros:** located in
hip, charming neighborhood with many bars and restaurants; reasonably priced with free off-street parking; free laundry and breakfast;
distinctive, charming decor. **Cons:** some rooms face busy Cesar Chavez
Boulevard; a 15-minute drive or 30-minute bus ride from Downtown.
⑤ *Rooms from: $120* ✉ *3860 S.E. Clinton St., Richmond, Southeast*
🖂 *503/206–6509, 877/600–6509* ⊕ *www.evermoreguesthouse.com*
⬌ *3 rooms, 3 suites* 🍽 *Breakfast* ✛ *H6.*

$$ 🛏 **Jupiter Hotel.** The hip, creative, and adventurous flock to this contem-
HOTEL porary boutique hotel, formerly a motor inn, adjacent to the Doug Fir
Lounge, a bar and restaurant that's also one of the city's most popular
concert venues. **Pros:** funky decor and vibe; trendy bar and music club
attached; easy access to Downtown. **Cons:** youthful; hipster personal-
ity isn't to everyone's taste; request a room on the "chill side" if you
want distance from the noisy patio/bar scene; thin walls between rooms.
⑤ *Rooms from: $164* ✉ *800 E. Burnside St., Central East Side, South-
east* 🖂 *503/230–9200, 877/800–0004* ⊕ *www.jupiterhotel.com* ⬌ *80
rooms, 1 suite* 🍽 *No meals* ✛ *H4.*

SOUTHWEST

$$$ 🛏 **River's Edge Hotel & Spa.** On the edge of Portland's recently developed
HOTEL South Waterfront District and just a 10- to 15-minute drive or bus ride
from Downtown, this tranquil boutique property is nestled among trees
along the meandering Willamette River. **Pros:** expansive river views;
most rooms have balconies; trails nearby for walking and jogging; full-
service spa on-site. **Cons:** few restaurants or businesses within walking distance; need a car or bus to get to Downtown; only valet ($25)
parking is available. ⑤ *Rooms from: $219* ✉ *0455 S.W. Hamilton Ct.,
South Waterfront, Southwest* 🖂 *503/802–5800, 888/556–4402* ⊕ *www.
riversedgehotel.com* ⬌ *81 rooms, 18 suites* 🍽 *Breakfast* ✛ *E6.*

NIGHTLIFE AND PERFORMING ARTS

Portland is quite the creative town. Every night top-ranked dance, theater, and musical performers take the stage somewhere in the city. Expect to find never-ending choices for things to do, from taking in true independent films, performance art, and plays, to checking out some of the Northwest's (and the country's) hottest bands at one of the city's many nightclubs or concert venues.

Given the city's unabashed passion for craft cocktails and beer, local wines, and artisanal coffee, it makes sense that Portland abounds with cool lounges, coffeehouses, and bars. Hard-core clubbing and dancing has a bit less of a following here than more casual barhopping, and Portlanders do like to combine noshing and sipping—you'll find an abundance of nightspots serving exceptional food (and often offering great happy-hour deals on victuals and drinks), and quite a few full-service restaurants with popular side bars and lounges. Nightlife and dining really overlap in the Rose City.

EVENT LISTINGS

"A&E, The Arts and Entertainment Guide," published each Friday in the *Oregonian* (⊕ *www.oregonlive.com*), contains listings of performers, productions, events, and club entertainment. *Willamette Week* (⊕ *wweek.com*), published free each Wednesday and widely available throughout the metropolitan area, contains similar, but hipper, listings. The *Portland Mercury* (⊕ *www.portlandmercury.com*), also free, is an even edgier entertainment publication distributed each Wednesday. The glossy newsstand magazine *Portland Monthly* (⊕ *www. portlandmonthlymag.com*) covers Portland culture and lifestyle and provides great nightlife, entertainment, and dining coverage for the city. The free monthly publication *Portland Family Magazine* (⊕ *www. portlandfamily.com*) has an excellent calendar of events for recreational and educational opportunities for families. PQ Monthly (⊕ *www. pqmonthly.com*) is the city's gay publication.

NIGHTLIFE

Portland has become something of a base for up-and-coming alternative-rock bands, which perform in clubs scattered throughout the city. Good jazz groups perform nightly in a handful of bars as well.

Portland's most diverting neighborhoods for barhopping are, not surprisingly, its favored dining districts, too—the West End, Pearl District, and Nob Hill on the west side of the Willamette River, within walking distance (or a streetcar ride) of Downtown hotels; Alberta Street, North Mississippi Avenue, East Burnside Street in the 20s, the Central East Side, Belmont Street, Hawthorne Boulevard, and Division Street on the East Side. Note that many of the restaurants listed in Where to Eat also double as highly popular nightspots; especially notable for sipping and socializing are Bluehour, Clyde Common, Departure, Interurban, Irving Street Kitchen, RingSide Steakhouse, Smallwares, and Veritable Quandary.

DOWNTOWN
BARS AND LOUNGES

Fodor'sChoice ★ **Driftwood Room.** Once your eyes adjust to the romantically dim lighting, you'll find a curved bar, leather banquette seating, and polished-wood ceilings and walls in this retro-chic bar in the Old Hollywood–themed Hotel deLuxe. The trendy cocktails are garnished with herbs culled from the hotel's garden. ■ TIP→ **The happy-hour food menu is one of the best in the city.** ✉ *Hotel deLuxe, 729 S.W. 15th Ave., Downtown* ☎ *503/820–2076* ⊕ *www.hoteldeluxeportland.com.*

Fodor'sChoice ★ **The Heathman Restaurant & Bar.** At the elegant Heathman Hotel, you can sip tea in the eucalyptus-paneled Tea Court or beer, wine, and cocktails in the marble bar. This is one of the city's most popular see-and-be-seen venues, especially before or after shows at nearby theaters and concert halls. ✉ *1001 S.W. Broadway, Downtown* ☎ *503/790–7752* ⊕ *www. heathmanrestaurantandbar.com.*

Huber's Cafe. The city's oldest restaurant (est. 1879) is notable for its old-fashioned feel and iconic Spanish coffee cocktail, which is set aflame at your table. The old bar in the back has great character. Huber's is on the ground floor of the historic Oregon Pioneer Building, which is being converted into an upscale boutique hotel with a planned 2015 opening, but Huber's will remain open during construction. ✉ *411 S.W. 3rd Ave., Downtown* ☎ *503/228–5686* ⊕ *www.hubers.com.*

Fodor'sChoice ★ **Multnomah Whiskey Library.** Smartly dressed mixologists roll drink carts around the seductively clubby room—with beam ceilings, wood panelling, leather club chairs, a wood-burning fireplace, and crystal chandeliers—pouring cocktails table-side. The emphasis, of course, is whiskey and bourbon—Multnomah has such an extensive collection in its "library" that bartenders need rolling ladders to access the bottles perched on the tall shelves lining the exposed-brick walls—but don't overlook the impressive food menu. ✉ *1124 S.W. Alder St., West End, Downtown* ☎ *503/954–1381* ⊕ *www.multnomahwhiskeylibrary.com.*

Raven & Rose. Popular with the after-work set as well as guests of Downtown hotels, this ornate Victorian two-level carriage house amid Downtown's office towers serves English-style pub fare and a worldly list of beers, wines, and cocktails in the Rookery Bar upstairs. Downstairs, you'll find a main dining room and a small lounge area. There's live music some evenings. ✉ *1331 S.W. Broadway, Downtown* ☎ *503/222–7673* ⊕ *www.ravenandrosepdx.com.*

Saucebox. A sophisticated crowd flocks here to enjoy colorful cocktails and trendy DJ music many evenings a week. The kitchen turns out consistently good pan-Asian fare. ✉ *214 S.W. Broadway, Downtown* ☎ *503/241–3393* ⊕ *www.saucebox.com.*

BREWPUBS AND MICROBREWERIES

First National Taphouse. Opened in fall 2014 near Portland State University—a section of Downtown surprisingly bereft of noteworthy bars—this outpost of a Eugene brewpub carries an exhaustive selection of some 30 beers on tap, plus another 400 or so by the bottle, along with wines, hard ciders, and spirits. Upscale pub fare is served, too, and the weekend brunch has quickly become popular. ✉ *1962 S.W. 5th Ave., Downtown* ☎ *971/703–4579* ⊕ *www.firstnationaltaphouse.com.*

COFFEEHOUSES

Case Study Coffee. A first-rate indie alternative to the scads of chain coffeehouses in Downtown, Case Study serves exceptional, house-roasted coffee in a variety of formats, from Chemex to Aeropress; they also make their own syrups and serve delicious drinking chocolates. Nibble delectable sweets from local bakeries Nuvrei and Petunia's (the latter is gluten-free). There are two additional locations in Northeast, as well as one in Hollywood and a newer one in Alberta. Other locations include 5347 N.E. Sandy Blvd. (Northeast) and 1422 N. E. Alberta St. (Northeast). ✉ *802 S.W. 10th Ave., Downtown* ☎ *503/475–3979* ⊕ *www.casestudycoffee.com* ✉ *5347 N.E. Sandy Blvd., Hollywood, Northeast* ☎ *503/477–8221* ⊕ *www.casestudycoffee.com.* ✉ *1422 N.E. Alberta St., Alberta District, Northeast* ☎ *503/477–8221* ⊕ *www. casestudycoffee.com*

Fodors Choice ★ **Heart Coffee.** Inside this sleek East Burnside coffeehouse, patrons sip coffees from Central America, South America, and Africa, and feast on *affogato* (homemade coconut ice cream topped with a shot of espresso) while admiring the rather elegant roasting equipment, which looks like a large-scale art installation. Finnish owner Wille Yli-Luoma brings a modern, minimalist aesthetic to this fiercely popular café. There's another location at 537 S.W. 12th Ave. (Downtown). ✉ *2211 E. Burnside St., Downtown* ☎ *503/206–6602* ⊕ *www.heartroasters.com* ✉ *537 S.W. 12th Ave., West End, Downtown* ☎ *503/224–0036* ⊕ *www. heartroasters.com.*

GAY AND LESBIAN

Casey's. Having moved from Old Town to a large, rather snazzy two-level space in Downtown, just a block or so from another popular LGBT hangout, the Silverado strip club, this festive gay video bar draws a mixed-age crowd for tempting happy-hour deals (daily 3–7 pm), karaoke, and assorted drinking games. ✉ *412 S.W. 4th Ave., Downtown* ☎ *503/505–9468* ⊕ *www.caseyspdx.net.*

Scandals. This low-key bar is the lone remaining LGBT hangout in the West End, which used to be the city's gay nightlife district (it's still a diverse, progressive neighborhood with plenty of mixed hangouts, but the city's gay bars are now mostly in Old Town). There's a small dance floor, a pool table, and light food service noon to closing. The plate-glass windows offer a view of Stark Street, and there's also seating along the sidewalk. ✉ *1125 S.W. Stark St., Downtown* ☎ *503/227–5887* ⊕ *www. scandalspdx.com.*

LIVE MUSIC

McMenamins Crystal Ballroom. With a 7,500-square-foot springy dance floor built on ball bearings to ramp up the energy, this historic former dance hall draws local, regional, and national acts every night but Monday. Past performers include Billy Idol, Jefferson Airplane, Emylou Harris, Death Cab for Cutie, and the Shins. ✉ *1332 W. Burnside St., Downtown* ☎ *503/225–0047* ⊕ *www.mcmenamins.com.*

PEARL DISTRICT
BARS AND LOUNGES

Fodor'sChoice **Teardrop Cocktail Lounge.** A swanky, see-and-be-seen bar in the heart
★ of the trendy Pearl District, Teardrop has earned a loyal following
for its creative cocktail menu. ✉ *1015 N.W. Everett St., Pearl District*
☎ *503/445–8109* ⊕ *www.teardroplounge.com.*

BREW PUBS AND MICROBREWERIES

Fodor'sChoice **BridgePort BrewPub & Restaurant.** Sample consistently good craft beers at
★ the oldest microbrewery in Portland, a beautiful brick-and-ivy building
that's long been a cornerstone of the Pearl Distirct. Free brewery tours
are given on Saturday; call for hours. ✉ *1313 N.W. Marshall St., Pearl
District* ☎ *503/241–3612* ⊕ *www.bridgeportbrew.com.*

Deschutes Brewery & Public House. The Portland branch of the Bend-based
Deschutes Brewery typically has more than 20 beers on tap, including
nationally acclaimed mainstays Mirror Pond Pale Ale, Inversion IPA,
and Black Butte Porter, plus seasonal and experimental brews. There's
an extensive menu of well-prepared pub fare, too. ✉ *210 N.W. 11th
Ave., Pearl District* ☎ *503/296–4906* ⊕ *www.deschutesbrewery.com.*

LIVE MUSIC

Fodor'sChoice **Jimmy Mak's.** Dubbed one of the world's "top 100 places to hear jazz"
★ by *DownBeat Magazine*, this old-school music club also serves Greek
and Middle Eastern dishes. ✉ *221 N.W. 10th Ave., Pearl District*
☎ *503/295–6542* ⊕ *www.jimmymaks.com.*

OLD TOWN
BARS AND LOUNGES

Davis Street Tavern. This convivial spot in an old brick building with
hardwood floors and beam ceilings offers cheerful service, late-night
dining, and one of the neighborhood's most popular happy hours. It's a
refreshingly refined yet friendly bar and tavern amid Old Town's many
rather rowdy clubs. ✉ *135 N.W. 5th Ave., Old Town* ☎ *503/505–5050*
⊕ *www.davisstreettavern.com.*

GAY AND LESBIAN

Fodor'sChoice **C.C. Slaughters Nightclub & Lounge.** The most popular gay and lesbian
★ dance club in the city, "C.C.'s" also has a quieter cocktail bar in
front called the Rainbow Room. ✉ *219 N.W. Davis St., Old Town*
☎ *503/248–9135* ⊕ *www.ccslaughterspdx.com.*

LIVE MUSIC

Roseland Theater. This spacious theater holds 1,400 people (standing-
room only except for the 21+ balcony seating area), primarily stages
rock, alternative, and blues shows. Past performers have included Miles
Davis, Pearl Jam, the Police, Bonnie Raitt, and Prince. ✉ *10 N.W. 6th
Ave., Old Town* ☎ *971/230–0033* ⊕ *www.roselandpdx.com.*

NOB HILL
BARS AND LOUNGES

Fodor'sChoice **The Fireside.** Warmed by an open fire pit and a roaring fireplace, and
★ decorated with lots of wood and leather, this cozy campfire-chic spot
on Nob Hill's retail strip offers one of the best happy hours in Northwest, wallet-friendly appetizers made from locally sourced ingredients,

and well-crafted cocktails. Try the Dillicious, made with rye whiskey, semidry vermouth, dill tincture, Kümmel liqueur, and lemon zest. ✉ *801 N.W. 23rd Ave., Nob Hill* ☎ *503/477–9505* ⊕ *www.pdxfireside.com.*

NORTH

BREWPUBS AND MICROBREWERIES

Prost! At the northern end of the hip North Mississippi retail and restaurant strip, Prost! is an airy, amber-lit, contemporary bar specializing in old-school German beers like Spaten Lager, Franziskaner Weissbier, and Erdinger Dunkel Weisse. Nosh on Bavarian pretzels and other Euro snacks or venture next door to one of the East Side's best food-cart pods, Mississippi Marketplace. ✉ *4237 N. Mississippi Ave., North* ☎ *503/954–2674* ⊕ *www.prostportland.com.*

LIVE MUSIC

Fodor'sChoice ★ **Mississippi Studios.** An intimate neighborhood music venue, with a seated balcony and old Oriental rugs covering the standing-room-only floor, Mississippi Studios offers high-quality live music performances every night of the week in a wide range of genres. Between sets, you can jump back and forth from the adjacent BarBar, a hip, comfortable bar with a delicious hamburger and a covered back patio. ✉ *3939 N. Mississippi, Boise, North* ☎ *503/288–3895* ⊕ *www.mississippistudios.com.*

NORTHEAST

BARS AND LOUNGES

Branch Whiskey Bar. Amid Alberta Street's offbeat galleries and indie cafés, candlelit and cozy Branch Whiskey Bar serves creative cocktails like the Branchattan—a blend of rye, Vya, Angostura bitters, and orange bitters, and well-crafted food, including expansive charcuterie boards, beef tartare, and seafood ceviche. ✉ *2926 N.E. Alberta St., Northeast* ☎ *503/206–6266* ⊕ *www.branchpdx.com.*

Fodor'sChoice ★ **The Bye and Bye.** An Alberta go-to specializing in creative drinks (sample the house favorite, the Bye and Bye, a refreshing concoction of peach vodka, peach bourbon, lemon, cranberry juice, and soda served in a Mason jar) and vegan fare, Bye and Bye has a big covered patio and a festive dining room. The owners also operate two other similarly trendy bars around town, Sweet Hereafter in Southeast and Jackknife at Downtown's Sentinel Hotel. ✉ *1011 N.E. Alberta St., Northeast* ☎ *503/281–0537* ⊕ *www.thebyeandbye.com.*

Fodor'sChoice ★ **Expatriate.** Opened in 2013 by Kyle Webster and his wife, celeb-chef partner Naomi Pomeroy of Beast (across the street), this intimate, candlelit spot has quickly gained a following for its balanced, boozy cocktails and addictively delicious Asian bar snacks, like curried-potato-and-English-pea samosas. Each of the eight nightly cocktails are meticulously crafted, but the Holding Patter—a mix of Laird's Bonded Apple Brandy, Priorat Vermut Natur, Luxardo Amaro Abano liqueur, and Peychaud's and Regan's bitters—is a house favorite. ✉ *5424 N.E. 30th Ave., Concordia, Northeast* ☎ *503/805–3750* ⊕ *www.expatriatepdx.com.*

Swift Lounge. The bird-themed Swift Lounge, an endearingly dive-y hipster hangout, offers a menu of Mason-jar cocktails inlcuding the Guilty Sparrow (citrus vodka, lemongrass, and house limoncello), the Stoned Finch (cucumber-infused vodka and house elderflower syrup), and the

Topless Robin (ginger-lemongrass-infused vodka and apricot brandy). You can order the drinks in two sizes—the 32-ounce "Fatty" or the 16-ounce "Sissy." The weekend "hangover brunch" is quite the scene. ⊠ *1932 N.E. Broadway, Sullivan's Gulch, Northeast* ☎ *503/288–3333* ⊕ *www.swiftloungepdx.com.*

COFFEEHOUSES

Barista. If you're looking to test-drive a few of Portland's best beans, this dapper café with other locations in Downtown, in the Pearl, and on N.E. Alberta is a great option. You'll find Stumptown, Coava, and other fine coffees, as well as a few craft beers and a small selection of high-quality chocolates and desserts. The high-ceilinged Alberta location is the most inviting, with plenty of indoor and outdoor seating. Other locations include 529 S.W. 3rd Ave. (Downtown), 539 N.W. 13th Ave. (Pearl District), and 823 N.W. 23rd Ave. (Nob Hill). ⊠ *1725 N.E. Alberta St., Alberta, Northeast* ☎ *503/274–1211* ⊕ *www.baristapdx.com.*

SOUTHEAST

BARS AND LOUNGES

Bar Avignon. Drop by this neighborhood wine bar on S.E. Division for one of the neighborhood's best happy hours, and to check out the impressive European-heavy wine selection; there are plenty of interesting bottles as well as more than 20 pours by the glass. The staff is friendly and knowledgeable, and the Northwest–French food menu consistently delivers. ⊠ *2138 S.E. Division St., Hosford-Abernethy, Southeast* ☎ *503/517–0808* ⊕ *www.baravignon.com.*

Fodor'sChoice **Coopers Hall.** Part of the Central East Side's burgeoning wine scene,
★ this urban winery and taproom is set inside a dramatic and spacious Quonset-hut structure, which was once home to an auto-repair shop. Order any of the outstanding wines produced on-site, or delve into the happily esoteric menu of unusual wines from all over the West Coast, with a few French varieties in the mix. The kitchen turns out seriously good food, too. ⊠ *404 S.E. 6th St., Central East Side, Southeast* ☎ *503/719–7000* ⊕ *www.coopershall.com.*

Double Dragon. Drop by this festive, low-lit bar for its sassy cocktails, such as the Burnt Reynolds (bourbon, Lapsang souchong honey, lemon, and orange bitters), scene-y crowd, and Saturday-night Baby Ketten Karaoke parties. Stay for the delish Asian bar food, including the eight-hour-braised pork-belly *banh mi* sandwiches and curried-coconut ramen with chicken and pork. ⊠ *1235 S.E. Division St., Hosford-Abernethy, Southeast* ☎ *503/230–8340* ⊕ *www.doubledragonpdx.com.*

Fodor'sChoice **Horse Brass Pub.** A laid-back beer-drinking crowd fills the venerable,
★ dark-wood Horse Brass Pub, as good an English-style pub as you will find in Portland, with more than 50 beers on tap (including some cask-conditioned varieties). ■**TIP**→ Try the fish-and-chips. ⊠ *4534 S.E. Belmont St., Sunnyside, Southeast* ☎ *503/232–2202* ⊕ *www.horsebrass.com.*

Fodor'sChoice **Sapphire Hotel.** In the lobby of a former brothel, the deep-red, candlelit
★ Sapphire Hotel serves cocktails, beer, and wine with an intimate, sultry atmosphere. There's a terrific food menu, too, served late and at bargain prices during happy hour. ⊠ *5008 S.E. Hawthorne Blvd., Hawthorne District, Southeast* ☎ *503/232–6333* ⊕ *www.thesapphirehotel.com.*

Fodor'sChoice
★

Southeast Wine Collective. This hive of boutique wine-making has an inviting tasting room–cum–wine bar in which you can sample the vinos of several up-and-coming producers. It's open until 10 most evenings, and the energy shifts from low-key tasting space to scene-y wine bar after about 5 pm. You could carve out a full meal from the extensive menu's tapas, salads, baguette sandwiches, and cheese and meats plates. ✉ *2425 S.E. 35th Pl., Richmond, Southeast* ☎ *503/208–2061* ⊕ *www. sewinecollective.com.*

Fodor'sChoice
★

Victory Bar. As beloved for its hefty venison burgers, chorizo spaetzle, and other stick-to-your-ribs bar victuals as for its impressive drinks selection, this dark corner bar with a pressed-tin ceiling is the definitive East Side hipster hangout, retaining a happily unfussy—almost dive-y—ambience in the face of Division Street's rapid transformation into a snazzy row of contemporary condos and A-list restaurants. ✉ *3652 S.E. Division St., Richmond, Southeast* ☎ *503/236–8755* ⊕ *www. thevictorybar.com.*

BREWPUBS AND MICROBREWERIES

Cascade Brewing. This laid-back brewpub and pioneer of the Northwest sour-beer movement is a good place for friends and sour-beer lovers to share tart flights of several varieties, including Blackcap Raspberry, Kriek, and potent (9.8% ABV) Sang Noir. You'll find 18 rotating taps, small plates and sandwiches to complement the sour beers, and ample outdoor seating. ✉ *939 S.E. Belmont St., Central East Side, Southeast* ☎ *503/265–8603* ⊕ *www.cascadebrewingbarrelhouse.com.*

Commons Brewery. This small, artisanal brewery, born in brewer Mike Wright's garage, maintained its small-batch, hands-on approach as it rapidly outgrew its first and second homes and even more rapidly earned a big reputation for exceptionally flavorful farmhouse-style ales. Wright's brews—inspired by European brewing traditions and crafted with local ingredients—have garnered many accolades; the fruit-forward Flemish Kiss and potent Bourbon Little Brother (aged in Heaven Hill bourbon barrels) are especially popular. Commons moved to this larger space, with a much-expanded tasting room, in early 2015. ✉ *628 S.E. Belmont St., Central East Side, Southeast* ☎ *503/343–5501* ⊕ *www.commonsbrewery.com.*

Hopworks Urban Brewery. A bicycle-themed microbrewery with deftly crafted beer, sandwiches, and pizzas, Hopworks Urban Brewery (HUB for short) occupies an industrial lodge-inspired building that's 100% renewably powered and water neutral. Hopworks BikeBar, located on the bike highway of North Williams, offers similar fare with the same bikey, eco-friendly vibe. ✉ *2944 S.E. Powell Blvd., Creston-Kenilworth, Southeast* ☎ *503/232–4677* ⊕ *www.hopworksbeer.com* ✉ *3947 N. Williams Ave., Boise, Northeast* ☎ *503/287–6258* ⊕ *www. hopworksbeer.com.*

COFFEEHOUSES

Fodor'sChoice
★

Coava Coffee Roasters. Located next door to the roastery, the light and open, bamboo wood–filled Coava Coffee Roasters offers some of the highest-quality single-origin, pour-over coffees in the city. A second branch opened in Hawthorne in 2014. ✉ *1300 S.E. Grand Ave.,*

2

Buckman, Southeast ☎ *503/894–8134* ⊕ *coavacoffee.com* ✉ *2631 S.E. Hawthorne Blvd., Hawthorne District, Southeast* ☎ *503/894–8134* ⊕ *coavacoffee.com.*

Stumptown Coffee Roasters. Stumptown Coffee Roasters has three cafés on the east side. At the original site (S.E. Division), organic beans are still roasted on a regular basis. At The Annex (S.E. Salmon), patrons can participate in "cuppings," or tastings, at 3 pm each day. ✉ *4525 S.E. Division St., Richmond, Southeast* ☎ *503/230–7702* ⊕ *stumptowncoffee.com* ✉ *100 S.E. Salmon St, Buckman, Southeast* ☎ *503/467–4123* ⊕ *stumptowncoffee.com.* ✉ *3356 S.E. Belmont St., Sunnyside, Southeast* ☎ *503/232–8889* ⊕ *stumptowncoffee.com*

Tao of Tea. With soft music and the sound of running water in the background, the Tao of Tea serves more than 80 loose-leaf teas as well as vegetarian snacks and sweets. The company also operates the tearoom inside Old Town's Lan Su Chinese Garden. ✉ *3430 S.E. Belmont St., Belmont District, Southeast* ☎ *503/736–0119* ⊕ *www.taooftea.com.*

Fodor's Choice ★ **Water Avenue Coffee.** Java aficionados serious about single-origin coffee favor this Central East Side roastery that sources its beans from top growers in Colombia, Ethiopa, and Indonesia, roasts on custom-built machines, and provides its house-roasted coffees to many restaurants and cafés around town. ✉ *1028 S.E. Water Ave., Central East Side, Southeast* ☎ *503/808–7084* ⊕ *www.wateravenuecoffee.com.*

DANCE CLUBS

Branx/Rotture. Legions of club goers of all styles and persuasions pour into these adjoining Central East Side nightclubs for arguably the best gay party in town—Blow Pony (fourth Saturday of each month), frequent live performances and shows by visiting DJs, and a variety of other parties and gatherings, most with a decided hipster vibe. Rotture (pronounced roh-TUR-ay) is on the upper level, and Branx is downstairs. ✉ *320 S.E. 2nd Ave., Southeast* ☎ *503/234–5683* ⊕ *www.branxpdx.com.*

GAY AND LESBIAN

Crush. A favorite gay hangout in Southeast, Crush serves up tasty food, strong cocktails, and DJ-fueled dance parties. The front section is mellow and good for conversation, while the back area contains a small but lively dance floor. ✉ *1400 S.E. Morrison St., Buckman, Southeast* ☎ *503/235–8150* ⊕ *www.crushbar.com* ⊗ *Closed Mon.*

LIVE MUSIC

Fodor's Choice ★ **Doug Fir Lounge.** Part retro diner and part log cabin, the Doug Fir serves food and booze and hosts DJs and live rock shows from both up-and-coming and established bands most nights of the week. It adjoins the trendy Hotel Jupiter. ✉ *830 E. Burnside St., Central East Side, Southeast* ☎ *503/231–9663* ⊕ *www.dougfirlounge.com.*

PERFORMING ARTS

For a city of this size, there is truly an impressive—and accessible—scope of talent from visual artists, performance artists, and musicians. The arts are alive, with outdoor sculptural works strewn around the city, ongoing festivals, and premieres of traveling Broadway shows. Top-named international acts, such as David Byrne, Arcade Fire, Joan Baez, and Mumford and Sons regularly include Portland in their worldwide stops.

PERFORMANCE VENUES

Fodor'sChoice **Arlene Schnitzer Concert Hall.** The 2,776-seat Arlene Schnitzer Concert
★ Hall, built in 1928 in an Italian rococo revival style, hosts rock concerts, choral groups, lectures, and concerts by the Oregon Symphony and others. ⊠ *Portland Center for the Performing Arts, 1037 S.W. Broadway, Downtown* ☎ *503/248-4335* ⊕ *www.portland5.com.*

Keller Auditorium. With 3,000 seats and outstanding acoustics, Keller Auditorium hosts performances by the Portland Opera and Oregon Ballet Theater, as well as country and rock concerts and touring Broadway shows. ⊠ *222 S.W. Clay St., Downtown* ☎ *503/248–4335* ⊕ *www.portland5.com.*

Portland'5 Centers for the Arts. The city's top performing arts complex hosts opera, ballet, rock shows, symphony performances, lectures, and Broadway musicals in its five venues *(⇨ Downtown in Exploring Portland)*. ⊠ *1111 S.W. Broadway, Downtown* ☎ *503/248–4335* ⊕ *www.portland5.com.*

Moda Center. This 21,000-seat facility, formerly known as the Rose Garden, is home to the Portland Trail Blazers basketball team and the site of other sporting events and rock concerts. It's right on the MAX light-rail line, just across from Downtown. ⊠ *Rose Quarter, 1 Center Ct., Lloyd District, Northeast* ☎ *503/797–9619* ⊕ *www.rosequarter.com.*

CLASSICAL MUSIC

The Oregon Symphony, established in 1896, is Portland's largest classical group—and one of the largest orchestras in the country.

CHAMBER MUSIC

Chamber Music Northwest. Some of the most sought-after soloists, chamber musicians, and recording artists from the Portland area and abroad perform here during the five-week summer concert series; performances take place at Reed College's Kaul Auditorium and the Lincoln Performance Hall at Portland State University. ☎ *503/294–6400* ⊕ *www.cmnw.org.*

OPERA

Portland Opera. This well-respected opera company performs five productions a year at Keller Auditorium. ⊠ *Keller Auditorium, 222 S.W. Clay St., Downtown* ☎ *503/241–1802, 866/739–6737* ⊕ *www.portlandopera.org.*

ORCHESTRAS

FAMILY **Oregon Symphony.** Established in 1896, the symphony is Portland's larg-
Fodor'sChoice est classical group—and one of the largest orchestras in the country.
★ Its season officially starts in September and ends in May, with concerts held at Arlene Schnitzer Concert Hall, but throughout the summer the orchestra and its smaller ensembles can be seen at Waterfront Park and Washington Park for special outdoor summer performances. It also presents about 40 classical, pop, children's, and family concerts each year. ☎ *503/228–1353, 800/228–7343* ⊕ *www.orsymphony.org.*

DANCE

Portland has a wonderful variety of both progressive and traditional dance companies. As part of their productions, many of these companies bring in international talent for choreography and guest performances.

BodyVox. Led by Emmy Award-winning choreographers, Body Vox performs energetic contemporary dance–theater works at its state-of-the-art space in the Pearl District. ✉ *1201 N.W. 17th Ave., Pearl District* ☎ *503/229–0627* ⊕ *www.bodyvox.com.*

Fodor's Choice **Northwest Dance Project.** Founded in 2004, this first-rate contemporary-★ dance company performs several shows—typically including a world premier or two—each season at different venues around town, including the Newmark Theatre and PSU's Lincoln Hall. ☎ *503/421–7434* ⊕ *www.nwdanceproject.org.*

Oregon Ballet Theatre. This respected company produces several classical and contemporary works a year, including a much-loved holiday *Nutcracker.* Most performances are at Keller Auditorium and the Portland Center for the Arts' Newmark Theatre. ☎ *503/222–5538, 888/922–5538* ⊕ *www.obt.org.*

FILM

The McMenimans "brew theaters" are a great place to catch a flick while chowing down and sipping on local beer. They are not-to-be-missed Portland landmarks when it comes to movie viewing in uniquely renovated buildings that avoid any hint of corporate streamlining.

If you're a film buff, be sure to check out the Northwest Film Center's calendar of events for special screenings and film festivals, with genres that include international, LGBT, and animation.

Fodor's Choice **Bagdad Theater.** Built in 1927, the stunningly restored, eminently quirky ★ Bagdad Theater shows first-run Hollywood films on a huge screen and serves pizza, burgers, sandwiches, and McMenamins ales. The Bagdad is a local favorite. ✉ *3702 S.E. Hawthorne Blvd., Hawthorne District, Southeast* ☎ *503/249–7474* ⊕ *www.mcmenamins.com.*

Hollywood Theatre. A landmark movie theater that showed silent films when it opened in 1926, the not-for-profit Hollywood Theatre screens everything from obscure foreign art films to old American classics and second-run Hollywood hits, and hosts an annual Academy Awards viewing party. ✉ *4122 N.E. Sandy Blvd., Hollywood District, Southeast* ☎ *503/281–4215* ⊕ *www.hollywoodtheatre.org.*

Kennedy School Theater. Furnished with couches and end tables, the Kennedy School Theater, which is located in a renovated elementary school that also contains a hotel, a restaurant, several bars, and a soaking pool, screens second-run and occasional Indie movies. ✉ *5736 N.E. 33rd Ave., Concordia, Northeast* ☎ *503/249–3983* ⊕ *www.mcmenamins.com.*

Laurelhurst Theater. With a classic neon sign out front, the historic Laurelhurst Theater serves beer and pizza and shows excellent second-run features and cult classics for only $4. ✉ *2735 E. Burnside St., Kerns, Northeast* ☎ *503/232–5511* ⊕ *www.laurelhursttheater.com.*

Living Room Theater. The sleek, upscale cinema, which has a lobby restaurant with a full bar, shows 3-D blockbuster, foreign, and independent films in cozy theaters furnished with spacious seats and moveable couches and tables. You can dine and drink from your seat. ⊠ *341 S.W. 10th Ave., West End, Downtown* ⊕ *pdx.livingroomtheaters.com.*

Fodor'sChoice   **Northwest Film Center.** Located adjacent to and operated by the Portland
★   Art Museum, the Northwest Film Center screens art films, documentaries, and independent features, and presents the three-week Portland International Film Festival every February. Films are shown at the Whitsell Auditorium, next to the museum. ⊠ *1219 S.W. Park Ave., Downtown* ☎ *503/221–1156* ⊕ *www.nwfilm.org.*

THEATER

From the largest of productions to the smallest of venues, theater comes to life in Portland year-round.

Artists Repertory Theatre. The theater company performs seven to nine productions a year including regional premieres, occasional commissioned works, and classics. ⊠ *1515 S.W. Morrison St., Downtown* ☎ *503/241–1278* ⊕ *www.artistsrep.org.*

Imago Theatre. One of Portland's most outstanding innovative theater companies, the Imago specializes in movement-based work for both young and old. ⊠ *17 S.E. 8th Ave., Buckman, Southeast* ☎ *503/231–9581* ⊕ *www.imagotheatre.com.*

FAMILY   **Northwest Children's Theater.** This long-running company presents four
Fodor'sChoice   shows during its fall–spring season, geared to both the toddler and teen
★   set. Performances are staged in the handsome Northwest Neighborhood Cultural Center in Nob Hill. ⊠ *1819 N.W. Everett St., Nob Hill* ☎ *503/222–4480.*

FAMILY   **Oregon Children's Theatre.** This kid-centric company puts on four to five shows a year for school groups and families at Downtown's Newmark and Winningstad theaters. ⊠ *1111 S.W. Broadway, Downtown* ☎ *503/228–9571* ⊕ *www.octc.org.*

Fodor'sChoice   **Portland Center Stage.** Housed in a handsomely restored 1891 armory,
★   Portland Center Stage puts on contemporary and classical works in the LEED-certified green building between September and June. ⊠ *Gerding Theater at the Armory, 128 N.W. 11th Ave., Pearl District* ☎ *503/445–3700* ⊕ *www.pcs.org.*

SPORTS AND THE OUTDOORS

Portlanders avidly gravitate to the outdoors and they're well acclimated to the elements year-round—including winter's wind, rain, and cold. Once the sun starts to shine in spring and into summer, the city fills with hikers, joggers, and mountain bikers, who flock to Portland's hundreds of miles of parks, paths, and trails. The Willamette and Columbia rivers are popular for boating and water sports. Locals also have access to a playground for fishing, camping, skiing, and snowboarding all the way through June, thanks to the proximity of Mt. Hood.

As for competitive sports, Portland is home to the Timbers, a major league soccer team with a devout local fan base, and NBA basketball's beloved Trail Blazers, who play at the Moda Center (aka Rose Quarter) arena, just across the Willamette River from Downtown.

PARTICIPANT SPORTS

BIKING

Biking is a cultural phenomenon in Portland—likely the most beloved mode of transportation in the city. Besides the sheer numbers of cyclists you see on roads and pathways, you'll find well-marked bike lanes and signs reminding motorists to yield to cyclists.

There are more than 320 miles of bicycle boulevards, lanes, and off-street paths in Portland. Accessible maps, specialized tours, parking capacity (including lockers and sheltered racks Downtown), and bicycle-only traffic signals at confusing intersections make biking in most neighborhoods easy. Cyclists can find the best routes by following green direction-and-distance signs that point the way around town, and the corresponding white dots on the street surface.

Cycling in Portland has evolved into a medium for progressive politics and public service. Several bike co-ops in the city are devoted to providing used bikes at decent prices, as well as to teaching bike maintenance and the economic and environmental benefits of becoming a two-wheel commuter. Check out the helpful Bike Portland (⊕ *www.bikeportland. org*) website for information on regularly scheduled bike events, cycling-related local news and advice, and referrals to reliable bike rental, sales, and repair shops.

BIKE RENTALS

Fat Tire Farm. For treks in Forest Park, rent mountain bikes at Fat Tire Farm, which is close to the park's Leif Erikson trailhead. The staff here really knows their stuff, from repair and maintenance help to advice on the best trails and routes. ⊠ *2714 N.W. Thurman St., Nob Hill* ☎ *503/222–3276* ⊕ *www.fattirefarm.com.*

Waterfront Bicycle Rentals. For jaunts along the Willamette River, Waterfront Bicycles has everything a visiting bicyclist needs. There is a variety of styles and sizes of bikes to outfit the entire family, including balance bikes for the little rider. Reservations can be made online at least 48 hours ahead. Guided bike tours are offered as well. ⊠ *10 S.W. Ash St., Suite 100, Downtown* ☎ *503/227–1719* ⊕ *www.waterfrontbikes.com.*

BIKE ROUTES

If you're a social rider, group rides set out from several local shops. Check the events pages of **Bike Gallery** (⊕ *www.bikegallery.com*), **River City Bicycles** (⊕ *www.rivercitybicycles.com*), and **Bike Portland** (⊕ *www. bikeportland.org*).

Bike paths line both sides of the **Willamette River** through Downtown, so you can easily make a mild, several-mile loop through Waterfront Park via the Steel, Hawthorne, or Sellwood bridges.

Though much of **Forest Park's** 70-plus miles of trails are reserved for hiking and nonbiking activities, there are 28 miles of single track mountain-biking trails and fire lanes open to biking, including Leif Erikson Drive, an 11-mile ride whose dense canopy occasionally gives way to river views. Along the park's trails you may come across old-growth forest as well as some of the park's more than 100 species of animals and birds. To reach the Leif Erikson trailhead, bike up steep Thurman Street or shuttle there via TriMet Bus 15. Maps and information on the trails can be found at ⊕ *www.forestparkconservancy.org.*

Department of Transportation. For information on bike routes and resources in and around Portland, visit the Department of Transportation website (look for the Active Transportation tab). You can download and view maps and learn about upcoming bike-related events and group rides. ☎ *503/823–5490* ⊕ *www.portlandoregon.gov/transportation.*

PARKS

The variety of Portland's parks ensures that there's something for just about everyone, from the world's smallest park (Mill Ends) to one of the largest urban natural areas in the country (Forest Park).

Fodor'sChoice ★ **Cathedral Park.** Whether it's the view of the imposing and stunning Gothic St. John's Bridge, which rises some 400 feet above the Willamette River, or the historic significance of Lewis and Clark having camped here in 1806, this park is divine. Though there's no church, the park gets its name from the picturesque arches supporting the bridge. It's rumored that the ghost of a young girl haunts the bridge, and that may be true, but if you're told that it was designed by the same man who envisioned the Golden Gate Bridge, that's just a popular misconception. Dog lovers, or those who aren't, should take note of the off-leash area. ⊠ *N. Edison St. and Pittsburg Ave., St. John's, North* ⊕ *www. portlandoregon.gov/parks.*

Council Crest Park. The highest point in Portland, at 1,073 feet, this 43-acre bluff-top patch of greenery is a superb spot to take in sunsets and sunrises. Along with nearly 180-degree views of the Portland metro area, a clear day also affords views of the surrounding peaks—Mt. Hood, Mt. St. Helens, Mt. Adams, Mt. Jefferson, and Mt. Rainier. A bronze fountain depicting a mother and child has been erected in the park twice; first in the 1950s and the second in the 1990s. The peaceful piece was stolen in the 1980s, uncovered in a narcotics bust 10 years later, and then returned to the park. Trails connect Council Crest with Marquam Nature Park and Washington Park. ■TIP→ **It's quite busy on weekends so visit on a weekday, if possible.** ⊠ *3400 Council Crest Dr., West Hills* ⊕ *www.portlandoregon.gov/parks.*

Peninsula Park & Rose Garden. The "City of Roses" moniker started here, at this park that harks back to another time. The city's oldest (1909) public rose garden (and the only sunken one) houses about 5,000 plantings of roses. The daunting task of deadheading all these flowers is covered in classes taught to volunteers twice a season. The bandstand is a historic landmark, and the last of its kind in the city. This 16-acre North Portland park also contains a 100-year-old fountain, Italian villa–inspired community center, playground, wading pool, tennis and volleyball courts, and picnic tables. ⊠ *700 N. Rosa Parks Way, Piedmont, North* ⊕ *www.portlandoregon.gov/parks.*

Fodor'sChoice ★ **Sauvie Island.** If it's a day to take advantage of gorgeous weather, then drive about a half hour northwest of Downtown to Sauvie Island. The

Walkers crossing the Hawthorne Bridge

island has a wildlife refuge, three beaches (including Collins Beach, which is clothing-optional), superb biking and hiking trails, and several farms offering "u-pick" bounty. To get to the beaches, take U.S. 30 north to Sauvie Island Bridge, and turn right; follow N.W. Sauvie Island Road to Reeder Road and follow signs. There's plenty of parking at the beaches, but a permit is required ($7 for a one-day permit, available at the general store at the base of the bridge). ⊠ *N.W. Sauvie Island Rd., across Sauvie Island bridge at U.S. 30, Sauvie Island* ⊕ *www.sauvieisland.org*.

FAMILY **Tryon Creek State Natural Area.** Portland is chock-full of parks, but this is the only state park within city limits. And at 670 acres, there's plenty of room for all its admirers. The area was logged starting in the 1880s, and the natural regrowth has produced red alder, Douglas fir, big leaf maple, and western red cedar, giving home to more than 50 bird species. The eastern edge has a paved trail, in addition to 14 miles of trails for bikes, hikers, and horses. Before heading to the trails, stop by the nature center to check out the exhibits and topographical relief map. ⊠ *11321 S.W. Terwilliger Blvd., Collins View, Southwest* ☎ *503/636–4398* ⊕ *www.tryonfriends.org* ⊗ *Daily 7 am–8 pm, Nature Center 9–4.*

SPECTATOR SPORTS

Since Portland isn't home to a large national football or baseball team, fans tend to show a lot of support for the NBA's Portland Trail Blazers and MLS's Portland Timbers.

BASKETBALL

Portland Trail Blazers. The NBA's Portland Trail Blazers play their 82-game season in the Moda Center (aka Rose Garden Arena), which can hold up to 20,000 spectators. The MAX train pulls up just a couple of blocks from the arena's front door. ✉ *Moda Center, 1 N. Center Ct., Rose Quarter, North* ☎ *503/797–9600* ⊕ *www.nba.com/blazers.*

SOCCER

Portland Timbers. Portland's major-league soccer team plays their 34-game season at the Downtown Jeld-Wen Field from March through October. The city has many ardent soccer fans known as the Timbers Army. Sitting near this group means a raucous time with drumming, chanting, and cheers. The MAX stops right by the stadium. ✉ *Jeld-Wen Field, 1844 S.W. Morrison St., Downtown* ☎ *503/553–5555* ⊕ *www.portlandtimbers.com.*

SHOPPING

The shopping landscape in Portland has changed significantly in recent years, perhaps not quite as dramatically as the much-buzzed-about culinary scene, but in similar (pardon the pun) fashion. Specifically, those same hip and indie-spirited neighborhoods around the city that have become hot spots for food and drink—areas like the Pearl District, Downtown West End, Alberta, North Mississippi, and Central East Side—are also enjoying a steady influx of distinctive, well-curated boutiques specializing in edgy fashion and jewelry, handcrafted home accessories and household goods, and artisanal foods.

The city's longstanding shopping hubs, including the Downtown core, Nob Hill, and the Hawthorne District continue to support a number of both established and up-and-coming retailers, too. Generally speaking, you'll find more of Portland's nationally known chain stores in these traditional commercial districts, especially around Downtown's Pioneer Courthouse Square, the Pearl District (particularly the lower half of the neighborhood, nearest Burnside Street), and along the lower blocks of Nob Hill's N.W. 23rd Avenue. Additionally, on the East Side, the prosaic but convenient Lloyd Center Mall and surrounding neighborhood has plenty of chain stores.

DOWNTOWN

CLOTHING

Fodor's Choice
★

Frances May. Located in the hip West End section of Downtown, this grandmother-and-granddaughter-owned clothing store is a favorite of stylish local men and women who come for that cool, understated, high-quality look (casual to dressy) that Portlanders are known for. You'll find made-in-America labels like Steven Alan and Rachel Comey as well as European faves like Acne and APC. The Alex Mill cashmere beanies and Carven women's pullovers and sweaters are especially popular during Portland's cool winters. ✉ *1013 S.W. Washington St., Downtown* ☎ *503/227–3402* ⊕ *www.francesmay.com.*

Mario's. Portland's best store for fine men's and women's clothing, Mario's carries designer lines by Prada, Dolce & Gabbana, Etro, and Loro Piana—among others. The store's buyers make regular trips to Italy in search of the latest fashions and trends. There's a *huge* shoe department, too. ⊠ *833 S.W. Broadway, Downtown* ☎ *503/227–3477* ⊕ *www.marios.com.*

Nike Portland. It's safe to assume that Nike's flagship retail store, just a short drive from the company's mammoth HQ campus in Beaverton, has the latest and greatest in swoosh-adorned products. The high-tech setting has athlete profiles, photos, and interactive displays. ⊠ *638 S.W. 5th Ave., Downtown* ☎ *503/221–6453* ⊕ *www.nike.com.*

FOOD

Cacao. Chocolate fiends and sweet-tooths get their fix at this inviting storefront shop and café in the West End, which also has a branch inside Downtown's natty Heathman Hotel. Browse the huge selection of ultrafine, single-origin, artisanal chocolates from around the world, or order a cup of luscious and satisfying house-made drinking chocolate. ⊠ *414 S.W. 13th Ave., Downtown* ☎ *503/241–0656* ⊕ *www. cacaodrinkchocolate.com.*

FAMILY

Fodor's Choice

★

Portland Farmers' Market. Running on Saturday mornings and early afternoons from March through December, this astoundingly large and diverse farmers' market carries not only Oregon's bounty of flowers and produce (look especially for berries in summer and stone fruits in fall) but also hazelnuts, cheese, delectable baked goods, wines and ciders, and other goodies. It's great for people-watching and souvenir shopping, and several stalls sell great food to eat on-site—be sure to come hungry. If you can't make the Saturday market, check the website for locations of smaller but still very popular versions of the market, held most days during the warmer months at various locations around town. ⊠ *South Park Blocks at S.W. Park Ave. and Montgomery St., Downtown* ☎ *503/241–0032* ⊕ *www.portlandfarmersmarket.org.*

GIFTS

Made in Oregon. This eclectic retail tribute to the Beaver State sells books, smoked salmon, artisanal chocolates, local wines, Pendleton woolen goods, carvings made of myrtle wood, and other products made in the state. There are numerous branches around the area, including Portland International Airport and all the larger shopping malls. ⊠ *Pioneer Place Mall, 340 S.W. Morrison St., Downtown* ☎ *503/241–3630, 866/257–0938* ⊕ *www.madeinoregon.com.*

HOUSEHOLD GOODS AND FURNITURE

Boys Fort. If the name of this colorful Downtown emporium brings back memories of hanging out with friends in a rad basement rec room, you'll likely love this offbeat store curated by designers R. Rolfe and Jake France. They've stocked this high-ceilinged shop with a mix of artful items for the hip dude's urban nest, including earthy-hued terra-cotta planters, model sailboats, and mounted wooden faux deer heads, plus old posters and games. ⊠ *902 S.W. Morrison St., Downtown* ☎ *503/567–1015* ⊕ *www.boysfort.com.*

Fodor's Choice **Canoe.** Form meets function at this stylish, contemporary boutique with
★ a carefully curated selection of clean-lined, modern goods and gifts for
every room in the home. You'll find curvy thick-glass bowls, modern
lamps with sheer paper shades, polished-stone trays, Bigelow natural-
bristle toothbrushes, and Chemex coffee kettles, with some goods produced locally and exclusively for Canoe, and others imported from Asia
and northern Europe. ⊠ *1136 S.W. Alder St., West End, Downtown*
☎ *503/889–8545* ⊕ *www.canoeonline.net.*

JEWELRY

The Real Mother Goose. Selling mostly handcrafted, unique artistic pieces,
current collections can include woodworking, furniture, blown glass
and jewelry. Dangling earrings that incorporate copper wire wrapped
around brilliant, colored glass are a customer favorite. The clothing
store next door, Changes Designs to Wear, is part of The Real Mother
Goose as well. ⊠ *901 S.W. Yamhill St., Downtown* ☎ *503/223–9510*
⊕ *www.therealmothergoose.com.*

MALLS AND DEPARTMENT STORES

Fodor's Choice **Union Way.** A modern take on an old-fashioned European shopping
★ arcade, this indoor alley—which opened in 2013—spans one block
from Stark to Burnside streets (right across the street from Powell's
Books) and contains about a dozen diverting boutiques, plus a branch of
Little T Bakery and the trendy Asian restaurant Boxer Ramen. Most of
these shops specialize in apparel and accessories, including Will Leather
Goods, Steven Alan eyewear, and Danner sports and outerwear, but
you'll also find Quin Candy shop and Spruce Apothecary. ⊠ *1022 W.
Burnside St., West End, Downtown* ☎ *503/922–0056.*

TOYS

Finnegan's Toys and Gifts. Downtown Portland's largest toy store,
Finnegan's stocks artistic, creative, educational, and other types of
toys. ⊠ *820 S.W. Washington St., Downtown* ☎ *503/221–0306* ⊕ *www.
finneganstoys.com.*

OLD TOWN/CHINATOWN

GIFTS

Hand-Eye Supply. One of a handful of intriguing shops that have opened
in Old Town in recent years, Hand-Eye specializes in work wear, studio
supplies, tools, and books. But before you write this place off as a purely
utilitarian resource, you should know that the buyers here have a keen eye
for beautifully designed goods. This is first and foremost an emporium
of cool lifestyle goods, including natty, gray, linen-cotton work aprons,
wood-handle Midori Hamono paring knives, bright-red Feuerhand camp
lanterns, and other stylish curiosities. ⊠ *427 N.W. Broadway, Old Town/
Chinatown* ☎ *503/575–9769* ⊕ *www.handeyesupply.com.*

MARKETS

Fodor's Choice **Portland Saturday Market.** The open-air Portland Saturday Market, which
★ has been going strong since 1976 and runs from March to Decem-
ber on weekends (including Sunday, despite the name), is a favorite
place to find one-of-a-kind, handcrafted home, garden, and clothing

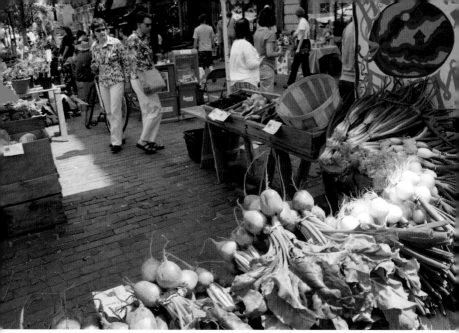
Farmers' markets in Portland offer fresh produce and other local goodies.

items—everything from T-shirts and souvenirs to high-quality sculptures and housewares. An impressive new pavilion, part of it covered, houses the more than 300 artisans. ■TIP→ **Don't confuse this crafts-oriented market with the equally popular Portland Farmers' Market, which takes place on Saturday on the campus of Portland State University.** ⊠ *Tom McCall Waterfront Park, 2 S.W. Naito Pkwy., adjacent to Burnside Bridge, Old Town/Chinatown* ☎ *503/222–6072* ⊕ *www. portlandsaturdaymarket.org.*

PEARL DISTRICT

BOOKS

Oblation Papers. Employing antique presses and old-world processes, this dapper shop in the Pearl District houses a paper mill, letterpress shop, and retail store where you can find one-of-a-kind cards, stationery, albums, and journals. The quality, handcrafted cards featuring vintage posters or images of local wildlife make wonderful keepsakes and gifts. ⊠ *516 N.W. 12th Ave., Pearl District* ☎ *503/223–1093* ⊕ *www. oblationpapers.com.*

Fodor's Choice ★ **Powell's City of Books.** The largest retail store of used and new books in the world (with more than 1.5 million volumes) covers an entire city block and rises three stories on the edge of the Pearl District. A local legend, and rightfully so, Powell's also carries rare and collectible books and contains a popular coffeehouse, World Cup. There are also branches in Portland International Airport as well as a large outpost in the heart of the Hawthorne District, with its own coffeehouse, Fresh

Pot. ⊠ *1005 W. Burnside St., Pearl District* ☎ *503/228–4651* ⊕ *www. powells.com.*

CLOTHING

Lizard Lounge. Shop until your caffeine levels drop at this expansive men's and women's fashion source in the Pearl, where staff will pour you a complimentary cup of Stumptown coffee as you browse that particularly Portland mix of hip and hipster chic. Lizard Lounge carries everything from major midrange brands like Levi's and Timberland to higher-end clubbing labels, like G-Star, Nudie Jeans, and Fetch Eyewear. There's also a good selection of gifts and household items, like Mast Brothers Chocolate and Portland-based Maak Soap Lab bath products. ⊠ *1323 N.W. Irving St., Pearl District* ☎ *503/416–7476* ⊕ *www. lizardloungepdx.com.*

Fodor'sChoice ★ **Mabel & Zora.** The owner of this chic Pearl destination for elegant ready-to-wear fashion, Tiffany Bean, carries her eponymous, widely acclaimed, and locally produced label as well as clothing, accessories, and jewelry from designers including Nic + Zoe, Lily Pulitzer, Trina Turk, and Michael Stars. If you're gearing up for a big night on the town, look no further. ⊠ *748 N.W. 11th Ave., Pearl District* ☎ *503/241–5696* ⊕ *www.mabelandzora.com.*

FOOD

Fodor'sChoice ★ **Smith Teamaker.** Tea drinkers rejoice: you don't have to resort to coffee just because you're in Portland. Proprietor and legendary tea guru Steve Smith launched two renowned companies, Stash Tea and Tazo, before opening his own company inside a former blacksmith shop on the northwestern edge of the Pearl District. At this handsome tea shop, you can see how the tea is made and packaged, shop teas and accessories, and then sample different varieties at a small tasting bar. Select a tea flight from a menu, try a tea latte, or work your way through an oxidation spectrum—from white to black. The sturdy, pastel-hued boxes in which Smith packages his exquisite, carefully sourced teas make great gifts. ⊠ *1626 N.W. Thurman St., Pearl District* ☎ *503/719–8752* ⊕ *www.smithtea.com.*

GALLERIES

Fodor'sChoice ★ **First Thursday.** This gallery walk the first Thursday of every month gives art appreciators a chance to check out new exhibits while enjoying music and wine. Typically, the galleries, which are largely located in the Pearl District, are open in the evening from 6 to 9, but hours vary. Be prepared for a lively scene including throngs of people, street musicians, and local art vendors, with much of the action along N.W. 13th Avenue between Hoyt and Kearney streets, which is pedestrian only during this event. ⊠ *Pearl District* ☎ *503/227–8519* ⊕ *www.explorethepearl.com.*

Quintana Galleries. The only Native American art gallery in Portland, Quintana focuses on Pacific Northwest Coast, Navajo, and Hopi art, pottery, and jewelry. ⊠ *124 N.W. 9th Ave., Pearl District* ☎ *503/223–1729, 800/321–1729* ⊕ *www.quintanagalleries.com.*

NOB HILL

CLOTHING

Sloan Boutique. Set among the several fine clothiers on the 700 and 800 blocks of N.W. 23rd Avenue, Sloan Boutique carries a good mix of affordable women's casual and fashion brands, including Kensie, Free People, Kut, and Franco Sarto. The boutique's adjoining space—PlaTform—carries a good selection of trendy shoes and accessories. Sloan has a second branch across the river in Hawthorne. ⊠ *738 N.W. 23rd Ave., Nob Hill* ☎ *503/222–6666* ⊕ *www.sloanpdx.com.*

GALLERIES

Laura Russo Gallery. A longtime staple of the Portland arts scene, the Laura Russo Gallery displays contemporary Northwest work of all styles, including landscapes and abstract expressionism. ⊠ *805 N.W. 21st Ave., Nob Hill* ☎ *503/226–2754* ⊕ *www.laurarusso.com.*

Twist. This huge space in Nob Hill is well stocked with contemporary American ceramics, glass, furniture, sculpture, and handcrafted jewelry often with a whimsical touch. ⊠ *30 N.W. 23rd Pl., Nob Hill* ☎ *503/224–0334* ⊕ *www.twistonline.com.*

GIFTS

Moonstruck Chocolate Cafe. Even without getting a nod from Oprah in her magazine, Moonstruck would still be known as a chocolatier extraordinaire. There are five cafés in the Portland metro area, including Downtown locations at Pioneer Place Mall and at S.W. Alder Street. All offer made-to-order hot chocolate, cocoa, shakes, and mochas, as well as truffles, chocolate bars, and dynamic holiday treats. ⊠ *526 N.W. 23rd Ave., Nob Hill* ☎ *503/542–3400* ⊕ *www.moonstruckchocolate.com.*

Stella's on 21st. At this colorful neighborhood shop, you'll find eccentric, artsy items for the home, including lamps, candles, and decorations, as well as jewelry. ⊠ *1108 N.W. 21st Ave., Nob Hill* ☎ *503/295–5930* ⊕ *www.stellason21st.com.*

JEWELRY

Gilt. Portland's premier estate and vintage jewelry destination occupies a dapper Craftsman bungalow along a fashionable stretch of Nob Hill's Northwest 23rd. Inside you'll find an ever-changing inventory of radiant gold and silver rings, bracelets, earrings, and necklaces, many inlaid with dazzling gems. The antique wedding and engagement rings are especially popular. Gilt's owner, Paula Bixel, is especially fond of Georgian and Victorian pieces. ⊠ *720 N.W. 23rd Ave., Nob Hill* ☎ *503/226–0629* ⊕ *www.giltjewelry.com.*

NORTH

FOOD

Fodor's Choice
★

The Meadow. Food writer Mark Bitterman knows a thing or two about salt—he's written two popular books on the subject, and he's the owner of this tiny purveyor of gourmet finishing salts, some of them smoked or infused with unusual flavors, like cherry and plums, or saffron. At this flagship location (there's a second Meadow in Nob Hill, and a third in

Manhattan's West Village) you can also purchase the additional magical touches you might need to create the perfect dinner party, from Oregon and European wines and vermouths, to fresh-cut flowers, aromatic cocktail bitters, and high-quality, single-origin chocolates. ⊠ *3731 N. Mississippi Ave., North* ☎ *503/288–4633* ⊕ *www.atthemeadow.com.*

HOUSEHOLD GOODS AND FURNITURE

Fodor'sChoice ★ **Beam & Anchor.** Set on a busy street corner several blocks from the North Side's trendy North Mississippi strip, this once-dilapidated warehouse houses an upstairs workshop for makers of artisanal goods and an inspiring downstairs retail space where proprietors Robert and Jocelyn Rahm sell a carefully curated selection of lifestyle goods for every room in the home, many of them produced locally—some as local as upstairs. Among the hipster treasures, look for warm and soft camp blankets and Navajo rugs with vibrant prints, women's jewelry in a variety of simple-but-beautiful styles, Portland Apothecary bath salts and soaps, and quite a few larger pieces of distinctive furniture. ⊠ *2710 N. Interstate Ave., Eliot, North* ☎ *503/367–3230* ⊕ *www.beamandanchor.com.*

TOYS

Fodor'sChoice ★ **Paxton Gate.** Here, science and biology mix with whimsy and imagination. You'll find everything from taxidermied scorpions and baby goats to ostrich eggs and ceramic chimes. It's a fascinating and strangely beguiling mix of goods, and not for the faint of heart. ⊠ *4204 N. Mississippi Ave., Boise, North* ☎ *503/719–4508* ⊕ *www.paxtongate.com.*

NORTHEAST

GALLERIES

Ampersand Gallery & Fine Books. Part art gallery, part store, this minimalist white-wall space on Alberta Street has monthly shows featuring edgy, contemporary art, and stocks a fascinating trove of photography and art books, vintage travel brochures, curious photography, pulp-fiction novels, and other printed materials of the sort you might find in a chest in a mysterious neighbor's attic. The owners also operate the cute Cord boutique next door, which stocks artfully designed household goods, from handcrafted soaps to aerodynamic coffeepots. ⊠ *2916 N.E. Alberta St., Alberta, Northeast* ☎ *503/805–5458* ⊕ *www. ampersandgallerypdx.com.*

FAMILY Fodor'sChoice ★ **Last Thursday Arts Walk.** The Alberta Arts District hosts an arts walk on the last Thursday of each month. This quirky procession along 15 blocks of one of the city's favorite thoroughfares for browsing art galleries, distinctive boutiques, and hipster bars and restaurants features street performers and buskers, crafts makers, and food vendors. The street is closed to traffic from 6 to 9:30 pm. ⊠ *N.E. Alberta St., Alberta Arts District, Northeast* ⊕ *www.lastthursdayonalberta.com.*

MUSIC

Fodor'sChoice ★ **Music Millennium.** The oldest record store in the Pacific Northwest, Music Millennium stocks a huge selection of new and used music in every possible category, including local punk groups. The store also hosts a number of in-store performances, often by top-name artists like Lucinda

Williams, Richard Thompson, Matthew Sweet, Sheryl Crow, and Randy Newman. ⊠ *3158 E. Burnside St., Laurelhurst, Southeast* ☎ *503/231–8926* ⊕ *www.musicmillennium.com.*

SOUTHEAST

CLOTHING

Herbivore Clothing. An animal-rights-minded shop in the Central East Side, Herbivore is a terrific resource if you're seeking clothing and accessories—from cotton-rayon tees and sweaters to braided canvas belts and wallets fashioned out of reclaimed bike and truck tubes—that have been created without the harm or use of animals. There's also a great selection of books on veganism, plus food, health-care products, and gifts. ⊠ *1211 S.E. Stark St., Central East Side, Southeast* ☎ *503/281–8638* ⊕ *www.herbivoreclothing.com.*

Fodor's Choice ★ **Machus.** This small, somewhat under-the-radar, upscale, men's clothier carries arguably the best selection of fashion-forward, emerging labels in the city. In addition to Machus's own private-label dress shirts and tees, check out the form-fitting, refreshingly unadorned Naked and Famous skinny jeans, stylish sportswear by Knomadik, and edgy, urbane bomber jackets and hoodies from ADYN. You won't find many—or any—pastels or bright prints in here; expect clean classics, with lots of blacks, grays, and whites. ⊠ *542 E. Burnside St., Central East Side, Southeast* ☎ *503/206–8626* ⊕ *www.machusonline.com.*

Fodor's Choice ★ **Mag-Big.** A tiny but impressively stocked boutique in a charming, old, Craftsman-style house that also houses the excellent Hazel Room café, Mag-Big is devoted to decorative items, fashion, jewelry, and crafts made by Portlanders. The selection is eclectic and fun—everything from handcrafted soaps made with local beer to geometric-shape brass necklaces. Clothing at Mag-Big is geared mostly to women. ⊠ *3279 S.E. Hawthorne Blvd., Hawthorne District, Southeast* ☎ *503/236–6120* ⊕ *www.magbig.com.*

Union Rose. For distinctive women's fashion and accessories designed and made in Portland, check out this boutique in up-and-coming Montavilla. Though there are scores of dresses for any season, including a very good selection of dresses and skirts in plus sizes, there's also plenty of everyday wear, like hoodies and hats. ⊠ *7909 S.E. Stark St., Montavilla, Southeast* ☎ *503/287–4242* ⊕ *www.unionrosepdx.com.*

GIFTS

Pastaworks. Fine charcuterie and cheeses, organic produce, and an exceptional selection of Italian wines, cookware, and fresh-made pastas and sauces are all sold at this spacious market in Hawthorne, adjoining Powell's Books for Home and Garden. There's a second location in Nob Hill. ⊠ *3735 S.E. Hawthorne Blvd., Hawthorne District, Southeast* ☎ *503/232–1010* ⊕ *www.pastaworks.com.*

HOUSEHOLD GIFTS AND FURNITURE

House of Vintage. This mammoth 13,000-square-foot shop, just down the street from one of the better Goodwill shops in the city, is de rigueur among vintage aficionados. Inside, you can rifle through the

WELCOME TO THE OREGON COAST

TOP REASONS TO GO

★ **Enjoy the beaches:**
The Oregon Coast has breathtaking beaches, from romantic stretches perfect for linking fingers with loved ones to creature-teeming tide pools great for exploring with kids. Hikers delight in the rugged trails that traverse the lush woodlands and stunning cliffs that flank many of the beaches.

★ **Shop for blown glass:**
Artisanal glass shops dot the coastline—at some, you can even craft your own colorful creations.

★ **Explore the dunes:**
Whether you're screaming in a dune buggy or scrambling over them on foot, southern Oregon's mountainous sand dunes bring out the kid in anyone who traverses them.

★ **Wine and dine:** You don't have to spend a lot to enjoy creatively prepared seafood, artisanal microbrews, and local wines. There's a nice balance between affordable no-frills fish shacks and increasingly sophisticated farm-to-table bistros.

North Coast. As the primary gateway for both Portlanders and those visiting from neighboring Washington, the north coast is the busiest stretch of Oregon coastline, although it's still rife with secluded coves and funky seaside hamlets. Its lighthouse-dotted shoreline stretches from the mouth of the Columbia River south to Pacific City. The 90-mile region includes the historic working-class fishing town of Astoria and its recent influx of hip cafés and restored hotels; family-friendly Seaside with its touristy but bustling boardwalk; art-fueled and refined Cannon Beach; laid-back and stunningly situated Manzanita Beach; and tiny Pacific City, where a colorful fleet of dories dots the wide, deep beach.

Central Coast. The 75-mile stretch from Lincoln City to Florence offers whale-watching, incomparable seafood, shell-covered beaches, candy confections, and close-up views of undersea life. At the north end, in Lincoln City visitors can indulge in gaming, shopping, golfing, and beachcombing. The harbor town of Depoe Bay is a center for whale-watching, and nearby Newport offers a stellar aquarium and science center. It's also home to one of Oregon's largest fishing fleets. The less-developed town of Yachats is a true seaside gem with astounding coastal views, where the only demands are to relax and enjoy. The cute town of Florence and its bustling downtown hugs the Siuslaw River—it's also the northern access point for the Oregon dunes.

South Coast. From the heart of Oregon dunes country in Reedsport to the southernmost Oregon town of Brookings, the 134-mile stretch of U.S. 101 is less touristy than points north, but still abundant with mesmerizing beaches, headlands, and coastal rain forests. Coos Bay and adjacent North Bend make up the region's largest population center. The beach town of Bandon is a world-class golfing destination that's also popular for beachcombing and lighthouse gazing. Ruggedly situated and low-key Port Orford has gorgeous beach landscapes and a growing arts scene, while Gold Beach, farther south, bathes in sunshine.

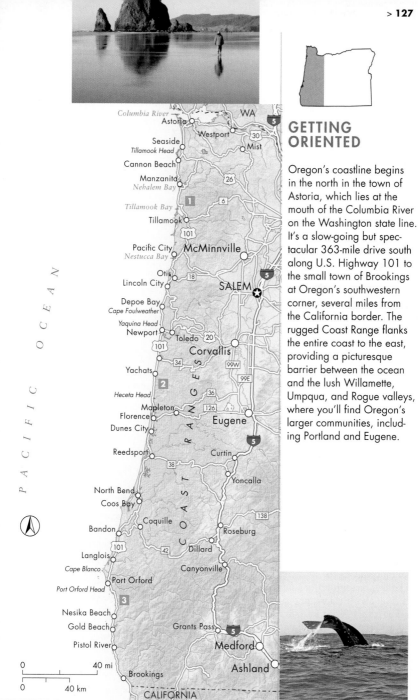

GETTING ORIENTED

3

Oregon's coastline begins in the north in the town of Astoria, which lies at the mouth of the Columbia River on the Washington state line. It's a slow-going but spectacular 363-mile drive south along U.S. Highway 101 to the small town of Brookings at Oregon's southwestern corner, several miles from the California border. The rugged Coast Range flanks the entire coast to the east, providing a picturesque barrier between the ocean and the lush Willamette, Umpqua, and Rogue valleys, where you'll find Oregon's larger communities, including Portland and Eugene.

EXPLORING OREGON'S BEST BEACHES

Oregon's 300 miles of public coastline is the backdrop for thrills, serenity, rejuvenation, and romance. From yawning expanses of sand dotted with beach chairs to tiny patches bounded by surf-shaped cliffs, the state's shoreline often draws comparisons to New Zealand.

(above) Surfing the Oregon Coast; (opposite page, top) Oregon Dunes National Recreation Area; (opposite page, bottom) Cannon Beach Sandcastle Contest

Most awe-inspiring are the massive rock formations just offshore in the northern and southern sections of the coast, breaking up the Pacific horizon. Beaches along the north coast, from Astoria to Pacific City, are perfect for romantic strolls on the sands. The central-coast beaches, from Lincoln City to Florence, are long and wide, providing perfect conditions for sunbathers, children, clam diggers, horseback riders, and surfers. The southern-coast beaches from Reedsport to Brookings are less populated, ideal for getting away from it all.

In late July and August the climate is kind to sun worshipers. During the shoulder months, keep layers of clothing handy for the unpredictable temperature swings. Winter can be downright blustery, a time that many seaside inns optimistically call "storm-watching season."

GLASS FLOATS: FINDERS KEEPERS

Since 1997, between mid-October and Memorial Day, more than 2,000 handcrafted glass floats made by local artists have been hidden along Lincoln City's 7½-mile public beach. If you happen to come upon one, call the local tourism office (☎ 800/452-2151) to register it, and find out which artist made it. While antique glass floats are extremely rare, these new versions make great souvenirs.

THE OREGON COAST'S BEST BEACHES

Cannon Beach. In the shadow of glorious **Haystack Rock,** this beach is wide, flat, and perfect for bird-watching, exploring tide pools, building sand castles, and romantic walks in the sea mist. Each June the city holds a **sand-castle contest,** drawing artists and thousands of visitors. The rest of the year the beach is far less populated. The dapper beachfront town has several of the region's swankiest hotels and finest restaurants, as well as spots for surfing, hiking, and beachcombing.

Pacific City. This beach is postcard perfect, with its colorful fleet of dories sitting on the sand. Dozens of them lie tilted in between early-morning fishing excursions to catch lingcod, surf perch, and rockfish. Like Cannon Beach, this town also has a huge (less famous) Haystack Rock that provides the perfect scenic backdrop for horseback riders, beach strollers, and people with shovels chasing sand-covered clams. With safe beach breaks that are ideal for beginners and larger peaks a bit to the south, this is also a great spot for surfers. Winterstorm-watchers love Pacific City, where winds exceeding 75 mph twist Sitka spruce, and tides deposit driftwood and logs on the beach.

Winchester Bay. One reason the Pacific Northwest isn't known for its

amusement parks is because nature hurls more thrills than any rattling contraption could ever provide. This certainly is true at **Oregon Dunes National Recreation Area.** Here riders of all-terrain vehicles (ATVs) will encounter some of the most radical slips, dips, hills, and chills in the nation. It is the largest expanse of coastal sand dunes in North America, extending for 40 miles, from Florence to Coos Bay. More than 1.5 million people visit the dunes each year. For those who just want to swim, relax, hike, and marvel at the amazing expanse of dunes against the ocean, there are spaces off-limits to motorized vehicles. Overlooking the beach is the gorgeous **Umpqua River Lighthouse.**

Samuel H. Boardman State Scenic Corridor. It doesn't get any wilder than this—or more spectacular. The 12-mile strip of forested, rugged coastline is dotted with smaller sand beaches, some more accessible than others. Here visitors will find the amazing **Arch Rock** and **Natural Bridges** and can hike 27 miles of the **Oregon Coast Trail.** Beach highlights include **Whaleshead Beach, Secret Beach,** and **Thunder Rock Cove,** where you might spot migrating gray whales. From the 345-foot-high **Thomas Creek Bridge** you can take a moderately difficult hike down to admire the gorgeous, jagged rocks off **China Beach.**

Updated by Andrew Collins

If you aren't from the Pacific Northwest, Oregon's spectacular coastline might still be a secret: it's less visited and talked about than California's coast, but certainly no less beautiful. But in recent decades, the state's reputation for scenic drives and splendid hikes, reasonably priced oceanfront hotels and vacation rentals, low-key towns with friendly, creative vibes, and consistently fresh and well-prepared seafood has garnered increased attention. The true draw here is the beaches, where nature lovers delight at their first sight of a migrating whale or a baby harbor seal sitting on a rock.

Oregon's coastline is open to all; not a grain of its 300 miles of white-sand beaches is privately owned. The coast's midsize towns and small villages (you won't find any large cities) are linked by U.S. 101, which runs the length of the state. It winds past sea-tortured rocks, brooding headlands, hidden beaches, historic lighthouses, and tiny ports. This is one of the most picturesque driving routes in the country, and it should not be missed. Embracing it is the vast, gunmetal-gray Pacific Ocean, which presents a range of moods with the seasons. On summer evenings it might be glassy, and reflect a romantic sunset. In winter the ocean might throw a thrilling tantrum for storm watchers sitting snug and safe in a beachfront cabin.

Active visitors indulge in thrills from racing up a sand dune in a buggy to making par at Bandon Dunes, one of the nation's finest links-style golf courses. Bicyclists pedal along misty coastline vistas, cruising past historic lighthouses. Hikers enjoy breezy, open trails along the sea as well as lush, evergreen-studded treks into the adjoining Coast Range. Boaters explore southern-coast rivers on jet boats while the more adventuresome among them shoot rapids on guided raft trips. If the weather turns, don't overlook indoor venues like the Oregon Coast Aquarium and Columbia River Maritime Museum.

Shoppers appreciate the several art galleries in Newport and Cannon Beach; for more family-oriented shopping fun, giggle in the souvenir shops of Lincoln City and Seaside while eating fistfuls of caramel corn or chewing saltwater taffy.

THE OREGON COAST PLANNER

WHEN TO GO

December through June are generally rainy months, but once the fair weather comes, coastal Oregon is one of the most gorgeous places on earth. July through September offer wonderful, dry days for beachgoers. Autumn is also a great time to visit, as the warm-enough weather is perfect for crisp beachcombing walks followed by hearty harvest meals paired with local ales.

Even with the rain, coastal winter and spring do have quite a following. Many hotels are perfectly situated for storm watching, and provide a romantic experience. Think of a toasty fire, sweet music, a smooth Oregon Pinot, and your loved one, settled in to watch the waves dance upon a jagged rocky stage.

FESTIVALS

If you're looking for one time of year to experience what friendly frivolity can be found on the coast, check out the **Cannon Beach Sandcastle Contest** in June—if you can find a room or a parking spot. Fans of opera and classical works flock to the increasingly popular **Astoria Music Festival** during the last two weeks of June. The **Newport Seafood and Wine Festival** occurs the last full weekend in February, and bills itself the premier seafood and wine event of the Oregon Coast. Dozens of wineries are represented at this expansive celebration, which also features myriad crafts and eateries. In Bandon each September the **Cranberry Festival** comprises a fair and parade.

GETTING HERE AND AROUND

By far the most practical way to reach and to explore the coast is by car. There's only one small regional airport with commercial service, the regional bus lines provide fairly slow and infrequent service from other parts of the state, and there's zero train service. Several two-lane state highways connect the central and northern sections of the coast with the state's two largest cities, Portland and Eugene; the southern portion of the coast is more remote and requires a longer drive.

AIR TRAVEL

From Portland, which has Oregon's largest airport, the drive is about two hours to Astoria and Cannon Beach, and 2½ hours to Lincoln City and Newport. If you're headed farther south, you have a few other options, including flying into the regional airport in Eugene, which is served by most major airlines and is a 90-minute drive from Florence; flying into the tiny Southwest Oregon Regional Airport in the coast town of North Bend, which is an hour south of Florence and 2½ hours north of Brookings; flying into Rogue Valley International Airport in Medford, which is a 2½-hour drive from Brookings and a three-hour drive from Bandon; and flying into Del Norte County

Airport in Crescent City, California, which is just a 30-minute drive south of Brookings.

Southwest Oregon Regional Airport has flights to Portland on SeaPort Airlines and to San Francisco on United Express. The airport has Hertz and Enterprise car-rental agencies as well as cab companies serving the area, including Coos Bay and Bandon.

There are a few shuttle services connecting the airports in Portland and Eugene to the coast, but these tend to be far less economical than renting a car. Caravan Airport Transportation runs a daily shuttle service from Portland International Airport to Lincoln City and on down to Yachats. OmniShuttle provides door-to-door van service from the Eugene airport to the central coast, from Florence down to around Bandon.

Contacts Caravan Airport Transportation ☎ 503/288–5102 ⊕ www. caravanairporttransportation.com. **OmniShuttle** ☎ 541/461–7959, 800/741–5097 ⊕ www.omnishuttle.com. **SeaPort Airlines** ☎ 888/573–2767 ⊕ www. seaportair.com. **Southwest Oregon Regional Airport** ✉ 1100 Airport La., North Bend ☎ 541/756–8531 ⊕ www.flyoth.com.

BUS TRAVEL

There is bus travel to the coast from Portland and Eugene, but this is a fairly slow and cumbersome way to explore the area. North by Northwest Connector is a nonprofit organization that coordinates travel among five rural transit services in the northwestern corner of the state. From its website, you can plan and book trips from Portland to Astoria, with connecting service between the two along the coast, stopping in Seaside, Cannon Beach, Manzanita, and other communities. Additionally, Northwest Point, operated by MTR Western bus line, has twice-daily bus service from Portland to Cannon Beach, and then up the coast to Astoria; Greyhound handles the company's reservations and ticketing. Porter Stage Lines connects Florence, Coos Bay, and Reedsport with Eugene every day except Saturday.

Contacts North by Northwest Connector ⊕ www.nworegontransit.org. **Northwest Point** ☎ 800/231–2222 ticketing through Greyhound, 541/484–4100 information ⊕ www.northwest-point.com. **Porter Stage Lines** ☎ 541/269–7183 ⊕ www.porterstageline.com.

CAR TRAVEL

Beautiful U.S. 101 hugs the entire Oregon coastline from Brookings near the California border in the south to Astoria on the Columbia River in the north. The road can be slow in places, especially where it passes through towns and curves over headlands and around coves. In theory, you could drive the entire 345-mile Oregon stretch of U.S 101 in a little under eight hours, but that's without stopping—and, of course, the whole point of driving the coast is stopping regularly to enjoy it. If you want to do a full road trip of the Oregon Coast, give yourself at least three days and two nights; that's enough time to see a few key attractions along the way, enjoy the many scenic viewpoints, and stop to eat and overnight in some small towns along the route.

Several two-lane roads connect key towns on the coast (Astoria, Cannon Beach, Tillamook, Lincoln City, Newport, Waldport, Florence,

Reedsport, and Bandon) with the major towns in the Willamette and Rogue valleys (Portland, Eugene, Roseburg). All these roads climb over the Coast Range, meaning the drives tend to be winding and hilly but quite picturesque. Keep in mind that winter storms in the mountains occasionally create slick conditions and even road closures. Always use numbered, paved state roads when crossing the mountains from the valley to the coast, especially in winter; what might appear to be a scenic alternative or shortcut on a map or GPS device is likely an unmaintained logging or forest road that leads through a secluded part of the mountains, without cell service.

RESTAURANTS

Deciding which restaurant has the best clam chowder is just one of the culinary fact-finding expeditions you can embark upon along the Oregon Coast. Chefs here take full advantage of the wealth of sturgeon, chinook, steelhead, and trout that abound in coastal rivers as well as the fresh rockfish, halibut, albacore, and lingcod caught in the Pacific. Fresh mussels, bay shrimp, and oysters are also standard fare in many establishments. Newport's bounty is its Dungeness crab. Razor clams also appear as a succulent addition to many restaurant menus along the coast. You'll find relatively few upscale dining options here, with most of these being in resorts, but quite a few midpriced urbane bistros emphasizing local seafood and seasonal produce have opened in recent years. They still tend to be casual, but with fine service, art-filled dining rooms, and prices more similar to what you'll find in Portland or Eugene. Most other restaurants tend to be low-key and affordable, many of them catering to both kids and adults. There are plenty of cozy brewpubs and clam shacks, and tasty fish-and-chips are easy to come by. In addition, many Oregon Coast restaurants focus heavily on locally produced wines, beers, and even spirits.

HOTELS

Compared with other coastal destinations in the United States, the Oregon Coast offers a pretty good value, although during high season in July and August, rates can get fairly steep at some higher-end inns and resorts, especially along the northern stretch of the coastline. Still, you can typically find clean but basic motels and rustic inns, often with beachfront locations, that have nightly rates well below $150, even in high season. Spring and fall rates often drop by 20% to 30%, and in winter—especially on weekdays—a hotel room that costs $250 in July might go for as little as $99. There are plenty of budget- and midpriced chains in larger towns, but for the most part, the lodging landscape is dominated by family-owned or independent motels and hotels, vacation rentals, and a smattering of distinctive B&Bs.

Properties in much of the north and central coast fill up fast in the summer, so book in advance. Many lodgings require a minimum two-night stay on a summer weekend. *Hotel reviews have been shortened. For full information, visit Fodors.com.*

WHAT IT COSTS IN U.S. DOLLARS			
$	**$$**	**$$$**	**$$$$**
Restaurants	Under $17	$17–$23	$24–$30	Over $30
Hotels	Under $151	$151–$200	$201–$250	Over $250

Restaurant prices are the average cost of a main course at dinner, or if dinner is not served, at lunch. Hotel prices are the lowest cost of a standard double room in high season.

VISITOR INFORMATION
Central Oregon Coast Association ☎ *541/265–2064, 800/767–2064* ⊕ *www.coastvisitor.com.* **Eugene, Cascades & Coast Visitor Center** ✉ *3312 Gateway St., Springfield* ☎ *541/484–5307, 800/547–5445* ⊕ *www. travellanecounty.org.* **Oregon Coast Visitors Association** ☎ *541/574–2679, 888/628–2101* ⊕ *www.visittheoregoncoast.com.*

NORTH COAST

This is the primary beach playground for residents of Portland, and in recent years, several sophisticated cafés and wine bars, colorful art galleries and boutiques, and smartly restored boutique hotels have opened along this stretch of the Oregon Coast. What distinguishes the region historically from other areas of the coast are its forts, its graveyard of shipwrecks, historic sites related to Lewis and Clark's early visit, and a town—Astoria—that is closer in look and misty temperament to Monterey, California, than any other city in the West. Just south, Cannon Beach and its several high-end hotels feels a bit swankier than any other town in the area.

Every winter Astoria celebrates fisherman poets: hardworking men and women who bare their souls as to what makes their relationship to Oregon's north-coast waters so magical. It's easy to understand their inspiration, whether in the incredibly tempestuous ocean or the romantic beaches.

ASTORIA

96 miles northwest of Portland.

The mighty Columbia River meets the Pacific at Astoria, the oldest city west of the Rockies and a bustling riverfront getaway with a creative spirit and urbane vibe. It is named for John Jacob Astor, owner of the Pacific Fur Company, whose members arrived in 1811 and established Fort Astoria. In its early days, Astoria was a placid amalgamation of small town and hardworking port city. With rivers rich with salmon, the city relied on its fishing and canning industries. Settlers built sprawling Victorian houses on the flanks of Coxcomb Hill; many of the homes have since been restored and used as backdrops in movies or been converted into bed-and-breakfast inns. In recent years the city itself has awakened, with a greater variety of trendy dining and lodging options, as well as a superb museum dedicated to the Columbia River.

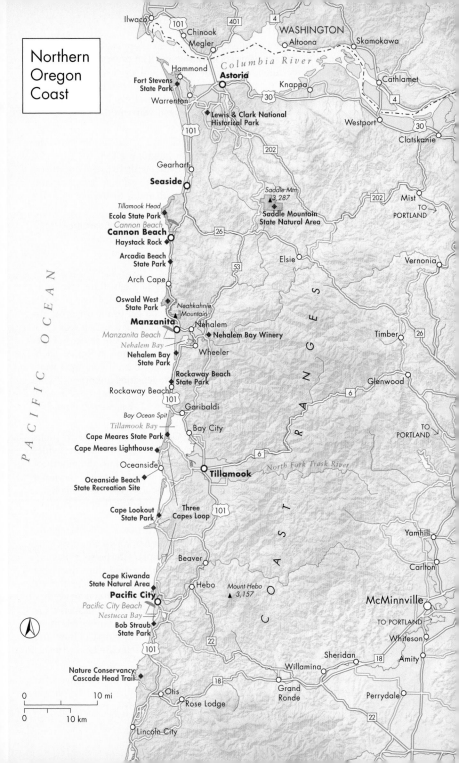

But Astoria still retains the soul of a fisherman's town, celebrated each February during its FisherPoets Gathering. The town of about 9,500 also has wonderful views from most areas and a richly forested backdrop to the east, yet it remains a working waterfront. There is little public beach access in the town proper; to reach the Pacific, you have to drive a few miles west to Fort Stevens in Warrenton.

GETTING HERE AND AROUND

The northernmost town on the Oregon Coast, Astoria is just across the Columbia River from southwestern Washington via U.S. 101 (over the stunning Astoria-Megler Bridge) and a two-hour drive from Portland on U.S. 30. It only takes about 20 extra minutes to get here from Portland via the more scenic route of U.S. 101 south and U.S. 26 east.

ESSENTIALS

Visitor Information Astoria-Warrenton Area Chamber of Commerce ⊠ 111 W. Marine Dr. ☎ 503/325–6311, 800/875–6807 ⊕ www.oldoregon.com.

EXPLORING

TOP ATTRACTIONS

Astoria Column. For the best view of the city, the Coast Range, volcanic Mt. Helens, and the Pacific Ocean, scamper up the 164 spiral stairs to the top of the Astoria Column. When you get to the top, you can throw a small wooden plane and watch it glide to earth; each year some 35,000 gliders are tossed. The 125-foot-high structure sits atop Coxcomb Hill, and was patterned after Trajan's Column in Rome. There are little platforms to rest on if you get winded, or, if you don't want to climb, the column's 500 feet of artwork, depicting important Pacific Northwest historical milestones, are well worth a study. ⊠ 16th St. S ☎ 503/325–2963 ⊕ www.astoriacolumn.org ☎ $2 per car ☉ Weekdays 9–5:30, weekends 9–5.

FAMILY
Fodor's Choice
★

Columbia River Maritime Museum. One of Oregon's best coastal attractions illuminates the maritime history of the Pacific Northwest and provides visitors with a sense of the perils of guiding ships into the mouth of the Columbia River. Vivid exhibits recount what it was like to pilot a tugboat and participate in a Coast Guard rescue on the Columbia River Bar. You can tour the actual bridge of a World War II–era U.S. Navy destroyer and the U.S. Coast Guard lightship *Columbia*. Also on display is a 44-foot Coast Guard motor lifeboat, artifacts from the region's illustrious riverboat heyday, and details about Astoria's seafood-canning history. One especially captivating exhibit displays the personal belongings of some of the ill-fated passengers of the 2,000 ships that have foundered here since the early 19th century. In addition, the theater shows an excellent documentary about the river's heritage as well as rotating 3-D films about sea life. At the east end of the property, the city's former railroad depot now houses the museum's Barbey Maritime Center, which offers classes and workshops on maritime culture and wooden boatbuilding. ⊠ 1792 Marine Dr. ☎ 503/325–2323 ⊕ www.crmm.org ☎ $12 ☉ Daily 9:30–5.

Flavel House. The Queen Anne-style mansion helps visitors imagine what life was like for the wealthy in late-19th-century Astoria. It rests on parklike grounds covering an entire city block and has been gorgeously restored, with its three-story octagon tower visible from throughout town. It was built for George Flavel, an influential Columbia River bar pilot and businessman who was one of the area's first millionaires. Visits start in the Carriage House interpretive center. ⊠ *441 8th St.* ☎ *503/325–2203* ⊕ *www.cumtux.org* ⊒ *$6* ⊙ *May–Sept., daily 10–5; Oct.–Apr., daily 11–4.*

FAMILY
Fodor's Choice
★

Fort Clatsop at Lewis and Clark National Historical Park. See where the 30-member Lewis and Clark Expedition endured a rain-soaked winter in 1805–06, hunting, gathering food, making salt, and trading with the local Clatsops, Chinooks, and Tillamooks. This memorial is part of the 3,200-acre Lewis and Clark National Historical Park and is a faithful replica of the log fort depicted in Clark's journal. The fort lies within a forested wonderland, with an exhibit hall, gift shop, film, and trails. Park rangers dress in period garb during the summer and perform such early-19th-century tasks as making fire with flint and steel. Hikers enjoy the easy 1½-mile Netul Landing trail and the more strenuous but still fairly flat 6½-mile Fort to Sea trail. ⊠ *92343 Fort Clatsop Rd., 6 miles southwest of downtown Astoria* ☎ *503/861–2471* ⊕ *www.nps.gov/lewi* ⊒ *$3* ⊙ *Mid-Jun.–Labor Day, daily 9–6; Labor Day–mid-Jun., daily 9–5.*

WORTH NOTING

Bumble Bee Cannery Museum. Drive or walk over the rickety (but actually completely sturdy) bridge onto historic Pier 39, which juts out into the Columbia River on the east side of downtown, to visit this small but interesting museum that occupies the oldest extant cannery building in Astoria. It was once operated by Bumble Bee Seafood, and some 30,000 cans of salmon were processed here annually during the plant's late-19th-century heyday. Exhibits and artifacts, including three vintage gill-net boats, some wonderful old photos, and equipment and cans tell the story of the town's—and facility's—canning history. Also on the pier is Coffee Girl café and Rogue Ales tavern. ⊠ *100 39th St.* ☎ *503/325–2502* ⊕ *www.canneryworker.org* ⊒ *Free* ⊙ *Daily 9–6.*

NEED A BREAK?

Coffee Girl. This cozy café inside a 19th-century cannery building on historic Pier 39 has big windows overlooking the river—you can always take your well-crafted espresso or latte with you for a stroll around the pier. Open until 4 pm each day, Coffee Girl also serves tasty quiches, pastries, soups, and grilled panini sandwiches. ⊠ *100 39th St.* ☎ *503/325–6900* ⊕ *www.thecoffeegirl.com.*

FAMILY
Fort Stevens State Park. This earthen fort at Oregon's northwestern tip was built during the Civil War to guard the Columbia River against attack. None came until World War II, when a Japanese submarine fired upon it. The fort still has cannons and an underground gun battery, of which tours are available in summer (call for details). The park has year-round camping, with full hookup sites and 15 yurts. There are also bike paths, boating, swimming, hiking trails, and a short walk to a gorgeous, wide beach where the corroded skeleton—or the tiny bit that remains of it—of the *Peter Iredale* pokes up through the sand. This century-old English four-master shipwreck is a reminder of the nearly

2,000 vessels claimed by these treacherous waters. ✉ *100 Peter Iredale Rd., 9 miles west of Astoria* ☎ *503/861–3170, 800/452–5687* ⊕ *www. oregonstateparks.org* ▭ *Day use $5 per vehicle* ☉ *Daily.*

FAMILY **Oregon Film Museum.** Housed in the old Clatsop County Jail, this small but engaging museum celebrates Oregon's long history of filmmaking and contains artifacts from and displays about prior productions. The location is apt because it was featured prominently in the famous cult film *The Goonies.* The state's film productions date back to 1908 for *The Fisherman's Bride.* Since then, Oregon has helped give birth to such classics as *The General, The Great Race, One Flew Over the Cuckoo's Nest, Paint Your Wagon, Animal House,* and *Twilight,* leading some to call the state Hollywood North. *Kindergarten Cop, The Ring II, Free Willy I* and *II,* and *Short Circuit* are among those filmed in Astoria. You can download an audio tour of filmed sites (or buy a tour CD for $2) from the Astoria-Warrenton Chamber of Commerce—it's a fun way to see the city's oft-unsung landmarks, especially during the annual Goonies festival, held in June. ✉ *732 Duane St.* ☎ *503/325–2203* ⊕ *www.oregonfilmmuseum.org* ▭ *$6* ☉ *May–Sept. daily 10–5; Oct.–Apr. daily 11–4.*

WHERE TO EAT

$ ✗ **Astoria Coffeehouse & Bistro.** A source of fine coffee drinks and baked
ECLECTIC goods, this cheerful storefront café has both sidewalk seating and a
Fodor'sChoice living-room-like interior decorated with old photos. The always-
★ bustling restaurant serves consistently well-prepared food, a mix of American classics and international treats. Try the decadent Monte Cristo sandwich at breakfast. Later in the day, highlights include tuna *poke* (salad) with mango and avocado, slow-roasted-beet salad with chèvre and apples, local-rockfish tacos with tomatillo salsa, and pad thai with fresh salmon. The fine drink selection makes this a favorite nightlife option, too. ⑤ *Average main: $15* ✉ *243 11th St.* ☎ *503/325–1787* ⊕ *www.astoriacoffeehouse.com.*

$ ✗ **Blue Scorcher Bakery Café.** "Joyful work, delicious food, and strong
CAFÉ community" is this family-friendly café's rallying cry. It serves up every-
FAMILY thing from *huevos scorcheros* (poached eggs with rice, beans, cheese, and salsa) and organic, handcrafted breads to a variety of foods using local, fair trade, and organic ingredients. The offerings change with the seasons, but there's always a vegan or gluten-free option. There's also a Pie-of-the-Month Club. Big windows overlook downtown and the Columbia River in the distance, and there's a children's play area. ⑤ *Average main: $8* ✉ *1493 Duane St.* ☎ *503/338–7473* ⊕ *www. bluescorcher.com* ☉ *No dinner.*

$$ ✗ **Bridgewater Bistro.** In the same complex as the Cannery Pier Hotel, this
PACIFIC stylish restaurant has great views of the river and bridge to Washington.
NORTHWEST Inside, high ceilings are supported by ancient fir timbers, and an extensive menu is strong on creative seafood and meat grills, including roasted spice-encrusted duck breast with cranberry-blackberry demi-glace, and seared wild local salmon with an arugula-strawberry salad and a star anise–balsamic vinaigrette. You'll also find more affordable burgers, pastas, and vegetarian options. There's a much-celebrated brunch on Sunday. ⑤ *Average main: $22* ✉ *20 Basin St., Suite A* ☎ *503/325–6777* ⊕ *www.bridgewaterbistro.com.*

$$ ✕ **Clemente's.** Serving some of the best seafood on the northern Oregon
SEAFOOD Coast, chefs Gordon and Lisa Clement have played a big role in Asto-
Fodor'sChoice ria's steady growth into a legitimate dining destination. Grounded in
★ the Mediterranean culinary traditions of Italy and the Adriatic Coast,
Clemente's inventive specials feature the freshest catches of that day,
from a succulent pan-seared local halibut with truffle salt and red-
pepper coulis to a hearty cioppino—all served up for reasonable prices.
Dungeness crab cakes stuffed with crab rather than breading, and wild
scallop fish-and-chips liven up a varied menu. The Clements have a
strong commitment to locally sourced ingredients and environmen-
tally friendly practices. ⑤ *Average main: $22* ✉ *1198 Commercial St.*
☎ *503/325–1067* ⊕ *www.clementesrestaurant.com* ☾ *No lunch Mon.*

$$ ✕ **Columbian Cafe.** Locals love this unpretentious diner that defies cat-
ECLECTIC egorization by offering inventive, fresh seafood, spicy vegetarian dishes,
and meats cured and smoked on the premises. Located next to the
quirky Voodoo Room bar and historic Columbian Theater, the café
serves simple food, such as crepes with broccoli, cheese, and homemade
salsa for lunch; grilled salmon and pasta with a lemon-cream sauce for
dinner. Colorful owner-chef Uriah Hulsey is usually on hand. Be sure
to come early as this place always draws a crowd. ⑤ *Average main: $23*
✉ *1114 Marine Dr.* ☎ *503/325–2233* ⊕ *www.columbianvoodoo.com/*
cafe ▭ *No credit cards* ☾ *Closed Mon. and Tues.*

WHERE TO STAY

$$$$ 🏨 **Cannery Pier Hotel.** From every room in this captivating property
HOTEL there's a gorgeous view of the mighty Columbia River flowing toward
Fodor'sChoice the Pacific Ocean, and it's almost hypnotic to watch the tugboats shep-
★ herding barges to and fro. **Pros:** amazing river views; great in-room
amenities; hotel hot tub and day spa. **Cons:** pricey; a bit of a walk
from downtown. ⑤ *Rooms from: $279* ✉ *10 Basin St.* ☎ *503/325–*
4996, 888/325–4996 ⊕ *www.cannerypierhotel.com* ⇆ *46 rooms, 8*
suites ❍| *Breakfast.*

$ 🏨 **Clementine's B& B.** This painstakingly restored 1888 Italianate Vic-
B&B/INN torian home is just a couple of blocks up the hill from Flavel House
Museum and a short walk from several fine restaurants and shops. **Pros:**
superb; multicourse breakfast included; handy downtown location.
Cons: the traditional lacy room decor isn't for everyone. ⑤ *Rooms from:*
$109 ✉ *847 Exchange St.* ☎ *503/325–2005* ⊕ *www.clementines-bb.*
com ⇆ *4 rooms, 1 suite* ❍| *Breakfast.*

$ 🏨 **Commodore Hotel.** An economical but stylish downtown boutique
HOTEL hotel, the Commodore has become a favorite with young and artsy
Fodor'sChoice souls from Portland and Seattle thanks to its vintage-chic aesthetic, large
★ wall murals and photos, and hip café off the lobby. **Pros:** hip ambience;
wallet-friendly rates; excellent Street 14 Coffee café on-site. **Cons:** least
expensive rooms share a bath; simple decor. ⑤ *Rooms from: $79* ✉ *258*
14th St. ☎ *503/325–4747* ⊕ *www.commodoreastoria.com* ⇆ *18 rooms,*
10 with shared bath ❍| *No meals.*

$ 🏨 **Hotel Elliott.** This atmospheric, five-story hotel stands in the heart of
HOTEL Astoria's historic district and retains the elegance of yesteryear, updated
with modern comforts like cozy underfloor heating in the bathrooms.
Pros: captures the city's historic ambience beautifully; every effort

made to infuse the rooms with upscale amenities; popular wine bar. **Cons:** some areas have a lingering smell of cigar smoke; no on-site dining. *⑤ Rooms from: $149 ⊠ 357 12th St. ☎ 503/325–2222 ⊕ www. hotelelliott.com ⟳ 21 rooms, 11 suites ⓧ Breakfast.*

NIGHTLIFE

Fodor'sChoice
★

Fort George Brewery. The spacious taproom and brewery set in a former 1920s auto showroom has plenty of indoor and outdoor seating where you can sample some of the best craft beers on the coast, including the Belgian-style Quick Wit or the oatmeal-infused Sunrise OPA, a light American pale ale. Plenty of seasonal brews appear on the menu as well, along with tasty pub fare. *⊠ 1483 Duane St. ☎ 503/325–7468 ⊕ www.fortgeorgebrewery.com.*

SHOPPING

Josephson's. One of the Oregon Coast's oldest commercial smokehouses, Josephson's uses alder for all processing and specializes in Pacific Northwest chinook and coho salmon. The mouthwatering fish that's smoked on the premises includes hot smoked pepper or wine-maple salmon, as well as smoked halibut, sturgeon, tuna, oysters, mussels, scallops, and prawns by the pound or in sealed gift packs. *⊠ 106 Marine Dr. ☎ 503/325–2190 ⊕ www.josephsons.com.*

SEASIDE

12 miles south of Astoria on U.S. 101.

As a resort town, Seaside has somewhat spruced up its kitschy, arcade-filled reputation and now supports a bustling tourist trade, with hotels, condominiums, and restaurants lining a traditional promenade. It still has fun games and plenty of carny noise to appeal to young people, but it has added plenty of classy getaways for adults, as well as some of the more affordable lodging options on this stretch of the coast. Only 90 miles from Portland, Seaside is often crowded, so it's not the place to come if you crave solitude. Peak times include mid- to late March, when hordes of teenagers descend on the town during spring break; and late June, when the annual Miss Oregon Pageant is in full swing. Just south of town, waves draw surfers to the Cove, a spot jealously guarded by locals.

GETTING HERE AND AROUND

Seaside is about a 90-minute drive from Portland via U.S 26 and a 20-minute drive south of Astoria on coastal U.S. 101.

VISITOR INFORMATION

Seaside Visitors Bureau *⊠ 7 N. Roosevelt Ave. ☎ 503/738–3097, 888/306–2326 ⊕ www.seasideor.com.*

WHERE TO EAT AND STAY

$

DINER

✕ **Firehouse Grill.** This bustling diner-style café in a former firehouse in downtown Seaside hits the mark with its hearty breakfast fare, including fluffy biscuits with gravy, cinnamon French toast, meat-loaf scrambles, and a couple of lighter options, such as house-made granola with fresh fruit. The excellent Sleepy Monk coffee from Cannon Beach is served, too, as are eye-opening Bloody Marys. Open only until early afternoon, the restaurant also turns out excellent burgers, panfried oysters, and halibut tacos at lunch. $ *Average main: $10* ✉ *841 Broadway* ☎ *503/717–5502* ⊘ *Closed Tues. and Wed. No dinner.*

$$ 🛏 **McMenamins Gearhart Hotel.** The quirky McMenamins group, which
HOTEL operates several historic and offbeat hotels around the state, opened this 18-room boutique inn on the upper floor of the Cape Cod–style Kelly House in 2012. **Pros:** short walk from beach; rooms have distinctive and arty flair; excellent 18-hole golf course. **Cons:** ocean view is blocked by condos across the street; not within walking distance of shopping and dining; restaurant on-site is just so-so. $ *Rooms from: $195* ✉ *1157 N. Marion Ave., 4 miles north of Seaside, Gearhart* ☎ *503/717–8159, 855/846–7583* ⊕ *www.mcmenamins.com/gearharthotel* ⤳ *18 rooms* ♚*No meals.*

$$ 🛏 **Rivertide Suites.** Although it's not right on the beach, the Rivertide's
HOTEL splendid accommodations are within walking distance of the town's
FAMILY best cuisine, shopping, and beach activities. **Pros:** contemporary; clean; near plenty of shopping and boardwalk activities. **Cons:** it's on a city river instead of the beach; rooms on lower floors have less of a view. $ *Rooms from: $169* ✉ *102 N. Holladay Dr.* ☎ *503/717–1100, 877/871–8433* ⊕ *www.rivertidesuites.com* ⤳ *70 rooms* ♚*Breakfast.*

$ 🛏 **Sandy Cove Inn.** This small, nicely maintained motel is fun and color-
HOTEL fully decorated, and it's just a block away from Seaside's promenade. **Pros:** near plenty of restaurants; distinctive room themes. **Cons:** not directly on the beach; funky rooms don't suit every taste. $ *Rooms from: $89* ✉ *241 Ave. U* ☎ *503/738–7473* ⊕ *www.sandycoveinn.net* ⤳ *13 rooms, 2 suites* ♚*No meals.*

SPORTS AND THE OUTDOORS

HIKING

Saddle Mountain State Natural Area. One of the most accessible mountain peaks in the Coast Range, 3,283-foot Saddle Mountain is reached via a challenging but beautiful 2½-mile climb, with a 1,603-foot elevation gain—the reward, on clear days, is a view of the ocean to the west and the Cascade peaks far to the east. Wear sturdy shoes, and be prepared for sections with steep upgrades. There's a zippy change in the altitude as you climb higher, but the wildflowers make it all worthwhile. The trailhead is well signed off of U.S. 26, the main highway from Portland to Cannon Beach and Seaside. ✉ *Saddle Mountain Rd., off U.S. 26, 20 miles east of Seaside and 70 miles west of Portland* ☎ *800/551–6949, 503/368–5943* ⊕ *www.oregonstateparks.org.*

CANNON BEACH

25 miles south of Astoria.

Cannon Beach is a mellow but relatively affluent town where locals and part-time residents—many of the latter reside in Portland—come to enjoy shopping and dining, the sea air, and the chance to explore the spectacular state parks at either end of the area: Ecola to the north and Oswald West to the south. Shops and galleries selling surfing gear, upscale clothing, local art, wine, coffee, and candies line Hemlock Street, Cannon Beach's main thoroughfare. In late June the town hosts the Cannon Beach Sandcastle Contest, for which thousands throng the beach to view imaginative and often startling works in this most transient of art forms. On the downside, this so-called Carmel of the Oregon Coast can be more expensive and crowded than other towns along U.S. 101.

GETTING HERE AND AROUND

It's a 90-minute drive east from Portland on U.S. 26 to reach Cannon Beach, which is a 10-minute drive south of Seaside. To make a scenic loop, consider returning to Portland by way of Astoria and U.S. 30 (about 2¼ hours) or Tillamook and Highway 6 (about 2½ hours).

ESSENTIALS

Visitor Information Cannon Beach Chamber of Commerce ⊠ *207 N. Spruce St., Cannon Beach* ☎ *503/436–2623* ⊕ *www.cannonbeach.org.*

EXPLORING

Haystack Rock. Towering over the broad, sandy beach is a gorgeous, 235-foot-high dome that is one of the most photographed natural wonders on the Oregon Coast. For safety and to protect birding habitats, people are not allowed to climb on the rock, but you can walk right up to its base at low tide. ⊠ *Cannon Beach.*

WHERE TO EAT

$$
IRISH
$$

✕ **Irish Table.** Adjacent to the Sleepy Monk café, this cozy restaurant with a timber-beam ceiling and warm lighting serves seasonal food with an Irish twist, such as potato-kale soup and its heralded Irish lamb stew. Other offerings include a perfect steak or delicate fresh halibut. Start with chicken-bacon chowder or the curried mussels, and soak up the sauce with slices of piping-hot soda bread. Naturally, there's a rich assortment of drinks, including Irish whiskey, and the wine list features plenty of noted Oregon options. It's a popular place, so be prepared to wait in summer and on weekends—reservations are available only for parties of four or more. ⑤ *Average main: $18* ⊠ *1235 S. Hemlock St.* ☎ *503/436–0708* ⊕ *www.theirishtablerestaurant.com* ☽ *Closed Wed. and Jan. No lunch.*

$
CAFÉ
Fodor's Choice
★

✕ **Sleepy Monk.** In a region renowned for artisan coffee, this small roaster brews some of the best espresso and coffee drinks in the state. Sleepy Monk attracts java aficionados on caffeine pilgrimages from near and far eager to sample its certified-organic, fair-trade beans. Local, fresh pastries are stacked high and there's also a good selection of herbal and green teas. The Irish Table restaurant next door is under the same management. ⑤ *Average main: $5* ⊠ *1235 S. Hemlock St.* ☎ *503/436–2796* ⊕ *www.sleepymonkcoffee.com* ☽ *Closed Wed. and Thurs. No dinner.*

$$$$
PACIFIC
NORTHWEST
Fodor's Choice
★

✕ **Stephanie Inn Dining Room.** As diners enjoy a romantic view of Haystack Rock, this luxe hotel's sophisticated, supremely romantic dining room prepares a new menu nightly, crafting exquisite dinners using fresh, local ingredients. Diners can expect dishes such as butternut squash risotto, cedar plank–roasted salmon, savory duck confit, and a lemon-curd tart with wild berry sauce. You can order a la carte or opt for the four-course prix-fixe, with or without wine pairings. There's an extensive regional and international wine list. The view, cuisine, and attentive service combine to make it one of the finest dining experiences in the Pacific Northwest. ⑤ *Average main: $43* ⊠ *2740 S. Pacific St.*

☏ *503/436–2221, 800/633–3466* ⊕ *www.stephanie-inn.com* ✍ *Reservations essential* ☽ *No lunch*.

$$$ ✗ **Wayfarer Restaurant.** The dazzling beach and ocean views, especially
AMERICAN at sunset, are just part of the story at this casually elegant restaurant
at the Surfsand Resort; it's also the top destination in town for a leisurely meal of tasty American food, including plenty of local seafood
options, such as sesame-breaded Pacific razor clams with jalapeño-lime
jelly, and Oregon-hazelnut-seared sole with a berry beurre blanc. If fish
isn't your game, consider the prodigious 22-ounce "tomahawk" rib-
eye steak with a Cabernet butter. There's a nice list of Oregon wines,
and breakfast—featuring several delicious Benedicts and omelets—is
offered daily. ⑤ *Average main: $29* ⊠ *1190 Pacific Dr.* ☏ *503/436–1108*
⊕ *www.wayfarer-restaurant.com.*

WHERE TO STAY

$ 🏨 **Ecola Creek Lodge.** With a quiet, shady courtyard just off the main
HOTEL road leading into the north side of town, this small, reasonably priced
1940s hotel offers 22 suites and rooms with a mix of configurations,
from two-bedroom units with kitchens to cozy standard rooms. **Pros:**
quiet setting; rooms come in wide range of layouts; good value. **Cons:**
not on the beach; slight walk from downtown shopping. ⑤ *Rooms
from: $124* ⊠ *208 5th St.* ☏ *503/436–2776, 800/873–2749* ⊕ *www.
ecolacreeklodge.com* ⬳ *9 rooms, 13 suites* ⦿ *No meals.*

$$$$ 🏨 **Ocean Lodge.** Designed to capture the feel of a 1940s beach resort, this
RESORT rustic but upscale lodge is perfect for special occasions and romantic get-
aways. **Pros:** beachfront location; spacious rooms; warm cookies deliv-
ered to rooms. **Cons:** expensive; balconies are shared with neighboring
rooms. ⑤ *Rooms from: $259* ⊠ *2864 S. Pacific St.* ☏ *503/436–2241,
888/777–4047* ⊕ *www.theoceanlodge.com* ⬳ *45 rooms* ⦿ *Breakfast.*

$$$$ 🏨 **Stephanie Inn.** One of the coastline's most beautiful views is paired
RESORT with one of its most splendid hotels, where the focus is firmly on
Fodor's Choice romance, superior service, and luxurious rooms. **Pros:** incredibly plush
★ accommodations; lots of little extras included; top-notch service. **Cons:**
among the highest rates of any hotel in the state; not for families with
younger children; some minimum-night stay requirements. ⑤ *Rooms
from: $479* ⊠ *2740 S. Pacific St.* ☏ *503/436–2221, 800/633–3466*
⊕ *www.stephanie-inn.com* ⬳ *27 rooms, 14 suites* ⦿ *Breakfast.*

$ 🏨 **Tolovana Inn.** Set on the beach at the quieter southern end of town, the
HOTEL large, rambling Tolovana Inn is one of the better-priced options in this
FAMILY tony seaside community, especially considering that most rooms enjoy
partial or full views of the Pacific. **Pros:** panoramic beach views; good mix
of layouts and room sizes; some units have kitchens. **Cons:** a 10-minute
drive from downtown shops; some rooms are relatively small. ⑤ *Rooms
from: $134* ⊠ *3400 S. Hemlock St.* ☏ *503/436–2211, 800/333–8890*
⊕ *www.tolovanainn.com* ⬳ *74 rooms, 103 suites* ⦿ *No meals.*

SHOPPING

Cannon Beach Art Galleries. The numerous art galleries that line Can-
non Beach's Hemlock Street are an essential part of the town's spirit
and beauty. A group of about a dozen galleries featuring beautifully
innovative works in ceramic, bronze, photography, painting, and other

mediums have collaborated to form the Cannon Beach Gallery Group. You'll find information about exhibits and special events on the website. ✉ *Hemlock St.* ⊕ *cbgallerygroup.com.*

SPORTS AND THE OUTDOORS

BEACHES

FAMILY   **Cannon Beach and Ecola State Park.** Beachcombers love Cannon Beach for
Fodor'sChoice   its often low foamy waves and the wide stretch of sand that wraps the
★   quaint community, making it ideal for fair-weather play or for hunting down a cup of coffee and strolling in winter. This stretch can get feisty in storms, however, which also makes Cannon Beach a good place to curl up indoors and watch the show. Haystack Rock rises 253 feet over the beach on the south side of downtown, one of 1,853 protected rocks that's part of the Oregon Ocean Island Wildlife Refuge, providing a nesting habitat for birds. Continue south past Tolovana Park—a playground located in the flood plain—to find the quiet side of Cannon Beach with a bevy of tide pools and few other souls. To the north of town, the beach gives way to Ecola State Park, a breathtakingly beautiful series of coves and rocky headlands where William Clark spotted a beached whale in 1806 and visitors still come to view them offshore during the twice-yearly migrations. From here, Sitka spruce and barbecues feature along the sands. There are a few excellent trails that hug the sometimes steep cliffs that rise above sand, including a 6-mile trail first traced by Lewis and Clark that runs from this spot all the way to Seaside. **Amenities:** parking; toilets. **Best for:** partiers; sunset; walking. ✉ *Ocean Ave.* ☎ *503/436–2844, 800/551–6949* ⊕ *www.cannon-beach. net* ✆ *Ecola State Park day use $5 per vehicle.*

MANZANITA

20 miles south of Cannon Beach.

Manzanita is a secluded and gorgeously situated seaside community with only a few more than 500 full-time residents—but a growing following among weekenders from the Willamette Valley means there's one of the highest number of vacation rentals along the northern Oregon Coast here. The village is on a sandy peninsula, peppered with tufts of grass, on the northwestern side of Nehalem Bay, a noted windsurfing destination. It's a fairly laid-back town, but its growing crop of notable restaurants and boutiques has made it increasingly popular with visitors, as has its proximity to beautiful Oswald West State Park.

GETTING HERE AND AROUND

Tiny Manzanita is an easy and picturesque 20-minute drive south of Cannon Beach on coastal U.S. 101; from Portland, it takes just under two hours to get here.

WHERE TO EAT AND STAY

$$$ ✕ **Blackbird.** Laid-back and decidedly causal downtown Manzanita
MODERN   received a significant culinary boost with the 2014 opening of this sophis-
AMERICAN   ticated, locavore-driven bistro. The menu changes often but might feature a salad of local greens, balsamic-soaked cherries, and smoked duck breast; roasted free-range chicken with kale, carrots, and spaetzle; or

tender beef tenderloin with potato gratin, sautéed Swiss chard, and red-wine jus—the fresh, uncomplicated food is attractively presented and sings with flavor. Save room for the rich dark-chocolate pot de crème topped with sea salt and caramel. Reservations are a good idea during busy times, as this intimate space has just a handful of tables plus several stools at the bar. $ *Average main: $25* ✉ *503 Laneda Ave.* ☏ *503/368–7708* ⊕ *www.blackbirdmanzanita.com* ☾ *Closed Sun. No lunch.*

$ ✕ **Bread and Ocean Bakery.** This small bakery with a handful of tables
CAFÉ inside and several more on the sunny patio is hugely popular for breakfast and lunch with the many folks who rent cottages in the friendly beach town; if it's crowded, consider taking your food to go—the beach is just a few blocks away. Start the morning with a slice of quiche or breakfast frittata. At lunchtime, tuck into a hefty deli sandwich, such as turkey with pear-apple compote and Gorgonzola on house-baked ciabatta. Fresh-baked breads, daily rotating side salads, decadent cinnamon rolls, Sleepy Monk coffee, gourmet sodas, craft beers, and local wines are sold, too. $ *Average main: $9* ✉ *154 Laneda Ave.* ☏ *503/368–5823* ⊕ *www.breadandocean.com* ▬ *No credit cards* ☾ *Closed Mon. and Tues. No dinner.*

$ ✕ **San Dune Pub.** Once just a neighborhood dive bar, this 1930s pub has
AMERICAN upped its game over the years and become a local magnet for delicious seafood, burgers, sweet-potato fries, grilled-cod tacos, oyster po'boys, and, on Tuesday, baby back ribs. Desserts are worth saving room for here—a few different fresh-fruit and cream pies are always featured. There are 17 beers on tap, regular live music ($5 cover charge), and a 50-inch screen for sports, so it's a one-stop shop. Patio seating on nicer days is a bonus, particularly if you've brought the dog along. $ *Average main: $14* ✉ *127 Laneda Ave.* ☏ *503/368–5080* ⊕ *www.sandunepub.com.*

$$$ 🛏 **Inn at Manzanita.** Shore pines around this 1987 Scandinavian struc-
B&B/INN ture give upper-floor patios a treehouse feel, and it's just half a block
FAMILY from the beach. **Pros:** tranquil ambience with a Japanese garden atmosphere; very light and clean; several rooms good for families. **Cons:** two-night minimum stay on weekends; can book up fast in summer. $ *Rooms from: $179* ✉ *67 Laneda Ave.* ☏ *503/368–6754* ⊕ *www.innatmanzanita.com* ⇗ *13 rooms, 1 suite* ❘❍❘ *No meals.*

SPORTS AND THE OUTDOORS
BEACHES
Manzanita Beach and Nehalem Bay State Park. The long stretch of white sand that separates the Pacific Ocean from the town of Manzanita is as loved a stretch of coastline as the next, its north side reaching into the shadows of Neahkanie Mountain, right where the mountain puts its foot in the ocean (the mountain itself, which makes for a great hike, lies within Oswald West State Park). The beach is frequented by vacationers, day-trippers, kite flyers, and dogs on its north end, but it extends a breezy 7 miles to the tip of Nehalem Bay State Park, which is accessible on foot over sand or by car along the road. At the south end of the park's parking lot, a dirt horse trail leads all the way to a peninsula's tip, a flat walk behind grassy dunes—you can book horseback rides from **Oregon Beach Rides** (☏ *971/237–6653* ⊕ *www.*

oregonbeachrides.com) which has a stable inside the park. Cross to the right for a secluded patch of windy sand on the ocean, or to the left for a quiet, sunny place in the sun on Nehalem Bay, out of the wind. **Amenities:** toilets. **Best for:** sunset; walking. ⊠ *Foot of Laneda Ave.* ☎ *503/368–5154, 800/551–6949* ⊕ *www.oregonstateparks.org* ⊠ *Nehalem Bay State Park day use $5 per vehicle.*

RECREATIONAL AREAS

Fodor's Choice
★

Oswald West State Park. Adventurous travelers will enjoy a sojourn at one of the best-kept secrets on the Pacific coast, at the base of Neahkahnie Mountain. Park in one of the two free lots on U.S. 101 and hike a half-mile trail to dramatic Short Sand Beach, aka "Shorty's," one of the top spots along the Oregon Coast for surfing. It's a spectacular beach with caves and tidal pools. There are several trails from the beach, all offering dazzling scenery; the relatively easy 2½-mile trail to Cape Falcon overlook joins with the Oregon Coast Trail and offers impressive views back toward Shorty's Beach. The arduous 5½-mile trail to the 1,680-foot summit of Neahkahnie Mountain (access the trailhead about 2 miles south of the parking lots marked only by a "hikers" sign, or get there via Short Sand Beach) provides dazzling views south for many miles toward the surf, sand, and mountains fringing Manzanita and, in the distance, Tillamook. Come in December or March and you might spot pods of gray whales. ⊠ *U.S. 101, 5 miles north of downtown Manzanita, Arch Cape* ☎ *800/551–6949* ⊕ *www.oregonstateparks.org* ⊠ *Free* ☉ *Daily dawn–dusk.*

HORSEBACK RIDING

FAMILY

Oregon Beach Rides. Saddle up for horseback rides at Nehalem Bay State Park, available Memorial Day through Labor Day weekends. Guides take you on a journey along the beach in Manzanita, and reserved rides can last from one to several hours. There's even a romantic sunset trot. It's appropriate for ages six and up. ⊠ *Nehalem Bay State Park, 9500 Sandpiper La., Nehalem* ☎ *971/237–6653* ⊕ *www.oregonbeachrides.com.*

TILLAMOOK

27 miles south of Manzanita.

More than 100 inches of annual rainfall and the confluence of three rivers contribute to the lush green pastures around Tillamook, probably best known for its thriving dairy industry and cheese factory. The Tillamook County Cheese Factory ships about 40 million pounds of cheese around the world every year. The town itself lies several miles inland from the ocean and doesn't offer much in the way of attractions, but it is the best jumping-off point for driving the dramatic **Three Capes Loop, which passes** over Cape Meares, Cape Lookout, and Cape Kiwanda and offers spectacular views of the ocean and coastline. The small village of Oceanside, just north of Cape Lookout, has several cute restaurants and shops.

GETTING HERE AND AROUND

Tillamook is a 90-minute drive from Portland on U.S. 26 to Highway 6. It's a winding, pretty, 45-minute drive south of Cannon Beach on U.S. 101, and a one-hour drive north of Lincoln City along the same coastal highway.

ESSENTIALS

VISITOR INFORMATION

Tillamook Chamber of Commerce ☎ *503/842–7525* ⊕ *www.GoTillamook. com.*

3

EXPLORING

FAMILY **Tillamook Cheese Factory.** In high season, hundreds of visitors stop by the largest cheese-making plant on the West Coast to watch the cheese-making process, enjoy free samples, and order delicious ice cream (try the marionberry) from the on-site parlor. Here the rich milk from the area's thousands of Holstein and brown Swiss cows becomes ice cream, butter, and cheddar and Monterey Jack cheeses. The self-guided cheese-making tours don't allow much interaction—you view the operations from a glassed-in mezzanine, but they're free. The store carries a variety of other specialty-food products, including smoked meats, chocolates, jams, and honeys. ⊠ *4175 U.S. 101 N* ☎ *503/815–1300, 800/542–7290* ⊕ *www.tillamookcheese.com* ⌨ *Free* ☉ *Labor Day–mid-June, daily 8–6; mid-June–Labor Day, daily 8–8.*

WHERE TO EAT

$$ ✕ **Roseanna's Cafe.** In a rustic 1915 building on the beach, this café is
SEAFOOD right opposite Three Arch Rock, a favorite resting spot for sea lions and puffins. The calm of the beach is complemented in the evening by candlelight and fresh flowers. The menu includes halibut or salmon cooked half a dozen ways, baked oysters, and Gorgonzola seafood pasta, and the meal's not complete without marionberry cobbler. $ *Average main: $21* ⊠ *1490 Pacific Ave., Oceanside* ☎ *503/842–7351* ⊕ *www.roseannascafe.com.*

SPORTS AND THE OUTDOORS

The **Three Capes Loop,** an enchanting 35-mile byway off U.S. 101, winds along the coast between Tillamook and Pacific City, passing three distinctive headlands—Cape Meares, Cape Lookout, and Cape Kiwanda. Bayocean Road heading west from Tillamook passes what was the thriving resort town of Bayocean, which washed into the sea more than 30 years ago. A road still crosses the levee to Bayocean, and along the beach on the other side you can find the remnants of an old hotel to the north. The panoramic views from the north end of the peninsula are worth the walk. A warm and windless road returns hikers on the bay side.

Cape Kiwanda State Natural Area. Huge waves pound the jagged sandstone cliffs and caves here, and the much-photographed, 327-foot-high **Haystack Rock** (not to be confused with the 235-foot-tall rock of the same name up in Cannon Beach) juts out of the Pacific Ocean to the south. Surfers ride some of the longest waves on the coast, hang gliders soar above the shore, and beachcombers explore tidal pools and take in unparalleled ocean views. ⊠ *Cape Kiwanda Dr., 1 mile north* *of Pacific City, Pacific City* ☎ *503/842–3182* ⊕ *www.oregonstateparks. org* ✉ *Free* ☉ *Daily sunrise–sunset.*

Cape Lookout State Park. Located about 8 miles south of the beach town Netarts, this park includes a moderately easy (though often muddy) 2-mile trail—marked on the highway as "wildlife viewing area"—that leads through giant spruces, western red cedars, and hemlocks, and ends with views of Cascade Head to the south and Cape Meares to the north. Wildflowers, more than 150 species of birds, and occasional whales throughout the summer months make this trail a favorite with nature lovers. The section of the park just north of the trail comprises a long, curving stretch of beach with picnic areas and campsites. ✉ *Cape Lookout Rd. at Netarts Bay Rd.* ☎ *503/842–4981* ⊕ *www.oregonstateparks. org* ✉ *Day use $5* ☉ *Daily dawn–dusk.*

Cape Meares State Park. On the northern tip of the Three Capes Loop is Cape Meares State Park. The restored **Cape Meares Lighthouse,** built in 1890 and open to the public April through October, provides a sweeping view over the cliff to the caves and sea lion rookery on the rocks below. A many-trunked Sitka spruce known as the Octopus Tree grows near the lighthouse parking lot. ✉ *3500 Cape Meares Loop, 10 miles west of Tillamook, Oceanside* ☎ *503/842–3182* ⊕ *www.oregonstateparks. org* ✉ *Free* ☉ *Park daily dawn–dusk. Lighthouse Apr.–Oct., daily 11–4.*

PACIFIC CITY

24 miles south of Tillamook.

There's a lot to like about Pacific City, not the least of which is that it's 3 miles off Oregon's busy coastal highway, U.S. 101. That means there's no backup at the town's only traffic light—a blinking-red, four-way stop in the center of town. There's just the quiet, happy ambience of a town whose 1,000-or-so residents live the good life in the midst of extraordinary beauty. There are a few notable dining and hotel options here, along with some wonderful opportunities for recreation. The beach at Pacific City is one of the few places in the state where fishing dories (flat-bottom boats with high, flaring sides) are launched directly into the surf instead of from harbors or docks. Pacific City's windy climes tend to keep even the summer months quieter than most.

GETTING HERE AND AROUND

Between Tillamook and Lincoln City, the unincorporated village of Pacific City is just off U.S. 101 on the south end of the beautiful Three Capes Loop. It is a two-hour drive from Portland on U.S. 26 to Highway 6, or a 75-minute drive from Salem via Highway 22.

ESSENTIALS

Visitor Information **Pacific City-Nestucca Valley Chamber of Commerce** ☎ *503/392–4340* ⊕ *www.pcnvchamber.org.*

WHERE TO EAT AND STAY

$
CAFÉ
FAMILY

✕ **Grateful Bread Bakery & Restaurant.** This airy and bright café uses the cod caught by the local dories for its fish-and-chips. Everything it makes is fresh and from scratch, including delicious breads, pastries, breakfasts, and pizzas. ⑤ *Average main: $9* ✉ *34805 Brooten Rd.* ☎ *503/965–7337* ⊘ *Closed Tues. and Wed. No dinner.*

$$ ✕ **Pelican Pub & Brewery.** This beer lover's favorite stands on the ocean-
AMERICAN   front by Haystack Rock. The microbrewery has garnered consider-
FAMILY   able kudos for its beers, including the Kiwanda Cream Ale and deep, rich Tsunami Stout, while the pub excels with creative comfort fare. Many entrées are infused with house-made beverages, such as pale-malt-crusted salmon and the root-beer float. The pub periodically hosts Brewers Dinners—splendid affairs that pair beers with Scottish, Greek, Italian, and Belgian cooking. Kids love the gourmet pizzas and children's menu. ⑤ *Average main: $17* ✉ *33180 Cape Kiwanda Dr.* ☎ *503/965–7007* ⊕ *www.yourlittlebeachtown.com/pelican.*

$$$$ ⌂ **Cottages at Cape Kiwanda.** For a memorable resort experience with a
RENTAL   glorious beach view, this complex has 18 units for rent that can sleep four or six people—perfect for families or that beach get-together with friends. **Pros:** upscale; comfortable; short walk from Pacific City eat-eries. **Cons:** the beach is lively, and tail-gating cars can be a fixture. ⑤ *Rooms from: $299* ✉ *33000 Cape Kiwanda Dr.* ☎ *866/571–0605* ⊕ *www.kiwandacottages.com* ⌫ *18 rooms* ⦿*No meals.*

$$$ ⌂ **Inn at Cape Kiwanda.** You won't find a weather-beaten beach cottage
RESORT   here—each of the 35 deluxe, fireplace-warmed rooms has a gorgeous
FAMILY   view of Haystack Rock. **Pros:** great views; light and contemporary rooms; terrific restaurants nearby. **Cons:** guests might get hit up with a sales pitch to buy a unit. ⑤ *Rooms from: $219* ✉ *33105 Cape Kiwanda Dr.* ☎ *888/965–7001, 503/965–7001* ⊕ *www.yourlittlebeachtown.com/ inn* ⌫ *33 rooms, 2 suites* ⦿*No meals.*

SPORTS AND THE OUTDOORS

BEACHES

Fodor'sChoice   **Pacific City beach.** The town's public beach sits between Cape Kiwanda
★   State Natural Area and Bob Straub State Park. Adjacent to Cape Kiwan-da's massive dune, it's a favorite for kids who often climb its bulk (by some estimates 500 feet) just for the thrill of sliding back down again. Hikers also get a thrill from the top, where the view opens on a tiny cove and tide pools below, and the walk down is infinitely easier than the climb. The beach is also popular with tailgaters—it's one of the few places on the Oregon Coast where it's legal to park your vehicle on the sand. Other parking is available off Cape Kiwanda Drive, near the Pelican Pub. For quieter outings, try the Bob Straub. **Amenities:** none. **Best for:** partiers; walking. ✉ *Cape Kiwanda Drive* ⊕ *www. pcnvchamber.org.*

RECREATIONAL AREAS

Fodor'sChoice   **Bob Straub State Park.** An often sand-blasting walk along the flat white-
★   sand beach leads down to the mouth of the Nestucca River, considered by many to be the best fishing river on the north coast. The beach along the Pacific is frequently windy, but it's separated from the stiller, warmer side of the peninsula by high dunes. Multiple trails cross the dunes into a forest that leads to small beaches on the Nestucca. Relax here with a book, and easily find stillness and sunshine. It's possible to skip the Pacific stroll all together, and find trails to the Nestucca straight from the parking lot, but it's hard to resist the views from the top of the dunes

at the Bob Straub. If you choose the ocean side, pitch your beach-camp in the dunes, not the flat sand, and you'll find respite from the some-times unrelenting wind. ✉ *Sunset Dr., just south of where Pacific Ave. crosses river* ☎ *503/842–3182* ⊕ *www.oregonstateparks.org* 🎫 *Free.*

CENTRAL COAST

This is Oregon's coastal playland, drawing families, shoppers, kite fly-ers, deep-sea fishing enthusiasts, surfers, and dune-shredding daredevils. Although it's a bit touristy and bisected by a rather tatty commercial stretch of U.S. 101, Lincoln City offers a wealth of shops devoted to souvenirs and knickknacks, and visitors can even blow their own glass float at a few local studios. Depoe Bay is popular for whale-watching excursions, and Newport is designated the Dungeness crab capital of the world. As you venture farther south, you'll roll through gorgeous and less developed Yachats and charming Florence to reach the iconic mountains of sand that fall within Oregon Dunes National Recreation Area. Even if you're not intent on making tracks in the sand, the dunes provide vast, unforgettable scenery.

LINCOLN CITY

16 miles south of Pacific City; 90 miles southwest of Portland.

Lincoln City is a captivating destination for families and lovers who want to share some time laughing on the beach, poking their fingers in tide pools, and trying to harness wind-bucking kites. Once a series of small villages, Lincoln City is a sprawling town without a center. But the endless tourist amenities make up for a lack of a small-coastal-town ambience. Clustered like barnacles on the offshore reefs are fast-food restaurants, gift shops, supermarkets, candy stores, antiques markets, dozens of motels and hotels, a factory-outlet mall, and a busy casino. Lincoln City is the most popular destination city on the Oregon Coast, but its only real geographic claim to fame is the 445-foot-long D River, stretching from its source in Devil's Lake to the Pacific; *Guinness World Records* lists the D as the world's shortest river.

GETTING HERE AND AROUND

Lincoln City is a two-hour drive from Portland on Highway 99W and Highway 18, and a 2½-hour drive south of Astoria along coastal U.S. 101.

ESSENTIALS

Visitor Information Lincoln City Visitors & Convention Bureau ✉ *801 S.W. U.S. 101, Suite 401* ☎ *541/996–1274, 800/452–2151* ⊕ *www.oregoncoast.org.*

WHERE TO EAT

$$$$ ╳ **Bay House.** Inside a charming bungalow, this restaurant serves meals
PACIFIC to linger over while you enjoy views across sunset-gilded Siletz Bay.
NORTHWEST The seasonal Pacific Northwest cuisine includes Dungeness crab cakes with roasted-chili chutney, fresh halibut Parmesan, and roast duckling with cranberry compote. Naturally, there's lamb, pork, and tasty fillets. There's lighter fare available in the lounge. The wine list is extensive,

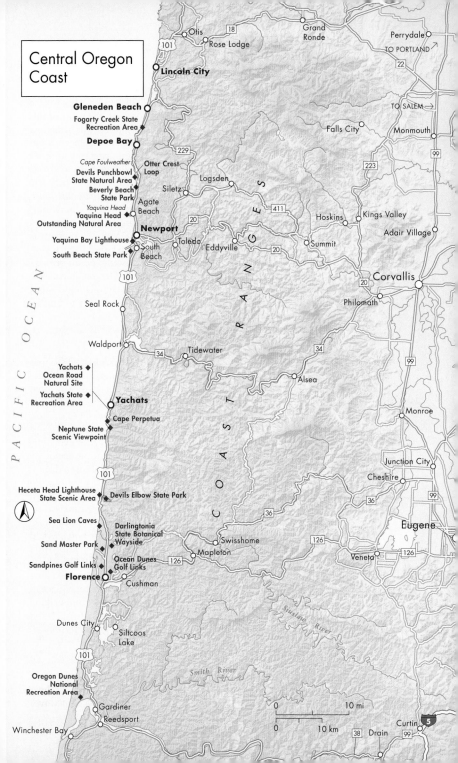

Central Oregon Coast

PACIFIC OCEAN

Otis
Rose Lodge
18
101
Grand Ronde
Perrydale
TO PORTLAND
22

Lincoln City

Gleneden Beach
Fogarty Creek State Recreation Area
Depoe Bay
229

Falls City
Monmouth
TO SALEM →
99
223

Cape Foulweather
Otter Crest Loop
Devils Punchbowl State Natural Area
Beverly Beach State Park
Logsden
Siletz
Agate Beach
Yaquina Head
Yaquina Head Outstanding Natural Area
Newport
Yaquina Bay Lighthouse
South Beach State Park
South Beach
Toledo
Eddyville
411
Hoskins
Kings Valley
Adair Village
Summit
20

Corvallis
20
Philomath
99

Seal Rock

Waldport
34
Tidewater
34

Yachats Ocean Road Natural Site
Yachats State Recreation Area
Yachats
Cape Perpetua
Neptune State Scenic Viewpoint
Alsea
Monroe

Heceta Head Lighthouse State Scenic Area
Devils Elbow State Park
Sea Lion Caves
Darlingtonia State Botanical Wayside
Sand Master Park
Sandpines Golf Links
Ocean Dunes Golf Links
Florence
Cushman
Swisshome
Mapleton
126
36
126
Veneta
Cheshire
Junction City
Eugene
126
36
99

Dunes City
Siltcoos Lake

Suslaw River

Oregon Dunes National Recreation Area
Gardiner
Reedsport
Winchester Bay
Smith River

Curtin
5
38
Drain
99

0   10 mi
0   10 km

and the service impeccable. $ *Average main: $33* ✉ *5911 S.W. U.S. 101* ☎ *541/996–3222* ⊕ *www.thebayhouse.org* ☽ *Closed Mon. and Tues. No lunch.*

$ ✕ **Beach Dog Café.** These are darn good dogs, dressed about 20 differ-
AMERICAN ent ways. You'll find everything from Coney, Philly, and Kosher to Hot
Fodor'sChoice Diggity. There's also a galaxy of dog photos adorning the walls of this
★ family-owned joint and its breakfasts have the morning crowds gathering. Roger and Sonja Seals offer a menu full of hearty potato dishes, scrambles, stuffed French toast, and delicious breakfast sandwiches. The apple potato pancake with sour cream and a Polish sausage is the keystone to any nutritious breakfast. $ *Average main: $9* ✉ *6042 S.E. U.S. 101* ☎ *541/996–3647* ▭ *No credit cards* ☽ *Closed Mon. and Tues. No dinner.*

$$ ✕ **Blackfish Café.** Owner and chef Rob Pounding serves simple-but-
SEAFOOD succulent dishes that blend fresh ingredients from local fishermen and
Fodor'sChoice gardeners. Before starting his own restaurant in 1999, Pounding was
★ the executive chef of acclaimed Salishan Lodge for nearly 15 years, winning top national culinary awards. His skillet-roasted, "ocean trolled" chinook salmon, basted with fennel lime butter, and Oregon blue-cheese potatoes are flavorful and perfect. The Blackfish Ding Dong dessert, with mixed-berry sauce and whipped cream, is the best way to finish a meal. $ *Average main: $20* ✉ *2733 N.W. U.S. 101* ☎ *541/996–1007* ⊕ *www.blackfishcafe.com* ☽ *Closed Tues.*

WHERE TO STAY

$ ▦ **Coho Oceanfront Lodge.** Set on a romantic cliff, the renovated Coho is
HOTEL a perfect hybrid of family-friendly lodging and a quiet, intimate hide-
FAMILY away for couples. **Pros:** great value; family-friendly; lots of nice in-room
Fodor'sChoice amenities. **Cons:** no restaurant. $ *Rooms from: $117* ✉ *1635 N.W.*
★ *Harbor Ave.* ☎ *541/994–3684* ⊕ *www.thecoholodge.com* ⤴ *33 studios, 32 suites* ⦿ *Breakfast.*

$ ▦ **Historic Anchor Inn.** This quirky bungalow might not be for everyone,
B&B/INN but for those who appreciate a warm, spirited inn with a decidedly inventive and whimsical touch, this is a remarkable find. **Pros:** a memorable, truly unique property; everything you need to explore Lincoln City. **Cons:** not on the beach; very quirky and rustic. $ *Rooms from: $89* ✉ *4417 S.W. U.S. 101* ☎ *541/996–3810* ⊕ *www.historicanchorinn. com* ⤴ *19 rooms* ⦿ *Breakfast.*

$$$ ▦ **Inn at Spanish Head.** Driving up to this upscale resort hotel, you'd
RESORT think it might be a fairly intimate place, but on further investigation you'll see that the property takes up the entire side of a bluff like a huge staircase. **Pros:** sweeping views of the ocean through floor-to-ceiling windows; good restaurant; easy beach access via elevator; great place to watch winter storms. **Cons:** pricey; isolated setting not within walking distance of many restaurants or shops. $ *Rooms from: $209* ✉ *4009 S.E. U.S. 101* ☎ *541/996–2161, 800/452–8127* ⊕ *www.spanishhead. com* ⤴ *68 rooms, 52 suites* ⦿ *Some meals.*

NIGHTLIFE

Chinook Winds Casino Resort. Oregon's only beachfront casino has a great variety of slot machines, blackjack, poker, keno, and off-track betting. The Rogue River Steakhouse serves a great fillet and terrific appetizers.

There's also the Siletz Bay Buffet, the Chinook Seafood Grill, a snack bar, and a lounge. An arcade keeps the kids busy while you are on the gambling floor. Big-name entertainers perform in the showroom. Players can take a break from the tables and enjoy a round of golf at the Chinook Winds Golf Resort next door. ⊠ *1777 N.W. 44th St.* ☎ *541/996–5825, 888/244–6665* ⊕ *www.chinookwindscasino.com.*

SHOPPING

Jennifer L. Sears Glass Art Studio. Blow a glass float or make a glorious glass starfish, heart, or fluted bowl of your own design (it costs $65 for a glass float). The studio's expert artisans will guide you every step of the way. It's a fun, memorable keepsake of the coast. ⊠ *4821 S.W. U.S. 101* ☎ *541/996–2569* ⊕ *www.jennifersearsglassart.com.*

Lincoln City Surf Shop. Darn right they surf on the Oregon Coast. Maybe the surfers are dressed from head to toe in wet suits, but they're riding some tasty waves just the same. At Lincoln City's oldest surf shop, there's equipment and apparel for purchase or rent. Lessons provide a great family activity, and rates include board, wet suits, hood, and booties. The shop also has a collection of kiteboards, skimboards, and skateboards. ⊠ *4792 S.E. U.S. 101* ☎ *541/996–7433* ⊕ *www. lcsurfshop.com.*

SPORTS AND THE OUTDOORS

BOATING

Devil's Lake State Recreation Area. Canoeing and kayaking are popular on this small lake just inland from the coast, also loved by coots, loons, ducks, cormorants, bald eagles, and grebes. Visitors can sign up in advance for popular kayaking tours in the summer, for which bird guides are provided. A campground has tent and RV sites as well as yurts. ⊠ *N.E. 6th St., just east of U.S. 101* ☎ *541/994–2002, 800/551–6949* ⊕ *www.oregonstateparks.org* ☉ *Daily.*

OFF THE
BEATEN
PATH

Nature Conservancy Cascade Head Preserve and trail. This dense, green trail winds through a rain forest where 100-inch annual rainfalls nourish 250-year-old Sitka spruces, mosses, and ferns. Emerging from the forest, hikers come upon grassy and treeless Cascade Head, an undulating maritime prairie. There are magnificent views down to the Salmon River and east to the Coast Range. Continuing along the headland, black-tailed deer often graze and turkey vultures soar in the strong winds. You need to be in fairly good shape for the first and steepest part of the hike, which can be done in about an hour (it's a little over 4 miles round-trip). The 270-acre area has been named a United Nations Biosphere Reserve. The website has detailed driving directions to reach the preserve. ⊠ *Savage Rd. at Headland Circle, 9 miles north of Lincoln City via U.S. 101, Otis* ⊕ *www.nature.org* ☐ *Free* ☉ *Upper trail closed Jan.–mid-July.*

GLENEDEN BEACH

7 miles south of Lincoln City.

Gleneden Beach is a small vacation town known primarily for the famed Salishan Resort, which is perched high above placid Siletz Bay. This expensive collection of guest rooms, vacation homes, condominiums, restaurants, golf fairways, tennis courts, and covered walkways blends into a forest preserve; if not for the signs, you'd scarcely be able to find it.

GETTING HERE AND AROUND

Little Gleneden Beach is a 10-minute drive south of Lincoln City via U.S. 101.

ESSENTIALS

Visitor Information Discover Newport ⊠ *555 S.W. Coast Hwy., Newport* ☎ *541/265–8801, 800/262–7844* ⊕ *www.discovernewport.com.*

EXPLORING

Lawrence Gallery at Salishan. The well-respected gallery has an informed staff that will guide you through the collections of work by Northwest artists, including paintings (pastels, oils, and watercolors), glassworks, bronze and metal, furniture, and ceramics and porcelain. ⊠ *7755 N. U.S. 101* ☎ *541/764–2318, 800/764–2318* ⊕ *www.lawrencegallery.net.*

WHERE TO EAT AND STAY

$$$
PACIFIC NORTHWEST

✕ **Side Door Café.** This dining room, set in an old brick and tile factory with a high ceiling, exposed beams, a fireplace, and many windows, shares its space with Eden Hall performance venue. The menu changes often—fresh preparations have included mushroom-crusted rack of lamb and broiled swordfish with citrus-raspberry vinaigrette over coconut-ginger basmati rice. ⑤ *Average main: $27* ⊠ *6675 Gleneden Beach Loop Rd.* ☎ *541/764–3825* ⊕ *www.sidedoorcafe.com* ۞ *Closed Mon. and Tues.*

$
RENTAL

Beachcombers Haven vacation rentals. This cluster of properties is right off the beach, and features spacious one-, two-, or three-bedroom accommodations, some with a hot tub or in-room Jacuzzi. **Pros:** very friendly; well-furnished units with full kitchens; near the beach. **Cons:** not especially fancy; two-night minimum. ⑤ *Rooms from: $149* ⊠ *7045 N.W. Glen* ☎ *541/764–2252, 800/428–5533* ⊕ *www.beachcombershaven. com* ⇰ *14 homes* ⑩ *No meals.*

$$$
RESORT

Salishan Lodge and Golf Resort. Secluded and refined, this upscale resort in a hillside forest preserve has long been revered as a luxury weekend getaway as well as a destination for tony corporate retreats, with plenty of reasons to stay on the property. **Pros:** very elegant; secluded resort with a terrific golf course; plenty of activities on the property. **Cons:** ocean views are few; service a bit hit-or-miss. ⑤ *Rooms from: $209* ⊠ *7760 N. U.S. 101* ☎ *541/764–3600, 800/452–2300* ⊕ *www.salishan. com* ⇰ *205 rooms* ⑩ *No meals.*

SPORTS AND THE OUTDOORS

GOLF

Salishan Golf Resort. With a layout designed by Peter Jacobsen, this par-71 course is a year-round treat for hackers and aficionados alike. The front nine holes are surrounded by a forest of old-growth timber, while the back nine holes provide old-school, links-style play. There's an expansive pro shop and a great bar and grill for relaxing after a "rough" day out on the links. ⊠ *7760 N. U.S. 101* ☎ *541/764–3600, 800/452–2300* ⊕ *www.salishan.com* ▨ *$119 on summer weekends.*

Salishan Golf Resort, Gleneden Beach

DEPOE BAY

5 miles south of Gleneden Beach.

Depoe Bay calls itself the whale-watching capital of the world. The small town was founded in the 1920s and named in honor of Charles DePoe of the Siletz tribe, who was named for his employment at a U.S. Army depot in the late 1800s. With a narrow channel and deep water, its tiny harbor is also one of the most protected on the coast. It supports a thriving fleet of commercial and charter fishing boats. The Spouting Horn, a natural cleft in the basalt cliffs on the waterfront, blasts seawater skyward during heavy weather.

GETTING HERE AND AROUND

Depoe Bay lies right between Newport and Lincoln City along U.S. 101—it's a 20-minute drive to either town.

ESSENTIALS

Visitor Information Depoe Bay Chamber of Commerce ⊠ *223 S.W. U.S. 101, Suite B* ☎ *541/765-2889, 877/485-8348* ⊕ *www.depoebaychamber.org.*

WHERE TO EAT AND STAY

$$$
PACIFIC
NORTHWEST
Fodor's Choice
★

✕ **Restaurant Beck.** Immensely talented chef-owner Justin Wills presents a short but memorable menu of creatively prepared, modern, Pacific Northwest cuisine each night in this romantic, contemporary dining room at the Whale Cove Inn. The menu changes regularly, with chef Wills sourcing largely from local farms, ranches, and fisheries. You might start with jasmine-tea-cured tuna crudo with jalapeño, citrus, garlic chips, and finger lime, followed by local rockfish served beside a bed of cannellini beans and bacon with grilled-kale-and-pine-nut pesto. Save room for dessert;

it's impressive here, with the Meyer lemon–and-almond pancake with figs, Italian plums, and honey-yogurt ice cream a particular standout. There are also great views from the large windows overlooking the cove and the Pacific. $ *Average main: $29 ⊠ Whale Cove Inn, 2345 U.S. 101* ☎ *541/765–3220* ⊕ *www.restaurantbeck.com* ⊗ *No lunch.*

$$
B&B/INN

🍴 **The Harbor Lights Inn.** This bed-and-breakfast overlooking tiny Depoe Bay Harbor provides a dreamy setting for watching boats and relaxing in a quaint atmosphere. **Pros:** small, quiet, and pretty; great breakfasts. **Cons:** on the water of the bay but no beach. $ *Rooms from: $139* ⊠ *235 S.E. Bay View Ave.* ☎ *541/765–2322, 800/228–0448* ⊕ *www. theharborlightsinn.com* ⟿ *13 rooms* �ΙΟΙ *Breakfast.*

$$$$
B&B/INN
Fodor's Choice
★

🍴 **Whale Cove Inn.** This small and exquisitely decorated inn overlooks the picturesque cove for which it's named and contains just eight spacious suites, each with a dazzling view of the water. **Pros:** astoundingly good restaurant; stunning building with cushy and spacious suites; fine ocean views. **Cons:** not a good fit for kids (only those 16 and over are permitted); quite pricey; not within walking distance of town. $ *Rooms from: $425* ⊠ *2345 U.S. 101* ☎ *541/765–4300, 800/628–3409* ⊕ *www. whalecoveinn.com* ⟿ *8 suites* ΙΟΙ *Breakfast.*

SPORTS AND THE OUTDOORS

RECREATIONAL AREAS

Fogarty Creek State Recreation Area. Bird-watching and viewing the tidal pools are the key draws here, but hiking and picnicking are also popular at this park found along U.S. 101. Wooden footbridges wind through the dense forest and tall cliffs rise above the beach. ⊠ *U.S. 101, 3 miles north of Depoe Bay* ☎ *800/551–6949, 541/265–4560* ⊕ *www. oregonstateparks.org* 🎫 *Free* ⊗ *Daily.*

NEWPORT

12 miles south of Depoe Bay.

Called the Dungeness crab capital of the world, Newport offers accessible beaches, a popular aquarium, the coast's premier performing-arts center, and a significant supply of both elegant and affordable accommodations and restaurants. Newport exists on two levels: the highway above, threading its way through the community's main business district, and the old Bayfront along Yaquina Bay below (watch for signs on U.S. 101). With its high-masted fishing fleet, well-worn buildings, seafood markets, art galleries, and touristy shops, Newport's Bayfront is an ideal place for an afternoon stroll. So many male sea lions in Yaquina Bay loiter near crab pots and bark from the waterfront piers that locals call the area the Bachelor Club. Visit the docks to buy fresh seafood or rent a kayak to explore the bay. In 2010 Newport was designated the National Oceanic and Atmospheric Administration's (NOAA) Pacific Marine Operations Center and a $38 million, 5-acre facility (and a port for four ships) opened a year later.

GETTING HERE AND AROUND

Newport is a 2½-hour drive from Portland by way of Interstate 5 south to Albany and U.S. 20 west; the town is a 40-minute drive south along U.S. 101 from Lincoln City, and a 75-minute drive north of Florence.

ESSENTIALS

Visitor Information Destination Newport ✉ *555 S.W. Coast Hwy.*
☎ *503/262–8801, 800/262–7844* ⊕ *www.discovernewport.com.*

TOURS

Marine Discovery Tours. Sealife cruises, departing throughout the day, are conducted on a 65-foot excursion boat *Discovery,* with inside seating for 49 people and two viewing levels. The cruise season is March through October. ✉ *345 S.W. Bay Blvd.* ☎ *800/903–2628, 541/265–6200* ⊕ *www.marinediscovery.com* ⊠ *From $36.*

EXPLORING

FAMILY **Hatfield Marine Science Center.** Interactive and interpretive exhibits at Oregon State University appeal to the kid in everyone. More than just showcasing sea life, the center contains exhibits and holds classes that teach the importance of scientific research in managing and sustaining coastal and marine resources. The staff regularly leads guided tours of the adjoining estuary. ✉ *2030 S. Marine Science Dr.* ☎ *541/867–0100* ⊕ *www.hmsc.oregonstate.edu* ⊠ *$5 suggested donation* ☉ *Memorial Day–Labor Day, daily 10–5; Labor Day–Memorial Day, Thurs.–Mon. 10–4.*

FAMILY **Oregon Coast Aquarium.** This 4½-acre complex brings visitors face to face with the creatures living in offshore and near-shore Pacific marine habitats: frolicking sea otters, colorful puffins, pulsating jellyfish, and even a 60-pound octopus. There's a hands-on interactive area for children, including tide pools perfect for "petting" sea anemones and urchins. The aquarium houses one of North America's largest seabird aviaries, including glowering turkey vultures. Permanent exhibits include *Passages of the Deep*, where visitors walk through a 200-foot underwater tunnel with 360-degree views of sharks, wolf eels, halibut, and a truly captivating array of sea life. Large coho salmon and sturgeon can be viewed in a naturalistic setting through a window wall 9-feet high and 20-feet wide. The sherbet-colored nettles are hypnotizing. ✉ *2820 S.E. Ferry Slip Rd.* ☎ *541/867–3474* ⊕ *www.aquarium.org* ⊠ *$19.95* ☉ *Summer, daily 9–6; winter, daily 10–5.*

FAMILY **Yaquina Head Lighthouse.** The tallest lighthouse on the Oregon Coast has been blinking its beacon since its head keeper first walked up its 114 steps to light the wicks on the evening of August 20, 1873. Next to the 93-foot tower is an interpretive center. Bring your camera and call ahead to confirm tour times. ✉ *N.W. Lighthouse Dr., off U.S. 101, 4 miles north of Newport* ☎ *541/574–3100* ⊕ *www.yaquinalights.org* ⊠ *Free. Donations suggested* ☉ *Thurs.–Tues. noon–3.*

WHERE TO EAT

$$ ✗ **Georgie's Beachside Grill.** This stand-alone restaurant for the Hallmark SEAFOOD Inns and Resorts serves up some wonderfully innovative dishes. From FAMILY the sea scallops blackened in house-mixed herbs to coconut shrimp Fodor'sChoice in pineapple salsa with chili slaw, the food here lives up to the ocean ★ view. Local ingredients are frequently mixed with tropical ones like the Dungeness crab cakes topped in mango salsa, and the plates are often layered—the bed of honey mustard-romaine is dressed apart from the blueberry barbecued salmon that lands on top. On the oceanside of Newport, Georgie's is one of few places in town with ocean views.

Oregon Coast Aquarium, Newport

Windows line a half-moon of table seating, and tiered booths mean even the back of the room has decent views. Georgie's is also extremely popular for its breakfasts. ⑤ *Average main: $19* ⊠ *744 S.W. Elizabeth St.* ☎ *503/265–9800, 888/448–4449* ⊕ *www.georgiesbeachsidegrill.com.*

$$ ✕ **Local Ocean Seafoods.** At this fish market and sleek grill on picturesque
SEAFOOD
FAMILY
Fodor'sChoice
★
Yaquina Bay, the operators purchase fish directly from more than 60 boats in the fishing fleet right outside and take the mission of locally sourced, sustainable seafood seriously. This is also one of few restaurants on the Oregon Coast that doesn't own a deep fryer—even the fish-and-chips are panfried. The menu includes such fish-lovers' fare as tuna mignon (bacon-wrapped albacore with pan-seared vegetables), panko-buttermilk-crusted oysters, and Fishwives Stew—a tomato broth stew loaded with both shell- and finfish, but come early, because it closes at 8 pm (9 in summer). From the bustling interior, there are views through windowed garage doors that roll up in summer. Those tempted to take home more than a doggie bag can dive into the fish case, where house-smoked offerings include a rare smoked black cod, and every fish comes with details about the boat that caught it. ⑤ *Average main: $20* ⊠ *213 S.E. Bay Blvd.* ☎ *514/574–7959* ⊕ *www.localocean.net.*

$$ ✕ **Panini Bakery.** The owner, who operates this local favorite bakery
CAFÉ
and espresso bar, prides himself on hearty and home-roasted meats, hand-cut breads, and friendly service. The coffee's organic, the eggs free-range, the orange juice fresh-squeezed, and just about everything is made from scratch. Take a seat inside, or, in good weather, streetside tables are a great place to view the Nye Beach scene. The café closes at 7 pm. ⑤ *Average main: $10* ⊠ *232 N.W. Coast Hwy.* ☎ *541/265–5033* ▭ *No credit cards.*

WHERE TO STAY

$$$ ⊞ **Inn at Nye Beach.** With a prime beachfront location in the historic
HOTEL   Nye Beach section of Newport, this chic, eco-friendly, boutique hotel
Fodor'sChoice   contains 22 rooms and suites. **Pros:** direct beach access and great views;
★   smartly furnished; contemporary rooms. **Cons:** the complimentary
breakfast is very limited (a full one costs extra); views not great from
some rooms. $ *Rooms from: $209* ⊠ *729 N.W. Coast St.* ☎ *541/265–*
2477, 800/480–2477 ⊕ *www.innatnyebeach.com* ⇆ *6 rooms, 16 suites*
⊠| *Breakfast.*

$ ⊞ **Newport Belle B&B.** This fully operational stern-wheeler is permanently
B&B/INN   moored at the Newport Marina, where guests have front-row seats to
all the boating activity around Yaquina Bay. **Pros:** one-of-a-kind lodg-
ing experience; great harbor views. **Cons:** not suitable for kids; need
a car to get into town. $ *Rooms from: $150* ⊠ *Dock H, 2126 S.E.*
Marine Science Dr. ☎ *541/867–6290* ⊕ *www.newportbelle.com* ⇆ *5*
rooms ⊘ *Closed Nov.–early Feb.* ⊠| *Breakfast.*

$ ⊞ **Sylvia Beach Hotel.** Make reservations far in advance for this 1913-
HOTEL   vintage beachfront hotel, where reading, writing, and conversation
eclipse technological hotel-room isolation. **Pros:** distinctive decor; great
place to disconnect. **Cons:** no TV, telephone, or Internet access; sharing
tables with other guests at mealtimes doesn't suit everyone; least expen-
sive rooms don't have ocean views. $ *Rooms from: $115* ⊠ *267 N.W.*
Cliff St. ☎ *541/265–5428, 888/795–8422* ⊕ *www.sylviabeachhotel.com*
⇆ *20 rooms* ⊠| *Breakfast.*

NIGHTLIFE AND THE PERFORMING ARTS

Fodor'sChoice   **Newport Symphony Orchestra.** The only year-round, professional sym-
★   phony orchestra on the Oregon Coast plays at the 400-seat Newport
Performing Arts Center, just a few steps away from the seashore in Nye
Beach. Adam Flatt is the music director and conductor, and actor and
narrator David Ogden Stiers serves as associate conductor. The orches-
tra performs a popular series of concerts in the Newport Performing
Arts Center September through May, and special events in the summer,
including its popular free community concert every July 4. ⊠ *777 W.*
Olive St. ☎ *541/574–0614* ⊕ *www.newportsymphony.org.*

SPORTS AND THE OUTDOORS

RECREATIONAL AREAS

Beverly Beach State Park. Seven miles north of Newport, this beachfront
park extends from Yaquina Head, where you can see the lighthouse,
to the headlands of Otter Rock. It's a great place to fly a kite, surf the
waves, or hunt for fossils. The campground is well equipped, with a
wind-protected picnic area and a yurt meeting hall. ⊠ *N.E. Beverly Dr.,*
off U.S. 101, 6 miles north of Newport ☎ *541/265–9278, 800/551–*
6949 ⊕ *www.oregonstateparks.org* ▱ *Free* ⊘ *Daily.*

Devil's Punchbowl State Natural Area. A rocky shoreline separates the day-
use area from the surf. It's a popular whale-watching site and has excel-
lent tidal pools. ⊠ *1st St., off U.S. 101, 8 miles north of Newport, Otter*
Rock ☎ *541/265–4560, 800/551–6949* ⊕ *www.oregonstateparks.org*
▱ *Free* ⊘ *Daily.*

Yaquina Head Outstanding Natural Area. Thousands of birds—cormorants, gulls, common murres, pigeon guillemots—make their home just beyond shore on Pinnacle and Colony rocks, and nature trails wind through fields of sea grass and wildflowers, leading to spectacular views. There is also an interpretive center and the historic Yaquina Head Lighthouse. ⊠ *750 N.W. Lighthouse Dr.* ☎ *541/574–3100* ⊕ *www.yaquinalights. org* ⊠ *Free; donations suggested* ☉ *Interpretive center June–early Sept., daily 9–4:30; mid-Sept.–May, daily 10–4:30.*

YACHATS

24 miles south of Newport.

The small town of Yachats (pronounced "yah-*hots*") is at the mouth of the Yachats River, and from its rocky shoreline, which includes the highest point on the Oregon Coast, trails lead to beaches and dozens of tidal pools. A relaxed alternative to the more touristy communities to the north, Yachats has all the coastal pleasures without the traffic: B&Bs and oceanfront hotels, some terrific restaurants, deserted beaches, tidal pools, surf-pounded crags, fishing, and crabbing.

GETTING HERE AND AROUND

Yachats lies between Newport and Florence on coastal U.S. 101—it's a 40-minute drive from either town, and a three-hour drive via Interstate 5 and Highway 34 from Portland.

ESSENTIALS

Visitor Information Yachats Visitors Center ⊠ *241 U.S. 101* ☎ *800/929–0477* ⊕ *www.yachats.org.*

WHERE TO EAT

$ | × **Bread and Roses Baking.** Artisan breads are handmade in small batches
BAKERY | here, along with pastries, muffins, scones, cookies, cinnamon rolls, and desserts. In the bright, yellow-cottage bakery you can also try the daily soup and sandwiches at lunchtime, or just while away the morning with pastries and good coffee. It's a couple of blocks from Yachats State Recreation Area and across the road from Yachats Commons Park. ■ TIP→ Let the kids out to play in the park, then settle in here for lunch. ⑤ *Average main: $10* ⊠ *238 4th St.* ☎ *541/547–4454* ☉ *No dinner.*

$$ | × **The Drift Inn.** This restaurant is a terrific find, with the best fresh razor
SEAFOOD | clams on the coast. Each night a musician plays to the crowd that sits
Fodor'sChoice | below a ceiling full of umbrellas, with views of the Yachats River where
★ | it meets the ocean. Family-friendly and lively, the Drift Inn features fresh seafood, juicy steaks, and other local meats and produce. The bar stools are usually crowded, and there's a great selection of Oregon craft brews and wines. ⑤ *Average main: $18* ⊠ *124 U.S. 101 N* ☎ *541/547–4477* ⊕ *www.the-drift-inn.com.*

$ | × **Luna Sea Fish House.** The freshest Dungeness crab around is one of the
SEAFOOD | seasonal attractions in this small weathered restaurant, coming straight from owner Robert Anthony's boat—he catches much of the fish served here using sustainable hook-and-kind methods for salmon, cod, and albacore tuna. And in season, he pots the crab seen bubbling in outdoor

kettles. Diners often eat family style here, bellied up to a few colorful tables. Fish-and-chips of all stripes, including clam and salmon, are served, but the fish tacos and a sinful dish called slumgullion—chowder baked with cheese and bay shrimp—are the most popular choices. The house special adds three cheeses to a bowl of thick, rich clam chowder, then tops it off with bay shrimp. You can also buy fresh fish here. $ *Average main: $12* ⊠ *153 N.W. U.S. 101* ☎ *541/547–4794, 888/547–4794* ⊕ *www.lunaseafishhouse.com.*

WHERE TO STAY

$$ HOTEL Fodor's Choice ★ ⊞ **Overleaf Lodge.** On a rocky shoreline at the north end of Yachats, this is a romantic place to enjoy a spectacular sunset in splendid comfort. **Pros:** best hotel in one of the coast's best communities; on-site full-service spa. **Cons:** no restaurant; exercise room is small; a bit of a walk from the action. $ *Rooms from: $200* ⊠ *280 Overleaf Lodge La.* ☎ *541/547–4885, 800/338–0507* ⊕ *www.overleaflodge.com* ➫ *54 rooms, 4 suites* ❙⊙❙ *Breakfast.*

SPORTS AND THE OUTDOORS

RECREATIONAL AREAS

Cape Perpetua Scenic Area. The highest lookout point on the Oregon Coast, Cape Perpetua towers 800 feet above the rocky shoreline. Named by Captain Cook on St. Perpetua's Day in 1778, the cape is part of a 2,700-acre scenic area popular with hikers, campers, beachcombers, and naturalists. General information and a map of several trails are available at the **Cape Perpetua Visitors Center,** on the east side of the highway, 2 miles south of Devil's Churn. The easy 1-mile **Giant Spruce Trail** passes through a fern-filled rain forest to an enormous 500-year-old Sitka spruce. Easier still is the marked Auto Tour; it begins about 2 miles north of the visitor center and winds through Siuslaw National Forest to the ¼-mile **Whispering Spruce Trail.** Views from the rustic rock shelter here extend 50 miles north to south, and some 40 miles out to sea. The **Cape Perpetua Interpretive Center,** in the visitor center, has educational movies and exhibits about the natural forces that shaped Cape Perpetua. ⊠ *2400 U.S. 101, 3 miles south of Yachats* ☎ *541/547–3289* ⊕ *www.fs.usda.gov/siuslaw* ➫ *Parking fee $5* ⊙ *Visitors Center: summer, daily 10–5; winter, daily 10–4.*

Neptune State Scenic Viewpoint. Visitors have fun searching for animals, watching the surf, or hunting for agates. The benches set above the beach on the cliff provide a great view of Cumming Creek. It's also a terrific spot for whale-watching. At low tide, beachcombers have access to a natural cave and tidal pools. ⊠ *U.S. 101, 4 miles south of Yachats* ☎ *800/551–6949, 541/547–3416* ⊕ *www.oregonstateparks. org* ➫ *Free* ⊙ *Daily.*

Yachats State Recreation Area. The public beach in Yachats is more like the surface of the moon than most other places, and certainly most beaches. A wooden platform overlooks the coastline, where the waves roll in sideways and spash over the rocks at high tide. As is the case throughout most of the town, the beach itself is paralleled by an upland walking trail and dotted with picnic tables, benches, and interpretive signs. Visit to spot the sea lions that frequent this stretch of coast. Or join the intrepid beachcombers who climb the rocks for a closer look at tide pools populated by sea urchins, hermit crabs, barnacles, snails, and sea stars. **Amenities:** parking; toilets. **Best for:** walking; sunset. ☒ *Ocean View Dr., off 2nd St. and U.S. 101* ☎ *800/551–6949, 541/867–7451* ⊕ *www.oregonstateparks.org.*

FLORENCE

25 miles south of Yachats; 64 miles west of Eugene.

Tourists and retirees have been flocking to Florence in ever-greater numbers in recent years. The restored riverfront Old Town has restaurants, antiques stores, fish markets, and other diversions, but what really makes the town so appealing is its proximity to remarkable stretches of coastline. Seventy-five creeks and rivers empty into the Pacific Ocean in and around Florence, and the Siuslaw River flows right through town. When the numerous nearby lakes are added to the mix, it makes for one of the richest fishing areas in Oregon. Salmon, rainbow trout, bass, perch, crabs, and clams are among the water's treasures. Fishing boats and pleasure crafts moor in Florence's harbor, forming a pleasant backdrop for the town's restored buildings. South of town, miles of white sand dunes lend themselves to everything from solitary hikes to rides aboard all-terrain vehicles.

GETTING HERE AND AROUND

It's a 75-minute drive west to Florence on Highway 126 from Eugene and a 40-minute drive south on U.S. 101 from Yachats. It takes about an hour to drive U.S. 101 south to Coos Bay, a stretch that takes in all of Oregon Dunes National Recreation Area.

ESSENTIALS

Visitor Information Florence Area Chamber of Commerce ☒ *290 U.S. 101* ☎ *541/997–3128* ⊕ *www.florencechamber.com.*

EXPLORING

FAMILY **Sea Lion Caves.** In 1880 a sea captain named Cox rowed a small skiff into a fissure in a 300-foot-high sea cliff. Inside, he was startled to discover a vaulted chamber in the rock, 125 feet high and 2 acres in size. Hundreds of massive sea lions—the largest bulls weighing 2,000 pounds or more—covered every available surface. Cox's discovery would become one of the Oregon Coast's premier attractions, if something of a tourist trap. An elevator near the cliff-top ticket office descends to the floor of the cavern, near sea level, where vast numbers of Steller's and California sea lions relax on rocks and swim about (their cute, fuzzy pups can be viewed from behind a wire fence). This is the only known hauling-out area and rookery for wild sea lions on the mainland in the Lower 48, and it's an awesome sight and sound. In spring and summer the mammals usually stay on the rocky ledges outside the cave; in fall and winter they move inside. You'll also see several species of seabirds here, including migratory pigeon guillemots, cormorants, and three varieties of gulls. Gray whales are visible during their northern and southern migrations, October–December and March–May. The gift shop has tasty fudge—try the jalapeño. ☒ *91560 U.S. 101, 10 miles north of* *downtown Florence* ☎ *541/547–3111* ⊕ *www.sealioncaves.com* ⊠ *$12* ⊙ *Daily 9–5.*

NEED A BREAK?

Siuslaw River Coffee Roasters. This small, homey business serves cups of drip-on-demand coffee—you select the roast and they grind and brew it on the spot. Beans are roasted on-site, muffins and breads are freshly baked, and a view of the namesake river can be savored from the deck out back. It closes at 5 pm. ⊠ *1240 Bay St.* ☎ *541/997–3443* ⊕ *www.coffeeoregon.com.*

WHERE TO EAT AND STAY

$$
SEAFOOD

✕ **Bridgewater Fishhouse.** Freshly caught seafood—20 to 25 choices nightly—is the mainstay of this creaky-floored, Victorian-era restaurant in Florence's Old Town. Whether you opt for patio dining during summer or lounge seating in winter, the eclectic fare of pastas, burgers, salads, and seafood-packed stews is consistently well-prepared. A live jazz band provides some foot-tapping fun many evenings, and the sounds otherwise trend toward reggae and southern influence. For a light snack, try the peel-and-eat shrimp and a cup of chowder in the restaurant's stylish Zebra Lounge. [$] *Average main: $18* ⊠ *1297 Bay St.* ☎ *541/997–1133* ⊕ *www.bridgewaterfishhouse.com* ⊙ *Closed Tues.*

$$
MODERN
AMERICAN

✕ **Homegrown Public House.** This bustling, intimate gastropub in Old Town Florence—a couple of blocks north of the riverfront—specializes in locally sourced, creatively prepared American fare and offers a well-chosen list of Oregon beers on tap, plus local spirits, iced teas, and kombucha. Stop by for lunch to enjoy the lightly battered albacore fish and hand-cut fries with tartar sauce, or a cheeseburger topped with Rogue blue and served with marinated vegetables and local greens. More substantial dinner options include grilled Carlton Farms pork loin over Parmesan polenta, and market fish of the day grilled over a bed of red quinoa, fennel, and arugula. An excellent brunch is served on Sunday. [$] *Average main: $17* ⊠ *294 Laurel St.* ☎ *541/997–4886* ⊕ *www.homegrownpub.com* ⊙ *Closed Mon.*

$$
SEAFOOD

✕ **Waterfront Depot Restaurant and Bar.** The detailed chalkboard menu says it all: from the fresh, crab-encrusted halibut to Bill's Flaming Spanish Coffee, this is a place serious about fresh food and fine flavors. Located in the old Mapleton train station, the atmospheric tavern has a great view of the Siuslaw River and the Siuslaw River Bridge. In the summer diners can enjoy patio seating right at the water's edge and chomp on the nice variety of tapas plates. [$] *Average main: $17* ⊠ *1252 Bay St.* ☎ *541/902–9100* ⊕ *www.thewaterfrontdepot.com* ⊙ *No lunch.*

$$$
B&B/INN
Fodor'sChoice
★

🏠 **Heceta Head Lighthouse B&B.** On a windswept promontory, this unusual late-Victorian property is one of Oregon's most remarkable bed-and-breakfasts, owned by the U.S. Forest Service and managed by two certified executive chefs. **Pros:** unique property with a magical setting; exceptionally good food. **Cons:** remote location; some rooms share a bath. [$] *Rooms from: $209* ⊠ *92072 U.S. 101, 12 miles north of Florence* ☎ *541/547–3696, 866/547–3696* ⊕ *www.hecetalighthouse.com* ⊷ *6 rooms, 4 with bath* ⊚ *Breakfast.*

$
B&B/INN

🏠 **River House Inn.** On the beautiful Siuslaw River, this property has terrific accommodations and is near quaint shops and restaurants in

Florence's Old Town. **Pros:** spacious rooms; great views from most rooms; close proximity to dining and shopping. **Cons:** not on the beach; interior style is a bit bland. $ *Rooms from: $119* ⊠ *1202 Bay St.* ☎ *541/997–3933, 888/824-2750* ⊕ *www.riverhouseflorence.com* ⤳ *40 rooms* �� *Breakfast.*

SPORTS AND THE OUTDOORS

RECREATIONAL AREAS

Fodor'sChoice
★
Heceta Head Lighthouse State Scenic Area. A ½-mile trail from the beachside parking lot leads to the oft-photographed Heceta Head Lighthouse built in 1894, whose beacon, visible for more than 21 miles, is the most powerful on the Oregon Coast. More than 7 miles of trails traverse the rocky landscape north and south of the lighthouse, which rises some 200 feet above the ocean. For a mesmerizing view of the lighthouse and Heceta Head, pull over at the scenic viewpoint just north of Sea Lion Caves. ⊠ *U.S. 101, 11 miles north of Florence, Yachats* ☎ *541/547–3416, 800/551–6949* ⊕ *www.oregonstateparks.org* ⤳ *Day use $5, lighthouse tours free* ⊙ *Lighthouse tours daily 11–3.*

FAMILY
Fodor'sChoice
★
Oregon Dunes National Recreation Area. The Oregon Dunes National Recreation Area is the largest expanse of coastal sand dunes in North America, extending for 40 miles, from Florence to Coos Bay. The area contains some of the best ATV riding in the United States and encompasses some 31,500 acres. More than 1.5 million people visit the dunes each year, and about 350,000 are ATV users. Honeyman Memorial State Park, 522 acres within the recreation area, is a base camp for dune-buggy enthusiasts, mountain bikers, hikers, boaters, horseback riders, and dogsledders (the sandy hills are an excellent training ground). There's a campground, too. The dunes are a vast playground for children, particularly the slopes surrounding cool **Cleawox Lake.** If you have time for just a quick scamper in the sand, stop by the Oregon Dunes Overlook off U.S. 101, 11 miles south of Florence and 11 miles north of Reedsport—it's on the west side of the road, just north of Perkins Lake. ⊠ *855 U.S. 101 (office), at Hwy. 38, Reedsport* ☎ *541/271–6000* ⊕ *www.fs.usda.gov/recarea/siuslaw/recreation* ⤳ *Day use $5* ⊙ *Office hours Sept.–May, weekdays 8–4:30; Jun.–Aug., Mon.–Sat. 8–4:30.*

FAMILY
Fodor'sChoice
★
Sandland Adventures. This outfitter provides everything you need to get the whole family together for the ride of their lives. Start off with a heart-racing dune-buggy ride with a professional that will take you careening up, over, down, and around some of the steepest sand in the Oregon Dunes National Recreation Area. After you're done screaming and smiling, Sandland's park has bumper boats, a go-kart track, a miniature golf course, and a small railroad. ⊠ *85366 U.S. 101* ☎ *541/997-8087* ⊕ *www.sandland.com.*

GOLF

Ocean Dunes Golf Links. A favorite of locals year-round, this course operated by Three Rivers Casino & Hotel is a straightforward 18 holes that reward great shots and penalize the poor ones. You won't find many sand bunkers, because the narrow course is surrounded by sand dunes. Instead, you'll encounter fairways winding about dunes lined with ball-swallowing gorse, heather, shore pines, and native sea grasses. Pot bunkers guard small greens, and play can get pretty frisky if the

Umpqua Sand Dunes in Oregon Dunes National Recreation Area

frequent wind picks up. However, the course is well drained and playable—even under the wettest conditions. ✉ *3345 Munsel Lake Rd.* ☎ *541/997–3232, 877/374–8377* ⊕ *www.threeriverscasino.com/golf* 🖅 *Summer green fees $99.*

Sandpines Golf Links. This Scottish Links–style course is playable year-round. Designed by Rees Jones, the outward nine is cut out of pine forest and near blue lakes; and the inward nine provides some undulating fun, with the rolling dunes at the forefront from tee to green. While challenging, the course is generous enough to provide a great day on the links for beginners and more polished players. Sandpines has a fully equipped practice area with a driving range, bunkers, and putting greens. ✉ *1201 35th St.* ☎ *800/917–4653, 541/997–1940* ⊕ *www. sandpines.com* 🖅 *Summer greens fees $79.*

HORSEBACK RIDING

C & M Stables. Ride year-round along the Oregon Dunes National Recreation Area. The area is rich with marine life, including sea lions, whales, and coastal birds. Sharp-eyed riders also might spot bald eagles, red-tailed fox, and deer. Rides range from hour-long trots to half-day adventures. Children must be at least eight years old for the beach ride or six years old for the dune trail rides. ✉ *90241 U.S. 101 N* ☎ *541/997–7540* ⊕ *www.oregonhorsebackriding.com* 🖅 *From $60.*

SANDBOARDING

Sand Master Park. Everything you need to sandboard the park's private dunes is right here: board rental, wax, eyewear, clothing, and instruction. The staff is exceptionally helpful, and will get beginners off on their sandboarding adventure with enthusiasm. However, what must be surfed, must first be hiked up, and so on. ✉ *5351 U.S. 101* ☎ *541/997–6006* ⊕ *www.sandmasterpark.com.*

SOUTHERN COAST

Outdoors enthusiasts find a natural amusement park along this gorgeous stretch of coast from Reedsport to Brookings. The northern portion has a continuation of the Oregon Dunes National Recreation Area, and is the location of its visitor center. The Umpqua Discovery Center is a perfect trip with (or without) the kids, to learn about the region's history and animals. In Bandon golfers flock to one of the most celebrated clusters of courses in the nation at Bandon Dunes. Lovers of lighthouses, sailing, fishing, crabbing, elk viewing, camping, and water sports may wonder why they didn't venture south sooner.

BAY AREA: COOS BAY AND NORTH BEND

27 miles south of Reedsport on U.S. 101.

The Coos Bay–Charleston–North Bend metropolitan area, collectively known as the Bay Area (population 27,000), is the gateway to rewarding recreational experiences. The town of Coos Bay lies next to the largest natural harbor between San Francisco Bay and Seattle's Puget Sound. A century ago, vast quantities of lumber cut from the Coast Range were milled in Coos Bay and shipped around the world. Coos Bay still has a reputation as a rough-and-ready port city, but with mill closures and dwindling lumber reserves it is looking to tourism and other industries for economic growth.

To see the best of the Bay Area, head west from Coos Bay on Newmark Avenue for about 7 miles to **Charleston.** Though it's a Bay Area community, this quiet fishing village at the mouth of Coos Bay is a world unto itself. As it loops into town, the road becomes the Cape Arago Highway and leads to several stunning oceanfront parks.

GETTING HERE AND AROUND
The area lies along a slightly inland stretch of U.S. 101 that's a 40-minute drive south of Reedsport and a 30-minute drive north of Bandon; from the Umpqua Valley and Interstate 5 corridor, Coos Bay is just under two hours' drive west from Roseburg on Highway 42.

Southwest Oregon Regional Airport in North Bend has commercial flights from Portland and San Francisco.

ESSENTIALS
Visitor Information Coos Bay–North Bend Visitors & Convention Bureau ✉ *50 Central Ave.* ☎ *541/269–0215, 800/824–8486* ⊕ *www.oregonsadventurecoast.com.*

EXPLORING
Cape Arago Lighthouse. On a rock island just offshore from Charleston near Sunset Bay State Park, this lighthouse has had several iterations; the first lighthouse was built here in 1866, but it was destroyed by storms and erosion. A second, built in 1908, suffered the same fate. The current white tower, built in 1934, is 44 feet tall and towers 100

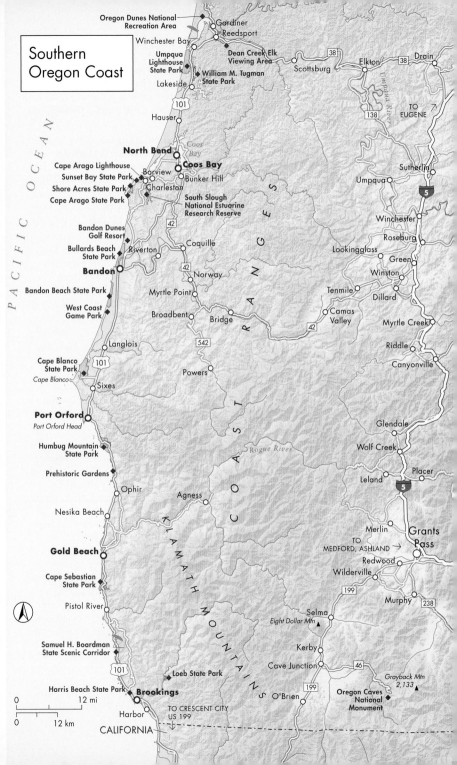

Southern Oregon Coast

PACIFIC OCEAN

Oregon Dunes National Recreation Area
Gardiner
Reedsport
Winchester Bay
Umpqua Lighthouse State Park
Dean Creek Elk Viewing Area
Scottsburg
Elkton
38
Drain
TO EUGENE
William M. Tugman State Park
Lakeside
Hauser
138
101
Coos Bay
Sutherlin
North Bend
Coos Bay
Barview
Bunker Hill
Umpqua
Winchester
5
Cape Arago Lighthouse
Sunset Bay State Park
Shore Acres State Park
Cape Arago State Park
Charleston
South Slough National Estuarine Research Reserve
Roseburg
Lookingglass
Green
42
Coquille
Winston
Bandon Dunes Golf Resort
Bullards Beach State Park
Riverton
42
Norway
Tenmile
Dillard
Bandon
Myrtle Point
Bandon Beach State Park
Broadbent
Bridge
Camas Valley
Myrtle Creek
West Coast Game Park
542
42
Langlois
Powers
Riddle
Cape Blanco State Park
101
Cape Blanco
Sixes
Canyonville
Port Orford
Port Orford Head
Glendale
Wolf Creek
Humbug Mountain State Park
Rogue River
Prehistoric Gardens
Leland
Placer
5
Ophir
Agness
Nesika Beach
Merlin
Grants Pass
Gold Beach
TO MEDFORD, ASHLAND →
Redwood
Cape Sebastian State Park
Wilderville
Pistol River
199
Murphy
238
Samuel H. Boardman State Scenic Corridor
Eight Dollar Mtn
Selma
101
Kerby
Grayback Mtn 2,133
Loeb State Park
Cave Junction
46
Harris Beach State Park
Brookings
199
O'Brien
Oregon Caves National Monument
Harbor
TO CRESCENT CITY US 199
CALIFORNIA

KLAMATH MOUNTAINS

COAST RANGES

0   12 mi
0   12 km

feet above the ocean. If you're here on a foggy day, listen for its unique foghorn. The lighthouse is connected to the mainland by a bridge. Neither is open to the public, but there's an excellent spot to view this lonely guardian and much of the coastline. From U.S. 101, take Cape Arago Highway to Gregory Point, where it ends at a turnaround, and follow the short trail. ⊠ *Cape Arago Highway, just north of Sunset Bay State Park, Charleston.*

Charleston Marina Complex. At this bustling marina 8 miles west of Coos Bay, there's a launch ramp, a store with tackle and marine supplies, a 110-space RV park, a motel, restaurants, and gift shops. Fishing charters also set out from here. ⊠ *4535 Kingfisher Dr., Charleston* ☎ *541/888–2548* ⊕ *www.charlestonmarina.com.*

Coos History Museum & Maritime Collection. The highlight here is a 1922 steam locomotive used in Coos County logging. On display are a formal 1900 parlor, a pioneer kitchen, and exhibits on Native American history, agriculture, and industry such as logging, shipping, and mining. As of this writing, the museum is in the midst of moving into a new 11,000-square-foot facility on the waterfront in downtown Coos Bay—it's expected to be completed by early 2015. ⊠ *N. Front St., just north of Marshfield Sun Printing Museum* ☎ *541/756–6320* ⊕ *www. cooshistory.org* ⊠ *$5* ۞ *Tues.–Sat. 10–5.*

South Slough National Estuarine Research Reserve. The reserve's fragile ecosystem supports everything from algae to bald eagles and black bears. More than 300 species of birds have been sighted at the reserve, which has an interpretive center with interesting nature exhibits, guided walks (summer only), and nature trails that give you a chance to see things up close. ⊠ *61907 Seven Devils Rd., 4 miles south of Charleston* ☎ *541/888–5558* ⊕ *www.oregon.gov/dsl/ssnerr* ⊠ *Free* ۞ *Trails daily dawn–dusk; interpretive center daily 10–4:30.*

WHERE TO EAT AND STAY

$

GERMAN

✗ **Blue Heron Bistro.** The specialty at this bustling downtown bistro is hearty German fare, but you'll also find a number of local seafood items, as well as sandwiches and lighter dishes, from panfried oysters to meatball sandwiches. The skylit, tile-floor dining room seats about 70 amid natural wood and blue linen. The seating area outside has blue awnings and colorful Bavarian window boxes that add a festive touch. Eighteen microbrews are available. ⑤ *Average main: $14* ⊠ *100 W. Commercial St., Coos Bay* ☎ *541/267–3933* ⊕ *www.blueheronbistro. com.*

$

SEAFOOD

✗ **Miller's at the Cove.** Often packed with local fishing and dock workers as well as tourists en route to and from Sunset Bay and nearby state parks, this lively and fun—if at times raucous—sports bar and tavern makes a great dinner or lunch stop for fresh seafood, pitchers of craft beer, and watching a game on TV. Favorites here include the fish-and-chips (available with local snapper or cod), oyster burgers, Dungeness crab melts, meatball subs, clam chowder, and Baja-style fish or crab tacos. ⑤ *Average main: $10* ⊠ *63346 Boat Basin Rd., Charleston* ☎ *541/808–2404* ⊕ *www.millersatthecove.com.*

$ 🏨 **Coos Bay Manor.** Built in 1912 on a quiet residential street, this
B&B/INN   15-room Colonial Revival manor is listed on the National Register of
Historic Places. **Pros:** very nicely kept and decorated; family-friendly.
Cons: in busy downtown Coos Bay; a 15-minute drive from the ocean.
⑤ *Rooms from: $145* ⊠ *955 S. 5th St.* ☎ *541/269–1224, 800/269–1224*
⊕ *www.coosbaymanor.com* ⇆ *5 rooms, 1 suite* ⃝⃝ *Breakfast.*

$ 🏨 **Mill Casino Hotel.** Even if you're not a big fan of gambling, this attrac-
RESORT   tive hotel near the waterfront in North Bend (a short distance north
of downtown Coos Bay) makes a handy and fairly economical base
for exploring this stretch of the coast. **Pros:** attractive, contemporary
rooms; location close to downtown dining and shopping; nice views
from rooms in tower. **Cons:** casino can be noisy and smoky. ⑤ *Rooms
from: $109* ⊠ *3201 Tremont Ave., North Bend* ☎ *541/756–8800,
800/953–4800* ⊕ *www.themillcasino.com* ⇆ *207 rooms, 10 suites*
⃝⃝ *No meals.*

SPORTS AND THE OUTDOORS

RECREATIONAL AREAS

Cape Arago State Park. The distant barking of sea lions echoes in the air
at a trio of coves connected by short but steep trails. The park overlooks
the **Oregon Islands National Wildlife Refuge,** where offshore rocks,
beaches, islands, and reefs provide breeding grounds for seabirds and
marine mammals, including seal pups (the trail is closed in spring to
protect them). ⊠ *End of Cape Arago Hwy., 1 mile south of Shore Acres
State Park* ☎ *800/551–6949, 541/888–3778* ⊕ *www.oregonstateparks.
org* ⃞ *Free* ☽ *Daily dawn–dusk. Trail closed Mar.–June.*

Fodor'sChoice   **Shore Acres State Park.** An observation building on a grassy bluff over-
★   looking the Pacific marks the site that held the mansion of lumber
baron Louis J. Simpson. The view over the rugged wave-smashed cliffs
is splendid, but the real glory of Shore Acres lies a few hundred yards
to the south, where an entrance gate leads into what was Simpson's
private garden. Beautifully landscaped and meticulously maintained, the
gardens incorporate formal English and Japanese designs. From March
to mid-October the grounds are ablaze with blossoming daffodils, rhododendrons, azaleas, roses, and dahlias. In December the garden is
decked out with a dazzling display of holiday lights. ⊠ *89526 Cape
Arago Hwy., 1 mile south of Sunset Bay State Park* ☎ *800/551–6949,
541/888–2472 info center, 541/888–3732* ⊕ *www.oregonstateparks.
org* ⃞ *$5 per vehicle day-use fee* ☽ *Daily 8–dusk.*

BANDON

25 miles south of Coos Bay.

Referred to by some who cherish its romantic lure as Bandon-by-the-
Sea, Bandon is both a harbor town and a popular vacation spot, famous
for its cranberry products and its artists' colony, complete with galleries
and shops. Two national wildlife refuges, Oregon Islands and Bandon
Marsh, are within the town limits. The Bandon Dunes links-style golf
courses are a worldwide attraction, often ranked among the top courses
in the nation.

Tiny Bandon bills itself as Oregon's cranberry capital—10 miles north of town you'll find acres of bogs and irrigated fields where tons of the tart berries are harvested every year. Each October there's the Cranberry Festival, featuring a parade and a fair.

GETTING HERE AND AROUND

Bandon, on U.S. 101, is a half-hour drive south of Coos Bay and North Bend, and a two-hour drive north up the coast from the California border; allow 4½ hours to get here from Portland.

ESSENTIALS

Visitor Information Bandon Chamber of Commerce ⊠ *300 2nd St.* ☎ *541/347–9616* ⊕ *www.bandon.com.*

EXPLORING

Bandon Historical Society Museum. In the old city hall building, this museum depicts the area's early history, including Native American artifacts, logging, fishing, cranberry farming, and the disastrous 1936 fire that destroyed the city. The well-stocked gift shop has books, knickknacks, jewelry, myrtlewood, and other little treasures. ⊠ *270 Fillmore St.* ☎ *541/347–2164* ⊕ *www.bandonhistoricalmuseum.org* ⊠ *$3* ⊙ *Daily 10–4.*

FAMILY
Fodor's Choice
★

Oregon Islands National Wildlife Refuge. Each of the colossal rocks jutting from the ocean between Bandon and Brookings is protected as part of this refuge, in total comprising a string of 1,853 rocks, reefs, islands, and two headland areas spanning 320 miles. Thirteen species of seabirds, totalling 1.2 million birds, nest here, and harbor seals, California sea lions, Steller sea lions, and Northern elephant seals also breed within the refuge. Coquille Point, a mainland unit of Oregon Islands Refuge, is one of many places to observe seabirds and harbor seals. The point overlooks a series of offshore rocks, and a paved trail that winds over the headland ends in stairways to the beach on both sides, allowing for a loop across the sand when tides permit. Visitors are encouraged to steer clear of harbor seals and avoid touching seal pups. A complete list of viewpoints and trails is available online. ⊠ *11th St. W and Portland Ave. SW, drive west to road's end for Coquille Point and parking* ☎ *541/347–1470* ⊕ *www.fws.gov/oregoncoast/oregonislands.*

West Coast Game Park Safari. The "walk-through safari" on 21 acres has free-roaming wildlife (it's the visitors who are behind fences); more than 450 animals and about 75 species, including lions, tigers, snow leopards, lemurs, bears, chimps, cougars, and camels, make it one of the largest wild-animal petting parks in the United States. The big attractions here are the young animals: bear cubs, tiger cubs, whatever is suitable for actual handling. ⊠ *46914 U.S. 101, 8 miles south of Bandon on U.S. 101* ☎ *541/347–3106* ⊕ *www.westcoastgameparksafari. com* ⊠ *$17.50* ⊙ *Mar.–Nov. and last week Dec., weekdays 9:30–5, weekends 9:30–5:30; Jan. and Feb., weekends 9:30–5.*

WHERE TO EAT

$$
SEAFOOD

✕ **Edgewaters Restaurant.** This second-story bar above Edgewaters Restaurant has some of the best west-facing views of the ocean from Bandon, and is among few properties in Old Town that don't face north toward the Coquille River. You can sometimes see whales from this spot during whale-watching season. It makes a great happy-hour stop with its tall ceilings, warm fireplace, and many windows. Downstairs, the main dining room also has large windows with views of the river. The menu features fresh seafood, pastas, creative salads, and even a sushi dish or two. ⑤ *Average main: $18* ⊠ *480 1st St.* ☎ *541/347–8500* ⊕ *www.edgewaters.net* ♁ *Closed Mon. No lunch Tues.–Thurs.*

$$$
PACIFIC
NORTHWEST
Fodor's Choice
★

× **The Loft Restaurant & Bar.** This hip eatery in Bandon's Old Town is notable for chef-owner Kali Fieger's innovative, modern spin on French basics. On the second floor of an old Port of Bandon property, The Loft's vaulted, wood-trimmed ceilings, three-sided view of the Coquille River, and classic wooden tables are all ingredients for an enjoyable meal. Every dish on the menu is as intentional as the next, prepared with thoughtful sauces, delicate chopping, and artful presentation, often combining unexpected flavors into single servings with fantastic results. You might start with grilled baby octopus with capers and chimichurri sauce, followed either by pan-seared sea scallops with shaved fennel, brown-butter hollandaise, and crisp root vegetables, or braised pork cheeks in an aromatic red-wine sauce. There's a deli, gourmet market, and wineshop on the ground floor, handy options for planning a beach picnic. ⑤ *Average main: $25* ⊠ *315 1st St.* ☎ *541/329–0535* ⊕ *www.theloftofbandon.com* ⤳ *0* ♁ *Closed Mon.–Wed. No lunch.*

$$$
MODERN
AMERICAN
Fodor's Choice
★

× **Lord Bennett's.** His lordship has a lot going for him: a cliff-top setting, a comfortable and spacious dining area in a dramatic contemporary building, sunsets visible through picture windows overlooking Face Rock Beach, and occasional live music on weekends. The modern American menu features plenty of local seafood; try the nut-crusted halibut, blackened red snapper with potato-horseradish crust, or wild prawns with garlic butter and sherry. Steaks and chops are offered, too. The weekend brunch is a big hit—consider reserving a table for this. ⑤ *Average main: $25* ⊠ *1695 Beach Loop Rd.* ☎ *541/347–3663* ⊕ *www.lordbennett.com* ♁ *No lunch Mon.–Thurs.*

$
SEAFOOD

× **Tony's Crab Shack & Seafood Grill.** Started in 1989 as a bait and tackle shop, Tony's Crab Shack has since become a staple of the Bandon boardwalk, popular with locals and visitors for its crab cakes, fish tacos, crab and bay shrimp sandwich, and smoked Alaskan sockeye. Open only until 6 pm, it's a reliable bet for lunch or perhaps very early dinner. ⑤ *Average main: $14* ⊠ *155 1st St.* ☎ *541/347–2875* ⊕ *tonyscrabshack.com.*

WHERE TO STAY

$
HOTEL
Fodor's Choice
★

☷ **Bandon Beach Motel.** As its owners like to proclaim, it's all about the view at this low-frills, exceptionally well-kept seaside motel set high on a bluff on Coquille Point and overlooking the smooth beach and rugged offshore rock formations below. **Pros:** terrific value; gorgeous beach views; run by a friendly and helpful family. **Cons:** basic rooms with few bells and whistles; 20-minute walk to downtown; often books up weeks in advance in summer. ⑤ *Rooms from: $105* ⊠ *1090 Portland Ave. SW* ☎ *541/347–9451, 866/945–0133* ⊕ *www.bandonbeachmotel. com* ⤳ *20 rooms* ⦙◎⦙ *No meals.*

$$$
RESORT
Fodor's Choice
★

Bandon Dunes Golf Resort. This golfing lodge provides a comfortable place to relax after a day on the links, with accommodations ranging from single rooms to four-bedroom condos, many with beautiful views of the famous golf course. **Pros:** if you're a golfer, this adds to an incredible overall experience; if not, you'll have a wonderful stay anyway. **Cons:** the weather can be wet and wild in the shoulder-season months. ⑤ *Rooms from: $230* ⊠ *57744 Round Lake Dr.* ☎ *541/347–4380, 888/345–6008* ⊕ *www.bandondunesgolf.com* ⇒ *186 rooms* ⑩ *Some meals.*

SPORTS AND THE OUTDOORS

RECREATIONAL AREA

Bullards Beach State Park. At this rugged park along the north bank of the Coquille River (just across from downtown Bandon but reached via a 3½-mile drive up U.S. 101), you can tour the octagonal **Coquille Lighthouse,** built in 1896 and no longer in use. From turnoff from U.S. 101, the meandering 2-mile drive to reach it passes through the Bandon Marsh, a prime bird-watching and picnicking area. The beach beside the lighthouse is a good place to search for jasper, agate, and driftwood—the firm sand is also popular for mountain biking. There's a campground with a wide variety of tent and RV sites. ⊠ *52470 U.S. 101, 2 miles north of Bandon* ☎ *800/452–5687, 541/347–2209* ⊕ *www.oregonstateparks.org* ⊠ *Free* ⊙ *Lighthouse: May–mid-Oct., daily 11–5.*

GOLF

Fodor's Choice
★

Bandon Dunes Golf Resort. This playland for the nation's golfing elite is no stranger to well-heeled athletes flying in to North Bend on private jets to play on the resort's four distinct courses, including the Old Macdonald course. The expectations at Bandon Dunes are that you will walk the course with a caddy—adding another refined, traditional touch. Greens fees range, according to season and other factors, from $245 to $310 a round from May to October, $75 to $220 other months. Caddy fees are determined by the player, but suggested fees are $80 to $100 per bag, per round. ⊠ *57744 Round Lake Dr.* ☎ *541/347–4380, 888/345–6008* ⊕ *www.bandondunesgolf.com.*

PORT ORFORD

30 miles south of Bandon.

The westernmost incorporated community in the contiguous United States, Port Orford is surrounded by forests, rivers, lakes, and beaches. The jetty at Port Orford offers little protection from storms, so every night the fishing boats are lifted out and stored on the docks. Commercial fishing boats search for crab, tuna, snapper, and salmon in the waters out of Port Orford, and diving boats gather sea urchins for Japanese markets. Visitors can fish off the Port Orford dock or the jetty for smelt, sardine, herring, lingcod, and halibut. Dock Beach provides beach fishing. The area is a favorite spot for sport divers because of the near-shore, protected reef, and for whale-watchers in fall and early spring.

GETTING HERE AND AROUND

Port Orford is a 30-minute drive south of Bandon and a one-hour drive north of Brookings along U.S. 101.

ESSENTIALS

Visitor Information **Port Orford Visitors Center** ✉ *520 Jefferson St.*
☎ *541/332–4106* ⊕ *www.portorford.org.*

EXPLORING

**OFF THE
BEATEN
PATH**

Prehistoric Gardens. As you round a bend between Port Orford and Gold Beach, you'll see one of those sights that make grown-ups groan and kids squeal with delight: a huge, open-jawed tyrannosaurus rex, with a green brontosaurus peering out from the forest beside it. You can view 23 other life-size dinosaur replicas on the trail that runs through the property. ✉ *36848 U.S. 101* ☎ *541/332–4463* ⊕ *www.prehistoricgardens.com* 💲 *$12* ☉ *Summer, daily 9–6; call for winter hrs.*

WHERE TO EAT AND STAY

$

SEAFOOD
FAMILY

✕ **Crazy Norwegians Fish and Chips.** This quirky and casual hole-in-the-wall in Port Orford excels at what they do: good old-fashioned fish-and-chips. With everything from shrimp to cod to halibut paired with fries, the Crazy Norwegians serve it up with a side of pasta salad or coleslaw. Dine in at wooden tables with the mostly family crowd or take it to go to nearby Battle Rock Park. 💲 *Average main: $12* ✉ *259 6th St.* ☎ *541/332–8601* ☉ *Closed Mon. and Tues.*

$$$

MODERN
AMERICAN
Fodor'sChoice
★

✕ **Redfish.** Two walls of windows allow diners at the stylish Redfish in downtown Port Orford spectacular ocean views, but the views inside are pretty inviting, too, from the modern artwork provided by sister establishment Hawthorne Gallery to the artfully presented and globally influenced food. Start with the Manila clams in lemongrass-coconut red-curry broth or the daily ceviche, before graduating to cedar-plank chinook salmon with mushroom risotto, or organic chicken with truffle grits, garlic-tomato marmalade, and broccoli rabe. The good-size portions make it possible to enjoy a moderately priced dinner here by ordering a couple of smaller plates. Weekend brunch items include crab cakes Benedict and a lingcod sandwich with spicy-pickle-tarragon aioli. 💲 *Average main: $25* ✉ *517 Jefferson St.* ☎ *541/366–2200* ⊕ *www.redfishportorford.com.*

$

HOTEL
FAMILY

🛏 **Castaway by the Sea.** This old-school motel operated by friendly proprietor Rockne Berge offers fantastic views from nearly every room, most of which have enclosed sun porches—the simplest and least expensive rooms open to an enclosed breezeway that takes in these same views. **Pros:** within walking distance of local restaurants; panoramic ocean views; reasonable rates. **Cons:** decor is a bit dated; not actually on the beach. 💲 *Rooms from: $95* ✉ *545 5th St.* ☎ *541/332–4502* ⊕ *www.castawaybythesea.com* 🛏 *9 rooms, 4 suites* ⦿ *No meals.*

$$$$

RESORT
Fodor'sChoice
★

🛏 **WildSpring Guest Habitat.** This rustic outpost in the woods above Port Orford blends all the comforts and privacy of a vacation rental with the services of a resort. **Pros:** relaxing, secluded, and private; gorgeous rooms; eco-conscious management. **Cons:** need to drive to the beach and stores. 💲 *Rooms from: $288* ✉ *92978 Cemetery Loop Rd.* ☎ *541/332–0977, 866/333–9453* ⊕ *www.wildspring.com* 🛏 *5 cabins* ⦿ *Breakfast.*

SPORTS AND THE OUTDOORS

RECREATIONAL AREAS

FAMILY **Battle Rock Park and Port Orford Heads State Park.** Stroll the mocha-colored sand and admire pristine Battle Rock right in the heart of downtown Port Orford. Named for a battle between white settlers and the Dene Tsut Dah that took place here in 1850, this spot sits just below Port Orford Heads State Park. Atop the bluff that is Port Orford Heads, a trail loops the rocky outcropping between the Pacific and the Port Orford Lifeboat Station, taking in the hillside below, from which crews once mounted daring rescues on the fierce sea. The lifeboat station and adjoining museum is open for tours Wednesday–Monday, 10–3:30. Their motto? "You have to go out; you don't have to come back." ⊠ *Port Orford Hwy.; follow signs from U.S. 101* ☎ *800/551–6949, 541/332–6774* ⊕ *www.oregonstateparks.org* ▣ *Free.*

> ### THE FAB 50
>
> U.S. 101 between Port Orford and Brookings, often referred to as the "fabulous 50 miles," soars up green headlands, some of them hundreds of feet high, and past a seascape of cliffs and sea stacks. The ocean is bluer and clearer—though not appreciably warmer—than it is farther north, and the coastal countryside is dotted with farms, grazing cattle, and small rural communities.

Cape Blanco State Park. Said to be the westernmost point in Oregon and perhaps the windiest—gusts clocked at speeds as high as 184 mph have twisted and battered the Sitka spruces along the 6-mile road from U.S. 101 to the **Cape Blanco Lighthouse.** The lighthouse, atop a 245-foot headland, has been in continuous use since 1870, longer than any other in Oregon. No one knows why the Spaniards sailing past these reddish bluffs in 1603 called them *blanco* (white). One theory is that the name refers to the fossilized shells that glint in the cliff face. Campsites at the 1,880-acre park are available on a first-come, first-served basis. Four cabins are available for reservation. ⊠ *91814 Cape Blanco Rd., off U.S. 101, 6 miles north of Port Orford, Sixes* ☎ *541/332–2973, 800/551–6949* ⊕ *www.oregonstateparks.org* ▣ *Day use and Hughes House tour free; lighthouse tour $2* ⊙ *Park daily; lighthouse and Hughes House Apr.–Oct., Wed.–Mon. 10–3:30.*

Humbug Mountain State Park. This secluded, 1,850-acre park, especially popular with campers, usually has warm weather, thanks to the nearby mountains that shelter it from ocean breezes. A 6-mile loop leads to the top of 1,756-foot Humbug Mountain, one the highest points along the state's coastline. It's a pretty, moderately challenging hike, but the summit is fairly overgrown and doesn't provide especially panoramic views. The campground has tent and RV sites. ⊠ *U.S. 101, 6 miles south of Port Orford* ☎ *541/332–6774, 800/551–6949* ⊕ *www.oregonstateparks.org.*

GOLD BEACH

28 miles south of Port Orford.

The fabled Rogue River is one of about 150 U.S. rivers to merit Wild and Scenic status from the federal government. From spring to late fall an estimated 50,000 visitors descend on the town to take one of the daily jet-boat excursions that roar upstream from Wedderburn, Gold Beach's sister city across the bay, into the Rogue River Wilderness Area. Black bears, otters, beavers, ospreys, egrets, and bald eagles are seen regularly on these trips.

Gold Beach is very much a seasonal town, thriving in summer and nearly deserted the rest of the year because of its remote location. It marks the entrance to Oregon's banana belt, where mild, California-like temperatures take the sting out of winter and encourage a blossoming trade in lilies and daffodils.

GETTING HERE AND AROUND
It's a 90-minute drive south along U.S. 101 from Coos Bay and North Bend to reach Gold Beach, which is a one-hour drive north of the California border.

ESSENTIALS
Visitor Information Gold Beach Visitors Center ⊠ *94080 Shirley La.* ☎ *541/247–7526, 800/525–2334* ⊕ *www.goldbeach.org.*

WHERE TO EAT

$$ ╳ **Anna's by the Sea.** Dining at Anna's by the Sea is like stepping into
MODERN one man's artisan universe: bowed and wood-trimmed ceilings, hand-
AMERICAN made cheeses, and blackberry honey lemonade, even a hydroponic herb garden, crafted by owner/head cook Peter Dower. The enchanting, intimate eatery seats only 18, six of those seats stools with a view into the kitchen. Diners get a dash of personality with their meal service, which offers such choices as wild shrimp in black truffle oil and seared albacore and chicken thighs in chanterelle gravy. A former wine retailer, Dower also stocks nearly 100 well-chosen wines and an Oregon Spirits Collection that's a menu standout. Dower is as much entertainer as curator of the restaurant, so drop in ready for the performance and the bistro's buoyant atmosphere. ⑤ *Average main: $20* ⊠ *29672 Stewart St.* ☎ *514/247–2100* ⊕ *www.annasbythesea.com* ☾ *No lunch.*

$ ╳ **The Port Hole Café.** A local staple in the old cannery building at the Port
AMERICAN of Gold Beach since 1995, this family business has been passed down
FAMILY a generation, and many of the employees are friends and relations who have been tied to it for years. This is a great place to experience local life in Gold Beach, and enjoy standard lunch or dinner fare by the sea. The café overlooks the mouth of the Rogue River, an area with great views but too blustery for outdoor dining. The bright interior is furnished with casual wooden tables and there are—you guessed it—portholes. Try the panko-breaded fish-and-chips and the blueberry pie, made from berries picked locally by a family friend. Beers from the town's excellent Arch Rock Brewing are served. ⑤ *Average main: $13* ⊠ *29975 Harbor Way* ☎ *541/247–7411* ⊕ *www.portholecafe.com.*

WHERE TO STAY

$ ⛺ **Pacific Reef and Resort.** This resort offers a little something for every-
HOTEL one: from comfy, clean, no-frills lodging in the original renovated 1950s
FAMILY hotel to modern two-story condos with expansive ocean views, king-size beds, full kitchens, and outdoor patios. **Pros:** luxurious condos; full kitchens. **Cons:** rocky beach; on a busy road. ⑤ *Rooms from: $89*

✉ *29362 Ellensburg Hwy. (U.S. 101)* ☎ *541/247–6658, 800/808–7263* ⊕ *www.pacificreefresort.com* ⤳ *39 units* ⏐◯⏐ *Breakfast.*

$$$$ ⌂ **Tu Tu' Tun Lodge.** Pronounced "too-*too*-tin," this renowned and rather
RESORT lavish resort is a slice of heaven on the Rogue River, and owner Kyle
Fodor's Choice Ringer is intent on providing his guests with a singular Northwest
★ experience. **Pros:** luxurious, beautifully outfitted rooms; exceptional
dining; peaceful location overlooking river. **Cons:** no TV; not well suited
for young kids; 15-minute drive from downtown. ⑤ *Rooms from:
$255* ✉ *96550 N. Bank Rogue River Rd., 7 miles east of Gold Beach*
☎ *541/247–6664, 800/864–6357* ⊕ *www.tututun.com* ⤳ *16 rooms, 2
suites, 2 cottages* ⏐◯⏐ *Breakfast.*

SPORTS AND THE OUTDOORS

BOATING

Jerry's Rogue Jets. These jet boats operate from May through September in the most rugged section of the Wild and Scenic Rogue River, offering 64, 81, and 104-mile tours. Whether visitors choose a shorter, 6-hour lower Rogue scenic trip or an 8-hour white-water trip, folks have a rollicking good time. Its largest vessels are 40-feet long and can hold 75 passengers. The smaller, white-water boats are 32-feet long and can hold 42 passengers. ✉ *29985 Harbor Way* ☎ *541/247–4571, 800/451–3645* ⊕ *www.roguejets.com.*

FISHING

Five Star Charters. Fishing charter trips range from a 4-hour bottom-fish outing to a full-day salmon, steelhead, or halibut charter. They offer all the tackle needed, and customers don't even need experience—they'll take beginners and experts. The outfit has four riverboats, including two drift boats and two powerboats, as well as two ocean boats. They operate year-round. ✉ *29957 Harbor Way* ☎ *541/247–0217, 888/301–6480* ⊕ *www.goldbeachadventures.com.*

RECREATIONAL AREAS

Cape Sebastian State Park. The parking lots at this scenic area are more than 200 feet above sea level. At the south parking vista you can see up to 43 miles north to Humbug Mountain. Looking south, you can see nearly 50 miles toward Crescent City, California, and the Point Saint George Lighthouse. A deep forest of Sitka spruce covers most of the park. There's a 1½-mile walking trail. ✉ *U.S. 101, 6 miles south of Gold Beach* ☎ *541/469–2021, 800/551–6949* ⊕ *www.oregonstateparks.org.*

**EN
ROUTE**
Between Gold Beach and Brookings you'll cross Thomas Creek Bridge, the highest span in Oregon. Take advantage of the off-road coastal viewing points along the 10-mile-long **Samuel H. Boardman State Scenic Corridor**—especially in summer, when highway traffic becomes heavy and rubbernecking can be dangerous.

Samuel H. Boardman State Scenic Corridor. This 12-mile corridor through beach forests and alongside rocky promontories and windswept beaches contains some of Oregon's most spectacular stretches of coastline, though seeing some of them up close sometimes requires a little effort. About 27 miles of the Oregon Coast Trail weaves its way through this area, a reach dominated by Sitka spruce trees that stretch up to 300 feet and by rocky coast interspersed with sandy beaches. Starting from the north, walk a short path from the highway turnoff to view Arch Rock. The path travels a meadow that blooms in spring time. Down the road, find **Secret Beach**—hardly a secret—where trails run from two parking lots into three separate beaches below. Visit at low tide to make your way through all three, including through a cave that connects to the third beach close to Thunder Rock. At **Thunder Rock**, just north of milepost 345 on U.S. 101, walk west for a 1-mile loop that traces inlets and headlands, edging right up to steep drops. Find the highest bridge in Oregon just south—the **Thomas Creek Bridge**—from which a moderately difficult trail extends to wide, sandy **China Beach**. Find some sun on China Beach, or continue south to walk the unusual sculpted sandstone at **Indian Sands**. Easy beach access is had at Whaleshead Beach, where shaded picnic tables shelter the view. From farther south at **Lone Ranch**, climb the grassy hillside to the top of **Cape Ferrelo** for a sweeping view of the rugged coastline, also a great spot for whale-watching in fall and summer. ⊠ *U.S. 101 between Gold Beach and Brookings* ☎ *800/551–6949, 541/469–2021* ⊕ *www.oregonstateparks.org* ⊠ *Free.*

BROOKINGS

27 miles south of Gold Beach on U.S. 101.

A startling 90% of the pot lilies grown in the United States come from a 500-acre area inland from Brookings. Mild temperatures along this coastal plain provide ideal conditions for flowering plants of all kinds—even a few palm trees, a rare sight in Oregon.

The town is equally famous as a commercial and sportfishing port at the mouth of the turquoise-blue Chetco River. Salmon and steelhead weighing 20 pounds or more swim here.

GETTING HERE AND AROUND

Brookings is the southernmost town on Oregon's coastal 101, just 10 miles north of the California border and a half-hour drive from Crescent City; it's a 2½-hour drive south on U.S. 101 from the Coos Bay and North Bend area. Allow about six hours to get here from Portland via Interstate 5 to Grants Pass and U.S. 199 to Crescent City.

VISITOR INFORMATION

Brookings Harbor Chamber of Commerce ⊠ *16330 Lower Harbor Rd.* ☎ *541/469–3181, 800/535–9469* ⊕ *www.brookingsharborchamber. com.*

WHERE TO EAT AND STAY

$ ✕ **Superfly Martini Bar & Grill.** The unusual name of this stylish little
AMERICAN bar and grill has nothing to do with the Curtis Mayfield '70s funk anthem—rather, owner Ryan Webster named this establishment, which is also an artisanal-vodka distillery, after a fishing fly. Appropriately, the bar serves first-rate cocktails, including a refreshing lemon-basil martini. But the food is tasty, too; consider the rare-seared yellowfin tuna over yakisoba noodles with lemon-zest wasabi, or the pulled-pork sandwich. The restaurant's breakfast is a good time to sample the Bloody Marys and a "monster" burrito with eggs, chorizo, and cheese.

WELCOME TO THE WILLAMETTE VALLEY AND WINE COUNTRY

TOP REASONS TO GO

★ **Swirl and sip:** Each region in the Willamette Valley offers some of the finest vintages and dining experiences found anywhere.

★ **Soar through the air:** Newberg's hot-air balloons will give you a bird's-eye view of Yamhill's wine country.

★ **Run rapids:** Feel the bouncing exhilaration and the cold spray of white-water rafting on the wild, winding McKenzie River outside Eugene.

★ **Walk on the wild side:** Hillsboro's Jackson Bottom Nature Preserve gives walkers a chance to view otters, beavers, herons, and eagles.

★ **Back the Beavers or Ducks:** Nothing gets the blood pumping like an Oregon State Beaver or University of Oregon Ducks football game.

1 North Willamette Valley. Most visitors begin their journey into wine country here, an area rich with upscale dining, shopping, the arts, and wineries. Close to Portland, North Willamette's communities provide all the amenities of urban life with a whole lot less concrete. Wine enthusiasts will relish the excellent vineyards in Beaverton, Hillsboro, and Forest Grove.

2 Yamhill County. This part of the state has undergone a renaissance in the past 20 years, as the world has beaten a path to its door, seeking the perfect Pinot. Many of the Willamette's highest-rated wineries are here. There are gorgeous inns, wine bars, and unforgettable restaurants providing a complete vacation experience.

3 Mid-Willamette Valley. Agriculture is the mainstay of this region; roadsides are dotted with fruit and veggie stands, and towns boast farmers' markets. The flat terrain is ideal for bicycle trips and hikes. The state capitol is Salem, and Oregon State University is in Corvallis.

4 South Willamette Valley. Here visitors soak in natural hot springs, hike in dense forest, run the rapids. Eugene, home to the University of Oregon, has a friendly, youthful vibe, which is enhanced by the natural splendor of the region.

GETTING ORIENTED

The Willamette Valley is a fertile mix of urban, rural, and wild stretching from Portland at the north to Cottage Grove at the south. It is bordered by the Cascade Range to the east and the Coast Range to the west. The Calapooya Mountains border it to the south and the mighty Columbia River runs along the north. Running north and south, Interstate 5 connects communities throughout the valley. In the mid-1800s the Willamette Valley was the destination of emigrants on the Oregon Trail, and today is home to about two-thirds of the state's population. The Willamette Valley is 150 miles long and up to 60 miles wide, which makes it Oregon's largest wine-growing region.

4

Updated
by Dave
Sandage

The Willamette (pronounced "wil-*lam*-it") Valley has become a wine lover's Shangri-La, particularly in the northern Yamhill and Washington counties between Interstate 5 and the Oregon Coast, a region that is not only carpeted with vineyards but encompasses small hotels and inns, cozy restaurants, and casual wine bars.

The valley divides two mountain ranges (the Cascade and Coast), and contains more than 200 wineries. The huge wine region is made up of six sub-appellations: Chehalem Mountains, Ribbon Ridge, Dundee Hills, Yamhill-Carlton, Eola-Amity Hills, and McMinnville. With its incredibly rich soil perfect for growing Pinot Noir, Pinot Gris, Chardonnay, and Riesling, the valley has received worldwide acclaim for its vintages. The region's farms are famous for producing quality fruits, vegetables, and cheeses that are savored in area restaurants. During spring and summer there are many roadside stands dotting the country lanes, and farmers' markets appear in most of the valley's towns. Also delicious are the locally raised lamb, pork, chicken, and beef. The valley also is a huge exporter of plants and flowers for nurseries, with a large number of farms growing ornamental trees, bulbs, and plants.

The valley definitely has an artsy, expressive, and fun side, with its wine and beer festivals, theater, music, crafts, and even ballooning. Many residents and visitors are serious runners and bicyclists, particularly in Corvallis and Eugene, so pay attention while driving.

The entire state is riveted by the collegiate rivalry between the Willamette Valley–based Oregon State Beavers in Corvallis and University of Oregon Ducks in Eugene. In these towns businesses think nothing of closing for the home football games, and getting a ticket to the "Civil War" game between the two is a feat in itself.

THE WILLAMETTE VALLEY AND WINE COUNTRY PLANNER

WHEN TO GO

July to October are the best times to wander the country roads in the Willamette Valley, exploring the grounds of its many wineries. Fall is spectacular, with leaves at their colorful peak in late October. Winters are usually mild, but they can be relentlessly overcast and downright rainy. Visitors not disturbed by dampness or chill will find excellent deals on lodging. In the spring rains continue, but the wildflowers begin to bloom, which pays off at the many gardens and nature parks throughout the valley.

FESTIVALS

International Pinot Noir Celebration. During the International Pinot Noir Celebration in late July and early August, wine lovers flock to McMinnville to sample fine regional vintages along with Pinot Noir from around the world. ⊠ *P.O. Box 1310800, McMinnville* ☎ *800/775–4762* ⊕ *www.ipnc.org.*

Oregon Bach Festival. Eugene hosts the world-class Oregon Bach Festival, with 18 summer days of classical music performances. ⊠ *1257 University of Oregon, Eugene* ☎ *541/346–5666, 800/457–1486* ⊕ *oregonbachfestival.com.*

Oregon State Fair. In late August and early September the Oregon State Fair in Salem has 8,000 things to do, see, and taste, ranging from carnival rides, top-name concert performances, animals, carnival-style games, and bodacious rides. ⊠ *2330 17th St. NE, Salem* ☎ *503/947–3247* ⊕ *oregonstatefair.org.*

Tigard Festival of Balloons. Look high in the sky for evidence of the colorful Tigard Festival of Balloons in June—hot-air balloons soar above the town throughout the weekend, launching from Cook Park. ⊠ *19600 S.W. Cipole Rd., Tualatin* ☎ *503/612–8213* ⊕ *www.tigardballoon.org.*

GETTING HERE AND AROUND

AIR TRAVEL

Portland's airport is an hour's drive east of the northern Willamette Valley. The **Aloha Express Airport Shuttle** and the **Beaverton Airporter** provide shuttle service. **Eugene Airport** is more convenient if you're exploring the region's southern end. It's served by Delta, Alaska/Horizon, American, and United/United Express. The flight from Portland to Eugene is 40 minutes. Smaller airports for private aircraft are scattered throughout the valley.

Rental cars are available at the Eugene airport from Budget, Enterprise, and Hertz. Taxis and airport shuttles will transport you to downtown Eugene for about $22. **Omni Shuttle** will provide shuttle service to and from the Eugene airport from anywhere in Oregon.

Air Contacts Aloha Express Airport Shuttle ☎ *503/356–8848* ⊕ *www.alohaexpressshuttle.com.* **Beaverton Airporter** ☎ *503/760–6565, 866/665–6965* ⊕ *www.beavertonairporter.com.* **Omni Shuttle** ☎ *541/461–7959, 800/741–5097* ⊕ *www.omnishuttle.com.*

BUS TRAVEL

Buses operated by Portland's **TriMet** network connect Forest Grove, Hillsboro, Beaverton, Tigard, Lake Oswego, and Oregon City with Portland and each other; light-rail trains operated by MAX run between Portland and Hillsboro. Many of the **Lane Transit District** buses will make a few stops to the outskirts of Lane County, such as McKenzie Bridge. All buses have bike racks. **Yamhill County Transit Area** (*YCTA* ☎ *503/472–0457* ⊕ *www.yctransitarea.org*) provides bus service for Yamhill County, with links to Hillsboro/MAX, Sherwood/TriMet, and Salem/SAMT.

Bus Contacts Lane Transit District (*LTD*). ☎ *541/682–6100* ⊕ *www.ltd.org*.

CAR TRAVEL

Interstate 5 runs north–south the length of the Willamette Valley. Many Willamette Valley attractions lie not too far east or west of Interstate 5. Highway 22 travels west from the Willamette National Forest through Salem to the coast. Highway 99 travels parallel to Interstate 5 through much of the Willamette Valley. Highway 34 leaves Interstate 5 just south of Albany and heads west, past Corvallis and into the Coast Range, where it follows the Alsea River. Highway 126 heads east from Eugene toward the Willamette National Forest; it travels west from town to the coast. U.S. 20 travels west from Corvallis. Rental cars are available from Budget (Beaverton), Enterprise, and Hertz (both Beaverton, Salem).

RESTAURANTS

The buzzwords associated with fine dining in this region are "sustainable," "farm-to-table," and "local." Fresh salmon, Dungeness crab, mussels, shrimp, and oysters are harvested just a couple of hours away on the Oregon Coast. Lamb, pork, and beef are local and plentiful, and seasonal game appears on many menus. Desserts made with local blueberries, huckleberries, raspberries, and marionberries should not be missed. But what really sets the offerings apart are the splendid local wines that receive worldwide acclaim.

Restaurants in the Willamette Valley are low-key and unpretentious. Expensive doesn't necessarily mean better, and locals have a pretty good nose for good value. Reasonably priced Mexican, Indian, Japanese, and Italian do very well. Food carts in the cities are a growing phenomenon. But there's still nothing like a great, sit-down meal at a cozy bistro for some fresh fish or lamb, washed down with a stellar Pinot Noir.

HOTELS

One of the great pleasures of touring the Willamette Valley is the incredible selection of small, ornate bed-and-breakfast hotels sprinkled throughout Oregon's wine country. In the summer and fall they can fill up quickly, as visitors come from around the world to enjoy wine tastings at the hundreds of large and small wineries. Many of these have exquisite restaurants right on the premises, with home-baked goods available day and night. There are plenty of larger properties located closer to urban areas and shopping centers, including upscale resorts with expansive spas, as well as national chains that are perfect for travelers who just need a place to lay their heads. *Hotel reviews have been shortened. For full information, visit Fodors.com.*

WHAT IT COSTS IN U.S. DOLLARS			
$	$$	$$$	$$$$
Restaurants	Under $17	$17–$24	$25–$30	Over $30
Hotels	Under $150	$150–$200	$201–$250	Over $250

Restaurant prices are the average cost of a main course at dinner or, if dinner is not served, at lunch. Hotel prices are the lowest cost of a standard double room in high season.

TOURS

Oregon Wine Tours and **EcoTours of Oregon** provide informative guided outings across the Willamette Valley wine country.

Contacts **EcoTours of Oregon** ✉ *503/475–0226, 888/868–7733* ⊕ *www. ecotours-of-oregon.com.* **Oregon Wine Tours** ✉ *503/681–9463* ⊕ *www. orwinetours.com.*

VISITOR INFORMATION

Contacts **Chehalem Valley Chamber of Commerce** ✉ *115 N. College St., Newberg* ✉ *503/538–2014* ⊕ *www.chehalemvalley.org.* **Oregon Wine Country/ Willamette Valley Visitors Association** ✉ *866/548–5018* ⊕ *www.oregonwinecountry.org.* **Travel Lane County** ✉ *754 Olive St., Eugene* ✉ *541/484–5307, 800/547–5445* ⊕ *www.eugenecascadescoast.org.* **Washington County Visitors Association** ✉ *12725 S.W. Millikan Way, Suite 210, Beaverton* ✉ *503/644–5555, 800/537–3149* ⊕ *www.oregonswashingtoncounty. com.*

NORTH WILLAMETTE VALLEY

Just outside Portland the suburban areas of Tigard, Hillsboro, and Forest Grove have gorgeous wineries, wetlands, rivers, and nature preserves. The area has a wealth of golfing, biking, and trails for running and hiking, and, appropriately, is home to the headquarters of Nike. From wetlands to residential neighborhoods, it's not unusual to spot red-tail hawks, beavers, and ducks on your route. Shopping, fine dining, and proximity to Portland make this a great area in which to begin your exploration of the Willamette Valley and the wine country.

EN ROUTE

Vineyard and Valley Scenic Tour. A 60-mile driving route through the lush Tualatin Valley runs between the city of Sherwood in the southern part of the valley and Helvetia at the northern end. The rural drive showcases much of Washington County's agricultural bounty, including many of the county's wineries and farms (some with stands offering seasonal fresh produce and/or U-pick), along with pioneer and historic sites, wildlife refuges, and scenic viewpoints of the Cascade Mountains. For more information, contact the **Washington County Visitors Association** (⊕ *www.oregonswashingtoncounty. com*). ⊕ *www.oregonswashingtoncounty.com/Discover-Wine-Country/ Scenic-Tour-Route.*

North Willamette Valley and Yamhill County

HILLSBORO

20 miles southwest of Portland.

Hillsboro offers a wealth of eclectic shops, preserves, restaurants, and proximity to the valley's fine wineries. In the past 20 years Hillsboro has experienced rapid growth associated with the Silicon Forest, where high-tech business found ample sprawling room. Several of Intel's industrial campuses are in Hillsboro, as are the facilities of other leading electronics manufacturers. Businesses related to the town's original agricultural roots remain a significant part of Hillsboro's culture and economy. Alpaca ranches, nurseries, berry farms, nut and fruit orchards, and numerous wineries are among the area's most active agricultural businesses.

GETTING HERE AND AROUND

Hillsboro is about a 45-minute drive west from Portland International Airport. The **Aloha Express Airport Shuttle** (☎ *503/356–8848* ⊕ *www. alohaexpressshuttle.com*) and the **Beaverton Airporter** (☎ *503/760–6565* ⊕ *www.beavertonairporter.com*) provide shuttle service.

From Downtown Portland it's a short 20-minute car ride, or visitors can ride the MAX light rail. The TriMet Bus Service connects to the MAX light rail in Hillsboro, with connections to Beaverton, Aloha, and other commercial areas.

EXPLORING

Hillsboro Saturday Market. Fresh local produce—some from booths, some from the backs of trucks—as well as local arts and crafts are on sale Saturdays from May through October. Live music is played throughout the day. The market is just a block from the light-rail line. ⊠ *Main St. between 1st and 3rd Aves.* ☎ *503/844–6685* ⊕ *www.hillsboromarkets. org.*

Fodor's Choice ★ **Ponzi Vineyards.** One of the founding families of Willamette Valley wine, Dick and Nancy Ponzi planted their original estate vineyard in 1970. While you can still visit the historic estate that looks out over these old vines, your best bet is to drop in at their new visitors facility at the winery just 12 miles south of Hillsboro. Here you'll find red and white flights of the current releases, as well as the occasional older vintage from the library. Enjoy tableside wine service indoors around the fireplace, or out on the covered terrace. Antipasti plates are a nice accompaniment to the wine. Pictures on the walls and displays provide a wonderful visual history of this winery that is still family owned and operated. The Ponzi family also launched the BridgePort Brewing Company in 1984, and runs a wine bar and restaurant in Dundee (⇨ *Dundee Bistro in Dundee*). ⊠ *19500 S.W. Mountain Home Rd., Sherwood* ☎ *503/628–1227* ⊕ *www.ponziwines.com* ☉ *Daily 11-5:30.*

FAMILY **Rice Northwest Museum of Rocks and Minerals.** Richard and Helen Rice began collecting beach agates in 1938, and over the years they developed one of the largest private mineral collections in the United States. The most popular item here is the Alma Rose rhodochrosite, a 4-inch red crystal. The museum (in a ranch-style home) also displays petrified wood from all over the world and a gallery of Northwest minerals—including specimens of rare crystallized gold. Tours are offered Saturdays at 2 pm. ✉ *26385 N.W. Groveland Dr.* ☎ *503/647–2418* ⊕ *www.ricenorthwestmuseum.org* 🖾 *$8* ⊗ *Wed.–Sun. 1–5.*

Washington County Museum and Historical Society. This impressive space on the second floor of the Hillsboro Civic Center houses a range of exhibits focusing on the history and culture of the area. Most of the exhibits include activities for children. ✉ *120 E. Main St.* ☎ *503/645–5353* ⊕ *www.washingtoncountymuseum.org* 🖾 *$6* ⊗ *Wed.–Sat. 10–5.*

WHERE TO EAT

$ | ✕**Mazatlan Mexican Restaurant.** Though this popular spot is hidden away
MEXICAN | in a small shopping mall, once you're inside and surrounded by stunning murals and ceramica you'll feel like you're in a charming village. Try the Mazatlan Dinner, a house specialty with sirloin, a chile relleno, and an enchilada, or *arroz con camarones*, prawns sautéed with vegetables. Save room for the flan or the *sopapillas* (fried dough). The kids' menu is a good value. ⑤ *Average main: $13* ✉ *20413 S.W. TV Hwy., Aloha* ☎ *503/591–9536* ⊕ *www.mazatlanmexicanrestaurant.com.*

$ | ✕**Syun Izakaya.** A large assortment of sushi and sashimi, soups, and
JAPANESE | salads are served in quiet surroundings in the basement of the old Hillsboro Library. Wonderful grilled and fried meats and vegetables are also available, accompanied by a vast sake selection. Be sure to look for the daily specials for superfresh and sometimes unusual selections. A nice assortment of small plates is served during happy hour, between 5 and 6 pm and from 9 to close. ⑤ *Average main: $13* ✉ *209 N.E. Lincoln St.* ☎ *503/640–3131* ⊕ *www.syun-izakaya.com* ⊗ *No lunch Sun.*

SPORTS AND THE OUTDOORS

The Tualatin, a slow, meandering river, flows into Hillsboro and along its length offers fantastic opportunities for paddlers who are new to the sport, as well those who are experienced.

RECREATIONAL AREAS

Cook Park. On the banks of the Tualatin River in Tigard, east of Hillsboro, this 79-acre park is where local suburbanites gather to enjoy a variety of outdoor activities, and plays host to the annual Festival of Balloons in June. The park has horseshoe pits, a fishing dock, small boat ramp, picnic shelters, and several walking trails and bike paths. Wildlife includes great blue herons and river otters. ✉ *17005 S.W. 92nd Ave., Tigard* ☎ *503/718–2641* ⊕ *www.tigard-or.gov.*

Jackson Bottom Wetlands Preserve. Several miles of trails in this 710-acre floodplain and woods are home to thousands of ducks and geese, deer, otters, beavers, herons, and eagles. Walking trails allow birders and other animal watchers to explore the wetlands for a chance to catch a glimpse of indigenous and migrating creatures in their own habitats. The **Education Center** has several hands-on exhibits, as well as a real bald eagle's nest that was rescued from the wild, and completely preserved (and sanitized) for public display. No dogs or bicycles are allowed. ✉ *2600 S.W. Hillsboro Hwy.* ☎ *503/681–6206* ⊕ *www. jacksonbottom.org* 🖾 *$2 suggested donation* ⊗ *Trails daily dawn–dusk, Education Center daily 10–4.*

FAMILY **L.L. "Stub" Stewart State Park.** This 1,654-acre, full-service park has hiking, biking, and horseback riding trails for day use or overnight camping. There are full hookup sites, tent sites, small cabins, and even a horse camp. Lush rolling hills, forests, and deep canyons are terrific for bird-watching, wildflower walks, and other relaxing pursuits. An 18-hole disc golf course winds its way through a dense forest. In case you don't know, in disc golf players throw a disc at a target and attempt to complete the course with the fewest throws. ✉ *30380 N.W. Hwy. 47, Buxton* ☎ *503/324–0606* ⊕ *www.oregonstateparks.org* ✉ *$5 for day use permit.*

Tualatin River Wildlife Refuge. This sanctuary for indigenous and migrating birds, waterfowl, and mammals is in Sherwood (about 18 miles south of Hillsboro). It is one of only a handful of national urban refuges in the United States and has restored much of the natural landscape common to western Oregon prior to human settlement. The refuge is home to nearly 200 species of birds, 50 species of mammals, 25 species of reptiles and amphibians, and a variety of insects, fish, and plants. It features an interpretive center, a gift shop, photography blinds, and restrooms. This restoration has attracted animals back to the area in great numbers, and with a keen eye, birders and animal watchers can catch a glimpse of these creatures year-round. In May the refuge hosts its Migratory Songbird Festival. ✉ *19255 S.W. Pacific Hwy., Tigard* ☎ *503/625–5944* ⊕ *www.fws.gov/tualatinriver* ☉ *Daily dawn–dusk; Wildlife Center, Tues.–Sun. 10–4.*

FOREST GROVE

24 miles west of Portland on Hwy. 8.

This small town is surrounded by stands of Douglas firs and giant sequoia, including the largest giant sequoia in the state. There are nearby wetlands, birding, the Hagg Lake Recreation Area, a new outdoor adventure park, and numerous wineries and tasting rooms. To get to many of the wineries, head south from Forest Grove on Highway 47 and watch for the blue road signs between Forest Grove, Gaston, and Yamhill. To the west of town, you'll find some of the oldest Pinot Noir vines in the valley at David Hill Winery.

GETTING HERE AND AROUND

Forest Grove is about an hour's drive west from Portland International Airport. The **Aloha Express Airport Shuttle** (☎ *503/356–8848* ⊕ *www. alohaexpressshuttle.com*) and the **Beaverton Airporter** (☎ *503/760–6565* ⊕ *www.beavertonairporter.com*) provide shuttle service.

From Downtown Portland it's a short 35-minute car ride with only a few traffic lights during the entire trip. TriMet Bus Service provides bus service to and from Forest Grove every 15 minutes, connecting to the MAX light rail 6 miles east in Hillsboro, which continues into Portland. Buses travel to Cornelius, Hillsboro, Aloha, and Beaverton.

ESSENTIALS

Forest Grove Chamber of Commerce ✉ *2417 Pacific Ave.* ☎ *503/357–3006* ⊕ *www.visitforestgrove.com.*

David Hill Vineyards and Winery, Forest Grove

EXPLORING

David Hill Vineyards and Winery. In 1965 Charles Coury came to Oregon from California and planted some of the Willamette Valley's first Pinot Noir vines on the site of what is now the David Hill Winery. The original farmhouse serves as the tasting room and offers splendid views of the Tualatin Valley. They produce Pinot Noir, some of which comes from the original vines planted by Coury, along with Chardonnay, Gewürztraminer, Merlot, Tempranillo, Pinot Gris, and Riesling. The wines are well made and pleasant, especially the eclectic blend called Farmhouse Red and the estate Riesling. ✉ *46350 N.W. David Hill Rd.* ☎ *503/992–8545* ⊕ *www.davidhillwinery.com* ⊙ *Daily 11–5.*

Elk Cove Vineyard. Founded in 1974 by Pat and Joe Campbell, this well-established winery covers 600 acres on four separate vineyard sites. The tasting room is set in the beautiful rolling hills at the foot of the Coast Range overlooking the vines. The focus is on Willamette Valley Pinot Noir, Pinot Gris, and Pinot Blanc. Be sure to also try the limited bottling of their Pinot Noir Rosé if they're pouring it. ✉ *27751 N.W. Olson Rd., Gaston* ☎ *503/985–7760, 877/355–2683* ⊕ *www.elkcove. com* 🍷 *$10* ⊙ *Daily 10–5.*

Montinore Estate. Locals chuckle at visitors who try to show off their French savvy when they pronounce it "Mont-in-or-ay." The estate, originally a ranch, was established by a tycoon who'd made his money in the Montana mines before he retired to Oregon; he decided to call his estate "Montana in Oregon." Montinore (no "ay" at the end) has 232 acres of vineyards, and its wines reflect the high-quality soil and fruit. Highlights include a crisp Gewürztraminer, a light Müller-Thurgau, an off-dry Riesling, several lush Pinot Noirs, and a delightful white blend called Borealis that's a perfect partner for Northwest seafood. The tasting-room staff is among the friendliest and most knowledgeable in Oregon wine country. ✉ *3663 S.W. Dilley Rd.* ☎ *503/359–5012, 888/359–5012* ⊕ *www.montinore.com* ⊗ *Daily 11–5.*

Pacific University. Founded in 1849, this is one of the oldest educational institutions in the western United States. Concerts and special events are held on the shady campus in the Taylor-Meade Performing Arts Center. ✉ *2043 College Way* ☎ *503/352–6151, 877/722–8648* ⊕ *www. pacificu.edu.*

SakéOne. After the founders realized that the country's best water supply for sake was in the Pacific Northwest, they built their brewery in Forest Grove in 1997. It's one of only six sake brewing facilities in America and produces award-winning sake under three labels, in addition to importing from partners in Japan. The tasting room offers three different flights, including one with a food pairing. Be sure to catch one of the tours, offered daily, where your guide will walk you through every phase of the sake-making process, from milling the rice to final filtration and bottling. ✉ *820 Elm St.* ☎ *503/357–7056, 800/550–7253* ⊕ *www. sakeone.com* ✇ *Free* ⊗ *Daily 11–5.*

WHERE TO STAY

$ 🖼 **McMenamins Grand Lodge.** On 13 acres of pastoral countryside, this
HOTEL converted Masonic rest home has accommodations that run from bunk-bed rooms to a three-room fireplace suite, with some nice period antiques in all. **Pros:** relaxed, friendly brewpub atmosphere. **Cons:** not as refined as some tourists would like; most rooms have shared bathrooms. ⑤ *Rooms from: $60* ✉ *3505 Pacific Ave.* ☎ *503/992–9533, 877/992–9533* ⊕ *www.mcmenamins.com/grandlodge* ➷ *77 rooms* ⑪ *No meals.*

SPORTS AND THE OUTDOORS

RECREATIONAL AREAS

Scoggin Valley Park and Henry Hagg Lake. This beautiful area in the Coast Range foothills has a 15-mile-long hiking trail that surrounds the lake. Bird-watching is best in spring. Recreational activities include fishing, boating, waterskiing, picnicking, and hiking, and a 10½-mile, well-marked bicycle lane parallels the park's perimeter road. ✉ *50250 S.W. Scoggins Valley Rd., Gaston* ☎ *503/846–8715* ⊕ *www.co.washington. or.us/hagglake* ✇ *$6* ⊗ *Mar.–Nov., daily sunrise–sunset.*

Tree to Tree Adventure Park. At the first public aerial adventure park in the Pacific Northwest—and only the second of its kind in the United States—the aerial adventure course features 19 zip lines and more than 60 treetop elements and obstacles. You can experience the thrills of moving from platform to platform (tree to tree) via wobbly bridges, tight ropes, Tarzan swings, and more. The courses range from beginner to extreme, with certified and trained instructors providing guidance to adventurers. "Woody's Ziptastic Voyage" zip-line tour features six extreme zip lines (including one that is 1,280 feet long), a bridge, and a 40-foot rappell. Harnesses and helmets are provided, and no open-toed shoes are allowed. Reservations are required. ✉ *2975 S.W. Nelson*

Rd., Gaston ☎ 503/357–0109 ⊕ tree2treeadventurepark.com ✈ Aerial park $48, zip tour $75 ⊙ Mar.–mid Nov., daily 9–3 hrs before sunset.

YAMHILL COUNTY

Yamhill County, at the northern end of the Willamette Valley, has a fortunate confluence of perfect soils, a benign climate, and talented winemakers who craft world-class vintages. In recent years several new wineries have been built in Yamhill County's hills, as well as on its flatlands. While vineyards flourished in the northern Willamette Valley in the 19th century, viticulture didn't arrive in Yamhill County until the 1960s and 1970s, with such pioneers as Dick Erath (Erath Vineyards Winery), David and Ginny Adelsheim (Adelsheim Vineyard), and David and Diana Lett (The Eyrie Vineyards). The focus of much of the county's enthusiasm lies in the Red Hills of Dundee, where the farming towns of Newberg, Dundee, Yamhill, and Carlton have made room for upscale bed-and-breakfasts, spas, wine bars, and tourists seeking that perfect swirl and sip.

The Yamhill County wineries are only a short drive from Portland, and the roads, especially Route 99W and Route 18, can be crowded on weekends—that's because these roads link suburban Portland communities to the popular Oregon Coast.

NEWBERG

24 miles south of Portland on Hwy. 99W.

Newberg sits in the Chehalem Valley, known as one of Oregon's most fertile wine-growing locations, and is called the Gateway to Oregon Wine Country. Many of Newberg's early settlers were Quakers from the Midwest, who founded the school that has become George Fox University. Newberg's most famous resident, likewise a Quaker, was Herbert Hoover, the 31st president of the United States. For about five years during his adolescence, he lived with an aunt and uncle at the Hoover-Minthorn House, now a museum listed on the National Register of Historic Places. Now the town is on the map for the nearby wineries, fine-dining establishments, and a spacious, spectacular resort, the Allison. St. Paul, a historic town with a population of about 325, is about 8 miles south of Newberg, and every July holds a professional rodeo.

GETTING HERE AND AROUND

Newberg is just under an hour's drive from Portland International Airport; **Caravan Airport Transportation** (☎ 541/994–9645 ⊕ www.caravanairporttransportation.com) provides shuttle service. The best way to visit Newberg and the Yamhill County vineyards is by car. Situated on Highway 99W, Newberg is 90 minutes from Lincoln City, on the Oregon Coast. Greyhound provides bus service to McMinnville.

EXPLORING
TOP ATTRACTIONS

Fodor's Choice ★ **Adelsheim Vineyard.** David Adelsheim is the knight in shining armor of the Oregon wine industry—tirelessly promoting Oregon wines abroad, and always willing to share the knowledge he has gained from his long viticultural experience. He and Ginny Adelsheim founded their pioneer winery in 1971. They make their wines from grapes picked on their 230 acres of estate vineyards, as well as from grapes they've purchased. Their Pinot Noir, Pinot Gris, Pinot Blanc, and Chardonnay all conform to the Adelsheim house style of rich, balanced fruit and long, clean finishes. They also make a spicy cool-climate Syrah from grapes grown just outside the beautiful tasting room. Tours are available by appointment. ⊠ *16800 N.E. Calkins La.* ☎ *503/538–3652* ⊕ *www.adelsheim. com* ☜ *$15* ☉ *Daily 11-4.*

Bergstrom Winery. Focusing on classic Oregon Pinot Noir and Chardonnay, this family-owned winery produces elegant and refined wines that represent some of the best the Willamette Valley has to offer. The tasting room is surrounded by the Silice vineyard, and offers beautiful views of several neighboring vineyards as well. French-trained winemaker Josh Bergstrom sources fruit from his estate vineyards and from several other local sites to produce a wide range of single-vineyard Pinots. Enjoy your tasting on the deck on a warm summer day. ⊠ *18215 N.E. Calkins La.* ☎ *503/554–0468* ⊕ *www.bergstromwines.com* ☜ *$20* ☉ *Daily 10–4.*

Penner-Ash Wine Cellars. Lynn Penner-Ash brings years of experience working in Napa and as Rex Hill's winemaker to the winery that she and her husband Ron started in 1998. Although focused primarily on silky Pinot Noir, Penner-Ash also produces very good Syrah, Viognier, and Riesling. From its hilltop perch in the middle of the Dussin vineyard, this state-of-the-art gravity-flow winery and tasting room offers commanding views of the valley below. ⊠ *15771 N.E. Ribbon Ridge Rd.* ☎ *503/554–5545* ⊕ *www.pennerash.com* ☉ *Daily 11–5.*

Rex Hill Vineyards. A few hundred feet off the busy highway, surrounded by conifers and overlooked by vineyards, Rex Hill seems to exist in a world of its own. The winery opened in 1982, after owners Paul Hart and Jan Jacobsen converted a former nut-drying facility. It produces first-class Pinot Noir, Pinot Gris, Chardonnay, Sauvignon Blanc, and Riesling from both estate-grown and purchased grapes. The tasting room has a massive fireplace, elegant antiques, and an absorbing collection of modern art. Another highlight is the beautifully landscaped garden, perfect for picnicking. ⊠ *30835 N. Hwy. 99W* ☎ *503/538–0666, 800/739–4455* ⊕ *www.rexhill.com* ☜ *$10* ☉ *Daily 10–5.*

WORTH NOTING

Aramenta Cellars. Owners Ed and Darlene Looney have been farming this land for more than 40 years. In 2000, they planted grape vines after keeping cattle on the property. The winery and tasting room are built on the foundation of the old barn, and Ed makes the wine while Darlene runs the tasting room. Of the 27 acres planted in vines, 20 acres are leased to Archrey Summit for their Looney Vineyard Pinot Noir, and the Looneys farm 7 acres for their own wines which have very limited distribution. If you're looking for a break from all the Pinot Noir, try the Tillie Claret—a smooth Bordeaux blend made with grapes from eastern Washington and southern Oregon. Aramenta offers a great opportunity to interact with farmers who have worked the land for several generations and to taste some great small production wine. ☒ *17979 N.E. Lewis Rogers La.* ☎ *503/538–7230* ⊕ *www.aramentacellars.com* ⊙ *Daily 10–4.*

Champoeg State Heritage Area. Pronounced "sham-*poo*-ee," this 615-acre state park on the south bank of the Willamette River is on the site of a Hudson's Bay Company trading post, granary, and warehouse that was built in 1813. This was the seat of the first provisional government in the Northwest. The settlement was abandoned after a catastrophic flood in 1861, then rebuilt and abandoned again after the flood of 1890. The park's wide-open spaces, groves of oak and fir, modern visitor center, museum, and historic buildings provide vivid insight into pioneer life. Tepees and wagons are displayed here, and there are 10 miles of hiking and cycle trails. ☒ *8239 Champoeg Rd. NE, St. Paul* ☎ *503/678–1251* ⊕ *www.oregonstateparks.org* ☒ *$5 per vehicle*

Fox Farm Vineyards. Conveniently located in downtown Newberg, this tasting room is a fun and easy stop if you're interested in trying fine wines from small producers that you won't likely find anywhere else. Winemaker Joe Dobbes produces small lots of Pinot Noir, Pinot Gris, Pinot Blanc, and Syrah. In addition to showcasing Fox Farm's own small-production wines, the tasting room will often pour an extra wine from one of several other boutique wineries in the area. Check the website for a schedule of live music and movie nights at the tasting room. ☒ *606 E. 1st St.* ☎ *503/538–8466* ⊕ *www.foxfarmvineyards. com* ⊙ *Daily noon–8.*

Hoover-Minthorn House Museum. In 1885 Dr. Henry Minthorn invited his orphan nephew Herbert "Bertie" Hoover to come west and join the Minthorn family in Newberg. Built in 1881, the restored frame house, the oldest and most significant of Newberg's original structures, still has many of its original furnishings, including the president's boyhood bed and dresser. Hoover maintained his connection to Newberg, and visited several times after his presidency. ☒ *115 S. River St.* ☎ *503/538–6629* ⊕ *www.thehoover-minthornhousemuseum.org* ☒ *$3* ⊙ *Mar.–Nov., Wed.–Sun. 1–4; Dec. and Feb., weekends 1–4.*

Raptor Ridge Winery. The huge windows in the new tasting room look out over the vines of their estate vineyard on the northeast slope of the Chehalem Mountains. If you keep a sharp eye, you may even catch a glimpse of the many raptors (red-tail hawks, sharp-shinned hawks, and kestrels) that give this small winery its name. Raptor Ridge specializes in single-vineyard Pinot Noirs that capture the sense of place of their estate vineyard as well as several other vineyards throughout the Willamette Valley. They also produce Chardonnay, Pinot Gris, and a very nice Tempranillo. During the summer, enjoy your tasting at a table on the outside deck that overlooks the vineyards. Tours of the winemaking facility are available by appointment. ☒ *18700 S.W. Hillsboro Hwy* ☎ *503/628–8463* ⊕ *www.raptoridge.com* ⊙ *Mid-Jan.–mid May* *and mid-Oct.–mid-Dec., Thurs.–Mon. 11–4; mid-May–mid-Oct., daily 11–4; mid-Dec.–mid-Jan., by appointment.*

Utopia Vineyard. Take a trip back in time to when the Oregon wine industry was much smaller and more intimate. Utopia owner and wine-maker Daniel Warnhius moved north from California looking for a vineyard site that would produce world-class Pinot Noir, and he found this location with the right combination of location, climate, and soil structure. In the tasting room, you're likely to be served by Daniel himself. In addition to several great Pinot Noirs, they also produce a bright, crisp Chardonnay, and a Pinot Noir Rosé. ⊠ *17445 N.E. Ribbon Ridge Rd.* ☎ *503/687–1671* ⊕ *utopiawine.com* ✉ *$10* ⊗ *May–Nov,. daily 11–6; Dec. –Apr., Sat. & Sun. 11-6.*

Vercingetorix. This small winery south of Newberg, which produces only Pinot Gris, Pinot Blanc, and Pinot Noir, is part of Willamette Farms, a grower of hazelnuts, trees, and wine grapes. The crisp, fruity Pinot Gris is especially worth seeking out. The winery has a half mile of Willamette River frontage, so you can claim a picnic table and keep your eyes peeled for wildlife (beavers, deer, ducks, geese, and raptors). ⊠ *8000 N.E. Parrish Rd.* ☎ *503/537–0799* ⊕ *www.vxvineyardwine. com* ⊗ *May–Nov., weekends 11–5.*

WHERE TO EAT AND STAY

$$$$

MODERN
AMERICAN

✕ **Jory.** This exquisite hotel dining room is named after one of the soils in the Oregon wine country. Chef Sunny Jin sources the majority of his ingredients locally, many from the on-site garden. The menu changes according to season, but always features fresh seafood (usually salmon and halibut), local lamb and pork, and an abundance of local veggies. Ask for a seat at the counter overlooking the open kitchen if you want to see the chefs in action. Naturally, the restaurant has an expansive wine list focused on Oregon wines. $ *Average main: $35* ⊠ *The Allison Inn, 2525 Allison La.* ☎ *503/554–2525, 877/294-2525* ⊕ *www.theallison. com* ⊗ *No lunch Sun.*

$$$$

RESORT

Fodor's Choice
★

⌂ **The Allison Inn & Spa.** At this luxurious, relaxing base for exploring the region's 200 wineries, each bright, comfortable room includes a gas fireplace, original works of art, a soaking tub, impressive furnishings, bay-window seats, and views of the vineyards from the terrace or balcony. **Pros:** outstanding on-site restaurant; excellent gym and spa facilities; located in the middle of wine country. **Cons:** not many nearby off-property activities other than wine tasting. $ *Rooms from: $350* ⊠ *2525 Allison La.* ☎ *503/554–2525, 877/294-2525* ⊕ *www.theallison. com* ⊷ *65 rooms, 20 suites.*

$$$

B&B/INN

⌂ **Le Puy, A Wine Valley Inn.** This beautiful wine country retreat caters to wine enthusiasts with amenities that include wine bars in each individually decorated room, along with hot tubs and gas fireplaces in some. **Pros:** beautiful surroundings; lots of nice architectural and decorative touches. **Cons:** a distance from sights other than wineries. $ *Rooms from: $225* ⊠ *20300 N.E. Hwy. 240* ☎ *503/554–9528* ⊕ *lepuy-inn. com* ⊷ *8 Rooms* ⦿⦿ *Breakfast.*

NIGHTLIFE AND THE ARTS

99W Drive-in. Ted Francis built this drive-in in 1953, and operated it until his death at 98; the business is now run by his grandson. The first film begins at dusk. ⊠ *3110 Portland Rd. (Hwy. 99W)* ☎ *503/538–2738* ⊕ *www.99w.com* ✉ *$8, vehicles with single occupant $12* ⊘ *Fri.–Sun.*

SPORTS AND THE OUTDOORS

BALLOONING

Hot-air balloon rides are nothing less than a spectacular, breathtaking thrill—particularly over Oregon's beautiful Yamhill County.

Vista Balloon Adventures. Enjoy floating gently above beautiful Oregon wine country as the sun rises behind the vines. Your FAA-licensed pilot will take the balloon up about 1,500 feet and can often steer the craft down to skim the water, then up to view hawk's nests. A brunch is served upon returning to the ground. ⊠ *1055 Commerce Pkwy.* ☎ *503/625–7385, 800/622–2309* ⊕ *www.vistaballoon.com* ✉ *$199 per person* ⊘ *Apr.–Sept., Fri.–Mon.*

DUNDEE

3 miles southwest of Newberg on Hwy. 99W.

Dundee used to be known for growing the lion's share (more than 90%) of the U.S. hazelnut crop. Today, some of Oregon's top-rated wineries are just outside Dundee, and the area is now best known for wine tourism and wine bars, bed-and-breakfast inns, and restaurants.

GETTING HERE AND AROUND

Dundee is just under an hour's drive from Portland International Airport; **Caravan Airport Transportation** (☎ *541/994–9645* ⊕ *www. caravanairporttransportation.com*) provides shuttle service.

What used to be a pleasant drive through quaint Dundee on Highway 99W now can be a traffic hassle, as it serves as the main artery from Lincoln City on the Oregon Coast to suburban Portland. Others will enjoy wandering along the 25 miles of Highway 18 between Dundee and Grande Ronde, in the Coast Range, which goes through the heart of the Yamhill Valley wine country.

EXPLORING

TOP ATTRACTIONS

Fodor's Choice ★ **Archery Summit Winery.** The winery that Gary and Nancy Andrus, owners of Pine Ridge winery in Napa Valley, founded in the 1990s has become synonomous with premium Oregon Pinot Noir. Because they believed that great wines are made in the vineyard, they adopted such innovative techniques as narrow spacing and vertical trellis systems, which give the fruit a great concentration of flavors. In addition to the standard flight of Pinot Noirs in the tasting room, you can call ahead and reserve a private seated tasting or a tasting paired with small bites or a tour of the winery and, weather permitting, a walk out to the vineyard. You're welcome to bring a picnic, and as at many Oregon wineries, you can bring your dog, too. ⊠ *18599 N.E. Archery Summit Rd., Dayton* ☎ *503/864–4300* ⊕ *www.archerysummit.com* ⊘ *Daily 10–4.*

Argyle Winery. A beautiful establishment, Argyle has its tasting room in a Victorian farmhouse set amid gorgeous gardens. The winery is tucked into a former hazelnut processing plant—which explains the Nuthouse label on its reserve wines. Since Argyle opened in 1987, it has consistently produced sparkling wines that are crisp on the palate, with an aromatic, lingering finish and bubbles that seem to last forever. And these sparklers cost about a third of their counterparts from California. The winery also produces Chardonnay, dry Riesling, Pinot Gris, and Pinot Noir. ⊠ *691 Hwy. 99 W* ☎ *503/538–8520, 888/427–4953* ⊕ *www. argylewinery.com* ⊙ *Daily 11–5.*

Fodor's Choice
★ **Domaine Drouhin Oregon.** When the French winery magnate Robert Drouhin ("the Sebastiani of France") planted a vineyard and built a winery in the Red Hills of Dundee back in 1987, he set local oenophiles abuzz. His daughter Veronique is now the winemaker and produces silky and elegant Pinot Noir and Chardonnay. Ninety acres of the 225-acre estate have been planted on a hillside to take advantage of the natural coolness of the earth and to establish a gravity-flow winery. No appointment is needed to taste the Oregon wines, but if you can plan ahead for the tour (reservations required), you can taste Oregon and Burgundy side-by-side. ⊠ *6750 N.E. Breyman Orchards Rd., Dayton* ☎ *503/864–2700* ⊕ *www.domainedrouhin.com* ⊙ *June–Sept.: daily 11–4; Oct.–May: Wed.–Sun. 11–4. Tours by appointment only.*

Winderlea. The tasting room looks over the acclaimed former Goldschmidt vineyard, first planted in 1974, and the view can be enjoyed on the outside deck on a warm summer day. Winemaker Robert Brittan crafts lush Pinot Noir and Chardonnay from several nearby vineyards in both single-vineyard offerings and blends from multiple vineyards. Proceeds from the tasting fee are donated to Salud, a partnership between Oregon winemakers and local medical professionals to provide healthcare services for Oregon's seasonal vineyard workers and their families. ⊠ *8905 N.E. Worden Hill Rd.* ☎ *503/554–5900* ⊕ *www.winderlea.com* ⊙ *Daily 11–4.*

WORTH NOTING

Dobbes Family Estate. Joe Dobbes makes a lot of wine, but he's definitly not a bulk winemaker. He provides custom wine-making services to many Oregon wineries that are too small to have their own winery or winemaker. But he also makes several lines of his own wine, ranging from his everyday "Wine By Joe" label to the premium Dobbes Family Estate label featuring great Pinot Noir, Syrah, Sauvignon Blanc, Viognier, and Grenache Blanc. In addition to a few single vineyard Pinot Noir bottlings, Dobbes focuses on blends from multiple vineyards to provide consistent, balanced, and interesting wines. Two different tasting fights are available in the tasting room, and seated tastings and tours can be arranged by appointment. ⊠ *240 S.E. 5th St.* ☎ *503/538–1141* ⊕ *www.joedobbeswines.com* ⊙ *Daily 11–6.*

Domaine Serene. This world-class winery in Dundee's Red Hills is a well-regarded producer of Oregon Pinot Noir and Chardonnay. Bring a picnic and enjoy the beautiful grounds of the estate. As an alternative to the standard drop-in tasting in the high-ceiling tasting room, call ahead

Continued on page 208

OREGON'S WINES: THEN AND NOW

Rex Hill Vineyards

THE EARLY YEARS

The French made wine first—French Canadians, that is. In the 1830s, retired fur trappers from the Hudson's Bay Company started to colonize the Willamette Valley and planted grapes on the south-facing buttes. They were followed by American settlers who made wine.

Although wine-making in the region-languished after these early efforts, it never quite vanished. A few wineries hung on, producing wines mainly for Oregonians of European descent.

It wasn't until the 1970s that the state's wine industry finally took off. Only after a group of young California winemakers started making vinifera wines in the Umpqua and Willamette Valleys and gained international acclaim for them, did Oregon's wines really take hold.

WINEMAKING TODAY

Today, Oregon's wine industry is racing ahead. Here the most prolific white and red grapes are Pinot Gris and Pinot Noir, respectively. Other prominent varietals include Riesling, Gewürztraminer, Viognier, Chardonnay, Carbernet Franc, and Syrah.

The wine industry in Oregon is still largely dominated by family and boutique wineries that pay close attention to quality and are often keen to experiment. That makes traveling and tasting at the source an always-interesting experience.

OREGON CERTIFIED SUSTAINABLE WINE

The latest trend in Oregon winemaking is a dedication to responsible grape growing and winemaking. When you see the Oregon Certified Sustainable Wine (OCSW) logo on the back of a wine bottle, it means the winery ensures accountable agricultural and winemaking practices (in conjunction with agencies such as USDA Organic, Demeter Biodynamic, the Food Alliance, Salmon-Safe, and Low Input Viticulture and Enology) through independent third-party certification. For more information on Oregon Certified Sustainable wines and participating wineries, check ⊕ www.ocsw.org.

WINE TASTING PRIMER

Ordering and tasting wine—whether at a winery, bar, or restaurant—is easy once you master a few simple steps.

LOOK AND NOTE

Hold your glass by the stem and look at the wine in the glass. Note its color, depth, and clarity.

For whites, is it greenish, yellow, or gold? For reds, is it purplish, ruby, or garnet? Is the wine's color pale or deep? Is the liquid clear or cloudy?

SWIRL AND SNIFF

Swirl the wine gently in the glass to intensify the scents, then sniff over the rim of the glass. What do you smell? Try to identify aromas like:

- **Fruits**—citrus, peaches, berries, figs, melon
- **Flowers**—orange blossoms, honey, perfume
- **Spices**—baking spices, pungent, herbal notes
- **Vegetables**—fresh or cooked, herbal notes

- **Minerals**—earth, steely notes, wet stones
- **Dairy**—butter, cream, cheese, yogurt
- **Oak**—toast, vanilla, coconut, tobacco
- **Animal**—leathery, meaty notes

Are there any unpleasant notes, like mildew or wet dog, that might indicate that the wine is "off?"

SIP AND SAVOR

Prime your palate with a sip, swishing the wine in your mouth. Then spit in a bucket or swallow.

Take another sip and think about the wine's attributes. Sweetness is detected on the tip of the tongue, acidity on the sides of the tongue, and tannins (a mouth-drying sensation) on the gums. Consider the body—does the wine feel light in the mouth, or is there a rich sensation? Are the flavors consistent with the aromas? If you like the wine, try to pinpoint what you like about it, and vice versa if you don't like it.

Take time to savor the wine as you're sipping it— the tasting experience may seem a bit scientific, but the end goal is your enjoyment.

WINE TOURING AND TASTING

Wine tasting at Argyle and Rex Hill

WHEN TO GO

In high season (June through October) and on weekends and holidays during much of the year, wine-country roads can be busy and tasting rooms are often crowded. If you prefer a more intimate tasting experience, plan your visit for a weekday.

To avoid the frustration of a fruitless drive, confirm in advance that wineries of interest will be open when you plan to visit.

Choose a designated driver for the day: Willamette wine-country roads are often narrow and curvy, and you may be sharing the road with bicyclists and wildlife as well as other wine tourists.

IN THE TASTING ROOM

Tasting rooms are designed to introduce newcomers to the pleasures of wine and to the wines made at the winery. At popular wineries you'll sometimes have to pay for your tasting, anything from a nominal $2 fee to $30 and up for a tasting that might include a glass you can take home. This fee is often deducted if you buy wine before leaving.

WHAT'S AN AVA?

AVAs (American Viticultural Areas) are geographic winegrowing regions that vaguely reflect the French concept of terroir, or "sense of place." The vineyards within a given AVA have similar characteristics such as climate, soil types, and/or elevation, which impart shared characteristics to the wines made from grapes grown in that area. AVAs are strictly geographic boundaries distinct from city or county designations. AVAs can also be subdivided into sub-AVAs; each of the AVAs mentioned here is actually part of the larger Willamette Valley AVA.

Each taste consists of an ounce or two. Feel free to pour whatever you don't finish into one of the dump buckets on the bar. If you like, rinse your glass between pours with a little water. Remember, those sips add up, so pace yourself. If you plan to visit several wineries, try just a few wines at each so you won't suffer from palate fatigue, when your mouth can no longer distinguish subtleties. It's also a good idea to bring a picnic lunch, which you can enjoy on the deck of a winery, taking in the surrounding wine country vistas.

FALL FOLIAGE

In autumn, Willamette Valley vineyards are particularly stunning as the leaves change color.

DAY TRIP FROM PORTLAND

With nearly 150 vineyards, the Chehalem Mountain and Ribbon Ridge AVAs offer widely varied soil types and diverse Pinot Noirs. The region is less than an hour away from Portland.

Ponzi Vineyards

CHEHALEM MOUNTAIN AND RIBBON RIDGE AVAS

❶ PONZI VINEYARDS

First planted in 1970, Ponzi has some of Oregon's oldest Pinot Noir vines. In addition to current releases, the tasting room sometimes offers older library wines. **Try:** *Arneis, a crisp Italian white varietal.*

✉ 19500 SW Mountain Home Rd., Sherwood

☎ 503/628–1227

🌐 www.ponziwines.com

❷ REX HILL VINEYARDS

Before grapevines, the Willamette Valley was widely planted with fruits and nuts. Enjoy classic Oregon Pinot Noir in this tasting room built around an old fruit and nut drying facility. **Try:** *dark and spicy Dundee Hills Pinot Noir.*

✉ 30835 N. Hwy. 99W, Newberg

☎ 800/739–4455

🌐 www.rexhill.com

❸ VERCINGETORIX (VX) VINEYARD

This 10-acre vineyard sits in the middle of a 210-acre farm near the Willamette River. The tasting room is in one of the barns; a relaxed, friendly atmosphere for sampling. **Try:** *crisp and refreshing Pinot Blanc.*

✉ 8000 N.E. Parrish Rd., Newberg

☎ 503/538–9895

🌐 www.vxvineyard.com

❹ FOX FARM VINEYARDS TASTING ROOM

In addition to offering their own wines, this multi-winery tasting room in downtown Newberg features samples from several small local producers. The menu changes periodically.

✉ 606 E. First St., Newberg

☎ 503/538–8466

🌐 www.foxfarmvineyards.com

❺ UTOPIA VINEYARD

The tasting room at this small Oregon winery is quite intimate—you'll likely be served by the winemaker himself. **Try:** *light and slightly sweet Rosé.*

✉ 17445 N.E. Ribbon Ridge Rd., Newberg

☎ 503/298–7841

🌐 www.utopiawine.com

Vercingetorix (VX) Vineyard

Adelsheim Vineyard

Rex Hill

Pinot Gris grapes

Map labels

219
Scholls Ferry Rd.
Winery La.
1
Scholls
15.7 mi
TO
PORTLAND ↗
Beef Bend Rd.
219
Scholls Sherwood Blvd.
Vista Hill
LeBeau Rd.
99W
CHEHALEM MOUNTAINS
Edy Rd.
Bell Rd.
Sherwood
Sunset Blvd.
Bell Rd.
23 mi
9
Quarty Rd.
Pleasant Hill Rd.
Ladd Hill
2
Haugen Rd.
21.1 mi
10
Newberg
Corral Cr.
4
99W
23.9 mi
219
Ladd Hill
Parrish Rd.
Wilsonville Rd.
5th St.
3
25.8 mi
Fox Farm Rd.

KEY
00 mi Driving distance from Portland

⑧ ARAMENTA CELLARS

A small, family-run operation that offers tastings in its winery, built on the foundation of an old barn. The on-site vineyard grows primarily Pinot Noir and Chardonnay. **Try:** *smooth and structured Tillie Claret.*

✉ 17979 N.E. Lewis Rogers La., Newberg
☎ 503/538–7230
⊕ www.aramentacellars.com

STOP FOR A BITE

⑨ JORY RESTAURANT

Located within the luxurious Allison Inn and Spa, Jory serves creative dishes that highlight the bounty of the Willamette Valley.

✉ 2525 Allison La., Newberg
☎ 503/554–2526
⊕ www.theallison.com

⑩ SUBTERRA

Casual fine dining in a wine cellar atmosphere underneath the Dark Horse wine bar. The menu features global cuisine and a good selection of local wines.

✉ 1505 Portland Rd., Newberg
☎ 503/538–6060
⊕ www.subterrarestaurant.com

⑥ ADELSHEIM VINEYARD

One of Oregon's older Pinot Noir producers, Adelsheim has just opened a new tasting room inside its modern winery, with friendly, knowledgeable employees. **Try:** *dark and smoky Elizabeth's Reserve Pinot Noir.*

✉ 16800 N.E. Calkins La., Newberg
☎ 503/538–3652
⊕ www.adelsheim.com

⑦ BERGSTROM WINERY

A beautiful tasting room, but the real high point here is the classic Oregon Pinot Noir sourced from several of its estate vineyards as well as other local sites. **Try:** *earthy Bergstrom Pinot Noir.*

✉ 18215 N.E. Calkins La., Newberg
☎ 503/554–0468
⊕ www.bergstromwines.com

TWO DAYS IN WINE COUNTRY

DAY 1

DUNDEE HILLS AVA

The Dundee Hills AVA is home to some of Oregon's best known Pinot Noir producers. Start your tour in the town of Dundee, about 30 miles southwest of Portland, then drive up into the red hills and enjoy the valley views from many wineries.

❶ ARGYLE WINERY

If you don't want to drive off the beaten path, this winery is right on Highway 99W in Dundee. They specialize in sparkling wines, but also make very nice still wines. **Try:** *crisp Brut Rosé.*

✉ 691 Hwy. 99 W, Dundee
☎ 503/538–8520
⊕ www.argylewinery.com

❷ PONZI WINE BAR

This tasting room close to Argyle has a nice selection of local wines. It's a good choice for those who want to sample a large selection side-by-side. **Try:** *bright and fruity Ponzi Pinot Gris.*

✉ 100 S.W. 7ᵗʰ St., Dundee
☎ 503/554–1500
⊕ www.ponziwines.com

❸ ARCHERY SUMMIT

An Oregon Pinot Noir pioneer, Archery Summit features memorable wines and equally pleasing views. Call in advance to schedule a tour of the winery and aging caves. **Try:** *dark and rich Premier Cuvée Pinot Noir.*

✉ 18599 NE Archery Summit Rd., Dayton
☎ 503/864–4300
⊕ www.archerysummit.com

❹ DOMAINE DROUHIN OREGON

Started in the late 1980s by the Drouhin family of Burgundy fame, this winery makes notable Oregon Pinot Noir, as well as Chardonnay. **Try:** *smooth and earthy Willamette Valley Pinot Noir.*

✉ 6750 Breyman Orchards Rd., Dayton
☎ 503/864–2700
⊕ www.domainedrouhin.com

❺ VISTA HILLS VINEYARD

The so-called Treehouse is arguably the most stunning tasting room in Oregon. Sample wine made from estate fruit on a deck that overlooks the vineyards of the Dundee Hills. **Try:** *fruity Treehouse Pinot Noir.*

✉ 6475 N.E. Hilltop La., Dayton
☎ 503/864–3200
⊕ www.vistahillsvineyard.com

DAY 2

YAMHILL-CARLTON AVA

To the west of the Dundee Hills AVA is the horseshoe-shaped Yamhill-Carlton AVA. Vineyards here are found on the slopes that surround the towns of Yamhill and Carlton. Carlton has become a center of wine tourism, and you could easily spend a day visiting tasting rooms in town.

❻ PENNER-ASH WINE CELLARS

This state-of-the-art winery and tasting room is atop a hill with an excellent view of the valley below. **Try:** *smooth and dark Shea Vineyard Pinot Noir.*

✉ 15771 N.E. Ribbon Ridge Rd., Newberg
☎ 503/554–5545
⊕ www.pennerash.com

KEY

📍 Driving distance from Portland
00 mi

Penner-Ash Wine Cellars

Ponzi Wine Bar

STOP FOR A BITE

⑦ LEMELSON VINEYARDS
Although it specializes in single-vineyard Pinot Noir, Lemelson also makes several crisp white wines. The deck overlooking the vineyards is perfect for picnics. **Try:** *crisp and fruity Riesling.*
- ✉ 12020 N.E. Stag Hollow Rd., Carlton
- ☎ 503/852-6619
- ⊕ www.lemelsonvineyards.com

⑧ TYRUS EVAN WINE
Well-known winemaker Ken Wright's second label features big reds. The tasting room is in the historic Carlton train station. **Try:** *bold and spicy Del Rio Claret.*
- ✉ 120 N. Pine St., Carlton
- ☎ 503/852-7070
- ⊕ www.tyrusevanwine.com

⑨ SCOTT PAUL WINES
In addition to making Oregon Pinot Noir, Scott Paul Wines also runs a Burgundy import company, allowing you to taste locally grown Pinot Noir alongside some of the best Burgundies. **Try:** *structured and elegant La Paulée Pinot Noir.*
- ✉ 128 S. Pine St., Carlton
- ☎ 503/852-7300
- ⊕ www.scottpaul.com

⑩ LENNÉ ESTATE
Lenné specializes in highly regarded Pinot Noir, although it's often pouring a couple of non-Pinot wines from other wineries as well. The tasting room in a small stone building overlooks the vineyards. **Try:** *complex and earthy Estate Pinot Noir.*
- ✉ 18760 Laughlin Rd., Yamhill
- ☎ 503/956-2256
- ⊕ www.lenneestate.com

⑪ THE HORSERADISH WINE AND CHEESE BAR
Located in downtown Carlton, The Horseradish offers a wide selection of local wines as well as cheese from around the world. The sandwiches and small plates make for a great quick lunch.
- ✉ 211 W. Main St., Carlton
- ☎ 503/852-6656
- ⊕ www.thehorseradish.com

⑫ DUNDEE BISTRO
A favorite of winemakers, Dundee Bistro serves seasonal local ingredients paired with Willamette Valley wines. Enjoy outdoor seating, or watch chefs work in the open kitchen inside.
- ✉ 100-A S.W. 7th St., Dundee
- ☎ 503/554-1650
- ⊕ www.dundeebistro.com

⑬ TINA'S
The warm and intimate Tina's features dishes made with seasonal ingredients, organic vegetables, and free-range meats. Stop by for lunch Tuesday–Friday, or nightly dinner.
- ✉ 760 Hwy. 99 W, Dundee
- ☎ 503/538-8880
- ⊕ www.tinasdundee.com

to reserve a tour or private seated tasting, which includes an extended flight of rare wines. ✉ *6555 N.E. Hilltop La., Dayton* ☎ *503/864–4600, 866/864-6555* ⊕ *www.domaineserene.com* ☽ *Daily 11–4.*

Erath Vineyards Winery. When Dick Erath opened one of Oregon's pioneer wineries more than a quarter century ago, he focused on producing distinctive Pinot Noir from grapes he'd been growing in the Red Hills since 1972—as well as full-flavored Pinot Gris, Pinot Blanc, Chardonnay, Riesling, and late-harvest Gewürztraminer. The wines are excellent and reasonably priced. In 2006 the winery was sold to Washington State's giant conglomerate Ste. Michelle Wine Estate. The tasting room is in the middle of the vineyards, high in the hills, with views in nearly every direction; the hazelnut trees that covered the slopes not so long ago have been replaced with vines. The tasting-room terrace, which overlooks the winery and the hills, is a choice spot for picnicking. Crabtree Park, next to the winery, is a good place to stretch your legs after a tasting. ✉ *9409 N.E. Worden Hill Rd.* ☎ *503/538–3318, 800/539–9463* ⊕ *www.erath.com* ☽ *Daily 11–5.*

Ponzi Wine Bar. Located right on the main highway between Portland and wine country, the Ponzi Wine Bar offers the opportunity to sample wines from both the Ponzi family and small local producers without straying far from the beaten path. The tasting menu features current releases of Ponzi wines, as well as a rotating selection of other local wines. If you've had enough wine for a while, you can also get snacks, Italian coffee, or a craft beer to enjoy in the comfortable tasting room. ✉ *100 S.W. 7th St.* ☎ *503/554–1500* ⊕ *ponziwines.com/our-locations/ wine-bar-dundee* ☽ *Daily 11–5.*

Sokol Blosser. One of Yamhill County's oldest wineries (it was established in 1971) makes consistently excellent wines and sells them at reasonable prices. Set on a gently sloping south-facing hillside and surrounded by vineyards, lush lawns, and shade trees, it's a splendid place to learn about wine. A demonstration vineyard with several rows of vines contains the main grape varieties and shows what happens to them as the seasons unfold. Winery tours are available by reservation as well as vineyard hikes and ATV tours during the summer. ✉ *5000 Sokol Blosser La., 3 miles west of Dundee off Hwy. 99W* ☎ *503/864–2282, 800/582–6668* ⊕ *www.sokolblosser.com* ☽ *Daily 10–4.*

Torii Mor Winery. Established in 1993, this winery makes small quantities of handcrafted Pinot Noir, Pinot Gris, and Chardonnay and is set amid Japanese gardens with breathtaking views of the Willamette Valley. The gardens were designed by Takuma Tono, the same architect who designed the renowned Portland Japanese Garden. The owners, who love all things Japanese, named their winery after the distinctive Japanese gate of Shinto religious significance; they added a Scandinavian *mor*, signifying "earth," to create an east-west combo: "earth gate." Jacques Tardy, a native of Nuits Saint Georges, in Burgundy, France, is the current winemaker. Under his guidance Torii Mor wines have become more Burgundian in style. ✉ *18323 N.E. Fairview Dr.* ☎ *800/839–5004* ⊕ *www.toriimorwinery.com* ☽ *Daily 11–5.*

Vista Hills Vineyard. The Treehouse tasting room here is arguably the most beautiful in Oregon. Step out onto the deck and enjoy the view from underneath the towering trees. Vista Hills is a bit different from its neighbors in that there is no winery but several well-known local winemakers create wine from the vineyard grapes to sell under the Vista Hills label. The result is a range of distinctive wine styles, all made from the same vineyard. Also available are Hawaiian chocolate and coffee from their sister farm in Kona. ⊠ *6475 Hilltop Ln., Dayton* ☎ *503/864–3200* ⊕ *www.vistahillsvineyard.com* ⊗ *Daily noon–5.*

White Rose Estate. Like many of its better-known neighbors in the Dundee Hills, White Rose Estate produces elegant Pinot Noir that reflects the land where it is grown. In addition to their own estate vineyard, they purchase grapes from several highly regarded vineyards around the Willamette Valley. They describe their wines as "neo-classical," using traditional techniques in the vineyard, and state-of-the-art equipment and handling in the winery. Somewhat unusual for Oregon, most of the wines have a fairly high percentage of whole clusters included during fermentation, giving the wines more complexity and a bit of spice. ⊠ *6250 N.E. Hilltop La., Dayton* ☎ *503/864–2328* ⊕ *www.whiteroseestate.com* ⊗ *Daily 11–5.*

WHERE TO EAT

$$
PACIFIC NORTHWEST

✕ **Babica Hen.** Breakfast is the headliner and is served until 2 pm at this second location of a popular Portland-area eatery. But don't worry: you can get a great lunch and dinner, too. They use fresh eggs from local pasture-raised chickens, and serve local pork, beef, and dairy products, and even produce from their own garden. The dinner menu changes frequently to reflect seasonal ingredients, and usually features local seafood and meats, along with a few familiar comfort dishes like meat loaf or chicken and dumplings. ⑤ *Average main: $18* ⊠ *1410 N. Hwy. 99 W* ☎ *503/538-7970* ⊕ *babicahencafe.com.*

$$$
CONTEMPORARY

✕ **Dundee Bistro.** The Ponzi wine family are capable restaurateurs as well and use Northwest organic foods such as Draper Valley chicken, Carlton Farms pork, and locally produced wines, fruits, vegetables, nuts, mushrooms, fish, and meats. Vaulted ceilings provide an open feeling inside, warmed by abundant fresh flowers and the works of local Oregon artists. ⑤ *Average main: $25* ⊠ *100-A S.W. 7th St.* ☎ *503/554–1650* ⊕ *www.dundeebistro.com.*

$
PACIFIC NORTHWEST

✕ **Red Hills Market.** Serving great sandwiches, salads, and pizza, this is the perfect stop for a quick lunch in the middle of a day of wine tasting, or a casual no-frills dinner at the end of the day. Many of the sandwiches feature locally made charcuterie and cheeses, and the pizzas range from traditional Margherita to a spicy chorizo, blue cheese, and arugula. In addition to wine, there are cocktails and a great selection of local and imported craft beers. There's also a market where you can stock up on snacks to keep you going for the rest of the day, and many of the menu items are available to go. ⑤ *Average main: $12* ⊠ *155 S.W. 7th St.* ☎ *971/832–8414* ⊕ *www.redhillsmarket.com.*

$$$ ✕ **Tina's.** Chef–proprietors Tina and David Bergen bring a powerful one-
FRENCH   two punch to this Dundee favorite that often lures Portlanders away
Fodor'sChoice   from their own restaurant scene. The couple shares cooking duties—
★   Tina does the baking and is often on hand to greet you, and David
brings his experience as a former caterer and employee of nearby Sokol
Blosser Winery to the table, ensuring that you have the right glass of
wine to match your course. Fish and game vie for attention on the
country-French menu: entrées might include grilled Oregon salmon or
Alaskan halibut, or a braised rabbit, local lamb, or tenderloin. Avail
yourself of any special soups, particularly if there's corn chowder in the
house. The lunch menu includes soup, sandwiches, and creative salads
with local, seasonal ingredients. Service is as intimate and laid-back as
the interior. A double fireplace divides the dining room, with heavy glass
brick shrouded by bushes on the highway side, so you're not bothered
by the traffic on Highway 99. ⑤ *Average main: $30* ✉ *760 Hwy. 99 W*
☎ *503/538–8880* ⊕ *www.tinasdundee.com* ☽ *No lunch Sat.–Mon.*

WHERE TO STAY

$$ 🛏 **Dundee Manor Bed and Breakfast.** This 1908-built traditional home
B&B/INN   on expansive grounds is filled with treasures and collectibles that add
Fodor'sChoice   intrigue to each themed room: African, Asian, European, and North
★   American. **Pros:** terrific amenities; lots of activities; attentive staff.
Cons: few rooms. ⑤ *Rooms from: $200* ✉ *8380 N.E. Worden Hill
Rd.* ☎ *503/554–1945, 888/262–1133* ⊕ *www.dundeemanor.com* ⇄ *4
rooms* ⑩ *Breakfast.*

$$ 🛏 **The Inn at Red Hills.** These spacious and extremely comfortable rooms,
HOTEL   each with its own layout, offer plenty of local flavor, from the materials
in the building, the wines served, and the ingredients used in the kitchen.
Pros: contemporary, stylish surroundings; close to many wineries. **Cons:**
located on the main highway through town rather than the country.
⑤ *Rooms from: $179* ✉ *1410 N. Hwy. 99 W* ☎ *503/538–7666* ⊕ *www.
innatredhills.com* ⇄ *18 rooms, 2 suites* ⑩ *No meals.*

YAMHILL-CARLTON

14 miles west of Dundee.

Just outside the small towns of Carlton and Yamhill are neatly combed
benchlands and hillsides, an American Viticultural Area (AVA) estab-
lished in 2004, and home to some of the finest Pinot Noir vineyards in
the world. Carlton has exploded with many small tasting rooms in the
past few years, and you could easily spend an entire day tasting wine
within three or four blocks. The area is a gorgeous quilt of nurseries,
grain fields, and orchards. Come here for the wine tasting, but don't
expect to find too much else to do.

GETTING HERE AND AROUND

Having your own car is the best way to explore this rural region of
Yamhill County, located a little more than an hour's drive from Portland
International Airport. The towns of Yamhill and Carlton are about an
hour's drive from Downtown Portland, traveling through Tigard, to
Newberg and west on Highway 240.

EXPLORING

TOP ATTRACTIONS

Lemelson Vineyards. This winery was designed from the ground up to be a no-compromises Pinor Noir production facility with an eye to Willamette Valley aesthetics, and the highlight is a diverse range of single-vineyard Pinot Noirs. But don't neglect the bright Pinot Gris and Riesling, perfect with seafood or spicy fare. The spacious high-ceiling tasting room is a great place to relax and take in the view through the floor-to-ceiling windows, or bring a picnic and enjoy the deck on a warm summer day. ✉ *12020 N.E. Stag Hollow Rd., Carlton* ☎ *503/852–6619* ⊕ *www.lemelsonvineyards.com* ⊘ *Thurs.–Mon. 11–4.*

Lenné Estate. The small stone building that houses the tasting room is surrounded by the estate vineyard and looks like something right out of Burgundy. Steve Lutz was looking for the perfect site to grow Pinot Noir and bought the property in 2000. In addition to offering his own rich and elegant estate Pinot Noirs for tasting, he often pours other varietals from other wineries. ✉ *18760 N.E. Laughlin Rd., Yamhill* ☎ *503/956–2256* ⊕ *www.lenneestate.com* ✍ *$10* ⊘ *Thurs.-Fri. 12:30–5, Sat.–Sun. 12–5.*

WORTH NOTING

Anne Amie Vineyards. Early wine country adopters Fred and Mary Benoit established this hilltop winery as Chateau Benoit in 1979. When the winery changed hands in 1999, it was renamed Anne Amie and has been concentrating on Pinot Blanc, Pinot Gris, and Pinot Noir, but still makes a dry Riesling. In addition, they also make Syrah and a Bordeaux blend from eastern Washington grapes. Both the tasting room and the picnic area have spectacular views across the hills and valleys of Yamhill County. ✉ *6580 N.E. Mineral Springs Rd., Carlton* ☎ *503/864–2991* ⊕ *www.anneamie.com* ⊘ *Open Mar.–Dec., daily 10–5; Jan.–Feb., Fri.–Sun. 10–5 or by appointment.*

Carlton Winemakers Studio. Oregon's first cooperative winery was specifically designed to house multiple small premium wine producers. This gravity-flow winery has up-to-date wine-making equipment as well as multiple cellars for storing the different makers' wines. You can taste and purchase bottles from the different member wineries: Andrew Rich, Asilda, Bachelder, Dukes Family Vineyard, Hamacher Wines, Lazy River Vineyard, Merriman Wines, Mad Violets, Omero, Retour Wine Co., Trout Lily Ranch, Utopia Vineyard, and Wahle Vineyards and Cellars. The emphasis is on Pinot Noir, but more than a dozen other types of wines are poured, from Cabernet Franc to Gewürztraminer to Mourvèdre on a rotating basis. The selection of wines available to taste changes every few days. ✉ *801 N. Scott St., Carlton* ☎ *503/852–6100* ⊕ *www.winemakersstudio.com* ⊘ *Daily 11–5.*

Ken Wright Cellars Tasting Room. Carlton's former train depot is now the tasting room for Ken Wright Cellars and his warm-climate label, Tyrus Evan. The winery specializes in single-vineyard Pinot Noirs, each subtly different from the next depending on the soil types and grape clones. The wines are poured side by side, giving you an opportunity to go back and forth to compare them. The Tyrus Evan wines are quite different from the Ken Wright Pinots: they are warm-climate varieties like Cabernet Franc, Malbec, Syrah, and red Bordeaux blends, from grapes Wright buys from vineyards in eastern Washington and southern Oregon. You can also pick up cheeses and other picnic supplies, as well as wine country gifts and souvenirs. ⊠ *120 N. Pine St., Carlton* ☎ *503/852–7010* ⊕ *www.kenwrightcellars.com* ⊙ *Daily 11–5.*

Scott Paul Tasting Room and Winery. Pinot Noir fans, listen up: this small spot in the center of Carlton not only makes Pinot Noir from Oregon grapes, but it also imports and sells Pinot Noirs from Burgundy (as well as grower Champagne). The mainstay Pinot Noirs made from local grapes are Audrey, the finest wine of the vintage, and La Paulée, a selection of the best lots of each vintage. In addition, they'll make several other Pinots customized to the widely variable growing conditions each year in Oregon. All are splendid examples of the wines that can be made from this great, challenging grape. The tasting room, a quaint redbrick building, is across the street from the winery. Tours are by appointment only. Wine seminars are offered periodically, and private guided tastings are available by appointment. ⊠ *128 S. Pine St., Carlton* ☎ *503/852–7300* ⊕ *www.scottpaul.com* ⊙ *Sat. noon–5.*

MCMINNVILLE

11 miles south of Yamhill on Hwy. 99 W.

The Yamhill County seat, McMinnville lies in the center of Oregon's thriving wine industry. There is a larger concentration of wineries in Yamhill County than in any other area of the state. Among the varieties are Chardonnay, Pinot Noir, and Pinot Gris. Most of the wineries in the area offer tours and tastings. McMinnville's downtown area, with a pleasantly disproportionate number of bookstores and art galleries for its size, is well worth exploring; many of the historic district buildings, erected 1890–1915, are still standing, and are remarkably well maintained.

GETTING HERE AND AROUND
McMinnville is a little more than an hour's drive from Downtown Portland; **Caravan Airport Transportation** (☎ *541/994–9645* ⊕ *www. caravanairporttransportation.com*) provides shuttle service to Portland International Airport. McMinnville is just 70 minutes from Lincoln City on the Oregon Coast, and 27 miles west of Salem.

ESSENTIALS
Visitor Information McMinnville Chamber of Commerce ⊠ *417 N.W. Adams St.* ☎ *503/472–6196* ⊕ *www.mcminnville.org.*

EXPLORING
FAMILY **Evergreen Aviation and Space Museum.** Howard Hughes' *Spruce Goose,* Fodor'sChoice the largest plane ever built and constructed entirely of wood, is on per-★ manent display, but if you can take your eyes off the giant you will also see more than 45 historic planes and replicas from the early years of flight and World War II, as well as the postwar and modern eras. Across the parking lot from the aviation museum is the space museum with artifacts that include a German V-2 rocket and a Titan missile, complete

with silo and launch control room. A water park (separate admission) has 10 waterslides, including one that starts at a Boeing 747-100 that sits on *top* of the building. The IMAX theater is open daily and features several different films each day. There's a museum store and two cafés, as well as ongoing educational programs and special events. ⊠ *500 N.E. Michael King Smith Way* ☎ *503/434–4185* ⊕ *www.evergreenmuseum. org* ⧄ *$25, includes IMAX movie* ☉ *Daily 9–5, closed holidays.*

The Eyrie Vineyards. When David Lett planted the first Pinot Noir vines in the Willamette Valley in 1965, he was setting in motion a series of events that has caused Willamette Valley Pinot Noir to be recognized as among the best in the world. Affectionately known as Papa Pinot, Lett, along with several other pioneering winemakers nurtured the Oregon wine industry to what it is today. Today David's son Jason Lett is now the winemaker and vineyard manager, and continues to make Pinot Noir, Pinot Gris, and Chadonnay that reflect the gentle touch that has always characterized Eyrie wines. In recent years, many small wineries have sprung up in the neighborhood around this historic winery. ⊠ *935 N.E. 10th Ave.* ☎ *503/472–6315, 888/440–4970* ⊕ *www.eyrievineyards.com* ☉ *Daily noon–5.*

4

NEED A BREAK?

Serendipity Ice Cream. Historic Cook's Hotel, built in 1886, is the setting for a true, old-fashioned ice-cream parlor experience. Try a sundae, and take home cookies made from scratch. If you don't feel like ice cream, the homemade soup is a great choice on a rainy day. ⊠ *502 N.E. 3rd St.* ☎ *503/474–9189* ⊕ *serendipityicecream.com.*

WHERE TO EAT AND STAY

$$$$
CONTEMPORARY

✕ **Joel Palmer House.** Wild mushrooms and truffles are the stars at this 1857 home, named after an Oregon pioneer, that is now on the National Register of Historic Places. There are three small dining rooms, each seating about 15 people. A popular starter is Heidi's three-mushroom tart, and while the menu changes seasonally, the mushroom tart, Joe's wild mushroom soup, and wild mushroom risotto with Oregon truffle oil are traditions that are always available. The standard dinner is a 3 course prix-fixe menu, but if you really, really like mushrooms, have your entire table order Chef Christopher's Mushroom Madness Menu, a six-course extravaganza. ⑤ *Average main: $50* ⊠ *600 Ferry St., Dayton* ☎ *503/864–2995* ⊕ *www.joelpalmerhouse.com* ☉ *Closed Sun. and Mon. No lunch.*

$$$
ITALIAN

✕ **Nick's Italian Cafe.** Famed for serving Oregon's wine country enthusiasts, this fine-dining venue is a destination for a special evening or lunch. Modestly furnished but with a voluminous wine cellar, Nick's serves spirited and simple food, reflecting the owner's northern Italian heritage. A five-course prix-fixe menu changes nightly with optional wine pairings. À la carte options are also available. ⑤ *Average main: $26* ⊠ *521 N.E. 3rd St.* ☎ *503/434–4471* ⊕ *www.nicksitaliancafe.com* ⧄ *Reservations essential.*

$
HOTEL

🏨 **Hotel Oregon.** Rooms in the former Elberton Hotel, built in 1905, have tall ceilings and high windows, are outfitted in late-Victorian furnishings, and filled with whimsical art—sometimes serene, often bizarre—as well as photos and sayings scribbled on the walls. **Pros:** inexpensive; casual and lively; plenty of food and drink on the premises. **Cons:** shared baths for most rooms; those seeking upscale ambience should look elsewhere. $ *Rooms from: $60* ⊠ *310 N.E. Evans St.* ☎ *503/472–8427, 888/472–8427* ⊕ *www.mcmenamins.com* ⇶ *42 rooms* ❑❘ *No meals.*

$$ 🅷 **Joseph Mattey House Bed & Breakfast.** The four upstairs rooms in this
B&B/INN   Queen Anne Victorian mansion are whimsically named after locally
Fodor'sChoice grown grape varieties and are decorated in keeping with the charac-
★   ter of those wines: crisp white furnishings in the Chardonnay Room, dark-wood pieces and reddish wine accents in the Pinot Noir room. **Pros:** refined bed-and-breakfast atmosphere. **Cons:** not many modern amenities in the rooms. $ *Rooms from: $170* ⊠ *10221 N.E. Mattey La., off Hwy. 99 W, ¼ mile south of Lafayette* ☎ *503/434–5058* ⊕ *www. matteyhouse.com* ⇶ *4 rooms* ❑❘ *Breakfast.*

NIGHTLIFE AND THE ARTS

Spirit Mountain Casino and Lodge. Located 24 miles southwest of McMinnville on Highway 18, this popular gambling getaway is owned and operated by the Confederated Tribes of the Grande Ronde Community of Oregon. The 90,000-square-foot casino has more than a thousand slots, as well as poker and blackjack tables, roulette, craps, Pai Gow poker, keno, bingo, and off-track betting. Big-name comedians and rock and country musicians perform in the 1,700-seat concert hall, and there's an arcade for the kids. Complimentary shuttle service from Portland and Salem is available. Dining options include an all-you-can-eat buffet, a deli, and a café. ⊠ *27100 S.W. Salmon River Hwy., Grand Ronde* ☎ *503/879–2350, 800/760–7977* ⊕ *spiritmountain.com.*

MID-WILLAMETTE VALLEY

While most of the wineries are concentrated in Washington and Yamhill counties, there are several finds in the Mid-Willamette Valley that warrant extending a wine enthusiast's journey. There are also flower, hops, berries, and seed gardens scattered throughout Salem, Albany, and Corvallis. The huge number of company stores concentrated on Interstate 5 will have you thinking about some new Nikes, and Oregon State University will have you wearing orange and black long after Halloween is over. Be aware that many communities in this region are little more than wide spots in the road. In these tiny towns you might find only a gas station, a grocery store, a church or two, and a school. Watch out for any "School Crossing" signs: Oregon strictly enforces its speed-limit laws.

SALEM

24 miles from McMinnville, south on Hwy. 99 W and east on Hwy. 22; 45 miles south of Portland on I–5.

The state capital has a rich pioneer history, but before that it was the home of the Calapooia Indians, who called it Chemeketa, which means "place of rest." Salem is said to have been renamed by missionaries.

Although trappers and farmers preceded them in the Willamette Valley, the Methodist missionaries had come in 1834 to minister to Native Americans, and they are credited with the founding of Salem. In 1842 they established the first academic institution west of the Rockies, which is now known as Willamette University. Salem became the capital when Oregon achieved statehood in 1859 (Oregon City was the capital of the Oregon Territory). Salem serves as the seat to Marion County as well as the home of the state fairgrounds. Government ranks as a major industry here, while the city's setting in the heart of the fertile Willamette Valley stimulates rich agricultural and food-processing industries. More than a dozen wineries are in or near Salem. The main attractions in Salem are west of Interstate 5 in and around the Capitol Mall.

GETTING HERE AND AROUND

Salem is located on Interstate 5 with easy access to Portland, Albany, and Eugene. **Hut Portland Airport Shuttle** (☎ *503/364–4444 ⊕ www. portlandairportshuttle.com*) provides transportation to Portland International Airport, which is one hour and 15 minutes away. Salem's McNary Field no longer has commercial airline service, but serves general aviation aircraft.

Bus transportation throughout Salem is provided by **Cherriot's** (⊕ *www. cherriots.org*). Amtrak operates regularly, and its train station is located at ✉ *500 13th Street SE.*

ESSENTIALS

Visitor Information Salem Convention & Visitors Center ✉ *181 High St. NE* ☎ *503/581–4325, 800/874–7012 ⊕ www.travelsalem.com.*

EXPLORING

TOP ATTRACTIONS

Oregon Garden. Just outside the town of Silverton is a gardener's oasis, showcasing the amazing botanical diversity of the Willamette Valley and Pacific Northwest. Open 365 days a year, the 80-acre garden features themed plots ranging from a conifer forest to medicinal plants. There is also a whimsical children's garden complete with a model train, and another garden featuring the agricultural bounty of the area. A free narrated tram tour operates from April to October, allowing visitors an overview of the garden before exploring on their own. ✉ *879 W. Main St., Silverton* ☎ *503/874–8100, 877/674–2733 ⊕ www.oregongarden. org* 🎫 *$11* ☾ *May–Sept., daily 9–6; Oct.–Apr., daily 10–4.*

Willamette Heritage Center at The Mill. Take a trip back in time and experience the story of Oregon's early pioneers and the industrial revolution. The **Thomas Kay Woolen Mill Museum** complex (circa 1889), complete with working waterwheels and millstream, looks as if the workers have just stepped away for a lunch break. Teasel gigging, napper flock bins, and the patented Furber double-acting napper are but a few of the machines and processes on display. The **Jason Lee House,** the **John D. Boon Home,** and the **Methodist Parsonage** are also part of the village. There is nothing grandiose about these early pioneer homes, the oldest frame structures in the Northwest, but they reveal a great deal about domestic life in the wilds of Oregon in the 1840s.

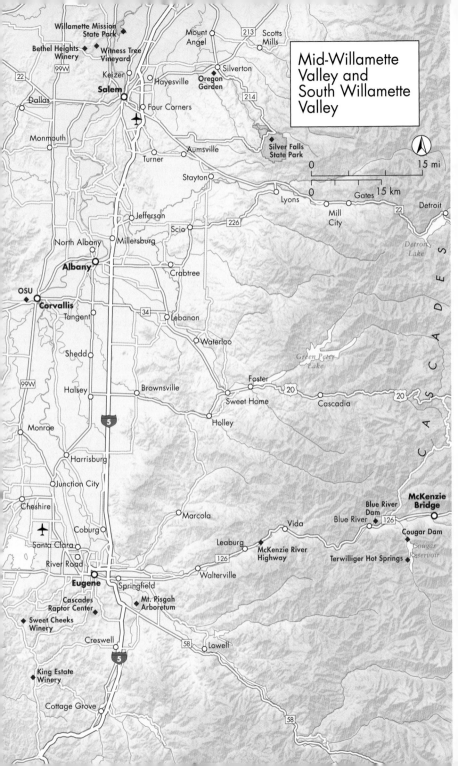

Mid-Willamette
Valley and
South Willamette
Valley

0 _____ 15 mi

0 _____ 15 km

Willamette Mission
State Park

Bethel Heights
Winery

Witness Tree
Vineyard

Keizer

Mount
Angel

213

Scotts
Mills

Silverton

Oregon
Garden

Hayesville

Salem

Four Corners

214

Dallas

22

99W

Monmouth

Turner

Aumsville

Silver Falls
State Park

Stayton

Lyons

Gates

Mill
City

Detroit

22

*Detroit
Lake*

Jefferson

Scio

226

Detroit

North Albany

Millersburg

Albany

Crabtree

OSU

Corvallis

Tangent

34

Lebanon

Waterloo

C A S C A D E S

Shedd

*Green Peter
Lake*

Halsey

Brownsville

Foster

20

Sweet Home

Cascadia

20

Holley

99W

Monroe

Harrisburg

Junction City

Marcola

Vida

Blue River
Dam

Blue River

126

**McKenzie
Bridge**

Cheshire

Coburg

Cougar Dam

Santa Clara

River Road

Leaburg

126

McKenzie River
Highway

Terwilliger Hot Springs

*Cougar
Reservoir*

Walterville

Eugene

Springfield

Cascades
Raptor Center

Mt. Pisgah
Arboretum

Sweet Cheeks
Winery

Creswell

5

58

Lowell

King Estate
Winery

58

Cottage Grove

✉ *1313 Mill St. SE* ☎ *503/585–7012* ⊕ *www.willametteheritage.org* ⌨ *$6* ⊙ *Mon.–Sat. 10–5.*

Witness Tree Vineyard. Named for the ancient oak that towers over the vineyard (it was used as a surveyor's landmark in the 1850s), this winery produces premium Pinot Noir made entirely from grapes grown on its 100-acre estate nestled in the Eola Hills northwest of Salem. The vineyard also produces limited quantities of estate Chardonnay, Viognier, Pinot Blanc, Dolcetto, and a sweet dessert wine called Sweet Signé. Tours are available by appointment. ✉ *7111 Spring Valley Rd. NW* ☎ *503/585–7874* ⊕ *www.witnesstreevineyard.com* ⊙ *May–Oct., Tues.–Sun. 11–5; Mar.–Apr. and Nov.–mid-Dec., Thurs.–Sun. 11–5.*

WORTH NOTING

FAMILY **Gilbert House Children's Museum.** This is a different kind of kids' museum; an amazing place to let the imagination run wild. Celebrating the life and the inventions of A.C. Gilbert, a Salem native who became a toy manufacturer and inventor, the historic houses included many themed interactive rooms along with a huge outdoor play structure. In addition to the children's activities, many beloved toys created by A.C. Gilbert are on display, including Erector sets and American Flyer trains. The wide range of indoor and outdoor interactive exhibits will appeal to children (and adults) of all ages. ✉ *116 Marion St. NE* ☎ *503/371–3631* ⊕ *www.acgilbert.org* ⌨ *$8* ⊙ *Mon.–Sat. 10–5, Sun. noon–5.*

Bethel Heights Vineyard. Founded in 1977, Bethel Heights was one of the first vineyards planted in the Eola Hills region of the Willamette Valley. It produces Pinot Noir, Chardonnay, Pinot Blanc, and Pinot Gris. The tasting room has one of the most glorious panoramic views of any winery in the state; its terrace and picnic area overlook the surrounding vineyards, the valley below, and Mount Jefferson in the distance. ✉ *6060 Bethel Heights Rd. NW* ☎ *503/581–2262* ⊕ *www. bethelheights.com* ⊙ *Feb.–Nov., Tues.–Sun. 11–5; Dec.–Jan., weekends 11–4.*

Bush's Pasture Park. These 105 acres of rolling lawn and formal English gardens include the remarkably well-preserved Bush House, an 1878 Italianate mansion at the park's far-western boundary. It has 10 marble fireplaces and virtually all of its original furnishings, and can be visited only on informative tours. Bush Barn Art Center, behind the house, exhibits the work of Northwest artists and has a sales gallery. ✉ *600 Mission St. SE* ☎ *503/363–4714* ⊕ *www.salemart.org* ⌨ *House $4* ⊙ *Gorunds: daily, dawn–midnight; house: Mar.–Dec. 23, Wed.–Sun., tours at 1, 2, 3, and 4.*

Elsinore Theatre. This flamboyant Tudor Gothic vaudeville house opened on May 28, 1926, with Edgar Bergen in attendance. Clark Gable (who lived in nearby Silverton) and Gregory Peck performed on stage. The theater was designed to look like a castle, with a false-stone front, chandeliers, ironwork, and stained-glass windows. It's now a lively performing arts center with a busy schedule of bookings, and there are concerts on its Wurlitzer pipe organ. ✉ *170 High St. SE* ☎ *503/375–3574* ⊕ *www.elsinoretheatre.com.*

Oregon Capitol building in Salem

Mount Angel Abbey. This Benedictine monastery on a 300-foot-high butte was founded in 1882 and is the site of one of two Modernist buildings in the United States designed by Finnish architect Alvar Aalto. A masterpiece of serene and thoughtful design, Aalto's library opened its doors in 1970, and has become a place of pilgrimage for students and aficionados of modern architecture. ⊠ *1 Abbey Dr., St. Benedict ✛ 18 miles from Salem; east on Hwy. 213 and north on Hwy. 214* ☎ *503/845–3030* ⊕ *www.mountangelabbey.org* ✉ *Free* ☉ *Mon.–Sat. 9–4:30.*

Oregon Capitol. A brightly gilded bronze statue of the *Oregon Pioneer* stands atop the 140-foot-high Capitol dome, looking north across the Capitol Mall. Built in 1939 with blocks of gray Vermont marble, Oregon's Capitol has an elegant yet austere neoclassical feel. East and west wings were added in 1978. Relief sculptures and deft historical murals soften the interior. Tours of the rotunda, the House and Senate chambers, and the governor's office leave from the information center under the dome. ⊠ *900 Court St. NE* ☎ *503/986–1388* ⊕ *www.leg.state.or.us* ✉ *Free* ☉ *Weekdays 8–5.*

WHERE TO EAT AND STAY

$$

ITALIAN

Fodor's Choice

★

✕ **DaVinci.** Salem politicos flock to this two-story downtown gathering spot for Italian-inspired dishes cooked in a wood-burning oven. No shortcuts are taken in the preparation, so don't come if you're in a rush. But if you're in the mood to linger over seafood and fresh pasta that's made on the premises, this may be your place. The wine list features a wide selection from the Northwest and Italy, and includes a good selection of wines by the glass. The staff is courteous and extremely professional, and there's live music most evenings. ⑤ *Average main:*

$24 ⊠ *180 High St. SE* ☎ *503/399–1413* ⊕ *www.davincisofsalem.com* ☾ *No lunch.*

$ 🛏**Grand Hotel in Salem.** Large rooms, with comfortable and luxurious
HOTEL furnishings, are the best in town, a good base for guests attending shows
and meetings at Salem Conference Center or touring the region. **Pros:**
spacious rooms; centrally located. **Cons:** some street noise; not a lot of
character. ⑤ *Rooms from: $139* ⊠ *201 Liberty St. SE* ☎ *503/540–7800,
877/540–7800* ⊕ *www.grandhotelsalem.com* ↻ *143 rooms, 50 suites*
⏀*Breakfast.*

$ 🛏**Oregon Garden Resort.** Bright, spacious, and tastefully decorated
RESORT rooms, each with a fireplace and a private landscaped patio or balcony,
neighbor the Oregon Garden (admission is included in the rates). **Pros:**
gorgeous grounds; luxurious rooms; pool and plenty of other amenities.
Cons: a distance from other activities. ⑤ *Rooms from: $110* ⊠ *895 W.
Main St., Silverton* ☎ *503/874–2500* ⊕ *www.oregongardenresort.com*
↻ *103 rooms* ⏀*Breakfast.*

SHOPPING

Reed Opera House. These days the 1869 opera house in downtown Salem
contains an eclectic collection of locally owned stores, shops, restaurants, bars, and bakeries, everything from art galleries to tattoo parlors.
Its Trinity Ballroom hosts special events and celebrations. ⊠ *189 Liberty
St. NE* ☎ *503/391–4481* ⊕ *www.reedoperahouse.com.*

Woodburn Company Stores. Located 18 miles north of Salem on Interstate 5 are more than 100 brand-name outlet stores, including Nike,
Calvin Klein, Bose, Gymboree, OshKosh B'Gosh, Ann Taylor, Levi's,
Chico's, Fossil, Forever 21, Polo, and Columbia Sportswear, and plenty
of places to eat. Chances are that someone in your traveling party
would enjoy burning an hour or three perusing these famous outlet
stores. ⊠ *1001 Arney Rd., Woodburn* ☎ *503/981–1900, 888/664–7467*
⊕ *www.woodburncompanystores.com* ☾ *Mon.–Sat. 10–9, Sun. 10–7.*

SPORTS AND THE OUTDOORS
RECREATIONAL AREAS

Silver Falls State Park. Hidden amid old-growth Douglas firs in the foothills of the Cascades, this is the largest state park in Oregon (8,700
acres). South Falls, roaring over the lip of a mossy basalt bowl into
a deep pool 177 feet below, is the main attraction here, but 13 other
waterfalls—half of them more than 100 feet high—are accessible to
hikers. The best time to visit is in the fall, when vine maples blaze with
brilliant color, or early spring, when the forest floor is carpeted with
trilliums and yellow violets. There are picnic facilities and a day lodge;
in winter you can cross-country ski. Camping facilities include tent and
trailer sites, cabins, and a horse camp. ⊠ *20024 Silver Falls Hwy. SE,
Sublimity* ☎ *503/873–8681, 800/551–6949* ⊕ *www.oregonstateparks.
org* ⊠ *$5 per vehicle* ☾ *Daily 8am–dusk.*

Willamette Mission State Park. Along pastoral lowlands by the Willamette
River, this serene park holds the largest black cottonwood tree in the
United States. A thick-barked behemoth by a small pond, the 275-year-
old tree has upraised arms that bring to mind J.R.R. Tolkien's fictional
Ents. Site of Reverend Jason Lee's 1834 pioneer mission, the park also

offers quiet strolling and picnicking in an old orchard and along the river. The Wheatland Ferry, at the north end of the park, began carrying covered wagons across the Willamette in 1844 and is still in operation today. ⊠ *Wheatland Rd., 8 miles north of Salem, I–5 Exit 263* ☏ *503/393–1172, 800/551–6949* ⊕ *www.oregonstateparks.org* ⊠ *$5 per vehicle* ☉ *Daily 8–5.*

ALBANY

20 miles from Salem, south on I–5 and west on U.S. 20.

Known as the grass-seed capital of the world, Albany has some of the most historic buildings in Oregon. Some 700 buildings, scattered over a 100-block area in three districts, include every major architectural style developed in the United States since 1850. The area is listed on the National Register of Historic Places. Eight covered bridges can also be seen on a half-hour drive from Albany. Oregon has the largest collection of covered bridges in the western United States, and the Willamette Valley has more than 34 of the wooden structures.

GETTING HERE AND AROUND
Albany is located on Interstate 5 with easy access to Portland, Salem, and Eugene. Portland International Airport is one hour, 40 minutes away, and the Eugene airport is one hour away to the south. Several shuttle services are available from both airports.

Albany Transit System provides two routes for intercity travel. The Linn-Benton loop system provides for transportation between Albany and Corvallis. Albany is served by Amtrak.

ESSENTIALS
Visitor Information Albany Visitors Association ⊠ *110 3rd Ave. SE* ☏ *541/928–0911, 800/526–2256* ⊕ *www.albanyvisitors.com.*

EXPLORING
Albany Historic Carousel and Museum. It's not often that you get to watch a carousel being built, but that's exactly what's happening here. Craftsmen and volunteers from the Albany area have come together to contribute thousands of hours to carving and painting a huge array of whimsical carousel creatures ranging from traditional horses to giant frogs and dragons. They hope to have the carousel in operation in 2016, but in the meantime you can enjoy watching the creations come together, as well as viewing many historical carousel artifacts in the museum. ⊠ *503 1st Ave. W* ☏ *541/791–3340* ⊕ *albanycarousel.com* ☉ *Thurs.–Tues. 10–4, Wed. 10–9.*

WHERE TO EAT
$

HUNGARIAN

✕ **Novak's Hungarian.** Since 1984, the Novak family has been a delightful fixture in Albany's dining scene. Whether you're ordering Hungarian hash and eggs in the morning or chicken paprika served over homemade Hungarian pearl noodles for dinner, you can't go wrong in this establishment. There's a huge assortment of desserts as well. On Sunday they serve brunch. Ⓢ *Average main: $14* ⊠ *2306 Heritage Way SE* ☏ *541/967–9488* ⊕ *www.novakshungarian.com* ☉ *No breakfast Mon.–Tues.*

$$

ECLECTIC

Fodor'sChoice

★

✕Sybaris. A rotating menu at this fine bistro in Albany's historic downtown changes monthly and features flavorful cuisine at reasonable prices. The restaurant strives to ensure that most of the ingredients, including the lamb, eggs, and vegetables, are raised within 10 miles. Even the huckleberries in the ice cream are gathered in secret locations by the restaurant's mushroom picker. The wine list includes worldwide classics, but is strong on local Oregon wines, too. ⑤ *Average main: $20* ✉ *442 1st Ave.* W ☎ *541/928–8157* ⊕ *www.sybarisbistro.com* ☾ *Closed Sun.–Mon. No lunch.*

CORVALLIS

4

10 miles southwest of Albany on U.S. 20.

To some, Corvallis is a brief stopping place along the way to Salem or Portland. To others, it's a small town that gives you a chance to escape the bigger cities. To still others, it's an academic and sports center, home to Oregon State University and its Beavers. Driving the area's economy are a growing engineering and high-tech industry, a burgeoning wine industry, and more traditional local agricultural crops, such as grass and legume seeds. The town and its environs offer plenty of outdoor activities as well as scenic attractions, from covered bridges to wineries and gardens.

GETTING HERE AND AROUND

Corvallis Transit System (CTS) operates eight bus routes throughout the city. **Hut Shuttle** (☎ *503/364–4444* ⊕ *www.portlandairportshuttle. com*) provides transportation between Corvallis and the Portland airport, located one hour, 53 minutes away. **OmniShuttle** (☎ *541/461–7959* ⊕ *www.omnishuttle.com*) provides transportation between Corvallis and the Eugene airport, 50 minutes away. Corvallis Municipal Airport is a public airport 4 miles south of the city.

ESSENTIALS

Visitor Information Corvallis Tourism ✉ *420 N.W. 2nd St.* ☎ *541/757–1544, 800/334–8118* ⊕ *www.visitcorvallis.com.*

EXPLORING

Oregon State University. It's a thrill to be on campus on game day, when students are a sea of orange and black cheering on their beloved Beavers. This 400-acre campus, west of the city center, was established as a land-grant institution in 1868. OSU has more than 26,000 students, many of them studying the university's nationally recognized programs in conservation biology, agricultural sciences, nuclear engineering, forestry, fisheries and wildlife management, community health, pharmacy, and zoology. ✉ *15th and Jefferson Sts.* ☎ *541/737–1000* ⊕ *oregonstate. edu.*

WHERE TO EAT AND STAY

$$$

LATIN AMERICAN

✕Del Alma. This multilevel waterfront eatery gives every table a nice view of the river and puts a modern spin on tapas, bringing unexpected flavors and textures to classic Latin food. The menu features both tapas and larger dishes, with a strong emphasis on seafood and beef. If you're not in the mood for meat, the chile relleno marries a mild poblano pepper with goat cheese and an amazing smoky salsa. They pride themselves on creative, Latin-inspired cocktails, and there's an extensive list of wines by the glass. ⑤ *Average main: $28* ⊠ *136 S.W. Washington Ave.* ☎ *541/753–2222* ⊕ *delalmarestaurant.com* ⊗ *Closed Sun. No lunch.*

$$$
MODERN
AMERICAN
Fodor'sChoice
★

✕ **Gathering Together Farm.** When spring arrives, it means that the organic farmers outside Philomath are serving their bounty. Fresh vegetables, pizzas, local lamb, pork, and halibut are frequent highlights on a menu that features simple fresh ingredients impeccably prepared. Local wines and tempting desserts make the evening perfect. If you don't see coppa (cured pork from the shoulder of the pig) on the menu, ask your server if the chef has any available. They can often add it to a dish, and it's fantastic. ⑤ *Average main: $25* ⊠ *25159 Grange Hall Rd., Philomath* ☎ *541/929–4270* ⊕ *www.gatheringtogetherfarm.com* ⌃ *Reservations essential* ⊗ *Closed Sun.–Mon. No breakfast Tues.–Fri., no lunch Sat., no dinner Tues., Wed., or Sat.*

$
B&B/INN

🛏 **Hanson Country Inn.** On a knoll overlooking the Willamette Valley, this 7,100-square-foot 1928 Dutch Colonial that was once headquarters of a poultry-breeding business now has a massive fireplace in the living room, many sitting areas, tall windows, and a sunporch with stained-glass windows and rattan furniture. **Pros:** flexible breakfast schedule; close to town. **Cons:** needs paint touch-up and minor maintenance. ⑤ *Rooms from: $135* ⊠ *795 S.W. Hanson St.* ☎ *541/752–2919* ⊕ *www. hcinn.com* ⌂ *5 suites, 1 cottage* ⏐◎⏐ *Breakfast.*

SPORTS AND THE OUTDOORS

RECREATIONAL AREAS

Fodor'sChoice
★

Siuslaw National Forest. The forest, starting just 2 miles from Corvallis and extending to the coast, includes the Oregon Dunes National Recreation Area and the Cape Perpetua Interpretive Center. Within the park is the highest point in the Coast Range, Mary's Peak (4,097 feet), offering panoramic views of the Cascades, the Willamette Valley, and the rest of the Coast Range. On a clear day you can see as far as the Pacific Ocean. There are several picnicking areas, more than 10 miles of hiking trails, and a small campground, as well as stands of noble fir and alpine meadows. You can access Mary's Peak from Highway 34 between Corvallis and Newport and the central coast. Several other major highways (Highways 26, 6, 18, 26, and 126) also run through the forest between the Willamette Valley and the coast, providing access to recreation areas. ⊠ *Forest office, 3200 S.W. Jefferson Way* ☎ *541/750–7000* ⊕ *www.fs.fed.us/r6/siuslaw* 💲 *$5 per vehicle at some recreation sites* ⊗ *Daily dawn–dusk.*

SWIMMING

Osborn Aquatic Center. This is not your ordinary lap pool. There are waterslides, a water channel, water cannons, and floor geysers. The indoor pools are open all year. ⊠ *1940 N.W. Highland Dr.* ☎ *541/766–7946* 💲 *$5* ⊗ *Daily, hours vary.*

SOUTH WILLAMETTE VALLEY

Lane County rests at the southern end of the Willamette Valley, encompassing Eugene, Springfield, Drain, McKenzie Bridge, and Cottage Grove. Visitors can enjoy a wide range of outdoor activities such as running, fishing, swimming, white-water rafting, and deep-woods hiking along the McKenzie River, while Eugene offers great food, shopping, and the arts. There are plenty of wineries to enjoy, too, as well as cheering on the Oregon Ducks. To the west lies the Oregon Dunes Recreation Area, and to the east are the beautiful central Oregon communities of Sisters, Bend, and Redmond.

EUGENE

63 miles south of Corvallis on I–5.

Eugene was founded in 1846, when Eugene Skinner staked the first federal land-grant claim for pioneers. Eugene is consistently given high marks for its "livability." As the home of the University of Oregon, a large student and former-student population lends Eugene a youthful vitality and countercultural edge. Full of parks and oriented to the outdoors, Eugene is a place where bike paths are used, pedestrians *always* have the right-of-way, and joggers are so plentiful that the city is known as the Running Capital of the World. Shopping and commercial streets surround the Eugene Hilton and the Hult Center for the Performing Arts, the two most prominent downtown buildings. During football season you can count on the U of O Ducks being the primary topic of most conversations.

GETTING HERE AND AROUND

Eugene's airport has rental cars, cabs, and shuttles that make the 15-minute trip to Eugene's city center. By train, Amtrak stops in the heart of downtown. Getting around Lane County's communities is easy with **Lane Transit District** (*LTD* ☎ *541/687–5555* ⊕ *www.ltd.org*) public transportation. Eugene is very bicycle-friendly.

ESSENTIALS

Visitor Information Eugene, Cascades and Coast Adventure Center ✉ *3312 Gateway St., Springfield* ☎ *541/484–5307, 800/547–5445* ⊕ *www. eugenecascadescoast.org.*

EXPLORING

TOP ATTRACTIONS

FAMILY **Cascades Raptor Center.** This birds-of-prey nature center and hospital hosts more than 30 species of birds. A visit is a great outing for kids, who can learn what owls eat, why and where birds migrate, and all sorts of other raptor facts. Some of the full-time residents include turkey vultures, bald eagles, owls, hawks, falcons, and kites. ✉ *32275 Fox Hollow Rd.* ☎ *541/485–1320* ⊕ *www.eraptors.org* ⚐ *$8* ⊙ *Apr.–Oct., Tues.–Sun. 10–6, Nov.–Mar., Tues.–Sun. 10–4.*

King Estate Winery. One of Oregon's largest producers is known for their crisp Pinot Gris and silky Pinot Noir and boasts the world's largest organic vineyard. The visitor center offers wine tasting and production tours, and the restaurant highlights local meats and organic produce grown in the estate gardens. ⊠ *80854 Territorial Rd.* ☎ *541/942–9874* ⊕ *www.kingestate.com* ⊘ *Daily 11–8.*

Ninkasi Brewing Company. Named after the Sumerian goddess of fermentation, Ninkasi has grown from a little startup in 2006 to a major supplier of craft beer. Its flagship beer, Total Domination IPA, is signature Northwest, with bold flavor and lots of hops. Visit the tasting room and enjoy a tasting flight or a pint, either indoors or on the patio. The beer menu changes often and includes a few hard-to-find limited-production beers. If you'd like a little food to go with your beer, you'll usually find one of Eugene's many food carts right there on the patio. Free brewery tours are offered daily. ⊠ *272 Van Buren St.* ☎ *541/344–2739* ⊕ *www.ninkasibrewing.com* ⊘ *Daily noon–10 pm.*

WORTH NOTING

5th Street Public Market. A former chicken-processing plant is the site of this popular shopping mall, filled with small crafts, art, and gifts stores. Dining includes sit-down restaurants, a wine bar, and the international diversity of the second-floor food esplanade. ⊠ *296 E. 5th Ave.* ☎ *541/484–0383* ⊕ *www.5stmarket.com* ⊘ *Shops Mon.–Sat. 10–7, Sun. 11–6.*

Alton Baker Park. This parcel of open land on the banks of the Willamette River is named after the late publisher of Eugene's newspaper, the *Register-Guard,* and is the site of many community events. Live music is performed in summer at the Cuthbert Amphitheater. There's fine hiking and biking on a footpath that runs along the river for the length of the park, and an 18-hole disc golf course. Also worth seeing is the Whilamut Natural Area, an open space with 13 "talking stones," each with an inscription. ⊠ *200 Day Island Rd.* ☎ *541/682–4906* ⊕ *www.altonbakerpark.com/.*

Jordan Schnitzer Museum of Art. Works from the 20th and 21st centuries are a specialty in these handsome galleries on the University of Oregon campus. They feature works by many leading Pacific Northwest artists, and European, Korean, Chinese, and Japanese works are also on view, as are 300 works commissioned by the Works Progress Administration in the 1930s and '40s. You can also view an ever-changing collection of important works from private collections by internationally recognized artists through the museum's Masterworks On Loan program. ⊠ *1430 Johnson La.* ☎ *541/346–3027* ⊕ *jsma.uoregon.edu* ⊒ *$5* ⊘ *Tues.–Sun. 11–5, Wed. 11–8.*

FAMILY **Mount Pisgah Arboretum.** This beautiful nature preserve near southeast Eugene includes extensive all-weather trails, educational programs for all ages, and facilities for special events. Its visitor center holds workshops and features native amphibian and reptile terraria; microscopes for exploring tiny seeds, bugs, feathers, and snakeskins; "touch me" exhibits; reference books; and a working viewable beehive. ⊠ *34901 Frank Parrish Rd.* ☎ *541/747–3817* ⊕ *www.mountpisgaharboretum.org* ⊒ *Parking $4* ⊘ *Park, daily dawn–dusk; visitor center, hours vary.*

FAMILY **Science Factory.** Formerly the Willamette Science and Technology Center (WISTEC), and still known to locals by its former name, Eugene's imaginative, hands-on museum assembles rotating exhibits designed for curious young minds. The adjacent **planetarium,** one of the largest in the Pacific Northwest, presents star shows and entertainment events. ✉ *2300 Leo Harris Pkwy.* ☎ *541/682–7888* ⊕ *www.sciencefactory.org* 🎫 *$4 for exhibit hall or planetarium, $7 for both* ☉ *Exhibit hall, Wed.– Sun. 10–4; planetarium, Sat.–Sun., shows at 10:30 and on the hour until 3; closed Oregon Ducks home football games.*

Sweet Cheeks Winery. This estate vineyard lies on a prime sloping hillside in the heart of the Willamette Valley appellation. It also supplies grapes to several award-winning wineries. Bring a picnic and enjoy the amazing view from the lawn outside the tasting room, or take advantage of the food available for purchase. Friday-night tastings are embellished with cheese pairings and live music. ✉ *27007 Briggs Hill Rd.* ☎ *541/349– 9463, 877/309–9463* ⊕ *www.sweetcheekswinery.com* ☉ *Sat.–Thurs. noon–6, Fri. noon–9.*

University of Oregon. The true heart of Eugene lies southeast of the city center at its university. Several fine old buildings can be seen on the 250-acre campus; **Deady Hall,** built in 1876, is the oldest. More than 400 varieties of trees grace the bucolic grounds, along with outdoor sculptures that include *The Pioneer* and *The Pioneer Mother.* The two bronze figures by Alexander Phimster Proctor were dedicated to the men and women who settled the Oregon Territory and less than a generation later founded the university. ✉ *1585 E. 13th Ave.* ☎ *541/346–1000* ⊕ *www.uoregon.edu.*

University of Oregon Museum of Natural and Cultural History. Relics on display are devoted to Pacific Northwest anthropology and the natural sciences. Highlights include the fossil collection of Thomas Condon, Oregon's first geologist, and a pair of 9,000-year-old sandals made of sagebrush. ✉ *1680 E. 15th Ave.* ☎ *541/346–3024* ⊕ *natural-history. uoregon.edu* 🎫 *$5* ☉ *Tues.–Sun. 11–5.*

WHERE TO EAT

$$
MODERN
AMERICAN

✕ **Café 440.** Putting a modern twist on classic comfort food, this airy, industrial-chic space features locally grown ingredients and a great local beer list. Along with updated classics like mac and cheese, burgers, and fish-and-chips, you'll find innovative versions of ahi *poke* (salad) and salmon cakes. Be sure and save room for one of the house-made dessert classics like crème brûlée or bread pudding. Enjoy live music every other Tuesday night, or try the wine-tasting flight on Wednesday nights. $ *Average main: $21* ✉ *440 Coburg Rd.* ☎ *541/505–8493* ⊕ *cafe440eugene. com* ☉ *No dinner Sun.*

$$
PACIFIC
NORTHWEST

✕ **Grit Kitchen and Wine.** You know you're in for local, seasonal ingredients when the chalkboard in this intimate place right across the street from the Ninkasi Brewery in Eugene's eccentric Whiteaker neighborhood lists nearly 20 local farmers and purveyors who are suppliers. The menu changes often, depending on what's in season. Eat inside and take advantage of the open kitchen to watch the chefs at work, or enjoy a pleasant outdoor dining experience on either of the two decks. The food is quintessential Northwest, featuring complex and unexpected flavors and a wide range of textures. You can order à la carte, or

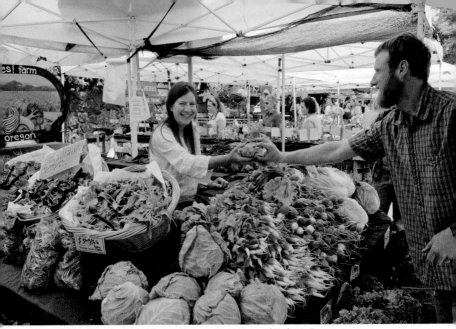

Fresh produce from Hey Bayles! Farm at the Lane County Farmers' Market in Eugene.

choose the Fixed Four, the weekly changing four-course feast; optional wine pairings are available. $ *Average main: $21* ✉ *1080 W. 3rd St.* ☎ *541/343–0501* ⊕ *gritkitchen.com* ⊙ *Closed Sun. and Mon. No lunch.*

$$$
FRENCH

✕ **Marché.** The name translates into "market," which is appropriate given the location in the bustling 5th Street Market, but also because this renowned Eugene restaurant works with more than a dozen local farmers to bring fresh, local organic food to the table. Specialties include salmon, halibut, sturgeon, and beef tenderloin, braised pork shoulders, and outstanding local oysters. The extensive wine list puts an emphasis on Oregon and France. There's also a Sunday brunch that offers amazing warm beignets. $ *Average main: $30* ✉ *296 E. 5th Ave.* ☎ *541/342–3612* ⊕ *www.marcherestaurant.com.*

$$$
ITALIAN

✕ **Ristorante Italiano.** The chef uses fresh local produce from the restaurant's own farm, but this bistro-style café across from the University of Oregon is best known for its authentic Italian cuisine, with a heavy emphasis on fresh local seafood. The menu changes according to the season, but staples include delicious salads and soups, ravioli, grilled chicken, pizza, and sandwiches. At dinner they feature daily lamb and seafood specials that are well worth asking about. The dining room, shaded by blossoming cherry trees in the spring, has a quiet, understated European feel, and there's outdoor seating on the patio in good weather. Breakfast and Sunday brunch are served. $ *Average main: $26* ✉ *754 E. 13th Ave.* ☎ *541/342–6963, 800/321–6963* ⊙ *No lunch Sat.*

WHERE TO STAY

$ 🏠 **Campbell House.** One of the oldest structures in Eugene, built in 1892, combines architectural details and a mixture of century-old antiques and reproductions to lend each of the rooms a distinctive personality. **Pros:** classic architecture; comfortable rooms; well-kept grounds. **Cons:** rooms lack some of the amenities of nearby hotels. *⑤ Rooms from: $129 ⊠ 252 Pearl St. ☎ 541/343–1119, 800/264–2519 ⊕ www. campbellhouse.com ⤳ 12 rooms, 6 suites ⏐◎⏐ Breakfast.*

B&B/INN

$$ 🏠 **C'est la Vie Inn.** Listed on the National Register of Historic Places, this 1891 Queen Anne Victorian bed-and-breakfast provides old-world comfort and modern-day amenities in its luxurious and romantic guest rooms. **Pros:** outstanding service and value. **Cons:** few rooms. *⑤ Rooms from: $150 ⊠ 1006 Taylor St. ⊕ cestlavieinn.com ⤳ 3 rooms, 1 suite ⏐◎⏐ Breakfast.*

B&B/INN
Fodor'sChoice
★

$ 🏠 **Excelsior Inn.** Quiet sophistication, attention to architectural detail, and rooms furnished in a refreshingly understated manner, each with a marble-and-tile bath and some with fireplaces, suggest a European inn. **Pros:** romantic accommodations; excellent service and restaurant. **Cons:** formal in a casual town. *⑤ Rooms from: $135 ⊠ 754 E. 13th Ave. ☎ 541/342–6963, 800/321–6963 ⊕ www.excelsiorinn.com ⤳ 14 rooms ⏐◎⏐ Breakfast.*

B&B/INN
Fodor'sChoice
★

$$ 🏠 **Valley River Inn.** At this sprawling inn on the banks of the Willamette River, some rooms have an outdoor patio or balcony, some have river or pool views, and concierge rooms have access to a private lounge. **Pros:** location on the river; lots of amenities; **Cons:** basic and fairly banal room decor, mediocre restaurant. *⑤ Rooms from: $159 ⊠ 1000 Valley River Way ☎ 541/743–1000, 800/543–8266 ⊕ www.valleyriverinn. com ⤳ 257 rooms.*

HOTEL

NIGHTLIFE AND THE ARTS

Hult Center for the Performing Arts. This is the locus of Eugene's cultural life. Renowned for the quality of its acoustics, the center has two theaters that are home to Eugene's symphony and opera. *⊠ 1 Eugene Center ☎ 541/682–5087 Administration, 541/682–5000 Tickets ⊕ www. hultcenter.org.*

Oregon Bach Festival. Conductor Helmuth Rilling leads the internationally known Oregon Bach Festival every summer. Concerts, chamber music, and social events—held mainly in Eugene at the Hult Center and the University of Oregon School of Music but also in Corvallis and Florence—are part of this three-week event. *⊠ 1787 Agate St. ☎ 541/682–5000 for tickets, 800/457–1486 for information ⊕ oregon-bachfestival.com.*

SPORTS AND THE OUTDOORS

BIKING AND JOGGING

The **River Bank Bike Path,** originating in Alton Baker Park on the Willamette's north bank, is a level and leisurely introduction to Eugene's topography. It's one of 120 miles of trails in the area. **Prefontaine Trail,** used by area runners, travels through level fields and forests for 1½ miles.

RECREATIONAL AREAS

FAMILY **Skinner Butte Park.** Rising from the south bank of the Willamette River, this forested enclave provides the best views of any of the city's parks; it also has the greatest historic cachet, since it was here that Eugene Skinner staked the claim that put Eugene on the map. Children can scale a replica of Skinner Butte, uncover fossils, and cool off under a rain circle. Skinner Butte Loop leads to the top of Skinner Butte, traversing sometimes difficult terrain through a mixed-conifer forest. ⊠ *248 Cheshire Ave.* ☎ *541/682–4800* 🎫 *Free* ☉ *Dawn–dusk.*

SKIING

Willamette Pass. With a summit 6,683 feet high in the Cascade Range, this pass packs an annual average snowfall of 430 inches and has access to 29 ski runs with a vertical drop of 1,563 feet. Four triple chairs and one six-person detachable service the downhill ski areas, and 13 miles of Nordic trails lace the pass. Facilities include a ski shop; day care; a bar and restaurant; and Nordic and downhill rentals, repairs, and instruction. ⊠ *Hwy. 58, 69 miles southeast of Eugene* ☎ *541/345–7669* ⊕ *www.willamettepass.com* ☉ *Wed.–Sun. 9–4 during ski season.*

SWIMMING

OFF THE
BEATEN
PATH

Waldo Lake. Nestled in old-growth forest, this mountain lake is famed as being remarkably clean and pristine. The lake is accessible only after a short hike, so bring comfortable shoes. ⊠ *Off Hwy. 58* ✛ *From Eugene, take Hwy. 58 to Oakridge and continue toward Willamette Pass; take Forest Road 5897 north 8 miles to the southern part of the lake, or 14 miles to the north portion.*

SHOPPING

Tourists coming to the Willamette Valley, especially to Eugene, can't escape without experiencing the **5th Street Public Market** in downtown Eugene. There are plenty of small crafts shops, and the food mall offers many cuisines, including vegetarian, pizza, and seafood.

Valley River Center. The largest shopping center between Portland and San Francisco has five department stores, including Macy's and JCPenney, plus 130 specialty shops and a food court. ⊠ *293 Valley River Center* ☎ *541/683–5513* ⊕ *www.valleyrivercenter.com.*

MCKENZIE BRIDGE

58 miles east of Eugene on Hwy. 126.

On the beautiful McKenzie River, lakes, waterfalls, and covered bridges surround the town of McKenzie Bridge and wilderness trails in the Cascades. Fishing, skiing, backpacking, and rafting are among the most popular activities in the area.

GETTING HERE AND AROUND

McKenzie Bridge is about an hour from Eugene, on Highway 126. It is just 38 miles from Hoodoo Ski Area, but its proximity can be deceiving if the snow is heavy. Bend also is close at 64 miles to the east.

4

EXPLORING

McKenzie River Highway. Highway 126, as it heads east from Eugene, is known as the McKenzie River Highway. Following the curves of the river, it passes grazing lands, fruit and nut orchards, and the small riverside hamlets of the McKenzie Valley. From the highway you can glimpse the bouncing, bubbling, blue-green McKenzie River, one of Oregon's top fishing, boating, and white-water rafting spots, against a backdrop of densely forested mountains, splashing waterfalls, and jet-black lava beds. The small town of McKenzie Bridge marks the end of the McKenzie River Highway and the beginning of the 26-mile McKenzie River National Recreation Trail, which heads north through the Willamette National Forest along portions of the Old Santiam Wagon Road.

OFF THE BEATEN PATH

McKenzie Pass. Just beyond McKenzie Bridge, Highway 242 begins a steep, 22-mile eastward climb to McKenzie Pass in the Cascade Range. The scenic highway, which passes through the Mt. Washington Wilderness Area and continues to the town of Sisters (⇨ *Central Oregon*), is generally closed November through June because of heavy snow. Novice motorists take note, this is not a drive for the timid: it's a challenging exercise in negotiating tight curves at quickly fluctuating, often slow speeds—the skid marks on virtually every turn attest to hasty braking—so take it slow, and don't be intimidated by cars on your tail itching to take the turns more quickly. The route is closed to trucks and large trailers and motor homes.

WHERE TO EAT AND STAY

$

AMERICAN

FAMILY

✕ **Takoda's Restaurant.** A popular roadside café serves burgers, sandwiches, great soups, salads, pizza, and daily specials. The burger selection includes not only beef, but seafood, chicken, turkey, and veggie options. If the weather is nice, sit outside in their beautiful garden area out back. A video game room keeps kids happy. $ *Average main: $10* ✉ *91806 Mill Creek Rd., Milepost 47.5 McKenzie Hwy., Blue River* ☎ *541/822–1153* ⊕ *www.takodasrainbow.com.*

$

RESORT

⌂ **Belknap Hot Springs Resort.** A pleasant lodge, with comfortable though not luxurious rooms, and a campground with both tent and trailer sites, are nestled onto the banks of the beautiful McKenzie River. **Pros:** hot springs; wooded location. **Cons:** 14-day cancellation policy; two-night minimum on weekends; trailers and motor homes detract from the rustic atmosphere. $ *Rooms from: $120* ✉ *59296 Belknap Springs Rd.* ☎ *541/822–3512* ⊕ *www.belknaphotsprings.com* ⥅ *19 rooms, 7 cabins* ⦿*Breakfast.*

$

B&B/INN

⌂ **Eagle Rock Lodge.** These wood-paneled rooms filled with quilts and antiques are surprisingly luxurious and provide a romantic, relaxing retreat in the woods. **Pros:** great location on the McKenzie River; comfortable atmosphere. **Cons:** a distance from non-outdoor activities. $ *Rooms from: $130* ✉ *49198 McKenzie Hwy., Vida* ☎ *541/822–3630, 888/773–4333* ⊕ *www.eaglerocklodge.com* ⥅ *8 rooms* ⦿*Breakfast.*

SPORTS AND THE OUTDOORS

GOLF

Tokatee Golf Club. Ranked one of the best golf courses in Oregon by *Golf Digest*, this 18-hole beauty is tucked away near the McKenzie River with views of the Three Sisters Mountains, native ponds, and streams. *Tokatee* is a Chinook word meaning "a place of restful beauty." The course offers a practice range, carts, lessons, rentals, a coffee shop and snack bar, and Wi-Fi. ⊠ *54947 McKenzie Hwy.* ☎ *541/822–3220, 800/452–6376* ⊕ *www.tokatee.com* ⊆ *18 holes $47; 9 holes $27.*

RECREATIONAL AREAS

Cougar Dam and Lake. Four miles outside McKenzie Bridge is the highest embankment dam ever built by the Army Corps of Engineers—452 feet above the streambed. The resulting reservoir, on the South Fork McKenzie River, covers 1,280 acres. The dam generates 25 megawatts of power, and includes a fish collection and sorting facility, and a temperature control tower to keep the downstream water at a suitable temperature for spawning. The public recreation areas are in the Willamette National Forest. You can visit the dam year-round, but some campgrounds are open only from April to September. ⊠ *Forest Rd. 19, Willamette National Forest* ☎ *541/822–3381* ⊆ *Free* ☉ *June–Sept., daily.*

Terwilliger Hot Springs (Cougar Hot Springs). Bring a towel and enjoy the soaking pools in this natural hot-springs area. Located an hour east of Eugene off Highway 126, the pools are a short hike from the parking area, and include a changing area. Soaking aficionados will find Terwilliger to be rustic, which many regard as an advantage, though the popularity of this beautiful spot can be a drawback. The pools are in a forest of old-growth firs and cedars, and just downstream is a beautiful lagoon complete with waterfall that is also suitable for swimming. Clothing is optional. ⊠ *Off Forest Rd. 19, Blue River* ☎ *541/822–3381* ⊆ *$6* ☉ *Dawn–dusk.*

Willamette National Forest. Stretching 110 miles along the western slopes of the Cascade Range, this forest boasts boundless recreation opportunities, including camping, hiking, boating, ATV riding, and winter sports. It extends from the Mt. Jefferson area east of Salem to the Calapooya Mountains northeast of Roseburg, encompassing 1,675,407 acres. ⊠ *3106 Pierce Pkwy., Suite D, Springfield* ☎ *541/225–6300* ⊕ *www.fs.usda.gov/willamette.*

WHITE-WATER RAFTING

FAMILY
Fodor's Choice
★

High Country Expeditions. Raft the white waters of the McKenzie River on a guided full- or half-day tour. You'll bounce through rapids, admire old-growth forest, and watch osprey and blue herons fishing. The outfit provides life jackets, splash gear, wet suits, booties (if requested), boating equipment, paddling instructions, river safety talk, a three-course riverside meal, and shuttle service back to your vehicle. Full day trips are $90, half-day trips $60. ⊠ *Belknap Hot Springs Resort, 59296 Belknap Springs Rd.* ☎ *541/822–8288, 888/461–7238* ⊕ *www.highcountryexpeditions.com.*

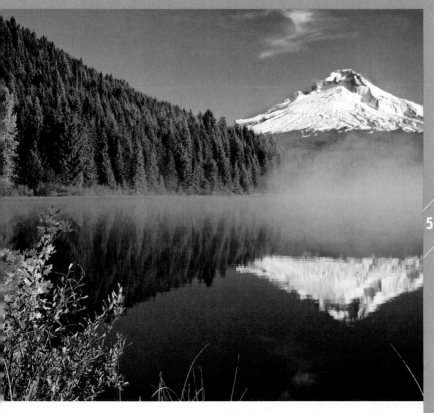

5

THE COLUMBIA RIVER GORGE AND MT. HOOD

WELCOME TO THE COLUMBIA RIVER GORGE AND MT. HOOD

TOP REASONS TO GO

★ **Outdoor rec mecca:** From kiteboarding in the Columbia River to mountain biking the slopes of Mt. Hood to hiking among the roaring waterfalls of the Gorge, this is a region tailor-made for adventure junkies.

★ **Historico-luxe:** Grand, distinctive landmarks like Timberline Lodge and the Columbia Gorge Hotel exude history and architectural distinction, offering some of the most memorable lodgings in the Northwest.

★ **Road-tripping:** This is a perfect region for backcountry driving through spectacular scenery—from Portland, you can make a full 250-mile loop through the Gorge out to Goldendale, Washington, returning to Hood River and then circling Mt. Hood to the south.

★ **Hop havens:** Oregon is the national seat of craft beer brewing, and the Gorge/Hood area has a fast-growing proliferation of taprooms, from Stevenson's tiny Walking Man Brewing to Pfriem, in Hood River.

1 Columbia River Gorge. The dams of the early 20th century transformed the Columbia River from the raging torrent that vexed Lewis and Clark in 1805 to the breathtaking but comparatively docile waterway that hosts kiteboarders and windsurfers today. Auto visitors have been scoping out the Gorge's picturesque bluffs and waterfalls for quite a while now—the road between Troutdale and The Dalles, on which construction began in 1913, was the country's first planned scenic highway.

2 Mt. Hood. Visible from 100 miles away, Mt. Hood (or simply "the Mountain," as some Portlanders call it) is the kind of rock that commands respect. It's holy ground for mountaineers, more than 10,000 of whom make a summit bid each year. Sightseers are often shocked by the summer snows, but skiers rejoice, keeping the mountain's resorts busy year-round. Mingle with laid-back powderhounds and other outdoorsy types in the hospitality villas of Welches and Government Camp.

GETTING ORIENTED

The mighty Columbia River flows west through the Cascade Range, past the Mt. Hood Wilderness Area, to Astoria. It's a natural border between Oregon and Washington to the north, and bridges link roads on both sides of the Gorge at Biggs Junction, The Dalles, Hood River, and Cascade Locks. The Gorge's watery recreation corridor stretches from Portland's east-ernmost suburbs past Hood River and The Dalles out to Maryhill and Goldendale, Washington. For portions of that drive, snowcapped Mt. Hood looms to the southwest. While the massive peak feels remote, the snowcapped heights are just 60 miles east of Portland. Hood River drains the mountain's north side, emptying into the Columbia at its name-sake town. Follow the river upstream and you'll trade the warm, low-elevation climes of the Gorge for the high country's tall pines and late-season snows.

Updated by Andrew Collins

Volcanoes, lava flows, Ice Age floodwaters, and glaciers were Nature's tools of choice when carving a breathtaking, nearly 100-mile landscape now called the Columbia River Gorge. Proof of human civilization here reaches back 31,000 years, and excavations near The Dalles have uncovered evidence that salmon fishing is a 10,000-year-old tradition in these parts. In 1805 Lewis and Clark discovered the Columbia River, the only major waterway that leads to the Pacific. Their first expedition was a treacherous route through wild, plunging rapids, but their successful navigation set a new exodus in motion.

Today the river has been tamed by a comprehensive system of hydroelectric dams and locks, and the towns in these parts are laid-back recreation hamlets whose residents harbor a fierce pride in their shared natural resources. Sightseers, hikers, and skiers have long found contentment in this robust region, officially labeled a National Scenic Area in 1986. They're joined these days by epicures scouring the Columbia's banks in search of farm-to-table cuisine, artisanal hop houses, and top-shelf vino. Highlights of the Columbia River Gorge include Multnomah Falls, Bonneville Dam, the rich orchard and vineyard land of Hood River, and Maryhill Museum of Art. Sailboaters, windsurfers, and kite-boarders take advantage of the blustery Gorge winds in the summer, their colorful sails decorating the waterway like windswept confetti.

To the south of Hood River are all the alpine attractions of the 11,250-foot-high Mt. Hood. With more than 2.2 million people living just up the road in greater Portland, you'd think this mountain playground would be overrun, but it's still easy to find solitude in the 300,000-acre wilderness surrounding the peak. Some of the world's best skiers take advantage of the powder on Hood, and they stick around in summertime for the longest ski season in North America at Palmer Snowfield, above Timberline Lodge.

THE COLUMBIA RIVER GORGE AND MT. HOOD PLANNER

WHEN TO GO

Winter weather in the Mt. Hood area is much more severe than in Portland and the Willamette Valley, and occasionally rough conditions permeate the Gorge, too. Rarely, Interstate 84 closes because of snow and ice. If you're planning a winter visit, be sure to carry plenty of warm clothes. High winds and single-digit temps are par for the course around 6,000 feet—the elevation of Timberline Lodge on Mt. Hood—in January. Note that chains are sometimes required for traveling over mountain passes.

Temperatures in the Gorge are mild year-round, rarely dipping below 30°F in winter and hovering in the high 70s in midsummer. As throughout Oregon, however, elevation is often a more significant factor than season, and an hour-long drive to Mt. Hood's Timberline Lodge can reduce those midsummer temps by 20–30 degrees. Don't forget that the higher reaches of Mt. Hood retain snow year-round.

In early fall, look for maple, tamarack, and aspen trees around the Gorge, bursting with brilliant red and gold color. No matter the season, the basalt cliffs, the acres of lush forest, and that glorious expanse of water make the Gorge one of the West's great scenic wonders.

FESTIVALS

Columbia Gorge Bluegrass Festival. One of the premier bluegrass fests in the West takes place in Stevenson, Washington, every fourth weekend in July. ⊕ *www.columbiagorgebluegrass.net.*

Hood River Hops Fest. In late September, beer lovers have the chance to sample some 60 hop-intensive beers in Hood River, which has become one of the top small towns in Oregon for craft brewing. ⊕ *www. hoodriver.org.*

Maryhill Winery Concert Series. About 20 minutes east of The Dalles on the Washington side of the Gorge, Maryhill Winery hosts summer concerts, drawing some nationally renowned rock and pop acts, in a cozy, 4,000-person amphitheater. ⊕ *www.maryhillwinery.com.*

Nicky USA's Wild About Game. This meat-centric food festival held in early September on Mt. Hood at Timberline Lodge features a competition among four top chefs each from Portland and Seattle. Guests can sample and vote on each dish and nibble and sip from a large marketplace of top Oregon purveyors, including cheese makers, charcuterie producers, wineries, and breweries. ⊕ *www.nickyusa.com/wag.*

Timberline Lodge Mountain Music Fest. This free single-day gathering at iconic Timberline Lodge takes place over Labor Day weekend and showcases top-name bluegrass bands from around the country. ⊕ *www. timberlinelodge.com/mountain-music-festival.*

GETTING HERE AND AROUND

The Columbia Gorge, which is easily accessed from Portland, is best explored by car. The same is generally true for the Mt. Hood area, but in season, the area ski resorts do have shuttle services from Portland and the airport. Even light exploring of the region, however, requires an automobile—take heart that the driving in these parts is scenic and relatively free of traffic. Just keep in mind that winter storms can result in road closures around Mt. Hood and, occasionally, even in the Gorge. It's just a 20-minute drive east of Portland to reach the beginning of the Columbia Gorge, in Troutdale. From Portland it's a one-hour drive to Hood River, a 90-minute drive to Mt. Hood, and a two-hour drive to Goldendale, Washington *(the farthest-away point covered in this chapter)*.

CAR TRAVEL

Interstate 84 is the main east–west route into the Columbia River Gorge, although you can also reach the area on the Washington side via slower but quite scenic Highway 14, which skirts the north side of the river. U.S. 26, which leads east from Portland, is the main route into the Mt. Hood area.

The scenic Historic Columbia River Highway (U.S. 30) from Troutdale to just east of Oneonta Gorge passes Crown Point State Park and Multnomah Falls. Interstate 84/U.S. 30 continues on to The Dalles. Highway 35 heads south from Hood River to the Mt. Hood area, intersecting with U.S. 26 near Government Camp. From Portland, the Columbia Gorge–Mt. Hood Scenic Loop is the easiest way to fully explore the Gorge and the mountain. Take Interstate 84 east to Troutdale and then follow U.S. 26 east to Mt. Hood, then take Highway 35 north to Hood River and Interstate 84 back to Portland. Or make the loop in reverse.

RESTAURANTS

A prominent locavore mentality pervades western Oregon generally, and low elevations around the Gorge mean long growing seasons for dozens of local producers. Fresh foods grown, caught, and harvested in the Northwest dominate menus in the increasingly sophisticated restaurants in the Gorge, especially in the charming town of Hood River, and up around Mt. Hood. Columbia River salmon is big, fruit orchards proliferate around Hood River, delicious huckleberries flourish in Mt. Hood National Forest, and the Gorge nurtures a glut of excellent vineyards. Additionally, even the smallest towns around the region have their own lively brewpubs with consistently tasty pub fare and tap after tap of craft ales. In keeping with the region's green and laid-back vibe, outdoor dining is highly popular.

HOTELS

The region is close enough that you could spend a day or two exploring the Gorge and Mt. Hood, using Portland hotels as your base. The best way to fully appreciate the Gorge, however, is to spend a night or two—look to Hood River and The Dalles for the largest selections of lodging options, although you'll also find some noteworthy resorts, motels, and B&Bs in some of the towns between Portland and Hood River, on both sides of the river. There are a couple of run-of-the-mill motels in Goldendale, but otherwise, you won't find any accommodations in the region east of The Dalles. The slopes of Mt. Hood are dotted with smart ski resorts, and towns like Government Camp and Welches have a mix of rustic and contemporary vacation rentals. The closer you are to Mt. Hood in any season, the earlier you'll want to reserve. With ski country working ever harder to attract summer patrons, Mt. Hood resorts like Timberline Lodge and Mt. Hood Skibowl offer some worthwhile seasonal specials. *Hotel reviews have been shortened. For full information, visit Fodors.com.*

WHAT IT COSTS IN U.S. DOLLARS				
	$	**$$**	**$$$**	**$$$$**
Restaurants	Under $17	$17–$23	$24–$30	Over $30
Hotels	Under $151	$151–$200	$201–$250	Over $250

Restaurant prices are the average cost of a main course at dinner or, if dinner is not served, at lunch. Hotel prices are the lowest cost of a standard double room in high season.

TOURS

EverGreen Escapes. The energetic crew at this highly respected tour operator provides both regularly scheduled and customizable tours of the Gorge (with themes that range from wine to hiking) and Mt. Hood, where options include hiking and snowshoeing. ☎ *503/252–1931, 866/203–7603* ⊕ *www.evergreenescapes.com* ✉ *From $135.*

Explore the Gorge. Customizable tours of the Gorge, Mt. Hood, and the Hood River Valley explore everything from the Lewis and Clark Trail to the region's microbreweries. ☎ *800/899–5676* ⊕ *www.explorethegorge. com* ✉ *From $180.*

Martin's Gorge Tours. Wine tours, waterfall hikes, and spring wildflower tours are among the popular trips offered by this Portland-based guide. ☎ *503/349–1323* ⊕ *www.martinsgorgetours.com* ✉ *From $49.*

Mt. Hood Adventure. The only outfitter on Mt. Hood that rents snowmobiles and offers snowmobile tours is also a well-respected tour company for snowshoe treks and sleigh rides in winter, and mountain hikes, biking trips, and boat excursions on area rivers—the shop is also a good place to buy gear and ask for advice on outdoorsy activities in the area. ✉ *88335 Government Camp Loop Rd., Government Camp* ☎ *503/715–2175* ⊕ *www.mthoodadventure.com* ✉ *Snowmobile tours from $189.*

VISITOR INFORMATION

Columbia River Gorge Visitors Association ☎ *509/427–8911* ⊕ *www.crgva. org.*

Mt. Hood Territory ☎ *800/424–3002* ⊕ *www.mthoodterritory.com.*

COLUMBIA RIVER GORGE

When glacial floods carved out most of the Columbia River Gorge at the end of the last Ice Age, they left behind massive, looming cliffs where the river bisects the Cascade mountain range. The size of the canyon and the wildly varying elevations make this small stretch of Oregon as ecologically diverse as anyplace in the state. In a few days along the Gorge you can mountain bike through dry canyons near The Dalles, hike through temperate rain forest in Oneonta Gorge, and take a woodland wildflower stroll just outside Hood River. At night you'll be rewarded with historic lodging and good food in one of a half-dozen mellow river towns. The country's second federally designated National Scenic Area remains exceptionally inviting.

HISTORIC COLUMBIA RIVER HIGHWAY

U.S. 30, paralleling I–84 for 22 miles between Troutdale and interstate Exit 35.

The oldest scenic highway in the United States is a construction marvel that integrates asphalt path with cliff, river, and forest landscapes. Paralleling the interstate, U.S. 30 climbs to forested riverside bluffs, passes half a dozen waterfalls, and provides access to hiking trails leading to still more falls and scenic overlooks. Completed in 1922, the serpentine highway was the first paved road in the Gorge built expressly for automotive sightseers. Technically, the Historic Columbia River Highway extends some 74 miles to The Dalles, but much of that is along modern Interstate 84—the 22-mile western segment is the real draw.

GETTING HERE AND AROUND

U.S. 30 heads east out of downtown Troutdale, but you can also access the route from Interstate 84 along the way, via Exit 22 near Corbett, Exit 28 near Bridal Veil Falls, Exit 31 at Multnomah Falls, and Exit 35, where it rejoins the interstate.

ESSENTIALS

Visitor Information Multnomah Falls Visitor Center ✉ *53000 E. Historic Columbia River Hwy., Exit 31 off I–84, 15 miles east of Troutdale, Bridal Veil* ☎ *503/695–2372* ⊕ *www.multnomahfallslodge.com.*

EXPLORING

FAMILY
Fodor's Choice
★

Multnomah Falls. A 620-foot-high double-decker torrent, the second-highest year-round waterfall in the nation, Multnomah is by far the most spectacular of the Gorge cataracts east of Troutdale. You can access the falls and Multnomah Lodge via a parking lot at Exit 31 off I–84, or via the Historic Columbia River Highway; from the parking area, a paved path winds to a bridge over the lower falls. A much steeper, though paved, 1.1-mile trail climbs to a viewing point overlooking the upper falls, and from here, unpaved but well-groomed trails join with others, allowing for as much as a full day of hiking in the mountains above the Gorge, if you're up for some serious but scenic trekking. Even the paved ramble to the top is fairly strenuous, but worth it to avoid the crowds that swarm the lower falls area in every season.

✉ *53000 E. Historic Columbia River Hwy., 15 miles east of Troutdale, Bridal Veil* ☎ *503/695–2376* ⊕ *www.multnomahfallslodge.com.*

Fodor's Choice   **Vista House at Crown Point.** A two-tier octagonal structure perched on
★   the edge of this 730-foot-high cliff offers unparalleled 30-mile views up and down the Columbia River Gorge. The building dates to 1917, its rotunda and lower level filled with displays about the Gorge and the highway. Vista House's architect Edgar Lazarus was the brother of Emma Lazarus, author of the poem displayed at the base of the Statue of Liberty. The property is part of the Crown Point State Scenic Corridor, which is administered by the Oregon State Parks office. ✉ *40700 E. Historic Columbia River Hwy., 10 miles east of Troutdale, Corbett* ☎ *503/695–2230, 800/551–6949* ⊕ *www.vistahouse.com* 🎟 *Free* ☉ *Daily 9–6.*

WHERE TO EAT AND STAY

$$ ✕ **Multnomah Falls Lodge.** Vaulted ceilings, stone fireplaces, and exqui-
AMERICAN   site views of Multnomah Falls are complemented by friendly service and reliably good American fare at this landmark restaurant, which is listed on the National Register of Historic Places. Consider the smoked salmon starter with apple-huckleberry compote, cod fish-and-chips, or the elk burger with aged Tillamook cheddar and garlic-sesame mayo. Breakfast favorites include the Hang Town fry oyster frittata with bacon, and the pancakes, available with marionberries, blueberries, or huckleberries. A particular pleaser for out-of-town guests, the champagne Sunday brunch is held 8–2. For a treat during warmer months, sit on the patio and get close to the falls without feeling a drop. ⑤ *Average main: $20* ✉ *53000 Historic Columbia River Hwy., Exit 31 off I-84, 15 miles east of Troutdale, Bridal Veil* ☎ *503/695–2376* ⊕ *www. multnomahfallslodge.com.*

$ ⛺ **McMenamins Edgefield.** Set in 74 acres of gardens, murals, orchards,
RESORT   and vineyards, this Georgian Revival manor that once housed the
Fodor's Choice   county poor farm is now operated by Northwest brewers and hospital-
★   ity innovators par excellence Mike and Brian McMenamin. **Pros:** plenty of eating and drinking choices; large variety of rooms and prices; great spa; on-site movie theater (only $3); live music events. **Cons:** this busy place can get pretty crowded; no TVs, phones, or air-conditioning in the rooms; most rooms share baths. ⑤ *Rooms from: $115* ✉ *2126 S.W. Halsey St.* ☎ *503/669–8610, 800/669–8610* ⊕ *www.mcmenamins.com* ⤳ *114 rooms, 20 with bath* ⑩ *No meals.*

SPORTS AND THE OUTDOORS

RECREATIONAL AREAS

Rooster Rock State Park. The most famous beach lining the Columbia River is right below Crown Point. Three miles of sandy beaches, panoramic cascades, and a large swimming area makes this a popular spot. True naturists appreciate that one of Oregon's two designated nude beaches is at the east end of Rooster Rock, and that it's not visible to conventional sunbathers—the area is especially popular with Portland's LGBT community. Rooster Rock is 9 miles east of Troutdale, and it's accessible only via the interstate. ✉ *I-84, Exit 25, 9 miles east*

of Troutdale, Corbett ☎ 503/695–2261 ⊕ www.oregonstateparks.org
Day use $5 per vehicle ⊙ Daily 7–dusk.

CASCADE LOCKS

7 miles east of Oneonta Gorge on Historic Columbia River Hwy. and I–84; 30 miles east of Troutdale on I–84.

In pioneer days, boats needing to pass the bedeviling rapids near the town of Whiskey Flats had to portage around them. The locks that gave the town its new name were completed in 1896, allowing waterborne passage for the first time. In 1938 they were submerged beneath the new Lake Bonneville when the Bonneville Lock and Dam became one of the most massive Corps of Engineers projects to come out of the New Deal. The town of Cascade Locks hung on to its name, though. A historic stern-wheeler still leads excursions from the town's port district, and the region's Native American tribes still practice traditional dip-net fishing near the current locks.

5

GETTING HERE AND AROUND

Cascade Locks is 45 miles east of Portland and 20 miles west of Hood River on Interstate 84. The town is also home to Bridge of the Gods ($1 toll), which is the only auto bridge crossing the Columbia River (it connects with Stevenson, Washington) between Portland and Hood River.

EXPLORING

FAMILY **Bonneville Dam.** President Franklin D. Roosevelt dedicated the first federal dam to span the Columbia in 1937. Its generators (visible from a balcony on a self-guided tour or up close during free guided tours offered daily in summer and on weekends the rest of the year) have a capacity of more than a million kilowatts, enough to supply power to more than 200,000 single-family homes. There's an extensive visitor center on Bradford Island, complete with underwater windows where gaggles of kids watch migrating salmon and steelhead as they struggle up fish ladders. The best viewing times are between April and October. In recent years the dwindling runs of wild Columbia salmon have made the dam a subject of much environmental controversy. ⊠ *Exit 40 from I–84, follow signs 1 mile to visitor center, Cascade Locks ☎ 541/374–8820 ⊕ www.nwp.usace.army.mil/Locations/ColumbiaRiver/Bonneville* *Free ⊙ Visitor center daily 9–5; powerhouse tours mid-June–Aug., daily at 11, 1, and 3; Sept.–mid-June, weekends at 11, 1, and 3.*

Cascade Locks Marine Park. This riverfront park is the home port of the 500-passenger stern-wheeler *Columbia Gorge*, which churns upriver, then back again, on one- and two-hour excursions through some of the Columbia River Gorge's most impressive scenery, mid-May to early October; brunch and dinner cruises are also available. The ship's captain discusses the Gorge's fascinating 40-million-year geology and pioneering spirits and legends, such as Lewis and Clark, who once triumphed over this very same river. The park itself, which includes a pedestrian bridge to leafy and tranquil Thunder Island, is a lovely spot for picnicking, and Thunder Island Brewing—at the north end of the park—serves first-rate craft beers. ⊠ *Marine Park, S.W. Portage Rd., Cascade Locks*

☎ *541/224–3900, 800/224–3901* ⊕ *www.portlandspirit.com* ⌦ *Cruises from $23* ⚓ *Reservations essential* ⊙ *Park open daily dawn–dusk; cruises May–Oct.*

WHERE TO EAT

$ ✕**Thunder Island Brewing.** Hikers, boaters, and others exploring the
AMERICAN Gorge gather at this laid-back, funky brewpub with several tables inside, as well as a large patio with picnic tables overlooking the Columbia River, Marine Park, and the little island for which the brewery is named. Order a glass of hoppy Pacific Crest Trail Pale Ale or malty Scotch Porter, and enjoy it with one of the light dishes from the short menu—the spinach-and-feta pasty, chicken-salad sandwich, and charcuterie, cheese, and smoked-fish plate are all excellent. Wine and hard cider are also served. ⑤ *Average main: $8* ⊠ *515 S.W. Portage Rd., Cascade Locks* ☎ *971/231–4599* ⊕ *www.thunderislandbrewing.com.*

SPORTS AND THE OUTDOORS

HIKING

Pacific Crest Trail. Cascade Locks bustles with grubby thru-hikers refueling along the 2,650-mile Canada-to-Mexico Pacific Crest Trail. Check out a scenic and strenuous portion of it, heading south from the trailhead at Herman Creek Horse Camp, just east of town. The route heads up into the Cascades, showing off monster views of the Gorge. Backpackers out for a longer trek will find idyllic campsites at Wahtum Lake, 14 miles south. You can also access the trail from the free parking area at Toll House Park, by the Bridge of the Gods. ⊠ *Off N.W. Forest La., 1 mile east of downtown, Cascade Locks* ☎ *541/308–1700* ⊕ *www. pcta.org.*

STEVENSON, WASHINGTON

Across the river from Cascade Locks via the Bridge of the Gods and 1 mile east on Hwy. 14.

With the Bridge of the Gods toll bridge spanning the Columbia River above the Bonneville Dam, Stevenson acts as a sort of "twin city" to Cascade Locks on the Oregon side. Tribal legends and the geologic record tell of the original Bridge of the Gods, a substantial landslide that occurred here sometime between AD 1000 and 1760, briefly linking the two sides of the Gorge before the river swept away the debris. The landslide's steel namesake now leads to tiny Stevenson, where vacationers traverse quiet Main Street, which has a few casual eateries and shops. Washington's Highway 14 runs through the middle of town, and since the cliffs on the Oregon side are more dramatic, driving this two-lane highway actually offers better views.

GETTING HERE AND AROUND

From the Oregon side of the Gorge, cross the Columbia River at the Bridge of the Gods ($1 toll).

ESSENTIALS

Visitor Information Skamania County Chamber of Commerce ⊠ *167 N.W. 2nd St., Stevenson* ☎ *509/427–8911, 800/989–9178* ⊕ *www.skamania.org.*

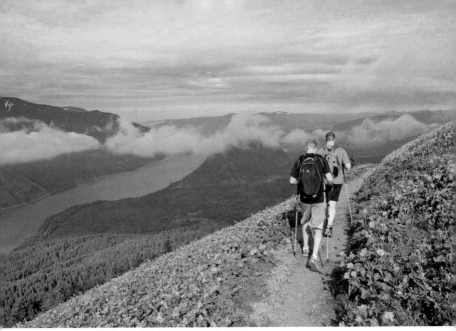
Dog Mountain Trail, Columbia River Gorge National Scenic Area

EXPLORING

FAMILY **Columbia Gorge Interpretive Center Museum.** A petroglyph whose eyes seem to look straight at you, "She Who Watches" or "Tsagaglalal" is the logo for this museum. Sitting among the dramatic basaltic cliffs on the north bank of the Columbia River Gorge, the museum explores the life of the Gorge: its history, culture, architecture, legends, and much more. Younger guests enjoy the reenactment of the Gorge's formation in the Creation Theatre, and the 37-foot-high fish wheel, a device like a mill wheel equipped with baskets for catching fish, from the 19th century. Historians appreciate studying the water route of the Lewis and Clark Expedition. There's also an eye-opening exhibit that examines current environmental impacts on the area. ⊠ *990 S.W. Rock Creek Dr.* ☎ *509/427–8211, 800/991–2338* ⊕ *www.columbiagorge.org* ◻ *$10* ⊘ *Daily 10–5.*

WHERE TO EAT AND STAY

$ ✕ **Big River Grill.** A tradition with hikers, bikers, fishermen, and scenic
AMERICAN drivers out exploring the Gorge, especially for weekend breakfast but also at lunch and dinnertime, this colorful roadhouse in the center of town is festooned with license plates, vintage signs, and kitschy artwork. Grab a seat at the counter or in one of the high-back wooden booths, and tuck into grilled wild salmon sandwich, chicken-fried chicken with eggs, home-style meat loaf with buttermilk-garlic mashed potatoes, and other hearty, reasonably priced fare. ⑤ *Average main: $14* ⊠ *192 S.W. 2nd St.* ☎ *509/427–4888* ⊕ *www.thebigrivergrill.com.*

$$ ✕ **Cascade Room at Skamania Lodge.** At Skamania Lodge's signature res-
PACIFIC taurant, with its stunning views of sky, river, and cliff scapes, chef
NORTHWEST Mark Henry, draws on local seafood and regionally sourced meats and
Fodor'sChoice produce, turning out dandy dishes like a Dungeness crab tower with
★ avocado, beet coulis, and basil oil; and braised lamb shank with an
aromatic Merlot sauce and buttermilk-mashed potatoes. There are sev-
eral lighter and less-pricey items, too, from burgers to wild-mushroom
risotto. The lavish Sunday Champagne brunch buffet draws patrons
from miles around. Henry also oversees the kitchen at the resort's sim-
pler and more casual River Rock café, which has both indoor and
outdoor seating with the same smashing views. ⑤ *Average main: $23*
✉ *Skamania Lodge, 1131 S.W. Skamania Lodge Way* ☎ *509/427–7700*
⊕ *www.skamania.com.*

$$$ ⛲ **Bonneville Hot Springs Resort and Spa.** At this modern resort on a
RESORT wooded tract just west of Stevenson, spacious rooms with upscale fur-
nishings allow guests to enjoy historic mineral springs and glorious
grounds. **Pros:** impressive architectural detail; the Pacific Crest Trail
passes directly through the property. **Cons:** the dull, boxy exterior
belies what's inside; rooms and public areas could use some updating. ⑤ *Rooms from: $209* ✉ *1252 E. Cascade Dr., North Bonneville*
☎ *509/427–7767, 866/459–1678* ⊕ *www.bonnevilleresort.com* ⤳ *78
rooms* ⦿ *No meals.*

$$$ ⛲ **Skamania Lodge.** This warm, woodsy lodge on an expansive, verdant
RESORT swath of forest and meadows impresses with a multitude of windows
FAMILY overlooking the surrounding mountains and Gorge, an outstanding
Fodor'sChoice array of recreational facilities, and handsome, Pacific Northwest–chic
★ accommodations, many with fireplaces and all with views. **Pros:** Just a
45-minute drive from Portland but feels secluded and totally relaxing;
plenty of fun outdoorsy activities; first-rate spa and dining facilities.
Cons: expensive for a large family; can get crowded—sometimes there's
a wait for a table in the dining room. ⑤ *Rooms from: $205* ✉ *1131
S.W. Skamania Lodge Way* ☎ *509/427–7700, 800/221–7117* ⊕ *www.
skamania.com* ⤳ *254 rooms* ⦿ *No meals.*

NIGHTLIFE AND THE ARTS

Walking Man Brewing. This sunshiny patio and cozy interior are great
spots for creative pizzas and sampling the dozen-or-so craft ales. After
a couple of pints of the strong Homo Erectus IPA and Knuckle Drag-
ger Pale Ale, you may go a little ape. Live music on summer weekends
skews twangy and upbeat. ✉ *240 S.W. 1st St.* ☎ *509/427–5520* ⊕ *www.
walkingmanbeer.com* ☼ *Closed Mon. and Tues.*

SPORTS AND THE OUTDOORS

RECREATIONAL AREA

Fodor'sChoice **Beacon Rock State Park.** For several hundred years this 848-foot rock was
★ a landmark for river travelers, including Native Americans, who rec-
ognized this point as the last rapids of the Columbia River. Lewis and
Clark are thought to have been the first white men to see the volcanic
remnant. Even most casual hikers can make the steep but safe trek up
to the top of the rock—allow about 45–60 minutes round-trip. More
serious hikers should head to the trailhead for Hamilton Mountain,

which is reached via a beautiful, though arduous, 8-mile ramble over a roaring waterfall, through dense temperate rain forest, and finally up to a 2,400-foot summit with breathtaking views up and down the Gorge. ⊠ *34841 Hwy. 14, 7 miles west of Bridge of the Gods, Skamania* ☎ *509/427–8265* ⊕ *www.parks.wa.gov* 💲 *$10 day pass.*

HOOD RIVER

20 miles east of Cascade Locks and 60 miles east of Portland on I–84.

This picturesque riverside community of about 7,200 residents affords visitors spectacular views both of the Columbia River and snowcapped Mt. Hood. More than 40 civic and commercial buildings date from 1893 to the 1930s, some of which are listed in the National Register of Historic Places.

Hood River is the dining and lodging hub of the Gorge, with an increasingly respected bounty of urbane farm-to-table restaurants, up-and-coming craft breweries and wine-tasting rooms, and diverting shops and art galleries. Little wonder this is one of the most popular weekend getaways among Portlanders, all the more so since the surrounding countryside abounds with orchards and vineyards, making it a favorite destination for fans of U-pick farmsteads and tasting rooms. Hood River wineries grow a broader range of grapes than Oregon's more famous Willamette Valley, and wine touring has become a favorite activity in the area.

GETTING HERE AND AROUND

Reach Hood River from Portland by driving 60 miles east on Interstate 84, or from Mt. Hood by heading 40 miles north on Highway 35.

ESSENTIALS

Visitor Information Hood River County Chamber of Commerce ⊠ *720 E. Port Marina Dr.* ☎ *541/386–2000, 800/366–3530* ⊕ *www.hoodriver.org.*

EXPLORING

Glassometry Studios. Artist and teacher Laurel Marie Hagner operates this colorful gallery and sculpture garden just off the Hood River Fruit Loop, near the village of Odell. You can admire the larger-than-life, riotously vibrant glass sculptures with a walk through the garden, watch live glass-blowing demonstrations (and take classes) in the studio, and browse the fanciful yet absolutely functional vases, bowls, drinking glasses, decanters, and decorative glass art in the studio. ⊠ *3015 Lower Mill Dr.* ☎ *541/354–3015* ⊕ *www.glassometry.com* 💲 *Free* ☺ *Wed.–Sun. 11–5.*

Fodor's Choice ★ **Gorge White House.** You'll find pretty much everything the Hood River Valley is famous for growing and being produced at this picturesque, century-old farm anchored by a Dutch Colonial farmhouse and surrounded by acres of U-pick flowers, apple and peach trees, and blackberry and blueberry bushes. After strolling through the farm fields, stop inside the main house to sample wines—the tasting room carries one of the largest selections of Columbia River wines in the region. Out back, there's a farm store, another tasting room serving local craft beer and cider, and a garden patio with seating and a food-truck-style

Vineyards in the Hood River Valley

café serving delicious strawberry salads, pulled-pork sandwiches, pear pizzas, and other light fare. ✉ *2265 Hwy. 35* ☎ *541/386–2828* ⊕ *www. thegorgewhitehouse.com* ⊗ *June–Sept., daily 10–7; Apr., May, and Oct., Fri.–Mon. 10–7.*

Fodor's Choice ★ **Marchesi Vineyards.** Somewhat unusual for the Pacific Northwest, this boutique winery with a small, airy tasting room and a verdant garden patio specializes in Italian varietals—Moscato, Primitivo, Dolcetto, Sangiovese, Barbera, Nebbiolo, and a few others. Owner Franco Marchesi hails from Italy's Piemonte regoin, and he's earned serious kudos for his finesse as a winemaker. ✉ *3955 Belmont Dr.* ☎ *541/386–1800* ⊕ *www. marchesivineyards.com* ⊗ *June–late Nov., daily 11–6; late Nov.–May, Fri.–Sun. 11–6.*

Mt. Hood Railroad. Scenic passenger excursions along a small rail line established in 1906 offer a picturesque and relaxing way to survey Mt. Hood and the Hood River Valley. Chug alongside the Hood River through vast fruit orchards before climbing up steep forested canyons, glimpsing Mt. Hood along the way. There are several trip options, from $30: a four-hour excursion (serves light concessions), dinner, brunch, and several themed trips, like murder-mysteries and Old West robberies. Exceptional service is as impressive as the scenery. ✉ *110 Railroad Ave.* ☎ *541/386–3556, 800/872–4661* ⊕ *www.mthoodrr.com* ⊗ *Mid-Apr.–late Oct.*

Viento Wines. Focused more on whites than most of the winemakers in the Gorge region, Viento has a stunning tasting room with vaulted ceilings, soaring windows, and a large patio overlooking the on-site vineyard of Riesling grapes. This is a lovely space for tasting and chatting with fellow oenophiles. Notable wines here include a crisp Grüner Velt-liner, a food-friendly Brut Rosé, and one of the better Oregon Pinot Noirs you'll find in the Hood River region. ⊠ *301 Country Club Rd.* ☎ *541/386–3026* ⊕ *www.vientowines.com* ⏱ *Daily 11–5.*

NEED A BREAK?
Doppio Coffee + Lounge. Sunshine fills the small dining room and outdoor seating area of this high-ceilinged, contemporary downtown coffee bar that serves fine espresso drinks as well as local wines and craft beers. It's great for light snacking—there's a nice selection of baked goods and fine chocolates—but there are also substantial grilled panini sandwiches, salads, and soups. ⊠ *310 Oak St.* ☎ *541/386–3000* ⊕ *www. doppiohoodriver.com* ⏱ *No dinner.*

Western Antique Aeroplane and Automobile Museum. Housed at Hood River's tiny airport (general aviation only), the museum's impressive, meticulously restored, propeller-driven planes are all still in flying condition. The antique steam cars, Model Ts, and sleek Depression-era sedans are road-worthy, too. Periodic car shows and an annual fly-in draw thousands of history buffs and spectators. ⊠ *1600 Air Museum Rd., off Hwy. 281* ☎ *541/308–1600* ⊕ *www.waaamuseum.org* 🎟 *$14* ⏱ *Daily 9–5.*

WHERE TO EAT

$$$ ✕ **Celilo Restaurant.** Refined and relaxing, this high-ceilinged restaurant
PACIFIC in a contemporary downtown building is popular both for dinner and
NORTHWEST enjoying a glass of local wine in the bar, which has both indoor and outdoor seating on colorful Oak Street. Chef Ben Stenn presents a seasonally changing menu of deftly crafted Pacific Northwest fare—order the cast-iron-skillet seafood-and-chorizo roast if it's on the menu, and also keep an eye out for house-preserved duck-leg confit with pickled green beans, pork-belly lardons, and organic greens. $ *Average main: $24* ⊠ *16 Oak St.* ☎ *541/386–5710* ⊕ *www.celilorestaurant.com.*

$$ ✕ **Nora's Table.** Chef Kathy Watson brings bold, world-beat flavors to
ECLECTIC this unpretentious but sophisticated downtown bistro that's also well
Fodor's Choice regarded for its Northwest-focused wine list. Mussels simmered in
★ Goan-style curry, local salmon with cannellini beans and Italian salsa verde, and New Mexico–style veggie enchiladas reflect the menu's varied approach. Nora's doesn't serve lunch, but is justly popular for breakfast, served only Friday–Sunday, and featuring the likes of Bombay-town fry with curried potatoes and vegetables, fried oysters, and poached eggs, and Louisiana-style eggs Benedict with tasso ham and grits. $ *Average main: $18* ⊠ *110 5th St.* ☎ *541/387–4000* ⊕ *www.norastable.com* ⏱ *No lunch.*

$$ ✕ **Solstice Wood Fire Cafe.** It can be hard to score a table on weekends in
PIZZA this snazzy space along the Hood River waterfront. What's all the fuss? Wood-fire-grilled pizzas with unusual toppings—such as the Cherry Girl, layered with local cherries, spicy chorizo, goat cheese, mozzarella, and marinara sauce—plus bountiful salads, wood-fired mac-and-cheese, and juicy burgers. The wood-fire oven comes into play for dessert, too, with classic s'mores. $ *Average main: $17* ⊠ *501 Portway Ave.* ☎ *541/436–0800* ⊕ *www.solsticewoodfirecafe.com.*

$$ **✕Stonehedge Gardens.** It's not just the cuisine that's out of this world,
AMERICAN this Columbia Gorge institution is of another time and place, sur-
Fodor'sChoice rounded by 7 acres of lush English-style gardens that gracefully frame
★ its multitude of stone terraces and trickling fountains. There's a *pet-
anque* (lawn bowling) court for quick predinner activity, and music on
Wednesday nights in summer draws a full house. Each of the four dining
rooms in the restored 1898 home has a distinct personality, from cozy to
verdant to elegant, but the tiered patio is where summer diners gather.
The kitchen tends toward the traditional side, specializing in classics like
steak Diane and filet mignon. Just when you think your meal is com-
plete, along comes the Flaming Bread Pudding. ⑤ *Average main: $23*
✉ *3405 Cascade Ave.* ☎ *541/386–3940* ⊕ *www.stonehedgeweddings.
com* ⊘ *No lunch.*

WHERE TO STAY

$$ ▦ **Best Western Plus Hood River Inn.** This low-slung, rambling hotel beside
HOTEL the Hood River Bridge offers some of the best river views of any hotel
in the Gorge, and many units have private balconies or patios on the
water; the deluxe accommodations have full kitchens, fireplaces, and
Jacuzzi tubs. **Pros:** riverfront location with great views; good restaurant
and lounge. **Cons:** tends to be a little pricey in summer; downtown
shopping and dining isn't within walking distance. ⑤ *Rooms from:
$169* ✉ *1108 E. Marina Way* ☎ *541/386–2200, 800/828–7873* ⊕ *www.
hoodriverinn.com* ⮑ *194 rooms* ⦿ *Breakfast.*

$$$ ▦ **Columbia Cliff Villas Hotel.** This elegant condo-style compound on a
HOTEL sheer cliff overlooking the Columbia River contains some of the plush-
FAMILY est accommodations in the region—units have one to three bedrooms,
Fodor'sChoice fireplaces, terraces or patios, stone-and-tile bathrooms, and fine lin-
★ ens. **Pros:** private apartment-style accommodations; great river views;
sophisticated decor and top-flight amenities. **Cons:** no restaurants or
fitness center on-site; pricey. ⑤ *Rooms from: $205* ✉ *3880 Westcliff
Dr.* ☎ *541/490–8081, 866/912–8366* ⊕ *www.columbiacliffvillas.com*
⮑ *37 suites* ⦿ *No meals.*

$ ▦ **Hood River Hotel.** In the heart of the lively and hip business district,
HOTEL steps from great restaurants and shops, this handsomely restored build-
ing has a grand, Old West facade, behind which are simple rooms with
tasteful period-style antiques and a few larger suites that have kitchen-
ettes and large sitting rooms. **Pros:** excellent downtown location; several
available adventure and romance packages; antiques-heavy interiors
have feel of a European inn. **Cons:** smallish rooms; no king-size beds;
rooms in back have great river views but tend to receive some freeway
noise. ⑤ *Rooms from: $129* ✉ *102 Oak St.* ☎ *541/386–1900, 800/386–
1859* ⊕ *www.hoodriverhotel.com* ⮑ *32 rooms, 9 suites* ⦿ *Breakfast.*

$$ ▦ **Sakura Ridge.** The five warm but sleekly furnished rooms of this con-
B&B/INN temporary lodge-style B&B on a 72-acre farm on the south side of
Fodor'sChoice town offer magical panoramas of Mt. Hood amid a welcome absence
★ of clutter. **Pros:** spectacular mountain views; rustic yet urbane decor;
lush gardens and orchards on the grounds. **Cons:** secluded location
is a 15-minute drive from downtown. ⑤ *Rooms from: $170* ✉ *5601
York Hill Rd.* ☎ *541/386–2636, 877/472–5872* ⊕ *www.sakuraridge.
com* ⮑ *5 rooms* ⦿ *Breakfast.*

5

$$
B&B/INN
$$

Villa Columbia B&B. The five guest rooms in this handsomely maintained 1911 Craftsman-style bed-and-breakfast are a tasteful but eclectic mix of older and newer pieces; all are named for famous Oregon rivers, and from the Columbia River room you're actually treated to a fine view of the Gorge. **Pros:** helpful, knowledgeable innkeepers; proximity to downtown galleries, restaurants, and brewpubs; decor is upscale but unfussy. **Cons:** river views are somewhat obstructed by trees and other houses; on a busy street. $ *Rooms from: $159* ⊠ *902 Oak St.* ☎ *541/386–6670* ⊕ *www.villacolumbia.com* ☞ *5 rooms* ¶○¶ *Breakfast.*

NIGHTLIFE AND THE ARTS

Brian's Pourhouse. A cute downtown cottage with a spacious deck serves excellent, eclectic food, but is even better known as a later-in-the-evening spot. It's the favored place in town to enjoy a cocktail or glass of wine and perhaps a sweet nosh—the Dutch apple pie with caramel sauce, whipped cream, and ice cream is memorable. ⊠ *606 Oak St.* ☎ *541/387–4344* ⊕ *www.brianspourhouse.com.*

Pfriem Family Brewers. Inside a striking new building on the Columbia River, Pfriem (pronounced "freem") is all about the marriage of Belgium's brewing traditions and Oregon's decidedly hoppy style. The brewery has quickly vaulted to the top echelon of Northwest craft beer makers, earning accolades for its heady Belgian Strong Blonde and one of the best IPAs in the state. The on-site restaurant serves stellar pub fare, too, including mussels and fries, vegan Moroccan stew, and house-made bratwurst. ⊠ *707 Portway Ave.* ☎ *541/321–0490* ⊕ *www. pfriembeer.com.*

SPORTS AND THE OUTDOORS

KAYAKING

Columbia Gorge Kayak School. Whether you want to practice your Eskimo roll in the safety of a pool, run the Klickitat River in an inflatable kayak, or try out a stand-up paddleboard on the Columbia, the Gorge's premier kayak guides can arrange the trip. Book online, by phone, or at the Kayak Shed downtown. ⊠ *6 Oak St.* ☎ *541/806–4190* ⊕ *www. gorgekayaker.com.*

WHITE SALMON, WASHINGTON

5 miles north of Hood River on Hwy. 14.

Tiny White Salmon, which sits on a bluff with commanding views of the Columbia River as well as the town of Hood River, is a good base for exploring the Washington side of the eastern end of the Gorge. A few noteworthy restaurants and shops in the village center cater to hikers, kayakers, and wine- and beer-tasting aficionados checking out this quieter but similar scenic counterpart to Hood River. Several first-rate wineries have opened in the rural communities just west and east of White Salmon along Highway 14.

GETTING HERE AND AROUND

You reach White Salmon by driving across the Hood River Bridge (toll $1), turning east onto Highway 14, and then north in the small village of Bingen onto Highway 141—it's just a 10-minute drive from Hood River.

ESSENTIALS

Mt. Adams Chamber of Commerce ✉ *1 Heritage Plaza, off Hwy. 14, just west of Hood River Bridge* ☎ *509/493–3630* ⊕ *www.mtadamschamber. com.*

EXPLORING

Aniche Cellars. This friendly boutique winery has one of the prettiest tasting-room settings in the area—it's high on Underwood Mountain, with outdoor seating that affords spectacular views looking east toward Hood River and deep into the Gorge. The cleverly named wines here—Puck, an Albarino–Pinot Gris blend; Three Witches, a Rhône-style blend of Cinsault, Carignan, and Counoise—are paired with little amuse-bouche-style nibbles, typically chocolate, prosciutto, or fruit. The winery is a 10-minute drive west of White Salmon. ✉ *71 Little Buck Creek Rd., Underwood* ☎ *360/624–6531* ⊕ *www.anichecellars. com* ☾ *Wed.–Sun. noon–6.*

Fodor'sChoice ★ **Syncline Wines.** The focus at this intimate winery is predominantly on elegant, full-bodied Rhône-style wines. The friendly, knowledgeable tasting-room has garnered plenty of awards for its aromatic Cuvée Elena Grenache-Syrah-Mourvedre blend, as well as a first-rate stand-alone Syrah, and several racy, dry whites—Picpoul, Grenache Blanc, Gruner Veltliner—that seem tailor-made for the Gorge's warm summer nights. Note that three other outstanding small wineries—Domaine Pouillon, Memaloose, and COR Cellars—are in the same rural town, 10 miles east of White Salmon. ✉ *111 Balch Rd., Lyle* ☎ *509/365–4361* ⊕ *www.synclinewine.com* ☾ *Thurs.–Sun. 11–6.*

WHERE TO EAT

$$
PACIFIC
NORTHWEST
Fodor'sChoice ★

✕ **Henni's Kitchen & Bar.** It's well worth venturing across the Columbia from Hood River to this jewel of a neighborhood tavern, which serves well-priced, creatively prepared international fare with a decided Northwest focus—think kale fritters with romesco sauce, Thai red curry with local flat-iron steak, and classic fish-and-chips. This is hearty comfort food, but with healthy and fresh ingredients. The bar serves terrific, innovative cocktails, and food prices during the weekday evening (5–6 pm) happy hour represent one of the best deals around. ⑤ *Average main: $18* ✉ *120 E. Jewett Blvd.* ☎ *509/493–1555* ⊕ *www. henniskitchenandbar.com* ☾ *No lunch.*

NIGHTLIFE

Everybody's Brewing. Head to this festive downtown brewpub for seriously impressive beers, with the potent Big Brother Imperial IPA (7.7% ABV) and orange-peel-enhanced Daily Bread Common Ale leading the way. There's live music many evenings, and tasty pub fare, too. ✉ *151 E. Jewett Blvd.* ☎ *509/637–2774* ⊕ *www.everybodysbrewing.com.*

SPORTS AND THE OUTDOORS

Wet Planet Whitewater. This outfitter just outside White Salmon offers half- and full-day white-water rafting trips on the White Salmon, Wind, Klickitat, Hood, and Tieton Rivers, which rank among some of the top waterways for this activity in the region. The Wind and Hood Rivers contain stretches of hairy Class IV–Class V rapids (previous experience is required), but the other trips are suitable for beginners. The company also offers kayaking instruction and trips. ⊠ *860 Hwy. 141, Husum* ☎ *509/493–8989, 877/390–9445* ⊕ *www.wetplanetwhitewater.com.*

THE DALLES

20 miles east of Hood River on I–84.

The Dalles lies on a crescent bend of the Columbia River where it narrows and once spilled over a series of rapids, creating a flagstone effect. French voyagers christened it *dalle,* or "flagstone." The Dalles is the seat of Wasco County and the trading hub of north-central Oregon. It gained fame early in the region's history as the town where the Oregon Trail branched, with some pioneers departing to travel over Mt. Hood on Barlow Road and the others continuing down the Columbia River. This may account for the small-town, Old West feeling that still permeates the area. Several historic Oregon moments as they relate to The Dalles' past are magnificently illustrated on eight murals painted by renowned Northwest artists, located downtown within short walking distance of one another.

GETTING HERE AND AROUND

From Hood River, it's a 22-mile drive east on Interstate 84 to reach The Dalles. Alternatively, you can take the slightly slower and more scenic Highway 14, on the Washington side of the Columbia, from White Salmon to U.S. 197, which leads you into town via The Dalles Bridge.

ESSENTIALS

Visitor Information The Dalles Area Chamber of Commerce ⊠ *404 W. 2nd St.* ☎ *541/296–2231, 800/255–3385* ⊕ *www.thedalleschamber.com.*

EXPLORING

FAMILY **Columbia Gorge Discovery Center–Wasco County Historical Museum.** Exhibits and artwork at this expansive, contemporary museum just off I–84 as you approach The Dalles from the west highlight the geological history of the Columbia Gorge, back 40 million years when volcanoes, landslides, and floods carved out the area. History exhibits focus on 10,000 years of Native American life and exploration of the region by white settlers, from Lewis and Clark to the early-20th-century engineers who developed the Historic Columbia River Highway. ⊠ *5000 Discovery Dr.* ☎ *541/296–8600* ⊕ *www.gorgediscovery.org* ⌑ *$9* ⊙ *Daily 9–5.*

Sunshine Mill Winery. You won't find many wineries situated in more unusual buildings than Quenett, which operates out of an early-1900s flour mill with huge grain elevators that soar over the southern end of The Dalles's downtown. Inside this dramatic old structure that nearly fell to the wrecking ball before winemakers James and Molli Martin bought it, you'll find the tasting room for Quenett, which produces first-rate Malbec, Viognier, Barbera, and a Chardonnay-Viognier-Sauvignon Blanc-Semillon blend. You can also order cheese boards and other snacks, and sample wines from the company's other line, Copa Di Vino, an inexpensive brand of single-serving table wines sold throughout the country. ⊠ *901 E. 2nd St.* ☏ *541/298–8900* ⊕ *www.sunshinemill.com* ⊙ *May–Oct., Sat.–Thurs. noon–6; Fri.–noon–7; call for winter hrs.*

WHERE TO EAT AND STAY

$ ✕ **Petite Provence.** This popular downtown bistro-bakery-dessertery,
CAFÉ which also has branches in Portland, serves delicious eggs, crepes, and croissants for breakfast; hot and cold sandwiches and salads for lunch, and fresh-baked pastries and breads (you can take a loaf home). For lunch, consider the Columbia River steelhead fillet with hazelnut-crust, served over sautéed leeks and roasted artichokes. The sparkling display case tempts with a goodly selection of napoleons, éclairs, tarts, and mousses. A good variety of local and French wines are available, too. $ *Average main: $8* ⊠ *408 E. 2nd St.* ☏ *541/506–0037* ⊕ *www.provencepdx.com* ⊙ *No dinner.*

$ 🛏 **Celilo Inn.** A prototypical retro motor lodge gone high-design, with
HOTEL exterior-entry rooms and a '50s light-up motel sign that disguise a
Fodor's Choice slick, boutique feel, commands a hilltop overlooking the Columbia
★ River and Dalles Dam. **Pros:** sexy design; terrific wine-touring packages; most rooms have great views. **Cons:** not all rooms have views; those on the far end feel very away from the front desk. $ *Rooms from: $119* ⊠ *3550 E. 2nd St.* ☏ *541/769–0001* ⊕ *www.celiloinn.com* 🛏 *46 rooms* ⦿ *No meals.*

$ 🛏 **Fairfield Inn & Suites.** Although it's part of Marriott's midrange brand,
HOTEL this four-story hotel a couple of blocks from Interstate 84 does have the brightest and most up-to-date rooms in the eastern end of the Gorge, with spacious work areas, comfy bedding, mini-refrigerators, microwaves, and marble-accent bathrooms. **Pros:** upscale rooms at reasonable prices; nice indoor pool and fitness center. **Cons:** bland location on the west side of town that's a bit of a long walk from downtown. $ *Rooms from: $107* ⊠ *2014 W. 7th St.* ☏ *541/769–0753, 800/306–1665* ⊕ *www.marriott.com* 🛏 *57 rooms, 23 suites* ⦿ *Breakfast.*

SPORTS AND THE OUTDOORS

RECREATIONAL AREAS

Mayer State Park. Views from atop the park's Rowena Crest bluff are knockout, especially during the March and April wildflower season, and there are a couple of fairly short and scenic hikes that lead from the bluff parking lot (off U.S. 30, 13 miles west of The Dalles, and 6 miles east of Mosier). The 3.5-mile (round-trip) trek up to McCall Point being especially scenic—it affords great views of Mt. Hood. The lower part of the park hugs the Columbia River and is accessed from I–84; here the activities include swimming, boating, fishing, and picnicking. ⊠ *Lower Mayer State Park access, Exit 76 off I–84* ☏ *800/551–6949* ⊕ *www.oregonstateparks.org* 🅿 *Day use $5 per vehicle* ⊙ *Daily.*

GOLDENDALE, WASHINGTON

34 miles northeast of The Dalles via Hwy. 14 and U.S. 97.

Although the actual town of Goldendale lies about 12 miles north of the Columbia River, this easygoing community is a good base for exploring the eastern end of the Gorge. It's home to one of the only notable restaurants in this vast but sparsely populated section of the Columbia River Valley, and it also has a couple of basic motels, a small downtown with a few funky cafés and shops, and the small but excellent Goldendale Observatory State Park. Views on the drive to Goldendale and in town itself are some of the most dramatic in the drier, eastern reaches of the Gorge—you'll see soaring white wind turbines lining the grassy bluffs and cliffs on both sides of the river, and along U.S. 97 as it leads into Goldendale, you can see the snowcapped summit of Washington's 12,281-foot Mt. Adams, which receives a little less attention than its southerly twin, Mt. Hood, but is actually taller and every bit as dramatic.

GETTING HERE AND AROUND

Although it's quickest to drive east along Interstate 84 and then north on U.S. 97 to reach Goldendale (a total of 34 miles) and the attractions around Maryhill, it takes only a few extra minutes and is far more scenic to cross the Columbia via The Dalles Bridge into Washington and drive east on Highway 14 to U.S. 97.

ESSENTIALS

Greater Goldendale Chamber of Commerce ✉ *903 E. Broadway St.* ☎ *509/773–3400* ⊕ *www.goldendalechamber.org.*

EXPLORING

FAMILY **Goldendale Observatory State Park.** This 5-acre park on a 2,100-foot-elevation bluff just north of Goldendale's compact downtown contains one of the nation's largest public telescopes, and the town's remote location, far from the lights of any cities, is ideal. Fascinating astronomy programs and sky-watching events are held during the day and evening, year-round. ✉ *1602 Observatory Dr.* ☎ *509/773–3141* ⊕ *www.goldendaleobservatory.com* 🎫 *$10 day pass* ☉ *Observatory, Apr.–Sept., Wed.–Sun. 1–11:30 pm; Oct.–Mar., Fri.–Sun. 1–9 pm.*

Fodor'sChoice ★ **Maryhill Museum of Art.** A wonderfully eclectic mix of artworks, including the largest assemblage of Rodin works outside France; posters, glasswork, and ephemera related to the modern-dance pioneer Loïe Fuller; an impressive cache of Native American artifacts; furniture and art that belonged to another Hill companion, Queen Marie of Romania; an art nouveau glass collection; and a large collection of mostly Victorian-era European and American landscape paintings: they're all housed within the walls of a grandiose mansion built rather improbably in the middle of nowhere by Sam Hill, the man who spearheaded the development of a scenic highway through the Columbia Gorge. The main Beaux-Arts building dates to 1914, and a daring, beautifully executed, LEED-certified modern wing, opened in 2012, extends from the back, with a terraced slope overlooking the Columbia River—it contains the museum café, a lovely spot for lunch. The extensive, harmoniously landscaped grounds include a sculpture garden and pathways along the Gorge rim. ⊠ *35 Maryhill Museum of Art Dr., off Hwy. 14, 3 miles west of junction with U.S. 97* ☎ *509/773–3733* ⊕ *www.maryhillmuseum.org* ⊠ *$9* ⊘ *Mid-Mar.–mid-Nov., daily 10–5.*

Maryhill Winery. Just down the road from Maryhill Museum, this large winery enjoys the same phenomenal views up and down the Gorge. The largest tasting room in the Gorge has a good-size gift shop as well as a market selling cheese, charcuterie, and other gourmet goodies. Maryhill produces dozens of wines at a variety of prices—the reserves, including stellar Cabernet Franc, Cabernet Sauvignon, Malbec, and Chardonnay, tend to earn most acclaim. In summer, the outdoor amphitheater on the grounds hosts a series of pop concerts—recent performers have included Jethro Tull, Peter Frampton, Styx, and Foreigner. ⊠ *9774 Hwy. 14* ☎ *509/773–1976* ⊕ *www.maryhillwinery.com* ⊘ *Daily 10–6.*

Stonehenge Memorial. Built by Maryhill Museum founder Sam Hill, this full-scale replica of England's legendary Neolithic stone creation was constructed in 1918 as the nation's first memorial to servicemen who perished in World War I. The memorial is a five-minute drive east of the museum, on a promontory overlooking the Columbia River. ⊠ *Stonehenge Dr., off Hwy. 14, just east of U.S. 97* ☎ *509/773–3733* ⊕ *www.maryhillmuseum.org* ⊠ *Free* ⊘ *Daily 7 am–dusk.*

WHERE TO EAT

$

MODERN

AMERICAN

Fodor's Choice

★

✕ **Glass Onion.** Visitors to small, unpretentious Goldendale will be surprised to find one of the culinary gems of the Columbia Gorge in the center of town, set within a cozy, beautifully restored house hung with local artwork. Chef Matt McGowan sources seasonal ingredients from local farms and purveyors, serves a great selection of local beers and wines, and keeps the price of everything on his menu at least $10 below what you'd pay in Hood River or Portland. Recent dishes from the regularly changing menu have included charcoal-grilled pork tenderloin with tomato jam and whole-grain mustard, and crispy Korean chicken wings with sweet-and-sour sauce and sesame seeds. Chocolate pot de crème with fresh blueberries and cream makes for a perfect ending. ⑤ *Average main: $13* ⊠ *604 S. Columbus Ave.* ☎ *509/773–4928* ⊕ *www.theglassonionrestaurant.com* ⊘ *Closed Sun.–Tues.*

MT. HOOD

The Multnomah tribe call Mt. Hood "Wy'East," named, according to popular legend, for a jealous lover who once sparred over a woman with his rival, Klickitat. When their fighting caught the Great Spirit's attention, Wy'East and Klickitat were transformed into two angry, smoke-bellowing mountains—one became Washington's Mt. Adams, the other became Mt. Hood. Wy'East has mellowed out a bit since then, but the mountain is still technically an active volcano, and it's had very minor, lava-free eruptive events as recently as the mid-1800s.

Today Mt. Hood is better known for the challenge it poses to climbers, its deep winter snows, and a dozen glaciers and snowfields that make skiing possible nearly year-round. Resort towns and colorful hospitality

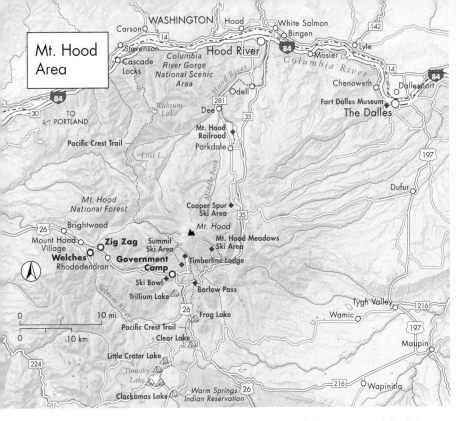

villages are arranged in a semicircle around the mountain, full of ski bars and rental cabins that host hordes of fun-loving Portlanders each weekend. In every direction from the postcard-perfect peak, the million-acre Mt. Hood National Forest spreads out like a big green blanket, and more than 300,000 acres of that are designated wilderness. Mule deer, black bears, elk, and the occasional cougar share the space with humans who come to hike, camp, and fish in the Pacific Northwest's quintessential wild ecosystem.

AROUND THE MOUNTAIN

About 60 miles east of Portland on I–84 and U.S. 26, and 42 miles south of Hood River via Hwy. 35 and U.S. 26.

Majestically towering 11,245 feet above sea level, Mt. Hood is what remains of the original north wall and rim of a volatile crater. Although the peak no longer spews ash or fire, active vents regularly release steam high on the mountain. The mountain took its modern moniker in 1792, when a crew of the British Royal Navy, the first recorded Caucasians sailing up the Columbia River, spotted it and named it after a famed British naval officer by the name of—you guessed it—Hood.

A snowboarder catches some air on Mt. Hood.

Mt. Hood offers the longest ski season in North America, with three major ski areas and some 30 lifts, as well as extensive areas for cross-country skiing and snowboarding. Many of the ski runs turn into mountain-bike trails in summer. The mountain is also popular with climbers and hikers. In fact, some hikes follow parts of the Oregon Trail, and signs of the pioneers' passing are still evident.

GETTING HERE AND AROUND

From Portland, U.S. 26 heads east into the heart of Mt. Hood National Forest, while Highway 35 runs south from Hood River along the mountain's east face. The roads meet 60 miles east of Portland, near Government Camp, forming an oblong loop with Interstate 84 and the Historic Columbia Gorge Highway. It's about a 75-minute drive from Downtown Portland to Government Camp via U.S. 26. Sea to Summit—call for timetables and pickup and drop-off sites—offers shuttle service from Portland International Airport and Downtown Portland hotels to all of the Mt. Hood resorts; the fare is $50 each way, with discounted lift-ticket and ski-rental packages available. Additionally, the **Mt. Hood Express** bus line operates daily and links the villages along the corridor—including Welches, Government Camp, and Timberline Lodge—to the Portland suburb of Sandy, which you can get to via TriMet commuter bus. This option is slower (it takes 2½ to 3 hours each way from the airport or Downtown to Timberline Lodge, for example) than a direct shuttle but costs just $2, plus $2.50 for TriMet bus fare to Sandy.

Contacts Mt. Hood Express ☎ 503/668–3466 ⊕ www.mthoodexpress.com. **Sea to Summit** ☎ 503/286–9333 ⊕ www.seatosummit.net.

ESSENTIALS

Visitor Information Mt. Hood Area Chamber of Commerce ☎ *503/622–3017* ⊕ *www.mthood.org.* **Mt. Hood National Forest Headquarters** ⊠ *16400 Champion Way, Sandy* ☎ *503/668–1700* ⊕ *www.fs.usda.gov/mthood.*

EXPLORING

Fodor'sChoice **Mt. Hood National Forest.** The highest spot in Oregon and the fourth-
★ highest peak in the Cascades, "the Mountain" is a focal point of the 1.1-million-acre forest, an all-season playground attracting around 3 million visitors annually. Beginning 20 miles southeast of Portland, it extends south from the Columbia River Gorge for more than 60 miles and includes more than 311,000 acres of designated wilderness. These woods are perfect for hikers, horseback riders, mountain climbers, and cyclists. Within the forest are more than 80 campgrounds and 50 lakes stocked with brown, rainbow, cutthroat, brook, and steelhead trout. The Sandy, Salmon, Clackamas, and other rivers are known for their fishing, rafting, canoeing, and swimming. Both forest and mountain are crossed by an extensive trail system for hikers, cyclists, and horseback riders. The **Pacific Crest Trail,** which begins in British Columbia and ends in Mexico, crosses at the 4,157-foot-high Barlow Pass. As with most other mountain destinations within Oregon, weather can be temperamental, and snow and ice may affect driving conditions as early as October and as late as June. Bring tire chains and warm clothes as a precaution.

Since this forest is close to the Portland metro area, campgrounds and trails are potentially crowded over the summer months, especially on weekends. If you're planning to camp, get info and permits from the Mt. Hood National Forest Headquarters. Campgrounds are managed by the U.S. Forest Service and a few private concessionaires, and standouts include a string of neighboring campgrounds on the south side of Mt. Hood: Trillium Lake, Still Creek, Timothy Lake, Little Crater Lake, Clackamas Lake, Summit Lake, Clear Lake, and Frog Lake. Each varies in what it offers and in price. The mountain overflows with day-use areas. From mid-November through April, all designated Winter Recreation Areas require a Sno-Park permit, available from the U.S. Forest Service and many local resorts and sporting goods stores. ⊠ *Headquarters, 16400 Champion Way, Sandy* ☎ *503/668-1700* ⊕ *www.fs.usda. gov/mthood* ⊠ *day pass $5–$7.*

WHERE TO EAT AND STAY

$$$$ ✕ **Cascade Dining Room.** Vaulted wooden beams and a wood-plank floor,
PACIFIC handcrafted furniture, and hand-woven drapes, and a lion-size stone fire-
NORTHWEST place set the scene in Timberline Lodge's esteemed restaurant, from which views of neighboring mountains are enjoyed, except when snow drifts cover the windows. The atmosphere is traditional and historic, but chef Jason Stoller Smith is a former wine-country *wunderkind* whose résumé includes orchestrating a salmon bake at the White House. The dinner menu's local/organic emphasis embraces, for example, cedar-plank steelhead with artichoke-polenta cake and saffron-tomato jus. The daily Taste of Oregon lunch buffet is itself worth the drive up— it highlights different seasonal ingredients and purveyors each week,

from Dungeness crab to local hazelnuts to Oregon cherries. Pick up a few culinary tips by attending a chef demonstration. $ *Average main: $34 ⊠ 27500 E. Timberline Rd., Timberline Lodge* ☎ *503/272–3104* ⊕ *www.timberlinelodge.com* ⌖ *Reservations essential.*

$$
RESORT
FAMILY
Fodor's Choice
★

☃ **Timberline Lodge.** Guest rooms are simple, rustic, and charming, but don't expect a cushy experience—the reason for staying here is the location and setting. **Pros:** a thrill to stay on the mountain itself; great proximity to all snow activity; amazing architecture. **Cons:** rooms are small and the least expensive ones have shared bathrooms; views from rooms are often completely blocked by snow in winter; carloads of tourists. $ *Rooms from: $155 ⊠ 27500 E. Timberline Rd., Timberline Lodge* ☎ *503/272–3311, 800/547–1406* ⊕ *www.timberlinelodge.com* ⇆ *70 rooms, 60 with bath* �‖ *Some meals.*

SPORTS AND THE OUTDOORS

DOWNHILL SKIING

Timberline Lodge & Ski Area. The longest ski season in North America unfolds at this full-service ski area, where the U.S. ski team conducts summer training. Thanks to the omnipresent Palmer Snowfield, it's the closest thing to a year-round ski area in the Lower 48 (it's typically closed for just a few weeks in September). Timberline is famous for its Palmer chairlift, which takes skiers and snowboarders to the high glacier for summer skiing. There are five high-speed quad chairs, one triple chair, and one double. The top elevation is 8,500 feet, with a 3,700-foot vertical drop, and the longest run is 3 miles. Facilities include a day lodge with fast food and a ski shop; lessons and equipment rental and repair are available. Parking requires a Sno-Park permit. The Palmer and Magic Mile lifts are popular with both skiers and sightseers. Timberline's long-awaited mountain-biking park is slated to open by summer 2015. ⊠ *27500 E. Timberline Rd., Timberline Lodge* ☎ *503/272–3311* ⊕ *www.timberlinelodge.com.*

GOVERNMENT CAMP

54 miles east of Portland on I–84 and U.S. 26, and 42 miles south of Hood River via Hwy. 35 and U.S. 26.

This alpine resort village with a bohemian vibe has several hotels and restaurants popular with visitors exploring Mt. Hood's ski areas and mountain-biking and hiking trails. "Govy" is also just a 12-mile drive up the hill from Welches, which also has restaurants and lodging.

WHERE TO EAT AND STAY

$
AMERICAN

✗ **Charlie's Mountain View.** Old and new ski swag plasters the walls, lift chairs function as furniture, and photos of famous (and locally famous) skiers and other memorabilia are as abundant as the menu selections. Open-flame-grilled steaks and hamburgers are worthy here, and the happy hour crowd shares plates piled high with waffle fries. When they're in season, try the apple dumplings. Charlie's is a local institution for powder hounds, and the fun, divey bar in back stays busy with ski bums and other lively degenerates. Live music packs them in on Friday and Saturday nights. $ *Average main: $9 ⊠ 88462 E. Government Camp Loop* ☎ *503/272–3333* ⊕ *www.charliesmountainview.com.*

5

$$ ✕ **Glacier Haus Bistro.** This lively, family-operated spot in the center of
EASTERN   Government Camp is a good bet for a simple snack and espresso drink
EUROPEAN   or a full meal. Pizzas and sandwiches are an option, but locals especially
love the Eastern European standards, such as Hungarian beef goulash,
Wiener schnitzel, and Bavarian sausages with sauerkraut and garlic-
mashed potatoes—the kind of cooking that'll provide you warmth and
comfort after a long day of skiing or hiking on the mountain. ⑤ *Average
main: $17* ✉ *88817 E. Government Camp Loop Rd.* ☎ *503/272–3471*
⊕ *www.glacierhaus.com* ☽ *Closed Mon.*

$ ✕ **Mt. Hood Brewing.** Producing finely crafted beers—Multorporter
AMERICAN   Smoked Porter, Ice Axe IPA, Highland Meadow Blond Ale, and oth-
ers—since the early '90s, this casual brewpub with stone walls, a fire-
place, and both booth and table seating buzzes in the early evening
for après-ski dining and drinking. It's popular for its creative comfort
food, including poutine with fontina cheese and peppercorn demi-glace,
cast-iron-skillet-baked fondue, Alsatian pizza topped with smoked ham
and crème fraîche, barbecue pulled-pork-and-porter sandwiches. Fin-
ish things off with a Tillamook Ice Cream root-beer or beer float—it's
especially good with the Hogsback Oatmeal Stout. ⑤ *Average main:
$13* ✉ *87304 E. Government Camp Loop* ☎ *503/272–3172* ⊕ *www.
mthoodbrewing.com.*

$$ ⛺ **Collins Lake Resort.** Comprising 66 poshly furnished chalets with
RESORT   fireplaces and dozens of other amenities, scattered around an alpine
FAMILY   lake, this contemporary, 28-acre compound is the cushiest accommo-
Fodor'sChoice   dations option in the Mt. Hood area. **Pros:** within walking distance of
★   Government Camp restaurants and bars; spacious layouts are ideal for
groups and families. **Cons:** steepest rates in town. ⑤ *Rooms from: $189*
✉ *88149 E. Creek Ridge Rd.* ☎ *503/928–3498, 800/234–6288* ⊕ *www.
collinslakeresort.com* ⇝ *66 condos* ⦿❘*No meals.*

SPORTS AND THE OUTDOORS
DOWNHILL SKIING

Fodor'sChoice   **Mt. Hood Meadows Ski Resort.** The mountain's largest resort has more
★   than 2,100 skiable acres, 85 runs, five double chairs, six high-speed
quads, a top elevation of 9,000 feet, a vertical drop of 2,777 feet, and
a longest run of 3 miles. If you're seeking varied, scenic terrain with
plenty of trails for all skiing abilities, this is your best choice among the
region's ski areas. Facilities include a day lodge, nine restaurants, two
lounges, a ski-and-snowboard school, a children's learning center with
daycar, and two ski shops with equipment rentals. ✉ *Hwy. 35, 10 miles
east of Government Camp* ☎ *503/337–2222* ⊕ *www.skihood.com.*

FAMILY   **Mt. Hood Skibowl.** The ski area closest to Portland is also known as
"America's largest night ski area," with 34 runs lighted each evening.
It has 960 skiable acres serviced by four double chairs and five surface
tows, a top elevation of 5,100 feet, a vertical drop of 1,500 feet, and a
longest run of 3½ miles. You can take advantage of two-day lodges, a
midmountain warming hut, four restaurants, and two lounges. Sleigh
rides are conducted, weather permitting, and a hugely popular tubing
and adventure park has several tubing hills, plus music, LED lights, and
a laser show. In summer the resort morphs into the Adventure Park at
Skibowl, with mountain biking, zip lines, bungee jumping, a five-story

free-fall Tarzan Swing, disc golf, and kid-friendly tubing and alpine slides. ⊠ *87000 E. U.S. 26* ☎ *503/272–3206* ⊕ *www.skibowl.com.*

SHOPPING

Govy General Store. Good thing this is a really nice grocery store, because it's the only one for miles around. Govy General stocks all the staples, plus a nice selection of gourmet treats like cheeses and chocolates. It's also a full-service liquor store and your one-stop shop for Mt. Hood sweatshirts, postcards, and other keepsake tchotchkes. Grab your Sno-Park permit here in winter. ⊠ *30521 E. Meldrum St.* ☎ *541/272–3107* ⊕ *www.govygeneralstore.com* ☼ *Daily 7 am–8 pm.*

WELCHES AND ZIGZAG

12 miles west of Government Camp and 40 miles east of Portland.

One of a string of small communities known as the Villages at Mt. Hood, Welches's claim to fame is that it was the site of Oregon's first golf course, built at the base of Mt. Hood in 1928. Another golf course is still going strong today, and summer vacationers hover around both towns for access to basic services like gas, groceries, and dining. Others come to pull a few trout out of the scenic Zigzag River or to access trails and streams in the adjacent Salmon–Huckleberry Wilderness.

GETTING HERE AND AROUND

Most of Welches is found just off U.S. 26, often called the Mt. Hood Corridor here, about 45 miles east of Portland.

WHERE TO EAT AND STAY

$$$
MODERN
AMERICAN

✕ **Altitude.** The flagship restaurant at the Resort at The Mountain aims for a sleek, modernist look in its glitzy—for the rustic Mt. Hood region at least—dining room with recessed lighting and contemporary art. Ask for a table by the row of large windows looking out over the resort's greenery. The kitchen ably handles standards like bacon-wrapped beef tenderloin with huckleberry sauce and hazelnut-crusted baked halibut, along with a few adventurous dishes like braised pork cheek with pickled shallots and pan-seared polenta. The adjacent lounge has fun, lighter fare (fish-and-chips, black-bean burgers), along with a few good specialty cocktails. ⑤ *Average main: $30* ⊠ *68010 E. Fairway Ave., Welches* ☎ *503/622–2214* ⊕ *www.altituderestaurant.com* ☼ *No lunch.*

$$
AMERICAN
Fodor's Choice
★

✕ **The Rendezvous Grill & Tap Room.** "Serious food in a not-so-serious place" is the slogan of this casual roadhouse with surprisingly sophisticated food—it's been a locals' favorite since it opened back in mid-'90s. For a joint many miles from the coast, the 'Vous sure does a nice job with seafood, turning out appetizing plates of sautéed shrimp, Willapa Bay oysters, Dungeness crab, and char-grilled wild salmon with roasted tomatoes and artichoke hash—steaks, burgers, and salads round out the menu. Grab a seat on the leafy patio in warm weather. In the adjacent taproom, ask about the seasonal, house-infused vodkas. ⑤ *Average main: $21* ⊠ *67149 E. U.S. 26, Welches* ☎ *503/622–6837* ⊕ *www.rendezvousgrill.net.*

$
RENTAL

▥ **The Cabins Creekside at Welches.** Affordability, accessibility to recreational activities, and wonderful hosts make these cabins with knotty-pine vaulted ceilings, log furnishings, and full-size kitchens a great lodging choice in the Mt. Hood area. **Pros:** Family-run; quiet, off-highway location; anglers will benefit from the Thurmans' fly-fishing savvy. **Cons:** No dining within walking distance; no cabin-side parking; simple but clean, functional furnishings. Ⓢ *Rooms from: $94* ✉ *25086 E. Welches Rd., Welches* ☎ *503/622–4275* ⊕ *www.mthoodcabins.com* ⇥ *10 cabins* �‖ *No meals.*

$$
RENTAL
🛉 **Mt. Hood Vacation Rentals.** Doggedly determined to ensure a great time for the two and four-pawed vacationer alike, this company welcomes the family pet into the majority of its homes/cabins/condos, yet the properties are still on the upscale side: you'll find fireplaces/wood-burning stoves, hot tubs, river views, and full kitchens. **Pros:** knowledgeable, hospitable staff; gorgeous homes nestled throughout the Mt. Hood area; many secluded sites; family- and pet-friendly. **Cons:** bring your own shampoo; two to five-night minimum. Ⓢ *Rooms from: $185* ✉ *67898 E. Hwy. 26, Welches* ☎ *866/921–1757* ⊕ *www.mthoodrentals. com* ⇥ *32 units* �‖ *No meals.*

$$
RESORT
🛉 **Resort at The Mountain.** In the evergreen-forest foothills of Mt. Hood, this expansive resort is popular year-round both with outdoorsy sorts and couples seeking romantic hideaways. **Pros:** every sport available; plenty of choices in room size. **Cons:** there will be crowds; may not appeal to those who are not fans of golf; grounds seem more designed for golf carts than pedestrians. Ⓢ *Rooms from: $179* ✉ *68010 E. Fairway Ave., Welches* ☎ *503/622–3101, 877/439–6774* ⊕ *www.theresort. com* ⇥ *157 rooms* �‖ *No meals.*

SPORTS AND THE OUTDOORS

GOLF

The Courses. The three 9-hole tracks at the Resort at the Mountain include the Pine Cone Nine, Oregon's oldest golf course, built on a rented hayfield in 1928—you can mix any combination of the three courses to complete a full 18-hole round. There's also a lighted 18-hole putting course that's popular with families and adults working on their short game. Check the website to review the club's dress code, or cover that T-shirt with a collared shirt from the pro shop. ✉ *68010 E. Fairway Ave., Welches* ☎ *503/622–3151, 877/439–6674* ⊕ *www. theresortcourses.com* 🏌 *Pine Cone: 9 holes. 3299 yds. Par 36. Foxglove: 9 holes. 3106 yds. Par 36. Thistle: 9 holes. 2956 yds. Par 34. Greens fee: $60 for 18 holes.*

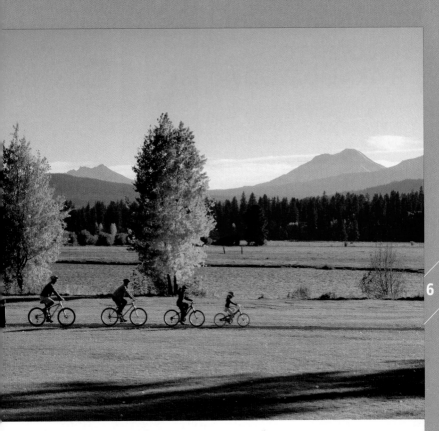

CENTRAL
OREGON

WELCOME TO CENTRAL OREGON

TOP REASONS TO GO

★ **Become one with nature:** Central Oregonians live on the flanks of the Cascade Range and are bracketed by rock formations, rivers, lakes, forests, ancient lava flows, and desert badlands. Bring your golf clubs, carabiners, snowboard, or camera, and explore deeper.

★ **Visit Bend:** Downtown Bend is lively and walkable, with a variety of appealing restaurants, galleries, and stores.

★ **Kick back at Sunriver:** This family-oriented resort has bike paths, river trails, an airstrip, horse stables, tennis courts, a golf course, and several restaurants.

★ **Check out the craft-brewing scene:** With two dozen breweries—and more on the horizon— you can discover nearly any type of beer that fits your tastes.

★ **Discover the Old West:** Cowboy towns, such as Sisters and Prineville, offer a glimpse into what life was like when the West was wild.

1 West Central Oregon. The western portion of central Oregon ranges from lush and green in the Cascades to dry and full of conifers down to the Deschutes River. It's the side with the ski areas, the high mountain lakes, most of the resorts, and the rushing waters. The region's largest town is Bend, and it straddles the forested west and the harshly beautiful east.

2 East Central Oregon. East of the Deschutes River this land is marked by rugged buttes, tough junipers, and bristly sagebrush. It's a place that still hugs the edge of the wilderness, with weathered barns, painted desert hills, a caldera holding two popular lakes, and some world-class rock climbing.

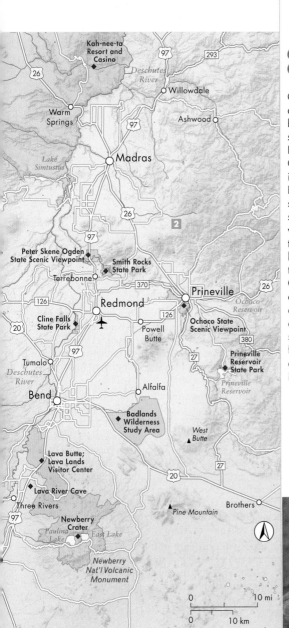

GETTING ORIENTED

Central Oregon provides a natural meeting place between the urban west side and the rural east side. It nestles neatly below the Columbia River basin and is drained by the Deschutes River, which flows from south to north. Skiers and snowboarders flock to winter sports areas on the western edge, anglers head to the Deschutes, the Metolius, and the Cascade Lakes, and climbers, campers, rockhounds, and wanderers explore the arid landscapes on the east side. Bend, the largest town for more than 120 miles in any direction, sits roughly in the center of this region.

6

Updated
by Kimberly
Bowker

After a day on the Sunriver bike paths, a first-time visitor from Europe shook her head. "This place is paradise," she declared. It's easy to see why she thought so. Central Oregon has snowfields so white they sharpen the edges of the mountains; canyons so deep and sudden as to induce vertigo; air so crisp that it fills the senses; water that ripples in mountain lakes so clear that boaters can see to the bottom, or rushes through turbulent rapids favored by rafters.

A region born of volcanic tumult is now a powerful lure for the adventurous, the beauty-seeking, and even the urbane—Bend has grown into a sophisticated city of 80,000-plus, a magnet for people retreating from larger, noisier city centers. For most visitors Bend is the sunny face of central Oregon, a haven for hikers, athletes, and aesthetes, but with the charm and elegance of much larger cities.

From Bend it's easy to launch to the attractions that surround it. To the northwest, Camp Sherman is a stunning place to fish for rainbow trout or kokanee. The Smith Rocks formation to the north draws climbers and boulderers, and, to the south, Lava Lands and the Lava River Caves fascinate visitors more than 6,000 years after they were chiseled out of the earth. The Oregon Badlands Wilderness to the east draws hikers and horseback riders wanting to connect with the untamed landscape. Lake Billy Chinook to the north is a startling oasis, where summer visitors drift in houseboats beneath the high walls of the Deschutes River canyon. The Deschutes River itself carries rafters of all descriptions, from young families to solo adventurers.

The area's natural beauty has brought it a diverse cluster of resorts, whether situated on the shores of high mountain lakes or cradling golf courses of startling green. They dot the landscape from the dry terrain around Warm Springs to the high road to Mt. Bachelor.

CENTRAL OREGON PLANNER

WHEN TO GO

Central Oregon is a popular destination year-round. Skiers and snow-boarders come from mid-December through March, when the powder is deepest and driest. During this time, guests flock to the hotels and resorts along Century Drive, which leads from Bend to Mt. Bachelor. In summer, when temperatures reach the upper 80s, travelers are more likely to spread throughout the region. But temperatures fall as the elevation rises, so take a jacket if you're heading out for an evening at the high lakes or Newberry Crater.

You'll pay a premium at the mountain resorts during ski season, and Sunriver and other family and golf resorts are busiest in summer. It's best to make reservations as far in advance as possible; six months in advance is not too early.

FESTIVALS

Bend Film Festival. This popular local film festival takes place in October. ⊠ *1000 N.W. Wall St., Suite 260, Bend* ☎ *541/388–3378* ⊕ *www. bendfilm.org.*

Bend Summer and Fall Festival. Downtown Bend is blocked off with food, crafts, art booths, and music in July and September. ⊠ *Box 1424, Bend* ☎ *541/508–4280* ⊕ *www.bendfestivals.com.*

Oregon Winterfest. February brings music, food, brews, wine, ice carving, and other winter sports to Bend's Old Mill District. ⊠ *Bend* ⊕ *www. oregonwinterfest.com.*

Sisters Rodeo. Multiple rodeo and community events, held annually for more than 70 years, take place over a weekend in June. ⊠ *67637 U.S. 20, south of Sisters* ☎ *541/549–0121, 800/827–7522* ⊕ *www. sistersrodeo.com.*

GETTING HERE AND AROUND

AIR TRAVEL

Visitors fly into **Redmond Municipal Airport–Roberts Field** (RDM), about 17 miles north of downtown Bend. Rental cars are available for pickup at the airport from several national agencies. The **Redmond Airport Shuttle** provides transportation throughout the region (reservations requested); a ride from the airport to downtown Bend costs about $35. Taxis are available at curbside, or can be summoned from the call board inside the airport. Portland's airport is 160 miles northwest of Bend.

Air Contacts Redmond Airport Shuttle ⊠ *Redmond* ☎ *541/382–1687, 888/664–8449* ⊕ *www.redmondairportshuttle.net.* **Redmond Municipal Airport–Roberts Field** (RDM). ⊠ *2522 S.E. Jesse Butler Circle, Redmond* ☎ *541/548–0646* ⊕ *www.flyrdm.com.*

BUS TRAVEL

The **Central Oregon Breeze,** a regional carrier, runs one bus a day each way between Portland and Bend, with stops in Redmond and Madras. **Cascades East Transit** is Bend's intercity bus service, and connects Redmond, La Pine, Madras, Prineville, Bend, and Sisters. Trips from the airport require reservations. **Greyhound** also serves the area with a shuttle that runs between Salem and Bend.

Bus Contacts Cascades East Transit ✉ *334 Hawthorn Ave., Bend* ☎ *541/385–8680, 866/385–8680* ⊕ *www.cascadeseasttransit.com.* **Central Oregon Breeze** ✉ *2045 N.E. Hwy. 20, Bend* ☎ *541/389–7469, 800/847–0157* ⊕ *www.cobreeze. com.* **Greyhound Bend** ✉ *334 N.E. Hawthorne Ave., Bend* ☎ *541/923–1732* ⊕ *www.greyhound.com.*

CAR TRAVEL

U.S. 20 heads west from Idaho and east from the coastal town of Newport into central Oregon. U.S. 26 goes southeast from Portland to Prineville, where it heads northeast into the Ochoco National Forest. U.S. 97 heads north from California and south from Washington to Bend. Highway 126 travels east from Eugene to Prineville; it connects with U.S. 20 heading south (to Bend) at Sisters. Major roads throughout central Oregon are well maintained and open throughout the winter season, although it's always advisable to have tire chains in the car. Some roads are closed by snow during winter, including Oregon 242. Check the **Oregon Department of Transportation's TripCheck** (⊕ *www.tripcheck. com*) or call **ODOT** (☎ *800/977–ODOT*).

RESTAURANTS

The center of culinary ambition is in downtown Bend, but good-to-excellent restaurants also serve diners in Sisters, Redmond, Prineville, and the major resorts. Styles vary, but many hew to the Northwest preference for fresh foods grown, caught, and harvested in the region.

Central Oregon also has many down-home places and family-friendly brewpubs, and authentic Mexican restaurants have emerged to win faithful followings in Prineville, Redmond, Madras, and Bend.

HOTELS

Central Oregon has lodging for every taste, from upscale resort lodges to an in-town brewpub village, eclectic bed-and-breakfasts, rustic Western inns, and a range of independent and chain hotels and motels. If you're drawn to the rivers, stay in a pastoral fishing cabin along the Metolius near Camp Sherman. If you came for the powder, you'll want a ski-snowboard condo closer to the mountain. For soaking up the atmosphere, you might favor one of downtown Bend's luxurious hotels, or Old St. Francis, the Catholic school–turned-brewpub village. *Hotel reviews have been shortened. For full information, visit Fodors.com.*

WHAT IT COSTS IN U.S. DOLLARS			
$	**$$**	**$$$**	**$$$$**
Restaurants	Under $17	$17–$24	$25–$30	Over $30
Hotels	Under $150	$150–$200	$201–$250	Over $250

Restaurant prices are the average cost of a main course at dinner, or if dinner is not served, at lunch. Hotel prices are the lowest cost of a standard double room in high season.

TOURS

Cog Wild. Bicycle tours are offered for people of all skill levels and interests. ✉ *255 Century Dr., Ste. 201, Bend* ☎ *541/385–7002* ⊕ *www. cogwild.com.*

Sun Country Tours. A longtime provider of raft and tube trips on central Oregon rivers offers rafting excursions that range from two hours to full days May through September. ☎ *541/382–6277* ⊕ *www. suncountrytours.com.*

Wanderlust Tours. Popular and family-friendly half-day or evening excursions are offered around Bend, Sisters, and Sunriver. Options include kayaking, canoeing, snowshoeing, and caving. ☎ *541/389–8359* ⊕ *www.wanderlusttours.com.*

VISITOR INFORMATION

Central Oregon Visitors Association ✉ *705 S.W. Bonnett Way, Suite 1000, Bend* ☎ *541/389–8799, 800/800–8334* ⊕ *www.visitcentraloregon.com.*

WEST CENTRAL OREGON

Sunshine, crisp pines, pure air, rushing waters, world-class skiing and snowboarding at Mt. Bachelor, destination golf resorts, a touch of the frontier West at Sisters, an air of sophistication in Bend—the forested side of central Oregon serves up many recreational flavors. The area draws young couples, seniors, families, athletes, and adventurers, all of whom arrive with a certain sense of purpose, but also with an appreciation for the natural world. Travelers will have no problem filling a week in central Oregon's western half with memorable activities, from rafting to enjoying some sensational meals.

BEND

160 miles southeast of Portland.

Bend, Oregon's largest city east of the Cascades, is once more one of the fastest-growing cities in the state, recovering abundantly from the hard-hitting recession. Construction has renewed and new businesses seem to open every day. The people of Bend continue to enjoy an enviable climate, proximity to skiing, dynamic lifestyle, and a reputation as a playground and recreational escape. At times it seems that everybody in Bend is an athlete or a brewer, but it remains a tolerant, welcoming town, conscious of making a good first impression. Bend's heart is an area of about four square blocks, centered on Wall and Bond streets. Here you'll find boutique stores, galleries, independent coffee shops, brewpubs, fine restaurants, lively nightlife establishments, and historic landmarks such as the Tower Theatre, built in 1940. A few traditional barbershops and taverns are also spread around, keeping it real.

Neighboring Mt. Bachelor, though hardly a giant among the Cascades at 9,065 feet, is blessed by an advantage over its taller siblings—by virtue of its location, it's the first to get snowfall, and the last to see it go. Inland air collides with the Pacific's damp influence, creating skiing

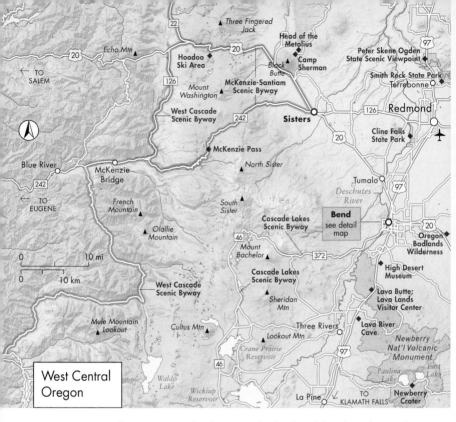

West Central Oregon

conditions immortalized in songs by local rock bands and raves from the ski press.

GETTING HERE AND AROUND

Portlanders arrive via car on U.S. 20 or U.S. 26, and folks from the mid-Willamette Valley cross the mountains on Oregon 126. Redmond Municipal Airport, 17 miles to the north, is an efficient hub for air travelers, who can rent a car or take a shuttle or cab into town. **Greyhound** also serves the area with a shuttle from Salem. The **Central Oregon Breeze,** a privately operated regional carrier, runs daily between Portland and Bend, with stops in Redmond and Madras. Bend is served by a citywide bus system called **Cascades East Transit,** which also connects to Redmond, La Pine, Sisters, Prineville, and Madras. To take a Cascades East bus between cities in central Oregon, reservations are not required but recommended. *For more on bus travel to and from Bend, see Getting Here and Around in the Central Oregon Planner.*

If you're trying to head out of or into Bend on a major highway during the morning or 5 pm rush, especially on U.S. 97, you may hit congestion. Parking in downtown Bend is free for the first two hours (three hours at the centrally located parking garage), or park for free in the residential neighborhoods just west of downtown. In addition to the car-rental counters at the airport, Avis, Budget, Enterprise, and Hertz also have rental locations in Bend.

ESSENTIALS

Visitor Information Bend Chamber of Commerce ✉ *777 N.W. Wall St., Ste. 200* ☎ *541/382–3221* ⊕ *www.bendchamber.org.* **Visit Bend/Bend Visitor Center** ✉ *750 N.W. Lava Rd.* ☎ *541/382–8048, 877/245–8484* ⊕ *www.visitbend. com.*

EXPLORING

FAMILY **Des Chutes Historical Museum.** Originally built as a schoolhouse in 1914 from locally quarried volcanic tuff, the museum is operated by the Deschutes County Historical Society. Exhibits depict historical life in the area, including a pioneer schoolroom, native artifacts, and relics from the logging, ranching, homesteading, and railroading eras. Outdoor heritage walks are conducted in the summer. ✉ *129 N.W. Idaho Ave.* ☎ *541/389–1813* ⊕ *www.deschuteshistory.org* ✑ *$5* ⊙ *Tues.–Sat. 10–4:30.*

Drake Park and Mirror Pond. At its western edge, downtown Bend slopes down to these 13 acres of manicured greensward and trees lining the edge of the Deschutes, attracting flocks of Canada geese as well as strollers from downtown. Various events, such as music festivals, occur in the park during the summer months. Note the 11-foot high wheel log skidder, harkening back to Bend's logging industry in the early 20th century, when four draft horses pulled the wheel to move heavy logs. ✉ *Bounded on the west by N.W. Brooks St. and Drake Park; N.W. Lava Rd on the east; N.W. Franklin Ave. to the south; and N.W. Greenwood Ave. to the north* ⊕ *www.downtownbend.org.*

FAMILY
Fodor's Choice
★
High Desert Museum. The West was actually wild, and this combo museum/zoo proves it. Kids will love the up-close-and-personal encounters with gila monsters, snakes, porcupines, birds of prey, Vivi the bobcat, and Snowshoe the lynx. Characters in costume take part in the Living History series, where you can chat with stagecoach drivers, boomtown widows, pioneers, homesteaders, and sawmill operators. Peruse the 110,000-square-feet of indoor and outdoor exhibits, such as Spirit of the West and a historic family ranch, to experience how the past can truly come alive. ✉ *59800 S. Hwy. 97, 7 miles south of downtown Bend* ☎ *541/382–4754* ⊕ *www.highdesertmuseum.org* ✑ *$15 May–Oct., $12 Nov.–Apr.* ⊙ *May–Oct., daily 9–5; Nov.–Apr., daily 10–4.*

Newberry National Volcanic Monument and Lava Lands. The last time hot lava flowed from Newberry Volcano was about 13 centuries ago. The north end of the monument has several large basalt flows, as well as the 500-foot **Lava Butte** cinder cone—a coal-black and scorched-red, symmetrical mound thrust from the depths 7,000 years ago. The cone is now home to the **Lava Lands Visitor Center,** which features interpretive exhibits that explain the volcanic and early human history of the area. **Lava River Cave,** a 1-mile-long lava tube, takes about 90 minutes to explore on your own with a lantern (available for rent, $4-$6). On the south end of the monument, an unpaved road leads to beautiful views from **Paulina Peak.** Along the shores of **Paulina Lake** and **East**

6

Lake, you can hike, fish, camp, or stay at the rustic resorts. The monument offers 100 miles of summer trails, and may be accessible during winter months, depending on snowmelt, for snowmobiling, snowshoeing, and skiing. ✉ 58201 S. Hwy. 97 ☎ 541/593–2421 ⊕ www.fs.usda. gov/centraloregon ⌲ $5 per vehicle ☉ Mid-May–mid-Oct., daily 9–5.

EN ROUTE

Cascade Lakes Scenic Byway. For about 90 miles, this forest-highway loop beginning and ending in Bend meanders past a series of high mountain lakes and is good for fishing, hiking, and camping in the summer months. (Much of the road is closed by snow during the colder months.) To find, take Century Drive/Oregon 372 out of Bend and follow it around Mt. Bachelor, and then U.S. 97 at La Pine to return. ⊕ www. visitbend.com.

WHERE TO EAT

$

AMERICAN

✕ **10 Barrel Brewing Co.** Attracting locals and travelers alike, this trendy brewpub supplies good beer and compatible food. Pizzas are hand tossed daily, salads are fresh, and sandwiches are varied. This is a popular place, so expect to wait during busy meal hours. Grab a table or stool in the bar for a cozier setting, and enjoy the windowed-garage doors that open to the Central Oregon sun on summer days and to patio fires on crisp winter nights. ⑤ Average main: $12 ✉ 1135 N.W. Galveston Ave. ☎ 541/678–5228 ⊕ www.10barrel.com.

Paulina and East Lakes in Newberry National Volcanic Monument

$ ✗ **Deschutes Brewery & Public House.** Bendites are fiercely loyal to their
AMERICAN city's original brewpub, established in 1988. Not only does the Brewery
bake its own bread and pizza dough (adding in its own spent grain),
it makes its sausages, sauces, mustards, dressings, soups, etc. House
favorites include the elk burger and fish-and-chips. Though the always-
popular Black Butte Porter is a Public House classic, Deschutes brews
a diverse lineup of craft beers, including such seasonals as Jubelale
(winter holidays) and Twilight Ale (summer). It is almost always hopping, and you may find yourself waiting to be seated, as there are
no reservations. However, time flies as you sip one of 19 Deschutes
beers on tap and people-watch the boisterous crowd while you wait.
$ *Average main: $12* ⊠ *1044 N.W. Bond St.* ☎ *541/382–9242* ⊕ *www.
deschutesbrewery.com.*

$ ✗ **Jackson's Corner.** This family-friendly community restaurant is housed
AMERICAN in an unassuming vintage building tucked into a neighborhood near
FAMILY downtown. The open, inviting space is a great place for casual gatherings, with live music Friday nights. The eclectic menu leans heavily on
locally grown and organic dishes. Order seasonal market salads, house-
made pasta dishes, or brick-oven pizza and sandwiches at the counter
to be served at your table. $ *Average main: $12* ⊠ *845 N.W. Delaware
Ave.* ☎ *541/647–2198* ⊕ *www.jacksonscornerbendor.com.*

$$ ✗ **Joolz.** "An insider's treasure," as one diner called it, serves vibrant
MIDDLE EASTERN Middle Eastern food with an Oregon flair. The chef, raised in Beirut,
is son of a Lebanese father and Oregonian mother (who is rumored to
still make the family's melt-in-your-mouth spiced date cake). Enjoy the
intimate and authentic ambience, including colorful drapes, while din-
ing on small dishes such as Oregon lamb meatballs, tabbouleh salad,

Central Oregon Brewery Boom

Central Oregon is not only home to gorgeous views and exciting outdoor activities, but a recent boom in breweries has turned the high desert into a haven for craft-beer lovers. With two-dozen breweries and counting, central Oregon only hit the map as a beer travel destination in recent years. Since the first microbrewery opened its doors in 1988 (Deschutes Brewery in downtown Bend), the industry has continued to grow and expand. Each brewery and brewpub approaches craft beer in an original manner, often supported by locals and a combination of live music, good food, unique marketing, experimental brews, and good ole standbys that keep pint glasses and growlers filled.

Residents may buoy the industry, but breweries in turn support the community. Local artists design labels, many beer proceeds go to neighborhood causes, and brews are continually concocted with local events and culture in mind.

BEND ALE TRAIL
Pick up a Bend Ale Trail brochure, or download the app, to guide you through Bend's 14 breweries. Stop at each brewery, have a taste or a pint, and receive a stamp in your passport. Once your passport is complete, drop by the Bend Visitor Center to receive your prize: a commemorative pint glass.

and cauliflower with tahini dipping sauce, or main plates such as a local free-range longhorn beef burger or Pacific seafood tagine. ⑤ *Average main: $17* ✉ *916 N.W. Wall St.* ☎ *541/388–5094* ⊕ *www.joolzbend. com* ☾ *No lunch.*

$ ✕ **McKay Cottage Restaurant.** This breakfast and lunch spot is housed
AMERICAN in a 1916 pioneer cottage that was home to a former state senator. Locals relax throughout its cozy rooms and spill over onto the porch and patio below. The menu is long on comfort food, including fresh scones and sticky buns, and servers are friendly and attentive. On your way out, you can pick up baked goods and coffee drinks at the to-go bakery. ⑤ *Average main: $12* ✉ *62910 O.B. Riley Rd.* ☎ *541/383–2697* ⊕ *www.themckaycottage.com* ☾ *No dinner.*

$$ ✕ **Pine Tavern.** Named for the Ponderosa pine tree growing through the
AMERICAN back dining room, this locally loved restaurant has been dishing up high-end meals in the heart of downtown Bend since 1936. Specialties include steaks, prime rib, pot pie, and other traditional American cuisine. Longtime regulars share the dining room with out-of-towners. In summertime, seek a spot on the patio—named Best Patio in Bend for multiple years—overlooking Mirror Pond and Drake Park. ⑤ *Average main: $21* ✉ *967 N.W. Brooks St.* ☎ *541/382–5581* ⊕ *www.pinetavern. com.*

$ ✕ **Spork.** Bend's favorite food cart–turned-restaurant offers a globally
INTERNATIONAL inspired and healthy menu with an intimate and trendy decor. Try Peruvian stir-fry, Thai steak salad, coconut green curry, or organic tofu tacos. Ingredients are local and fresh, and practices are eco-conscious. ⑤ *Average main: $10* ✉ *937 N.W. Newport Ave.* ☎ *541/390–0946* ⊕ *www.sporkbend.com.*

$
AMERICAN
Fodor'sChoice
★

✕**The Victorian Café.** In a renovated house on the west side of Bend, this breakfast and lunch place offers a wide selection of surprising combinations of eggs Benedict, such as the Caribbean Benedict with Cuban seasoned ham, mango, and black beans. Weekly mouthwatering specials may include deep-fried graham cracker–crusted Texas toast filled with mascarpone. With local accolades for Best Breakfast in Bend for many years, the restaurant is also known for its homemade applesauce and scones. There's often a long wait on weekends, so order a Bloody Mary or a "Man-mosa" (a mimosa in a pint glass) and enjoy around the outdoor fireplace. ⑤ *Average main: $16* ✉ *1404 N.W. Galveston Ave.* ☎ *541/382–6411* ⊕ *www.victoriancafebend.com* ⊗ *No dinner.*

$$
AMERICAN
Fodor'sChoice
★

✕**Zydeco Kitchen & Cocktails.** The blended menu of Northwest specialties and Cajun influences has made this restaurant (named after a style of Creole music) a very popular spot. On the menu, fillet medallions, chicken, and pasta sit alongside jambalaya and redfish dishes. The owners emphasize the preparation of fresh, organic foods and provide a gluten-free selection. The bar is trendy, but welcoming. In warm weather, ask to sit on the patio. Bonus: Kids eat free on Sunday. ⑤ *Average main: $23* ✉ *919 N.W. Bond St.* ☎ *541/312–2899* ⊕ *www.zydecokitchen.com* ⊗ *No lunch weekends.*

OFF THE
BEATEN
PATH

Cowboy Dinner Tree. Seventy miles south of Sunriver you'll find an authentic barbecue cook firing up a genuine taste of the Old West for dinner. Oregonians will tell you that the "true cowboy cut" 30-ounce steak or whole chicken over an open flame, plus all the fixings, is more than worth the trip. Don't expect to plug in your laptop: there's no electricity, nor is alcohol served, nor credit cards accepted. If you are making a day out of it, detour to Fort Rock State Natural Area to hike around a prehistoric volcanic tuff emerging from the flat horizon, and explore a nearby cave home to the oldest sandals ever discovered. If you journey from afar, lodging is available in rustic buckaroo bunkhouses. Plates are $28.00 per adult, $10.25 for kids 7–13; kids 6 and under free. Reservations required. ✉ *County Rd. 4-12/Forest Service Rd. 28, Silver Lake* ☎ *541/576–2426* ⊕ *www.cowboydinnertree.net.*

WHERE TO STAY

$$
B&B/INN

Lara House Lodge. Located in a manicured residential neighborhood across from Drake Park, guests will feel at home at this historically grand and cherished Bend house. **Pros:** clean lines and an uncluttered feel; downtown is a short walk away; wine hour every night. **Cons:** no pets or kids; can be crowded during peak travel times; check-in only 4–6 or by prior arrangement. ⑤ *Rooms from: $195* ✉ *640 N.W. Congress St.* ☎ *541/388–4064, 800/766–4064* ⊕ *www.larahouse.com* ⤳ *6 rooms* ⑩ *Breakfast.*

$$
RESORT

Old St. Francis School. This charming and fun outpost in a restored 1936 Catholic schoolhouse has classrooms turned into lodging quarters, restaurant and bars, a brewery, a stage, a mosaic-tile soaking pool, and a movie theater with couches and food service. **Pros:** a self-contained destination village, yet only footsteps from downtown Bend and Drake Park; kids and pets welcome. **Cons:** few modern appliances. ⑤ *Rooms from: $155* ✉ *700 N.W. Bond St.* ☎ *541/382–5174, 877/661–4228* ⊕ *www.mcmenamins.com* ⤳ *19 rooms* ⑩ *No meals.*

6

$$$$
HOTEL
Fodor'sChoice
★

The Oxford Hotel. Stepping into the sleek, high-ceilinged lobby tells you you've found a new kind of accommodations in central Oregon, with stylish Northwest interiors and elegantly spacious rooms. **Pros:** generous and environmentally sustainable amenities; luxurious spa and fitness room; loaner bikes, iPods, and Breedlove guitars; exceptional service. **Cons:** on the exterior, property appears inconspicuously wedged into a half block on the edge of downtown. $ *Rooms from: $279* ⊠ *10 N.W. Minnesota Ave.* ☎ *877/440–8436* ⊕ *www.oxfordhotelbend.com* ↘ *59 rooms* ⦿ *No meals.*

$$$
RESORT
FAMILY
Fodor'sChoice
★

Sunriver Resort. Central Oregon's premier family playground and luxurious destination resort encapsulates so many things that are distinctive about central Oregon, from the mountain views and winding river, to the biking, rafting, golfing, skiing, and family or romantic getaways that live up to the resort's tagline of "the start of something unforgettable." **Pros:** many activities for kids and adults; much pampering in elegant lodge facilities; close to The Village at Sunriver. **Cons:** when visitors throng the shops, restaurants, and bike paths, it can feel as if an entire city has relocated here. $ *Rooms from: $229* ⊠ *17600 Center Dr., 15 miles south of Bend on Hwy. 97, Sunriver* ☎ *800/801–8765* ⊕ *www.sunriver-resort.com* ↘ *245 rooms, 284 houses* ⦿ *No meals.*

NIGHTLIFE

900 Wall Restaurant and Bar. In a historic corner brick building on a downtown Bend crossroads, this sophisticated restaurant and bar serves hundreds of bottles and about 50 different wines by the glass, earning it the Wine Spectator Award of Excellence. ⊠ *900 N.W. Wall St.* ☎ *541/323–6295* ⊕ *www.900wall.com.*

Bend Brewing Company. Another local brewery, founded in 1995, BBC (as it is affectionately called by locals) offers about 10 different types of beers on tap. It's located on the second floor above the brewpub, where diners and drinkers can look up through windows to the tanks above. Since space is limited for brewing, BBC focuses not on the quantity of beer, but the quality. Tours are available by appointment only. ⊠ *1019 N.W. Brooks St.* ☎ *541/383–1599* ⊕ *www.bendbrewingco.com.*

Deschutes Brewery. Central Oregon's first and most famous brewery produces and bottles its beer in this facility separate from the popular brewpub. Built in 1993 and expanded in 2004, it now distributes beer to more than half the country, as well to Canada. Take a free tour between 1 and 4 pm every day; be sure to make reservations online or by phone since groups fill quickly. The tour ends in the tasting room and gift shop, where participants get to try samples of the fresh beer. ⊠ *901 S.W. Simpson Ave.* ☎ *541/385–8606* ⊕ *www.deschutesbrewery.com.*

Level 2. After a day of shopping, or before concert-going at the ampitheater, sip on a perfectly mixed cocktail at this trendy Old Mill District urban-esque lounge. The rich chai martini is a delectable winter treat. ⊠ *360 S.W. Powerhouse Dr.* ☎ *541/323–5382* ⊕ *www.bendlevel2.com.*

Sunriver Resort

SPORTS AND THE OUTDOORS

BIKING

U.S. 97 north to the Crooked River Gorge and Smith Rock and the route along the **Cascade Lakes Highway** out of Bend provide bikers with memorable scenery and a good workout. **Sunriver** has more than 30 miles of paved bike paths.

Hutch's Bicycles. Road, mountain, and kids' bikes can be rented at this shop as well as a location at 725 N.W. Columbia St. ⊠ *820 N.E. 3rd St.* ☎ *541/382–6248 3rd St. shop, 541/382–9253 Columbia St. shop* ⊕ *www.hutchsbicycles.com.*

BOATING

A popular summer activity is floating the Deschutes River at your own pace.

Riverbend Park. In Bend, rent an inner tube at Riverbend Park from a kiosk operated from Memorial Day to Labor Day by **Sun Country Tours** *(⇨ see Tours in the Central Oregon Planner)* and float an hour and a half downriver to Drake Park, where you can catch a shuttle back for a minimal cash fee. ⊠ *799 S.W. Columbia St.* ☎ *541/389–7275* ⊕ *www.bendparksandrec.org.*

Tumalo Creek Kayak & Canoe. Rent a kayak or stand-up paddleboard and enter the river from the store's backyard, but be prepared to paddle upriver before a leisurely float downstream. ⊠ *805 S.W. Industrial Way* ☎ *541/317–9407* ⊕ *tumalocreek.com.*

RECREATIONAL AREAS

Deschutes National Forest. This 1½-million-acre forest has 20 peaks higher than 7,000 feet, including three of Oregon's five highest mountains, more than 150 lakes, and 500 miles of streams. If you want to park your car at a trailhead, some of the sites require a Northwest Forest Pass; day-use passes are also needed May through September at many locations for boating and picnicking. Campgrounds (fees payable) are operated by a camp host. ⊠ *63095 Deschutes Market Rd.* ☎ *541/383–5300* ⊕ *www.fs.usda.gov/centraloregon* ⊠ *Park pass $5.*

SKIING

Many Nordic trails—more than 165 miles of them—wind through the Deschutes National Forest.

FAMILY **Mt. Bachelor.** This alpine resort area has 60 percent of downhill runs that are rated advanced or expert, with the rest geared for beginner and intermediate skiers and snowboarders. One of 10 lifts takes skiers all the way to the mountain's 9,065-foot summit. One run has a vertical drop of 3,265 feet for thrill-seekers, and the longest of the 88 runs is 4 miles. Facilities and services include equipment rental and repair, a ski school, retail shop, and day care; you can enjoy seven restaurants, three bars, and six lodges. Other activities include cross-country skiing, a tubing park, sled-dog rides, snowshoeing, and in summer, hiking, biking, disc golfing, and chairlift rides. The 35 miles of trails at the **Mt. Bachelor Nordic Center** are for all abilities.

During the offseason, the lift to the **Pine Marten Lodge** provides sightseeing, stunning views, and fine sunset dining. Visitors can play disc golf on a downhill course that starts near the lodge. At the base of the mountain, take dry-land dog sled rides with four-time Iditarod musher Rachael Scdoris. ⊠ *13000 S.W. Century Dr.* ☎ *541/382–7888, 800/829–2442* ⊕ *www.mtbachelor.com* ⊠ *Lift tickets $47–$79 per day; kids 5 and under free* ☉ *Nov.–May, daily 9–4, or as weather allows.*

SHOPPING

In addition to Bend's compact downtown, the Old Mill District draws shoppers from throughout the region. Chain stores and franchise restaurants have filled in along the approaches to town, especially along U.S. 20 and U.S. 97.

Cowgirl Cash. This funky western outfitter buys and sells vintage boots and western apparel. You never know exactly what you'll find, but you can expect a fair share of leather, turquoise, silver, and, always, boots. It's a quirky and welcome feature of the downtown scene but closed Thursday–Sunday in the winter. ⊠ *924 N.W. Brooks St.* ☎ *541/678–5162* ⊕ *www.cowgirlcashbend.com.*

Dudley's BookShop Café. This independent bookseller offers Wi-Fi, a small café, and seating areas that attract interesting people who meet amidst new and used books to participate in all kinds of activites, from tango classes to philosophical debates. ⊠ *135 N.W. Minnesota Ave.* ☎ *541/749–2010* ⊕ *www.dudleysbookshopcafe.com.*

Goody's. If the aroma of fresh waffle cones causes a pause on your downtown stroll, you've probably hit one of Central Oregon's favorite soda fountain and candy shops. Try the Oreo cookie ice cream, a local favorite, or the homemade chocolate. If you purchase a stuffed toy animal that calls the store home, expect for it to smell sweetly for weeks to come. ⊠ *957 N.W. Wall St.* ☎ *541/389–5185* ⊕ *www. goodyschocolates.com.*

Newport Avenue Market. In business for more than 20 years, this culinary mecca not only offers a large selection of organic and gourmet foods, but also sells items such as high-end kitchen supplies and humorous gifts. Pick up a pair of squirrel underwear—it's as small as you might expect. ⊠ *1121 N.W. Newport Ave.* ☎ *541/382–3940* ⊕ *www. newportavemarket.com.*

Old Mill District. Bend was once the site of one of the world's largest sawmill operations, with a sprawling industrial complex along the banks of the Deschutes. In recent years the abandoned shells of the old factory buildings have been transformed into an attractive shopping center, a project honored with national environmental awards. National chain retailers can be found here, along with restaurants, boutiques, a 16-screen multiplex and IMAX movie theater, and the Les Schwab Amphitheater that attracts nationally renowned artists, local bands, and summer festivals. ⊠ *450 S.W. Powerhouse Dr.* ☎ *541/312–0131* ⊕ *www.theoldmill.com.*

SISTERS

21 miles northwest of Bend.

If Sisters looks as if you've stumbled into the Old West, that's entirely by design. The town fathers—or perhaps we should say "sisters"—strictly enforce an 1800s-style architecture. Rustic cabins border ranches on the edge of town, and you won't find a stoplight on any street. Western storefronts give way to galleries, the century-old hotel now houses a restaurant and bar, and a bakery occupies the former general store. Although its population is just a little more than 2,000, Sisters increasingly attracts visitors as well as urban runaways who appreciate its tranquillity and charm. If you're driving over from the Willamette Valley, note how the weather seems to change to sunshine when you cross the Cascades at the Santiam Pass and begin descending toward the town.

Black Butte, a perfectly conical cinder cone, rises to the northwest. The Metolius River/Camp Sherman area to the west is a special find for fly-fishermen and abounds with springtime wildflowers.

GETTING HERE AND AROUND

Travelers from Portland and the west come to Sisters over the Santiam Pass on Oregon 126. This is also the route for visitors who fly into Redmond Municipal Airport, rent a car, and drive 20 miles west. Those coming from Bend drive 21 miles northwest on U.S. 20. **Cascades East,** a regional bus carrier, runs routes between Sisters and the Redmond airport by reservation.

ESSENTIALS

Visitor Information Sisters Chamber of Commerce ⊠ *291 E. Main Ave.* ☎ *541/549–0251* ⊕ *www.sisterscountry.com.*

EXPLORING

Camp Sherman. Surrounded by groves of whispering yellow-bellied ponderosa pines, larch, fir, and cedars and miles of streamside forest trails, this small, peaceful resort community of about 250 full-time residents (plus a few stray cats and dogs) is part of a designated conservation area. The area's beauty and natural resources are the big draw: the spring-fed Metolius River prominently glides through the community. In the early 1900s Sherman County wheat farmers escaped the dry summer heat by migrating here to fish and rest in the cool river environment, making Camp Sherman one of the first destination resorts in central Oregon. As legend has it, to help guide fellow farmers to the spot, devotees nailed a shoebox top with the name "camp sherman" to a tree at a fork in the road. Several original buildings still stand from the early days, including some cabins, a schoolhouse, and a tiny railroad chapel. The "action" is at the Camp Sherman Store & Fly Shop, built in 1918, adjacent to the post office. ⊠ *25451 S.W. Forest Service Rd. 1419, 10 miles northwest of Sisters on U.S. 20, 5 miles north on Hwy. 14.* ☎ *541/595–6711* ⊕ *www.campshermanstore.com* ⊙ *June–Aug., Mon.–Thurs. 8–7, Fri.–Sat. 8–8, Sun. 8–6; Sept. hours vary; Oct.–May, Fri.–Sat. 9–5, Sun. 9–4.*

NEED A BREAK? | **Sisters Bakery.** In a rustic Western-looking former general store built in 1925, Sisters Bakery turns out high-quality pastries, doughnuts, and specialty breads from 5 am–5 pm. The bakery serves Bend's Strictly Organic coffee, and harkens back to a time when doughnuts were simple and tasty. Cash and checks only. ⊠ *251 E. Cascade St.* ☎ *541/549–0361* ⊕ *www. sistersbakery.com.*

WHERE TO EAT

$
AMERICAN

✕ **The Depot Café.** A railroad theme prevails at this main-street rustic café. A miniature train circles above as the kitchen dishes out sandwiches, salads, and dinner specials. Sit inside next to the rough-wood walls or out back on the deck. ⑤ *Average main: $15* ⊠ *250 W. Cascade St.* ☎ *541/549–2572* ⊕ *www.sistersdepot.com* ⊙ *Closed Tues.; no breakfast weekdays.*

$$$
FRENCH
Fodor's Choice
★

✕ **Jen's Garden.** "Everything is beautiful and delicious" one diner said about this top-class restaurant that offers a three-course prix-fixe option, as well as traditional five-course meal in an intimate cottage setting. In keeping with the European custom of small servings, the courses are deliberately integrated so that the flavors complement each other in a vibrant and sometimes daring manner. The menu changes often to incorperate seasonal specialites and fresh products, with choices for each course: summer vegetable and wild mushroom gnocchi, basil-scented Oregon bay shrimp and chilled corn soup, braised beef cheek ragout, olive oil cake with mascarpone icing. If one particular dish tantalizes the senses, ordering à la carte is also an option. ⑤ *Average main: $27* ⊠ *403 E. Hood Ave.* ☎ *541/549–2699* ⊕ *www.intimatecottagecuisine. com* ⚐ *Reservations essential* ⊙ *No lunch* ⊙ *Closed Mon. and Tues. in fall and spring, and for a few weeks around Thanksgiving and after Valentine's Day.*

\$\$\$ ✕**Kokanee Café.** The remarkable restaurant near the banks of the Meto-
AMERICAN lius River draws diners from across the mountains to sample artful
Fodor's Choice Northwest dishes at this homey hideaway with a paneled dining room
★ and warm-weather porch. Local lamb, fresh fish, and vegetarian options
are presented with creative elegance. As if brilliant appetizers, entrées
and full bar weren't enough, sample the house-made desserts. ⑤ *Average main: $25* ✉ *25545 S.W. Forest Service Rd. 1419, Camp Sherman*
☎ *541/595–6420* ⊕ *www.kokaneecafe.com* ⚓ *Reservations essential*
♥ *Closed Nov.–Apr. No lunch.*

\$ ✕**The Open Door.** Serving simple and light Italian fare, such as panini
ITALIAN and flatbread pizzas, this quaint and cozy restaurant offers a different
homemade pasta dish every night for dinner. The interior is an eclectic mix of mismatched tables and chairs, the restaurant and wine bar
opens into Clearwater Gallery & Framing, which displays Northwest
artwork. An outdoor patio is open in the summer, but since the indoor
eating space is small and fills quickly, come early for lunch or try to
make reservations for dinner. If the place is busy on a winter's eve, you
may find yourself eating in the gallery among paintings and pottery.
⑤ *Average main: $12* ✉ *303 W. Hood Ave.* ☎ *541/549–4994* ⊕ *www.
theclearwatergallery.com* ♥ *Closed Tues. in fall and winter.*

\$ ✕**Sno Cap Drive In.** Since 1945, this burger joint has been serving iconic
AMERICAN burgers, sandwiches, fries, milk shakes, and ice cream to residents and
visitors. Be prepared for long lines out the doors, as travelers driving
across the mountain often plan to stop here for lunch. Inside there
are a few tables and checkered curtains, and outdoor seating with
umbrellas is available. ⑤ *Average main: $8* ✉ *380 W. Cascade Ave.*
☎ *541/549–6151.*

WHERE TO STAY

\$\$ 🏨**FivePine Lodge.** At this authentic, luxury, Western-style resort resem-
RESORT bling a forest lodge, high-end furnishings were built by Amish crafts-
Fodor's Choice men. **Pros:** top-quality amenities, like the Kohler waterfall tubs; peaceful
★ atmosphere, but conviently located on the fringes of downtown Sis-
ter; every detail and pleasure is considered, including the softest sheets
and towels seemingly available. **Cons:** only slightly set back from
U.S. 20, where traffic is sometimes heavy; some cabins are close to
neighbors. ⑤ *Rooms from: $189* ✉ *1021 Desperado Trail* ☎ *541/549–
5900, 866/974–5900* ⊕ *www.fivepinelodge.com* ⟲ *8 rooms, 24 cabins*
🍴| *Breakfast.*

\$\$\$\$ 🏨**The Lodge at Suttle Lake.** Presiding over the eastern side of Suttle Lake,
RESORT with supersized wooden architecture and whimsical charm, this Grand
Cascadian style getaway offers 11 lodge rooms that are big on luxury,
with fireplaces and glorious lake or forest views, and six waterfront
cabins. **Pros:** peaceful setting in luxurious accomodations; accessibility
to varied sports in all seasons; various rooms and prices. **Cons:** no air-
conditioning in summer; cell reception is spotty. ⑤ *Rooms from: $263*
✉ *13300 U.S. Hwy. 20, 13 miles northwest of Sisters* ☎ *541/595–2628*
⊕ *www.thelodgeatsuttlelake.com* ⟲ *11 rooms, 14 cabins* 🍴| *No meals.*

\$\$\$\$ 🏨**Metolius River Resort.** Each of the immaculate, individually owned
RENTAL cabins that nestle amid the pines and aspen at this peaceful resort has
splendid views of the sparkling Metolius River, decks furnished with

6

Adirondack chairs, a full kitchen, and a fireplace. **Pros:** privacy; cabins feel like home—a very luxurious home; fall asleep and wake up to the sound of the river. **Cons:** no additional people (even visitors) allowed; no cell-phone service; bring supplies on winter weekdays when Camp Sherman closes down. ⑤ *Rooms from: $265* ✉ *25551 S.W. Forest Service Rd. 1419, Camp Sherman* ✛ *Off U.S. 20, northeast 10 miles from Sisters, turn north on Camp Sherman Rd., stay to left at fork (1419), and then turn right at the only stop sign* ☎ *800/818–7688, 541/595–6281* ⊕ *www.metoliusriverresort.com* ↬ *11 cabins* ⦿*No meals.*

NIGHTLIFE AND THE ARTS

Bronco Billy's Ranch Grill and Saloon. Pass through the swinging saloon doors into this Old West watering hole, originally built more than a century ago as the Hotel Sisters. Head to the bar, which is decorated with a mural of cancan dancers, weathered saddles hanging on the wall, and a mounted stuffed buffalo head. The saloon beckons to both residents and travelers alike. ✉ *190 E. Cascade Ave.* ☎ *541/549–7427* ⊕ *www.broncobillysranchgrill.com.*

Three Creeks Brewing Co. Currently Sisters' only brewery, Three Creeks offers a selection of beers at its brewing facility and brewpub that play on Northwest culture and the outdoor lifestyle. It's currently in the middle of an expansion project and plans to start canning its beers to further promote a convenient relationship between craft beer and the great outdoors. The brewery is visible from the brewpub and tours are available by appointment, although plans are in motion to formalize a touring schedule. The brewpub, with 10 of its beers on tap, also serves a wide range of food. Order a frothing pint of the popular Knotty Blonde, or the clever Stonefly Rye, and perhaps even sign up for in-house educational classes to learn more about beers. ✉ *721 Desperado Ct.* ☎ *541/549–1963* ⊕ *www.threecreeksbrewing.com.*

SHOPPING

Don Terra Artworks. This gallery represents local artists and craftspeople. You'll find stone sculptures, pottery, jewelry, glass, paintings, and photography. ✉ *103 E. Hood Ave.* ☎ *541/549–1299* ⊕ *www.donterra.com* ☾ *Closed Tues.–Thurs. Jan.–Mar.*

Paulina Springs Books. Select a book from the discounted staff recommendation table, or from categories such as history, outdoor recreation, field guides, regional, science, and fiction. Sisters' leading independent bookstore also sells toys and games, and has a substantial young readers section. ✉ *252 W. Hood Ave.* ☎ *541/549–0866* ⊕ *www.paulinasprings.com.*

Stitchin' Post. Owned by a mother and daughter team, the famous knitting, sewing, and quilting store opened its doors in 1975. The spacious store not only inspires the senses with colorful fabric, patterns and yarns, but also conducts classes throughout the year. The Sisters Outdoor Quilt Show, annually held the second Saturday of July, is the largest in the world and intertwines its origins with the store's early years. ✉ *311 W. Cascade St.* ☎ *541/549–6061* ⊕ *www.stitchinpost.com.*

SPORTS AND THE OUTDOORS

FISHING

Fly-fishing the Metolius River attracts anglers who seek a challenge.

Camp Sherman Store & Fly Shop. This local institution, center of life in the riverside community, sells gear and provides information about where and how best to fish. ⊠ *25451 Forest Service Rd.1419, Camp Sherman* ☎ *541/595–6711* ⊕ *www.campshermanstore.com.*

Fly and Field Outfitters. This large supplier of gear also sets anglers up with expert guides. ⊠ *35 S.W. Century Dr., Bend* ☎ *866/800–2818* ⊕ *www. flyandfield.com.*

RECREATIONAL AREAS

Metolius Recreation Area. On the eastern slope of the Cascades and within the 1.6-million-acre Deschutes National Forest, this bounty of recreational wilderness is drier and sunnier than the western side of the mountains, giving way to bountiful natural history, outdoor activities, and wildlife. There are spectacular views of jagged, 10,000-foot snow-capped Cascade peaks, looming high above the basin of an expansive evergreen valley clothed in pine.

Five miles south of **Camp Sherman** (⇨ *See Exploring listings*), (two miles to head waters) the dark and perfectly shaped cinder cone of **Black Butte** rises 6,400 feet. At its base the **Metolius River** springs forth. Witness the birth of this "instant" river by walking a short paved path embedded in ponderosa forest, eventually reaching a viewpoint with the dramatic snow-covered peak of **Mt. Jefferson** on the horizon. At this point, water gurgles to the ground's surface and pours into a wide trickling creek cascading over moss-covered rocks. Within feet it funnels outward, expanding its northerly flow; becomes a full-size river; and meanders east alongside grassy banks and a dense pine forest to join the Deschutes River downstream. Within the 4,600-acre area of the Metolius and along the river, there are ample resources for camping, hiking, biking, and floating. Enjoy fly-fishing for rainbow, brown, and bull trout in perhaps the best spot within the Cascades. ⊠ *Off Hwy. 20, 9 miles northwest of Sisters, Camp Sherman* ⊕ *www.metoliusriver.org.*

SKIING

Hoodoo Ski Area. On a 5,703-foot summit, this winter sports area has more than 800 acres of skiable terrain. With 32 runs and five lifts, skiers of all levels will find suitable thrills. Upper and lower Nordic trails are surrounded by silence, and an inner-tube run and night skiing round out the range of activites. At a 60,000-square-foot lodge at the mountain's base you can take in the view, grab a bite, shop, or rest your weary feet. The ski area has kids' activities and child-care services available. Lift tickets range from $10 to $51, depending on the type and day. ⊠ *U.S. 20, 20 miles northwest of Sisters* ☎ *541/822–3799* ⊕ *www.hoodoo.com.*

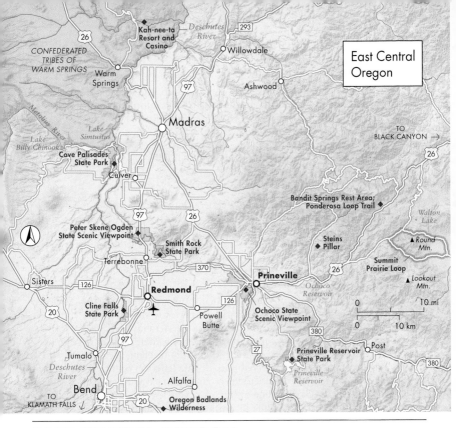

EAST CENTRAL OREGON

East of the Cascades, central Oregon changes to desert. The land is austere, covered mostly in sage and juniper, with a few hardy rivers and great extrusions of lava, which flowed or was blasted across the prehistoric landscape. In recent years resorts have emerged to draw west-side residents weary of the rain. They come over to bask in the sun and to soak up the feeling of the frontier, reinforced by ranches and resilient towns like Redmond and Prineville. They also come to fish and boat on the man-made lakes near Culver and Prineville.

REDMOND

20 miles east of Sisters, 17 miles northeast of Bend.

Redmond sits at the western end of Oregon's high desert, a handful of miles from the Deschutes River and within minutes of several lakes. It is a place where desert ranches meet runways, as it serves as the regional hub for air travel. It is the town nearest to Eagle Crest Resort and Smith Rock, a magnet for rock climbers. As with Deschutes County, Redmond has experienced rapid growth in the state during the past 10 years, largely owing to a dry and mild climate and year-round downhill and cross-country skiing, fishing, hiking, mountain biking, and rockhounding. Still, this is no gentrified resort town à la Bend, as a stroll through the compact and historic downtown will attest. A few blocks of vintage buildings remain, but north–south traffic hustles through the city core, with most residents in neighborhoods strung out to the west. Centennial Park is a small but attractive open space with fountains and an expansive lawn, aspen trees, flowers, and a kiosk selling drinks and ice cream. The park is a great place for the kids to play in the splash fountain on a hot summer's day. A clock tower contains a time capsule buried in 2010, marking the centennial celebration of Redmond's founding.

GETTING HERE AND AROUND

A couple of highways—U.S. 97 and Oregon 126—cross in Redmond. U.S. 97 carries travelers north and south to Washington and California, and Highway 126 runs between Sisters in the west to Prineville in the east. If you're driving on U.S. 26 from Portland, stop at **The Museum at Warm Springs** (☎ *541/553–3331* ⊕ *www.museumatwarmsprings.org*) at the Confederated Tribes of Warm Springs Reservation for a look at Native American artifacts and history. Taxis and the **Redmond Airport Shuttle** ferry travelers to the Redmond Municipal Airport. Two bus lines, the **Central Oregon Breeze** and **Cascades East Transit,** serve Redmond. The Central Oregon Breeze links Bend, Redmond, Madras, and Portland, and Cascades East runs buses to and from Redmond and Madras, Prineville, and Bend. Passengers should call to ensure a ride.

ESSENTIALS

Visitor Information Redmond Chamber of Commerce and Convention Visitor's Bureau ✉ *446 S.W. 7th St.* ☎ *541/923–5191* ⊕ *www. visitredmondoregon.com.*

EXPLORING

OFF THE BEATEN PATH

The Cove Palisades State Park. Many people who drive through this part of north central Oregon are more intent on their distant destinations than on the arid landscape they're passing through. But venture down the two-lane roads to this mini Grand Canyon of red-rock cliffs and gorges 14 miles west of small-town Madras. On a clear day a column of snow-capped Cascades peaks lines the horizon during the drive from town. Lake Billy Chinook, a glittering oasis amid the rocks, snakes through the park. It's formed by the Deschutes, Metolius, and Crooked rivers.

The park is accessible year-round, but high season is summertime, when families camp on the lakeshore and houseboats drift unhurriedly from cliff to cleft. The lake is renowned for its wildlife, from the lake's bull trout to turkey vultures that fill the sky with their cries. Nature lovers also flock to the park in February for the annual eagle watch. The Crooked River Day Use Area is the most immediately accessible part of the park, a great place to cast a line into the water, launch a boat, or raid your picnic basket. Nearby is the Cove Palisades Marina, where you can rent fishing and houseboats, clean fish, and buy sandwiches and boat supplies, including kids' water toys.

In addition to 10 miles of hiking trails, the Cove Palisades has a driving loop around its craggy rim. Near the Ship Rock formation, you may

Rock climbing in Smith Rock State Park

see petroglyphs carved into a boulder by indigenous people who moved through the area centuries ago.

Two full-service campgrounds have full hookups, electrical sites with water, and tent sites, boat slips, and cabins. ⊠ *7300 Jordan Rd., Off U.S. 97, 27 miles north of Redmond, Culver* ☎ *541/546–3412, 800/551–6949, 800/452–5687* ⊕ *www.oregonstateparks.org* ⌫ *Day use $5 per vehicle.*

Peter Skene Ogden Scenic Viewpoint. Even the most seasoned traveler may develop vertigo peering from the cliff top into a deep river canyon. It is a view that gives insight into why Oregon's high desert looks the way it does, with sheer drops and austere landscapes. You'll want to take pictures, but hang on to your camera. ⊠ *U.S. 97 N, 9 miles north of Redmond* ☎ *800/551–6949* ⊕ *www.oregonstateparks.org.*

WHERE TO EAT AND STAY

$$$
STEAKHOUSE
✕ **Brickhouse.** An elegant dining experience in Redmond can be found at this wood-tables and brick-wall restaurant, which specializes in steaks and chops but also offers attractive plates of seafood, especially shellfish. You can get lost in the list of cocktails and wines from Oregon and around the world. ⑤ *Average main: $30* ⊠ *412 S.W. 6th St.* ☎ *541/526–1782* ⊕ *www.brickhousesteakhouse.com* ⊘ *Closed Sun. and Mon. No lunch.*

$$
MEXICAN FUSION
✕ **Diego's Spirited Kitchen.** Near the "Redmond Est. 1910" sign that straddles downtown 6th Street, this fusion restaurant serves both Mexican and classic American dishes. Answer to "senorita" and "senor" as the bartender hand-squeezes limes for fresh margaritas while considering the good ol' five-way grilled ham and cheese sandwich, or the more

adventurous pork carnitas raviolis. $ *Average main: $20* ✉ *447 S.W. 6th St.* ☎ *541/316–2002.*

$$ ✕**Terrebonne Depot.** An old train depot is the setting for a meal that can
AMERICAN   match the stunning views of the Smith Rock cliffs. Offering an array of reasonably priced, tasty dishes, the kitchen plays it straight down the middle with nicely seasoned salmon, chicken, and pasta. You can also get lunch baskets to take with you on the climb. Service is friendly, and the menu is a cut above what you'd expect in this off-the-beaten-track location. The view allows you to reflect on the climb you've just made—or will inspire you to embark on one. $ *Average main: $18* ✉ *400 N.W. Smith Rock Way* ☎ *541/548–5030* ⊕ *www.terrebonnedepot.com* ⊘ *Closed Tues. year-round and Mon. Labor Day–Memorial Day.*

$ ⛺**Eagle Crest Resort.** On high-desert grounds covered with juniper and
RESORT   sagebrush, accommodations include vacation rental houses as well as
FAMILY   rooms and suites, some with fireplaces, clustered in a single building. **Pros:** a full-service resort with a spa, three 18-hole golf courses, restaurants; great for kids; pet-friendly. **Cons:** there can be crowds, kids, and pets; clean but not luxurious. $ *Rooms from: $129* ✉ *1522 Cline Falls Hwy., 5 miles west of Redmond* ☎ *541/923–2453, 888/306–9643* ⊕ *www.eagle-crest.com* ⇱ *100 rooms, 70 town houses* ⦿*No meals.*

NIGHTLIFE

Wild Ride Brewing Co. One of Redmond's newer breweries, Wild Ride is located on a block at the edge of downtown; you might spot the food carts first, where patrons can grab a bite to eat and then enjoy their meal in the brewery's taproom or the outdoor seating area. As you sample a beer, look at the pint glass and read the tag line: "What's Your Wild Ride?" The brewery focuses its theme on various "wild rides"—from motorcycles to skiing to rock climbing. In warmer months, the garage doors to the brewery open and expose the shining steel tanks inside. A full day of tours is offered once a month, or individual tours are available by appointment. ✉ *332 S.W. 5th St.* ☎ *541/516–8544* ⊕ *www. wildridebrew.com.*

SPORTS AND THE OUTDOORS

RECREATIONAL AREAS

Cline Falls State Park. Picnicking and fishing are popular at this nine-acre rest area commanding scenic views on the Deschutes River. You'll feel free from civilization here. ✉ *Hwy. 126, 4 miles west of Redmond* ☎ *800/551–6949* ⊕ *www.oregonstateparks.org.*

ROCK CLIMBING

Fodor'sChoice ★   **Smith Rock State Park.** Eight miles north of Redmond, this park is world famous for rock climbing, with hundreds of routes of all levels of difficulty. A network of trails serves both climbers and families dropping in for the scenery. In addition to the stunning rock formations, the Crooked River, which helped shape these features, loops through the park. You might spot golden eagles, prairie falcons, mule deer, river otters, and beavers. Due to the environmental sensitivity of the region, the animal leash law is strongly enforced. It can get quite hot in midsummer, so most prefer to climb in the spring and fall. The stunning scenery—specifically, a view of the river curving through the high rocks—was adopted by Deschutes Brewery for its Twilight Summer Ale label. ⊠ *9241 N.E. Crooked River Dr., Off U.S. 97* ☎ *541/548–7501, 800/551–6949* ⊕ *www.oregonstateparks.org* ⊠ *Day use $5 per vehicle.*

Smith Rock Climbing Guides. Professionals with emergency medical training take visitors to the Smith Rock formation for climbs of all levels of difficulty; they also supply equipment. Guided climbs—you meet at Smith Rock—can run a half day or full day, and are priced according to the number of people. ⊠ *Smith Rock State Park, Terrebonne* ☎ *541/788–6225* ⊕ *www.smithrockclimbingguides.com.*

PRINEVILLE

18 miles east of Redmond.

Prineville is the oldest town in central Oregon, and the only incorporated city in Crook County. Tire entrepreneur Les Schwab founded his regional empire here, and it remains a key hub for the company. Recently, Facebook and Apple chose Prineville as the location for new data centers. Surrounded by verdant ranch lands and the purplish hills of the Ochoco National Forest, Prineville will likely interest you chiefly as a jumping-off point for some of the region's more secluded outdoor adventures. The area attracts thousands of anglers, boaters, sightseers, and rockhounds to its nearby streams, reservoirs, and mountains. Rimrocks nearly encircle Prineville, and geology nuts dig for free agates, limb casts, jasper, and thunder eggs. Downtown Prineville consists of a handful of small buildings along a quiet strip of Highway 26, dominated by the Crook County Courthouse, built in 1909. Shopping and dining opportunities are mostly on the basic side.

GETTING HERE AND AROUND

Travelers approaching Prineville from the west on Oregon 126 descend like a marble circling a funnel, dropping into a tidy grid of a town from a high desert plain. It's an unfailingly dramatic way to enter the seat of Crook County, dominated by the courthouse on Northeast Third Street, aka Highway 26, the main drag. Prineville is 19 miles east of Redmond Municipal Airport. If you're coming to Prineville from the airport, it's easiest to rent a car and drive. However, two bus lines, **Central Oregon Breeze** and **Cascades East Transit,** run routes.

ESSENTIALS

Visitor Information Ochoco National Forest Office ⊠ *3160 N.E. 3rd St.* ☎ *541/416–6500* ⊕ *www.fs.usda.gov/centraloregon.* **Prineville-Crook County Chamber of Commerce and Visitor Center** ⊠ *185 N.E. 10th St.* ☎ *541/447–6304* ⊕ *www.visitprineville.org.*

EXPLORING

A.R. Bowman Memorial Museum. A tough little stone building (it was once a bank, and banks out here needed to be solid) is the site of the museum of the Crook County Historical Society. The 1910 edifice is on the National Register of Historic Places, with the inside vault and teller cages seemingly untouched. Prominent in the museum are old guns, relics from the lumber mills, and Native American artifacts that define early Prineville. A recent expansion houses a research library and life-size representations of an Old West street. ⊠ *246 N. Main St.* 🕾 *541/447–3715* ⊕ *www.bowmanmuseum.org* ⌲ *Free* ⊗ *Memorial Day–Labor Day, weekdays 10–5, weekends 11–4; Labor Day–Dec. and Feb.–Memorial Day, Tues.–Fri. 10–5, Sat. 11–4. Closed Jan.*

Ochoco Viewpoint. This is a truly fantastic scenic overlook that commands a sweeping view of the city, including the prominent Crook County Courthouse built in 1909, and the hills, ridges, and buttes beyond. ⊠ *U.S. Hwy. 126, ½ mile west of Prineville.*

WHERE TO EAT AND STAY

$$
STEAKHOUSE
✕ **Barney Prine's Steakhouse & Saloon.** Prineville is home to a startlingly appealing restaurant and saloon named after one of the town's founders. It's a good place to get a filet mignon, pepper steak, slow-smoked prime rib, 1-pound ribeye steak, or other cuts. Chicken, pasta, seafood, and sometimes wild game are also on the menu. The waitstaff is cheerful and attentive, and the ambience is part frontier western, part contemporary. ⑤ *Average main: $18* ⊠ *389 N.W. 4th St.* 🕾 *541/362–1272* ⊕ *www.barneyprines.com* ⊗ *No lunch.*

$
DINER
✕ **Tastee Treet.** Open since 1957, this local establishment is renowned for its traditional burgers, hand-cut french fries, and milk shakes. Saunter up to the horseshoe-shaped counter to sit on swiveling stools and chat with locals, or talk with out-of-towners, some of whom never miss a chance to drop by while passing through. Claim a red-and-white leather booth for the family, a table on the patio, or pick up an order from the drive-through. Hearty breakfast plates, such as hamburger steak and eggs, are available until 11 am, when the menu switches to sandwiches, burgers, chili cheese fries, and other "Tastee Eats." ⑤ *Average main: $9* ⊠ *493 N.E. 3rd St.* 🕾 *541/447–4165.*

$$$
RESORT
Fodor's Choice
★
🏨 **Brasada Ranch.** Enjoy a luxurious guest-ranch resort with spacious suites and cabins with fireplaces and decks, all offering authentic Western experiences and pristine modern amenities in the midst of exquisite views on 1,800 acres. **Pros:** extremely helpful staff help to make nearly anything possible; superb range of on-site facilities and activities; serene beauty and stunning mountain horizons. **Cons:** not all units have hot tubs; morning light seeps through wood-slatted shades. ⑤ *Rooms from: $249* ⊠ *16986 S.W. Brasada Ranch Rd., Powell Butte* 🕾 *866/373–4882* ⊕ *www.brasada.com* 🛏 *8 suites, 63 cabins* ⦿ *No meals.*

SPORTS AND THE OUTDOORS

FISHING

It's a good idea to check the **Oregon Department of Fish and Wildlife**'s (⊕ *ww.dfw.state.or.us*) recreation report before you head out.

Ochoco Reservoir. This lake is annually stocked with fingerling trout, and you might also find a rainbow, bass, or brown bullhead tugging on your line. ⊠ *Hwy. 26, 6 miles east of Prineville* 🕾 *541/447–1209* ⊕ *www.ccprd.org* ⌲ *Campsites $16.*

HIKING

Pick up maps at the Ochoco National Forest office for trails through the nearly 5,400-acre **Bridge Creek Wilderness** and the demanding Black Canyon Trail (11½ miles one way with a hazardous river crossing in spring) in the **Black Canyon Wilderness.** The 1½-mile **Ponderosa Loop Trail**

6

follows an old logging road through ponderosa pines growing on hills. In early summer wildflowers take over the open meadows. The trailhead begins at Bandit Springs Rest Area, 29 miles east of Prineville on U.S. 26. A 2-mile, one-way trail winds through old-growth forest and mountain meadows to **Steins Pillar**, a giant lava column with panoramic views; be prepared for a workout on the trail's poorly maintained second half, and allow at least three hours for the hike. To get to the trailhead, drive east 9 miles from Prineville on U.S. 26, head north (to the left) for 6½ miles on Mill Creek Road (also signed as Forest Service Road 33), and head east (to the right) on Forest Service Road 500.

RECREATIONAL AREAS

Ochoco National Forest. Twenty-five miles east of the flat, juniper-dotted countryside around Prineville, the landscape changes to forested ridges covered with tall ponderosa pines and Douglas firs. Sheltered by the diminutive Ochoco Mountains and with only about a foot of rain each year, the national forest, established in 1906 by President Theodore Roosevelt, manages to lay a blanket of green across the dry, high desert of central Oregon. This arid landscape—marked by deep canyons, towering volcanic plugs, and sharp ridges—goes largely unnoticed except for the annual influx of hunters during the fall. The Ochoco, part of the old Blue Mountain Forest Reserve, is a great place for camping, hiking, biking, and fishing in relative solitude. In its three wilderness areas—Mill Creek, Bridge Creek, and Black Canyon—it's possible to see elk, wild horses, eagles, and even cougars. ⊠ *Office, 3160 N.E. 3rd St. (U.S. 26)* ☎ *541/416–6500* ⊕ *www.fs.usda.gov/recmain/ochoco* ⊗ *Daily; office open weekdays 8–4:30.*

Oregon Badlands Wilderness. This 29,000-acre swath of Oregon's high desert was designated a national wilderness in 2009, following the longtime advocacy of Oregonians enamored by its harshly beautiful landscape riven by ancient lava flows and home to sage grouse, pronghorn antelope, and elk. Motorized vehicles are prohibited, but visitors can ride horses on designated trails and low-impact hikers are welcome. Bring a camera to capture the jagged rock formations, birds, and wildflowers. ⊠ *BLM Office, 3050 N.E. 3rd St. (U.S. 26)* ☎ *541/416–6700* ⊕ *www.blm.gov/or/wilderness/badlands.*

Prineville Reservoir State Park. Mountain streams flow out of the Ochoco Mountains and join together to create the Crooked River, which is dammed near Prineville. Bowman Dam on the river forms this park, where recreational activities include boating, swimming, fishing, hiking, and camping. Some anglers return here year after year, although temperatures can get uncomfortably hot and water levels relatively low by late summer. The reservoir is known for its bass, trout and crappie, with fly-fishing available on the Crooked River below Bowman Dam. ⊠ *19020 S.E. Parkland Dr.* ☎ *541/447–4363, 800/452–5687* ⊕ *www. oregonstateparks.org* ⊠ *Campsites $21–$31.*

SKIING

Bandit Springs Rest Area. A network of cross-country trails starts here. Designed for all levels of skiers, the trails traverse areas near the Ochoco Divide and have great views. ⊠ *U.S. 26, 29 miles east of Prineville.*

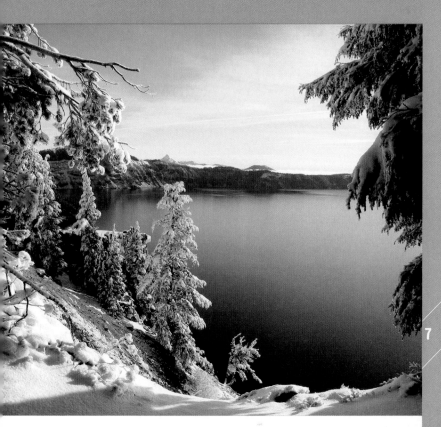

CRATER LAKE
NATIONAL PARK

WELCOME TO CRATER LAKE NATIONAL PARK

TOP REASONS TO GO

★ **The lake:** Cruise inside the caldera basin and gaze into the extraordinary sapphire-blue water of the country's deepest lake.

★ **Native land:** Enjoy the rare luxury of interacting with totally unspoiled terrain.

★ **The night sky:** Billions of stars glisten in the pitch-black darkness of an unpolluted sky.

★ **Splendid hikes:** Accessible trails spool off the main roads and wind past colorful bursts of wildflowers and cascading waterfalls.

★ **Camping at its best:** Pitch a tent or pull up a motor home at Mazama Campground, a beautifully situated, guest-friendly, and well-maintained campground.

1 Crater Lake. The focal point of the park is this nonrecreational, scenic lake known for its deep-blue hue.

2 Wizard Island. Visitors can take boat rides to this protruding landmass rising from the western section of Crater Lake; it's a great place for a hike or a picnic.

3 Mazama Village. This is your best bet for stocking up on snacks, beverages, and fuel in the park; it's about 5 miles from Rim Drive.

4 Cleetwood Cove Trail. The only safe, designated trail to hike down the caldera and reach the lake's edge is on the rim's north side off Rim Drive.

GETTING ORIENTED

Crater Lake National Park covers 183,224 acres. Located in southern Oregon less than 100 miles from the California border, it's surrounded by several Cascade Range forests, including the Winema and Rogue River national forests. Of the nearby towns, Klamath Falls is closest at 60 miles south of the park; Ashland and Medford, to the southwest, are approximately 80 miles and 90 miles from the lake, respectively, with Roseburg the farthest away at 110 miles northwest of the park.

KEY	
🏠	Ranger Station
▲	Campground
🛏	Picnic Area
🍴	Restaurant
🏨	Lodge
🥾	Trailhead
🚻	Restrooms
⇗	Scenic Viewpoint
------	Walking/Hiking Trails

PCT Parking

TO
ROSEBURG

TO →
BEND

North Entrance Station

Boundary Springs

Pumice
Desert

North Entrance Rd.

Pacific Crest National Scenic Trail

North Junction

Steel
Bay

Cleetwood
Cove

Cleetwood
Cove Trail

Rim Trail

Deepest point
below lake surface:
-1,943 ft

Grotto
Cove

Rim Dr.

Scott Bluffs

The Watchman
8,013 ft

Watchman
Trail

Wizard
Island

*Crater
Lake*

Cloudcap
Bay

Cloudcap Overlook

Mount Scott
8,929 ft

Pacific Crest Trail

Discovery Point

Rim Village

Crater Lake
Lodge

Danger
Bay

Phantom Ship
Overlook

Mount Scott
Trail

TO
MEDFORD
←AND ASHLAND

Sun
Notch

Steel Visitor Center

Vidae
Falls

Rim Dr.

Grayback Dr.
(one way)

Annie Spring
Entrance Station

Lost
Creek

Mazama Village

Grayback

Crater Peak

Grayback Ridge

Pinnacles
Overlook

Pumice
Flat

TO
KLAMATH FALLS

0   3 mi

0   3 km

Updated by Christine Vovakes

The pure, crystalline blue of Crater Lake astounds visitors at first sight. More than 5 miles wide and ringed by cliffs almost 2,000 feet high, the lake was created approximately 7,700 years ago, following Mt. Mazama's fiery explosion. Days after the eruption, the mountain collapsed on an underground chamber emptied of lava. Rain and snowmelt filled the caldera, creating a sapphire-blue lake so clear that sunlight penetrates to a depth of 400 feet (the lake's depth is 1,943 feet). Today it's both the clearest and deepest lake in the United States—and the ninth deepest in the world.

CRATER LAKE PLANNER

WHEN TO GO

The park's high season is July and August. September and early October tend to draw smaller crowds. From October through June, the entire park virtually closes due to heavy snowfall. The road is kept open just to the rim in winter, except during severe weather.

FESTIVALS

Oregon Shakespeare Festival. More than 400,000 Bard lovers descend on Ashland (90 miles from Crater Lake) for the annual Oregon Shakespeare Festival. Plays run from February to November in three theaters; peak season is July, August, and September. ☎ 541/482–4331 ⊕ *www. osfashland.org.*

PLANNING YOUR TIME

CRATER LAKE IN ONE DAY

Begin at **Steel Visitor Center,** where interpretive displays and a short video introduce you to the story of the lake's formation and its unique characteristics. Then circle the crater's rim by heading northeast on **Rim Drive,** allowing an hour to stop at overlooks—check out the Phantom

Ship rock formation in the lake—before you reach **Cleetwood Cove Trail** trailhead, the only safe and legal access to the lake. If you're up to the strenuous challenge, hike down the trail to reach the dock, and hop aboard one of the **tour boats** for a two-hour lake tour with a park ranger as your guide. If you have time, add on a trip to **Wizard Island** for a picnic lunch.

Back on Rim Drive, continue around the lake, stopping at the **Watchman Trail** for a short but steep hike to this peak above the rim, which affords not only a splendid view of the lake, but a broad vista of the surrounding southern Cascades. Wind up your visit at **Crater Lake Lodge**—allow time to wander the lobby of the 1915 structure perched on the rim. Dinner at the lodge restaurant, overlooking the lake and the Cascade sunset, caps the day.

GETTING HERE AND AROUND

Most of the park is accessible only in late June or early July through mid-October. The rest of the year, snow blocks all park roadways and entrances except Highway 62 and the access road to Rim Village from Mazama Village. Rim Drive is typically closed because of heavy snowfall from mid-October to mid-June and sometimes as late as early July; you could encounter icy conditions any month of the year, particularly in early morning.

PARK ESSENTIALS

PARK FEES AND PERMITS

Admission to the park, good for seven days, is $10 per car, or $5 per motorcycle, bicycle, or pedestrian. Backcountry campers and hikers must obtain a free wilderness permit at Rim Visitor Center or Steel Visitor Center for all overnight trips.

PARK HOURS

Crater Lake National Park is open 24 hours a day year-round; however, snow closes most park roadways October through June. Lodging and dining facilities usually are open from late May to mid-October. The park is in the Pacific time zone.

CELL-PHONE RECEPTION

Cell-phone reception in the park is unreliable. You'll find public telephones at Crater Lake Lodge and outside the Mazama Village Camper Store.

RESTAURANTS

There are a few casual eateries and convenience stores within the park. For fantastic upscale dining on the caldera's rim, head to the Crater Lake Lodge.

HOTELS

Crater Lake's summer season is relatively brief, and the park's main lodge is generally booked with guest reservations a year in advance. If you don't snag one, check availability as your trip approaches—cancellations are always possible. Outside the park are options in Prospect, Klamath Falls, Roseburg, Medford, and Ashland. *Hotel reviews have been shortened. For full information, visit Fodors.com.*

WHAT IT COSTS IN U.S. DOLLARS			
	$	**$$**	**$$$**	**$$$$**
Restaurants	Under $13	$13–$20	$21–$30	Over $30
Hotels	Under $101	$101–$150	$151–$200	Over $200

Restaurant prices are the average cost of a main course at dinner, or if dinner is not served, at lunch. Hotel prices are the lowest cost of a standard double room in high season.

VISITOR INFORMATION

PARK CONTACT INFORMATION

Crater Lake National Park ☎ *541/594–3000* ⊕ *www.nps.gov/crla.*

VISITOR CENTERS

Rim Visitor Center. In summer you can obtain park information here, take a ranger-led tour, or stop into the nearby Sinnott Memorial, with a small museum and a 900-foot view down to the lake's surface. In winter, snowshoe walks are offered on weekends and holidays. The Rim Village Gift Store and cafeteria are the only services open in winter. ⊠ *Rim Dr. on the south side of the lake, 7 miles north of Annie Spring entrance station* ☎ *541/594–3090* ⊕ *www.nps.gov/crla* ⊗ *Late May–late-Sept., daily 9:30–5.*

Steel Visitor Center. Open year-round, the information center is part of the park's headquarters; you'll find restrooms and a first-aid station here. There's also a small post office and a shop that sells books, maps, and postcards. In the auditorium, a 22-minute film, *Crater Lake: Into the Deep*, describes the lake's formation and geology, and explores the area's cultural history. ⊠ *Rim Dr., 4 miles north of Annie Spring entrance station* ☎ *541/594–3100* ⊕ *www.nps.gov/crla* ⊗ *Early Apr.– early Nov., daily 9–5; mid-Nov.–early Apr., daily 10–4.*

EXPLORING

For most visitors, the star attractions of Crater Lake are the lake itself and the breathtakingly situated Crater Lake Lodge. Other park highlights include the natural, unspoiled beauty of the forest and the geological marvels that you can access along the Rim Drive.

SCENIC DRIVES

Fodor'sChoice ★ **Rim Drive.** Take this 33-mile scenic loop for views of the lake and its cliffs from every conceivable angle. The drive alone is at least two hours long; frequent stops at overlooks and short hikes can easily stretch this to a half day. Be aware that Rim Drive is typically closed due to heavy snowfall from mid-October to mid-June, and icy conditions can be encountered any month of the year, particularly in early morning. ⊠ *Drive begins at Rim Village, 7 miles from Annie Spring entrance station along Munson Valley Rd.* ⊕ *To get to Rim Dr. from the park's north entrance, access the north entrance road via either Rte. 230 or Hwy. 138, and follow it for about 10 miles.* ⊕ *www.nps.gov/crla.*

HISTORIC SITES

Fodor's Choice
★

Crater Lake Lodge. First built in 1915, this classic log-and-stone structure still boasts the original lodgepole-pine pillars, beams, and stone fireplaces. The lobby, fondly referred to as the Great Hall, serves as a warm, welcoming gathering place where you can play games, socialize with a cocktail, or gaze out of the many windows to view spectacular sunrises and sunsets by a crackling fire. ⊠ *Rim Village, just east of Rim Visitor Center* ⊕ *www.craterlakelodges.com.*

SCENIC STOPS

Cloudcap Overlook. The highest road-access overlook on the Crater Lake rim, Cloudcap has a westward view across the lake to Wizard Island and an eastward view of Mt. Scott, the volcanic cone that is the park's highest point, just 2 miles away. ⊠ *2 miles off Rim Dr., 13 miles northeast of Steel Visitor Center* ⊕ *www.nps.gov/crla.*

Discovery Point. This overlook marks the spot at which prospectors first spied the lake in 1853. Wizard Island is just northeast, close to shore. ⊠ *Rim Dr., 1½ miles north of Rim Village* ⊕ *www.nps.gov/crla.*

Mazama Village. In summer a campground, motor inn, amphitheater, gas station, post office, and small store are open here. No gasoline is available in the park from mid-October to mid-May. Snowfall determines when the village and its facilities open and close for the season. ⊠ *Mazama Village Rd., off Hwy. 62, near Annie Spring entrance station* 🕾 *541/594–2255, 888/774–2728* ⊕ *www.craterlakelodges.com* ☉ *Mid- to late-May and late Sept.–mid-Oct., daily 10–5; June–early Sept., daily 7 am–9 pm; early Sept.–late Sept., daily 8–8.*

Phantom Ship Overlook. From this point you can get a close look at Phantom Ship, a rock formation that resembles a schooner with furled masts and looks ghostly in fog. ⊠ *Rim Dr., 7 miles northeast of Steel Visitor Center* ⊕ *www.nps.gov/crla.*

Pinnacles Overlook. Ascending from the banks of Sand and Wheeler creeks, unearthly spires of eroded ash resemble the peaks of fairy-tale castles. Once upon a time, the road continued east to a former entrance. A path now replaces the old road and follows the rim of Sand Creek (affording more views of pinnacles) to where the entrance arch still stands. ⊠ *5 miles northeast of Steel Visitor Center, then 7 miles east on Pinnacles Spur Rd.* ⊕ *www.nps.gov/crla.*

Sun Notch. It's a moderate ¼-mile hike through wildflowers and dry meadow to this overlook, which has views of Crater Lake and Phantom Ship. Mind the cliff edges. ⊠ *Rim Dr., 4.4 miles east of Steel Visitor Center, east side of the lake* ⊕ *www.nps.gov/crla.*

Wizard Island. To get here, hike down the steep Cleetwood Cove Trail (and back up on your return) and board the tour boat (⇨ *Educational Offerings)* for a two-hour ride ($52) with the option of a half or full day stay on the island. Bring a picnic. If you're in top shape, take the very strenuous 2-mile hike that begins at the boat dock and steeply ascends over rock-strewn terrain to Wizard Summit and a path around the 90-foot-deep crater at the top. A more moderate hike is the 1.8-mile

Wildlife in Crater Lake

CLOSE UP

Two primary types of fish swim beneath the surface of Crater Lake: kokanee salmon and rainbow trout. It's estimated that hundreds of thousands of kokanee inhabit the lake, but because boating and recreational access is so limited they elude many would-be sportsman. Kokanees average about 8 inches in length, but they can grow to nearly 18 inches. Rainbow trout are larger than the kokanee but are less abundant in Crater Lake. Trout—including bull, Eastern brook, rainbow, and German brown—swim in the park's many streams and rivers; they usually remain elusive because these waterways flow near inaccessibly steep canyons.

Remote canyons shelter the park's elk and deer populations, which can sometimes be seen at dusk and dawn feeding at forest's edge. Black bears and pine martens—cousins of the short-tailed weasel—also call Crater Lake home. Birds such as hairy woodpeckers, California gulls, red-tailed hawks, and great horned owls are more commonly seen in summer in forests below the lake.

---

trek on a rocky trail along the shore of the island. ⊠ *Via Cleetwood Cove Trail to Wizard Island dock* ☎ *541/594–2255, 888/774–2728* ⊕ *www.craterlakelodges.com* ☉ *Daily late June–mid-Sept.*

EDUCATIONAL OFFERINGS

RANGER PROGRAMS

FAMILY **Boat Tours.** The most extensively used guided tours in Crater Lake are on the water, aboard launches that carry 37 passengers on a two-hour tour accompanied by a ranger. The boats circle the lake; two of the eight daily boats stop at Wizard Island, where you can get off and reboard a minimum of three hours later, or six hours later if you catch the morning boat. The first tour leaves the dock at 9:30 am; the last departs at 3:30 pm. To get to the dock you must hike down Cleetwood Cove Trail, a strenuous 1.1-mile walk that drops 700 feet; only those in excellent physical shape should attempt the hike. Bring adequate water with you. Purchase boat-tour tickets at Crater Lake Lodge, at the top of the trail or through advance reservations. Restrooms are available at the top and bottom of the trail. ⊠ *Cleetwood Cove Trail, off Rim Dr., 11 miles north of Rim Village on the north side of the lake* ☎ *541/594–2255, 888/774–2728* ⊕ *www.craterlakelodges.com* 🎫 *$37; $52 with island drop-off* ☉ *Late June–mid-Sept., daily.*

FAMILY **Junior Ranger Program.** Kids ages 6–12 learn about Crater Lake while earning either a Junior Ranger patch or badge in daily sessions during summer months at the Rim Visitor Center, and year-round at the Steel Visitor Center. Pick up free activity booklets at either visitor center. ☎ *541/594–3100* ⊕ *www.nps.gov/crla.*

SPORTS AND THE OUTDOORS

FISHING

Fishing is allowed in the lake, but you may find the experience frustrating—in such a massive body of water, the problem is finding the fish. Try your luck near the Cleetwood Cove boat dock, or take poles on the boat tour and fish off Wizard Island. Rainbow trout and kokanee salmon lurk in Crater Lake's aquamarine depths, and some grow to enormous sizes. You don't need a state fishing license, but to protect the lake's pristine waters, use only artificial bait as opposed to live worms. Private boats are prohibited on the lake.

HIKING

EASY

Castle Crest Wildflower Trail. This short half-mile loop that passes through a spring-fed meadow is one of the park's flatter hikes. Wildflowers burst into full bloom here in July. *Easy.* ⊠ *Across the street from Steel Visitor Center parking lot, East Rim Dr.* ⊕ *www.nps.gov/crla.*

Godfrey Glen Trail. This 1-mile loop trail is an easy stroll through an old-growth forest with canyon views. Its dirt path is accessible to wheelchairs with assistance. *Easy.* ⊠ *2.4 miles south of Steel Visitor Center* ⊕ *www.nps.gov/crla.*

MODERATE

Annie Creek Canyon Trail. This somewhat strenuous 1.7-mile hike loops through a deep stream-cut canyon, providing views of the narrow cleft scarred by volcanic activity. This is a good area to look for flowers and deer. *Moderate.* ⊠ *Mazama Campground, behind ampitheater, between D&E campground loops; Mazama Village Rd., near Annie Spring entrance station* ⊕ *www.nps.gov/crla.*

Boundary Springs Trail. If you feel like sleuthing, take this moderate 5-mile round-trip hike to the headwaters of the Rogue River. The trail isn't always well marked, so a detailed trail guide is necessary. You'll see streams, forests, and wildflowers along the way before discovering Boundary Springs pouring out of the side of a low ridge. *Moderate.* ⊠ *Pullout on Hwy. 230, near milepost 19, about 5 miles west of the junction with Hwy. 138* ⊕ *www.nps.gov/crla.*

Watchman Peak Trail. This is one of the best hikes in the park. Though it's less than a mile each way, the trail climbs more than 400 feet—not counting the steps up to the actual lookout, which has great views of Wizard Island and the lake. *Moderate.* ⊠ *Watchman Overlook, 3.8 miles northwest of Rim Village on Rim Dr., west side of the lake* ⊕ *www.nps.gov/crla.*

DIFFICULT

Cleetwood Cove Trail. This strenuous 2.2-mile round-trip hike descends 700 feet down nearly vertical cliffs along the lake to the boat dock. Be in top shape before you take this one. *Difficult.* ⊠ *Cleetwood Cove* *trailhead, Rim Dr., 11 miles north of Rim Village, north side of the lake ⊕ www.nps.gov/crla.*

FodorśChoice **Mt. Scott Trail.** This strenuous 5-mile
★ round-trip trail takes you to the park's highest point—the top of Mt. Scott, the oldest volcanic cone of Mt. Mazama, at 8,929 feet. The average hiker needs 90 minutes to make the steep uphill trek—and nearly 60 minutes to get down. The trail starts at an elevation of about 7,450 feet, so the climb is not extreme but does get steep in spots. Views of the lake and the

broad Klamath Basin are spectacular. *Difficult.* ⊠ *14 miles east of Steel Visitor Center on Rim Dr., east side of the lake, across from the road to Cloudcap Overlook* ⊕ *www.nps.gov/crla.*

Pacific Crest Trail. You can hike a portion of the Pacific Crest Trail, which extends from Mexico to Canada and winds through the park for 33 miles. For this prime backcountry experience, catch the trail off Highway 138 about a mile east of the north entrance, where it heads south and then toward the west rim of the lake and circles it for about 6 miles, then descends down Dutton Creek to the Mazama Village area. You'll need a detailed map for this hike; check online or with the PCT association. *Difficult.* ⊠ *Pacific Crest Trail parking lot, north access road off Hwy. 138, 2 miles east of the Hwy. 138–north entrance road junction* ⊕ *www.nps.gov/crla.*

SKIING

There are no maintained ski trails in the park, although some backcountry trails are marked with blue diamonds or snow poles. Most cross-country skiers park at Rim Village and follow a portion of West Rim Drive toward Wizard Island Overlook (4 miles). The road is plowed to Rim Village, but it may be closed temporarily due to severe storms. Snow tires and chains are essential. The park's online brochure (available at ⊕ *www.nps.gov/crla*) lists additional trails and their length and difficulty.

SWIMMING

Swimming is allowed in the lake, but it's not advised. Made up entirely of snowmelt, Crater Lake is very cold—about 45°F to 56°F in summer. The lagoons on Wizard Island and at Cleetwood Cove are your best choices—but only when the air temperature rises above 80°F, which is rare. If you're able to brave the cold, though, you can say that you've taken a dip in the deepest lake in the United States.

WHERE TO EAT

$$
AMERICAN
FAMILY

✕ **Annie Creek Restaurant.** At this family-friendly dining spot you'll find pizza and pasta along with chicken, beef, and fish entrées. Less expensive sandwich selections are available, plus a breakfast menu. The outdoor seating area is surrounded by towering pine trees. $ *Average main: $16* ✉ *Mazama Village Rd., near Annie Spring entrance station* ☎ *541/594–2255* ⊕ *www.craterlakelodges.com* ☉ *Closed mid-Sept.–late May.*

PEST ALERT

Early summer snowmelt often creates watery breeding areas for large groups of mosquitoes. Bring lots of insect repellent in June and July, and expect mosquito swarms in the early morning and at sunset. They can also be a problem later in the summer in campgrounds and on the Cleetwood Cove Trail, so pack repellent if you plan on camping or hiking.

$$$
AMERICAN
Fodor's Choice
★

✕ **Dining Room at Crater Lake Lodge.** Virtually the only place where you can dine well once you're in the park, the lodge emphasizes fresh, regional Northwest cuisine. The dining room is magnificent, with a large stone fireplace and views of Crater Lake's clear-blue waters. Breakfast and lunch are enjoyable here, but the evening menu is the main attraction, with tempting delights such as wild Alaskan salmon, pork loin with apple compote, steak, and vegetarian offerings. An extensive wine list tops off the gourmet experience. No reservations accepted for breakfast and lunch, but they're essential for dinner. $ *Average main: $30* ✉ *Crater Lake Lodge, 1 Lodge Loop Rd., Rim Village* ☎ *541/594–2255* ⊕ *www.craterlakelodges.com* ⌂ *Reservations essential* ☉ *Closed mid-Oct.–late May.*

PICNIC AREAS

Rim Drive. About a half-dozen picnic-area turnouts encircle the lake; all have good views, but they can get very windy. Most have pit toilets, and a few have fire grills, but none have running water. ✉ *Rim Dr.*

Rim Village. This is the only park picnic area with running water. The tables are set behind the visitor center, and most have a view of the lake below. There are flush toilets inside the visitor center. ✉ *Rim Dr. on the south side of the lake, 7 miles north of Annie Spring entrance station.*

Wizard Island. The park's best picnic venue is on Wizard Island; pack a lunch and book yourself on one of the early-morning boat tour departures, reserving space on an afternoon return. There are no formal picnic areas and just pit toilets, but you'll discover plenty of sunny, protected spots where you can have a quiet meal and appreciate the astounding scene that surrounds you. The island is accessible by boat tour only (⇨ *Educational Offerings*). ✉ *Wizard Island, Crater Lake.*

WHERE TO STAY

$$
HOTEL

▥ **The Cabins at Mazama Village.** In a wooded area 7 miles south of the lake, this complex is made up of several A-frame buildings and has mostly modest rooms with two queen beds and a private bath. **Pros:** clean

CLOSE UP

Best Campgrounds in Crater Lake

Both tent campers and RV enthusiasts will enjoy the heavily wooded and well-equipped setting of Mazama Campground. Drinking water, showers, and laundry facilities help ensure that you don't have to rough it too much. Lost Creek Campground is much smaller, with minimal amenities and a more "rustic" Crater Lake experience.

Lost Creek Campground. The 16 small, remote tent sites here are usually available on a daily basis from late May to early October, depending on snow; in July and August arrive early to secure a spot. ⊠ *3 miles south of Rim Rd. on Pinnacles Spur Rd. at Grayback Dr.* ☎ *541/594–3100.*

Mazama Campground. This campground is set well below the lake caldera in the pine and fir forest of the Cascades not far from the main access road (Highway 62). About half the spaces are pull-throughs, some with electricity; no hookups are available. The best tent spots are on some of the outer loops above Annie Creek Canyon. ⊠ *Mazama Village, near Annie Spring entrance station* ☎ *541/594–2255, 888/774–2728* ⊕ *www.craterlakelodges.com.*

and well-kept facility. **Cons:** lots of traffic into adjacent campground. Ⓢ *Rooms from: $144* ⊠ *Mazama Village, near Annie Spring entrance station* ☎ *541/594–2255, 888/774–2728* ⊕ *www.craterlakelodges.com* ⬎ *40 rooms* ⊗ *Closed mid-Oct.–late May* ⦿| *No meals.*

$$$ **HOTEL** 🏛 **Crater Lake Lodge.** The period feel of this 1915 lodge on the caldera's rim is reflected in its lodgepole-pine columns, gleaming wood floors, and stone fireplaces in the common areas. **Pros:** ideal location for watching sunrise and sunset reflected on the lake. **Cons:** very difficult to reserve rooms; some rooms have tubs only, no shower. Ⓢ *Rooms from: $167* ⊠ *Rim Village, east of Rim Visitor Center, 1 Lodge Loop Rd., Crater Lake* ☎ *541/594–2255, 888/774–2728* ⊕ *www.craterlakelodges.com* ⬎ *71 rooms* ⊗ *Closed mid-Oct.–mid-May* ⦿| *No meals.*

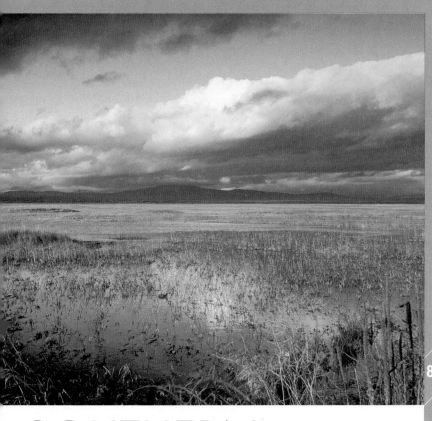

SOUTHERN OREGON

WELCOME TO SOUTHERN OREGON

TOP REASONS TO GO

★ **Discover the other wine regions:** The underrated Umpqua and Rogue River wine regions offer picturesque pastoral views and numerous tasting rooms.

★ **Go underground:** Explore deep into mysterious underground chambers and marble caves at Oregon Caves National Monument.

★ **Savor Shakespeare:** The acclaimed Oregon Shakespeare Festival draws drama lovers to Ashland nine months a year, presenting a wide variety of both classic and contemporary theater.

★ **Enjoy quaint towns:** Southern Oregon's own throwback to the Old West, Jacksonville abounds with well-preserved buildings while Ashland claims one of the prettiest downtowns in the state.

★ **Get wet and wild:** Each fall more than 1 million waterfowl descend upon Klamath Basin National Wildlife Refuge Complex. The Rogue River is Oregon's white-water-rafting capital, and the entire region is laced with stunning hiking trails.

1 Umpqua Valley. Known increasingly for its up-and-coming wineries, including award-winning Abacela, this valley is home to historic Oakland, Roseburg and its family-friendly Wildlife Safari park, and the Umpqua River Scenic Byway, a particularly scenic route to Crater Lake.

2 Rogue Valley. This fertile, mild-temperature region that extends from Grants Pass southeast through Medford and down to Ashland takes in the most populous communities in the area—it's also the gateway for reaching Klamath Falls, to the east, and the remote but fascinating Oregon Caves National Monument to the southwest. The Oregon Shakespeare Festival and an abundance of historic buildings have turned Ashland into a hub of arts, culture, and fine bed-and-breakfasts. Grants Pass, which also has a lively downtown dining and shopping district, is the launch point for some of the best white-water rafting around, while Medford and historic Jacksonville are surrounded by vineyards and farms that produce some of the state's tastiest local edibles, from pears to Pinot Gris.

Umpqua River Scenic Byway

138

1

Umpqua River

Chemult

Diamond Lake

97

230

138

Crater Lake

Union Creek

62

7

232

Prospect

97

Crater Lake National Park

62

Kirk

62

Fort Klamath

Shady Cove

Klamath Agency

Butte Falls

Chiloquin

Eagle Point

Upper Klamath Lake

Lakecreek

140

Medford

140

97

Phoenix

Aspen Lake

Talent

Howard Prairie Lake

Altamont

Ashland

Klamath Falls

5

66

Siskiyou

66

Keno

Midland

Worden

39

Hornbrook

0   20 mi
0   20 km

GETTING ORIENTED

To locals, southern Oregon really refers to the south-western corner of the state, encompassing the Rogue and several other river valleys that lie between the Coast and Cascade mountain ranges, from a little north of Roseburg down to the California bor-der. The area is due south of Eugene and the Willamette Valley, and has a lush, hilly, and fertile terrain that lends itself perfectly to agriculture and wine-making. Towns in the valleys, such as Ashland and Roseburg, have eleva-tions ranging from about 500 to 2,000 feet, while peaks to the east, in the Cascade Range, rise as high as 9,000 feet. This area is also the gateway to Crater Lake National Park—many visitors to that park overnight in Medford or Ashland, which are about 85 miles away.

8

Updated
by Andrew
Collins

Southern Oregon begins where the verdant lowlands of the Willamette Valley give way to a complex collision of mountains, rivers, and ravines. The intricate geography of the "Land of Umpqua," as the area around Roseburg is somewhat romantically known, signals that this is territory distinct from neighboring regions to the north, east, and west.

Wild rivers—the Rogue and the Umpqua are legendary for fishing and boating—and twisting mountain roads venture through the landscape that saw Oregon's most violent Indian wars and became the territory of a self-reliant breed. "Don't-Tread-on-Me" southern Oregonians see themselves as markedly different from fellow citizens of the Pacific Wonderland. In fact, several early-20th-century attempts to secede from Oregon (in combination with Northern California) and proclaim a "state of Jefferson" survive in local folklore and culture. That being said, Ashland and parts of the surrounding area have gradually become more progressive and urbane in recent decades, as wineries, art galleries, and stylish restaurants continue to proliferate. The mix of folks from all different political, social, and stylistic bents is a big part of what makes southern Oregon so interesting—and appealing.

Some locals describe this sun-kissed, sometimes surprisingly hot landscape as Mediterranean; others refer to it as Oregon's banana belt. It's a climate built for slow-paced pursuits and a leisurely outlook on life, not to mention agriculture—the region's orchards, farms, and increasingly acclaimed vineyards have lately helped give southern Oregon cachet among food and wine aficionados. The restaurant scene has grown partly thanks to a pair of big cultural draws, Ashland's Oregon Shakespeare Festival and Jacksonville's open-air, picnic-friendly Britt Festivals concert series.

Roseburg, Medford, and Klamath Falls are also all popular bases for visiting iconic Crater Lake National Park *(⇨ see Chapter 7)*, which lies at the region's eastern edge, about two hours away by car. Formed nearly 8,000 years ago by the cataclysmic eruption of Mt. Mazama, this stunningly clear-blue lake is North America's deepest.

SOUTHERN OREGON PLANNER

WHEN TO GO

Southern Oregon's population centers, which all lie chiefly in the valleys, tend to be warmer and quite a bit sunnier than Eugene and Portland to the north, receiving almost no snow in winter and only 2 to 3 inches of rain per month. In summer, temperatures regularly climb into the 90s, but the low humidity makes for a generally comfortable climate. This makes most of the region quite pleasant to visit year-round, with spring and fall generally offering the best balance of sunny and mild weather.

The exceptions, during the colder months, are southern Oregon's mountainous areas to the east and west, which are covered with snow from fall through spring. Some of the roads leading from the Umpqua and Rogue Valleys up to Crater Lake are closed because of snow from mid-October through June, making summer the prime time to visit.

FESTIVALS

Fodor's Choice ★ **Oregon Shakespeare Festival.** From mid-February to early November, more than 100,000 Bard-loving fans descend on Ashland for some of the finest Shakespearean productions you're likely to see outside of Stratford-upon-Avon—plus works by Ibsen, Williams, and contemporary playwrights. Between June and October plays are staged in the 1,200-seat Elizabethan Theatre, an atmospheric re-creation of the Fortune Theatre in London; the 600-seat Angus Bowmer Theatre, a state-of-the-art facility typically used for five different productions in a single season; and the 350-seat New Theater, which mostly hosts productions of new or experimental work. The festival generally operates close to capacity, so it's important to book ahead. ⊠ *15 S. Pioneer St., Ashland* ☎ *541/482–4331* ⊕ *www.osfashland.org.*

Winter Wings Festival. Each February nature enthusiasts flock to the Klamath Basin for the Winter Wings Festival, the nation's oldest birding festival. ⊠ *Box 354, Klamath Falls* ☎ *877/541–2473* ⊕ *winterwingsfest.org.*

GETTING HERE AND AROUND

AIR TRAVEL

Medford's Rogue Valley International Airport (MFR) is the state's third-largest facility, with direct flights to Denver, Los Angeles, Phoenix, Portland, Salt Lake City, San Francisco, and Seattle, and service by Allegiant, Alaska, Delta, and United. Most national car-rental branches are at the airport. A few taxi and shuttle companies provide transportation from the airport to other towns in the area; these are used mostly by locals, as a car is the only practical way to explore this relatively rural part of Oregon. The one exception is Ashland, where many attractions, restaurants, and accommodations are within walking distance. Cascade Airport Shuttle offers door-to-door service from the airport to Ashland for about $30 to $35. Among taxi companies, Valley Cab serves the Rogue Valley region, with fares costing $3 base per trip, plus $2.50 per mile thereafter.

8

Roseburg is a 75-mile drive from Oregon's second-largest airport, in Eugene (EUG). Ashland is about 300 miles south of the state's largest airport, in Portland, and 350 miles north of San Francisco. Although it's often cheaper to fly into these larger airports than it is to Medford, what you lose in gas costs, time, and inconvenience will likely outweigh any savings.

Contacts **Cascade Airport Shuttle** ☎ *541/488–1998, 888/760–7433* ⊕ *www. cascadeshuttle.com.* **Rogue Valley International Airport** ☎ *541/772–8068* ⊕ *www.jacksoncountyor.org/airport.* **Valley Cab** ☎ *541/772–1818* ⊕ *www. myvalleycab.com.*

CAR TRAVEL

Unquestionably, your best way to explore the region is by car, although most of Ashland's key attractions, hotels, and dining are downtown and within walking distance of one another. Interstate 5 runs north–south the length of the Umpqua and Rogue River Valleys, linking Roseburg, Grants Pass, Medford, and Ashland. Many regional attractions lie not too far east or west of Interstate 5. Jacksonville is a short drive due west from Medford. Highway 138 winds scenically along the Umpqua River east of Roseburg to the less-visited northern end of Crater Lake National Park. Highway 140 leads from Medford east to Klamath Falls, which you can reach from Bend via U.S. 97.

RESTAURANTS

Southern Oregon's dining scene varies greatly from region to region, with the more tourism-driven and upscale communities of Ashland, Jacksonville, and Grants Pass leading the way in terms of sophisticated farm-to-table restaurants, hip coffeehouses, and noteworthy bakeries and wine bars. Other larger towns in the valleys, including Roseburg and Medford, have grown in culinary stature and variety of late, while Klamath Falls and Cave Junction have few dining options of note. In the former communities you'll find chefs emphasizing Oregon-produced foods; Oregon wines, including many from the Rogue and Umpqua Valleys, also find their way onto many menus.

HOTELS

Ashland has the region's greatest variety of distinctive lodgings, from the usual low- to midpriced chain properties to plush B&Bs set in restored Arts and Crafts and Victorian houses. Nearby Jacksonville also has several fine, upscale inns. Beyond that, in nearly every town in southern Oregon you'll find two or three interesting B&Bs or small hotels, and in any of the communities along Interstate 5—including Roseburg, Grants Pass, and Medford—a wide variety of chain motels and hotels. Rooms in this part of the state book up earliest in summer, especially on weekends. If you're coming to Ashland or Jacksonville, try to book at least a week or two ahead. Elsewhere, you can usually find a room in a suitable chain property on less than a day's notice. *Hotel reviews have been shortened. For full information, visit Fodors.com.*

WHAT IT COSTS IN U.S. DOLLARS				
	$	**$$**	**$$$**	**$$$$**
Restaurants	Under $17	$17–$23	$24–$30	Over $30
Hotels	Under $151	$151–$200	$201–$250	Over $250

Restaurant prices are the average cost of a main course at dinner or, if dinner is not served, at lunch. Hotel prices are the lowest cost of a standard double room in high season.

TOURS

Hellgate Jetboat Excursions. You'll see some of Oregon's most magnificent scenery on these excursions, which depart from the Riverside Inn in Grants Pass. The 36-mile round-trip runs through Hellgate Canyon and takes two hours. There is also a five-hour, 75-mile round-trip from Grants Pass to Grave Creek, with a stop for a meal on an open-air deck (cost of meal not included). Trips are available May through September, conditions permitting. ☎ *541/479–7204, 800/648–4874* ⊕ *www.hellgate.com* ✉ *From $40.*

Wine Hopper Tours. Getting to know the region's more than 125 wineries can be a challenge to visitors, especially when you factor in having to drive from tasting room to tasting room. This outfitter with knowledgeable guides leads seven-hour tours leaving daily from Ashland, Medford, and Jacksonville—the day includes a tour of a winery, picnic lunch, and tasting at a few of the area's top producers. ☎ *541/476–9463, 855/550–9463* ⊕ *www.winehoppertours.com* ✉ *From $79.*

VISITOR INFORMATION

Southern Oregon Visitors Association ⊕ *www.southernoregon.org.*

UMPQUA VALLEY

The northernmost part of southern Oregon, beginning about 40 miles south of Eugene and the Willamette Valley, the rural and sparsely populated Umpqua Valley is the gateway to this part of the state's sunny and relatively dry climate. As you drive down Interstate 5 you'll descend through twisting valleys and climb up over scenic highlands. In summer you can follow the dramatic Umpqua River Scenic Byway (Highway 138) east over the Cascades to access Crater Lake from the north—it's the prettiest route to the lake. Within the Umpqua Valley, attractions are relatively few, but this area has several excellent wineries, some of the best river fishing in the Northwest, and one of the region's top draws for animal lovers, the Wildlife Safari park.

ROSEBURG

73 miles south of Eugene on Interstate 5.

Fishermen the world over hold the name Roseburg sacred. The timber town on the Umpqua River attracts anglers in search of a dozen popular fish species, including bass, brown and brook trout, and chinook, coho, and sockeye salmon. The native steelhead, which makes its run to the sea in the summer, is king of them all.

The north and south branches of the Umpqua River meet up just north of Roseburg. The roads that run parallel to this river provide spectacular views of the falls, and the North Umpqua route also provides access to trails, hot springs, and the Winchester fish ladder. White-water rafting is also popular here, although not to the degree that it is farther south in the Rogue Valley.

About 80 miles west of the northern gateway to Crater Lake National Park and in the Hundred Valleys of the Umpqua, Roseburg produces innovative, well-regarded wines. Wineries are sprouting up throughout the mild, gorgeous farm country around town, mostly within easy reach of Interstate 5.

GETTING HERE AND AROUND

Roseburg is the first large town you'll reach driving south from Eugene on Interstate 5. It's also a main access point into southern Oregon via Highway 138 if you're approaching from the east, either by way of Crater Lake or U.S. 97, which leads down from Bend. And from the North Bend–Coos Bay region of the Oregon Coast, windy but picturesque Highway 42 leads to just south of Roseburg. It's a 75-mile drive north to Eugene's airport, and a 95-mile drive south to Rogue Valley Airport in Medford. Attractions in the region are spread over a large area—a car is a must.

ESSENTIALS

Visitor Information Roseburg Visitors & Convention Bureau ✉ *410 S.E. Spruce St.* ☏ *541/672–9731, 800/444–5584* ⊕ *www.visitroseburg.com.*

EXPLORING

Fodor'sChoice ★ **Abacela Vineyards and Winery.** The name derives from an archaic Spanish word meaning "to plant grapevines," and that's exactly what this winery's husband-wife team did not so very long ago. Abacela released its first wine in 1999 and has steadily established itself as one of the state's most acclaimed producers—one of the best outside the Willamette Valley. Hot-blooded Spanish Tempranillo is Abacela's pride and joy, though inky Malbec and torrid Sangiovese also highlight a repertoire heavy on Mediterranean varietals. ✉ *12500 Lookingglass Rd.* ☏ *541/679–6642* ⊕ *www.abacela.com* ☉ *June–Oct., daily 11–6; Nov.–May, daily 11–5.*

Douglas County Museum. One of the best county museums in the state surveys 8,000 years of human activity in the region. The fossil collection is worth a stop, as is the state's second-largest photo collection, numbering more than 24,000 images, some dating to the 1840s. ✉ *123 Museum Dr.* ☏ *541/957–7007* ⊕ *www.umpquavalleymuseums. org* ☞ *$5* ☉ *Tues.–Sat. 10–5.*

FAMILY
Fodor'sChoice ★ **Wildlife Safari.** Come face-to-face with some 500 free-roaming animals at the 600-acre drive-through wildlife park. Inhabitants include alligators, bobcats, cougars, gibbons, lions, giraffes, grizzly bears, Tibetan yaks, cheetahs, Siberian tigers, and more than 100 additional species. There's also a petting zoo, a miniature train, and elephant rides. The admission price includes two same-day drive-throughs. This nonprofit

Wine production in southern Oregon

zoological park is a respected research facility with full accreditation from the American Zoo and Aquarium Assocation, with a mission to conserve and protect endangered species through education and breeding programs. ⊠ *1790 Safari Rd., Winston* ☎ *541/679–6761* ⊕ *www. wildlifesafari.net* ⊠ *$18* ☉ *Mid-Mar.–Oct., daily 9–5; Nov.–mid-Mar., daily 10–4.*

WHERE TO EAT AND STAY

$$
AMERICAN
✕ **Brix 527.** This handsome downtown American bistro with exposed-brick walls, curving leather banquettes, and high ceilings serves reasonably priced breakfast and lunch fare daily, and somewhat more upscale dinners. There's also a convivial lounge, and an impressive wine, beer, and cocktail list available in either space. Start the day with blueberry–lemon zest pancakes or eggs Benedict topped with wild salmon. Highlights from the evening menu include the fusion-y chicken artichoke-spinach nachos, and blackened, rare-seared ahi tuna steak. Several more affordable sandwiches, burgers, and salads are available, too. ⑤ *Average main: $20* ⊠ *527 S.E. Jackson St.* ☎ *541/440–4901* ⊕ *www.brix527.com* ☉ *No dinner Sun.*

$$
B&B/INN
Fodor's Choice
★
▦ **The Steamboat Inn.** The world's top fly-fishermen converge at this secluded forest inn, high in the Cascades above the emerald North Umpqua River; others come simply to relax in the reading nooks or on the broad decks of the riverside guest cabins nestled below soaring fir trees and surrounded by verdant gardens. **Pros:** good option if en route to Crater Lake; access to some of the best fishing in the West; great escape. **Cons:** extremely far from civilization. ⑤ *Rooms from: $195* ⊠ *42705 N. Umpqua Hwy., 38 miles east of Roseburg on Hwy. 138,*

near Steamboat Creek, Idleyld Park ☎ *541/498–2230, 800/840–8825* ⊕ *www.thesteamboatinn.com* ⇝ *8 cabins, 5 cottages, 2 suites, 5 houses* ⦿*No meals.*

SPORTS AND THE OUTDOORS

FISHING

You'll find some of the best river fishing in Oregon along the Umpqua, with smallmouth bass, shad, steelhead, salmon (coho, chinook, and sockeye), and sturgeon—the biggest reaching 10 feet in length—among the most prized catches. In addition to the Steamboat Inn, several out-fitters in the region provide full guide services, which typically include all gear, boats, and expert leaders. There's good fishing in this region year-round, with sturgeon and steelhead at their best during the colder months, chinook and coho salmon thriving in the fall, and most other species prolific in spring and summer.

Big K Guest Ranch. Set along a 10-mile span of the upper Umpqua River near Elkton (about 35 miles north of Roseburg), Big K is a pastoral 2,500-acre guest ranch. The accommodations are geared primarily to groups and corporate retreats, but the ranch offers individual fishing packages starting at $400 per person, per day (meals and lodging included), with three- and four-night deals available at a better rate. Adventures include fly-fishing for smallmouth bass and summer steelhead, as well as spin-casting and drift-boat fishing. ✉ *20029 Hwy. 138 W., Elkton* ☎ *541/584–2295* ⊕ *www.big-k.com.*

Oregon Angler. One of the state's most respected and knowledgeable guides, Todd Hannah, specializes in jet-boat and drift-boat fishing excursions along the famed "Umpqua Loop," an 18-mile span of river that's long been lauded for exceptional fishing. Full-day trips start at $200 per person. ✉ *1037 Maupin Rd., Elkton* ☎ *800/428–8585* ⊕ *www.theoregonangler.com.*

RAFTING

There's thrilling Class III and higher white-water rafting along the North Umpqua River, with several outfitters providing trips ranging from a few hours to a few days throughout the year.

North Umpqua Outfitters. Since 1987, this trusted provider has offered both half- and full-day rafting and kayaking trips along the frothy North Umpqua. ✉ *P.O. Box 158, Idleyld Park* ☎ *888/454–9696* ⊕ *www.nuorafting.com.*

ROGUE VALLEY

Encompassing the broad, curving, southeasterly swath of towns from Grants Pass through Medford down to Ashland, the mild and sun-kissed Rogue Valley is southern Oregon's main population center, and also where you'll find the bulk of the region's lodging, dining, shopping, and recreation.

Interstate 5 cuts through the valley en route to Northern California, but venture away from the main thoroughfare to see what makes this part of Oregon so special, including the superb—if underrated—wineries.

Kayaking Rainey Falls on the Rogue River

With warmer temperatures, this area is conducive to many more varietals than the Willamette Valley—from reds like Syrah, Tempranillo, and Cabernet Sauvignon to increasingly well-known old-world whites like Viognier and Pinot Gris. Foodies are drawn to the region's abundance of local food producers, from nationally acclaimed cheese makers and chocolatiers to farms growing juicy pears, blackberries, and cherries. Access to excellent food has helped turn the small but artsy city of Ashland into one of Oregon's top restaurant destinations, with nearby communities also growing in culinary cachet. Additionally, the area's reputation for performing arts, which manifests itself in the famed Oregon Shakespeare Festival in Ashland and Britt Music Festival in historic Jacksonville, continues to grow.

Flanked by 1.8-million-acre Rogue–Siskiyou National Forest, which has rangers' offices near Grants Pass and Medford, the Rogue Valley is a hub of outdoor recreation, from fishing and white-water rafting along its clear rivers to mountain biking, hiking, and even skiing in the higher elevations—peaks in the Cascade Range, to the east, rise to nearly 10,000 feet. Klamath Falls lies technically a bit east of the Rogue Valley but shares the region's abundance of unspoiled wilderness and opportunities for getting in touch with nature.

GRANTS PASS

70 miles south of Roseburg on I–5.

"It's the Climate!" So says a confident 1950s vintage neon sign presiding over Josephine County's downtown. Grants Pass bills itself as Oregon's white-water capital: the Rogue River, preserved by Congress in 1968 as a National Wild and Scenic River, runs right through town. Downtown Grants Pass is a National Historic District, a stately little enclave of 19th-century brick storefronts housing a mix of folksy businesses harking back to the 1950s and newer, trendier cafés and boutiques. It's all that white water, however, that compels most visitors—and not a few moviemakers (*The River Wild* and *Rooster Cogburn* were both filmed here). If the river alone doesn't serve up enough natural drama, the sheer rock walls of nearby Hellgate Canyon rise 250 feet.

GETTING HERE AND AROUND

Grants Pass is easily reached from elsewhere in the region via Interstate 5, and it's also where U.S. 199 cuts southwest toward Oregon Caves National Monument and, eventually, the northernmost section of California's coast (as well as the northern sections of Redwood National Park). Many visitors to the southern Oregon coastline backtrack inland up U.S. 199 to create a scenic loop drive, ultimately intersecting with Interstate 5 at Grants Pass. Medford's airport is a 30-mile drive south.

ESSENTIALS

Visitor Information Grants Pass Tourism ⊠ *198 S.W. G St.* ☎ *800/547–5927, 541/450–6180* ⊕ *www.visitgrantspass.org.*

EXPLORING

Fodor's Choice
★

Troon Vineyards. Few winemakers in southern Oregon have generated more buzz than Troon, whose swank tasting room and winery is patterned after a French country villa. Troon produces relatively small yields of exceptional wines more typical of Sonoma than Oregon (Cabernet Sauvignon, Zinfandel, and Syrah are the heavy hitters), but they also plant less typical U.S. varietals, such as Viognier and Cabernet Franc. The winery is 14 miles southeast of downtown Grants Pass, in the northern edge of the Applegate Valley. ⊠ *1475 Kubli Rd.* ☎ *541/846–9900* ⊕ *www.troonvineyard.com* ⊗ *Late May–early Sept., daily 11–6; early Sept.–late May, daily 11–5.*

WHERE TO EAT

$
AMERICAN
Fodor's Choice
★

Ma Mosa's. Sustainability is the name of the game at this lively café spot in downtown Grants Pass, with a cozy dining room of colorfully painted tables and mismatched chairs, and a large adjacent patio with picnic tables and lush landscaping—it's pet-friendly out here, too. The kitchen sources from local farms and purveyors to create beer-battered fried chicken and waffles, kale Caesar salads, and line-caught-fish tacos with seasonal slaw and housemade salsa. Mimosa's are, as you might guess, a favorite drink throughout the day, and beer lover's will always find a few rotating taps of mostly Oregon craft brews. ⑤ *Average main: $10* ⊠ *118 N.W. E St.* ☎ *541/479–0236* ⊕ *www.mamosas. com* ⊗ *Closed Mon. No dinner Tues.*

$$
MODERN
AMERICAN

Roux 26. Set in the handsome, vintage Grants Pass Steam Laundry building—a brick-red beauty with a light-filled, solarium-style dining room—this casually upscale neighborhood bistro and bar offers an extensive and eclectic menu of well-crafted modern American fare. Start things off, perhaps, with an order of the addictively good garlic truffle fries or the citrus-shrimp salad with heirloom cherry tomatoes, avocado, and cotija cheese. Worthy main dishes include several thin-crust pizzas, fettucine with spicy habanero chilis and smoked chicken, and the classic Southern favorite, shrimp-and-grits with tomato-corn salsa and house-chili oil. ⑤ *Average main: $17* ⊠ *234 S.W. 5th St.* ☎ *541/507–1234* ⊕ *www.roux26.com* ⊗ *Closed Sun. and Mon.*

$
WINE BAR

Twisted Cork Wine Bar. With a mission to showcase southern Oregon's fast-growing reputation for acclaimed vino, this dapper, art-filled space has lent a bit of urbane sophistication to downtown Grants Pass. In addition to pouring varietals from throughout the Umpqua and Rogue Valleys, Twisted Cork carries wines from more than 115 wineries throughout the Northwest, along with a few from California. The menu focuses on small plates ideal for sharing—fruit-and-cheese plates, cured meats—as well as creative and quite affordable larger plates, including pomegranate-cinnamon flank steak, ginger-glazed salmon, and wild-mushroom flatbread with butternut-mint hummus. There's a nice list of local ports, too. ⑤ *Average main: $15* ⊠ *210 S.W. 6th St.* ☎ *541/295–3094* ⊕ *www.thetwistedcorkgrantspass.com* ⊗ *Closed Sun. and Mon.*

WHERE TO STAY

$
HOTEL

Lodge at Riverside. The pool and many rooms overlook the Rogue River as it passes through downtown, and all but a few rooms, furnished with stylish country house–inspired armoires, plush beds, and

8

oil paintings, have private balconies or patios; suites have river-rock fireplaces and Jacuzzi tubs. **Pros:** central location; beautiful modern furnishings; attractively landscaped pool overlooks Rogue River. **Cons:** among the highest rates in town; no restaurant on-site. $ *Rooms from: $145* ⊠ *955 S.E. 7th St.* ☎ *541/955–0600, 877/955–0600* ⊕ *www. thelodgeatriverside.com* ⇆ *29 rooms, 4 suites* ⊙ *Breakfast.*

$$$

B&B/INN

Fodor'sChoice

★

⊤ **Weasku Inn.** Pacific Northwest–inspired art, handmade furnishings, and fine fabrics fill a rambling timber-frame home overlooking the Rogue River, 11 handsomely outfitted cabins, and an A-frame bungalow to create the most luxurious accommodations between Ashland and Eugene. **Pros:** set directly on the Rogue River; impeccably decorated; fireplaces in many rooms. **Cons:** it's a 10-minute drive east of downtown; among the highest rates in the region. $ *Rooms from: $202* ⊠ *5560 Rogue River Hwy.* ☎ *541/471–8000, 800/493–2758* ⊕ *www. weaskuinn.com* ⇆ *5 rooms, 12 cabins* ⊙ *Breakfast.*

SPORTS AND THE OUTDOORS

RAFTING

Fodor'sChoice

★

More than a dozen outfitters guide white-water rafting trips along the Rogue River in and around Grants Pass. In fact, this stretch of Class III rapids ranks among the best in the West. The rafting season lasts from about July through August and often into September, and the stretch of river running south from Grants Pass, with some 80 frothy rapids, is exciting but not treacherous, making it ideal for novices, families, and others looking simply to give this enthralling activity a try.

Orange Torpedo Trips. One of the most reliable operators on the Rogue River offers half-day to several-day trips, as well as relaxed dinner-and-wine float trips along a calmer stretch of river. ⊠ *210 Merlin Rd., Merlin* ☎ *541/479–5061, 866/479–5061* ⊕ *www.orangetorpedo.com.*

Rogue River Raft Trips. If you're up for an adventure that combines rafting with overnight accommodations, consider booking one of these exciting excursions that run along a 44-mile stretch of the Rogue River. They last for four days and three nights, with options for both lodge and camping stays along the way. ⊠ *8500 Galice Rd., Merlin* ☎ *800/826–1963, 541/476–3825* ⊕ *www.rogueriverraft.com.*

RECREATIONAL AREAS

Rogue River–Siskiyou National Forests, Grants Pass. In the Klamath Mountains and the Coast Range of southwestern Oregon, the 1.8-million-acre forest contains the 35-mile-long Wild and Scenic section of the Rogue River, which races through the Wild Rogue Wilderness Area, and the Illinois and Chetco Wild and Scenic Rivers, which run through the 180,000-acre Kalmiopsis Wilderness Area. Activities include white-water rafting, camping, and hiking, but many hiking areas require trail-park passes. ⊠ *Off U.S. 199* ☎ *541/618–2200* ⊕ *www.fs.fed.us/r6/rogue-siskiyou.*

Valley of the Rogue State Park. A 1¼-mile hiking trail follows the bank of the Rogue, the river made famous by novelist and fisherman Zane Grey. There's a campground along 3 miles of shoreline with full RV hookups as well as yurts. There are picnic tables, walking trails, playgrounds, and restrooms. The park is 12 miles east of downtown Grants

Pass. ✉ *3792 N. River Rd., Gold Hill* ☎ *541/582–1118, 800/551–6949* ⊕ *www.oregonstateparks.org* ⊙ *Daily.*

MEDFORD

30 miles southeast of Grants Pass on I–5.

Medford is the professional, retail, trade, and service center for eight counties in southern Oregon and Northern California. As such, it offers more professional and cultural venues than might be expected for a city of its size (with a population of about 80,000). The workaday downtown has shown signs of gentrification and rejuvenation in recent years, and in the outskirts you'll find several major shopping centers and the famed fruit and gourmet-food mail-order company Harry & David.

Lodging tends to be cheaper in Medford than in nearby (and easily accessible) Ashland or Jacksonville, although cookie-cutter chain properties dominate the hotel landscape. It's also 71 miles southwest of Crater Lake and 80 miles northeast of the Oregon Caves, making it an affordable and convenient base for visiting either.

GETTING HERE AND AROUND

Medford is in the heart of the Rogue Valley on I–5, and is home to the state's third-largest airport, Rogue Valley International. A car is your best way to get around the city and surrounding area.

ESSENTIALS

Visitor Information Medford Visitors & Convention Bureau ✉ *1314 Center Dr.* ☎ *541/776–4021, 800/469–6307* ⊕ *www.visitmedford.org.*

EXPLORING

Butte Creek Mill. This 1872 water-powered gristmill, which is 12 miiles north of Medford, is listed in the National Historic Register and still produces whole-grain food products, which you can buy at the country store here. There's also a modest display of antiques. ✉ *402 Royal Ave. N, Central Point* ☎ *541/826–3531* ⊕ *www.buttecreekmill.com* ▨ *Free* ⊙ *Mon.–Sat. 9–5, Sun. 11–5.*

Crater Rock Museum. Jackson County's natural history and collections of the Roxy Ann Gem and Mineral Society are on display at this quirky, 12,000-square-foot museum in Central Point (6 miles northwest of Medford). Fossils, petrified wood, fluorescent rocks, and precious minerals from throughout Oregon and elsewhere in the West are included, plus works of glass by renowned artist Dale Chihuly. ✉ *2002 Scenic Ave., Central Point* ☎ *541/664–6081* ⊕ *www.craterrock.com* ▨ *$5* ⊙ *Tues.–Sat. 10–4.*

EdenVale Winery. Four miles southwest of downtown Medford amid a bucolic patch of fruit orchards, this winery and tasting room, called the Rogue Valley Wine Center, adjoins a rather grand 19th-century white-clapboard farmhouse surrounded by flower beds and vegetable gardens. Inside the tasting room you can sample and buy not only EdenVale's noted reds and late-harvest whites but also other respected labels from vineyards throughout the region. ✉ *2310 Voorhies Rd.* ☎ *541/512–2955* ⊕ *www.edenvalewines.com* ⊙ *Mar.–Oct., Mon.–Thurs. 11–6,*

Fri.–Sat. 11–7, Sun. 11–5; Nov.–Feb., Mon.–Thurs. 11–5, Fri.–Sat. noon–6, Sun. noon–4.

WHERE TO EAT AND STAY

$$
TAPAS
✕ **Elements Tapas Bar.** A touch of urbane sophistication and a taste of impressively authentic Spanish fare—these are the draws of this handsome tapas restaurant in downtown Medford's turn-of-the-20th-century "Goldy" building. Owner Chris Dennett set out to create a space that's fun for groups of friends, where sharing and conversation are encouraged. Pass around plates of mussels in romesco sauce, apricot-braised-pork empanadas, chorizo-studded Andalucian paella, and lamb-sausage flatbread, while sampling selections from the lengthy beer and cocktail menus. Food is served till at least 11 nightly, and there's a great Sunday brunch. $ *Average main: $20* ⌂ *101 E. Main St.* ☎ *541/779–0135* ⊕ *www.elementsmedford.com* ⊗ *No lunch.*

$
BURGER
✕ **Jaspers Cafe.** This cute road-house-style building a few miles northwest of downtown Medford has made a name for itself serving obscenely large, decadently topped, and deliciously crafted burgers. Polish off the Jasperado, wth chorizo, salsa verde, and a fried egg, and you probably won't be experiencing any hunger pains for the rest of the day—especially if you add a side of sweet potato fries or pork pot stickers. Veggie and game (from lamb to antelope to kangaroo) burgers are offered, too. Although potentially a dinner option, keep in mind that Jaspers closes between 6 and 8 pm, depending on the night of week. $ *Average main: $7* ⌂ *2739 N. Pacific Hwy.* ☎ *541/776–5307* ⊕ *www.jasperscafe.com.*

$
HOTEL
▦ **Best Western Horizon Inn.** Convenient to downtown, Bear Creek Park, and the freeway, this midpriced, comfortable Best Western motel is set around a large outdoor pool and contains 122 rooms with tasteful blond-wood furniture, tan armchairs with ottomans, and decent-quality—if run-of-the-mill—bedding and towels. **Pros:** nice pool and fitness center for a midrange motel; central location; clean and updated room. **Cons:** cookie-cutter decor; on a busy road. $ *Rooms from: $89* ⌂ *1154 E. Barnett Rd.* ☎ *541/779–5085, 800/452–2255* ⊕ *www.bestwesternoregon.com* ⤳ *122 rooms* |⊙| *Breakfast.*

$
HOTEL
▦ **Rodeway Inn–Medford.** If you're on a budget and seeking a simple and immaculately clean base camp, check into this friendly, family-run '50s vintage motor court on the city's south side. **Pros:** vintage charm; convenient to sights in Medford as well as Jacksonville and Ashland. **Cons:** few amenities and luxuries; rather dated (though that's part of the charm). $ *Rooms from: $60* ⌂ *901 S. Riverside Ave.* ☎ *541/776–9194, 877/424–6423* ⊕ *www.rodewayinn.com* ⤳ *40 rooms* |⊙| *Breakfast.*

NIGHTLIFE AND THE ARTS

Jefferson Spirits. This hip newcomer is helping to spur downtown Medford's ongoing renaissance by creating a sophisticated, stylish environment for hobnobbing and enjoying creative craft cocktails, like the locally inspired Rogue Pear, with whiskey, pear, and a splash of lemon juice. The owners have plans to develop their own microdistillery and will continue to carry a fine selection of premium booze, local and international wines, and mostly Oregon beers. ⌂ *404 E. Main St.* ☎ *541/622–8190* ⊕ *www.jeffersonspirits.com.*

SPORTS AND THE OUTDOORS

FISHING

With close access to some of the best freshwater fishing venues in the Northwest, Medford has several companies that lead tours and provide gear.

Carson's Guide Service. Based 22 miles north of Medford along Highway 62 (going toward Crater Lake), Carson's provides expert instruction and knowledge of many of the area's rivers, including the Rogue, Umpqua, Coquille, Elk, and Chetco, as well as several lakes. Steelhead, salmon, shad, and smallmouth bass are the most common catches. ⊠ *595 Ragsdale Rd., Trail* ☎ *541/261–3279* ⊕ *www.fishwithcarson.com.*

HIKING

Fodor'sChoice
★

Table Rock. One of the best venues for hiking in the Rogue Valley comprises a pair of monolithic rock formations that rise some 700 to 800 feet above the valley floor about 10 miles north of Medford and just a couple of miles north of TouVelle State Park. Operated by a partnership between the Bureau of Land Management and the Nature Conservancy, the Table Rock formations and surrounding 4,864 acres of wilderness afford panoramic valley views from their summits. You reach Lower Table Rock by way of a moderately challenging 2-mile trail, and Upper Table Rock via a shorter (1-mile) and less-steep route. The trailheads to these formations are a couple of miles apart—just follow the road signs from Table Rock Road, north of TouVelle State Park (reached from Exit 33 of Interstate 5). ⊠ *Off Table Rock Rd., Central Point* ☎ *541/618–2200* ⊕ *www.blm.gov.*

RAFTING

Medford is close to a number of the region's great white-water-rafting rivers, including the famed Rogue River. Both overnight and day trips are offered by several outfitters.

Rogue Klamath River Adventures. This popular outfitter for guided whitewater rafting trips as well as fishing adventures (for salmon and steelhead) throughout the area also offers boating excursions on inflatable kayaks. The company visits a great variety of waterways, from fairly gentle but scenic Class II rivers to wild and exciting Class V rapids. ☎ *541/779–3708, 800/231–0769* ⊕ *www.rogueklamath.com.*

RECREATIONAL AREAS

Rogue River–Siskiyou National Forest, Medford. Covering 2 million acres, this immense tract of wilderness woodland has fishing, swimming, hiking, and skiing. Motorized vehicles and equipment—even bicycles—are prohibited in the 113,000-acre Sky Lakes Wilderness, south of Crater Lake National Park. Its highest point is the 9,495-foot Mt. McLoughlin. Access to most of the forest is free, but there are fees at some trailheads. ⊠ *Off Hwy. 140* ☎ *541/618–2200* ⊕ *www.fs.fed.us/r6/rogue-siskiyou.*

OFF THE
BEATEN
PATH

Rogue River Views. Nature lovers who want to see the Rogue River at its loveliest can take a side trip to the Avenue of the Boulders, Mill Creek Falls, and Barr Creek Falls, off Highway 62, near Prospect, which is about 45 miles northeast of Medford—it's a scenic one-hour drive, and it's on the way to Crater Lake. Here the wild waters of the upper Rogue

8

foam past volcanic boulders and the dense greenery of the Rogue River National Forest. ⊠ *Hwy. 62, Prospect.*

FAMILY **Rogue Valley Family Fun Center.** You'll find an impressive array of kids' games and recreation at this complex just off Exit 33 of Interstate 5 (about 5 miles north of Medford). Miniature golf, batting cages, a golf driving range, bumper boats, and go-karts are among the offerings, and there's also a video arcade and game room. ⊠ *1A Peninger Rd., Central Point* ☎ *541/664–4263* ⊕ *www.rvfamilyfuncenter.com.*

SHOPPING

Harry & David. Famous for their holiday gift baskets, Harry & David is based in Medford and offers hour-long tours of its huge facility on weekdays at 9:15, 10:30, 12:30, and 1:45. The tours cost $5 per person, but the fee is refunded if you spend a minimum of $40 in the mammoth Harry & David store, great for snagging picnic supplies to carry with you on any winery tour. Reservations are recommended, as space is limited. ⊠ *1314 Center Dr.* ☎ *541/864–2278, 877/322–8000* ⊕ *www. harryanddavid.com.*

Fodor'sChoice **Lillie Belle Farms.** Next door to Rogue River Creamery, this artisan choc-
★ olatier handcrafts outstanding chocolates using local, often organic ingredients. A favorite treat is the Smokey Blue Cheese ganache made with Rogue River blue, but don't overlook the dark-chocolate–marionberry bonbons (made with organic marionberries grown on-site) or the delectable hazelnut chews. Most unusual, however, is the chocolate-covered bacon. Yes, you read that correctly—the bacon is coated in chipotle and brown sugar, hand-dipped in chocolate, and sprinkled with sea salt. ⊠ *211 N. Front St., Central Point* ☎ *541/664–2815* ⊕ *www. lilliebellefarms.com.*

Fodor'sChoice **Rogue Creamery.** Just a few miles up the road from Medford in the little
★ town of Central Point, you'll find one of the nation's most respected cheese makers, started in 1935 by Italian immigrants. Current owners Cary Bryant and David Gremmels bought the company in 2002, and promptly won one of the highest honors for cheese making, the London World Cheese Award. You can purchase any of the company's stellar cheeses here, from Smokey Blue to a lavender-infused cheddar, and you can watch the production through a window on most days. There's a wine-tasting room that carries vintages by a few local vineyards; the best nearby place to enjoy a picnic is the small neighborhood park a few blocks north at Laurel and North 6th streets. ⊠ *311 N. Front St., Central Point* ☎ *541/664–1537, 866/396–4704* ⊕ *www.roguecreamery.com.*

JACKSONVILLE

5 miles west of Medford on Hwy. 238.

This perfectly preserved town founded in the frenzy of the 1851 gold rush has served as the backdrop for several western flicks. It's easy to see why. Jacksonville is one of only eight towns corralled into the National Register of Historic Places lock, stock, and barrel. These days, living-history exhibits offering a glimpse of pioneer life and the world-renowned Britt Festivals of classical, jazz, and pop music are the draw, rather than gold. Trails winding up from the town's center lead to the festival amphitheater, mid-19th-century gardens, exotic madrona groves, and an intriguing pioneer cemetery.

GETTING HERE AND AROUND

Most visitors to Jacksonville come by way of Medford, 5 miles east, on Highway 238—it's a scenic drive over hilly farmland and past vineyards. Alternatively, you can reach the town coming the other way on Highway 238, driving southeast from Grants Pass. This similarly beautiful drive through the Applegate Valley takes about 45 minutes.

ESSENTIALS

Visitor Information **Jacksonville Visitor Center** ⊠ *185 N. Oregon St.* ☎ *541/899–8118* ⊕ *www.jacksonvilleoregon.org.*

EXPLORING

FAMILY

Fodor's Choice

★

Jacksonville Cemetery. A trip up the winding road—or, better yet, a hike via the old cart track marked Catholic access—leads to the resting place of the clans (the Britts, the Beekmans, and the Orths) that built Jacksonville. You'll also get a fascinating, if sometimes unattractive, view of the social dynamics of the Old West: older graves (the cemetery is still in use) are strictly segregated, Irish Catholics from Jews from Protestants. A somber granite plinth marks the pauper's field, where those who found themselves on the losing end of gold-rush economics entered eternity anonymously. The cemetery closes at sundown. ⊠ *Oregon St., follow signs from downtown* ☎ *541/826–9939* ⊕ *www.friendsjvillecemetery.org.*

Valley View Vineyard. Perched on a bench in the scenic Applegate Valley, you can sample acclaimed Chardonnay, Viognier, Rousanne, Merlot, Tempranillo, Pinot Noir, and Cabernet Franc while soaking up some of the best views in southern Oregon. The valley's especially sunny, warm climate produces highly acclaimed vintages. Founded in the 1850s by pioneer Peter Britt, the vineyard was reestablished in 1972. A restored pole barn houses the winery and tasting room. ⊠ *1000 Upper Applegate Rd., 10 miles southwest of downtown* ☎ *541/899–8468, 800/781–9463* ⊕ *www.valleyviewwinery.com* �l *Daily 11–5.*

WHERE TO EAT AND STAY

$$

SOUTHERN

✕ **Back Porch Bar & Grill.** For an excellent, midpriced alternative to Jacksonville's more upscale eateries, head to this roadhouse-style clapboard building six blocks northeast of the town's historic main drag. Authentic central Texas–style barbecue is served here: char-grilled red-hot sausage, slow-cooked pork ribs, chicken-fried steak, and ½-pound burgers, plus a few dishes to remind you that you're in Oregon, including wild local salmon baked with Cajun spices. ⑤ *Average main: $18* ⊠ *605 N. 5th St.* ☎ *541/899–8821* ⊕ *www.backporchbbqinc.com.*

$$

PACIFIC

NORTHWEST

✕ **Déjà Vu Bistro.** This classy but unpretentious wine bar and bistro resides inside downtown Jacksonville's historic McCully House Gardens inn. Chef Bill Prahl is a strong adherent of using seasonal ingredients. Some notable dishes that reflect his talent and philosophy include a summertime starter of pan-roasted Brussels sprouts, heirloom cherry tomatoes, crumbled goat cheese, and balsamic, and the entrée of coffee-rubbed flat-iron steak with local green beans, roasted red potatoes, and

8

stone-ground mustard sauce. The natty wine bar makes an inviting spot for a pre-dinner sip. $ *Average main: $20 ⊠ 240 E. California St.* ☎ *541/899–1942* ⊕ *www.dejavubistrowinebar.com* ⊘ *Closed Mon. and Tues. No lunch.*

$$$
ECLECTIC
Fodor'sChoice
★
✕ **Gogi's.** Many visitors overlook this small, low-key restaurant just down the hill from Britt Gardens—it's a favorite of foodies and locals, and word is out about the artful presentation and innovative style of chef-owner Gabriel Murphy's sophisticated international cuisine. The menu changes regularly, but has featured a tower of roasted beets and chèvre topped with toasted walnuts and a balsamic-truffle reduction, followed by prosciutto-wrapped quail with cauliflower, asparagus, and roasted mushrooms. The wine list is small but discerning. If you're in town on a Sunday, do not miss the super brunch. $ *Average main: $26 ⊠ 235 W. Main St.* ☎ *541/899–8699* ⊕ *www.gogisrestaurant.com* ⊘ *Closed Mon. and Tues. No lunch Wed.–Sat.*

$$
B&B/INN
🛏 **Jacksonville Inn.** The spotless pioneer period antiques and the wealth of well-chosen amenities (fireplaces, saunas, whirlpool tubs, double steam showers) at this 1861-vintage inn evoke what the Wild West might have been had Martha Stewart been in charge. **Pros:** in heart of downtown historic district; one of the town's most historically significant buildings; very good restaurant on-site. **Cons:** rather old-fashioned decor for some tastes. $ *Rooms from: $159 ⊠ 175 E. California St.* ☎ *541/899–1900, 800/321–9344* ⊕ *www.jacksonvilleinn.com* ⤶ *8 rooms, 4 cottages* ⋈ *Breakfast.*

$
B&B/INN
Fodor'sChoice
★
🛏 **TouVelle House B&B.** This six-bedroom inn set inside a grand 1916 Craftsman-style home a few blocks north of Jacksonville's tiny commercial strip manages that tricky balance between exquisite and comfy. **Pros:** situated on a gentle bluff surrounded by beautiful gardens; downtown dining is a 5-minute walk away; knowledgeable and friendly hosts. **Cons:** a couple of rooms require climbing two flights of stairs to third floor. $ *Rooms from: $135 ⊠ 455 N. Oregon St.* ☎ *541/899–8938, 800/846–8422* ⊕ *www.touvellehouse.com* ⤶ *6 rooms* ⋈ *Breakfast.*

SHOPPING

Jacksonville's historic downtown has several engaging galleries, boutiques, and gift shops. It's best just to stroll along California Street and its cross streets to get a sense of the retail scene.

Jacksonville Barn Co. This colorful shop specializes in both antiques and contemporary home decor, from Victorian pieces that have come from many nearby estates to modern garden accessories and country-house furnishings. ⊠ *150 S. Oregon St.* ☎ *541/702–0307* ⊕ *www.jacksonvillebarnco.com.*

Jacksonville Mercantile. The racks of this gourmet-food store abound with sauces, oils, vinegars, jams, and tapenades. Watch for Lillie Belle Farms lavender–sea salt caramels, and the shop's own private-label Merlot-wine jelly. ⊠ *120 E. California St.* ☎ *541/899–1047* ⊕ *www.jacksonvillemercantile.com.*

Ashland's Main Street

ASHLAND

20 miles southeast of Jacksonville and 14 miles southeast of Medford on I–5.

As you walk Ashland's twisting hillside streets, it seems like every house is a restored Victorian operating as an upscale B&B, though that's not nearly all there is to this town: the Oregon Shakespeare Festival attracts thousands of theater lovers to the Rogue Valley every year, from late February to early November (though tourists don't start showing up en masse until June). That influx means that Ashland is more geared toward the arts, more eccentric, and more expensive than its size (about 21,000 people) might suggest. The mix of well-heeled theater tourists, bohemian students from Southern Oregon University, and dramatic show folk imbues the town with some one-of-a-kind cultural frissons. The stage isn't the only show in town—skiing at Mt. Ashland and the town's reputation as a secluded getaway and growing culinary destination keep things hopping year-round.

GETTING HERE AND AROUND

Ashland is the first town you'll reach on Interstate 5 if driving north from California, and it's the southernmost community in this region. You can also get here from Klamath Falls by driving west on winding but dramatic Highway 66. Cascade Airport Shuttle offers door-to-door service from the airport to Ashland for about $30 to $35. A car isn't necessary to explore downtown and to get among many of the inns and restaurants, but it is helpful if you're planning to venture farther afield or visit more than one town, which most visitors do.

ESSENTIALS

Visitor Information Ashland Chamber of Commerce and Visitors Information Center ⊠ *110 E. Main St.* ☎ *541/482–3486* ⊕ *www.ashlandchamber.com.*

EXPLORING

Fodor'sChoice ★ **Lithia Park.** The Elizabethan Theatre overlooks this park, a 93-acre jewel that is Ashland's physical and psychological anchor. The park is named for the town's mineral springs, which supply a water fountain by the band shell as well as a fountain on the town plaza—be warned that the slightly bubbly water has a strong and rather disagreeable taste. Whether thronged with colorful hippie folk and picnickers on a summer evening or buzzing with joggers and dog walkers in the morning, Lithia is a well-used, well-loved, and well-tended spot. On summer weekend mornings the park plays host to a '60s-ish artisans' market. Each June the Oregon Shakespeare Festival opens its outdoor season by hosting the Feast of Will in the park, with music, dancing, bagpipes, and food. Tickets ($15) are available through the festival box office (☎ *541/482–4331* ⊕ *www.osfashland.org*). ⊠ *W. Fork and S. Pioneer Sts.* ⊕ *www.ashland.or.us.*

Schneider Museum of Art. At the edge of the Southern Oregon University campus, this museum includes a light-filled gallery devoted to special exhibits by Oregon, West Coast, and international artists. The permanent collection has grown considerably over the years, and includes pre-Columbian ceramics and works by such notables as Alexander Calder, George Inness, and David Alfaro Siqueiros. Hallways and galleries throughout the rest of the 66,000-square-foot complex display many works by students and faculty. ⊠ *1250 Siskiyou Blvd.* ☎ *541/552–6245* ⊕ *www.sou.edu/sma* ⊠ *$5* ⊙ *Mon.–Sat. 10–4.*

Weisinger's Winery. Although downtown Ashland has wine bars and tasting rooms, the only major winery of note here is Weisinger's, which set up shop in 1988 and is set a few miles south of town on a hilltop with broad views of the surrounding mountains. Specialties here include a fine Cabernet Franc, a well-respected Petit Blanc, and a nicely balanced Tempranillo. ⊠ *3150 Siskiyou Blvd.* ☎ *541/488–5989, 800/551–9463* ⊕ *www.weisingers.com* ⊙ *May–Sept., daily 11–6; Oct.–Apr., Wed.–Sun. 11–5.*

WHERE TO EAT

$$$

PACIFIC NORTHWEST

Fodor'sChoice ★

✕ **Alchemy.** Meticulous attention to detail, with regard both to preparation and presentation, are hallmarks of this refined contemporary Pacific Northwest restaurant inside the plush Winchester Inn, just a few blocks from the Shakespeare Festival theaters. Typically artful creations from the seasonal menu include a starter of goat cheese gnocchi seared in brown butter with chorizo and mint-compressed apricots, and a tender 14-day dry-aged Oregon filet mignon cooked *sous vide* and sunchoke purée, sautéed root vegetables, and a radish–watercress–Serrano ham salad. Alchemy serves only dinner and a well-attended Sunday brunch, where you might try a hash of duck confit, sunnyside-up egg, crispy fingerling potatoes, and cranberry-citrus cream sauce. Additionally, lighter fare—flatbread pizzas, pork-belly burgers, baked Brie with onion-fennel jam and bourbon-orange marmalade—are offered in the more casual bistro. $ *Average main: $28* ⊠ *Winchester Inn, 35 S. 2nd*

St. ☎541/488–1115 ⊕ *www.alchemyashland.com* ⊙ *Closed Mon.– Tues. No lunch Wed.–Sat.*

$$$
ECLECTIC
Fodor'sChoice
★

✕ **Amuse.** Northwest-driven French cuisine here is infused with seasonal, organic meat and produce. Chef-owners Erik Brown and Jamie North prepare a daily-changing menu. You might sample braised cheek and grilled tenderloin of pork with herb spaetzle, Savoy cabbage, and pomegranate molasses, or truffle-roasted game hen with kale and tarragon jus. Try your best to save room for the warm hazelnut crepes filled with banana ganache and topped with brandy whipped cream. If you're craving pastries during the day, stop by the sister establishment, Mix Sweet Shop, a few blocks away on North Main Street. ⑤ *Average main: $28* ⊠ *15 N. 1st St.* ☎ *541/488–9000* ⊕ *www.amuserestaurant. com* ⊙ *Closed Mon. and Tues. No lunch.*

$
AMERICAN
Fodor'sChoice
★

✕ **Morning Glory.** Breakfast reaches new heights in an eclectically furnished, blue Craftsman-style bungalow across the street from Southern Oregon University. The extraordinarily good food emphasizes breakfast fare—omelets filled with crab, artichokes, Parmesan, and smoked-garlic cream; Tandoori tofu scrambles with cherry-cranberry chutney; lemonpoppy waffles with seasonal berries; and cranberry-hazelnut French toast with lemon butter. Expect a wait on weekend mornings, especially for a table on the good-weather patio; it's first-come, first-served. ⑤ *Average main: $11* ⊠ *1149 Siskiyou Blvd.* ☎ *541/488–8636* 🥢*Reservations not accepted* ⊙ *No dinner.*

$$
MODERN
AMERICAN

✕ **Peerless Restaurant & Bar.** This cosmopolitan, neighborhood bistro and wine bar anchors the up-and-coming Railroad District, on the north side of downtown, just a few blocks from Main Street and the Shakespeare theaters. It's adjacent to the Peerless Hotel, a stylish little property with the same creative spirit and hipster vibe of the restaurant. Regulars here come as much for the well-crafted cocktails and thoughtful wine list as for the consistently tasty locally sourced American food. Start with the Manila clams in a broth of pernod, garlic confit, and smoked bacon, before tucking into a plate of sage-rubbed roast chicken, or baked ziti with sweet corn, chunks of lobster, and three cheeses. Desserts are the one spendy item on the menu, but they're delicious, too. ⑤ *Average main: $19* ⊠ *265 4th St.* ☎ *541/488–6067* ⊕ *www.peerlesshotel.com* ⊙ *Closed Sun. and Mon. No lunch.*

WHERE TO STAY

The Oregon Shakespeare Festival has stimulated one of the most extensive networks of B&Bs in the Northwest—more than 25 in all. High season for Ashland-area bed-and-breakfasts is between June and October.

Ashland B&B Network. The network provides referrals and has an online booking system for about two dozen of the town's top inns. ⊕ *www. stayashland.com.*

$$$
B&B/INN

▦ **Ashland Creek Inn.** Every plush suite in this converted mill has a geographic theme—the Normandy is outfitted with rustic country French prints and furniture, while Moroccan, Danish, and New Mexican motifs are among the designs in other units—and each sitting room– bedroom combo has its own entrance, a full kitchen or kitchenette, and a deck just inches from burbling Ashland Creek. **Pros:** exceptionally good breakfasts; peaceful but central location; enormous suites. **Cons:** spendy for this part of the state; limited common areas. ⑤ *Rooms from: $245* ✉ *70 Water St.* ☎ *541/482–3315* ⊕ *www.ashlandcreekinn.com* ⮐ *10 suites* ❏*◯❙ Breakfast.*

$$ ⛨ **Ashland Springs Hotel.** Ashland's stately 1925 landmark hotel towers
HOTEL seven stories over the center of downtown, with 70 rooms done with a preponderance of gentle fall colors and unconventional decor—think French-inspired botanical-print quilts and lampshades with leaf designs. **Pros:** rich with history; upper floors have dazzling mountain views; the excellent Larks restaurant is on-site. **Cons:** central location translates to some street noise and bustle; some rooms are on the small side. ⑤ *Rooms from: $199* ✉ *212 E. Main St.* ☎ *541/488–1700, 888/795– 4545* ⊕ *www.ashlandspringshotel.com* ⮐ *70 rooms* ❏*◯❙ Breakfast.*

$$ ⛨ **Chanticleer Inn.** At this courtly, 1920 Craftsman-style bed-and-break-
B&B/INN fast, owner Ellen Campbell has given the rooms a tasteful, contem-
Fodor'sChoice porary flair with muted, nature-inspired colors and Arts and Crafts
★ furnishings and patterns. **Pros:** rooms all have expansive views of the Cascade Mountains; only eco-friendly products are used. **Cons:** it's intimate and homey, so fans of larger and more anonymous lodgings may prefer a bigger inn or hotel. ⑤ *Rooms from: $160* ✉ *120 Gresham St.* ☎ *541/482–1919, 800/898–1950* ⊕ *www.ashland-bed-breakfast.com* ⮐ *6 rooms* ❏*◯❙ Breakfast.*

$$$ ⛨ **The Winchester Inn.** These rooms and suites have character and rest-
B&B/INN ful charm—some have fireplaces, refrigerators, and wet bars, and pri-
FAMILY vate exterior entrances, and most are well-suited to having one or two children in the room. **Pros:** the adjacent Alchemy wine bar and restaurant serve outstanding international fare; one of the more child-friendly B&Bs in town; surrounded by lush gardens. **Cons:** among the more expensive lodgings in town. ⑤ *Rooms from: $225* ✉ *35 S. 2nd St.* ☎ *541/488–1113, 800/972–4991* ⊕ *www.winchesterinn.com* ⮐ *11 rooms, 8 suites* ❏*◯❙ Breakfast.*

NIGHTLIFE AND THE ARTS

With its presence of college students, theater types, and increasing numbers of tourists (many of them fans of local wine), Ashland has developed quite a festive nightlife scene. Much of the activity takes place at bars inside some of downtown's more reputable restaurants in the center of town.

Fodor'sChoice **Caldera Tap House.** In addition to operating a full-service restaurant at
★ their brewing facility out at 590 Clover Lane, just off Interstate 5, exit 14, this highly acclaimed Ashland craft-beer maker with wide distribution throughout the Northwest also has this tap room downtown. Here you can sample the signature Hopportunity Knocks IPA, Old Growth Imperial Stout, and an extensive selection of tasty apps, burgers, and pub fare. ✉ *31 Water St.* ☎ *541/482–7468* ⊕ *www.calderabrewing.com.*

Tabu. This Nuevo Latino restaurant keeps busy with revelers into the later hours. Live comedy, reggae, salsa, and other entertainment takes place most Thursday through Saturday nights. ✉ *76 N. Pioneer St.* ☎ *541/482–3900* ⊕ *www.tabuashland.com.*

SPORTS AND THE OUTDOORS

MULTISPORT OUTFITTERS

Adventure Center. This respected Ashland company offers "mild to wild" outdoor expeditions, including white-water rafting, fishing, and bike excursions. ⊠ *40 N. Main St.* ☎ *541/488–2819, 800/444–2819* ⊕ *www. raftingtours.com.*

RAFTING

Noah's River Adventures. This long-running outfitter provides white-water rafting and wilderness fishing trips throughout the region—the company can lead single- or multiple-day adventures along the mighty Rogue River as well as just across the border, in Northern California, on the Salmon and Scott Rivers. ⊠ *53 N. Main St.* ☎ *800/858–2811* ⊕ *www.noahsrafting.com.*

SKIING

Mt. Ashland Ski Area. This winter-sports playground in the Siskiyou Mountains is halfway between San Francisco and Portland. The ski runs average more than 280 inches of snow each year. There are 23 trails, virtually all of them intermediate and advanced, in addition to chute skiing in a glacial cirque called the bowl. Two triple and two double chairlifts accommodate a vertical drop of 1,150 feet; the longest of the runs is 1 mile. Facilities include rentals, repairs, instruction, a ski shop, a restaurant, and a bar. A couple of days a week, usually Thursday and Friday, there's also lighted twilight skiing until 9 pm. Anytime of year the drive up the twisting road to the ski area is incredibly scenic, affording views of 14,162-foot Mt. Shasta, some 90 miles south in California. ⊠ *Mt. Ashland Access Rd., off Exit 6 from I–5, 18 miles southwest of downtown* ☎ *541/482–2897* ⊕ *www.mtashland. com* ⊒ *Lift ticket $46* ⊙ *Nov.–Apr., daily 9–4; twilight skiing, Jan.– mid-Mar., Thurs. and Fri. 3–9.*

SHOPPING

Dagoba Organic Chocolate. A few miles' drive south of town you'll find the retail outlet of this company that produces those small, handsomely packed, superfine chocolate bars sold in fancy-food shops and groceries throughout the country. Although Hershey Company now owns the company, Dagoba was founded in Ashland, and its operation remains here, where a small retail shop—open weekdays only—sells its goods. ⊠ *1105 Benson St.* ☎ *866/608–6944* ⊕ *www.dagobachocolate.com.*

KLAMATH FALLS

65 miles east of Ashland via Hwy. 66; 75 miles east of Medford via Hwy. 140.

Often overlooked by visitors traveling the Interstate 5 corridor, the greater Klamath Falls area is one of the most beautiful parts of Oregon. The small (about 20,000 people), if not especially exciting, city of Klamath Falls stands at an elevation of 4,100 feet, on the southern shore of Upper Klamath Lake. The highest elevation in Klamath County is the peak of Mt. Scott, at 8,926 feet. There are more than 82 lakes and streams in Klamath County, including Upper Klamath Lake, which covers 133 square miles.

The Klamath Basin, with its six national wildlife refuges, hosts the largest wintering concentration of bald eagles in the contiguous United States and the largest concentration of migratory waterfowl on the continent. Each February nature enthusiasts from around the world flock here for the Winter Wings Festival, the nation's oldest birding festival.

The Nature Conservancy has called the basin a Western Everglades, because it is the largest wetland area west of the Mississippi. But humans have significantly damaged the ecosystem through farming and development. More than 25% of vertebrate species in the area are now endangered or threatened. As recently as the 1980s, about 6 million birds used the area every year; today that number is down to 2 to 3 million. Environmental organizations are working to reverse some of the damage.

GETTING HERE AND AROUND
Klamath Falls lies along U.S. 97, one of the Northwest's main north–south routes—it's a prime stop between Bend, 140 miles north, and Weed, California, about 70 miles south. You can also get here from the Rogue Valley, either by way of Highway 66 from Ashland or Highway 140 from Medford, which is home to the nearest airport (about a 90-minute drive).

ESSENTIALS
Visitor Information Discover Klamath ⊠ *205 Riverside Dr.* ☎ *541/882–1501, 800/445–6728* ⊕ *www.discoverklamath.com.*

EXPLORING
Fodor'sChoice ★ **Klamath Basin National Wildlife Refuge Complex.** As many as 1,000 bald eagles make Klamath Basin their rest stop, amounting to the largest wintering concentration of these birds in the contiguous United States. Located along the Pacific Flyway bird migration route, the nearly 40,000 acres of freshwater wetlands in the refuge complex serve as a stopover for nearly 1 million waterfowl in the fall. Any time of year is bird-watching season; more than 400 species of birds—including about 15 types of raptors—have been spotted in the Klamath Basin. For a leisurely ramble by car take the tour routes in the Lower Klamath and Tule Lake Refuges. There's a superb bookstore at the visitor center. ⊠ *Visitor Center, 4009 Hill Rd., 27 miles south of Klamath Falls via Hwy. 39, Tulelake, California* ☎ *530/667–2231* ⊕ *www.fws.gov/refuge/ Tule_Lake* ⊡ *Free* ☉ *Visitor center: weekdays 8–4:30, weekends 9–4.*

WHERE TO EAT AND STAY
$$ AMERICAN ⤬ **Basin Martini Bar.** Although the name of this swell-elegant storefront spot in the heart of the downtown historic district suggests an option for evening cocktails, the bar is just as well regarded for its reliably tasty dinner fare—New York strip steaks, burgers topped with Crater Lake blue cheese, and bacon-wrapped scallops are among the highlights. There's seating in a handful of comfy booths or at stools along the modern bar. The creative drinks are notable, too—consider the lemon-basil martini. ⑤ *Average main: $17* ⊠ *632 Main St.* ☎ *541/884–6264* ☉ *No lunch.*

$$ RESORT FAMILY ⛺ **Running Y Ranch Resort.** Golfers rave about the Arnold Palmer–designed course at this 3,600-acre Holiday Inn resort situated in a juniper-and-ponderosa–shaded canyon overlooking Upper Klamath Lake. **Pros:** kids enjoy an indoor pool; walkers and joggers have 8

miles of paved trails. **Cons:** may be a bit too far off the beaten path for some. $ *Rooms from: $154* ✉ *5500 Running Y Rd., 8 miles north of Klamath Falls, Klamath Falls* ☎ *541/850–5500, 800/569–0029* ⊕ *www. runningy.com* ⌁ *82 rooms, 43 houses* ⦶ *No meals.*

SPORTS AND THE OUTDOORS

MULTISPORT OUTFITTERS

The Ledge Outdoor Store. For advice, gear, clothing, books, and maps for hiking, birding, mountaineering, canoeing, camping, and fishing throughout the area, visit this extensively stocked shop in downtown Klamath Falls, which carries all kinds of equipment, and also offers guided fly-fishing trips. ✉ *369 S. 6th St.* ☎ *541/882–5586.*

BOATING

Birding & Boating. For a chance to enjoy the beauty of Klamath Lake while also observing the region's abundant birdlife, rent a sailboat, canoe, or kayak from this outfit with a prime spot on the lake and a staff that can offer expert advice on wildlife-viewing. You can also fish from a dock on the lake. ✉ *658 Front St.* ☎ *541/885–5450* ⊕ *www. birdingandboating.com.*

CAVE JUNCTION

30 miles southwest of Grants Pass via U.S. 199, 60 miles west of Jacksonville via Hwy. 238 and U.S. 199.

One of the least populated and most pristine parts of southern Oregon, the town of Cave Junction and the surrounding Illinois Valley attract outdoors enthusiasts of all kinds for hiking, backpacking, camping, fishing, and hunting. Expect rugged terrain and the chance to view some of the tallest Douglas fir trees in the state. Other than those passing through en route from Grants Pass to the Northern California coast via U.S. 199, most visitors come here to visit the Oregon Caves National Monument, one of the world's only marble caves (formed by erosion from acidic rainwater). Sleepy Cave Junction makes an engaging little base camp, its main drag lined with a handful of quirky shops, short-order restaurants, and gas stations.

GETTING HERE AND AROUND

Cave Junction lies along U.S. 199, the main road leading from Grants Pass. You can also reach Cave Junction by heading west from Jacksonville on Highway 238 to U.S. 199. From Cave Junction, head east on Highway 46 to reach Oregon Caves National Monument. Cave Junction is about a 75-minute drive southwest of Medford's regional airport. Alternatively, the small airport (served by United Airlines, with service from San Francisco) in Crescent City, California, is the same distance.

ESSENTIALS

Visitor Information Illinois Valley Chamber of Commerce ✉ *201 Caves Hwy. (Hwy. 46), just off U.S. 199* ☎ *541/592–3326* ⊕ *www.cavejunction.com.*

EXPLORING

Bridgeview Vineyard and Winery. The producers of the well-distributed and reasonably priced Blue Moon wines (known especially for Riesling, Chardonnay, Pinot Gris, and Merlot), as well as more premium vintages

8

such as Black Beauty Syrah and a very nice reserve Pinot Noir, established the winery in 1986, and—despite considerable skepticism from observers—have gone on to tremendous success. There's a second tasting room, open summer only, in the Applegate Valley, near Grants Pass. ✉ *4210 Holland Loop Rd.* ☎ *541/592–4688, 877/273–4843* ⊕ *www. bridgeviewwine.com* ⊘ *Daily 11–4.*

Fodor's Choice   **Oregon Caves National Monument.** Marble caves, large calcite formations,
★   and huge underground rooms shape this rare adventure in geology. Guided cave tours take place on the hour in late spring and fall, and every half hour June through August. The 90-minute half-mile tour is moderately strenuous with low passageways, twisting turns, and more than 500 stairs; children must be at least 42 inches tall to go on the tour. Cave tours aren't given in winter. Aboveground, the surrounding valley holds an old-growth forest with some of the state's largest trees. ⚠ **Park officials say that GPS coordinates for the caves often direct drivers onto a mostly unpaved forest service road meant for four-wheel-drive vehicles. Instead, follow Highway 46 off U.S. 199 at Cave Junction, which is also narrow and twisty in parts; RVs or trailers over 32 feet not advised.** ✉ *19000 Caves Hwy. (Hwy. 46), 20 miles east of U.S. 199* ☎ *541/592–2100* ⊕ *www.nps.gov/orca* ✄ *Entrance to park, free; tours $8.50* ⊘ *Late Apr.–late May, and mid-Oct.–early Nov., daily 10–4; late May–early Sept., daily 9–6; early Sept.–mid-Oct., daily 9–4.*

WHERE TO STAY

$ ⌂ **Oregon Caves Chateau.** This six-story wood-frame lodge, virtually
HOTEL   unchanged since it was built in 1934, has a rustic authenticity and steep
FAMILY   gabled roofs, while the simple rooms, all with their original furnishings, have canyon or waterfall views. **Pros:** on the grounds of the national monument; historic and funky personality; wonderfully tranquil setting. **Cons:** no-frills rooms; no Internet or phones (and very limited cell reception); location well out of the way if you're visiting the caves. ⑤ *Rooms from: $109* ✉ *20000 Caves Hwy.* ☎ *541/592–3400, 877/245–9022* ⊕ *www.oregoncaveschateau.com* ⇄ *23 rooms* ⊘ *Closed Oct.–mid-May* ⎰⎱ *No meals.*

$ ⌂ **Out 'n' About.** You sleep among the leaves in the tree houses of this
B&B/INN   extraordinary resort—the highest is 37 feet from the ground, one has
FAMILY   an antique claw-foot bath, and another has separate kids' quarters connected to the main room by a swinging bridge. **Pros:** kids love the Swiss Family Robinson atmosphere; it truly feels at one with the surrounding old-growth forest; amazingly quiet and peaceful. **Cons:** accommodations are extremely rustic; some units don't have bathrooms; two-night minimum during week and three-night minimum weekends during spring to fall. ⑤ *Rooms from: $120* ✉ *300 Page Creek Rd.* ☎ *541/592–2208* ⊕ *www.treehouses.com* ⇄ *15 tree houses, 1 cabin* ⎰⎱ *Breakfast.*

9

SEATTLE

WELCOME TO SEATTLE

TOP REASONS TO GO

★ **Examine Seattle's architecture:** Chihuly Garden and Glass is conveniently located at the base of the Space Needle, which you can visit or just admire from below.

★ **Appreciate art:** Visit the Seattle Art Museum and make time for a stroll in SAM's Olympic Sculpture Park on the Elliott Bay waterfront.

★ **Drink coffee:** Seattle may be the birthplace of Starbucks, but there is also a variety of other excellent local chains.

★ **Cheer beer:** Seattle is so obsessed with it that the city's annual Beer Week actually lasts for two.

★ **Indulge in fresh seafood:** First gawk at all the fabulous local produce and seafood at the Pike Place Market, and then visit some of Seattle's renowned restaurants to eat it.

★ **Stroll the "Republic of Fremont":** This pretty neighborhood is where you'll find boutiques, restaurants, a scenic canal-side path, the Theo Chocolate Factory, and the Fremont Troll.

1 Downtown and Belltown. Skyscrapers are here, along with most of the city's hotels and many popular spots, including the waterfront, Pike Place Market, and Seattle Art Museum. Just north of Downtown, Belltown is home to the Olympic Sculpture Park.

2 Seattle Center, South Lake Union, and Queen Anne. Queen Anne, north of Belltown, rises up from Denny Way to the Lake Washington Ship Canal. At the bottom are the Space Needle, the Seattle Center, and the EMP museum. South Lake Union has the REI superstore, lakefront, and some eateries and hotels.

3 Pioneer Square. Seattle's oldest neighborhood has lovely redbrick and sandstone buildings, plus numerous galleries and antiques shops.

4 International District. This is a fun place to shop and eat. The stunning Wing Luke Museum and Uwajimaya shopping center anchor the neighborhood.

5 First Hill. There is one must-see here: the Frye Art Museum.

6 Capitol Hill. The Hill has two faces: young and sassy and elegant and upscale. It has fantastic restaurants and nightlife.

7 Fremont. There is a mix of pricey boutiques and yummy restaurants here; up the hill, residential Phinney Ridge includes the Woodland Park Zoo.

8 Ballard. The main attraction is the Hiram M. Chittenden Locks. This historically Scandinavian neighborhood is beloved for its eateries, trendy shops, and farmers' market.

GETTING ORIENTED

Hemmed in by mountains, hills, and multiple bodies of water, Seattle is anything but a linear, grid-lined city. Twisty, turny, and very long, the city can be baffling to navigate, especially if you delve into its residential neighborhoods—and you should. Water makes the best landmark. Both Elliott Bay and Lake Union are pretty hard to miss. When you are trying to get your bearings Downtown, Elliott Bay is a much more reliable landmark than the Space Needle. Remember that Interstate 5 bisects the city (north–south). The major routes connecting the southern part of the city to the northern part are Interstate 5, Aurora Avenue/Highway 99, 15th Avenue NW (Ballard Bridge), and Westlake (Fremont Bridge) and Eastlake avenues. Streets in the Seattle area generally travel east to west, whereas avenues travel north to south.

9 **Wallingford.** At the ship canal is the wonderful waterfront Gas Works Park. Its booming commercial strip along North 45th Street has a few excellent restaurants.

10 **The "U District."** The university's surrounding neighborhood can be both gritty and charming, with loads of ethnic restaurants and a large student population.

11 **West Seattle.** West Seattle's California Avenue has some lovely shops and restaurants. Gorgeous Alki Beach offers views of the Seattle skyline.

12 **Eastside.** East of Lake Washington, the Eastside suburbs are home to Microsoft. Bellevue is the most citylike, with its own skyline, an art museum, and high-end shops and restaurants.

Updated by
AnnaMaria
Stephens

Seattle is a city of many neighborhoods: eclectic, urban, outdoorsy, artsy, gritty, down-to-earth, or posh—it's all here, from the quirky character of the Seattle Waterfront and the eccentric "Republic of Fremont," to hipsters walking baby carriages past aging mansions on Capitol Hill. There's something for just about everyone within this vibrant Emerald City.

Indeed, part of Seattle's diversity lies in the topography: the city is a feat of environmental engineering. When the Denny party arrived on its shores, "Seattle" was a series of densely forested valleys covered by Douglas fir, Western hemlock, and red cedar. Where SoDo (the stadium district south of Downtown) currently is was nothing but mudflats. Pioneer Square was actually an island of sorts where Duwamish tribespeople crossed to the mainland over sandbars.

Once Seattle started to grow, its residents literally changed the landscape. Massive Denny Hill once occupied the Belltown neighborhood, but it simply had to go. The multistage "regrade" started in 1899 and was completed 32 years later. The Denny Hill Regrade was just one of dozens of projects; another equally ambitious earth-moving mission was the construction of the canal that links Lake Washington to Puget Sound. Today, the city is once again moving a lot of earth around with the construction of a light rail line across the city; it's changing the look, feel, and energy of neighborhoods as a result.

It's hard to think of Seattle as anything but natural, though. After all, the city owes much of its appeal to its natural features—the myriad hills that did survive settlement offer views of mountain ranges and water, water, water. Outside Downtown and other smaller commercial cores, Seattle's neighborhoods fan out in tangles of tree-lined streets. Massive parks like Discovery, Magnuson, and Washington Park Arboretum make Seattle one of the greenest and most livable cities in the nation. From the peaks of the Olympics or Cascades to an artistically

A steel sculpture by Richard Serra at the Olympic Sculpture Park

landscaped garden in front of a classic Northwest bungalow, nature is in full effect every time you turn your head.

SEATTLE PLANNER

WHEN TO GO

Unless you're planning an all-indoor museum trip, Seattle is most enjoyable May through October. June can be surprisingly rainy, but July through September is almost always dry, with warm days reaching into the mid-70s and 80s; nights are cooler, though it doesn't get dark until 9 or 10 pm. Although the weather can be dodgy, spring (particularly April) and fall are also excellent times to visit, as lodging and tour costs are usually much lower (and the crowds much smaller). In winter, the days are short, dark, and wet, but temperatures rarely dip below the low 40s and winter events—especially around the holidays—are plentiful.

FESTIVALS

■TIP→ The Seattle Convention and Visitors Bureau has a full calendar of events at ⊕ *www.visitseattle.org/cultural*. Foodies will want to hit up **Taste Washington** (spring ⊕ *www.tastewashington.org*) for the best of food and wine, as well as **Bite of Seattle** (July ⊕ *www.biteofseattle.com*), the Northwest Chocolate Festival (September ⊕ *www.nwchocolate. com*) and Seattle International Beer Fest (July ⊕ *www.seattlebeerfest. com*). The **Seattle International Film Festival** presents more than 200 features (May–June ⊕ *www.siff.net*).

Music lovers have three major events to keep them happy: **Bumbershoot** (September ⊕ *bumbershoot.org*) is Seattle's premier music festival, packed with major acts, as well as dance and theater, while Northwest Folklife Festival (May ⊕ *www.nwfolklife.org*) is a free, family-friendly event featuring folk music and dance from around the globe. Hipsters will want to check out Capitol Hill Block Party (July ⊕ *www. capitolhillblockparty.com*) for the best indie pop, rock, hip-hop, and alt-country.

The **Seattle Pride Festival** (June ⊕ *www.seattlepride.org*) has the Northwest's biggest gay, lesbian, and transgender pride parade. A local favorite, the quirky Fremont Fair Summer Solstice Parade (June ⊕ *www. fremontfair.org*) provides a glimpse into the true character of the city. **Seafair** (July–August ⊕ *www.seafair.com*) is the biggest summer festival; hydroplane races are just one major event.

GETTING HERE AND AROUND

AIR TRAVEL

The major gateway is Seattle–Tacoma International Airport (SEA), known locally as Sea-Tac. The airport is south of the city and reasonably close to it—non-rush-hours trips to Downtown sometimes take less than a half hour. Sea-Tac is a midsize, modern airport that is usually pleasant to navigate. Charter flights and small carriers, such as Kenmore Air, that operate shuttle flights between the cities of the Pacific Northwest land at Boeing Field, which is between Sea-Tac and Seattle.

AIRPORT TRANSFER You can take Sound Transit's **Link Light Rail** (⊕ *www.soundtransit. org*), which will take you right to Downtown in 35 minutes for just $2.75. Trains depart every 7, 10, or 15 minutes, depending on the time of day and run from 5 am to 1 am Monday through Saturday and 6 am to midnight on Sunday.

BIKING AND WALKING

Biking is popular but still something of a cult endeavor, thanks to a shortage of safe bike routes and some daunting hills. Check out ⊕ *www. ridethecity.com/seattle*. Walking is fun, though distances and rain can sometimes get in the way. Several neighborhoods—from Pioneer Square to Downtown, or from Belltown to Queen Anne, for example—are close enough to each other that even hills and moisture can't stop walkers.

BUS TRAVEL

The bus system will get you anywhere you need to go, although some routes require a time commitment and several transfers. Within the Downtown core, however, the bus is efficient and affordable, with off-peak fares starting at $2.25, while an unlimited regional day pass can be purchased for $9. The Trip Planner (⊕ *tripplanner.kingcounty.gov*) is a useful resource for finding routes. If you plan to travel primarily by bus during your visit, purchase a reloadable ORCA Smart Card; it's an extra $5 but makes riding the bus a cinch.

CAR TRAVEL

Access to a car is *almost* a necessity if you want to explore the residential neighborhoods beyond their commercial centers. Before you book a car for city-only driving, keep in mind that many high-end hotels offer complimentary town-car service around Downtown and the immediate areas. Parking can cost upwards of $40 per night in the urban center

The best advice about driving in Seattle is to avoid driving during rush hour whenever possible, and always allow for more time than you think you'll need. Check ⊕ *www.wsdot.com/traffic/seattle* for bridge and road closures and live traffic updates.

FERRY TRAVEL

Ferries are a major part of Seattle's transportation network, and they're the only way to reach such points as Vashon Island and the San Juans. You'll get outstanding views of the skyline and the elusive Mt. Rainier from the ferry to Bainbridge. Whale-watching and ferry-ride vacation packages like those offered by the *Victoria Clipper* can be booked in advance. The Washington State Ferries to Puget Sound and San Juan Islands rarely accept reservations (only on international sailings to Sidney, British Columbia, for example), so be sure to plan island travel thoughtfully: leave enough time in your schedule to arrive at the piers early—and to wait for the next ferry if you're last in line. Check the VesselWatch page at ⊕ *wsdot.com/ferries* for live cams and wait times, which can take hours on nice days and holiday weekends.

LIGHT-RAIL TRAVEL

Sound Transit's Central Link Light Rail (⊕ *www.soundtransit.org*)— the first link of which was completed in 2009—will eventually provide what the buses can't: an efficient way to go north–south in this vertically oriented city. (Fare: $2.50)

MONORAIL TRAVEL

Built for the 1962 World's Fair, the monorail (⊕ *www.seattlemonorail. com*) is the shortest transportation system in the city. It runs from Westlake Center (on 5th and Pike) to Seattle Center. But this is great for visitors who plan to spend a day at the Space Needle and the Seattle Center's museums. (Fare: $4.50 round-trip)

SEATTLE STREETCAR TRAVEL

The second-shortest system in the city (⊕ *www.seattlestreetcar.org*) was built to connect Downtown to South Lake Union (directly east of Seattle Center). It runs from Westlake and Olive to the southern shore of Lake Union (Fare: $2.50). In 2014, the city laid tracks for the new First Hill line, a major transportation initiative that connects Pioneer Square with Capitol Hill.

TAXI TRAVEL

Though the city is testing out an expanded taxi-license program, Seattle still has a much smaller taxi fleet than most major cities do. Taking a cab is not a major form of transportation in the city, and you'll find that rates run higher here. Most people take cabs only to and from the airport and when they go out partying on weekends. You'll often be able to hail cabs on the street in Downtown, but anywhere else, you'll have to call. Expect long waits on Friday and Saturday nights. Two major cab companies are **Yellow Cab** (☎ *206/622–6500*) and **Farwest** (☎ *206/622–1717*).

Many locals rely on ride-sharing companies like Lyft (⊕ *www.lyft. com*), Sidecar (⊕ *www.side.cr*), and Uber (⊕ *www.uber.com*) to get around town. Just check prices before you book a lift with your phone app, as costs can rise and fall according to demand. Another option is Car2Go (⊕ *www.car2go.com*), which—for a membership fee and a per-mile charge—lets you locate and borrow a tiny SmartCar. You can park and leave it just about anywhere—even at Seattle parking meters without paying.

TRAIN TRAVEL

Amtrak tickets to Portland and Vancouver, BC, sell out on summer weekends, and last-minute fares can be quite expensive.

VISITOR INFORMATION

Contact the **Seattle Visitors Bureau and Convention Center** (⊕ *www. visitseattle.org* ☎ *206/461–5800*) for help with everything from sightseeing to booking spa services. You can also follow its Twitter feed (⊕ *twitter.com/seattlemaven*). The main visitor information center is Downtown, at the Washington State Convention and Trade Center on 8th Avenue and Pike Street; it has a full-service concierge desk open daily 9 to 5 (in summer; weekdays only in winter). There's also an info booth at Pike Place Market.

EXPLORING

Each of Seattle's neighborhoods has a distinctive personality, and taking a stroll, browsing a bookstore, or enjoying a cup of coffee can feel different in every one. It's the adventure of exploring that will really introduce you to the character of Seattle.

DOWNTOWN AND BELLTOWN

Except for the busy areas around the Market and the piers, and the always-frenetic shopping district, a lot of Downtown can often seem deserted, especially at night. Still, while it may not be the soul of the city, it's definitely the heart, and there's plenty to do—nearly all of it easily reachable by foot. There's the city's premier art museum, the eye-popping Rem Koolhaas–designed Central Library, lively Pike Place Market, the West Coast's tallest Ferris wheel, and a major shopping corridor along 5th Avenue and down Pine Street. And, of course, there's the water: Elliott Bay beckons from every crested hill.

Belltown is Downtown's younger sibling, just north of Virginia Street (up to Denny Way) and stretching from Elliott Bay to 6th Avenue. Not so long ago, Belltown was home to some of the most unwanted real estate in the city. Today, Belltown is increasingly hip, with luxury condos, trendy restaurants, bustling bars, and a number of boutiques. (Most of the action happens between 1st and 4th avenues and between Bell and Virginia streets.) You can still find plenty of evidence of its edgy past—including a gallery exhibiting urban street art, a punk-rock vinyl shop, and a major indie rock music venue that was a cornerstone of the grunge scene—but today Belltown is almost unrecognizable to long-term residents.

Fodor'sChoice
★ **Olympic Sculpture Park.** An outdoor branch of the Seattle Art Museum is a favorite destination for picnics, strolls, and quiet contemplation. Nestled at the edge of Belltown with views of Elliott Bay, the gently

sloping green space features native plants and walking paths that wind past bigger-than-life public artwork. On sunny days, the park frames an astounding panorama of the Olympic Mountains, but even the grayest afternoon casts a favorable light on the site's sculptures. The grounds are home to works by such artists as Richard Serra, Louise Bourgeois, and Alexander Calder, whose bright-red steel "Eagle" sculpture is a local favorite (and a nod to the bald eagles that sometimes soar above). "Echo," a 46-foot-tall elongated girl's face by Spanish artist Jaume Plensa, is a beautiful and bold presence on the waterfront. The park's PACCAR Pavilion has a gift shop, café, and information about the artworks. ⊠ *2901 Western Ave., between Broad and Bay Sts., Belltown* ☎ *206/654–3100* ⊕ *www.seattleartmuseum.org/visit/osp* ☜ *Free* ⊙ *Park, daily sunrise–sunset; PACCAR Pavilion, Mar.–Sept., daily 10–5; Nov.–Feb., weekends 10–4.*

FAMILY

Fodor'sChoice

★

Pike Place Market. One of the nation's largest and oldest public markets dates from 1907, when the city issued permits allowing farmers to sell produce from parked wagons. At one time the market was a madhouse of vendors hawking their produce and haggling with customers over prices; now you might find fishmongers engaging in frenzied banter and hilarious antics, but chances are you won't get them to waver on prices. There are many restaurants, bakeries, coffee shops (including the flagship Starbucks), lunch counters, and ethnic eateries. Go to Pike Place hungry and you won't be disappointed. The flower market is also a must-see—gigantic fresh arrangements can be found for less than $10. Strap on some walking shoes and enjoy the market's many corridors, where you'll find specialty-food items, quirky gift shops, tea, honey, jams, comic books, beads, eclectic crafts, and cookware. ⊠ *Pike Pl. at Pike St., west of 1st Ave., Downtown* ☎ *206/682–7453* ⊕ *www.pikeplacemarket.org* ⊙ *Market opens daily for breakfast at 6 am; fresh produce and fish open 7 am–6 pm; merchants open 10 am–6 pm; restaurants and bars last call, 1:30 am.*

9

A GOOD
COMBO

If you plan to spend the morning exploring Pike Place Market or the Seattle Art Museum, but still have energy for a walk, head north into the Belltown neighborhood, grab lunch to go at Macrina Bakery, and stroll down to the Olympic Sculpture Park: views, works of art, and chairs aplenty await.

FAMILY

Fodor'sChoice

★

Seattle Aquarium. Located right at the water's edge, the Seattle Aquarium is one of the nation's premier aquariums. Among its most engaging residents are the sea otters—kids, especially, seem able to spend hours watching the delightful antics of these creatures and their river cousins. In the Puget Sound Great Hall, "Window on Washington Waters," a slice of Neah Bay life, is presented in a 20-foot-tall tank holding 120,000 gallons of water. The aquarium's darkened rooms and large, lighted tanks brilliantly display Pacific Northwest marine life. The "Life on the Edge" tide pools re-create Washington's rocky coast and sandy beaches—kids can touch the starfish, sea urchins, and sponges. Huge glass windows provide underwater views of the harbor seal exhibit; go up top to watch them play in their pools. ■ TIP➔ If you're visiting in fall or winter, dress warmly—the Marine Mammal area is outside on the waterfront and catches all those chilly Puget Sound breezes.

Downtown Seattle and Environs

The café serves Ivar's chowder and kid-friendly food like burgers and chicken fingers; the balcony has views of Elliott Bay. ✉ *1483 Alaskan Way, Pier 59, Downtown* ☎ *206/386–4300* ⊕ *www.seattleaquarium.org* 💲 *$21.95; children 4–12 $14.95* ⊙ *Daily 9:30–6 (last entry at 5 pm).*

Seattle Art Museum. Sculptor Jonathan Borofsky's several-stories-high "Hammering Man" greets visitors to SAM, as locals call this pride of the city's art scene. The genre-spanning museum features plenty of free public space. The first floor includes the SAM's fantastic gift shop, a café that focuses on local ingredients, and spaces for drop-in workshops where the whole family can get creative. ✉ *1300 1st Ave., Downtown* ☎ *206/654–3100* ⊕ *www.seattleartmuseum.org* 💲 *Suggested donation $19.50; fee for special exhibition* ⊙ *Wed. and weekends 10–5, Thurs. and Fri. 10–9; closed Mon. and Tues. Free on First Thursdays.*

Seattle Great Wheel. At 175 feet tall, on a clear day this giant Ferris wheel perched on the very edge of Downtown's Pier 57 offers a spectacular panorama of Seattle and its surroundings—not to mention a jaw-dropping view of the water below. Cozy up in one of 42 climate-controlled gondolas and enjoy the approximately 12-minute ride—or three full revolutions. For a splurge, a ride in the glass-bottomed VIP car comes with a glass of champagne at the end. ✉ *1301 Alaskan Way, Downtown* ☎ *206/623–8607* ⊕ *seattlegreatwheel.com* 💲 *$13* ⊙ *July–Sept., Sun.–Thurs. 10 am–11 pm, Fri. and Sat. 10 am–midnight; Oct.–Jun., Mon.–Thurs. 11–10, Fri. 11 am–midnight; Sat. 10 am–midnight, Sun. 10–10.*

Fodor'sChoice ★ **The Seattle Public Library.** The hub of Seattle's 27-branch library system is a stunning jewel of a building that stands out against the concrete jungle of Downtown. Designed by renowned Dutch architect Rem Koolhaas and Joshua Ramus, this 11-story structure houses more than 1 million books, a language center, terrific areas for kids and teens—plus hundreds of computers with Internet access, an auditorium, a "mixing chamber" floor of information desks, and a café. The building's floor plan is anything but simple; stand outside the beveled glass-and-metal facade of the building and you can see the library's floors zigzagging upward. Tours are self-guided via a laminated sheet you can pick up at the information desk; there's also a number you can call on your cell phone for an audio tour. The reading room on the 10th floor has unbeatable views of the city and the water, and the building has Wi-Fi throughout. Readings and free film screenings happen on a regular basis; check the website for more information. ✉ *1000 4th Ave.,*

The stunning Seattle Central Library

Downtown ☎ *206/386–4636* ⊕ *www.spl.org/locations/central-library* ⊗ *Mon.–Thurs. 10–8, Fri. and Sat. 10–6, Sun. noon–6.*

SEATTLE CENTER, SOUTH LAKE UNION, AND QUEEN ANNE

Almost all visitors make their way to Seattle Center at some point, to visit the Space Needle or other key Seattle sites like the EMP building, the Pacific Science Center, or the stunning new Chihuly Garden and Glass. The neighborhoods that bookend Seattle Center couldn't be more different: Queen Anne is all residential elegance (especially on top of the hill), while South Lake Union, once completely industrial, is quickly becoming Seattle's next hot neighborhood.

TOP ATTRACTIONS

Fodor's Choice
★
Chihuly Garden and Glass. Just steps from the base of the Space Needle, fans of Dale Chihuly's glass works will be delighted to trace the artist's early influences—neon art, Native American Northwest Coast trade baskets, and Pendleton blankets, to name a few—to the vibrant chandelier towers and architectural glass installations he is most known for today. There are eight galleries total, plus the 40-foot-tall Glasshouse and an outdoor garden, which serves as a backdrop for colorful installations that integrate with a dynamic Northwest landscape, including native plants and a 500-year-old western cedar that washed up on the shores of Neah Bay. Chihuly, who was born and raised in Tacoma, was actively involved in the design of the exhibition as well as the whimsical Collections Cafe, where you'll find Chihuly's quirky personal collections on display—everything from tin toys to vintage cameras to antique shaving brushes. Indeed, so many of his personal touches are

MARIJUANA LEGALIZATION

In 2012, Washington voted to legalize recreational marijuana, one of the first two states in the United States to blaze such a groundbreaking trail. Washington debuted its first pot stores in the summer of 2014, and—as in Colorado—things haven't rolled out quite as smoothly as hoped. Because of strict regulations, supply levels have remained chronically low, while licensed vendors have struggled to set up shop. In fact, only one Seattle pot shop managed to open on the day sales commenced—and it had to close up early. Add in the high taxes—a 25% excise tax plus a 9.5% sales tax—and legalized weed hasn't been quite as big a draw (or moneymaker) as lawmakers had hoped. In fact, one *New York Times* editorial suggested that legalized marijuana was destined to become little more than a tourist novelty in Washington.

But that's good news for tourists who'd like to try it! If you're so inclined, it's a good idea to do a bit of research first. Check sites like ⊕ *leafly.com* or ⊕ *weedmaps.com* to locate stores and check on what strains they carry. You must be 21 or up with a valid ID to purchase marijuana in Washington. You can buy or possess an ounce of flower at a time, or up to 16 ounces of marijuana-infused edibles. When it comes to consumption, treat it like booze. Don't partake in public, and don't get high and drive. If you'd like a guided introduction to Emerald City's green offerings, check out Kush Tourism (⊕ *www.kushtourism.com*), which can also help visitors find weed-friendly lodging.

part of the exhibition space, you can almost feel his presence in every room (look for the guy with the unruly hair and the black eyepatch). Chihuly is kid-friendly for all but the littlest ones. ✉ *305 Harrison St., under the Space Needle, Seattle Center* ☎ *206/753–4940* ⊕ *www. chihulygardenandglass.com* ✉ *$21; $31 for a two-time pass* ⊙ *Daily 11–7; extended hours in summer.*

FAMILY
Fodor's Choice
★

EMP Museum. Seattle's most controversial architectural statement is the 140,000-square-foot complex designed by architect Frank Gehry, who drew inspiration from electric guitars to achieve the building's curvy metallic design. It's a fitting backdrop for rock memorabilia from the likes of Bob Dylan and the grunge-scene heavies. ✉ *325 5th Ave. N, between Broad and Thomas Sts., Seattle Center* ☎ *206/770–2700* ⊕ *www.empsfm.org* ✉ *$20 weekdays, $22 weekend* ⊙ *Daily 10–5.*

FAMILY
Fodor's Choice
★

Pacific Science Center. If you have kids, this nonprofit science center in the heart of Seattle is a must-visit, home to more than 200 indoor and outdoor hands-on exhibits, two IMAX theaters, a Laser Dome, a butterfly house, and a state-of-the-art Planetarium. The dinosaur exhibit—complete with moving robotic reproductions—is a favorite, and tots can experiment with water at the ever-popular stream table. Machines analyze human physiology in the *Body Works* exhibit. When you need to warm up, The Tropical Butterfly House is 80 degrees and home to colorful butterflies from South and Central America, Africa, and Asia; other creatures live in the Insect Village and saltwater tide-pool areas. IMAX movies, Planetarium shows, Live Science Shows, and Laser

Dome rock shows run daily. Look for the giant white arches near the Space Needle and make a day of the surrounding sights. ■TIP➔ **Pacific Science Center offers a number of lectures, forums, and "Science Cafes" for adults, plus a variety of educational programs for kids, including camp-ins, monthly parents' night outs, workshops, and more. See website for schedule information.** ✉ *200 2nd Ave. N, Seattle Center* ☎ *206/443–2001* ⊕ *www.pacsci.org* 🎫 *Center $19.50, IMAX $9, laser shows $6–$9.75, combined museum/IMAX $23.50* ⊙ *Mon.–Fri. 10–5, weekends 10–6.*

FAMILY **Space Needle.** Over 50 years old, Seattle's most iconic building is as quirky and beloved as ever. The distinctive, towering, 605-foot-high structure is visible throughout much of Seattle—but the view from the inside out is even better. A less-than-one-minute ride up to the observation deck yields 360-degree vistas of Downtown Seattle, the Olympic Mountains, Elliott Bay, Queen Anne Hill, Lake Union, and the Cascade Range. Built for the 1962 World's Fair, the Needle has educational kiosks, interactive trivia game stations for kids, and the glass-enclosed SpaceBase store and Pavilion spiraling around the base of the tower. The top-floor SkyCity restaurant is "revolutionary" (literally—watch the skyline revolve as you dine) and the elevator trip and observation deck are complimentary with your reservation. ■TIP➔ **If the forecast says you may have a sunny day during your visit, schedule the Needle for that day!** If you can't decide whether you want the daytime or nighttime view, for an extra ten bucks you can buy a ticket that allows you to visit twice in one day. (Also look for package deals with Chihuly Garden and Glass.) ✉ *400 Broad St., Seattle Center* ☎ *206/905–2100* ⊕ *www.spaceneedle.com* 🎫 *$21* ⊙ *Daily 9 am–midnight.*

WORTH NOTING

FAMILY **Bill & Melinda Gates Foundation Visitor Center.** The Bill and Melinda Gates Foundation has some lofty goals, and it's here, across the street from Seattle Center, where you get to witness their plans in action. Exhibits are thought-provoking and interactive, inviting you to offer up your own solutions to complex global problems like poverty and climate change. The "Innovation & Inspiration" gallery is the most fun, providing dozens of creative activities for visitors of all ages. ✉ *440 5th Ave N., South Lake Union* ☎ *206/709–3100* ⊕ *www.visitorcenter. gatesfoundation.org* 🎫 *Free* ⊙ *Tues.–Sat. 10–5.*

FAMILY **The Children's Museum, Seattle.** If you're traveling with kids, you already know that a good children's museum is like gold at the end of a rainbow. This colorful, spacious museum, located on the lower level of The Armory in the heart of Seattle Center, provides hours of exploration and fun. Enter through a Northwest wilderness setting, with winding trails, hollow logs, and a waterfall. From there, you can explore the Global Village where rooms with kid-friendly props show everyday life in Ghana, the Philippines, and Japan. Cog City is a giant game of pipes, pulleys, and balls; kids can also test their talent in a mock recording studio. There's a small play area for toddlers and plenty of crafts to keep everyone engaged. ✉ *305 Harrison St., Seattle Center* ☎ *206/441–1768* ⊕ *www.thechildrensmuseum.org* 🎫 *$8.25* ⊙ *Weekdays 10–5, weekends 10–6.*

Continued on page 352

PIKE PLACE MARKET
Nine Acres of History & Quirky Charm

With more than a century of history tucked into every corner and plenty of local personality, the Market is one spot you can't miss. Office workers hustle past cruise-ship crowds to take a seat at lunch counters that serve anything from pizza to piroshkies to German sausage. Local chefs plan the evening's menu over stacks of fresh, colorful produce. At night, couples stroll in to canoodle by candlelight in tucked-away bars and restaurants. Sure, some residents may bemoan the hordes of visitors, and many Seattleites spend their dollars at a growing number of neighborhood farmers' markets. But the Market is still one of Seattle's best-loved attractions.

The Pike Place Market dates from 1907. In response to anger over rising food prices, the city issued permits for farmers to sell produce from wagons parked at Pike Place. The impromptu public market grew steadily, and in 1921 Frank Goodwin, a hotel owner who had been quietly buying up real estate around Pike Place for a decade, proposed to build a permanent space.

More than 250 businesses, including 70 eateries. Breathtaking views of Elliott Bay. A pedestrian-friendly central shopping arcade that buzzes to life each day beginning at 6:30 AM. Strumming street musicians. Cobblestones, flying fish, and the very first Starbucks. Pike Place Market—the oldest continuously operated public market in the United States and a beloved Seattle icon—covers all the bases.

The Market's vitality ebbed after World War II, with the exodus to the suburbs and the rise of large supermarkets. Both it and the surrounding neighborhoods began to deteriorate. But a group of dedicated residents, led by the late architect Victor Steinbrueck, rallied and voted the Market a Historical Asset in the early 1970s. Years of subsequent restoration turned the Market into what you see today.

Pike Place Market is many buildings built around a central arcade (which is distinguished by its huge red neon sign).

Shops and restaurants fill buildings on Pike Place and Western Avenue. In the main arcade, dozens of booths sell fresh produce, cheese, spices, coffee, crafts, and seafood—which can be packed in dry ice for flights home. Farmers sell high-quality produce that helps to set Seattle's rigorous dining standards. The shopkeepers who rent store spaces sell art, curios, clothing, beads, and more. Most shops cater to tourists, but there are gems to be found.

EXPLORING THE MARKET

TOP EATS

❶ THE PINK DOOR. This adored (and adorable) Italian eatery is tucked into Post Alley. Whimsical decor, very good Italian food (such as the scrumptious *linguine alla vongole*), and weekend cabaret and burlesque make this gem a must-visit.

❷ LE PANIER. It's a self-proclaimed "Very French Bakery" and another Seattle favorite. The pastries are the main draw, but sandwiches on fresh baguettes and stuffed croissants offer more substantial snacks.

❸ PIROSHKY PIROSHKY. Authentic piroshky come in both standard varieties (beef and cheese) and Seattle-influenced ones (smoked salmon with cream cheese). There are plenty of sweet piroshky, too, if you need a sugar fix.

❹ CAMPAGNE. This French favorite and its charming attached café have you covered, whether you want a quick Croque Madame for lunch, a leisurely and delicious weekend brunch, or a white-tablecloth dinner.

❺ BEECHER'S. Artisanal cheeses—and mac-n-cheese to go—make this a spot Seattleites will brave the crowds for.

❻ THREE GIRLS BAKERY. This tiny bakery turns out piles of pastries and sandwiches on their fresh-baked bread (the baked salmon is a favorite).

❼ MATT'S IN THE MARKET. Matt's is the best restaurant in the Market, and one of the best in the city. Lunch is casual (try the catfish po'boy), and dinner is elegant, with fresh fish and local produce showcased on the small menu. Reservations are essential.

❽ DAILY DOZEN DONUTS. Mini-donuts are made fresh before your eyes and are a great snack to pick up before you venture into the labyrinth.

❾ MARKET GRILL. This no-frills counter serves up the market's best fish sandwiches and a great clam chowder.

❿ CHUKAR CHERRIES. Look for handmade confections featuring—but not restricted to—local cherries dipped in all sorts of sweet, rich coatings.

TOP SHOPS

⓫ MARKET SPICE TEA. For a tin of the Market's signature tea, Market Spice Blend, which is infused with cinnamon and clove oils, seek out Market Spice shop on the south side of the main arcade.

⓬ PIKE & WESTERN WINE SHOP. The Tasting Room in Post Alley may be a lovely place to sample Washington wines, but Pike and Western is the place where serious oenophiles flock.

⓭ THE TASTING ROOM. With one of the top wine selections in town, the Tasting Room offers Washington wines for the casual collector and the experienced connoisseur. Stop by the bar for large or small pours before you buy.

⑭ WORLD SPICE. Glass jars are filled with spices and teas from around the world here: Buy by the ounce or grab a pre-packaged gift set as a souvenir.

⑮ LEFT BANK BOOKS. A collective in operation since 1973, this tiny bookshop specializes in political and history titles and alternative literature.

⑯ THE ORIGINAL STARBUCKS. At 1912 Pike Place, you'll find the tiny store that opened in 1971 and started an empire. The shop is definitely more quaint and old-

timey than its sleek younger siblings, and it features the original, uncensored (read: bare-breasted) version of the mermaid logo.

⑰ THE SPANISH TABLE. Though not technically in the Market, this amazing specialty store is nearby. It's the Spanish equivalent of DeLaurenti's, and carries hard-to-find cured meats and cheeses plus a nice stock of sweets and clay cookware like cazuelas.

⑱ RACHEL'S GINGER BEER. The flagship store for Seattle's

wildly popular ginger beer serves up delicious variations on its homemade brew, including boozy cocktails.

⑲ PAPPARDELLE'S PASTA. There's no type of pasta you could dream up that isn't already in a bin at Pappardelle's.

⑳ DELAURENTI'S. This amazing Italian grocery has everything from fancy olive oil to digestifs and wine to meats and fine cheeses.

TOP EXPERIENCES

Pike Place Flowers

Pike Place Fish Co.

Market buskers

FISHMONGERS. There are four spots to visit if you want to see some serious fish: Pike Place Fish Co. (where the fish-throwers are—look for the awestruck crowds); City Fish (the place for fresh crab); Pure Food Fish Market (selling since 1911); and Jack's Fish Spot.

FLOWER STALLS. Flower growers, many of them Hmong immigrants, dot the main arcade. The gorgeous, seasonal bouquets are among the market's biggest draws.

PILES OF PRODUCE. The bounty of the agricultural valleys just outside Seattle is endless. In summer, seek out sweet peaches and Rainier cherries. In fall, look for cider made from Yakima Valley apples. There are dozens of produce vendors, but Sosio's and Manzo Brothers have been around the longest.

BUSKERS. The market has more than 240 street entertainers in any given year; the parade of Pacific Northwest hippie quirkitude is entertainment in itself.

POST ALLEY. There are some great finds in the alley that runs the length of the Market, paralleling First Avenue, from the highbrow (The Tasting Room) to the very lowbrow (the Gum Wall, a wall speckled with discarded gum supposedly left by people waiting in line at the Market Theater).

GHOSTS. If you listen to local lore, Pike Place Market may be the most haunted spot in Seattle. The epicenter seems to be 1921 First Avenue, where Butterworths & Sons Undertakers handled most of Seattle's dead in the early 1900s. You might see visitors sliding flowers into the building's old mail slot.

***SLEEPLESS IN SEATTLE* STOP.** Though it's been more than a decade since Rob Reiner and Tom Hanks discussed dating mores at the bar of The Athenian Inn, tourists still snap pictures of the corner they occupied. Look for the bright red plaque declaring: TOM HANKS SAT HERE.

A DAY AT THE MARKET

6:30 AM Delivery vans and trucks start to fill the narrow streets surrounding Pike Place Market. Vendors with permanent stalls arrive to stack produce, arrange flowers, and shovel ice into bins for displaying salmon, crab, octopus, and other delicacies.

7:30 AM Breakfast is served! ■ **TIP→ For freshly made pastries head to Three Girls and Le Panier.**

9 AM Craftspeople vying for day stalls sign in and are assigned spots based on seniority.

10 AM Craftspeople set up Down Under —the levels below the main arcade—as the main arcade officially opens. The Heritage Center on Western Avenue opens. Market tours ($10) start at the information booth. ■ **TIP→ Make reservations for market tours at least a day in advance; call ☎ 206/774-5249.**

11 AM The Market madness begins. In summer, midday crowds make it nearly impossible to walk through the street-level arcades. ■ **TIP→ Head Down Under where things are often a bit quieter.**

12 PM–2 PM Lunch counters at places like the Athenian Inn and the Market Grill fill up.

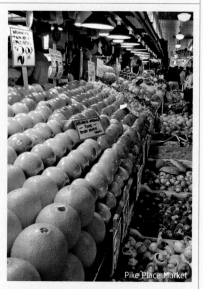

Pike Place Market

5 PM Down Under shops close and the cobblestones are hosed down. (The Market closes at 6 PM Mon.–Sat. and 5 PM on Sun.)

7 PM–2 AM Patrons fill the tables at the Alibi Room, Zig Zag Café, the Pink Door, Matt's at the Market, and Maximilien's.

RACHEL THE PIG

Rachel, the 550-lb bronze pig that greets marketgoers at the main entrance on Pike and 1st Avenue, is a popular photo stop. But she's also a giant piggy bank that contributes up to $9,000 per year to the Market Foundation. Rachel was sculpted by Georgia Gerber, of Whidbey Island, and was named for the 750-pound pig that won the 1985 Island County Fair.

PARKING

There are numerous garages in the area, including one affiliated with the market itself (the Public Market Parking Garage at 1531 Western Ave.), at which you can get validated parking from many merchants; some restaurants offer free parking at this garage after 5 PM. You'll also find several pay lots farther south on Western Ave. and north on 1st Ave. Street parking is next to impossible to find midday. From Downtown hotels, the Market is easy to reach on foot or on city buses in the "Ride Free Zone."

FAMILY

Fodor's Choice

★

Discovery Park. You won't find more spectacular views of Puget Sound, the Cascades, and the Olympics. Located on Magnolia Bluff, northwest of Downtown, Seattle's largest park covers 534 acres and has an amazing variety of terrain: shaded, secluded forest trails lead to meadows, saltwater beaches, sand dunes, a lighthouse, and two miles of protected beaches. The North Beach Trail, which takes you along the shore to the lighthouse, is a must-see. Head to the South Bluff Trail to get a view of Mt. Rainier. The park has several entrances—if you want to stop at the visitor center to pick up a trail map before exploring, use the main entrance at Government Way. The North Parking Lot is much closer to the North Beach Trail and to Ballard and Fremont, if you're coming from that direction. First-come, first-serve beach parking passes for the disabled, elderly, and families with small children are available at the Learning Center. ■TIP➔ **Note that the park is easily reached from Ballard and Fremont. It's easier to combine a park day with an exploration of those neighborhoods than with a busy Downtown itinerary.** ⊠ *3801 W. Government Way, Magnolia* ✛ *From Downtown, take Elliot Ave. W (which turns into 15th Ave. W), and get off at the Emerson St. exit and turn left onto W. Emerson. Make a right onto Gilman Ave. W (which eventually becomes W. Government Way). As you enter the park, the road becomes Washington Ave.; turn left on Utah Ave.* ☎ *206/386–4236* ⊕ *seattle.gov/parks/environment/discovery.htm* ✎ *Free* ⊙ *Park open daily 6 am–11 pm, visitor center Tues.–Sun. 8:30–5.*

FAMILY

Museum of History & Industry. Located in the Lake Union Park's converted Naval Reserve Building, the 20,000-square-foot MOHAI offers visitors an in-depth slice of regional history. Permanent exhibitions include the Center for Innovation, which showcases Seattle's role as a place where innovation and entrepreneurship flourish; the exhibit is supported by a $10 million gift from Jeff Bezos, founder and CEO of Seattle-based Amazon.com (which has its corporate headquarters a few blocks away). Special temporary exhibitions examine everything from chocolate to stories of Jewish merchants in Washington State. ⊠ *860 Terry Avenue N., at Lake Union Park, South Lake Union* ☎ *206/324–1126* ⊕ *www.seattlehistory.org* ✎ *$17, free 1st Thurs. of month (excluding special exhibitions)* ⊙ *Daily 10–5, 1st Thurs. of month 10–8.*

PIONEER SQUARE

The Pioneer Square district, directly south of Downtown, is Seattle's oldest neighborhood. It attracts visitors with elegantly renovated (or in some cases replica) turn-of-the-20th-century redbrick buildings and art galleries. It's the center of Seattle's arts scene, and the galleries in this small neighborhood are a large part of the sights. In recent years, a growing number of new restaurants and businesses have opened, giving the neighborhood fresh appeal to locals and tourists alike.

Bill Speidel's Underground Tour. Present-day Pioneer Square is actually one story higher than it used to be. After the Great Seattle Fire of 1889, Seattle's planners regraded the neighborhood's streets, which had been built on filled-in tide lands and regularly flooded. The result? There is now an intricate and expansive array of subterranean passageways and

The Pioneer Square skyline is dominated by historic Smith Tower.

basements beneath Pioneer Square, and Bill Speidel's Underground Tour is the only way to explore them. Speidel was an irreverent historian, PR man, and former *Seattle Times* reporter who took it upon himself to preserve historic Seattle, and this tour is packed with his sardonic wit and playful humor. It's very informative, too—if you're interested in the general history of the city or salty anecdotes about Seattle's early denizens, you'll appreciate it that much more. Younger kids will probably be bored, as there's not much to see at the specific sites, which are more used as launching points for the stories. ■TIP➡ **Comfortable shoes, a love for quirky historical yarns, and an appreciation of bad puns are musts.** Several tours are offered daily, and schedules change month to month: call or visit the website for a full list of tour times. ✉ *608 1st Ave., Pioneer Square* ☎ *206/682–4646* ⊕ *www.undergroundtour.com* ✆ *$18* ☉ *May–Sept., dailt 9–7; Oct.–Apr., daily 10–6.*

Foster/White Gallery. One of the Seattle art scene's heaviest hitters has digs as impressive as the works it shows: a century-old building with high ceilings and 7,000 square feet of exhibition space. Works by internationally acclaimed Northwest masters Kenneth Callahan, Mark Tobey, Alden Mason, and George Tsutakawa are on permanent display. ✉ *220 3rd Ave. S, Pioneer Square* ☎ *206/622–2833* ⊕ *www.fosterwhite. com* ✆ *Free* ☉ *Tues.–Sat. 10–6.*

Fodor's Choice ★ **G. Gibson Gallery.** Vintage and contemporary photography is on exhibit in this elegant corner space, including work by the likes of Michael Kenna, Walker Evans, Jule Blackman, Lori Nix, and JoAnn Verburg. The gallery also shows contemporary paintings, sculpture, and mixed-media pieces. The gallery's taste is always impeccable and shows rotate every six weeks. ✉ *300 S. Washington St., Pioneer Square* ☎ *206/587–4033* ⊕ *www.ggibsongallery.com* ✉ *Free* ☺ *Wed.–Sat. 11–5 and Tues. by appointment.*

Fodor's Choice ★ **Greg Kucera Gallery.** One of the most important destinations on the First Thursday gallery walk, this gorgeous space is a top venue for national and regional artists. Be sure to check out the outdoor sculpture deck on the second level. If you have time for only one gallery visit, this is the place to go. You'll see big names that you might recognize—along with newer artists—and the thematic group shows are always thoughtful and well presented. ✉ *212 3rd Ave. S., Pioneer Square* ☎ *206/624–0770* ⊕ *www.gregkucera.com* ✉ *Free* ☺ *Tues.–Sat. 10:30–5:30.*

Occidental Park. This shady, picturesque cobblestone park is the geographical heart of the historic neighborhood—on first Thursdays it's home to a variety of local artisans setting up makeshift booths. Grab a sandwich or pastry at the Grand Central Bakery (arguably the city's finest artisanal bakery) and get in some good people-watching at the outdoor patio. Note that this square is a spot where homeless people congregate; you're likely to encounter more than a few oddballs. The square is best avoided at night. ✉ *Occidental Ave. S and S. Main St., Pioneer Square.*

Smith Tower. When this iconic landmark opened on July 4, 1914, it was the tallest office building outside New York City and the fourth tallest building in the world. (It remained the tallest building west of the Mississippi for nearly 50 years.) The Smith Tower Observation Deck on the 35th floor is an open-air wraparound deck providing panoramic views of the surrounding historic neighborhood, ball fields, the city skyline, and the mountains on clear days. The ride to the Observation Deck is via a manually-operated elevator (the last on the West Coast) and the ground floor was recently restored and returned to its original 1914 footprint as part of a $28 million restoration. ✉ *506 2nd Ave. S, Pioneer Square* ☎ *206/622–4004* ⊕ *www.smithtower.com* ✉ *$7.50* ☺ *May–Sept., daily 10–7; Oct.–Apr., daily 10–5.*

Stonington Gallery. You'll see plenty of cheesy tribal art knockoffs in tourist-trap shops, but this elegant gallery will give you a real look at the best contemporary work of Northwest Coast and Alaska tribal members (and artists from these regions working in the native style). Three floors exhibit wood carvings, paintings, sculpture, and mixed-media pieces from the likes of Robert Davidson, Joe David, Preston Singeltary, Susan Point, and Rick Barto. ✉ *119 S. Jackson St., Pioneer Square* ☎ *206/405–4040* ⊕ *www.stoningtongallery.com* ✉ *Free* ☺ *Weekdays 10–6, Sat. 10–5:30, Sun. noon–5.*

INTERNATIONAL DISTRICT

Bright welcome banners, 12-foot fiberglass dragons clinging to lampposts, and a traditional Chinese gate confirm you're in the International District. The I.D., as it's locally known, is synonymous with delectable dining—it has many inexpensive Chinese restaurants (this is the neighborhood for barbecued duck and all manner of dumplings), but the best eateries reflect its Pan-Asian spirit: Vietnamese, Japanese, Malay,

Filipino, Cambodian. With the endlessly fun Uwajimaya shopping center, the gorgeously redesigned Wing Luke Museum, and several walking tours to choose from, you now have something to do in between bites.

A GOOD COMBO

For a great day of walking and exploring, start your day with breakfast at Pike Place Market, then bus, cab, or stroll down 1st Avenue to Pioneer Square (you'll pass SAM en route—another option!). After visiting some art galleries (which generally open between 10:30 and noon) and stopping at any of the neighborhood's coffee shops (such as Zeitgeist or Grand Central Bakery), walk southeast to the International District for some retail therapy at Uwajimaya and a visit to the Wing Luke Museum. Then cab it back to your hotel.

Kubota Garden. A serene 20 acres of streams, waterfalls, ponds, and rock outcroppings were created by Fujitaro Kubota, a 1907 emigrant from Japan. The gardens on the Seattle University campus and the Japanese Garden at the Bloedel Reserve on Bainbridge Island are other examples of his work. The garden, a designated historical landmark of the city of Seattle, is free to visitors and tours are self-guided, though you can go on a docent-led tour on the fourth Saturday of every month, April through October, at 10 am. ⊠ *9817 55th Ave. S, Mt. Baker* ⊹ *From I–5, take Exit 158 and turn left toward Martin Luther King Jr. Way; continue up the hill on Ryan Way. Turn left on 51st Ave. S, then right on Renton Ave. S and right on 55th Ave. S to the parking lot.* ☎ *206/684–4584* ⊕ *www. kubota.org* ⊟ *Free* ☾ *Open daily during daylight hours.*

FAMILY

Fodor'sChoice

★

Uwajimaya. This huge, fascinating Japanese supermarket is a feast for the senses. A 30-foot-long red Chinese dragon stretches above colorful mounds of fresh produce and aisles of delicious packaged goods—colorful sweets and unique savory treats from countries throughout Asia. A busy food court serves sushi, Japanese bento-box meals, Chinese stir-fry combos, Korean barbecue, Hawaiian dishes, Vietnamese spring rolls, and an assortment of teas and tapioca drinks. You'll also find authentic housewares, cosmetics (Japanese-edition Shiseido), toys (Hello Kitty) and more. There's also a fantastic branch of the famous Kinokuniya bookstore chain, selling many Asian-language books. The large parking lot is free for one hour with a minimum $7.50 purchase or two hours with a minimum $15 purchase—don't forget to have your ticket validated by the cashiers. ⊠ *600 5th Ave. S, International District* ☎ *206/624–6248* ⊕ *www.uwajimaya.com* ☾ *Mon.–Sat. 8 am–10 pm, Sun. 9–9.*

FAMILY

Fodor'sChoice

★

Wing Luke Museum of the Asian Pacific American Experience. The only museum in the United States devoted to the Asian Pacific American experience provides a sophisticated and often somber look at how immigrants and their descendants have transformed (and been transformed by) American culture. The evolution of the museum has been driven by community participation—the museum's library has an oral history lab, and many of the rotating exhibits are focused around stories from longtime residents and their descendants. Museum admission includes a guided walk and talk tour through the East Kong Yick building, where scores of immigrant workers from China, Japan, and

9

A striking show at Greg Kucera Gallery

the Philippines first found refuge in Seattle. ✉ *719 S. King St., International District* ☎ *206/623–5124* ⊕ *www.wingluke.org* ✉ *$12.95, free 1st Thurs. and 3rd Sat. of month* ☾ *Tues.–Sun. 10–5.*

FIRST HILL

Smack between Downtown and Capitol Hill, First Hill is an odd mix of sterile-looking medical facilities (earning it the nickname "Pill Hill"), old brick buildings that look like they belong on a college campus, and newer residential towers. The main draws of the neighborhood are the Frye Art Museum, which is well worth a detour, and the fantastic historic Sorrento Hotel.

Frye Art Museum. In addition to its beloved permanent collection—predominately 19th- and 20th-century pastoral paintings—the Frye hosts eclectic and often avant-garde exhibits, putting this elegant museum on par with The Henry in the U-District. No matter what's going on in the stark, brightly lighted back galleries, it always seems to blend well with the permanent collection, which is rotated regularly. Thanks to the legacy of Charles and Emma Frye, the museum is always free, and parking is free as well. ✉ *704 Terry Ave., First Hill* ☎ *206/622–9250* ⊕ *www.fryemuseum.org* ✉ *Free* ☾ *Tues.–Sat. 11–5 (Thurs. until 8), Sun. noon–5.*

CAPITOL HILL

The Hill has two faces: on one side, it's young and edgy, full of artists, musicians, and students. Tattoo parlors and coffeehouses abound, as well as thumping music venues and bars. On the other side, it's elegant and upscale, with tree-lined streets, 19th-century mansions, and John Charles Olmsted's Volunteer Park and the Seattle Asian Art Museum. Converted warehouses, modern high-rises, colorfully painted two-story homes, and brick mansions all occupy the same neighborhood. There are parks aplenty and cute, quirky shops to browse, including one of the best bookstores in the city.

> **GALLERY WALKS**
>
> It's fun to simply walk around Pioneer Square and pop into galleries. South Jackson Street to Yesler between Western and 4th Avenue South is a good area. The first Thursday of every month, galleries stay open late for First Thursday Art Walk, a neighborhood highlight. Visit ⊕ *www.firstthursdayseattle.com.*

Volunteer Park and the Seattle Asian Art Museum. Nestled amongst the grand homes of North Capitol Hill sits this 45-acre grassy expanse that's perfect for picnicking, sunbathing (or stomping in rain puddles), and strolling. You can tell this is one of the city's older parks by the size of the trees and the rhododendrons, many of which were planted more than a hundred years ago. The Olmsted Brothers, the premier landscape architects of the day, helped with the final design in 1904; the park has changed surprisingly little since then. In the center of the park is the **Seattle Asian Art Museum (SAAM, a branch of the Seattle Art Museum)**, housed in a 1933 art moderne–style edifice. It fits surprisingly well with the stark plaza stretching from the front door to the edge of a bluff, and with the lush plants of Volunteer Park. The museum's collections include thousands of paintings, sculptures, pottery, and textiles from China, Japan, India, Korea, and several Southeast Asian countries. ⊠ *Park entrance, 1400 East Prospect St., Capitol Hill* ☎ *206/654–3100 museum, 206/684–4743 conservatory* 🖾 *Park free; museum $7, free 1st Thurs. (all day), 2nd Thurs. (5–9), and 1st Sat. (families)* ☉ *Park daily sunrise–sunset; museum Wed.–Sun. 10–5 (Thurs. until 9); conservatory Tues.–Sun. 10–4.*

FAMILY

Fodor's Choice

★

Washington Park Arboretum. As far as Seattle's green spaces go, this 230-acre arboretum is arguably the most beautiful. On calm weekdays, the place feels really secluded. The seasons are always on full display: in warm winters, flowering cherries and plums bloom in its protected valleys as early as late February, while the flowering shrubs in Rhododendron Glen and Azalea Way bloom March through June. In autumn, trees and shrubs glow in hues of crimson, pumpkin, and lemon; in winter, plantings chosen specially for their stark and colorful branches dominate the landscape. March through October, visit the peaceful **Japanese Garden**, a compressed world of mountains, forests, rivers, lakes, and tablelands. The pond, lined with blooming water irises in spring, has turtles and brightly colored koi. An authentic Japanese teahouse is reserved for tea ceremonies and instruction on the art of

9

serving tea (visitors who would like to enjoy a bowl of tea and sweets can purchase a $7 "Chado" tea ticket at the garden ticket booth). The Graham Visitors Center at the park's north end has descriptions of the arboretum's flora and fauna (which include 130 endangered plants), as well as brochures, a garden gift shop, and walking-tour maps. Free tours are offered most of the year; see website for schedule. ✉ *2300 Arboretum Dr. E, Capitol Hill* ☎ *206/543–8800 arboretum, 206/684–4725 Japanese garden* ⊕ *www.depts.washington.edu/uwbg* ✉ *Free, Japanese garden $6* ⊙ *Park open daily 7 am–sunset; visitor center daily 10–4. Japanese garden May–Aug., daily 10–8, hrs vary seasonally, call to confirm.*

FREMONT AND PHINNEY RIDGE

For many years, Fremont enjoyed its reputation as Seattle's weirdest neighborhood, home to hippies, artists, bikers, and rat-race dropouts. But Fremont has lost most of its artist cachet as the stores along its main strip turned more upscale, and rising rents sent many longtime residents reluctantly packing (many to nearby Ballard). On weekend nights, the so-called Downtown strip sometimes looks like one big party, as a bunch of bars draw in a young crowd. Mostly residential Phinney Ridge, above Fremont, is home to the wonderful Woodland Park Zoo; it also shares the booming commercial street of Greenwood Avenue North with its neighbor to the north, Greenwood. Although not as strollable as similar districts in Fremont or Ballard, Greenwood Avenue has a lot of boutiques, coffee shops, and restaurants that range from go-to diner food to pricey Pacific Northwest.

FAMILY **Theo Chocolate Factory.** If it weren't for a small sign on the sidewalk pointing the way, you'd never know that Fremont has its own chocolate factory. Theo has helped to boost the Northwest's growing artisan chocolate scene and has taken the city by storm, thanks to high-quality chocolate creations. Theo uses only organic, Fair Trade cocoa beans, usually in high percentages—yielding darker, less-sweet, and more complex flavors than some of their competitors. You'll see Theo chocolate bars for sale in many local businesses, from coffee shops to grocery stores. Stop by the factory to buy exquisite "confection" truffles—made daily in small batches—with unusual flavors like basil-ganache, lemon, fig-fennel, and burnt sugar. The super-friendly staff is known to be generous with samples. You can go behind the scenes as well: informative, yummy tours are offered daily; reservations aren't always necessary, but it's a good idea to reserve ahead, particularly on weekends. ✉ *3400 Phinney Ave. N, Fremont* ☎ *206/632–5100* ⊕ *www.theochocolate.com* ✉ *Tour $10* ⊙ *Store daily 10–6. Daily tours on the half hour 10:30–4:30, except for 1:30.*

FAMILY **Woodland Park Zoo.** Ninety-two acres are divided into bioclimatic zones here, allowing many animals to roam freely in habitat areas. A jaguar exhibit is the center of the Tropical Rain Forest area, where rare cats, frogs, and birds evoke South American jungles. The Humboldt penguin exhibit is environmentally sound—it uses geothermal heating and cooling to mimic the climes of the penguins' native home, the coastal areas of Peru. With authentic thatch-roof buildings, the African Village has a replica schoolroom overlooking animals roaming the savanna; the Elephant Forest trail takes you through the Thai Village; and the Northern Trail winds past rocky habitats where brown bears, wolves, mountain goats, and otters scramble and play. The Reserve Zoomazium is a nature-themed indoor playspace for toddlers and young kids, and the Woodland Park Rose Garden (free; located near the zoo's South Entrance) is always a hit. ⌧ *5500 Phinney Ave. N, Phinney Ridge* ☏ *206/548–2000* ⊕ *www.zoo.org* ✉ *Oct.–Apr. $12.75, May–Sept. $18.75* ⊘ *Oct.–Apr., daily 9:30–4; May–Sept., daily 9:30–6.*

BALLARD

Ballard is Seattle's sweetheart. This historically Scandinavian neighborhood doesn't have major sights outside of the Hiram M. Chittenden Locks, though it's also home to one of Seattle's most beloved and beautiful public beaches, Golden Gardens Park, which looks out at panoramic views of the Puget Sound and Olympic Mountains. The water is too cold for swimming, but Golden Gardens features picnic areas, hiking trails, and a wetland marsh where visitors might see a variety of ducks, geese, eagles and blackbirds. The Ballard Avenue Historic District is a place to check out lovely old buildings, along with a happening nightlife, shopping, and restaurant scene. Every Sunday, rain or shine, Ballard hosts one of the best farmers' markets in town.

FAMILY

Fodor'sChoice

★

Hiram M. Chittenden Locks. There's no doubt—there's something intriguing and eerie about seeing two bodies of water, right next to each, at different levels. The Hiram M. Chittenden Locks (also known as "Ballard Locks") are an important passage in the 8-mile Lake Washington Ship Canal that connects Puget Sound to freshwater Lake Washington and Lake Union. In addition to boat traffic, the locks see an estimated half-million salmon and trout make the journey from saltwater to fresh each summer, with the help of a fish ladder.

Families picnic beneath oak trees in the adjacent 7-acre Carl S. English Botanical Gardens; various musical performances (from jazz bands to chamber music) serenade visitors on summer weekends; and steel-tinted salmon awe spectators as they climb a 21-step fish ladder en route to their freshwater spawning grounds—a heroic journey from the Pacific to the base of the Cascade Mountains.

In the 1850s, when Seattle was founded, Lake Washington and Lake Union were inaccessible from the tantalizingly close Puget Sound. The city's founding fathers—most notably, Thomas Mercer in 1854—began dreaming of a canal that would connect the freshwater lakes and the sound. The lure of freshwater moorage and easier transport of timber and coal proved powerful, but it wasn't until 1917 that General Hiram M. Chittenden and the Army Corps of Engineers completed the Lake Washington Ship Canal and the locks that officially bear his name. More than 90 years later, the locks are still going strong. Tens of thousands of boaters pass through the locks each year, carrying more than a million tons of commercial products—including seafood, fuel, and building materials.

Guided tours of the locks are available departing from the visitor's center; however, plaques by the locks will give you plenty of information if you don't have time for a tour. ⊠ *3015 N.W. 54th St., Ballard ✥ From Fremont, head north on Leary Way NW, west on N.W. Market St., and south on 54th St.* ☎ *206/783-7059* ⊕ *www.seattle.gov/tour/locks.htm* ▭ *Free* ⊙ *Locks daily 7 am–9 pm; visitor center Thurs.–Mon. 10–4 (extended in summer). Call for free tour information.*

WALLINGFORD

The laid-back neighborhood of Wallingford is directly east of Fremont—the boundaries actually blur quite a bit. There are several lovely parks and residential streets brimming with colorful Craftsman houses. The main drag, 45th Street NW, has an eclectic group of shops, from a gourmet beer store to an erotic bakery to a Hawaiian merchant, along with a few great coffeehouses, and several notable restaurants.

FAMILY **Gas Works Park.** Far from being an eyesore, the hulking remains of an
Fodor'sChoice old 1907 gas plant actually lends quirky character to the otherwise
★ open, hilly, 20-acre park. Get a great view of Downtown Seattle while seaplanes rise up from the south shore of Lake Union; the best vantage point is from the zodiac sculpture at the top of a very steep hill, so be sure to wear appropriate walking shoes. This is a great spot for couples and families alike; the sand-bottom playground has monkey bars, wooden platforms, and a spinning metal merry-go-round. Crowds throng to picnic and enjoy outdoor summer concerts, movies, and the July 4th fireworks display over Lake Union. ■ TIP→ Gas Works can easily be reached on foot from Fremont Center, via the waterfront Burke-Gilman Trail. ⊠ *2101 N. Northlake Way, at Meridian Ave. N (the north end of Lake Union), Wallingford* ⊙ *Daily 6 am–10 pm.*

UNIVERSITY DISTRICT

The U District, as everyone calls it, is the neighborhood surrounding the University of Washington (UW or "U Dub" to locals). The campus is extraordinarily beautiful (especially in springtime, when the cherry blossoms are flowering), and the Henry Art Gallery, on its western edge, is one of the city's best small museums. Beyond that, the appeal of the neighborhood lies in its variety of cheap, delicious ethnic eateries, its proximity to the waters of Portage and Union Bays and Lake Washington, and its youthful energy.

FAMILY **Burke Museum of Natural History and Culture.** Founded in 1899, the Burke is the state's oldest museum, featuring exhibits that survey the natural history of the Pacific Northwest. Highlights include artifacts from Washington's 35 Native American tribes, dinosaur skeletons, and dioramas depicting the traditions of Pacific Rim cultures. An adjacent ethnobotanical garden is planted with species that were important to the region's Native American communities. Check out the schedule for family events and adult classes. ⊠ *University of Washington campus, 17th Ave. NE and N.E. 45th St., University District* ☎ *206/543-5590*

⊕ *www.burkemuseum.org* ⊠ *$10, free 1st Thurs. of month* ⊙ *Daily 10–5, 1st Thurs. of each month 10–8.*

Fodor'sChoice **Henry Art Gallery.** This large gallery is perhaps the best reason to take
★ a side trip to the U District and consistently presents sophisticated and thought-provoking contemporary work. Exhibits pull from many different genres and include mixed media, photography, and paintings. Richard C. Elliott used more than 21,500 bicycle and truck reflectors of different colors and sizes in his paintings that fit into the sculpture alcoves on the exterior walls of the museum; in another permanent installation, *Light Reign,* a "Skyspace" from artist James Turrell, an elliptical chamber allows visitors to view the sky. More than a few people have used this as a meditation spot; at night the chamber is illuminated by thousands of LED lights. ⊠ *University of Washington campus, 15th Ave. NE and N.E. 41st St., University District* ☎ *206/543–2280* ⊕ *www.henryart.org* ⊠ *$10* ⊙ *Tues.–Fri. 8–4, weekends 10:30–2.*

WEST SEATTLE

Cross the bridge to West Seattle and it's another world altogether. Jutting out into Elliott Bay and Puget Sound, separated from the city by the Duwamish waterway, this out-of-the-way neighborhood covers most of the city's western peninsula—and, indeed, it has an identity of its own. In summer, throngs of people hang out at Alki Beach—Seattle's taste of California—while others head for the trails and playgrounds of Lincoln Park to the west.

FAMILY **Alki Point and Beach.** In summer, this is as close to California as Seattle
Fodor'sChoice gets—and some hardy residents even swim in the cold, salty waters of
★ Puget Sound here (water temperature ranges from 46 to 56 degrees F). This 2½-mile stretch of sand has views of the Seattle skyline and the Olympic Mountains, and the beachfront promenade is especially popular with skaters, joggers, strollers, and cyclists. Year-round, Seattleites come to build sand castles, beachcomb, and fly kites; in winter, storm-watchers come to see the crashing waves. Facilities include drinking water, grills, picnic tables, phones, and restrooms; restaurants line the street across from the beach. ■TIP→ **To get here from Downtown, take either I-5 south or Highway 99 south to the West Seattle Bridge (keep an eye out, as this exit is easy to miss) and exit onto Harbor Avenue SW, turning right at the stoplight.** Alki Point is the place where David Denny, John Low, and Lee Terry arrived in September 1851, ready to found a city. The Alki Point Lighthouse dates from 1913. One of 195 Lady Liberty replicas found around the country lives near the 2700 block of Alki Avenue SW. Miss Liberty (or Little Liberty) is a popular meeting point for beachfront picnics and dates. ⊠ *1702 Alki Ave. SW, West Seattle.*

OFF THE BEATEN PATH
The Museum of Flight. Boeing, the world's largest builder of aircraft, was founded in Seattle in 1916. This facility at Boeing Field, close to Sea-Tac airport, houses one of the city's best museums, and it's especially fun for kids, who can climb in many of the aircraft and pretend to fly, make flight-related crafts, or attend special programs. The Red Barn, Boeing's original airplane factory, houses an exhibit on the history of

flight. The Great Gallery, a dramatic structure designed by Ibsen Nelson, contains more than three-dozen vintage airplanes. The Personal Courage Wing showcases World War I and World War II fighter planes, and the Charles Simonyi Space Gallery is home to the NASA Full Fuselage Space Shuttle Trainer. ☒ *9404 E. Marginal Way S, Tukwila* ⚓ *Take I–5 south to Exit 158, turn right on Marginal Way S* ☎ *206/764–5720* ⊕ *www.museumofflight.org* ⛴ *$19* ⊗ *Daily 10–5; 1st Thurs. of every month, free from 5–9 pm.*

THE EASTSIDE

The suburbs east of Lake Washington can easily supplement any Seattle itinerary. The center of East King County is Bellevue, a fast-growing city with its own Downtown core, high-end shopping, and a notable dining scene. Kirkland, north of Bellevue, has a few shops and restaurants (including fabulous Café Juanita) plus lakefront promenades. Redmond and Issaquah, to the northeast and southeast respectively, are gateways to greenery. Woodinville, north of Redmond, is the ambassador for Washington State's wine industry, with many wineries and tasting rooms. Redmond itself is home to Microsoft's gigantic campus.

WHERE TO EAT

Use the coordinate (⚓ B2) at the end of each listing to locate a site on the corresponding map.

Thanks to inventive chefs, first-rate local produce, adventurous diners, and a bold entrepreneurial spirit, Seattle has become one of the culinary capitals of the nation. Fearless young chefs have stepped in and raised the bar. Nowadays, fresh and often foraged produce, local seafood, and imaginative techniques make the quality of local cuisine even higher.

Seattle's dining scene has been stoked like a wildfire by culinary rock stars who compete on shows like *Iron Chef* and *Top Chef* and regularly dominate "best of" lists. Seattle chefs have won big in the prestigious James Beard competition—empire-builder Tom Douglas has even been named the national "Best Restaurateur." The city is particularly strong on New American, French, and Asian cuisines. Chefs continuously fine-tune what can best be called Pacific Northwest cuisine, which features fresh, local ingredients. Think nettles and mushrooms foraged in nearby forests; colorful berries, apples, and cherries grown by Washington State farmers; and outstanding seafood from the cold northern waters of the Pacific Ocean, like wild salmon, halibut, oysters, Dungeness crab, and geoduck. Seattle boasts quite a few outstanding bakeries, too, whose breads and desserts you'll see touted on many menus.

For a truly local experience, be sure to try at least one of Seattle's famous food trucks—the city's roving casual restaurants routinely make national "best of" lists. They're parked all over the city and serve up everything from authentic po'boys to Native American flatbreads to sushi, crepes, and vegan fare. Among the very best are El Camion, Marination Nation, Maximus/Minimus, and Where Ya At Matt.

Prices in the reviews are the average cost of a main course at dinner or, if dinner is not served, at lunch.

WHAT IT COSTS IN U.S. DOLLARS			
$	$$	$$$	$$$$
RESTAURANTS Under $16	$16–$24	$25–$32	Over $32

Restaurant prices are the average cost of a main course at dinner or, if dinner is not served, at lunch.

DOWNTOWN AND BELLTOWN

$$ ✕ **Boat Street Café & Kitchen.** Tables at this French–meets–Nantucket bistro often fill up with couples at night, but the lunchtime scene runs the gamut from Downtown office workers to tourists. Food is understated, fresh, and simply divine. Start with raw oysters and a crisp glass of white wine, followed by mousse pate and bibb lettuces salad, or a plate of the famous housemade pickles. Entrées, too, take advantage of whatever is in season, so expect anything from Washington pork rib chop to sockeye with fava beans. Monday through Sunday, brunch and lunch are served 10:30–2:30. ⑤ *Average main: $16* ⊠ *3131 Western Ave., Belltown* ☎ *206/632–4602* ⊕ *www.boatstreetcafe.com* ⊗ *No dinner Sun.–Mon.* ✛ *C3.*

MODERN
AMERICAN
Fodor's Choice
★

$$$ ✕ **Lola.** Tom Douglas dishes out his signature Northwest style, spiked with Greek and Mediterranean touches—another huge success for the local celebrity chef. Try a sensational tagine of suckling pig with shishito pepper; wood-grilled salmon; a variety of meat kebabs; and scrumptious spreads including hummus, tzatziki, and *harissa* (a red-pepper concoction). Booths are usually full at this bustling, dimly lighted restaurant, which anchors the Hotel Ändra. The fabulous weekend brunches are inventive: try Tom's Big Breakfast—octopus, mustard greens, cumin-spiced yogurt, bacon, and an egg. If you still have room, there are made-to-order doughnuts, too. ⑤ *Average main: $25* ⊠ *2000 4th Ave., Belltown* ☎ *206/441–1430* ✛ *E4.*

MEDITERRANEAN
Fodor's Choice
★

$ ✕ **Macrina Bakery.** One of Seattle's favorite bakeries is also popular for breakfast and brunch and an excellent place to take a delicious break on your way to or from the Olympic Sculpture Park. With its perfectly executed breads and pastries—from Nutella brioche and ginger cookies to almond croissants and dark-chocolate, sugar-dusted brownies—it's become a true Belltown institution. You can also wait for a table and have a larger breakfast or lunch—sandwiches, quiches, and salads are all yummy and fresh. There are also locations in SoDo and Queen Anne. ⑤ *Average main: $7* ⊠ *2408 1st Ave., Belltown* ☎ *206/448–4032* ⊕ *www.macrinabakery.com* ✛ *D4.*

BAKERY

$$$ ✕ **Matt's in the Market.** Your first dinner at Matt's is like a first date you hope will never end. One of the most beloved of Pike Place Market's restaurants, Matt's is now owned by Dan Bugge, who continues to value intimate dining, fresh ingredients, and superb service. An expansion nearly doubled the number of seats, and some tables are now held for walk-ins. You can perch at the bar for pints and a delicious pulled

PACIFIC
NORTHWEST
Fodor's Choice
★

9

BEST BETS FOR SEATTLE DINING

With so many restaurants to choose from, how to decide where to eat? Fodor's writers and editors have selected their favorite restaurants by price, cuisine, and experience in the Best Bets lists *below*. In the first column, Fodor's Choice properties represent the "best of the best" in every price category. Other favorites are listed by price category, cuisine, and experience.

Fodor's Choice ★

Anchovies & Olives, $$, p. 370

Boat Street Café & Kitchen, $$, p. 363

Café Juanita, $$$$, p. 375

Cascina Spinasse, $$$, p. 370

La Carta de Oaxaca, $, p. 374

Lark, $$$, p. 371

Lola, $$$, p. 363

Ma'ono, $$, p. 375

Matt's in the Market, $$$, p. 363

Monsoon, $$$, p. 371

Poppy, $$$, p. 371

Salumi Cured Meats, $, p. 368

Shiro's Sushi Restaurant, $$$, p. 365

Sitka & Spruce, $$$, p. 372

By Price

$

Café Presse, p. 370

Delancey, p. 374

Espresso Vivace, p. 368

Green Leaf, p. 369

La Carta de Oaxaca, p. 374

Macrina Bakery, p. 363

Salumi Cured Meats, p. 368

Victrola Coffee Roasters, p. 373

$$

Anchovies & Olives, p. 370

Boat Street Café & Kitchen, p. 363

How to Cook a Wolf, p. 368

Joule, p. 373

Ma'ono, p. 375

Palace Kitchen, p. 365

Quinn's, p. 371

Tamarind Tree, p. 369

$$$

Cascina Spinasse, p. 370

Lark, p. 371

Lola, p. 363

Matt's in the Market, p. 363

Monsoon, p. 371

Poppy, p. 371

Shiro's Sushi Restaurant, p. 365

Sitka & Spruce, p. 372

$$$$

Café Juanita, p. 375

Canlis, p. 365

Crush, p. 370

By Cuisine

ASIAN

Joule, $$, p. 373

Monsoon, $$$, p. 371

Tamarind Tree, $$, p. 369

ITALIAN

Café Juanita, $$$$, p. 375

Cascina Spinasse, $$$, p. 370

Il Corvo, $, p. 368

How to Cook a Wolf, $$, p. 368

Salumi Cured Meats, $, p. 368

LATIN

La Carta de Oaxaca, $, p. 374

MEDITERRANEAN

Lola, $$$, p. 363

PACIFIC NORTHWEST

Canlis, $$$$, p. 365

Matt's in the Market, $$$, p. 363

Ma'ono, $$, p. 375

Palace Kitchen, $$, p. 365

SEAFOOD

Anchovies & Olives, $$, p. 370

Seastar Restaurant and Raw Bar, $$$$, p. 368

Westward, $$, p. 373

Best by Experience

BRUNCH

Café Presse, $, p. 370

Lola, $$$, p. 363

Monsoon, $$$, p. 371

LATE-NIGHT DINING

Café Presse, $, p. 370

MOST ROMANTIC

Boat Street Café & Kitchen, $$, p. 363

Canlis, $$$$, p. 365

Lark, $$$, p. 371

pork or hot grilled-tuna sandwich or a cup of gumbo, or be seated at a table—complete with vases filled with flowers from the market—for a seasonal menu that synthesizes the best picks from the restaurant's produce vendors and an excellent wine list. Dinner entrées always include at least one catch of the day—perhaps a whole fish in saffron broth or Alaskan halibut with pea vines. ⑤ *Average main: $32* ⊠ *94 Pike St., Downtown* ☎ *206/467–7909* ⊕ *www.mattsinthemarket.com* ⊘ *Closed Sun.* ✛ *D4.*

$$
PACIFIC
NORTHWEST

✕ **Palace Kitchen.** The star of this chic yet convivial Tom Douglas eatery may be the 45-foot bar, but the real show takes place in the giant open kitchen at the back. Wood-grilled chicken wings, olive poppers, Penn Cove mussels, roast-pork ravioli, and a nightly selection of cheeses vie for your attention on the ever-changing menu of small plates. The half-pound Palace Burger Royale is one of the city's best, and there are always a few entrées, mouthwatering desserts, and a rotisserie special from the apple-wood grill. If it's after 10 pm, ask about Palace Kitchen's secret late-night breakfast menu. ⑤ *Average main: $22* ⊠ *2030 5th Ave., Belltown* ☎ *206/448–2001* ⊕ *www.tomdouglas.com* ⊘ *No lunch* ✛ *D4.*

$$$
JAPANESE
Fodor'sChoice
★

✕ **Shiro's Sushi Restaurant.** Shiro Kashiba is the most famous sushi chef in Seattle; he's been in town for more than 40 years, and still occasionally takes the time to helm the sushi bar at his popular restaurant. If you get a seat at the sushi bar in front of Shiro, don't be shy—this is one place where ordering omakase (chef's choice) is a must. Willfully unconcerned with atmosphere, this simple spot is a real curiosity amid Belltown's chic establishments, though it does seem to be charging Belltown prices for simpler pleasures like teriyaki and tempura dinners. New fans have been drawn in by the documentary film *Jiro Dreams of Sushi,* which features Shiro's Tokyo mentor, Jiro Ono; one of Jiro's other protégés, Daisuke Nakazawa, now works at Shiro's, where he's training to take over as Kashiba's successor. ⑤ *Average main: $28* ⊠ *2401 2nd Ave., Belltown* ☎ *206/443–9844* ⊕ *www.shiros.com* ⊘ *No lunch* ✛ *D4.*

SOUTH LAKE UNION AND QUEEN ANNE

$$$$
PACIFIC
NORTHWEST

✕ **Canlis Restaurant.** Canlis has been setting the standard for opulent dining in Seattle since the 1950s and although there are no longer kimono-clad waitresses, the food, the wine, the practically clairvoyant service, and the views overlooking Lake Union are still remarkable. Executive chef Jason Franey (formerly of Manhattan's acclaimed Eleven Madison Park) maintains the restaurant's signature insistence on the finest meat and the freshest produce but he has also refreshed the menu—which offers traditional multicourse and tasting options. The famous Canlis Salad of romaine, bacon, Romano cheese, and mint is always a crowd-pleaser, but the entrées are the stars here: 14-day dry-aged roasted duck breast accompanied by orange chutney, fennel, and caramelized cipollini onion, or perhaps halibut with tomato fondue and artichokes. If the dining room seems too formal, the bar menu is more wallet-friendly and you don't need a reservation. ⑤ *Average main: $48* ⊠ *2576 Aurora Ave. N, Queen Anne* ☎ *206/283–3313* ⊕ *www.canlis.com* ⬧ *Reservations essential* ⬩ *Jacket required* ⊘ *Closed Sun. No lunch* ✛ *D1.*

9

$ | **✕ Espresso Vivace.** A cozy and large outpost of the famed Capitol Hill
CAFÉ | roaster, the Vivace coffee shrine in South Lake Union is right across from the REI megastore and amid a growing number of hip boutiques and design shops. Grab a seat, order an expertly prepared espresso beverage, and munch on a small variety of snacks—this is a perfect stop after an exhausting jaunt through REI and before you head out to the next adventure. ⑤ *Average main: $3* ✉ *227 Yale Ave. N., South Lake Union* ☎ *206/388–5164* ⊕ *www.espressovivace.com* ✛ *F3.*

$$ | **✕ How to Cook a Wolf.** This sleek eatery—complete with loads of trendy
ITALIAN | young couples perched at its tables—"pays homage to M. F. K. Fisher and her philosophy of taking simple ingredients and transforming them into culinary splendor." As you would expect then, fresh, artisanal ingredients are the focus. Starters run the gamut from cured-meat platters, to roasted almonds, pork terrine, chicken-liver mousse, and arugula salad, while tasty mains focus on simple handmade pastas—orecchiette with sausage, garlic, and ricotta. Fresh skate with brown butter and capers or quail with saffron aioli are examples of the rustic-chic Italian-inspired dishes chef Ethan Stowell has perfected in his various eateries around town. This restaurant is worth the trip even if you're far from Queen Anne. ⑤ *Average main: $16* ✉ *2208 Queen Anne Ave. N, Queen Anne* ☎ *206/838–8090* ⊕ *www.ethanstowellrestaurants.com* ◔ *No lunch* ✛ *C1.*

$$$$ | **✕ Seastar Restaurant and Raw Bar.** Nestled in the Pan Pacific Hotel com-
SEAFOOD | plex on the southern edge of South Lake Union, this sleek and spacious restaurant is known for its extensive happy hour. The raw bar features sushi and such delicacies as Thai seafood salad, giant black tiger prawns, ceviche, and a Northwest oyster sampler. Delicious tempura rolls, hamburger sliders, and cedar-plank salmon are all popular. Order a chilled white wine and get comfortable in one of the spacious booths. ⑤ *Average main: $35* ✉ *Pan Pacific Hotel, 2121 Terry Ave., South Lake Union* ☎ *206/462–4364* ⊕ *www.seastarrestaurant.com* ◔ *No lunch Sat. or Sun.* ✛ *E3.*

PIONEER SQUARE

$ | **✕ Il Corvo.** It may be a Pioneer Square hole-in-the-wall, but Il Corvo
ITALIAN | serves up some of the best pasta in town. Experienced chef Mike Easton left the cooking line at higher-end restaurants to found this lunch-only (11 am to 3 pm), cash-only collection of family-style tables where he prepares a few inexpensive handmade dishes each day using antique pasta-makers and artisanal, seasonal ingredients—perhaps squid-ink perciatelli with anchovy-toasted bread crumbs or pappardelle *alla Bolognese*. The short chalkboard menu usually features an antipasto or two, as well. ⑤ *Average main: $9* ✉ *217 James St., Pioneer Square* ☎ *206/538–0999* ⊕ *www.ilcorvopasta.com* ⌕ *Reservations not accepted* ◔ *Closed weekends. No dinner* ✛ *E5.*

$ | **✕ Salumi Cured Meats.** The lines are long for hearty, unforgettable sand-
ITALIAN | wiches filled with superior house-cured meats and all other sorts of
Fodor's Choice | goodies at this shoebox shop owned by Gina Batali—sister of famed
★ | New York chef Mario Batali—and founded by their dad Armandino. The oxtail sandwich special is unbeatable, but if it's unavailable or sold

out (as specials often are by the lunchtime peak) order a salami, bresaola, porchetta, meatball, sausage, or lamb prosciutto sandwich with onions, peppers, cheese, and olive oil. Most people opt for takeout, though there is limited indoor seating. ⑤ *Average main: $9* ⊠ *309 3rd Ave. S, Pioneer Square* ☎ *206/621–8772* ⊕ *www.salumicuredmeats. com* ⊗ *Closed Sat.–Mon. No dinner* ✛ *E5.*

INTERNATIONAL DISTRICT

$ ✕ **Green Leaf Vietnamese Restaurant.** Locals pack this friendly café for
VIETNAMESE the expansive menu of fresh, well-prepared Vietnamese staples. The quality of the food—the spring rolls, *báhn xèo* (the Vietnamese version of an omelet), and lemongrass chicken are just a few standouts—and reasonable prices would be enough to make it an instant I.D. favorite. With mood lighting and stylish bamboo touches, Green Leaf also proves you don't have to sacrifice ambience to get cheap, authentic Asian food in Seattle. The staff greets everyone as though they're regulars—and there are plenty of regulars, enough to fill the small space. ■TIP➜ **If it's packed, try the Belltown branch, a large space with a full bar and late-night hours, at 2800 First Ave.** ⑤ *Average main: $11* ⊠ *418 8th Ave. S, International District* ☎ *206/340–1388* ⊕ *www.greenleaftaste. com* ✛ *F5.*

$$ ✕ **Tamarind Tree.** Wildly popular with savvy diners from all across the
VIETNAMESE city, this Vietnamese haunt on the eastern side of the I.D. *really* doesn't look like much from the outside, especially because the entrance is through a grungy parking lot (which it shares with Sichuanese Cuisine restaurant). Once you're inside, though, the elegantly simple, large, and warm space is extremely welcoming. The food is the main draw—try the spring rolls, which are stuffed with fresh herbs, fried tofu, peanuts, coconut, jicama, and carrots; authentic *bánh xèo*; spicy, authentic pho; the signature "seven courses of beef"; and, to finish, grilled banana cake with warm coconut milk. Service is attentive, but the waits can be long, even with reservations. ⑤ *Average main: $21* ⊠ *1036 S. Jackson St., International District* ☎ *206/860–1404* ⊕ *www. tamarindtreerestaurant.com* ✛ *F6.*

CAPITOL HILL

$$$$ ✕ **Altura.** A hand-carved cedar angel statue watches over diners at this
ITALIAN lively spot, where chef-owner Nathan Lockwood lends a Northwest focus to Italian cuisine. The weekly seasonal menu is presented as prix-fixe, but technically dishes are available à la carte as well. It's hard to go wrong with any of the starters or pastas: you might begin with a crudo misto of geoduck (a variety of clam) and scallops with dollops of urchin roe, then move on to pappardelle with braised tripe and oxtail ragu. Mains may include black cod with fragrant shavings of foraged matsutake mushrooms. Service is hyper-solicitous but the atmosphere is more casual and loud than you might expect given the price tag. ⑤ *Average main: $33* ⊠ *617 Broadway E, Capitol Hill* ☎ *206/402–6749* ⊕ *www.alturarestaurant.com* ⌘ *Reservations essential* ⊗ *Closed Sun. and Mon. No lunch* ✛ *F2.*

9

$$
SEAFOOD
Fodor's Choice
★

✕ **Anchovies & Olives.** Artful lighting, an exposed kitchen, a well-edited Italian and Northwest wine list, and a lively small bar are the backdrop for some of the best, and most elegant, seafood dishes in the city at this sophisticated Ethan Stowell restaurant in the ground floor of a residential high-rise at the eastern end of the Pike–Pine Corridor. Appetizer plates are small and easily shared, while mains from the changing menu might include mackerel with cauliflower and radicchio; skate wing with asparagus and saffron leeks; clams with pine nuts and hot pepper; and octopus with corona beans and fennel. The "oyster power hour," from 5 to 6 pm, Sunday through Thursday, is popular for $1 oysters and drink specials. Dinner reservations are highly recommended. ⑤ *Average main: $24* ✉ *1550 15th Ave., at Pine St., Capitol Hill* ☎ *206/838–8080* ⊕ *ethanstowellrestaurants.com/anchoviesandolives* ⊙ *No lunch* ✛ *G4.*

$
FRENCH

✕ **Café Presse.** Two distinct rooms create plenty of space at this French bistro just off the Pike–Pine Corridor, where you can get such Parisian fare as pressed chicken with greens; a *croque madame*; mussels with french fries; pan-roasted quail with sautéed potatoes and apples; and simple cheese platters with slices of baguette. This is the spot to order some red table wine and people-watch. A quirky, low-key vibe pervades this beloved Capitol Hill haunt, thanks in part to Seattle University, which is just steps away. It's equally good for early birds and night owls, open from the 7 am *petit dejeuner* until 2 am. Reservations are only accepted for dinner. ⑤ *Average main: $15* ✉ *1117 12th Ave., Capitol Hill* ☎ *206/709–7674* ⊕ *www.cafepresseseattle.com* ✛ *F4.*

$$$
ITALIAN
Fodor's Choice
★

✕ **Cascina Spinasse.** Squeeze into this postage stamp–size eatery with its cream-colored lace curtains and true Italian soul—and come hungry, because chef Jason Stratton knows how to make pasta. It's made fresh daily and comes with such sauces and fillings as lamb or rabbit ragu, roasted carrot and goat cheese, or duck confit. *Secondi* options can range from braised pork belly with cabbage to stewed venison served over polenta. The dessert selections are lovely; a favorite is *panna cotta* with cardoon flower honey. With the friendly service and dynamite grappa, amaro, and an Italian-focused wine selection, you likely won't mind paying the price, even if the restaurant is loud and small. Reservations are recommended. For a well-crafted apertif, start out next door at Stratton's companion bar-eatery, Artusi (✉ *1535 14th Ave.*) ⑤ *Average main: $26* ✉ *1531 14th Ave., Capitol Hill* ☎ *206/251–7673* ⊕ *www. spinasse.com* ⊙ *Closed Tues. No lunch* ✛ *G4.*

$$$$
MODERN
AMERICAN

✕ **Crush.** Occupying a converted two-story house, this sleek restaurant helmed by James Beard Award–winning chef Jason Wilson may have you thinking that you're Downtown, not on the southeastern edge of Capitol Hill. The food is very good, even sublime: braised short ribs are Crush's signature dish, and they're so delicious that the menu could begin and end right there. Seafood dishes are also superbly executed, such as seared sea scallops with baby leeks and porcini. Despite the clamor for a table on the weekend, servers remain serene and you'll never be rushed out the door. For a budget-minded taste of Wilson's wizardry, go for happy hour. ⑤ *Average main: $34* ✉ *2319 E. Madison St., Madison Park* ☎ *206/302–7874* ⊕ *www.chefjasonwilson.com* ✍ *Reservations essential* ⊙ *Closed Mon., no lunch* ✛ *H3.*

$$$
MODERN
AMERICAN
Fodor'sChoice
★

✕ Lark. The Central Agency Building, a converted 1917 warehouse with 25-foot ceilings, is the setting for mouthwateringly delicious small plates to share—you'll want to sample as much as possible. The expert servers can help you choose from an impressive wine list, and will happily help you decide from a menu divided into cheese; vegetables and grains; charcuterie; fish; meat; and, of course, dessert. Seasonally inspired dishes may include chicken-liver parfait with grilled ramps; carpaccio of yellowtail with preserved lemons; veal sweetbreads with black truffle; and poached organic egg with chorizo. For dessert try the Theo-chocolate madeleines, which come wrapped in a white napkin with a small pot of dipping chocolate. Reservations recommended, though the new location will have a full bar, easing the wait for walk-ins. ■TIP→ **Be sure to check out the building's other foodie-friendly offerings.** Ⓢ *Average main: $28* ⊠ *952 E. Seneca St., Capitol Hill* ☎ *206/323–5275* ⊕ *www.larkseattle.com* ☉ *Closed Mon. No lunch* ✢ *G3.*

$$$
VIETNAMESE
Fodor'sChoice
★

✕ Monsoon. With a recent expansion that nearly doubled its space—and added an elegant tiled bar—this serene Vietnamese restaurant on a tree-lined residential stretch of Capitol Hill is a better bet than ever. Upscale fare blending Vietnamese and Pacific Northwest elements includes wild gulf prawns with lemongrass, catfish clay pot with fresh coconut juice and green onion, and lamb with fermented soybeans and sweet onions. Homemade ice creams include lychee and mango, but the restaurant's most famous dessert is the coconut crème caramel. The wine cellar has nearly 250 varieties, including many French selections. ■TIP→ **The weekend brunch—which serves traditional Vietnamese offerings, dim sum, and "colonial" favorites like French toast and eggs en cocotte—is divine.** Ⓢ *Average main: $25* ⊠ *615 19th Ave. E, Capitol Hill* ☎ *206/325–2111* ⊕ *www.monsoonrestaurants.com* ✢ *G3.*

$$$
MODERN
AMERICAN
Fodor'sChoice
★

✕ Poppy. Jerry Traunfeld's bright, airy restaurant on the northern end of Broadway is a feast for the senses, with funky design details, friendly staff, and a happening bar area. Start with one of the many interesting cocktails and an order of eggplant fries with sea salt and honey; then peruse the menu, which offers small plates and *thali* of various sizes—the idea is inspired by the Indian thali meal, in which a selection of different dishes is served in small compartments on a large platter, though the food here is mainly seasonal New American cuisine with occasional Asian accents. Dinner might include items like braised Wagyu beef cheek with ginger, rhubarb pickles, onion-poppy naan, and roasted halibut with saffron leeks. The concept may be gimmicky but somehow each small-portioned delight seems better than the last. Ⓢ *Average main: $28* ⊠ *622 Broadway E., Capitol Hill* ☎ *206/324–1108* ⊕ *www.poppyseattle.com* ☉ *No lunch* ✢ *F2.*

$$
BRITISH

✕ Quinn's. Capitol Hill's coolest gastropub has friendly bartenders, an *amazing* selection of beers on tap (with the West Coast and Belgium heavily represented), an extensive list of whiskey, and an edgy menu of good food, which you can enjoy at the long bar or at a table on either of the two floors of the industrial-chic space. Spicy fried peanuts and country-style rabbit pâté are good ways to start—then you can choose from Painted Hills beef tartare with pumpernickel crisps, perfect marrow bones with baguette and citrus jam, or a cheese plate.

9

A pared-down pub menu is also available from 3 pm to midnight or later. The folks here take their libations seriously, so feel free to chat up the bartenders about their favorites. $ *Average main: $17* ✉ *1001 E. Pike St., Capitol Hill* ☏ *206/325–7711* ⊕ *www.quinnspubseattle.com* ⌦ *Reservations not accepted* ⊘ *No lunch* ✛ *F4.*

$$$
BRASSERIE

✕ **Red Cow.** One of the latest from restaurateur Ethan Stowell—and a well-received departure from his usual Italian fare—this new French brasserie in beautiful tree-lined Madrona serves up excellent house-made charcuterie and expertly prepared grass-finished beef. A 10-minute trip from Downtown or Capitol Hill, Red Cow is a bustling modern space with knowledgeable, personable servers. Start with a selection of the restaurant's many nose-to-tail delicacies, such as lamb terrine, beef marrow, or a chicken-liver mousse so exquisite you'll want to scrape up every last bit of it with a side of frites. Beef cuts range from a flavorful hanger steak to a splurge-worthy New York strip from Mishima Ranch; if you can't decide on one classic sauce (béarnaise, compound butter, red-wine reduction, and horseradish cream), ask for a sampling of all four. Other entrées include fresh local shellfish and a succulent half roast chicken. A well-curated wine list—several bottles cost less than $40—features French imports alongside a noteworthy selection of Northwest whites and reds. $ *Average main: $30* ✉ *1423 34th Ave., Madrona* ☏ *206/454–7932* ⊘ *No lunch* ✛ *H4.*

$$$
MODERN
AMERICAN
Fodor'sChoice
★

✕ **Sitka & Spruce.** James Beard Award–winner Matthew Dillon helms this popular restaurant at Capitol Hill's Melrose Market. Romantic, chic, friendly, and cutting edge all at once, S&S is a heaven for foodies—try to snag a table at the large butcher block that extends from the chef's kitchen for a view of the cooks at work. Choose from seasonally-rotating offerings such as king bolete mushrooms with blistered fava beans, whole baby turnips in tarragon with house-made yogurt with za'atar spice, and deliciously tender charcoal-grilled chicken served with rye berries grown in nearby Winthrop. The sourdough bread baked at Dillon's Georgetown project, The Corson Building, is a deal even at $5.50 (fancy butters and spreads included). Mondays the menu is given over to inventive guest chefs. ■TIP➔ Read more about the hip Melrose Market—home to a fishmonger, butcher, and more—in the shopping section. $ *Average main: $29* ✉ *1531 Melrose Ave., Capitol Hill* ☏ *206/324–0662* ⊕ *www.sitkaandspruce.com* ✛ *E4.*

$
AMERICAN

✕ **Skillet Diner.** Diner fare takes a modern turn on Capitol Hill at this stylishly retro, brick-and-mortar version of one of the city's preeminent food trucks. Skillet's hot, strong coffee is made with beans from the local Fonté micro-roastery, while their burgers are ridiculously savory, topped with signature "bacon jam" and blue cheese (max out the decadence with a side of cheesy poutine). A kale Caesar salad and a fried chicken "sammy" sporting a fennel seed crust are other signs you're not in the '50s anymore. Sit on counter stools or in comfy avocado-green booths, but allow plenty of time—while service is cheerful and prompt, lunch-hour and weekend breakfast waits are lengthy. ■TIP➔ A second location in Ballard usually isn't quite as slammed. $ *Average main: $14* ✉ *1400 E. Union, Capitol Hill* ☏ *206/512–2000* ⊕ *www. skilletstreetfood.com* ⌦ *Reservations not accepted* ✛ *G4.*

$ × **Victrola Coffee Roasters.** Victrola is probably the most loved of Capitol
CAFÉ Hill's many coffeehouses, and it's easy to see why: the sizable space is
lovely—the walls are hung with artwork by local painters and photographers—the coffee and pastries are fantastic, the baristas are skillful,
and everyone, from soccer moms to indie rockers, is made to feel like
this neighborhood spot exists just for them. If 15th Avenue E is too far
off the beaten path for you, there are also branches at 310 East Pike
Street (☎ 206/462–6259), between Melrose and Bellevue, as well as
in Beacon Hill. $ *Average main: $3* ✉ *411 15th Ave. E, Capitol Hill*
☎ *206/462–6259* ⊕ *www.victrolacoffee.com* ⌖ *G3.*

FREMONT

$$ × **Joule.** Married chef/owners Rachel Yang and Seif Chirchi have wowed
KOREAN Seattle diners with their French-fusion spins on Asian cuisine here and
at nearby Revel. Joule's nouvelle take on a Korean steak house serves
meat options like Wagyu bavette steak with truffled pine nuts and short
rib with Kalbi and grilled kimchi. Non-meat menu items include Chinese broccoli with walnut pesto and mackerel with green curry cilantro
crust and black currant, while a weekend brunch buffet goes slightly
more mainstream with a fruit and pastry buffet, as well as entrées like
oatmeal-stuffed porchetta. ■**TIP**➜ **If Joule is packed, try The Whale
Wins (from award-winning Boat Street chef Renee Erickson) next door.
Both are part of the very cool Fremont Collective building.** $ *Average
main: $19* ✉ *3506 Stone Way N, Fremont* ☎ *206/632–1913* ⊕ *www.
joulerestaurant.com* ☾ *No lunch* ⌖ *D1.*

$$ × **Revel.** Adventurous enough for the most committed gourmands but
ASIAN FUSION accessible enough to be a neighborhood lunchtime favorite, Revel starts
with Korean street food and shakes it up with a variety of influences,
from French to Americana. Noodle dishes at this popular, sleek spot (try
for a counter seat overlooking the open kitchen) might feature smoked
tea noodles with roast duck or seaweed noodles with Dungeness crab,
while irresistibly spicy dumplings might be stuffed with bites of short
ribs, shallots, and scallions, or perhaps chickpeas, roasted cauliflower,
and mustard yogurt. Plates are small enough so that you can save room
for one of the playful desserts riffing off Junior Mints or butterscotch
pudding. $ *Average main: $22* ✉ *403 N. 36th St., Fremont* ☎ *206/547–
2040* ⊕ *www.revelseattle.com* ⌖ *D1.*

$$ × **Westward.** Between the stunning lakefront setting, fabulously fresh
SEAFOOD seafood, and clever nautical decor, this place has made a huge splash in
Seattle's dining scene. The attention to detail borders on fanatical—the
restaurant's designer even earned the title "Director of Vibe"—from
the diorama-filled bar backdrop to the outdoor deck with picnic tables,
striped umbrellas, and a fire pit. Start with freshly shucked oysters at
Westward's popular oyster bar, and move on to baked gigante beans and
braised Anderson Ranch lamb shoulder pulled out of a wood-burning
oven and served with tzatziki and pita. The hot spot on Lake Union
has earned national accolades for its ambience and tasty food. An all-
day weekend menu and Adirondack beach chairs make it all the more
inviting. $ *Average main: $22* ✉ *2501 N. Northlake Way, Wallingford*

9

☎ *206/552–8215* ⊕ *www.westwardseattle.com* ☾ *No lunch weekdays* ✛ *F1.*

BALLARD

$ ✕ **Café Besalu.** A slice of France here in Ballard, this small, casual bak-
BAKERY   ery gets patrons from across the entire city, thanks to its *I-swear-I'm-
in-Paris* croissants—they are buttery, flaky perfection. Weekend lines
are long, but if you score a table, you'll be in heaven. You can also, of
course, take pastries to go, which is perfect if you're en route to Golden
Gardens. Apple turnovers, *pain au chocolat,* decent espresso drinks,
quiches, and sandwiches round out the offerings. Note that Besalu is a
bit north of downtown Ballard on 24th Avenue, but the walk is worth it.
■ TIP➔ Besalu has twice-yearly weekly closures, usually after Christmas and around July 4, so call ahead. $ *Average main: $8* ⊠ *5909 24th
Ave. NW, Ballard* ☎ *206/789–1463* ⊕ *www.cafebesalu.com* ☾ *Closed
Mon. and Tues.* ✛ *D1.*

$ ✕ **Delancey.** Brandon Pettit spent years developing his thin-but-chewy
PIZZA   pizza crust, and the final product has made him a contender for the
city's best pies. Pettit himself is often manning the wood-fired oven at
this sweetly sophisticated little spot north of downtown Ballard that he
owns with wife Molly Wizenberg (author of the popular "Orangette"
food blog). Neighborhood families and far-flung travelers alike line up
before opening time for seasonal pizzas topped with anything from
fresh sausage and local clams to blistered padron peppers and crimini
mushrooms. The small wine list is well edited and elegant; desserts are
simple but inspired—the homemade chocolate chip cookie with sea salt
is delish. ■ TIP➔ Long wait? Pop next door to charming Essex, the couple's artisanal cocktail bar. $ *Average main: $14* ⊠ *1415 N.W. 70th St.,
Ballard* ☎ *206/838–1960* ⊕ *www.delanceyseattle.com* ☾ *Closed Mon.
and Tues. No lunch* ✛ *D1.*

$ ✕ **Hot Cakes.** A few savory dishes are available at this Ballard "cak-
CAFÉ   ery," but consider passing on the chicken pot pie in favor of the grilled
chocolate sandwich. Autumn Martin, formerly head chocolatier at Theo
Chocolate, specializes in creative, high-quality desserts (including vegan
options) such as a "s'mores" molten chocolate cake with house-made
marshmallows and caramel, and cookies with house-smoked chocolate chips. Thick, rich milk shakes come in gourmet seasonal flavors
like Meyer lemon with lavender, or grown-up "boozy" shakes like
smoked chocolate and scotch. Hot Cakes is open late night, too. A
few long communal tables make for casual dining. ■ TIP➔ The company's take-and-bake Mason-jar desserts make a great gift. $ *Average
main: $9* ⊠ *5427 Ballard Ave. NW, Ballard* ☎ *206/420–3431* ⊕ *www.
getyourhotcakes.com* ⤳ *Reservations not accepted* ✛ *D1.*

$ ✕ **La Carta de Oaxaca.** True to its name, this low-key, bustling Ballard
MEXICAN   favorite serves traditional Mexican cooking with Oaxacan accents. The
Fodor's Choice   *mole negro* is a must, served with chicken or pork; another standout
★   is the *albondigas* (a spicy vegetable soup with meatballs). The menu
is mostly small plates, which works to your advantage because you
won't have to choose just one savory dish. The small, casual space has
an open kitchen enclosed by a stainless-steel bar, the walls are covered

in gorgeous black-and-white photos. It gets very crowded on weekends and stays busy until late, though if you have a small party you usually don't have to wait too long for a table. $ *Average main: $15* ✉ *5431 Ballard Ave. NW, Ballard* ☎ *206/782–8722* ⊕ *www.lacartadeoaxaca. com* ⊙ *Closed Sun. No lunch Mon.* ✛ *D1.*

$$$

MODERN ITALIAN

✕ **Staple & Fancy.** The "Staple" side of this Ethan Stowell restaurant at the south end of Ballard Avenue might mean ethereal gnocchi served with corn and chanterelles, or a whole grilled branzino. But visitors to the glam remodeled historic brick building are best served by going "Fancy," meaning the chef's choice dinner where diners are asked about allergies and food preferences, then presented with several courses (technically four, but the appetizer usually consists of a few different plates) of whatever the cooks (often including Stowell himself) are playing with on the line that night—cured meats, salads made with exotic greens, handmade pastas, seasonal desserts. You won't know what's coming next, but it's usually remarkably good. $ *Average main: $28* ✉ *4739 Ballard Ave. NW, Ballard* ☎ *206/789–1200* ⊕ *www.ethanstowellrestaurants. com* ⊙ *No lunch* ✛ *E1.*

$$

SEAFOOD

✕ **The Walrus and the Carpenter.** Chef-owner Renee Erickson was inspired by the casual oyster bars of Paris to open this bustling shoebox of a restaurant on the south end of Ballard Avenue (in the rear of a historic brick building, behind Staple & Fancy). Seats fill fast at the zinc bar and the scattered tall tables where seafood fans slurp on fresh-shucked kusshis and shigokus and other local oysters, but the menu also offers refined small plates like grilled sardines with shallots and walnuts or roasted greengage plums in cream. ■TIP→ **Arrive soon after the 4 pm opening or you may be in for an exceptionally long wait. Check out Erickon's tiny Barnacle bar next door if you decide to stick it out.** $ *Average main: $24* ✉ *4743 Ballard Ave. NW, Ballard* ☎ *206/395–9227* ⊕ *www.thewalrusbar.com* ⚖ *Reservations not accepted* ✛ *E1.*

9

WEST SEATTLE

$$

PACIFIC NORTHWEST

Fodor's Choice

★

✕ **Ma'ono Fried Chicken & Whiskey.** A quietly hip vibe pervades this culinary beacon in West Seattle, where the vast bar surrounds an open kitchen. Diners of all stripes relish the Hawaiian spin on fresh and high-quality Pacific Northwest bounty. Chef Mark Fuller's famous fried chicken dinners are offered nightly, while his saiman soup with smoked ham broth, house-made noodles, mustard cabbage, and fish cake could cure any hangover. Spam musubi, Portuguese sweet bread, and other sides showcase expertly made but down-to-earth foods. There are some two-dozen whiskeys and a short cocktail list. $ *Average main: $18* ✉ *4437 California Ave. SW, West Seattle* ☎ *206/935–1075* ⊕ *www. maono.springhillnorthwest.com* ⊙ *No lunch weekdays* ✛ *D6.*

THE EASTSIDE

$$$$

ITALIAN

Fodor's Choice

★

✕ **Café Juanita.** There are so many ways for a pricey "destination restaurant" to go overboard, making itself nothing more than a special-occasion spectacle, but Café Juanita manages to get everything just right. This Kirkland space is refined without being overly posh, and the food—much of which has a Northern Italian influence—is also perfectly balanced. One bite of lauded chef Holly Smith's tender saddle of Oregon lamb with baby artichokes, fava beans, and lemon emulsion and you'll be sold. The daily fish specials are almost always worth the plunge, and the restaurant is extremely accommodating for gluten-free guests. With advance notice, she'll craft individualized tasting menus at Table 2 with its view of the kitchen. To top it all off, the restaurant has an excellent wine list. ⑤ *Average main: $35* ✉ *9702 N.E. 120th Pl., Eastside, Kirkland* ☎ *425/823–1505* ⊕ *www.cafejuanita.com* ✍ *Reservations essential* ☽ *Closed Mon. No lunch* ✛ *D6.*

$$$$

PACIFIC NORTHWEST

✕ **The Herbfarm.** You might consider fasting before dining at the Herbfarm. It's prix-fixe only and you'll get nine courses—dinner takes at least four hours and includes six fine wines (you might also want to arrange for transportation there and back). The dining room itself is reminiscent of a country estate, but before you tuck in, you'll be treated to a delightful tour of the herb garden. The set menus change roughly every other week, with clever themes like the 100-mile dinner where even the salt is harvested from local waters (if you have dietary restrictions, it's essential to call ahead). With all products coming from the restaurant's farm (including heritage pigs), or from other regional growers and suppliers, you can expect uber-fresh ingredients, including rarities like Ozette potatoes and Roy's Calais flint corn. Book a room at elegant Willows Lodge to make a true getaway of it. ⑤ *Average main: $189* ✉ *14590 N.E. 145th St., Eastside, Woodinville* ☎ *425/485–5300* ⊕ *www.theherbfarm.com* ✍ *Reservations essential* ☽ *Closed Mon.– Wed. No lunch* ✛ *D1.*

WHERE TO STAY

Use the coordinate (✛ B2) at the end of each listing to locate a site on the corresponding map. Prices in the reviews are the lowest cost of a standard double room in high season.

Hotel reviews have been shortened. For full information, visit Fodors. com.

Much like the eclectic city itself, Seattle's lodging offers something for everyone. There are grand, ornate vintage hotels; sleek and elegant modern properties; green hotels with yoga studios and enough bamboo for an army of pandas; and cozy bed-and-breakfasts with sweet bedspreads and home-cooked breakfasts. Travelers who appreciate the anonymity of high-rise chains can comfortably stay here, while guests who want to feel like family can find the perfect boutique inn to lay their heads.

WHAT IT COSTS IN U.S. DOLLARS			
$	**$$**	**$$$**	**$$$$**
HOTELS	Under $180	$180–$265	$266–$350	Over $350

Hotel prices are the lowest cost of a standard double room in high season.

WHERE SHOULD I STAY?

	Neighborhood Vibe	Pros	Cons
Downtown and Belltown	Downtown is central, with the hottest hotels with water views. If you're a fan of galleries and bars, stay in Belltown.	A day in Downtown and Belltown can take you from the Seattle Art Museum to Pike Place Market.	Parking can be pricey and hard to come by. This is not your spot if you want a quiet, relaxing respite.
Seattle Center, South Lake Union, and Queen Anne	Queen Anne boasts great water views and easy access to Downtown. South Lake Union can feel industrial.	Seattle Center's many festivals (such as Bumbershoot) means you'll have a ringside seat.	You'll be away from the key Downtown sights. Parking can be difficult.
Capitol Hill	One of Seattle's oldest and quirkiest neighborhoods, Capitol Hill has cozy accommodations.	A great place to stay if you want to mingle with creative locals in great bookstores and cafés.	If you're uncomfortable with the pierced, tattooed, or LGBT set, look elsewhere.
Fremont and Ballard	From the Woodland Park Zoo to the locks, these funky neighborhoods are excellent jumping-off points.	These quintessential Seattle 'hoods are a short trek from Downtown and have restaurants and shops.	The only lodgings to be found in Fremont are B&Bs—book ahead.
Green Lake	Laid-back and wonderfully situated near the Woodland Park Zoo and Gas Works Park.	Outdoorsy types will love the proximity to Green Lake, a great place to stroll or jog.	You won't find anything trendy here, and, after a few days, you'll have seen everything.
University District	It offers everything you'd expect from a college area—from bookstores to ethnic food.	If you're renting a car, this area offers centrality with a lower price tag for parking.	The homeless and college kids populate University Avenue ("The Ave."). Not much in the way of sightseeing.
West Seattle	In summer, West Seattle can feel a lot like Southern California: it's a fun place to stay.	Alki Beach and Lincoln Park are fun, plus great restaurants and shopping on California Avenue.	You'll need a car to stay in this very removed 'hood. The only way in or out is over a bridge.
The Eastside	Proximity to high-end malls, Woodinville wineries, and Microsoft.	Woodinville is wine HQ; Kirkland offers cute boutiques; and Bellevue is a shopping mecca.	If you're here to experience Seattle, stick to the city. Traffic is a total nightmare.

DOWNTOWN AND BELLTOWN

$ **Ace Hotel.** The Ace is a dream come true for both penny-pinching HOTEL hipsters and folks who appreciate unique minimalist decor, with such Fodor's Choice touches in the rooms as army-surplus blankets, industrial metal sinks, ★ and street art breaking up any notion of austerity; the cheapest rooms share bathrooms, which have enormous showers. **Pros:** ultratrendy but with some of the most affordable rates in town; good place to meet other travelers; free Wi-Fi. **Cons:** half the rooms have shared bathrooms; not for people who want pampering; neighborhood rife with panhandlers; lots of stairs to get to lobby. $ *Rooms from: $109* ⊠ *2423*

BEST BETS FOR SEATTLE LODGING

Fodor's offers a selective listing of lodging experiences at every price range. Here, we've compiled our top recommendations by price and experience. The very best properties are designated in the listings with the Fodor's Choice logo.

Fodor's Choice ★

11th Avenue Inn Seattle Bed & Breakfast, $, p. 382

Ace Hotel, $, p. 377

Arctic Club Seattle, $$$, p. 379

Chelsea Station Inn Bed & Breakfast, $$, p. 383

The Fairmont Olympic Hotel, $$$$, p. 379

Four Seasons Hotel Seattle, $$$$, p. 379

Greenlake Guest House, $, p. 383

Hotel 1000, $$$, p. 380

Hotel Ändra, $$, p. 380

Hotel Ballard, $$, p. 383

Hotel Monaco, $$, p. 380

Hyatt at Olive 8, $$$$, p. 380

Inn at El Gaucho, $$, p. 381

Inn at the Market, $$$, p. 381

Mayflower Park Hotel, $$, p. 381

Pan Pacific Hotel Seattle, $$$, p. 382

Shafer Baillie Mansion Bed & Breakfast, $$, p. 382

Sorrento Hotel, $$$, p. 381

By Price

$

11th Avenue Inn Seattle Bed & Breakfast, p. 382

Ace Hotel, p. 377

Gaslight Inn, p. 382

Green Tortoise Backpacker's Hotel, p. 379

Greenlake Guest House, p. 383

$$

Chelsea Station Inn Bed & Breakfast, p. 383

Hotel Ändra, p. 380

Hotel Ballard, p. 383

Hotel Max, p. 380

Hotel Monaco, p. 380

Inn at El Gaucho, p. 381

Maxwell Hotel, p. 382

Mayflower Park Hotel, p. 381

Shafer Baillie Mansion Bed & Breakfast, p. 382

$$$

Arctic Club Seattle, p. 379

Hotel 1000, p. 380

Inn at the Market, p. 381

Pan Pacific Hotel Seattle, p. 382

Sorrento Hotel, p. 381

$$$$

Alexis Hotel, p. 379

The Fairmont Olympic Hotel, p. 379

Four Seasons Hotel Seattle, p. 379

Hotel Vintage, p. 380

Hyatt at Olive 8, p. 380

By Experience

BEST VIEWS

Four Seasons Hotel Seattle, $$$$, p. 379

Inn at the Market, $$$, p. 381

GREEN FOCUS

The Fairmont Olympic Hotel, $$$$, p. 379

Hotel Monaco, $$, p. 380

Hyatt at Olive 8, $$$$, p. 380

Pan Pacific Hotel Seattle, $$$, p. 382

HOT SCENE

Ace Hotel, $, p. 377

Four Seasons Hotel Seattle, $$$$, p. 379

Hotel Ändra, $$, p. 380

Hotel Max, $$, p. 380

Motif Seattle, $$$, p. 381

BEST SPA

Four Seasons Hotel Seattle, $$$$, p. 379

Hotel 1000, $$$, p. 380

Hyatt at Olive 8, $$$$, p. 380

MOST KID-FRIENDLY

The Fairmont Olympic Hotel, $$$$, p. 379

Four Seasons Hotel Seattle, $$$$, p. 379

Hotel Monaco, $$, p. 380

Motif Seattle, $$$, p. 381

Pan Pacific Hotel Seattle, $$$, p. 382

1st Ave., Belltown ☎ *206/448–4721* ⊕ *www.acehotel.com* ⮌ *14 standard rooms, 14 deluxe rooms* ⫶◯⫶ *No meals* ✦ *D4.*

$$$$ ⊞ **Alexis Hotel.** Two historic buildings near the waterfront use exposed
HOTEL   brick, walls of windows, and nouveau-baroque touches to appeal to
aesthetes and modern romantics, and ornate leather chairs and wood-
burning fireplaces recall a different era. **Pros:** great service; close to
waterfront; unique, beautiful rooms; suites aren't prohibitively expensive. **Cons:** small lobby; not entirely soundproofed against old building
and city noise; some rooms can be a bit dark. ⑤ *Rooms from: $585*
✉ *1007 1st Ave., Downtown* ☎ *206/624–4844, 888/850–1155* ⊕ *www.
alexishotel.com* ⮌ *88 rooms, 33 suites* ⫶◯⫶ *No meals* ✦ *E5.*

$$$ ⊞ **The Arctic Club Seattle.** From the Alaskan-marble-sheathed foyer and
HOTEL   the antique walrus heads to the Northern Lights Dome room with its
Fodor'sChoice   leaded glass ceiling to fun touches like trunks for bedside tables, the
★   Arctic Club pays homage to an era of Gold Rush opulence. **Pros:** cool,
unique property; great staff; light rail and bus lines just outside the door.
Cons: not in the heart of Downtown; rooms are a bit dark; style may
be off-putting for travelers who like modern hotels; charge for Wi-Fi.
⑤ *Rooms from: $289* ✉ *700 3rd Ave., Downtown* ☎ *206/340–0340,
800/445–8667* ⊕ *thearcticclubseattle.com* ⮌ *118 rooms, 2 suites* ⫶◯⫶ *No
meals* ✦ *E5.*

$$$$ ⊞ **The Fairmont Olympic Hotel.** With marble floors, brocade chairs, mas-
HOTEL   sive chandeliers, and sweeping staircases, this old-world hotel personi-
FAMILY   fies class and elegance, with guest rooms that are lovely and light filled,
Fodor'sChoice   with French Country touches like pastel wallpaper and floral patterns.
★   **Pros:** great location; excellent service; fabulous on-site dining and ame-
nities. **Cons:** not much in the way of views; may be a little too old-
school for trendy travelers ⑤ *Rooms from: $389* ✉ *411 University St.,
Downtown* ☎ *206/621–1700, 888/363–5022* ⊕ *www.fairmont.com/
seattle* ⮌ *232 rooms, 218 suites* ⫶◯⫶ *No meals* ✦ *E4.*

$$$$ ⊞ **Four Seasons Hotel Seattle.** Just south of the Pike Place Market and
HOTEL   steps from the Seattle Art Museum, this Downtown gem is polished
FAMILY   and elegant, with Eastern accents and plush furnishings in comfortable
Fodor'sChoice   living spaces in which Pacific Northwest materials, such as stone and
★   fine hardwoods, take center stage. **Pros:** fantastic location with amaz-
ing views of Elliott Bay; large rooms with luxurious bathrooms with
deep soaking tubs; lovely spa. **Cons:** Four Seasons regulars might not
click with this modern take on the brand; street-side rooms not entirely
sound-proofed; some room views are partially obscured by industrial
sites. ⑤ *Rooms from: $575* ✉ *99 Union St., Downtown* ☎ *206/749–
7000, 800/332-3442* ⊕ *www.fourseasons.com/seattle* ⮌ *134 rooms, 13
suites* ⫶◯⫶ *No meals* ✦ *E5.*

$ ⊞ **Green Tortoise Backpacker's Hotel.** This Seattle institution is still con-
HOTEL   sidered by many to be the best deal in town—and even if you don't
own a backpack and the word "hostel" gives you the heebie-jeebies,
the impressive cleanliness makes the Tortoise an option for anyone
on a budget who doesn't mind sacrificing a little privacy. **Pros:** cheap-
est lodging in town; great place to make instant friends from around
the globe; across the street from Pike Place Market; great bike rental
program; free day storage. **Cons:** street noise; thin walls; if you don't

9

like the communal experience this isn't for you. ⑤ *Rooms from: $32* ✉ *105½ Pike St., Downtown* ☎ *206/340–1222* ⊕ *www.greentortoise. net* ⤹ *30 rooms without en suite bath* ⑪ *Breakfast* ✛ *D4.*

$$$
HOTEL
FAMILY
Fodor's Choice
★

Hotel 1000. Chic and modern yet warm and inviting, these luxurious tech-savvy rooms are full of surprising touches, including large soaking tubs that fill from the ceiling—and a cute yellow rubber ducky and bubbles for bathtime. **Pros:** useful high-tech gadgets; virtual golf club and spa; hotel is hip without being alienating. **Cons:** rooms can be dark; a small percentage of rooms without views look out on a cement wall. ⑤ *Rooms from: $289* ✉ *1000 1st Ave., Downtown* ☎ *206/957–1000, 877/315-1088* ⊕ *www.hotel1000seattle.com* ⤹ *101 rooms, 19 suites* ⑪ *No meals* ✛ *E5.*

$$
HOTEL
Fodor's Choice
★

Hotel Ändra. Scandinavian sensibility and clean, modern lines define this sophisticated hotel on the edge of Belltown, where rooms have dark fabrics and woods, with a few bright accents and geometric prints. **Pros:** hangout-worthy lobby lounge; hip vibe; excellent service; spacious rooms. **Cons:** some street noise; not family-friendly. ⑤ *Rooms from: $229* ✉ *2000 4th Ave., Belltown* ☎ *206/448–8600, 877/448–8600* ⊕ *www.hotelandra.com* ⤹ *93 rooms, 4 studios, 22 suites* ⑪ *No meals* ✛ *E4.*

$$
HOTEL

Hotel Max. Stylish rooms are on the small side, but clean and smartly designed, with a generous desk space and cool art from locals throughout the historic 1926 building, providing a hip, slightly more upscale alternative to the Ace. **Pros:** cool vibe including a craft-beer hour; clean, bright rooms at a reasonable price; walking distance to Downtown. **Cons:** can be noisy; really tiny elevator. ⑤ *Rooms from: $189* ✉ *620 Stewart St., Downtown* ☎ *206/728–6299, 866/986–8087* ⊕ *www. hotelmaxseattle.com* ⤹ *163 rooms* ⑪ *No meals* ✛ *E4.*

$$
HOTEL
FAMILY
Fodor's Choice
★

Hotel Monaco. It only takes one glimpse of the gorgeous modern-global lobby to know that this stylish boutique hotel in the heart of Downtown is a standout, and rooms carry on the image, with a palette of soft reds and gunmetal grays, beds topped with Frette linens, floor-to-ceiling drapes in a Turkish motif, and floor lamps that recall telescopes. **Pros:** near Pike Place Market and the Space Needle; welcoming public spaces; one of the best happy hours in town. **Cons:** some street-facing rooms can be a little noisy; small gym. ⑤ *Rooms from: $239* ✉ *1101 4th Ave., Downtown* ☎ *206/621–1770, 800/715-6513* ⊕ *www.monaco-seattle.com* ⤹ *152 rooms, 37 suites* ⑪ *No meals* ✛ *E5.*

$$$$
HOTEL

Hotel Vintage. Each of the stylish rooms—some of which boast marvelous views of Seattle's iconic public library—feature a vineyard-inspired palette of burgundy, taupe, and green hues, with a focus on unique interior design. **Pros:** friendly staff; beautiful, quiet rooms; caters to wine lovers; close to shopping, theaters, and the Convention Center. **Cons:** a short-but-steep uphill walk from Downtown could be tough on some travelers; small lobby; small bathrooms. ⑤ *Rooms from: $529* ✉ *1100 5th Ave., Downtown* ☎ *206/624–8000, 800/853–3914* ⊕ *www. hotelvintage-seattle.com* ⤹ *124 rooms, 1 suite* ⑪ *No meals* ✛ *E5.*

$$$$
HOTEL
Fodor's Choice
★

Hyatt at Olive 8. In a city known for environmental responsibility, being the greenest hotel in town is no small feat, and green is rarely this chic—rooms have floor-to-ceiling windows flooding the place with light along with enviro touches like dual-flush toilets, fresh-air vents, and low-flow showerheads. **Pros:** central location; superb amenities; environmental responsibility; wonderful spa. **Cons:** standard rooms have showers only; guests complain of hallway and traffic noise; translucent glass bathroom doors offer little privacy; fee for Wi-Fi. ⑤ *Rooms from: $359* ✉ *1635 8th Ave., Downtown* ☎ *206/695–1234, 800/233–1234* ⊕ *www.olive8.hyatt.com* ↗ *331 rooms, 15 suites* ¶⊙¶ *No meals* ⊹ *E4.*

$$ ⚏ **Inn at El Gaucho.** Hollywood Rat Pack enthusiasts will want to move
B&B/INN right in to these swank, retro-style, ultrachic suites done in dark wood
Fodor'sChoice with buttery leather furniture, upstairs from Belltown's beloved El Gau-
★ cho steak house and the Big Picture—a fabulous movie theater with a full bar. **Pros:** unique aesthetic; some rooms have great views; location; warm, helpful staff. **Cons:** steep stairs with no elevator; some rooms only have showers; no outdoor spaces; rooms are (purposely) dark; no on-site fitness center. ⑤ *Rooms from: $249* ✉ *2505 1st Ave., Belltown* ☎ *206/728–1133, 866/354–2824* ⊕ *www.elgaucho.com* ↗ *17 suites* ¶⊙¶ *No meals* ⊹ *D4.*

$$$ ⚏ **Inn at the Market.** From its heart-stopping views and comfortable
B&B/INN rooms to the fabulous location and amazing fifth-floor deck perched
Fodor'sChoice above Puget Sound, this is a place you'll want to visit again and again.
★ **Pros:** outstanding views from most rooms; steps from Pike Place Market; fantastic service; complimentary town-car service for Downtown locations. **Cons:** little common space; being in the heart of the action means some street noise. ⑤ *Rooms from: $315* ✉ *86 Pine St., Downtown* ☎ *206/443–3600, 800/446–4484* ⊕ *www.innatthemarket.com* ↗ *63 rooms, 7 suites* ¶⊙¶ *No meals* ⊹ *D4.*

$$ ⚏ **Mayflower Park Hotel.** Comfortable, old-world charm in the center of
HOTEL the action comes with sturdy antiques, Asian accents, brass fixtures, and
Fodor'sChoice florals. **Pros:** central Downtown location; quiet; good value; direct con-
★ nection to the airport via Light Rail and Seattle Center via the Monorail; great service. **Cons:** rooms are small; no pool. ⑤ *Rooms from: $229* ✉ *405 Olive Way, Downtown* ☎ *206/623–8700, 800/426–5100* ⊕ *www.mayflowerpark.com* ↗ *160 rooms, 29 suites* ¶⊙¶ *No meals* ⊹ *E4.*

$$$ ⚏ **Motif Seattle.** These rooms just a few blocks from Pike Place Market
HOTEL are clean and contemporary, and the higher they are, the better the sweeping views of Elliott Bay and the Olympic Mountains. **Pros:** fancy views for a more reasonable price than most; lively atmosphere; family-friendly. **Cons:** lower floors near Frolick restaurant can be noisy until late; small bathrooms. ⑤ *Rooms from: $285* ✉ *1415 5th Ave., Downtown* ☎ *206/971–8000, 855/515–1144* ⊕ *www.motifseattle.com* ↗ *319 rooms* ¶⊙¶ *No meals* ⊹ *E4.*

$$$ ⚏ **Sorrento Hotel.** If you're the type who owns a smoking jacket, names
HOTEL aged Scotch as your poison, or wants to pretend you're on the set of a
Fodor'sChoice period piece, look no further than this Italianate hotel built in 1909—
★ though guest rooms are as light as the common areas are dark, with only a few tasseled pillows and antique furnishings. **Pros:** serene and classy; fantastic service; great restaurant; fabulous beds; free Downtown car service. **Cons:** not central; rooms are a bit small (though corner suites are commodious). ⑤ *Rooms from: $285* ✉ *900 Madison St., First*

9

Hill ☎ *206/622–6400, 800/426–1265* ⊕ *www.hotelsorrento.com* ⤴ *34 rooms, 42 suites* ⏐◯⏐ *No meals* ✛ *F4.*

SOUTH LAKE UNION AND QUEEN ANNE

$$ **The Maxwell Hotel.** Colorful and funky rooms, with argyle-print chairs
HOTEL and outlines of chandeliers painted on the walls, are *the* choice for visitors frequenting the Seattle Center for opera or the ballet, or going to Teatro Zinzanni, whose huge, colorful tent is just steps from the hotel. **Pros:** free parking and shuttle; complimentary bikes; some rooms have great views of the Space Needle. **Cons:** hotel is on a busy street; pool and gym are tiny; guests complain of low water pressure. ⑤ *Rooms from: $249* ⌧ *300 Roy St., Queen Anne* ☎ *206/286–0629, 866/866–7977* ⊕ *www.themaxwellhotel.com* ⤴ *139 rooms* ⏐◯⏐ *No meals* ✛ *D2.*

$$$ **Pan Pacific Hotel Seattle.** One of the best-looking hotels in Seattle is
HOTEL a chic treat for travelers, from the stylish and comfortable modern
FAMILY rooms to the impressive views of the Space Needle and Lake Union.
Fodor'sChoice **Pros:** away from tourist throngs; feels more luxurious than it costs;
★ destination-worthy on-site drinks and dining; award-winning sustainability efforts. **Cons:** long walk to Downtown (though streetcar access and the hotel's free car service help with that); bathroom design isn't the most private. ⑤ *Rooms from: $350* ⌧ *2125 Terry Ave., South Lake Union* ☎ *206/264–8111* ⊕ *www.panpacific.com/seattle* ⤴ *130 rooms, 23 suites* ⏐◯⏐ *No meals* ✛ *E3.*

CAPITOL HILL

$ **11th Avenue Inn Seattle Bed & Breakfast.** The closest B&B to Down-
B&B/INN town offers all the charm of a classic bed-and-breakfast (exquisitely
Fodor'sChoice styled with antique beds and Oriental rugs) with the convenience of
★ being near the action. **Pros:** unpretentious take on classic B&B; free on-site parking; oozes vintage charm; wonderful owner and staff. **Cons:** although most guests are courteous, sound does carry in old houses; no kids under 12. ⑤ *Rooms from: $159* ⌧ *121 11th Ave. E, Capitol Hill* ☎ *206/720–7161* ⊕ *www.11thavenueinn.com* ⤴ *9 rooms* ⏐◯⏐ *Breakfast* ✛ *F3.*

$ **Gaslight Inn.** Rooms here range from a crow's nest with peeled-log fur-
B&B/INN niture and Navajo-print fabrics to a more traditional suite with Arts and Crafts–style furnishings, a fireplace, and stained-glass windows. **Pros:** great art collection; house and rooms are quite spacious; pool; Wi-Fi. **Cons:** breakfast is unimpressive; street parking not always easy to find. ⑤ *Rooms from: $108* ⌧ *1727 15th Ave., Capitol Hill* ☎ *206/325–3654* ⊕ *www.gaslight-inn.com* ⤴ *6 rooms with private bath; 2 rooms with shared bath* ⏐◯⏐ *Breakfast* ✛ *G3.*

$$ **Shafer Baillie Mansion Bed & Breakfast.** The opulent guest rooms and
B&B/INN suites on the second floor are large, with private baths, antique fur-
Fodor'sChoice nishings, Oriental rugs, huge windows, and lush details like ornate
★ four-poster beds; third-floor rooms, while lovely, have a more contemporary country feel, but still have private baths and large windows. **Pros:** wonderful staff; great interior and exterior common spaces; free Wi-Fi; location. **Cons:** no elevator and the walk to the third floor might

be hard for some guests; while children are allowed, some guests say the mansion isn't kid-friendly. ⑤ *Rooms from: $199* ✉ *907 14th Ave. E, Capitol Hill, Sea-Tac* ☎ *800/985–4654* ⊕ *www.sbmansion.com* ⇨ *6 rooms; 2 suites* ¹⊙¹ *Breakfast* ✛ *G2.*

FREMONT

$$ ⊞ **Chelsea Station Inn Bed & Breakfast.** The four huge suites in this 1920s
B&B/INN brick colonial have distressed hardwood floors with colorful rugs, deco-
Fodor's Choice rative fireplaces, sleeper sofas, contemporary furnishings, and a soft,
★ modern color palette, and are a convenient and luxurious jumping-off point for all the north end has to offer. **Pros:** great, unobtrusive host; huge rooms and 1½ bathrooms per suite; fabulous breakfasts and complimentary snacks. **Cons:** far from Downtown; no TVs; no elevator. ⑤ *Rooms from: $265* ✉ *4915 Linden Ave. N, Fremont* ☎ *206/547–6077* ⊕ *www.chelseastationinn.com* ⇨ *4 suites* ¹⊙¹ *Breakfast* ✛ *D1.*

GREEN LAKE

$ ⊞ **Greenlake Guest House.** Outdoorsy types, visitors who want to stay
B&B/INN in a low-key residential area, and anyone who wants to feel pampered
Fodor's Choice and refreshed will enjoy these charming rooms with such amenities as
★ private baths with jetted tubs, fluffy robes, gas fireplaces, and heated tile floors, across the street from beautiful Green Lake. **Pros:** views; thoughtful amenities and wonderful hosts; can accommodate kids over four years old; short walk to restaurants. **Cons:** 5 miles from Downtown; on a busy street. ⑤ *Rooms from: $179* ✉ *7630 E. Green Lake Dr. N, Green Lake* ☎ *206/729–8700, 866/355–8700* ⊕ *www. greenlakeguesthouse.com* ⇨ *4 rooms* ¹⊙¹ *Breakfast* ✛ *F1.*

BALLARD

$$ ⊞ **Hotel Ballard.** A historic sandstone building features a modern gray-
HOTEL and-yellow palette that melds historical details with design accents that
Fodor's Choice nod to the neighborhood's Scandinavian heritage, and many rooms
★ include views of waterways and the Olympic Mountains; eight rooftop suites are especially inviting. **Pros:** in the heart of Ballard; $15 self-park; free use of large gym with saltwater pool; fireplaces and soaking tubs in suites. **Cons:** not close to the majority of Seattle attractions. ⑤ *Rooms from: $239* ✉ *5216 Ballard Ave., Ballard* ☎ *206/789–5012* ⊕ *www. hotelballard.com* ⇨ *20 rooms, 8 suites* ¹⊙¹ *No meals* ✛ *D1.*

NIGHTLIFE

Seattle's amazing musical legacy is well known, but there's more to the arts and nightlife scenes than live music. In fact, these days, there are far more swanky bars and inventive pubs than music venues in the city. To put it bluntly, Seattle's a dynamite place to drink. You can sip overly ambitious and ridiculously named specialty cocktails in trendy lounges, get a lesson from an enthusiastic sommelier in a wine bar or restaurant, or swill cheap beer on the patio of a dive bar. Though some places have very specific demographics, most Seattle bars are egalitarian, drawing loyal regulars of all ages.

The music scene is still kicking—there's something going on every night of the week in nearly every genre of music.

In addition to its bars, Downtown and Belltown in particular have notable restaurants with separate bar areas. ■TIP➔ Nearly all of Tom Douglas's restaurants have busy after-work and weekend bar scenes, as do trendy hotel restaurants. Most restaurants have impressive bar menus, and food is often served until 11 pm, midnight, or even 1 am in some spots.

DOWNTOWN AND BELLTOWN

BARS AND LOUNGES

Alibi Room. Well-dressed locals head to this hard-to-find wood-paneled bar to sip double martinis while taking in views of Elliott Bay or studying the scripts, handbills, and movie posters that line the walls. The lower level is more crowded and casual. It's an ever-cool yet low-key, intimate place. Stop by for a drink or a meal, or stay to listen and dance to live music. Happy hour—daily noon to 6—is quiet and a good respite from the market. ✉ 85 Pike St., in Post Alley, at Pike Place Market, Downtown 📞 206/623–3180 ⊕ www.seattlealibi.com.

Black Bottle. This sleek and sexy gastro-tavern makes the northern reaches of Belltown look good. The interior is simple but stylish, with black chairs and tables and shiny wood floors. It gets crowded on nights and weekends with a laid-back but often dressed-up clientele. A small selection of beers on tap and a solid wine list (with Washington, Oregon, California, and beyond well represented) will help you wash down the sustainably sourced pub snacks, including house-smoked wild boar ribs, pork belly with kimchi, and oysters on the half shell. ✉ 2600 1st Ave., Belltown 📞 206/441–1500 ⊕ www.blackbottleseattle.com.

Purple Café and Wine Bar. Wine lovers come for the massive selection—the menu boasts 80 wines by the glass and some 600 bottles—but this place deserves props for its design, too. Despite the cavernous quality of the space and floor-to-ceiling windows, all eyes are immediately drawn to the 20-foot tower ringed by a spiral staircase that showcases thousands of bottles. Full lunch and dinner menus feature American and Pacific Northwest fare—the lobster mac 'n' cheese is especially tasty—and servers know their ideal pairings. ✉ 1225 4th Ave., Downtown 📞 206/829–2280 ⊕ www.thepurplecafe.com.

Spur. The inventive small plates and carefully planned drink menu make this a very popular nightspot and a favorite with foodies. The decor, which pays subtle photographic homage to the pioneers, fishermen, and outlaws of Seattle's past, is also a draw. Sip a bourbon-infused cocktail and munch on stellar crostini with salmon or veal sweetbreads. Spur can be a bit spendy, so it may make sense to save your visit for happy hour (Sunday to Thursday 5 to 7) or for a late-night snack (it serves a special pairing menu from 11 to 1:30). ✉ 113 Blanchard St., Belltown 📞 206/728–6706 ⊕ www.spurseattle.com.

Fodor'sChoice ★ **Zig Zag Café.** A mixed crowd of mostly locals hunts out this unique spot at Pike Place Market's Street Hill Climb (a nearly hidden stairwell leading down to the piers). In addition to pouring a perfect martini, Zig Zag features a revolving cast of memorable cocktails. A very simple, ho-hum food menu includes cheese and meat plates, bruschetta, soup, salad, olives, and nuts. A small patio is the place to be on a summery happy-hour evening. Zig Zag is friendly—retro without being obnoxiously ironic—and very Seattle, with the occasional live music show to boot. ⊠ *1501 Western Ave., Downtown* ☎ *206/625–1146* ⊕ *zigzagseattle.com.*

LIVE MUSIC

Fodor'sChoice ★ **The Crocodile.** The heart and soul of Seattle's music scene since 1991 has hosted the likes of Nirvana, Pearl Jam, and Mudhoney, along with countless other bands. There's a reason *Rolling Stone* once called the 525-person Crocodile one of the best small clubs in America. Nightly shows are complemented by cheap beer on tap and pizza right next door at Via Tribunali. All hail the Croc! ⊠ *2200 2nd Ave., Belltown* ☎ *206/441–7416* ⊕ *www.thecrocodile.com.*

Dimitriou's Jazz Alley. Seattleites dress up to see nationally known jazz artists at Dimitriou's. The cabaret-style theater, where intimate tables for two surround the stage, runs shows nightly. Those with reservations for cocktails or dinner, served during the first set, receive priority seating. ⊠ *2033 6th Ave., Downtown* ☎ *206/441–9729* ⊕ *www.jazzalley.com.*

Showbox. Just across from Pike Place Market, this venue—which turned 75 in 2014—is a great spot to see some pretty big-name acts. The acoustics are decent, the room's small enough that you don't feel like you're miles away from the performers, and the bar areas flanking the main floor provide some relief if you don't want to join the crush in front of the stage. Another branch, **Showbox SoDo** (⊠ *1700 1st Ave. S, SoDo*), is named for its location south of Downtown; the converted warehouse, larger than the original, features big national acts. ⊠ *1426 1st Ave., Downtown* ☎ *206/628–3151* ⊕ *www.showboxonline.com.*

THEATER

Paramount Theatre. Built in 1928 as a venue for early talkies and vaudeville acts, this lovely Beaux-Arts movie palace—which features an original Wurlitzer theatre pipe organ—now mostly hosts concerts, as well as the occasional comedy, dance, or Broadway event. ■ TIP→ **Seattle Theatre Group (STG Presents) also operates the Moore and the Neptune, both old Seattle theaters with terrific music-and-beyond lineups.** ⊠ *907 Pine St., Downtown* ☎ *206/682–1414* ⊕ *www.stgpresents.org.*

QUEEN ANNE

MUSIC CLUBS

Teatro ZinZanni. There's dinner theater, and then there's Seattle's famous, over-the-top—and totally entertaining—five-course feast with a circus on the side. Featuring vaudeville, comedy, music and dance, the themed shows change every few months, but ZinZanni, in the heart of Seattle Center, remains a reliable favorite for locals and tourists alike.

Tickets start at $99. ✉ *222 Mercer St., Queen Anne* ☎ *206/802–0015* ⊕ *dreams.zinzanni.org.*

PIONEER SQUARE

BARS AND LOUNGES

Collins Pub. The best beer bar in Pioneer Square features 22 rotating taps of Northwest (including Boundary Bay, Chuckanut, and Anacortes) and California beers and a long list of bottles from the region. Its upscale pub menu features local and seasonal ingredients—try the grilled lamb chops or the Parmesan risotto cakes with your pint. ✉ *526 2nd Ave., Pioneer Square* ☎ *206/623–1016* ⊕ *www.thecollinspub.com.*

Sake Nomi. Whether you're a novice or expert, you'll appreciate the authentic offerings here. The shop and tasting bar is open until 10 pm Tuesday through Saturday and from noon to 6 on Sunday. Don't be shy—have a seat, try a few of the rotating samples, and ask a lot of questions. Sake can be served up in a variety of temperatures and styles. ✉ *76 S. Washington St., Pioneer Square* ☎ *206/467–7253* ⊕ *www.sakenomi.us.*

CAPITOL HILL

BARS AND LOUNGES

Garage Billiards. Built in 1928, this former auto-repair shop is now a large, happening, chrome-and-vinyl pool hall, restaurant, and bar. The large garage doors are thrown wide open on warm evenings, making it a pleasurable alternative to other, more cramped places. There are 18 tournament pool tables and a small bowling alley. The place is 21 and over only. ✉ *1130 Broadway Ave., Capitol Hill* ☎ *206/322–2296* ⊕ *www.garagebilliards.com.*

Linda's Tavern. Welcome to one of the Hill's iconic dives—and not just because it was allegedly the last place Kurt Cobain was seen alive. The interior has a vaguely Western theme, but the patrons are pure Capitol Hill indie-rockers and hipsters. The bartenders are friendly, the burgers are good (brunch is even better), and the always-packed patio is one of the liveliest places to grab a happy-hour drink. ✉ *707 E. Pine St., Capitol Hill* ☎ *206/325–1220* ⊕ *www.lindastavern.com.*

The Pine Box. The clever name is just one reason to visit this beer hall housed in a former funeral home on the corner of Pine Street. The churchlike interior is stately, with soaring ceilings, dark woodwork, and custom furniture made from huge Douglas fir timbers found in the basement—they were supposedly used to shelve coffins many years ago. The place is rumored to be haunted, but that doesn't stop a trendy crowd from congregating to sample from 30-plus taps of craft beer and a menu of wood-fired pizza and entrées like herbed lamb loin and pancetta scallops. Or get your morning drink on at the weekend brunch. ✉ *1600 Melrose Ave., Capitol Hill* ☎ *206/588–0375* ⊕ *www.pineboxbar.com.*

Fodor'sChoice ★ **Sun Liquor Lounge.** If you adore creative handcrafted cocktails, add this intimate Capitol Hill haunt to your must-visit list. Friendly bartenders sling exceptional drinks mixed with fresh-squeezed juices and house-made ingredients like shrubs—flavorful "drinking vinegars" that first became popular in colonial America—and aromatic bitters. They even make and sell their own hooch. A few years ago, Sun Liquor opened a nearby distillery, which produces the company's flagship Hedge Trimmer Gin, among others. ■TIP➔ **The lounge is a much cozier place to hang out, but the same specialty cocktails are served up at the distillery, along with a lunch menu (**⊠ **512 East Pike).** ⊠ *607 Summit Ave. E, Capitol Hill* ☎ *206/860–1130* ⊕ *www.sunliquor.com.*

BREWPUBS

Elysian Brewing Company. Worn booths and tables are scattered across the bi-level warehouse space of this Capitol Hill mainstay, where the beers are a good representation of the thriving brewing scene in the Northwest. Always on tap are the hop-heavy Immortal IPA, the rich Perseus Porter, and the crisp Elysian Fields Pale Ale. The food (burgers, fish tacos, sandwiches, salads) is decent, too. This is a favorite of Seattleites and Capitol Hill residents and a laid-back alternative to the more trendy haunts and lounges in the area. ⊠ *1221 E. Pike St., Capitol Hill* ☎ *206/860–1920* ⊕ *www.elysianbrewing.com.*

LIVE MUSIC

Neumo's. Once one of the grunge era's iconic clubs (when it was Moe's) has managed to reclaim its status as a staple of the Seattle rock scene, despite being closed for a six-year stretch. And it is a great rock venue: acoustics are excellent, and the roster of cutting-edge indie rock bands is the best in the city. That said, it's one of the most uncomfortable places in town to see a show (sight lines throughout the club can be terrible). It's also stuffy and hot during sold-out shows. ⊠ *925 E. Pike St., Capitol Hill* ☎ *206/709–9467* ⊕ *www.neumos.com.*

FREMONT AND GREENWOOD

BARS AND LOUNGES

Brouwer's. It may look like a trendy Gothic castle, but in fact this is heaven for Belgian-beer lovers. A converted warehouse is home to a top selection of suds, which are provided by the owners of Seattle's best specialty-beer shop, Bottleworks. Brouwer's serves plenty of German and American/Northwest beers, too, as well as English, Czech, and Polish selections. A menu of surprisingly good sandwiches, frites, and Belgian specialties help to lay a pre-imbibing foundation (remember that most Belgian beers have a higher alcohol content). Before settling on a seat downstairs, check out the balcony and the cozy parlor room. ⊠ *400 N. 35th St., Fremont* ☎ *206/267–2437* ⊕ *www.brouwerscafe.com.*

Chuck's Hop Shop. Were it not for the picnic tables and rotating food trucks routinely parked outside, this place might look like just another corner convenience store. In fact, that's precisely what it used to be before owner Chuck transformed it into one of North Seattle's favorite spots for sampling craft beer and hanging out for hours. With nearly 40 taps, Chuck's features an especially good selection of IPAs and ciders on draft, many of local origin. Families love this extremely kid-friendly spot—there's an ice-cream counter, ample seating and a stack of board games inside—and so do the dogs that get plenty of head pats and a big cookie, if you ask. Chuck's also offers a huge selection of bottled beers from all over the world, including gluten- and alcohol-free options. ■TIP→ **Sticking to the Capitol Hill area? Chuck's now has a second location (⊠ 2001 E. Union St.).** ⊠ *656 N.W. 85th St., Greenwood* ☎ *206/297–6212* ⊕ *www.chucks85th.com.*

Quoin. Even if you're not staying for dinner at the neighboring Revel—a Korean fusion restaurant that's won raves for its dumplings, rice, and noodle dishes—this sliver of a bar is worth a visit. Bartenders make a fantastic cocktail, and Quoin offers a much more intimate and stylish experience than other Fremont spots. There's also an outdoor deck with bench seating around a fire pit. ⊠ *403 N. 36th St., Fremont* ☎ *206/547–2040.*

BREWPUBS

Hale's Ales. One of the city's oldest craft breweries, opened in 1983, produces unique English-style ales, cask-conditioned ales and nitrogen-conditioned cream ales, plus a popular Mongoose IPA. The pub serves a full menu and has a great view of the fermenting room. Order a taster's flight if you want to try everything. ⊠ *4301 Leary Way NW, Fremont* ☎ *206/706–1544* ⊕ *www.halesbrewery.com.*

BALLARD

BARS AND LOUNGES

The Noble Fir. A rotating selection of great beer, cider, and wine and a truly varied crowd are just part of the appeal of this popular bar. Like many (most?) Seattleites, the husband-and-wife owners are outdoorsy—and it shows in the rustic-modern interior, which includes a library-like seating area stocked with large trail maps, as well as hundreds of travel books. The Noble Fir serves a few simple snacks, like cheese and charcuterie, in case you feel like settling in and planning your next big adventure. ⊠ *5316 Ballard Ave., Ballard* ☎ *206/420–7425* ⊕ *www.thenoblefir.com.*

Ocho. Blink and you'll miss it, and that would be a shame, because this tiny corner hotspot crafts some of the finest cocktails in town. Try the Donkey Tongue, made with chili-infused tequila, cucumber, pomegranate liqueur, and lemon, or the San Miguel, a refreshing concoction of gin, St. Germain, lemon, and rhubarb bitters. Dimly lit and loud, Ocho only has a few tables and bar seats, and it fills up fast with a mixed crowd that flocks here for the drinks and top-notch Spanish tapas. It's usually possible to snag a table without a wait during the weekend happy hour from noon to 6. Come summer, the slender sidewalk patio is an ideal spot for soaking up the sun and people-watching. ⊠ *2325 N.W. Market St., Ballard* ☎ *206/784–0699* ⊕ *www.ochoballard.com.*

The Peoples Pub. Head to this Ballard institution to see what locals love about this unpretentious neighborhood. The pub (a dining room and a separate bar in the back) isn't much to look at—a lot of wood paneling, simple wood tables and chairs, and some unfortunate floral upholstery—but it has a *Prost*-worthy selection of German beers and one delicious fried pickle. True to its name, Peoples draws an interesting cross section of the neighborhood, from the young and trendy to old-school fishermen. ⊠ *5429 Ballard Ave. NW, Ballard* ☎ *206/783–6521* ⊕ *www.peoplespub.com.*

Portalis. Serious oenophiles gather around communal tables and at the long bar to sample wines from around the world in this cozy, brick-lined bar. It's a full-service retail shop as well, so you can pick up a few bottles to take home. Though it's a bit stuffy for the neighborhood, it's a nice alternative to the frenetic scene on the upper part of Ballard Avenue. ⊠ *5205 Ballard Ave. NW, Ballard* ☎ *206/783–2007* ⊕ *www.portaliswines.com.*

Reuben's Brews. Ballard, former home to Redhook Brewing (one of America's very first craft beers, now based in Woodinville), has become quite the suds-friendly enclave over the past few years, with a number of startup breweries opening in the neighborhood's former industrial buildings. Reuben's, helmed by a British expat who started home brewing after years of being awed by Seattle's beer scene, is a favorite among serious beer geeks, with particularly outstanding IPAs and rye varieties. Make an afternoon of it and walk (or ride) to a few other nearby breweries. Some best bets: the bike-themed Peddler Brewing (⊠ *1514 N.W. Leary Way*), Stoup Brewing (⊠ *108 N.W. 52nd Street*), and Hilliard's Beer (⊠ *1550 N.W. 49th Street*). Many are kid-friendly. ⊠ *1406 N.W. 53rd St., Ballard* ☎ *206/784–2859* ⊕ *www.reubensbrews.com.*

LIVE MUSIC

Tractor Tavern. Seattle's top spot for roots music and alt-country has a large, dimly lighted hall with all the right touches—wagon-wheel fixtures, exposed-brick walls, and a cheery staff. The sound system is outstanding. ⊠ *5213 Ballard Ave. NW, Ballard* ☎ *206/789–3599* ⊕ *www.tractortavern.com.*

SPORTS AND THE OUTDOORS

9

The question in Seattle isn't "do you exercise?" Rather, it's "how do you exercise?" Athleticism is a regular part of most people's lives here, whether it's an afternoon jog, a sunrise rowing session, a lunch-hour bike ride, or an evening game of Frisbee.

The Cascade Mountains, a 60-minute drive east, have trails and peaks for alpinists of all skill levels. Snoqualmie Pass attracts downhill skiers and snowboarders, and cross-country skiing and snowshoeing are excellent throughout the Cascades. To the west of the city is Puget Sound, where sailors, kayakers, and anglers practice their sports. Lake Union and Lake Washington also provide residents with plenty of boating, kayaking, fishing, and swimming opportunities. Farther west, the Olympic Mountains beckon adventure-seeking souls to their unspoiled wilderness.

Spectator sports are also appreciated here, from the UW Huskies (Go Dawgs!) to the Sonics, Seattle's beloved pro soccer team. And let's not forget the Seahawks, the 2014 Super Bowl champs.

PARKS INFORMATION

King County Parks and Recreation. This agency manages many of the parks outside city limits. ⊠ *201 S. Jackson, Suite 700, Downtown* ☎ *206/477–4527 information* ⊕ *www.kingcounty.gov/recreation/parks.aspx.*

Seattle Parks and Recreation Department. To find out whether an in-town park baseball diamond or tennis court is available, contact the Seattle Parks and Recreation Department, which is responsible for most of the parks, piers, beaches, playgrounds, and courts within city limits. The department issues permits for events, arranges reservations for facilities, and staffs visitor centers and naturalist programs. ⊠ *100 Dexter Ave. N, Seattle Center* ☎ *206/684–4075* ⊕ *www.seattle.gov/parks.*

Washington State Parks. The state manages several parks and campgrounds in greater Seattle. ⊠ *1111 Israel Rd. SW, Olympia* ☎ *360/902–8844 for general information, 888/226–7688 for campsite reservations* ⊕ *www.parks.wa.gov.*

BASEBALL

Seattle Mariners. The Seattle Mariners play at **Safeco Field,** a retractable-roof stadium where there really isn't a bad seat in the house. One local sports columnist referred to the $656 million venue—which finished $100 million over budget—as "the guilty pleasure." You can purchase tickets through Ticketmaster or StubHub; online or by phone from Safeco Field (to be picked up at the Will Call); in person at Safeco's box office (no surcharges), which is open daily 10–6; or from the Mariners team store at 4th Avenue and Stewart Street in Downtown. Priced dynamically based on day and opponent, the cheap seats start at $10; better seats cost $45 to $82, and the best seats go for upwards of $400. ⊠ *1st Ave. S and Atlantic St., SoDo* ☎ *206/346–4000* ⊕ *seattle. mariners.mlb.com.*

BIKING

Biking is probably Seattle's most popular sport. Thousands of Seattleites bike to work, and even more ride recreationally, especially on weekends. In the past, Seattle wasn't a particularly bike-friendly city. But the city government has adopted a sweeping Bicycle Master Plan that calls for 118 new miles of bike lanes, 19 miles of bike paths, and countless route signs and lane markings throughout the city by 2017. The plan can't erase the hills, though—only masochists should attempt Queen Anne Hill and Phinney Ridge. Fortunately, all city buses have easy-to-use bike racks (on the front of the buses, below the windshield) and drivers are used to waiting for cyclists to load and unload their bikes. If you're not comfortable biking in urban traffic—and there is a lot of urban traffic to contend with here—you can do a combination bus-and-bike tour of the city or stick to the car-free Burke-Gilman Trail.

Seattle drivers are fairly used to sharing the road with cyclists. With the exception of the occasional road-rager or clueless cell-phone talker, drivers usually leave a generous amount of room when passing; however, there are biking fatalities every year, so be alert and cautious,

Bicyclists ride along Lake Washington in the Seattle-to-Portland (STP) event.

especially when approaching blind intersections, of which Seattle has many. You must wear a helmet at all times (it's the law) and be sure to lock up your bike—bikes do get stolen, even in quiet residential neighborhoods.

The Seattle Parks Department sponsors Bicycle Sundays on various weekends from May through September. On these Sundays, a 4-mile stretch of Lake Washington Boulevard—from Mt. Baker Beach to Seward Park—is closed to motor vehicles. Many riders continue around the 2-mile loop at Seward Park and back to Mt. Baker Beach to complete a 10-mile, car-free ride. Check with the **Seattle Parks and Recreation Department** (☎ 206/684–4075 ⊕ *www.seattle.gov/parks/bicyclesunday*) for a complete schedule.

The trail that circles **Green Lake** is popular with cyclists, though runners and walkers can impede fast travel. The city-maintained **Burke-Gilman Trail**, a slightly less congested path, follows an abandoned railroad line 14 miles roughly following Seattle's waterfront from Ballard to Kenmore, at the north end of Lake Washington. (From there, serious cyclists can continue on the Sammamish River Trail to Marymoor Park in Redmond; in all, the trail spans 42 miles between Seattle and Issaquah.) **Discovery Park** is a very tranquil place to tool around in. **Myrtle Edwards Park**, north of Pier 70, has a two-lane waterfront path for biking and running. The **islands of the Puget Sound** are also easily explored by bike (there are rental places by the ferry terminals), though keep in mind that Bainbridge, Whidbey, and the San Juans all have some tough hills.

King County has more than 100 miles of paved and nearly 70 miles of unpaved routes, including the Sammamish River, Interurban, Green

River, Cedar River, Snoqualmie Valley, and Soos Creek trails. For more information, contact the **King County Parks and Recreation** office (☎ 206/296–8687).

RENTALS

Montlake Bicycle Shop. This shop a mile south of the University of Washington and within easy riding distance of the Burke-Gilman Trail rents mountain bikes, road bikes, basic cruisers, and tandems. Prices range from $35 to $90 for the day, with discounts for longer rentals (credit card hold required). If you find yourself on the Eastside, you can rent a bike from its Kirkland branch. ☒ 2223 24th Ave. E, Montlake ☎ 206/329–7333 ⊕ www.montlakebike.com ☒ Kirkland Bicycle Shop, 208 Kirkland Ave., Kirkland ☎ 425/828–3800 ⊕ www.montlakebike. com.

BOATING AND KAYAKING

Fodor's Choice ★ **Agua Verde Cafe & Paddle Club.** Start out by renting a kayak and paddling along either the Lake Union shoreline, with its hodgepodge of funky-to-fabulous houseboats and dramatic Downtown vistas, or Union Bay on Lake Washington, with its marshes and cattails. Afterward, take in the lakefront as you wash down some Mexican food (halibut tacos, anyone?) with a margarita. Kayaks and stand-up paddleboards are available March through October and are rented by the hour—$17 for singles, $22 for doubles. It pays to paddle midweek: the third hour is free on weekdays. ☒ 1303 N.E. Boat St., University District ☎ 206/545–8570 ⊕ www.aguaverde.com.

Alki Kayak Tours & Adventure Center. For a variety of day-long guided kayak outings—from a Seattle Sunset Sea Kayak Tour to an Alki Point Lighthouse Tour—led by experienced, fun staff, try this great outfitter in West Seattle. In addition to kayaks, you can also rent skates, fishing boats, and longboards here. Custom sea-kayaking adventures can be set up, too. To rent a kayak without a guide, you must be an experienced kayaker; otherwise, sign up for one of the fascinating guided outings (the popular sunset tour is $49 per person). ☒ 1660 Harbor Ave. SW, West Seattle ☎ 206/953–0237 ⊕ kayakalki.com.

The Center for Wooden Boats. Located on the southern shore of Lake Union, Seattle's free maritime heritage museum is a bustling community hub. Thousands of Seattleites rent rowboats and small wooden sailboats here every year; the Center also offers workshops, demonstrations, and classes. Rentals for non-members range from $24 to $40 per hour. There's also a $20 skills-check fee for sailing. Free half-hour guided sails and steamboat rides are offered on Sunday from 2 to 4 (arrive an hour early to reserve a spot). ☒ 1010 Valley St., Lake Union ☎ 206/382–2628 ⊕ www.cwb.org.

Green Lake Boat Rental. This shop is the source for canoes, paddleboats, sailboats, kayaks, sailboards, and rowboats to take out on Green Lake's calm waters. On beautiful summer afternoons, however, be prepared to spend most of your time dealing with traffic, both in the parking lot and on the water. Fees are $18 an hour for paddleboats, single kayaks, rowboats, and sailboards, $25 an hour for sailboats. Don't confuse

Agua Verde Paddle Club and Café

this place with the Green Lake Small Craft Center, which offers sailing programs but no rentals. ✉ *7351 E. Green Lake Dr. N, Green Lake* ☎ *206/527–0171* ⊕ *www.greenlakeboatrentals.net.*

Northwest Outdoor Center. This center on Lake Union's west side rents one- or two-person kayaks (it also has a few triples) by the hour or day, including equipment and basic or advanced instruction. The hourly rate is $14 for a single and $20 for a double (costs are figured in 10-minute increments after the first hour). If you want to find your own water, NWOC offers "to-go" kayaks. In summer, reserve at least three days ahead. NWOC also runs guided trips to the Nisqually Delta and Chuckanut Bay, as well as sunset tours near Golden Gardens Park and moonlight tours of Portage Bay. ✉ *2100 Westlake Ave. N, Lake Union* ☎ *206/281–9694* ⊕ *www.nwoc.com.*

FOOTBALL

Seattle Seahawks. If you heard the earth rumbling on Feb. 2, 2014, it was probably just Seattle. The entire city went nuts when their beloved team trounced the Denver Broncos and won the Super Bowl. Now it's harder than ever to get tix to see the Seattle Seahawks play in their $430-million arena, the state-of-the-art **Qwest Field.** Single-game tix go on sale in late July or early August, and all home games sell out quickly. They're expensive, too, leading the NFL in starting prices at $99 for the cheap seats. The average ticket ask-price averages more like $400. Note that traffic and parking are both nightmares on game days; try to take public transportation—or walk the mile from Downtown. **Fun local trivia:** The number 12—look around and you'll see it everywhere—refers to Seattle's "12th Man" phenomenon. The squad consists of 11 players and the fans are the 12th man. Just how serious are the Seahawks fans to earn such a title? The stadium gets so loud that it literally generates earthquakes. ⊠ *800 Occidental Ave. S., SoDo* ☎ *425/203–8000* ⊕ *www.seahawks.com.*

GOLF

Gold Mountain Golf Complex. Most people make the trek to Bremerton to play the Olympic Course, a beautiful and challenging par 72 that is widely considered the best public course in Washington. The older, less-sculpted Cascade Course is also popular; it's better suited to those new to the game. There are four putting greens, a driving range, and a striking clubhouse with views of the Belfair Valley. Prime-time greens fees are $35 to $44 for the Cascade and $49 to $69 for the Olympic. Carts are $32. You can drive all the way to Bremerton via I–5, or you can take the car ferry to Bremerton from Pier 52. The trip will take roughly an hour and a half no matter which way you do it, but the ferry ride (60 minutes) might be a more pleasant way to spend a large part of the journey. Note, however, that the earliest departure time for the ferry is 6 am, so this option won't work for very early tee times. ⊠ *7263 W. Belfair Valley Rd., Bremerton* ☎ *206/464–1175* ⊕ *www.goldmt.com.*

Jefferson Park. This golf complex has views of the city skyline *and* Mt. Rainier. The par-27, 9-hole course has a lighted driving range with heated stalls that's open from dusk until midnight. And the 18-hole, par-72 main course is one of the city's best. Greens fees are $40 on weekends and $35 on weekdays for the 18-hole course; you can play the 9-hole course for $8.50 daily. Carts are $28 and $14, and $5 buys you a bucket of 30 balls at the driving range. You can book tee times online up to 10 days in advance or by phone up to 7 days in advance. ⊠ *4101 Beacon Ave. S, Beacon Hill* ☎ *206/762–4513* ⊕ *www.seattlegolf.com.*

HIKING

■ **TIP→** Within Seattle city limits, the best nature trails can be found in Discovery Park, Lincoln Park, Seward Park, and at the Washington Park Arboretum. Some trailheads require parking permits, but they're marked and you can usually pay on-site.

Cougar Mountain Regional Wildland Park. This spectacular park in the "Issaquah Alps" has more than 36 miles of hiking trails and 12 miles of bridle trails within its 3,000-plus acres. The Indian Trail, believed to date back 8,000 years, was part of a trade route that Native Americans used to reach North Bend and the Cascades. Thick pine forests rise to spectacular mountaintop views; there are waterfalls, deep caves, and the remnants of a former mining town. Local residents include deer, black bears, bobcats, bald eagles, and pileated woodpeckers, among many other woodland creatures. ⊠ *18201 S.E. Cougar Mountain Dr., Issaquah* ✛ *From Downtown Seattle take I-90 East; follow signs to park beyond Issaquah* ⊙ *Daily 8 am–dusk.*

Mt. Si. This thigh-buster is where mountaineers train to climb grueling Mt. Rainier. Mt. Si offers a challenging hike with views of a valley (slightly marred by the suburbs) and the Olympic Mountains in the distance. The main trail to Haystack Basin, 8 miles round-trip, climbs some 4,000 vertical feet, but there are several obvious places to rest or turn around if you'd like to keep the hike to 3 or 4 miles. Note that solitude is in short supply here—this is an extremely popular trail thanks to its proximity to Seattle. On the bright side, it's one of the best places to witness the local hikers and trail-runners in all their weird and wonderful splendor. ⊠ *North Bend* ⊹ *Take I–90 East to Exit 31 (towards North Bend). Turn onto North Bend Way and then make a left onto Mt. Si Rd. and follow that road to the trailhead parking lot.* ⊕ *www.mountsi.com.*

Fodor's Choice
★ **Snow Lake.** Washington State's most popular wilderness trail may be crowded at times, but the scenery and convenience of this hike make it a classic. Though very rocky in stretches—you'll want to wear sturdy shoes—the 8-mile round trip sports a relatively modest 1,300-foot elevation gain; the views of the Alpine Lakes Wilderness are well worth the sweat. The glimmering waters of Snow Lake await hikers at the trail's end; summer visitors will find abundant wildflowers, huckleberries, and wild birds. ⊠ *Snoqualmie Pass* ⊹ *Take I–90 East to Exit 52 (toward Snoqualmie Pass West). Turn left (north), cross under the freeway, and continue on to the trailhead, located in parking lot at the Alpental Ski Area.* ⊕ *www.wta.org/go-hiking/hikes/snow-lake-1.*

WALKING TOURS

Taking a tour is a great way to see the city if you have specific interests or limited time.

Market Ghost Tours. These weekend tours around the Pike Place Market weave in local ghost stories, eerie history, and fun facts about the market and its haunted places. ⊠ *1410 Post Alley, Downtown* ☎ *206/805–0195* ⊕ *www.seattleghost.com.*

Savor Seattle Food Tours. Two- to three-hour culinary walking tours around town include a Chocolate Indulgence tour, a Gourmet Seattle tour (with stops at fine restaurants to meet chefs, and tasty meals with wine and beer pairings); and a Pike Place Market walking tour led by a local guide. ⊠ *1st Ave. and Pike St., Downtown* ☎ *888/987–2867* ⊕ *www.savorseattletours.com.*

SHOPPING

Shopping in Seattle is something best done gradually. Don't expect to find it all in one or two days' worth of blitz shopping tours. Downtown is the only area that allows for easy daylong shopping excursions. Within a few blocks along 4th and 5th avenues, you'll find the standard chains (Anthropologie, H&M, Old Navy, Sephora, Urban Outfitters), along with Nike's flagship store, and a few more glamorous high-end stores (Escada, Louis Vuitton). Downtown is also where you'll find department stores like Nordstrom, Macy's, and Barneys New York.

Belltown and Pioneer Square are also easy areas to patrol—most stores of note are within a few blocks.

To find many of the stores that are truly special to Seattle—such as boutiques featuring handmade frocks from local designers, independent record stores run by encyclopedic-minded music geeks, cozy used-book shops that smell of paper and worn wood shelves—you'll have to branch out to Capitol Hill, Queen Anne, and northern neighborhoods like Ballard. Shopping these areas will give you a better feel for the character of the city and its quirky inhabitants, all while you score that new dress or nab gifts for your friends.

DOWNTOWN AND BELLTOWN

BOOKS AND PRINTED MATERIAL

Fodor's Choice
★
Peter Miller Architectural & Design Books and Supplies. Aesthetes and architects haunt this shop, which is stocked floor to ceiling with all things design. Rare, international architecture, art, and design books mingle with high-end products from Alessi and Iittala; sleek notebooks, bags, portfolios, and drawing tools round out the collection. This is a great shop for quirky, unforgettable gifts, like a Black Dot sketchbook, an Arne Jacobsen wall clock, or an aerodynamic umbrella. ⊠ *2326 2nd Ave., Belltown* ☎ *206/441–4114* ⊕ *www.petermiller.com.*

CHOCOLATE

Fodor's Choice
★
Fran's Chocolates. A Seattle institution (helmed by Fran Bigelow) has been making quality chocolates for decades. Its world-famous salted caramels are transcendent—a much-noted favorite of the Obama family, in fact—as are delectable truffles, which are spiked with oolong tea, single malt whiskey, or raspberry, among other flavors. This shop is housed in the Four Seasons on 1st Avenue—how very elegant, indeed! ⊠ *1325 1st Ave., Downtown* ☎ *206/682–0168* ⊕ *www.franschocolates.com.*

CLOTHING

Alhambra. Sophisticated, casual, and devastatingly feminine, this pricey boutique delivers quality, European-style looks for women of all ages. Pop into the Moorish-inspired shop for a party dress, elegant jewelry, or separates, and be sure to check out the house line, designed by the owners. ⊠ *101 Pine St., Downtown* ☎ *206/621–9571* ⊕ *www. alhambrastyle.com.*

Arc'teryx. Technical clothing doesn't get more fashionable than this obsessively designed and extremely durable outerwear and gear. The first U.S. outpost of a growing Canadian cult brand based in Vancouver, this 2,300-square-foot flagship store caters to devoted outdoorsy types with deep pockets. ⊠ *400 Pike St., Downtown* ☎ *206/462–6058* ⊕ *www.arcteryx.com.*

Karan Dannenberg Clothier. A favorite of Seattle executives and sophisticates, this boutique stocks classy, modern clothing for women—including designs by local Cameron Levin—and doesn't bow to useless trends. The staff is very knowledgeable, and offers wardrobe consulting for their customers—they'll even make house calls to critique your closets in a What Not to Wear–style evaluation. Shop here for perfect jeans,

TOP SPOTS TO SHOP

Shopping becomes decidedly less fun when it involves driving around and circling for parking. You're better off limiting your all-day shopping tours to one of several key areas than planning to do a citywide search for a particular item. The following areas have the greatest concentration of shops and the greatest variety.

5th and 6th Avenues, Downtown. Depending on where you're staying, you may not need to drive to this area, but if you do, the parking garage at Pacific Place mall (at 600 Pine Street) always seems to have a space somewhere. Tackling either Pacific Place or the four blocks of 5th and 6th avenues between Olive Way and University Street will keep you very busy for a day.

1st Avenue, Belltown. From Wall Street to Pine Street, you'll find clothing boutiques, shoe stores, and some sleek home- and architectural-design stores. First Avenue and Pike Street brings you to the Pike Place Market. There are numerous pay parking lots on both 1st and 2nd avenues.

Pioneer Square. Walk or bus here if you can. Art galleries are the main draw, along with some home-decor and rug shops. If you do drive, many pay lots in the neighborhood participate in the "Parking Around the Square" program, which works with local businesses to offer shoppers validated parking; the website ⊕ www.pioneersquare.org lists the lots and stores that offer it.

International District. Parking in the I.D. can be hit or miss depending on the time of day. It's best if you can walk here from Downtown or take a quick bus ride over. If you do drive, go directly to the Uwajimaya parking lot. It validates for purchases, and it's a safe bet you'll be buying something here.

Pike–Pine Corridor, Capitol Hill. The best shopping in the Hill is on Pike and Pine Streets between Melrose Avenue and 10th Avenue East. Most of the stores are on Pike Street; Pine's best offerings are clustered on the western end of the avenue between Melrose and Summit. There are pay lots on Pike Street (near Broadway) and one on Summit by East Olive Way (next to the Starbucks).

Fremont and Ballard. Start in Fremont's small retail center, which is mostly along 36th Street. You may be able to snag street parking. After you've exhausted Fremont's shops, it's an easy drive over to Ballard. Ballard Avenue and N.W. Market Street are chockablock with great boutiques. Finding parking in Ballard can be tricky on weekends, but it's possible.

9

business attire, or glamorous formal wear. ⊠ 2232 1st Ave., Belltown ☎ 206/441–3442 ⊕ karandannenberg.com.

Mario's. Known for fabulous service and designer labels, this high-end boutique treats every client like a superstar. Men shop the ground floor for Armani, Etro, and Zegna; women ascend the ornate staircase for Prada, Emilio Pucci, and Lanvin. A freestanding Hugo Boss boutique sells the sharpest tuxedos in town. ⊠ 1513 6th Ave., Downtown ☎ 206/223–1461 ⊕ www.marios.com.

Pirkko. Fans of Scandinavian fashion and home decor will adore this little boutique just outside Pike Place Market. Specializing in Finnish design, Pirkko stocks a covetable selection of Marimekko—the brand's iconic graphic prints adorn clothing, handbags, and home accessories—along with Ilse Jacobsen, Iittala, Hasbeens, and more. ⊠ *1407 1st Ave., Downtown* ☎ *206/223–1112* ⊕ *www.pirkko.com.*

DEPARTMENT STORES

Fodor'sChoice
★

Nordstrom. Seattle's own retail giant sells quality clothing, accessories, cosmetics, jewelry, and lots of shoes—in keeping with its roots in footwear—including many hard-to-find sizes. Peruse the various floors for anything from trendy jeans to lingerie to goods for the home. A sky bridge on the store's fourth floor will take you to Pacific Place Shopping Center. Deservedly renowned for its impeccable customer service, the busy Downtown flagship has a concierge desk and valet parking. ■ TIP➔ **The Nordstrom Rack store at 1st Avenue and Spring Street, close to Pike Place Market, has great deals on marked-down items.** ⊠ *500 Pine St., Downtown* ☎ *206/628–2111* ⊕ *shop.nordstrom.com.*

GIFTS AND HOME DECOR

FAMILY
Fodor'sChoice
★

Schmancy. Weird and wonderful, this toy store is more surreal art funhouse than FAO Schwarz. Pick up a crocheted zombie (with a cute little bow), a felted Ishmael's whale, your very own Hugh Hefner figurine—or how about a pork-chop pillow? With collectibles from cult favorites Plush You!, Kidrobot, and Lovemongers, this quirky shop is full of surprises. Warning: Sense of humor required. ⊠ *1932 2nd Ave., Downtown* ☎ *206/728–8008* ⊕ *www.schmancytoys.com.*

Sur La Table. Need a brass-plated medieval French duck press? You've come to the right place. Culinary artists and foodies have flocked to this popular Pike Place Market destination since 1972. The chain's flagship shop is packed to the rafters with many thousands of kitchen items, including an exclusive line of copper cookware, endless shelves of baking equipment, tabletop accessories, cookbooks, and a formidable display of knives. ⊠ *84 Pine St., Downtown* ☎ *206/448–2244* ⊕ *www. surlatable.com.*

MUSIC

Singles Going Steady. If punk rock is more to you than anarchy symbols sewn on Target sweatshirts, then stop here. Punk and its myriad subgenres on CD and vinyl are specialties, though they also stock rockabilly, indie rock, and hip-hop. It's a nice foil to the city's indie-rock-dominated record shops, and a good reminder that Belltown is still more eclectic than its rising rents may indicate. ⊠ *2219 2nd Ave., Belltown* ☎ *206/441–7396.*

OUTDOORS CLOTHING AND EQUIPMENT

Patagonia. If the person next to you on the bus isn't wearing North Face, he or she is probably clad in Patagonia. This popular and durable brand excels at functional outdoor wear—made with earth-friendly materials such as hemp and organic cotton—as well as technical clothing hip enough for mountaineers or urban hikers. The line of whimsically patterned fleece wear for children is particularly cute. ⊠ *2100 1st Ave., Belltown* ☎ *206/622–9700* ⊕ *www.patagonia.com.*

WINE AND SPECIALTY FOODS

Fodor'sChoice **DeLaurenti Specialty Food and Wine.** Attention foodies: Clear out your
★ hotel mini-bars and make room for delectable treats from DeLaurenti.
And, if you're planning any picnics, swing by here first. Imported meats
and cheeses crowd the deli cases, and packaged delicacies pack the
aisles. Stock up on hard-to-find items like truffle-infused olive oil or
excellent Italian vintages from the wine shop upstairs. Spring travelers
will also want to stop by DeLaurenti's nosh nirvana, called Cheesefest,
in May. ⊠ *Pike Place Market, 1435 1st Ave., Downtown* ☎ *206/622–
0141* ⊕ *www.delaurenti.com.*

Pike and Western Wine Shop. These folks have spent nearly four decades
carving out a reputation as one of the best wine markets in the city. With
more than 1,000 wines personally selected from the Pacific Northwest
and around the world, this shop offers expert advice from friendly
salespeople. ⊠ *1934 Pike Pl., Downtown* ☎ *206/441–1307* ⊕ *www.
pikeandwestern.com.*

SOUTH LAKE UNION

OUTDOORS CLOTHING AND EQUIPMENT

Fodor'sChoice **REI.** The enormous flagship for Recreational Equipment, Inc. (REI)
★ has an incredible selection of outdoor gear—polar-fleece jackets, wool
socks, down vests, hiking boots, raingear, and much more—as well as
its own 65-foot climbing wall. The staff is extremely knowledgeable;
there always seems to be enough help on hand, even when the store
is busy. You can test things out on the mountain-bike test trail or in
the simulated rain booth. REI also rents gear such as tents, sleeping
bags, skis, snowshoes, and backpacks. Bonus: The outdoor behemoth
offers an hour of free parking. ⊠ *222 Yale Ave. N, South Lake Union*
☎ *206/223–1944* ⊕ *www.rei.com.*

QUEEN ANNE

BOOKS AND MUSIC

FAMILY **Queen Anne Book Company.** This beloved Seattle bookstore is well known
for its friendly, knowledgeable staff and extensive book selection. Pop in
for children's storytelling sessions on the third Sunday of every month,
or browse at night and catch one of the many author events. After
you grab your new books, slip into El Diablo, the cute coffee shop
adjacent to the bookstore. ⊠ *1811 Queen Anne Ave. N, Queen Anne*
☎ *206/283–5624* ⊕ *www.queenannebooks.com.*

CLOTHING

Peridot Boutique. Strapless animal-print pocket dresses, retro gingham
tops, and ruffly skirts abound in this contemporary women's boutique
in lower Queen Anne. The prices are reasonable, the accessories are
abundant, and local designers are represented as well. ⊠ *532 Queen
Anne Ave. N, Queen Anne* ☎ *206/687–7130* ⊕ *www.peridotboutique.
wordpress.com.*

9

WINE AND SPECIALTY FOODS

McCarthy & Schiering Wine Merchants. One of the best wine shops in the city is attitude-free and offers an amazing selection of wines from around the world. Check out the selection of local wines to experience the true flavor of the Northwest. ✉ *2401B Queen Anne Ave. N, Queen Anne* ☎ *206/282–8500* ⊕ *www.mccarthyandschiering.com.*

PIONEER SQUARE

ANTIQUES AND COLLECTIBLES

Cuttysark Nautical Antiques. Named for the famous Scottish tea clipper, Cuttysark is filled to the brim with nautical memorabilia: antique navigational instruments, signal flags, clocks, lanterns, ships' wheels, telegraphs, binnacles, and other decorative items, along with books and ship models. It's worth wandering through even if you don't know your bow from your stern. ✉ *320 1st Ave., Pioneer Square* ☎ *206/262–1265* ⊕ *www.cuttyantiques.com.*

ART AND GIFTS

Agate Designs. Amateur geologists, curious kids, and anyone fascinated by fossils and gems should make a trip to this store that's almost like a museum (but a lot more fun). Between the 500 million-year-old fossils and the 250-pound amethyst geodes, there's no shortage of eye-popping items on display. ✉ *120 1st Ave. S, Pioneer Square* ☎ *206/621–3063* ⊕ *www.agatedesigns.com.*

Glass House Studio. Seattle's oldest glassblowing studio and gallery lets you watch fearless artisans at work in the "hot shop." Some of the best glass artists in the country work out of this shop, and many of their impressive studio pieces are for sale, along with around 40 other Northwest artists represented by the shop. ✉ *311 Occidental Ave. S, Pioneer Square* ☎ *206/682–9939* ⊕ *www.glasshouse-studio.com.*

BOOKS AND TOYS

FAMILY   **Magic Mouse Toys.** Since 1977, this two-story, 7,000-square-foot shop in the heart of Pioneer Square has been supplying families with games, toys, puzzles, tricks, candy, and figurines. They claim a professional child runs this friendly store—and it shows. ✉ *603 1st Ave., Pioneer Square* ☎ *206/682–8097* ⊕ *www.magicmousetoys.com.*

CLOTHING AND ACCESSORIES

Filson. Seattle's flagship Filson store is a shrine to meticulously well-made outdoor wear for men and women. The hunting lodge–like decor of the space, paired with interesting memorabilia and pricey, made-on-site clothing, makes the drive south of Pioneer Square worth it (we recommend catching a cab, not hoofing it). The attention to detail paid to the plaid vests, oil-treated rain slickers, and fishing outfits borders on the fetishistic. ✉ *1555 4th Ave. S, Pioneer Square* ☎ *206/622–3147* ⊕ *www.filson.com.*

Velouria. The ultimate antidote to mass-produced, unimaginative women's clothes can be found in this exquisitely feminine shop where independent West Coast designers rule. Much on offer is one-of-a-kind: handmade, '70s-inspired jumpsuits; romantic, demure eyelet dresses;

and clever screen-printed tees. Superb bags, delicate jewelry, and fun cards and gifts are also on display. It's worth a look just to check out all the wearable art. ✉ *145 S. King St., Pioneer Square* ☎ *206/788–0330* ⊕ *shopvelouria.tripod.com.*

CAPITOL HILL

BOOKS AND MUSIC

Elliott Bay Book Company. A major reason to visit this landmark bookstore—formerly a longtime haunt in Pioneer Square, hence the name—is the great selection of Pacific Northwest history books and fiction titles by local authors, complete with handwritten recommendation cards from the knowledgeable staff. A big selection of bargain books, underground parking, lovely skylights, and an appealing café all sweeten the deal—and the hundreds of author events held every year mean that nearly every day is an exciting one for dropping by. ✉ *1521 10th Ave., Capitol Hill* ☎ *206/624–6600* ⊕ *www.elliottbaybook.com.*

Wall of Sound. If you're on the hunt for Japanese avant-rock on LP, antiwar spoken word, spiritual reggae with Afro-jazz undertones, or old screen-printed show posters, you've found the place. Obscure, experimental, adventurous, and good? Wall of Sound probably has it. ✉ *315 E. Pine St., Capitol Hill* ☎ *206/441–9880* ⊕ *www.wosound.com.*

CLOTHING

Le Frock. It may look like just another overcrowded consignment shop, but among the racks of Seattle's classiest vintage and consignment store you'll find classic steals for men and women from Burberry, Fendi, Dior, Missoni, and the like. Contemporary looks from Prada, Gucci, and Chanel round out the collection. ✉ *317 E. Pine St., Capitol Hill* ☎ *206/623–5339* ⊕ *www.lefrockonline.com.*

The Red Light Clothing Exchange. Nostalgia rules in this cavernous space filled with well-organized, good-quality vintage clothing. Fantasy outfits from decades past are arranged by era or by genre. There's plenty of denim, leather, and disco threads alongside cowboy boots and eveningwear. ✉ *312 Broadway E, Capitol Hill* ☎ *503/963–8888* ⊕ *redlightclothingexchange.com.*

Totokaelo. Style mavens (including men) who wouldn't be caught dead in fleece flock to this fashion-forward cult boutique, which stocks edgy lines like Marni, Maison Martin Margiela, Rachel Comey, Acne Studios, and Dries Van Noten. The gorgeously spare space—a converted 1940s auto shop—plays blank canvas for the covetable clothing and shoes, as well as the store's smartly curated selection of "art-objects," such as lighting, textiles, ceramics, linens, and art, along with eye-catching pieces from Totokaelo's in-house furniture brand. ✉ *1523 10th Ave., Capitol Hill* ☎ *206/623–3582* ⊕ *www.totokaelo.com.*

FOOTWEAR

Edie's Shoes. Super-comfy, effortlessly cool shoes can be found at this small, carefully planned shop. Plop down on the big purple couch and try on trendy but sensible footwear by Camper, Onitsuka Tiger, Biviel, Tretorn, and Tsubo. You won't find any outrageous designs or one-of-a-kind items here, but it does have a great selection of favored brands in perhaps a few more styles than you'd find at Nordstrom. ✉ *319 E. Pine St., Capitol Hill* ☎ *206/839–1111* ⊕ *www.ediesshoes. com.*

GIFTS AND HOME DECOR

Area 51. Anything might materialize in this 10,000-square-foot industrial space, from Eames replicas to clever coffee mugs, but the mix of retro-inspired new items and vintage finds all looks like it's straight out of a handbook of the design trends from the middle of the last century. ✉ *401 E. Pine St., Capitol Hill* ☎ *206/568–4782* ⊕ *www.area51seattle. com.*

NuBe Green. An emphasis on recycled goods and sustainability is the mission of this well-presented store anchoring a corner of the Oddfellows Building. All items are sourced and made in the United States, including linens, candles, glass art, and even dog beds made from old jeans. Our favorite items are by local **Alchemy Goods** (⊕ *www.alchemygoods. com*), which recycles bicycle tubes, reclaimed vinyl mesh, and seat belts into distinctively cool wallets and messenger bags. ✉ *921 E. Pine St., Capitol Hill* ☎ *206/402–4515* ⊕ *www.nubegreen.com.*

SPECIALTY FOODS

Melrose Market. Seattle is famously foodie-friendly, and this historic triangular building packs several of the city's best culinary shops under one roof. Browse and sample artisanal meats, cheeses, shellfish, and liquor, all with locavore leanings. Unlike Pike Place, the relatively pint-size Melrose is more a hipster haunt than a tourist trap: Anthony Bourdain and the Seattle *Top Chef* contestants have been spotted here. ✉ *1501–1535 Melrose Ave., Capitol Hill* ⊕ *melrosemarketseattle.com.*

FREMONT

CLOTHING

Les Amis. Women whose sartorial leanings go beyond low-rise jeans will adore the sophisticated dresses, gorgeous handknits, and the makings of great work outfits here, much of it from Europe and Japan. Younger fashionistas come here, too, for unique summer skirts and ultrasoft T-shirts. Everyone seems to love the whimsical lingerie collection. Les Amis carries some top designers, such as Dosa, Isabel Marant, and Nanette Lepore. ✉ *3420 Evanston Ave. N, Fremont* ☎ *206/632–2877* ⊕ *www.lesamis-inc.com.*

OUTDOOR CLOTHING

evo. For outdoor gear with an edgy vibe, locals head to evo, which specializes in snow sports gear and also carries a solid selection of hip street clothes for men and women. You'll find everything you need to shred Washington's big mountains in style, from fat powder skis and snowboards with wild graphics to flashy ski jackets and thick woolen beanies. Occupying a two-level space at the Fremont Collective building, evo also has a gallery space that hosts art shows. ■**TIP→ Traveling with skateboarders? Seattle's only indoor skate park, All Together Skate**

Park, is right next door. ⊠ *3500 Stone Way N, Fremont* ☎ *206/973–4470* ⊕ *www.evo.com.*

BALLARD

BOOKS AND MUSIC

FAMILY **Secret Garden Bookshop.** Named after the Francis Hodgson Burnett classic, this cozy shop has been delighting readers for 34 years. A favorite of teachers, librarians, and parents, the store stocks a wide array of imaginative literature and thoughtful nonfiction for all ages; their children's section is particularly notable. ⊠ *2214 N.W. Market St., Ballard* ☎ *206/789–5006* ⊕ *www.secretgardenbooks.com.*

CLOTHING AND ACCESSORIES

FAMILY **Clover.** What's easily the cutest children's store in town carries wonderful handcrafted wooden toys, European figurines, works by local artists, and a variety of swoon-worthy, perfectly crafted little clothes. Even shoppers without children will be smitten—it's hard to resist the vintage French Tintin posters, knit-wool cow dolls, and classic figurines. ⊠ *5333 Ballard Ave. NW, Ballard* ☎ *206/782–0715* ⊕ *www.clovertoys.com.*

THE EASTSIDE

CENTERS AND MALLS

FAMILY **The Bellevue Collection.** In this impressive trifecta of shopping centers, you'll find just about any chain store you've heard of (and some that you haven't). Bellevue Square alone has more than 200 stores, including Nordstrom, Macy's, Pottery Barn, Crate & Barrel, Aveda, Banana Republic, Coach, 7 For All Mankind, Build-a-Bear, and Helly Hansen. The Square's wide walkways and benches, its many children's clothing stores, the first-floor play area, and a children's museum on the third floor make this a great place for kids, too. You can park for free in the attached garage. Take the sky bridge to Lincoln Center, to catch a flick at their 16-screen cinema, organize your life at The Container Store, or sample an assortment of other retail and several popular chain restaurants. Bellevue Place, across from Lincoln Center, hosts a variety of retail along with the ever-popular Daniel's Broiler. ⊠ *Bellevue Way, 575 Bellevue Sq., Bellevue* ☎ *425/454–8096* ⊕ *www.bellevuesquare.com.*

The Shops at the Bravern. If you have some serious cash to burn, the sleek, upscale Bravern might be the Eastside spot for you. With high-end shops like Neiman Marcus, Hermès, Brooks Brothers, Jimmy Choo, Salvatore Ferragamo, and Louis Vuitton, it's tempting to empty your wallet—but save room for a spa treatment at the Elizabeth Arden Red Door Spa or a meal at Northwest favorite Wild Ginger. Valet and complimentary parking (with validation) are available. ⊠ *11111 N.E. 8th St., Bellevue* ☎ *425/456–8780* ⊕ *www.thebravern.com.*

9

SIDE TRIPS FROM SEATTLE: THE PUGET SOUND ISLANDS

The islands of Puget Sound—particularly Bainbridge, Vashon, and Whidbey—are easy and popular day trips for Seattle visitors, and riding the Washington State ferries is half the fun. There are a few classic inns and B&Bs in the historic towns of Langley and Coupeville if you want to spend the night. It's definitely worth planning your trip around mealtimes, because the islands of Puget Sound have top-notch restaurants serving local foods—including locally grown produce, seafood, and even island-raised beef. On Vashon Island, Sea Breeze farm's restaurant La Boucherie is at the top of the locavore pack; Bainbridge, Whidbey, and the San Juans also have a myriad of small farms and charming restaurants worth a visit. Seafood is a big draw: local crab, salmon, and shellfish should be on your not-to-miss list, including the world-renowned Penn Cove mussels from Whidbey Island.

Whidbey Island has the most spectacular natural attractions, but it requires the biggest time commitment to get to (it's 30 miles northwest of Seattle). Bainbridge is the most developed island—it's something of a moneyed bedroom community—with higher-end restaurants and shops supplementing its natural attractions. It's also the easiest to get to—just hop on a ferry from Pier 52 on the Downtown Seattle waterfront. Vashon is the most pastoral of the islands—if you don't like leisurely strolls, beachcombing, or bike rides, you might get bored there quickly. Bainbridge and Whidbey get tons of visitors in summer. Though you'll be able to snag a walk-on spot on the ferry, spaces for cars can fill up, so arrive early. Whidbey is big, so you'll most likely want to tour by car (you can actually drive there, too, as the north end of the island is accessible via Deception Pass), and a car is handy on Bainbridge as well, especially if you want to tour the entire island or visit spectacular Bloedel Reserve. Otherwise, Bainbridge is your best bet if you want to walk on the ferry and tour by foot.

BAINBRIDGE ISLAND

10 minutes west of Seattle by ferry.

Of the three main islands in Puget Sound, Bainbridge has by far the largest population of Seattle commuters. Certain parts of the island are dense enough to have rush-hour traffic problems, while other areas retain a semirural, small-town vibe. Longtime residents work hard to keep parks and protected areas out of the hands of condominium builders, and despite the increasing number of stressed-out commuters, the island still has resident artists, craftspeople, and old-timers who can't be bothered to venture into the big city. Though not as dramatic as Whidbey or as idyllic as Vashon, Bainbridge always makes for a pleasant day trip.

The ferry, which departs from the Downtown terminal at Pier 52, drops you off in the charming village of Winslow. Along its compact main street, Winslow Way, it's easy to while away an afternoon among the antiques shops, art galleries, bookstores, and cafés. There are two bike-rental shops in Winslow, too, if you plan on touring the island on two wheels. Getting out of town on a bike can be a bit nerve-racking, as the traffic to and from the ferry terminal is thick, and there aren't a lot of dedicated bike lanes, but you'll soon be on quieter country roads. Be sure to ask for maps at the rental shop, and if you want to avoid the worst of the island's hills, ask the staff to go over your options with you before you set out.

Many of the island's most reliable dining options are in Winslow, or close to it. You'll also find the delightful Town & Country supermarket on the main stretch if you want to pick up some provisions for a picnic, though you can also easily do that in Seattle at the Pike Place Market before you get on the ferry.

GETTING HERE AND AROUND

Unless you're coming from Tacoma or points farther south, or from the Olympic Peninsula, the only way to get to Bainbridge is via the ferry from Pier 52 Downtown. Round-trip fares start at $7.70 per person; round-trip fare for a car and driver is $32.80. Crossing time is 35 minutes. If you confine your visit to the village of Winslow, as many visitors do, then you won't need anything other than a pair of walking shoes. Out on the island, besides driving or biking, the only way to get around is on buses provided by Kitsap Transit. Fares are only $2 one way, but note that since routed buses are for commuters, they may not drop you off quite at the doorstep of the park or attraction you're headed to. Be sure to study the route map carefully or call Kitsap at least a day in advance of your trip to inquire about its Dial-A-Ride services.

Contacts Kitsap Transit ☏ *800/501–7433* ⊕ *www.kitsaptransit.com.*

ESSENTIALS

Visitor Information Bainbridge Chamber of Commerce. The Chamber operates a visitor kiosk just outside the ferry terminal near the taxi area, as well as a visitor center at 395 Winslow Way E. ☏ *206/842–3700* ⊕ *www. bainbridgechamber.com.*

EXPLORING

Bainbridge Island Studio Tour. Twice a year (the second weekend in August and the first weekend in December), the island's artists and craftspeople are in the spotlight when they put their best pieces on display for these three-day events, and you can buy anything from watercolors to furniture directly from the artists. Even if you can't make the official studio tours, check out the website, which has maps and information on studios and shops throughout the island, as well as links to artists' websites. Many of the shops have regular hours, and you can easily put together your own tour. ⊕ *www.bistudiotour.com.*

Fodor's Choice ★ **Bloedel Reserve.** This 150-acre internationally recognized preserve is a stunning mix of natural woodlands and beautifully landscaped gardens—including a moss garden, Japanese garden, a reflection pool, and the impressive former Bloedel estate home. Dazzling rhododendrons and azaleas bloom in spring, and Japanese maples colorfully signal autumn's arrival. Picnicking is not permitted, and you'll want to leave the pooch behind—pets are not allowed on the property, even if they

9

Bloedel Reserve, Bainbridge Island

stay in the car. Check the website's events page for special events, lectures, and exhibits. ⊠ *7571 N.E. Dolphin Dr., 6 miles west of Winslow, via Hwy. 305* ☎ *206/842–7631* ⊕ *www.bloedelreserve.org* ✉ *$15* ☉ *Sept.–May, Tues.–Sun. 10–4; Jun.–Aug., Tues.–Weds. 10–4, Thurs.–Sun. 10–6.*

Fort Ward Park. On the southwest side of the island is this lovely and tranquil 137-acre park. There are 2 miles of hiking trails through forest, a long stretch of (sometimes) sun-drenched rocky beach, several picnic tables, and even a spot for scuba diving. Along with views of the water and the Olympic Mountains, you might be lucky and get a peek of Mt. Rainier—or of the massive sea lions that frequent the near-shore waters. A loop trail through the park is suitable for all ability levels, and will take you past vestiges of the park's previous life as a military installation. ⊠ *Fort Ward Hill Rd. NE* ✛ *Take Hwy. 305 out of Winslow; turn west on High School Rd. and follow signs to park* ☎ *206/842–3931* ⊕ *www.biparks.org/parksandfacilities/pkftward.html* ☉ *Daily 8–dusk.*

WHERE TO EAT

$ × **Blackbird Bakery.** A great place to grab a cup of coffee and a snack
BAKERY before exploring the island serves up rich pastries and cakes along with quiche, soups, and a good selection of teas and espresso drinks. Though there is some nice window seating that allows you to watch the human parade on Winslow Way, the place gets very crowded, especially when the ferries come in, so you might want to take your order to go. Ⓢ *Average main: $5* ⊠ *210 Winslow Way E, Winslow* ☎ *206/780–1322* ⊕ *www.blackbirdbakery.com* ▭ *No credit cards* ☉ *No dinner.*

$$ ✕ **Café Nola.** This is the best option on the island for something a little
BISTRO fancier than pub grub or picnic fare. The bistro setting is pleasant, with
pale yellow walls, white tablecloths, and jazz music, and there's a small
patio area for alfresco dining. The food is basically American and Euro-
pean comfort cooking with a few modern twists. The lunch menu offers
salads, burgers, and sandwiches, such as an open-faced Dungeness crab
melt on foccacia or a fresh king salmon sandwich with red pepper aioli.
At dinner, classics like pan-seared scallops and roasted pork shoulder
steal the show. The restaurant is within walking distance of the main
ferry terminal. $ *Average main: $22* ✉ *101 Winslow Way E, Winslow*
☎ *206/842–3822* ⊕ *www.cafenola.com.*

$ ✕ **Harbor Public House.** An 1881 estate home overlooking Eagle Harbor
SEAFOOD was renovated to create this casual pub and restaurant at Winslow's
Harbor Marina, where a complimentary boat tie-up is available for pub
patrons. Local seafood—including steamed mussels, clams, and oyster
sliders—plus burgers, fish-and-chips, and poutine are typical fare, and
there are 12 beers on tap. This is where the kayaking and pleasure-
boating crowds come to dine in a relaxed, waterfront setting. When
the sun shines, the harbor-front deck is the place to be, and things get
raucous during the first Tuesday night open-mike sessions. $ *Average
main: $15* ✉ *231 Parfitt Way SW, Winslow* ☎ *206/842–0969* ⊕ *www.
harbourpub.com.*

VASHON ISLAND

20 minutes by ferry from West Seattle.

Vashon is the most peaceful and rural of the islands easily reached from
the city, home to fruit growers, commune-dwelling hippies, rat-race
dropouts, and Seattle commuters.

Biking, beachcombing, picnicking, and kayaking are the main activi-
ties here. A tour of the 13-mile-long island will take you down country
lanes and past orchards and lavender farms. There are several artists'
studios and galleries on the island, as well as a small commercial dis-
trict in the center of the island, where a farmers' market is a highlight
every Saturday from May to October. The popular Strawberry Festival
takes place every July.

GETTING HERE AND AROUND

Washington State Ferries leave from Fauntleroy in West Seattle (about 9
miles southwest of Downtown) for the 20-minute ride to Vashon Island.
The ferry docks at the northern tip of the island. Round-trip fares are
$5.20 per person or $22.05 for a car and driver. A water taxi also goes
to Vashon from Pier 50 on the Seattle waterfront, but it's primarily
for commuters, operating only on weekdays during commuter hours.
One-way fares are $5. There's limited bus service on the island; the
best way to get around is by car or by bicycle (bring your own or rent
in Seattle. Note that there's a huge hill as you immediately disembark
the ferry dock and head up to town). The site ⊕ *www.vashonchamber.
com* is also a good source of information.

9

ESSENTIALS

Visitor Information Vashon-Maury Island Chamber of Commerce. The office is open Monday–Saturday 10 to 3. ⊠ *17141 Vashon Highway SW, across from Ober Park, Vashon Island* ☎ *206/463–6217* ⊕ *www.vashonchamber.com.*

EXPLORING

Jensen Point and Burton Acres Park. Vashon has many parks and protected areas. This park, on the lush Burton Peninsula overlooking Quartermaster Harbor, is home to 64 acres of secluded hiking and horseback riding trails. The adjacent Jensen Point, a 4-acre shoreline park, has picnic tables, a swimming beach, and kayak and paddleboard rentals (May through September). ⊠ *8900 S.W. Harbor Dr., Vashon Island* ⊹ *From the ferry terminal, take Vashon Hwy. SW to S.W. Burton Dr. and turn left. Turn left on 97 Ave. SW and follow it around as it becomes S.W. Harbor Dr.* ⊕ *www.vashonparkdistrict.org.*

Point Robinson Park. You can stroll along the beach, which is very picturesque thanks to **Point Robinson Lighthouse**. The lighthouse is typically open to the public from noon to 4 on Sundays during the summer; call to arrange a tour or rent out the keeper's quarters by the week. ⊠ *3705 S.W. Pt. Robinson Rd., Vashon Island* ☎ *206/463–9602* ⊕ *www.vashonparkdistrict.org.*

Vashon Allied Arts. The best representative of the island's diverse arts community presents monthly exhibits and events that span all mediums, including dance, chamber music, and art lectures. The gallery's exhibits rotate monthly, featuring local and Northwest artists, and Heron's Nest (⊠ *17600 Vashon Hwy. SW* ☎ *206/463–5252*), the affiliated gift shop in town, is where you'll find fine art and handcrafted items by local artists. ⊠ *19704 Vashon Hwy.* ☎ *206/463–5131* ⊕ *www.vashonalliedarts.org* ⊗ *Weekdays 10–5, Sat. noon–5.*

WHERE TO EAT

$$
AMERICAN
× **Hardware Store.** This all-day restaurant's unusual name comes from its former life as a mom-and-pop hardware shop—it occupies the oldest commercial building on Vashon, and certainly looks like a relic from the outside. Inside, you'll find a charming restaurant that's a cross between a bistro and an upscale diner. The cuisine is "Northwest Americana," with breakfast highlights like rustic French toast and smoked salmon Benedict; sandwiches, salads, and burgers for lunch, and for dinner, hearty old standbys like buttermilk fried chicken, pasta, meat loaf, and grilled salmon. Almost everything on the menu can be made gluten-free. A decent wine list focuses on Northwest and Californian wines. ⑤ *Average main: $16* ⊠ *17601 Vashon Hwy. SW, Vashon Island* ☎ *206/463–1800* ⊕ *www.thsrestaurant.com.*

$$$$
FRENCH
× **La Boucherie.** As the retail and restaurant side of the "beyond organic" Sea Breeze Farm, this much-discussed outpost of ultralocal cuisine serves meats, poultry, and produce grown on or very close to the property. As a result, the menu is highly seasonal (changing twice weekly), but it always highlights Vashon's growers and farmers. The charcuterie plate is one of their most popular starters; it features all the pâtés they make in-house. Foodies who flock here swear by the pork chops, too. You can order off the à la carte menu but the six course prix-fixe is the

way to go. It's a tiny spot; reservations are essential. $ *Average main: $38* ✉ *17635 100th Ave. SW, Vashon Island* ☎ *206/567–4628* ⊕ *www. seabreezefarm.net* ⚑ *Reservations essential* ⊗ *Closed Sun.–Wed.*

$ ✕ **May Kitchen + Bar.** Here's another reason for city dwellers to hop a
THAI ferry to come to Vashon for dinner. This is where sophisticated foodies
Fodor's Choice swoon over delectable and highly authentic Thai dishes. The ambi-
★ ence is scene-y (atypical for Vashon): dark with fully paneled walls
in mahogany and teak—wood that owner May Chaleoy had shipped
from Thailand, where it previously lived in the interior of a 150-year-
old home. Reservations are highly recommended. $ *Average main: $15*
✉ *17614 Vashon Hwy. SW, Vashon Island* ☎ *206/408–7196* ⊕ *www. maykitchen.com* ⊗ *Closed Mon.–Tues. No lunch.*

WHIDBEY ISLAND

*20 minutes by ferry from Mukilteo (20 miles north of Seattle) to Clin-
ton, at the southern end of Whidbey Island, or drive north 87 miles to
Deception Pass at the north end of the island.*

Whidbey is a blend of low pastoral hills, evergreen and oak forests,
meadows of wildflowers (including some endemic species), sandy
beaches, and dramatic bluffs with a few pockets of unfortunate suburban sprawl. It's a great place for a scenic drive, viewing sunsets over
the water, taking ridge hikes that give you uninterrupted views of the
Strait of Juan de Fuca, walking along miles of rugged seaweed-strewn
beaches, and for boating or kayaking along the protected shorelines of
Saratoga Passage, Holmes Harbor, Penn Cove, and Skagit Bay.

The best beaches are on the west side, where wooded and wildflower-
bedecked bluffs drop steeply to sand or surf—which can cover the
beaches at high tide and can be unexpectedly rough on this exposed
shore. Both beaches and bluffs have great views of the shipping lanes
and the Olympic Mountains. Maxwelton Beach, with its sand, driftwood, and amazing sunsets, is popular with the locals. Possession Point
includes a park and a beach, but it's best known for its popular boat
launch. West of Coupeville, Ft. Ebey State Park has a sandy spread and
an incredible bluff trail; West Beach is a stormy patch north of the fort
with mounds of driftwood. At 35 miles long, Whidbey's island vibe is
split between north and south; the historic southern and central towns
of Langley and Coupeville are quaint and offer the most to do; Clinton
(near the ferry terminal) isn't much of a destination, nor is the sprawling navy town of Oak Harbor farther north. Yet Deception Pass at the
island's northern tip offers the most jaw-dropping splendor, so plan
enough time to visit both ends of the island. One fun way to see it all is
to arrive via the Clinton ferry and drive back to Seattle via Deception
Pass, or vice versa.

GETTING HERE AND AROUND

You can reach Whidbey Island by heading north from Seattle on Interstate 5, west on Route 20 onto Fidalgo Island, and south across Deception Pass Bridge. The Deception Pass Bridge links Whidbey to Fidalgo
Island. From the bridge it's just a short drive to Anacortes, Fidalgo's
main town and the terminus for ferries to the San Juan Islands. It's

9

easier—and more pleasant—to take the 20-minute ferry trip from Mukilteo (30 miles northwest of Seattle) to Clinton, on Whidbey's south end, as long as you don't time your trip on a Friday evening, which could leave you waiting in the car line for hours. Fares are $4.80 per person for walk-ons (round-trip) and $10.30 per car and driver (one way). Be sure to look at a map before choosing your point of entry; the ferry ride may not make sense if your main destination is Deception Pass State Park. Buses on Whidbey Island, provided by Island Transit, are free. Routes are fairly comprehensive, but keep in mind that Whidbey is big—it takes at least 35 minutes just to drive from the southern ferry terminal to the midway point at Coupeville—and if your itinerary is far-reaching, a car is your best bet.

Contact Island Transit ☎ *800/240–8747* ⊕ *www.islandtransit.org.*

ESSENTIALS

Visitor Information Central Whidbey Chamber of Commerce. The Chamber's website provides a great list of resources, from lodging to shopping, restaurants, and local events. ✉ *107 S. Main St., Coupeville* ☎ *360/678–5434* ⊕ *www.centralwhidbeychamber.com.* **Langley Chamber of Commerce.** Start off the "Langley Loop"—an 8-mile scenic driving or biking tour—at the Chamber offices, which will point you in the right direction for South Whidbey's eclectic mix of restaurants, galleries, wineries, and markets. ✉ *208 Anthes Ave., Langley* ☎ *360/221–6765* ⊕ *www.visitlangley.com.*

LANGLEY

The historic village of Langley, 7 miles north of Clinton on Whidbey Island, is above a 50-foot-high bluff overlooking Saratoga Passage, which separates Whidbey from Camano Island. A grassy terrace just above the beach is a great place for viewing birds on the water or in the air. On a clear day you can see Mt. Baker in the distance. Upscale boutiques selling art, glass, jewelry, books, and clothing line 1st and 2nd streets in the heart of town.

WHERE TO EAT AND STAY

$$
BISTRO
✕ **Prima Bistro.** Langley's most popular gathering spot occupies a second-story space on 1st Street, right above the Star Store Grocery. Northwest-inspired French cuisine is the headliner here; classic bistro dishes like steak frites, salade niçoise, and confit of duck leg are favorites. Penn Cove mussels and oysters are always popular. The wine list is by far the best in town. The bistro's outdoor deck offers views of Saratoga Passage, Camano Island, and beyond, and ample heat lamps ensure that guests enjoy the beauty of Whidbey summer's night. Live music every Thursday night and a daily happy hour from 3 to 6 pm keeps locals and tourists coming back for more. ⑤ *Average main: $20* ✉ *201½ 1st St.* ☎ *360/221–4060* ⊕ *www.primabistro.com.*

$$$$
B&B/INN
Fodor's Choice
★
⌂ **Inn at Langley.** In a concrete-and-wood Frank Lloyd Wright–inspired structure, perching on a bluff above the beach just steps from the center of town, elegant, Asian-inspired guest rooms have dramatic marine and mountain views. **Pros:** island luxury; lovely views; amazing restaurant. **Cons:** some rooms can be on the small side; decor is starting to feel slightly dated. ⑤ *Rooms from: $390* ✉ *400 1st St.* ☎ *360/221–3033* ⊕ *www.innatlangley.com* ⇗ *28 rooms* ⦿ *Breakfast.*

$$ | ☖ **Saratoga Inn.** At the edge of Langley, this cedar-shake, Nantucket-style
B&B/INN | inn with cozy decor and fireplaces in every room, is a short walk from
the town's shops and restaurants; it overlooks the waters of Saratoga
Passage and the stunning North Cascades. **Pros:** breathtaking views;
cozy interiors. **Cons:** a bit rustic; some small bathrooms. ⑤ *Rooms
from: $205* ✉ *201 Cascade Ave.* ☎ *360/221–5801, 800/698–2910*
⊕ *www.saratogainnwhidbeyisland.com* ⇄ *15 rooms, 1 carriage house*
⑩ *Breakfast.*

SHOPPING

Brackenwood Gallery. At this gallery known for its fine art and well-known
Pacific Northwest artists, you can see pieces by Georgia Gerber, a famed
island sculptor whose bronze pieces are regionally famous; Western-
themed paintings and prints by Bruce Morrow; exquisite stone sculpture
by Sharon Spencer; and Northwest landscape paintings by Pete Jordan.
✉ *302 1st St.* ☎ *360/221–2978* ⊕ *www.brackenwoodgallery.com.*

Moonraker Books. Langley's independent bookshop, an institution since
1972, stocks a wonderful and eclectic array of fiction, nonfiction, cookbooks—and, according to the owners, "books you didn't even know
you wanted until you stepped inside." ✉ *209 1st St.* ☎ *360/221–6962.*

Museo. This contemporary fine art gallery focused on Northwest and
regional artists is known for its glass art, sculpture, and handcrafted
jewelry. Artist receptions are held on the first Saturday of each month
from 5 to 7 pm. ✉ *215 1st St.* ☎ *360/221–7737* ⊕ *www.museo.cc*
⊗ *Wed.–Mon. 11–5; Tues. by appointment.*

GREENBANK

About halfway up Whidbey Island, 14 miles northwest of Langley, is
the hamlet of Greenbank, home to a loganberry farm encircled by views
of the Olympic and Cascade Ranges.

EXPLORING

FAMILY | **Greenbank Farm.** You can't miss the huge, chestnut-color, two-story barn
with the wine vat out front—the centerpiece to this picturesque, 125-
acre property. Greenbank's loganberry wines and dessert wines (for
which they are famous) can be sampled daily in the tasting room. The
adjacent Whidbey Pies Café creates gourmet sandwiches, soups, and
pies, all of which disappear quickly as visitors head for the scattered
picnic tables. There's also a specialty cheese shop. Bring your dog (or
horse!) and walk the scenic meadow trails. Besides wildlife, be on the
lookout for the herd of fluffy alpacas raised on-site by the Whidbey
Island Alpacas company. The 1904 barn, which once housed a winery,
is now a community center for farmers' markets, concerts, flea markets,
and other events, including the famous Loganberry Festival each July.
✉ *765 Wonn Rd.* ☎ *360/678–7700* ⊕ *www.greenbankfarm.com* ⌑ *Free*
⊗ *Grounds daily, dawn–dusk; businesses daily, noon–5.*

Meerkerk Rhododendron Gardens. The 53-acre Meerkerk Rhododendron
Gardens contain 1,500 native and hybrid species of rhododendrons
and more than 100,000 spring bulbs on 10 acres of display gardens
with more than 4 miles of nature trails. The flowers are in full bloom
in April and May; summer flowers and fall color provide interest later
in the year. The 43 remaining acres are kept wild as a nature preserve.

This Historic Ferry House is part of Ebey's Landing National Historic Reserve on Whidbey Island.

Leashed pets are permitted on the gravel paths. ⊠ *Hwy. 525 and Resort Rd., Hilton Head Island* ☎ *360/678–1912* ⊕ *www.meerkerkgardens. org* ✉ *$5* ⊘ *Daily 9–4.*

WHERE TO STAY

$$
B&B/INN

🏨 **Guest House Cottages.** Surrounded by 25 secluded wooded acres, each of these six private cabins, resembling cedar-sided barns with towering stone chimneys, comes with a feather bed, a Jacuzzi, country antiques, a kitchen, and a fireplace. **Pros:** lots of privacy and amenities; good location between Langley and Coupeville. **Cons:** strict cancellation policy of 21 days; basic breakfast foods are provided but you have to make your own. ⑤ *Rooms from: $235* ⊠ *24371 State Route 525 E, Christianson Rd.* ☎ *360/678–3115, 800/997–3115* ⊕ *www.guesthouselogcottages. com* ✈ *6 cabins* ⑪ *Some meals.*

COUPEVILLE

Restored Victorian houses grace many of the streets in quiet Coupeville, Washington's second-oldest city, on the south shore of Penn Cove, 12 miles north of Greenbank. It also has one of the largest national historic districts in the state, and has been used for filming movies depicting 19th-century New England villages. Stores above the waterfront have maintained their old-fashioned character. Captain Thomas Coupe founded the town in 1852. His house was built the following year, and other houses and commercial buildings were built in the late 1800s. Even though Coupeville is the Island County seat, the town has a laid-back, almost 19th-century air.

EXPLORING

FAMILY

Fodor'sChoice

★

Ebey's Landing National Historic Reserve. The reserve encompasses a sand-and-cobble beach, bluffs with dramatic views down the Strait of Juan de Fuca, two state parks (⇨ *Ft. Casey and Ft. Ebey; see separate listings*), and several privately held pioneer farms homesteaded in the early 1850s. The first and largest reserve of its kind holds nearly 400 nationally registered historic structures (including those located within the town of Coupeville), most of them from the 19th century. Miles of trails lead along the beach and through the woods. Cedar Gulch, south of the main entrance to Ft. Ebey, has a lovely picnic area in a wooded ravine above the beach. ⊕ *From Hwy. 20, turn south on Main St. in Coupeville. This road turns into Engles Rd. as you head out of town. Turn right on Hill Rd. and follow it to the reserve.* ⊕ *www.nps.gov/ebla.*

Ft. Casey and Keystone State Park. The 467-acre Ft. Casey State Park, on a bluff overlooking sweeping views of Strait of Juan de Fuca and the Port Townsend ferry landing, was one of three forts (the "Triangle of Death") built after 1890 to protect the entrance to Admiralty Inlet from a naval invasion. Look for the concrete gun emplacement and a couple of 8-inch "disappearing" guns. The charming Admiralty Head Lighthouse Interpretive Center is north of the gunnery emplacements. There are also grassy picnic sites, rocky fishing spots, waterfront campsites, and a boat launch. A Washington State Discover Pass is required (⊞ *$30/year or $10/day* ⊕ *www.discoverpass.wa.gov*). Once you're done exploring the park, take the ferry from here to Port Townsend for a quick side trip or long lunch. ⊠ *2 miles west of Rte. 20* ☎ *360/678–4519* ⊕ *www.parks.wa.gov/parks* ⊞ *Discover Pass required; $30/year or $10/day* ⊙ *Park open daily 8 am–dusk; lighthouse hrs vary by season, usually open 11–5.*

Ft. Ebey State Park. In late May and early June, Ft. Ebey State Park blazes with native rhododendrons. West of Coupeville on Point Partridge, it has 3 miles of shoreline, campsites in the woods, trails to the headlands, a freshwater lake for fishing, World War II gun emplacements, wildflower meadows, spectacular views down the Strait of Juan de Fuca, and miles of hiking and biking trails. A Washington State Discover Pass is required. ⊠ *3 miles west of Rte. 20* ☎ *360/678–4636* ⊕ *www.parks.wa.gov* ⊞ *Washington State Discover Pass required ($30/year or $10/day)* ⊙ *Daily sunrise–sunset.*

FAMILY

Island County Historical Museum. Collections include Ice Age relics, mammoth remains, and a strong Native American collection, including cedar dugout canoes. The square-timber **Alexander Blockhouse** outside dates from 1855. Note the squared logs and dovetail joints of the corners—no overlapping log ends. This construction technique was favored by many Western Washington pioneers. ⊠ *908 N.W. Alexander St.* ☎ *360/678–3310* ⊞ *$3* ⊙ *May–Sept., Mon.–Sat. 10–5, Sun. 11–5; Oct.–Apr., Mon.–Sat. 10–4, Sun. 11–4.*

WHERE TO EAT AND STAY

$$

PACIFIC

NORTHWEST

✕ **Christopher's on Whidbey.** This warm and casual place is in a house one block from the waterfront. The menu features many Whidbey favorites, including local mussels and clams, and such flavorful fare as raspberry

Woodinville Wineries

Walla Walla wine country is too far to go from Seattle if you've only got a few days; instead, check out Woodinville's excellent wineries. It's only about 22 miles from Seattle's city center. You'll need a car unless you sign up for a guided tour. Check out ⊕ www.woodinvillewinecountry.com for a full list of wineries and touring maps.

WINERIES

There are more than 50 wineries in Woodinville, though most of them don't have tasting rooms. This list provides a good survey, from the big guys to the smallest boutique producers:

Chateau Ste. Michelle (⊠ *14111 N.E. 145th St.* ⊕ *www.ste-michelle.com*) is the grande dame of the Woodinville wine scene, and perhaps the most recognizable name nationwide. Guided tours of the winery and grounds (which do include a château) are available daily 10:30–4:30. The tasting room is open daily 10–5. Check the website for special events like dinners and concerts.

Columbia Winery (⊠ *14030 N.E. 145th St.* ⊕ *www.columbiawinery. com*) is another major player with a grand house anchoring its winery. Columbia's tasting room is open Sunday–Tuesday 11–6 and Wednesday–Saturday 11–7. Regular tastings are $10 and private tastings are available for $25 per person.

Novelty Hill–Januik (⊠ *14710 Woodinville-Redmond Rd. NE* ⊕ *www. noveltyhilljanuik.com*) is often described as the most Napa-esque experience in Woodinville. The tasting room (open daily 11–5) for these sister wineries is sleek and modern. Themed tastings are $7–$10 per person. Brick-oven pizza is available on weekends.

Ross Andrew (⊠ *14810 N.E. 145th St., No. A-2* ⊕ *www.rossandrewwinery. com*) is a newcomer that is already at the top of many enthusiasts' lists for Cabs and Syrah from Columbia Valley grapes and Pinot Blanc and Pinot Gris from Oregon grapes. The tasting room is open Thursday–Monday noon–5 (Saturday until 6).

---

barbecued salmon, bacon-wrapped pork tenderloin with mushrooms, Penn Cove seafood stew, and linguine with a smoked-salmon cream sauce. The wine list is extensive. $ *Average main: $21* ⊠ *103 N.W. Coveland* ☎ *360/678–5480* ⊕ *www.christophersonwhidbey.com* ⊗ *Closed Mon.*

$$$
SEAFOOD
Fodor's Choice
★

✕ **The Oystercatcher.** A dining destination for foodies from across the Northwest is renowned for its local-inspired cuisine. The simple menu is heavily influenced by fresh, in-season ingredients. Owners Joe and Jamie Martin have crafted an intimate, romantic dining space in the heart of town, and the restaurant's wine list is stellar. $ *Average main: $28* ⊠ *901 Grace St. NW* ☎ *360/678–0683* ⊕ *www.oystercatcherwhidbey. com* ⊗ *Closed Mon. and Tues. No lunch weekdays.*

$
B&B/INN

⬚ **Captain Whidbey Inn.** Over a century old, this venerable historic lodge on a wooded promontory offers a special kind of old-world romance and charm now rarely found, with gleaming log-walled rooms and suites. **Pros:** private cabins with hot tubs; rustic yet comfortable. **Cons:** poor soundproofing in the main motel; shared bathrooms. $ *Rooms from: $107* ⊠ *2072 Captain Whidbey Inn Rd., off Madrona Way* ☎ *360/678–4097, 800/366–4097* ⊕ *www.captainwhidbey.com* ⤺ *29 rooms, 2 suites, 4 cabins.*

$

B&B/INN

▢ **Compass Rose Bed and Breakfast.** Inside this stately 1890 Queen Anne Victorian on the National Register of Historic Places, a veritable museum of art, artifacts, and antiques awaits you. **Pros:** wonderful hosts; great breakfast; full of interesting antiques and collectibles. **Cons:** only two rooms, so it gets booked up fast. $ *Rooms from: $115* ⊠ *508 S. Main St.* ☎ *360/678–5318* ☎ *800/237–3881* ⊕ *www.compassrosebandb.com* ⤺ *2 rooms* ▭ *No credit cards* ❛❍❜ *Breakfast.*

OAK HARBOR

Oak Harbor, about 10 miles north of Coupeville, is the least attractive and least interesting part of Whidbey—it mainly exists to serve the Whidbey Island Naval Air Station, and has none of the historic or pastoral charm of the rest of the island. It is, however, the largest town on the island and the one closest to Deception Pass State Park. If you need to stock up on provisions, you'll find all the big-box stores here, in addition to major supermarkets. In town, the marina, at the east side of the bay, has a picnic area with views of Saratoga Passage and the entrance of Penn Cove.

FAMILY **Deception Pass State Park.** The biggest draw of the park is the historic two-lane Deception Pass Bridge connecting Whidbey Island to Fidalgo Island, about 9 miles north of Oak Harbor. Park the car and walk across in order to get the best views of the dramatic saltwater gorges and churning whirlpools below. Then, spend a few hours walking the 19 miles of rocky shore and beaches, exploring three freshwater lakes, or walking along the many forest and meadow trails. ⊠ *Rte. 20, 9 miles north of Oak Harbor* ☎ *360/675–2417* ⊕ *www.parks.wa.gov* ⤳ *Day pass $10 per vehicle; annual Discovery Pass $30 (valid at all state parks); campsite fees vary* ⊘ *Apr.–Sept., daily 6:30 am–dusk; Oct.– Mar., daily 8 am–dusk.*

WASHINGTON CASCADE MOUNTAINS AND VALLEYS

With Tacoma, Olympia, and Mt. St. Helens

WELCOME TO WASHINGTON CASCADE MOUNTAINS AND VALLEYS

TOP REASONS TO GO

★ **Take flight:** See a Boeing in mid-construction or a World War II chopper up close at Everett's Paine Field.

★ **Tiptoe through the tulips:** Bike past undulating fields of tulips and other spring blooms in La Conner and Mount Vernon.

★ **Hang in glass houses:** Check out Dale Chihuly's biomorphic sculptures at Tacoma's Museum of Glass.

★ **View a volcano:** Visit Johnston Ridge Observatory, for an eerily close view of Mt. St. Helens.

★ **Paddle around Puget Sound:** Rent a kayak to explore the charming seaside communities of Poulsbo or Gig Harbor.

1 Cascade Foothills and Snohomish County. Short jaunts off the Interstate 5 highway include attending a county fair in Puyallup and winding down a day of hiking or biking near Snoqualmie Pass with a snack in the cute town of Snoqualmie. North of Seattle are two notable port towns, Edmonds and Everett. Edmonds has more of a seaside vibe, with waterfront parks and trendy downtown restaurants, and a ferry terminal serving the islands of Puget Sound. Everett, on the other hand, is devoted to flight, with a Boeing factory tour and a collection of vintage airplanes its main attractions.

2 Bellingham and Skagit Valley. The laid-back, outdoorsy college town of Bellingham is about as close as this area comes to bustle. Although not as tranquil as the central part of the state, the area is about picturesque roads less traveled: the farm roads that connect La Conner and Mount Vernon and the bike and hiking paths that wind through state parks.

3 Kitsap Peninsula. Exploring Bremerton's collection of naval vessels is a favorite family activity. The smaller, less industrial port

towns provide beach parks plus glimpses of the region's Scandinavian and logging pasts—a nice snapshot of coastal Washington life that's more accessible than the Olympic Peninsula.

4 Tacoma and Olympia. Immortalized in song by Neko Case as the "dusty old jewel in the South Puget Sound," Tacoma is shining far more brightly these days, with a walkable waterfront that includes several impressive museums and a burgeoning restaurant scene. Farther south is the capital city Olympia, which is the perfect mix of quirky and stately.

5 Mt. Rainier Environs. Washington's rugged southern Cascades region is famous for two massive volcanic peaks, Mt. Rainier and Mt. St. Helens. Small, remote towns are strung along winding, forested country highways that meander through this dramatic area within day-tripping distance of Olympia and Tacoma, even Seattle.

GETTING ORIENTED

Most of the major towns are along—or not far from—the Interstate 5 corridor, stretching from the capital city of Olympia, 60 miles south of Seattle, and on north to Bellingham, 90 miles north of Seattle and the last city of any size before the Canadian border. Many of the cities along the route are ports on Puget Sound. There's even more waterfront out on the Kitsap Peninsula, which is sandwiched between this corridor and the Olympic Peninsula. Three other outlying areas include the western edge of the Skagit Valley, an important agricultural area; Snoqualmie, in the foothills of the Cascades east of Seattle via Interstate 90; and the towns around Mt. Rainier and Mt. St. Helens, which are south of Seattle and just east of the Interstate 5 corridor.

10

Updated
by Andrew
Collins

The San Juan Islands, the Olympic Peninsula, and the great swaths of midstate wilderness provide Washington's favorite photo ops, but there are plenty of adventures that don't require traveling on ferries or bumping along Forest Service roads.

Up and down Interstate 5 you'll find most of the state's major cities: the ports of Tacoma, Olympia, and Bellingham each have enough cultural and outdoorsy attractions to warrant an overnight or two.

Slightly farther afield you'll find smaller towns with some very specific draws: Poulsbo's proud Norwegian heritage, Port Gamble's painstakingly preserved mill-town vibe, Everett's enthusiasm for all things flight related, whether crafted by Boeing or not, and North Bend and Snoqualmie's breathtaking alpine scenery and friendly feel. And south of Mt. Rainier, towns like Packwood and Ashford in the Cascades offer rugged scenery and jumping-off points for visiting both Rainier and Mt. St. Helens.

Exploring this part of the state, encompassing so many distinct geographical areas like the Kitsap Peninsula and the western fringe of the Skagit Valley, can bring you from industrial areas to tulip fields in one day. From naval warships to thundering falls, there's a lot to see within two hours of Seattle.

WASHINGTON CASCADE MOUNTAINS AND VALLEYS PLANNER

WHEN TO GO

The climate throughout the Interstate 5 corridor, from the Skagit Valley down through Tacoma and Olympia, largely matches that of Seattle, with cool and damp winters (with low temperatures in the upper 30s) and largely dry and sunny summers, with temperatures in the 70s and low 80s. The more favorable weather of late spring through mid-October brings the largest crowds to the region. Rainy winter brings lower hotels rates—and on the Kitsap Peninsula or up in Bellingham and the Skagit Valley, can be charmingly stormy—ideal for cozying up by the fireplace in a toasty room. In the Snoqualmie area, skiing and other winter sports are popular from December through April, when heavy snows come, although the towns in the foothills receive more rain than snow. In the towns up around Mt. Rainier and Mt. St. Helens, winter snow often brings temporary road closures, and many restaurants, lodges, and attractions are closed or have limited hours from mid-fall through mid-spring; it's definitely wise to check forecasts and call ahead if venturing into the Cascades at this time.

FESTIVALS AND EVENTS

Skagit Valley Tulip Festival. June brings monthlong celebration of these iconic flowers that bloom in their millions throughout Mount Vernon and La Conner. ☎ *360/428–5959* ⊕ *www.tulipfestival.org.*

Washington State Fair. This fair in September brings thousands of visitors daily over two weeks to Puyallup, a suburb just south of Seattle and southeast of Tacoma, and features concerts, a rodeo, art and cultural exhibits, agricultural shows, and amusement rides. ☎ *253/845–1771* ⊕ *www.thefair.com.*

GETTING HERE AND AROUND

AIR TRAVEL

Seattle-Tacoma International Airport (Sea-Tac), 15 miles south of Seattle, is the hub for this region. There are several regional airports, but the only one that sees much action is Bellingham's International Airport, which has direct flights to and from Seattle as well as Denver, Honolulu, Las Vegas, Oakland, Phoenix, Portland, and several other cities. This small airport is a hub between northwestern Washington and Canada and serves as link to Bellingham's ferry terminal for cruises to British Columbia and beyond.

Contacts Bellingham International ✉ *1801 Roeder Ave., Bellingham* ☎ *360/676–2500* ⊕ *www.portofbellingham.com.*

AIRPORT TRANSFERS

Shuttle Express provides scheduled ride-share service hourly from Sea-Tac Airport to all the cities and larger towns *in this chapter*. Bremerton–Kitsap Airporter shuttles passengers from Sea-Tac to points in Tacoma, Bremerton, Port Orchard, Gig Harbor, and Poulsbo ($16–$26 one way). The Capital Aeroporter connects Sea-Tac with Olympia ($36 one way) and Tacoma ($31 one way). The Airporter Shuttle/Bellair Charters makes numerous trips daily between Sea-Tac and Bellingham ($37 one way), with a few stops in between; and between Sea-Tac and North Bend ($21 one way), continuing on to Yakima

Contacts Airporter Shuttle/Bellair Charters ☎ *866/235–5247* ⊕ *www. airporter.com.* **Bremerton–Kitsap Airporter** ☎ *360/876–1737* ⊕ *www. kitsapairporter.com.* **Capital Aeroporter** ☎ *360/754–7113, 800/962–3579* ⊕ *www.capair.com.* **Shuttle Express** ☎ *425/981–7000* ⊕ *www.shuttleexpress. com.*

10

BOAT AND FERRY TRAVEL

Washington State Ferries ply Puget Sound, with routes between Seattle and Bremerton and between Edmonds and Kingston on the Key Peninsula.

BUS TRAVEL

Greyhound Lines and Northwestern Trailways cover Washington and the Pacific Northwest. From Seattle, Greyhound connects to Tacoma, Olympia, Bellingham, and several other cities in the region. Pierce County Transit provides bus service around Tacoma. *For more on bus travel throughout the region, see Travel Smart.*

Contacts Pierce County Transit ☎ *253/581–8000* ⊕ *www.piercetransit.org.*

CAR TRAVEL

Interstate 5 runs south from the Canadian border through Seattle, Tacoma, and Olympia to Oregon and California. Interstate 90 begins in Seattle and runs east through North Bend all the way to Idaho. U.S. 2 meanders east, parallel to Interstate 90, from Everett to Spokane. Highways 7 and 167 connect the Tacoma area with the Puyallup suburbs and towns around Mt. Rainier. U.S. 101 begins northwest of Olympia and traces the coast of the Olympic Peninsula.

TRAIN TRAVEL

Amtrak's Cascades line serves Centralia, Tacoma, Olympia, Seattle, Edmonds, Everett, Mount Vernon, and Bellingham. Sound Transit's Sounder trains (commuter rail, weekdays only) connect Seattle with Edmonds, Mukilteo, and Everett; and Seattle with Tacoma and Puyallup as well as a few other suburbs.

TRAVELING FROM SEATTLE

Tacoma, Bremerton, and Everett are good choices for day trips. Tacoma is only 30–40 minutes by car or train from Seattle; Bremerton and Everett are also easy to reach in under an hour, plus seeing their major attractions (exhibits on naval and flight history, respectively) doesn't require an overnight. Just don't get stuck driving the Interstate 5 corridor during weekday rush hours or on Sunday night in summer—the chaotic and heavy traffic will sour any outing.

Snoqualmie is also easily visited in a day, as it's close to Seattle, but because it's a popular base for outdoor recreation, many visitors overnight here.

Olympia is far enough from Seattle—technically it's only about 60 miles, but during the day you'll nearly always hit traffic, so expect a solid 1½ hours in the car—that it's often better for an overnight visit or as a stop on the way to the southern part of the Olympic Peninsula (Ocean Shores or Moclips, for example). You can pick up U.S. 101 on the outskirts of the city. Olympia is also a good leg-stretch between Seattle and Portland and can be part of an itinerary to Mount Rainier National Park or Mount St. Helens National Volcanic Monument—it's a good idea to spend the night near these parks if planning a visit, as they're a good drive from Seattle, and you'll want to get an early start if planning a hike or driving along these winding, narrow forest roads.

RESTAURANTS

Olympia and especially Tacoma have increasingly hip and sophisticated dining scenes, with everything from laid-back cafés to seasonally driven restaurants with water views. After those cities, Gig Harbor and Bellingham have the best food scenes—they're not terribly big, but support fine little crops of notable restaurants. You'll also find good brewpubs and indie coffeehouses in most of the larger towns in the area. Edmonds also has a growing bounty of exceptional eateries.

On the road, refueling takes place at country-style cafés, farm stands, and kitschy or specialty shops like the '50s-style sweets shops of Port Gamble and Snoqualmie or the Norwegian bakeries of Poulsbo. None of these is in short supply, and many eateries, however small, pride themselves on using local ingredients.

HOTELS

Many of the towns listed are easy day trips from Seattle, so staying there is always an option. On the other hand, hotel rates are nearly always lower outside Seattle. Tacoma, Olympia, and Bellingham have the widest variety of accommodations, with pricey hotels, midrange chains, and bed-and-breakfasts. Almost all but the smallest rural towns have midrange chain motels; towns lacking those, like Port Gamble, have at least one B&B. The only truly great luxury resort in the region is the Salish Lodge in Snoqualmie. There are a few other noteworthy hotels in these parts—the Murano in Tacoma, the Chrysalis Inn in Bellingham, and some fine B&Bs elsewhere—but relatively prosaic chains dominate the lodging landscape. *Hotel reviews have been shortened. For full information, visit Fodors.com.*

WHAT IT COSTS IN U.S. DOLLARS				
	$	**$$**	**$$$**	**$$$$**
Restaurants	Under $16	$16–$23	$24–$30	Over $30
Hotels	Under $100	$100–$175	$176–$250	Over $250

Restaurant prices are the average cost of a main course at dinner, or if dinner is not served, at lunch. Hotel prices are the lowest cost of a standard double room in high season.

10

CASCADE FOOTHILLS AND SNOHOMISH COUNTY

Flanking the Interstate 5 corridor are gateway towns to the scenically beautiful areas north and east of Seattle: Snoqualmie and North Bend are tried-and-true pit stops for hikers, bikers, and skiers heading over Snoqualmie Pass. The town of Snoqualmie is itself day-trip-worthy, with its stuck-in-time downtown full of vintage railroad cars, and beautiful, easily accessed falls.

The towns north of Seattle are a mixed bag. Edmonds and Everett, both close to Seattle, are important commuter hubs. Edmonds has a major ferry terminal and the more sophisticated dining and shopping scenes.

Everett has slightly more tourist appeal because of its connection to Boeing and the great airplane-related attractions its Paine Field supports.

SNOQUALMIE

28 miles east of Seattle.

Spring and summer snowmelt turn the Snoqualmie (sno-*qual*-mie) River into a thundering torrent at **Snoqualmie Falls,** the sweeping cascades that provided the backdrop for the *Twin Peaks* opening montage. The water pours over a 268-foot rock ledge (100 feet higher than Niagara Falls) to a 65-foot-deep pool. These cascades, considered sacred by the Native Americans, are Snoqualmie's biggest attraction. A 2-acre park and observation platform afford views of the falls and the surrounding area. The 3-mile round-trip River Trail winds through trees and over open slopes to the base of the cascades.

GETTING HERE AND AROUND

To reach Snoqualmie from Seattle, take Interstate 90 east to Exit 27. The Old Town area of Snoqualmie is very compact and walkable; the falls and Salish Lodge are a mile north of Old Town.

EXPLORING

FAMILY **Northwest Railway Museum.** Vintage cars line a paved path along Railroad Avenue, with signs explaining the origin of each engine, car, and caboose on display, and more history and memorabilia exhibited inside the former waiting room of the stunning restored Snoqualmie depot. Several times a day, on weekends only, a train made of cars built in the mid-1910s for the Spokane, Portland, and Seattle Railroad travels between Snoqualmie Depot and North Bend. The 75-minute (round-trip) excursion passes through woods, past waterfalls, and around patchwork farmland. Crowds of families pack the winter Santa Train journeys and the midsummer Railroad Days rides, when a helicopter drops balloons and prizes over the annual parade. ⊠ *Snoqualmie Depot, 38625 S.E. King St.* 🕾 *425/888–3030* ⊕ *www.trainmuseum. org* 🖙 *Depot free; rides $18* ☉ *Depot daily 10–5; rides weekends only.*

WHERE TO EAT AND STAY

$ ╳ **Snoqualmie Taproom & Brewery.** This bustling, spacious Old Town
AMERICAN brewpub and casual restaurant is renowned for its craft beers, including a much-acclaimed Steam Train Porter, named for the town's historic rail line. Food-wise, expect a nice range of hearty hot and cold sandwiches (the smoked turkey, provolone, jalapeño, and chipotle mayo on rosemary bread has plenty of kick), plus a nice variety of 12-inch pizzas. The Greek pie, with feta, kalamatas, artichokes, roasted red peppers, and pesto is a favorite. 🖇 *Average main: $9* ⊠ *8032 Falls Ave. SE* 🕾 *425/831–2357* ⊕ *www.fallsbrew.com.*

$$$ 🏨 **Salish Lodge.** The stunning, chalet-style lodge sits right over Sno-
RESORT qualmie Falls and eight rooms have gorgeous views of the cascades,
Fodor's Choice while others have a river panorama. **Pros:** right on the falls; exceptional,
★ sophisticated restaurants; great spa. **Cons:** resort fee; not within easy walking distance of Old Town. 🖇 *Rooms from: $219* ⊠ *6501 Railroad*

Ave. SE ☎ *206/888–2556* ⊕ *www.salishlodge.com* ⤴ *80 rooms, 4 suites* ⦿ *No meals.*

SPORTS AND THE OUTDOORS

FAMILY
Fodor'sChoice
★

The Summit at Snoqualmie. This winter sports destination, 53 miles east of Seattle and about 25 miles east of North Bend, combines the Alpental, Summit West, Summit East, and Summit Central ski areas along Snoqualmie Pass. Spread over nearly 2,000 acres at elevations of up to 5,400 feet, the facilities include 65 ski trails (85% of them intermediate and advanced), 24 chairlifts, and two terrain parks. Those seeking tamer pursuits can head to the Summit Nordic Center, with groomed trails and a tubing area. Shops, restaurants, lodges (none of which are slope-side), and ski schools are connected by shuttle vans; there's even child care. For a different take on the mountains, head up to the pass after dinner; this is one of the nation's largest night-skiing areas. Full-day lift tickets, good for any of the four mountains, start at $62. ⊠ *1001 Hwy. 906, exit 52 off I–90, Snoqualmie Pass* ☎ *425/434–7669, 206/236–1600 snow conditions* ⊕ *www.summitatsnoqualmie. com* ☼ *Oct.–Apr.*

EDMONDS

45 miles northwest of Snoqualmie, 15 miles north of Seattle.

This charming, somewhat suburban small city just north of Seattle has a waterfront lined by more than a mile of boutiques and restaurants, seaside parks and attractions, and a string of broad, windswept beaches. Just beyond is the small but lively downtown area, where you can wander into hip cafés and wineshops, peruse attractive antiques stores and chic galleries, and browse the colorful Summer Market, which runs Saturday 9 to 3 from late June to early October. The early-evening Third Thursday Art Walk—one of the state's largest such events—shows off the work of local artists, and a long list of events and festivals takes place year-round. On the east side of Puget Sound, Edmonds is also a gateway to the Kitsap Peninsula, as ferries from here connect to Kingston.

GETTING HERE AND AROUND

From Seattle, take Interstate 5 north to Highway 104 west, which leads downtown and to the ferry terminal.

ESSENTIALS

Visitor Information Edmonds Chamber of Commerce ⊠ *120 5th Ave. N* ☎ *425/776–6711* ⊕ *edmondswa.com.*

EXPLORING

Edmonds Historical Museum. The lower level of this museum is the place to find out about local legends and traditions; rotating exhibits upstairs touch on everything from local art to regional and maritime history. The museum's Summer Garden Market sells handmade and hand-grown items on Saturdays from 9 to 3 from late June through early October. ⊠ *118 5th Ave. N* ☎ *425/774–0900* ⊕ *www.historicedmonds.org* 🖾 *$5* ☼ *Wed.–Sun. 1–4.*

10

The Summit at Snoqualmie

Edmonds Underwater Park. Perhaps the best-known dive site in Puget Sound besides the Narrows Bridge area has 27 acres of sunken structures and developed dive trails. It's immediately north of the ferry landing at the foot of Main Street. The adjacent Brackett's Landing Park—where there's parking—has trails, picnic areas, and restrooms. ✉ *Brackett's Landing Park, Main St. and Railroad Ave., next to ferry terminal* ☎ *425/771–0230* ⊕ *www.edmondswa.gov.*

FAMILY **Olympic Beach.** Get your dinner to go and watch the sun go down behind Whidbey Island and the Olympic Mountains at this lovely waterfront park. The Olympic Beach fishing pier attracts anglers all year and public art dots the landscape. In summer, a visitor station (open weekends noon–5) is a great place to pick up local info; kids like exploring the marine touch tank. ✉ *200 Admiral Way* ☎ *425/775–1344* ⊕ *www. edmondswa.gov.*

WHERE TO EAT

$$ ✕ **Bar Dojo.** Although it's a couple of miles east of downtown in a strip
ASIAN FUSION mall, this trendy place has quickly established itself as a hot spot for creative, often complex modern Asian fare, with an emphasis on local ingredients. The early-evening and late-night happy hours are hugely popular, with great bargains on food and drinks. Pork belly ramen and fried soft-shell crab with tuna poke are stars among the noodle bowls, but also consider the grilled lemongrass chicken with a white wine–oyster sauce. Save room for the banana tarte tatin. There's a popular brunch on weekends. ⑤ *Average main: $18* ✉ *8404 Bowdoin Way* ☎ *425/967–7267* ⊕ *www.bardojo.com* ⊗ *Closed Mon. No lunch weekdays.*

$$ ✕ **Epulo Bistro.** Darkly lighted, smartly furnished, and urbane, this hip
MEDITERRANEAN spot in the heart of downtown serves seasonally driven Mediterranean
Fodor'sChoice food with plenty of Northwestern influences. It's very easy to make
★ a meal here of several tantalizing small plates, like sautéed brussels
sprouts with bacon, chili, and garlic and Penn Cove mussels with saf-
fron, orange, and leeks. But there are plenty of tasty main dishes to
consider, too, including braised-beef short rib with garlic-mashed pota-
toes. Wood-fired pizzas are another stellar option. ⑤ *Average main: $21*
✉ *526 Main St.* ☎ *425/678–8680* ⊕ *epulobistro.com* ⊗ *Closed Mon.
No lunch.*

$$ ✕ **Girardi's Osteria Italiana.** Coming here is like walking into an elegant
ITALIAN yet comfortable Italian kitchen, where every space beneath the high,
peaked ceiling glows with warm country colors and muted light. Small
tables, with gleaming glass and white linens, are set on polished-wood
floors and tucked in near exposed-brick walls, and there's additional
seating on a breezy patio. The menu is an induction into the Italian dining experience, with such entrées as *anitra della casa* (pan-seared duck
breast on herb polenta) and *vitello del capitano* (veal medallions in a
Madeira wine sauce). Come Monday and Tuesday for half-price bottled
wines, and look for seasonal wine-tasting dinners focused on specific
regions of Italy. ⑤ *Average main: $19* ✉ *504 5th Ave. S* ☎ *425/673–
5278* ⊕ *www.girardis-osteria.com.*

WHERE TO STAY

$$ ⊡ **Best Western Plus Edmonds Harbor Inn.** In downtown Edmonds, this inn
HOTEL has as much country style and luxury as you're likely to find in a chain
property, with comfortable rooms updated in modern, easy-on-the-eyes
beiges and earth tones; some have fireplaces, kitchens, or oversize jet-
ted bathtubs. **Pros:** proximity to the waterfront and downtown dining;
only 1½ blocks from the Kingston ferry terminal. **Cons:** no beach views.
⑤ *Rooms from: $112* ✉ *130 W. Dayton St.* ☎ *425/771–5021, 800/441–
8033* ⊕ *www.bwedmondsharborinn.com* ⊷ *91 rooms* ⊙⊢ *Breakfast.*

SPORTS AND OUTDOORS

DIVING

Underwater Sports. This in-town shop offers scuba instruction, equip-
ment rentals, and underwater tours of the park. ✉ *264 Railroad Ave.,
Edmonds* ☎ *425/771–6322* ⊕ *www.underwatersports.com.*

10

EVERETT

19 miles north of Edmonds.

Much of this industrial town, the county seat of suburban Snohomish
County, sits high on a bluff above Port Gardner Bay and the Snohom-
ish River. The waterfront was once lined by so many lumber, pulp, and
shingle mills that Everett proudly called itself "the city of smokestacks."
Downtown Everett has many elegant old commercial buildings dating
from the period when John D. Rockefeller heavily invested in the fledg-
ing town, hoping to profit from the nearby Monte Cristo mines—which
turned out to be a flop. Another scheme failed when James J. Hill made
Everett the western terminus of the Great Northern Railroad, hoping to

turn it into Puget Sound's most important port. Everett is best known for the Boeing Aircraft plant and for having the second-largest Puget Sound port (after Seattle). The naval station here is home to the U.S.S. *Nimitz* aircraft carrier and a support flotilla of destroyers and frigates.

The pleasant waterfront suburb of Mukilteo, about 5 miles southeast of Everett, is the main departure point for ferries to Clinton, on Whidbey Island. The old lighthouse and waterfront park are fun to explore. An important Native American treaty was signed in 1855 at nearby Point Elliott.

Marysville, 6 miles north of Everett, was set up as a trading post in 1877. Pioneers exchanged goods with the Snohomish people, who once occupied southeastern Whidbey Island and the lower Snohomish Valley. Settlers drained and diked the lowlands, raised dairy cows, planted strawberry fields, cleared the forests, and in no time a thriving community was established. Marysville kept to itself for a century, until the Interstate 5 freeway was built; today it's a thriving community and the home of the popular Tulalip (Too-*lay*-lip) Casino.

GETTING HERE AND AROUND

Everett is best explored by car; take Interstate 5 north to Exit 192.

Contact **Sound Transit** ☎ 800/201–4900 ⊕ www.soundtransit.org.

ESSENTIALS

Visitor Information **Snohomish County Tourism Bureau** ⊠ *Visitor center at Future of Flight, 8415 Paine Field Blvd., Mukilteo* ☎ *425/348–5802, 888/338–0976* ⊕ *www.snohomish.org.*

EXPLORING

The Flying Heritage Collection. Housed within a 51,000-square-foot airport hangar, this spectacular gathering of unique vintage aircraft belongs to local tycoon Paul Allen, who began collecting and restoring rare planes in 1998. The selections run the full length of 20th-century military history, including pieces from the two world wars and other international battles. A favorite plane is the P-51D Mustang from World War II. Tours are self-guided; exhibits help to explain the collection. In summer, try to time your visit for one of the Free Fly Days, when pilots are on-site to fly some of the craft as part of monthly maintenance. ⊠ *Paine Field, 3407 109th St. SW* ☎ *206/342–3404* ⊕ *www.flyingheritage.com* 🎫 *$14* ⊙ *Late May–early Sept., daily 10–5; mid-Sept.–mid-May, Tues.–Sun. 10–5.*

Fodor'sChoice

★ **Future of Flight Aviation Center & Boeing Tour.** This facility showcases the Boeing Everett line (747, 767, 777, and 787), and the 98-acre site holds the world's largest building—so big that it often creates its own weather system inside. You can see planes in various stages of production on a 90-minute tour and spend time in the Future of Flight gallery, with cutaways of airplane fuselages, exhibits on the inner workings of navigation and hydraulic systems, and interactive exhibits that let you design your own commercial airliner. It also has a café. Note that there are no bathroom breaks on the tour, and no purses, cameras, cell phones, or children under 48 inches tall are permitted. The tour includes a lot of walking and some stair-climbing, but the facility can accommodate people with mobility issues with advance arrangements. Reserving tour tickets a day in advance is recommended if you need a specific tour time, but same-day tickets are always available. ✉ *8415 Paine Field Blvd., Mukilteo* ☎ *425/438–8100, 800/464–1476 reservations* ⊕ *www. futureofflight.org* 🖼 *$18* ⊘ *Facility daily 8:30–5:30, tours hourly 9–3.*

FAMILY **Imagine Children's Museum.** This engaging spot for kids is on a pioneer homestead built in the 1800s. Interactive exhibits and crafts are part of the fun; wee ones love the magic school bus as well. ✉ *1502 Wall St.* ☎ *425/258–1006* ⊕ *www.imaginecm.org* 🖼 *$9.80* ⊘ *Tues.–Wed. 9–5, Thurs.–Sat. 10–5, Sun. 11–5.*

FAMILY **Jetty Island.** Open in summer only, this is a 2-mile-long, sand-fringed offshore haven full of wildlife and outdoor opportunities. Seasonal programs include guided walks, bonfires, and midsummer Jetty Island Days festivities. A ferry (reservation recommended to avoid lines) provides round-trip transportation. ✉ *West end of 10th St., off W. Marine View Dr.* ☎ *425/257–8304* ⊕ *www.ci.everett.wa.us* 🖼 *$2 ferry fare* ⊘ *Early July–early Sept., ferries depart jetty on the half hr; Mon.–Thurs. and Sun. 10–5:30, Fri.–Sat. 10–8.*

Museum of Flight Restoration Center. At this branch of Seattle's Museum of Flight, vintage planes are restored by a volunteer staff who simply love bringing vintage aircraft back to life. You can wander among the mix of delicate and behemoth planes on a leisurely, self-guided tour at Paine Field. ✉ *2909 100th St. SW, Bldg. C-72* ☎ *425/745–5150* ⊕ *www. museumofflight.org/restoration* 🖼 *$5* ⊘ *June–Aug., Tues.–Sat. 9–4; Sept.–May, Tues.–Thurs. and Sat. 9–4.*

WHERE TO EAT AND STAY

$$$
SEAFOOD
✕ Anthony's Homeport. Tucked into chic Marina Village, this elegant waterfront outlet of a popular Washington-based seafood chain has large windows opening to a panorama of Port Gardner Bay. In summer, sunsets appear to ooze into the water. The specials, which change daily, might include meaty Dungeness crab, wild chinook salmon, and other sea creatures caught just offshore, and the clam chowder is justly renowned. Desserts are fabulous, especially those crafted from the state's succulent berries and fruits. ⑤ *Average main: $24* ✉ *1726 W. Marine View Dr.* ☎ *425/252–3333* ⊕ *www.anthonys.com.*

$
AMERICAN
✕ The Sisters. This funky breakfast and lunch café in Everett Public Market is as popular now as when it opened in 1983. Perhaps that's because the blueberry or pecan hotcakes, rich soups, and overflowing sandwiches are as good as ever. Eye-opening espresso drinks start the morning; homemade ice cream is a perfect end to the afternoon. Breakfast is served all day. ⑤ *Average main: $7* ✉ *2804 Grand St.* ☎ *425/252–0480* ⊕ *www.thesistersrestaurant.com* ⊘ *Closed weekends. No dinner.*

$$
HOTEL
⛉ Inn at Port Gardner. Stroll along the marina and you'll encounter this gray, warehouse-style structure, which wraps around a cozy, contemporary-style hotel where accommodations are enhanced with water views. **Pros:** right on the waterfront; close to area restaurants; nice patio and lobby. **Cons:** no pool; rooms are lovely but of the standard chain-hotel variety. ⑤ *Rooms from: $110* ✉ *1700 W. Marine Dr.* ☎ *425/252–6779,*

10

Boeing Everett Facility

888/252–6779 ⊕ www.innatportgardner.com ⌐27 rooms, 6 suites
¶○¶ Breakfast.

PUYALLUP

35 miles south of Seattle, 10 miles southeast of Tacoma.

Set before the towering forests and snowfields of Mt. Rainier is Puyallup
(pyoo-*al*-lup), one of western Washington's oldest towns. The Puyallup
Fair attracts all of western Washington to its carnival rides, performers, produce, and animals. The annual event is held at the fairgrounds
on the northwest end of town each September. The Spring Fair and
Daffodil Festival (known as "The Little Puyallup") is another beloved
event that takes place each April. These special events are really the
only reason to make a detour to Puyallup unless you need a leg-stretch
or a bite to eat on your way elsewhere. The downtown area is pleasant
enough and has a few boutiques and restaurants, as well as a growing
numbers of antiques dealers, but doesn't have enough charm to warrant a special visit.

GETTING HERE AND AROUND

To reach Puyallup, take Interstate 5 south to Interstate 405 north and
then Route 167 south.

EXPLORING

FAMILY **Northwest Trek Wildlife Park.** This spectacular, 435-acre wildlife park 35
miles south of Puyallup is devoted to native creatures of the Pacific
Northwest. Walking paths wind through natural surroundings—so
natural that in 1998 a cougar entered the park and started snacking

on the deer (it was finally trapped and relocated to the North Cascades). See beavers, otters, and wolverines; get close to wolves, foxes, coyotes; and observe several species of big cats and bears in wild environments. Admission includes a 50-minute tram ride through fields of wandering moose, bighorn sheep, elk, bison, and mountain goats. The most adventurous way to see the park is via one of five zip lines, which traverse the park canopy—rides are available early May through late September. ✉ *11610 Trek Dr. E., Eatonville* ☎ *360/832–6117* ⊕ *www.nwtrek.org* ✍ *$19.75* ⊗ *Hours vary seasonally; call ahead.*

FAMILY **Pioneer Farm Museum and Ohop Indian Village.** This living history museum, 23 miles south of Puyallup, provides a look at pioneer and Native American life. Kids can learn how to hunt and fish in a realistic tribal village, grind grain, milk a cow, churn butter, and do other old-fashioned chores. A trading post shows the commodities of earlier eras. One-hour tours are available through both the farm and village. ✉ *7716 Ohop Valley Rd. E, Eatonville* ☎ *360/832–6300* ⊕ *www.pioneerfarmmuseum. org* ✍ *Farm $9, village $8.50* ⊗ *Mid-June–early Sept., daily 11–4; mid-Mar.–mid-June and early Sept.–late Nov., weekends 11–4.*

WHERE TO EAT

$ ✕ **Powerhouse Brewery and Restaurant.** The interior of what was once a
AMERICAN   railroad powerhouse is adorned with glass insulators and high-voltage signs. About a dozen brews are served—some brewed on the premises and others from a sister brewery. The pub fare includes salads, pizzas, burgers, sandwiches, and pastas. Ⓢ *Average main: $13* ✉ *454 E. Main Ave.* ☎ *253/845–1370* ⊕ *www.powerhousebrewpub.com.*

BELLINGHAM AND SKAGIT VALLEY

Many people drive right past places like La Conner, Mount Vernon, or Bellingham on their way west to the San Juans, east to the Cascades, or north to the Canadian border. But between Everett and Canada are some lovely miles of coastline, some impressive parkland, and charming farm towns—all of which are fairly easy to access from Interstate 5. Collectively, the towns that anchor the northwestern edge of the state are seriously underappreciated: La Conner is a pleasantly laid-back farming community, and Mount Vernon is a riverfront town with some great festivals. Between the two towns are the best of the Skagit Valley flower farms, which do draw big crowds in spring when the tulips bloom. Bellingham is a progressive, scenic town with a fun and quirky vibe that's popular with artists, outdoorsy types, and hipsters. Any one of these towns makes a good stopover on other itineraries.

10

LA CONNER

14 miles southeast of Anacortes, 68 miles north of Seattle.

Morris Graves, Kenneth Callahan, Guy Anderson, Mark Tobey, and other painters set up shop in La Conner in the 1940s, and the village on the Swinomish Channel (Slough) has been a haven for artists ever since. In recent years the community has become increasingly popular as a regional weekend escape—it's a fairly short drive from Seattle, but it feels refreshingly far from the bustle.

La Conner has several historic buildings near the waterfront or a short walk up the hill—use the stairs leading up the bluff, or go around and walk up one of the sloping streets—as well as several inviting shops and restaurants. In summer the village can become a bit congested with people and cars, and parking can be hard to find. The flat land around La Conner makes for easy biking along levees and through the tulip fields. You'll see plenty of fields and farms, and a major attraction in fall and summer are farm stands selling local produce.

GETTING HERE AND AROUND

The center of La Conner is roughly 12 miles west of Interstate 5 (from Seattle, take Exit 221 for Highway 534). The town is very close to both Anacortes, where ferries depart for the San Juan Islands, and the northern tip of Whidbey Island. A car is by far the best way to reach and explore the area. In summer bike rentals ($30 for a half day; $40 per day) are available at the Port of Skagit Marina in La Conner from Tulip Country Bike Tours.

Contact La Conner Chamber of Commerce ✉ *511 Morris St., Suite 3* ☎ *360/466–4778, 888/642–9284* ⊕ *www.lovelaconner.com.*

EXPLORING

Museum of Northwest Art. Here in this striking, modern building you can view some 2,500 works of regional creative minds past and present, painters, sculptors, photographers, and other artists. Soaring spaces, circular exhibit rooms, a glass gallery, and a broad spiral staircase add to the free-form feeling of the displays. The small shop sells examples of what you see in the exhibits. ✉ *121 S. 1st St.* ☎ *360/466–4446* ⊕ *www. museumofnwart.org* 🔖 *Free* ☾ *Sun. and Mon. noon–5, Tues.–Sat. 10–5.*

Skagit County Historical Museum. This hilltop museum surveys domestic life in early Skagit County and Northwest Coastal Native American history. There's an interesting gallery showcasing goods commonly found in the region's early general stores, and rotating exhibits interpret the different aspects of the community's rich heritage. ✉ *501 4th St.* ☎ *360/466–3365* ⊕ *www.skagitcounty.net/museum* 🔖 *$5* ☾ *Tues.– Sun. 11–5.*

WHERE TO EAT

$

CAFÉ

Fodor's Choice

★

✕ Calico Cupboard. A local favorite, this storefront bakery with branches nearby in Anacortes and Mount Vernon, too, turns out some of the best pastries in Skagit County, plus big portions of tasty breakfast and lunch fare. Lunches focus on fresh and creative salads, soups, and burgers; while huge and hearty breakfasts may leave you with little need for lunch—the roasted butternut-squash hash and migas are a couple of favorites. Buy goodies at the take-out counter for a picnic adventure. If dining on-site, grab a seat on the back deck overlooking the river. ⑤ *Average main: $10* ✉ *720 S. 1st St.* ☎ *360/466–4451* ⊕ *www. calicocupboardcafe.com* ☾ *No dinner.*

$$

AMERICAN

✕ La Conner Channel Grill. This casually trendy and dapper spot with a pubby vibe, varnished-wood tables, and a lively bar scene has earned a popular following for fresh, deftly prepared seafood and steaks. Pecan-baked local wild salmon, panko-crusted panfried oysters, and filet mignon are favorites, and the burgers are a nice option for a lighter, less-spendy meal. ⑤ *Average main: $22* ✉ *110 N. 1st St.* ☎ *360/466–3800* ⊕ *www.laconnerrestaurant.com* ☾ *Closed Tues. No lunch.*

WHERE TO STAY

$$
B&B/INN

⌂ **Armstrong House.** A white picket fence surrounds this stately, three-story, early-20th-century country house about a mile east of downtown La Conner, and the large rooms are tastefully furnished with a mix of antiques and newer pieces; one has a sunken hot tub and another has a claw-foot tub. **Pros:** great value; lovely views of the countryside; friendly staff; soft robes. **Cons:** downtown shops and restaurants a 20-minute walk away. ⑤ *Rooms from: $130* ✉ *1075 Chilberg Rd., Mount Vernon* ☎ *360/466–4578* ⊕ *www.queenofthevalleyinn.com* ⇄ *4 rooms, 1 cottage* ❘⊙❘ *Breakfast.*

$$$
HOTEL
Fodor's Choice
★

⌂ **Channel Lodge.** Most of the smartly furnished contemporary rooms here, done in subdued gray tones with wooden trim and gas fireplaces, overlook the narrow Swinomish Channel. **Pros:** big stone fireplace in lobby; rustic charm wrapped around sleek modern amenities; lovely waterfront setting and views. **Cons:** some rooms don't overlook water. ⑤ *Rooms from: $179* ✉ *205 N. 1st St.* ☎ *360/466–1500, 888/466–4113* ⊕ *www.laconnerlodging.com/channel-lodge* ⇄ *39 rooms, 3 suites* ❘⊙❘ *Breakfast.*

$$
HOTEL
FAMILY

⌂ **La Conner Country Inn.** At this rambling motel-style property all the spacious rooms have private outdoor entrances, high, vaulted ceilings, gas fireplaces, refrigerators, and pleasant country-style furnishings; several have whirlpool baths. **Pros:** spacious rooms, most with more than one bed; good value; quiet but central location. **Cons:** rooms are a slightly odd mix of country coziness and chain hotel. ⑤ *Rooms from: $139* ✉ *107 S. 2nd St.* ☎ *360/466–1500, 888/466–4113* ⊕ *www.laconnerlodging.com/country-inn* ⇄ *27 rooms, 1 suite* ❘⊙❘ *Breakfast.*

$$
B&B/INN
Fodor's Choice
★

⌂ **Wild Iris.** The garden-laced exterior is a sprawling model of a Victorian-style inn, and the elegantly decorated interior begins with a river-rock fireplace and extends to spacious rooms done with soft, colorful fabrics and polished wood accents. **Pros:** beautiful and tastefully decorated rooms; great in-room amenities (plush linens, DVD library, CD players) considering the decent rates; excellent breakfast. **Cons:** the least expensive rooms are quite small. ⑤ *Rooms from: $129* ✉ *121 Maple Ave.* ☎ *360/466–1400, 800/477–1400* ⊕ *www.wildiris.com* ⇄ *4 rooms, 12 suites* ❘⊙❘ *Breakfast.*

10

MOUNT VERNON

11 miles northeast of La Conner.

This attractive riverfront town, the county seat of Skagit County and founded in 1871, is surrounded by dairy pastures, vegetable fields, and bulb farms—the town is famous for its annual Tulip Festival in April, when thousands of people visit to admire the floral exuberance. After a giant logjam on the lower Skagit was cleared, steamers began churning up the river, and Mount Vernon soon became the major commercial center of the Skagit Valley, a position it has never relinquished. Rising above downtown and the river, 972-foot-high Little Mountain is a city park with a view. It used to be an island until the mudflats were filled in by Skagit River silt. Glacial striations in rocks near the top of the mountain, dating from the last continental glaciation (10,000–20,000 years ago), were made when the mountain (and all of the Puget Sound region) was covered by some 3,500 feet of ice.

GETTING HERE AND AROUND

The best way to reach Mount Vernon is by car, taking Interstate 5 north to any of several exits right in town. In Mount Vernon Interstate 5 connects with Highway 536, which then merges with Highway 20 toward Anacortes.

Tulip Country Bike Tours arranges spring trips through the tulip fields, starting at $65 per person. In summer, tours take in other Skagit Valley sights like berry farms and Padilla Bay. You can also rent bikes for $40 per day.

Contacts Mount Vernon Chamber of Commerce ✉ *301 W. Kincaid St.* ☎ *360/428–8547* ⊕ *www.mountvernonchamber.com.* **Tulip Country Bike Tours** ☎ *360/424–7461* ⊕ *www.countrycycling.com.*

EXPLORING

Bay View State Park. Adjoining the small waterfront community of the same name, this scenic 25-acre park has a campground in the woods and picnic tables on the low grassy bluff above the bay. Canoers and kayakers take note: Padilla Bay runs almost dry at low tide, when water is restricted to a few creek-like tidal channels. ✉ *10905 Bay View–Edison Rd.* ☎ *360/757–0227* ⊕ *www.parks.wa.gov* 🎫 *Day pass $10 per vehicle; annual Discovery Pass $30 (valid at all state parks)* ⊙ *Daily 8 am–dusk.*

Little Mountain Park. Atop the eponymous mountain at the southeastern edge of town, this 522-acre park, which rises to nearly 1,000 feet above sea level, has great views of the Skagit Valley (especially in March and April, when the daffodils and tulips are in full bloom), the San Juan Islands, and the distant Olympic Mountains. ✉ *Little Mountain Rd., off E. Blackburn Rd., 4 miles southeast of downtown* ☎ *360/336–6213* ⊕ *www.mountvernonwa.gov* 🎫 *Free* ⊙ *Daily dawn–dusk.*

Padilla Bay National Estuarine Reserve. At this serene wildlife preserve, the Breazeale Interpretive Center has great birding: there are black Brant (or Brent) geese, raptors, peregrine falcons, and bald eagles. Trails lead into the woods and to a rocky beach, with more good bird-watching opportunities. The 2¼-mile Padilla Bay Trail starts at the south end of Bayview; look for signs directing you to the parking area, which is away from the water off the east side of the road. ✉ *10441 Bayview–Edison Rd.* ☎ *360/428–1558* ⊕ *www.padillabay.gov* 🎫 *Free* ⊙ *Grounds daily; interpretive center Wed.–Sun. 10–5.*

Roozengaarde. This 1,200-acre estate was established by the Roozen family and Washington Bulb Company in 1985—it's the world's largest family-owned tulip-, daffodil-, and iris-growing business. Fifteen acres of greenhouses are filled with multicolored blossoms, and more than 200,000 bulbs are planted in the show gardens each fall. The Skagit Valley Tulip Festival, held in April, is the main event, when the flowers pop up in neat, brilliant rows across the flat land, attracting thousands of sightseers. The garden and store are open year-round, and the staff and website are full of helpful advice for both novice and experienced gardeners. ⊠ *15867 Beaver Marsh Rd.* ☎ *360/424–8531, 800/732–3266* ⊕ *www.tulips.com* 🖅 *Free* ☉ *Mon.–Sat. 9–6, Sun. 11–4.*

WHERE TO EAT

$$$
ITALIAN
✕ **Il Grainaio.** Tucked deep into the town's historic Old Granery, amid displays of century-old farming equipment, is this cozy and rustic place where dark-wood floors, small tables, and lantern-like lighting provide the authentic ambience of a local trattoria. The waitstaff is quick and knowledgeable, bringing out enormous pasta bowls, seafood salads, and pan-fried eggplant or salmon. Excellent wines garnish the tables, and desserts are simple and rich. Slip in early on weekends, when dinners bustle with groups. ⑤ *Average main: $25* ⊠ *100 E. Montgomery St.* ☎ *360/419–0674* ⊕ *www.granaio.com* ☉ *No lunch weekends.*

$
CAFÉ
FAMILY
Fodor's Choice
★
✕ **Rexville Grocery.** From Ben & Jerry's to Pocky sticks to local microbrews, Rexville is one well-stocked country store, with a great mix of everyday and gourmet snacks and drinks. There's a small café with a patio encircled by trees, vines, and blooming thistle. On weekends, you can sit down for a breakfast (served until noon) of scrambles or pancakes; the rest of the week, stop in for a sandwich or salad. You could put together quite a good picnic basket here. On Sundays from spring through fall, there's a farmers market out front. ⑤ *Average main: $10* ⊠ *19271 Best Rd.* ☎ *360/466–5522* ⊕ *www.rexvillegrocery.com* ☉ *No dinner.*

BELLINGHAM

29 miles northwest of Mount Vernon.

The fishing port and college community of Bellingham has steadily transformed itself from a rough-and-tumble blue-collar town to the arts, retirement, and pleasure-boating capital of Washington's northwest corner. Downtown abounds with cafés, microbreweries, specialty shops, and galleries, and the waterfront—dominated by lumber mills and shipyards in the early 1900s—is gradually morphing into a string of parks with connecting trails. College students and professors from Western Washington University make up a sizable part of the town's population and contribute to its laid-back intellectual climate. The lushly green bay front, creeks meandering through town, and Lakes Whatcom and Padden attract wildlife like deer, raccoons, river otters, beavers, ducks, geese, herons, bald eagles, and the occasional cougar.

GETTING HERE AND AROUND

From Seattle, Bellingham is nearly a straight shot on Interstate 5 north (Exit 253 gets you into the center of town).

Amtrak's Cascades train stops in Bellingham on its way to Vancouver, B.C. Greyhound buses also serve Bellingham from Seattle, as does the Airporter Shuttle from Sea-Tac and Downtown Seattle. The low-cost

10

Bolt Bus is another handy option, connecting with both Seattle and Vancouver, B.C.

Biking is popular in and around Bellingham, which has a series of designated bike paths and park trails. The city of Bellingham has a good high-res bike-route map that can be downloaded from its website.

The Coast Millennium Trail will eventually connect Skagit and Whatcom counties to British Columbia. So far, about 15 miles of the 50-mile trail are open to bikes and walkers. Fairhaven Bike & Ski rents road bikes, full-suspension bikes, and standard mountain bikes starting at $55 per day.

Contacts Bellingham Whatcom County Tourism ✉ *904 Potter St.* ☎ *360/671–3990, 800/487–2032* ⊕ *www.bellingham.org.* **City of Bellingham Bike Routes** ⊕ *www.cob.org/services/transportation.* **Fairhaven Bike & Ski** ☎ *360/733–4433* ⊕ *www.fairhavenbike.com.*

EXPLORING

TOP ATTRACTIONS

Fodor'sChoice
★
Chuckanut Drive. Highway 11, also known as Chuckanut Drive, was once the only highway accessing Bellingham from the south. The drive begins in Fairhaven, reaches the flat farmlands of the Samish Valley near the village of Bow, and joins up with I–5 at Burlington, in Skagit County; the full loop can be made in a couple of hours. For a dozen miles this 23-mile road winds along the cliffs above beautiful Chuckanut and Samish Bays. It twists its way past the sheer sandstone face of Chuckanut Mountain and crosses creeks with waterfalls. Turnouts are framed by gnarled madrona trees and pines and offer great views of the San Juan Islands. Bald eagles cruise along the cliffs or hang out on top of tall firs. Drive carefully: the cliffs are so steep in places that closures resulting from rock slides occasionally occur in winter. ✉ *Hwy. 11, starting in Fairhaven at 12th St. and Old Fairhaven Pkwy.*

Fairhaven. Just shy of 3 miles south of downtown Bellingham and at the beginning of Chuckanut Drive (Highway 11), this historic district was an independent city until 1903 and still retains its distinct identity as an intellectual and artistic center. The beautifully restored 1890s redbrick buildings of the Old Fairhaven District, especially on Harris Avenue between 10th and 12th streets, house restaurants, galleries, and specialty boutiques. On the north side of the district, Boulevard Park is a beautiful swath of greenery fronting Bellingham Bay, with access to the South Bay biking and pedestrian path. ⊕ *www.fairhaven.com.*

Fairhaven Marine Park. This long, sandy beach at the foot of Harris Avenue a few blocks south of Bellingham Cruise Terminal is a good place to launch sea kayaks. A rough trail runs south from the park along the railroad tracks to pebble beaches and rocky headlands, where you'll find clams, summer blackberries, and splendid views of Lummi Island. ✉ *Foot of Harris Ave., Bellingham.*

Larrabee State Park. South of Chuckanut Bay along the Whatcom–Skagit county line, this rugged 2,683-acre tract is one of the state's most scenic and popular parks. It straddles a rocky shore that has quiet, sandy coves and runs high up along the slopes of Chuckanut Mountain. Even though the mountain has been logged repeatedly, some of it is still wilderness. Miles of trails lead through ferny fir and maple forests to hidden lakes, caves, and cliff-top lookouts from which you can see all the way to the San Juan Islands. At the shore there's a sheltered boat launch; you can go crabbing here or watch the birds—and the occasional harbor seal—that perch on the offshore rocks. The area west of Chuckanut Drive has picnic tables as well as tent and RV sites with hookups, which are open all year. ⊠ *245 Chuckanut Dr.* ☎ *360/676–2093* ⊕ *www.parks. wa.gov* 🖃 *Day pass $10 per vehicle; annual Discovery Pass $30 (valid at all state parks)* ☉ *Daily dawn–dusk.*

FAMILY
Fodor's Choice
★
Whatcom Museum. Bellingham's art and history museum comprises three buildings near one another downtown. At its centerpiece is the Lightcatcher, a LEED-certified (Leadership in Energy and Environmental Design) building with a 180-foot-long translucent wall. Rotating shows are presented here, as are permanent collections of contemporary Northwest artists. The second building, Bellingham's 1892 former city hall, is a redbrick structure that was converted into a museum in 1941—it completed a dramatic renovation in 2010 and contains historic exhibits. The third building, the Syre Education Center, contains a photographic archive. The museum's restaurant, TwoFifty Flora, is in the Lightcatcher and garners raves for its creative farm-to-table lunch fare. ⊠ *250 Flora St.* ☎ *360/778–8930* ⊕ *www.whatcommuseum.org* 🖃 *$10* ☉ *Lightcatcher Building: Wed.–Fri. and Sun. noon–5 (open to 8 pm Thurs.), Sat. 10–5. Old City Hall: Thurs.–Sun. noon–5. Syre Education Center: call for hrs.*

Woods Coffee Boulevard Park. This bay-front outpost of a popular northwestern Washington coffeehouse chain has a cozy dining room with high-back chairs and large windows overlooking Bellingham Bay—in warm weather, you can enjoy your vanilla latte, yogurt parfait, breakfast sandwich, or white-chocolate–raspberry scone on the patio. With its peaceful setting in leafy Boulevard Park, this is a popular spot with bikers and strollers using the Bay Trail, which passes right outside the door. ⊠ *470 Bayview Rd.* ☎ *360/738–4771* ⊕ *www.thewoodscoffee.com.*

WORTH NOTING

Bellingham Cruise Terminal. This massive brick building surrounded by gardens dispatches daily ferries to Alaska as well as tour boats to the San Juan Islands and whale-watching ships. There's terrific wildlife-watching right off the docks and adjacent shoreline, where sea lions, and otters frolic out in the water as great blue herons, cormorants, and harlequin ducks bob on the surface. The Community Boating Center right by the terminal is a good place to launch sea kayaks. ⊠ *355 Harris Ave.* ☎ *360/676–2500* ⊕ *www.portofbellingham.com.*

Bloedel Donovan Park. The only public access in Bellingham to rippling, 14-mile-long Lake Whatcom is at its north end, in this park about a 10-minute drive east of downtown. Locals swim in the sheltered waters of a cove, but you might find the water a bit cold. If so, spend some time trying to spot beavers, river otters, ducks, great blue herons, and yellow pond lilies at Scudder Pond, which is another 100 feet west (reached by trail from a parking area at Northshore and Alabama). ⊠ *2214*

10

Electric Ave. ☎ *360/778–7000* ⊕ *www.cob.org/services/recreation* ⊘ *Daily dawn–dusk.*

FAMILY   **Maritime Heritage Park.** Down a flight of steps behind the Whatcom Museum's 1892 City Hall building, this park pays tribute to Bellingham's fishing industry. Self-guided Marine Heritage Center tours take you through a salmon's life cycle, winding past hatcheries, aquarium tanks, and fish ladders. A boardwalk route from Holly Street leads to the ponds and a waterfall, where Bellingham was founded in 1852, when it was then known as Whatcom. Note that salmon runs occur annually around September and October. ⊠ *500 W. Holly St.* ☎ *360/778–7000* ⊕ *www.cob.org/services/recreation* ⊠ *Free* ⊘ *Daily 6 am–10 pm.*

WHERE TO EAT

$ ✕ **Boundary Bay Brewery & Bistro.** Long a top venue in downtown Bel-
AMERICAN   lingham, both for sampling distinctive, well-crafted microbrews and
Fodor'sChoice   enjoying big portions of delicious pub fare, this convivial spot occu-
★   pies a vintage former garage—the huge central door is rolled open in warm weather, and there's also a good-size side patio. Boundary garners high marks among beer lovers for its ruby-red Scottish ale, smooth oatmeal stout, and rotating seasonal ales. From the food menu, you won't go wrong with the Bavarian-style pretzels (served with spicy brown mustard), smoked-clam chowder, beer-barbecue-sauce pizzas, and char-grilled lamb burger. ⑤ *Average main: $14* ⊠ *1107 Railroad Ave.* ☎ *360/647–5593* ⊕ *www.bbaybrewery.com.*

$ ✕ **Chuckanut Brewery & Kitchen.** Even if you're not a beer aficionado,
AMERICAN   this spacious, chatter-filled brewpub in a modern industrial build-
FAMILY   ing near Whatcom Creek and the Maritime Heritage Center is a ter-
        rific, affordable option for lunch or dinner, and the good kids' menu makes it a family-friendly choice. The brewery's acclaimed beers play a role in many of the kitchen's top dishes, from the Reuben sandwich with beer-braised corned beef to the "beerbq" chicken pizzas. The Chuckanut bread pudding makes a fine ending. Among the beers, the smoky porter and extra-dry British-style IPA both have plenty of fans. ⑤ *Average main: $12* ⊠ *601 W. Holly St.* ☎ *360/752–3377* ⊕ *www. chuckanutbreweryandkitchen.com.*

$$$ ✕ **Fork at Agate Bay.** It's a scenic 20-minute drive east from downtown to
PACIFIC   reach this intimate but lively contemporary bistro near the north shore
NORTHWEST   of Lake Whatcom, where chef-owners John and Gina Russell emphasize
Fodor'sChoice   local, seasonal ingredients in creating some of the most creative and art-
★   fully presented fare in the region. In the evening, you might start with an heirloom-tomato-and-lump-crab salad with chèvre, mizuna greens, and balsamic vinaigrette, before continuing on to a perfectly grilled hanger steak with roasted-garlic-and-cauliflower purée, kale "lollipops," and a cherry-shallot demi-glace. Breakfast and lunch are served on week-ends—try the North Carolina–barbecue pulled pork with eggs and a biscuit, accompanied by a Sparkling Fork cocktail (Prosecco, aromatic bitters, raw-sugar cube, and lemon). ⑤ *Average main: $25* ⊠ *2530 N. Shore Rd.* ☎ *360/733–1126* ⊕ *www.theforkatagatebay.com* ⊘ *Closed Mon. and Tues. No lunch Wed.–Fri.*

$ ✕ **Harris Avenue Café.** Occupying a light-filled, cheerfully painted late-
CAFÉ   Victorian building a few blocks from the port and train station in

Fairhaven, this hugely popular breakfast and lunch spot adjoins an inviting little coffeehouse (Tony's), which is a nice option for lighter snacking and fueling up on espresso. In the main café, which has patio dining in summer, you can kick off a day of exploring with a filling Sitka omelet (smoked salmon, feta, roasted garlic, tomatoes, and pesto). Lunch options include the Matterhorn Burger, topped with mushrooms and Swiss cheese, and a poached pear salad with candied pecans and fresh wild salmon. The café closes at 2, but Tony's remains open till 6 pm. ⑤ *Average main: $10* ✉ *1101 Harris Ave.* ☎ *360/738–0802* ⊕ *www.harrisavecafe.com* ☾ *No dinner.*

$ ✕ **Old World Deli.** Epicureans flock to this bustling, high-ceilinged deli
DELI and specialty market in the heart of downtown for generously portioned sandwiches, salads, and charcuterie and cheese plates fashioned out of Portland's famed Olympic Provisions and Seattle's vaunted Salumi. The hot-pressed sub with mortadella, capicola, sopressata, fontina cheese, tomato, pepperoncini, and arugula on an Italian roll tastes right out of the best Little Italy neighborhoods of any big East Coast city. The shelves lining the dining room are stocked with hard-to-find imported and regional wines, plus fine sauces, nuts, chips, and chocolates. You can enjoy a casual early dinner on Thursday through Saturdays, when the deli is open until 8. ⑤ *Average main: $9* ✉ *1228 N. State St.* ☎ *360/738–2090* ⊕ *www.oldworlddeli1.com* ☾ *Closed Sun.*

$$$$ ✕ **Oyster Bar.** Above the shore on a steep, wooded bluff, this intimate
SEAFOOD restaurant in the village of Bow is regionally famous for what may be
Fodor's Choice the best marine view from any Washington restaurant. People come here
★ to dine and watch the sun set over the islands to the west or to watch the full moon reflect off the waters of Samish Bay. The menu changes regularly, so it's hard to predict what you might find, but the oyster bar, along with the refined seafood dishes (including a delectable oyster fry with parmesan breadcrumb crust and sour-apple aioli), wild game, and pastas never disappoint—and there are well-chosen wines to complement every dish. ⑤ *Average main: $35* ✉ *2578 Chuckanut Dr., 22 miles south of Bellingham, Bow* ☎ *360/766–6185* ⊕ *www.theoysterbar.net.*

WHERE TO STAY

$$$ 🛏 **Chrysalis Inn and Spa at the Pier.** In a long, gray, gabled building rising
HOTEL above the waterfront between downtown and Fairhaven, the lobby is
Fodor's Choice warmed by dark woods and a large fireplace, and light-filled, contem-
★ porary rooms have fireplaces and offer the cushiest accommodations in town. **Pros:** utterly relaxing; great water views from most rooms; first-rate on-site restaurant and spa. **Cons:** some noise from train track behind the hotel. ⑤ *Rooms from: $215* ✉ *804 10th St.* ☎ *360/756–1005, 888/808–0005* ⊕ *www.thechrysalisinn.com* ⇄ *34 rooms, 9 suites* ❖ *Breakfast.*

$$$ 🛏 **Fairhaven Village Inn.** On a slight bluff overlooking Fairhaven Village
B&B/INN Green and just up the street from Port of Bellingham's south termi-
nal, this charming, historic inn overlooks Bellingham Bay; the bayview rooms have balconies and gas fireplaces, and a suite has French doors dividing a bedroom and sitting area. **Pros:** interesting part of town with good shops, galleries, and restaurants; convenient for Chuckanut Scenic Drive and the university; staff is helpful and knowledgeable. **Cons:**

10

two-night minimum stay at certain times. ⑤ *Rooms from: $179* ⊠ *1200 10th St.* ☎ *360/733–1311, 877/733–1100* ⊕ *www.fairhavenvillageinn. com* ⌁ *21 rooms, 1 suite* ⊚⍬ *Breakfast.*

$$$ ⚇ **Hotel Bellwether.** Bellingham's original waterfront hotel overlooks the
HOTEL entrance to bustling Squalicum Harbor, and its luxurious rooms have gas fireplaces, plush bathrooms with jetted tubs and separate glassed-in showers, and private balconies for lounging and dining. **Pros:** beautiful bay views; large private dock; wide variety of room configurations. **Cons:** can get crowded with groups and weddings; one of the more expensive options in town. ⑤ *Rooms from: $205* ⊠ *Squalicum Harbor Marina, 1 Bellwether Way* ☎ *360/392–3100, 877/411–1200* ⊕ *www. hotelbellwether.com* ⌁ *50 rooms, 16 suites* ⊚⍬ *Breakfast.*

$$ ⚇ **MoonDance B&B.** This handsomely restored 1930s lodge-style home
B&B/INN with tastefully and quirkily furnished guest rooms is surrounded by colorful gardens and sits on the western shore of pristine Lake Whatcom—it's one of the most tranquil settings of any lodging in the area. **Pros:** expansive lake views; kayaks on-site; one family-friendly room can accommodate two adults and two children. **Cons:** 5 miles east of downtown; two-night minimum during busy times. ⑤ *Rooms from: $135* ⊠ *4737 Cable St.* ☎ *360/927–2599* ⊕ *www.bellinghambandb. com* ⌁ *4 rooms, 1 suite* ⊚⍬ *Breakfast.*

$$ ⚇ **Silver Reef Hotel Casino and Spa.** This modern casino hotel just out-
RESORT side the small town of Ferndale—10 miles northwest of Bellingham— has spacious and well-maintained rooms and a slew of amenities that include a full-service spa, an indoor pool, slots and table games, a showroom, and nearly a dozen restaurants and bars. **Pros:** lots of entertainment and dining options on-site; pretty favorable rates considering the nice rooms. **Cons:** a 20-minute drive from downtown Bellingham; casino vibe not for everyone; many rooms face a large parking lot. ⑤ *Rooms from: $149* ⊠ *4876 Haxton Way, Ferndale* ☎ *866/383–0777, 360/543–7169* ⊕ *www.silverreefcasino.com/* ⌁ *199 rooms, 5 suites* ⊚⍬ *No meals.*

NIGHTLIFE AND PERFORMING ARTS

Aslan Brewing. One of the newer of Bellingham's fast-growing number of highly regarded craft breweries occupies a sleek downtown building with soaring glass walls, an open floor plan, and plenty of sidewalk seating. The brewmasters here specialize in flavorful, small-batch beers, like faintly ginger-accented Irie Eyes Red Ale, and a rich, chocolaty dark lager called Cascadian. Part of the fun here is the bar food, including a rather decadent waffle-fry poutine, hefty bacon-bison burgers, and Chocolate Stout soft-serve ice cream topped with candied barley. ⊠ *1330 N. Forest St.* ☎ *360/778–2088* ⊕ *www.aslanbrewing.com.*

The Local. This old-school downtown pub with a modern vibe and first-rate beer and food was opened by a trio of Western Washington University graduates who also happen to be talented beer makers (they own Menace Brewing). As you might guess, this laid-back spot with a conversation-friendly decibel level has a great list of rotating taps, featuring craft beers from throughout the Northwest. The locally driven food is tasty, too, from fried chicken and waffles during the popular weekend brunches to late-night pork-belly tacos and fish-and-chips. ✉ *1427 Railroad Ave.* ☎ *360/306–3731.*

Mt. Baker Theatre. The state's largest performing arts center north of Seattle occupies a restored vaudeville-era (1927) theater with a 110-foot-tall Moorish tower and a lobby fashioned after a Spanish galleon. It's home to the Whatcom Symphony Orchestra and is also a venue for movies, musicals, and headline performers. ✉ *104 N. Commercial St.* ☎ *360/734–6080* ⊕ *www.mountbakertheatre.com.*

Up and Up Tavern. This relaxed, endearingly dive-y spot for a beer has been serving Bellingham's colorful mix of local workers, college students, and folks passing through town since the 1930s. ✉ *1234 N. State St.* ☎ *360/733–9739.*

SPORTS AND THE OUTDOORS
WHALE-WATCHING
Island Mariner Cruises. This long-respected tour company conducts whale-watching, nature, and sunset cruises around Bellingham Bay and on out to the San Juans. ✉ *2621 S. Harbor Loop Drive* ☎ *360/734–8866, 877/734–8866* ⊕ *www.orcawatch.com.*

San Juan Cruises. This popular whale-watching excursion company sails around Bellingham Bay and out to the San Juan Islands, where there's a stop for lunch and exploring in Friday Harbor on San Juan Island. Under the right conditions, the views of whales and sunsets cannot be beat. ✉ *Bellingham Cruise Terminal, 355 Harris St., Suite 104* ☎ *360/738–8099, 800/443–4552* ⊕ *www.whales.com.*

KITSAP PENINSULA

Branching off the southeastern edge of the Olympic Peninsula, the Kitsap Peninsula has Puget Sound on one side and the Hood Canal on the other. Though the Kitsap doesn't possess the great wild beauty of the Olympic Peninsula, it does have several charming waterfront towns with beach parks, kayaking, and sailing opportunities, as well as a serene setting. Bremerton is the most developed (and least attractive) city on the peninsula, but it's home to a navy base, and its waterfront has many naval museums and retired ships to crawl around on. Gig Harbor's marinas, on the other hand, are full of pretty sailboats—it's the town that has the most to offer in terms of tourist amenities. Outside of these main cities, Poulsbo and Port Gamble get the most attention. The former is a pilgrimage point for anyone interested in tracing the Norwegian influence in the Pacific Northwest, and the latter is a twee little town made up mostly of historic buildings.

GIG HARBOR

10 miles northwest of Tacoma.

One of the most picturesque and accessible waterfront cities on Puget Sound, Gig Harbor has a neat, circular bay dotted with sailboats and fronted by hills of evergreens and million-dollar homes. Expect spectacular views all along the town's winding, 2-mile, bay-side walkway, which is intermittently lined by boat docks, quirky shops, cozy cafés, and broad expanses of open water.

The bay was a storm refuge for the 1841 survey team of Captain Charles Wilkes, who named the area after his small gig (boat). A decade later Croatian and Scandinavian immigrants put their fishing, lumber, and boatbuilding skills to profitable use, and the town still has strong seafaring traditions. By the 1880s, steamboats carried passengers and goods between the harbor and Tacoma, and auto ferries plied the narrows between the cities by 1917.

The town winds around the waterfront, centering at the intersection of Harborview Drive and Pioneer Way, where shops, art galleries, and restaurants often attract more foot traffic than vehicles. From here, Harborview makes a long, gentle curve around the bay toward the renovated Finholm Market building, which has shops, docks, a restaurant, kayak rentals, and more views. A Gig Harbor Historical Society self-guided walk brochure covers 49 sights (see if you can spot the 16 metal salmon sculptures, designed by local artists, placed in front of sights around town).

Surrounding Gig Harbor, pine forests and open woods alternate with rolling pastures; it's enjoyable scenery (even on rainy days) during the 10-minute drive to Fox Island. Crossing the Fox Island Bridge over Echo Bay, you'll see stunning views of the Olympic Mountains to the right and the Tanglewood Lighthouse against a backdrop of Mt. Rainier to the left. Tanglewood Island, the small drop of forest on which the Tanglewood Lighthouse sits, was once a Native American burial ground known as Grav Island. At low tide the boat ramp and boulder-strewn beach next to the bridge are scattered with stranded saltwater creatures.

GETTING HERE AND AROUND

From Seattle, the fastest way (if there's no traffic) to Gig Harbor is to take Interstate 5 south through Tacoma to Highway 16 toward Bremerton. A slightly longer approach—in minutes, not miles—is to take the ferry from the West Seattle terminal to the Southworth landing on the Kitsap Peninsula and take Highway 160 west to Route 16 south. Taking the ferry from Seattle to Bremerton also works—you'd take Highway 3 south to Route 16.

ESSENTIALS

Visitor Information Gig Harbor Chamber of Commerce ✉ *3125 Judson St.* ☎ *253/851–6865* ⊕ *www.gigharborchamber.com.*

EXPLORING

Gig Harbor Museum. An excellent collection of exhibits here describes the city's maritime history, and there are photo archives, video programs, and a research library focusing on the area's pioneer and Native American ancestors. The facilities include a one-room, early-20th-century schoolhouse and a 65-foot, 1950s purse seiner, a type of fishing vessel from the community's famous seafaring fleets. News clippings and videos about "Galloping Gertie," a bridge over the Tacoma Narrows that famously collapsed in 1940, are particularly eerie. ✉ *4121 Harborview Dr.* ☎ *253/858–6722* ⊕ *www.harborhistorymuseum.org* 🖃 *$7*

Gig Harbor

⊘ *Mid-Apr.–Dec., Tues.–Sun. 10–5; Jan.–mid-Apr., Wed.–Sat. 10–4, Sun. noon–4.*

Kopachuck State Park. A10-minute drive from Gig Harbor, this is a wonderful beachcombing area at low tide. Native American tribes once fished and clammed here, and you can still see people trolling the shallow waters or digging deep for razor clams in season. Children and dogs alike delight in discovering huge Dungeness crabs, sea stars, and sand dollars. Picnic tables and walking trails are interspersed throughout the steep, forested hills, and the campground is always full in summer. ⊠ *11101 56th St. NW* ☏ *253/265–3606* ⊕ *www.parks.wa.gov* ⊘ *Day pass $10 per vehicle; annual Discovery Pass $30 (valid at all state parks)* ⊘ *Daily 8–dusk.*

WHERE TO EAT

$$$
MODERN
AMERICAN
Fodor'sChoice
★

✕ **Brix 25.** Simple seafood dishes and classic European fare are beautifully presented in this cozy, glass-fronted setting at the base of Harborview Drive and the Gig Harbor bay. Dinners are elaborate affairs that feature seafood—perhaps Thai curry and coconut steamed mussels—and dishes such as the Brix Signature Boeuf Bourguignon or Osso Bucco–style lamb shank. Tempting desserts include an array of sugary cakes, sorbets, and cobblers, and there's a fine wine to match every course. Seasonal events include chef-hosted, multicourse dinners, and great deals on food and drink are offered during the daily (except Saturdays) happy hour in the bar. ⑤ *Average main: $26* ⊠ *7707 Pioneer Way* ☏ *253/858–6626* ⊕ *www.harborbrix.com* ⊘ *No lunch.*

$
MEXICAN

✕ **El Pueblito.** The mariachi music, cilantro and chili pepper scents from the kitchen, and a waitstaff that chats in Spanish are reminiscent of a compact cantina south of the border. Huge portions of better-than-average Mexican dishes and frothy margaritas are served amid much gaiety. The adjacent bar is a lively late-night hangout on weekends. There's a second branch in Port Gamble. $ *Average main: $13* ✉ *3226 Harborview Dr.* ☎ *253/858–9077* ⊕ *www.elpueblitorestaurant.com.*

$$ ✕ **JW.** This elegant yet unfussy downtown bistro is one of Gig Harbor's
PACIFIC top picks for memorable dinners. The kitchen turns out creative, sea-
NORTHWEST sonally driven fare—starters of honey-almond prawns, and duck-confit sliders, followed by seared sea scallops with candied bacon, and wild boar Bourguignon with sweet onions, carrots, fennel, and peppercorn sauce. The flourless dark-chocolate torte with white-chocolate ganache is worth preserving your appetite for, and the terrific wine list focuses on Washington and Oregon. JW doesn't cater to diners under the age of 21. $ *Average main: $22* ✉ *4107 Harborview Dr.* ☎ *253/858–3529* ⊕ *www.jwgigharbor.com* ⊗ *Closed Mon. No lunch.*

WHERE TO STAY

$$ ⊞ **Inn at Gig Harbor.** The city's largest hotel is a four-story midrange
HOTEL property that looks and feels a bit like a cookie cutter chain, but many of its rooms have Mt. Rainier views, and suites have a fireplace or jetted tub. **Pros:** lodge-style ambience; professional staff; good, affordable restaurant on-site. **Cons:** no pool; rates can get steep during busy summer periods. $ *Rooms from: $159* ✉ *3211 56th St. NW* ☎ *253/858–1111, 800/795–9980* ⊕ *www.innatgigharbor.com* ⇌ *52 rooms, 12 suites* ⦿| *Breakfast.*

$$ ⊞ **Maritime Inn.** On a hill across from Jersich Park and the docks, these
HOTEL individually decorated and themed rooms have unfussy, contemporary furnishings and gas fireplaces, and nearly every one overlooks the water; several have decks. **Pros:** right on the waterfront; friendly staff and highly personal service. **Cons:** front rooms absorb traffic noise. $ *Rooms from: $155* ✉ *3112 Harborview Dr.* ☎ *253/858–1818, 888/506–3580* ⊕ *www.maritimeinn.com* ⇌ *15 rooms* ⦿| *Breakfast.*

SPORTS AND THE OUTDOORS

SAILING AND BOATING

Gig Harbor Rent-a-Boat. Look here to rent powerboats, kayaks, pedal boats, and stand-up paddleboards. ✉ *8829 N. Harborview Dr.* ☎ *253/858–7341* ⊕ *www.gigharborrentaboat.com.*

BREMERTON

18 miles west of Seattle by ferry, 68 miles southwest of Seattle by road, 25 miles north of Gig Harbor by road.

Nearly surrounded by water, and with one of the largest navy bases on the West Coast, Bremerton is a workaday city of about 30,000 with several attractions that center on the waterfront and its gardens, fountains, and ferry docks dwarfed by massive warships. Away from the waterfront, and especially around the ferry terminal, Bremerton looks a bit depressed in some parts. The western Charleston neighborhood, which had been run-down for years until some recent revitalization efforts, has the most going on, with a few art galleries and restaurants. Bremerton appeals primarily to fans of naval history and machinery.

GETTING HERE AND AROUND

From Seattle, Washington State Ferries provides regular hour-long service to Bremerton. The many navy sights are close to the ferry terminal, but Bremerton is best explored by car. You can also drive here via Gig Harbor—from Seattle, it takes a little over 90 minutes.

ESSENTIALS

Visitor Information Bremerton Area Chamber of Commerce ⌧ *286 4th St.* ☎ *360/479-3579* ⊕ *www.bremertonchamber.org.*

EXPLORING

Bremerton Marina. This waterfront expanse, lining the glistening blue bay between the warships and ferry docks, is the place to walk, bicycle, picnic, run through fountains in summer, and watch a mass of sailboats and military craft pass through the calm waters. It's an especially good place for spotting the host of birds and marine life around the docks. ⌧ *Off Washington Ave.* ⊕ *www.portofbremerton.org.*

Kitsap County Historical Society Museum. Pioneer artifacts, nautical items, and a collection of old photographs are on show. The staff plans such special children's events as costume dress-up sessions and treasure hunts for the first Friday of the month, when the museum is open late in conjunction with the town's monthly Art Walk. ⌧ *280 4th St.* ☎ *360/479-6226* ⊕ *www.kitsaphistory.org* ⌧ *$4* ⊙ *Tues.–Sat. 10–4, Sun. noon–4.*

FAMILY **Naval Undersea Museum.** A 15-minute drive north of Bremerton (not far from Poulsbo), this museum is fronted by a can't-miss sight: the 88-ton *Trieste II* submarine, which dove to the deepest spot in the ocean (the Marianas Trench) in 1960. In the main building are exhibits on torpedoes, diving equipment, model submarines, and mines. ⌧ *1 Garnett Way, Keyport* ☎ *360/396–4148* ⊕ *www.navalunderseamuseum.org* ⌧ *Free* ⊙ *May–Sept., daily 10–4; Oct.–Apr., Wed.–Mon. 10–4.*

FAMILY **Puget Sound Navy Museum.** One of Bremerton's several maritime-related attractions, right on the waterfront near the ferry terminal, brings American naval history to life through war photos, ship models, historic displays, and American and Japanese war artifacts. ⌧ *251 1st St.* ☎ *360/479–7447* ⊕ *www.pugetsoundnavymuseum.org* ⌧ *Free* ⊙ *May–Sept., Mon.–Sat. 10–4, Sun. 1–4; Oct.–Apr. closed Tues.*

FAMILY **USS Turner Joy.** This vintage navy destroyer, berthed along the marina near the ferry docks, is open for self-guided tours. Allow about 90 minutes to walk through the narrow passages to view the cafeteria, medical office, barbershop, prison cell, cramped bunk rooms, and captain's quarters. ⌧ *300 Washington Beach Ave.* ☎ *360/792–2457* ⊕ *ussturnerjoy.org* ⌧ *$12* ⊙ *Mar.–Oct., daily 10–5; Nov.–Feb., Fri.–Sun. 10–4.*

WHERE TO EAT AND STAY

$$ ✕ **Boat Shed.** At this deliberately rustic waterfront restaurant, diners
SEAFOOD share a casual, seaside camaraderie as they slurp up clam chowder, steamed clams, and mussels, plus larger plates of creatively prepared seafood grills and pastas—cioppino, wasabi-spiced fresh halibut, and smoked-salmon linguine are some of the best bets. Sailors, who enjoy free boat moorage, arrive early for the famed Sunday brunch. ⑤ *Average main: $21* ⌧ *101 Shore Dr.* ☎ *360/377–2600.*

10

$ ⌂**Flagship Inn.** Although it's a budget spot, rooms here have pri-
HOTEL   vate balconies overlooking Oyster Bay and the Olympic Mountains.
Pros: the price is right; nice views. **Cons:** place could use an update—
some furnishings are worn. ⑤ *Rooms from: $75* ⊠ *4320 Kitsap Way*
☏ *360/479–6566, 800/447–9396* ⊕ *www.flagship-inn.com* ⤳ *29 rooms*
⏀ *Breakfast.*

$$ ⌂ **Hampton Inn & Suites Bremerton.** Its splashy waterfront location—right
HOTEL   in the center of the city marina, adjacent to the Bremerton Harborside
Conference Center and just a block from the ferry terminal—makes
this large, modern hotel a bit more interesting than your usual mid-
range chain property. **Pros:** reliable chain hotel; good location. **Cons:**
not much personality ⑤ *Rooms from: $139* ⊠ *150 Washington Ave.*
☏ *360/405–0200, 800/426–7866* ⊕ *hamptoninn3.hilton.com* ⤳ *105*
rooms, 21 suites ⏀ *Breakfast.*

POULSBO

19 miles north of Bremerton, 12 miles northwest of Bainbridge Island.

Velkommen til Poulsbo (*pauls*-bo), a charming village on lovely Liberty
Bay. Soon after it was settled by Norwegians in the 1880s, shops and
bakeries sprang up along Front Street, as did a cod-drying facility to
produce the Norwegian delicacy called lutefisk. Although it's no longer
produced here commercially, lutefisk is still served at holiday feasts.
Front Street is crammed with authentic Norwegian bakeries, eclectic
Scandinavian crafts shops, small boutiques and bookstores, and art
galleries. Norwegian flags flutter from the eaves of the town's chalet-
style buildings. Grassy Liberty Bay Park is fronted by a network of
slender docks where seals and otters pop in and out of the waves. One
of the town's biggest events is the annual May Viking Festival (⊕ *www.*
vikingfest.org), complete with Viking tents and weapons, costumed
locals, and a lively parade.

GETTING HERE AND AROUND

To reach Poulsbo from Seattle, it's easiest to take the Washington State
Ferries to Bainbridge Island and drive 12 miles from there via Highway
305 north across the Agate Pass Bridge. If you're driving up the Kitsap
Peninsula, head north from Bremerton about 19 miles up Highway 3.

ESSENTIALS

Visitor Information Greater Poulsbo Chamber of Commerce ⊠ *19351 8th*
Ave., Suite 108 ☏ *360/779–4848, 877/768–5726* ⊕ *www.poulsbochamber.com.*

EXPLORING

FAMILY   **Poulsbo Marine Science Center.** Right along the shoreline and the edge of
Liberty Bay Park, the center is raised above the water and jam-packed
with exhibits of local sea creatures. An inter-tidal touch tank lets kids
feel sea anemones, sea urchins, and starfish, while other displays house
crabs, jellyfish, and plants. Puppets, puzzles, murals, and videos help
youngsters learn more about what they see. Don't miss the giant Pacific
octopus in a 2,000-gallon tank beneath the center. A small gift shop
fronts the building, and the center organizes special activities during

Poulsbo festivals. ⊠ *18743 Front St. NE* ☎ *360/598–4460* ⊕ *www. poulsbomsc.org* 🍽 *Free* ⊘ *Thurs.–Sun. 11–4.*

WHERE TO EAT AND STAY

$$ ✕ **Paella Bar.** Respected local chef Kim Tomlinson, who also helms the
TAPAS kitchen at adjacent and similarly excellent Burrata Bistro, serves richly
flavorful, Pacific Northwest–inspired Spanish tapas at this warmly
lighted spot in downtown Poulsbo that's popular for both afternoon
and late-night happy hour as well as for lunch and dinner. Paella is,
of course, the big star here—it's studded with fresh local seafood. But
you could also easily make a fine meal of delicious tapas, including
achiote-marinated beef short ribs over golden polenta, cod fritters with
chipotle aioli, and roasted brussels sprouts with pancetta and man-
chego cheese. ⑤ *Average main: $18* ⊠ *19006 Front St.* ☎ *360/930–8446*
⊕ *www.burratabistro-paellabar.com.*

$$ ⌂ **Green Cat Guest House.** A few miles north of downtown Poulsbo on
B&B/INN the way to Port Gamble, this dashing B&B with steep gabled roof has a
funky vibe, whimsical artwork, and a striking design, along with rooms
decorated with a mix of Mission and Arts and Crafts pieces. **Pros:** completely peaceful and enchanting setting; distinctive furnishings; good
proximity both to Poulsbo and Port Gamble. **Cons:** not within walking
distance of downtown; a bit remote. ⑤ *Rooms from: $119* ⊠ *25819
Tytler Rd. NE* ☎ *360/779–7569* ⊕ *www.greencatbb.com* 🛏 *3 rooms,
1 suite* ⎟⊙⎟ *Breakfast.*

SHOPPING

Sluys Bakery. Rhyme it with "pies" and you'll sound like a local when
you enter the town's most famous bakery. Gorgeous Norwegian pastries, braided bread, and *lefse* (traditional Norwegian round flatbread)
line the shelves. Kids often beg for one of the decorated cookies or
frosted doughnuts displayed at eye level. There's only strong coffee and
milk to drink, and there are no seats, but you can grab a bench along
busy Front Street or take your goodies to the waterfront at Liberty Bay
Park. ⊠ *18924 Front St.* ☎ *360/779–2798.*

PORT GAMBLE

6 miles northeast of Poulsbo.

Residents from the opposite side of America founded Port Gamble
around a sawmill in 1853; hence its New England–style architecture mimicking founder Captain William Talbot's hometown of East
Machias, Maine. Its setting amid the Kitsap Peninsula's tall stands of
timber brought in great profits, but the mill was later destroyed by fire,
and much of the forest has disappeared. A walk through town takes
you past the 1870 St. Paul's Episcopal Church as well as the Thompson
House, thought to be the state's oldest continuously lived-in home, and
a handful of shops and restaurants. The town also stages a popular
medieval-inspired June Faire each summer. This is also an excellent
hiking area, with numerous backcountry trails throughout.

10

GETTING HERE AND AROUND

Port Gamble is just 6 miles from Poulsbo via Highway 3 and Highway 104.

EXPLORING

FAMILY

Fodor's Choice

★

Port Gamble Historic Museum. Beneath the town's quaint General Store, the Smithsonian-designed Port Gamble Historic Museum takes you through the region's timber heyday. Highlights include artifacts from the Pope and Talbot Timber Company, which built the town, and realistic ship's quarters. Above the General Store, the **Of Sea and Shore Museum** is open daily and houses more than 25,000 shells as well as displays on natural history. Kids love the weird bug exhibit. In between visits stop at the General Store for souvenirs or a huge ice-cream cone or hand-dipped milkshake, or stay for lunch or dinner in the acclaimed restaurant in the back of the building. ⊠ *32400 Rainier Ave. NE* ☎ *360/297–8078* ⊕ *portgamble.com/visitin/museum* ⊠ *Historic Museum $4, Shell Museum free* ☉ *May–Sept., daily 9:30–5; Oct.–Apr., Fri.–Sun. 11–4.*

WHERE TO EAT

$

AMERICAN

✕ **Taste Port Gamble.** The sunny yellow exterior of this colonial home provides a lovely front for this elegant spot that's a tearoom and sandwich shop. Enjoy specials like cream tea (with scones and cream), or take chocolate high tea with finger sandwiches and chocolate fondue. This is also a popular stop for lunch or Sunday brunch. The adjacent artisanal chocolate shop whips up homemade dark- and white-chocolate truffles, as well as a variety of molded chocolate candies. ⑤ *Average main: $12* ⊠ *32279 N.E. Rainier Ave.* ☎ *360/297–4225* ⊕ *www.tasteportgamble.com* ☉ *Closed Mon.–Tues. No dinner.*

TACOMA AND OLYMPIA

A trip south down Interstate 5 quickly yields two important port cities: Tacoma, and Olympia, the state capital. Although Olympia is more practiced in winning over visitors with its tidy legislative campus and laid-back charms, Tacoma has steadily followed suit with an ambitious revitalization plan and a growing number of hip restaurants, lounges, and shops. Both have the same good foundation to work with: beautiful waterfront locations with historic cores and lots of adjacent parkland, and Tacoma has an especially notable bounty of first-rate museums.

TACOMA

25 miles southeast of Gig Harbor, 34 miles southwest of Seattle.

After decades of decline, Tacoma has been steadily undergoing a renaissance in recent years, with development around the waterfront and in other parts of downtown showing dramatic progress—a number of urbane galleries, bars, and restaurants have popped up around Union Station and nearby blocks. Several of the Victorian homes in the charming Stadium Hill neighborhood, high on a hill overlooking Commencement Bay, have been converted to bed-and-breakfast inns. Still, even on the busiest nights, Tacoma can seem a little quiet considering its population of 202,000. In this sense, proximity to Seattle is both a blessing and a curse, as locals still tend to drive there for a big night on the town.

Tacoma's got character, however, and it does have plenty to fill a day or two. The museums (which are vastly underrated), waterfront promenade, lush and expansive Point Defiance Park, and attractive old neighborhoods make for a very pleasant side trip or overnight adventure. The waterfront stretches west from the busy port, past the city and Puget Sound islands to the cliff-lined Tacoma Narrows. Renovated 19th-century homes, pretty beaches, and parks pocket the outskirts, and a young, diverse population gives the city a spirited character. The city's convenient setting provides easy access to Seattle to the north; Mt. Rainier to the southeast; Olympia to the south; and the Kitsap and Olympic Peninsulas to the west.

Tacoma was the first Puget Sound port connected by train to the East, and its economy was once based on the railroad. Old photos show tall-masted windjammers loading at the City Waterway, whose storage sheds were promoted by local boosters as the "longest warehouse under one continuous roof in the world." The city's shipping industry certainly weathered the tests of time, as Tacoma is roughly tied with Seattle as the largest container port in the Northwest.

GETTING HERE AND AROUND

Tacoma is close enough to Seattle that many people commute in both directions. It's a straight 30-mile shot down Interstate 5 to Exit 133 toward the city center. Tacoma is served by Greyhound and Amtrak, with connections north to Seattle and beyond, as well as south to Olympia. Tacoma is also served by Sound Transit's commuter rail, though trains are limited to rush hours.

If you're not planning to go too far out of the downtown core—just seeing the museums and the waterfront—you don't absolutely need a car to get around, as Amtrak and Greyhound let you off within a few blocks of each other in the Dome district (by the Tacoma Dome, on Puyallup Avenue). From here, you can catch Sound Transit's free Link Light Rail, which will get you to the museums, restaurants, and hotels of the downtown core.

10

ESSENTIALS

Visitor Information Tacoma Regional Convention & Visitors Bureau
✉ *Tacoma Convention Center, 1500 Broadway* ☎ *253/284–3254, 800/272–2662* ⊕ *www.traveltacoma.com.*

EXPLORING

TOP ATTRACTIONS

Foss Waterway Seaport. With its beautiful setting right along the Thea Foss waterfront, the turn-of-the-20th-century, wharf-style structure—with a dashing new glass facade—is easily reached along a walk by the bay. Inside the enormous timber building, a museum devoted to the city's waterfront heritage contains displays about the history of Tacoma's brisk shipping business. Extensive exhibits cover boat-making, importing and exporting, and the development of the waterfront. Photos and relics round out the exhibits, and children's activities are staged regularly. ✉ *705 Dock St.* ☎ *253/272–2750* ⊕ *www. fosswaterwayseaport.org* 🎫 *$8* ⊘ *Wed.–Sat. 10–4, Sun. noon–4.*

FAMILY
Fodor's Choice
★
LeMay—America's Car Museum. About 350 meticulously restored automobiles, from some of the world's earliest models to brassy muscle cars from the late '60s, are displayed in this sleek, striking museum on the south side of downtown. It's one of the most impressive car museums in the country, with engaging exhibits on Route 66, alternative-fuel cars, NASCAR, and other aspects of automobile culture and history. The cars here were collected by the late Harold LeMay, whose entire inventory of some 4,000 autos is recognized by the *Guinness Book of World Records* as the largest privately owned collection in the world. Highlights include a 1906 Cadillac Model M, a 1926 Rolls-Royce Silver Ghost, a 1930 Lincoln L Brougham, a 1953 Citroen 2CV, a 1960 Corvette, and a 1963 Studebaker Avanti. The café serves diner classics. ✉ *2702 E. D St.* ☎ *253/779–8490, 877/902–8490* ⊕ *www.lemaymuseum.org* 🎫 *$16* ⊘ *Daily 10–5.*

Fodor's Choice
★
Museum of Glass. The showpiece of this spectacular, 2-acre combination of delicate and creative exhibits is the 500-foot-long Chihuly Bridge of Glass, a tunnel of glorious color and light that stretches above I–705. Cross it from downtown to reach the building grounds, which sit above the bay and next to a shallow reflecting pool dotted with large

Chihuly Bridge of Glass, Tacoma

modern-art sculptures. Inside, you can wander through the quiet, light-filled galleries, take a seat in the theater-like Hot Shop—with its soaring conical roof—to watch glass-blowing artists, or try your own hand at arts and crafts in the studio. You'll also find a souvenir shop and café. ✉ *1801 E. Dock St.* ☎ *253/284–4750, 866/468–7386* ⊕ *www. museumofglass.org* 💲 *$12* ⊘ *Late May–early Sept., Mon.–Sat. 10–5, Sun. noon–5; early Sept.–mid-May, Wed.–Sat. 10–5, Sun. noon–5.*

★

Point Defiance Park. Jutting into Commencement Bay, this hilly, 765-acre park surrounds Five Mile Drive with lush picnicking fields and patches of forest. Hiking trails, bike paths, and numerous gardens draw crowds year-round, particularly during summer festivals such as the Taste of Tacoma, in June. The park begins at the north end of Pearl Street as you drive toward the Point Defiance Ferry Terminal, where vehicles depart for Vashon Island just across the sound. A one-way road branches off the ferry lane, past a lake and picnic area, a rose garden, a spectacular 22-acre rhododendron garden, and a Japanese garden, finally winding down to the beach.

A half-mile past the gardens is **Owen Beach,** a driftwood-strewn stretch of pebbly sand near the ferry dock and a wonderful place for beach-combing and sailboat-watching. Kayak rentals and concessions are available in summer. Continue around the looping drive, which offers occasional views of the narrows. Cruise slowly to take in the scenes—and watch out for joggers and bikers. ✉ *5400 N. Pearl St.* ⊕ *www. metroparkstacoma.org/point-defiance-park.*

Point Defiance Zoo & Aquarium. One of the Northwest's finest collections of regional and international species, this winding and hilly

10

site includes tigers, elephants, tapirs, and gibbons in the Asian Forest Sanctuary, where paw-print trails lead between lookouts so even the smallest tots can spot animals. The aquariums are also fun to explore, including a glass-walled, floor-to-ceiling shark tank; seahorse room; touch-tank marine area; and open-topped, two-level Pacific Northwest reef display. Other areas house such cold-weather creatures as beluga whales, Arctic foxes, polar bears, and penguins. Thirty-minute animal shows, run two to four times daily, let different creatures show off their skills. The fantastic playground area has friendly farm animals running between the slides, and seasonal special events include a Halloween trick-or-treat night and the famous nightly Zoolights holiday displays around Christmas. On weekends, weather permitting, camel rides are offered. ⊠ *Point Defiance Park, 5400 N. Pearl St.* ☎ *253/305–1000* ⊕ *www.pdza.org* ⊠ *$17* ⊘ *Mar.–Oct., daily 9:30–5, Nov.–Feb., Thurs.– Mon. 9:30–4; hrs vary so call ahead or check website.*

Ft. Nisqually. This restored Hudson's Bay Trading Post—a British outpost on the Nisqually Delta in the 1830s—was moved to Point Defiance in 1935. The compound houses a trading post, granary, blacksmith's shop, bakery, and officers' quarters. Docents dress in 1850s attire and demonstrate pioneer skills like weaving and loading a rifle. Queen Victoria's birthday in August is a big event, and eerie candlelight tours run throughout October. ⊠ *5400 N. Pearl St.* ☎ *253/591–5339* ⊕ *www.fortnisqually.org* ⊠ *$7* ⊘ *Late May–early Sept., daily 11–5; early May–late May and early Sept.–late Sept., Wed.–Sun 11–5; Oct.– Apr., Wed.–Sun. 11–4.*

Tacoma Art Museum. Adorned in glass and steel, this Antoine Predock masterpiece wraps around a beautiful garden. Inside, you'll find paintings, ceramics, sculptures, and other creations dating from the 18th century to the present. Look for the many glass sculptures by Dale Chihuly—especially the magnificent, flame-color *Mille Fiori* (Thousand Flowers) glass garden. ⊠ *1701 Pacific Ave.* ☎ *253/272–4258* ⊕ *www. tacomaartmuseum.org* ⊠ *$10* ⊘ *Wed.–Sun. 10–5.*

Washington State History Museum. Adjacent to Union Station, and with the same opulent architecture, Washington's official history museum presents interactive exhibits and multimedia installations about the exploration and settlement of the state. Some rooms are filled with Native American, Inuit, and pioneer artifacts, while others display logging and railroad relics. The upstairs gallery hosts rotating exhibits, and summer programs are staged in the outdoor amphitheater. ⊠ *1911 Pacific Ave.* ☎ *253/272–3500* ⊕ *www.washingtonhistory.org* ⊠ *$11* ⊘ *Summer, Tues.–Sun. 10–5; winter, Wed.–Sun. 10–5.*

WORTH NOTING

FAMILY **Children's Museum of Tacoma.** Fun activities for little ones take place at this hands-on, state-of-the-art museum where areas for exploration are broken down into a variety of "playscapes"—woods, water, voyager, Becka's Studio, invention, and reflection. Snacks are served in Café Play. ⊠ *1501 Pacific Ave.* ☎ *253/627–6031* ⊕ *www.playtacoma.org* ⊠ *Donation suggested* ⊘ *Wed.–Sun. 10–5.*

Karpeles Manuscript Library Museum. Housed in the former American Legion hall and across from Wright Park, the museum showcases rare and unpublished letters and documents by notables who have shaped history. Themes of the rotating exhibits have included the correspondence from the family of Presidents John and John Quincy Adams and Einstein's theory of relativity. ⊠ *407 S. G St.* ☎ *253/383–2575* ⊕ *www. rain.org/~karpeles* ⊠ *Free* ☾ *Tues.–Fri. 10–4.*

Tacoma-Narrows Bridge. A mile-wide waterway is the boundary between the Tacoma hills and the rugged bluffs of the Kitsap Peninsula. From the twin bridges that span it, the view plunges hundreds of feet down to roiling green waters, which are often busy with barge traffic or obscured by fog. The original bridge, "Galloping Gertie," famously twisted itself to death and broke in half during a storm in 1940—it's now the world's largest man-made reef, and is a popular dive site. Its mint-green replacement and a sister bridge opened in 2007. Note: The $5.50 toll is for eastbound cars only; westbound it's free from Tacoma into Gig Harbor. ⊠ *Hwy. 16 at N. Jackson Ave.*

WHERE TO EAT

$$$
SEAFOOD

× **Cliff House Restaurant.** For an unforgettable scene, witness the ocean panorama from this 1925 landmark restaurant's Rainier Room when there's a full moon. On any clear day, you'll likely get a view of Mt. Rainier across the bay. Clubby, curved banquettes provide the best positioning, but the cozier tables tucked in between offer more intimacy. When the succulent steaks, seafood, and wild game are served, your attention is turned away from the views. Entrées include Northwest seafood stew in a tomato-garlic broth, and boneless rib-eye steak with a green-peppercorn demi-glace. ⑤ *Average main: $26* ⊠ *6300 Marine View Dr.* ☎ *253/927–0400* ⊕ *cliffhousetacoma.com.*

$$
SEAFOOD
Fodor's Choice
★

× **Duke's Chowder House.** One of several popular seafood restaurants along Ruston Way, overlooking Tacoma's picturesque Commencement Bay, Duke's is part of a regional chainlet that can be counted on for serving some of the freshest and most creative fare of the bunch—it's not just about the view here, although the tables on the patio do offer dazzling panoramas. Chowder fans having a tough time deciding what to try might want to order the "full fleet" sampler, with small servings of clam, lobster, crab bisque, chicken-corn, and Northwest seafood varieties. Other notable dishes include the greens with crab cakes and Laura Chenel goat cheese, and pan-seared wild salmon with a balsamic-infused beurre blanc. ⑤ *Average main: $20* ⊠ *3327 Ruston Way* ☎ *253/752–5444* ⊕ *www.dukeschowderhouse.com.*

$
NORTHERN
ITALIAN

× **Europa Bistro.** Set in the middle of the genial and hip Proctor retail and restaurant district, on the city's north side (not too far from Point Defiance), this charming, affordable neighborhood spot focuses on authentic northern Italian recipes, but with an emphasis on seasonal ingredients. The convivial, if sometimes a bit noisy, dining room has tile floors and rows of polished-wood tables, at which regulars feast on traditional panfried zucchini with goat cheese and crostini, slow-roasted lamb over pappardelle noodles, seafood risotto, and thin-crust pizzas. There's an extensive list of Italian wines. ⑤ *Average main: $13*

10

✉ *2515 N. Proctor St.* ☎ *253/761–5660* ⊕ *www.europabistro.net* ◐ *No lunch Sun.*

$$
ASIAN
Fodor'sChoice
★

✕**Indochine.** The elegant, pan-Asian conglomeration of sounds, scents, and sights takes place in a sleekly modern yet darkly cozy space. Black-leather seats, curving banquettes, and steely metal accents set off plush red curtains and pavilion tables. The taste-dazzling array of Thai, Chinese, Indian, and Japanese cuisines includes curries, stir-fries, soups, and seafood. Standouts include coconut and galangal chicken soup and the Oceans Five seafood platter. ⑤ *Average main: $21* ✉ *1924 Pacific Ave.* ☎ *253/272–8200* ⊕ *indochinedowntown.com* ◐ *Closed Sun.*

$$
MODERN
AMERICAN
Fodor'sChoice
★

✕**Marrow Kitchen & Bar.** A culinary hot spot in the trendy 6th Avenue business district, Marrow occupies an urbane, storefront space with light-wood banquettes and tables and modern lighting, the sort of sleek look that's becoming increasingly commonplace in this up-and-coming city. Owned by the same talented team behind Hilltop Kitchen, this swish spot serves creative cocktails and superb, beautifully plated mod-American food, including foie-gras mousse waffles and the signature burger topped with white cheddar, harissa barbecue sauce, bacon, and a fried duck egg. It's a great late-night option, too—open until midnight. ⑤ *Average main: $19* ✉ *2717 6th Ave.* ☎ *253/267–5299* ⊕ *www.marrowtacoma.com* ◐ *Closed Sun. and Mon. No lunch.*

$$
PACIFIC
NORTHWEST

✕**Over The Moon Cafe.** Tucked down an alley near Wright Park, the Theater District, and several popular antiques shops, this quirky and cozy neighborhood bistro serves first-rate Northwest-influenced Italian fare, including bounteous salads and creative grills. It's worth seeking out this art-filled space with exposed-brick walls for such delectable fare as slow-cooked chicken ragu over rigatoni, and pan-seared, bourbon-glazed salmon fillet. Desserts, including banana pie with chocolate-fudge sauce, are a major draw. ⑤ *Average main: $20* ✉ *709 Opera Alley* ☎ *253/284–3722* ⊕ *www.overthemooncafe.net* ◐ *Closed Sun. and Mon.*

$$$
MODERN
AMERICAN

✕**Pacific Grill.** With its clubby interior, huge wine list, and proximity to downtown hotels and attractions, it's easy to see how this flashy restaurant is a favorite for special occasions and high-end business meals. Here you can expect a menu of contemporary variations on seafood and steak, including Columbia River steelhead with a maple-balsamic glaze, and New York steak with red flannel hash and a red wine sauce; vegetarians shouldn't pass up the unusual roasted cauliflower "steak" served with olive gremolata, tomatoes, orange, and capers. Terrific happy hour deals are offered on weekday afternoons. ⑤ *Average main: $29* ✉ *1502 Pacific Ave.* ☎ *253/627–3535* ⊕ *www.pacificgrilltacoma.com* ◐ *No lunch weekends.*

$
HOT DOG
Fodor'sChoice
★

✕**Red Hot.** The first thing you notice upon walking inside this bustling tavern and hot-dog joint are the dozens of beer taps hanging from the ceiling, each one representing a particular ale that's been poured here. Indeed, this quirky spot is a must for beer lovers, with plenty of interesting varieties on tap and available by the bottle, from Northwest craft brews to Belgian Trappist tripels. But it's the dogs and brats that set Red Hot apart from your usual beer barn—the kitchen here serves up the classics, like a Chicago-style beef version topped with mustard, relish, and celery salt, as well as unusual versions, like the Hosmer Hound, which is slathered in peanut butter and crowned with crispy bacon. German-style bratwurst and vegan dogs are served, too. $ *Average main: $5* ⊠ *2914 6th Ave.* ☎ *253/779–0229* ⊕ *www.redhottacoma.com.*

$

SOUTHERN

Fodor'sChoice

★

× **Southern Kitchen.** Sure, it's awfully far north to be specializing in down-home Southern cooking, but this bustling, casual spot on Tacoma's north side, a little west of Wright Park, serves remarkably authentic and absolutely delicous soul food. In the morning, regulars swing by for heaping plates of chicken-fried steak with grits and eggs, or home-made biscuits and gravy. Later, move on to fried catfish strips with a side of hush puppies, Texas-style hand-trimmed brisket, and hot-links sandwiches. Dinners come with corn cakes and lots of tasty sides—and do save room for the sweet potato pie. Note that the restaurant closes on the early side most evenings, usually around 8 pm. $ *Average main: $12* ⊠ *1716 6th Ave.* ☎ *253/627–4282* ⊕ *www.southernkitchen-tacoma.com.*

WHERE TO STAY

$$

B&B/INN

Chinaberry Hill. Original fixtures and stained-glass windows are among the grace notes in this 1889 Queen Anne–style house on a tree-lined street, where accommodations come with shining wood floors, antique feather beds dressed in fine-quality linens, and ornate desks. **Pros:** wraparound porch with vast bay views; in the Stadium Historic District. **Cons:** creaks and quirks of a century-old mansion; 20- to 30-minute walk from downtown attractions. $ *Rooms from: $149* ⊠ *302 Tacoma Ave. N* ☎ *253/272–1282* ⊕ *www.chinaberryhill.com* ⌁ *1 room, 4 suites, 1 cottage* |○| *Breakfast.*

$$

HOTEL

Courtyard Marriott Tacoma Downtown. Although set in the late-19th-century Waddell Building, this Marriott has spacious, modern rooms outfitted in bright Northwest colors with lots of 21st-century touches, and you'll find an upscale restaurant and bar. **Pros:** reliable chain hotel in historic building; steps from convention center and museums; full-service spa. **Cons:** rooms get street noise; can get little pricey for a midrange chain hotel; parking fee. $ *Rooms from: $149* ⊠ *1515 Commerce St.* ☎ *253/591–9100* ⊕ *www.marriott.com* ⌁ *156 rooms, 6 suites* |○| *Breakfast.*

$$

B&B/INN

Green Cape Cod Bed & Breakfast. At this 1929 house in a residential neighborhood only blocks from the historic Proctor shopping district rooms come with frilly linens and beautiful antiques. **Pros:** cozy, roman-tic rooms; lovely, historic neighborhood. **Cons:** need a car to get down-town $ *Rooms from: $145* ⊠ *2711 N. Warner St.* ☎ *253/752–1977, 866/752–1977* ⊕ *www.greencapecod.com* ⌁ *3 rooms* |○| *Breakfast.*

$$$

HOTEL

Fodor'sChoice

★

Hotel Murano. Named for the Venetian island where some of the world's best glass is created, this big hotel with an intimate ambience centers around exhibits by world-famous glass artists and offers rooms done in black and white with fiery accents. **Pros:** stylish rooms with beautiful art; luxury amenities; top-flight service. **Cons:** no pool; park-ing fee. $ *Rooms from: $179* ⊠ *1320 Broadway Plaza* ☎ *253/238–8000, 888/862–3255* ⊕ *www.hotelmuranotacoma.com* ⌁ *319 rooms, 10 suites* |○| *Breakfast.*

10

$$$
HOTEL

⊤ **Silver Cloud Inn.** Tacoma's only waterfront hotel juts right out into the bay along picturesque Ruston Way and the historic Old Town area, with fairly functional rooms, but posh suites that have plush carpets, overstuffed chairs, fireplaces, and corner hot tubs and hang out over the water. **Pros:** waterside locale; Ruston Way walking paths and restaurants nearby; free parking. **Cons:** summer traffic; compact rooms—it's worth splurging for a suite. $ *Rooms from: $199* ⊠ *2317 N. Ruston Way* ☎ *253/272–1300, 866/820–8448* ⊕ *www.silvercloud.com* ⇄ *90 rooms* ⦿ *Breakfast.*

$$$$
B&B/INN

⊤ **Thornewood Castle Inn and Gardens.** Spread over four lush acres along beautiful American Lake, this 27,000-square-foot, Gothic Tudor–style mansion built in 1908 has hosted two American presidents, William Howard Taft and Theodore Roosevelt, and surrounds current guests with medieval stained-glass windows, gleaming wood floors, large mirrors, antiques, fireplaces, and hot tubs. **Pros:** castlelike ambience; lively events. **Cons:** one of the more expensive properties in the area; in a sort of no-man's-land between Tacoma and Fort Lewis. $ *Rooms from: $325* ⊠ *8601 N. Thorne La. SW, 12 miles south of Tacoma, Lakewood* ☎ *253/589–9052* ⊕ *www.thornewoodcastle.com* ⇄ *2 rooms, 7 suites, 3 apartments* ⦿ *Breakfast.*

NIGHTLIFE AND PERFORMING ARTS

PERFORMING ARTS

Cultural activity in Tacoma centers on the Broadway Center for the Performing Arts, and on and around Broadway between 9th and 10th streets.

NIGHTLIFE

Fodor's Choice
★

Hilltop Kitchen. Although this stylish but casual north end bistro is a terrific dining option (don't miss the lamb *barbacoa* [Caribbean barbecue] tacos with mango mustard and cotija cheese), the scene comes alive, especially during the evenings. The talented bartenders pour such creative concoctions as the Single Dad (tequila, genepy, cachaca, lime, and amaro) and the Discipline Problem (rum with blackberry drinking vinegar and Mexican yogurt, served up). ⊠ *913 Martin Luther King Jr. Way* ☎ *253/327–1397* ⊕ *www.hilltopkitchen.com* ⊙ *Closed Sun.*

Jazzbones. This classy no-cover, no-fuss, just-great-music joint is on the Sixth Avenue strip, with live jazz on stage every night. There's a good restaurant here, too, serving eclectic Southern-inspired American food, and—a bit surprisingly—a popular sushi bar. ⊠ *2803 6th Ave.* ☎ *253/396–9169* ⊕ *www.jazzbones.com.*

The Mix. Tacoma has a sizable, increasingly visible gay community, and this friendly, welcoming bar with a nice-size dance floor and fun karaoke parties is the top nightspot among LGBT folks. It's in the heart of the Theater District. ⊠ *635 St. Helens Ave.* ☎ *253/383–4327* ⊕ *www.themixtacoma.com.*

Swiss Pub. This lively pub inside a historic building has microbrews on tap, pool tables, and bands on stage Thursday through Saturday. Monday brings free admission for live blues night, and there's karaoke on Wednesday. The place is best early in the evening before the bands start playing—it can get pretty loud and rambunctious in here as the evening goes on. ⊠ *1904 S. Jefferson Ave.* ☎ *253/572–2821* ⊕ *www. theswisspub.com.*

1022 South. You can't claim to have a sophisticated nightlife scene until someone in a vest is mixing artisanal cocktails, and 1022 South is Tacoma's top spot for fine drinks made with unusual infusions (nettles, yerba mate), housemade liqueurs and colas, and premium liquors with hipster cachet (Portland's Aviation gin, for example). Daily happy hour is 4 to 8 pm, and the kitchen produces nosh-worthy nibbles, from cheese plates to burgers. ⊠ *1022 S. J St.* ☎ *253/627–8588* ⊕ *www.ten22southj.com.*

SHOPPING

Tacoma's top shopping districts are Antique Row, along Broadway at St. Helen's Street, where upscale shops sells everything from collectibles to vintage paraphernalia, and the Proctor District, in the north end, where many specialty shops do business.

OLYMPIA

30 miles southwest of Tacoma.

Olympia has been the capital of Washington since 1853, the beginning of city and state. It is small for the capital city of a major state, but that makes it all the more pleasant to visit. The old and charming downtown area is compact and easy on the feet, stretching between Capitol Lake and the gathering of austere government buildings to the south, the shipping and yacht docks around glistening Budd Inlet to the west, the colorful market area capping the north end of town, and Interstate 5 running along the eastern edge. There are small, unexpected surprises all through town, from pretty, little half-block parks and blossoming miniature gardens to clutches of Thai and Vietnamese restaurants and antiques shops. The imposing state capitol, finished in 1928, is set above the south end of town like a fortress, framed by a skirt of granite steps. The monumental 287-foot-high dome is the fourth-largest masonry dome in the world (only St. Peter's in Rome, St. Paul's in London, and the national Capitol in the other Washington are larger).

GETTING HERE AND AROUND

From Seattle, take Interstate 5 south to Exit 105—this is an easy city to drive and park in, and a car is your best way around. Both Greyhound and Amtrak serve Olympia, but the Amtrak station is 8 miles away, so from Seattle, if you're not driving, taking the bus is actually more convenient, as the bus station is centrally located and the sights are clustered around downtown.

ESSENTIALS

Visitor Information Olympia Visitor and Convention Bureau ⊠ *103 Sid Snyder Ave. SW* ☎ *360/704–7544, 877/704–7500* ⊕ *www.visitolympia.com.*

EXPLORING

TOP ATTRACTIONS

Capitol Campus. These attractive grounds, sprawling around the buildings perched above the Capitol Lake bluffs, contain memorials, monuments, rose gardens, and Japanese cherry trees. The 1939 conservatory is open year-round on weekdays from 8 to 3 and also on weekends in summer. Directly behind the legislative building, the modern state library has exhibits devoted to Washington's history. Free 45-minute tours from the visitor center take you around the area. If you want to see state government in action, the legislature is in session for 30 or 60 days from the second Monday in January, depending on whether it's an even- or odd-numbered year. ✉ *Capitol Way, between 10th and 14th Aves.* ☎ *360/902–8880 tour information* ⊕ *www.des.wa.gov* ✉ *Free* ⊙ *Campus tours daily on the hr, 10–3 weekdays and 11–3 weekends.*

FAMILY   **Hands On Children's Museum.** This fun spot in a handsome, modern building just off Marine Drive overlooking East Bay is where children can touch, build, and play with all sorts of crafts and exhibits. Dozens of interactive, cleverly designed stations include an art studio and a special gallery for kids four and under. During the city's First Friday art walks the museum is open late and stages special programs and events. ✉ *414 Jefferson St. NW* ☎ *360/956–0818* ⊕ *www.hocm.org* ✉ *$10.95* ⊙ *Tues.–Sat. 10–5, Mon.–Sun. 11–5.*

Percival Landing Waterfront Park. Framing nearly an acre of landscaped desert gardens and bird-watching areas, this lovely waterfront spot stretches along a 1-mile boardwalk through a beachy section of the Ellis Cove coastline. To the south are yachts bobbing in the water at the wooden docks and the waterfront Anthony's restaurant; to the north are the shipyards and cargo cranes; and to the east is the market. In the center is an open space with an outdoor stage for summer shows, music, and festivals. You can see it all from three stories up by climbing the winding steps of the viewing tower, where open benches invite visitors to relax and enjoy the outlook. ✉ *4th Ave. to Thurston Ave.* ☎ *360/753–8380* ⊕ *olympiawa.gov/community/parks/percival-landing* ✉ *Free* ⊙ *Daily dawn–dusk.*

WORTH NOTING

Olympia Farmers' Market. Neat, clean, and well-run, this expanse of covered fruit, vegetable, pastry, and craft stalls at the north end of town includes organic produce. You'll also find all sorts of oddities such as ostrich eggs, button magnets, and glass sculptures. With a dozen tiny ethnic eateries tucked in between the vendors, it's also a terrific place to grab a bite and then walk over to the waterfront area. ✉ *700 N. Capitol Way* ☎ *360/352–9096* ⊕ *www.olympiafarmersmarket.com* ✉ *Free* ⊙ *Apr.–Oct., Thurs.–Sun. 10–3; Nov. and Dec., weekends 10–3.*

The Olympic Flight Museum. Housed in a hangar at the Olympic Regional Airport south of town, this museum brings to life an ever-changing collection of vintage aircraft. Important pieces include a colorful P-51D Mustang, a sleek BAC-167 Strikemaster, and a serious-looking AH-1S Cobra helicopter. On the annual schedule are winter lectures, weekly tours, monthly flights, and the Gathering of Warbirds event each June. The shop sells a model of just about everything you see on-site. ✉ *7637 Old Hwy. 99 SE* ☎ *360/705–3925* ⊕ *www.olympicflightmuseum.com* ✉ *$7* ⊙ *May–Sept., daily 11–5; Oct.–Dec., Tues.–Sun. 11–5; Jan.–Apr., Wed.–Sun. 11–5.*

Priest Point Park. This leafy tract is a beautiful section of protected shoreline and wetlands. Thick swaths of forest and glistening bay views are the main attractions, with picnic areas and playgrounds filling in the open spaces. The 3-mile **Ellis Cove Trail,** with interpretive stations, bridges, and nature settings, runs right through the Priest Point Park area and around the Olympia coast. ⊠ *East Bay Dr.* ☎ *360/753–8380* ⊕ *olympiawa.gov/community/parks/parks-and-trails/priest-point-park.*

FAMILY **Wolf Haven International.** Guided tours of this 80-acre wolf sanctuary are given every hour on the hour and run about 50 minutes, during which docents explain the recovery programs and visitors can view the wolves. You must join a tour. Note that it's worth taking a look at the website before visiting—the sanctuary has a few rules regarding conduct and photography (certain zoom lenses can only be used on special photography tours). Most important, parents should know that although the sanctuary can be a wonderful place for kids, it does not provide as much stimulation as a typical zoo and may bore kids with short attention spans. ⊠ *3111 Offut Lake Rd. SE* ✛ *From Olympia, take I–5 south to Exit 99 and follow signs east for 7 miles* ☎ *800/448–9653* ⊕ *www. wolfhaven.org* ☞ *$12* ⊗ *Apr.–Sept., Mon. and Wed.–Sat. 10–4, Sun. noon–4; Oct.–mid-Feb. and last 2 wks of Mar., Sat. 10–4, Sun. noon–4.*

WHERE TO EAT

$$$ ✕ **Dockside Bistro & Wine Bar.** The marina views are just part of the appeal
PACIFIC of this bright, modern bistro overlooking West Bay. It's the innova-
NORTHWEST tive, beautifully presented Asia-meets-Northwest cuisine of chef Laurie Nguyen that has foodies buzzing, not to mention friendly and efficient service and a stellar wine list. The food here focuses strongly on what's local and organic, with Totten Inlet steamer clams in white wine, and local elk rib-eye carpaccio with juniper berries and green papaya salad starring among the starters. Worthy picks among the main dishes include pear-Gorgonzola ravioli with wild prawns, and seared sea scallops with a light watercress-saffron cream. ⑤ *Average main: $24* ⊠ *501 Columbia St. NW* ☎ *360/956–1928* ⊕ *www.docksidebistro.com* ⊗ *Closed Mon. No lunch Sun.*

$ ✕ **Fish Tale BrewPub.** This long-running microbrewery and tavern in a
AMERICAN slightly industrial section of downtown has a bustling, open dining room with mounted fish on the walls and a quieter section of outdoor seating along the sidewalk. It's a funky and fun standby for big portions of pub standards—nachos, smoked wild salmon platters, black-bean burgers, fish-and-chips, and a much beloved Mudshark Porter dark-chocolate cheesecake. The ales are well crafted—try the Winterfish Organic Seasonal Ale during the cooler months, or cool off with a light Organic Blonde Ale on a hot summer night. ⑤ *Average main: $13* ⊠ *515 Jefferson St. SE* ☎ *360/943–3650* ⊕ *www.fishbrewing.com.*

$$ ✕ **Mercato.** Tucked into a glitzy, glass-front office building on a sunny
MEDITERRANEAN corner across from the Farmers' Market, the aptly named restaurant brings an Italian countryside ambience to this relaxed neighborhood. Tables line up against sponge-painted gold walls decorated with a series of Patés Baroni posters, with tiny stained-glass lamps lighting the scene. Specialties include the *piadina* sandwiches, slices of warmed flatbread slathered with such cold fillings as smoked duck on spinach vinaigrette, along with thin-crust pizzas, creative pastas and risottos, and hearty

10

grills. $ *Average main: $18* ✉ *111 Market St. NE* ☎ *360/528–3663* ⊕ *www.mercatoristorante.com.*

WHERE TO STAY

$$

HOTEL

🛏 **Doubletree Olympia Hotel.** These polished rooms nestle right up to Budd Inlet just a couple of blocks from the Farmers' Market and are done with plush fabrics in deep charcoals, golds, and beiges and come with such splashy bonuses as corner jetted tubs and chaises longues. **Pros:** great rates considering size and look of rooms; lots of amenities; indoor pool open 24 hours. **Cons:** pedestrian hotel appearance. $ *Rooms from: $149* ✉ *415 Capitol Way N* ☎ *360/570–0555, 855/610–8733* ⊕ *www.hilton.com* ⇥ *102 suites* �‖ *Breakfast.*

$$

B&B/INN

🛏 **Swantown Inn.** Antiques and lace ornament every room of this stylish, peak-roofed Victorian inn, built as a mansion in 1893 and then used for many years as a boardinghouse. **Pros:** 19th-century feel, but modern and business-friendly. **Cons:** a 20- to 30-minute walk to downtown. $ *Rooms from: $139* ✉ *1431 11th Ave. SE* ☎ *360/753–9123* ⊕ *www.swantowninn.com* ⇥ *3 rooms, 1 suite* �‖ *Breakfast.*

SHOPPING

Fodor'sChoice

★

Batdorf & Bronson Dancing Goats Coffee Bar. Here is a local roaster (also with branches in metro Atlanta, Georgia) that can stand up to the best of Seattle's coffeehouses. Several spacious and sleek shops, including this one across from the Farmers' Market, pair the best beans with just-baked pastries and tasty sandwiches. The tasting room up the street at 200 Market is in the roastery. You can sample about a half dozen of Batdorf's favorite blends Wednesday through Sunday from 9 to 4. ✉ *111 Market St. NE* ☎ *360/528–5555* ⊕ *www.dancinggoats.com.*

MT. RAINIER ENVIRONS

The Cascade Mountains south of Snoqualmie Pass are more heavily eroded than those to the north and generally not as high. But a few peaks do top 7,000 feet, and two volcanic peaks are taller than any of the state's northern mountains. Mt. Adams is more than 12,000 feet high, and Mt. Rainier rises to more than 14,000 feet. The third of the southern peaks, Mt. St. Helens, blew its top in 1980, transforming it from 9,677 to 8,365 feet in elevation.

This is a rural part of the state with just a handful of fairly small towns that make good bases for visiting both Mt. Rainier and Mt. St. Helens— these include Ashford, which offers the only year-round access to and services near Mt. Rainier; the mountain village of Packwood, just below White Pass; and tiny Mossyrock, which lies between the alpine lakes of Riffe and Mayfield. Right on Interstate 5, about midway between Portland and Seattle, the town of Centralia—which has a historic downtown and a handful of antiques shops—makes a handy base or stopover. Here you'll find a few distinctive lodging and dining options, plus a plethora of chain properties just off the interstate.

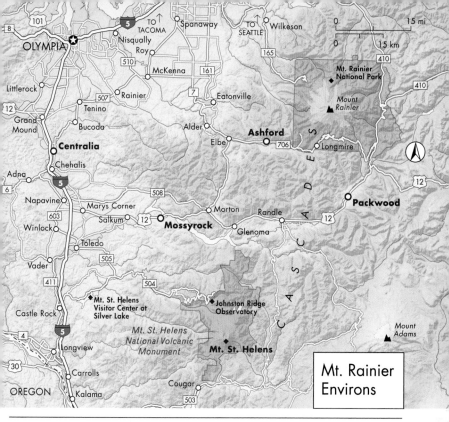

Mt. Rainier
Environs

ASHFORD

85 miles south of Seattle, 130 miles north of Portland.

Adjacent to the Nisqually (Longmire) entrance to Mount Rainier National Park, Ashford draws around 2 million visitors every year. Long a transit route for local aboriginal tribes, its more recent history began when it became a logging terminal on the rail line and developed into a tourism hot spot with lodges, restaurants, groceries, and gift shops along Highway 706.

GETTING HERE AND AROUND

Ashford is easiest to reach from Seattle via Interstate 5 southbound to Highway 7, then driving southeast to Highway 706. An alternate route is via Interstate 5 southbound to Highway 167, then continuing south to Highway 161 through Eatonville to Highway 7, then east to Highway 706. From Portland, follow Interstate 5 northbound, then head east on Highway 12 to Morton and north via Highway 7 to Highway 706.

EXPLORING

FAMILY **Mt. Rainier Scenic Railroad and Museum.** This trip takes you through lush forests and across scenic bridges, covering 14 miles of incomparable beauty. Trains depart from Elbe, 11 miles west of Ashford, then bring passengers to a lovely picnic area near Mineral Lake before returning.

Seasonal theme trips, such as the Great Pumpkin Express and the Snowball Express, are also available. Back at the station in Mineral Lake, guests can tour the museum containing old train memorabilia and artifacts, as well as exhibits on the area's old railroad camps, which served as the hub of logging operations by rail. ⊠ *349 Mineral Creek Rd., Mineral* ☎ *360/569–2588, 888/783–2611* ⊕ *www.mrsr.com* ⊠ *Rides $29, museum $10 (free with train ride),* ☉ *Mid-May–Oct., weekends (also Thurs. and Fri. in summer); some seasonal trips in Dec. and Mar.*

WHERE TO EAT

$$$
AMERICAN

✕ **Alexander's Country Inn & Restaurant.** This woodsy country inn serves some of the best food in the area. Ceiling fans and wooden booths lining the walls add a touch of whimsy to the 1912 building. Try the steak or trout—freshly caught from the pond on the grounds. The homemade bread is fantastic, and the blackberry pie is a must for dessert. Dine inside or outside on a patio overlooking a waterfall. Box lunches for adventurers are available. ⑤ *Average main: $24* ⊠ *37515 Hwy. 706 E, Ashford* ☎ *360/569–2323, 800/654–7615* ⊕ *www.alexanderscountryinn.com* ☉ *No lunch Mon.–Thurs.*

$
AMERICAN
FAMILY
Fodor's Choice
★

✕ **Copper Creek Restaurant.** This good old-fashioned roadhouse, with rough-hewn fir floors and knotty-pine walls, is nestled beneath soaring pine trees along the main road to Mt. Rainier from Eatonville. It's been a favorite lunch and dinner stop since it opened in the 1940s, and these days park goers still come by in droves to fill up on hearty, straightforward American comfort fare, such as biscuits and gravy in the morning, and bacon–blue cheese burgers and wild Alaskan salmon with blackberry vinaigrette in the evening. Be sure to save room for the blackberry pie à la mode. The restaurant is part of a rustic inn with standard rooms and cabin rentals. ⑤ *Average main: $15* ⊠ *35707 Hwy. 706, Ashford* ☎ *360/569–2799* ⊕ *www.coppercreekinn.com* ☉ *Closed Tues. and Wed. in winter.*

$
AMERICAN
FAMILY

✕ **Scaleburgers.** Once a 1939 logging-truck weigh station, the building is now a popular restaurant serving homemade hamburgers, fries, and shakes. Eat outside on tables overlooking the hills and scenic railroad. ⑤ *Average main: $6* ⊠ *54109 Mountain Hwy. E, 11 miles west of Ashford, Elbe* ☎ *360/569–2247* ⊟ *No credit cards* ☉ *Limited hrs in winter; call ahead.*

WHERE TO STAY

$$
B&B/INN

⌂ **Alexander's Country Inn.** At this top-notch lodging just a mile from Mount Rainier's Nisqually entrance, antique furnishings and fine linens lend romance to rooms in the main building; there are also two adjacent guesthouses. **Pros:** luxurious amenities, especially considering moderate rates; on-site day spa; serving guests since 1912 and also home to one of the region's most popular restaurants. **Cons:** lots of breakables means it's not great for children. ⑤ *Rooms from: $130* ⊠ *37515 Hwy. 706 E, 4 miles east of Ashford, Ashford* ☎ *360/569–2323, 800/654–7615* ⊕ *www.alexanderscountryinn.com* ⇱ *12 rooms, 2 3-bedroom houses* ❙⦿❙ *Breakfast.*

$$
HOTEL

⌂ **Nisqually Lodge.** Though these accommodations a few miles west of Mount Rainier National Park are of the standard motel-room variety, crackling flames from the massive stone fireplace lend warmth and cheer

Mt. Rainier was named after British admiral Peter Rainier in the late 18th century.

to the great room. **Pros:** spacious rooms; central to mountain activities and just a few miles from park; the price is right. **Cons:** no frills. $ *Rooms from: $120* ⊠ *31609 Hwy. 706 E* ☎ *360/569–8804, 888/674–3554* ⊕ *www.nisqually.whitepasstravel.com* ⇝ *24 rooms* ¶◎¶ *Breakfast.*

$ **Wellspring.** Deep in the woods outside Ashford, the accommodations here include tastefully designed log cabins, tent cabins, a tree house, and a room in a greenhouse. **Pros:** unique lodging with a wide range of prices, depending on the room; some options good for groups; relaxing spa and hot soaking tubs. **Cons:** limited amenities; some units are closed in winter. $ *Rooms from: $95* ⊠ *54922 Kernehan Rd., Ashford* ☎ *360/569–2514* ⊕ *www.wellspringspa.com* ⇝ *5 rooms, 6 cabins, 3 tent cabins, 1 cottage, 1 tree house, 1 lodge* ¶◎¶ *Breakfast.*

B&B/INN

$ **Whittaker's Bunkhouse Motel.** Inexpensive bunk spaces (available May–September) as well as large private rooms and a cottage are comfortable and come with a communal hot tub, a welcome amenity after a day of recreation. **Pros:** inexpensive; convenient; historical draw for mountain buffs. **Cons:** no frills in most rooms; bunk room shares bathrooms. $ *Rooms from: $90* ⊠ *30205 Hwy. 706 E* ☎ *360/569–2439* ⊕ *www. whittakersbunkhouse.com* ⇝ *20 rooms, 1 12-bed bunk room, 1 cottage* ¶◎¶ *No meals.*

HOTEL

PACKWOOD

25 miles southeast of Ashford via Skate Creek Rd. (closed in winter).

Its location, between Mt. Rainier and Mt. St. Helens, makes this delightful mountain village on U.S. 12 an attractive destination for those who plan to explore the nearby wilderness areas.

MT. ST. HELENS

One of the most prominent peaks in the Northwest's rugged Cascade Range, Mount St. Helens National Volcanic Monument affords visitors an up close look at the site of the most destructive volcanic blast in U.S. history.

Just 55 miles northeast of Portland, and 155 miles southeast of Seattle, this once soaring, conical summit stood at 9,667 feet above sea level. Then, on May 18, 1980, a massive eruption launched a 36,000-foot plume of steam and ash into the air and sent nearly 4 million cubic yards of debris through the Toutle and Cowlitz river valleys. The devastating eruption leveled a 230-square-mile area, claiming 57 lives and more than 250 homes. The mountain now stands at 8,365 feet, and a horseshoe-shape crater—most visible from the north—now forms the scarred summit. A modern highway carries travelers to within about 5 miles of the summit, and the surrounding region offers thrilling opportunities for climbing, hiking, and learning about volcanology.

BEST TIME TO GO

It's best to visit from mid-May through late October, as the last section of Spirit Lake Highway, Johnston Ridge Observatory, and many of the park's forest roads are closed the rest of the year. The other visitor centers along the lower sections of the highway are open year-round, but overcast skies typically obscure the mountain's summit in winter.

PARK HIGHLIGHTS

Ape Cave. The longest continuous lava tube in the continental U.S., Ape Cave is one of the park's outstanding attractions. The lower route is an easy hour-long hike; the upper route is challenging and takes about three hours. Be sure to bring your own light source and warm clothing—temperatures in the cave don't rise above the mid-40s. In high season ranger-led walks are sometimes available; inquire at the **Apes' Headquarters** (☎ 360/449–7800), which is off Forest Service road 8303, 3 miles north of the junction of Forest Roads 83 and 90. Although Ape Cave is open year-round, the headquarters closes from November through April. ⊠ Cougar ☎ 360/449–7800 ⊕ www.fs.usda.gov/mountsthelens.

Johnston Ridge Observatory. The visitor center closest to the summit is named for scientist David Johnston, who was killed by the mountain's immense lateral blast, and stands at the end of the park's Spirit Lake Highway. Inside are fascinating exhibits on the mountain's geology, instruments measuring volcanic and seismic activity, and a theater that shows a riveting film that recounts the 1980 eruption. Several short trails afford spectacular views of the summit. ⊠ 2400 Spirit Lake Hwy., Toutle ☎ 360/274–2140 ⊕ www.fs.usda.gov ⊙ Mid-May–early Nov., daily 10–6.

Spirit Lake Highway. Officially known as Highway 504, this twisting, turning paved road rises some 4,000 feet from the town of Castle Rock (just off I-5, Exit 49) to within about 5 miles of the Mt. St. Helens summit. Along this road are several visitor centers that interpret the region's geology and geography, and several turnouts afford views of the destruction wrought upon the Toutle and Cowlitz river valleys. Don't miss the **Mt. St. Helens Visitor Center at Silver Lake** (⊠ Hwy. 504, 5 miles east of I-5 ☎ 360/274–0962 ⊕ www.parks.wa.gov) in Seaquest State Park, which shows chilling video footage of the eruption, contains superb exhibits on the region's geologic beginnings, and houses a scale model of the mountain that you can actually climb through.

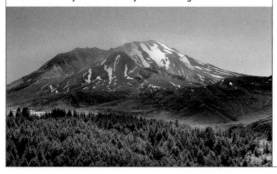

STAY THE NIGHT

Mt. St. Helens is in a remote area. You'll find a handful of chain motels in Kelso and Longview, about 10 to 15 miles south.

🛏 **Lewis River B&B.** In Woodland, 30 miles south of Castle Rock but right on Highway 503, the gateway for approaching great Mt. St. Helens hiking from the south, the charming Lewis River B&B is a terrific lodging option. The five rooms have upscale, contemporary furnishings, and most overlook the scenic Lewis River. ⊠ 2339 Lewis River Rd., Woodland ☎ 360/225–8630 ⊕ www.lewisriverbedandbreakfast.com .

✕ **Patty's Place at 19 Mile House.** For a memorable meal midway up Spirit Lake Highway, drop by this rustic roadhouse with a veranda overlooking the North Fork Toutle River—burgers are a specialty, and be sure to save room for the fresh-fruit cobblers. ⊠ 9440 Spirit Lake Hwy., Kid Valley ☎ 360/274–8779, 888/342–1420 ⊙ Limited hrs in winter; call ahead.

10

GETTING HERE AND AROUND

From Seattle (about 120 miles away), take Interstate 5 south to Highway 167 near Renton, then south via Highway 161 through Eatonville and southeast on Highway 7 through Morton, then east on U.S. 12. Packwood is about 140 miles from Portland via Interstate 5 northbound to Exit 68, then 64 miles east via U.S. 12 (also called the White Pass Scenic Byway).

ESSENTIALS

Visitor Information Destination Packwood Association ⊠ *103 Main St. E, Packwood* ☎ *360/494–2223* ⊕ *www.destinationpackwood.com.*

EXPLORING

Goat Rocks Wilderness. The crags in Gifford Pinchot National Forest, south of Mt. Rainier, are aptly named. You often see mountain goats here, especially when you hike into the backcountry. Goat Lake is a particularly good spot for viewing these elusive creatures. See the goats without backpacking by taking Forest Road 21 to Forest Road 2140, south from U.S. 12. The goats will be on Stonewall Ridge looming up ahead of you. ⊠ *NF-21 and NF-2140, Randle* ☎ *360/891–5000* ⊕ *www.fs.usda.gov/giffordpinchot.*

WHERE TO STAY

$ ⛾ **Cowlitz River Lodge.** A lodge-like construction and a large stone fireHOTEL place in the great room add some character—a good thing, since guest rooms have standard motel furniture and bedding. **Pros:** convenient location to scenic areas; knowledgeable staff. **Cons:** no pool; no restaurant; rooms are basic motel-style. ⑤ *Rooms from: $80* ⊠ *13069 U.S. 12* ☎ *360/494–4444, 888/305–2185* ⊕ *www.escapetothemountains.com* ⇆ *31 rooms* ⦿ *Breakfast.*

$ ⛾ **Mountain View Lodge.** Rooms here have pine paneling, and some have HOTEL log furniture, microwaves, and refrigerators; family suites have fireFAMILY places and sleep six. **Pros:** roomy accommodations (some with kitchens); close to ski resort; friendly and helpful owners; rock-bottom rates. **Cons:** no restaurant on-site. ⑤ *Rooms from: $55* ⊠ *13163 U.S. Hwy. 12* ☎ *360/494–5555, 877/277–7192* ⊕ *www.mtvlodge.com* ⇆ *23 rooms* ⦿ *No meals.*

MOSSYROCK

45 miles west of Packwood.

Another great outdoors destination, with opportunities for camping, fishing and boating in abundance, Mossyrock is a charming small town with two lakefront parks. The large lakes—Riffe and Mayfield—were created in the 1960s when dams were constructed for generating electricity, and Tacoma Power (which generates the power) stocks the lakes with fish. At Mayfield Lake there are also a state park and a privately owned marina and resort.

GETTING HERE AND AROUND

Mossyrock is reached from Portland or Seattle via Interstate 5, Exit 68, then 21 miles east via U.S. 12 (also called the White Pass Scenic Byway).

EXPLORING

DeGoede Bulb Farm. Just outside town, fields of tulips and other flowers grown at the DeGoede Bulb Farm provide a colorful backdrop along U.S. 12. Stroll through the manicured show gardens year-round. ✉ *409 Mossyrock Rd. W.* ☎ *360/983–9000* ⊕ *www.degoedebulb.com* ✆ *Free* ⊙ *Mar.–Aug., Mon.–Sat. 9–6; Sept.–Feb., Mon.–Sat. 9–5.*

Ike Kinswa State Park. This serene 454-acre preserve on the north side of Mayfield Lake is about 4 miles from Mossyrock. Many of the forested campsites provide a nice sense of seclusion, and some lake-view spots are situated for prime sunset views. Five cabins have electricity and bunk beds, but no bathrooms. There's year-round camping, two boat ramps, hiking trails, and fishing (including the challenging tiger muskie, stocked from a nearby hatchery). The park is named after a Cowlitz tribe that lived in this area; their burial grounds are nearby. ✉ *873 Harmony Rd., Silver Creek* ☎ *360/983–3332* ⊕ *www.parks.wa.gov* ✆ *$10 day pass* ⊙ *Summer, daily 6:30–dusk; winter, daily 8:30–dusk.*

Mayfield Lake Park. At this park right off U.S. 12, 4 miles west of Mossyrock, you'll find a handy boat launch. Camping spots are especially scenic, with lake views, forest settings, and even lakefront spots. Fish for trout, bass, and coho salmon. ✉ *180 Beach Rd.* ☎ *360/985–2364, 888/502–8690* ✆ *Parking $5* ⊙ *Daily; camping mid-Apr.–mid-Oct.*

Mossyrock Park. Fish, camp, and boat at this park on Riffe Lake, just a few miles east of town. The lake is stocked with cutthroat, rainbow and brown trout, coho salmon, steelhead, and bass. ✉ *202 Ajlune Rd.* ☎ *360/983–3900, 888/502–8690* ✆ *Parking $5.*

WHERE TO STAY

$$$

B&B/INN

Fodor's Choice

★

Adytum Retreat. The two suites here, equipped with fireplaces and all sorts of other amenities, are all about luxury in nature—set on a hill on nearly 16 acres of forested grounds, the castle-like home, with its stone front, towers, and 75 windows, faces Mayfield Lake and the valleys below. **Pros:** amazing views; beautiful grounds; unique amenities. **Cons:** a bit of a drive to restaurants and shopping. ⑤ *Rooms from: $180* ✉ *186 Skyview Dr.* ☎ *360/983–8008* ⊕ *www.adytumsanctuary. com* ⤴ *2 suites* ⑩ *Breakfast.*

10

CENTRALIA

Centralia is 35 miles northwest of Mossyrock.

Centralia (sen-*trail*-ya) was founded by George Washington, a freed slave from Virginia, who faced serious discrimination in several states and territories before settling here in 1852. The town has a well-maintained historic business district. In a park just off Interstate 5 stand the Borst Blockhouse (built during the 1855–56 Indian Wars) and the elegant Borst farmhouse. Centralia is an antiques-hunter's paradise, with some 350 dealers in several malls. It's also known for its numerous murals depicting the region's history. Pick up a brochure about the murals at the Centralia Train Depot. Six miles to the south is the sister city of Chehalis (sha-*hay*-liss), where there's a historical museum and the Chehalis–Centralia Steam Train.

GETTING HERE AND AROUND

Centralia is almost halfway between Seattle (85 miles north) and Portland (92 miles south) via Interstate 5, and coming by car is the only sensible option for anyone wanting to explore the area.

EXPLORING

FAMILY **Chehalis–Centralia Railroad & Museum.** Through scenic landscapes and over covered bridges, the authentic engines of the Chehalis–Centralia Steam Train will carry you on rails originally laid for logging. The line runs through farmland and rolling hills, and crosses several wooden bridges. There's a 12-mile round-trip ride and an 18-mile ride, plus dinner trains and special events. ⊠ *1101 S.W. Sylvenus St., Chehalis* ☎ *360/748–9593* ⊕ *www.steamtrainride.com* ✉ *$14–$17; dinner train $44* ☉ *Memorial Day–Labor Day, weekends 1 and 3; call for dinner train and events schedule.*

WHERE TO EAT AND STAY

$$
PACIFIC
NORTHWEST
Fodor's Choice
★

✕ **Mackinaw's Restaurant.** In a vintage redbrick building in downtown Chehalis, a 10-minute drive south of Centralia, you'll find the region's most sophisticated restaurant, where chef Laurel Khan produces consistently imaginative, fresh Pacific Northwest fare at reasonable prices. The seasonally driven menu changes daily but might feature a starter of grilled flatbread topped with Dungeness crab, herbed goat cheese, and tomato-pepper jam, followed by Parmesan-crusted whitefish with a light lemon-dill sauce, or sliced duck breast with a black-cherry-and-walnut reduction—it's pretty urbane fare for this laid-back, down-home part of Washington. The beer and wine lists are commendable, too. ⑤ *Average main: $20* ⊠ *545 N. Market St., Chehalis* ☎ *360/740–8000* ⊕ *www.mackinawsrestaurant.com* ☉ *Closed Sun. and Mon. No lunch.*

$$$
RESORT
FAMILY

Great Wolf Lodge. With nearly 400 spacious rooms, some with bunk beds and log-cabin-style forts geared to kids, this activity-focused, rustic-contemporary, lodge-style resort is the largest accommodation in the region. **Pros:** huge indoor water park and plenty of other activities for kids; easy access from freeway; the staff seem to have a good time. **Cons:** avoid this one if you're seeking a quiet, adults-oriented getaway; freeway setting; somewhat high rates. ⑤ *Rooms from: $199* ⊠ *20500 Old Hwy. 99 SW* ☎ *360/273–7718, 800/640–9653* ⊕ *www.greatwolf.com/grandmound* ⤴ *398 rooms* ⦿ *No meals.*

$
HOTEL

McMenamins Olympic Club Hotel & Theater. When it opened in 1908, the Olympic Club was an exclusive gentlemen's resort; now it's owned by microbrewery moguls the McMenamin brothers, and, along with European-style rooms with king, queen, or bunk beds and share bathrooms down the hall, includes a restaurant, bar, pool hall, and vintage movie theater. **Pros:** restored historic facility complete with its own theater; inexpensive rates and restaurant. **Cons:** nearby train tracks may prove too noisy for light sleepers; shared bathrooms; small rooms. ⑤ *Rooms from: $75* ⊠ *112 N. Tower Ave.* ☎ *360/736–5164, 866/736–5164* ⊕ *www.mcmenamins.com* ⤴ *27 rooms with shared bath* ⦿ *No meals.*

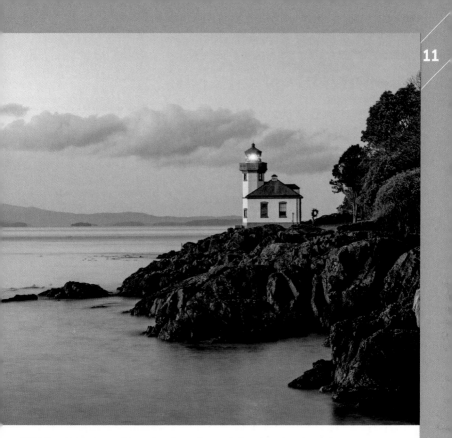

THE SAN JUAN
ISLANDS

WELCOME TO
THE SAN JUAN ISLANDS

TOP REASONS
TO GO

★ **Whale watch:** Spot whales and other marine life from a tour boat or sea kayak.

★ **Taste local flavors:** Talented chefs have turned Orcas and San Juan Islands into hot spots for sophisticated, locavore-driven cuisine.

★ **Gallery hop:** Dozens of acclaimed artists live year-round or seasonally in the San Juans, and you can find their work in studio galleries and group cooperatives throughout the islands.

★ **Indulge in a spa day:** Work out the kayaking or hiking kinks with a massage at the lovely seaside Rosario Resort and Spa on Orcas Island.

★ **Bike beautiful terrain:** Rent a bike and cycle the scenic, sloping country roads—Lopez Island has the gentlest terrain for this activity.

1 Lopez Island. The smallest, least populated, and most tranquil of the main islands is a largely rural and wonderfully restive place with a handful of charming cafés, a few inns, and traffic-free roads ideal for biking.

2 Orcas Island. The rugged and hilly terrain contains the highest point in the San Juans and is the largest in the archipelago, although the pace is easygoing and relaxed. The main village of Eastsound, however, contains a number of sophisticated restaurants and galleries, and you'll find several fine eateries, inns, and boutique resorts elsewhere on this verdant island.

3 San Juan Island. The political seat and commercial center of the archipelago, and the only one of the islands with direct ferry service to British Columbia, is home to the bustling town of Friday Harbor, which abounds with good shopping, cheery cafés, and a mix of midpriced and luxury inns and small hotels. Aside from cultural activities, you'll enjoy fine beaches, great roads for biking, and marinas that rent kayaks and boats. Still, even in summer, you'll discover plenty of quiet, secluded areas on the island.

GETTING ORIENTED

Spending time on the San Juans is all about connecting with the sea, although there's plenty to see and do—especially on the two largest islands—away from the water, from mountain hiking to sophisticated gallery-hopping. A trip to the San Juans requires a bit of travel, planning, and expense, but visitors nevertheless flock here to spot whales, go kayaking, chill out in endearingly informal inns, and dine on creative, surprisingly urbane cuisine. The most popular boating activity is whale-watching, but each island has its share of parks, bluffs, and coastline to explore. The San Juan Islands are part of the same archipelago as the Gulf Islands of British Columbia—they're actually far closer to Victoria, BC, than they are to Seattle. The closest mainland Washington city is Anacortes, about 90 minutes north of Seattle.

Updated by Andrew Collins

The waters of the Pacific Northwest's Salish Sea, between mainland Washington and Vancouver Island, contain hundreds of islands, some little more than rocky reefs, others rising to nearly 2,500 feet. Among these, the San Juans are considered by many to be the loveliest.

About 100 miles northwest of Seattle, these romantic islands abound with breathtaking rolling pastures, rocky shorelines, and thickly forested ridges, and their quaint villages draw art lovers, foodies, and city folk seeking serenity. Inns are easygoing and well-appointed, and many restaurants are helmed by highly talented chefs emphasizing local ingredients.

Each of the San Juans maintains a distinct character, though all share in the archipelago's blessings of serene farmlands, unspoiled coves, blue-green or gray tidal waters, and radiant light. Offshore, seals haul out on sandbanks and orcas patrol the deep channels. Since the late 1990s, gray whales have begun to summer here, instead of heading north to their arctic breeding grounds; you may see the occasional minke or humpback whale frolicking in the kelp.

There are 176 named islands in the archipelago. Sixty are populated (though most have only a house or two), and 10 are state marine parks, some of which are accessible only to kayakers navigating the Cascadia Marine Trail.

The San Juan Islands have valleys and mountains where eagles soar, and forests and leafy glens where the tiny island deer browse. Even a species of prickly pear cactus (*Opuntia fragilis*) grows here. Beaches can be of sand or shingle (covered in small pebbles). The islands are home to ducks and swans, herons and hawks, otters and whales. The main draw is the great outdoors, but there's plenty to do once you've seen the whales or hiked. Each island, even tiny Lopez, has at least one commercial center, where you'll find shops, restaurants, and history museums. Not surprisingly, many artists take inspiration from the dramatic surroundings, and each island has a collection of galleries; Friday Harbor even has an impressive sculpture park and art museum. Lavender and alpaca farms, spas and yoga studios, whale museums and lighthouse tours—the San Juans have a little bit of everything.

THE SAN JUAN ISLANDS PLANNER

WHEN TO GO

This part of Washington has a mild, maritime climate. Winter temperatures average in the low 40s, while summer temps hover in the mid 70s. July and August are by far the most popular months to visit the three main islands—they can get busy during this time, with resorts, boating tours, and ferries often at capacity. To beat the crowds and avoid the worst of the wet weather, visit in late spring or early fall—September and early October can be fair and stunningly gorgeous, as can May and early June. Hotel rates are generally lower everywhere during these shoulder seasons—and even lower once often drizzly winter starts.

■TIP→ Orcas, Lopez, and San Juan islands are extremely popular in high season; securing hotel reservations in advance is essential. Car lines for the ferries during this time can be very long. If you're traveling light and plan to stay put in one place in the islands, consider walking or biking on. Lot parking at Anacortes is $10 per day and $40 per week in summer and half that October–April.

FESTIVALS

August: The Orcas Island Chamber Music Festival (☎ 866/492–0003 ⊕ www.oicmf.org) comprises more than two weeks of "classical music with a view." These concerts are immensely popular with chamber-music fans around the Pacific Northwest.

October: Artstock (☎ 360/378–6550 ⊕ www.artstocksanjuanisland.com) is a weekend-long festival of open-studio and gallery art tours and receptions taking place in Friday Harbor during the first weekend of October. The entire month is Savor the San Juans (☎ 360/378-3277 ⊕ www.visitsanjuans.com/savor), which consists of an islands-wide series of food-related events and gatherings celebrating local food and culinary products.

GETTING HERE AND AROUND

AIR TRAVEL

Port of Friday Harbor is the main San Juan Islands airport, but there are also small airports on Lopez, Shaw, and Orcas Islands. Seaplanes land on the waterfront at Friday Harbor and Roche Harbor on San Juan Island; Rosario Resort, Deer Harbor, and West Sound on Orcas Island; and Fisherman Bay on Lopez Island. Daily scheduled flights link the San Juan Islands with mainland airports at Anacortes, Bellingham, and both Seattle-Tacoma International Airport and Boeing Field near Seattle. Some airlines also offer charter services.

If traffic and ferry lines really aren't your thing, consider hopping aboard a seaplane for the quick flight from Seattle. **Kenmore Air** offers several daily departures from Lake Union, Lake Washington, Boeing Field, and Sea-Tac. Flying isn't cheap—around $120–$160 each way—but the scenic, hour-long flight is an experience in itself. Flights on **San Juan Airlines** from Bellingham and Anacortes run about $75 each way.

Air Contacts Kenmore Air. This is a regular provider of flights from Downtown Seattle to Orcas, San Juan, and Lopez islands. ⊠ *Kenmore Air Harbor, 6321 N.E. 175th St., Kenmore* ☎ *425/486–1257, 866/435–9524* ⊕ *www.kenmoreair.com.* **San Juan Airlines.** This is a reliable option for daily flights to the islands from Bellingham and Anacortes. ⊠ *4167 Mitchell Way, Bellingham* ☎ *800/874–4434* ⊕ *www.sanjuanairlines.com.*

CAR TRAVEL

Most visitors arrive by car, which is the best way to explore these mostly rural islands comprehensively, especially if you plan on visiting for more than a couple of days. You can also park your car at the Anacortes ferry terminal ($10 per day or $40 per week high season, and half that fall through spring), as fares are cheaper and lines much shorter for passengers without cars. B&B owners can often pick guests up at the ferry terminal by prior arrangement, and you can rely on bikes and occasional taxis or on-island car or moped rentals (on San Juan and Orcas) for getting around. Also, in summer, a shuttle bus makes its way daily around San Juan Island and on weekends on Orcas and Lopez islands. From Seattle, it's a 90-minute drive via Interstate 5 north and Highway 20 west to reach Anacortes.

Island roads are narrow and often windy, with one or two lanes. Slow down and hug the shoulder when passing another car on a one-lane road. Expect rough patches, potholes, deer and rabbits, bicyclists, and other hazards—plus the distractions of sweeping water views. There are a few car-rental agencies on San Juan and Orcas, with daily rates running about $60 to $100 in summer, and as much as 25% less off-season. You'll likely save money renting a car on the mainland, even factoring in the cost of ferry transport (which in high season is about $40 to $60 for a standard vehicle including driver, plus around $13 per passenger, depending on which island you're headed to).

Rental Car Contacts M and W Rental Cars. This agency has an office on San Juan Island and also rents cars by arrangement on Orcas Island. ⊠ *725 Spring St., Friday Harbor* ☎ *360/376–5266 Orcas, 360/378–2794 San Juan* ⊕ *www. sanjuanauto.com.* **Orcas Island Rental Cars.** This agency on Orcas Island rents both cars and vans; staff will leave a car off for you at the Orcas ferry landing. ⊠ *P.O. Box 208, Orcas Island* ☎ *360/376–7433* ⊕ *www.orcasislandshuttle.com.* **Susie's Mopeds.** This company with offices on San Juan Island in both Friday Harbor and Roche Harbor rents cars and mopeds. ⊠ *125 Nichols St., Friday Harbor* ☎ *360/378–5244, 800/532–0087* ⊕ *www.susiesmopeds.com.*

FERRY TRAVEL

The Washington State Ferries system can become overloaded during peak travel times, leading to lengthy waits at the Anacortes terminal for passengers bringing their vehicles aboard. Thankfully, as of press time, the company is planning to implement a long-awaited reservations system, which should make it far easier to plan trips and avoid lines. With or without a reservation, always arrive at least 45 minutes ahead of your departure. Without reservations, plan to arrive as much as two hours ahead on summer weekends or holidays, when you can also expect heavier road traffic reaching Anacortes. You'll find information on the Washington State Ferries website on up-to-minute wait times as well as tips on which ferries tend to be the most crowded. It's rarely a problem to get a walk-on spot, although arriving a bit early to ensure you get a ticket is wise. ⇨ *For more information, see Getting Here and Around in individual islands below.*

Ferry Contacts Washington State Ferries. These state-operated ferries depart from Anacortes, about 75 miles north of Seattle, for the San Juan Islands. That same ferry service also connects the San Juans to one another, and San Juan Island with Sidney, BC, near Victoria. ⊠ *2100 Ferry Terminal Rd., Anacortes* ☎ *206/464–6400, 888/808–7977* ⊕ *www.wsdot.wa.gov/ferries.*

RESTAURANTS

The San Juans have myriad small farms and restaurants serving local foods and fresh-harvested seafood, and culinary agritourism—visiting local farmers, growers, and chefs at their places of business—is on the rise.

HOTELS

With the exception of Lopez Island, which has just a handful of rather homey inns, accommodations in the San Juans can be quite plush. Rosario Resort & Spa on Orcas Island and Roche Harbor Resort on San Juan Island are favorite spots for special-occasion splurges, and both islands have seen an influx of either new or luxuriously updated inns in recent years. These places often have perks like lavish breakfasts and on-site outfitters and tour operators. *Hotel reviews have been shortened. For full information, visit Fodors.com.*

WHAT IT COSTS IN U.S. DOLLARS			
$	**$$**	**$$$**	**$$$$**
Restaurants	Under $17	$17–$24	$25–$30	Over $30
Hotels	Under $150	$150–$225	$226–$300	Over $300

Restaurants prices are the average cost of a main course at dinner, or if dinner is not served, at lunch. Hotel prices are the cost of a standard double room in high season.

VISITOR INFORMATION

Look to the San Juan Islands Visitors Bureau for general information on all the islands—the website is very useful.

San Juan Islands Visitors Bureau ⊠ *The Technology Center, 640 Mullis St., Suites 210–211, Friday Harbor* ☎ *360/378–3277, 888/468–3701* ⊕ *www. visitsanjuans.com.*

LOPEZ ISLAND

45 minutes by ferry from Anacortes.

Known affectionately as "Slow-pez," the closest significantly populated island to the mainland is a broad, bay-encircled bit of terrain set amid sparkling blue seas, a place where cabin-like homes are tucked into the woods, and boats are moored in lonely coves. Of the three San Juan Islands with facilities to accommodate overnight visitors, Lopez has the

San Juan
Islands

smallest population (approximately 2,200), and with its old orchards, weathered barns, and rolling green pastures, it's the most rustic and least crowded in the archipelago. Gently sloping roads cut wide curves through golden farmlands and trace the edges of pebbly beaches, while peaceful trails wind through thick patches of forest. Sweeping country views make Lopez a favorite year-round biking locale, and except for the long hill up from the ferry docks, most roads and designated bike paths are easy for novices to negotiate.

The only settlement is Lopez Village, really just a cluster of cafés and boutiques, as well as a summer market and outdoor theater, visitor information center, and grocery store. Other attractions—such as seasonal berry-picking farms, small wineries, kitschy galleries, intimate restaurants, and one secluded bed-and-breakfast—are scattered around the island.

GETTING HERE AND AROUND

The Washington State Ferries crossing from Anacortes take about 45 minutes; round-trip fares are about $13 per person, $40 for a car and driver. One-hour flights from Seattle cost about $120 to $160 each way. You can get around the island by car (bring your own—there are no rentals) or bike; there are bike-rental facilities by the ferry terminal.

ESSENTIALS

Visitor Information Lopez Island Chamber of Commerce ✉ *Lopez Rd., at Tower Rd., Lopez Island* ☎ *360/468–4664* ⊕ *www.lopezisland.com.*

EXPLORING

Lopez Island Historical Museum. Artifacts from the region's Native American tribes and early settlers include some impressive ship and small-boat models and maps of local landmarks. You can also listen to fascinating digital recordings of early settlers discussing life on Lopez Island. ✉ *Weeks Rd. and Washburn Pl., Lopez Island* ☎ *360/468–2049* ⊕ *www.lopezmuseum.org* ☉ *May–Sept., Wed.–Sun. noon–4; or by appointment.*

Lopez Island Vineyard. This popular winery is spread over 6 acres on Fisherman Bay Road and has a tasting room right in the heart of Lopez Village. The vineyards and orchards yield estate-grown white wines, including Madeleine Angevine and Siegerrebe; sweet wines using raspberries, blackberries, and other local fruits; and a number of reds sourced from eastern Washington's Yakima Valley, including Malbec, Cabernet Sauvignon, and Sangiovese. ✉ *724 Fisherman Bay Rd., Lopez Island* ☎ *360/468–3644* ⊕ *www.lopezislandvineyards.com* 🎫 *Free* ☉ *July–Aug., Wed.–Sun. noon–5; limited days Mar.–June and Sept.–Dec., call ahead.*

Fodor'sChoice
★
Shark Reef Sanctuary. A quiet forest trail along beautiful Shark Reef leads to an isolated headland jutting out above the bay. The sounds of raucous barks and squeals mean you're nearly there, and eventually you may see throngs of seals and seagulls on the rocky islets across from the point. Bring binoculars to spot bald eagles in the trees as you walk, and to view sea otters frolicking in the waves near the shore. The trail starts at the Shark Reef Road parking lot south of the airport, and it's a 15-minute walk to the headland. ✉ *Shark Reef Rd.* ↔ *2 miles south of Lopez Island Airport* 🎫 *Free* ☉ *Daily dawn–dusk.*

Spencer Spit State Park. Set on a spit along the Cascadia Marine Trail for kayakers, this popular spot for summer camping is on former Native American clamming, crabbing, and fishing grounds. A variety of campsites are available, from primitive tent sites to full hookups. This is one of the few Washington beaches where cars are permitted. ✉ *521 A. Bakerview Rd., Lopez Island* ☎ *360/468–2251* ⊕ *www.parks.wa.gov/ parks* 🎫 *$10 day pass* ☉ *Mar.–Oct., daily 8–dusk.*

WHERE TO EAT AND STAY

$$$
PACIFIC
NORTHWEST
Fodor'sChoice
★
✕ **Bay Café.** Boats dock right outside this pretty waterside house at the entrance to Fisherman Bay. In winter, sunlight streams into the window-framed dining room; in summer you can relax on the wraparound porch before a gorgeous sunset panorama. The menu is highlighted by regionally sourced meats and seafood, including sea scallop risotto with porcinis, leeks, and crème fraîche, and grilled rib eye with a green-peppercorn demi-glace, which is best enjoyed with a side of bacon-studded roasted brussels sprouts. Homemade sorbet and a fine

crème caramel are among the desserts. ⑤ *Average main: $25* ⊠ *9 Old Post Rd.* ☎ *360/468–3700* ⊕ *www.bay-cafe.com* ⊙ *Closed Oct.–May Mon.–Tues. No lunch Mon.–Thurs.*

$ ✕ **Holly B's Bakery.** Tucked into a small, cabin-like strip of businesses set

BAKERY   back from the water, this cozy, wood-paneled bakery is a source of delicious fresh ham-and-Gruyere croissants, marionberry scones, slices of pizza, and other savory and sweet treats. Sunny summer mornings bring diners out onto the patio, where kids play and parents relax. ⑤ *Average main: $6* ⊠ *Lopez Plaza, Lopez Rd.* ☎ *360/468–2133* ⊕ *www. hollybsbakery.com* ▭ *No credit cards* ⊙ *Closed Dec.–Mar. No dinner.*

$ ✕ **Vita's Wildly Delicious.** At this gourmet market and wineshop (open

CAFÉ   primarily during the daytime but until 8 pm on Friday), the proprietors create a daily-changing assortment of prepared foods and some made-to-order items, such as Reuben panini sandwiches. Other favorites include Dungeness crab cakes, hearty meat loaf, lobster mac and cheese, and an assortment of tempting desserts. You order at the counter and can then enjoy your meal either to go or on the colorful garden patio. ⑤ *Average main: $10* ⊠ *77 Village Rd.* ☎ *360/468–4268* ⊕ *www. vitaswildlydelicious.com* ⊙ *Closed Sun. and Mon. No dinner.*

$$ ▦ **Edenwild Inn.** In this large Victorian-style farmhouse, surrounded by

B&B/INN   gardens and framed by Fisherman Bay, large rooms are each painted or papered in different pastel shades and furnished with simple antiques; some have claw-foot tubs and brick fireplaces. **Pros:** bicycles provided; nice breakfast buffet using local produce; handy location close to village restaurants. **Cons:** few in-room amenities (no TVs); some guests have reported uneven service. ⑤ *Rooms from: $190* ⊠ *132 Lopez Rd.* ☎ *360/468–3238, 800/606–0662* ⊕ *www.edenwildinn.com* ⤳ *5 rooms, 3 suites* �ⓧ *Breakfast.*

$$ ▦ **Mackaye Harbor Inn.** This former sea captain's house, built in 1904,

B&B/INN   rises two stories above the beach at the southern end of the island and

Fodor'sChoice   accommodates guests in cheerfully furnished rooms with golden-oak

★   and brass details and wicker furniture; three have views of MacKaye Harbor. **Pros:** fantastic water views; mountain bikes (free) and kayaks (reasonable daily fee) available; friendly and attentive hosts. **Cons:** on far end of the island; several miles from the ferry terminal and airport; some bathrooms are across the hall from rooms. ⑤ *Rooms from: $175* ⊠ *949 MacKaye Harbor Rd., Lopez Island* ☎ *360/468–2253, 888/314– 6140* ⊕ *www.mackayeharborinn.com* ⤳ *4 rooms, 1 suite* ⓧ *Breakfast.*

SPORTS AND THE OUTDOORS

BIKING

Mountain-bike rental rates start at around $7 an hour and $30 a day. Reservations are recommended, particularly in summer.

Lopez Bicycle Works. At the marina 4 miles from the ferry, this full-service operation can bring bicycles to your door or the ferry. In addition to cruisers and mountain bikes, the shop aslo rents tandem and recumbent bikes. ⊠ *2847 Fisherman Bay Rd.* ☎ *360/468–2847* ⊕ *www. lopezbicycleworks.com.*

SEA KAYAKING

Cascadia Kayaks. This company rents kayaks for half days or full days The outfitter also organizes half-day, full-day, and two- to three-day guided tours. Hour-long private lessons are available, too, if you need a little coaching before going out on your own. ✉ *135 Lopez Rd., Lopez Island* ☎ *360/468–3008* ⊕ *www.cascadiakayaks.com.*

Lopez Island Sea Kayak. Open May–September at Fisherman Bay, this outfitter has a huge selection of kayaks, both plastic and fiberglass touring models. Rentals are by the hour or day, and the company can deliver kayaks to any point on the island for an additional fee. ✉ *2845 Fisherman Bay Rd., Lopez Island* ☎ *360/468–2847* ⊕ *www.lopezkayaks.com.*

ORCAS ISLAND

75 minutes by ferry from Anacortes.

Orcas Island, the largest of the San Juans, is blessed with wide, pastoral valleys and scenic ridges that rise high above the neighboring waters. (At 2,409 feet, Orcas's Mt. Constitution is the highest peak in the San Juans.) Spanish explorers set foot here in 1791, and the island is actually named for their ship—not for the black-and-white whales that frolic in the surrounding waters. The island was also the home of Native American tribes, whose history is reflected in such places as Pole Pass, where the Lummi people used kelp and cedar-bark nets to catch ducks, and Massacre Bay, where in 1858 a tribe from southeast Alaska attacked a Lummi fishing village.

Today farmers, fishermen, artists, retirees, and summer-home owners make up the population of about 4,500. Houses are spaced far apart, and the island's few towns typically have just one major road running through them. Low-key resorts dotting the island's edges are evidence of the thriving local tourism industry, as is the gradual but steady influx of urbane restaurants, boutiques, and even a trendy late-night bar in the main village of Eastsound. The beauty of this island is beyond compare; Orcas is a favorite place for weekend getaways from the Seattle area any time of the year, as well as one of the state's top settings for summer weddings.

The main town on Orcas Island lies at the head of the East Sound channel, which nearly divides the island in two. More than 20 small shops and boutiques here sell jewelry, pottery, and crafts by local artisans, as well as gourmet edibles, from baked goods to chocolates.

GETTING HERE AND AROUND

The Washington State Ferries crossing from Anacortes to Orcas Village, in the island's Westsound area, takes about 75 minutes; round-trip fares are about $13 per person, $50 for a car and driver. One-hour flights from Seattle cost about $120 to $160 each way. Planes land at Deer Harbor, Eastsound, Westsound, and at the Rosario Resort and Spa.

The best way to get around the island is by car—bikes will do in a pinch, but the hilly, curvy roads that generally lack shoulders make cycling a bit risky. Most resorts and inns offer transfers from the ferry terminal.

ESSENTIALS

Visitor Information Orcas Island Chamber of Commerce ⊠ *65 N. Beach Rd., Eastsound* ☎ *360/376–2273* ⊕ *www.orcasislandchamber.com.*

EXPLORING

Moran Museum at Rosario. This 1909 mansion that forms the centerpiece of Rosario Resort was constructed as the vacation home of Seattle shipping magnate and mayor Robert Moran. On the second floor is this fascinating museum that spans several former guest rooms and includes old photos, furniture, and memorabilia related to the Moran family, the resort's history, and the handsome ships built by Moran and his brothers. A highlight is the music room, which contains an incredible two-story 1913 aeolian pipe organ and an ornate, original Tiffany chandelier. Renowned musician Christopher Peacock discusses the resort's history and performs on the 1900 Steinway grand piano daily (except Sunday) at 4 pm in summer, and on Saturday at 4 the rest of the year. The surrounding grounds make for a lovely stroll, which you might combine with lunch or a cocktail in one of the resort's water-view restaurants. ⊠ *1400 Rosario Rd., Eastsound* ☎ *360/376–2222* ⊕ *www. rosarioresort.com/history.htm* ⊠ *Free* ⊗ *Daily 9 am–9 pm.*

NEED A BREAK?

Brown Bear Baking. You might make it a point to get to this wildly popular village bakery by late morning—come midafternoon, many of the best treats are sold out. Delectables here include flaky almond-coated bear paw pastries, rich Croque Monsieur sandwiches, hubcap-sized "Sasquatch" cookies, Tuscan olive bread, and moist blueberry muffins. Dine on the garden patio on sunny days. ⊠ *29 N. Beach Rd., Eastsound* ☎ *360/855–7456* ⊕ *www.facebook.com/brownbearbaking.*

FAMILY
Fodor's Choice ★

Moran State Park. This pristine patch of wilderness comprises 5,252 acres of hilly, old-growth forests dotted with sparkling lakes, in the middle of which rises the island's highest point, 2,409-foot Mt. Constitution. A drive to the summit affords exhilarating views of the islands, the Cascades, the Olympics, and Vancouver Island, and avid hikers enjoy the strenuous but stunning 7-mile round-trip trek from rippling Mountain Lake to the summit (some 38 miles of trails traverse the entire park). The observation tower on the summit was built by the Civilian Conservation Corps in the 1930s. In summer, you can rent boats to paddle around beautiful Cascade Lake. ⊠ *Mt. Constitution Rd., Olga* ☎ *360/376–2326* ⊕ *www.parks.wa.gov/parks* ⊠ *$10 day pass* ⊗ *Daily dawn–dusk.*

Orcas Island Historical Museum. Surrounded by Eastsound's lively shops and cafés, this museum comprises several reassembled and relocated late-19th-century pioneer cabins. An impressive collection of more than 6,000 photographs, documents, and artifacts tell the story of the island's Native American and Anglo history, and in an oral-history exhibit longtime residents of the island talk about how the community has evolved over the decades. The museum also operates the 1888 Crow Valley Schoolhouse, which is open on summer Wednesdays and Saturdays;

Rosario Point at Rosario Resort, on Orcas Island in the San Juans

call the museum for exact hours and directions. ⊠ *181 N. Beach Rd.,
Eastsound* ☎ *360/376–4849* ⊕ *www.orcasmuseum.org* ✉ *$5* ☉ *Late
May–early Oct., Wed.–Sun. 11–4; mid-Oct.–mid-May, Sat. 11–4.*

Fodor's Choice
★

Turtleback Mountain Preserve. A more peaceful, less crowded hiking and
wildlife-watching alternative to Moran State Park, this 1,576-acre
expanse of rugged ridges, wildflower-strewn meadows, temperate rain
forest, and lush wetlands is one of the natural wonders of the archipelago.
Because the San Juan County Land Bank purchased this land in 2006,
it will be preserved forever for the public to enjoy. There are 8 miles of
well-groomed trails, including a steep trek up to 1,519-foot-elevation
Raven Ridge and a windy hike to Turtlehead Point, a soaring bluff with
spectacular views west of San Juan Island and Vancouver Island beyond
that—it's an amazing place to watch the sunset. You can access the preserve either from the North Trailhead, which is just 3 miles southwest
of Eastsound on Crow Valley Road, or the South Trailhead, which is 3
miles northeast of Deer Harbor off Wild Rose Lane—check the website for a trail map and detailed directions. ⊠ *North Trailhead parking,
Crow Valley Rd., just south of Crow Valley Schoolhouse, Eastsound*
☎ *360/378–4402* ⊕ *www.sjclandbank.org/turtle_back.html* ✉ *Free.*

WHERE TO EAT

$$

PACIFIC
NORTHWEST

Fodor's Choice
★

✕ **Doe Bay Cafe.** Most of the tables in this warmly rustic dining room at
Doe Bay Resort overlook the tranquil body of water for which the café
is named. This is a popular stop for breakfast, lunch, or dinner before
or after hiking or biking in nearby Moran State Park—starting your day
off with an olive oil–poached local duck egg with spicy slow-cooked

greens, smoked mushrooms, and grits will provide you with plenty of fuel for recreation. The kitchen uses ingredients foraged from the lush resort garden (tours are available) in such artful, healthy dinner creations as crisp-skinned wild salmon with onion-port jam, dandelion greens, salsify-chevre-quinoa cakes, and walnuts; and Northwest-style pho with king oyster mushrooms, seasonal veggies, baked tofu, spot prawns, and rice noodles. ⓢ *Average main: $20 ⊠ 107 Doe Bay Rd., Olga* ☎ *360/376–8059* ⊕ *www.doebay.com/cafe.html* ⊗ *Closed Tues.– Wed. Limited hours Oct.–May; call ahead.*

$ ✕**Hogstone's Wood Oven.** An intimate, minimalist space with large win-
PIZZA   dows and just a handful of tables, this hip locavore-minded pizza joint
Fodor'sChoice   serves wood-fired pies with creative toppings—consider the one with
★   new potatoes, crispy pork fat, chickweed, cultured cream, and uncured garlic. The bounteous, farmers' market–sourced salads are another strength, and the wine list, with varietals from the Northwest and Europe, is exceptional. The bad news? Reservations aren't accepted, and the wait on weekend evenings can be 45 minutes or more. ⓢ *Average main: $16 ⊠ 460 Main St., Eastsound* ☎ *360/376–4647* ⊕ *www. hogstone.com* ⊗ *Closed Tues. and Wed. (and some additional days in winter; call first). No lunch.*

$$$ ✕**Inn at Ship Bay.** This restaurant at this stylish, contemporary inn just
PACIFIC   a mile from Eastsound offers among the most memorable dining expe-
NORTHWEST   riences on the island. Tucked into a renovated 1869 farmhouse, the dining room and bar serve food that emphasizes local, seasonal ingredients. Island greens, fruits, and seafood are served alongside a regionally focused wine list, and the results are spectacular. Notable dishes include sea scallops with bacon-potato hash and lemon aioli, and local roasted pork with creamy garlic farro, sweet onions, rhubarb, and wilted greens. Even the bread is memorable; the restaurant serves housemade sourdough from a starter that's more than 100 years old. ⓢ *Average main: $25 ⊠ 326 Olga Rd.* ☎ *360/376–5886* ⊕ *www.innatshipbay.com* ⊗ *Closed Sun. and Mon. and mid-Dec.–mid-Mar. No lunch.*

$ ✕**The Kitchen.** Seating at this casual, affordable Asian restaurant adja-
ASIAN   cent to the distinctive boutiques of Prune Alley is in a compact dining room or, when the weather is nice, at open-air picnic tables in a tree-shaded yard. The pan-Asian food here is filling and simple, using local seafood and produce, with plenty of vegetarian options. Start with a steaming cup of Thai-style hot-and-sour soup. Then consider one of the hearty wraps with tofu or local pork and greens, seeds, veggies, pickled cabbage, and lemon-garlic dressing; or the rice cakes topped with salmon, crispy kale, and your choice of sauce: ginger-wasabi-soy, teriyaki, peanut-lime-miso, or coconut-curry. Note that dinner service ends at 8 pm. ⓢ *Average main: $8 ⊠ 249 Prune Alley, Eastsound* ☎ *360/376–6958* ⊕ *www.thekitchenorcas.com* ⊗ *Closed Sun.*

$$ ✕**Madrona Bar & Grill.** Situated on the Eastsound waterfront, this pub-
PACIFIC   style eatery serves classic Northwest cuisine: panfried local oysters,
NORTHWEST   Dungeness crab cakes, Angus beef burgers, and grilled wild coho salmon. But what really stands out here is the atmosphere. A vaulted ceiling with exposed wooden beams gives the little space some serious personality, a small patio is ideal during warm summer nights, and a

rotating cast of microbrews on tap complement the restaurant's spectacular water views. $ *Average main: $18* ⊠ *310 Main St., in the Porter Building., Eastsound* ☎ *360/376–7171* ⊕ *www.madronabarandgrill.com.*

$$ ✕ **Mijitas.** A bustling family-friendly Mexican restaurant with a cozy
MEXICAN dining room and a sprawling shaded garden patio is helmed by Raul
FAMILY Rios, who learned to cook during his years growing up outside Mexico City. The flavorful food here isn't entirely authentic—expect a mix of Mexican and Mexican-American dishes, many featuring local ingredients. The tender braised short ribs in blackberry mole sauce and red-snapper tacos are justly popular, and there's a good selection of margaritas and beers, too. $ *Average main: $17* ⊠ *310 A St., Eastsound* ☎ *360/376–6722* ☾ *No lunch.*

WHERE TO STAY

$$ ⛭ **Inn on Orcas Island.** Innkeepers Jeremy Trumble and John Gibbs
B&B/INN welcome guests to their handsome, contemporary, adults-only inn, with spacious, plush rooms in the main house and two in separate outbuildings. **Pros:** among the most opulent accommodations on the island; serene setting; delicious breakfasts (and fresh-baked chocolate chip cookies); overlooking the northern tip of Deer Harbor and within walking distance of the community's bustling marina. **Cons:** 20-minute drive from Eastsound shopping and dining; steep rates. $ *Rooms from: $215* ⊠ *114 Channel Rd., Deer Harbor* ☎ *360/376–5227* ⊕ *www.theinnonorcasisland.com* ⤴ *1 room, 3 suites, 2 cottages* ❑ *Breakfast.*

$ ⛭ **Outlook Inn.** This nice range of accommodations in the center of East-
HOTEL sound includes small budget-oriented rooms with twin beds and shared
Fodor'sChoice bathrooms, rooms with queen or double beds, and rambling bay-view
★ suites with gas fireplaces, kitchenettes, and two-person Jacuzzi tubs. **Pros:** steps from Eastsound dining and shops (and great restaurant on-site); superfriendly and helpful staff; broad mix of prices. **Cons:** in-town location can be a little noisy; only some rooms have water view. $ *Rooms from: $99* ⊠ *171 Main St., Eastsound* ☎ *360/376–2200, 888/688–5665* ⊕ *www.outlookinn.com* ⤴ *24 rooms, 14 with shared bath, 16 suites* ❑ *No meals.*

$$ ⛭ **Rosario Resort and Spa.** Shipbuilding magnate Robert Moran built this
RESORT Arts and Crafts–style waterfront mansion in 1909, and it is now the
FAMILY centerpiece of a 40-acre resort that comprises several different buildings
Fodor'sChoice with sweeping views of Cascade Bay and Rosario Point—accommoda-
★ tions range from moderately priced standard guest rooms to deluxe one- and two-bedroom suites with fireplaces, decks, and full kitchens. **Pros:** gorgeous, peaceful location; new management has immensely improved service and continues to upgrade the rooms; first-rate spa and several dining options. **Cons:** often busy with weddings and special events; some accommodations still show a little wear and could use updating. $ *Rooms from: $159* ⊠ *1400 Rosario Rd., Eastsound* ☎ *360/376–2222, 800/562–8820* ⊕ *www.rosarioresort.com* ⤴ *16 rooms, 51 suites* ❑ *No meals.*

$$ ⛭ **Turtleback Farm Inn.** Eighty acres of meadow, forest, and farmland in
B&B/INN the shadow of Turtleback Mountain surround these pleasant and homey

rooms in the carefully restored late-19th-century green-clapboard farmhouse and the newer cedar Orchard House. **Pros:** lovely grounds to stroll through; peaceful location, smartly furnished rooms. **Cons:** not near the water; two-night minimum in high season. ⑤ *Rooms from: $165* ✉ *1981 Crow Valley Rd.* ☎ *360/376–3914, 800/376–4914* ⊕ *www.turtlebackinn.com* ⌁ *11 rooms* ⓘⓞⓘ *Breakfast.*

$$
RESORT
FAMILY

⌂ **West Beach Resort.** This old-school cottage compound with a dazzling beachfront location on the island's northwest shore, just a 10-minute drive from Eastsound, is a good value for families and groups of friends—most of these compact, rustic cottages sleep four to six guests, and all have kitchens. **Pros:** many cabins are right on the beach; great for families and groups; good value, especially considering these water views. **Cons:** furnishings in some cottages are a bit dated and basic; no restaurants within walking distance. ⑤ *Rooms from: $185* ✉ *190 Waterfront Way, Eastsound* ☎ *360/376–2240, 877/937–8224* ⊕ *www. westbeachresort.com* ⌁ *21 cottages* ⓘⓞⓘ *No meals.*

NIGHTLIFE

The Barnacle. This quirky hole-in-the-wall bar with an insider-y, speakeasy vibe is across the lawn from the Kitchen restaurant, and has developed a cult following for its sophisticated, well-made craft cocktails—many infused with house-made bitters and local herbs and berries—and interesting wines. On this quiet, early-to-bed island, it's a nice late-night option. Light tapas are served, too. ✉ *249 Prune Alley, Eastsound* ☎ *206/679–5683.*

Island Hoppin' Brewery. Set in an otherwise inauspicious industrial area near the airport, this craft brewery and taproom (open nightly till 9 pm) has quickly earned a reputation throughout the archipelago—and even on the mainland as far away as Seattle—for well-made beers, including the faintly citrusy Elwha Rock IPA and the silky Old Salts Brown Ale. Smoked salmon, cheese and crackers, and a few other snacks are sold in the homey taproom. ✉ *33 Hope La., Eastsound* ☎ *360/376–6079* ⊕ *www.islandhoppinbrewery.com.*

SPORTS AND THE OUTDOORS

BICYCLES AND MOPEDS

Mountain bikes rent for about $30 per day or $100 per week. Tandem, recumbent, and electric bikes rent for about $50 per day. Mopeds rent for $20 to $30 per hour or $70 per day. Three-wheel, two-passenger electric Scootcars rent for about $50 per hour or $155 per day.

Orcas Moped Rentals. You can rent mopeds, three-wheel Scootcars, and bicycles at this agency by the ferry landing. ✉ *65 Orcas Hill Rd., Eastsound* ☎ *360/376–5266* ⊕ *www.orcasmopeds.com.*

Wildlife Cycles. This trusty shop rents bikes and can recommend great routes all over the island. ✉ *350 N. Beach Rd., Eastsound* ☎ *360/376–4708* ⊕ *www.wildlifecycles.com.*

BOATING AND SAILING

Orcas Boat Rentals. You can rent a variety of sailboats, outboards, and skiffs for full- and half-day trips, as well as book custom charter cruises, with this company. ✉ *5164 Deer Harbor Rd., Deer Harbor* ☎ *360/376–7616* ⊕ *www.orcasboats.com.*

West Beach Resort Marina. This is a good option for renting motorized boats, kayaks and canoes, and fishing gear on the island's northwest shore. The resort is also a popular spot for divers, who can fill their tanks here. ✉ *190 Waterfront Way, Eastsound* ☎ *360/376–2240, 877/937–8224* ⊕ *www.westbeachresort.com.*

SEA KAYAKING

All equipment is usually included in a rental package or tour. One-hour trips cost around $30; three-hour tours, about $70; and day tours, $100 to $125.

Orcas Outdoors Sea Kayak Tours. This outfitter offers one-, two-, and three-hour journeys, as well as day trips, overnight tours, and rentals. ✉ *Orcas Ferry Landing, Eastsound* ☎ *360/376–4611* ⊕ *www.orcasoutdoors.com.*

Shearwater Kayak Tours. This established company holds kayaking classes and runs three-hour, day, and overnight tours from Rosario, Deer Harbor, West Beach, and Doe Bay resorts. ✉ *138 N. Beach Rd., Eastsound* ☎ *360/376–4699* ⊕ *www.shearwaterkayaks.com.*

WHALE-WATCHING

Cruises, which run about four hours, are scheduled daily in summer and once or twice weekly at other times. The cost is around $80 to $100 per person, and boats hold 20 to 40 people. Wear warm clothing and bring a snack.

Deer Harbor Charters. This eco-friendly tour company (the first in the San Juans to use biodiesel) offers whale-watching cruises around the island straits, with departures from both Deer Harbor Marina and Rosario Resort. Outboards and skiffs are also available, as is fishing gear. ✉ *Deer Harbor Rd., Deer Harbor* ☎ *360/376–5989, 800/544–5758* ⊕ *www.deerharborcharters.com.*

Eclipse Charters. In addition to tours that search around Orcas Island for whale pods and other sea life, this charter company offers lighthouse tours. ✉ *Orcas Island Ferry Landing, Eastsound* ☎ *360/376–6566* ⊕ *www.orcasislandwhales.com.*

SHOPPING

Crow Valley Pottery. Since 1959 this gallery with a lovely wooded setting has exhibited beautiful and distinctive ceramics, metalworks, blown glass, and sculptures; there's also a second branch in Eastsound's village center at 269 Eastman Road. ✉ *2274 Orcas Rd., Eastsound* ☎ *360/376–4260* ⊕ *www.crowvalley.com.*

Kathryn Taylor Chocolates. This sweet sweetshop in Eastsound village sells the creative bonbons (pistachio-fig, black raspberry) of Kathryn Taylor. It's also a good stop for ice cream and Stumptown coffee drinks. ✉ *109 N. Beach Rd., Eastsound* ☎ *360/376–1030* ⊕ *www.kathryntaylorchocolates.com.*

Fodor'sChoice
★ **Orcas Island Pottery.** A stroll through the historic house, outbuildings, and gardens of this enchanting arts complex on a bluff overlooking President Channel and Waldron Island is more than just a chance to browse beautiful pottery—it's a great spot simply to relax and soak up the views. More than a dozen regular and guest potters exhibit and sell their wares here, everything from functional dinnerware and mugs to fanciful vases and wall hangings. ✉ *338 Old Pottery Rd., Eastsound* ☎ *360/376–2813* ⊕ *www.orcasislandpottery.com.*

SAN JUAN ISLAND

45 minutes by ferry from Orcas Island, 75–90 minutes by ferry from Anacortes or Sidney, BC (near Victoria).

San Juan is the cultural and commercial hub of the archipelago that shares its name. Friday Harbor, the county seat, is larger and both more vibrant and crowded than any of the towns on Orcas or Lopez, yet San Juan still has miles of rural roads, uncrowded beaches, and rolling woodlands. It's easy to get here, too, making San Juan the preferred destination for travelers who have time to visit only one island.

Lummi Indians were the first settlers on San Juan, with encampments along the north end of the island. North-end beaches were especially busy during the annual salmon migration, when hundreds of tribal members would gather along the shoreline to fish, cook, and exchange news. Many of the Lummi tribe were killed by smallpox and other imported diseases in the 18th and 19th centuries. Smallpox Bay was where tribal members plunged into the icy water to cool the fevers that came with the disease.

The 18th century brought explorers from England and Spain, but the island remained sparsely populated until the mid-1800s. From the 1880s Friday Harbor and its newspaper were controlled by lime-company owner and Republican bigwig John S. McMillin, who virtually ran San Juan Island as a personal fiefdom from 1886 until his death in 1936. The town's main street, rising from the harbor and ferry landing up the slopes of a modest hill, hasn't changed much in the past few decades, though the cafés, inns, and shops have become increasingly urbane.

GETTING HERE AND AROUND
With ferry connections from both Anacortes and Sidney, BC (on Vancouver Island, near Victoria), San Juan is the most convenient of the islands to reach, and the island is easily explored by car; public transportation and bicycles also work, but require a bit more effort. However, if you're staying in Friday Harbor, you can get from the ferry terminal to your hotel as well as area shops and restaurants easily on foot.

AIR TRAVEL One-hour flights from Seattle to San Juan Airport, Friday Harbor, or Roche Harbor cost about $120 to $160 each way.

BUS TRAVEL   San Juan Transit & Tours operates shuttle buses daily from mid-May to mid-September. Hop on at Friday Harbor, the main town, to get to all the island's significant points and parks, including the San Juan Vineyards, Krystal Acres Alpaca Ranch, Lime Kiln Point State Park, and Snug Harbor and Roche Harbor resorts. Different buses call on different stops, so be sure to check the schedule before you plan your day. Tickets are $5 one way, or $15 for a day pass.

Contact San Juan Transit & Tours ⊠ *Cannery Landing, Friday Harbor* ☎ *360/378–8887* ⊕ *sanjuantransit.com.*

BOAT AND   The Washington State Ferries crossings from Anacortes to Friday Har-
FERRY TRAVEL   bor takes about 75 to 90 minutes; round-trip fares are about $13 per person, $60 for a car and driver. It's about the same distance from Sidney, BC, on Vancouver Island—this service is available twice daily in summer and one daily spring and fall (there's no BC service in winter). Round-trip fares are about $25 per person, $90 for car and driver. Clipper Navigation operates the passenger-only *Victoria Clipper* jet catamaran service between Pier 69 in Seattle and Friday Harbor. Boats leave Seattle daily mid-May–early September (and also on weekends through the end of September) at 7:45 am and return from Friday Harbor at 4:30 pm; reservations are strongly recommended. The journey costs $65 to $70 round-trip, depending on the day. Clipper also offers optional whale-watching excursions, too, which can be combined ferry passage.

Contacts Clipper Navigation ☎ *206/448–5000 in Seattle, 800/888–2535 in the U.S.* ⊕ *www.clippervacations.com.*

ESSENTIALS

The San Juan Island Chamber of Commerce has a visitor center (open daily 10 to 4) in Friday Harbor where you can grab brochures and ask for advice.

Visitor Information San Juan Island Chamber of Commerce ⊠ *135 Spring St., Friday Harbor* ☎ *360/378–5240* ⊕ *www.sanjuanisland.org.*

EXPLORING

TOP ATTRACTIONS

FAMILY   **Lime Kiln Point State Park.** To watch whales cavorting in Haro Strait, head
Fodor'sChoice   to these 36 acres on San Juan's western side just 6 miles from Friday
★   Harbor. A rocky coastal trail leads to lookout points and a little white 1919 lighthouse. The best period for sighting whales is from the end of April through August, but a resident pod of orcas regularly cruises past the point. This park is also a beautiful spot to soak in a summer sunset, with expansive views of Vancouver Island and beyond. ⊠ *1567 Westside Rd.* ☎ *360/378–2044* ⊕ *www.parks.wa.gov/parks* ☞ *$10 day pass* ☉ *Daily 8 am–dusk; lighthouse tours May–Sept. at 3 and 5.*

Pelindaba Lavender Farm. Wander a spectacular 20-acre valley smothered with endless rows of fragrant purple-and-gold lavender blossoms. The oils are distilled for use in therapeutic, botanical, and household products, all created on-site. The farm hosts the very popular San Juan Island Lavender Festival in late July. If you can't make it to the farm, stop at the outlet in the Friday Harbor Center on First Street, where you can buy their products and sample delicious lavender-infused baked goods, ice cream, and beverages. ✉ *33 Hawthorne La., Friday Harbor* ☎ *360/378–4248, 866/819–1911* ⊕ *www.pelindabalavender. com* 🖃 *Free* ⊗ *May–Oct., daily 9:30–5:30; Apr. and Oct., Wed.–Sun. 9:30–5:30.*

FAMILY

Fodor's Choice

★

Roche Harbor. It's hard to believe that fashionable Roche Harbor at the northern end of San Juan Island was once the most important producer of builder's lime on the West Coast. In 1882 John S. McMillin gained control of the lime company and expanded production. But even in its heyday as a limestone quarrying village, Roche Harbor was known for abundant flowers and welcoming accommodations. McMillin transformed a bunkhouse into private lodgings for his invited guests, who included such notables as Teddy Roosevelt. The guesthouse is now the Hotel de Haro (part of the ⇨ *Roche Harbor Resort*), which displays period photographs and artifacts in its lobby. The staff has maps of the old quarry, kilns, and the Mausoleum, an eerie Greek-inspired memorial to McMillin.

McMillin's heirs operated the quarries and plant until 1956, when they sold the company to the Tarte family. Although the old lime kilns still stand below the bluff, the company town has become a posh resort. Locals say it took two years for the limestone dust to wash off the trees around the harbor. McMillin's former home is now a restaurant, and workers' cottages have been transformed into comfortable visitors' lodgings. With its rose gardens, cobblestone waterfront, and well-manicured lawns, Roche Harbor retains the flavor of its days as a hangout for McMillin's powerful friends—especially since the sheltered harbor is very popular with well-to-do pleasure boaters. ✉ *End of Roche Harbor Road* ⊕ *www.rocheharbor.com.*

FAMILY

Fodor's Choice

★

San Juan Island National Historic Park. Fortifications and other 19th-century military installments commemorate the Pig War, in which the United States and Great Britain nearly went into battle over their respective claims on the San Juan Islands. The dispute began in 1859 when an American settler killed a British soldier's pig, and escalated until roughly 500 American soldiers and 2,200 British soldiers with five warships were poised for battle. Fortunately, no blood was spilled, and the disagreement was finally settled in 1872 in the Americans' favor, with Kaiser Wilhelm I of Germany as arbitrator.

The park comprises two separate areas on opposite sides of the island. English Camp, in a sheltered cove of Garrison Bay on the northern end, includes a blockhouse, a commissary, and barracks. A popular (though steep) hike is to the top of Young Hill, from which you can get a great view of northwest side of the island. American Camp, on the southern end, has a visitor center and the remains of fortifications; it stretches along driftwood-strewn beaches. Many of the American Camp's walking trails are through prairie; in the evening, dozens of rabbits emerge from their warrens to nibble in the fields. Great views greet you from the top of the Mt. Finlayson Trail—if you're lucky, you might be able to see Mt. Baker and Mt. Rainier along with the Olympics. From June to August you can take guided hikes and see reenactments of 1860s-era military life. ⊠ *Park headquarters, 125 Spring St., American Camp, 6 miles southeast of Friday Harbor; English Camp, 9 miles northwest of Friday Harbor, Friday Harbor* ☎ *360/378–2240* ⊕ *www.nps.gov/ sajh* ⊠ *Free* ☉ *American Camp visitor center, June–Aug., daily 8:30–5; Sept.–May, Wed.–Sun. 8:30–4:30. English Camp visitor center, June– Aug., daily 9–5; grounds open daily dawn–11 pm.*

San Juan Islands Museum of Art. Previously known as the Visual Arts Museum, this facility now generally referred to as the IMA presents rotating art shows and exhibits with an emphasis on island and Northwest artists. The museum moved into a sleek, angular, contemporary permanent building in late 2014. ⊠ *540 Spring St., Friday Harbor* ☎ *360/370–5050* ⊕ *www.sjima.org* ⊠ *Free* ☉ *Thurs.–Sun. 11–5.*

FAMILY **San Juan Islands Sculpture Park.** At this serene 20-acre park near Roche Harbor, you can stroll along winding trails to view more than 125 colorful, in many cases large-scale sculptures spread amid freshwater and saltwater wetlands, open woods, blossoming fields, and rugged terrain. The park is also a haven for birds; more than 120 species nest and breed here. It's a great spot for picnicking, and dogs are welcome. ⊠ *Roche Harbor Rd., just before entrance to Roche Harbor Resort, Roche Harbor* ⊕ *www.sjisculpturepark.com* ⊠ *$5* ☉ *Daily dawn–dusk.*

WORTH NOTING

FAMILY **Krystal Acres Alpaca Farm.** Kids and adults love admiring the more than 70 alpacas from South America at this sprawling 80-acre ranch on the west side of the island. The shop in the big barn displays beautiful, high-quality clothing and crafts, all handmade from alpaca hair. ⊠ *152 Blazing Tree Rd., Friday Harbor* ☎ *360/378–6125* ⊕ *www.krystalacres. com* ⊠ *Free* ☉ *Apr.–Dec., daily 10–5; Jan.–Mar., daily 11–4.*

FAMILY **Whale Museum.** A stairwell painted with a life-size underwater mural leads you into a world filled with models of whales and whale skeletons, recordings of whale sounds, and videos of whales. Head around to the back of the first-floor shop to view maps of the latest orca pod trackings in the area. ⊠ *62 1st St. N, Friday Harbor* ☎ *360/378–4710* ⊕ *www. whale-museum.org* ⊠ *$6* ☉ *Daily 9–6.*

WHERE TO EAT

$$ ✕ **Backdoor Kitchen.** This local favorite has become well-known beyond
ECLECTIC the San Juans, thanks to the stellar service and inventive, globally
Fodor's Choice inspired cuisine and craft cocktails. As the name might indicate, it's
★ a bit hard to find, tucked in an elegant courtyard a few blocks uphill from the water. Star dishes include pan-seared scallops with ginger-sake beurre blanc, and pork chops topped with a poblano–goat cheese sauce and served with caramelized onions and smoked bacon. Local greens and produce are used often, and the Northwest-heavy wine list cements the Backdoor's status as a regional gem. Backdoor serves dinner only except for its popular "Noodle Bowl Monday" lunches. ⑤ *Average main: $21* ⊠ *400b A St., Friday Harbor* ☎ *360/378–9540* ⊕ *www. backdoorkitchen.com* ☉ *Closed Mon.–Tues. and additional days in winter; call off-season. No lunch except Mon.*

$$$
PACIFIC
NORTHWEST
Fodor'sChoice
★

✕ **The Bluff.** Talented chef Aaron Rock brings enthusiasm, creativity, and dedication to local ingredients to the lunch and dinner menus at this stylish, contemporary restaurant at Friday Harbor House hotel. The burger, with Gruyère cheese and spicy aioli, is one of the best in town, but don't overlook the more ambitious dishes, such as pork-belly *arancini* (risotto balls) with chopped parsley and garlic, and local halibut accompanied by grilled garlic scape, bulgur wheat, heirloom baby carrots, and kabocha-squash cream. There's an impressive cocktail and wine list, and tempting desserts include a rosemary-apple tart with whisky-apricot preserve. Chef Rock also presents Lunch n' Learn daytime cooking demonstrations, weekly farm dinners, and other foodie-favored events. ⑤ *Average main: $26* ⊠ *130 West St., Friday Harbor* ☎ *360/378–8455* ⊕ *www.fridayharborhouse.com* ⊙ *Closed Mon. and Tues.*

$$
AMERICAN

✕ **Cask and Schooner.** This convivial pub decked out with nautical trappings and steps from the ferry terminal serves reliably filling, tasty, English-inspired pub fare with contemporary twists. Among the popular dishes are spicy braised short ribs with mashed potatoes and horseradish crème and a lamb burger with tomato chutney, watercress, and feta. Anglophiles appreciate classics like cod fish-and-chips, shepherd's pie, and bangers and mash. On weekend mornings, this is a fine option for brunch. ⑤ *Average main: $18* ⊠ *1 Front St., Friday Harbor* ☎ *360/378–2922* ⊕ *www.caskandschooner.com.*

$$$$
PACIFIC
NORTHWEST

✕ **Duck Soup Inn.** Blossoming vines thread over the cedar-shingled walls and inside, island-inspired paintings and a flagstone fireplace are the background for creative meals served at comfortable booths. Everything is made from scratch daily, from the sourdough bread to the ice cream. You might start with crispy five-spice duck confit with hoisin-plum sauce; or perhaps Jones Family Farm Manila clams from Lopez Island steamed with pancetta and sherry. For a second course, consider the Vietnamese crepe with pork confit, wild prawns, bull kelp pickles, herbs, romaine lettuce, and Himalayan blackberry *nuoc cham* dipping sauce; or roasted-eggplant croquettes with garlic hummus, cucumber-mint yogurt, and toasted walnuts. An excellent selection of Northwest, Californian, and European wines is also on hand. ⑤ *Average main: $34* ⊠ *50 Duck Soup La., off Roche Harbor Rd., Friday Harbor* ☎ *360/378–4878* ⊕ *www.ducksoupinn.com* ⊙ *Closed Mon. and Nov.–Mar.; also some other weekdays spring and fall; call ahead. No lunch.*

$
ECLECTIC

✕ **Ernie's Cafe.** Ask a local for the best lunch recommendation in town, and you may be surprised by the answer—plenty of folks will send you to this casual diner at the airport, fun as much for watching planes take off and land as for the laid-back, friendly vibe and delicious, casual fare. You'll find a few Asian dishes on the menu, including Korean-style *bulgogi* (grilled marinated beef) and hearty noodle bowls, plus diner classics like hefty cheeseburgers, breakfast sandwiches, and flaky popovers. ⑤ *Average main: $9* ⊠ *744 Airport Circle Dr., Friday Harbor* ☎ *360/378–6605* ⊙ *Closed weekends. No dinner.*

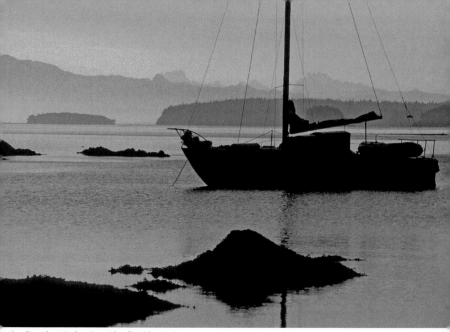

A solitary boat in San Juan Island's Friday Harbor

WHERE TO STAY

HOTEL **Birdrock Hotel.** The range of spiffy lodging options ranges from affordably priced if compact rooms that have private baths down the hall to downright cushy two-bedroom suites with gas fireplaces, spacious sitting rooms, pitched ceilings, and terrific harbor views. **Pros:** handy downtown Friday Harbor location; tasteful, unfussy furnishings; great value. **Cons:** central location means some street noise and crowds. ⑤ *Rooms from: $139* ⊠ *35 1st St., Friday Harbor* ☎ *360/378–5848, 800/352–2632* ⊕ *www.birdrockhotel.com* ⤴ *10 rooms, 5 suites* ⦿ *Breakfast.*

$$$

HOTEL

Fodor's Choice

★

Friday Harbor House. At this bluff-top getaway with floor-to-ceiling windows, sleek, modern wood furnishings and fabrics in beige hues fill the rooms, all of which have gas fireplaces, deep jetted tubs, and at least partial views of the marina, ferry landing, and San Juan Channel below (be sure to request a marina-view room at booking). **Pros:** Great views; excellent restaurant; steps from downtown shopping and dining. **Cons:** limited views from some rooms. ⑤ *Rooms from: $264* ⊠ *130 West St., Friday Harbor* ☎ *360/378–8455, 866/722–7356* ⊕ *www.fridayharborhouse.com* ⤴ *23 rooms* ⦿ *Breakfast.*

$$

HOTEL

Fodor's Choice

★

Island Inn at 123 West. There's a pretty striking mix of accommodations styles at this cosmopolitan complex that tumbles down a hillside overlooking Friday Harbor, from intimate Euro-style rooms that lack exterior windows to expansive suites with water views to ginormous bi-level penthouses with two bedrooms, private decks, gorgeous full kitchens, and astounding views. **Pros:** penthouse suites are great for luxurious family getaways; Euro-style standard rooms are a good deal;

handy in-town location. **Cons:** suites are quite spendy; standard rooms have no outlooks. $ *Rooms from: $209* ⊠ *123 West St., Friday Harbor* ☎ *360/378–4400, 877/512–9262* ⊕ *www.123west.com* ⊃ *5 rooms, 11 suites* ¶⊙¶ *No meals.*

$$ ⚹ **Kirk House Bed and Breakfast.** Rooms are all differently decorated in
B&B/INN   this 1907 Craftsman bungalow, the summer home of steel magnate Peter Kirk: the Garden Room has a botanical motif, the sunny Trellis Room is done in soft shades of yellow and green, and the Arbor Room has French doors leading out to the garden. **Pros:** gorgeous house full of stained glass and other lovely details; within walking distance of town. **Cons:** occasional noise from nearby airport; a couple of the rooms are on the small side. $ *Rooms from: $205* ⊠ *595 Park St., Friday Harbor* ☎ *360/378–3757, 800/639–2762* ⊕ *www.kirkhouse.net* ⊃ *4 rooms* ¶⊙¶ *Breakfast.*

$$ ⚹ **Roche Harbor Resort.** This sprawling resort, with accommodations
RESORT   ranging from historic hotel rooms to contemporary condos, occupies the site of the lime works that made John S. McMillin his fortune in the late 19th century. **Pros:** lots of different options for families and groups; very convenient for boaters; beautiful grounds. **Cons:** condos have less character and are far from the resort; a bit isolated from the rest of the island if you don't have a car; standard rooms in Hotel de Haro have private baths down the hall. $ *Rooms from: $200* ⊠ *248 Reuben Memorial Dr., Roche Harbor* ☎ *360/378–2155, 800/451–8910* ⊕ *www.rocheharbor.com* ⊃ *16 rooms, 18 suites, 9 cottages, 20 condos* ¶⊙¶ *No meals.*

$$$ ⚹ **Snug Harbor Resort.** At this popular cottage resort and marina on
RESORT   the northwest side of the island, all the units were completely rebuilt
FAMILY   in 2014 with tall windows overlooking the water, high ceilings, well-equipped kitchens, knotty-pine wood paneling, gas fireplaces, and private decks. **Pros:** beautiful, contemporary decor; quiet location; nice views of the harbor. **Cons:** no pets; 20-minute drive from Friday Harbor; expensive. $ *Rooms from: $289* ⊠ *1997 Mitchell Bay Rd., Friday Harbor* ☎ *360/378–4762* ⊕ *www.snugresort.com* ⊃ *16 cottages* ¶⊙¶ *No meals.*

SPORTS AND THE OUTDOORS

BEACHES

San Juan County Park. You'll find a wide gravel beachfront at this park 10 miles west of Friday Harbor, overlooking waters where orcas often frolic in summer, plus grassy lawns with picnic tables and a small campground. **Amenities:** parking (free); toilets. **Best for:** walking. ⊠ *380 Westside Rd., Friday Harbor* ☎ *360/378–8420* ⊕ *www.co.san-juan. wa.us.*

South Beach at American Camp. This 6-mile public beach on the southern end of the island is part of San Juan Island National Historical Park. **Amenities:** parking (free); toilets. **Best for:** solitude; walking. ⊠ *Off Cattle Point Road* ⊕ *www.nps.gov/sajh.*

11

BICYCLES

You can rent standard, mountain, and BMX bikes for $40 to $50 per day or $175 to $235 per week. Tandem, recumbent, and electric bikes rent for about $70 to $80 per day.

Island Bicycles. This full-service shop rents bikes. ⊠ *380 Argyle Ave., Friday Harbor, Friday Harbor* ☎ *360/378–4941* ⊕ *www.islandbicycles. com.*

BOATING AND SAILING

At public docks, high-season moorage rates are $1 to $2 per foot (of vessel) per night.

Port of Friday Harbor. The marina at the island's main port offers guest moorage, vessel assistance and repair, bareboat and skippered charters, overnight accommodations, and wildlife and whale-watching cruises. ⊠ *204 Front St., Friday Harbor* ☎ *360/378–2688* ⊕ *www. portfridayharbor.org.*

Roche Harbor Marina. The marina at Roche Harbor Resort has a fuel dock, pool, grocery, and other guest services. ⊠ *248 Reuben Memorial Dr., Roche Harbor* ☎ *360/378–2155* ⊕ *www.rocheharbor.com.*

Snug Harbor Resort Marina. This well-located marina adjoins a popular, upscale small resort. It provides van service to and from Friday Harbor and rents small powerboats. ⊠ *1997 Mitchell Bay Rd., Friday Harbor* ☎ *360/378–4762* ⊕ *www.snugresort.com.*

SEA KAYAKING

You'll find many places to rent kayaks in Friday Harbor, as well as outfitters providing classes and tours. Be sure to make reservations in summer. Three-hour tours run about $70 to $90, day tours cost around $100 to $110, and overnight tours start around $125 per day. Equipment is always included in the cost.

Crystal Seas Kayaking. Sunset trips and multisport tours that might include biking, kayaking, yoga, and camping are among the options with this respected guide company. ⊠ *40 Spring St., Friday Harbor* ☎ *360/378–4223, 877/732–7877* ⊕ *www.crystalseas.com.*

Discovery Sea Kayaks. This outfitter offers both sea-kayaking adventures, including sunset trips and multiday excursions, and whale-watching tours. ⊠ *185 1st St. S, Friday Harbor* ☎ *360/378–2559, 866/461–2559* ⊕ *www.discoveryseakayak.com.*

San Juan Kayak Expeditions. This reputable company has been running kayaking and camping tours in two-person kayaks since 1980. ⊠ *85 Front St., Friday Harbor* ☎ *360/378–4436* ⊕ *www.sanjuankayak.com.*

Sea Quest Expeditions. Kayak eco-tours with guides who are trained naturalists, biologists, and environmental scientists are available through this popular outfitter. ⊠ *Friday Harbor* ☎ *360/378–5767, 888/589–4253* ⊕ *www.sea-quest-kayak.com.*

WHALE-WATCHING

Whale-watching expeditions typically run three to four hours and cost around $90 per person. ■TIP→ **For the best experience, look for tour companies with small boats that carry under 30 people.** Bring warm clothing even if it's a warm day.

Island Adventures. Two San Juan tours operate out of Anacortes per day from June through August—you'll get right up next to the orcas. ⊠ *1801 Commercial Ave., Anacortes* ☎ *360/293–2428, 800/465–4604* ⊕ *www.island-adventures.com.*

San Juan Cruises. Full-day whale-watching adventure cruises out of Bellingham include lunch and a two-hour stop at Friday Harbor and are offered on May weekends and daily from June through late September. These trips depart Bellingham at 9:30 am and return at 5:30 pm. Two-night overnight trips to the islands are also sometimes available. ⊠ *Bellingham Cruise Terminal, 355 Harris Ave., Fairhaven, Bellingham* ☎ *360/738–8099, 800/443–4552* ⊕ *www.whales.com.*

San Juan Excursions. Whale-watching cruises are offered aboard a converted 1941 U.S. Navy research vessel. ⊠ *2 Spring St., Friday Harbor* ☎ *360/378–6636, 800/809–4253* ⊕ *www.watchwhales.com.*

Western Prince Cruises. Narrated whale-watching tours last three to four hours. ⊠ *1 Spring St., Friday Harbor* ☎ *360/378–5315, 800/757–6722* ⊕ *www.orcawhalewatch.com.*

SHOPPING

Friday Harbor is the main shopping area, with dozens of shops selling a variety of art, crafts, and clothing created by residents, as well as a bounty of island-grown produce.

Arctic Raven Gallery. The specialty here is Northwest native art, including scrimshaw and wood carvings. ⊠ *130 S. 1st St., Friday Harbor* ☎ *360/378–3433* ⊕ *www.arcticravengallery.com.*

San Juan Island Farmers Market. From mid-April through late October, this open-air market with more than 30 vendors selling local produce and crafts takes place at Friday Harbor Brickworks on Saturdays from 10 to 1. The market is also open once or twice a month on Saturdays in winter; check the website for the schedule. ⊠ *150 Nichols St., Friday Harbor* ⊕ *www.sjifarmersmarket.com.*

San Juan Vineyards. This winery 3 miles north of Friday Harbor has a tasting room and gift shop, and organizes such special events as a harvest festival in October and November barrel tastings. Noteworthy varietals here include Pinot Gris, Riesling Sangiovese, and Cabernet Franc. ⊠ *3136 Roche Harbor Rd., Friday Harbor* ☎ *360/378–9463* ⊕ *www.sanjuanvineyards.com.*

Waterworks Gallery. This respected gallery represents about 30 eclectic, contemporary artists, from painters to jewelers. ⊠ *315 Argyle St., Friday Harbor* ☎ *360/378–3060* ⊕ *www.waterworksgallery.com.*

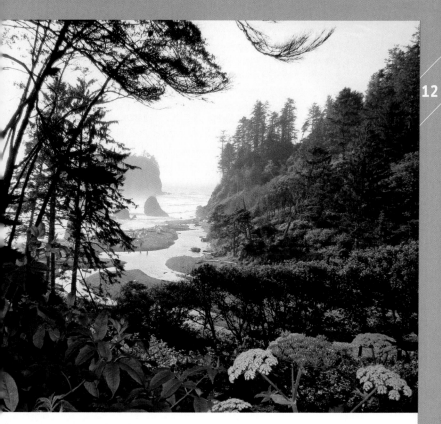

OLYMPIC
NATIONAL PARK

WELCOME TO OLYMPIC NATIONAL PARK

TOP REASONS TO GO

★ **Exotic rain forest:** A rain forest in the Pacific Northwest? Indeed, Olympic National Park is one of the few places in the world with this unique temperate landscape.

★ **Beachcombing:** Miles of rugged, spectacular coastline hemmed with sea stacks and tidal pools edge the driftwood-strewn shores of the Olympic Peninsula.

★ **Nature's hot tubs:** A dip in Sol Duc's natural geothermal mineral pools offers a secluded spa experience in the wooded heart of the park.

★ **Lofty vistas:** The hardy can hike up meadowed foothill trails or climb the frosty peaks throughout the Olympics—or just drive up to Hurricane Ridge for endless views.

★ **A sense of history:** Native American history is key to this region, where eight tribes have traditional ties to the parklands— there are 12,000 years of human history to explore.

1 Coastal Olympic. Here the Pacific smashes endlessly into the rugged coastline, carving out some of the park's most memorable scenes in the massive, rocky sea stacks and islets just offshore. Back from the water are beaches and tide pools full of sea stars, crabs, and anemones.

12

2 **The Rain Forest.**
Centered on the Hoh, Queets, and Quinault river valleys, this is the region's most unique landscape. Fog-shrouded Douglas firs and Sitka spruces, some more than 300 feet tall, huddle in this moist, pine-carpeted area, shading fern- and moss-draped cedars, maples, and alders.

3 **The Mountains.** Craggy gray peaks and snow-covered summits dominate the skyline. Low-level foliage and wildflower meadows make for excellent hiking in the plateaus. Even on the sunniest days, temperatures are brisk. Some roads are closed in winter months.

4 **Alpine Meadows.** In midsummer, the swath of colors is like a Monet canvas spread over the landscape, and wildlife teems among the honeyed flowers. Trails are never prettier, and views are crisp and vast.

GETTING ORIENTED

The Olympic Peninsula's elegant snowcapped and forested landscape is edged on all sides by water: to the north the Strait of Juan de Fuca separates the United States from Canada, a network of Puget Sound bays laces the east, the Chehalis River meanders along the southern end, and the massive gray Pacific Ocean guards the west side.

KEY	
📍	Ranger Station
⛺	Campground
🔻	Picnic Area
🍴	Restaurant
🏠	Lodge
🥾	Trailhead
🚻	Restrooms
⇗	Scenic Viewpoint
-----	Walking/Hiking Trails

Updated by
Shelley Arenas

A spellbinding setting is tucked into the country's far-northwestern corner, within the heart-shaped Olympic Peninsula. Edged on all sides by water, the forested landscape is remote and pristine, and works its way around the sharpened ridges of the snowcapped Olympic Mountains. Big lakes cut pockets of blue in the rugged blanket of pine forests, and hot springs gurgle up from the foothills. Along the coast the sights are even more enchanting: wave-sculpted boulders, tidal pools teeming with sea life, and tree-topped sea stacks.

OLYMPIC PLANNER

WHEN TO GO

Summer, with its long stretches of sun-filled days, is prime touring time for Olympic National Park. June through September are the peak months; Hurricane Ridge, the Hoh Rain Forest, Lake Crescent, and Ruby Beach are bustling by 10 am.

Late spring and early autumn are also good bets for clear weather; anytime between April and October, you'll have a good chance of fair skies. Between Thanksgiving and Easter, it's a toss-up as to which days will turn out fair; prepare for heavy clouds, rain showers, and chilly temperatures, then hope for the best.

Winter is a great time to visit if you enjoy isolation. Locals are usually the only hardy souls during this time, except for weekend skiers heading to the snowfields around Hurricane Ridge. Many visitor facilities have limited hours or are closed from October to April.

12

FESTIVALS AND EVENTS

MAY **Irrigation Festival.** For more than 100 years, the people of Sequim have been celebrating the irrigation ditches that brought life-giving water here. Highlights of the nine-day festival include a beauty pageant, logging demonstrations, arts and crafts, a classic car show, a strongman competition, parades, and a picnic. ⊕ *www.irrigationfestival.com.*

JUNE–AUGUST **Centrum Summer Arts Festival.** This summer-long lineup of concerts and workshops is held at Fort Worden State Park, a 19th-century army base near Port Townsend. ☎ *360/385–3102* ⊕ *www.centrum.org.*

JUNE–SEP-TEMBER **Olympic Music Festival.** A variety of classical concerts are performed in a renovated barn on weekends from late June through early September; picnic on the farm while you listen. ☎ *360/732–4800* ⊕ *www.olympicmusicfestival.org.*

JULY **Forks Old-Fashioned Fourth of July.** A salmon bake, parade, demolition derby, arts and crafts exhibits, kids activities, and plenty of fireworks mark Forks' weekend-long celebration. ☎ *360/374–2531, 800/443–6757* ⊕ *www.forkswa.com.*

Sequim Lavender Farm Faire. Held the same weekend as the long-running Sequim Lavender Festival, this newer event features guided farm tours and a free festival in the park. ☎ *360/681–7532* ⊕ *www.sequimlavender.org.*

Sequim Lavender Festival. Mid-month, a street fair and free self-guided farm tours celebrate Sequim's many fragrant lavender fields. ☎ *360/681–3035* ⊕ *www.lavenderfestival.com.*

SEPTEMBER **Wooden Boat Festival.** Hundreds of antique boats sail into Port Townsend for the weekend; there's also live music, education programs, and demonstrations. ☎ *360/385–3628* ⊕ *www.woodenboat.org.*

PLANNING YOUR TIME

OLYMPIC IN ONE DAY

Start at the **Lake Quinault Lodge,** in the park's southwest corner. From here, drive a half hour into the Quinault Valley via **South Shore Road.** Tackle the forested **Graves Creek Trail,** then head up **North Shore Road** to the Quinault Rain Forest Interpretive Trail. Next, head back to U.S. 101 and drive to **Ruby Beach,** where a shoreline walk presents a breathtaking scene of sea stacks and sparkling, pink-hued sands.

Forks, and its **Timber Museum,** are your next stop; have lunch here, then drive 20 minutes to the beach at **La Push.** Next, head to **Lake Crescent,** around the corner to the northeast, where you can rent a boat, take a swim, or enjoy a picnic next to the sparkling teal waters. Drive through **Port Angeles** to **Hurricane Ridge;** count on an hour's drive from bottom to top if there aren't too many visitors. At the ridge, explore the visitor center or hike the 3-mile loop to **Hurricane Hill,** where you can see over the entire park north to Vancouver Island and south past Mt. Olympus.

GETTING HERE AND AROUND

You can enter the park at a number of points, but since the park is 95% wilderness, access roads do not penetrate far. The best way to get around and to see many of the park's top sites is on foot.

BOAT TRAVEL

Ferries provide another unique (though indirect) link to the Olympic area from Seattle; contact **Washington State Ferries** (☎ *800/843–3779, 206/464–6400* ⊕ *www.wsdot.wa.gov/ferries*) for information.

BUS TRAVEL

Grays Harbor Transit runs buses on weekdays only from Aberdeen, Hoquiam, and Forks to Amanda Park, on the west end of Lake Quinault. Jefferson Transit operates a Forks–Amanda Park route Monday through Saturday.

Bus Contacts Grays Harbor Transit ☎ *360/532–2770, 800/562–9730* ⊕ *www.ghtransit.com.* **Jefferson Transit** ☎ *800/371–0497, 360/385-4777* ⊕ *www.jeffersontransit.com.*

CAR TRAVEL

U.S. 101 essentially encircles the main section of Olympic National Park, and a number of roads lead from the highway into the park's mountains and toward its beaches. You can reach U.S. 101 via Interstate 5 at Olympia, via Route 12 at Aberdeen, or via Route 104 from the Washington State Ferries terminals at Bainbridge or Kingston.

PARK ESSENTIALS

ADMISSION FEES AND PERMITS

Seven-day vehicle admission fee is $15; an annual pass is $30. Individuals arriving on foot, bike, or motorcycle pay $5. An overnight wilderness permit, available at visitor centers and ranger stations, is $5 (covers registration of your party for up to 14 days), plus $2 per person per night. A frequent-hiker pass, which covers all wilderness-use fees, is $30 per year. Fishing in freshwater streams and lakes within Olympic National Park does not require a Washington state fishing license; however, anglers must acquire a salmon-steelhead punch card when fishing for those species. Ocean fishing and harvesting shellfish and seaweed require licenses, which are available at sporting goods and outdoor supply stores.

ADMISSION HOURS

Six park entrances are open 24/7; gate kiosk hours (for buying passes) vary according to season and location, but most are staffed during daylight hours. Olympic National Park is in the Pacific time zone.

CELL-PHONE RECEPTION

Note that cell reception is sketchy in wilderness areas. There are public telephones at the Olympic National Park Visitor Center, Hoh River Rain Forest Visitor Center, and lodging properties within the park— Lake Crescent, Kalaloch, and Sol Duc Hot Springs. Fairholm General Store also has a phone.

RESTAURANTS

The major resorts are your best bets for eating out in the park. Each has a main restaurant, café, and/or kiosk, as well as casually upscale dinner service, with regional seafood, meat, and produce complemented by a range of microbrews and good Washington and international wines. Reservations are either recommended or required.

Outside the park, small, easygoing cafés and bistros line the main thoroughfares in Sequim, Port Angeles, and Port Townsend, offering cuisine that ranges from hearty American-style fare to more eclectic local flavor.

HOTELS

Major park resorts run from good to terrific, with generally comfortable rooms, excellent facilities, and easy access to trails, beaches, and activity centers. Midsize accommodations, like Sol Duc Hot Springs Resort, are often shockingly rustic—but remember, you're here for the park, not for the rooms.

The towns around the park have motels, hotels, and resorts for every budget. For high-priced stays with lots of perks, base yourself in the new coastal community of Seabrook (near Pacific Beach). Sequim and Port Angeles have many attractive, friendly B&Bs, plus lots of inexpensive chain hotels and motels. Forks is basically a motel town, with a few guesthouses around its fringes. *Hotel reviews have been shortened. For full information, visit Fodors.com.*

WHAT IT COSTS IN U.S. DOLLARS			
$	**$$**	**$$$**	**$$$$**
Restaurants	Under $12	$12–$20	$21–$30	Over $30
Hotels	Under $100	$100–$150	$151–$200	Over $200

Restaurant prices are the average cost of a main course at dinner, or if dinner is not served, at lunch. Hotel prices are the lowest cost of a standard double room in high season.

VISITOR INFORMATION

PARK CONTACT INFORMATION

Olympic National Park ⊠ *Olympic National Park Visitor Center, 3002 Mount Angeles Rd., Port Angeles* ☎ *360/565–3130* ⊕ *www.nps.gov/ olym.*

VISITOR CENTERS

Hoh Rain Forest Visitor Center. Pick up park maps and pamphlets, permits, and activities lists in this busy, woodsy chalet; there's also a shop and exhibits on natural history. Several short interpretive trails and longer wilderness treks start from here. ⊠ *Hoh Valley Rd., 31 miles south of Forks, Forks* ☎ *360/374–6925* ⊕ *www.nps.gov/olym/planyourvisit/ visitorcenters.htm* ☉ *Mid-June–Labor Day, daily 9–5; early-Sept.–mid-June, Fri.–Sun. 10–4.*

Hurricane Ridge Visitor Center. The upper level of this visitor center has exhibits and nice views; the lower level has a gift shop and snack bar. Guided walks and programs start in late June. In winter, find details on the surrounding ski and sledding slopes and take guided snowshoe walks. ⊠ *Hurricane Ridge Rd.* ☎ *360/565–3131* ⊕ *www.nps.gov/olym/ planyourvisit/visitorcenters.htm* ☉ *May–Dec., daily 9–dusk; late-Dec.– Apr., Fri.–Sun. 9–4 (if road is open).*

Olympic National Park Visitor Center. This modern, well-organized facility, staffed by park rangers, provides everything: maps, trail brochures, campground advice, weather forecasts, listings of wildlife sightings, educational programs and exhibits, information on road and trail closures, and a gift shop. ✉ *3002 Mount Angeles Rd., Port Angeles* ☎ *360/565–3130* ⊕ *www.nps.gov/olym/planyourvisit/visitorcenters. htm* ☉ *May–Sept., daily 9–4; Oct.–Apr., daily 10–4.*

South Shore Quinault Ranger Station. The National Forest Service's ranger station near the Lake Quinault Lodge has maps, campground information, and program listings. ✉ *353 S. Shore Rd., Quinault* ☎ *360/288–2525* ⊕ *www.fs.usda.gov/main/olympic/home* ☉ *Year-round, weekdays 8–4:30; Memorial Day–Labor Day, also open weekends 9–4.*

Wilderness Information Center (WIC). Located behind Olympic National Park Visitor Center, this facility provides all the information you'll need for a trip in the park, including trail conditions, safety tips, and weather bulletins. The office also issues camping permits, takes campground reservations, and rents bear-proof food canisters. ✉ *3002 Mount Angeles Rd., Port Angeles* ☎ *360/565–3100* ⊕ *www.nps.gov/ olym/planyourvisit/wic.htm* ☉ *May–Aug., Sun.–Thurs. 7:30–6, Fri.– Sat. 7:30–7; Sept. daily 8–5; Oct.–Apr., daily 8–4.*

EXPLORING

Most of the park's attractions are found either off U.S. 101 or down trails that require hikes of 15 minutes or longer. The West Coast beaches are linked to the highway by downhill tracks; the number of cars parked alongside the road at the start of the paths indicates how crowded the beach will be.

SCENIC DRIVES

Port Angeles Visitor Center to Hurricane Ridge. The premier scenic drive in Olympic National Park is a steep ribbon of curves, which climbs from thickly forested foothills and subalpine meadows into the upper stretches of pine-swathed peaks. At the top, the visitor center at Hurricane Ridge has some truly spectacular views over the heart of the peninsula and across the Strait of Juan de Fuca. (Backpackers note wryly that you have to hike a long way in other parts of the park to get the kinds of views you can drive to here.) A mile past the visitor center, there are picnic tables in open meadows with photo-worthy views of the mountains to the east. Hurricane Ridge also has an uncommonly fine display of wildflowers in spring and summer. In winter, vehicles must carry chains and the road is usually open Friday–Sunday only (call first to check conditions). ⊕ *www.nps.gov/olym.*

HISTORIC SITES

La Push. At the mouth of Quileute River, La Push is the tribal center of the Quileute Indians. In fact, the town's name is a variation on the French *la bouche,* which means "the mouth." Offshore rock spires known as sea stacks dot the coast here, and you may catch a glimpse of bald eagles nesting in the nearby cliffs. ✉ *Rte. 110, 14 miles west of Forks, La Push* ⊕ *www.nps.gov/olym/planyourvisit/upload/Mora.pdf.*

Lake Ozette. The third-largest glacial impoundment in Washington anchors the coastal strip of Olympic National Park at its north end. The small town of Ozette, home to a coastal tribe, is the trailhead for two of the park's better one-day hikes. Both 3-mile trails lead over board-walks through swampy wetland and coastal old-growth forest to the ocean shore and uncrowded beaches. ⊠ *At the end of Hoko-Ozette Rd., 26 miles southwest of Hwy. 112 near Sekiu, Ozette* ☎ *360/963–2725 Ozette Ranger Station* ⊕ *www.nps.gov/olym/planyourvisit/visiting-ozette.htm.*

SCENIC STOPS

Fodor'sChoice
★

Hoh River Rain Forest. South of Forks, an 18-mile spur road links Highway 101 with this unique temperate rain forest, where spruce and hemlock trees soar to heights of more than 200 feet. Alders and big-leaf maples are so densely covered with mosses they look more like shaggy prehis-toric animals than trees, and elk browse in shaded glens. Be prepared for precipitation; the region receives 140 inches or more each year. The visitor center is open daily mid-June through Labor Day from 9 to 5, and Friday through Sunday from 10 to 4 in other months. ⊠ *From Hwy. 101, at about 20 miles north of Kalaloch, turn onto Upper Hoh Rd. 18 miles east to Hoh Rain Forest Visitor Center* ☎ *360/374–6925* ⊕ *www.nps.gov/olym/planyourvisit/visiting-the-hoh.htm.*

Fodor'sChoice
★

Hurricane Ridge. The panoramic view from this 5,200-foot-high ridge encompasses the Olympic range, the Strait of Juan de Fuca, and Van-couver Island. Guided tours are given in summer along the many paved and unpaved trails, where wildflowers and wildlife such as deer and marmots flourish. ⊠ *Hurricane Ridge Rd., 17 miles south of Port Ange-les* ☎ *360/565–3130 visitor center* ⊕ *www.nps.gov/olym/planyourvisit/ visiting-hurricane-ridge.htm* ☉ *Visitor center open daily in summer; on days road is open rest of year.*

Kalaloch. With a lodge, a huge campground, miles of coastline, and easy access from the highway, this is a popular spot. Keen-eyed beachcomb-ers may spot sea otters just offshore; they were reintroduced here in 1970. ⊠ *Hwy. 101, 32 miles northwest of Lake Quinault, Kalaloch* ☎ *360/565–3130 Olympic National Park visitor info* ⊕ *www.nps.gov/ olym/planyourvisit/visiting-kalaloch-and-ruby-beach.htm.*

Lake Crescent. Visitors see Lake Crescent as Highway 101 winds along its southern shore, giving way to gorgeous views of teal waters rippling in a basin formed by Tuscan-like hills. In the evening, low bands of clouds caught between the surrounding mountains often linger over its reflective surface. ⊠ *Hwy. 101, 16 miles west of Port Angeles and 28 miles northeast of Forks* ☎ *360/565–3130 ONP Visitor Info* ⊕ *www. nps.gov/olym/planyourvisit/visiting-lake-crescent.htm.*

Lake Quinault. This glimmering lake, 4½ miles long and 300 feet deep, is the first landmark you'll reach when driving the west-side loop of U.S. 101. The rain forest is thickest here, with moss-draped maples and alders, and towering spruce, fir, and hemlock. Enchanted Valley, high up near the Quinault River's source, is a deeply glaciated valley that's closer to the Hood Canal than to the Pacific Ocean. A scenic loop drive circles

12

Plants and Wildlife in Olympic

Along the high mountain slopes hardy cedar, fir, and hemlock trees stand tough on the rugged land; the lower montane forests are filled with thickets of silver firs; and valleys stream with Douglas firs and western hemlock. The park's famous temperate rain forests are on the peninsula's western side, marked by broad western red cedars, towering red spruces, and ferns festooned with strands of mosses and patchwork lichens. This lower landscape is also home to some of the Northwest's largest trees: massive cedar and Sitka spruce near Lake Quinault can measure more than 700 inches around, and Douglas firs near the Queets and Hoh Rivers are nearly as wide.

These landscapes are home to a variety of wildlife, including many large mammals and 15 creatures found nowhere else in the world. Hikers often come across Roosevelt's elk, black-tailed deer, mountain goats, beavers, raccoons, skunks, opossums, and foxes; Douglas squirrels and flying squirrels populate the heights of the forest. Less common are black bears (most prevalent from May through

August); wolves, bobcats, and cougars are rarely seen. Birdlife includes bald eagles, red-tailed hawks, osprey, and great horned owls. Rivers and lakes are filled with freshwater fish, while beaches hold crabs, sea stars, anemones, and other shelled creatures. Get out in a boat on the Pacific to spot seals, sea lions, and sea otters—and perhaps a pod of porpoises, orcas, or gray whales.

Beware of jellyfish around the shores—beached jellyfish can still sting. In the woods, check for ticks after every hike and after each shower. Biting nasties include black flies, horseflies, sand fleas, and the ever-present mosquitoes. Yellow-jacket nests populate tree hollows along many trails; signs throughout the Hoh Rain Forest warn hikers to move quickly through these sections. If one or two chase you, remain calm and keep walking; these are just "guards" making sure you're keeping away from the hive. Poison oak is common, so familiarize yourself with its appearance. Bug repellent, sunscreen, and long pants and sleeves will go a long way toward making your experience more comfortable.

the lake and travels around a section of the Quinault River. ⊠ *Hwy. 101, 38 miles north of Hoquiam* ☎ *360/288–2444 for Quinault Rain Forest ranger station* ⊕ *www.nps.gov/olym/planyourvisit/visiting-quinault.htm* ☉ *Ranger station open daily in summer; weekends rest of year.*

Second and Third Beaches. During low tide these flat, driftwood-strewn expanses are perfect for long afternoon strolls. Second Beach, accessed via an easy forest trail through Quileute lands, opens to a vista of Pacific Ocean and sea stacks; Third Beach offers a 1.3-mile forest hike for a warm-up before reaching the sands. ⊠ *Hwy. 101, 32 miles north of Lake Quinault* ☎ *360/565–3130 ONP Visitor Info line* ⊕ *www.nps. gov/olym.*

Sol Duc. Sol Duc Valley is one of those magical places where all the Northwest's virtues seem at hand: lush lowland forests, sparkling river

scenes, salmon runs, and serene hiking trails. Here, the popular Sol Duc Hot Springs area includes three attractive sulfuric pools ranging in temperature from 98°F to 104°F. ⊠ *Sol Duc Rd., south of U.S. 101, 12 miles past the west end of Lake Crescent* ☎ *360/565–3130 ONP Visitor Info Line* ⊕ *www.nps.gov/olym/planyourvisit/visiting-the-sol-duc-valley.htm.*

Staircase. Unlike the forests of the park's south and west sides, Douglas fir is the dominant tree on the east slope of the Olympic Mountains. Fire has played an important role in creating the majestic forest here, as the Staircase Ranger Station explains in interpretive exhibits. ⊠ *At end of Rte. 119, 15 miles from U.S. 101 at Hoodsport* ☎ *360/877–5569 Staircase Ranger Station* ☉ *Daily 9–4 in summer; hours vary in other seasons.*

EDUCATIONAL OFFERINGS

CLASSES AND SEMINARS

NatureBridge. This rustic educational facility offers talks and excursions focusing on park ecology and history. Trips range from canoe trips to camping excursions, with a strong emphasis on family programs. ⊠ *111 Barnes Point Rd., Port Angeles* ☎ *360/928–3720* ⊕ *www.naturebridge. org/olympic-national-park.*

RANGER PROGRAMS

Junior Ranger Program. Anyone can pick up the booklet at visitor centers and ranger stations and follow this fun program, which includes assignments to discover park flora and fauna, ocean life, and Native American lore. Kids get a badge when they turn in the finished work. ☎ *360/565–3130* ⊕ *www.nps.gov/olym/forkids/beajuniorranger.htm.*

SPORTS AND THE OUTDOORS

BEACHCOMBING

The wild, shell-strewn Pacific coast teems with tide pools and crustaceans. Crabs, sand dollars, anemones, sea stars, and all sorts of shellfish are exposed at low tide, when flat beaches can stretch out for hundreds of yards. The most easily accessible sand-strolling spots are Rialto, Ruby, First, and Second beaches, near Mora and La Push, and Kalaloch Beach and Fourth Beach in the Kalaloch stretch.

The Wilderness Act and the park's code of ethics instruct visitors to leave all nonliving materials where they are for others to enjoy.

BIKING

The rough gravel car tracks to some of the park's remote sites were meant for four-wheel-drive vehicles, but can double as mountain-bike routes. The Quinault Valley, Queets River, Hoh River, and Sol Duc River roads have bike paths through old-growth forest. Graves Creek Road, in the southwest, is a mountain-bike path; Lake Crescent's north side is also edged by the bike-friendly Spruce Railroad Trail. More bike tracks run through the adjacent Olympic National Forest. Note that U.S. 101 has heavy traffic and isn't recommended for cycling, although the western side has broad roads with beautiful scenery and can be biked off-season. Bikes are not permitted on foot trails.

TOURS AND OUTFITTERS

All Around Bikes. This bike, gear, and repair shop is a great resource for advice on routes around the Olympic Peninsula. Bike rentals cost $30 per half day, $50 all day, and $60 for 24 hours. ✉ *150 W. Sequim Bay Rd., Sequim* ☎ *360/681–3868* ⊕ *www.allaroundbikes.com.*

Sound Bike & Kayak. This sports outfitter rents and sells bikes, kayaks, and related equipment. ✉ *120 E. Front St., Port Angeles* ☎ *360/457–1240* ⊕ *www.soundbikeskayaks.com.*

CLIMBING

At 7,980 feet, Mt. Olympus is the highest peak in the park and the most popular climb in the region. To attempt the summit, climbers must register at the Glacier Meadows Ranger Station. Mt. Constance, the third-highest Olympic peak at 7,743 feet, has a well-traversed climbing route that requires technical experience; reservations are recommended for the Lake Constance stop, which is limited to 20 campers. Mt. Deception is another possibility, though tricky snows have caused fatalities and injuries in the last decade. Climbing season runs from late June through September. Note that crevasse skills and self-rescue experience are highly recommended. Climbers must register with park officials and purchase wilderness permits before setting out. The best resource for climbing advice is the Wilderness Information Center in Port Angeles.

TOURS AND OUTFITTERS

Alpine Ascents. This company offers a backpacking and wilderness navigation course in the Olympic ranges. ✉ *109 W. Mercer St., Seattle* ☎ *206/378–1927* ⊕ *www.alpineascents.com.*

Mountain Madness. Adventure through the rain forest to the glaciated summit of Mt. Olympus on a 5-day trip, offered several times per year. ☎ *800/328–5925, 206/937–8389* ⊕ *www.mountainmadness.com.*

FISHING

There are numerous fishing possibilities throughout the park. Lake Crescent is home to cutthroat and rainbow trout, as well as petite kokanee salmon; Lake Cushman, Lake Quinault, and Ozette Lake have trout, salmon, and steelhead. As for rivers, the Bogachiel and Queets have steelhead salmon in season. The glacier-fed Hoh River is home to chinook salmon April to November, and coho salmon from August through November; the Sol Duc River offers all five species of salmon, plus cutthroat and steelhead trout. Rainbow trout are also found in the Dosewallips, Elwha, and Skykomish rivers. Other places to go after salmon and trout include the Duckabush, Quillayute, Quinault, and Salmon Rivers. A Washington state punch card is required during salmon-spawning months; fishing regulations vary throughout the park. Licenses are available from sporting goods and outdoor supply stores.

TOURS AND OUTFITTERS

Bob's Piscatorial Pursuits. This company, based in Forks, offers salmon and steelhead fishing trips around the Olympic Peninsula from October through April. ☎ *866/347–4232* ⊕ *www.piscatorialpursuits.com.*

HIKING

Know your tides, or you might be trapped by high water. Tide tables are available at all visitor centers and ranger stations. Remember that a wilderness permit is required for all overnight backcountry visits.

EASY

FAMILY

Fodor's Choice

★

Hoh River Trail. From the Hoh Visitor Center, this rain-forest jaunt takes you into the Hoh Valley, wending its way for 17.4 miles alongside the river, through moss-draped maple and alder trees and past open meadows where elk roam in winter. *Easy.* ⊠ *Hoh Visitor Center, 18 miles east of U.S. 101* ⊕ *www.nps.gov/olym/planyourvisit/hoh-river-trail.htm.*

Hurricane Ridge Meadow Trail. A ¼-mile alpine loop, most of it wheelchair-accessible, leads through wildflower meadows overlooking numerous vistas of the interior Olympic peaks to the south and a panorama of the Strait of Juan de Fuca to the north. *Easy.* ⊠ *Hurricane Ridge Rd., 17 miles south of Port Angeles* ⊕ *www.nps.gov/olym/planyourvisit/ visiting-hurricane-ridge.htm.*

MODERATE

FAMILY

Cape Alava Trail. Beginning at Ozette, this 3-mile boardwalk trail leads from the forest to wave-tossed headlands. *Moderate.* ⊠ *End of the Hoko-Ozette Rd., 26 miles south of Hwy. 112, west of Sekiu,, Ozette* ⊕ *www.nps.gov/olym/planyourvisit/visiting-ozette.htm.*

Graves Creek Trail. This 6-mile-long moderately strenuous trail climbs from lowland rain forest to alpine territory at Sundown Pass. Due to spring floods, a fjord halfway up is often impassable in May and June. *Moderate.* ⊠ *End of S. Shore Rd., 23 miles east of U.S. 101* ⊕ *www. nps.gov/olym.*

FAMILY

Fodor's Choice

★

Sol Duc River Trail. The 1.5-mile gravel path off Sol Duc Road winds through thick Douglas fir forests toward the thundering, three-chute Sol Duc Falls. Just 0.1 miles from the road, below a wooden platform over the Sol Duc River, you'll come across the 70-foot Salmon Cascades. In late summer and autumn, thousands of salmon negotiate 50 miles or more of treacherous waters to reach the cascades and the tamer pools near Sol Duc Hot Springs. The popular 6-mile **Lovers Lane Loop Trail** links the Sol Duc falls with the hot springs. You can continue up from the falls 5 miles to the **Appleton Pass Trail,** at 3,100 feet. From there you can hike on to the 8.5-mile mark, where views at the High Divide are from 5,050 feet. *Moderate.* ⊠ *Sol Duc Rd., 12 miles south of U.S. 101* ⊕ *www.nps.gov/olym/planyourvisit/sol-duc-river-trail.htm.*

Sol Duc Trail

DIFFICULT

High Divide Trail. A 9-mile hike in the park's high country defines this trail, which includes some strenuous climbing on its last 4 miles before topping out at a small alpine lake. A return loop along High Divide wends its way an extra mile through alpine territory, with sensational views of Olympic peaks. This trail is only for dedicated, properly equipped hikers who are in good shape. *Difficult.* ⊠ *End of Sol Duc River Rd., 13 miles south of U.S. 101* ⊕ *www.nps.gov/olym/planyourvisit/high-divide-loop.htm.*

KAYAKING AND CANOEING

Lake Crescent, a serene expanse of teal-color waters surrounded by deep-green pine forests, is one of the park's best boating areas. Note that the west end is for swimming only; no speedboats are allowed here.

Lake Quinault has boating access from a gravel ramp on the north shore. From U.S. 101, take a right on North Shore Road, another right on Hemlock Way, and a left on Lakeview Drive. There are plank ramps at Falls Creek and Willoughby campgrounds on South Shore Drive, 0.1 mile and 0.2 mile past the Quinault Ranger Station, respectively.

WHERE TO EAT

$$$
AMERICAN

✕ **Creekside Restaurant.** A tranquil country setting and ocean views at Kalaloch Lodge's restaurant create the perfect backdrop for savoring local dinner specialties like grilled salmon, fresh shellfish, and quinoa-stuffed chicken breast. Tempting desserts include local berry crisp and chocolate walnut pie. Note that seating is every half hour after 5, and reservations are recommended. Hearty breakfasts and sandwich-style lunches are more casual. $ *Average main: $24* ✉ *157151 Hwy. 101, Forks* ☎ *866/525–2562, 360/962–2271* ⊕ *www.thekalalochlodge.com/ Dine.aspx.*

$$$
AMERICAN

✕ **Lake Crescent Lodge.** Part of the original 1916 lodge, the fir-paneled dining room overlooks the lake; you won't find a better spot for sunset views. Hearty breakfast selections include biscuits and gravy, omelets and scrambles made with cage-free eggs, and raspberry-filled French toast. Dinner entrées include grilled salmon, seared weathervane scallops, filet mignon, pork shank, and roasted chicken breast. A good Northwest-wine list complements the menu. Note that meals are only offered during set hours, but a more casual menu of appetizers, sandwiches, burgers, and desserts is available from the lounge all day for dining in the lobby or out on the Sun Porch. $ *Average main: $29* ✉ *416 Lake Crescent Rd., Port Angeles* ☎ *360/928–3211* ⊕ *www. olympicnationalparks.com/activities/dining.aspx* ☉ *Closed Jan.–Apr.*

$$$
AMERICAN

✕ **The Springs Restaurant.** The main Sol Duc Hot Springs Resort restaurant is a rustic, fir-and-cedar paneled dining room surrounded by trees. In summer big breakfasts are turned out daily 7:30 to 10:30; dinner is served between 5 and 9:30 (lunch and snacks are available 11 to 4 at the Poolside Deli). Evening choices include Northwest seafood, rotisserie chicken, burgers, and steaks. $ *Average main: $24* ✉ *12076 Sol Duc Rd., at U.S. 101, Port Angeles* ☎ *360/327–3583* ⊕ *www. olympicnationalparks.com/activities/dining.aspx* ☉ *Closed mid-Oct.– late Mar.*

PICNIC AREAS

All Olympic National Park campgrounds have adjacent picnic areas with tables, some shelters, and restrooms, but no cooking facilities. The same is true for major visitor centers, such as Hoh Rain Forest. Drinking water is available at ranger stations, interpretive centers, and inside campgrounds.

East Beach Picnic Area. Set on a grassy meadow overlooking Lake Crescent, this popular swimming spot has six picnic tables and vault toilets. ✉ *East Beach Rd., at far east end of Lake Crescent, off Hwy. 101, 17 miles west of Port Angeles.*

Rialto Beach Picnic Area. Relatively secluded at the end of the road from Forks, this is one of the premier day-use areas in the park's Pacific coast segment. This site has 12 picnic tables, fire grills, and vault toilets. ✉ *Rte. 110, 14 miles west of Forks.*

WHERE TO STAY

$$$$ **Kalaloch Lodge.** Overlooking the Pacific, Kalaloch has cozy lodge
HOTEL   rooms with sea views and separate cabins along the bluff. **Pros:** ranger
tours nearby; clam digging; supreme storm watching in winter. **Cons:**
no Internet and most units don't have TVs; some units are two blocks
from main lodge; cabins can smell musty or like pets. $ *Rooms from:*
$202 ✉ 157151 U.S. 101, Forks ☎ 360/962–2271, 866/662–9928
⊕ www.thekalalochlodge.com ⇗ 10 lodge rooms, 7 motel rooms, 3
motel suites, 42 cabins ¶○¶ *No meals.*

$$$ **Lake Crescent Lodge.** Deep in the forest at the foot of Mt. Storm King,
HOTEL   this 1916 lodge has a variety of comfortable accommodations, from
basic rooms with shared baths to spacious two-bedroom fireplace cot-
tages. **Pros:** gorgeous setting; free wireless access in the wilderness.
Cons: no laundry; Roosevelt Cottages must be booked a year in advance
for summer stays. $ *Rooms from: $178 ✉ 416 Lake Crescent Rd., Port*
Angeles ☎ 360/928–3211, 888/723–7127 ⊕ www.lakecrescentlodge.
com ⇗ 30 motel rooms, 17 cabins, 5 lodge rooms with shared bath
⊗ Closed Jan.–Apr. ¶○¶ *No meals.*

$$$$ **Lake Quinault Lodge.** On a lovely glacial lake in Olympic National
HOTEL   Forest, this beautiful early-20th century lodge complex is within
walking distance of the lakeshore and hiking trails in the spectacular
old-growth forest. **Pros:** hosts summer campfires with s'mores; family-
friendly ambience; year-round pool. **Cons:** no TV in some rooms; lake
is sometimes closed to fishing and boating; some units are noisy and not
very private. $ *Rooms from: $219 ✉ 345 South Shore Rd., Quinault*
☎ 360/288–2900, 800/562–6672 ⊕ www.olympicnationalparks.com
⇗ 92 rooms ¶○¶ *No meals.*

$ **Log Cabin Resort.** This rustic resort has an idyllic setting at the north-
HOTEL   east end of Lake Crescent with lodging choices that include A-frame
chalet units, standard cabins, small camper cabins, motel units, and RV
sites with full hookups. **Pros:** boat rentals available on-site; convenient
general store; pets allowed in some cabins. **Cons:** cabins are extremely
rustic; no plumbing in the camper cabins; no TVs. $ *Rooms from: $99*
✉ 3183 E. Beach Rd., Port Angeles ☎ 888/896–3818, 360/928–3325
⊕ www.olympicnationalparks.com ⇗ 4 rooms, 24 cabins, 22 RV sites,
4 tent sites ⊗ Closed Oct.–late May ¶○¶ *No meals.*

$$$ **Sol Duc Hot Springs Resort.** Deep in the brooding forest along the Sol
HOTEL   Duc River and surrounded by 5,000-foot-tall mountains, the main draw
of this remote 1910 resort is the pool area, with soothing mineral baths
and a freshwater swimming pool. **Pros:** nearby trails; peaceful setting;
some units are pet-friendly. **Cons:** units are dated; no air-conditioning;
pools get crowded. $ *Rooms from: $172 ✉ 12076 Sol Duc Hot Springs*
Rd. ☎ 888/476–5382 ⊕ www.olympicnationalparks.com ⇗ 27 cabins,
1 suite ⊗ Closed mid-Oct.–late Mar. ¶○¶ *No meals.*

12

CLOSE UP

Best Campgrounds in Olympic

Note that only a few places take reservations; if you can't book in advance, you'll have to arrive early to get a place. Each site usually has a picnic table and grill or fire pit, and most campgrounds have water, toilets, and garbage containers; for hookups, showers, and laundry facilities, you'll have to head into the towns. Firewood is available from camp concessions, but if there's no store you can collect dead wood within 1 mile of your campsite. Dogs are allowed in campgrounds, but not on most trails or in the backcountry. Trailers should be 21 feet long or less (15 feet or less at Queets Campground) though a few campgrounds can accommodate up to 35 feet. There's a camping limit of two weeks. Nightly rates run $12–$18 per site.

If you have a backcountry pass, you can camp virtually anywhere throughout the park's forests and shores. Overnight wilderness permits are $5—plus $2 per person per night—and are available at visitor centers and ranger stations. Note that when you camp in the backcountry, you must choose a site at least ½ mile inside the park boundary.

Elwha Campground. The larger of the Elwha Valley's two campgrounds, this is one of Olympic's year-round facilities. ⊠ *Elwha River Rd., 7 miles south of U.S. 101* ☎ *No phone.*

Kalaloch Campground. Kalaloch is the biggest and most popular Olympic campground, and it's open all year. Its vantage of the Pacific is unmatched on the park's coastal stretch. ⊠ *U.S. 101, ½ mile north of Kalaloch Information Station, Olympic National Park* ☎ *360/962–2271 for group bookings.*

Lake Quinault Rain Forest Resort Village Campground. Stretching along the south shore of Lake Quinault, this RV campground has many recreation facilities, including beaches, canoes, ball fields, and horseshoe pits. The 31 RV sites, which rent for $30 per night, are open year-round, but bathrooms are closed in winter. ⊠ *3½ miles east of U.S. 101, South Shore Rd., Lake Quinault* ☎ *360/288–2535, 800/255–6936* ⊕ *www.rainforestresort.com.*

Mora Campground. Along the Quillayute estuary, this campground doubles as a popular staging point for hikes northward along the coast's wilderness stretch. ⊠ *Rte. 110, 13 miles west of Forks* ☎ *No phone.*

Ozette Campground. Hikers heading to Cape Alava, a scenic promontory that is the westernmost point in the Lower 48 states, use this lakeshore campground as a jumping-off point. ⊠ *Hoko-Ozette Rd., 26 miles south of Hwy. 112* ☎ *No phone.*

Sol Duc Campground. Sol Duc resembles virtually all Olympic campgrounds save one distinguishing feature—the famed hot springs are a short walk away. ⊠ *Sol Duc Rd., 11 miles south of U.S. 101* ☎ *360/327–3534.*

Staircase Campground. In deep woods away from the river, this campground is a popular jumping-off point for hikes into the Skokomish River Valley and the Olympic high country. ⊠ *Rte. 119, 16 miles northwest of U.S. 101* ☎ *No phone.*

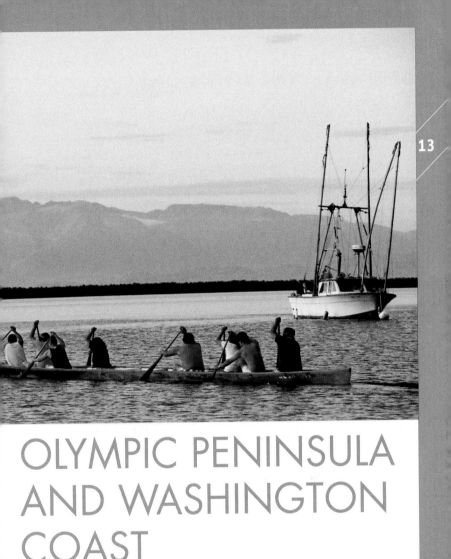

OLYMPIC PENINSULA AND WASHINGTON COAST

WELCOME TO OLYMPIC PENINSULA AND WASHINGTON COAST

TOP REASONS TO GO

★ **Soak up the scene in Port Townsend:** Washington's Victorian seaport is home to artists, boat lovers, foodies, and one of the state's best loved parks, Fort Worden.

★ **Go fly a kite:** The weeklong Washington State International Kite Festival draws kite fliers from around the world, who also pay a visit to the World Kite Museum.

★ **Inhale the aroma of lavender:** Pick your own in the fields surrounding Sequim, which grow an abundance of this fragrant herb.

★ **Meet the Makah:** Exhibits at the impressive Makah Cultural Center complex display authentic scenes of early life in the Northwest.

★ **Enjoy the great outdoors at Hurricane Ridge:** Drive to the top of this spectacular ridge for splendid summer hikes and winter snow sports.

1 Northeastern Olympic Peninsula. On the northeastern tip by the restored Victorian seaport of Port Townsend, this part of the peninsula is less remote than its northwestern counterpart. Here, the protected waters of Hood Canal meet the Strait of Juan de Fuca, providing a backdrop for boatbuilding, bird-watching, sailing and—at the turn of the 19th century—shanghaiing. Farther west, bucolic farmland abounds in the rain shadow surrounding Sequim. Port Angeles provides a launchpad for skiing, snowboarding, hiking, and biking at Hurricane Ridge, one of the most easily accessible parts of Olympic National Park.

2 Northwestern Olympic Peninsula. Driftwood-strewn secluded beaches and dense old-growth forests, featuring enormous ferns and moss-dripping evergreens, rule the rain-soaked west end. Marked by waterfalls, rivers, mountain lakes, and lodges, this part of the peninsula is home to Cape Flattery, the most northwesterly edge of the contiguous United States, and the old logging town of Forks, the setting for the fictional *Twilight* series.

3 Washington Coast. The communities along this stretch of Pacific coastline range from the new Cape Cod–style homes in the master-planned development of Seabrook, where bikes and flip-flops provide the preferred means of transportation, to Ocean Shores and Westport, guarding the entry to Grays Harbor. Tucked inside are the historic lumber and fishing towns of Hoquiam and Aberdeen, hometown of Nirvana front man Kurt Cobain and home port of the *Lady Washington*. The state's official ship offers dockside tours as well as sail training.

4 Long Beach Peninsula. Bookended by two state parks and bounded in part by the Pacific Ocean and the Columbia River, this narrow stretch of land offers a series of ocean-side retreats, oyster farms, cranberry bogs, and beach after beach to comb. Kite flying, kayaking, horseback riding, clam digging, and winter-storm watching are also popular pastimes. At the southern tip, Cape Disappointment is anything but, with two lighthouses, stunning views, 8 miles of hiking trails, and the Lewis and Clark Interpretative Center.

Neah

Ozette Lake

La Push

Olympic National Park

PACIFIC OCEAN

0 — 20 mi
0 — 20 km

CANADA

Juan de Fuca

Sekiu

112

Joyce

Port
Angeles

Dungeness

Port
Townsend

ppho

101

Sequim

1

Forks

Blyn

13

Quilcene

Olympic
National
Park

Brinnon

GETTING
ORIENTED

Kalaloch

Quinault Lake

101

Eldon

It's little wonder that the
Olympic Peninsula, marked
by the majestic Olympic
Mountains, contains many of
the last places to be explored
in the contiguous United
States, let alone the Pacific
Northwest. Even today, people must drive or sail around
this mass of land—there's
no direct route through the
rugged and remote north-
western arm of Washington
state. But this is no deterrent.
It's a popular playground
for anglers, birders, hikers,
snowboarders and snowsho-
ers, skiers, surfers, and sailors. A ferry ride west across
Puget Sound from Seattle,
it's bordered by the Pacific
Ocean on the west, the Strait
of Juan de Fuca on the north,
and the Hood Canal on the
east. Seaports and beaches
hug its shores, but the wilderness—waterfalls, rain forests,
hot springs, lakes, rivers,
ridges, and peaks—lies at
the heart of this mysteri-
ously beautiful place.

Amanda Park

Quinault

109

Neilton

Hoodsport

Taholah

Skokomish

oclips

abrook

101

109 3

Copalis
Beach
cean City

Copalis Crossing

New London

McCleary

108

8

Ocean
Shores

North
Bay

Aberdeen

Elma

Hoquiam

12

Montesano

ays Harbor

Westport

105

Melbourne

12

Grayland

105

Grand Mound

5

Raymond

Bay Center

Doty

Chehalis

Oysterville

101

Frances

6

Napavine

Ocean Park

Nemah

Winlock

Willapa Bay

103

Vader

Long Beach

4

Naselle

Grays River

5

Seaview

Ilwaco

Chinook

4

Megler

Skamokawa

Castle Rock

OREGON

Updated
by Adriana
Janovich

Wilderness envelops most of the Olympic Peninsula, an unrefined and enchanting place that promises craggy, snow-capped peaks, pristine evergreen forests, and driftwood-covered coastlines. This is a wonderland where the scent of saltwater and pine hang in the air and the horizon sometimes seems to make the entire world appear to be shades of blue and green. Historic lighthouses, seaports, and tidal pools trim its shores and a majestic mountain range rises up from its heart.

The Olympic Mountains form the core of the peninsula, skirted by saltwater on three sides. The area's highest point, Mt. Olympus, stands nearly 8,000 feet above sea level. It's safeguarded in the 922,000-acre Olympic National Park (⇨ *see Chapter 12*), along with much of the extraordinary interior landscape. Several thousand acres more are protected in the Olympic National Forest. The peninsula also encompasses seven Native American reservations, five wilderness areas, five national wildlife refuges, the world's largest unmanaged herd of Roosevelt elk, and some of the wettest and driest areas in the coastal Pacific Northwest. The mountains catch penetrating Pacific storms, bringing an average annual rainfall of about 140 inches to the lush western river valleys and rain forests. The drier northeastern slopes of the peninsula's rain shadow see about 16 inches of precipitation per year, creating an ideal climate for the lavender that's grown commercially here.

Most residents live on the edges of the peninsula, anchored at its southwestern corner by Grays Harbor, named for Captain Robert Gray. He became the first European-American to enter the harbor in 1792. From there, the coast extends north along the Washington Coast to Cape Flattery and Neah Bay on the Makah Indian Reservation, then stretches to the Victorian seaport of Port Townsend, on the tip of the Quimper Peninsula, a narrow, crooked elbow of land at the northeastern end of the larger land mass. Rugged terrain and few roads limit interior accessibility to backpackers and climbers. But the 330-mile outer loop of U.S. 101 offers breathtaking forest, ocean, and mountain vistas as well as rest stops at a variety of colorful outposts along the way.

OLYMPIC PENINSULA AND WASHINGTON COAST PLANNER

WHEN TO GO

Visitors trek to the Olympic Peninsula year-round, but summer is prime touring time for this outdoors-lovers' paradise. June through September, when it's least likely to rain, is busiest. Beaches, campgrounds, and downtown areas bustle during the sun-filled summer months, and festivals attract additional crowds. This is also the time of peak lodging rates.

Early and late spring and fall are likely to be less crowded, and in many cases the shoulder season also promises less expensive hotel rates. Anytime between April and October, there's a good chance of clear skies, even if temperatures dip. The rest of the year, prepare for heavy clouds, rain showers, and chilly temperatures.

Accommodations tend to fill up year-round on festival and holiday weekends. Some museums and other tourist attractions close or operate on a limited schedule in winter, when unrelenting storms pound Washington's Pacific coast. Mid-October through mid-March, pummeling waves crash into sea stacks and outcroppings, and wind speeds of up to 60 mph send rain spitting sideways. Winter-storm watchers, weekend skiers and snowboarders heading to Hurricane Ridge, and locals are usually the only hardy souls around this time of the year. For some, that—coupled with off-season lodging rates—is a draw.

FESTIVALS AND EVENTS

The region has a number of festivals and events that are worth planning for.

Great Port Townsend Bay Kinetic Sculpture Race. Since 1983, contestants have been racing human-powered contraptions through sand, mud, neighborhoods, and saltwater in the hope of winning the most coveted prize: the Mediocrity Award for finishing in the middle of the pack. The race takes place the first weekend in October. Festivities include safety tests, a parade, and a "Kween Koronation Kostume Ball" on Saturday night. ⊠ *Port Townsend* ☎ *360/379–4972* ⊕ *ptkineticrace.org.*

Irrigation Festival. Sequim has been celebrating the introduction of irrigation water to its once-parched prairie since 1896. The fest, held in May, features an antique-car show, art show, logging show, street fair, pageant, parade, dance, community breakfast and Strongman Showdown, in which competitors put their muscles to the test in events like the arm-over-arm truck pull, log press, and car lift. ⊠ *Sequim* ☎ *360/683–6197* ⊕ *irrigationfestival.com.*

Port Townsend Film Festival. Founded in 1999 by Rocky Friedman, owner and operator of the town's 1907 Rose Theatre, this mid-September fest features onstage discussions with Hollywood stars, a variety of documentary and narrative films, and the ever-popular outdoor screenings on Taylor Street in front of the movie house. ⊠ *Port Townsend* ☎ *360/379–1333* ⊕ *www.ptfilmfest.com.*

Sequim Lavender Festival. A street fair and free self-guided farm tours celebrate Sequim's many fragrant lavender fields in July. ⊠ *Sequim* ☎ *360/681–3035* ⊕ *www.lavenderfestival.com.*

Wooden Boat Festival. Hundreds of wooden boats sail into the Bay of Port Townsend each September for a weekend of demonstrations, presentations, tours, and sea shanties. Believed to be the largest gathering of its kind on the West Coast, the festival is sponsored by the Wooden Boat Foundation, part of the Northwest Maritime Center, which holds on-the-water programming for adults and youths all year. ⊠ *Port Townsend* ☎ *360/385–3628* ⊕ *www.nwmaritime.org/wooden-boat-foundation/ wooden-boat-festival.*

GETTING HERE AND AROUND

AIR TRAVEL

Port Angeles is the major northern gateway to the Olympic Peninsula, while Olympia is the major entry point in the south. Kenmore Air connects Port Angeles with Boeing Field, near Seattle. Fairchild International Airport, the largest on the Olympic Peninsula, is 6 miles southwest of Port Angeles off U.S. 101 (take Airport Road north from U.S. 101). Jefferson County Airport, a small charter-flight base, is 4 miles southwest of Port Townsend off Highway 19.

Contacts Fairchild International Airport ⊠ *1402 Fairchild International Airport Rd., Port Angeles* ☎ *360/417–3433 Airport manager, 866/435–9524 Kenmore Air* ⊕ *www.portofpa.com.* **Jefferson County International Airport** ⊠ *310 Airport Rd., Port Townsend* ☎ *360/385–2323, 360/385–0656* ⊕ *www. portofpt.com.*

AIRPORTS AND TRANSFERS

Olympic Bus Lines, a Greyhound affiliate, transports passengers twice daily from Port Angeles, Discovery Bay, and Port Townsend to Sea-Tac Airport ($49) and downtown Seattle ($39).

Contacts Olympic Bus Lines ☎ *360/417–0700, 800/457–4492* ⊕ *www. olympicbuslines.com.*

BOAT AND FERRY TRAVEL

Washington State Ferries offer the most direct route from Seattle to the Olympic Peninsula. Fares vary seasonally. Walk-ons pay less than vehicles with a driver and other passengers. A ferry from Whidbey Island takes travelers to downtown Port Townsend.

Nearby ferry terminals in Edmonds, Kingston, and Bremerton also provide access to the Olympic Peninsula. From Port Angeles, travelers can reach Victoria, British Columbia, on the M.V. *Coho*, which makes 1½-hour Port Angeles–Victoria crossings four times daily from mid-May through mid-October and twice daily the rest of the year (except when it's docked for maintenance, from mid-January through mid-March). Rates are $62 per car and driver, $17.50 per passenger, and $6.50 per bike; travelers can reserve ahead online or by telephone for an additional fee. *Coho,* operated by Black Ball Transport, departs from the ferry terminal at the foot of Laurel Street.

Contacts Black Ball Ferry Line ☎ *360/457–4491 in Port Angeles, 250/386–2202 in Victoria* ⊕ *www.ferrytovictoria.com.*

CAR TRAVEL

U.S. 101, the main thoroughfare around the Olympic Peninsula, is a two-lane, well-paved highway. Rural back roads are blacktop or gravel, and tend to have potholes and get washed out during rains. In winter, landslides and wet weather frequently close roads. Highway 112 heads west from U.S. 101 at Port Angeles to Neah Bay. Highway 113 winds north from U.S. 101 at Sappho to Highway 112. Highway 110 travels west from U.S. 101 at Forks to La Push. Highway 109 leads west from U.S. 101 at Hoquiam to Copalis Beach, Moclips, and Taholah. Highway 8 heads west from Olympia and connects with U.S. 12, which travels west to Aberdeen. From the Hood Canal Bridge, State Routes 19 and 20 branch off State Route 104 to Port Townsend, Discovery Bay, and Sequim.

RESTAURANTS

Port Townsend reigns as the foodie capital of the Olympic Peninsula, where Pacific Northwest coastal cuisine prevails. For a small town, it features an impressive collection of casual yet upscale dining options, some with sweeping bay views. Influences include Mediterranean, Latin, and Southern American cooking. Many restaurants and pubs offer straight-from-the-farm organic herbs and vegetables as well as locally crafted artisanal breads and cheeses and, of course, shellfish and salmon from local waters.

The entire Olympic Culinary Loop—from Port Townsend, Sequim, Port Angeles, and Forks to the Long Beach Peninsula(⊕ *www. olympicculinaryloop.com*)—is best known for its seafood, fresh from local bays and inlets or wild caught in the Pacific Ocean by local fishermen. Many restaurants along the route feature fish-and-chips, chowders, oyster or salmon burgers, crab cakes, cioppino, clams, and mussels. The peninsula also offers many family-friendly and downhome eateries, from hearty burger and breakfast joints to authentic Thai, Japanese, and Mexican restaurants.

HOTELS

The Olympic Peninsula offers an array of lodging options, from Cape Cod–style cottages and rustic cabins to midrange motels, timber-lined lodges, and Victorian-mansions-turned-bed-and-breakfasts. Many offer beach access or views of the water or mountains—or both. It's most difficult to find rooms during holidays and festivals. Winter and shoulder seasons typically offer the most economical prices. Skiers, snowboarders, and day hikers headed to Hurricane Ridge might opt to use Port Angeles as their home base. For gourmands, history buffs, and maritime enthusiasts, Port Townsend offers numerous Victorian-themed B&Bs and hotels as well as inns and motels with bay views. Those seeking peace and quiet might consider accommodations in Sequim. The Washington Coast and Long Beach Peninsula are the best destinations for winter-storm watchers and beachcombers. *Hotel reviews have been shortened. For full information, visit Fodors.com.*

WHAT IT COSTS IN U.S. DOLLARS				
	$	**$$**	**$$$**	**$$$$**
Restaurants	Under $16	$16–$23	$24–$30	Over $30
Hotels	Under $150	$150–$200	$201–$250	Over $250

Restaurant prices are the average cost of a main course at dinner, or if dinner is not served, at lunch. Hotel prices are the lowest cost of a standard double room in high season.

VISITOR INFORMATION

Contacts North Olympic Peninsula Visitor and Convention Bureau ⊠ *Port of Port Angeles, 338 W. 1st St., Suite 104, Port Angeles* ☎ *360/452–8552, 800/942–4042* ⊕ *www.olympicpeninsula.org.* **Discover Your Northwest.** Formerly known as the Northwest Interpretive Association, this nonprofit operates a bookshop in the Olympic National Park Visitor Center with maps, guides and other useful information for navigating public lands in the Pacific Northwest. ⊠ *3002 Mt. Angeles Rd., Port Angeles* ☎ *360/565–3195* ⊕ *www. nwpubliclands.com.* **Olympic National Forest** ⊠ *1835 Blacklake Blvd. S.W., Olympia* ☎ *360/956–2400 Olympia Office, 360/765–2200 Hood Canal Ranger District, Quilcene, 360/374–6522 Pacific Ranger District North, Forks, 360/288–2525 Pacific Ranger District South, Quinault* ⊕ *www.fs.usda.gov/olympic.*

NORTHEASTERN OLYMPIC PENINSULA

The northeastern shelf of the Olympic Peninsula is easily accessible, making it a favorite getaway for Seattleites and other Washingtonians who live along the urban corridor that follows the north–south ribbon of Interstate 5. The restored Victorian seaport of Port Townsend at the peninsula's northeastern tip is a mere hour-and-45-minute drive from Seattle, including a scenic half-hour ferry ride across Puget Sound. The town is small—some 9,000 people live here—but it's teeming with activity. With its thriving arts scene, main street lined with galleries and boutiques, rich maritime heritage, upscale eateries, and variety of festivals, PT—as locals call it—offers plenty to do. Travelers could easily spend an entire weekend in this town alone. But, farther west, past Discovery Bay, bucolic farmland abounds in the rain shadow surrounding Sequim, home of the Olympic Game Farm and Dungeness Spit, a 5-mile sandy finger of shoreline topped with a wide, wishbone-shaped beach that juts into the Strait of Juan de Fuca. An 1857 lighthouse, which allows families to serve as lighthouse keepers for a week at a time, stands guard at the north end of the wishbone. At the western edge of this corner of the peninsula, Port Angeles provides a launchpad for skiing, snowboarding, hiking, and biking at Hurricane Ridge, one of the most easily accessible parts of Olympic National Park. It also offers ferry service to Victoria, British Columbia, sweeping views of the Strait of Juan de Fuca, and a chance for *Twilight* fans to relive some of their favorite scenes, including dinner at La Bella Italia, the restaurant that served as the backdrop for Bella and Edward's first date.

PORT TOWNSEND

99 miles north from Olympia.

On a peninsula—the small, crooked arm of the Quimper on the northeastern tip of the larger, torch-shaped Olympic—Port Townsend is a place where the modern meets the Victorian, maritime trades meet the arts, and the sun sets over the water. Its inhabitants are a collection of artists, writers, retirees, musicians, mariners, and "shed boys," a term coined in the early 2000s for the mostly single men who live here off the grid. For all of them Port Townsend remains a city of dreams. These knit-cap and Carhartt-wearing residents are well traveled and highly educated. It's not unusual to find waitresses, bartenders, and students at the boat school who have willingly given up more lucrative positions in larger cities to live here, in the most picturesque gateway to the Olympic Peninsula.

Ship captains from around the world once sailed into this port, known for its parlors of ill repute, saloons, shanghaiing, and other mid-19th century waterfront shenanigans. In fact, it was developed into two separate urban centers: the waterfront, which catered to hard-drinking sailors and other adventurers, and uptown, on the cliff above the bay, where merchants and permanent residents lived and raised their families away from the riffraff. The refined Victorian-era women who once shunned Water Street, the main drag through downtown, would likely want to be seen there now. The once rough-and tumble thoroughfare has given way to art galleries and antiques stores, trendy boutiques, coffeehouses, pubs, upscale eateries, and public docks.

Officially settled in 1851, Port Townsend was dubbed the "City of Dreams" because of the early idea that it would become the largest harbor on the West Coast with help from the impending railroad. Instead, the railroad opted for the east side of Puget Sound and the former boomtown experienced a bit of a bust. But the spirit of the town's maritime community and idea that open water lies just off the horizon continue to tinge this place with a certain romance.

GETTING HERE AND AROUND

From Downtown Seattle, Port Townsend is reached via the Washington State Ferries to Bainbridge Island, then north on State Route 305, north on State Route 3, west on State Route 104, and north on State Route 19, which connects to State Route 20 and takes travelers into town. From Edmonds (north of Seattle via Interstate 5), take the Washington State Ferries to Kingston, then travel west via Highway 104 and north via State Route 19. Both routes run roughly an hour and 45 minutes, not including ferry waits. From Olympia and points south, there are two routes northbound: U.S. 101 and Highway 14. Both take about two hours.

GUIDED TOURS

Port Townsend Walking Tours. The Jefferson County Historical Society conducts hour-long walking tours of Port Townsend on weekends from June through September for $10. ✉ *540 Water St.* ☎ *360/385–1003* ⊕ *www.jchsmuseum.org.*

ESSENTIALS

Visitor Information Jefferson County Chamber of Commerce and Visitor Information Center ✉ 440 12th St. ☎ 360/385–7869 administrative office, 360/385–2722 visitor information office, 888/365–6978 visitor information office ⊕ jeffcountychamber.org.

EXPLORING

FAMILY **Chetzemoka Park.** A lovely gazebo is the hallmark of this gem of a city park, a perfect place to picnic perched atop a bluff overlooking Admiralty Inlet. The 6 well-maintained acres also feature a pond, footbridge, swings, other playground equipment, and a whimsical, trellis-covered pathway that teems with blooms in spring. The Port Townsend Summer Band performs concerts in the park. Access the sliver of beach below via a short footpath. ✉ *Jackson and Blaine Sts.* ☎ *360/379–5096 Public Works* ⊕ *www.cityofpt.us/parks.htm.*

Fire Bell Tower. Set high along the bayside bluffs, the tower is recognizable by its pyramid shape and red paint job. Built in 1890 to hold a 1,500-pound brass alarm bell, the 75-foot wooden structure was once the key alert center for local volunteer firemen. A century later it's considered one of the state's most valuable historic buildings. Reach the tower by climbing the steep set of stairs behind Haller Fountain at the end of Taylor Street. The tenth-of-an-acre plot also holds a park bench and five parking spots. ✉ *Jefferson and Tyler Sts., Uptown* ☎ *360/385–1003* ⊕ *www.jchsmuseum.org.*

FAMILY **Fort Worden State Park.** With hiking trails, restored—and rentable—Victorian officers' houses, and pre-World War I-era bunkers, this historic 434-acre park provides myriad outdoor activities along with a step back in time. Built on Point Wilson in 1896 to guard the mouth of Puget Sound, the old fort is now a magical place for both children and adults to explore. A sandy beach leads to the graceful 1913 Point Wilson Lighthouse. Memory's Vault, hidden in the hill above the inlet, features works from local poet Sam Hamill as well as a place to contemplate. Touch tanks at Port Townsend Marine Science Center on the pier offer an up close look at sea life. The fort also hosts kayaking tours, conferences, camping, an artillery museum, and music festivals in an old military balloon-hangar-turned-performing-arts-pavilion. ✉ *200 Battery Way* ☎ *360/385–4730, 360/344–4400* ⊕ *www.parks.wa.gov/ fortworden* 🎫 *Day pass: $10 per vehicle; annual Discovery Pass $30 (valid at all state parks)* ⊘ *Daily dawn–dusk.*

Northwest Maritime Center. The myriad traditions and trades of the Pacific Northwest's seafaring history are explained here, with special emphasis on the importance of Port Townsend as one of only three Victorian-era seaports on the country's register of National Historic Sites. It's the core of the Point Hudson district and the center of operations for the Wooden Boat Foundation, which stages the annual Wooden Boat

13

Festival early each September. The center has interactive exhibits, hands-on sailing training, boatbuilding workshops, a wood shop, and a pilot house where you can test navigational tools. The boardwalk, pier, and sandy beach that front the buildings are laced with marine life, and are the perfect points to launch a kayak or watch sloops and schooners gliding along the coast. The chandlery features a variety of nautical gifts and gear, from brass fittings and rigging supplies to galley wares, illustrated knot books, and boats-in-a-bottle. In a well-lighted back corner overlooking the bay, Velocity Coffee Bar sells espresso and baked goods from 6:30 am to 5 pm Monday through Saturday. ✉ *431 Water St.* ☎ *360/385–3628, 360/379–5383* ⊕ *www.nwmaritime.org* 🗓 *Free* ⊘ *Weekdays 9–5.*

Port Townsend Marine Science Center. Along the waterfront at Fort Worden State Park, the center is divided into two sections. The marine lab and aquarium building, in a former World War II military storage facility at the end of a pier, houses numerous aquarium displays, as well as touch tanks with sea stars, crabs, and anemones. The separate, on-shore Natural History Exhibit Center is filled with displays detailing the region's geography and marine ecology. Beach walks, nature camps, cruises, and day camps run throughout the summer, and there's a Low Tide Festival each July. ✉ *520 Battery Way* ☎ *360/385–5582, 800/566–3932* ⊕ *www.ptmsc.org* 🗓 *$5* ⊘ *Mid-June–early Sept., Wed.–Mon. 11–5; early Sept.–Nov. and late Mar.–mid-June, Fri.–Sun. noon–4 (marine lab and aquarium building by appointment only Dec.–Mar.).*

WHERE TO EAT

$$
INTERNATIONAL

✕ **Alchemy Bistro & Wine Bar.** This upscale eatery overlooking Haller Fountain offers a blend of Italian, Spanish, and French favorites alongside Pacific Northwest fare, including succulent salmon, oysters, and mussels. Start with rich, creamy stuffed poblano peppers, or oyster stew with leeks, ginger, garlic and fresh tarragon in the well-lighted, casually elegant main dining room. Entrées include a selection of salads, seafood, and pastas as well as the often-requested Drunken Rabbit, slow-cooked in red wine with garlic, carrots, and onions. Sunday brunch features wild salmon Benedict, crêpes with fresh berry compote and marscapone, crème brûlée French toast, and endless mimosas, and there's an evening "small bites" menu in the intimate bar with deep-red walls. ⑤ *Average main: $22* ✉ *842 Washington St.* ☎ *360/385–5225* ⊕ *alchemybistroandwinebar.com.*

$$
PACIFIC
NORTHWEST

✕ **The Belmont.** The town's only remaining 1880s saloon is tucked into the line of brickfront buildings along the seaport's main street. Tall, waterfront windows let in light and afford broad bay views, which make a perfect backdrop to the innovative seafood dishes and Pacific Northwest fare. Dig into a pound of mussels or clams or a combination poached in a pesto cream sauce, a char-grilled salmon filet topped with Dungeness crab and béarnaise sauce, or the "three-masted" filet mignon topped with Dungeness crab, three prawns and béarnaise sauce. A bar on the mezzanine overlooks Water Street for people-watching. The second floor is a hotel with Victorian furnishings to match the history and architecture. ⑤ *Average main: $20* ✉ *925 Water St.* ☎ *360/385–3007* ⊕ *www.thebelmontpt.com.*

Victorian building, Port Townsend

$ ✕ **Blue Moose Cafe.** Comfortable, cozy, and a bit off-the-wall, this is
AMERICAN one of the best places in Port Townsend to go for a generous, hearty,
and unfussy breakfast or lunch. It's popular with locals—especially
sailors and shipwrights who work in the surrounding Port Townsend
Boat Haven. Comfort food, such as thick pancakes and amply stuffed
omelets, burgers, and sandwiches, is served with a quirky sense of
humor. The "This Ain't No Atkins Special" consists of biscuits and
thick gravy with corned-beef hash. Weekend breakfasts are bustling,
but you can help yourself to a mug of drip coffee while you wait. $ *Average main: $10* ⊠ *311 Haines Pl., in the Port Townsen Boat Haven*
☎ *360/385–7339* ⊟ *No credit cards* ⊗ *No dinner.*

$ ✕ **Cellar Door.** The entrance to this eclectic subterranean space can be dif-
CONTEMPORARY ficult to spot—at the bottom of a Tyler Street staircase. There you'll find
a sophisticated yet casual wine and cocktail bar that melds vintage Victorian with a rustic industrial feel and sense of whimsy (concrete floors,
reclaimed wood, antiques). Catering to the after-hours crew, it offers
contemporary bites, handcrafted cocktails, and a distinctly steampunk
vibe. Specials like bread crumb–encrusted mac and cheese in tarragon
béchamel sauce or pork tenderloin with roasted parsnips can be eaten
at the force-rusted steel bar or in any of the intimate nooks. Most of
the sodas, syrups, bitters, and infusions are made in-house. Quick bites
include latke cakes, stuffed dates with house-cured bourbon bacon,
beef or lamb sliders. $ *Average main: $13* ⊠ *940 Water St., entrance
on Tyler St.* ☎ *360/385–6959* ⊕ *www.cellardoorpt.com* ⊗ *Closed Tues.
and Wed. No lunch.*

$$$ ✕ **Fins Coastal Cuisine.** This spacious, second-floor Pacific Northwest-
SEAFOOD style dining room, set above the main street and picturesque bay,

provides a perfect setting to sample fresh catch, from appetizers like Dungeness crabcakes and calamari to full dinners of succulent, beautifully presented shellfish and salmon. Look for mains like creamy but not too thick clam chowder with a hint of white wine and thyme, Dungeness crab rigatoni with sweet corn sauce, macadamia crusted halibut, and traditional cioppppino. The menu also features locally harvested oysters, mussels, and clams. Housemade pickles garnish dishes, and housemade simple syrups and infused vodkas add something special to a wide selection of spirits. In warm weather, dine on the terrace, which overlooks the incoming and outgoing ferries and sailboats. $ *Average main: $25* ✉ *1019 Water St.* ☎ *360/379–3474* ⊕ *www.finscoastal.com.*

$$ ✕**Fountain Café.** Artwork lines the walls of the small, funky café tucked
ECLECTIC inside a historic clapboard building a block off the main drag, where seafood and pasta dishes carry Mediterranean, Morrocan, Indian, Thai, and Pacific Northwest influences. Start with panfried oysters or mussels and clams in a pesto-Chardonnay broth. Chicken marsala and paella are mainstays. Full-bodied Pacific Northwest and Italian wines as well as simple sweets like tiramisu and gingerbread round out the menu. Most of the art on the walls is for sale, and the café is included on the town's monthly gallery walks. $ *Average main: $18* ✉ *920 Washington St.* ☎ *360/385–1364* ⌱ *Reservations not accepted.*

$ ✕**Hanazono Asian Noodle.** The regular menu at this small, long, thin,
JAPANESE authentic Japanese noodle house includes three types of egg noodles—ramen, *yakisoba*, and *champon*—as well as rice, soba and udon noodles in a variety of soups, stir-fries, and salads. The restaurant also serves sushi rolls, *donburi* (rice bowl dish), bento, and daily specials. Start with tofu fries, miso soup, seaweed salad, spring rolls, or *gyoza* (handmade potstickers stuffed with cabbage, pork, and green onion). Finish with green tea or ginger ice cream, green tea tiramisu, or cheesecake. Don't be surprised if you have to wait for a table; the place gets packed. $ *Average main: $9* ✉ *225 Taylor St.* ☎ *360/385–7622* ⊕ *hanazonoasiannoodle.com* ⊘ *Closed Mon.*

$$ ✕**Lanza's Ristorante.** Intimate and romantic, this small uptown eatery
ITALIAN has been a local institution for 30 years and exudes the warmth of Italy with welcoming and gracious staff, generous portions, and authentic, old-country recipes. Share the ample antipasto platter while waiting for pizza or pasta, from classic spaghetti and meatballs to ravioli Florentine, penne with sausage, mushrooms and spinach, and a rich, creamy linguini *luna*. Specialty dishes include rack of lamb, chicken Marsala, and chicken picatta. A Port Townsend institution for nearly 30 years, Lanza's is popular with locals and there's usually a crowd, especially on weekends, when live music adds to the ambience. Reservations are recommended. Save room for tiramisu. $ *Average main: $18* ✉ *1020 Lawrence St., Uptown* ☎ *360/379–1900* ⊕ *www.lanzaspt.com* ⊘ *Closed Sun. and Mon. No lunch.*

$ ✕**Owl Sprit Cafe.** Tucked into a small space on a side street on the edge
PACIFIC of downtown, this cozy and eclectic little gem uses locally sourced,
NORTHWEST organic ingredients in its variety of grilled sandwiches, burritos, tacos, soups, salads, sliders, and the popular, hand-cut haystack onion rings. Breakfast includes French toast, tostadas, eggs on toast, and biscuits

and gravy. For dinner, there are burgers and pastas, like the preserved-lemon linguine with smoked salmon, artichoke hearts, peas, and goat cheese. Vegetarian, vegan, and gluten-free options are available. A colorful owl mural on the back wall watches over the dining room, full of plants, patterned tablecloths, and local works of art. $ *Average main: $14* ✉ *218 Polk St.* ☎ *360/385–5275* ⊕ *www.owlsprit.com.*

$$$ ✕ **Sweet Laurette Café and Bistro.** Paris meets the Pacific Northwest in
BISTRO   this uptown bistro. Starting out as a pâtissierie in 2001, it still serves
Fodor's Choice   espresso and baked treats in its cozy, French-inspired coffee shop, but
★   don't forego a full meal in the lavender-lined courtyard or casually elegant, intimate dining room, with chocolate-colored wainscoting and pistachio-tinted walls. The menu is classic French bistro with a fresh, contemporary, farm-to-table flair—chef-owner Laurette Feit sources her ingredients, including grass-fed beef, organic eggs, and wild king salmon, from local farmers and fishermen. Exquisitely presented entrées—think lamb shanks with creamy polenta; steak au poivre; king salmon topped with black olive and sun-dried tomato butter—feature beautifully-balanced flavors, colors, and textures. Profiteroles, flourless chocolate torte, and crème brûlée are signature desserts. Breakfast and lunch selections are equally accomplished. $ *Average main: $25* ✉ *1029 Lawrence St., Uptown* ☎ *360/385–4886* ⊕ *www.sweetlaurette. com* ☾ *Closed Mon. and Tues.*

$ ✕ **Waterfront Pizza.** This longtime pizza place regularly wins the best
PIZZA   pizza category in the local newspaper's annual awards. The sourdough crust is generously covered with all kinds of toppings. Try the Waterfront, with sausage, pepperoni, mushrooms, and olives. Sit in the small, upstairs dining room overlooking the town's main street and share a whole pie with table service. Or, order a slice to go at the walk-up counter on the ground floor and enjoy it on the small beach nearby. $ *Average main: $10* ✉ *951 Water St.* ☎ *360/385–6629.*

WHERE TO STAY

$ ⌂ **Ann Starrett Mansion.** Gables, turrets, and gingerbread trim decorate
B&B/INN   this glorious 1889 mansion, with well-appointed, unique rooms, all
Fodor's Choice   beautifully decorated and furnished with antiques. **Pros:** sweeping
★   views; a short walk to downtown and uptown restaurants and shops; a chance to experience Victorian elegance. **Cons:** no breakfast; no elevator. $ *Rooms from: $115* ✉ *744 Clay St.* ☎ *360/385–3205, 800/321–0644* ⊕ *www.starrettmansion.com* ⇆ *8 rooms, 2 cottages* ⦿ *No meals.*

$$ ⌂ **Bishop Victorian Hotel.** This brick inn abounds with 19th-century ele-
B&B/INN   gance and thoughtful service, and most of the one- and two-bedroom suites, adorned with lush, floral fabrics, antiques, and authentic brass features, have garden, mountain, or water views, as well as fireplaces. **Pros:** Victorian flair with contemporary conveniences; a stone's throw from the waterfront, restaurants, boutiques, and coffee shops; congenial staff; some kitchenettes. **Cons:** no elevator. $ *Rooms from: $157* ✉ *714 Washington St.* ☎ *360/385–6122, 800/824–4738* ⊕ *www. bishopvictorian.com* ⇆ *16 suites* ⦿ *Breakfast.*

$ ⌂ **Manresa Castle.** This expansive, imposing, hillside mansion, built in
HOTEL   1892 for Port Townsend's first mayor, has lots of Victorian character—wood trim, antique furniture, high ceilings, patterned wallpaper, and

lace curtains covering tall windows—and some sweeping views of the bay. **Pros:** staying in a real slice of history. **Cons:** somewhat of a spooky vibe (ask the staff about reported ghost sightings). ⑤ *Rooms from: $109* ⊠ *651 Cleveland St.* ☎ *360/385–5750, 800/732–1281* ⊕ *www.manresacastle.com* ⇋ *30 rooms, 9 suites* ⦿ *Breakfast.*

$

Old Consulate Inn. Perched on a bluff above the bay, this elegant, red, turreted Victorian mansion with a sweeping veranda and surrounded by park-like gardens features well-appointed view rooms, three with claw-foot tubs and one that's dog-friendly. **Pros:** gourmet breakfast; gorgeous grounds and views; quiet; a real stepping-back-in-time experience. **Cons:** no children under 14; no elevator. ⑤ *Rooms from: $110* ⊠ *313 Walker St.* ☎ *360/385–6753, 800/300–6753* ⊕ *www.oldconsulate.com* ⇋ *5 rooms, 3 suites* ⦿ *Breakfast.*

B&B/INN

Fodor's Choice
★

$

Palace Hotel. In a former bordello that retains its 19th-century grandeur, light-filled rooms, many named for the women who used to work here, feature 14-foot ceilings and elegant period furnishings like hand-carved dressers, wrought-iron bed frames, and big claw-foot bathtubs. **Pros:** a feeling of participating in a bit of Port Townsend's history; a stone's throw from restaurants, boutiques, and bars. **Cons:** might not suit travelers who don't appreciate Victorian charm. ⑤ *Rooms from: $99* ⊠ *1004 Water St.* ☎ *360/385–0773, 800/962–0741* ⊕ *www.palacehotelpt.com* ⇋ *19 rooms, 17 with bath* ⦿ *No meals.*

B&B/INN

$

The Swan Hotel. Tucked at the end of the downtown thoroughfare, this balcony-encased, four-story hotel features well-lighted, airy, hand-somely furnished rooms with gorgeous sea views or, on the northside, overlooking the Point Hudson Marina. **Pros:** central location; majestic views; comfortable and cozy; suite is good for small groups. **Cons:** no breakfast; small, often crowded parking lot, with an alternative lot a few blocks away. ⑤ *Rooms from: $130* ⊠ *216 Monroe St.* ☎ *360/379–1840, 800/824–4738* ⊕ *www.theswanhotel.com* ⇋ *8 rooms, 1 suite, four cottages* ⦿ *No meals.*

B&B/INN

$

Tides Inn. The multistory, peak-roofed inn resembles an expansive beach house, and it's set on the water near the ferry dock with a nice variety of lodgings, from small, basic, cabin-type budget rooms to more spacious units with mini-refrigerators, microwaves, jetted tubs, and balconies. **Pros:** beach locale, with beautiful bay views; reasonable price; one of the few hotels in town with an elevator. **Cons:** need to book far in advance for festivals and summer weekends; three rooms don't have a sea view. ⑤ *Rooms from: $89* ⊠ *1807 Water St.* ☎ *360/385–0595, 800/822–8696* ⊕ *www.tides-inn.com* ⇋ *23 rooms, 21 suites* ⦿ *Breakfast.*

HOTEL

$

Washington Hotel. With its keyless entry and modern interiors, this small hotel on the second floor of a historic building in the heart of downtown caters to the independent traveler. **Pros:** stylish city feel in a small-town environment; central location. **Cons:** no lobby; not the best choice for travelers who require 24-hour concierge services. ⑤ *Rooms from: $109* ⊠ *825 Washington St.* ☎ *360/774–0213* ⊕ *washingtonhotelporttownsend.com* ⇋ *4 rooms* ⦿ *No meals.*

HOTEL

13

NIGHTLIFE

Port Townsend Brewing Company. Boatyard workers and beer enthusiasts congregate at this casual and cozy Boat Haven brewery to enjoy a pint and bowl of peanuts (and not worry about dropping the spent shells on the floor). There's an outdoor beer garden during warmer months. Proprietors Kim and Guy Sands opened the brewery in 1997 with only two beers. About 10 are now on the menu, including the award-winning Boatyard Bitter, Port Townsend Pale Ale, and Hop Diggidy, a classic Northwest-style IPA. The brewery closes early evening, so nightlife seekers might want to make this one of their first stops. ✉ *330 10th St., Port Townsend Boat Haven* ☎ *360/385–9967* ⊕ *www. porttownsendbrewing.com.*

Pourhouse. A gathering place for local and out-of-town beer enthusiasts features a dozen rotating taps, 200 bottles and cans of beer and hard cider, and wines by the glass. During warmer months, the bayside beer garden has sweeping views of the Cascade and Olympic Mountains and nearby boat haven. There are picnic tables, a pétanque court, and a concrete table for table tennis. Some snacks—like charcuterie or cheese plates—are served, you can bring your own takeout, or order from one of the many in-town eateries that will deliver full meals; menus are available in the taproom. Most Friday and Saturday nights in summer, there's live music outside in the "Impound Lot." ✉ *2231 Washington St.* ☎ *360/379–5586* ⊕ *www.ptpourhouse.com.*

Sirens. The upper floor of a historic sandstone building on Port Townsend's main street provides breathtaking bay views and regularly books West Coast rockabilly, alternative country, blues, jazz, and rock bands on weekends. Fiddlers jam here Tuesday nights, and Wednesday open mike nights are a local tradition. Microbrews and handcrafted cocktails quench thirst, and there's a menu of hearty Pacific Northwest-inspired pub food, from pastas and burgers to salads and innovative seafood dishes. If there's a free table, opt to sit on the back upper or lower deck overlooking the water. ✉ *832 Water St.* ☎ *360/379–1100* ⊕ *www.sirenspub.com.*

Starlight. This third-floor room in the Silverwater Cafe, a collaboration with the next-door Rose Theatre, allows moviegoers aged 21 and over the chance to watch a film and enjoy wine (by the glass or bottle), beer, a cocktail, dessert, or an array of Mediterranean antipasti. ✉ *237 Taylor St.* ☎ *360/385–6448.*

SHOPPING

Port Townsend brims with antiques stores, art galleries, clothing boutiques, consignment shops, vintage and New Age-y bookstores, and upscale maritime, kitchen, home design, and gift shops. Water and Washington Streets, which run parallel to the bay, are lined with storefronts. So are their block-long offshoots, cut off by the cliff that separates downtown from uptown. More stores are located uptown on Lawrence Street near an enclave of Victorian houses. To reach them, walk up the Terrace Steps behind Haller Fountain at Washington and Taylor Streets. Along the way, plenty of pubs, coffeehouses, and eateries provide tired shoppers a place to revive and rest their feet.

Conservatory Coastal Home. With an array of upscale seaside luxe living essentials and soy candles (hand-poured on-site in small batches in scents like sailcloth, fog, moss, and water) this high-ceilinged, brick-walled home-design and gift boutique smells as good and it looks. A variety of air plants in recycled glass terrariums are always in stock. Look for furniture fashioned from reclaimed wood, nautical-themed throw pillows, jewelry, and seashells. ⊠ *639 Water St.* ☎ *360/385–3857* ⊕ *www.conservatorycoastalhome.com.*

get-a-bles. An eclectic range of supplies makes this little shop as interesting and fun as the name suggests. There are eat-a-bles and drink-a-bles—sandwiches, cheese, pickles, pretzels, nuts, hard cider, soda, and beer—and gift-a-bles such as locally-roasted coffee, gourmet salts, handmade sugar scrubs and soaps, toys, and flasks. ⊠ *810 Water St.* ☎ *360/385–5560* ⊕ *www.getablespt.com.*

Lively Olive Tasting Bar. Sample more than 30, often flavor-infused, varieties of oil and vinegar at this new and bright specialty shop along the town's main street. Offerings include balsamic vinegars in flavors of dark chocolate, black mission fig, and honey-ginger, and olive oils in black truffle and blood orange. The shop also sells gourmet pastas. ⊠ *929 Water St.* ☎ *360/385–3993* ⊕ *livelyolive.com.*

Maestrale. East meets West in this specialty shop that imports fabrics, furniture, jewelry, and other handicrafts from India, Indonesia, Thailand, Nepal, and China. ⊠ *821 Water St.* ☎ *360/385–5565* ⊕ *maestraleimports.com.*

Mt. Townsend Creamery. Watch cheesemakers at work while sampling artisanal offerings like the ale-washed Off Kilter or popular Seastack. The creamery, founded in 2007, uses cows' milk from a single, local herd to make not quite a dozen diferent kinds of cheese. ⊠ *338 Sherman St.* ☎ *360/379-0895* ⊕ *www.mttownsendcreamery.com.*

Pane d'Amore. Pick up a baguette, chocolate-chip cookie, or cinnamon bun at this top-notch bakery, tucked into a small storefront in the heart of the uptown district. ⊠ *617 Tyler St.* ☎ *360/385–1199* ⊕ *panedamore. com.*

Port Townsend Antique Mall. Three-dozen dealers at the two-story Port Townsend Antique Mall sell merchandise ranging from pricey Victorian collectors' items to cheap flea-market kitsch. ⊠ *802 Washington St.* ☎ *360/379–8069.*

Port Townsend Farmers' Market. Port Townsend is proud of its farm-to-table food movement and visitors can witness and share in the region's bounty at the farmers' market. Approximately 70 vendors, including some 40 farmers, showcase their fare—fresh produce, flash-frozen salmon, artisanal foods and baked goods, crafts, and handmade soaps and salves. The market is open Saturday 9–2 April–December and also on Wednesday 3–6 July–late September. ⊠ *Tyler St. and Lawrence St., Uptown* ☎ *360/379–9098* ⊕ *jeffersoncountyfarmersmarket.org.*

William James Bookseller. Used and out-of-print books covering all fields—with an emphasis on nautical, regional history, and theology titles—are arrayed from floor to ceiling of this jam-packed gem of a bookstore. ✉ *829 Water St.* ☎ *360/385–7313.*

SPORTS AND THE OUTDOORS

BIKING

The nearest place to go biking is Fort Worden State Park, but you can range as far afield as Fort Flagler, the lower Dungeness trails (no bikes are allowed on the spit itself), or across the water to Whidbey Island.

The Broken Spoke. This bike retail, repair, and rental shop in the heart of downtown promotes cycling at all levels. ✉ *230 Taylor St.* ☎ *360/379–1295* ⊕ *www.thebrokenspokept.blogspot.com.*

P. T. Cyclery. Mountain bikes are available for rent here, and the shop repairs flats and can advise you on where to start your journey. ✉ *252 Tyler St.* ☎ *360/385–6470* ⊕ *www.ptcyclery.com.*

BOAT CRUISES

Puget Sound Express. This company runs summer speedboat connections between Port Townsend and Friday Harbor from May through September (boats depart from Port Townsend at 9, arriving in Friday Harbor at noon; the return trip departs from Friday Harbor at 2:30 and arrives back in Port Townsend at 5. Four-hour guaranteed-sighting whale-watching trips depart from Friday Harbor at 10 and 2:30 May–late September to view orcas (killer whales) and at 11 from mid-March–end April to see migrating gray whales. Whale-watching trips are subject to a minimum number of passengers. ✉ *227 Jackson St., at the Point Hudson Marina* ☎ *360/385–5288* ⊕ *www.pugetsoundexpress.com* ✉ *Trips and tours from $85.*

KAYAKING

PT Outdoors. Located at Fort Worden State Park and open seasonally, this company offers kayaking classes and guided trips. Waterfront tours are $60; three-hour tours to Bird Island are $100; specialty tours can also be arranged with at least a week's advance notice. All tours require reservations. Single touring kayaks rent for $25 per hour; double touring kayaks rent for $40 per hour. ✉ *Fort Worden State Park, 200 Battery Way* ☎ *360/379–3608* ⊕ *www.ptoutdoors.com.*

SEQUIM

31 miles west of Port Townsend.

Sequim (pronounced *skwim*), incorporated in 1913, is a pleasant old mill town and farming center between the northern foothills of the Olympic Mountains and the southeastern stretch of the Strait of Juan de Fuca. With lots of sunshine, lovely views, and neat, quiet blocks, it's also a popular place to retire. Sequim's walkable downtown, marked by a historic grain elevator, features a variety of gift and other shops. A few miles to the north is the shallow and fertile Dungeness Valley, which enjoys some of the lowest rainfall in western Washington. Fragrant purple lavender flourishes in local fields. East of town, scenic Sequim Bay is home to the John Wayne Marina. The actor, who navigated local waters aboard his yacht, *Wild Goose,* donated land for the marina in 1975, four years before his death.

GETTING HERE AND AROUND

Sequim is about two hours from Seattle, via the Seattle–Bainbridge Island or Edmonds–Kingston ferries and U.S. 101. It's served by Clallam Transit to local Olympic Peninsula towns, and Olympic Bus Lines to Silverdale, Seattle, and Sea-Tac International Airport.

Contacts Clallam Transit ☎ *360/452–4511, 800/858–3747* ⊕ *www.clallamtransit.com.* **Olympic Bus Lines** ☎ *360/417–0700, 800/457–4492* ⊕ *www.olympicbuslines.com.*

ESSENTIALS

Visitor Information Sequim Chamber of Commerce ✉ *1192 E. Washington St.* ☎ *360/683–6197, 800/737–8462* ⊕ *www.sequimchamber.com.*

EXPLORING

Fodor's Choice ★ **Dungeness Spit.** Curving 5½ miles into the Strait of Juan de Fuca, the longest natural sand spit in the United States is a wild, beautiful section of shoreline. More than 30,000 migratory waterfowl stop here each spring and fall, but you'll see plenty of birdlife any time of year. The entire spit is part of the **Dungeness National Wildlife Refuge.** Access it through the **Dungeness Recreation Area,** which serves as a portal to the shoreline. ✉ *554 Voice of America Rd., entrance 3 miles north from U.S. 101, 4 miles west of Sequim* ☎ *360/457–8451 wildlife refuge* ⊕ *www.clallam. net/Parks/Dungeness.html* 🖃 *$3 per family* ⏱ *Daily dawn–dusk.*

Dungeness Lighthouse. At the end of the Dungeness Spit is the towering white 1857 Dungeness Lighthouse; tours are available, though access is limited to those who can hike or kayak out 5 miles to the end of the spit. Guests also have the opportunity to serve as lighthouse keepers for a week at a time. An adjacent, 64-site camping area, on the bluff above the Strait of Juan de Fuca, is open February through September. ✉ *Entrance 3 miles north of Hwy. 101 via Kitchen Dick Rd.* ☎ *360/683–6638* ⊕ *www.newdungenesslighthouse.com.*

FAMILY **Olympic Game Farm.** This 200-acre property—part zoo, part safari—is Sequim's biggest attraction after the Dungeness Spit. For years, the farm's exclusive client was Walt Disney Studios, and many of the animals here are the offspring of former movie stars. On the hour-long, drive-through tour, which covers some 84 acres of the picturesque property, be prepared to see large animals like buffalo surround your car and lick your windows. You'll also see zebras, llamas, lynx, lions, elk, Tibetan yak, emu, bobcat, Siberian and Bengal tigers, and Kodiak and black bears, among other animals. Facilities also include an aquarium, a studio barn with movie sets, a snack kiosk, and a gift shop. Guests are allowed to feed the uncaged animals (with wheat bread only), except for the buffalo and elk at the entrance gates, but must stay in their vehicles at all times. Even sunroofs must remain locked. ✉ *1423 Ward Rd.* ☎ *360/683–4295, 800/778–4295* ⊕ *www.olygamefarm.com* 🖃 *Drive-through tour $12 per adult and $11 per child; mini guided walking tour $5* ⏱ *Summer, daily 9–5 (open until 6 Sat.); winter daily 9–3; spring and fall daily 9–4.*

Railroad Bridge Park. Set along a beautifully serene, 25-acre stretch of the Dungeness River, the park is centered on a lacy ironwork bridge

The Dungeness National Wildlife Refuge

that was once part of the coastal line between Port Angeles and Port Townsend. Today the park shelters a pristine river environment. The River Walk hike-and-bike path leads from the River Center educational facility, on the banks of the Dungeness, into the woods, and a horseback track links Runnion Road with the waterway. In summer, families picnic at the River Shed pavilion, students participate in science programs at the Dungeness River Audubon Society office, and locals come to watch performances at the River Stage amphitheater. There are free guided bird walks every Wednesday morning from 8:30 to 10:15. You'll find the park 2 miles west of town, and a five-minute drive from the coast. ⊠ *2151 Hendrickson Rd.* ☎ *360/681–4076* ⊕ *www. dungenessrivercenter.org* ✉ *Free* ☉ *Park, daily dawn–dusk. Audubon office Tues.–Sat. 10–4, Sun. noon–4.*

Sequim Farmers Market. You'll find honey, lavender, sea glass jewelry, pottery, and locally grown produce in abundance at this Saturday market, a tented affair with lots of color and live music, open from 9 to 3 between early May and late October. ⊠ *Cedar St., between Seal St. and 2nd Ave.* ☎ *360/460–2668* ⊕ *www.sequimmarket.com.*

WHERE TO EAT

$$

ECLECTIC

⤬ **Alder Wood Bistro.** An inventive menu of local and organic dishes makes this one of the most popular restaurants in Sequim. Pizzas from the wood-fired oven include unique creations, like the chicken pesto with organic chicken, basil pesto, blue cheese, black olives, toasted walnuts, pickled red onions, and mozzarella. Some feature Mt. Townsend Creamery cheeses. The menu's sustainably harvested seafood selections highlight whatever is in season, from black cod and mussels to oysters and salmon; they also get the wood-fire treatment. Even the bacon-wrapped meat loaf features local beef, along with buttermilk mashed potatoes and greens. For dessert, try the organic seasonal frangipane fruit tart or panna cotta. On warmer days, enjoy alfresco dining in the pretty garden courtyard. ⑤ *Average main: $18* ✉ *139 W. Alder St* ☎ *360/683–4321* ⊕ *www.alderwoodbistro.com* ⊘ *Closed Sun. and Mon. No lunch.*

$$ ✕**Dockside Grill.** With tremendous views of John Wayne Marina and
PACIFIC Sequim Bay, this is a fun place to watch boats placidly sail by. The
NORTHWEST casual yet elegant menu includes Dungeness crab fritters, steamed clams, cedar-plank salmon, bouillabaisse, cioppino, and pasta. The kitchen also serves up excellent steak, surf-n-turf *poutine* (fried shrimp and beef tips, served on fries with cheese and a Cabernet demi-glace), and a duck confit burger. ⑤ *Average main: $18* ✉ *2577 W. Sequim Bay Rd.* ☎ *360/683–7510* ⊕ *www.docksidegrill-sequim.com* ⊘ *Closed Mon. and Tues.*

$ ✕**Nourish.** The greenhouse-enclosed restaurant and patio café over-
PACIFIC look one of the region's oldest lavender and herb farms and feature an
NORTHWEST ever-evolving, seasonally inspired menu, specializing in the garden-to-plate experience. There are carefully crafted smoothies, soups, salads, sandwiches, and pastas and burgers, and the house-made sodas are a particular treat. A variety of vegetarian, vegan, and gluten-free options are available. There's open mike Wednesday nights and brunch on Sundays. ⑤ *Average main: $14* ✉ *101 Provence View La.* ☎ *360/797–1480* ⊕ *www.nourishsequim.com* ⊘ *Closed Mon.*

$ ✕**Oak Table Café.** Carefully crafted breakfasts and lunches, made with
AMERICAN high-grade, fresh ingredients, are the focus of this well-run, family-friendly eatery, a Sequim institution since 1981. Breakfast is served throughout the 7 am–3 pm open hours; on Sunday, when the large, well-lighted dining room is especially bustling, it's the only meal, and the selection is extensive. Thickly sliced bacon and eggs are a top-seller, but the restaurant is best known for its creamy blintzes, golden-brown waffles, crepes, and variety of pancakes, particularly the cinnamon-y sweet soufflé-style apple pancake. Egg dishes include eggs Nicole—a medley of sautéed mushrooms, onions, spinach, and scrambled eggs served over an open-face croissant and covered with hollandaise sauce. Lunches include burgers, salads, and sandwiches. ⑤ *Average main: $12* ✉ *292 W. Bell St.* ☎ *360/683–2179* ⊕ *www.oaktablecafe.com* ⊘ *No dinner. No lunch Sun.*

WHERE TO STAY

$$$ ⊡**Holiday Inn Express & Suites Sequim.** Modern rooms done in sooth-
HOTEL ing green-and-tan Pacific Northwest color schemes come with lots of perks, including an indoor pool, hot tub, fitness center, and 24-hour business center. **Pros:** easily accessible from the highway; next door to café. **Cons:** not right in town center; some complaints about high summer rates and noise. ⑤ *Rooms from: $201* ✉ *1441 E. Washington St.* ☎ *360/681–8756, 800/315–2621* ⊕ *www.hiexpress.com* ⊅ *77 rooms, 19 suites* ⍾ *Breakfast.*

$$ ▦ **Red Caboose Getaway.** Vintage metal railcars form the centerpiece
B&B/INN of this bed-and-breakfast, where guests can experience the romance
Fodor'sChoice of the rails and sleep in luxury cabooses, each with a different theme.
★ **Pros:** unique style; great breakfast. **Cons:** no children under 12.
⑤ *Rooms from: $175* ✉ *24 Old Coyote Way* ☎ *360/683–7350* ⊕ *www.
redcaboosegetaway.com* ⇨ *6 suites* ⓧ *Breakfast.*

$ ▦ **Sequim Bay Lodge.** This sprawling, modern hotel on 17 acres is as
HOTEL resort-style as you'll get for the area, with rooms done in pastel florals
and set above woodland views; most of the suites have a fireplace or
balcony. **Pros:** good value; suites are convenient for families; varied
room styles; helpful staff. **Cons:** not too fancy; interior design is some-
what dated. ⑤ *Rooms from: $79* ✉ *268522 U.S. 101* ☎ *360/683–0691,
800/622–0691* ⊕ *www.sequimbaylodge.com* ⇨ *54 rooms* ⓧ *Breakfast.*

PORT ANGELES

17 miles west of Sequim.

Sprawling along the hills above the deep-blue Strait of San Juan de Fuca,
Port Angeles is the crux of the Olympic Peninsula's air, sea, and land
links. The once largely blue-collar logging and fishing town is capped
off at the water's edge by a gathering of hotels, restaurants, shops, and
attractions, all set around the modern marina and the sandy swath of
Hollywood Beach. With a population of about 19,000, the town is
the largest on the Olympic Peninsula and a major gateway to Olympic
National Park. Summer foot traffic is shoulder-to-shoulder downtown
with hopefuls rushing to ferries, vacationers strolling the waterfront,
locals relaxing at outdoor cafés, and *Twilight* fans retracing steps of
their favorite characters (Port Angeles served as a backdrop for several
scenes in the popular series). Other fans flock here, too; Port Angeles
is the last place writer Raymond Carver lived, and it remains home to
his widow, the poet Tess Gallagher, who was born here.

It didn't start out this way, though, as the seasonal crowds have only
been a phenomenon since the 1950s. The area was first settled by the
Hoh, Makah, Quileute, Quinault, and S'Klallam tribes, and others had
little reason to visit until a Greek navigator named Apostolos Valeria-
nus—aka Juan de Fuca—sailed into the strait in 1610. In 1791 Span-
ish explorer Juan Francisco de Eliza followed him and named it Puerto
de Nuestra Señora de Los Angeles, or Port of Our Lady of the Angels.
George Vancouver shortened the name to Port Angeles in 1792, and
the site was settled by pioneers in 1856. In the century that followed,
Port Angeles became a timber-mill town, a military base, and a key
regional fishing port.

GETTING HERE AND AROUND
Port Angeles is about two hours from Seattle via the Seattle–Bainbridge
Island and Edmonds–Kingston ferries and Highway 104; it's about 17
miles west of Sequim on U.S. 101. It's served by Clallam Transit to local
Olympic Peninsula towns, and Olympic Bus Lines to Silverdale, Seattle,
and Sea-Tac airport. Kenmore Air runs flights between Port Angeles and
Boeing Field, near Seattle.

Contacts **Clallam Transit** ☎ 360/452–4511, 800/858–3747 ⊕ www. clallamtransit.com. **Olympic Bus Lines** ☎ 360/417–0700, 800/457–4492 ⊕ www.olympicbuslines.com.

ESSENTIALS

Visitor Information Port Angeles Regional Chamber of Commerce ✉ 121 E. Railroad Ave. ☎ 360/452–2363 ⊕ www.portangeles.org.

EXPLORING

Port Angeles Fine Arts Center. This small, sophisticated museum is inside the former home of late artist and publisher Esther Barrows Webster, one of Port Angeles's most energetic and cultured citizens; displays are modern, funky, and intriguing. Outside, Webster's Woods Art Park is dotted with oversize sculptures set before a vista of the city and harbor. Exhibitions emphasize the works of emerging and well-established Pacific Northwest artists. ✉ 1203 W. Lauridsen Blvd. ☎ 360/457–3532 ⊕ www.pafac.org ⌲ Free ⊗ Mar.–Nov., Thurs.–Sun. 11–5; Dec.–Feb., Thurs.–Sun. 10–4 and by appointment; Art Park daily sunrise–sunset.

WHERE TO EAT

$$
PACIFIC NORTHWEST

✕ **The Bushwhacker.** More than three decades of excellent surf-and-turf keep the locals coming back to this big, friendly Northwest-style place just east of the city. Families gather to dig into huge cuts of meat or seafood dishes, while other tasty fare includes jam-packed seafood fettucine, sandwiches, wraps, and build-your-own, half-pound "Whacker" burgers. A salad and soup bar comes with every meal—but save room for decadent desserts like triple berry cobbler with ice cream. $ *Average main: $18* ✉ 1527 E. 1st St. ☎ 360/457–4113 ⊕ www.bushwhackerpa. com.

$$$$
FRENCH

✕ **C'est Si Bon.** The interior design as well as the food is far more Euro-savvy than is typical on the Olympic Peninsula. A fanciful dining room is done up in bold red hues, with crisp white linens, huge oil paintings, and glittering chandeliers; the spacious solarium takes an equally formal approach. A changing menu highlights housemade French onion soup, escargots, *magret de canard* (duck breast) with berry sauce, Dungeness crab soufflé, filet mignon, and rack of lamb. The wine list is superb, with French, Australian, and Northwest choices to pair with everything. $ *Average main: $32* ✉ 23 Cedar Park Rd. ☎ 360/452–8888 ⊕ www. cestsibon-frenchcuisine.com ⌲ Reservations essential ⊗ Closed Mon. No lunch.

$$
SEAFOOD

✕ **Dupuis Restaurant.** Flower-filled gardens surround this kitschy little log cabin, painted a cheery yellow and blue and trimmed with bright flower boxes. One of the dining rooms was a tavern in the 1920s and still evokes the feeling of a bygone era. Close-set tables in the cozy, country-style, wood-panelled main dining room are lit by small chandeliers. Antiques and knickknacks abound. Seafood reigns the menu; look for grilled local fish, like king salmon, as well as steamed crabs, crab cakes, panfried oysters, oyster stew, seafood gnocchi, and prawns with pesto and pasta. This is a culinary highlight of a trip to Port Angeles. $ *Average main: $18* ✉ 256861 U.S. 101 ☎ 360/457–8033 ⊗ Closed Mon. No lunch.

13

WHERE TO STAY

$$$
B&B/INN
Fodor'sChoice
★

☉ **Colette's Bed & Breakfast.** A contemporary oceanfront mansion set on a 10-acre sanctuary of gorgeous gardens offers more space, service, and luxury than any other property in the area, with water-view suites that have fireplaces, patios, and two-person spa tubs. **Pros:** water views extend to Victoria, BC; discreet personal service. **Cons:** does not cater to families. ⑤ *Rooms from: $205* ✉ *339 Finn Hall Rd., 10 miles east of town* ☎ *360/457–9197, 888/457–9777* ⊕ *www.colettes.com* ⤵ *5 suites* ❢⊙❢ *Breakfast.*

$$$
B&B/INN

☉ **Domaine Madeleine.** Luxurious accommodations perched on 5 acres on a bluff above the Strait of Juan de Fuca have either impressionist or Asian accents, fireplaces, and water and mountain views. **Pros:** the mosaic of colorful waterfront blossoms; abundant wildlife; well-appointed rooms; beautifully presented gourmet breakfast. **Cons:** no children under 12. ⑤ *Rooms from: $205* ✉ *146 Wildflower La., 8 miles east of town* ☎ *360/457–4174, 888/811–8376* ⊕ *www.domainemadeleine.com* ⤵ *4 rooms, 1 cottage* ❢⊙❢ *Breakfast.*

$$
B&B/INN

☉ **Five Sea Suns Bed & Breakfast.** Just steps from town, within gardens that have won awards, this cozy 1926 inn overlooks the mountains and the bay and offers elegant rooms, each with the theme of a time of year: the four seasons plus an Indian summer. **Pros:** lovely garden setting close to town; home-baked chocolate-chip cookies; top-notch hospitality. **Cons:** on a busy street; no children under 12; strict 14-day cancellation policy. ⑤ *Rooms from: $160* ✉ *1006 S. Lincoln St.* ☎ *360/452–8248, 800/708–0777* ⊕ *www.seasuns.com* ⤵ *5 rooms* ❢⊙❢ *Breakfast.*

$$
B&B/INN
Fodor'sChoice
★

☉ **Sea Cliff Gardens Bed & Breakfast.** A gingerbread-style porch fronts this antiques-furnished waterfront Victorian home on 2 acres of landscaped grounds, and all the exquisitely appointed guest rooms have fireplaces and panoramic water views through large picture windows. **Pros:** sumptuous accommodations with stunning views; gorgeous flower gardens have been featured in a national commercial; very romantic setting. **Cons:** a bit off the beaten path. ⑤ *Rooms from: $185* ✉ *397 Monterra Dr.* ☎ *360/452–2322, 800/880–1332* ⊕ *www.seacliffgardens.com* ⤵ *5 suites* ❢⊙❢ *Breakfast.*

SPORTS AND THE OUTDOORS

BEACHES

FAMILY
Ediz Hook. At the western end of Port Angeles, this long natural sand spit protects the harbor from big waves and storms. The Hook is a fine place to take a walk along the water and watch shore- and seabirds, and to spot the occasional seal, orca, or gray whale. It's also a popular dive spot. From downtown, take Front Street west and follow it as it meanders past the shuttered lumber mill. **Amenities:** toilets. **Best for:** walking; sunset. ✉ *Ediz Hook Rd., off west end of Marine Dr..*

KAYAKING

Olympic Raft & Kayak. White-water and scenic float trips are conducted on the Hoh and Elwha Rivers, and the Sound Dive Center has scuba certification classes, dive equipment, and tours around the region, including Lake Crescent. ✉ *123 Lake Aldwell Rd.* ☎ *360/452–1443* ⊕ *www.raftandkayak.com.*

NORTHWESTERN OLYMPIC PENINSULA

It takes travelers more time to reach the remote, rugged, and rain-soaked west end of the Olympic Peninsula, but unspoiled beaches, old-growth forests, and mountain lakes make for a spectacular geographic pilgrimage. This is where the forest meets the ocean and the wilderness runs into the water. It's lush, green, and wet, a land of fallen trees, ferns, moss-covered rocks, sea stacks, saltwater spray, and smoked salmon. Surfers seek out the coastline near Neah Bay, immortalized in Robert Sullivan's 2000 book *A Whale Hunt*, documenting the Makah Nation's quest to reclaim its cultural heritage. Artifacts from an ancient fishing village at the tribe's museum and cultural center offer an opportunity to learn about the people whose ancestors lived for thousands of years off the land and sea. Nearby, in the old logging town of Forks, fans can celebrate the setting of the fictional *Twilight* series, and Cape Flattery offers views from the most northwesterly edge of the contiguous United States.

13

NEAH BAY

15 miles northwest of Sekiu.

One of the oldest villages in Washington, Neah (pronounced *nee*-ah) Bay is surrounded by the Makah Reservation at the northwestern tip of the Olympic Peninsula. It's a quiet, seldom-visited seaside settlement of one-story homes, espresso stands, and bait shops stretched along about a mile of gravelly coastal road, which parallels the glistening, boat-filled bay. Stroll along the docks to watch boot-clad fishermen and shaggy canines motoring out on warped and barnacled vessels, and peer into the oil-stained water for views of anemones, shellfish, and sea lions. The rocky bulkhead rises behind the marina; look beyond that to view sunsets and Cape Flattery, the northwesternmost point in the contiguous United States.

Explorer James Cook named the cape in 1778 when his ship missed the fog-smothered Strait of Juan de Fuca and landed here instead. In 1792 Spanish mariners established a short-lived fort, the first European settlement in what is now Washington State. The local Makah tribe is more closely related to the Nootka of Vancouver Island, just across the water, than to any Washington tribe. Like their ancestors, they embark on whale hunts by canoe, a right guaranteed by treaty, although fleets of kayaks skimming through the calm bay are all you're likely to see during your visit.

GETTING HERE AND AROUND

Neah Bay is quite remote, accessed only by Highway 112 west of Sekiu (about a half-hour drive).

EXPLORING

FAMILY
Fodor's Choice
★

Makah Cultural and Research Center. Thousands of Makah art pieces and artifacts, many eons old, fill a space done in low lights and rich timbers and divided into an easy route of intriguing exhibits. The centerpiece is a full-size cedar longhouse, complete with hand-woven baskets, fur skins, cattail wool, grass mats on the bed planks, and a background of

Makah Indian art

tribal music. Another section houses full-size whaling and seal-hunting canoes and weapons. Other areas show games, clothing, crafts, and relics from the ancient Ozette Village mudslide. The small shop stocks a collection of locally made art pieces, books, and crafts; plan to spend some time looking around. This is as impresssive a museum as you'd find in any major city, and should be a stop on any itinerary in the region. ⌧ *1880 Bayview Ave.* ☎ *360/645–2711* ⊕ *www.makah.com* ⌧ *$5* ⏱ *Daily 10–5 (unless harsh weather forces closure).*

Makah National Fish Hatchery. Here visitors can view chinook salmon as they make their way over fish ladders to the hatchery's spawning area. Spawning months are October through December, and the salmon are released in late April. Smaller numbers of coho and chum salmon as well as steelhead trout also populate the hatchery. Call to find out the best times to see hatchery activity. From Neah Bay, follow signs south for 7 miles. ⌧ *897 Hatchery Rd.* ☎ *360/645–2521* ⊕ *www.fws.gov/ makahnfh* ⌧ *Free* ⏱ *Daily 7:30–4.*

WHERE TO STAY

$ 🏨 **Inn at Neah Bay.** This three-story, sky-gray chalet above the Strait of
B&B/INN   Juan de Fuca is done in Pacific Northwest style, trimmed with timber and a fringe of colorful flowers, and offers a range of basic but comfortable accommodations, each with different décor. **Pros:** there's a fire pit and barbecue grill for guests; owners also run a charter fishing and marine tour service; well-suited for anglers, budget travelers and families. **Cons:** children 12 and up. ⑤ *Rooms from: $110* ⌧ *1562 Hwy. 112, Sekiu* ☎ *360/374–2225* ⊕ *www.theinnatneahbay.com* ⇥ *2 rooms, 2 suites* ⏍ *Breakfast.*

FORKS

49 miles south of Neah Bay.

The former logging town of Forks is named for two nearby river junctions: the Bogachiel and Calawah Rivers merge west of town, and a few miles farther they are joined by the Soleduck to form the Quileute River, which empties into the Pacific at the Native American village of La Push. Forks is a small, quiet gateway town for Olympic National Park's Hoh River valley unit. The surrounding countryside is exceptionally green, with an annual precipitation of more than 100 inches. As the setting for the popular *Twilight* movie series, the town has become a favorite destination for fans in recent years, and Bella's Birthday Weekend, in October, has plenty of *Twilight*-related events.

13

GETTING HERE AND AROUND

From the Seattle area, Forks is about 3½ hours via the Seattle–Bainbridge Island and Edmonds–Kingston ferries and U.S. 101 west; it's about an hour past Port Angeles. Coming from the south, U.S. 101 north from Aberdeen to Forks takes about two hours. Clallam Transit runs from Forks to Port Angeles and other north peninsula towns. West Jefferson Transit provides service between Forks and Lake Quinault, including a stop at Kalaloch.

GUIDED TOURS

Peak 6 Tours and Gift Shop. Here you'll find gear and information for hiking, biking, camping, climbing, and sightseeing on the Olympic Peninsula. Guided hikes cost about $50 per day. ⊠ *4883 Upper Hoh Rd.* ☎ *360/374–5254.*

ESSENTIALS

Visitor Information Forks Chamber of Commerce ⊠ *1411 S. Forks Ave.* ☎ *360/374–2531, 800/443–6757* ⊕ *www.forkswa.com.*

EXPLORING

Big Cedar. Thought to be the world's largest, this monumental cedar tree stands 178 feet tall and is 19 feet 5 inches in diameter. Area loggers left it standing when they realized just how enormous it really was. The tree is off Nolan Creek Road. From U.S. 101, turn right onto Highway N1000 for 1.3 miles, then turn right onto N1100 for 2.4 miles. Turn right again onto N1112 for 0.4 miles, and then turn right once more for 0.1 miles. ⊠ *Forks.*

WHERE TO EAT

$ ✕ **Forks Coffee Shop.** This modest restaurant on the highway in downtown Forks serves home-style, classic American fare. From 5 am to 8 pm you can dig into giant pancakes and Sol Duc scrambles (eggs, sausage, hash browns, and veggies tumbled together). At lunch there's a choice of soups, salads, and hot and cold sandwiches, which the waitstaff will bag for pickup if you're on the run. Dinner specials come with free trips to the salad bar and include entrées like baby back ribs and grilled Hood Canal oysters. Top off the meal with a home-baked treat, like a slice of flaky-crust pie made with locally grown marionberries, blueberries, strawberries, cherries, or apples. Don't come here looking for espresso,

DINER

though; this is a drip-coffee kind of place. $ *Average main: $8* ✉ *241 Forks Ave.* ☎ *360/374–6769.*

$ ✕ **Plaza Jalisco.** On the outside you can tell it was once a gas station, but
MEXICAN   head past the painted Mexican bandit statue and suddenly you're in a colorful world south of the border. Desert colors, ceramic bells, hand-painted masks, and hand-knit blankets decorate the small, airy dining room, where locals gather to down heaping plates of rice, beans, and meat-filled burritos. Frothy and potent margaritas are the big draw on weekends. This is a prime budget stop, where the home-cooked flavors and low prices keep both your stomach and your wallet full. $ *Average main: $9* ✉ *90 N. Forks Ave.* ☎ *360/374–3108.*

WHERE TO STAY

$ ⊡ **Manitou Lodge.** If seclusion, quiet, and relaxation are what you seek,
B&B/INN   visit this cedar lodge in the rain forest, where five lodge rooms of varying sizes and two suites in the adjacent cottage have cedar paneling, handmade quilts, driftwood headboards, and oak furnishings; the large Sacagawea room even has a fireplace. **Pros:** guests are welcomed with cookies in their rooms; coffee and snacks are served in the great room; some lodgings are family-friendly. **Cons:** no TV, phones, or cell-phone service, though there is Wi-Fi. $ *Rooms from: $139* ✉ *813 Kilmer Rd.* ☎ *360/374–6295* 🖶 *360/374–7495* ⊕ *www.manitoulodge.com* ⇥ *5 rooms, 2 cottage suites, 2 cabins, 2 tent sites* �‖ *Breakfast.*

WASHINGTON COAST

The communities along this stretch of Pacific coastline range from quiet and secluded getaways to busy beach towns, especially during the summer months when highways in and out of towns can become congested with vacationers. Pacific Beach and Moclips to the north are a little more remote and less crowded than their southern counterparts. Ocean Shores is one of the busier beaches, with horseback riders, kite flyers, go-carts, dune buggies, and beachcombers all competing for space. Although the sun shines here in summer, it gets gusty on the beach at any time of year, so don't forget your windbreaker and polar fleece.

COPALIS BEACH

74 miles west of Olympia.

A Native American village for several thousand years, this small coastal town at the mouth of the Copalis (pronounced coh-*pah*-liss) River was settled by European-Americans in the 1890s. The beach here is known locally for its innumerable razor clams, which can be gathered by the thousands each summer, and for its watchtowers, built between 1870 and 1903 to spot and stalk sea otters—the animals are now protected by Washington state law. The first oil well in the state was dug here in 1901, but it proved to be unproductive. However, some geologists still claim that the continental shelf off the Olympic Peninsula holds major oil reserves.

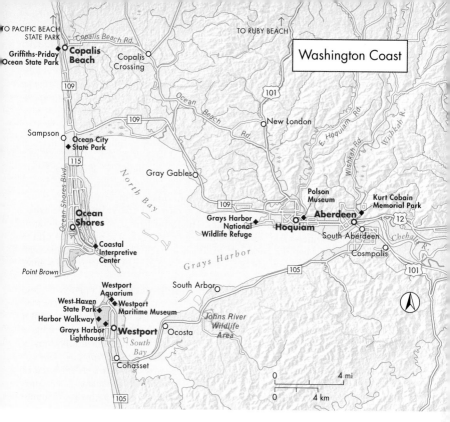

GETTING HERE AND AROUND

Copalis Beach is about 30 miles from Aberdeen, via Highway 109. Bus service is provided by Grays Harbor Transit.

Contact Grays Harbor Transit ☎ 360/532–2770, 800/562–9730 ⊕ www. ghtransit.com.

EXPLORING

Griffiths-Priday Ocean State Park. You can hike or ride horses in this 364-acre marine park stretching more than a mile along both the Pacific Ocean and the Copalis River. A boardwalk crosses low dunes to the broad, flat beach. The Copalis Spit section of the park is a designated wildlife refuge for thousands of snowy plover and other bird life. There is no camping at this park, but there's plenty of picnicking, bird-watching, mountain biking, fishing, clamming, kite-flying, and beach-combing. ⊠ 3119 Hwy. 109 ☎ 360/902–8844 ⊕ www.parks.wa.gov/parks 🔁 Day pass $10 per vehicle; annual Discovery Pass $30 (valid at all state parks) ⊙ Daily dawn–dusk.

Pacific Beach State Park. Between Copalis Beach and the town of Moclips, this is a lovely spot for walking, surf-perch fishing, and razor-clam digging. There's also excellent fishing for sea-run cutthroat trout in the Moclips River—but be careful not to trespass onto Native American land, as the Quinault Reservation starts north of the river. The 10-acre park has developed tent and RV sites, as well as a few primitive beach-front campsites. **Amenities:** parking (free); toilets. **Best for:** solitude; sunset; walking. ✉ *49 2nd St., Hwy. 109 S, 5 miles north of Copalis Beach* ☎ *360/276–4297* ⊕ *www.parks.wa.gov* 🔗 *Day pass $10 per vehicle; annual Discovery Pass $30 (valid at all state parks); camping $12–$37* ⊙ *Daily dawn–dusk.*

WHERE TO EAT AND STAY

$

PACIFIC

NORTHWEST

× **Mill 109 Restaurant and Pub.** A perch atop a hillside in the master-planned beach community of Seabrook is the setting for Pacific Northwest entrées and contemporary American pub fare. Look for ample burgers and hot sandwiches, fish tacos, fish-and-chips, and thick and creamy clam chowder for lunch and dinner. For breakfast, there are thick slices of crème brûlée French toast and crab cakes eggs Benedict. Water is served in Mason jars. The feel is light, comfortable, modern, and somewhat maritime, with large vintage photos of the area on the walls. There's a good selection of wine, craft beer, and cocktails, too. ⑤ *Average main: $14* ✉ *5 W. Myrtle La., Pacific Beach* ☎ *360/276-4884* ⊕ *www.mill109.com.*

$

RESORT

🏨 **Sandpiper Beach Resort.** These no-frills studios and one-, two-, and three-bedroom suites, all but one with a fireplace, are on a secluded beach 3 miles south of Moclips, and are great for getting away from it all and immersing yourself in nature. **Pros:** spacious lodgings; right on the beach; affordable. **Cons:** not for technology-dependent folks; no on-site restaurant; some walls are paper-thin. ⑤ *Rooms from: $79* ✉ *4159 Hwy. 109, Pacific Beach* ☎ *360/276–4580, 800/567-4737* ⊕ *www.sandpiper-resort.com* 🔁 *24 suites, 4 cabins* ⦿ *No meals.*

$$$$

RENTAL

FAMILY

Fodor'sChoice

★

🏨 **Seabrook Cottage Rentals.** Crushed seashells line pathways through-out this charming collection of some 250 newer Cape Cod–style homes, more than half of which are available to rent and include the Beach Camp, a collection of modern and cozy cabins surrounding a shared fire pit. **Pros:** recreational activities and beach within walking distance; homes are new with many amenities; some are pet-friendly. **Cons:** there is ongoing construction; cleaning fee added to all stays; limited nearby services outside of village. ⑤ *Rooms from: $269* ✉ *4275 State Rte. 109, Pacific Beach* ☎ *360/276–0265, 877/779–9990* ⊕ *www.seabrookcottagerentals.com* 🔁 *138 cottages* ⦿ *No meals.*

SPORTS AND THE OUTDOORS

Ruby Beach. Named for the rosy fragments of garnet that color its sands, this is one of the peninsula's most beautiful stretches of coastline. A short trail leads to the wave-beaten sands, where sea stacks, caves, rock cairns, tidal pools, and bony driftwood make it a favorite place for beachcombers, artists, and photographers. It's 28 miles south of Forks, off U.S. 101. **Amenities:** toilets. **Best for:** sunset; walking. ✉ *Kalaloch.*

OCEAN SHORES

10 miles south of Copalis Beach.

Ocean Shores, a long stretch of resorts, restaurants, shops, and attractions, sits on the northern spit that encloses Grays Harbor. The whole area was planned by housing developers in the 1960s, and with its broad, flat, white beach, shallow surf, and sunset panoramas, it's been a favorite seaside getaway since. Come summer, dune buggies and go-carts buzz up and down the sand road, weaving around clusters of horses trotting tourists over the dunes. Colorful kites flap overhead, dogs romp in the waves, and tide pools are filled with huge orange Dungeness crabs, live sand dollars, and delicate snails, to the delight of small children. It's no tropical haven, however, as summer can bring chilly breezes, and the water never warms up much for swimming—jackets are mandatory even in July. A fog of sea mist often blows in during the late afternoon, and in winter massive thunderstorms billow onto land directly before the line of coastal hotels. An indoor pool and in-room fireplace are coveted amenities year-round in this cool climate, and well worth the added expense.

GETTING HERE AND AROUND

Ocean Shores is the closest developed ocean-beach town to Seattle; it's about a 2½-hour drive via Interstate 5 south to Olympia then west via U.S. 101 and north via Highway 109. The traffic through Aberdeen and Hoquiam can slow to a crawl on busy summer weekends; try especially to avoid heading back east on Sunday or holiday afternoons. Grays Harbor Transit serves the community locally.

Contact Grays Harbor Transit ☎ 360/532–2770, 800/562–9730 ⊕ www. ghtransit.com.

ESSENTIALS

Visitor Information Ocean Shores/North Beach Chamber of Commerce ✉ 873 Point Brown Ave. NW, Suite 1, Oak Harbor ☎ 360/289–2451 ⊕ www. oceanshores.org.

EXPLORING

Coastal Interpretive Center. A great stormy-day educational spot for families, the center highlights the seaside environment, local history, and Native American traditions. Displays include tsunami debris, artifacts from the founding of the city, and Native American basketry. Reproduction seabirds, whale bones, and a vast shell collection let you examine the shoreline wildlife up close. ✉ 1033 Catala Ave. SE ☎ 360/289–4617 ⊕ interpretivecenter.org 🍴 Free ☺ Apr.–Sept., daily 11–4; Oct.–Mar., weekends 11–4.

WHERE TO EAT

$ ✗ **Bennett's Fish Shack.** This is unfussy, family-friendly, casual coastal din-
SEAFOOD ing. Look for crowd-pleasers like the crab cakes, clam chowder, hand-breaded halibut, and fish tacos. A few different burgers are also on the menu at this informal and relaxed eatery. $ Average main: $15 ✉ 105 W. Chance a la Mer ☎ 360/289–2847 ⊕ www.bennettsdining.com.

$$ ✗ **Galway Bay Irish Restaurant, Pub and Gifts.** Steak and traditional Irish
IRISH fare are served at this dimly lit eatery, anchored by a corner fireplace and decorated with old church pews. The fare is decidedly Irish: beef in Guinness stew, soda bread, corned beef, steak in a Bailey's reduction, and a Blarney burger with Swiss cheese on a warm bun. Jameson and Bushmills line the top shelf of the back bar, along with a variety of other Irish whiskeys. Friendly barkeeps and Irish music add to the

atmosphere, and the place hosts one of the largest Irish music festivals around in late October, with more than 30 bands on 10 stages at three venues. To get to the back, covered patio—where there are darts and Guinness paraphernalia—walk through an oversized can of Guinness that doubles as a door. In the adjacent gift shop, you can buy a Guinness T-shirt, sweatshirt, ball cap, or other Celtic imports. ⑤ *Average main: $20 ⊠ 880 Pt. Brown Ave. NE ☎ 360/289–2300 ⊕ www. galwaybayirishpub.com.*

$$
SEAFOOD

✕ **Mike's Steak and Seafood Restaurant.** At this must-stop in Ocean Shores, wander through the small, roadside seafood stand to see what's cooking before you sit down in the adjacent restaurant. Everything served is fresh-caught, and salmon is smoked on the premises. Italian specialties like puttanesca round out the menu, which includes burgers and fish-and-chips for lunch. Dinner specialties include whole Dungeness crab that diners pick out from the live-crab tank, crab-stuffed prawns, pepper pear prawns, and smoked salmon linguini. One of the best ways to sample it all is in the tomato-based cioppino. ⑤ *Average main: $18 ⊠ 830 Point Brown Ave. NE ☎ 360/289–0532 ⊕ www. oceanshoresseafood.com.*

$
AMERICAN

✕ **Ocean Beach Roasters.** Espresso, beer, and a variety of sweet baked goods—including memorable cinnamon rolls and lemon bars—are available; for lunch, there are soups, quiches, and hearty sandwiches, like capicola with fresh mozzarella, spinach, and pesto, and turkey croissants with provolone, spinach, and Roma tomatoes. The shop roasts its own coffee beans and also offers wine tastings. There's live music on Saturday nights and open mike on Thursday. ⑤ *Average main: $6 ⊠ 841 Pt. Brown Ave. ☎ 360/289–3100 ⊕ oceanbeachroasters.com ⊗ No dinner.*

WHERE TO STAY

$$$
RESORT

🛏 **Quinault Beach Resort & Casino.** A half mile of dunes and wild beach grasses surrounds this enormous resort, where shades of green, gray, and gold appear throughout the rooms, all with 10-foot ceilings, gas fireplaces, and twin bathroom sinks. **Pros:** grand rooms; upscale setting; on-site spa and dining. **Cons:** gambling crowds can be rowdy. ⑤ *Rooms from: $201 ⊠ 78 Hwy. 115 ☎ 360/289–5001, 888/461–2214 ⊕ www. quinaultbeachresort.com ➷ 150 rooms, 9 suites ⊙ No meals.*

$$
HOTEL

🛏 **Shilo Inn.** Framed by a Pacific Ocean seascape to the west and a dune-covered state park to the south, this all-suites hotel houses guests in large, modern units that include a living area, fireplace, and a balcony overlooking the beach. **Pros:** great location; attractive lobby; lots of amenities. **Cons:** lots of tourists, families, and groups make hallways noisy late and early; rates spike during summer and special events. ⑤ *Rooms from: $189 ⊠ 707 Ocean Shores Blvd. ☎ 360/289–4600, 800/222–2244 ⊕ www.shiloinns.com ➷ 113 suites ⊙ No meals.*

SPORTS AND THE OUTDOORS

Ocean Shores Beaches. Six miles of wide, public, sandy beaches line a peninsula trimmed by the Pacific Ocean on the west and Grays Harbor on the east. With five access roads, it's possible to find secluded sections along the state's most visited beach destination. Highest tides occur in July and December, the latter when winter-storm watching is at its peak. Motor vehicles are allowed on **City Beach**, a popular place for clam-digging and kite-flying. **Ocean City State Park**, a 170-acre oceanfront park 2 miles north in Hoquiam, has year-round camping. Several hotels and resorts line the beach, including the **Quinault Beach Resort & Casino** and the **Shilo Inn** *(⇨ See Where to Stay)*; trails provide access. **Amenities:** food and drink; parking; showers; toilets. **Best for:** solitude; sunrise; sunset; walking. ⊠ *Sand Dune Ave. SW and off Duck Lake Dr. SE* ☎ *360/289–2451* ⊕ *oceanshores.org.*

13

HOQUIAM

21½ miles east of Ocean Shores.

Hoquiam (pronounced *hoh*-quee-ahm) is a historic lumber town near Aberdeen and the mouth of the Hoquiam River. Both river and town were named with the Chehalis word meaning "hungry for wood." The town was settled in the mid-19th century, around the same time as Aberdeen, and is now a major Grays Harbor port for cargo and fishing vessels. Its industries include canneries and manufacturers of wood products and machine tools.

GETTING HERE AND AROUND
Hoquiam is about an hour from Olympia via U.S. 101. Grays Harbor Transit serves Hoquiam and neighboring towns.

Contact Grays Harbor Transit ☎ *360/532–2770, 800/562–9730* ⊕ *www. ghtransit.com.*

ESSENTIALS
Visitor Information Grays Harbor Chamber of Commerce ⊠ *506 Duffy St., Aberdeen* ☎ *360/532–1924, 800/321–1924* ⊕ *www.graysharbor.org.*

EXPLORING
Grays Harbor National Wildlife Refuge. In fall and spring, this refuge, established in 1990, is a perfect place to observe the multitude of migrating shorebirds that visit the area. Keep your binoculars handy as you stroll along the 1,800-foot-long boardwalk, and make sure to stop at the visitor center's shop and bookstore. ⊠ *Airport Way, west of Hoquiam via Hwy. 109 and Paulson Rd.* ☎ *360/753–9467* ⊕ *www.fws.gov/ graysharbor* ⊡ *$3 per family* ☉ *Park: daily dawn–dusk; visitor center: Wed.–Sun. 9–4.*

The Polson Museum. A 26-room mansion built in 1924 is filled with artifacts and mementos relating to Grays Harbor's past. You can walk through the remodeled dining room, kitchen, and living room, where an exhibit traces the history of tall ships in the Pacific Northwest. Upstairs is the logging exhibit, with a replica Little Hoquiam Railroad; a period-costume room; and the Polson children's room and dollhouse. Outside you can wander the riverside grounds, which have exotic trees and a rose garden. ⊠ *1611 Riverside Ave.* ☎ *360/533–5862* ⊕ *www. polsonmuseum.org* ⊡ *$4 for adults, $10 for families* ☉ *Jan.–Aug., Wed.–Sat. 11–4, Sun. noon–4.*

WHERE TO EAT

$
PACIFIC
NORTHWEST

× **8th Street Ale House.** Comforting Pacific Northwest pub fare abounds at this long, narrow, and dimly lit eatery, where there's an ample selection of regional beer on tap and service is friendly. Look for pizza, seafood, and appetizers like deep-fried pickles, beer-battered mushrooms, crab cakes, or a pound of clams. Fish-and-chips, sandwiches and burgers, like the Naughty Nellie with American and Swiss cheese and crushed red pepper, round out the menu. There's a small beer garden in back, more seating out front, open mike night on Wedneaday, and trivia on Tuesdays. $ *Average main: $10* ⊠ *207 8th St.* ☎ *360/612–3455* ⊕ *www.8thstreetalehouse.com.*

ABERDEEN

4 miles east of Hoquiam.

The pretty town of Aberdeen, on Grays Harbor at the mouth of the Chehalis River, is known for its lovely harbor, spread glittering and gray along the west edge of town, where the bay bobs with sailboats and speed cruisers. Vast swaths of lumberyards are broken up by towering cranes, which transport the massive timbers onto immense metal barges. Forested hills serve as a backdrop to town, promising a picturesque entry into the Olympic Peninsula to the north. The town is also dotted with the classic, century-old mansions built by shipping and timber barons of the 20th century. Walking tours provide looks at some of the largest and most beautiful homes as well as local highlights from some of the town's best-known former residents, including Bill Boeing and Kurt Cobain.

GETTING HERE AND AROUND

Aberdeen is 4 miles east of Hoquiam and is served by Grays Harbor Transit.

Contact Grays Harbor Transit ☎ *360/532–2770, 800/562–9730* ⊕ *www. ghtransit.com.*

EXPLORING

Kurt Cobain Memorial Park. This pocket park, dedicated in 2011 along the muddy banks of the Wishkah River, pays homage to grunge legend and Nirvana front man Kurt Cobain, who grew up in a modest home two blocks from here. A guitar sculpture, lyrics to "Something in the Way," and other remembrances—like an empty instrument-stand sculpture identified as the musician's air guitar—mark the quiet spot that fans still seek out 20 years after the rock star's death. Some leave messages on the park bench and picnic table as well as under the bridge. ⊠ *E. 2nd St., under the Young Street Bridge.*

Lady Washington. Tall, billowing white sails in the harbor mark the presence of this replica of the 1750s coastal freighter from Boston that in 1792, under the command of famous explorer Captain Robert Gray, was the first American vessel to reach the northwest American coast. The replica was famously converted into the multimasted HMS *Interceptor* sloop for the 2002 Disney movie *Pirates of the Caribbean.* Its main base is the Grays Harbor Historic Seaport, but you'll find the vessel at local coastal towns throughout the region, where it's open for self-guided tours. Three-hour cruises include the hands-on "Adventure Sail" and a mock "Battle Sail" war between two vessels, and if you're at least 18 you can volunteer as a deckhand for multiday trips. The free **Seaport Learning Center**, a 214-acre site spread across the harbor and surrounding wetlands, runs tours on two historic longboats, and schedules monthly boatbuilding, rope-climbing, and marine-trade programs for families and students. ⊠ *712 Hagara St.* ☎ *360/532–8611, 800/200–5239* ⊕ *historicalseaport.org* ✍ *Tours by donation; sailings $40–$60.*

13

Morrison Riverfront Park Walk. For a general look at the lay of Aberdeen, follow this 1½-mile-long, paved walkway to the 40-foot-wide Compass Rose mosaic, inlaid at the confluence of the Wishkah and Chehalis rivers. ⊠ *1404 Sargent Blvd.*

WHERE TO EAT AND STAY

$ ✕ **Amoré Pizza and Pasta.** Pizza comes in three sizes—small, medium, and large—at this Italian eatery across the street from the historic D&R Theatre in the heart of downtown Aberdeen. Jumbo cheese or spinach ravioli, seafood risotto, amply stuffed calzones, and chicken or veal marsala or piccata round out the menu. Starters include a pound of steamed clams or tomato-basil soup, decorated with an artful pesto "A." For dessert, there's cannoli or tiramisu. ⑤ *Average main: $15* ⊠ *116 W. Heron St.* ☎ *360/533–2442.*

ITALIAN

$ ✕ **Billy's.** This bar and grill used to be the most popular saloon and brothel in town, and the restaurant has a collection of prints recalling those bawdy days. Even the establishment's name was taken from the saloon's notorious original owner, Billy Ghol. It's said his ghost haunts the premises. Standard fare includes generous burgers, soups and salads, but you can go exotic with grilled yak, and food is served until 11 pm. If you're really hungry and looking for a challenge, try the Billy's Belt Buster, a burger with four patties, cheese, and bacon. ⑤ *Average main: $11* ⊠ *322 E. Heron St.* ☎ *360/533–7144.*

AMERICAN

$$ ✕ **Rediviva.** *Rediviva* means renewed or revived, and much of the material—wood, metal, and glass—in the interior has been repurposed for an effect that is intimate, elegant, rustic yet refined, modern, and somewhat nautical. Edison-style lighting and blown glass floats mix with steel cable in what is perhaps the most cosmopolitan eatery around the region, where the focus is on fresh, seasonal and locally sourced ingredients from the Olympic Peninsula and the Washington Coast. Look for rum-spiced smoked duck, charbroiled black and bleu oysters, roasted cod, baked mussels and litteneck clams, and winter kale or roasted beet root salads. The menu mentions the locale of each creative and thoughtfully prepared entrée. A well-selected regional wine list and handcrafted cocktails are available as well. ⑤ *Average main: $22* ⊠ *118 E. Wishkah St.* ☎ *360/637–9259* ⊕ *redivivarestaurant.com* ☾ *Closed Sun.*

PACIFIC NORTHWEST

$ ⌂ **A Harbor View Inn.** You can see the harbor from every room in this 1905 Colonial Revival–style mansion with old-fashioned rooms, three with fireplaces, where handmade quilts cover king-size beds with antique headboards. **Pros:** special packages available; gourmet breakfast served in the sunroom overlooking the harbor; feeling of stepping back in

B&B/INN

time. **Cons:** not for those who don't enjoy an abundance of Victoriana. ⑤ *Rooms from: $129* ✉ *111 W. 11th St.* ☎ *360/533–7996, 877/533–7996* ⊕ *www.aharborview.com* ⇆ *4 rooms, 1 suite* ⦿ *Breakfast.*

WESTPORT

21 miles southwest of Aberdeen.

Westport is a bay-front fishing village on the southern spit that helps protect the entrance to Grays Harbor from the fury of the Pacific Ocean. Numerous charter companies based here offer salmon, lingcod, rockfish, and albacore fishing trips, as well as whale-watching tours. If you're not taking a cruise, you can stand on Westport's beach to look for gray whales migrating southward in November and December, toward their breeding grounds in Baja California, and northward in April and May, toward their feeding grounds in the Bering Sea. The serene beach is perfect for walking, surfing, or kite flying—although it's too dangerous for swimming and too cold for sunbathing. In winter it's one of the best spots on the coast to watch oncoming storms.

GETTING HERE AND AROUND

Westport is about a half-hour southwest of Aberdeen via Highway 105. Grays Harbor Transit serves the town.

Contact Grays Harbor Transit ☎ *360/532–2770, 800/562–9730* ⊕ *www.ghtransit.com.*

ESSENTIALS

Visitor Information Westport-Grayland Chamber of Commerce ✉ *2985 S. Montesano* ☎ *360/268–9422, 800/345–6223* ⊕ *www.westportgrayland-chamber.org.*

EXPLORING

Harbor Walkway. A 2-mile-long paved promenade winds along the sandy beach between Grays Harbor Lighthouse and West Haven State Park. ✉ *Ocean Ave.*

FAMILY **Westport Aquarium.** Exhibits of local marine life include a wolf eel, an octopus, and a dog shark. Touch tanks let you feel shells, starfish, anemones, and other sea creatures. You can even hand-feed two seals. ✉ *321 Harbor St.* ☎ *360/268–7070* ⊕ *westportaquarium.weebly.com* 🎟 *$5.50* ⊗ *Thurs.–Mon, 10–4, and by appointment.*

Westport Maritime Museum. A former Coast Guard station houses displays of historic photos, equipment, clothing, and other relics from the life-saving service and such local industries as fishing, logging, and cranberry farming. Among the exhibits is a collection of sea-mammal bones, and the 17-foot-tall Destruction Island Lens, a lighthouse beacon that was built in 1888 and weighs almost 6 tons. The octagonal **Grays Harbor Lighthouse**, a 107-foot structure built in 1898, is the tallest on the Washington coast. It stands near the museum and adjacent to Westport Light State Park, a day-use area with picnic tables and a beach. A tour of the lighthouse base is included with museum admission; it costs extra to climb to the top. ✉ *2201 Westhaven Dr.* ☎ *360/268–0078* ⊕ *www.westportmaritimemuseum.com* 🎟 *$5, includes lighthouse base (extra*

$5 to climb to the top) ☉ *Apr.–Sept., daily 10–4; Oct.–Mar., Fri.–Mon. noon–4; lighthouse closed Dec. and Jan.*

WHERE TO STAY

$ | 🏨 **Chateau Westport Motel.** These large rooms with contemporary furni-
HOTEL | ture (some with fireplaces and kitchenettes) are near the dunes and are
perfect for families who want a base near the beach. **Pros:** guests 21 and
older receive a voucher for free wine and cheese tasting at local winery.
Cons: rooms facing parking lot can be noisy; two-night minimum stay
some holiday weekends. ⑤ *Rooms from: $129* ✉ *710 Hancock Ave.*
☎ *360/268–9101, 800/255–9101* ⊕ *www.chateauwestport.com* ⤳ *104
rooms* ⑩ *Breakfast.*

13

NIGHTLIFE

Westport Brewing. This brewery makes 19 styles of craft beer, like the
Wetsuit Wheat, Plank Island Porter, Neptune's Imperial India Pale Ale,
and Cranberry Stout. If you're not sure where to start, try the ample
sampler in the casual tasting room, overlooking the beer-making operations. Or, opt for a picnic table with an umbrella in the lovely, well-
maintained garden. ✉ *118 W. Pacific Ave.* ☎ *503/702–7520* ⊕ *www.
westportbrewing.com* ☉ *Closed Tues. and Wed.*

SPORT AND THE OUTDOORS

Westport Beaches. At the southern mouth of Grays Harbor, **Westhaven
State Park** encompasses some 80 acres, including oceanfront and easy
pedestrian access to the beach. A 1 -mile concrete boardwalk crosses
the dunes, connecting Westhaven with the 212-acre **Westport Light
State Park**, adjacent to the historic Westport Lighthouse, built in 1898.
Farther south, the 172-acre **Twin Harbors State Park** provides another
stretch of Pacific coastline, popular for clamming, bird-watching, and
beachcombing. **Amenities:** parking (fee); showers; toilets. **Best for:** solitude; sunrise; sunset; walking. ✉ *St. Park Access Rd., off N. Montesano
St.* ☎ *360/268–9422* ⊕ *www.westportwa.com.*

LONG BEACH PENINSULA

Long Beach Peninsula stretches north from Cape Disappointment,
where the mighty Columbia River meets the stormy waters of the Pacific
Ocean. The peninsula has vast stretches of sand dunes, friendly beach
towns, dank cranberry bogs, and forests and meadows. To the east the
peninsula shelters Willapa Bay, once known as Shoalwater Bay because
it runs almost dry at low tide. It's a prime oyster habitat, producing
more of the creatures than any other estuary in the country.

Seas beneath the cliffs of Cape Disappointment are so turbulent that
several explorers, from James Cook to George Vancouver, mistook
the river's mouth for surf breaking on a wild shore. Many ships have
crossed (and many have come to grief) here since American sea captain Robert Gray sailed into the river on May 11, 1792, and named it
after his ship.

The 28-mile-long, uninterrupted stretch of sand that runs along the
peninsula's ocean shore is a great place to beachcomb. Don't even think

about swimming here, however. Though surfers in wet suits brave the waves in some areas, the water is too cold and the surf too rough for most people; hypothermia, shifting sands underfoot, and tremendous undertows account for several drownings each year.

The peninsula is a great place to hike, bike, and bird-watch. Lakes and marshes attract migrating birds, among them trumpeter swans. Long Island, in southeastern Willapa Bay, has a stand of old-growth red cedar trees, home to spotted owls, marbled murrelets (a western seabird), elks, and black bears. The island is accessible only by private boat (the boat ramp is on the bay's eastern shore).

GETTING HERE AND AROUND

The Long Beach peninsula is a little more than three hours from Seattle via Interstate 5 south to Olympia and then southwest via U.S. 101. From Portland, the drive takes about 2¼ hours via Interstate 5 north to Kelso then west via Highway 30. Pacific Transit buses serve the towns of Aberdeen, Bay Center, Chinook, Ilwaco, Long Beach, Nahcotta, Naselle, Ocean Park, Oysterville, South Bend, Surfside, Raymond, and Astoria, Oregon.

Contact Pacific Transit ☎ 360/642-9418 ⊕ www.pacifictransit.org.

ILWACO

170 miles southwest of Seattle, 109 miles northwest of Portland, OR.

Ilwaco (ill-*wah*-co) has been a fishing port for thousands of years, first as a Native American village and later as an American settlement. A 3-mile scenic loop winds past Cape Disappointment State Park (formerly Fort Canby State Park) to North Head Lighthouse and through the town. The colorful harbor is a great place for watching gulls and boats. Lewis and Clark camped here before moving their winter base to the Oregon coast at Fort Clatsop.

EXPLORING

FAMILY

Fodor's Choice ★

Cape Disappointment State Park. The cape, named in 1788 by Captain John Meares, an English fur trader who had been unable to find the Northwest Passage, with its treacherous sandbar—the so-called graveyard of the Pacific—has been the scourge of sailors since the 1800s. More than 250 ships have sunk after running aground on its ever-shifting sands. The 1,882-acre park (formerly Fort Canby) was an active military installation until 1957. Emplacements for the guns that once guarded the Columbia's mouth remain, some of them hidden by dense vegetation. Trails lead to stunning beaches and eagles can sometimes be seen on the cliffs. All of the park's 240 campsites have stoves and tables; some have water, sewer, and electric hookups. The park also has three lightkeepers' residences (houses) available for rent, as well as 14 yurts and three cabins. Exhibits at the park's **Lewis & Clark Interpretive Center** tell the tale of the duo's 8,000-mile round-trip expedition. Displays include artwork, journal entries, and other items that elaborate on the Corps of Discovery, which left Wood River, Illinois, in 1804, arrived at Cape Disappointment in 1805, and got back to Illinois in 1806. A ½-mile-long path from the center leads to the Cape Disappointment Lighthouse. Built in 1856, it's the oldest lighthouse on the West Coast that's still in use. ⊠ *Robert Gray Dr., 2½ miles southwest of Ilwaco off U.S. 101* ☎ *360/642–3029, 360/642–3078* ⊕ *www.parks. wa.gov* ⊠ *Day pass $10 per vehicle; annual Discovery Pass $30 (valid at all state parks); interpretive center $5; campsites $21–$28* ☉ *Daily dawn–dusk; interpretive center: daily 10–5.*

Columbia Pacific Heritage Museum. Dioramas and miniatures of Long Beach towns illustrate the history of southwestern Washington, and other displays cover Native Americans; the influx of traders, missionaries, and pioneers; and the contemporary workers of the fishing, agriculture, and forest industries. The original Ilwaco Freight Depot and a Pullman car from the Clamshell Railroad highlight rail history. ⊠ *115 S.E. Lake St., off U.S. 101* ☎ *360/642–3446* ⊕ *columbiapacificheritage-museum.org* ⊠ *$5; free on Thurs.* ☉ *Tues.–Sat. 10–4, Sun. noon–4.*

North Head Lighthouse. Built in 1898, this lighthouse was needed to help skippers sailing from the north, who couldn't see the Cape Disappointment Lighthouse. Stand high on a bluff above the pounding surf here, amid the windswept trees, for superb views of the Long Beach Peninsula. Lodging is available in the Lighthouse Keepers' Residence. ⊠ *North Head Lighthouse Rd., 2 miles from Cape Disappointment via*

13

Spur 100 Rd. ☎ *360/642–3029* ⊕ *www.parks.wa.gov/241/North-Head-Lighthouse* ⌨ *$2.50* ⊗ *Hrs vary; call for info.*

WHERE TO EAT AND STAY

$

DINER

✕ **Don's Portside Café and Pizzeria.** This local favorite, two blocks from the dock and boat launch, is known for its breakfasts (it opens at 4 am on weekends during fishing season) and its lunches of biscuits and gravy, soups, and pies—all of them homemade. Pizza is also on the menu, along with burgers and platter cakes, pancakes the size of a platter. ⑤ *Average main: $10* ⊠ *303 Main St. SE* ☎ *360/642–3477* ⊗ *No dinner.*

$

SEAFOOD

✕ **Imperial Schooner.** This is the place to go for fish-and-chips, fried shrimp, clam chowder, and grilled oysters. Overlooking the Port of Ilwaco marina, it serves six varieties of local Willapa Bay oysters, including chicken-fried, and Angels and Devils on Horseback (wrapped in bacon). Thursday is oyster day, with varying specials. ⑤ *Average main: $12* ⊠ *107 3rd St. SE* ☎ *360/642–0541.*

$$$

B&B/INN

⊡ **China Beach Retreat.** Between the port of Ilwaco and Cape Disappointment State Park, this secluded and comfortable B&B filled with antiques, original art, and handcrafted furniture is surrounded by serene wetlands and has wonderful views of Baker's Bay and the mouth of the Columbia River. **Pros:** secluded, back-to-nature setting; tideflat views will keep bird-watchers enthralled. **Cons:** breakfast served at sister property, Shelburne Inn, 5 miles away (but it's sumptuous and complimentary). ⑤ *Rooms from: $201* ⊠ *222 Robert Gray Dr.* ☎ *360/642–2442* ⊕ *www.chinabeachretreat.com* ⤲ *3 rooms, 1 cottage* ⑩ *Breakfast.*

SPORTS AND THE OUTDOORS

FISHING AND WHALE-WATCHING

Gray whales pass the Long Beach Peninsula twice a year: December to February, on their migration from the Arctic to their winter breeding grounds in Californian and Mexican waters, and March to May, on the return trip north. The view from the **North Head Lighthouse** is spectacular. ◾**TIP**➔ **The best time for sightings is in the morning, when the water is calm and overcast conditions reduce the glare.** Look on the horizon for a whale blow—the vapor, water, or condensation that spouts into the air when the whale exhales. If you spot one blow, you're likely to see others: whales often make several shorter, shallow dives before a longer dive that can last as long as 10 minutes.

The fish that swim in the waters near Ilwaco include salmon, rock cod, lingcod, flounder, perch, sea bass, and sturgeon. Charters generally cost from $100 to $200 per person.

Port of Ilwaco. Free tide charts are available from the port; check the website for information about fishing season and clam-digging dates. ⊠ *Ilwaco* ☎ *360/642–3143* ⊕ *www.portofilwaco.com.*

SEAVIEW

3 miles north of Ilwaco.

Seaview, an unincorporated town, has 750 year-round residents and several homes that date from the 1800s. The Shelburne Inn, built in

Cape Disappointment State Park

1896, is on the National Register of Historic Places. In 1892 U.S. Senator Henry Winslow Corbett built what's now the Sou'wester Lodge.

WHERE TO EAT AND STAY

$$
× **42nd Street Cafe and Bistro.** Inspired and creative yet unpretentious, this cozy, cheerful place serves gourmet comfort food at its best. Make a meal of small plates like fried green tomatoes, Dungeness crab beignets, or Willapa Bay clams steamed in Heffewiezen with lemon, garlic, chili flakes, and parsley. Dinner entrées—such as ravioli stuffed with butternut squash and gorgonzola, eight-hour pot roast, and lemon crab and shrimp fettuccine—come with house-baked bread, marionberry conserve, corn relish, and seasonal local vegetables. Razor clams and panfried oysters are available for breakfast, lunch, and dinner. Rich chocolate rum truffle cheesecake and a lighter mini mint chocolate sorbet are popular desserts. The excellent wine list has Pacific Northwest labels. $ *Average main: $20* ⊠ *4201 Pacific Hwy.* ☎ *360/642–2323* ⊕ *www.42ndstreetcafe.com.*

PACIFIC
NORTHWEST
Fodor's Choice
★

$
☐ **Shelburne Inn.** A white picket fence and lovely gardens surround a Victorian hotel that's been continuously operating since it was built in 1896 and offers distinctly decorated rooms, full of fresh flowers, antiques, fine-art prints, wrought-iron beds, vintage wardrobes, and a variety of colors and patterns. **Pros:** excellent breakfast; historic appeal; attentive service. **Cons:** no in-room phones or TVs; some rooms are rather small. $ *Rooms from: $139* ⊠ *4415 Pacific Way* ☎ *360/642–2442, 800/466–1896* ⊕ *www.theshelburneinn.com* ⊄ *14 rooms* ⊚| *Breakfast.*

B&B/INN
Fodor's Choice
★

$
☐ **Sou'wester Lodge.** For a bohemian and iconic Pacific Northwest experience, try these eclectic accommodations—beach cottages, a fleet of

RESORT

vintage travel trailers just behind the beach, three large bedrooms, or second-floor suites converted from space that once housed a ballroom—at the 1892 summer retreat of Henry Winslow Corbett, a Portland magnate and U.S. senator. **Pros:** one-of-a-kind lodgings; interesting history; good for bohemian and budget travelers; involved and attentive owner. **Cons:** not for luxury seekers; some rooms don't have private baths. $ *Rooms from: $73* ⊠ *3728 J Pl.* ☎ *360/642–2542* ⊕ *www.souwesterlodge.com* ⇨ *3 rooms without bath, 4 suites, 4 cottages, 12 trailers.*

LONG BEACH

½ mile north of Seaview.

Long Beach bears a striking resemblance to Brooklyn's Coney Island in the 1950s. Along its main drag, which stretches southwest from 10th Street to Bolstadt Street, you'll find everything from cotton candy and hot dogs to go-carts and bumper cars.

EXPLORING

Cranberry Museum. Here, visitors can learn about more than a century of cranberry cultivation in this area, take a self-guided walking tour through the bogs, try some cranberry tea, and buy cranberry products to take home. ⊠ *2907 Pioneer Rd.* ☎ *360/642–5553* ⊕ *www.cranberrymuseum.com* ☑ *Free* ⊗ *Apr.–mid-Dec., daily 10–5.*

FAMILY **Discovery Trail.** Created to memorialize Lewis and Clark's explorations here in 1805–06, the 8-mile Discovery Trail traces the explorers' moccasin steps from Ilwaco to north Long Beach, overlooking sandy dunes and beachfront. Access the trail from the beach parking lots on Sid Snyder Drive or Bolstad Street in Long Beach. Parking is also available at the Beard's Hollow lot in Cape Disappointment State Park. ⊠ *Long Beach* ☎ *800/451–2542* 🖥 *360/642–3900* ⊕ *www.funbeach.com.*

FAMILY **Long Beach Boardwalk.** The ½-mile-long wooden boardwalk runs through the dunes parallel to the beach, and is a great place for strolling, bird-watching, or just sitting and listening to the wind and the roar of the surf. It's ¼ mile west of downtown, between Bolstad Avenue and Sid Snyder Drive. ⊠ *Long Beach* ⊕ *funbeach.com.*

FAMILY **Marsh's Free Museum.** If you've got kids in your group, or simply an appreciation of oddities, be sure to visit this quirky museum that's best known for "Jake the Alligator Man." Marsh's is filled with plenty of other curiousities, like real shrunken heads, skeletons, and an eight-legged lamb. ⊠ *400 S. Pacific Ave.* ☎ *360/642–2188* ⊕ *www.marshsfreemuseum.com* ☑ *Free* ⊗ *Daily 9–6, later in summer.*

World Kite Museum and Hall of Fame. Each August Long Beach hosts the Washington State International Kite Festival; the community is also home to the Northwest Stunt Kite Championships, a competition held each June. At the only U.S. museum focused solely on kites and kiting, you can view an array of kites and learn about kite making and history. ⊠ *303 Sid Snyder Dr. SW* ☎ *360/642–4020* ⊕ *www.worldkitemuseum.com* ☑ *$5* ⊗ *May–Sept., daily 11–5; Oct.–Apr., Fri.–Tues. 11–5.*

WHERE TO EAT AND STAY

$$
SEAFOOD
✕ **Dooger's Seafood and Grill.** Locals will urge you to eat here—listen to them. The place serves seafood from 11 am to 9 pm in winter, and until 10 on summer weekends. The ample portions come with potatoes, shrimp-topped salad, and garlic toast. Clam chowder and fish-and-chips are popular lunch choices. Dinner entrées, served all day, include crab legs, razor clams, lobster tail, halibut, and salmon: panfried, poached, grilled, or Cajun-style. Ⓢ *Average main: $18* ✉ *900 Pacific Hwy. S.* ☎ *360/642–4224* ⊕ *doogersseafood.com.*

$
RENTAL
FAMILY
Anchorage Cottages. Along a western ridge of the Long Beach Peninsula, these cozy cottages with fireplaces and unobstructed views of the dunes have been accommodating beach getaways since the early 1950s. **Pros:** pretty gardens and courtyard; affordable; near the beach. **Cons:** not very private; town is a mile away. Ⓢ *Rooms from: $90* ✉ *2209 Boulevard Ave. N* ☎ *800/646–2351, 360/642–2351* ⊕ *www. theanchoragecottages.com* ⌁ *10 cottages* ⦿*No meals.*

$$
B&B/INN
Boreas Bed and Breakfast. Antiques and books fill this vintage 1920s beach house, where rooms have balconies or decks and ocean views, a jetted spa tub sits in an enclosed glass-and-cedar gazebo overlooking the ocean, and a private path leads through the dunes to the shore. **Pros:** great breakfast; helpful innkeepers; on the Lewis and Clark Trail. **Cons:** no bathtubs in three rooms; not for families. Ⓢ *Rooms from: $179* ✉ *607 N. Ocean Beach Blvd.* ☎ *360/642–8069, 888/642–8069* ⊕ *www.boreasinn.com* ⌁ *5 suites, 3 with shower only* ⦿*Breakfast.*

$
RESORT
FAMILY
Breakers Motel and Condominiums. Each of the contemporary one- and two-bedroom condominiums here has a private balcony or patio, and many also have fireplaces and exceptional views of the dunes and the surf. **Pros:** very family-friendly, with lots of activities. **Cons:** units are individually owned, so style and quality differ. Ⓢ *Rooms from: $129* ✉ *210 26th St. NW* ☎ *360/642–4414, 800/219–9833* ⊕ *www. breakerslongbeach.com* ⌁ *144 rooms* ⦿*No meals.*

$
HOTEL
Our Place at the Beach. This older, pet-friendly motel is both quiet and convenient, and styles vary from basic, budget accommodations with a queen bed to family suites that sleep eight and have kitchens. **Pros:** cheerful, accommodating staff; reasonably priced; five-minute walk from the beach, restaurants, and shops. **Cons:** thin walls and somewhat dated interiors in some units. Ⓢ *Rooms from: $104* ✉ *1309 S. Ocean Beach Blvd.* ☎ *360/642–3793, 800/538–5107* ⊕ *www. ourplacelongbeach.weebly.com* ⌁ *26 rooms* ⦿*Breakfast.*

SPORTS AND THE OUTDOORS

BEACHES

Long Beach. The Long Beach Peninsula consists of 28 continuous miles of broad sandy beach, which fills with kite-flyers, sand-castle builders, sunbathers, bicyclists, horseback riders, and drivers during summer months. Watch out for horses, cars, and other motor vehicles—some sections are open for driving year round, while other parts don't allow it in summer; the speed limit on the sand is 25 mph. Bonfires are also allowed. Bring a windbreaker—strong gusts are common near the water, which remains consistently frigid throughout the year. **Amenties:**

toilets. **Best for:** solitude; sunrise; sunset; walking. ✉ *West off State Rte. 103* ☎ *360/642–2400* ⊕ *funbeach.com.*

GOLF

Peninsula Golf Course. There are two 9-hole, par-33 courses here, on Long Beach's northern edge. Greens fees are $18 for 9 holes and $25 for 18 holes. After 2 pm, it's all-you-can-play for $20. ✉ *9604 Pacific Hwy.* ☎ *360/642–2828* ⊕ *peninsulagolfcourse.com.*

HORSEBACK RIDING

Back Country Wilderness Outfitters. One- and two-hour horseback rides are offered here for $25 per hour. The Ribeye Ride, which lasts nearly four hours, comes with a steak dinner on the beach and costs $85. ✉ *409 Sid Snyder Dr.* ☎ *360/642–2576.*

NORTH CASCADES NATIONAL PARK

WELCOME TO NORTH CASCADES NATIONAL PARK

TOP REASONS TO GO

★ **Pure wilderness:** Nearly 400 miles of mountain and meadow trails immerse hikers in pristine natural panoramas, with sure sightings of bald eagles, deer, elk, and other wildlife.

★ **Majestic glaciers:** The North Cascades are home to several hundred moving ice masses, more than half the glaciers in the United States.

★ **Splendid flora:** A bright palette of flowers blankets the hillsides in midsummer, while October's colors paint the landscape in vibrant autumn hues.

★ **Thrilling boat rides:** Lake Chelan, Lake Ross, and the Stehekin River are the starting points for kayaking, white-water rafting, and ferry trips.

★ **19th-century history:** Delve into the state's farming, lumber, and logging pasts in clapboard towns and homesteads around the park.

1 North Unit. The park's creek-cut northern wilderness, centered on snowy Mt. Challenger, stretches north from Highway 20 over the Picket Range toward the Canadian border. It's an endless landscape of pine-topped peaks and ridges.

2 South Unit. Hike lake-filled mountain foothills in summer to take in vistas of blue skies and flower-filled meadows. Waterfalls and wildlife are abundant here.

3 Ross Lake National Recreation Area. Drawing a thick line from British Columbia all the way down to the North Cascades Scenic Highway, placid Ross Lake is edged with pretty bays that draw swimmers and boaters.

4 Lake Chelan National Recreation Area. Ferries steam between small waterfront towns along this pristine waterway, while kayakers and hikers follow quiet trails along its edges. This is one of the Northwest's most popular summer escapes, with nature-bound activities and rustic accommodations.

14

GETTING ORIENTED

The park rises upward from the massive Cascade Range seen northeast of Seattle, widening in a swath of snow-covered peaks all the way to the Canadian border. The broad Skagit River and many large creeks cut through the valleys; most end in the long arm of Lake Chelan in the south or in the snakelike expanse of Ross Lake at the park's northern edge. Even in summer, valleys can start the day shrouded in fog; it's best to drive the highway west to east in afternoon. A morning start is a good choice coming the other way. The most sensational scenery, however, is reached by hiking to one of the high park passes or mountain lookouts.

KEY

- 🚻 Ranger Station
- 🏕 Campground
- ⛱ Picnic Area
- 🍴 Restaurant
- 🏨 Lodge
- 🚶 Trailhead
- 🚻 Restrooms
- ⇗ Scenic Viewpoint
- ----- Walking/Hiking Trails

Updated by
Shelley Arenas

Countless snow-clad mountain spires dwarf narrow glacial valleys in this 505,000-acre expanse of the North Cascades, which encompasses three diverse natural areas. North Cascades National Park is the core of the region, flanked by Lake Chelan National Recreation Area to the south and Ross Lake National Recreation Area to the north; all are part of the Stephen T. Mather Wilderness Area. It's a spectacular gathering of snowy peaks, glacial meadows, plunging canyons, and cold, deep-blue lakes. Traditionally the lands of several Native American tribes, it's fitting that it's still completely wild—and wildlife-filled.

NORTH CASCADES PLANNER

WHEN TO GO

The spectacular, craggy peaks of the North Cascades—often likened to the Alps—are breathtaking anytime. Summer is peak season, especially along the alpine stretches of Highway 20; weekends and holidays can be crowded. Summer is short and glorious in the high country, extending from snowmelt (late May to July, depending on the elevation and the amount of snow) to early September.

The North Cascades Highway is a popular autumn drive in September and October, when the changing leaves put on a colorful show. The lowland forest areas, such as the complex around Newhalem, can be visited almost any time of year. These are wonderfully quiet in early spring or late autumn on mild, rainy days. Snow closes the North Cascades Highway from November through mid-April.

PLANNING YOUR TIME

NORTH CASCADES IN ONE DAY

The **North Cascades Highway,** with its breathtaking mountain and meadow scenery, is one of the most memorable drives in the United States. Although many travelers first head northeast from Seattle into the park and make this their grand finale, if you start from Winthrop, at the south end of the route, traffic is lighter and there's less morning fog. Either way, the main highlight is **Washington Pass,** the road's highest point, where an overlook affords a sensational panorama of snow-covered peaks.

Rainy Pass, where the road heading north drops into the west slope valleys, is another good vantage point. Old-growth forest begins to appear, and after about an hour you reach **Gorge Creek Falls overlook** with its 242-foot cascade. Continue west to Newhalem and stop for lunch, then take a half-hour stroll along the **Trail of the Cedars.** Later, stop at the **North Cascades Visitor Center** and take another short hike. It's an hour drive down the Skagit Valley to Sedro-Woolley, where bald eagles are often seen along the river in winter.

GETTING HERE AND AROUND

CAR TRAVEL

Highway 20, the North Cascades Highway, splits the park's north and south sections. The gravel Cascade River Road, which runs southeast from Marblemount, peels off Highway 20; Sibley Creek/Hidden Lake Road (USFS 1540) turns off Cascade River Road to the Cascade Pass trailhead. Thornton Creek Road is another rough four-wheel-drive track. For the Ross Lake area in the north, the unpaved Hozomeen Road (Silver–Skagit Road) provides access between Hope, British Columbia, and Silver Lake and Skagit Valley provincial parks. From Stehekin, the Stehekin Valley Road continues to High Bridge, Car Wash Falls, Bridge Creek, and Cottonwood campgrounds—although seasonal floods may cause washouts. Note that roads are narrow and closed from October to June, many sights are off the beaten path, and the scenery is so spectacular that, once you're in it, you'll want to make more than a day trip.

PARK ESSENTIALS

PARK FEES AND PERMITS

There are no entrance fees to the national park and no parking fees at trailheads on park land. A Northwest Forest Pass, required for parking at Forest Service trailheads, is $5 per vehicle for one calendar day or $30 for one year. A free wilderness permit is required for all overnight stays in the backcountry; these are available in person only. Dock permits for boat-in campgrounds are also $5 per day. Passes and permits are sold at visitor centers and ranger stations around the park area.

PARK HOURS

The park never closes, but access is limited by snow in winter. Highway 20 (North Cascades Highway), the major access to the park, is partially closed from mid-November to mid-April.

CELL-PHONE RECEPTION

Cell-phone reception in the park is unreliable. Public telephones are found at the North Cascades Visitor Center and Skagit Information Center in Newhalem, and the Golden West Visitor Center and North Cascades Stehekin Lodge in Stehekin.

RESTAURANTS

There are no formal restaurants in North Cascades National Park, just a lakeside café at the North Cascades Environmental Learning Center. The only other place to eat out is in Stehekin, at the Stehekin Valley Ranch dining room, North Cascades Lodge at Stehekin, or the Stehekin Pastry Company; all serve simple, hearty, country-style meals and sweets. Towns within a few hours of the park on either side have a few small eateries, and a few lodgings have small dining rooms with skilled chefs who craft high-end meals of locally grown products, matched with extensive wine lists. Otherwise, don't expect fancy decor or gourmet frills—just friendly service and generally delicious homemade stews, roasts, grilled fare, soups, salads, and baked goods.

HOTELS

Accommodations in North Cascades National Park are rustic, cozy, and comfortable. Options range from plush Stehekin lodges and homey cabin rentals to spartan Learning Center bunks and campgrounds. Expect to pay roughly $50 to $200 per night, depending on the rental size and the season. Book at least three months in advance, or even a year for popular accommodations in summer. Outside the park are numerous resorts, motels, bed-and-breakfasts, and even overnight boat rentals in Chelan, Concrete, Glacier, Marblemount, Sedro-Woolley, Twisp, and Winthrop. *Hotel reviews have been shortened. For full information, visit Fodors.com.*

WHAT IT COSTS IN U.S. DOLLARS				
	$	$$	$$$	$$$$
Restaurants	Under $12	$12–$20	$21–$30	Over $30
Hotels	Under $100	$100–$150	$151–$200	Over $200

Restaurant prices are the average cost of a main course at dinner, or if dinner is not served, at lunch. Hotel prices are the lowest cost of a standard double room in high season.

TOURS

North Cascades Institute (NCI). Come here for information on park hiking, wildlife watching, horseback riding, climbing, boat rentals, and fishing, as well as classroom education and hands-on nature experiences. Guided tours staged from the center include mountain climbs, pack-train excursions, and float trips on the Skagit and Stehekin Rivers. Choices range from forest ecology and backpacking trips to explorations of the Cascades hot springs. There's also a research library, a dock on Diablo Lake, an amphitheater, and overnight lodging. ⊠ *1940 Diablo Dam Rd., Diablo* ☎ *360/854–2599 Headquarters, 206/526–2599 Environmental Learning Center* ⊕ *www.ncascades.org.*

VISITOR INFORMATION
PARK CONTACT INFORMATION
North Cascades National Park ⊠ *810 Rte. 20, Sedro-Woolley* ☎ *360/854–7200* ⊕ *www.nps.gov/noca.*

VISITOR CENTERS
Chelan Ranger Station. The base for the Chelan National Recreation Area and Wenatchee National Forest has an information desk and a shop selling regional maps and books. ⊠ *428 W. Woodin Ave., Chelan* ☎ *509/682–4900* ⊕ *www.nps.gov/noca/planyourvisit/visitorcenters. htm* ⊗ *Weekdays 7:45–4:30.*

Glacier Public Service Center. This office doubles as a headquarters for the Mt. Baker–Snoqualmie National Forest; it has maps, a book and souvenir shop, and a permits desk. The center is also right on the way to some of the park's main trailheads. ⊠ *10091 Mt. Baker Hwy., Glacier* ☎ *360/599–2714* ⊕ *www.nps.gov/noca/planyourvisit/visitorcenters. htm* ⊗ *Late May, Fri.–Mon. 8–4:30; June–mid-Oct., daily 8–4:30; mid-Oct.–mid-May, weekends 9–3.*

Golden West Visitor Center. Rangers here offer guidance on hiking, camping, and other activities, as well as audiovisual and children's programs and bike tours. There's also an arts-and-crafts gallery. Maps and concise displays explain the layered ecology of the valley, which encompasses in its length virtually every ecosystem in the Northwest. Campers can pick up free backcountry permits. Note that access is by floatplane, ferry, or trail only. ⊠ *Stehekin Valley Rd., ¼ mile north of Stehekin Landing, Stehekin Valley Rd., Stehekin* ☎ *360/854–7365* ⊕ *www.nps. gov/noca/planyourvisit/visitorcenters.htm* ⊗ *Mid-Oct.–Nov. and mid-Mar.–Apr., Mon., Wed., and Fri. 12:30–1:30; May weekdays 12:30–2, weekends 10–2; Memorial Day–Sept., daily 8:30–5; early Oct.–mid-Oct., daily 10–2.*

North Cascades Park & Forest Information Center. This is the park's major administrative center and the place to pick up passes, permits, and information about current conditions. ⊠ *810 Rte. 20, Sedro-Woolley* ☎ *360/854–7200* ⊕ *www.nps.gov/noca/planyourvisit/visitorcenters. htm* ⊗ *Mid-Oct.–mid-May, weekdays 8–4:30; mid-May–mid-Oct., daily 8–4:30.*

North Cascades Visitor Center. The main visitor facility for the park complex has extensive displays on the surrounding landscape. Learn about the history and value of old-growth trees, the many creatures that depend on the rain-forest ecology, and the effects of human activity on the ecosystem. Park rangers frequently conduct programs; check bulletin boards for schedules. ⊠ *Milepost 120, North Cascades Hwy., Newhalem* ☎ *206/386–4495* ⊕ *www.nps.gov/noca/planyourvisit/ visitorcenters.htm* ⊗ *Mid-May–Jun., daily 9–5; Jul. and Aug., daily 9–6; Sept. and Oct., daily 9–5.*

Wilderness Information Center. The main stop to secure backcountry and climbing permits for North Cascades National Park and the Lake Chelan and Ross Lake recreational areas, this office has maps, a bookshop, and nature exhibits. If you arrive after hours, there's a self-register permit stop outside. ⊠ *Off milepost 105.9, N. Cascades Hwy., 7280*

14

Ranger Station Rd., Marblemount ☎ *360/854–7245* ⊕ *www.nps.gov/ noca/planyourvisit/visitorcenters.htm* ⊘ *May–Jun. and Sept.–mid-Oct., Sun.–Thurs. 8–4:30, Fri. and Sat. 7–6; Jul.–Aug., Sun.–Thurs. 7–6, Fri. and Sat. 7–8.*

EXPLORING

SCENIC DRIVES

North Cascades Highway. Also known as Highway 20, this classic scenic route first winds through the green pastures and woods of the upper Skagit Valley, the mountains looming in the distance. Beyond Concrete, a former cement-manufacturing town, the highway climbs into the mountains, passes the Ross and Diablo dams, and traverses Ross Lake National Recreation Area. Here several pullouts offer great views of the lake and the surrounding snowcapped peaks. From June to September, the meadows are covered with wildflowers, and from late September through October, the mountain slopes flame with fall foliage. The pinnacle point of this stretch is 5,477-foot-high Washington Pass: look east, to where the road descends quickly into a series of hairpin curves between Early Winters Creek and the Methow Valley. Remember, this section of the highway is closed from roughly November to April, depending on snowfall, and sometimes closes temporarily during the busy summer season due to mudslides from storms. From the Methow Valley, Highway 153 takes the scenic route along the Methow River's apple, nectarine, and peach orchards to Pateros, on the Columbia River; from here, you can continue east to Grand Coulee or south to Lake Chelan. ⊕ *www.cascadeloop.com.*

> **PLANTS AND WILDLIFE IN NORTH CASCADES**
>
> Bald eagles are present year-round along the Skagit River and the lakes—in December, hundreds flock to the Skagit to feed on a rare winter salmon run, and remain through January. Spring and early summer bring black bears to the roadsides in the high country. Deer and elk can often be seen in early morning and late evening, grazing and browsing at the forest's edge. Other mountain residents include beaver, marmots, pika, otters, skunks, opossums, and smaller mammals, as well as forest and field birds.

HISTORIC SITES

Buckner Homestead. Dating from 1889, this restored pioneer farm includes an apple orchard, farmhouse, barn, and many ranch buildings. One-hour ranger-guided tours of the property, now maintained by a nonprofit foundation, are offered on weekends in July and August; otherwise, you can pick up a self-guided tour booklet from the drop box. ⊠ *Stehekin Valley Rd., 3½ miles north of Stehekin Landing, Stehekin* ⊕ *www.bucknerhomestead.org* ⊘ *June–Sept., daily 9–5.*

SCENIC STOPS

Gorge Powerhouse/Ladder Creek Falls and Rock Gardens. A powerhouse is a powerhouse, but the rock gardens overlooking Ladder Creek Falls, 7 miles west of Diablo, are beautiful and inspiring. ⊠ *North Cascades Hwy., 2 miles east of North Cascades Visitor Center, Newhalem* ☎ *360/854–2589* ⊕ *www.seattle.gov/light/tours/skagit/* ⌕ *Free* ☉ *May–Sept., daily dawn to dusk.*

Fodor'sChoice ★ **Stehekin.** One of the most beautiful and secluded valleys in the Pacific Northwest, Stehekin was homesteaded by hardy souls in the late 19th century. It's actually not a town, but rather a small community set at the scenic northwest end of Lake Chelan, and it's accessible only by boat, floatplane, or trail. Year-round residents—there's about 100 of them—enjoy a wildnerness lifestyle. They have intermittent outside communications, boat-delivered supplies, and just two-dozen cars among them—vehicles must be barged in, after all. Even on a peak summer season day, only around 200 visitors make the trek here. ⊠ *Stehekin* ⊕ *www.stehekin.com.*

RANGER PROGRAMS

In summer, rangers conduct programs at the visitor centers, where you also can find exhibits and other park information. At the North Cascades Visitor Center (in Newhalem) you can learn about rain-forest ecology, while at the Golden West Visitor Center (in Stehekin) there's an arts-and-crafts gallery as well as audiovisual and children's programs. Check center bulletin boards for schedules.

SPORTS AND THE OUTDOORS

BIKING

Mountain bikes are permitted on highways, unpaved back roads, and a few designated tracks around the park; however, there is no biking on footpaths. Ranger stations have details on the best places to ride in each season, as well as notes on spots that are closed due to weather, mud, or other environmental factors. It's $27 round-trip to bring a bike on the Lake Chelan ferry to Stehekin.

OUTFITTERS

Discovery Bikes. You can rent mountain bikes at a self-serve rack in front of the Stehekin Log office in Stehekin. Helmets are included. ⊠ *5-minute walk from boat landing, Stehekin Valley Rd, Stehekin* ☎ *509/682–3014* ⊕ *www.stehekindiscoverybikes.com* ⌕ *$4 per hr, $15 per half day, $20 per day, $25 per 24 hrs; $35 for Ranch breakfast ride.*

BOATING

The boundaries of North Cascades National Park touch two long and sinewy expanses: Lake Chelan in the far south, and Ross Lake, which runs toward the Canadian border. Boat ramps, some with speed- and sailboat, paddleboat, kayak, and canoe rentals, are situated all around

Lake Chelan, and passenger ferries cross between towns and campgrounds. Hozomeen, accessible via a 39-mile dirt road from Canada, is the boating base for Ross Lake; the site has a large boat ramp, and a boat taxi makes drops at campgrounds all around the shoreline. Diablo Lake, in the center of the park, also has a ramp at Colonial Creek. Gorge Lake has a public ramp near the town of Diablo.

HIKING

⚠ Black bears are often sighted along trails in the summer; do not approach them. Back away carefully, and report sightings to the Golden West Visitor Center. Cougars, which are shy of humans and well aware of their presence, are rarely sighted in this region. Still, keep kids close and don't let them run too far ahead or lag behind on a trail. If you do spot a cougar, pick up children, have the whole group stand close together, and make yourself look as large as possible.

EASY

FAMILY **Happy Creek Forest Walk.** Old-growth forests are the focus of this kid-friendly boardwalk route, which loops just 0.3 miles through the trees right off the North Cascades Highway. Interpretive signs provide details about flora along the way. *Easy.* ⊠ *Trailhead at milepost 135, North Cascades Hwy.* ⊕ *www.nps.gov/noca.*

Rainy Pass. An easy and accessible 1-mile paved trail leads to Rainy Lake, a waterfall, and glacier-view platform. *Easy.* ⊠ *Trailhead off Hwy. 20, 38 miles east of visitor center at Newhalem* ⊕ *www.nps.gov/noca.*

River Loop Trail. Take this flat and easy, 1.8-mile, wheelchair-accessible trail down through stands of huge, old-growth firs and cedars toward the Skagit River. *Easy.* ⊠ *Trailhead near North Cascades Visitor Center* ⊕ *www.nps.gov/noca/planyourvisit/newhalem-area-trails.htm.*

Sterling Munro Trail. Starting from the North Cascades Visitor Center, this popular introductory stroll follows a short 300-foot path over a boardwalk to a lookout above the forested Picket Range peaks. *Easy.* ⊠ *Milepost 120, near Newhalem Creek Campground* ⊕ *www.nps.gov/ noca/planyourvisit/newhalem-area-trails.htm.*

Trail of the Cedars. Only 0.3 miles long, this trail winds its way through one of the finest surviving stands of old-growth western red cedar in Washington. Some of the trees on the path are more than 1,000 years old. *Easy.* ⊠ *Trailhead near North Cascades Visitor Center, milepost 120, Hwy. 20, Newhalem* ⊕ *www.nps.gov/noca/planyourvisit/ newhalem-area-trails.htm.*

MODERATE

Fodor's Choice **Cascade Pass.** This extremely popular 3.7-mile, four-hour trail is known
★ for stunning panoramas from the great mountain divide. Dozens of peaks line the horizon as you make your way up the fairly flat, hairpin-turn track, the scene fronted by a blanket of alpine wildflowers from July to mid-August. Arrive before noon if you want a parking spot at the trailhead. *Moderate.* ⊠ *Trailhead at end of Cascade River Rd., 14 miles from Marblemount* ⊕ *www.nps.gov/noca/planyourvisit/cascade-pass-trail.htm.*

Diablo Lake Trail. Explore nearly 4 miles of waterside terrain on this route, which is accessed from the Sourdough Creek parking lot. An excellent alternative for parties with small hikers is to take the Seattle City Light Ferry one way. *Moderate.* ⊠ *Trailhead at milepost 135, Hwy. 20* ⊕ *www.nps.gov/noca.*

DIFFICULT

Thornton Lakes Trail. A 5-mile climb into an alpine basin with three pretty lakes, this steep and strenuous hike takes about five to six hours round-trip. *Difficult.* ⊠ *Trailhead off Hwy. 20, 3 miles west of Newhalem, Thornton Lake Rd. and Hwy. 20* ⊕ *www.nps.gov/noca/planyourvisit/ thornton-lake-trail.htm.*

HORSEBACK RIDING

Many hiking trails and backwoods paths are also popular horseback-riding routes, particularly around the park's southern fringes.

TOURS AND OUTFITTERS

Cascade Corrals. This subsidiary of Stehekin Outfitters organizes 2½-hour horseback trips to Coon Lake and full-day rides (lunch included) to Moore Point and Bridge Creek. English- and western-style riding lessons are also available. Reservations are taken at the Courtney Log Office at Stehekin Landing. Some rides depart from the Landing, others from Stehekin Valley Ranch. ⊕ *www.cascadecorrals.com* ☎ *$55–$150* ⊗ *June–mid-Sept., half-day rides daily at 8:15 and 2:15.*

KAYAKING

The park's tangles of waterways offer access to remote areas inaccessible by road or trail; here are some of the most pristine and secluded mountain scenes on the continent. Bring your own kayak and you can launch from any boat ramp or beach; otherwise, companies in several nearby towns and Seattle suburbs offer kayak and canoe rentals, portage, and tours. The upper basin of Lake Chelan (at the park's southern end) and Ross Lake (at the top edge of the park) are two well-known kayaking expanses, but there are dozens of smaller lakes and creeks between. The Stehekin River also provides many kayaking possibilities.

TOURS AND OUTFITTERS

Ross Lake Resort. The resort rents kayaks, motor boats, and canoes, and offers portage service for exploring Ross Lake. A water-taxi service is also available; the resort is not accessible by road. ⊠ *503 Diablo St., Rockport* ☎ *206/386–4437, 206/708–3980 off-season (Jan.–May)* ⊕ *www.rosslakeresort.com.*

Stehekin Valley Ranch. Kayak tours of the upper estuary of Lake Chelan are offered daily at 10 am. ⊠ *Stehekin Valley Rd., 3½ miles from Stehekin Landing, Stehekin* ☎ *509/682–4677, 800/536–0745* ⊕ *www. stehekinvalleyranch.com* ☎ *$40* ⊗ *June–Sept.*

14

RAFTING

June through August is the park's rafting season, with family-friendly rafting trips (Classes II and III) run through the Skagit River.

TOURS AND OUTFITTERS

North Cascades River Expeditions. June through October, North Cascades River Expeditions focuses on regional rivers; trips are offered on the Upper Skagit year-round. ☎ 800/634–8433 ⊕ *www.riverexpeditions. com.*

Orion River Expeditions. Introductory, family-oriented floats are offered in August on the Skagit River for ages 6 and up. More lively white-water tours run on other area rivers April through September. ☎ 509/548–1401, 800/553–7466 ⊕ *www.orionexp.com.*

Wildwater River Guides. Half-day rafting excursions on the Skagit River depart from Goodell Creek Campground near Newhalem, from March through September. The mild waters are great for beginners and families. ✉ *Goodell Creek Campground, Newhalem* ☎ 509/470–8558, 800/522–9453 ⊕ *www.wildwater-river.com.*

WINTER SPORTS

Mt. Baker, just off the park's far northwest corner, is one of the Northwest's premier skiing, snowboarding, and snowshoeing regions—the area set a world record for most snow in a single season during the winter of 1998–99 (1,140 inches). The Mt. Baker Highway (Route 542) cuts through the slopes toward state sno-parks; Salmon Ridge Sno-Park, 46 miles east of Bellingham at exit 255, has groomed trails and parking. Mt. Baker Ski Area, 17 miles east of the town of Glacier, has eight chairlifts and access to backcountry skiing; its season runs roughly from November to April.

Mt. Baker. Off the park's northwest corner, this is the closest winter-sports area, with facilities for downhill and Nordic skiing, snowboarding, and other recreational ventures. The main base is the town of Glacier, 17 miles west of the slopes, where lodging is available. Equipment rental and food service are on-site. ✉ *Hwy. 542, 52 miles east of Bellingham, Glacier* ☎ 360/734–6771, 360/671–0211 for snow reports ⊕ *www.mtbaker.us* ✉ *All-day lift ticket weekdays $51, weekends and holidays $56* ⊘ *Nov.–Apr.*

WHERE TO EAT

$
CAFÉ

✕ **Stehekin Pastry Company.** As you enter this lawn-framed timber chalet, you're immersed in the tantalizing aromas of a European bakery. Glassed-in display cases are filled with trays of homemade baked goods, and the pungent espresso is eye-opening. Sit down at a window-side table and dig into an over-filled sandwich or rich bowl of soup—and don't forget dessert: we're guessing you'll never taste a better slice of pie, made with fruit fresh-picked from local orchards. Although it's outside town, the shop is conveniently en route to Rainbow Falls. ⑤ *Average main: $5* ✉ *Stehekin Valley Rd., about 2 miles north of Stehekin*

CLOSE UP

Best Campgrounds in North Cascades

Tent campers can choose between forest sites, riverside spots, lake grounds, or meadow spreads encircled by mountains. Here camping is as easy or challenging as you want to make it; some campgrounds are a short walk from ranger stations, while others are miles from the highway. Note that many campsites, particularly those around Stehekin, are completely remote and without road access anywhere, so you have to walk, boat, ride a horse, or take a floatplane to reach them. Most don't accept reservations, and spots fill up quickly May through September. If there's no ranger on-site, you can often sign yourself in—and always check in at a ranger station before you set out overnight. Note that some areas are occasionally closed due to flooding, forest fires, or other factors.

Lake Chelan National Recreation Area. Many backcountry camping areas are accessible via park shuttles or boat. All require a free backcountry permit. Purple Point, the most popular campground due to its quick access to Stehekin Landing, has six tent sites, bear boxes, and nearby road access. ⊠ *Stehekin Landing, Stehekin* ☎ *360/854-7365.*

Landing, Stehekin ☎ *509/682-7742* ⊕ *www.stehekinpastry.com* ☐ *No credit cards* ⊘ *Closed Mon.–Thurs. and mid-Oct.–Memorial Day.*

$$
AMERICAN ✕ **Restaurant at Stehekin Valley Ranch.** Meals in the rustic log ranch house, served at polished wood tables, include buffet dinners of steak, ribs, hamburgers, salad, beans, and dessert. Note that breakfast is served 7 to 9, lunch is noon to 1, and dinner is 5:30 to 7. Show up later than that and you'll find the kitchen is closed. If you want to enjoy a drink with your meal, you can bring your own alcohol—it's not otherwise served. For guests not staying at the ranch, dinner reservations are required and transportation from the Stehekin Landing costs $6. ⑤ *Average main: $18* ⊠ *Stehekin Valley Rd., 9 miles north of Stehekin Landing, Stehekin* ☎ *509/682-4677, 800/536-0745* ⊕ *www.stehekinvalleyranch.com* ⤳ *Reservations essential* ☐ *No credit cards* ⊘ *Closed Oct.–mid-June.*

PICNIC AREAS

Developed picnic areas at both Rainy Pass (Highway 20, 38 miles east of the park visitor center) and Washington Pass (Highway 20, 42 miles east of the visitor center) have a half-dozen picnic tables, drinking water, and pit toilets. The vistas of surrounding peaks are sensational at these two overlooks. More picnic facilities are located near the visitor center in Newhalem and at Colonial Creek Campground, 10 miles east of the visitor center on Highway 20.

WHERE TO STAY

$$
HOTEL 🏨 **North Cascades Lodge at Stehekin.** Crackling fires and Lake Chelan views are provided both in standard rooms in the Alpine House, with its shared lounge and lakeside deck, and in larger rooms in the Swiss Mont building, with private decks overlooking the water. **Pros:** on the

water; recreation center with pool table; tent-to-tent hiking excursions; kayaking. **Cons:** no air-conditioning; TV is only available in the recreation building; out of range of cell-phone service. ⑤ *Rooms from: $128* ⊠ *955 Stehekin Valley Rd., Stehekin* ☎ *509/682–4494* ⊕ *www. lodgeatstehekin.com* ⇥ *28 rooms, 1 house* ⍥ *No meals.*

$$$ ⊡ **Silver Bay Inn Resort.** Perched on a slip of land at the head of Lake
B&B/INN Chelan, Silver Bay's accommodations feature water and mountain views; all have their own kitchens. **Pros:** hot tub vistas; free use of boats and bikes. **Cons:** summertime mosquitoes; five-night minimum in summer; not for families with kids under 12. ⑤ *Rooms from: $195* ⊠ *Silver Bay Rd., Stehekin* ☎ *509/670–0693* ⊕ *www.silverbayinn.com* ⇥ *1 room, 2 cabins, 1 house* ⍟ *Closed Nov.–May* ⍥ *No meals.*

$$$$ ⊡ **Stehekin Valley Ranch.** Alongside pretty meadows at the edge of pine
B&B/INN forest, this rustic ranch is a center for hikers and horseback riders, who stay in barnlike cabins with cedar paneling, tile floors, and a private bath, or canvas-roof tent cabins with bunk beds, kerosene lamps, and shared bathrooms. **Pros:** many activities; free vehicle use with kitchen cabins. **Cons:** no bathrooms in tent cabins. ⑤ *Rooms from: $250* ⊠ *Stehekin Valley Rd., 9 miles north of Stehekin Landing, Stehekin* ☎ *509/682–4677, 800/536–0745* ⊕ *www.stehekinvalleyranch. com* ⇥ *7 tent cabins (shared bathroom), 8 cabins* ⍟ *Closed Oct.–mid-June* ⍥ *All meals.*

NORTH CENTRAL WASHINGTON

WELCOME TO NORTH CENTRAL WASHINGTON

TOP REASONS TO GO

★ **Winter sports:** The nonprofit Methow Valley Sport Trails Association maintains 120 miles of groomed trails in the North Cascades during winter, when the region is also busy with snowmobiling, heli-skiing, snowshoeing, and other winter sports.

★ **Summer sports:** The groomed trails of winter are used for mountain biking, trail running, and hiking when the snow melts. Mountain lakes, ridges, and rivers also provide a perfect playground.

★ **Cascade Loop:** Visitors to the North Cascades don't *have* to be athletic. This scenic byway circles through the mountains, offering some 400 miles of stunning sights.

★ **The Old West:** With its wagon wheels, wooden sidewalks, false fronts, and hitching posts, riverside Winthrop gives a glimpse into frontier days.

★ **The Old World:** The Bavarian-style mountain town of Leavenworth lights up for the holidays, Oktoberfest, and its annual accordion festival.

1 North Cascades.
West of Washington Pass, Highway 20 winds around the northern shore of Diablo Lake and southern tip of Ross Lake, continuing through the former cement-manufacturing town of Concrete and fertile Skagit Valley pastures. The route offers breathtaking views of snowcapped peaks, summer wildflowers, and fall foliage. Snowfall closes the pass from November to April, cutting the valley off from Okanogan County, which includes Old West–style Winthrop and the riverfront town of Twisp in the Methow Valley.

2 Central Cascades.
This picturesque region encompasses not only the resort town and fjord-like lake Chelan, but also the Bavarian-style village of Leavenworth and Wenatchee, self-proclaimed "Apple Capital of Washington," surrounded by orchards. Bordered by the Columbia River to the east, this stretch offers the ultimate in outdoor experiences, from boating and mountain biking to hiking and fishing, as well as plenty of outposts at which to relax and recoup.

GETTING ORIENTED

Former logging towns, nestled in the shadow of Mt. Baker to the north, line the upper ring of the Cascade Loop, encircling a vast series of national forests fanning north and east from Seattle. The ridges and valleys of the Cascade Range form the heart of this region, a mecca for skiers, snowshoers, white-water river rafters, campers, hikers, mountain bikers, and other adventurers drawn to its natural beauty. Fjord-like Lake Chelan reaches into the wilderness from the eastern edge of the loop, providing a gateway to the secluded outpost of Stehekin, accessible only by boat or plane or on foot. The alpine area is anchored by the orchards surrounding Wenatchee to the southeast, where the Columbia River forms a natural border between north-central and eastern Washington.

15

Updated
by Adriana
Janovich

Wilderness embraces much of north-central Washington, replete with old timber towns, cascading creeks, glacial peaks, and low-hanging valleys dusted with wildflowers. The region's natural beauty creates a feeling of journeying to an out-of-the-way, rural retreat. This is the quintessential outdoors, a place of snowcapped summits, sparkling lakes, evergreen forests, and—despite the remote outpost of Stehekin and a road closure that walls off the east and west in winter—surprising accessibility.

Because of the depth of their glaciated valleys, the North Cascades are uncommonly reachable. One of the most popular drives in the state encircles the region, from the old lumber towns of Sedro-Woolley and Marblemount to the northwest, over Washington Pass to Mazama, where the family-run country store is a must-stop for a bowl of soup and baked goods, through the riverside stops of Twisp and Winthrop to the northeast. Both towns boast riverfront brewpubs with live music on summer weekends as well as good selections of craft beer. Farther south, the resort community of Chelan, on the southern tip of a pristine, 50-mile, glacier-fed lake of the same name, chalks up some 300 days of sunshine per year. The lake stretches 1½ miles at its widest and descends 1,486 feet at its deepest. Bavarian-style Leavenworth, 23 miles northwest of Wenatchee, bustles with shopping and a variety of festivals, including an annual Oktoberfest celebration.

Most permanent residents live along the loop, on ranches and orchards and in pocket-sized towns, all gateways to the northern ridges of the Cascade Range. In winter, these peaks, which climb 4,000 to 9,000 feet and higher, have the greatest measured snowfall in North America—more than 80 feet in high places on the western slopes. Washington Pass closes in November, cutting off the Cascade Loop until April, but the region remains accessible via Interstate 90. Still, when Highway 20 reopens in spring, travelers on both sides line up, waiting to be among the first to travel back over the byway.

NORTH CENTRAL WASHINGTON PLANNER

WHEN TO GO

With its evergreen foothills, impressive peaks, and general accessibility, the North Cascades—often likened to the Alps—is a popular destination year-round. Skiers, snowboarders, and snowshoers come here from December through March, relaxing après-ski in the area's lodges, small hotels, and bed-and-breakfasts. With Washington Pass closed, however, winter visitors have to take alternative routes, making some otherwise easily accessible destinations and accommodations seem out-of-the-way. Still, almost all lowland forest areas and valleys can be visited any time of year. Summer peak season extends from snowmelt (late May through July, depending on elevation) to early September. Many annual visitors to Lake Chelan book lodging for the following summer before leaving. Weekends and holidays can get crowded with hikers, backpackers, boaters, anglers, white-water rafters, and other outdoors enthusiasts.

In the fall, when the North Cascades glow with crimson, saffron, and rust-colored foliage against a backdrop of its evergreen trees, the Cascade Loop is a popular route. Leaf-peepers who don't mind the rainy days of late autumn can enjoy otherwise mild temperatures and a quieter drive. Early spring also offers peace and quiet as well as the promise of alpine air. Many hotels and other lodging options offer economical shoulder-season pricing.

FESTIVALS AND EVENTS

If you want to match your visit up with a local event, there are highlights in each season.

Christkindlmarkt and Christmas Lighting Festival. Old-world holiday traditions blend with modern rituals to turn downtown Leavenworth into a glittering holiday wonderland, complete with carriage rides, carols, sledding, tree-lighting, children's activities, and other festivities. ✉ *Leavenworth* ☎ *509/548–5807* ⊕ *www.christkindlmarktleavenworth.com.*

Lake Chelan Winterfest Fire and Ice. Held during two weekends in January, this festival features a chili cook-off, music, winter ale tasting, a fun run, ice slide, wine walk, polar bear dip, children's activities, and ice sculpture. ✉ *Chelan* ☎ *509/682–3503* ⊕ *www.lakechelanwinterfest.com.*

Leavenworth International Accordion Celebration. Sponsored by the Northwest Accordion Society, this June fest features jam sessions, competitions, concerts, workshops, vendors, and free accordion lessons. ✉ *Leavenworth* ⊕ *www.accordioncelebration.org.*

Maifest. Enjoy traditional German dancing, including an intricate old-world maypole dance, as well as a lederhosen contest and parade flower-decked Bavarian-style village of Leavenworth. As the name suggests, it takes place in May. ✉ *Leavenworth* ☎ *509/548–5807* ⊕ *www.leavenworth.org.*

15

Oktoberfest. Show off your "chicken dance" and other oom-pah moves in Leavenworth at one of the most exuberant stateside celebrations of this German beer festival, complete with German food, German music, German dancing and, of course, beer. Needless to say, it's in October. Lodging fills up fast this festive weekend; some participants book rooms a year in advance. ⊠ *Leavenworth* ☏ *509/548–5807* ⊕ *www.leavenworthoktoberfest.com.*

Winthrop Rhythm and Blues Fest. The Blues Ranch, 1 mile west of Winthrop, is the venue for this nonprofit, volunteer-run July music festival—an outdoor Methow Valley tradition. ⊠ *Winthrop* ☏ *509/997–3837* ⊕ *www.winthropbluesfestival.com.*

GETTING HERE AND AROUND

AIR TRAVEL

In addition to the regular commercial service to and from Seattle, small craft make it easy to get around this far-flung region.

Catlin Flying Service. This Twisp-based company offers direct flights to Chelan, Winthrop, Stehekin, and Seattle's Boeing Field. Private flights, including scenic mountain flights, are also available for up to five passengers. ⊠ *P. O. Box 427, Twisp* ☏ *509/997–4602, 866/445–2359, 509/429–2697 pilot's cell* ⊕ *www.catlinflyingservice.com.*

Pangborn Memorial Airport. Commercial flights from Sea-Tac International Airport to Wenatchee's airport are available through Horizon Air. ⊠ *1 Pangborn Dr., East Wenatchee* ☏ *509/884–2494* ⊕ *www.pangbornairport.com.*

CAR TRAVEL

From the Skagit Valley towns of Mount Vernon and Burlington, about 65 miles north of Seattle on Interstate 5, take Highway 20, the North Cascades Highway, east through Sedro-Woolley, Concrete, and Marblemount. From April to November, when Washington Pass is open, continue to Winthrop and Twisp, then use State Route 153 to get to Chelan, and U.S. 97—with a short jaunt on U.S. 2 heading west—to get to Leavenworth and Wenatchee. An hour and a half to the south, U.S. 97 connects with Interstate 90 at Ellensburg, about an hour and 45 minutes from Seattle.

From Seattle, take Interstate 90 to U.S. 97 to Wenatchee and Leavenworth—with a short jaunt on U.S. 2 heading east—to Chelan. From there, State Route 153 takes travelers north to Highway 20 through Twisp and Winthrop, and—from April to November—west over Washington Pass, through Marblemount, Concrete, Sedro-Woolley, and Burlington, where it connects with Interstate 5, Washington's main north–south artery.

From Everett, about 28 miles north of Seattle on Interstate 5, take U.S. 2 east through Gold Bar, Index, Stevens Pass, and the Alpine Lakes Wilderness to Leavenworth and Wenatchee.

RESTAURANTS

This region has a good range of dining options, from American pub fare to fine dining, and many incorporate locally grown and produced ingredients, including organic produce, beef, chicken, eggs, and artisanal breads and cheeses. Around the region, there are low-key, affordable, and unpretentious eateries—coffee shops, bakeries, brewpubs, diners, and restaurants.

Wenatchee is the largest city in the North Cascades and features the most variety when it comes to dining. It's home to the most ethnically diverse cuisine in the region, including several Mexican restaurants as well as Italian, Thai, Japanese, Chinese, and others. The self-proclaimed "Apple Capital of Washington," this is the place to try to the fruit in a variety of forms, sweet and savory.

Bavarian-themed Leavenworth offers a number of restaurants specializing in traditional German fare as well as Southern barbecue and American pub fare. Wine enthusiasts might want to make a stop in the Lake Chelan region, home to some two-dozen wineries. Craft-beer lovers won't want to miss the riverfront breweries in both Winthrop and Twisp.

HOTELS

15

Accommodations in the North Cascades range from rustic cabins and basic motels to charming bed-and-breakfasts, riverside inns, intimate hotels, and upscale mountain resorts, most featuring first-rate hospitality. Many also have picturesque mountain, lake, or river views. Book well in advance for holiday and summer weekends, particularly during festivals and events. Winter and shoulder seasons tend to feature lower prices. Look for package deals online at many establishments. *Hotel reviews have been shortened. For full information, visit Fodors.com.*

WHAT IT COSTS IN U.S. DOLLARS			
$	$$	$$$	$$$$
Restaurants	Under $16	$16–$23	$24–$30	Over $30
Hotels	Under $150	$150–$200	$201–$250	Over $250

Restaurant prices are the average cost of a main course at dinner or, if dinner is not served, at lunch. Hotel prices are the lowest cost of a standard double room in high season.

NORTH CASCADES

This is a backpacker's paradise, the perfect place to take a hike, enjoy winter snow sports, and go white-water rafting or fishing. In fall, the changing leaves provide a colorful backdrop along the Cascade Loop, one of the state's most popular scenic byways. In summer, the valleys and slopes are blanketed with wildflowers. The towns of Twisp and Winthrop—the latter with an appealing Old West feel—provide launch pads to the great outdoors, easily accessible from every corner of this gorgeous region, marked by snowcapped peaks and low-hanging valleys.

GLACIER

113 miles north of Seattle.

The canyon village of Glacier, just outside the Mt. Baker–Snoqualmie National Forest boundary, has a few shops, cafés, and lodgings. Highway 542 winds east from Glacier into the forest through an increasingly steep-walled canyon. It passes 170-foot-high Nooksack Falls, about 5 miles east of Glacier, and travels up the north fork of the Nooksack River and the slopes of Mt. Baker to a ski area, which is bright with huckleberry patches and wildflowers in summer.

GETTING HERE AND AROUND

Glacier is about two hours and 15 minutes from Seattle. Take Interstate 5 north to Exit 230 at Burlington; go east 6 miles on Highway 20 then north via Highway 9, then northeast via Highway 542.

EXPLORING

Mt. Baker–Snoqualmie National Forest. A vast forest, including much of the mountain and forest land around North Cascades National Park, has many trails, but because the snowline is quite low in Washington State, the upper ridges and mountains are covered by snow much of the year. This makes for a short hiking, climbing, and mountain-biking season, usually from mid-July to mid-September or October—but winter brings skiing and snowmobiling. The wildflower season is also short, but it's spectacular; expect fall color by late August or early September. The 10,778-foot-high, snow-covered volcanic dome of **Mt. Baker** is visible from much of Whatcom County and from as far north as Vancouver and as far south as Seattle. ⊠ *Ranger Station: 1405 Emens Ave. N, Darrington* ☎ *360/783–6000 Everett office, 800/627–0062 toll free, 360/436–1155 Darrington Ranger District office, 206/470–4060 Outdoor Recreation Information* ⊕ *www.fs.fed.us/r6/mbs* ⊠ *$5 for day pass, $30 for annual pass* ☉ *Daily 24 hrs.*

WHERE TO STAY

$$
B&B/INN
⊡ **The Inn at Mt. Baker.** Nestled into the upper Cascades, this stately country home offers airy spaces with vaulted ceilings and sweeping mountain panoramas. **Pros:** easy to find; European-style luxuries; recreation packages can be arranged. **Cons:** simple room style can seem sparse; no children under 16; strict cancellation policy. ⑤ *Rooms from: $165* ⊠ *8174 Mt. Baker Hwy., at milepost 28* ☎ *360/599–1776, 877/567–5526* ⊕ *www.theinnatmtbaker.com* ⇄ *5 rooms* ⑩ *Breakfast.*

$
B&B/INN
⊡ **Kale House Bed & Breakfast.** The charming home gleams with polished wood and large windows, which look out to knobby apple trees and a weeping willow. **Pros:** small and inviting; lovely gardens; lots of art. **Cons:** no children or pets. ⑤ *Rooms from: $125* ⊠ *201 Kale St., Everson* ☎ *360/966–7027* ⊕ *www.kalehouse.net* ⇄ *2 rooms* ⑩ *Breakfast.*

$
RENTAL
⊡ **The Logs at Canyon Creek.** Rustic, timber-lined two-bedroom cabins have full kitchens, plus living rooms with rock fireplaces—your wood is even provided. **Pros:** your home in the woods; great ski access. **Cons:** a long drive from civilization; three-night minimum stay in summer. ⑤ *Rooms from: $135* ⊠ *7577 Canyon View Dr., 3½ miles northwest of Glacier off Mt. Baker Hwy., Deming* ☎ *360/599–2711* ⊕ *www.thelogs.com* ⇄ *5 cabins, 3 chalets* ▭ *No credit cards* ⑩ *No meals.*

SPORTS AND THE OUTDOORS

Mt. Baker Ski Area. Here you can snowboard and ski downhill or cross-country from roughly November to the end of April. The area set a world snowfall record in winter 1998–99. Ski and snowboard equipment is available to rent. ⊠ *17 miles east of Glacier at end of Hwy. 542* ☎ *360/734–6771, 360/671–0211 snow reports* ⊕ *www.mtbakerskiarea.com* ⊠ *Lift ticket $49 weekdays, $54 weekends and holidays.*

SEDRO-WOOLLEY

42 miles southwest of Glacier.

On its way east from Interstate 5, Highway 20 skirts Burlington and Sedro-Woolley, the latter a former mill and logging town now considered the gateway to the Cascades. Fronted by a huge black steam engine, the settlement has a bit of an old downtown and a smattering of Tar Heel culture, as it was settled by pioneer loggers and farmers from North Carolina. It also has an institute that arranges trips into North Cascades National Park, and a nearby park headquarters.

15

GETTING HERE AND AROUND

Sedro-Woolley is about one hour, 20 minutes from Seattle via Interstate 5 north to Burlington (Exit 230), then 5 miles east via Highway 20.

ESSENTIALS

Visitor Information Sedro-Woolley Chamber of Commerce ⊠ *714-B Metcalf St.* ☎ *360/855–1841, 888/225–8365* ⊕ *www.sedro-woolley.com.*

EXPLORING

Lake Whatcom Railway. The steam-powered train makes short jaunts through the woods 11 miles north of Sedro-Woolley. Excursions run in July and August and during special events, such as the Christmas train rides with Santa in December. During peak weekends, tours depart at noon and children pay half price. Note that the schedule changes seasonally. ⊠ *Hwy. 9, Wickersham* ☎ *360/595–2218* ⊕ *www.lakewhatcomrailway.com* ⊠ *$25* ⊗ *Call for hrs.*

WHERE TO STAY

$ 🖾 **Three Rivers Inn.** This pleasant two-story motel, where each room has
HOTEL   a deck or a balcony overlooking the manicured lawn or courtyard with a seasonal pool and hot tub, is a handy place to stay on the way to or from North Cascades National Park. **Pros:** rooms are equipped with microwaves and refrigerators; seasonal swimming pool; pet-friendly. **Cons:** no elevator; basic interior design. ⑤ *Rooms from: $120* ⊠ *210 Ball St., Sedro-Woolley* ☎ *360/855–2626, 800/221–5122* ⊕ *www.thethreeriversinn.com* ⊅ *40 rooms* ⦿ *Breakfast.*

WINTHROP

87 miles east of Marblemount, 128 miles east of Sedro-Woolley.

Before the cowboys came, the Methow Valley was a favorite gathering place for Native American tribes, who dug the plentiful and nutritious bulbs and hunted deer while their horses fattened on the tall native grasses. For wayward pioneers who came later, the cool, glacier-fed streams provided welcome relief on hot summer days, and the rich fields were a starting point for vast crops and orchards. The 1800s saw the burgeoning riverside settlement of Winthrop grow into a cattle-ranching town, whose residents inspired some of Owen Wister's colorful characters in his novel *The Virginian.* In 1972, inspired by Leavenworth's Bavarian theme, Winthrop business owners enacted a plan to restore its Old West feel, and many of the original, turn-of-the-20th-century buildings still stand.

Getting to town through the Washington countryside is a picturesque drive, with endless vistas of golden meadows, neatly sown crop fields, and rustic old barn frames. In winter the land is a crisp blanket of glittering frost; in summer little fruit-and-vegetable stands pop up along the back roads. Massive tangles of blackberry bushes produce kumquat-size fruit you can eat right off the vines, and the pungent aroma of apples pervades the breezes in autumn. Flat roads, small towns, incredible views, and plenty of camping spots make this the perfect weekend wandering territory by bike, car, or motorcycle.

GETTING HERE AND AROUND

When the North Cascades Highway is open, Winthrop can be reached via that scenic route; it takes about three hours, 45 minutes from Seattle. The rest of the year, it will take about an extra hour via Stevens Pass (U.S. 2) or Snoqualmie Pass (Interstate 90 then Highway 970 to Highway 2) to Wenatchee then north via Highways 97, 153, and 20. From Spokane, Winthrop is about 3½ hours west via Highway 2, then Highways 174, 17, 97, 153, and 20.

ESSENTIALS

Visitor Information Winthrop Chamber of Commerce ✉ *202 Hwy. 20* ☎ *509/996–2125* ⊕ *www.winthropwashington.com.*

WHERE TO EAT

$$$$
PACIFIC
NORTHWEST

✗ **Dining Room at Sun Mountain Lodge.** In a sylvan hilltop setting overlooking the Methow Valley, intimate tables and a woodsy interior design set the scene for an extraordinary dining experience. The upscale Pacific Northwest cuisine is based on often-organic, locally grown, raised, caught, and crafted ingredients, providing for exquisite flavors to match the artful presentation and elegant yet unpretentious atmosphere. Delicacies include chicken curry soup, melt-in-your-mouth pork chops, eggplant gateaux, and beef tenderloin with foie gras and potato tart. The dessert menu has many tempting choices, including a duo of vanilla and mocha brûlée, individual apple pie with house-made vanilla bean ice cream, and Chocolate Fantasy—a quintet of chocolate delights. The 5,000-bottle wine cellar is one of the best and most extensive in the region. $ *Average main: $38* ✉ *604 Patterson Lake Rd., Winthrop* ☎ *509/996–2211* ⊕ *www.sunmountainlodge.com/dining* ☾ *Closed Sun.–Thurs. in winter and spring; closed late-Oct.–early Dec. and Mar.–early Apr. No lunch.*

$
MODERN IRISH

✗ **Kelly's at Wesola Polana.** Young and gregarious Steven Kelly, a transplant from Ireland, serves hearty Irish fare like bangers and mash, shepherd's pie, and Irish stew as well as American pub grub and Spanish wines and appetizers. Dishes feature seasonal local ingredients and offer sustenance for winter skiers and summer hikers and cyclists heading for the miles of groomed trails that run past the place (trail passes are available here). The breakfast fry-up features organic eggs, local sausage links, grilled tomato, and traditional Irish *boxty* (potato pancakes) or roasted potatoes. There's an expanding wine list as well as a wide selection of imported bottled beers. A deck and lawn seating are available in warmer weather, and there's a fenced dog-run nearby. $ *Average main: $12* ✉ *18381 Hwy. 20, Winthrop* ☎ *509/996–9804* ⊕ *www.kellys-wesolapolana.com* ☾ *Closed Mon.–Wed.*

$
AMERICAN

✗ **Old Schoolhouse Brewery.** Located in a red-painted building designed to resemble an old, one-room schoolhouse, this family-run craft brewpub sits between the town's main drag and the river. Live music plays on the outdoor stage in the beer garden on the banks of the Chewuch River on summer weekend nights. Seating is also available on the back deck, affectionately dubbed "The Hangover," as well as indoors in the long, one-room pub. While waiting for big burgers, fish-and-chips, baked mac and cheese, or a succulent pork sandwich, sip an Epiphany Pale, Hooligan Stout, or Ruud Awakening IPA, the latter named for

15

the family that owns the place. $ *Average main: $12* ✉ *155 Riverside Ave.* ☎ *509/996–3183* ⊕ *www.oldschoolhousebrewery.com* ☉ *Closed Tues. and Wed. in winter.*

WHERE TO STAY

$$$
RESORT
Fodor's Choice
★

Freestone Inn. At the heart of the 120-acre, historic Wilson Ranch, amid more than 2 million acres of forest, this upscale mountain retreat embraces the pioneer spirit in spacious rooms, suites, and wood-paneled cabins snuggled up to Early Winters Creek. **Pros:** gorgeous scenery; myriad activities; close to North Cascades National Park (17 miles west). **Cons:** limited cell-phone and TV service; some resort amenities may be limited in shoulder season. $ *Rooms from: $225* ✉ *31 Early Winters Dr., about 14 miles northwest of Winthop, Mazama* ☎ *509/996–3906, 800/639–3809* ⊕ *www.freestoneinn.com* ⟿ *10 rooms, 7 suites, 15 cabins, 4 lodges* ◎| *Breakfast.*

$
B&B/INN

Methow Valley Inn. Run with family-style friendliness, this historic country inn with lovely gardens has guest rooms furnished with antiques and decorated with Scandinavian quilts and other old-world influences. **Pros:** gorgeous gardens in summer; lovely holiday decorations in winter; superb cleanliness. **Cons:** no bathtubs; no in-room TVs; some shared bathrooms; no children under 12 unless you rent the entire inn. $ *Rooms from: $89* ✉ *234 E. 2nd Ave., about 9 miles south of Winthrop, Twisp* ☎ *509/997–2253* ⊕ *www.methowvalleyinn.com* ⟿ *7 rooms, 5 with private bath, 1 suite* ◎| *Breakfast.*

$
RENTAL

Rolling Huts. There's camping, and then there are the Rolling Huts. **Pros:** gorgeous views; serene setting; interesting architecture. **Cons:** limited cell-phone service; portable toilets and water faucets outside each hut. $ *Rooms from: $135* ✉ *18381 Hwy. 20, about 14 miles northwest of Winthrop on State Rte. 20, Mazama* ☎ *509/996–4442* ⊕ *www.rollinghuts.com* ⟿ *6 huts* ◎| *No meals.*

$$$
RESORT
Fodor's Choice
★

Sun Mountain Lodge. The stunning North Cascades and all its attractions are the stars of this outdoor-oriented resort set 3,000-feet up in the foothills, with luxurious accommodations, spectacular mountain views, and a range of activities that make it a year-round destination, whether the peaks are covered in snow or wildflowers. **Pros:** stunning setting; a wide array of outdoor activities year-round; panoramic views; award-winning dining; warm hospitality. **Cons:** limited cell service; roundabout route from Seattle in winter. $ *Rooms from: $235* ✉ *604 Patterson Lake Rd., Winthrop* ☎ *509/996–2211, 800/572–0493* ⊕ *www.sunmountainlodge.com* ⟿ *86 rooms, 10 suites, 16 cabins* ☉ *Closed late-Oct.–early Dec. and Mar.–early Apr.* ◎| *Breakfast.*

$$
HOTEL
Fodor's Choice
★

Twisp River Suites. These chic, comfortable, and contemporary rooms and condominium-style suites are on the banks of the Twisp River, lined by ponderosa pine and frequented by bald eagles. **Pros:** riverfront views; sleek and modern mountain feel, next door to a popular brewpub. **Cons:** not too much to do in the little town of Twisp. $ *Rooms from: $199* ✉ *140 W. Twisp Ave., Twisp* ☎ *509/997–0100, 855/784–8328* ⊕ *www.twispriversuites.com* ⟿ *5 rooms, 8 suites* ◎| *Breakfast.*

Sun Mountain Lodge

SPORTS AND OUTDOORS

MULTI-SPORT OUTFITTERS

North Cascades Mountain Guides. This outfitter provides guided days of backcountry skiing ($375) and rock climbing ($175 half day, $310 full day) or a half day of each ($340), as well as mountaineering courses, ice-climbing expeditions, and more. ✉ *48 Lost River Rd., Mazama* ☎ *509/996–3194* ⊕ *www.ncmountainguides.com.*

HIKING

Methow Valley Ranger District. Miles of hiking trails, including the famed Pacific Crest Trail, abound in the wilderness surrounding Winthrop. The ranger district has information about trails and conditions in the Okanogan-Wenatchee National Forest. ✉ *24 W. Chewuch Rd.* ☎ *509/996–4003* ⊕ *www.fs.usda.gov/okawen/.*

RAFTING

Outdoor Adventures. Beginning and experienced paddlers are welcome on rafting trips through the rapids of the Methow River. Half-day excursions are $85. ☎ *800/282–4043* ⊕ *outdooradventurecenter.com.*

SKIING

Methow Valley Sport Trails Association. The Methow Valley boasts one of the most extensive groomed cross-country ski trail systems in the nation. Fat bikes and snowshoes are also allowed. When there's no snow, the trails are open to dirt bikers and are said to be some of the best for dirt biking in the state. ✉ *309 Riverside Ave.* ☎ *509/996–3287 office, 509/996–3860 trail conditions* ⊕ *www.mvsta.com.*

North Cascade Heli-Skiing. If they can afford it, experienced skiers looking for fresh powder can get dropped off in virgin, backcountry snow by a

Stehekin River Valley

helicopter for one day of runs ($1,200) or three days in a row ($3,200). Three- or four-night yurt trips are also available ($1,250 and $1,400). ⊠ *31 Early Winters Dr., at the Freestone Inn, Mazama* ☎ *509/996–3272* ⊕ *www.heli-ski.com.*

CENTRAL CASCADES

Lake Chelan, with its sparkling glacier-fed waters, is one of Washington's longtime favorite destinations. Temperatures soar at this mountain lake in the summer, when vacationers flock to its shores. The remote outpost of Stehekin, not accessible by any road, hugs its northern end. To the south, the Bavarian-style town of Leavenworth hosts numerous festivals, along with outdoor fun and plenty of bratwurst. Wenatchee, known for the apples plucked from its local orchards, and Cashmere, with its candied aplets and cotlets, anchor the region's southeast corner. Like its North Cascades neighbor, this area is also good for hiking, backpacking, fishing, rafting, skiing, and other winter snow sports.

CHELAN

181 miles east of Seattle.

Lake Chelan, a sinewy, 50½-mile-long fjord—Washington's deepest lake—works its way from the town of Chelan, at its south end, to Stehekin, at the far northwest edge. The scenery is unparalleled, the flat blue water encircled by plunging gorges, with a vista of snow-slathered mountains beyond. No roads access the lake except for the shoreline around Chelan, so a floatplane or boat is needed to see the whole thing. Resorts dot the warmer eastern shores. Its northwestern end, at Stehekin, just penetrates North Cascades National Park. South of the lake, 9,511-foot Bonanza Peak is the tallest nonvolcanic peak in Washington.

Today Chelan serves as the favorite beach resort of western Washingtonians. In summer Lake Chelan is one of the hottest places in Washington, with temperatures often soaring above 100°F. The mountains surrounding the 50½-mile-long fjord-like lake rise from a height of about 4,000 feet near Chelan to 8,000 and 9,000 feet near the town of Stehekin, at the head of the lake.

GETTING HERE AND AROUND

From Seattle it takes about three hours, 15 minutes to reach Chelan by either Highway 2 (Stevens Pass) or Interstate 90 (Snoqualmie Pass) then north via Highway 97. From Spokane it's about three hours via Highways 2 and 17.

ESSENTIALS

Visitor Information Lake Chelan Chamber of Commerce ⊠ *102 E. Johnson Ave.* ☎ *509/682–3503* ⊕ *www.lakechelan.com.*

Purple Point Information Center. Rangers here offer guidance on hiking and camping and information about the national parks and recreation areas. This is a good place to pick up permits and passes. Maps and concise displays explain the complicated ecology of the valley, which encompasses in its length virtually every ecosystem in the Northwest. Hours vary in spring and fall. ⊠ *Stehekin Valley Rd., ¼ mile north of Stehekin Landing, Stehekin* ☎ *360/856–5700* ☉ *Mid-Mar.–mid-Oct., daily 8:30–5.*

EXPLORING

Lake Chelan Boat Co. The *Lady of the Lake II* makes journeys from May to October, departing Chelan at 8:30 and returning at 6 ($40.50 round-trip). The *Lady Express*, a speedy catamaran, runs between Stehekin, Holden Village, the national park, and Lake Chelan year-round; schedules vary with the seasons. Tickets are $61 round-trip. The vessels also can drop off and pick up at lakeshore trailheads. ⊠ *1418 Woodin Ave., Chelan* ☎ *509/682–4584, 888/682–4584* ⊕ *www.ladyofthelake.com.*

Lake Chelan State Park. Right on the lake and 9 miles west of Chelan on the opposite (less crowded) shore, this 127-acre park with 6,000 feet of shoreline is a favorite hangout for folks from the cool west side of the Cascades who want to soak up some sun. There are docks, a boat ramp, RV sites with full hookups, and lots of campsites for those who prefer a less "citified" approach to camping. ⊠ *7544 S. Lakeshore Rd., U.S. 97A, west to South Shore Dr. or Navarre Coulee Rd.* ☎ *360/902–8844, 509/687–3710* ⊕ *www.parks.wa.gov* ☜ *Day pass $10 per vehicle, annual Discovery Pass $30 (valid at all state parks), camping $20–$42* ☉ *Memorial Day–Labor Day, daily 6:30 am–10 pm.*

Twenty-Five Mile Creek State Park. Directly north of Lake Chelan State Park, this park also abuts the lake's eastern shore. It has many of the same facilities as the Chelan park, including a modern marina that offers easier access to the lake's upper reaches, and because it's the more remote of the two, it's often less crowded. ✉ *20530 South Lakeshore Rd.* ☎ *509/687–3610, 800/452–5687* ⊕ *www.parks.wa.gov* ◯ *Apr.– Sept., daily dawn–dusk.*

WHERE TO STAY

$$$$
RESORT
▢ **Campbell's Resort.** This long-established lakeshore landmark has 8 acres of landscaped grounds and 1,200 feet of pristine sandy beach-front, and every room has a balcony or patio with lake views and at least a microwave and refrigerator; some have kitchens and fireplaces. **Pros:** lots of activities as well as tranquil spaces; private beach; lake and mountain views; low off-season rates. **Cons:** very busy high sea-son. ⑤ *Rooms from: $275* ✉ *104 W. Woodin Ave.* ☎ *509/682–2561, 800/553–8225* ⊕ *www.campbellsresort.com* ↩ *170 rooms* ❚◯❚ *No meals.*

$$$$
RENTAL
▢ **The Lake House at Chelan.** Just across the street from lakeshore Don Morse Park you'll find these sophisticated and impeccable condominium-style rental units with one or three bedrooms and full modern kitchens, fireplaces, and decks or patios. **Pros:** modern and immaculate; family-friendly; year-round pool; reasonable shoulder and off-season rates; secured underground parking. **Cons:** some traf-fic noise from State Route 150, which fronts the property; no restau-rant or bar on-site. ⑤ *Rooms from: $299* ✉ *402 W. Manson Highway* ☎ *509/293–5982, 877/293–5982* ⊕ *www.lakehousechelan.com* ↩ *40 condominiums* ❚◯❚ *No meals.*

$$$
HOTEL
Fodor'sChoice
★
▢ **Lake View Hotel.** In the heart of Chelan's historic downtown overlook-ing a riverfront park, you'll find deluxe rooms in warm, earthen tones featuring high ceilings, wrought-iron balconies, skylights, and lake and river views. **Pros:** sophisticated feel; prime location. **Cons:** not suitable for families; no on-site parking; $50 cancellation fee, or 50% of first night if canceled within two weeks. ⑤ *Rooms from: $225* ✉ *104 E. Woodin Ave.* ☎ *509/682–1334* ⊕ *chelanhotel.com* ↩ *12 rooms* ❚◯❚ *No meals.*

STEHEKIN

44 miles northwest of Chelan.

Fodor'sChoice
★
One of the most beautiful and secluded valleys in the Pacific North-west, Stehekin was homesteaded by hardy souls in the late 19th cen-tury. It's actually not a town, but rather a small community set at the scenic northwest end of Lake Chelan, and it's accessible only by boat, floatplane, or trail. Year-round residents—there are about a hundred of them—enjoy a wilderness lifestyle. They have intermittent outside com-munications, boat-delivered supplies, and just two dozen cars among them—vehicles must be barged in, after all. Even on a peak summer season day, only around 200 visitors make the trek here.

GETTING HERE AND AROUND

The only way to get to Stehekin is by boat, plane, or on foot; most visi-tors make the trip by boat, including the ferries operated by the Lake Chelan Boat Co. *(see above).*

EXPLORING

Buckner Homestead. Dating from 1889, this restored pioneer farm includes an apple orchard, farmhouse, barn, and many ranch buildings. One-hour ranger-guided tours of the property, now maintained by a nonprofit foundation, are offered on weekends in July and August; otherwise, you can pick up a self-guided tour booklet from the drop box. ⊠ *Stehekin Valley Rd., 3½ miles north of Stehekin Landing, Stehekin* ⊕ *www.bucknerhomestead.org* ☉ *June–Sept., daily 9–5.*

WHERE TO EAT

$
CAFÉ

✕ **Stehekin Pastry Company.** As you enter this lawn-framed timber chalet, you're immersed in the tantalizing aromas of a European bakery. Glassed-in display cases are filled with trays of homemade baked goods, and the pungent espresso is eye-opening. Sit down at a window-side table and dig into an over-filled sandwich or rich bowl of soup—and don't forget dessert: we're guessing you'll never taste a better slice of pie, made with fruit fresh-picked from local orchards. Although it's outside town, the shop is conveniently en route to Rainbow Falls. ⑤ *Average main: $5* ⊠ *Stehekin Valley Rd., about 2 miles north of Stehekin Landing, Stehekin* ☎ *509/682–7742* ⊕ *www.stehekinpastry.com* ⊟ *No credit cards* ☉ *Closed Mon.–Thurs. and mid-Oct.–Memorial Day.*

$$
AMERICAN

✕ **Restaurant at Stehekin Valley Ranch.** Meals in the rustic log ranch house, served at polished wood tables, include buffet dinners of steak, ribs, hamburgers, salad, beans, and dessert. Note that breakfast is served 7 to 9, lunch is noon to 1, and dinner is 5:30 to 7. Show up later than that and you'll find the kitchen is closed. If you want to enjoy a drink with your meal, you can bring your own alcohol—it's not otherwise served. For guests not staying at the ranch, dinner reservations are required and transportation from the Stehekin Landing costs $6. ⑤ *Average main: $18* ⊠ *Stehekin Valley Rd., 9 miles north of Stehekin Landing, Stehekin* ☎ *509/682–4677, 800/536–0745* ⊕ *www.stehekinvalleyranch.com* ⌂ *Reservations essential* ⊟ *No credit cards* ☉ *Closed Oct.–mid-June.*

WHERE TO STAY

$
HOTEL

🏨 **North Cascades Lodge at Stehekin.** Crackling fires and Lake Chelan views are provided both in standard rooms in the Alpine House, with its shared lounge and lakeside deck, and in larger rooms in the Swiss Mont building, with private decks overlooking the water. **Pros:** on the water; recreation center with pool table; tent-to-tent hiking excursions; kayaking. **Cons:** no air-conditioning; TV is only available in the recreation building; out of range of cell-phone service. ⑤ *Rooms from: $128* ⊠ *955 Stehekin Valley Rd., Stehekin* ☎ *509/682–4494* ⊕ *www.lodgeatstehekin.com* ⇆ *28 rooms, 1 house* ⏽⏽ *No meals.*

$$$
B&B/INN

🏨 **Stehekin Valley Ranch.** Alongside pretty meadows at the edge of pine forest, this rustic ranch is a center for hikers and horseback riders, who stay in barnlike cabins with cedar paneling, tile floors, and a private bath, or canvas-roof tent cabins with bunk beds, kerosene lamps, and shared bathrooms. **Pros:** many activities; free vehicle use with kitchen cabins. **Cons:** no bathrooms in tent cabins. ⑤ *Rooms from: $250* ⊠ *Stehekin Valley Rd., 9 miles north of Stehekin Landing, Stehekin* ☎ *509/682–4677, 800/536–0745* ⊕ *www.stehekinvalleyranch.*

com ↝ *7 tent cabins (shared bathroom), 8 cabins* ⊘ *Closed Oct.–mid-June* ⫝̸ *All meals.*

SPORTS AND THE OUTDOORS

On a scenic half-day raft trip you can traverse the lower section of the Stehekin River, which winds through cottonwood and pine forest, from Yawning Glacier on the slopes of Magic Mountain southeast to Lake Chelan.

Stehekin Valley Ranch Activities. The popular ranch is a good launch-pad for mountain biking, day hiking, and fishing, and offers kayaking ($40) and horseback riding ($60 half day, $135 full day). There's a free shuttle from Stehekin Landing. ⊠ *Stehekin Valley Rd., 9 miles from Stehekin Landing, Stehekin* ☏ *509/682–4677, 800/536–0745* ⊕ *stehekinvalleyranch.com.*

Mountain bikers also make their way into this rugged terrain.

Stehekin Discovery Bikes. Bikes can be rented for $4 per hour or $25 for 24 hours. The $35 Ranch Breakfast Ride is a popular package; riders are transported to Stehekin Valley Ranch for custom breakfasts, then explore the valley at their own pace. ⊠ *Stehekin Valley Rd., 5-minute walk from the boat landing, Stehekin* ⊕ *stehekindiscoverybikes.com.*

WENATCHEE

39 miles southwest of Chelan.

Wenatchee (we-*nat*-chee), the county seat of Chelan County, is an attractive city in a shallow valley at the confluence of the Wenatchee and Columbia rivers. Surrounded by orchards, Wenatchee is known as the "Apple Capital of Washington." Downtown has many old commercial buildings as well as apple-packing houses where visitors can buy locally grown apples by the case (at about half the price charged in supermarkets). The paved Apple Valley Recreation Loop Trail runs on both sides of the Columbia River. It crosses the river on bridges at the northern and southern ends of town and connects several riverfront parks. The Wenatchee section is lighted until midnight.

The town was built on an ancient Wenatchi tribal village, which may have been occupied as long as 11,000 years ago, as recent archaeological finds of Clovis hunter artifacts suggest. (The Clovis hunters, also known as Paleo-Indians, were members of the oldest tribes known to have inhabited North America.)

GETTING HERE AND AROUND

Horizon Air serves Wenatchee's Pangborn Memorial Airport. Amtrak's Empire Builder, which runs from Chicago to Seattle, stops in Wenatchee; Greyhound Bus Lines serves the town, too. From Seattle it's about a 2½-hour drive to Wenatchee via Highway 2 or Interstate 90 and Highway 97; from Spokane it takes about three hours via Highway 2 or Interstate 90.

ESSENTIALS

Visitor Information Wenatchee Chamber of Commerce ⊠ *1 S. Wentachee Ave.* ☎ *509/662–2116, 800/572–7753* ⊕ *www.wenatcheevalley.org.* **Wenatchee Valley Convention and Visitor Bureau** ⊠ *1 S. Wenatchee Ave., Ste. 100* ☎ *800/572–7753* ⊕ *wenatchee.org.*

EXPLORING

Aplets and Cotlets/Liberty Orchards Co., Inc. Surrounded by snowcapped mountain peaks, Cashmere, 11 miles northwest of Wenatchee, is one of Washington's oldest towns, founded by Oblate missionaries back in 1853, when the Wenatchi and their vast herds of horses still roamed free over the bunch grasslands of the region. Some of the great Wenatchi leaders are buried in the mission cemetery. Today Cashmere is the apple, apricot, and pear capital of the Wenatchee Valley. Aplets and Cotlets/ Liberty Orchards Co., Inc. was founded by two Armenian brothers who escaped the massacres of Armenians by Turks early in the 20th century, settled in this peaceful valley, and became orchardists. When a marketing crisis hit the orchards in the 1920s, the brothers remembered dried-fruit confections from their homeland, re-created them, and named them aplets (made from apples) and cotlets (made from apricots). Sales took off almost immediately, and today aplets and cotlets are known as the combination that made Cashmere famous. Free samples are offered during the 15-minute tour of the plant. If production isn't taking place, be sure to watch the video in the candy shop, which displays memorabilia and usually has specially priced confections. ⊠ *117 Mission Ave., Cashmere* ☎ *509/782–2191* ⊕ *www.libertyorchards.com* ⊠ *Free* ☉ *Apr.–Dec., daily 8:30–5:30; Jan.–Mar., weekdays 8:30–4:30; tours every 20 mins with some exceptions for breaks.*

Okanogan-Wenatchee National Forest. More than 4 million acres of pines extend from the eastern slopes of the Cascades to the crest of the Wenatchee Mountains and north to Lake Chelan. Camping, hiking, boating, fishing, hunting, and picnicking are popular activities. ⊠ *215 Melody La.* ☎ *509/664–9200* ⊕ *www.fs.fed.us/r6/wenatchee* ⊠ *$5 daily parking pass, or $30 Northwest Forest Pass* ☉ *Daily 24 hrs.*

Rocky Reach Dam. There's a museum and visitor center here, as well as picnic tables and elaborately landscaped grounds. The Gallery of the Columbia has the pilothouse of the late-19th-century Columbia River steamer *Bridgeport,* Native American tools and replica dwellings, and loggers' and railroad workers' tools. The Gallery of Electricity has exhibits making a case for why dams are good for us. ⊠ *U.S. 97A N, about 10 miles north of Wenatchee* ☎ *509/663–7522* ⊕ *www. chelanpud.org/visitor-center.html* ⊠ *Free* ☉ *Park, daily dawn–dusk; museum, daily 8:30–5; visitor center, daily 8:30–5:30.*

Wenatchee Valley Museum & Cultural Center. Displays include local Native American and pioneer artifacts, the story of the Washington apple industry, and the 1931 landing of the first-ever flight across the Pacific. Children enjoy the hands-on area and the model railway. There are also Northwest artist exhibits. ⊠ *127 S. Mission St.* ☎ *509/888–6240* ⊕ *www.wvmcc.org* ⊠ *$5, free on first Fri. of month* ☉ *Tues.–Sat. 10–4 (open until 7 on first Fri. of month).*

15

WHERE TO EAT

$ ✕**Anjou Bakery.** Located on the edge of a pear orchard, this easily
BAKERY   accessible bakeshop boasts an industrial–vintage-farmhouse feel and
the best breads and pastries in the region—from bread pudding and
almond meringue cookies to lemon cheesecake, muffins, and a rustic
apricot or pear Danish. Enjoy an espresso or European-style sandwich
(baguette, butter, cured meats, cheeses) at a picnic table indoors or on
the sunny patio anchored by a modern, concrete water feature and lots
of lavender. ⑤ *Average main: $6* ✉ *3898 Old Monitor Rd., Cashmere*
☎ *509/782–4360* ⊕ *www.anjoubakery.com* ☉ *Closed Mon.–Wed. No
dinner.*

$ ✕**Badger Mountain Brewing.** A large window lets guests sneak a peek at
BARBECUE   the brewing operation while quenching their thirst with some two-dozen
taps and enjoying generous pulled-pork sandwiches and other barbe-
cue staples (slaw, corn bread, baby back ribs), provided by the on-site
Country Boy's Southern Style BBQ. ⑤ *Average main: $8* ✉ *1 Orondo
Ave.* ☎ *509/888–2234, 509/667–7427* ⊕ *www.countryboysbbq.com*
☉ *Closed Sun. and Mon.*

$ ✕**Bob's Classic Brass and Brew.** A classic hot-pink car on a pedestal in
BURGER   the parking lot beckons diners to this longtime burger joint, where
another car is positioned to look as though it's coming through the
roof. This casual, sometimes noisy eatery serves up a variety of burgers
with fries and onion rings, plus prime rib, teriyaki skewers, overstuffed
sandwiches, and wraps, salads, and pasta dishes. Different happy hour
specials are offered almost every day. ⑤ *Average main: $10* ✉ *110 2nd
St.* ☎ *509/663–3954.*

$$ ✕**Garlini's Napoletana.** This casually elegant and romantic Italian eat-
ITALIAN   ery is known for its pastas and wood-fired pizzas. You can start with
steamed clams, bruschetta, or tomato-Gorgonzola bisque. If you're not
in the mood for pizza, there's cannelloni, lasagna, chicken Milanese, and
other standards. On Sunday, it's happy hour all day in the bar. ⑤ *Aver-
age main: $18* ✉ *212 5th St.* ☎ *509/884–1707* ⊕ *garlinisrestaurant.com.*

$ ✕**McGlinn's Public House.** This popular public house, with its exposed-
AMERICAN   brick walls and high, wood-beam ceilings goes beyond traditional pub
fare (that's available, too) with an ample variety of starters, specialty
salads, pastas, and entrées like wild Alaskan salmon and steak. Wash
it all down with one of the craft beers on tap. But don't forget dessert;
there's beer-bread strawberry shortcake, peanut-butter pie, apple crisp
with vanilla ice cream, and more. ⑤ *Average main: $15* ✉ *111 Orondo
Ave.* ☎ *509/663–9073* ⊕ *www.mcglinns.com.*

$$ ✕**Shakti's.** The small, two-level restaurant and bar has twinkling white
ECLECTIC   lights that create a romantic ambience, and an eclectic menu that offers
several pasta dishes as well as steak and seafood. A charming garden
is open during the warmer months for patio dining. ⑤ *Average main:
$20* ✉ *218 N. Mission St.* ☎ *509/662–3321* ⊕ *www.shaktisfinedining.
com* ☉ *Closed Sun.*

$$$$ ✕**The Windmill.** The comfortable old roadhouse, gamely topped by a
AMERICAN   windmill, was built in 1931. Here it's all about home-style food, particularly steak: famous entrées include whiskey pepper steak (pepper-
coated New York strip sautéed, flamed with whiskey, and finished

with mushrooms in a rich demi-glace), slow-roasted prime rib, and marinated tenderloin chunks, flamed with cognac. Seafood isn't to be overlooked, either; try the salmon with herbed butter and white wine, jumbo tempura prawns, or prawn sauté. Can't decide? The surf-and-turf dinner includes tenderloin and lobster tail. If you still have room after the entrée, splurge on a piece of fresh-baked pie or cheesecake, and wash it all down with a regional wine. ⑤ *Average main: $35* ⊠ *1501 N. Wenatchee Ave.* ☎ *509/665–9529* ⊙ *No lunch.*

WHERE TO STAY

$

HOTEL

Coast Wenatchee Center Hotel. A skywalk links these tidy and comfortable rooms to a convention center, a bonus for travelers on business, but there are enough facilities and amenities, including indoor and outdoor pools, to appeal to vacationing families, too. **Pros:** convenient access to local sights and activities; suites have kitchenettes. **Cons:** standard hotel atmosphere. ⑤ *Rooms from: $129* ⊠ *201 N. Wenatchee Ave.* ☎ *509/662–1234, 800/716–6199* ⊕ *www.wenatcheecenter.com* ⌁ *147 rooms* ⦿ *Breakfast.*

$$

B&B/INN

Warm Springs Inn & Winery. Roses planted along the driveway lead you to this 1917 mansion, set amid 10 acres of gardens, with rooms filled with a tasteful selection of art and antiques; some look out onto the Wenatchee River. **Pros:** charming, quiet setting; wine tasting. **Cons:** wedding bookings fill rooms far in advance. ⑤ *Rooms from: $165* ⊠ *1611 Love La.* ☎ *509/662–5863* ⊕ *www.warmspringsinn.com* ⌁ *5 rooms, 1 suite* ⦿ *Breakfast.*

SHOPPING

Pybus Public Market. Located in a renovated warehouse along the Columbia River, this market offers specialty food products, fresh produce from nearby farms, artisanal cheeses, seafood, coffee, gelato, and charcuterie, as well as a few restaurants and gift shops. It's been likened to an eastern Washington version of the much larger and older Pike Place Market in Seattle. ⊠ *7 N. Worthen Ave.* ☎ *509/888–3900* ⊕ *www. pybuspublicmarket.org.*

SPORTS AND THE OUTDOORS

SKIING

Mission Ridge Ski Area. Four lifts, 33 downhill runs, powder snow, and some 30 miles of marked cross-country trails make Mission Ridge one of Washington's most popular ski areas. There's a 2,100-foot vertical drop, and the snowmaker scatters whiteness from the top to bottom slopes during the season. Snowboarding is allowed. Lift tickets cost $55 per day. ⊠ *7500 Mission Ridge Rd.* ☎ *509/663–6543, 800/374–1693 snow conditions* ⊕ *www.missionridge.com* ⊙ *mid-Nov.–Apr., Thurs.– Mon. 9–4 (daily during school breaks).*

LEAVENWORTH

23 miles northwest of Wenatchee, 118 miles northeast of Seattle.

Leavenworth is a favorite weekend getaway for Seattle folks, and it's easy to see why: the charming (if occasionally *too* cute) Bavarian-style village, home to good restaurants and attractive lodgings, is a hub for some of the Northwest's best skiing, hiking, rock climbing, rafting, canoeing, and snowshoeing.

A railroad and mining center for many years, Leavenworth fell on hard times around the 1960s, and civic leaders, looking for ways to capitalize on the town's setting in the heart of the Central Cascade Range, convinced shopkeepers and other businesspeople to maintain a gingerbread-Bavarian architectural style in their buildings. Today, even the Safeway supermarket and the Chevron gas station adhere to the theme. Restaurants prepare Bavarian-influenced dishes, candy shops sell Swiss-style chocolates, and stores and boutiques stock music boxes, dollhouses, and other Bavarian items.

GETTING HERE AND AROUND

From Seattle, Leavenworth can be reached by either of Washington's most-developed mountain passes—Stevens (Highway 2) or Snoqualmie (Interstate 90, then a short jog up Highway 97/Blewett Pass); either takes about 2½ hours. From Spokane, traveling west via Highway 2 takes about 3½ hours. Amtrak's Empire Builder now makes daily trips from Spokane and Seattle to Leavenworth, and Greyhound Bus Lines also serves the town.

ESSENTIALS

Visitor Information Leavenworth Chamber of Commerce ☎ *509/548–5807* ⊕ *www.leavenworth.org.*

EXPLORING

Leavenworth Upper Valley Museum. Settled into the 19th-century, barn-style Big Haus, this museum evokes pioneer days in the Cascades. The riverside grounds, where Arabian stallion were once put to graze, now host Audubon programs that take advantage of plentiful bird sightings. Exhibits highlight the lives and times of the Field family, local Native American tribes, and other prominent residents of Leavenworth and the Upper Wenatchee Valley. ⊠ *347 Division St.* ☎ *509/548–0728* ⊕ *www.uppervalleymuseum.org* ⊒ *$3* ☼ *Apr.–Oct., Wed.–Sun. 10–5; Nov.–Mar., Thurs.–Sun. 10–4.*

Nutcracker Museum and Shop. Nearly 6,000 modern and antique nutcrackers — some of them centuries old — are displayed in the upstairs museum and sold downstairs in a popular shop that stocks nutcrackers of all sizes and in the likeness of all kinds of characters. ⊠ *735 Front St.* ☎ *509/548–4573, 800/892–3989* ⊕ *www.nutcrackermuseum.com and www.nussknackerhaus.com* ⊒ *$2.50* ☼ *Museum, May–Oct. daily 1–5; Nov.–Apr. weekends 2–5; store, daily 10–5.*

Red Tail Canyon Farm. Arrange for group hay rides aboard a horse-drawn wagon through a peaceful valley and tree farm from April through October (10-person minimum, $150, reservations required). The experience includes a barbecue cookout. In winter, sleigh rides are offered through the woods, and you can warm up with hot cocoa by a campfire afterward ($17.50 per person). ⊠ *11780 Freund Canyon Rd.* ☎ *509/548–4512, 800/678–4512* ⊕ *www.redtailcanyonfarmleavenworth.com.*

Holiday season in Leavenworth

WHERE TO EAT

$$ ✕ **Andreas Keller German Restaurant.** Merry "oompah" music bubbles out
GERMAN from marching accordion players at this fun-focused dining hub, where
the theme is "Germany without the Passport." Laughing crowds lap up
strong, cold brews and feast on a selection of brat-, knack-, weiss-, and
mettwursts, Polish sausage, Wienerschnitzel and Schnitzel Cordon Bleu,
all nestled into heaping sides of sauerkraut, tangy German potato salad,
and thick, dark rye bread. Get a taste of it all with the sampler plate—
and save room for the knockout apple strudel. Note that service can be
slow at times, so just sit back and enjoy the ambience. You just might
get called to stand up and do the "chicken dance." $ *Average main: $17*
✉ *829 Front St.* ☎ *509/548–6000* ⊕ *www.andreaskellerrestaurant.com.*

$$ ✕ **Bären Haus.** The cuisine at this spacious, noisy, and often crowded
GERMAN beer hall–style room may not be haute, but the generous servings will
appeal to hungry travelers. Fill up on basic American and German fare
in the large dining room, located in a historic corner building with a
high ceiling and exposed brick walls. For lunch and dinner, there are
burgers and fries, sandwiches, pizza, and pasta, as well as bratwurst,
schnitzel, German sausage, stuffed cabbage rolls, and potato pancakes.
For dessert, try German apple or German chocolate cake. $ *Average
main: $17* ✉ *208 9th St.* ☎ *509/548–4535* ⊕ *www.barenhaus.com*
🕓 *No breakfast weekdays (except most holidays).*

$$ ✕ **Cafe Mozart.** This elegant upstairs eatery resembles a central Euro-
ECLECTIC pean town house, capturing the essence of *Gemütlichkeit* (coziness)
in the way the small dining rooms are decorated and the drapes are
cut. The wine cellar, visible from the intimate dining room, is quite
extensive for a restaurant of its size. Authentic aromas drift from the

kitchen, too, promising superb, well-constructed dishes that will not disappoint. Start, perhaps, with cold-smoked Norwegian salmon on a potato pancake, followed by a "symphony of schnitzels" (veal or pork topped with a choice of sauces), duck breast in a ruby port reduction with sautéed Bing cherries, or rainbow trout fillet with toasted almond butter. Almond cream-filled marzipan torte, apple strudel, or a "chorus of crêpes" might conclude the meal. A pianist plays during weekend dinners. $ *Average main: $20* ✉ *829 Front St., upstairs* ☎ *509/548–0600* ⊕ *www.cafemozartrestaurant.com.*

$ ╳ **Carlos 1800 Mexican Grill and Cantina.** At this light, bright, and casual
MODERN spot the usual fare includes tacos, enchiladas, burritos, and fajitas, as
MEXICAN well as entrées with a Yucatecan influence, such as green mole and *pipian* sauce (made from pumpkin and sesame seeds, peanuts, and chili peppers). The specialty is *conchinita pibil,* or pork marinated in achiote paste and sour-orange juice, then cooked in a banana leaf. There are also several prawn dishes as well as fish tacos. $ *Average main: $14* ✉ *633 Front St.* ☎ *509/888–0265* ⊕ *carlos1800.com.*

$ ╳ **Gustav's Grill and Beer Garden.** Traditional Bavarian pub food meets
GERMAN Pacific Northwest cuisine at this Leavenworth landmark, topped with a distinctive onion dome and anchored by a large river-rock fireplace. Munch on German sausage, an array of gourmet burgers, sandwiches, and salads. When the weather's nice, enjoy one of 30 beers on the sun-soaked deck with spectacular mountain views. When it's cold, come inside and play board games by the fire. $ *Average main: $10* ✉ *617 Hwy. 2* ☎ *509/548–4509* ⊕ *www.gustavsleavenworth.com.*

$ ╳ **Icicle Brewing Company.** Enjoy a cold Bootjack IPA, Dirtyface Amber,
AMERICAN or Priebe Porter at a picnic table in the lively beer garden overlooking the town's main drag. Inside, check out stainless-steel fermentation tanks or play a board game while you quench your thirst. $ *Average main: $5* ✉ *935 Front St.* ☎ *509/548–2739* ⊕ *www.iciclebrewing.com.*

$$ ╳ **Pavz Cafe Bistro.** This cozy, long, narrow room has only eight tables
ECLECTIC and serves up an eclectic mix of Pacific Northwest and European fare— from seafood, steak, and pasta to soups, salads, and sandwiches. But the signature dishes here are the savory and sweet crepes. Choose from portobello mushroom, topped with blue cheese, cream sauce, and walnuts; spicy Italian, with sausage, roasted red peppers, basil, ricotta, and four cheeses—it's thick and baked, resembling lasagna; and the Black Forest ham, with cremini mushrooms, béchamel sauce, and Parmesan and mozzarella cheeses. On the sweet side, there are hazel nougat, mango, and strawberry crepes as well as assorted cakes and other desserts. $ *Average main: $17* ✉ *833 Front St.* ☎ *509/548–2103* ⊕ *pavz-cafe.com.*

$$ ╳ **South.** An innovative menu of modern, Latin-inspired dishes provides
LATIN AMERICAN a nice—and spicy—change from all the Bavarian food in town. Enjoy sweet-potato and roasted poblano chili enchiladas, Yucatan chicken rojo, and Oaxacan black mole with chicken or pork, and be sure to take a trip to the salsa bar. It's not all south-of-the-border, though. While there's no Wienerschnitzel on the menu, there is German sausage and the popular South burger. The children's menu includes tacos, quesadillas, and even prawns, and oranges can be substituted for chips. More

than two-dozen kinds of tequila and a margarita infused with basil are among the drink choices. $\boxed{\text{\$}}$ *Average main: $17* ⊠ *913 Front St.* ☎ *509/888–4328* ⊕ *www.southleavenworth.com.*

$$$

ITALIAN

Fodor'sChoice

★

✕ **Visconti's.** This castle-like establishment provides fine Italian dining paired with one of the region's most extensive wine lists. For lunch, there's pizza and panini. At dinner, whet your appetite with an antipasti platter of cheeses and house-made salamis and sausages, then move on to such pastas as clam linguine or bone-in rib-eye steak and wild Alaskan sockeye salmon. The enterprise also includes Cured, a ground-floor meat shop with sausages and other meats; Viadolce Gelato, which sells flavors from almond to tiramisu; and Leavenworth Sausage Garten, a walk-up counter with picnic-table seating, craft beer, and sausages. $\boxed{\text{\$}}$ *Average main: $24* ⊠ *636 Front St.* ☎ *509/548–1213* ⊕ *www. viscontis.com.*

WHERE TO STAY

$$

B&B/INN

🏨 **Abendblume Pension.** Wonderful views of the mountains and Leavenworth Valley are afforded from each room's private balcony, and the many fireplaces and carved-wood walls and ceilings of this Bavarian-style country chalet give it an authentic alpine feel. **Pros:** very romantic; Bavarian breakfast is authentic and ample; exceptional hospitality. **Cons:** fills up quickly during festivals; strict cancellation policy. $\boxed{\text{\$}}$ *Rooms from: $159* ⊠ *12570 Ranger Rd., ¾ mile from downtown* ☎ *509/548–4059, 800/669–7634* ⊕ *www.abendblume.com* ⌁ *7 rooms* ⦿| *Breakfast.*

$$

RESORT

FAMILY

🏨 **Icicle Village Resort.** This nearly 7-acre, easily accessible resort has an array of amenities, including two outdoor pools, and attractive rooms and suites decorated with modern, mountain-chic flair. **Pros:** lots of on-site activities; very kid-friendly; full, hot breakfast buffet included, even for condominium guests. **Cons:** no room service (the restaurant offers takeout); it's nearly a mile walk along the highway to downtown shops and restaurants (cruiser bicycles are available to make the distance seem shorter). $\boxed{\text{\$}}$ *Rooms from: $152* ⊠ *505 Hwy. 2* ☎ *800/961–0162, 509/888–2776* ⊕ *www.iciclevillage.com* ⌁ *112 rooms, 9 suites, 27 condominiums* ⦿| *Breakfast.*

$$

HOTEL

FAMILY

🏨 **Linderhof Inn.** One of the best-value lodgings in town offers rooms that are basic yet modern and comfortable, with all the usual amenities and a bit of chintz added for character. **Pros:** seasonal pool; across the street from town and shopping; rooms all have microwaves; family-friendly. **Cons:** prices increase during Christmas, Oktoberfest, and festivals. $\boxed{\text{\$}}$ *Rooms from: $155* ⊠ *690 U.S. 2* ☎ *509/548–5283, 800/828–5680* ⊕ *www.linderhof.com* ⌁ *34 rooms* ⦿| *Breakfast.*

$$$$

B&B/INN

🏨 **Mountain Home Lodge.** This contemporary mountain inn, where peeled-pine and vine-maple furniture fill the rooms, is built of sturdy cedar and redwood and sits on a 20-acre alpine meadow with breathtaking Cascade Mountains views. **Pros:** pristine luxury; high-quality sports and activities. **Cons:** tough winter transportation; some rooms on the small side. $\boxed{\text{\$}}$ *Rooms from: $360* ⊠ *8201 Mountain Home Rd., 3 miles south of Leavenworth* ☎ *509/548–7077, 800/414–2378* ⊕ *www. mthome.com* ⌁ *10 rooms, 2 cabins* ⦿| *Breakfast.*

15

$$$ |🛏 **Run of the River.** This intimate, relaxed mountain inn stands on the
B&B/INN banks of the Icicle River near Leavenworth, placing the rustic rooms, with timber furnishings, private outside entrances, and decks, close to nature. **Pros:** close to town; abundant healthy breakfasts; lots of outdoor activities. **Cons:** a bit off the beaten path. ⑤ *Rooms from: $230* ⊠ *9308 E. Leavenworth Rd.* ☎ *509/548–7171, 800/288–6491* ⊕ *www.runoftheriver.com* ⇝ *6 rooms, 1 lodge* |◎| *Breakfast.*

$$$$ |🛏 **Sleeping Lady Mountain Resort.** Fall asleep on a hand-hewn log bed under
RESORT a down comforter along the banks of Icicle Creek at this quiet and scenic retreat in the heart of the Cascade Mountains, where lodge-like rooms are light and airy, with lots of wood accents. **Pros:** plenty of activities as well as peace and quiet; spectacular setting and scenery. **Cons:** it's a 10-minute drive into downtown Leavenworth; rooms do not have TVs, which may be a plus. ⑤ *Rooms from: $255* ⊠ *7375 Icicle Rd.* ☎ *509/548–6344* ⊕ *www.sleepinglady.com* ⇝ *58 rooms* |◎| *Some meals.*

SHOPPING

The Cheesemonger's Shop. Pick up a snack or the makings of a picnic at this lively basement-level cheese shop, where applewood-smoked chedder is the number one seller, and you'll be offered a sample as soon as one of the mongers makes eye contact. ⊠ *819 Front St.* ☎ *509/548–9011, 877/888–7389* ⊕ *www.cheesemongersshop.com.*

Homefires Bakery. Tucked inside a back corner of Dan's Food Market, which is easily accessible off the highway and offers ample parking, this homey little bakery turns out delicious breads, muffins, cookies, cakes, and pastries. Take a cinnamon roll or berry pie—and espresso—to go. You can satisfy your sweet tooth here daily from 6 am to 10 pm. ⊠ *1329 U.S. 2* ☎ *509/548–7362* ⊕ *www.homefiresbakery.com.*

Schocolat. Tucked in the back of the high-end home-decor and gourmet-kitchen store **Ganz Klasse,** which offers handcrafted wooden cutting boards, table linens, and porcelain pieces, **Schocolat** sells fine handcrafted chocolates in flavors like Raspberry Crown, with raspberry purée and Chambord; Earl Grey, with double bergamot tea; and Golden Cinnamon, with milk chocolate ganache, gold flecks, and Goldschläger Swiss cinnamon schnapps. ⊠ *834 Front St.* ☎ *509/548–7274* ⊕ *www.schocolat.com.*

SPORTS AND THE OUTDOORS

HIKING

The Leavenworth Ranger District has more than 320 miles of scenic trails, among them Hatchery Creek, Icicle Ridge, the Enchantments, Tumwater Canyon, Fourth of July Creek, Snow Lake, Stuart Lake, and Chatter Creek. Both of the following sell the Northwest Forest Pass ($5 day pass; $30 annual pass), which is required year-round for parking at trailheads and for camping in the upper Chiwawa Valley.

Lake Wenatchee Ranger Station. Updates on trails and fire closures are available here. ⊠ *22976 Hwy. 207* ☎ *509/763–3103* ⊕ *www.wta.org.*

Leavenworth Ranger District. Contact this district office for information on area hikes. ⊠ *600 Sherburne St.* ☎ *509/548–6977* ⊕ *www.leavenworth.org.*

HORSEBACK RIDING

Eagle Creek Ranch. Rent horses by the hour, or take daylong rides (including lunch) or overnight pack trips ($26–$65) at this ranch. Seasonal sleigh rides are also available ($16–$35). ☒ *7951 Eagle Creek Rd., 8 miles northwest of Leavenworth* ☎ *509/548–7798* ⊕ *www.eaglecreek.ws.*

Icicle Outfitters & Guides. You can enjoy 2- to 4-mile trail rides ($28–$55.50 per person) here, or daylong rides with lunch ($172), even two- to seven-day custom deluxe pack trips (starting at $200). ☒ *7373 Icicle Creek Rd.* ☎ *800/497–3912, 509/669–1518* ⊕ *www. icicleoutfitters.com.*

Mountain Springs Lodge. Horseback rides from 50 minutes to all day ($27–$135) long are offered here, as well as daytime sleigh rides ($24 or $26), moonlight dinner sleigh rides ($69), breakfast sleigh rides ($39), and snowmobile tours lasting one to five hours ($69–$265), including a moonlight dinner ride ($179). ☒ *19115 Chiwawa Loop Rd.* ☎ *509/763–2713, 800/858–2276* ⊕ *www.mtsprings.com.*

SKIING

More than 20 miles of cross-country ski trails lace the Leavenworth area.

Leavenworth Ski Hill. In winter enjoy a Nordic ski jump, snowboarding, tubing, and really great downhill and cross-country skiing here. In summer, come for the wildflowers or to catch the Leavenworth Summer Theatre's production of *The Sound of Music.* The ski hill is 1 mile north of downtown Leavenworth. The Play All Day Pass is $27; there's also a Nordic Day Pass ($16), an Alpine Day Pass ($16), and a Tubing Pass ($17). ☒ *Ski Hill Dr.* ☎ *509/548–5477* ⊕ *www.skileavenworth.com.*

Loup Loup Ski Bowl. Lift tickets at this small ski area, where you can downhill or telemark ski, cost $45 on weekends or holidays, and $40 on weekdays. ☒ *Off Hwy. 20, 20 miles east of town, Twisp* ☎ *509/557–3401 office, 509/557–3405 conditions* ⊕ *www.skitheloup.com.*

Stevens Pass. There's snowboarding and cross-country skiing here as well as 37 major downhill runs and slopes for skiers of every level. Lift tickets cost $67. Summer weekends, it's open for biking. ☒ *U.S. 2, Summit Stevens Pass, 51 miles west of Leavenworth, Skykomish* ☎ *206/812–4510* ⊕ *www.stevenspass.com.*

WHITE-WATER RAFTING

Rafting is popular from March to July; the prime high-country runoff occurs in May and June. The Wenatchee River, which runs through Leavenworth, is considered one of the best white-water rivers in the state—a Class III on the International Canoeing Association scale.

Alpine Adventures. Challenging white-water and relaxing river floats through spectacular scenery are the options here. A Wenatchee River white-water trip with lunch costs $84; a scenic Wenatchee River float (lunch included) is $79. The Methow River drift is $89. An Icicle River run (no lunch) is $49 and fills up fast. ☎ *800/723–8386, 509/470–7762* ⊕ *www.alpineadventures.com.*

Blue Sky Outfitters. Half- and full-day rafting trips on the Methow and Wenatchee rivers are offered by this outfitter. ☒ *Cashmere*

15

Riverside Park, Cashmere ☎ *206/938–4030, 800/228–7238* ⊕ *www. blueskyoutfitters.com.*

Leavenworth Outdoor Center. Rent tubes, rafts, kayaks, paddleboards, and bicycles at this shop, which provides a shuttle to the launch point along the Wenatchee River, and even outfits your pet pooch with a life jacket for a float downstream. ✉ *321 9th St.* ☎ *509/548–8823* ⊕ *www. leavenworthoutdoorcenter.com.*

Osprey Rafting Co. This outfitter offers 4½-hour trips on the Wenatchee River for $78.56, which includes wet suits and booties, transportation, and a barbecue lunch; there's a $50, two-hour trip for travelers short on time. ✉ *9342 Icicle Rd.* ☎ *509/548–6800, 888/548–6850* ⊕ *www. ospreyrafting.com.*

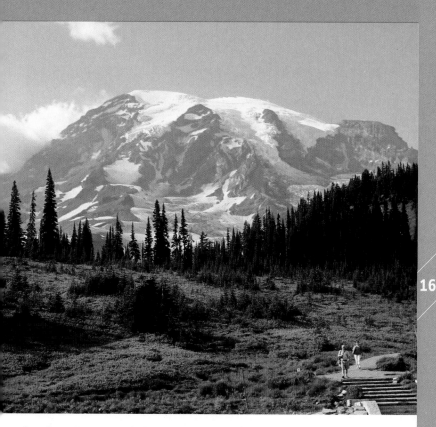

MOUNT RAINIER
NATIONAL PARK

WELCOME TO MOUNT RAINIER NATIONAL PARK

TOP REASONS TO GO

★ **The mountain:** Some say Mt. Rainier is the most magical mountain in America. At 14,411 feet, it is a popular peak for climbing, with more than 10,000 attempts per year—half of which are successful.

★ **The glaciers:** About 35 square miles of glaciers and snowfields encircle Mt. Rainier, including Carbon Glacier and Emmons Glacier, the largest glaciers by volume and area, respectively, in the continental United States.

★ **The wildflowers:** More than 100 species of wildflowers bloom in the park's high meadows; the display dazzles from midsummer until the snow falls.

★ **Fabulous hiking:** More than 240 miles of maintained trails provide access to old-growth forest, river valleys, lakes, and rugged ridges.

★ **Unencumbered wilderness:** Under the provisions of the 1964 Wilderness Act and the National Wilderness Preservation System, 97% of the park is preserved as wilderness.

1 Longmire. Inside the Nisqually Gate, explore Longmire historic district's museum and visitor center, ruins of the park's first hotel, or the nature loop. Nearby, delicate footbridges span the thundering Christine and Narada Falls.

2 Paradise. The park's most popular destination is famous for wildflowers in summer and skiing in winter. Skyline Trail is one of many hiking routes that crisscross the base of the mountain; the larger of the two park lodges is also here.

3 **Ohanapecosh.** Closest to the southeast entrance and the town of Packwood, the old-growth trees of the Grove of the Patriarchs are a must-see. Another short trail around nearby Tipsoo Lake has great views.

4 **Sunrise and White River.** This side of the park is easy to visit in summer if you enter from the east side, but it's a long drive from the southwest entrance. Sunrise is the highest stretch of road in the park and a great place to take in the alpenglow—reddish light on the peak of the mountain near sunrise and sunset. Mount Rainier's premier mountain-biking area, White River, is also the gateway to more than a dozen hiking trails.

5 **Carbon River and Mowich Lake.** Near the Carbon River Entrance Station is a swath of temperate forest, but to really get away from it all, follow the windy gravel roads to remote Mowich Lake.

GETTING ORIENTED

The jagged white crown of Mt. Rainier is the showpiece of the Cascades and the focal point of this 337-square-mile national park. The most popular destination in the park, Paradise, is in the southern region; Ohanapecosh, the Grove of the Patriarchs, and Tipsoo Lake are in the southeastern corner. Mount Rainier National Park's eastern and northern areas are dominated by wilderness. The snowy folds of the Cascade mountain range stretch out from this Washington park; Seattle is roughly 50 miles north and the volcanic ruins of Mt. St. Helens 100 miles south.

16

Map labels

Huckleberry Creek

SOURDOUGH MOUNTAINS

SUNRISE RIDGE

410

White River

Mather Memorial Parkway

Pacific Crest Trail

Sunrise
Visitor Center

4 **White River**
White River Entrance

GOVERNORS RIDGE

BOAT ISLAND MOUNTAIN

410

410

Tipsoo Lake

123

Wonderland Trail

COWLITZ DIVIDE

3

0   2 mi
0   2 km

Grove of the Patriarchs
Stevens Canyon Entrance

Visitor Center

123

Updated by
Shelley Arenas

Like a mysterious, white-clad chanteuse, veiled in clouds even when the surrounding forests and fields are bathed in sunlight, Mt. Rainier is the centerpiece of its namesake park. The impressive volcanic peak stands at an elevation of 14,411 feet, making it the fifth-highest peak in the Lower 48 states. Nearly 2 million visitors a year enjoy spectacular views of the mountain and return home with a lifelong memory of its image.

The mountain holds the largest glacial system in the contiguous United States, with more than two-dozen major glaciers. On the lower slopes you find silent forests made up of cathedral-like groves of Douglas fir, western hemlock, and western red cedar, some more than 1,000 years old. Water and lush greenery are everywhere in the park, and dozens of thundering waterfalls, accessible from the road or by a short hike, fill the air with mist.

MOUNT RAINIER PLANNER

WHEN TO GO

Rainier is the Puget Sound's weather vane: if you can see it, skies will be clear. Visitors are most likely to see the summit July through September. Crowds are heaviest in summer, too, meaning the parking lots at Paradise and Sunrise often fill before noon, campsites are reserved months in advance, and other lodgings are reserved as much as a year ahead.

True to its name, Paradise is often sunny during periods when the lowlands are under a cloud layer. The rest of the year, Rainier's summit gathers lenticular clouds whenever a Pacific storm approaches; once the peak vanishes from view, it's time to haul out rain gear. The rare periods of clear winter weather bring residents up to Paradise for cross-country skiing.

PLANNING YOUR TIME
MOUNT RAINIER IN ONE DAY

The best way to get a complete overview of Mount Rainier in a day is to enter via Nisqually and begin your tour by browsing in **Longmire Museum.** When you're done, get to know the environment in and around Longmire Meadow and the overgrown ruins of Longmire Springs Hotel on the 0.5-mile **Trail of the Shadows** nature loop.

From Longmire, Highway 706 East climbs northeast into the mountains toward Paradise. Take a moment to explore gorgeous **Christine Falls,** just north of the road, 1½ miles past Cougar Rock Campground, and **Narada Falls,** 3 miles farther on; both are spanned by graceful stone footbridges. Fantastic mountain views, alpine meadows crosshatched with nature trails, a welcoming lodge and restaurant, and the excellent **Jackson Memorial Visitor Center** combine to make lofty Paradise the primary goal of most park visitors. One outstanding (but challenging) way to explore the high country is to hike the 5-mile round-trip **Skyline Trail** to Panorama Point, which rewards you with stunning 360-degree views.

Continue eastward on Highway 706 East for 21 miles and leave your car to explore the incomparable, thousand-year-old **Grove of the Patriarchs.** Afterward, turn your car north toward White River and **Sunrise Visitor Center,** where you can watch the alpenglow fade from Mt. Rainier's domed summit.

GETTING HERE AND AROUND
CAR TRAVEL

The Nisqually entrance is on Highway 706, 14 miles east of Route 7; the Ohanapecosh entrance is on Route 123, 5 miles north of U.S. 12; and the White River entrance is on Route 410, 3 miles north of the Chinook and Cayuse Passes. These highways become mountain roads as they reach Rainier, winding up and down many steep slopes, so cautious driving is essential: use a lower gear, especially on downhill sections, and take care not to overheat brakes by constant use. These roads are subject to storms any time of year and are repaired in the summer from winter damage and washouts.

Side roads into the park's western slope are narrower, unpaved, and subject to flooding and washouts. All are closed by snow in winter except Highway 706 to Paradise and Carbon River Road, though the latter tends to flood near the park boundary. (Route 410 is open to the Crystal Mountain access road entrance.)

Park roads have a maximum speed of 35 mph in most places, and you have to watch for pedestrians, cyclists, and wildlife. Parking can be difficult during peak summer season, especially at Paradise, Sunrise, Grove of the Patriarchs, and at the trailheads between Longmire and Paradise; arrive early if you plan to visit these sites. All off-road-vehicle use—4X4 vehicles, ATVs, motorcycles, snowmobiles—is prohibited in Mount Rainier National Park.

16

PARK ESSENTIALS
PARK FEES AND PERMITS
The entrance fee of $15 per vehicle and $5 for those on foot, motorcycle, or bicycle is good for seven days. Annual passes are $30. Climbing permits are $45 per person per calendar year. Wilderness camping permits ($20 per party, up to 12 people; valid for 14 days) must be obtained for all backcountry trips and overnight climbs; advance reservations are highly recommended.

PARK HOURS
Mount Rainier National Park is open 24/7 year-round, but with limited access in winter. Gates at Nisqually (Longmire) are staffed year-round during the day; facilities at Paradise are open daily from late May to mid-October; and Sunrise is open daily July to early September. During off-hours you can buy passes at the gates from machines that accept credit and debit cards. Winter access to the park is limited to the Nisqually entrance, and the Jackson Memorial Visitor Center at Paradise is open on weekends and holidays in winter. The road from Longmire to Paradise is closed Tuesday and Wednesday during the winter; the Paradise snow-play area is open Thursday to Monday when there is sufficient snow.

CELL-PHONE RECEPTION
Cell-phone reception is unreliable throughout much of the park, although access is clear at Paradise, Sunrise, and Crystal Mountain. Public telephones are at all park visitor centers, at the National Park Inn at Longmire, and at Paradise Inn at Paradise.

RESTAURANTS
A limited number of restaurants are inside the park, and a few worth checking out lie beyond its borders. Mount Rainier's picnic areas are justly famous, especially in summer, when wildflowers fill the meadows. Resist the urge to feed the yellow pine chipmunks darting about.

HOTELS
The Mount Rainier area is remarkably bereft of quality lodging. Rainier's two national park lodges, at Longmire and Paradise, are attractive and well maintained. They exude considerable history and charm, especially Paradise Inn, but unless you've made summer reservations a year in advance, getting a room can be a challenge. Dozens of motels, cabin complexes, and private vacation home rentals are near the park entrances; while they can be pricey, the latter are convenient for longer stays. *Hotel reviews have been shortened. For full information, visit Fodors.com.*

WHAT IT COSTS IN U.S. DOLLARS			
$	**$$**	**$$$**	**$$$$**
Restaurants	Under $13	$13–$20	$21–$30	Over $30
Hotels	Under $101	$101–$150	$151–$200	Over $200

Restaurant prices are the average cost of a main course at dinner, or if dinner is not served, at lunch. Hotel prices are the lowest cost of a standard double room in high season.

VISITOR INFORMATION
PARK CONTACT INFORMATION
Mount Rainier National Park ✉ *55210 238th Ave. East, Ashford* ☎ *360/569–2211, 360/569–6675* ⊕ *www.nps.gov/mora.*

VISITOR CENTERS
Jackson Memorial Visitor Center. High on the mountain's southern flank, this center houses exhibits on geology, mountaineering, glaciology, and alpine ecology. Multimedia programs are staged in the theater; there's also a snack bar and gift shop. This is the park's most popular visitor destination, and it can be quite crowded in summer. ✉ *Hwy. 706 E, 19 miles east of Nisqually park entrance* ☎ *360/569–6571* ⊕ *www.nps.gov/mora/planyourvisit/paradise.htm* ⊙ *June 15–Sept. 1, daily 10–7; Sept. 2–14, daily 10–6; mid-Sept. 15–mid-Oct., daily 10–5; late Oct.–early Jun., weekends 10–5.*

Longmire Museum and Visitor Center. Glass cases inside this museum preserve the park's plants and animals, including a stuffed cougar. Historical photographs and geographical displays provide a worthwhile overview of the park's history. The adjacent visitor center has some perfunctory exhibits on the surrounding forest and its inhabitants, as well as pamphlets and information about park activities. ✉ *Hwy. 706, 10 miles east of Ashford, Longmire* ☎ *360/569–6575* ⊕ *www.nps.gov/mora/planyourvisit/longmire.htm* 🎟 *Free* ⊙ *July–mid-Oct., daily 9–5; mid-Oct.–June, daily 9–4:30.*

Sunrise Visitor Center. Exhibits at this center explain the region's sparser alpine and subalpine ecology. A network of nearby loop trails leads you through alpine meadows and forest to overlooks that have broad views of the Cascades and Rainier. The visitor center has a snack bar and gift shop. ✉ *Sunrise Rd., 15 miles from the White River park entrance* ☎ *360/663–2425* ⊕ *www.nps.gov/mora/planyourvisit/sunrise.htm* ⊙ *Early Jul.–early Sept, daily 10–6.*

PLANTS AND WILDLIFE IN MOUNT RAINIER

Wildflower season in the meadows at and above timberline is mid-July through August. Large mammals like deer, elk, black bears, and cougars tend to occupy the less accessible wilderness areas of the park and thus elude the average visitor; smaller animals like squirrels and marmots are easier to spot. The best times to see wildlife are at dawn and dusk at the forest's edge. Fawns are born in May, and the bugling of bull elk on the high ridges can be heard in late September and October, especially on the park's eastern side.

16

EXPLORING

SCENIC DRIVES

Chinook Pass Road. Route 410, the highway to Yakima, follows the eastern edge of the park to Chinook Pass, where it climbs the steep, 5,432-foot pass via a series of switchbacks. At its top, take in broad views of

Rainier and the east slope of the Cascades. The pass usually closes for the winter in November. ⊕ *www.wsdot.wa.gov/traffic/passes/chinook.*

Mowich Lake Road. In the northwest corner of the park, this 24-mile mountain road begins in Wilkeson and heads up the Rainier foothills to Mowich Lake, traversing beautiful mountain meadows along the way. Mowich Lake is a pleasant spot for a picnic. The road is open mid-July to mid-October. ⊕ *www.nps.gov/mora/planyourvisit/carbon-and-mowich.htm.*

Paradise Road. This 9-mile stretch of Highway 706 winds its way up the mountain's southwest flank from Longmire to Paradise, taking you from lowland forest to the ever-expanding vistas of the mountain above. Visit on a weekday if possible, especially in peak summer months, when the road is packed with cars. The route is open year-round though there may be some weekday closures in winter. From November through April, all vehicles must carry chains.

Sunrise Road. This popular (and often crowded) scenic road carves its way 11 miles up Sunrise Ridge from the White River Valley on the northeast side of the park. As you top the ridge there are sweeping views of the surrounding lowlands. The road is open late June to October.

HISTORIC SITES

National Park Inn. Even if you don't plan to stay overnight, you can stop by year-round to view the architecture of this inn, built in 1917 and on the National Register of Historic Places. While you're here, relax in front of the fireplace in the lounge, stop at the gift shop, or dine at the restaurant. ⊠ *Longmire Visitor Complex, Hwy. 706, 10 miles east of Nisqually entrance, Longmire* ☎ *360/569–2411* ⊕ *www.mtrainierguestservices.com/accommodations/national-park-inn.*

SCENIC STOPS

Christine Falls. These two-tiered falls were named in honor of Christine Louise Van Trump, who climbed to the 10,000-foot level on Mt. Rainier in 1889 at the age of 9, despite having a crippling nervous-system disorder. ⊠ *Next to Hwy. 706, about 2½ miles east of Cougar Rock Campground.*

Fodor's Choice ★ **Grove of the Patriarchs.** Protected from the periodic fires that swept through the surrounding areas, this small island of 1,000-year-old trees is one of Mount Rainier National Park's most memorable features. A 1½-mile loop trail heads through the old-growth forest of Douglas fir, cedar, and hemlock. ⊠ *Rte. 123, west of the Stevens Canyon entrance* ⊕ *www.nps.gov/mora/planyourvisit/ohanapecosh.htm.*

Narada Falls. A steep but short trail leads to the viewing area for these spectacular 168-foot falls, which expand to a width of 75 feet during peak flow times. In winter the frozen falls are popular with ice climbers. ⊠ *Along Hwy. 706, 1 mile west of the turnoff for Paradise, 6 miles east of Cougar Rock Campground* ⊕ *www.nps.gov/mora.*

FAMILY **Tipsoo Lake.** The short, pleasant trail that circles the lake—ideal for families—provides breathtaking views. Enjoy the subalpine wildflower meadows during the summer months; in early fall there is an abundant supply of huckleberries. ⊠ *Off Cayuse Pass east on Hwy. 410* ⊕ *www. nps.gov/mora/planyourvisit/sunrise.htm.*

EDUCATIONAL OFFERINGS

RANGER PROGRAMS

FAMILY **Junior Ranger Program.** Youngsters ages 6 to 11 can pick up an activity booklet at a visitor center and fill it out as they explore the park. When they complete it, they can show it to a ranger and receive a Mount Rainier Junior Ranger badge. ⊠ *Visitor Centers* ☎ *360/569–2211* ⊕ *www. nps.gov/mora/forkids/index.htm* ✉ *Free.*

Ranger Programs. Park ranger-led activities include **guided snowshoe walks** in the winter (most suitable for those older than 8) as well as **evening programs** during the summer at Longmire/Cougar Rock,

> ### FLOOD DAMAGE
>
> Harsh winter weather and heavy spring rains cause road damage and closings every year. Those with the most snow and storm debris usually include Carbon River Road, Stevens Canyon Road, Westside Road to Dry Creek, and Highway 706 from Longmire to Paradise. ■ TIP→ Before your trip, confirm site and road openings with one of the park's visitor centers.

Ohanapecosh, and White River campgrounds, and at the Paradise Inn. Evening talks may cover subjects such as park history, its flora and fauna, or interesting facts on climbing Mt. Rainier. There are also daily guided programs that start at the Jackson Visitor Center, including meadow and vista walks, tours of the Paradise Inn, and a morning ranger chat. ⊠ *Visitor Centers* ☎ *360/569–2211* ⊕ *www.nps.gov/mora/ planyourvisit/rangerprograms.htm* ✉ *Free.*

SPORTS AND THE OUTDOORS

MULTISPORT OUTFITTERS

RMI Expeditions. Reserve a private hiking guide through this highly regarded outfitter, or take part in its one-day mountaineering classes (mid-May through late September), where participants are evaluated on their fitness for the climb and must be able to withstand a 16-mile round-trip hike with a 9,000-foot gain in elevation. The company also arranges private cross-country skiing and snowshoeing guides. ⊠ *30027 Hwy. 706 E, Ashford* ☎ *888/892–5462, 360/569–2227* ✉ *360/569– 2982* ⊕ *www.rmiguides.com* ✉ *$1,006 for four-day package.*

Whittaker Mountaineering. You can rent hiking and climbing gear, skis, snowshoes, snowboards, and other outdoor equipment at this all-purpose Rainier Base Camp outfitter, which also arranges for private cross-country skiing and hiking guides. ⊠ *30027 Hwy. 706 E, Ashford* ☎ *800/238–5756* ✉ *360/569–2982* ⊕ *www.whittakermountaineering. com.*

16

BIRD-WATCHING

Be alert for kestrels, red-tailed hawks, and, occasionally, golden eagles on snags in the lowland forests. Also present at Rainier, but rarely seen, are great horned owls, spotted owls, and screech owls. Iridescent rufous hummingbirds flit from blossom to blossom in the drowsy summer lowlands, and sprightly water ouzels flutter in the many forest creeks. Raucous Steller's jays and gray jays scold passersby from trees, often darting boldly down to steal morsels from unguarded picnic tables. At higher elevations, look for the pure white plumage of the white-tailed ptarmigan as it hunts for seeds and insects in winter. Waxwings, vireos, nuthatches, sapsuckers, warblers, flycatchers, larks, thrushes, siskins, tanagers, and finches are common throughout the park.

HIKING

Although the mountain can seem remarkably benign on calm summer days, hiking Rainier is not a city-park stroll. Dozens of hikers and trekkers annually lose their way and must be rescued—and lives are lost on the mountain each year. Weather that approaches cyclonic levels can appear quite suddenly, any month of the year. All visitors venturing far from vehicle access points, with the possible exception of the short loop hikes listed here, should carry day packs with warm clothing, food, and other emergency supplies.

EASY

Nisqually Vista Trail. Equally popular in summer and winter, this trail is a 1¼-mile round-trip through subalpine meadows to an overlook point for Nisqually Glacier. The gradually sloping path is a favorite venue for cross-country skiers in winter; in summer, listen for the shrill alarm calls of the area's marmots. *Easy.* ⊠ *Trailhead at Jackson Memorial Visitor Center, Rte. 123, 1 mile north of Ohanapecosh, at the high point of Hwy. 706* ⊕ *www.nps.gov/mora/planyourvisit/paradise.htm.*

Sourdough Ridge Trail. The mile-long loop of this self-guided trail takes you through the delicate subalpine meadows near the Sunrise Visitor Center. A gradual climb to the ridgetop yields magnificent views of Mt. Rainier and the more distant volcanic cones of Mt. Baker, Mt. Adams, and Glacier Peak. *Easy.* ⊠ *Access trail at Sunrise Visitor Center, Sunrise Rd., 15 miles from the White River park entrance* ⊕ *www.nps.gov/ mora/planyourvisit/day-hiking-at-mount-rainier.htm.*

Trail of the Shadows. This ¾-mile loop is notable for its glimpses of meadowland ecology, its colorful soda springs (don't drink the water), James Longmire's old homestead cabin, and the foundation of the old Longmire Springs Hotel, which was destroyed by fire around 1900. *Easy.* ⊠ *Trailhead at Hwy. 706, 10 miles east of Nisqually entrance* ⊕ *www.nps.gov/mora/planyourvisit/day-hiking-at-mount-rainier.htm.*

MODERATE

Fodor's Choice ★ **Skyline Trail.** This 5-mile loop, one of the highest trails in the park, beckons day-trippers with a vista of alpine ridges and, in summer, meadows filled with brilliant flowers and birds. At 6,800 feet, Panorama Point, the spine of the Cascade Range, spreads away to the east, and Nisqually

Glacier tumbles downslope. *Moderate.* ⊠ *Jackson Memorial Visitor Center, Rte. 123, 1 mile north of Ohanapecosh at the high point of Hwy. 706* ⊕ *www.nps.gov/mora/planyourvisit/skyline-trail.htm.*

Van Trump Park Trail. You gain an exhilarating 2,200 feet on this route while hiking through a vast expanse of meadow with views of the southern Puget Sound. The 5.8-mile track provides good footing, and the average hiker can make it up and back in five hours. *Moderate.* ⊠ *Hwy. 706 at Christine Falls, 4.4 miles east of Longmire* ⊕ *www.nps. gov/mora/planyourvisit/van-trump-trail.htm.*

DIFFICULT

Fodor's Choice ★

Wonderland Trail. All other Mt. Rainier hikes pale in comparison to this stunning 93-mile trek, which completely encircles the mountain. The trail passes through all the major life zones of the park, from the old-growth forests of the lowlands to the alpine meadows and goat-haunted glaciers of the highlands—pick up a mountain-goat sighting card from a ranger station or visitor center if you want to help in the park's effort to learn more about these elusive animals. Wonderland is a rugged trail; elevation gains and losses totaling 3,500 feet are common in a day's hike, which averages 8 miles. Most hikers start out from Longmire or Sunrise and take 10–14 days to cover the 93-mile route. Snow lingers on the high passes well into June (sometimes July); count on rain any time of the year. Campsites are wilderness areas with pit toilets and water that must be purified before drinking. Only hardy, well-equipped, and experienced wilderness trekkers should attempt this trip, but those who do will be amply rewarded. Wilderness permits are required, and reservations are strongly recommended. *Difficult.* ⊠ *Longmire Visitor Center, Hwy. 706, 17 miles east of Ashford; Sunrise Visitor Center, Sunrise Rd., 15 miles west of the White River park entrance* ⊕ *www. nps.gov/mora/planyourvisit/the-wonderland-trail.htm.*

16

MOUNTAIN CLIMBING

Climbing Mt. Rainier is not for amateurs; each year, adventurers die on the mountain, and many become lost and must be rescued. Near-catastrophic weather can appear quite suddenly, any month of the year. If you're experienced in technical, high-elevation snow, rock, and ice-field adventuring, Mt. Rainier can be a memorable adventure. Climbers can fill out a climbing card at the Paradise, White River, or Carbon River ranger stations and lead their own groups of two or more. Climbers must register with a ranger before leaving and check out on return. A $45 annual climbing fee applies to anyone heading above 10,000 feet or onto one of Rainier's glaciers. During peak season it is recommended that climbers make their camping reservations ($20 per site) in advance; reservations are taken by fax and mail beginning in mid-March on a first-come, first-served basis (find the reservation form at ⊕ *www.nps. gov/mora/planyourvisit/wilderness-permit.htm*).

SKIING AND SNOWSHOEING

Mount Rainier is a major Nordic ski center for cross-country and tele-mark skiing. Although trails are not groomed, those around Paradise are extremely popular. If you want to ski with fewer people, try the trails in and around the Ohanapecosh–Stevens Canyon area, which are just as beautiful and, because of their more easterly exposure, slightly less subject to the rains that can douse the Longmire side, even in the dead of winter. Never ski on plowed main roads, especially around Paradise—the snowplow operator can't see you. Rentals aren't available on the eastern side of the park.

Deep snows make Mount Rainier a snowshoeing pleasure. The Paradise area, with its network of trails, is the best choice. The park's east-side roads, Routes 123 and 410, are unplowed and provide other good snowshoeing venues, although you must share the main routes with snowmobilers.

Paradise Snowplay Area and Nordic Ski Route. Sledding on flexible sleds (no toboggans or runners), inner tubes, and plastic saucers is allowed only in the Paradise snow-play area adjacent to the Jackson Visitor Center. The area is open when there is sufficient snow, usually Thursday through Monday from late December through mid-March. The easy, 3½-mile Paradise Valley Road Nordic ski route begins at the Paradise parking lot and follows Paradise Valley/Stevens Canyon Road to Reflection Lakes. Equipment rentals are available at Whittaker Mountaineering in Ashford or at the National Park Inn's General Store in Longmire. ✉ *Adjacent to the Jackson Visitor Center at Paradise* ☎ *360/569–2211* ⊕ *www.nps.gov/mora/planyourvisit/winter-recreation.htm.*

TOURS AND OUTFITTERS

General Store at the National Park Inn. The store at the National Park Inn in Longmire rents cross-country ski equipment and snowshoes. It's open daily in winter, depending on snow conditions. ✉ *National Park Inn, Longmire* ☎ *360/569–2411* ⊕ *www.mtrainierguestservices.com/activities-and-events/winter-activities/cross-country-skiing.*

WHERE TO EAT

$$$
ECLECTIC
✕ **National Park Inn Dining Room.** Photos of Mt. Rainier taken by top photographers adorn the walls of this inn's large dining room, a bonus on the many days the mountain refuses to show itself. Meals are simple but tasty: pot roast with yukon gold mashed potatoes, rainbow trout, cedar plank salmon, and blackberry cobbler à la mode. For a hearty start to the day, try the country breakfast or oatmeal brûlée. ⑤ *Average main: $23* ✉ *Hwy. 706, Longmire* ☎ *360/569–2411* ⊕ *www.mtrainierguestservices.com* ⌖ *Reservations not accepted.*

$
AMERICAN
FAMILY
✕ **Paradise Camp Deli.** Grilled meats, sandwiches, salads, and soft drinks are served daily from May through early October and on weekends and holidays during the rest of the year. ⑤ *Average main: $9* ✉ *Jackson Visitor Center, Paradise Rd. E, Paradise* ☎ *360/569–2400* ⊕ *www.mtrainierguestservices.com* ⌖ *Reservations not accepted* ⊙ *Closed weekdays early Oct.–Apr.*

$$$ ✕ **Paradise Inn.** Where else can you enjoy Sunday brunch in a historic,
AMERICAN heavy-timbered lodge halfway up a mountain? Tall windows provide terrific views of Rainier, and the warm glow of native wood permeates the large dining room. The lunch menu is simple and healthy—four kinds of burgers (black bean, chicken, bison, and beef), salads, and the like. For dinner, there's nothing like a hearty plate of the inn's signature bourbon buffalo meat loaf. ⑤ *Average main: $24* ⊠ *E. Paradise Rd., near Jackson Visitor Center, Paradise* ☎ *360/569–2275* ⊕ *www.mtrainierguestservices.com* ⚑ *Reservations not accepted* ⊘ *Closed Oct.–late May and daily 9:30–noon, 2–5:30.*

$ ✕ **Sunrise Day Lodge Food Service.** A cafeteria and grill serve inexpensive
AMERICAN hamburgers, chili, and hot dogs from early July to early September.
FAMILY ⑤ *Average main: $9* ⊠ *Sunrise Rd., 15 miles from the White River park entrance* ☎ *360/663–2425* ⊕ *www.mtrainierguestservices.com* ⚑ *Reservations not accepted* ⊘ *Closed early Sept.–early July.*

PICNIC AREAS

Park picnic areas are open July through September only.

Paradise Picnic Area. This site has great views on clear days. After picnicking at Paradise, you can take an easy hike to one of the many waterfalls in the area—Sluiskin, Myrtle, or Narada, to name a few. ⊠ *Hwy. 706, 11 miles east of Longmir.*

Sunrise Picnic Area. Set in an alpine meadow that's filled with wildflowers in July and August, this picnic area provides expansive views of the mountain and surrounding ranges in good weather. ⊠ *Sunrise Rd., 11 miles west of the White River entrance.*

16

WHERE TO STAY

$$$ ⊡ **National Park Inn.** A large stone fireplace warms the common room
HOTEL of this country inn, the only one of the park's two inns that's open year-round. **Pros:** classic ambience; open all year. **Cons:** jam-packed in summer; must book far in advance; some rooms have shared bath. ⑤ *Rooms from: $165* ⊠ *Longmire Visitor Complex, Hwy. 706, 6 miles east of Nisqually entrance, Longmire* ☎ *360/569–2275, 855/755–2275* ⊕ *www.mtrainierguestservices.com* ⌘ *25 rooms, 18 with bath* ⍾ *No meals.*

$$$ ⊡ **Paradise Inn.** With its hand-carved Alaskan cedar logs, burnished
HOTEL parquet floors, stone fireplaces, Indian rugs, and glorious mountain
Fodor'sChoice views, this 1917 inn is a classic example of a national park lodge. **Pros:**
★ central to trails; pristine vistas; nature-inspired details. **Cons:** noisy in high season; rooms in main lodge have shared bathrooms. ⑤ *Rooms from: $170* ⊠ *E. Paradise Rd., near Jackson Visitor Center, Paradise* ☎ *360/569–2275, 855/755–2275* ⊕ *www.mtrainierguestservices.com* ⌘ *121 rooms* ⊘ *Closed Oct.–mid-May* ⍾ *No meals.*

Best Campgrounds in Mount Rainier

Three drive-in campgrounds are in the park—Cougar Rock, Ohanapecosh, and White River—with almost 500 sites for tents and RVs. None have hot water or RV hookups. The more primitive Mowich Lake Campground has 10 walk-in sites for tents only. For backcountry camping, get a free wilderness permit at a visitor center. Primitive sites are spaced at 7- to 8-mile intervals along the Wonderland Trail.

Cougar Rock Campground. A secluded, heavily wooded campground with an amphitheater, Cougar Rock is one of the first to fill up. Reservations are accepted for summer only. ✉ *2½ miles north of Longmire* ☎ 877/444–6777.

Mowich Lake Campground. This is Rainier's only lakeside campground.

At 4,959 feet, it's also peaceful and secluded. ✉ *Mowich Lake Rd., 6 miles east of park boundary* ☎ *360/569–2211.*

Ohanapecosh Campground. This lush, green campground in the park's southeast corner has an amphitheater and self-guided trail. It's one of the first campgrounds to open for the season. ✉ *Rte. 123, 1½ miles north of park boundary* ☎ 877/444–6777.

White River Campground. At an elevation of 4,400 feet, White River is one of the park's highest and least wooded campgrounds. Here you can enjoy campfire programs, self-guided trails, and partial views of Mt. Rainier's summit. ✉ *5 miles west of White River entrance* ☎ *360/569–2211.*

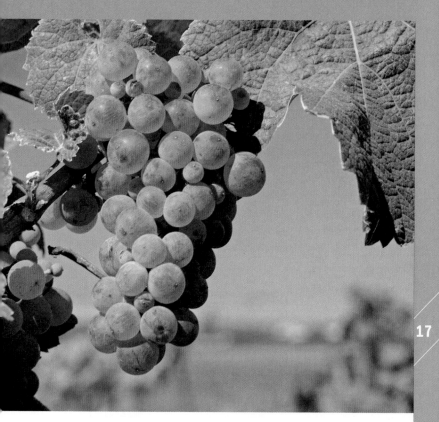

WASHINGTON WINE COUNTRY

Yakima River Valley

WELCOME TO WASHINGTON WINE COUNTRY

TOP REASONS TO GO

★ **Stay at a spectacular mountain lodge:** The Lodge at Suncadia is one of Washington's premier resorts. Golfers, cross-country skiers, hikers, and families will enjoy this terrific lodge in the beautiful Cascade Mountains.

★ **Delve into Washington history:** Yakima Valley Museum is one of the finest collections in the state, with plenty of history of the real West.

★ **Sip fine wine:** Yakima Valley may be the state's finest wine region, with more than 70 wineries producing excellent yields.

★ **Eat at a classic diner:** There happen to be two terrific diners in wine country. The Red Horse Diner in Ellensburg is more than a hamburger joint: it's a restaurant and museum all in one, built around a mid-1900s Mobil gas station. And Miner's Drive-In, a Yakima icon, serves great old-fashioned hamburgers, fries, and shakes in a truly vintage setting.

1 Northern Yakima River Valley. Just 80 miles from Seattle over the Cascade Mountains, the historic mining towns of Roslyn and Cle Elum offer quaint shops and one very plush resort. Golf, fishing, hiking, biking, cross-country skiing, and more are readily available in this region. As you follow the Yakima River down past Ellensburg to Yakima, you'll see how irrigation turns a virtual desert into one of the most agriculturally rich regions in the nation. Yakima is the shopping and entertainment hub of the region.

2 Southern Yakima River Valley. From Yakima, which touts itself as the gateway to wine country, visitors can choose from more than 70 wineries, as well as fresh fruits and vegetables of all kinds. The area is one of the most agriculturally diverse in the country, with some outstanding restaurants. History is rich here as well. The Yakama Indian Reservation occupies much of the land, and the history of its people can be seen in several museums around the region, including the museum at the Yakama Nation Cultural Center in Toppenish.

GETTING ORIENTED

The Yakima River Valley encompasses a region of south-central Washington that starts just east of Snoqualmie Pass in the Kittitas Valley. It includes the forested eastern slopes and the foothills of the Central Cascades, from Chinook and White Pass all the way down through the Yakima Valley near Benton City. Two interstates meet in Ellensburg. Interstate 90 links Seattle to Cle Elum and Ellensburg before heading east toward Spokane. Interstate 82 branches south off Interstate 90 just east of Ellensburg, and runs through the Yakima Valley to the so-called Tri-Cities (Richland, Pasco, and Kennewick). U.S. 97 is the primary link from Ellensburg north (Wenatchee, Canada's Okanagan Valley) and from Yakima south toward central Oregon.

17

Updated by
Rob Phillips

The Yakima River binds a region of great contrasts. Snow-capped volcanic peaks and evergreen-covered hills overlook a natural shrub steppe turned green by irrigation. Famed throughout the world for its apples and cherries, its wine and hops, this fertile landscape is also the ancestral home of the Yakama people from whom it takes its name.

The river flows southeasterly from its source in the Cascade Mountains near Snoqualmie Pass. Between the college town of Ellensburg, at the heart of the Kittitas Valley, and Yakima, the region's largest city, the river cuts steep canyons through serried, sagebrush-covered ridges before merging with the Naches River. Then it breaks through Union Gap to enter its fecund namesake, the broad Yakima Valley. Some 200 miles from its birthplace, the river makes one final bend around vineyard-rich Red Mountain before joining the mighty Columbia River at the Tri-Cities.

Broad-shouldered Mt. Adams is the sacred mountain of the Yakama people. The 12,276-foot-tall mountain marks the western boundary of their reservation, second largest in the Pacific Northwest. As they have for centuries, wild horses run free through the Yakama Nation and can be seen feeding along Highway 97 south of Toppenish. Deer and elk roam the evergreen forests, eagles and ospreys soar overhead.

Orchards and vineyards dominate Yakima Valley's agricultural landscape. Cattle and sheep ranching initially drove the economy; apples and other produce came with the engineering of irrigation canals and outlets in the 1890s. The annual asparagus harvest begins in April, followed by cherries in June; apricots and peaches ripen in early to midsummer. Hops are ready by late August and exported throughout the world for the brewing of beer; travelers may see the bushy vines spiraling up fields of twine. The apple harvest runs from late summer through October.

The valley's real fame, however, rests on its wine grapes, which have a growing reputation as among the best in the world. Concord grapes were first planted here in the 1960s, and they still take up large tracts of land. But vinifera grapes, the noble grapes of Europe, now dominate the local wine industry. Merlot and white Burgundies boosted the region, and Syrah is often regarded as the grape of the future. There are fine Cabernets, Grenaches, Rieslings, Chardonnays, Gewürztraminers, Sémillons, Sauvignon Blancs, Chenin Blancs, and Muscats, as well as such lesser-known varietals as Sangioveses, Nebbiolos, and Lembergers.

WASHINGTON WINE COUNTRY PLANNER

WHEN TO GO

Much of the area is considered high desert, with annual rainfall of just 7 inches a year. But in winter, in the higher elevations, it is quite common to have snow on the ground from November until March. This is a decidedly four-season region, with wet, cool, windy springs, beautiful warm summer days, and gorgeous falls with colors to match those of any Northeastern state. Best time to visit is April through October, unless, of course, you're looking to ski, snowboard, or snowmobile.

The main wine-tasting season begins in late April and runs to the end of the fall harvest in November. Winery hours vary in winter, when you should call ahead before visiting. The Yakima Valley Winery Association (⊕ *www.wineyakimavalley.org*) publishes a map-brochure that lists wineries with tasting-room hours. Most are owned and managed by unpretentious enthusiasts, and their cellar masters are often on hand to answer questions.

GETTING HERE AND AROUND

AIR TRAVEL

Although major airlines serve the region's two airports, most people fly into Seattle or Portland, Oregon, and drive to the area.

Tri-Cities Airport has a similar schedule from Seattle, a 60-minute trip, with additional nonstop connections to Denver, Portland, and Salt Lake City. Both Yakima and the Tri-Cities are served by Horizon. The Tri-Cities are also served by Delta and United. *For detailed information on airlines that service the region, see Air Travel in Travel Smart.*

Airports Tri-Cities Regional Airport. This small airport is convenient to Grandview, Prosser, and Benton City. ⊠ *3601 N. 20th Ave., Pasco* ☎ *509/547–6352* ⊕ *www.portofpasco.org.* **Yakima International Airport** ⊠ *2300 W. Washington Ave., 4 miles southeast of downtown, Yakima* ☎ *509/575–6149* ⊕ *www. yakimaairterminal.com.*

Transfers Taxis and public transit are available at both airports. **Airporter Shuttle.** There are five daily round-trips from Sea-Tac Airport (between Seattle and Tacoma) to the Yakima Airport ($42.50 in either direction), or downtown Yakima ($40) with stops in Downtown Seattle, Cle Elum ($30), and Ellensburg ($35). Trips from the Downtown Seattle Convention Center are five dollars more each way. ☎ *866/235–5247* ⊕ *www.airporter.com.*

Airport Transportation Diamond Cab. From Yakima Airport, this company will take you pretty much anyplace in Washington State. ☎ *509/453–3113.*

17

CAR TRAVEL

The Yakima Valley Highway, which turns into Wine Country Road just south of Sunnyside, is a reliable, off-the-beaten-track alternative to Interstate 82 for wine-country visits; but it can be slow, especially through towns, or if farm machinery is on the road. Because of unmarked turns and other potential hazards, it's wise to stick to the freeway after dark. Gas stations in towns, and at major freeway intersections, are typically open well after dark.

Major car rental companies in the area include **Avis** (☎ *509/469–4543 Yakima*), **Budget** (☎ *509/248–6767 Yakima*), **Enterprise** (☎ *509/494–7111 Yakima, 509/925–5040 Ellensburg*), and **Hertz** (☎ *509/452–9965 Yakima*). Hertz and Budget are available at Yakima International Airport.

RESTAURANTS

National fast-food chains, local eateries, and some fine-dining restaurants can be found scattered throughout the region, or sometimes right alongside one another. As a huge agricultural area, the Yakima Valley supplies many of its local restaurants with fresh fruits and vegetables in season. Yakima Valley wines are a staple at virtually all the fine-dining establishments. Pacific Northwest seafood (particularly salmon) is another staple of the region. South-central Washington also has a fair share of Mexican food, from taco wagons to fine Mexican restaurants.

HOTELS

Two major freeways, Interstate 90 and Interstate 82, pass through the cities of Ellensburg and Yakima, where you'll find the highest concentration of lodgings. A few independent motels are available, but the majority are independently operated under familiar chain names. At the far northeastern end of the region sits Suncadia Resort, offering possibly the finest accommodations in the area. Several bed-and-breakfasts are also available, particularly in the lower Yakima Valley, near the plethora of wineries in the area. It is always prudent to call ahead for reservations, but the busiest tourist times include the third week in April, for Spring Barrel Tasting, and from Memorial Day through Labor Day. *Hotel reviews have been shortened. For full information, visit Fodors.com.*

WHAT IT COSTS IN U.S. DOLLARS			
$	**$$**	**$$$**	**$$$$**
Restaurants	Under $17	$17–$23	$24–$30	Over $30
Hotels	Under $130	$130–$200	$201–$250	Over $250

Restaurant prices are the average cost of a main course at dinner or, if dinner is not served, at lunch. Hotel prices are the lowest cost of a standard double room in high season

TOURS

Lifelong residents run Yakima Valley Tours' custom agricultural, historical, wine-tasting, and adventure-sports tours. Accent! Tours has informative trips to area wineries. Bus companies such as A & A

Motorcoach, and limo services, including Moonlit Ride, conduct charter tours of the Yakima area.

Tour Contacts A & A Motorcoach ✉ *2410 S. 26th Ave., Yakima* ☎ *509/575–3676* ⊕ *www.aamotorcoach.com.* **Accent! Tours** ✉ *1017 S. 48th Ave., Suite C, Yakima* ☎ *509/575–3949, 800/735–0428* ⊕ *www.accenttours.com.* **Moonlit Ride Limousine** ✉ *3908 River Rd., Yakima* ☎ *509/575–6846* ⊕ *www. moonlitride.com.* **Yakima Valley Tours** ✉ *551 N. Holt Rd.* ☎ *509/985–8628, 509/840–4777* ⊕ *www.yakimavalleytours.com.*

VISITOR INFORMATION

Wine Yakima Valley Association ☎ *509/965–5201, 800/258–7270* ⊕ *www. wineyakimavalley.org.*

Yakima Valley Visitor Information Center ✉ *101 Fair Ave., Exit 34 off I–82, Yakima* ☎ *509/573–3388, 800/221–0751* ⊕ *www.visityakima.com.*

NORTHERN YAKIMA RIVER VALLEY

In the upper Kittitas Valley, tucked between the Cascade Mountains to the west and the rugged, snowcapped Sawtooth Mountains to the east, visitors will find the newest in championship golf courses, resort amenities, and fine dining. Plentiful shops, restaurants, museums, and outdoor activities make this one of the most diverse regions of the state. The old-time coal mining towns of Roslyn and Cle Elum are being discovered by more and more travelers seeking good food, fun, and relaxation. The college town of Ellensburg, home of the annual Ellensburg Rodeo on Labor Day, offers a variety of entertainment, restaurants, and hotels. Through it all runs the Yakima River, the lifeblood of this agricultural region, and one of Washington's best trout-fishing rivers.

The city of Yakima is the region's hub, offering all kinds of shopping, including a new Cabela's Outdoor Store and, thanks to a newly refurbished downtown core district, many new restaurants, wineries, and nightlife options. Thousands of acres of orchards, producing cherries, apricots, peaches, pears, plums, nectarines, and apples, surround the city. In spring and summer, outdoors enthusiasts flock here to hike, bike, canoe, raft, swim, and fish. Winter sports enthusiasts delight in the multitude of cross-country skiing, snowshoeing, and snowmobiling options, along with downhill skiing at White Pass.

CLE ELUM

86 miles southeast of Seattle.

A former railroad, coal, and logging town, Cle Elum (pronounced "klee *ell*-um") now caters to travelers stopping for a breath of air before or after tackling Snoqualmie Pass. It's also home to the ever-growing Suncadia Resort, possibly Washington's finest destination resort. Roslyn, a former coal-mining town just 3 miles northwest of Cle Elum, gained notoriety as the stand-in for the fictional Alaskan village of Cicely on the 1990s TV show *Northern Exposure*. A map locating sites associated with filming is available from the city offices at First Street and Pennsylvania Avenue. Roslyn is also notable for its 28 ethnic cemeteries. Established by communities of miners in the late 19th and early 20th centuries, they are clustered on a hillside west of town.

GETTING HERE AND AROUND

Cle-Elum is hard to miss; it's just off Interstate 90. Exit 80 will get you to Suncadia Resort. Exit 84 will put you at the west end of Cle Elum, placing you in the business district if you're approaching from Seattle and points west. Exit 85 will deliver you into the eastern boundaries of Cle Elum, but will also put you directly in the business district. Most of the amenities are found within the city limits of Cle Elum and Roslyn.

WHERE TO EAT

$ ✕ **The Cle Elum Bakery.** A local institution, this establishment has been
BAKERY doing business from the same spot since 1906. Delectable treats from fresh-baked donuts and pastries to a fabulous sticky bun–cinnamon roll are available daily. Lunch is served behind the bakery. $ *Average main: $5* ✉ *501 E. 1st St.* ☎ *509/674–2233* ⊕ *www.cleelumbakery.com* ☽ *No dinner.*

$ ✕ **MaMa Vallone's Steak House and Inn.** Set in a building constructed in
ITALIAN 1906, the upscale but rustic Western look makes the perfect style for this cozy and informal restaurant that once was a boarding house for unmarried miners. Guests dine at antique tables, and the works of several local artists hang on the walls. In addition to steaks and prime rib prepared daily, many Italian family recipes are featured on the menu. *Bagna calda* (a bath of olive oil, garlic, anchovies, and butter for dredging vegetables and meat) and pasta dishes, such as the tomato-based *fagioli* (soup with vegetables and beans), attract diners from as far away as Seattle. $ *Average main: $13* ✉ *302 W. 1st St.* ☎ *509/674–5174* ⊕ *www.mamavallones.com* ☽ *No lunch.*

$ ✕ **Sunset Café and Loose Wolf Lounge.** Since 1936 this Western-themed
AMERICAN restaurant has been serving breakfast delectables that include Texas-sized cinnamon rolls made on-site. At other meals, homemade Italian dishes share a lengthy menu with traditional American favorites, such as hamburgers and fried chicken. $ *Average main: $12* ✉ *318 E. 1st St.* ☎ *509/674–2241.*

WHERE TO STAY

$ ⊞ **Econo Lodge-Cle Elum Mountain Inn.** Interiors are simple, but the
HOTEL large rooms are well kept and provide home-away-from-home comfort with many amenities. **Pros:** clean, affordable rooms; kitchenettes are an added convenience. **Cons:** no-frills motel; no pool. $ *Rooms from: $95* ✉ *906 E. 1st St.* ☎ *509/674–2380, 888/674–3975* ⊕ *www. econolodgecleelum.com* ⤳ *43 rooms* ⏸ *Breakfast.*

$ ⊞ **Iron Horse Inn Bed and Breakfast.** What was once a boardinghouse for
B&B/INN rail workers (1909–74) is now a comfortable country inn owned by the daughter and son-in-law of a one-time lodger. **Pros:** unique lodging experience; on the National Registry of Historic Places. **Cons:** some rooms share bathrooms. $ *Rooms from: $100* ✉ *526 Marie Ave., South Cle Elum* ☎ *509/674–5939, 800/228–9246* ⊕ *www.ironhorseinnbb. com* ⤳ *11 rooms, 8 with bath* ⏸ *Breakfast.*

$$$$ ⊤ **The Lodge at Suncadia.** In the middle of two of the region's premier
RESORT golf courses, this great stone-and-wood lodge blends beautifully with
FAMILY its mountain and forest surroundings, and the elegant rooms, most
Fodor's Choice with gas fireplaces, maintain a rustic, homespun appeal. **Pros:** intimate
★ mountain-retreat environment; golfing, fly-fishing, cross-country skiing,
and hiking just minutes away. **Cons:** costs can quickly add up for a family visit. $ *Rooms from: $309* ⊠ *3320 Suncadia Trail* ☎ *509/649–6400,
866/904–6300* ⊕ *www.suncadia.com* ⊃ *254 rooms* ⦿ *No meals.*

SHOPPING

Owens Meats. The Owens family established this marvelous smokehouse
in 1887 and has been running it ever since. No processed meats here—
just the freshest smoked and cured meats around, including beef jerky
that is addictive. ⊠ *502 E. 1st St.* ☎ *509/674–2530* ⊕ *owensmeats.com.*

ELLENSBURG

24 miles southeast of Cle Elum.

This university town is one of the state's friendliest and most easygoing places. "Modern" Ellensburg had its origin in a July 4 fire that
engulfed the original city in 1889. Almost overnight, Victorian brick
buildings rose from the ashes; many still stand, though their functions
have changed. Stroll downtown to discover art galleries, comfortable
cafés, secondhand-book and -record stores, an old-fashioned hardware
store, and one antiques shop after another.

One of central Washington's biggest events is the Ellensburg Rodeo,
held Labor Day weekend. On the national circuit since the 1920s, the
rodeo has a year-round headquarters on Main Street, where you can
buy tickets and souvenirs. You can also get a bird's-eye view of the
rodeo grounds from Reed Park, in the 500 block of North Alder Street.

GETTING HERE AND AROUND

Ellensburg is adjacent to Interstate 90, with two exits that will take you
right to gas, fast food, and lodging. Follow Main Street north and it will
put you into the heart of downtown and Central Washington University.

ESSENTIALS

Visitor Information Kittitas County Chamber of Commerce ⊠ *609 N. Main
St.* ☎ *509/925–2002, 888/925–2204* ⊕ *www.kittitascountychamber.com.*

EXPLORING

Central Washington University. The nearly 11,000 students here enjoy a
pleasant, tree-shaded campus marked by tasteful redbrick architecture.
On the 8th Avenue side are several handsome buildings dating from the
university's founding in 1891 as the State Normal School. Near the center of campus is a serene Japanese garden. The Sarah Spurgeon Gallery,
in Randall Hall, features the work of regional and national artists as
well as students and faculty. ⊠ *400 E. University Way* ☎ *509/963–1111
⊕ www.cwu.edu* ⊠ *Free* ⊙ *Tours weekdays 10–2*

Clymer Museum of Art. Half the museum houses a collection of works by
painter John Clymer (1907–89), an Ellensburg native who was one of
the most widely published illustrators of the American West, focusing

his oils and watercolors on wildlife and traditional lifestyles. The other half features other well-known and aspiring Western and wildlife artists. ⊠ *416 N. Pearl St.* ☎ *509/962–6416* ⊕ *www.clymermuseum.org* ⊠ *Free* ☉ *Weekdays 10–5, Sat. 10–2.*

FAMILY **Dick and Jane's Spot.** Nestled in suburbia is the area's most peculiar attraction. The home of artists Dick Elliott and Jane Orleman is a continuously growing whimsical sculpture: a collage of 20,000 bottle caps, 1,500 bicycle reflectors, and other bits. Their masterpiece stands on private property near downtown, but it's still possible to see the recycled creation from several angles; sign the guestbook mounted on the surrounding fence. ⊠ *101 N. Pearl St.* ☎ *509/925–3224* ⊕ *www. reflectorart.com.*

Olmstead Place State Park. This park and 217-acre working farm encompasses the grounds of an original pioneer farm built in 1875. A 1-mile interpretive trail links eight buildings, including a barn and schoolhouse. During harvest time, the park holds threshing bees, demonstrating historic farming practices. ⊠ *N. Ferguson Rd., ½ mile south of Kittitas Hwy., 4 miles east of Ellensburg* ☎ *509/925–1943* ⊕ *www. parks.wa.gov* ⊠ *Free; parking $10* ☉ *Apr.–Oct., 6:30 am–dusk; Nov.– Mar., 8 am–dusk.*

WHERE TO EAT

$ ✕ **Cornerstone Pie.** Set near the CWU campus and decorated with repur-
PIZZA   posed, reclaimed, and even historic artifacts, this casual place revolves around one central piece, a wood-fire pizza oven. Out of that oven come pies and grinders with a focus on local and seasonal ingredients. The bar features a nice rotation of Pacific Northwest wines and beers to help wash them down. $ *Average main: $12* ⊠ *307 E. 5th Ave.* ☎ *509/933–3600* ⊕ *www.cornerstonepie.com* ☉ *No lunch.*

$ ✕ **The Palace Cafe.** Hungry travelers and locals have enjoyed good food
AMERICAN   here since 1892, and now choose from a solid menu with standard varieties of steaks, burgers, chicken, and pasta, served in a Western setting. The specialty is a prawn strawberry salad, and the chicken linguine is excellent. $ *Average main: $14* ⊠ *323 Main St.* ☎ *509/925–2327* ⊕ *www.thepalacecafe.net.*

$ ✕ **Red Horse Diner.** Step back in time to a 1930s-era service station. Now,
AMERICAN   however, the service includes specialty sandwiches, shakes, and more.
Fodor's Choice   While you wait for your burger and fries, check out the hundreds of
★   old metal signs and advertisements that enhance the vintage appeal of this classic burger joint. $ *Average main: $10* ⊠ *1518 W. University Way* ☎ *509/925–1956* ⊕ *www.redhorsediner.com.*

$$ ✕ **Valley Cafe.** Meals at this vintage art deco eatery consist of Mediter-
CONTEMPORARY   ranean bistro-style salads, pastas, and other plates. Featured dinner entrées include pork tenderloin, seared ahi tuna, and chicken Marsala. An impressive wine list offers dozens of Yakima Valley options. Owner Greg Beach also owns the wine shop next door. $ *Average main: $22* ⊠ *105 W. 3rd Ave.* ☎ *509/925–3050.*

$$ ✕ **Yellow Church Café.** Built in 1923 as a Lutheran church, this house of
AMERICAN   culinary worship now offers seating in the nave or choir loft. Soups, salads, sandwiches, pastas, and home-baked goods are served, as well as

Yakima Valley Museum

dinner specials. Breakfast is popular on weekends. $ *Average main: $18* ⊠ *111 S. Pearl St.* ☎ *509/933–2233* ⊕ *www.theyellowchurchcafe.com.*

WHERE TO STAY

$$ ⬚ **Best Western Lincoln Inn and Suites.** A spacious hostelry one block
HOTEL off Ellensburg's main north–south arterial offers travelers plenty of elbow room in rooms with separate sitting areas and lots of amenities and services. **Pros:** pool; free breakfast. **Cons:** a bit more expensive than the competition. $ *Rooms from: $130* ⊠ *211 W. Umptanum Rd.* ☎ *509/925–4244, 866/925–4288* ⊕ *www.bestwestern.com* ⬎ *55 rooms* ❙⊙❙ *Breakfast.*

YAKIMA

38 miles south of Ellensburg.

The gateway to Washington wine country is sunny Yakima (pronounced *yak*-imah), home to more than 90,000 people within the city limits and another 25,000 in the surrounding area. Spread along the west bank of the Yakima River just south of its confluence with the Naches River, Yakima is a bustling community with lovely parklands and a downtown in the midst of revitalization. Downtown street improvements with period lighting, trees, and planters have created a fresh new "old" feel.

Yakima was settled in the late 1850s as a ranching center where Ahtanum Creek joins the Yakima River, on the site of earlier Yakama tribal villages at present-day Union Gap. When the Northern Pacific Railroad established its terminal 4 miles north in 1884, most of the town literally picked up and moved to what was then called "North Yakima."

Yakima's Mission-style Northern Pacific Depot (1912) is the highlight of its historic North Front Street. Four blocks east is the ornate Capitol Theatre, built in 1920. The former vaudeville and silent-movie hall is now a performing arts center. Opposite is Millennium Plaza, a public art installation that celebrates the importance of water to the Yakima Valley. Residents and visitors alike enjoy year-round natural beauty in the heart of Yakima, thanks to the city's ongoing restoration and preservation of the Yakima Greenway. The nature area and trails stretch from Selah Gap to Union Gap, and west along the Naches River.

Yakima is also home to the Central Washington State Fair, the original state fair of Washington. Drawing over 300,000 people from all over the Northwest, the annual fair, held in late September, is the showcase for the agricultural bounty of the area and provides big-name entertainment and all the unique and delicious "fair" fare.

GETTING HERE AND AROUND

Yakima can be reached via air and road. The Yakima International Airport offers commercial flights to and from Seattle daily, and also welcomes private flights from all over. Interstate 82 from Ellensburg to the Tri-Cities and beyond, runs right through the city limits. Highways 12 and 410, known as White and Chinook Pass, pass on either side of Mt. Rainier and connect with Interstate 82 at Yakima, as does Highway 97, which brings travelers from Oregon and points south.

Yakima is the only city in the region with a public transportation system.

Yakima City Transit. Buses operate weekdays 6:15 am to 6:45 pm and Saturday from 8:45 to 6:45 at half-hour intervals on eleven routes. The one-way fare is a dollar. ☎ *509/575–6175* ⊕ *www.yakimatransit.org.*

ESSENTIALS

Visitor Information Yakima Valley Visitors and Convention Bureau ✉ *10 N. 8th St.* ☎ *800/221-0751* ⊕ *www.visityakima.com.*

EXPLORING

Gilbert Cellars. In downtown Yakima's historic district, this tasting room serves up selections from the family vineyards, specializing in blends of Rhone varietals and an unoaked Chardonnay. Local craft beers are also available, as well as small plates to accompany your favorite vintage. The downtown location makes the tasting room an ideal place to meet before a night on the town, or to enjoy a glass of wine after dinner. ✉ *5 N. Front St.* ☎ *509/249–9049* ⊕ *www.gilbertcellars.com* ☾ *Mon.– Thurs. noon–9, Fri. noon–11, Sat. noon–10, Sun. noon–5.*

Naches Heights Vineyard. Just a few miles west of Yakima, this winery is located in Washington's newest wine-growing area. Set among organic and biodynamic vineyards, the tasting room has ample seating inside, where you may catch some live music while contemplating their wines. The winery features blends in both red and white. ✉ *250 Ehler Rd., south of Hwy. 12* ☎ *855/648–9463* ⊕ *www.nhvwines.com.* ☾ *Winter: Thurs.–Mon. 11–7; summer: Sun., Mon., Thurs. 11–7, Weds. 6–9, Fri.– Sat. 11–9.*

Yakima Area Arboretum. Just off Interstate 82, this parklike swath features hundreds of different plants, flowers, and trees. A Japanese garden and

Yakima Valley Wineries

Columbia River

182

82

West Richland

Richland

Hedges Cellars

Sunset Rd.

224

Kiona Vineyards Winery

Blackwood Canyon Vintners

Terra Blanca

De Moss Rd.

Benton City

Kiona

Yakima River

82

Kestrel Vintners

221

Thurston Wolfe

Hanks Rd.

VineHeart

Chinook Wines

Hinzerling Rd.

Hogue Cellars

Prosser

Desert Wind Winery

221

Willow Crest Winery

Snipes Rd.

Pontin del Roza

Hinzerling Vineyards

Yakima River Winery

Wine Country Rd.

Grandview

Tucker Cellars

Sunnyside Canal

Sunnyside

240

Cold River

Columbia River

Rattlesnake Hills

241

Sunnyside Hwy.

12

82

22

Horizon's Edge Winery

E. Zillah Dr.

Outlook Rd.

Granger

Yakima Valley Hwy.

Silver Lake Winery at Rosa Hills

Maison de Padgett

Paradisos del Sol

Porteus Vineyards

Highland Dr.

Claar Cellars

Gurley Rd.

24

Hyatt Vineyards

Wineglass Cellars

Bonair Winery

Buena

Zillah

22

Moxee City

Yakima Ridge

Gilbert Cellars

Yakima

82

12

97

Wapato

220

Toppenish

22

97

Toppenish River

Sattus Creek

YAKAMA INDIAN RESERVATION

Naches Heights Vineyards

10 miles

10 kilometers

0

a wetland trail are highlights. The arboretum sits alongside the Yakima River and the 10-mile-long Yakima Greenway, a paved path that links a series of riverfront parks. ✉ *1401 Arboretum Dr., off Nob Hill Blvd.* ☎ *509/248–7337* ⊕ *www.ahtrees.org* 🎫 *Free* ☉ *Daily dawn–dusk.*

FAMILY **Yakima Valley Museum.** Exhibits here focus on Yakama native, pioneer, and 20th-century history, ranging from horse-drawn vehicles to a "neon garden" of street signs. Highlights include a fully operating 1930s soda fountain and a model of Yakima native and Supreme Court Justice William O. Douglas's Washington, D.C., office. Other visiting and rotation exhibits are also scheduled throughout the year. ✉ *2105 Tieton Dr.* ☎ *509/248–0747* ⊕ *www.yakimavalleymuseum.org* 🎫 *$5* ☉ *Mon.–Sat. 10–5.*

WHERE TO EAT

$$ ✕ **Gasperetti's.** John Gasperetti's restaurant keeps an elegant low pro-
ITALIAN file in a high-traffic area north of downtown. Moderately priced pasta dishes share the menu with a short list of special weekly dinners—meat or seafood entrées with organically grown local produce. The cellar has an excellent selection of wines, including Italian varietals. Ⓢ *Average main: $20* ✉ *1013 N. 1st St.* ☎ *509/248–0628* ⊕ *www. gasperettisrestaurant.com* ☉ *Closed Sun. No lunch Sat.*

$ ✕ **Miner's Drive-In.** This Yakima icon (actually located in Union Gap) is
AMERICAN a must-visit for many travelers coming to or through Yakima. It's an
FAMILY authentic 1940s hamburger joint that has expanded from a traditional drive-in to a family sit-down diner. There are plenty of great-tasting items on the menu, from salads to fish-and-chips, but the real crowd pleaser is the giant "Big Miner"—an old-fashioned burger that knocks any chain burger out of the park. Add a huge basket of fries and a shake, and chances are you'll be full for most of your day. Ⓢ *Average main: $10* ✉ *2415 S. 1st St., Union Gap* ☎ *509/457–8194.*

$ ✕ **Rooster's Diner.** Soda jerks at the Yakima Valley Museum's café make
AMERICAN shakes and sundaes plus soups, hot dogs, and sandwiches while a period Wurlitzer spins 1930s big-band records. Ⓢ *Average main: $8* ✉ *Yakima Valley Museum, 2105 Tieton Dr.* ☎ *509/457–9810* ⊕ *www. roostersdiner.net* 🚫 *Reservations not accepted* ☉ *Closed Sun.–Mon.*

$ ✕ **Santiago's.** Elegant and charming, Jar and Deb Arcand's skylit estab-
MEXICAN lishment puts a new spin on Mexican dishes. For chili verde, chunks of pork loin are slow-cooked in jalapeño sauce; the Yakima apple-pork mole is prepared with chocolate and cinnamon. Ⓢ *Average main: $15* ✉ *111 E. Yakima Ave.* ☎ *509/453–1644* ⊕ *www.santiagos.org* ☉ *Closed Sun. No lunch Sat.*

$$ ✕ **Second Street Grill.** This hub for Yakima's rejuvinated nightlife is
AMERICAN located in the heart of downtown. Century-old bare brick walls hung with huge black-and-white photographs and HDTVs provide the setting, and the menu has a similar mix of old and new, featuring a wide array of salads, pastas, and steaks, with a bit of Asian flair thrown in. The restaurant's bar is a happy-hour destination (3 to 6 pm) and a late night hot spot on the weekends, with live music on Saturday. During the warmer months, sidewalk seating is available and recommended as long as the weather isn't too warm. Ⓢ *Average main: $19* ✉ *28 N. 2nd St.* ☎ *509/469–1486* ⊕ *www.secondstreetgrill.com.*

WHERE TO STAY

$$
B&B/INN
🛏 **Birchfield Manor.** The valley's most luxurious accommodations are on a plateau just east of Yakima, where the old manor houses the restaurant and five traditionally furnished upstairs rooms, while a newer, more private cottage contains rooms with such amenities as steam-sauna showers and gas fireplaces. **Pros:** a unique experience for this region; good restaurant on-site. **Cons:** a little difficult to find; restaurant only open three nights a week. *⑤ Rooms from: $170 ✉ 2018 Birchfield Rd., just south of Hwy. 24 ☎ 509/452–1960, 800/375–3420 ⊕ www. birchfieldmanor.com ⤴ 11 rooms* ❘⊙❘ *Breakfast.*

$
HOTEL
🛏 **Hilton Garden Inn.** Modern, spacious, and comfortably furnished rooms in the heart of downtown are some of the city's finest upscale lodgings. **Pros:** one block from the convention center and within walking distance of dozens of shops; restaurant on-site; indoor pool. **Cons:** in the midst of the concrete jungle. *⑤ Rooms from: $125 ✉ 402 E. Yakima Ave. ☎ 509/454–1111 ⊕ hiltongardeninn3.hilton.com ⤴ 111 rooms, 3 suites* ❘⊙❘ *Breakfast.*

$
HOTEL
🛏 **North Park Lodge.** Rustic, outdoor designs combine with premium comfort to provide overstuffed leather furniture and handsome wood furniture, adding to the appeal of these very inviting guest quarters and lounges. **Pros:** quiet and affordable, with plenty of room for the family; indoor pool. **Cons:** 8 miles from Yakima. *⑤ Rooms from: $100 ✉ 659 N. Wenas Rd., Selah ☎ 509/698–6000 ⊕ www.northparklodge.com ⤴ 53 rooms* ❘⊙❘ *Breakfast.*

SPORTS AND THE OUTDOORS

GOLF

Apple Tree Golf Course. This beautiful course cut through the apple orchards of West Yakima and is rated as one of the state's top 10. The signature hole on the 18-hole, par-72 course is Number 17, shaped like a giant apple surrounded by a lake. Greens fees run $45–$85. *✉ 8804 Occidental Rd. ☎ 509/966–5877 ⊕ www.appletreeresort.com.*

SKIING

White Pass Ski Area. A full-service ski area 50 miles west of Yakima toward Mt. Rainier is the home mountain of former Olympic medalists Phil and Steve Mahre. Eight lifts serve 47 trails on a vertical drop of 1,500 feet from the 6,000-foot summit. Here you'll find condominiums, a gas station, grocery store, and snack bar. Open woods are popular with cross-country skiers and summer hikers. *✉ 48935 U.S. 12 ☎ 509/672–3101 ⊕ www.skiwhitepass.com.*

NIGHTLIFE AND THE ARTS

Bale Breaker Brewing Company. While central Washington is known for its wine production, less well-known is the fact that the vast majority of hops grown in the United States come from the Yakima Valley. This brewery is situated in the middle of hop yards, and uses the hops that grow right out the back door for its brews. Take a peek out back to check out the brewing operations, enjoy the grassy outdoor seating on a sunny day, or just hang out in the taproom for a taste of the local produce—in beer form. Weekends often bring live music and food trucks serving a variety of cuisines. ⊠ *1801 Birchfield Rd.* ☏ *509/424-4000* ⊕ *www.balebreaker.com.*

Johnson Orchards. This company has been growing and selling fruit— including cherries, peaches, apples, and pears—to the public since 1904. ⊠ *4906 Summitview Ave.* ☏ *509/966–7479.*

Valley Mall. Central Washington's largest shopping center has all kinds of specialty shops and three major department stores: Sears, Kohls, and Macy's. The area surrounding the mall is the main retail area for the region, featuring several national retailers within a mile radius. Sportsmen and women flock to the Cabela's outdoor store. ⊠ *2529 Main St., off I-82, exit 36, Union Gap* ☏ *509/453–8233.*

Yakima Farmers' Market. Produce vendors gather in downtown Yakima every Sunday, June through October, for this well-stocked market. At other times, roadside stands and farms welcome visitors. Best bets for roadside produce are west of town on Highway 12, and south on Highway 97. ⊠ *Yakima Ave. and 3rd St., Downtown.*

SOUTHERN YAKIMA RIVER VALLEY

The lower Yakima Valley encompasses hundreds of thousands of acres both on and off the Yakama Indian Reservation and includes several small towns. Agriculture is the name of the game in this part of the lower valley, where everything from apples to zucchinis are grown. Throughout the summer visitors buy or pick all kinds of fresh vegetables and fruits in season. In early May the asparagus grows to cutting height, and soon after that it's time for the cherries to be harvested. Basically, it's one harvest after the next, culminating with apples in late October. Growing conditions also make this area the hot spot for wine-grape growing, and where there are grapes, there are wineries. The vines of some 70 wineries now carpet the Yakima Valley, with many of the best wines in the country coming from these vintners. The history of this region stretches back hundreds of years from the time of the Native American Yakama people and early white settlers. Much of this history can be seen in several museums around the region, including the museum at the Yakama Nation Cultural Center in Toppenish.

ZILLAH

15 miles southeast of Yakima.

The south-facing slopes above Zillah, a tiny town named after the daughter of a railroad manager, are covered with orchards and vineyards. Several wineries are in or near the community; more are near Granger, 6 miles southeast.

GETTING HERE AND AROUND

The outskirts of Zillah, which is growing to include many new businesses, sits right on Interstate 82, southeast of Yakima. Downtown Zillah is just up the hill a half mile or so.

EXPLORING
TOP ATTRACTIONS

Bonair Winery. After years of amateur wine-making in California, the Puryear family began commercial wine production in their native Yakima Valley in 1985. Bonair offers a large tasting room reminiscent of a European chalet that sits among the vineyards, and a duck pond that was voted one of Washington's best places for a kiss. Visit the tasting room and you will likely meet the winemaker, Gail Puryear, or his wife, the "wine goddess" Shirley. Bonair makes Cabernets, Cabernet Francs, Chardonnays, Gewürztraminer Port, Merlots, Rieslings, and more. Visitors are welcome to picnic here, and vineyard and production tours are available by appointment. ⊠ *500 S. Bonair Rd.* ☎ *509/829–6027* ⊕ *www.bonairwine.com* ☉ *Mar.–Oct., daily 10–5; Nov.–Feb., daily noon–5.*

Claar Cellars. This family-owned estate is right off Interstate 82 at Exit 52 and has one of the highest visitor numbers of any Yakima Valley winery. Claar produces a variety of wines, including some ice wines, Sangiovese, and rare varieties such as Corneauxcopia (a blended variety) and Fouled Anchor Port, which includes cherries, raisins, honey, and maple syrup. It also produces traditional Merlots, Cabernets, Chardonnays, Sauvignon Blancs, and Rieslings. The grapes come from vineyards in the White Bluffs region, so while the tasting room is easily accessible, it is separated from the vineyards. ⊠ *1001 Vintage Valley Pkwy.* ☎ *509/829–6810* ⊕ *www.claarcellars.com* ☉ *Feb.–Nov., Fri.–Mon. 10–6.*

Hyatt Vineyards. Leland and Linda Hyatt's 97 acres of estate vineyards have long been well respected locally for Merlot and Cabernet Sauvignon, and lately those wines have been attracting national attention. Their late-harvest Riesling is also worth tasting. The tasting room is well-appointed, the staff has wide knowledge of local viniculture, and the spacious, well-manicured grounds are nice for picnicking. On clear days there are spectacular views of the Yakima Valley, Mt. Adams, and the Cascade Mountains. ⊠ *2020 Gilbert Rd., off I–82 Exit 52* ☎ *509/829–6333* ⊕ *www.hyattvineyards.com* ☉ *Daily 11–5.*

WORTH NOTING

Horizon's Edge Winery. With a spectacular view of the Yakima Valley, Mt. Adams, and Mt. Rainier, it is easy to see where Horizon's Edge got its name. The winery makes sparkling wine, Chardonnay, Pinot Noir, Merlot, Cabernet Sauvignon, and Muscat Canelli. ⊠ *4530 E. Zillah Dr., east of Yakima Valley Hwy.* ☎ *509/829–6401* ⊕ *www.horizonsedgewinery. com* ☉ *Mar.–Nov., Thurs.–Mon. 11–5.*

Maison de Padgett Winery. A small family produces specialized handcrafted wines in a beautiful winery highlighted by adjoining European-style gardens. Groups of 10 or more should call ahead. ⊠ *2231 Roza Dr., at Highland Dr.* ☎ *509/829–6412* ⊕ *www.maisondepadgettwinery. com* ☉ *Mar.–Nov., Thurs.–Mon. 11–5; Dec.–Feb., by appointment.*

Paradisos del Sol. At this family-owned winery, operated by veteran wine-grower Paul Vandenberg, the tasting room is a part of the family farmhouse, surrounded by orchards, vineyards, and chickens. Unlike many area winemakers, the Vandenbergs focus as much on growing the

17

grapes as turning them into wine. Various blends, both white and red, highlight the wine selections. ✉ *3230 Highland Dr.* ☎ *509/829–9000* ⊕ *www.paradisosdelsol.com* ☉ *Daily 11–6.*

Portteus Vineyards. One of the early Yakima Valley wineries, established in 1981, is beloved by red-wine drinkers. Production includes Cabernet Sauvignon and Franc, Merlot, Malbec, Syrah, Zinfandel, and Port—as well as a robust Chardonnay. Family run, the tasting room is staffed by the second generation of the Portteus family. Grapes are grown at 1,440-foot elevation on 47 acres above Zillah. ✉ *5201 Highland Dr.* ☎ *509/829–6970* ⊕ *www.portteus.com* ☉ *Daily 10–5.*

Silver Lake at Roza Hills. Bands serenade picnickers on summer weekends on what the winery calls their "viniferanda," above their historic estate high in the Rattlesnake Hills. With both a large deck and well-manicured lawn with a soothing fountain, visitors are afforded views of the Cabernets, Merlots, Chardonnays, Rieslings, and other vintages in production in the valley below. Sundays in August bring live music and salmon dinners, and the tasting room offers wide views as well. ✉ *1500 Vintage Rd., off Highland Dr.* ☎ *509/829–6235* ⊕ *www. silverlakewinery.com* ☉ *Apr.–Nov., daily 10–5; Dec.–Mar., Thurs.– Mon. 11–4.*

Wineglass Cellars. This small winery got its name from an unusual collection of antique wine glasses. In the interest of quality and priority, the winery produces limited lots of Merlot, Cabernet Sauvignon, Chardonnay, and port. ✉ *206 N. Bonair Rd.* ☎ *509/829–3011* ⊕ *www. wineglasscellars.com* ☉ *Mid-Feb.–Nov., Fri.–Sun. 10:30–5.*

WHERE TO STAY

$
HOTEL
Vintage Valley Inn. Large, comfortable rooms, a business center, gym, and an indoor pool and spa make this stop just a few steps from Claar Cellars ideal for wine lovers and families alike. **Pros:** right on the freeway, and the only motel within miles. **Cons:** potential freeway-traffic noise. ⑤ *Rooms from: $100* ✉ *911 Vintage Valley Pkwy.* ☎ *509/829–3399, 800/501–5433* ⊕ *www.vintagevalleyinn.com* ↘ *40 rooms* ¶◎¶ *Breakfast.*

TOPPENISH

17 miles southeast of Yakima.

This intriguing small town with a rustic Old West sensibility lies within the Yakama Reservation and blends history and culture, art and agriculture. You can't miss the 70 colorful murals that adorn the facades and exterior walls of businesses and homes. Commissioned since 1989 by the Toppenish Mural Association and done in a variety of styles by regional artists, they commemorate the town's history and Western spirit. Tours in a horse-drawn covered wagon leave from the association's office on Toppenish Avenue.

Desert Wind Winery, Prosser

GETTING HERE AND AROUND
Jump on Highway 97 out of Yakima, and the four-lane road will take you through Wapato and right to Toppenish. Or follow the signs from Interstate 82 at Zillah. From Oregon and points south Highway 97 also brings you right to Toppenish over Status Pass.

ESSENTIALS
Visitor Information Toppenish Chamber of Commerce ✉ *504 S. Elm St.* ☎ *509/865-3262, 800/863-6375* ⊕ *www.visittoppenish.com.*

EXPLORING

FAMILY **American Hop Museum.** The Yakima Valley grows 75% of the nation's hops and 25% of the world's, and the industry's story is well told at this museum. Exhibits describe the history, growing process, and unique biology of the plant, a primary ingredient in beer. ✉ *22 S. B St.* ☎ *509/865-4677* ⊕ *www.americanhopmuseum.org* 🎫 *$3* ⊙ *Early May–late Sept., Wed.–Sat. 10–4, Sun. 11–4.*

Fort Simcoe Historical State Park. The residential quarters of an 1856 army fort, 30 miles west of Toppenish, look like a Victorian summer retreat. Exhibits focus on relations between the Yakama people—in the heart of whose reservation the fort stands—and American settlers. ✉ *5150 Ft. Simcoe Rd.* ☎ *509/874-2372* ⊕ *www.parks.wa.gov* 🎫 *Free* ⊙ *Apr.–Oct., daily 6:30 am–dusk.*

Yakama Nation Cultural Center. This six-building complex has a fascinating museum of tribal history and culture, including costumes, basketry, beadwork, and reconstructions of traditional lodges. Tribal dances and other cultural events are often staged in the Heritage Theater; the complex also includes a gift shop, library, and restaurant. ⊠ *Buster Dr. at U.S. 97* ☏ *509/865–2800* ⊕ *www.yakamamuseum.com* 🎫 *$6* ⊙ *Weekdays 8–5, weekends 9–5.*

SUNNYSIDE

14 miles southeast of Zillah.

The largest community in the lower Yakima Valley and the hometown of astronaut Bonnie Dunbar, Sunnyside runs along the sunny southern slopes of the Rattlesnake Hills.

GETTING HERE AND AROUND

Interstate 82 runs right past Sunnyside as it threads its way down through the Lower Yakima Valley. Three exits put you at either end, and in the middle of Sunnyside.

ESSENTIALS

Visitor Information Sunnyside Chamber of Commerce ⊠ *451 S. 6th St.* ☏ *509/837–5939, 800/457–8089* ⊕ *www.sunnysidechamber.com.*

EXPLORING

Tucker Cellars. The Tucker family came to the Yakima Valley as share-croppers during the Great Depression. They became successful farmers and were among the first to grow vinifera grapes on a commercial scale. Dean and Rose Tucker founded the winery in 1981, now a family operation involving their four children. Tucker plantings include Riesling, Pinot Noir, Gewürztraminer, Chenin Blanc, Chardonnay, and Muscat Canelli. Attached to the Tucker Cellars tasting room is the family's produce stand, which sells some of the Yakima Valley's best seasonal fruits and vegetables. There's a picnic area. ⊠ *70 Ray Rd.* ☏ *509/837–8701* ⊕ *www.tuckercellars.net* ⊙ *Daily 10–5.*

WHERE TO EAT AND STAY

$
MEXICAN
✕ **El Conquistador.** The bright, lively colors and clean, modern-Mexican interior belie the aging facade of this quaint eatery. The menu ranges from burritos, fajitas, and enchiladas mole to shrimp sautéed with green peppers and onions and served with a tangy salsa. Egg dishes are also on the menu, as are some unique Mexican salads and soups. Handcrafted clay masks on the walls add a festive flair. ⑤ *Average main: $10* ⊠ *612 E. Edison Ave.* ☏ *509/839–2880.*

$
AMERICAN
✕ **Snipes Mountain Microbrewery & Restaurant.** In an imposing log structure that resembles a hunting or ski lodge, the lower valley's oldest and largest brewpub is a grand restaurant with fare ranging from burgers and wood-fired pizzas to pasta dishes, fresh king salmon cooked on an alder plank, prime rib, and rack of lamb. Head brewer Chad Roberts makes handcrafted beers, using locally grown hops, of course. ⑤ *Average main: $15* ⊠ *905 Yakima Valley Hwy.* ☏ *509/837–2739* ⊕ *www.snipesmountain.com.*

$
B&B/INN
🛏 **Sunnyside Inn Bed & Breakfast.** At this two-house inn, built in 1919 as a doctor's residence and office, nine rooms have whirlpool tubs, several have small sunrooms, and all have private entrances. **Pros:** in the heart of wine country; a short drive to several different wineries; free Wi-Fi in rooms. **Cons:** immediate surroundings are not the most appealing.

Hogue Cellars, Prosser

$ *Rooms from: $100* ✉ *800–804 E. Edison Ave.* ☎ *509/839-5557, 800/221-4195* ⊕ *www.sunnysideinn.com* ⤴ *12 rooms* ⍾| *Breakfast.*

PROSSER

13 miles southeast of Sunnyside.

On the south bank of the Yakima River, Prosser feels like small-town America of the 1950s. The seat of Benton County since 1905, it has a 1926 courthouse. In 2005, Prosser's Horse Heaven Hills, on the Columbia River's north slope, became Washington's seventh federally recognized wine region.

GETTING HERE AND AROUND

On the lower end of the Yakima Valley, Prosser sits alongside Interstate 82 as it works its way to Benton City and then on to the Tri-Cities (Richland/Kennewick/Pasco). Two exits put you at either end of town.

ESSENTIALS

Visitor Information Prosser Chamber of Commerce ✉ *1230 Bennett Ave.* ☎ *509/786-3177, 866/343-5101* ⊕ *www.prosserchamber.com.*

EXPLORING

TOP ATTRACTIONS

Desert Wind Winery. An expansive tasting room housed in an elegant Southwestern-style building featuring a vast patio overlooking the Yakima River is one of the highlights of any wine tour in the valley. Tasters will delight in Sémillon, Barbera, Ruah, Viognier, and various other unique wine selections. Just off I-82, the winery also includes Mojave, a small restaurant (open Wednesday–Saturday), and a gift shop with Yakima Valley food products and gift items. Also available on the second floor are four luxury guest suites. ✉ *2258 Wine Country Rd.* ☎ *509/786–7277* ⊕ *www.desertwindwinery.com* ☉ *Daily 11–5.*

Hogue Cellars. Founded in 1982, one of the largest wineries in the state has earned multiple awards for its wines. The gift shop carries the winery's famous pickled beans and asparagus as well as Cabernet Sauvignon, Merlot, Chenin Blanc, Rieslings, and Fumé Blanc, among other wines. ✉ *Prosser Wine and Food Park, 2800 Lee Rd.* ☎ *509/786–6108* ⊕ *www.hoguecellars.com* ☉ *Mar.–Nov., daily 10–5; Dec.–Feb., daily 11–4.*

Kestrel Vintners. Although visiting this winery, in the Port of Benton's Prosser Wine and Food Park, doesn't necessarily rank as a great sensory pleasure, tasting the wines does. Kestrel is one of the Yakima Valley's premium wineries and makes mainly reds (Cabernet Sauvignon, Merlot, Syrah), as well as some white (Chardonnay, Viognier), from grapes—some of them estate-grown—that are deliberately stressed to increase the intensity of their flavors. The tasting room sells cheeses and deli items to go with the wines. ✉ *2890 Lee Rd., in Prosser Wine and Food Park* ☎ *509/786–2675* ⊕ *www.kestrelwines.com* ☉ *Daily 11–5.*

WORTH NOTING

Chinook Wines. This small house winery is run by Kay Simon and Clay Mackey, vintners known for their dry wines, including Merlot, Chardonnay, Sémillon, and Sauvignon Blanc. The tasting room is within the original farm buildings, and there's a shady picnic area outside. ✉ *Wittkopf Loop at Wine Country Rd.* ☎ *509/786–2725* ⊕ *www. chinookwines.com* ☉ *May–Oct., weekends noon–5, or by appointment.*

Hinzerling Vineyards. The place that's billed as the valley's first winery specializes in dessert and appetizer wines, including Port, Sherry, and Muscat. Vintner Mike Wallace is one of the state's wine pioneers: he planted his first Prosser-area vines in 1972, and established the small winery in 1976. ✉ *1520 Sheridan Ave., at Wine Country Rd.* ☎ *509/786–2163* ⊕ *www.hinzerling.com* ☉ *Daily 11–4.*

Pontin del Roza. This vintner named for its owners, the Pontin family, and the grape-friendly slopes irrigated by the Roza Canal, produces Italian-style Sangioveses and Pinot Grigios, as well as Rieslings, Chenin Blancs, Chardonnays, Sauvignon Blancs, and Cabernet Sauvignons. ✉ *35502 N. Hinzerling Rd., 3½ miles north of Prosser* ☎ *509/786–4449* ⊕ *www. pontindelroza.com* ☉ *Daily 10–5.*

Thurston Wolfe. Established in 1987, one of the region's highest regarded wineries features Wade Wolfe's unusual blends of specialty wines, including a white Pinot Gris–Viognier, for instance, and a red mix of Zinfandel, Syrah, Lemberger, and Turiga. One of their popular varieties is Sweet Rebecca, an orange Muscat. ✉ *Prosser Wine and Food Park, 588 Cabernet Ct.* ☎ *509/786–3313* ⊕ *www.thurstonwolfe.com* ☉ *Apr.–early Dec., Thurs.–Sun. 11–5.*

VineHeart. This pleasant boutique winery offers a buttery Riesling, a raspberry-toned Sémillon, a Lemberger, and a Sangiovese, as well as Zinfandel, Cabernet Sauvignon, and Syrah. ✉ *44209 N. McDonald*

Yakima Valley vineyard

Rd., 7 miles northeast of Prosser ☎ *509/973–2993* ⊕ *www.vineheart. com* ☉ *Mon. and Thurs.–Sat. 9–5, Sun. 11–5.*

Willow Crest Winery. David Minick founded his small winery in 1995 and offers a Tuscan-themed tasting room that pours its own award-winning Syrah, as well as Cabernet Franc and Pinot Gris. There's also a café on site, open for lunch May through October. ⊠ *Vintners Village, 590 Merlot Dr.* ☎ *509/786–7999* ⊕ *www.willowcrestwinery.com* ☉ *Daily 11–5.*

Yakima River Winery. Another of the pioneer wineries in the valley, established by John and Louise Rauner in 1977, specializes in barrel-aged reds and a memorable Port. ⊠ *143302 N. River Rd., 1½ miles south of Wine Country Rd.* ☎ *509/786–2805* ⊕ *www.yakimariverwinery.com* ☉ *Daily 10–5.*

WHERE TO STAY

$

B&B/INN

🏛 **Vintners Inn.** You'll think you have time-warped back to the turn of the 20th century when you arrive at this 1905 Queen Anne that has been remodeled into a farmhouse-style B&B, with two cozy rooms with private baths. **Pros:** Hinzerling Winery right next door; central location. **Cons:** bathrooms only have tubs, no showers; three blocks from railroad track, so occasional train noise at night; no TV. Ⓢ *Rooms from: $90* ⊠ *1520 Sheridan Ave.* ☎ *509/786–2163, 800/727–6702* ⊕ *www. hinzerling.com* ⮂ *2 rooms* ⌾ *Breakfast.*

BENTON CITY

16 miles east of Prosser.

The Yakima River zigzags north, making a giant bend around Red Mountain and the West Richland district before pouring into the Columbia River. Benton City—which, with a mere 3,000 residents, is hardly a city—is on a bluff west of the river facing vineyard-cloaked Red Mountain. High-carbonate soil, a location in a unique high-pressure pocket, and geographical anomalies have led to this district's being given its own appellation. You can access the wineries from Highway 224.

GETTING HERE AND AROUND

You'll find Benton City just off Interstate 82 about halfway between Prosser and Richland. One exit takes off from the interstate and funnels traffic into the little town and to Highway 224.

EXPLORING

Blackwood Canyon Vintners. Winemaker Michael Taylor Moore freely admits he's pushing the edge, meticulously crafting wines by hand, in the traditional European style of yesteryear. He shuns modern filters, pumps, and even sulfites, and carefully avoids pesticides. Chardonnays, Sémillons, Merlots, Cabernets, and late-harvest wines age *sur lies* (on their sediment) for as long as eight years before release. ⊠ *53258 N. Sunset Rd.* ☎ *509/588–7124* ⊕ *www.blackwoodwine.com* ☉ *Daily 10–6.*

Hedges Cellars. This spectacular hillside château winery dominates upper Red Mountain and produces robust red wines. The estate blends Cabernet Sauvignon, Cabernet Franc, Merlot, Syrah, and the reserve blends are superb. ⊠ *53511 N. Sunset Rd.* ☎ *509/588–3155* ⊕ *www.hedgesfamilyestate.com* ☉ *Apr.–Nov., weekends 11–5 or by appointment.*

Kiona Vineyards Winery. John Williams planted the first grapes on Red Mountain in 1975, made his first wines in 1980, and produced the first commercial Kiona Lemberger, a light German red, in the United States. Today Williams's recently constructed 10,000-square-foot tasting room features a 180-degree view of Red Mountain and the Rattlesnake Hills. Kiona also produces premium Riesling, Chenin Blanc, Chardonnay, Cabernet Sauvignon, Merlot, Syrah, Sangiovese, and dessert wines. You can picnic on the patio and, in addition to the wines, a range of meats and cheeses can be purchased. ⊠ *44612 N. Sunset Rd.* ☎ *509/588–6716* ⊕ *www.kionawine.com* ☉ *Daily noon–5.*

Terra Blanca. It's named for the calcium carbonate in its soil—Terra Blanca is Latin for "white earth"—and from this unique soil grow wine grapes that produce such specialties as Syrah, Merlot, Cabernet Sauvignon, and Chardonnay. ⊠ *34715 N. Demoss Rd.* ☎ *509/588–6082* ⊕ *www.terrablanca.com* ☉ *Daily 11–6 (from 10 am Apr.–Oct.).*

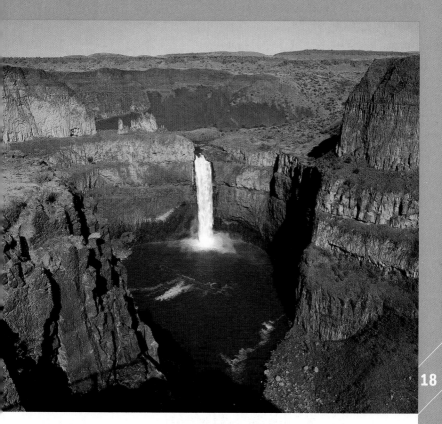

SPOKANE
AND EASTERN
WASHINGTON

Visit Fodors.com for advice, updates, and bookings

WELCOME TO SPOKANE AND EASTERN WASHINGTON

TOP REASONS TO GO

★ **Historic lodgings:** Take a step back in time. Visit the historic hotels and inns in Spokane, Walla Walla, and Dayton, which have been updated with modern amenities and high-tech touches, yet retain the flavor of yesteryear.

★ **Natural wonders:** Get off the beaten path to experience the unique waters of Soap Lake, see the cliffs and canyons along the Columbia River, and hike in national forests.

★ **Wineries:** Explore the many wineries in Walla Walla, Tri-Cities, and Spokane.

★ **Family attractions:** Slip in a little education on your family vacation by visiting pioneer museums, then play at water parks and Spokane's sprawling Riverfront Park.

1 **Southeastern Washington.** In the wide-open areas of the Walla Walla and Columbia Valleys, hillsides are covered with rows of grapevines and wind turbines. Lodging, restaurants, museums, and wine-tasting opportunities can be found in Walla Walla and the Tri-Cities.

2 **Spokane.** The second-largest city in Washington is home to one of the state's best hotels, the restored Davenport, and several other historic lodgings. There are numerous restaurants, museums, and notable parks.

3 **Grant County.** The highway through central Washington's desert lands can seem long and boring, but the farmers of Grant County's irrigated lands perk things up a bit with crop signs in the fences and lighted holiday displays. Venture off the main route to discover the stunning Cave B Resort by the Columbia River, see pioneer-history displays in Ephrata, and experience the healing waters of Soap Lake.

4 **Northeastern Washington.** Travelers to this region will find the "Eighth Technological Wonder of the World"—the Grand Coulee Dam—which features a daily laser light show in summer. Further exploration brings you to the Colville and Okanogan national forests, and the small towns of Grand Coulee, Coulee City, Omak, and Colville.

GETTING ORIENTED

The main route through eastern Washington is Interstate 90. Coming from the west, as you leave the Cascade Mountains and its foothills behind, the terrain turns to desert and sagebrush, before crossing over the Columbia River and reaching the irrigated areas where fields of crops grow. In this area's barren, dry lands a new type of farming has emerged—wind farms with giant turbines that transform the landscape and provide electricity. The southeast part of the state offers a more verdant setting—rolling hills and fields where rain helps produce abundant crops of grains and wine grapes. The northeast part of the state is flanked by three mountain ranges (Selkirk, Okanogan, and Kettle River), which are considered foothills of the Rocky Mountains; this area is rich with lakes, rivers, cliffs, and meadows, and home to diverse wildlife.

18

Updated by
Shelley Arenas

The Columbia Plateau was created by a series of lava flows that were later deeply cut by glacial floods. Because its soil is mostly made up of alluvial deposits and windblown silt (known to geologists as loess), it's very fertile. But little annual rainfall means that its vast central section—more than 30,000 square miles from the foothills of the Cascades and the northeastern mountains east to Idaho and south to Oregon—has no forests. In fact, except for a few scattered pine trees in the north, oaks in the southwest, and willows and cottonwoods along creeks and rivers, it has no trees.

This treeless expanse is part of an even larger steppe and desert region that runs north into Canada and south to California and the Sea of Cortez. There is water, however, carried from the mountains by the great Columbia and Snake Rivers and their tributaries. Irrigation provides the region's cities with shrubs, trees, and flowers, and its fields bear a great variety of crops: asparagus, potatoes, apples, peaches, alfalfa, sweet corn, wheat, lentils, and much more. This bounty of agriculture makes the region prosperous, and provides funds for symphony halls and opera houses, theaters, art museums, and universities.

Southeast of the Columbia Plateau lies a region of rolling hills and fields. Farmers of the Palouse region and of the foothills of the Blue Mountains don't need to irrigate their fields, as rain here produces record crops of wheat, lentils, and peas. It's a blessed landscape, flowing green and golden under the sun in waves of loam. In the Walla Walla Valley the traditional crops of wheat and sweet onions remain, but more than 1,800 acres of grapes now supply more than 100 wineries that have opened in the past few decades. The region is not only fertile, it is historically significant as well. The Lewis and Clark expedition passed through the Palouse in 1805, and Walla Walla was one of the earliest settlements in the Inland Northwest.

The northeastern mountains, from the Okanogan to the Pend Oreille Valley, consist of granite peaks, glaciated cliffs, grassy uplands, and sunlit forests. Few Washingtonians seem to know about this region's attractions, however. Even at the height of the summer its roads and trails are rarely crowded.

The hidden jewel of these mountains is the Sanpoil River Valley, which is a miniature Yosemite Valley, with vertical rock walls rising 2,000–3,000 feet straight from the river, their height accentuated by the narrowness of the canyon. The valley has no amenities, and is still in the possession of its original owners, the Native Americans of the Colville Reservation, who have preserved its beauty. These wild highlands have few visitor facilities. Towns in the Okanogan Valley and the regional metropolis of Spokane, on the fringes of the region, offer more services.

SPOKANE AND EASTERN WASHINGTON PLANNER

WHEN TO GO

Eastern Washington has four distinct seasons, with generally very hot summers and sometimes very snowy winters. Recreational activities are geared to the specific season, with several downhill ski resorts open for skiing and snowboarding, and Nordic skiing available in the national forests, too. In summer, water activities on the lakes and rivers are popular, and there are many places to pursue hiking, backpacking, cycling, fishing, and hunting. Eastern Washington rarely feels crowded, though popular campgrounds may fill in summer. Lodging rates tend to be higher between Memorial Day and Labor Day, so visiting off-season can reduce costs. Spring and fall are both beautiful seasons to explore the region. In smaller towns certain attractions are open only from May through September, so call ahead to plan visits to sights. Also call well in advance to make reservations during college special-event weekends in Pullman and Walla Walla.

FESTIVALS AND EVENTS

The region's rich bounty of viniculture and agriculture is celebrated with festivals throughout the year.

Bloomsday. On the first Sunday of May, more than 40,000 runners course 12 km (7½ miles) through downtown Spokane and the northwest part of the city. ✉ *Spokane* ☎ *509/838–1579* ⊕ *www.bloomsdayrun.org.*

Farmer Consumer Awareness Day. Farms and processing plants in Quincy throw an open house for a weekend every mid-September so consumers can get a closer look at where their food comes from. There are exhibits, a farmers' market, food booths, tours of farms, processors, and geology sites, and lots of other events. ✉ *Quincy* ☎ *509/787–4246* ⊕ *www. quincyfarmerconsumer.com.*

Green Bluff Growers Festivals. The association of small farms and food stands in Green Bluff (about 20 miles northeast of downtown Spokane) presents several festivals as orchard fruits come into season. Strawberries are celebrated in late June and early July, while the Cherry Festival runs two weekends in July, the Peach Festival mid-August through Labor Day, and the Apple Festival weekends from late September through late October. ⊠ *Hwy. 2 and Green Bluff Rd., Colbert* ⊕ *www. greenbluffgrowers.com.*

Hoopfest. The last weekend in June, basketball mania descends on downtown Spokane as Hoopfest comes to town, a mega tournament with nearly 7,000 teams and 27,000 players playing 3-on-3 basketball on 450 courts over 40 city blocks. It's the world's largest event of its type, with more than 225,000 fans in attendance. ⊠ *Spokane* ☎ *509/624–2414* ⊕ *www.spokanehoopfest.net.*

Pig Out in the Park. Locals and tourists flock to Riverfront Park over Labor Day to gorge on yummy food and nonstop live music. ⊠ *Riverfront Park, 507 N. Howard St., Spokane* ☎ *509/879–0826* ⊕ *www. spokanepigout.com.*

Spokane Lilac Festival. Parades and other events honor the flower that gives Spokane the moniker "Lilac City." ⊠ *Spokane* ☎ *509/535–4554* ⊕ *www.spokanelilacfestival.org.*

Walla Walla Wine Festivals. The Walla Walla Valley Wine Alliance coordinates Spring Release Weekend, the first weekend in May; Celebrate Walla Walla Wines, for a weekend in mid-June; Fall Release Weekend, the first weekend in November; and Holiday Barrel Tasting, the first weekend in December. Events include wine tasting, tours, winemaker dinners, music, and arts festivals. ⊠ *Walla Walla* ☎ *509/526–3117* ⊕ *www.wallawallawine.com.*

GETTING HERE AND AROUND

AIR TRAVEL

Spokane International Airport is the main hub for air travel in eastern Washington. Smaller airports include Pullman, Tri-Cities, Walla Walla, and Lewiston, Idaho (across the border from Clarkston). Spokane International Airport is served by Alaska, Delta, and Southwest; the Tri-Cities Airport is served by Allegiant, Delta, Horizon, and United. Horizon serves the smaller regional airports.

Contacts Lewiston-Nez Perce County Airport ⊠ *406 Burrell Ave., Lewiston, Idaho* ☎ *208/746–4471* ⊕ *www.golws.com.* **Spokane International Airport** ⊠ *9000 W. Airport Dr., Spokane* ☎ *509/455–6455* ⊕ *www.spokaneairports. net.* **Tri-Cities Airport** ⊠ *3601 N. 20th Ave., Pasco* ☎ *509/547–6352* ⊕ *www. portofpasco.org.*

CAR TRAVEL

Interstate 90 is the most direct route from Seattle to Spokane over the Cascade Mountains (Snoqualmie Pass). U.S. 2 (Stevens Pass), an alternate route, begins north of Seattle near Everett, and passes through Wenatchee and Coulee City. South of Interstate 90, U.S. 395 leads to the Tri-Cities from the east; the Tri-Cities can also be accessed via Interstate 82 from the west. Past the Tri-Cities, continue on Interstate 82 then U.S. 12 to reach Walla Walla. U.S. 195 traverses southeastern Washington to Pullman. Leave U.S. 195 at Colfax, heading southwest on Highway 26 and then 127, and finally U.S. 12 to Dayton and Walla

Walla. Gas stations along the main highways cater to truckers, and some are open 24 hours.

RESTAURANTS

Nearly every small town in eastern Washington has at least one fast-food drive-through for a quick meal on the go, but choosing a slower pace will reward visitors with an authentic dining experience that often doesn't cost much more. Local diners and cafés are great spots for getting a hearty breakfast of traditional favorites like farm-fresh eggs or biscuits and gravy. Somewhat surprisingly, several of the small towns have outstanding dining options, too. At many restaurants there's an emphasis on locally grown, organic foods. With the region's many farms, it's easy to source produce, grains, poultry, meat, and dairy items, and some restaurants have their own gardens on-site for the freshest produce of all. Spokane has a good diversity of cuisines and some highly acclaimed restaurants, but up-and-coming Walla Walla is also becoming a mecca for foodies and wine lovers.

HOTELS

Family-owned motels and budget chains are prevalent in small towns like Colville, Grand Coulee, Moses Lake, Omak, Pullman, and Soap Lake. More of these properties are updating their amenities to include modern touches such as flat-screen TVs; others can feel dated, but at least the prices are reasonable, except during special events when demand spikes create rate hikes. Several pleasant bed-and-breakfasts with friendly innkeepers are found in Spokane, Walla Walla, Dayton, and Uniontown (near Pullman), but with no more than six suites at each it's usually necessary to call ahead for a reservation. There are several historic hotels built in the early 1900s and restored in recent years that are definitely worth visiting in Spokane, Walla Walla, and Dayton. The Inn at Abeja, just outside Walla Walla on a historic farm site, offers unique, high-end lodging. A stay at the Cave B Resort by the Columbia River—in one of its cliff houses, cavern rooms, or luxury yurts—is a recommended destination experience, too. *Hotel reviews have been shortened. For full information, visit Fodors.com.*

WHAT IT COSTS IN U.S. DOLLARS			
$	$$	$$$	$$$$
Restaurants	Under $18	$18–$24	$25–$30	Over $30
Hotels	Under $151	$151–$200	$201–$250	Over $250

Restaurant prices are the average cost of a main course at dinner, or if dinner is not served, at lunch. Hotel prices are the lowest cost of a standard double room in high season.

SOUTHEASTERN WASHINGTON

The most populated area in this region is the Tri-Cities—Pasco, Kennewick, and Richland. Each town has its own character, but their proximity makes it easy to access an array of services and attractions like local wineries and pleasant riverfront parks. The town of Walla Walla has a historic downtown shopping district with innovative restaurant choices, wine-tasting rooms, elegant B&Bs, and the impressive Marcus Whitman Hotel. Just outside town, wineries in bucolic country settings are as enjoyable for picnickers as for serious wine connoisseurs. If you continue east and north on quiet two-lane highways you'll discover Dayton, another historic small town, and Pullman, home of Washington State University.

RICHLAND

202 miles southeast of Seattle, 145 miles southwest of Spokane.

Richland is the northernmost of the three municipalities along the bank of the Columbia River known as the Tri-Cities (the others are Pasco and Kennewick). Founded in the 1880s, Richland was a pleasant farming village until 1942, when the federal government built a nuclear reactor on the nearby Hanford Nuclear Reservation. The Hanford site was instrumental in the building of the Tri-Cities, and still plays a major role in the area's economy. In recent years this has also become a major wine-producing area. You can find more than 100 wineries within a 50-mile radius, many with tasting rooms.

GETTING HERE AND AROUND

The Tri-Cities Airport in Pasco is served by Allegiant, Delta, Horizon, and United. Taxis and rental cars are available there. Some hotels also offer an airport shuttle. Greyhound Bus Lines and Amtrak's Empire Builder both stop in Pasco. Ben Franklin Transit serves all three cities. By car, Interstate 82 is the main east–west highway; from Ritzville or Spokane, take Highway 395 to reach the Tri-Cities; from Ellensburg and Yakima, take Highway 82 south and east.

Contact **Ben Franklin Transit** ☎ 509/735–5100 ⊕ www.bft.org.

ESSENTIALS

Visitor Information **City of Richland** ⊠ 505 Swift Blvd. ☎ 509/942–7390 ⊕ www.ci.richland.wa.us. **Tri-Cities Visitor and Convention Bureau.** For winery information and maps, contact Tri-Cities Visitor and Convention Bureau. ⊠ 7130 W. Grandridge Blvd., Ste. B, Kennewick ☎ 800/254–5824, 509/735–8486 ⊕ www.visittri-cities.com.

EXPLORING

Barnard Griffin Winery and Tasting Room. Owners Rob Griffin and Deborah Barnard offer a variety of fine wines, including excellent Merlot and Cabernet. The art gallery adds class to the wine-tasting experience. ⊠ 878 Tulip La. ☎ 509/627–0266 ⊕ www.barnardgriffin.com ⊙ Daily 10–5; wine bar Wed.–Sat. 4–9.

Bookwalter Winery. Next door to Barnard Griffin Winery, Bookwalter produces red wines aged in French oak barrels and whites that are 100% stainless-steel fermented. The classic Merlot is celebrated. Blends are prevalent in both reds and whites. The on-site restaurant, Fiction, features small plates like prosciutto flatbread with pears, six types of salad, and heartier fare such as steaks, burgers, and salmon. ⊠ 894 Tulip La. ☎ 509/627–5000 ⊕ www.bookwalterwines.com ☎ $10 tasting fee; applied toward wine purchase $35 or more ⊙ Sun.–Tues. 11–10, Wed.–Sat. 11–11.

The REACH (The Hanford Reach Interpretive Center). Here's the place to learn about the Hanford Reach National Monument, an area that encompasses the Hanford Reach of the Columbia River and greater Columbia Basin and surrounds the former site of the Hanford Nuclear Reservation. The interpretive center highlights the region's history, culture, science and technology, natural resources and agriculture, and arts. The exhibit area has permanent exhibits on the Columbia Basin Project's irrigated agriculture, the history of the atomic age and Hanford's contribution to ending World War II, and the Columbia River's role in producing electrical power. Special events include tours, classes, and culinary events highlighting the area's wineries and agriculture. The 18-acre setting on the Columbia River includes outdoor exhibits, a nature trail, and a stage where concerts are held in the summer. ⊠ 1943 Columbia Park Trail ☎ 509/943–4100 ⊕ www.visitthereach.org ☎ $8 ⊙ Tues.–Sat. 9–5, Sun. noon–5.

18

WHERE TO EAT AND STAY

$$$ ✕ **Anthony's at Columbia Point.** For years the Anthony's chain has been
SEAFOOD known for fine waterfront dining in western Washington; since 2004
the Tri-Cities has had its own Anthony's on the Columbia River water-
front. Seafood is the specialty—even the appetizers are fish-focused,
including panfried Willapa Bay oysters and fresh Puget Sound mussels.
Dungeness crab (whole, in fettuccine, or in crab cakes), Idaho rainbow
trout, char-grilled Alaskan halibut, and several steaks are among the
many entrée offerings. Anthony's weekday sunset four-course dinners
are especially popular. ⑤ *Average main: $25* ⊠ *550 Columbia Point Dr.*
☎ *509/946–3474* ⊕ *www.anthonys.com.*

$ ✕ **Atomic Ale Brewpub and Eatery.** The staff is friendly at this small, casual
AMERICAN brewpub, which serves mainly house-brewed beers. The delicious piz-
zas are cooked in a wood-fired oven; sandwiches, salads, and soups
(including potato, made with the in-house brew) are also fine. Des-
sert choices get clever names to match the nuclear theme, including
Plutonium Porter chocolate containment cake and B-Reactor brownie.
Local memorabilia is displayed throughout the restaurant, and the his-
tory of the Hanford nuclear plant is depicted in photos on the walls.
⑤ *Average main: $16* ⊠ *1015 Lee Blvd.* ☎ *509/946–5465* ⊕ *www.*
atomicalebrewpub.com.

$ ☷ **Red Lion Hotel Richland Hanford House.** The best of these standard-issue
HOTEL motel-style rooms overlook the Columbia River, and all have access
to the riverfront park and trails along the levee. **Pros:** nice location;
free airport shuttle; favorite of Hanford contractors. **Cons:** older hotel,
though some rooms have been updated; can get noisy with larger groups
and teams. ⑤ *Rooms from: $129* ⊠ *802 George Washington Way*
☎ *509/946–7611, 800/733–5466* ⊕ *www.redlion.com* ⤴ *142 rooms,*
7 suites ⁙⊙⁙ *Breakfast.*

$ ☷ **Shilo Inn Suites Hotel.** Rooms are simple in style yet they come with cof-
HOTEL feemakers, microwaves, refrigerators, fold-down ironing units, and free
FAMILY unlimited local and long-distance calls. **Pros:** excellent value; convenient
riverfront location. **Cons:** rooms by outdoor pool can be noisy; property
needs updating; no elevators. ⑤ *Rooms from: $109* ⊠ *50 Comstock St.*
☎ *509/946–4661, 800/222–2244* ⊕ *www.shiloinns.com* ⤴ *151 rooms,*
13 suites ⁙⊙⁙ *Breakfast.*

PASCO

10 miles east of Richland.

Tree-shaded Pasco, a college town and the Franklin County seat, is an
oasis of green on the Columbia River near a site where the Lewis and
Clark expedition made camp in 1805. The city began as a railroad
switchyard and now has a busy container port. The neoclassical Frank-
lin County Courthouse (1907) is worth a visit for its fine marble interior.

The Pasco Basin has first-rate vineyards and wineries and some of the
state's most fertile land. You can purchase the regional bounty at the
farmers' market, held downtown every Wednesday and Saturday morn-
ing during the growing season.

GETTING HERE AND AROUND

The Tri-Cities Airport is in Pasco; Allegiant, Delta, Horizon, and United operate there. Taxis and rental cars are both available and some hotels offer an airport shuttle. Ben Franklin Transit serves all three cities. By car, Interstate 82 is the main east–west highway; from Ritzville or Spokane, take Highway 395 to reach the Tri-Cities; from Ellensburg and Yakima, take Interstate 82 south and east.

Contact Ben Franklin Transit ☎ 509/735–5100 ⊕ www.bft.org.

ESSENTIALS

Visitor Information City of Pasco ☎ 509/544–3080 ⊕ www.pasco-wa.gov.

EXPLORING

Franklin County Historical Museum. Here you'll find numerous items illustrating local history, including Native American artifacts. Revolving exhibits have featured the Lewis and Clark expedition, the railroad, World War II, agriculture, and aviation. ⊠ 305 N. 4th Ave. ☎ 509/547–3714 ⊕ www.franklincountyhistoricalsociety.org ☜ Donations accepted ⊙ Tues.–Fri. noon–4.

Sacajawea State Park. At the confluence of the Snake and Columbia Rivers, this park occupies the site of Ainsworth, a railroad town that flourished from 1879 to 1884. It's named for the Shoshoni woman who guided the Lewis and Clark expedition over the Rocky Mountains and down the Snake River. The 284-acre day-use park has an interpretive center and a large display of Native American tools. A beach, boat launch, picnic area, and children's playground round out the facilities; sand dunes, marshes, and ponds are great for watching wildlife. ⊠ 2503 Sacajawea Park Rd., off U.S. 12, 5 miles southeast of Pasco ☎ 509/545–2361 ⊕ www.parks.wa.gov ☜ Day pass $10 per vehicle; annual Discovery Pass $30 (valid at all state parks) ⊙ Apr.–Oct., 6:30 am–dusk.

WHERE TO EAT AND STAY

$$$ ✕ **Bin 20 Steak and Seafood Restaurant.** A nice selection of wine, many

AMERICAN from Washington State, accompanies signature dishes that include the Bin 20 wedge salad and rib-eye steak with a choice of four sauces. Crème brûlée doughnuts are a unique and popular dessert item. Happy hour runs 4 to 7 Monday through Thursday. ⑤ Average main: $30 ⊠ 2525 N. 20th St. ☎ 509/544–3939 ⊕ www.bin20.com ⊙ No lunch.

$ ⌂ **Red Lion Hotel Pasco.** Most of these functional rooms, in three sepa-

HOTEL rate wings of low-rise buildings, have either a patio or balcony, and the outdoor pool area and spacious, open lobby are attractive. **Pros:** good service; spacious rooms; two restaurants on-site. **Cons:** very large hotel, so some rooms can be a long walk from the lobby. ⑤ Rooms from: $129 ⊠ 2525 N. 20th St. ☎ 509/547–0701 ⊕ www.redlion.com ⬟ 279 rooms, 10 suites ⑩ No meals.

18

KENNEWICK

3 miles southwest of Pasco, directly across the Columbia River.

In its 100-year history, Kennewick (*ken*-uh-wick) evolved from a railroad town to a farm-supply center and then to a bedroom community for Hanford workers and a food-processing capital for the Columbia Basin. The name Kennewick translates as "grassy place," and Native Americans had winter villages here long before Lewis and Clark passed through. Arrowheads and other artifacts aside, the 9,000-year-old skeleton of Kennewick Man has been studied by scientists at the University of Washington to determine whether its features are Native American or, as some claim, Caucasian.

GETTING HERE AND AROUND
The Tri-Cities Airport is in nearby Pasco, served by Allegiant, Delta, Horizon, and United. Taxis and rental cars are available and some hotels offer an airport shuttle. Ben Franklin Transit serves all three cities. By car, Interstate 82 is the main east–west highway; from Ritzville or Spokane, take Highway 395 to reach the Tri-Cities; from Ellensburg and Yakima, take Interstate 82 south and east.

ESSENTIALS
Visitor Information City of Kennewick ☎ 509/585–4266 ⊕ www. go2kennewick.com.

EXPLORING
TOP ATTRACTIONS
Badger Mountain Vineyard. A beautiful view of the valley and wine made without pesticides or preservatives is what you'll find here. Badger Mountain was the first wine-grape vineyard in Washington State to be certified organic. ⊠ 1106 N. Jurupa St. ☎ 800/643–9463 ⊕ www. badgermtnvineyard.com ⊙ Daily 10–5.

Columbia Park. Adjacent to the Columbia River, this is one of Washington's great parks. Its 4½-mile-long riverfront has boat ramps, a golf course, picnic areas, playgrounds (including an aquatic one), train ride, ropes course, and family fishing pond. In summer, hydroplane races are held here. ⊠ Columbia Trail Dr., between U.S. 240 and the Columbia River ☎ 509/585–4293 ⊕ www.go2kennewick.com.

McNary National Wildlife Refuge. More than 200 species of birds have been identified here, and many waterfowl make it their winter home. But the 15,000 acres of water and marsh, croplands, grasslands, trees, and shrubs are most enjoyable in spring and summer. The Environmental Education Center features hands-on exhibits. A self-guided 2-mile trail winds through the marshes, and a cabin-like blind hidden in the reeds allows you to watch wildlife up close. Other recreation includes boating, fishing, hiking, and horseback-riding. ⊠ 64 Maple Rd., ¼ mile east of U.S. 12, south of Snake River Bridge, Burbank ☎ 509/546–8300 ⊕ www.fws.gov/refuge/McNary ☑ Free ⊙ Daily during daylight hrs. Headquarters Mon.–Thurs. 8–4:30, Fri. 8–3:30.

WORTH NOTING
East Benton County Historical Museum. The entire entryway to the museum is made of petrified wood. Photographs, agricultural displays, petroglyphs, and a large collection of arrowheads interpret area history. Kennewick's oldest park, Keewaydin, is across the street. ⊠ 205 Keewaydin Dr. ☎ 509/582–7704 ⊕ www.ebchs.org ☑ Free ⊙ Tues.–Sat. noon–4.

Ice Harbor Lock and Dam. At 103 feet, the single-lift locks here are among the world's highest. ✉ *2763 Monument Dr., about 12 miles southeast of Kennewick, Burbank* ☏ *509/547–7781* ⊕ *www.nww.usace.army. mil/Locations/DistrictLocksandDams/IceHarborLockandDam.aspx* ✉ *Free* ☉ *Visitor center Apr.–Oct., daily 9–4:30.*

WHERE TO EAT AND STAY

$$$

AMERICAN

✕ **The Cedars.** A perch right on the edge of the Columbia River provides beautiful views and a 200-foot dock for boaters coming to dine. A deck is open seasonally, and it's popular as an after-work gathering place. The menu includes top-quality steaks, pasta, and poultry. Shellfish are also on the menu, as well as several kinds of fresh fish, including salmon, halibut, swordfish, and ahi tuna. The fish are available with a choice of sauces and the option to be prepared blackened in Cajun spices in a cast iron skillet. An extensive wine list features many local labels. Save room for the house-made mud pie. ⑤ *Average main: $28* ✉ *355 Clover Island Dr.* ☏ *509/582–2143* ⊕ *www.cedarsrest.com* ☉ *No lunch.*

$

HOTEL

☗ **Red Lion Columbia Center.** Talk about convenience: these well-kept, up-to-date rooms, all with microwaves, are next to a regional shopping mall and a few blocks from the convention center. **Pros:** handy location; good value; seasonal pool. **Cons:** no full-service restaurant (many at the nearby mall); best for business guests. ⑤ *Rooms from: $139* ✉ *1101 N. Columbia Center Blvd.* ☏ *509/783–0611, 800/733–5466* ⊕ *www. redlion.com* ⇆ *153 rooms, 9 suites* ⚭ *No meals.*

WALLA WALLA

52 miles southeast of Kennewick.

18

Walla Walla, founded in the 1850s on the site of a Nez Perce village, was Washington's first metropolis. As late as the 1880s its population was larger than that of Seattle. Walla Walla occupies a lush green valley below the rugged Blue Mountains. Its beautiful downtown boasts old residences, green parks, and the campus of Whitman College, Washington's oldest institution of higher learning.

A successful downtown restoration has earned Walla Walla high praise. The heart of downtown, at 2nd and Main streets, looks as pretty as it did 60 years ago, with beautifully maintained old buildings and newer structures designed to fit in. Walla Walla's Main Street is the winner of the "Great American Main Street Award" from the National Trust for Historic Preservation. Residents and visitors come here to visit shops, wineries, cafés, and restaurants.

West of town, the green Walla Walla Valley—famous for asparagus, sweet onions, cherries, and wheat—has emerged as Washington's premier viticultural region. Tall grain elevators mark Lowden, a few miles west of Walla Walla, a wheat hamlet that now has several wineries.

GETTING HERE AND AROUND

Coming from points west, Walla Walla is reached via Interstate 82 east of the Tri-Cities, then Highway 12, which is still a two-lane highway in places but has recently been expanded west of Walla Walla and into the town. From Spokane and the northeast, travel is all by two-lane highway, going south on Highway 195 to Colfax, then southwest via Highways 26 and 127 to Highway 12, then continuing south through Dayton and Waitsburg. Horizon Air runs two daily flights (one on Saturday) each way between Walla Walla and Seattle.

Contacts Walla Walla Regional Airport ⊠ *45 Terminal Loop Rd.* ☎ *509/525–3100* ⊕ *www.wallawallaairport.com.*

ESSENTIALS

Visitor Information Walla Walla Valley Chamber of Commerce ⊠ *29 E. Sumach St.* ☎ *509/525–0850* ⊕ *www.wvchamber.com.*

EXPLORING

TOP ATTRACTIONS

FAMILY **Fort Walla Walla Museum.** On 15 acres at Fort Walla Walla Park, a 17-building pioneer village depicts the region's life in the 1800s, and four halls house military, agricultural, and penitentiary exhibits. ⊠ *755 Myra Rd.* ☎ *509/525–7703* ⊕ *www.fortwallawallamuseum.org* ☜ *$7* ⊗ *Apr.–Oct., daily 10–5; Nov.–Dec., daily 10–4; Jan.–Mar., weekdays 10–4.*

L'Ecole No. 41. Housed in the lower floors of a circa-1915 schoolhouse, this winery produces outstanding Sémillon and Merlot, among other wines. The tasting room is in one of the old classrooms, and details like chalkboards and books add to the ambience. ⊠ *41 Lowden School Rd., Lowden* ☎ *509/525–0940* ⊕ *www.lecole.com* ⊗ *Daily 10–5.*

Sinclair Estate Vineyards. This downtown tasting room for one of Walla Walla's newest wineries offers Syrah, Merlot, and Chardonnay. Owners Tim and Kathy Sinclair also own Vine and Roses Bed and Breakfast, and their love for French antiques and fine art is evident in the elegant tasting room. There's even a grand piano and live music on Friday evening, with no cover charge. ⊠ *109-B E. Main St.* ☎ *509/876–4300* ⊕ *www.sinclairestatevineyards.com* ⊗ *Thurs.–Mon. 10–5.*

Three Rivers Winery. This winery just off U.S. 12 and surrounded by vineyards produces premium Cabernet Sauvignon, Merlot, Malbec, Sauvignon Blanc, Chardonnay, and Riesling. It has a nice tasting room, a gift shop, summer concerts, and a 3-hole golf course. ⊠ *5641 Old Hwy. 12* ☎ *509/526–9463, 866/485–7566* ⊕ *www.threeriverswinery. com* ⊗ *Daily 10–5.*

Waterbrook Winery. The tasting room, part of a facility on 75 acres, has an indoor-outdoor feel, with a spacious patio and outdoor fireplace, hillside views, and natural landscaping and ponds. Waterbrook is best known for Merlot, Chardonnay, and Cabernet. ⊠ *10518 W. U.S. Hwy. 12* ☎ *509/522–1262* ⊕ *www.waterbrook.com* ⊗ *Sun.–Thurs. 11–6, Fri.–Sat. 11–7.*

FAMILY **Whitman Mission National Historic Site.** This is a reconstruction of Waiilatpu Mission, a Presbyterian outpost established on Cayuse lands in 1836. The park preserves the foundations of the mission buildings, a short segment of the Oregon Trail, and, on a nearby hill, the graveyard where the Native American victims of an 1847 measles epidemic and subsequent uprising are buried. ⊠ *328 Whitman Mission Rd., 7 miles*

L'Ecole No. 41 winery

west of downtown ☎ *509/522–6360, 509/529–2761* ⊕ *www.nps.gov/ whmi* ✉ *Free* ⊙ *Daily 8–430; visitor center open March–Dec., Wed.– Sun. 9–4.*

Woodward Canyon Winery. Lovers of fine wines make pilgrimages to this winery 12 miles west of Walla Walla, for the superb Cabernet Sauvignon, Chardonnay, and Merlot. The winery occasionally produces other varietals and also has a second label, Nelms Road, that focuses on younger and more affordable red wines. The Reserve House restaurant is open for lunch from Thursday through Sunday seasonally, pairing Woodward Canyon's wines with farm-to-table menus that feature locally grown produce, artisanal cheeses, and entrées like smoked duck breast and seared halibut. ✉ *11920 W. U.S. 12, Lowden* ☎ *509/525– 4129* ⊕ *www.woodwardcanyon.com* ⊙ *Daily 10–5.*

WORTH NOTING

Canoe Ridge Vineyards. Owned by Precept Wine, this vineyard produces Merlot, Cabernet Sauvignon, Chardonnay, Pinot Gris, and a red blend. The tasting room is in Walla Walla's historic Engine House. ✉ *1102 W. Cherry St.* ☎ *509/525–1843* ⊕ *www.canoeridgevineyard.com* ⊙ *Daily 11–5.*

Pioneer Park. Planted with native and exotic flowers and trees, this turn-of-the-20th-century park has a fine aviary. It was originally landscaped by sons of Frederick Law Olmsted, who designed New York City's Central Park. ✉ *E. Alder St. and Division St.* ⊕ *www.ci.walla-walla.wa.us.*

Seven Hills Winery. Here, owner Casey McClellan makes well-balanced Cabernet Sauvignon, Malbec, and several white wines, too. The winery is in Walla Walla's historic Whitehouse-Crawford building. ✉ *212 N.*

3rd Ave. ☎509/529–7198, 877/777–7870 ⊕ www.sevenhillswinery. com ☉ Mon.–Sat. 10–5, Sun. 10–2.

Whitman College. Large, tree-lined lawns surround the many beautiful 19th-century stone and brick structures of the Whitman College campus. The school began as a seminary in 1859 and became a college in 1883. ⊠ *345 Boyer Ave. ☎509/527–5111 ⊕ www.whitman.edu.*

WHERE TO EAT

$
CAFÉ

✕ **Olive Marketplace & Cafe.** Kick back and enjoy good food in a casual environment in this two-level downtown café. Between pouring its first cup of coffee at 8 am and the last glass of wine from the wine bar before closing at 9 pm, the café serves reasonably-priced and varied items. The breakfast menu ranges from classics like eggs Benedict to contemporary dishes like maple-braised pork belly sweet potato hash and poached eggs with polenta cakes. The all-day menu includes hearty meals like adobo-braised beef enchiladas and chicken curry, along with sandwiches, salads, and seasonal soups. Flatbread pizzas are popular, too, including the unique prosciutto and grape, smoked salmon, or spicy adobo braised beef with jalapenos varieties. There's free live music every Thursday night. ⑤ *Average main: $14 ⊠ 21 E. Main St. ☎509/526–0200 ⊕ www.olivemarketplaceandcafe.com.*

$$$
ITALIAN
Fodor's Choice
★

✕ **T. Maccarones.** Italian food with a very contemporary flare is the draw at "T-Mac's," along with the neighborly feel of the small, two-level restaurant. It's the kind of place that quickly becomes a favorite for locals. Customers are often greeted personally by friendly owner Tom Maccarone, a native of Walla Walla. Chef Gerry Meza's menu focuses on bold flavors and fresh, local, and organic ingredients for dishes like Upper Dry Creek lamb with seared scallops, cider-braised pork shank, and grilled octopus salad. The T-Mac and Cheese is rich and delicious; desserts are baked in-house. ⑤ *Average main: $28 ⊠ 4 N. Colville St. ☎509/522–4776 ⊕ www.tmaccarones.com.*

$$$
AMERICAN
Fodor's Choice
★

✕ **Whitehouse-Crawford Restaurant.** In a former wood mill, this restaurant has gained a reputation for quality and excellence, thanks to chef Jamie Guerin. Local is the watchword here, where hamburgers are made with grass-fed beef from Blue Valley Meats, and more than a dozen nearby purveyors supply produce, cheese, meat, eggs, and coffee. Try the Painted Hills beef tenderloin steak, roasted sockeye salmon, grilled grass-fed flat-iron steak, or roasted pork loin with chutney, and save room for the house-made ice cream or the rich twce-baked chocolate cake for dessert. The extensive wine list features many Walla Walla Valley winemakers. ⑤ *Average main: $29 ⊠ 55 W. Cherry St. ☎509/525– 2222 ⊕ www.whitehousecrawford.com ☉ Closed Tues. No lunch.*

WHERE TO STAY

$$
B&B/INN

▦ **Green Gables Inn.** One block from the Whitman College campus, this 1909 Arts and Crafts-style mansion sits among flowering plants and shrubs on a quaint, tree-lined street and offers charming guest rooms individually decorated with Victorian antiques. **Pros:** mini-refrigerators in rooms are a nice touch; pretty setting; good room amenities for a B&B. **Cons:** two-night minimum stay on weekends. ⑤ *Rooms from:*

$165 ✉ 922 Bonsella St. ☎ 509/876–4373 ⊕ www.greengablesinn.com ➵ 4 rooms, 1 suite ⃝❙ Breakfast.

$$$$
B&B/INN
Fodor's Choice
★

🏨 **Inn at Abeja.** Thirty-five acres of gardens, lawns, and vineyards surround this turn-of-the-20th-century farm; the high-end details of the incredibly stylish, beautifully furnished guest cottages and suites, attentive and friendly service, and gated entrance all contribute to an experience of serene, relaxing, secluded luxury. **Pros:** beautiful grounds; spacious accommodations, some with kitchens; private tours of the on-site winery, which is not open to the public. **Cons:** closed from early-December through February; book early as it fills up fast, especially with repeat guests. ⑤ Rooms from: $265 ✉ 2014 Mill Creek Rd. ☎ 509/522–1234 ⊕ www.abeja.net/inn ➵ 4 cottages, 3 suites ⦿ Closed mid-Dec.–Feb. ⃝❙ Breakfast.

$$
HOTEL
Fodor's Choice
★

🏨 **Marcus Whitman Hotel.** This 1928 hotel is *the* landmark in downtown Walla Walla, and guest quarters include spacious two-room parlor suites and spa suites in the historic tower building—adorned with Renaissance-style Italian furnishings and lots of amenities, these rooms are well worth the splurge. **Pros:** range of accommodations available; downtown location; full breakfast buffet and parking included. **Cons:** no pool; no bathtubs in historic rooms. ⑤ Rooms from: $155 ✉ 6 W. Rose St. ☎ 509/525–2200, 866/826–9422 ⊕ www.marcuswhitmanhotel.com ➵ 127 rooms, 16 suites ⃝❙ Breakfast.

$$$
B&B/INN
Fodor's Choice
★

🏨 **Vine and Roses Bed & Breakfast.** An 1893 Victorian just a block from Pioneer Park has been extravagantly renovated to create an oasis of luxury and grace with quiet, secluded suites decorated with French antiques and equipped with gas fireplaces, deep soaking tubs (some with jets), and separate walk-in showers. **Pros:** free tastings at the Sinclairs' other business, Sinclair Estate Vineyards; rooms are very quiet and private; breakfast features herbs and produce from the garden. **Cons:** as with many B&Bs, this isn't a place to bring kids. ⑤ Rooms from: $229 ✉ 516 S. Division St. ☎ 509/876–2113 ⊕ www.vineandroses.com ➵ 5 suites ⃝❙ Breakfast.

DAYTON

31 miles northeast of Walla Walla.

The tree-shaded county seat of Columbia County is the kind of Currier & Ives place many people conjure up when they imagine the best qualities of rural America. This tidy town has 117 buildings listed on the National Register of Historic Places, including the state's oldest railroad depot and courthouse.

GETTING HERE AND AROUND

Dayton is northeast of Walla Walla via Highway 12. From the Spokane area, take Highway 195 to Colfax, then veer southwest via Highways 26 and 127 before reaching Highway 12 and continuing into the town.

EXPLORING

Dayton Historical Depot Society. At Washington's oldest standing depot, the society houses exhibits illustrating the history of Dayton and surrounding communities. ✉ 222 E. Commercial Ave. ☎ 509/382–2026

⊕ *www.daytonhistoricdepot.org* ✉ *Free* ⊙ *May–Oct., Wed.–Sat. 10–5 (closed noon–1); Nov.–Apr., Wed.–Sat. 11–4.*

OFF THE
BEATEN
PATH

Palouse Falls State Park. Just north of its confluence with the Snake River, the Palouse River gushes over a basalt cliff higher than Niagara Falls and drops 198 feet into a steep-walled basin. Those who are sure-footed can hike to an overlook above the falls, which are at their fastest during spring runoff in March. Just downstream from the falls at the Marmes Rock Shelter, remains of the earliest-known inhabitants of North America, dating back 10,000 years, were discovered by archaeologists. The park has 11 primitive campsites, open year-round, but with no water September through April. ⊠ *Palouse Falls Rd. and State Route 261, 38 miles north of Dayton* ☎ *509/646–9218* ⊕ *www.parks. wa.gov/559/Palouse-Falls* ✉ *Day pass $10 per vehicle; annual Discovery Pass $30 (valid at all state parks)* ⊙ *Summer, daily 6:30 am–dusk; winter, daily 8 am–dusk.*

WHERE TO EAT AND STAY

$$$

FRENCH

✕ **Patit Creek Restaurant.** The chef turns out inspired beef, duck, and lamb dishes at this small café, which has been a favorite southeastern Washington eatery for more than 30 years. Portobello mushroom saltimbocca is a popular vegetarian option. Not only can the food be truly sublime, but the service is also excellent. The wine list is short, but has some rare Walla Walla Valley vintages. ⑤ *Average main: $30* ⊠ *725 E. Dayton Ave.* ☎ *509/382–2625* ⊙ *Closed Sun.–Tues. No lunch Sat.*

$$

AMERICAN

✕ **Weinhard Café.** The past seems to echo through this restaurant, which is across the street from the Weinhard Hotel in what was once a pharmacy. At breakfast/brunch, don't miss the signature French toast, made with orange cardamom challah bread. Try a panini sandwich for lunch; for dinner, the rib-eye steak with a Cabernet-infused butter and au gratin potatoes and local seasonal vegetable, or the ratatouille risotto with Walla Walla sweet onions are good bets. Raspberry-rhubarb pie and coconut-lemon pie are dessert favorites. The menu changes frequently to highlight seasonal specialties and local purveyors. ⑤ *Average main: $20* ⊠ *258 E. Main St.* ☎ *509/382–1681* ⊕ *www.weinhardcafe.com* ⊙ *Closed Mon., brunch only Sun.*

$

HOTEL

🏨 **Weinhard Hotel.** Echoes of the Old West ring through this hotel, built as a saloon and lodge in the late 1800s by the nephew of beer baron Henry Weinhard, and where rooms have modern amenities but period antiques. **Pros:** friendly, attentive service; rooms reflect the history of the era but have modern features. **Cons:** some street noise from rooms that face highway; no elevator. ⑤ *Rooms from: $125* ⊠ *235 E. Main St.* ☎ *509/382–4032* ⊕ *www.weinhard.com* ⇆ *15 rooms* ⦿| *Breakfast.*

PULLMAN

75 miles south of Spokane.

This funky, liberal town—home of Washington State University—is in the heart of the rather conservative Palouse agricultural district. The town's freewheeling style can perhaps be explained by the fact that most of the students come from elsewhere in Washington.

The Palouse River, the upper course of which flows though the town, is an exception among Washington rivers: because of the high erosion rate of the light Palouse loess soils it usually runs muddy, almost like a gruel during floods (most Washington rivers run clear, even after major storms). The 198-foot-high Palouse Falls farther downstream, near Washtucna, dramatically drop as a thin sheet of water into a steep box canyon.

GETTING HERE AND AROUND

Horizon Air flies into the local airport, where taxis and rental cars are available to get you to your destination. Most of the hotels have free airport shuttles, too. Pullman is reached via Highway 195, about 75 miles from Spokane.

Pullman-Moscow Regional Airport ⊠ *3200 Airport Complex N* ☎ *509/338–3223* ⊕ *www.flypuw.com.*

ESSENTIALS

Visitor Information Pullman Chamber of Commerce ⊠ *415 N. Grand Ave.* ☎ *509/334–3565, 800/365–6948* ⊕ *www.pullmanchamber.com.*

EXPLORING

Kamiak Butte County Park. The 3,640-foot-tall butte is part of a mountain chain that was here long before the lava flows of the Columbia Basin erupted millions of years ago. The park has great views of the Palouse hills and Idaho's snowcapped peaks to the east, as well as seven primitive campsites, a picnic area, and a 1-mile trail to the top of the butte. ⊠ *902 Kamiak Butte Park Rd., 12 miles north of Pullman, Palouse* ☎ *509/397–6238* ⊕ *www.whitmancounty.org* 🖾 *Free; campsite $15* ⊗ *Daily 7–dusk.*

Washington State University. Opened in 1892 as the state's agriculture school, Washington State University today sprawls almost all the way to the Idaho state line. To park on campus, pick up a parking pass in the Security Building on Wilson Road. ⊠ *1 S.E. Stadium Way* ☎ *509/335–3564* ⊕ *www.wsu.edu* 🖾 *Free* ⊗ *Daily.*

Ferdinand's. On weekdays between 9:30 and 4:30, you can pop into Ferdinand's, a soda fountain-cheese shop in the food-science building, to buy Aged Cougar Gold, a cheddar-type cheese in a can. ⊠ *2035 N.E. Ferdinand's La.* ☎ *509/335–2141* ⊕ *creamery.wsu.edu/* ⊗ *Closed weekends, holidays, school breaks.*

Museum of Art. The small Museum of Art has lectures, as well as exhibitions that might include turned-wood art, Native American art, or landscaping displays. ⊠ *WSU Fine Arts Center, Wilson Rd. and Stadium Way* ☎ *509/335–1910* ⊕ *museum.wsu.edu* 🖾 *Free* ⊗ *School year, Mon.–Wed., Fri., and Sat. 10–4, Thurs. 10–7; summer Tues.–Fri. 12–4.*

Charles R. Conner Museum of Zoology. This museum has the finest collection of stuffed birds and mammals and preserved invertebrates in the Pacific Northwest; more than 700 are on display. ⊠ *Abelson Hall, Library Rd. and College Ave.* ☎ *509/335–3515* ⊕ *sbs.wsu.edu/connermuseum* 🖾 *Free* ⊗ *Daily 8–5.*

18

WHERE TO EAT AND STAY

$ ✕ **Basilio's Italian Café.** In the heart of downtown, Basilio's serves up
ITALIAN   such classics as pasta, lasagna, and chicken parmigiana in addition
to an assortment of sandwiches and pizzas. Gaze at scenic downtown
from the sidewalk seating area. $ *Average main: $8* ⊠ *337 E. Main St.*
☎ *509/334–7663* ⊕ *www.basiliospullman.com.*

$ ✕ **Sella's Calzone and Pastas.** Made daily from scratch, the calzones are
PIZZA   always fresh at this cozy storefront. The most popular is the Coug (pep-
peroni, mushrooms, and black olives), followed by Gourmet (artichoke
hearts, sundried tomatoes, and pesto sauce). Pizzas, sandwiches, pastas, and salads are also served. A daily lunch special includes a small
calzone with salad or soup. $ *Average main: $10* ⊠ *1115 E. Main St.*
☎ *509/334–1895.*

$ 🏠 **Churchyard Inn.** Registered as a national and state historic site, this
B&B/INN   1905 Flemish-style inn, 15 miles southeast of Pullman in Uniontown,
was once a parish house for the adjacent church; some of the homey, traditionally furnished rooms have views of the countryside, and one suite
has its own kitchen. **Pros:** welcoming and helpful innkeeper; interesting
history; quiet and scenic. **Cons:** no a/c or TVs in most rooms. $ *Rooms
from: $95* ⊠ *206 St. Boniface St., Uniontown* ☎ *509/229–3200* ⊕ *www.
churchyardinn.com* ⤴ *5 rooms, 2 suites* ⦿| *Breakfast.*

SPOKANE

75 miles north of Pullman, 282 miles east of Seattle.

Washington's second-largest city, Spokane (spo-*can,* not spo-*cane*) takes
its name from the Spokan tribe of Salish Native Americans. It translates
as "Children of the Sun," a fitting name for this sunny city. It's also a
city of flowers and trees, public gardens, parks, and museums. Known
as the "Capital of the Inland Empire," Spokane is the cultural and
financial center of the Inland Northwest.

Spokane began as a Native American village at a roaring waterfall
where each autumn salmon ascended in great numbers. American settlers built a sawmill at the falls in 1873. Several railroads arrived after
1881, and Spokane soon became the transportation hub of eastern
Washington. In 1885 Spokane built the first hydroelectric plant west of
the Mississippi. Downtown boomed after the fire of 1889, as the city
grew rich from mining ventures in Washington, Idaho, and Montana,
and from shipping the wheat grown on the Palouse hills.

Until they were cleared away for the 1974 World's Fair, bridges and
railroad trestles hid Spokane's magnificent falls from view. Today they
form the heart of downtown's Riverfront Park, and the city rises from
the falls in a series of broad terraces to the valley's rim. Urban parks are
among Spokane's assets. The dry, hot summers here make it easy to plan
golf, fishing, and hiking excursions; long, snowy winters provide nearly
five months to enjoy skiing, snowboarding, and sledding.

Spokane

18

GETTING HERE AND AROUND

AIRPORT
TRANSFERS
Many hotels offer a free airport shuttle service. Spokane Transit runs between the airport and downtown, every half hour 6 am–6 pm (then hourly until 11 pm) weekdays, and hourly on weekends: 6 am–9 pm Saturday and 8–7 Sunday; the 20-minute bus ride costs $1.50. Wheatland Express has shuttle service between the Spokane Airport and Pullman and Moscow, Idaho. Reservations are recommended; the cost is $38 one way. City Cab serves the Spokane area. Metered fares run about $2.50 a mile. A taxi ride from the Spokane airport to downtown costs about $20.

Contacts City Cab ☎ *509/455–3333* ⊕ *www.spokanecitycab.com.* **Spokane Transit Authority** ☎ *509/328–7433* ⊕ *www.spokanetransit.com.* **Wheatland Express** ☎ *509/334–2200, 800/334–2207* ⊕ *www.wheatlandexpress.com.*

BUS TRAVEL
Spokane has an extensive local bus system. The fare is $1.50; exact change or a token is required. Pick up schedules, maps, and tokens at the bus depot or the Plaza, the major downtown transfer point.

Contacts The Plaza ✉ *Bus Shop at the Plaza, 701 W. Riverside Ave.* ☎ *509/456–7277* ⊕ *www.spokanetransit.com.*

CAR TRAVEL
Spokane can be reached by Interstate 90 from the east or west. U.S. 395 runs north from Spokane to Colville and the Canadian border.

Downtown Spokane is laid out along a true grid: streets run north–south, avenues east–west; many are one way. Spokane's heaviest traffic is on Interstate 90 between Spokane and Spokane Valley on weekday evenings. Metered parking is available on city streets; there are also several downtown lots.

TRAIN TRAVEL Amtrak's Empire Builder runs daily between Spokane and Seattle and between Spokane and Portland, stopping at points in between (including Ephrata and Pasco). Reservations are recommended. Round-trip fares vary depending on season; $110 is an average fare between Seattle and Spokane.

ESSENTIALS

Visitor Information Spokane Area Visitors Information ✉ *801 W. Riverside, Ste. 301* ☎ *509/624–1341, 888/776–5263* ⊕ *www.visitspokane.com.*

EXPLORING

TOP ATTRACTIONS

Cathedral of St. John the Evangelist. This architectural masterpiece, considered one of America's most important and beautiful Gothic cathedrals, was constructed in the 1920s with sandstone from Tacoma and Boise and limestone from Indiana. The cathedral's renowned 49-bell carillon has attracted international guest musicians. ✉ *127 E. 12th Ave.* ☎ *509/838–4277* ⊕ *www.stjohns-cathedral.org* 🎟 *Free* ☉ *Weekdays 9–4; guided tours Wed., Fri., and Sat. 11–2.*

FAMILY **Manito Park and Gardens.** A pleasant place to stroll in summer, this
Fodor's Choice 90-acre park has a formal Renaissance-style garden, conservatory, Japa-
★ nese garden, duck pond, and rose and perennial gardens. A café is open daily in summer and Friday–Sunday in the off-season. Snowy winters find its hills full of sledders and its frozen pond packed with skaters. ✉ *1702 S. Grand Blvd.* ☎ *509/625–6200* ⊕ *spokaneparks.org* 🎟 *Free* ☉ *Summer, daily 4 am–11 pm, winter, daily 5 am–10 pm; Japanese garden Apr.–Oct., daily 8 am to ½ hr before dusk.*

FAMILY **Mobius Kids Children's Museum.** Spokane's museum for children is in the lower level of River Park Square and has six interactive galleries for hands-on learning. Exhibits include a miniature city with safety education features, an art studio, a science exhibit called Geotopica, a forest-themed play area for infants and toddlers, and a stage with theater equipment and costumes. A partner facility, Mobius Science Center, is across the street. ✉ *808 W. Main Ave.* ☎ *509/321–7121* ⊕ *www.mobiusspokane.org* 🎟 *$7; $15 combined same-day admission with Mobius Science Center* ☉ *Tues.–Sat. 10–5, Sun. 11–5.*

FAMILY **Mobius Science Center.** Across the street from Mobius Kids Children's Museum, the 26,000-square-foot center has 65 interactive science and technology exhibits and also presents special events, camps, and educational programs. ✉ *811 W. Main Ave.* ☎ *509/321–7133* ⊕ *www.mobiusspokane.org* 🎟 *$10; $15 combined same-day admission with Mobius Kids Children's Museum* ☉ *Tues.–Sat. 10–6; Sun. 11–5.*

FAMILY **Northwest Museum of Arts and Culture.** Affectionately referred to as the MAC, the museum is in an impressive six-level glass-and-wood

A GOOD TOUR

Begin your tour of Spokane west of downtown at the **Finch Arbore-tum** on Woodland Boulevard off Sunset Boulevard. From the arbore-tum, head east on Sunset Boule-vard, left on Chestnut Street, and left on First Avenue to get to the **Northwest Museum of Arts and Culture.** Riverside Avenue, a block north of First Avenue, leads east to **Riverfront Park.** From here you can see Spokane Falls. If you have kids in tow, make a stop before or after the park at **Mobius Kids,** the children's museum in River Park Square shopping center. Across the street, check out the new **Mobius Science Center.** About a mile south of downtown off Grand Boule-vard is the **Cathedral of St. John the Evangelist,** and the pleasant **Manito Park and Gardens** are about six blocks south of here.

If you have time to venture out of the city, head north on Division Street, which becomes U.S. 2

(Newport Highway) to **Cat Tales Zoological Park,** about 13 miles from downtown. From here a 2-mile drive east will take you to **Townshend Cellar,** where you can sample Columbia Valley and huckle-berry wines (open Friday–Sunday, noon–6). Drive through the country-side another 10 miles south to reach **Arbor Crest Wine Cellars** and its pleasant views of the Spokane River. From here, head north to Interstate 90 for the 6-mile drive back to downtown.

TIMING

You could easily drive the in-city route in an hour. Plan to spend a half day at Riverfront Park and two hours at the Northwest Museum of Arts and Culture, with at least a half hour to an hour for stops at the other sights. For the destinations outside the city, figure on driving about 1½ hours round-trip from downtown and making half-hour stops at each site.

structure. It has an audiovisual display and artifacts that trace Spo-kane's history as well as a fine Native American collection that includes baskets and beadwork of the Plateau nation. Wander the adjacent Vic-torian, the Campbell House, to admire the interior or view mining-era exhibits; guided tours are offered four times a day (register in advance when you arrive at the museum). ✉ 2316 W. 1st Ave. ☎ 509/456–3931 ⊕ www.northwestmuseum.org ≦ $10 ⊗ Wed.–Sun. 10–5 (until 8 pm on 1st Fri. of month).

FAMILY

Fodor's Choice

★

Riverfront Park. The 100-acre park is what remains of Spokane's Expo '74. Sprawling across several islands in the Spokane River, near the falls, the park was developed from old railroad yards, where the stone clock tower of the former Great Northern Railroad Station, built in 1902, stands in sharp architectural contrast to the Expo '74 building. One of the modernist buildings houses an IMAX theater, and the opera house occupies the former Washington State pavilion. The outdoor Ice Palace is open mid-October through March. A children's train chugs around the park in summer, and a 1909 carousel, hand-carved by master builder Charles I.D. Looff, is a local landmark. Another icon here is the giant red slide shaped like a Radio Flyer wagon. Other attractions include a sky ride over Spokane falls, mini-golf, and amusement rides. ✉ 507

Riverfront Park

N. Howard St. ☎ 509/625–6600 ⊕ www.spokaneriverfrontpark.com
⌨ Park free, fees for some attractions ⊗ Park, daily 4 am–midnight;
attraction hrs vary.

WORTH NOTING

Arbor Crest Wine Cellars. On the grounds of the eclectic, 1924 mansion
of Royal Riblet, the inventor of a square-wheel tractor and the poles
that hold up ski lifts, you can sample Arbor Crest wines, enjoy the
striking view of the Spokane River below, or meander through the
impeccably kept grounds (the house isn't open to tours). Enjoy Sunday
evening concerts (5:30 pm–sunset) from mid-May through September.
Local musicians perform Thursday evenings in summer, too. ⊠ 4705 N.
Fruithill Rd. ☎ 509/927–9463 ⊕ www.arborcrest.com ⊗ Daily noon–5;
extended hrs in summer.

FAMILY **Cat Tales Zoological Park.** Among the large cats living at this zoo are
lions, tigers, ligers (a combination of lion and tiger), leopards, pumas,
and lynxes. Guided tours give background information on the animals.
There's also a petting zoo. ⊠ 17020 N. Newport Hwy., 12 miles north
of I–90, Mead ☎ 509/238–4126 ⊕ www.cattales.org ⌨ $10 ⊗ May–
Sept., Tues.–Sun. 10–6; Oct.–Apr., Tues.–Sun. 10–4.

Finch Arboretum. This mile-long green patch along Garden Springs Creek
has an extensive botanical garden with more than 2,000 labeled trees,
shrubs, and flowers. Follow the walking tour on well-manicured paths
along the creek, or follow your whim—depending on the season—
through flowering rhododendrons, hibiscus, magnolias, dogwoods,
hydrangeas, and more. ⊠ 3404 W. Woodland Blvd. ☎ 509/624–4832
⊕ spokaneparks.org ⌨ Free ⊗ Daily dawn–dusk.

Townshend Cellar. A drive to the Green Bluff countryside leads wine lovers to this small winery and its tasting room. It's won awards for its Cabernet Sauvignon, and also produces Merlot, Chardonnay, Syrah, and several blends, offering more than 20 wines. Berries from nearby Idaho are used in huckleberry Port and sparkling wine. ⊠ *8022 E. Greenbluff Rd., 13 miles northeast of Spokane, Colbert* ☎ *509/238–1400* ⊕ *www.townshendcellar.com* ⊘ *Fri.–Sun. noon–6.*

EN ROUTE

Eastern Washington University. The tree-shaded Cheney campus has six original buildings that are on the National Register of Historic Places, but most of the 300-acre campus consists of post–World War II concrete-and-glass structures. ⊠ *526 5th St., about 20 miles west of Spokane, Cheney* ☎ *509/359–6200* ⊕ *www.ewu.edu.*

Gallery of Art. Changing exhibits of works by local and nationally known artists are on show here throughout the school year, and year-end exhibitions showcase student works. ⊠ *140 Art Bldg., Cheney* ☎ *509/359–2494* ⊕ *www.ewu.edu/cale/programs/art/gallery.xml* ⊠ *Free* ⊘ *Weekdays, 9–5.*

WHERE TO EAT

$$$
SEAFOOD
✕ **Clinkerdagger.** In a former flour mill with great views of the Spokane River, Clink's has been a Spokane institution since 1974. The seafood, steaks, and prime rib are excellent; the Maytag blue cheese salad and beer-battered fish and chips are both popular at lunch. Some favorite dessert choices include a bananas Foster sundae, seasonal fruit crisp, and key lime pie. Prices can tend to make this more of a special-occasion destination, though savings can be had during happy hour, which runs daily from 3 to 6 and also 9 to close on Friday and Saturday. ⑤ *Average main: $28* ⊠ *621 W. Mallon Ave.* ☎ *509/328–5965* ⊕ *www. clinkerdagger.com* ⊘ *No lunch Sun.*

$
AMERICAN
✕ **Elk Public House.** This casual eatery in the relaxed Browne's Addition neighborhood, west of downtown, serves pub food such as grilled lamb sandwiches, burgers, soft tacos, salads, and a spicy gumbo, together with a good selection of microbrews, most from the Northwest. A copper bar stands along one wall, backed by a mirror, giving the interior a saloon-like appearance. Grab an outdoor table in summer if you can. ⑤ *Average main: $10* ⊠ *1931 W. Pacific Ave.* ☎ *509/363–1973* ⊕ *www. wedonthaveone.com.*

$
DINER
FAMILY
Fodor's Choice
★
✕ **Frank's Diner.** Right off the Maple Street Bridge, this is the state's oldest railroad-car restaurant. Built as an observation car in 1906, it has original light fixtures, stained-glass windows, and mahogany details. Breakfast is the specialty here, and portions are large; for dinner there's such comfort food as turkey with mashed potatoes, meat loaf, and chicken-fried steak. Everything is made from scratch. The North Spokane branch (⊠ *10929 N. Newport Highway* ☎ *509/465–2464*) is housed in a luxury Pullman car built in 1913. ⑤ *Average main: $10* ⊠ *1516 W. 2nd Ave.* ☎ *509/747–8798* ⊕ *www.franksdiners.com.*

$$$
ECLECTIC
✕ **Latah Bistro.** Tucked into a strip mall in south Spokane near Qualchan Golf Course, Dave and Heather DuPree's neighborhood restaurant serves a diverse menu that changes frequently and may include

18

pasta or fresh seafood. Try the glazed pork tenderloin with Yukon potato purée or shrimp fettuccine with English peas, grape tomatoes, and squash. Pizzas, including one topped with housemade fennel sausage, are baked in a wood-burning oven. Save room for dessert and try the pumpkin-bread pudding or the "bucket of love" (gluten-free flourless mini-chocolate cakes dusted with spices). Sunday brunch features varied choices, from English toffee pecan waffles to egg-topped pizza. ⑤ *Average main: $25* ✉ *4241 S. Cheney–Spokane Rd.* ☎ *509/838–8338* ⊕ *www.latahbistro.com.*

$$$
ECLECTIC
Fodor's Choice
★

✕ **Luna.** You'll find inventive approaches to classics here, many items are gluten-free, and fresh ingredients are grown in the restaurant's garden. Weekend brunch has such treats as Italian cassoulet with poached eggs, bacon and mushroom crepes, and brioche French toast with macerated fruits. The luscious desserts are worth a visit on their own—especially the six-layer coconut cake (featured in *Bon Appetit* magazine) and shortbread-topped fruit crisp baked in the wood-fired oven. Luna is especially known for its extensive wine list, with more than 900 vintages, and has a wine bar as well. The rose terrace and courtyard are open in summer. ⑤ *Average main: $25* ✉ *5620 S. Perry St.* ☎ *509/448–2383* ⊕ *www.lunaspokane.com.*

$$$
SEAFOOD

✕ **Milford's Fish House.** This brick and terra-cotta tile structure was built in 1925, and the terrazzo floor and tin ceiling are relics of that era. The interior's exposed brick walls and wood details, lit by candles, create a romantic environment in which to enjoy the wide array of seafood dishes and steaks. Everything is fresh here, and it is hard to predict what the menu will include, but you might find such offerings as tuna, cod, salmon, snapper, mahimahi, clams, and prawns. Panfried oysters are a house specialty. ⑤ *Average main: $27* ✉ *719 N. Monroe St.* ☎ *509/326–7251* ⊕ *www.milfordsfishhouse.com* ☉ *Closed Mon. No lunch.*

$$$
ECLECTIC

✕ **Mizuna Restaurant.** Fresh flowers and redbrick walls lend color and charm to this downtown eatery. Grilled Idaho rainbow trout is served with shiitake mushroom risotto and grilled baby bok choy; New York strip steak comes with gorgonzola-thyme latkes and basil green beans. Local produce is the inspiration for such scrumptious vegetarian fare as white cheddar–and-apple salad and red bell peppers stuffed with quinoa. Vegan and gluten-free options are extensive. Mizuna's cheese plate gets rave reviews and goes well with the Northwest wines highlighted in the wine bar. Dessert specialties include vegan carrot cake and flourless chocolate cake. The patio is open for outdoor dining May through September. ⑤ *Average main: $26* ✉ *214 N. Howard St.* ☎ *509/747–2004* ⊕ *www.mizuna.com* ☉ *No lunch Sun.*

$
AMERICAN

✕ **Post Street Ale House.** Adjacent to Hotel Lusso, this casual eatery offers standard pub fare like fish-and-chips, burgers, and sausage dogs, and several kinds of pasta and salads, too. Two kinds of ribs are on the menu—braised short ribs and baby back ribs. The "After 10" menu (available from 10 pm until closing) includes fried pickles, wings, sandwiches, burgers, and desserts for the "late night munchies." More than 25 beers are on tap. ⑤ *Average main: $12* ✉ *1 N. Post St.* ☎ *509/789–6900* ⊕ *www.davenporthotelcollection.com/our-hotels/hotel-lusso/dining/.*

$$ ✕**Rock City Grill.** This upbeat place, which is close to Riverfront Park,
ITALIAN has excellent pastas and gourmet wood-fired pizzas, including their
FAMILY most popular, the Thai, with marinated chicken and prawns. Other
specialties include Greek chicken and Jack Daniels whiskey steak. The
extensive gluten-free menu features pizza and pasta. Expect some kid-
ding around from the outgoing staff, who will make sure your soft
drinks and lemonades never go empty. Save room for such desserts as
tiramisu and the Italian favorite, spumoni ice cream. If you love Thai
peanut sauce, take some home; it's available by the bottle. There are
late-night pizza specials after 9, and on Sunday there's an all-day happy
hour in the bar. $ *Average main: $19* ✉ *808 W. Main St.* ☎ *509/455–
4400* ⊕ *www.rockcitygrill.com.*

$$$ ✕**Sante Restaurant and Charcuterie.** Spectacular French cuisine that isn't
FRENCH too rich and saucy is the focus here. The charcuterie board brings to
mind an outdoor picnic, with cheese, jam, mustard, and a baguette;
paté made of duck and chicken is also accompanied by a baguette. For
a heartier meal, try the apple-braised pork with kale, grass-fed beef, or
tofu herb risotto with root vegetables. There is even a kids' menu with
such delights as croque monsieur and green eggs and ham. If there's
a wait to be seated, consider browsing in Auntie's Bookstore right
next door. $ *Average main: $26* ✉ *404 W. Main St.* ☎ *509/315–4613*
⊕ *www.santespokane.com* ◷ *No dinner Sun.–Tues.*

$ ✕**Steelhead Bar & Grill.** This casual pub-style eatery, housed in one of
AMERICAN Spokane's many older brick buildings, has an urban contemporary
FAMILY vibe, with lots of burnished-metal artwork by local artists. About a
dozen beers are on tap, but there's also a decent kids' menu with the
usual favorites. Sandwiches and burgers make this a handy place for
lunch; kebabs, steak, and halibut-and-chips are heartier fare at dinner. Reservations are not accepted on Friday and Saturday nights.
$ *Average main: $17* ✉ *218 N. Howard St.* ☎ *509/747–1303* ⊕ *www.
steelheadbarandgrille.com.*

$ ✕**The Wandering Table.** Chef Adam Hegsted will create your meal based
MODERN on what is in season, and is likely to include some of the unique house
AMERICAN standards, such as deviled eggs with maple-bacon filling, baby kale
salad with edible dirt, and bacon-wrapped bacon sliders. These and
other small plates make this a popular spot for both a light lunch and
tapas-style dinner; there are also a few full-plate options like Idaho
fried trout with jasmine rice, wood-roasted chicken, and green pepper,
steak, and potatoes. Save room for the unique desserts, including goat
cheesecake and olive oil–dark chocolate gelato. $ *Average main: $16*
✉ *1242 W. Summit Pkwy.* ☎ *509/443–4410* ⊕ *www.thewanderingtable.
com* ◷ *No lunch Sun. and Mon.*

WHERE TO STAY

$$ ▥**The Davenport Hotel & Tower.** Two buildings on opposite sides of the
HOTEL street—one historic, the other a 21-floor modern tower—make up
FAMILY Washington State's fourth-largest hotel and one of its best, with ele-
Fodor'sChoice gant accommodations and a plethora of amenities. **Pros:** main hotel's
★ historical restoration is a marvel to see; abundant resort-like ameni-
ties; experienced service. **Cons:** no coffeemakers or minibars in rooms;

18

no bathtubs in Tower rooms. ⑤ *Rooms from: $175* ✉ *10 S. Post St.* ☎ *509/455–8888, 800/899–1482* ⊕ *www.davenporthotel.com* ⊅ *563 rooms, 48 suites* ⦿| *No meals.*

$ ⊡ **Hotel Lusso.** European furnishings and many modern amenities,
HOTEL including flat-screen TVs, provide an intimate and elegant getaway, enhanced by the Italian marble floor, archways, and fountains of the lobby. **Pros:** small and intimate; access to pool. **Cons:** no coffeemakers or minibars; some rooms face an alley and other buildings. ⑤ *Rooms from: $139* ✉ *808 W. Sprague Ave.* ☎ *509/747–9750, 800/899–1482* ⊕ *www.hotellusso.com* ⊅ *36 rooms, 12 suites* ⦿| *No meals.*

$ ⊡ **Marianna Stolz House.** Across from Gonzaga University on a tree-
B&B/INN lined street, this American Foursquare home built in 1908 is listed on Spokane's historical register and is decorated with leaded-glass china cabinets, Renaissance Revival armchairs, and original dark-fir wood-work. **Pros:** convenient location; friendly innkeeper. **Cons:** shared bath-room for some rooms. ⑤ *Rooms from: $115* ✉ *427 E. Indiana Ave.* ☎ *509/483–4316, 800/978–6587* ⊕ *www.mariannastoltzhouse.com* ⊅ *4 rooms, 2 with bath* ⦿| *Breakfast.*

$$ ⊡ **Red Lion Hotel at the Park.** These conventional yet comfortable busi-
HOTEL ness-hotel style rooms are adjacent to Riverfront Park and just a two-
FAMILY block walk from the downtown shopping district. **Pros:** pool area is popular with families; location is great; good service. **Cons:** very large hotel so gets crowded; rooms that face atrium-style lobby are noisy (those in two newer wings are quieter). ⑤ *Rooms from: $152* ✉ *303 W. North River Dr.* ☎ *509/326–8000, 800/733–5466* ⊕ *www.redlion. com* ⊅ *400 rooms, 25 suites* ⦿| *No meals.*

$ ⊡ **Stratford Suites.** Ten minutes from downtown, these spacious apart-
HOTEL ment-style suites have full kitchens, one or two bedrooms, and mod-ern style and many amenities, including computers, printers, and fax machines in some. **Pros:** friendly staff; free fresh-baked cookies in the evening; pet-friendly. **Cons:** no pool; no restaurant on-site; front desk isn't staffed 24 hours. ⑤ *Rooms from: $129* ✉ *11808 W. Center La., 9 miles west of Spokane, Airway Heights* ☎ *509/321–1600, 888/705–8877* ⊕ *www.stratfordsuites.com* ⊅ *60 suites* ⦿| *No meals.*

NIGHTLIFE AND PERFORMING ARTS

NIGHTLIFE

Gibliano Brothers. Every Thursday through Saturday pianists duke it out on the ivories, playing both popular and offbeat tunes—and, of course, they take requests. Trivia Night is held every Tuesday and there's kara-oke on Wednesday nights. ✉ *718 W. Riverside Ave.* ☎ *509/315–8765* ⊕ *giblianobrothers.com.*

Underground 15. In this steampunk/industrial-themed bar something happens every night—open mike on Monday, karaoke on Tuesday and Wednesday, and live music of all genres on weekends. The bar has a few video and pinball games, and self-play trivia on one of the TVs. There's a limited food menu of flatbreads and bar snacks. ✉ *15. S. Howard St.* ☎ *509/868–0358.*

PERFORMING ARTS

Interplayers Theatre. This professional theater company presents eight main stage productions from September through May; they also offer occasional concerts and participate in downtown Spokane's "First Friday" monthly events. ✉ *174 S. Howard St.* ☎ *509/455–7529* ⊕ *www. interplayerstheatre.org.*

The Knitting Factory Concert House. National acts, ranging from Matisyahu to Twenty One Pilots, are hosted in this 1,500-seat venue. ✉ *919 W. Sprague Ave.* ☎ *509/244–3279* ⊕ *sp.knittingfactory.com.*

Spokane Civic Theatre. The long-running community theater presents musicals and dramas on two stages from September through June. ✉ *1020 N. Howard St.* ☎ *509/325–2507* ⊕ *www.spokanecivictheatre. com.*

Spokane Symphony. Classical and pops concerts are presented from September through May in the newly restored historic Martin Woldson Theater at The Fox, plus special events such as the *Nutcracker* at the INB Performing Arts Center, free outdoor concerts at city parks in summer, and chamber music in the Davenport Hotel. ✉ *Fox Theater, 1001 W. Sprague* ☎ *509/624–1200* ⊕ *www.spokanesymphony.org.*

SHOPPING

Flour Mill. When it was built in 1895, the mill was a huge technical innovation. Today it's home to shops, restaurants, and an event center. The mill sits virtually atop the falls, north of the river. ✉ *621 W. Mallon Ave.*

River Park Square. Upscale shopping here includes Nordstrom, Apple, Williams-Sonoma, Pottery Barn, The North Face, and other national retailers—more than 30 stores in all. Several restaurants are here or nearby, and there's a 20-screen movie theater. ✉ *808 W. Main St.* ⊕ *www.riverparksquare.com.*

18

SPORTS AND THE OUTDOORS

GOLF

Hangman Valley. This 18-hole, par-72 course, has greens fees of $29 weekdays, $31 weekends. ✉ *2210 E. Hangman Valley Rd.* ☎ *509/448–1212* ⊕ *www.spokanecounty.org/parks.*

Indian Canyon. On the slope of a basalt canyon, this 18-hole course has great views of North Spokane and Mt. Spokane. The greens fees are $29 weekdays, $32 weekends. ✉ *4304 W. West Dr.* ☎ *509/747–5353* ⊕ *www.spokanegolf.org.*

Liberty Lake. This course is near MeadowWood, so avid golfers can visit both and play 36 holes. The greens fees are $29 weekdays, $31 weekends. ✉ *24403 E. Sprague Ave., Liberty Lake* ☎ *509/255–6233* ⊕ *www. spokanecounty.org/parks.*

MeadowWood. This is a Scottish-style course that has been ranked in Washington's top 10 municipal courses. Greens fees are $29 weekdays, $31 weekends. ✉ *24501 E. Valleyway Ave., Liberty Lake* ☎ *509/255–9539* ⊕ *www.spokanecounty.org/parks.*

HIKING

The hills around Spokane are laced with trails, almost all of which connect with 37-mile-long **Centennial Trail,** which winds along the Spokane River. Beginning in Nine Mile Falls, northwest of Spokane, the well-marked trail ends in Idaho. Maps are available at the visitor center at 201 West Main Street. Northwest of downtown at **Riverside State Park,** a paved trail leads through a 17-million-year-old fossil forest in Deep Creek Canyon. From there it's easy to get to the western end of the Centennial Trail by crossing the suspension bridge at the day-use parking lot; trails heading both left and right will lead to the Centennial.

SKIING

49° North. An hour north of Spokane in the Colville National Forest, this is a 2,325-acre family-oriented resort. Lift tickets cost $52 to $57; snowboards and ski package rentals are about $35. ⊠ *U.S. 395, 3311 Flowery Trail Rd., Chewelah* ☎ *509/935–6649, 866/376–4949* ⊕ *www. ski49n.com.*

Mt. Spokane. This modest downhill resort, 28 miles northeast of downtown Spokane, has a 2,000-foot drop and 10 miles of groomed cross-country ski trails. Snowshoeing and tubing are also options. There's night skiing Wednesday–Saturday. Lift tickets cost $39 to $52. A Discover Pass is required on all vehicles ($10 for one day or $30 annually) and is valid at all Washington State Parks. A Sno-Park permit is also required for parking at nordic skiing trailheads. ⊠ *29500 N. Mt. Spokane Park Dr., Mead* ☎ *509/238–2220* ⊕ *www.mtspokane.com.*

GRANT COUNTY

If you travel along the Interstate at 70-plus mph, it might seem that this area is mainly a lot of crop fields and a single town with a big lake. But slow the pace a bit and get off the beaten path to discover family-friendly activities in Moses Lake, including a lively water park and lakefront park for swimming on hot summer days. North in the town of Ephrata, local history is depicted in a pioneer village. Soap Lake is a body of water like no other, with bubbly, mineral-rich water that has been purported to have healing effects for more than a century. Closer to the Columbia River just west of Quincy, the award-winning Gorge Amphitheatre hosts concerts through the summer. Adjacent to the Gorge is the not-to-be-missed Cave B Resort, which has luxurious accommodations, fabulous river and canyon views, an estate winery, pool, spa, fine dining, and upscale yurts.

MOSES LAKE

105 miles west of Spokane.

The natural lake from which this sprawling town takes its name seems to be an anomaly in the dry landscape of east-central Washington. But ever since the Columbia Basin Project took shape, there's been water everywhere. Approaching Moses Lake from the west on Interstate 90, you'll pass lushly green irrigated fields; to the east lie vast stretches of wheat. The lakes of this region have more shorebirds than Washington's ocean beaches. Potholes Reservoir is an artificial lake that supports as much wildlife as does the Columbia Wildlife Refuge. The Winchester Wasteway, west of Moses Lake, is a great place to paddle a kayak or canoe and watch birds as you glide along the reedy banks. The airfield north of town was once a major Air Force base, and now serves as a training facility for airline pilots.

GETTING HERE AND AROUND

Moses Lake straddles Interstate 90; it's about 100 miles from Spokane and 175 miles from Seattle. To the north, Highway 17 connects Moses Lake to Ephrata and points north, including Soap Lake and Coulee City.

ESSENTIALS

Visitor Information Moses Lake Area Chamber of Commerce ⊠ *324 S. Pioneer Way* ☎ *509/765–7888, 800/992–6234* ⊕ *www.moseslake.com.*

EXPLORING

Columbia National Wildlife Refuge. A great number of birds are attracted to this reserve: hawks, falcons, golden eagles, ducks, sandhill cranes, herons, American avocets, black-necked stilts, and yellow-headed and red-winged blackbirds. The refuge is also home to beavers, muskrats, badgers, and coyotes. ⊠ *7 miles northwest of Othello via McMahon Rd. to Morgan Lake Rd.; about 20 miles southeast of Moses Lake, Othello* ☎ *509/546–8300* ⊕ *www.fws.gov/columbia* ⊠ *Free* ☉ *Daily 5–dusk.*

Moses Lake. Claw-shaped, 38-foot-deep, 18-mile-long Moses Lake is filled by Crab Creek—which originates in the hills west of Spokane—with three side branches known as Parker Horn, Lewis Horn, and Pelican Horn. The city of Moses Lake sprawls over the peninsulas formed by these "horns," and can therefore be a bit difficult to get around. This is the state's second-largest lake. ⊠ *Hwy. 17, off I–90.*

Moses Lake Museum and Art Center. Fossils collected all over North America, including prehistoric land and marine animals, are exhibited here. Regional artists are also featured. ⊠ *Moses Lake Civic Center, 401 S. Balsam St.* ☎ *509/764–3830* ⊕ *www.cityofml.com* ⊠ *Free* ☉ *Mon.–Sat. 11–5.*

Potholes State Park. This park is 25 miles southwest of Moses Lake on the west side of O'Sullivan Dam. Camping and boating, as well as fishing for trout, perch, and walleye, are popular diversions. ⊠ *6762 Hwy. 262 E, Othello* ☎ *360/902–8844, 888/226–7688* ⊕ *www.parks. wa.gov/568/Potholes* ⊠ *Day pass $10 per vehicle; annual Discovery Pass $30 (valid at all state parks); campsite $20–$42, cabins $59–$79* ☉ *Daily: summer, 6:30–dusk; winter, 8–dusk.*

FAMILY **Surf 'n Slide Water Park.** This is a great place to cool off from the hot central Washington sunshine, with an Olympic-sized pool, two 200-foot waterslides, a tube slide, a "baby octopus" slide, and diving boards. ⊠ *McCosh Park, 401 W. 4th Ave.* ☎ *509/764–3805* ⊕ *www.cityofml. com* ⊠ *$10* ☉ *Early-June–Aug., Mon.–Thurs. 11–6:30, Fri.–Sun. 11–7; Memorial Day and Labor Day, weekends, 11–7.*

18

WHERE TO EAT AND STAY

$$ ✕ **Michael's on the Lake.** In the late afternoon golden rays of sunset wash
AMERICAN over the dining room and deck at this lakeside restaurant. Indulge in prime rib or Parmesan-crusted halibut over linguine, or go for the lighter soups and sandwiches. Small plates include blacked tuna tacos and kale maple bacon salad. Chocolate lovers will appreciate the dessert menu with choices like mile-high mud pie, half-baked chocolate chip cookies, and chocolate banana bread pudding. Unique appetizers, including ginger chicken lettuce wraps and fried polenta, are half price during happy hour, daily 4 to 6 and 9 to close. ⑤ *Average main: $22 ⊠ 910 W. Broadway Ave.* ☎ *509/765–1611* ⊕ *www.michaelsonthelake.com.*

$$ ✕ **Porter House Steakhouse.** The current owners of one of Moses Lake's
STEAKHOUSE oldest restaurants set out with the goal, ably achieved, of making it a
FAMILY favorite family and group gathering place. As the name implies, steaks are the main event here, ranging from an 8-oz. sirloin to 24-oz. porterhouse. There's even a 4-oz. steak on the kids' menu. Complementing the beef entrées are a variety of chicken, seafood, and pasta dishes. Check out the house-made desserts, including Texas sheet cake and bread pudding with vanilla ice cream. ⑤ *Average main: $22 ⊠ 217 N. Elder St.* ☎ *509/766–0308* ⊕ *www.porterhousesteakhouse.net* ⊙ *No lunch on Sun.*

$$ ⯑ **Comfort Suites.** Spacious and comfortable rooms, considered suites
HOTEL because there's a sitting area separate from the beds, shine with modern style and conveniences. **Pros:** clean and modern; nice pool; friendly service. **Cons:** no restaurant; prices steep during some events. ⑤ *Rooms from: $169 ⊠ 1700 E. Kittleson Rd.* ☎ *509/765–3731, 877/424–6423* ⊕ *www.comfortsuites.com* ⯇ *60 suites* ⦿*Breakfast.*

SHOPPING

Moses Lake Farmers Market. Vendors come here each Saturday from May–October to sell fresh produce and handmade arts and crafts. ⊠ *McCosh Park (next to aquatic center), Dogwood St.* ☎ *509/750–7831* ⊕ *www. moseslakefarmersmarket.com* ⊙ *May–Oct., Sat. 8–1.*

QUINCY

34 miles northwest of Moses Lake.

On the fences along Interstate 90 to Gorge and north on Highway 281 to Quincy, crop-identification signs highlight what the Quincy Valley is known for: agriculture. From Thanksgiving to New Year's Eve, these same fields are filled with Christmas motion-light displays, powered by electricity from farmers' irrigation lines—a delightful sight for highway travelers in the dark winter nights. Agriculture hasn't always been king in this area. Though the rich soils attracted many settlers after the railroad made the region accessible in the early 1900s, several serious droughts proved that Mother Nature could not be relied on to water the crops consistently. In the mid-1930s the federal government began to assist with irrigation plans, and by the early 1950s the first systems were in place.

Today the area has 200,000 irrigable acres growing corn, alfalfa, wheat, potatoes, seed, apples, and more. An annual Farmer Consumer

Awareness Day is held the second Saturday of September, with farm tours, entertainment, food, arts and crafts, and plenty of fresh produce. Tourism is also growing here, with visitors from across the state and beyond coming to summer concerts at the Gorge Amphitheatre, touring wineries between Quincy and Wenatchee, and hiking and climbing near the Columbia River.

GETTING HERE AND AROUND

Quincy is 11 miles north of Interstate 90's Exit 149, via Highway 281. It's about two hours, 45 minutes from Seattle and two hours, 30 minutes from Spokane.

EXPLORING

Gorge Amphitheatre. This 27,500-seat amphitheater has won accolades as best outdoor concert venue due to its fine acoustics and stunning vistas of the Columbia River—a setting compared to the Grand Canyon's. Set in one of the sunniest parts of the state, the concert season runs from May to September. Concertgoers often overnight at the adjacent campground or at motels and hotels in Quincy, Moses Lake, and Ellensburg. ⊠ *754 Silica Rd. NW, Gorge* ☎ *509/785–6262.*

WHERE TO EAT AND STAY

$ ✕ **The Grainery.** Quincy farmers David and Harriet Weber opened their café to feature their own farm products, including the grains used for breads and the scrumptious pastries baked in-house. Locals stop in for espresso and giant cinnamon rolls to start their day. Menu items change to reflect what's in season, such as the strawberry summer salad and hearty vegetable soups. A wide selection of paninis and deli sandwiches are served with salad or chips and a mini-cookie. Some Friday nights live music plays in the spacious, brightly decorated, country-cozy setting. $ *Average main: $9* ⊠ *101 E St. SE* ☎ *509/797–7240* ⊕ *www.grainerycafe.biz* ⊘ *Closed Sun. No dinner.*

CAFÉ
FAMILY

$$$$ ⊞ **Cave B Estate Winery and Resort.** Washington's first destination winery resort is built on (and into) ancient basalt cliffs 900 feet above the Columbia River; its 15 cliffhouses, cavern (with 12 rooms), and inn all designed to blend into the natural environment and offer casually elegant, comfortable accommodations with fireplaces, soaking tubs, and other luxuries. **Pros:** fantastic place to stargaze; secluded; gorgeous accommodations. **Cons:** expensive during Gorge Amphitheatre events; no local meal options besides on-site restaurant. $ *Rooms from: $259* ⊠ *344 Silica Rd. NW* ☎ *509/787–8000, 888/785–2283* ⊕ *www.cavebresort.com* ⟿ *12 rooms, 18 suites, 25 yurts* ⊘ *Closed mid-Dec.–mid-Feb.; yurts closed Nov.–Mar.* ❏ *Breakfast.*

RESORT
Fodor'sChoice
★

EPHRATA

18 miles northeast of Quincy.

Ephrata (e-*fray*-tuh), a pleasant, small farm town and the Grant County seat, is in the exact center of Washington. It was settled quite early because its abundant natural springs made it an oasis in the dry steppe country of the Columbia Basin. Native Americans visited the springs, as did cattle drovers after American ranchers stocked the open range.

Ephrata began to grow after the Great Northern Railroad established a terminal here in 1892. Cattlemen took advantage of the railroad to round up and ship out thousands of wild horses that roamed the range. The last great roundup was held in 1906, when the remaining 2,400 horses of a herd that once numbered some 25,000 were corralled and shipped off.

GETTING HERE AND AROUND

Ephrata is about 20 miles north of Moses Lake via Highway 17. Continuing north on the highway leads to the town of Soap Lake, then past state parks, up to Coulee City.

EXPLORING

Grant County Courthouse. Built in the 1920s, the redbrick courthouse has a facade framed by white columns and a majestic set of stairs. Although it may seem antique from the exterior, the building has a unique and progressive feature: it's heated by thermal springs. ⊠ *35 C St. NW* ☎ *509/754–2011* ⊕ *www.grantcountywa.gov* ☉ *Weekdays 8–5.*

FAMILY **Grant County Historical Museum and Village.** More than 30 pioneer-era buildings have been brought here from other parts of Grant County. They include a blacksmith forge, saloon, barber shop, and printing office. ⊠ *742 Basin St. N* ☎ *509/754–3334* ⊠ *$3.50* ☉ *May–Sept., Mon., Tues. and Thurs.–Sat. 10–5, Sun. 1–4.*

Soap Lake. The water is high in dissolved carbonates, sulfates, and chlorides, but even though the lake has long been famous for its mineral waters and therapeutic mud baths, the eponymous small town has never quite succeeded as a resort—perhaps because the miraculous waters have been heavily diluted by irrigation waters. But agriculture is much more profitable anyway, and many other beautiful recreation areas are nearby. ⊠ *6 miles north of Ephrata, Soap Lake* ⊕ *www.soaplakecoc. org.*

WHERE TO STAY

$ ⊞ **Inn at Soap Lake.** At this inn opened in 1915 during Soap Lake's hey-
B&B/INN   day as a destination for health treatments, most rooms have a soaking tub with the natural mineral-rich water on tap, along with contemporary furnishings and modern amenities. **Pros:** beautifully landscaped gardens; private beach has lounge chairs; cozy lobby. **Cons:** no pool; registration desk is not staffed, but management is on-site. $ *Rooms from: $62* ⊠ *226 Main Ave. E, Soap Lake* ☎ *509/246–1132, 800/557– 8514* ⊕ *www.innsoaplake.com* ⇲ *20 rooms, 8 cottages* ❤ *No meals.*

$ ⊞ **Notaras Lodge.** The spacious rooms at this four-building lodge on
HOTEL   the shore of Soap Lake are individually decorated; all have a rustic
FAMILY   log-style construction. **Pros:** room style is very unusual and fun; helpful staff; interesting grounds. **Cons:** not all rooms have lake views. $ *Rooms from: $85* ⊠ *13 Canna St., Soap Lake* ☎ *509/246–0462* ⊕ *www.notaraslodge.com* ⇲ *8 rooms, 7 suites* ❤ *No meals.*

Cave B Estate Winery and Resort

NORTHEASTERN WASHINGTON

A technological marvel, the Grand Coulee Dam took nearly a decade to build in the 1930s. Its fascinating history is on display at the year-round visitor center, where tours are also available. The dam created a 150-mile-long lake; several campgrounds surround it and recreational activities abound. Farther north, the Colville and Okanogan National Forests comprise three mountain ranges that are foothills of the Rockies. These wild areas teem with wildlife and natural beauty, yet remain pristine and uncrowded. The small towns of Omak and Colville provide basic services for travelers and a couple of excellent restaurants.

COULEE DAM NATIONAL RECREATION AREA

60 miles northeast of Ephrata, 239 miles northeast of Seattle, 87 miles northwest of Spokane.

Grand Coulee Dam is the one of the world's largest concrete structures. At almost a mile long, it justly deserves the moniker "Eighth Technological Wonder of the World." Beginning in 1932, 9,000 men excavated 45 million cubic yards of rock and soil and dammed the Grand Coulee, a gorge created by the Columbia River, with 12 million cubic yards of concrete—enough to build a sidewalk the length of the equator. By the time the dam was completed in 1941, 77 men had perished and 11 towns were submerged under the newly formed Roosevelt Lake. The waters backed up behind the dam turned eastern Washington's arid soil into fertile farming land, but not without consequence: salmon-fishing stations that were a source of food and spiritual identity for Native Americans were destroyed. Half the dam was built on the Colville Indian Reservation on the north shore of the Columbia; the Colville tribes later received restitution in excess of $75 million from the U.S. government.

In 1946 most of Roosevelt Lake and the grassy and pine woodland hills surrounding it were designated the Coulee Dam National Recreation Area. Crown Point Vista, about 5 miles west of Grand Coulee on Highway 174, may have the best vantage for photographs of the dam, Roosevelt Lake, Rufus Woods Lake (below the dam), and the town of Coulee Dam.

After nightfall from Memorial Day through September the dam is transformed into an unlikely entertainment complex by an extravagant, free laser light show. After 25 years of the same show, a new one called "One River, Many Voices" debuted in 2014 with a more contemporary, high-tech style and oral histories of the dam project. The audio portion is broadcast on 90.1 FM. Show up early to get a good seat. The show starts at 10 pm Memorial Day through July, 9:30 pm in August, and 8:30 pm in September.

GETTING HERE AND AROUND
From Ephrata, take Highway 17 north to reach Grand Coulee. From the Spokane area, U.S. 2 and Highway 174 is the most direct route.

ESSENTIALS

Visitor Information Grand Coulee Dam Area Chamber of Commerce ⊠ *17 Midway Ave.* ☎ *509/633–3074* ⊕ *www.grandcouleedam.org.*

EXPLORING

Colville Indian Reservation. Highway 155 passes through the Colville Indian Reservation, one of the largest reservations in Washington, with about 7,700 enrolled members of the Colville Confederated Tribes. This was the final home for Chief Joseph and the Nez Perce, who fought a series of fierce battles with the U.S. Army in the 1870s after the U.S. government enforced a treaty that many present-day historians agree was fraudulent. Chief Joseph lived on the Colville Reservation until his death in 1904. There's a memorial to him off Highway 155 east of the town of Nespelem, 17 miles north of the dam; four blocks away (two east and two north) is his grave. You can drive through the reservation's undeveloped landscape, and except for a few highway signs you'll feel like you've time-traveled to pioneer days. The **Colville Tribal Museum** (*512 Mead Way, Coulee Dam, 509/633–0751, open daily 8:30–5*) is worth a visit. ⊠ *Coulee Dam* ⊕ *www.colvilletribes.com/tourism.php*

FAMILY **Grand Coulee Dam Visitor Center.** Colorful displays about the dam, a 13-minute film on the site's geology and the dam's construction, and information about the 30-minute laser light show (held nightly from Memorial Day weekend through September) are here. The U.S. Bureau of Reclamation, which oversees operation and maintenance of the dam, conducts tours year-round, weather and maintenance schedules permitting. You can also pick up a self-guided historical walking tour that will take you from the visitors center through the old part of town, across the bridge, and into the old engineers' town. ⊠ *Hwy. 155, south of Coulee Dam, Coulee Dam* ☎ *509/633–9265* ⊕ *www.usbr.gov/pn/grandcoulee* ⅏ *Free* ☉ *Late May–July, daily 8:30 am–11 pm; Aug., daily 8:30 am–10:30 pm; Sept., daily 8:30 am–9:30 pm; Oct.–late May, 9–5.*

Lake Roosevelt National Recreation Area. The 150-mile-long lake was created by the Columbia River when it was backed up by Grand Coulee Dam. Several Native American villages, historic sites, and towns lie beneath the waters. ⊠ *Headquarters, 1008 Crest Dr., Coulee Dam* ☎ *509/754–7800* ⊕ *www.nps.gov/laro* ⅏ *Free; camping $10 May–Sept., $5 Oct.–Apr.* ☉ *Daily 24 hrs.; office weekdays 8–4.*

Steamboat Rock State Park. Here, a 2,200-foot-high flat-topped lava butte rises 1,000 feet above Banks Lake, the 31-mile-long irrigation reservoir filled with water from Lake Roosevelt by giant pumps and siphons. Water is distributed from the south end of the lake throughout the Columbia Basin. The state park has campsites, three cabins, a swimming area, and boat ramps. In summer it's popular with boaters and anglers, and in winter there's Nordic skiing, snowshoeing, and ice fishing. ⊠ *51052 Hwy. 155, 16 miles north of Coulee City, Electric City* ☎ *360/902–8844, 888/226–7688* ⊕ *www.parks.wa.gov/590/ Steamboat-Rock* ⅏ *Day pass $10 per vehicle; annual Discovery Pass $30 (valid at all state parks); campsites $20–$42, cabins $$69–79* ☉ *Daily 6:30–dusk.*

18

Fodor's Choice ★ **Sun Lakes-Dry Falls State Park.** A high point in the coulee, this park has campgrounds, picnic areas, boat rentals, and a state-run golf course that attracts visitors year-round; in summer the lakes bristle with boaters. From the bluffs on U.S. 2, west of the dam, you can get a great view over this enormous canyon. To the north, the banks of the lake are hemmed in by cliffs. At Dry Falls, the upstream erosion of the canyon caused by the floods stops. Below Dry Falls, steep, barren cliffs—some 1,000 feet high—rise from green meadows, marshes, and blue lakes bordered by trees. Most of the water is irrigation water seeping through the porous rock, but the effect is no less spectacular. Eagles and ravens soar along the cliffs, while songbirds, ducks, and geese hang out in the bottomlands.

South of the Sun Lakes, the landscape turns even wilder. The coulee narrows and the cliffs often look like they are on fire, an illusion created by the bold patterns of orange and yellow lichens. The waters of the lakes change, too. The deep blue waters of the small lakes below Dry Falls are replaced by lapis lazuli in the Sun Lakes and turn milky farther south. Presentations at the park's interpretive center at Dry Falls survey the area's geology, and an excellent film describes the great floods. ⊠ *34875 Park Lake Rd. NE, Coulee City* ☎ *360/902–8844, 888/226–7688* ⊕ *www.parks.wa.gov/298/Sun-Lakes-Dry-Falls* ⊠ *Day pass $10 per vehicle; annual Discovery Pass $30 (valid at all state parks); camping $20–$42* ⊙ *Summer, daily 6:30–dusk; winter, daily 8–dusk; visitor center May–Aug. daily 9–6, hrs vary off season.*

WHERE TO EAT AND STAY

$
DINER
× **Flo's Cafe.** One mile south of the dam, this diner dishes up heaps of local color along with loggers' food: biscuits and gravy, corned-beef hash, hamburgers, chicken-fried steak, and chef's salads. Flo's is open for breakfast but closes at 1, so look elsewhere if you want a late lunch. $ *Average main: $8* ⊠ *316 Spokane Way* ☎ *509/633–3216* ⊙ *No dinner.*

$
HOTEL
Columbia River Inn. The well-appointed rooms all have private decks at this inn across the street from Grand Coulee Dam, with easy access to hiking trails and fishing. **Pros:** rooms have microwaves and refrigerators; pretty location. **Cons:** basic rooms on the small side; some visitors have complained about noise. $ *Rooms from: $110* ⊠ *10 Lincoln St., Coulee Dam* ☎ *509/633–2100, 800/633–6421* ⊕ *www. columbiariverinn.com* ⊄ *34 rooms, 1 suite* ⊙ *No meals.*

OMAK

52 miles northwest of Grand Coulee Dam.

Omak is a small mill and orchard town in the beautifully rustic Okanogan Valley of north-central Washington. Lake Omak to the southeast, on the Colville Reservation, is part of an ancient channel of the Columbia River, which ran north prior to the last ice age before turning south at Omak in what is now the lower Okanogan Valley.

For years Omak has been criticized by animal lovers for its mid-August Omak Stampede and Suicide Race. During the annual event, wild horses race down a steep bluff and across the Okanogan River. Some horses have been killed and riders seriously injured. Many of the riders are from the Colville Reservation, and elders defend the race as part of Native American culture. Despite the detractors, more spectators attend the event each year.

GETTING HERE AND AROUND

Omak can be reached from the west via Highway 20 from the Methow Valley area. From Ephrata, head north via Highway 17, then Highway 97. From Grand Coulee Dam, take WA 155N.

EXPLORING

FAMILY **Okanogan County Historical Museum.** Okanogan pioneer life is portrayed in the displays here, and there's a replica of an Old West town. Outside are Okanogan's oldest building, a 19th-century log cabin, and antique farm equipment. ✉ *1410 2nd Ave. N, Okanogan* ☎ *509/422–4272* ⊕ *okanoganhistory.org* ☜ *$2* ☉ *Memorial Day weekend–Labor Day, daily 10–4; otherwise by appointment.*

Okanogan National Forest. This is a region of open woods, meadows, and pastoral river valleys in the Okanogan highlands. There's lots of wildlife: deer, black bears, coyotes, badgers, bobcats, cougars, grouse, hawks, and golden eagles. Campgrounds are scattered throughout the region. There are 11 Sno-Parks with groomed trails for snowmobilers, and open areas for cross-country skiing. Ski areas are at Loup Loup Pass (Nordic and alpine) and Sitzmark (alpine only). ✉ *Okanogan Valley office, 1240 S. 2nd Ave., Okanogan* ☎ *509/826–3275* ⊕ *www.fs.fed. us/r6/oka* ☜ *Free; permits required at Sno-Parks* ☉ *Office: weekdays 7:30–4.*

WHERE TO EAT AND STAY

$$ ✕ **Breadline Cafe.** For more than 30 years, Breadline has been a top ECLECTIC destination for dinner and live music in the Okanogan Valley. A varied Fodor'sChoice menu highlights local organic produce, locally raised natural Angus ★ beef, crepes, and seafood. You'll find Cajun dishes such as jambalaya, as well as an around-the-world assortment of cuisines, including Italian and Greek. Enjoy the breakfast buffet on Saturday. The bakery features a daily cupcake and other pastries and breads for take-out; or indulge in a decadent dessert with your meal, including brandied bread pudding and soda fountain treats like banana splits and sundaes. There's even ice cream sodas with lemoncello and other liqueurs. ⑤ *Average main: $16* ✉ *102 S. Ash St.* ☎ *509/826–5836* ⊕ *www.breadlinecafe.com* ☉ *Closed Sun. and Mon. No breakfast Tues.–Fri.*

$ ⌂ **Omak Inn.** At this motel just off U.S. 97, all rooms are "mini-suites," HOTEL with a separate sitting area, and there's a small patio and an expansive lawn for relaxing in the summer. **Pros:** most rooms have microwaves and refrigerators; close to restaurants. **Cons:** room style is basic; no elevator. ⑤ *Rooms from: $80* ✉ *912 Koala Dr.* ☎ *509/826–3822, 800/204–4800* ⊕ *www.omakinnwa.com* ➥ *66 rooms* �101 *Breakfast.*

18

COLVILLE

115 miles east of Omak.

This small town, the seat of Stevens County, sits in a valley surrounded by lakes, forests, and mountains. The town has many well-maintained old houses and a pleasant, well-to-do atmosphere.

GETTING HERE AND AROUND

Colville is a direct drive north of Spokane via Highway 395.

ESSENTIALS

Visitor Information Colville Chamber of Commerce ✉ *986 S. Main St., Ste. B* ☎ *509/684–5973* ⊕ *www.colville.com.*

EXPLORING

Colville National Forest. This vast region encompasses mountains, forests, and meadows in the state's northeast corner. Here the desert area ends, and three mountain ranges (Selkirks, Kettle River, and Okanogan)—considered foothills of the Rocky Mountains—traverse the region from north to south. It's a beautiful, wild area, where only the river bottoms are dotted with widely spaced settlements and where the mountains (with an average height of about 4,500 feet) are largely pristine. The streams abound with trout, and the forests with deer and black bears. This is perfect backpacking country, with many trails to remote mountain lakes. ✉ *Forest Service office, 765 S. Main St.* ☎ *509/684–7000* ⊕ *www.fs.usda.gov/colville* ✆ *Free* ☉ *Daily dawn–dusk.*

FAMILY **Keller Heritage Center.** Visitors here can see a farmstead, lookout tower, trappers' cabins, blacksmith shop, sawmill, and museum. ✉ *700 N. Wynne St.* ☎ *509/684–5968* ⊕ *www.stevenscountyhistoricalsociety.org* ✆ *$5* ☉ *May, daily 1–4; June–Sept., Mon.–Thurs. 10–4, Fri.–Sun. 1–4; Oct.–Apr., by appointment.*

WHERE TO EAT AND STAY

$

PACIFIC
NORTHWEST
Fodor's Choice
★

×**Lovitt Restaurant.** Occupying a 1908 farmhouse, it's no surprise that the emphasis here is on farm-fresh ingredients, and owners Norman and Kristen Six are sincerely committed to localized sourcing. Their original Lovitt Restaurant in Chicago won numerous accolades, and their talents have been well received here since their move back to where Norman grew up. The menu is driven by what's in season, but expect to find at least one vegetarian dish, as well as steak and burgers made from grass-fed beef. Flatbread starters come with toppings like Cougar Gold cheese and Dry Fly Gin–cured salmon. Chocolate bonbons with homemade ice cream are a favorite dessert item. In summer, enjoy outside dining with views of the bucolic Colville Valley. ⑤ *Average main: $16* ✉ *149 Hwy. 395 S* ☎ *509/684–5444* ⊕ *www.lovittrestaurant.com* ☉ *Closed Sun.–Tues. No lunch.*

$

HOTEL

⌂ **Benny's Colville Inn.** At this comfortable family motel nestled in a pristine valley between the Kettle River and Selkirk mountain ranges, larger king suites have both hot tubs and fireplaces, and there's an indoor lap pool and spa. **Pros:** family-owned; friendly staff; very affordable. **Cons:** can be noisy; older, budget-priced rooms are small. ⑤ *Rooms from: $69* ✉ *915 S. Main St.* ☎ *509/684–2517, 800/680–2517* ⊕ *www.colvilleinn. com* ➪ *101 rooms, 4 suites* ⭤ *Breakfast.*

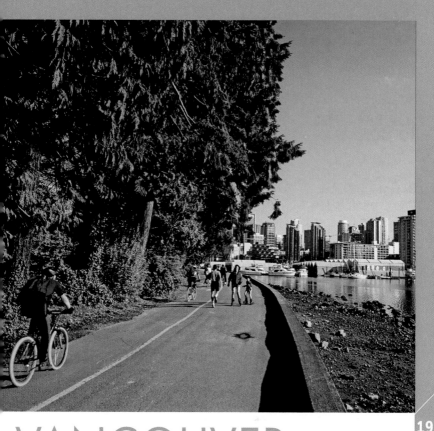

VANCOUVER
AND VICTORIA

WELCOME TO
VANCOUVER AND VICTORIA

TOP REASONS
TO GO

★ **Stanley Park:** The views, the activities, and the natural wilderness beauty here are quintessential Vancouver.

★ **Granville Island:** Ride the mini-ferry across False Creek to the Granville Island Public Market, where you can shop for delicious lunch fixings; eat outside when the weather's fine.

★ **Museum of Anthropology at the University of British Columbia:** The phenomenal collection of First Nations art and cultural artifacts, and the incredible backdrop, make this a must-see.

★ **The Journey here:** Yes, getting here is one of the best things about Victoria: whether by ferry meandering past the Gulf or San Juan Islands, by floatplane (try to travel at least one leg this way), or on a whale-watching boat, getting to Victoria from the mainland is memorable.

★ **Butchart Gardens:** Nearly a million and a half visitors can't be wrong—these lavish gardens north of town live up to the hype.

1 Vancouver. Many people say that Vancouver is the most gorgeous city in North America, and situated as it is, between mountains and water, it's hard to disagree. The Vancouver area actually covers a lot of ground, but the central core—Downtown, Gastown, Yaletown, Chinatown, Stanley Park, and Granville Island—is fairly compact. An excellent public transportation system makes getting around a snap. When in doubt, remember that the mountains are north.

2 Victoria. British Columbia's capital city, Victoria, is a lovely, walkable city with waterfront paths, lovely gardens, fascinating museums, and splendid 19th-century architecture. In some senses remote, it's roughly midway between Vancouver and Seattle and about three hours by car and ferry from either city.

British Columbia

GETTING ORIENTED

Most of Vancouver is on a peninsula, which makes it compact and easy to explore on foot. To get your bearings, use the mountains as your "true north" and you can't go too far wrong. Victoria, at the southern tip of Vancouver Island, is farther south than most of Canada, giving it the mildest climate in the country, with virtually no snow and less than half the rain of Vancouver. The names can get confusing so here's what to to remember: the city of Victoria is on Vancouver Island (not Victoria Island). The city of Vancouver is on the British Columbia mainland, not on Vancouver Island, or on Victoria Island (which isn't in British Columbia but rather way up north, spanning parts of Nunavut and the Northwest Territories).

19

Updated By Carolyn B. Heller, Chloë Ernst, and Sue Kernaghan

Set on Canada's West Coast, Vancouver and Victoria blend urban sophistication and multicultural vitality with spectacular settings near mountains, ocean, and rain forest.

Both cities are famously livable: Vancouver gleams with towering skyscrapers; the smaller Victoria charms with its historic waterfront. To see the appeal, stroll and bike in Vancouver's Stanley Park, eat fresh seafood, sip cocktails, browse boutiques, and visit renowned museums and gardens. Sure, it rains out here, but take a cue from the laid-back locals in their chic, all-weather clothes. Vancouver is a delicious juxtaposition of urban sophistication and on-your-doorstep wilderness adventure. The mountains and seascape make the city an outdoor playground for hiking, skiing, kayaking, cycling, and sailing—and so much more—while the cuisine and arts scenes are equally diverse, reflecting the makeup of Vancouver's ethnic (predominantly Asian) mosaic. Victoria, British Columbia's photogenic capital, is a walkable, livable seaside city of fragrant gardens, waterfront paths, engaging museums, and beautifully restored 19th-century architecture. In summer, the Inner Harbour—Victoria's social and cultural center—buzzes with visiting yachts, horse-and-carriage rides, street entertainers, and excursion boats heading out to visit pods of friendly local whales.

VANCOUVER

More than 8 million visitors each year come to Vancouver, Canada's third-largest metropolitan area. Because of its peninsula location, traffic flow is a contentious issue. Vancouver is wonderfully walkable, especially in the Downtown core. The mild climate, exquisite natural scenery, and relaxed outdoor lifestyle keep attracting residents, and the number of visitors is increasing for the same reasons. People often get their first glimpse of Vancouver when catching an Alaskan cruise, and many return at some point to spend more time here.

PLANNING

MAKING THE MOST OF YOUR TIME

If you don't have much time in Vancouver, you'll probably still want to spend at least a half day in Stanley Park. A couple of hours at the Granville Island Public Market are also a must—plan to have breakfast or lunch, and, if you have time, check out the crafts stores. Walking the Downtown core is a great way to get to know the city. Start at Canada Place and head east to Gastown and Chinatown; that's a good half day. Then head north to Yaletown, perhaps for a glass of wine and dinner. If you're traveling with children, make sure to check out Science World, Grouse Mountain, and the Capilano Suspension Bridge or Lynn Canyon. For museums, adults and older children love the displays of Northwest Coast First Nations art at the Museum of Anthropology. The Bill Reid Gallery also has an impressive collection of aboriginal art.

GETTING HERE AND AROUND

Central Vancouver is extremely walkable and the public transit system—a mix of bus, ferry, and SkyTrain (a fully automated rail system)—is efficient and easy to use. The hop-on, hop-off Vancouver Trolley buses circle the city in a continuous loop and are a great way to see the sites—especially on a rainy day; the same company runs the seasonal Stanley Park Shuttle.

Contacts Vancouver Trolley Company. ☎ 604/801–5515 ⊕ www. vancouvertrolley.com.

BUS AND RAPID-TRANSIT TRAVEL

TransLink, Metro Vancouver's public transport system, includes bus service, a rapid transit system called SkyTrain, and a 400-passenger commuter ferry (SeaBus) that connects Downtown to the North Shore.

In 2015 TransLink is expected to introduce a new electronic Compass Card system for single fare tickets or stored-value cards, to be purchased at station vending machines before boarding. You "tap in" your ticket or card to the electronic reader when you board the bus, SkyTrain, or SeaBus; you "tap out" when you exit, which subtracts the fare from your card. Until then you can still buy single-fare tickets; day passes (good across all zones) and discounted FareSaver tickets (sold in books of 10, at outlets such as 7-Eleven, Safeway, and London Drugs) can also be purchased. Tickets for bus travel require exact change at time of embarkation, while Sky-Train and SeaBus tickets are purchased from machines (correct change isn't necessary). Tickets, which are valid for 90 minutes and allow travel in any direction on the buses, SkyTrain, or SeaBus, must be carried with you as proof of payment. Both the ticket fares and the new Compass Card fares are based on zones: one zone (C\$2.75), two zones (C\$4), or three zones (C\$5.50). Travel within the Vancouver city limits is a one-zone trip; traveling between Vancouver and the North Shore or from Vancouver to Richmond is two zones. The Compass Card will also have a day pass available if you're planning to use the system frequently in one day (C\$9.75, good all day across all zones).

19

You'll be able to board a bus without a Compass Card or electronic ticket; just pay your fare as you enter (exact change required). However a Compass Card gives you free transfers between the bus and either the SkyTrain or the SeaBus; if you pay cash, your ticket is good on the bus only.

■ TIP➔ SkyTrain is convenient for transit between Downtown, BC Place Stadium, Pacific Central Station, Science World, and Vancouver International Airport. SeaBus is the fastest way to travel between Downtown and the North Shore (there are bus connections to Capilano Suspension Bridge and Grouse Mountain).

Contacts TransLink. ☎ 604/953–3333 ⊕ www.translink.ca.

FERRY TRAVEL

Twelve-passenger Aquabus Ferries and False Creek Ferries bypass busy bridges and are a key reason why you don't need a car in Vancouver. Both of these are private commercial enterprises—not part of the TransLink system—that provide passenger services between key locales on either side of False Creek. Single-ride tickets range from C$3.25 to C$5.50 depending on the route; day passes are C$15–C$16. Aquabus Ferries connections include The Village (Science World and the Olympic Village), Plaza of Nations, Granville Island, Stamp's Landing, Spyglass Place, Yaletown, David Lam Park, and the Hornby Street dock. False Creek Ferries provides service between the Aquatic Centre on Beach Avenue, Granville Island, Science World, Stamp's Landing, and Vanier Park. The large SeaBus ferries travel between Waterfront Station and Lonsdale Quay in North Vancouver. TransLink tickets valid on the city's buses and subways are also good for the SeaBus.

EXPLORING VANCOUVER

The city's Downtown core includes the main business district between Robson Street and the Burrard Inlet harbor front; the West End that edges up against English Bay; Stanley Park; trendy Yaletown; and Gastown and Chinatown, which are the oldest parts of the city. Main Street, which runs north–south, is roughly the dividing line between the east and west sides. The entire Downtown district sits on a peninsula bordered by English Bay and the Pacific Ocean to the west; by False Creek to the south; and by Burrard Inlet, the city's working port, to the north, where the North Shore Mountains loom.

DOWNTOWN AND THE WEST END

Vancouver's compact Downtown juxtaposes historic architecture with gleaming brand-new buildings. There are museums and galleries to visit, as well as top-notch shopping, most notably along Robson Street, which runs into the city's West End. The harbor front, with the green-roofed convention center, has a fabulous water's edge path all the way to Stanley Park—walk along here to get a feel for what Vancouver is all about.

DOWNTOWN
TOP ATTRACTIONS

Fodor's Choice
★

Bill Reid Gallery. Named after one of British Columbia's preeminent artists, Bill Reid (1920–98), this small aboriginal gallery is as much a legacy of Reid's works as it is a showcase of current First Nations artists. Displays include wood carvings, jewelry, print, and sculpture, and programs often include artist talks and themed exhibitions such as basket weaving. Reid is best known for his bronze statue *The Spirit of Haida Gwaii, The Jade Canoe* —measuring 12 feet by 20 feet; the original is an iconic meeting place at the Vancouver International Airport, and its image is on the back of the Canadian $20 bill. More Bill Reid pieces are at the Museum of Anthropololgy. ⊠ *639 Hornby St., Downtown, Vancouver* ☏ *604/682–3455* ⊕ *www.billreidgallery.ca* ⊠ *C$10* ⊗ *Wed.–Sun. 11–5.*

QUICK
BITES

Bella Gelateria. If you're strolling around Downtown, take note of this tiny shop tucked into a corner of the Fairmont Pacific Rim Hotel building. Bella Gelateria makes its gelato the old-fashioned Italian way, changing the selection of 24 flavors every day (not the night before) from fresh natural ingredients. These treats don't come cheap, but they're delicious. ⊠ *1001 W. Cordova St., Downtown, Vancouver* ☏ *604/569–1010* ⊕ *www.bellagelateria.com.*

Robson Street. Running from the Terry Fox Plaza outside BC Place Stadium down to the West End, Robson is Vancouver's busiest shopping street, where fashionistas hang out at see-and-be-seen sidewalk cafés, high-end boutiques, and chain stores. Most of the designer action takes place between Jervis and Burrard Streets and that's also where you can find buskers and other entertainers in the evenings. ⊠ *Vancouver* ⊕ *www.robsonstreet.ca.*

Vancouver Art Gallery. Canadian painter Emily Carr's haunting evocations of the British Columbian hinterland are among the attractions at western Canada's largest art gallery. Carr (1871–1945), a grocer's daughter from Victoria, BC, fell in love with the wilderness around her and shocked middle-class Victorian society by running off to paint it. Her work accentuates the mysticism and danger of BC's wilderness, and records the diminishing presence of native cultures during that era (there's something of a renaissance now). The gallery, which also hosts touring historical and contemporary exhibitions, is housed in a 1911 courthouse that Canadian architect Arthur Erickson redesigned in the early 1980s as part of the Robson Square redevelopment. Stone lions guard the steps to the parklike Georgia Street side; the main entrance is accessed from Robson Square or Hornby Street. ⊠ *750 Hornby St., Downtown, Vancouver* ☏ *604/662–4719* ⊕ *www.vanartgallery.bc.ca* ⊠ *C$20 (with tax C$21); higher for some exhibits; by donation Tues. 5–9* ⊗ *Wed.–Mon. 10–5, Tues. 10–9.*

FAMILY **Vancouver Lookout!** Resembling a flying saucer stuck atop a high-rise, the 553-foot-high Vancouver Lookout has fabulous views of Vancouver. A glass elevator whizzes you up 50 stories to the circular observation deck, where knowledgeable guides point out the sights and give a (free) tour every hour on the hour. On a clear day you can see Vancouver Island and

19

STANLEY PARK
Stanley Park

Stanley Park Dr.
Park Ln.

Chilco St.
Gilford St.
Denman St.
Bidwell St.
Cardero St.
Nicola St.
Broughton St.
Haro St.
Robson St.
Barclay St.
Nelson St.
Melville St.
W. Georgia St.
Alberni St.

WEST END

Pendrell St.
Davie St.
Burnaby St.
Harwood St.
Beach Ave.

English Bay

Comox St.
Jervis St.
Bute St.
Thurlow St.

DOWNTOWN

Nelson Park

Helmcken St.
Davie St.

N

0   1/4 mi
0   1/4 km

Beach Ave.

Sunset Beach Park

Vanier Park

McNichol Ave.

12
11 10

Drake St.
Pacific St.

Maple St.
Cypress St.

KITSILANO

Burrard St. Bridge

GRANVILLE ISLAND

Granville St. Bridge

Vancouver Downtown, Gastown, Chinatown, Yaletown, and Kitsilano

Burrard Inlet

Coal Harbor Rd.

W.Hastings St.
W.Pender St.

Canada Place Way

WATERFRONT

Coal Harbour Rd.

Portside Park

GASTOWN

W.Cordova St.

W.Hastings St.

W.Pender St.

W.Georgia St.

Dunsmuir St.

GRANVILLE

BURRARD

Burrard St.

Hornby St.

Howe St.

Granville St.

Seymour St.

Richards St.

Homer St.

Hamilton St.

Smithe St.

Cambie St.

Beatty St.

Nelson St.

YALETOWN

SKYTRAIN

Cambie St.

Water St.

Alexander St.

E. Powell St.

Cordova St.

Abbott St.

Hastings St.

Pender St.

CHINATOWN

Columbia St.

Main St.

Carrall St.

Keefer St.

STADIUM

Union St.

Georgia St.

Columbia St.

Main St.

Expo Blvd.

Pacific Blvd. South

Cambie St. Bridge

Marinaside Ct.

Hamilton St.

False Creek

MAIN STREET

① ② ③ ④ ⑤ ⑥ ⑦ ⑧ ⑨

KEY

SeaBus

Mt. Baker in Washington State. The top-floor restaurant (*604/669–2220, www.topofvancouver.com*) makes one complete revolution per hour; the elevator ride up is free for diners. Tickets are good all day, so you can visit in daytime and return for another look after dark. ⊠ *555 W. Hastings St., Downtown, Vancouver* ☎ *604/689–0421* ⊕ *www.vancouverlookout. com* ⊠ *C$15.75* ☉ *May–mid-Oct., daily 8:30 am–10:30 pm; mid-Oct.– Apr., Mon.–Thurs. 9–9, Fri.–Sun. 9 am–9:30 pm.*

WEST END

Robson Street, Vancouver's prime shopping boulevard, runs from Downtown into the West End, a partly residential and partly commercial district. The West End has Vancouver's prettiest streetscapes and harks back to the early 1930s when it housed the affluent middle class: trees are plentiful, gardens are lushly planted, and homes and apartment buildings exude the character of that era. There are lots of restaurants and cafés along the main arteries: Robson, Denman, and Davie streets.

STANLEY PARK

A 1,000-acre wilderness park, only blocks from the Downtown section of a major city, is a rare treasure and Vancouverites make use of it to bike, walk, jog, in-line skate, and go to the beach.

TOP ATTRACTIONS

Prospect Point. At 211 feet, Prospect Point is the highest point in the park and provides striking views of the Lions Gate Bridge (watch for cruise ships passing below), the North Shore, and Burrard Inlet. There's also a year-round souvenir shop, a snack bar with terrific ice cream, and a restaurant. From the seawall, you can see where cormorants build their seaweed nests along the cliff ledges. ⊠ *Stanley Park, Vancouver.*

Stanley Park Seawall. Vancouver's seawall path includes a 9-km (5½-mile) paved shoreline section within Stanley Park. It's one of several car-free zones in the park and it's popular with walkers and cyclists. If you have the time (about a half day) and the energy, strolling the entire seawall is an exhilarating experience. It extends an additional mile east past the marinas, cafés, and waterfront condominiums of Coal Harbour to Canada Place in Downtown, so you could start your walk or ride from there. From the south side of the park, the seawall continues for another 28 km (17 miles) along Vancouver's waterfront to the University of British Columbia, allowing for a pleasant, if ambitious, day's bike ride. Along the seawall, cyclists must wear helmets and stay on their side of the path. Within Stanley Park, cyclists must ride in a counterclockwise direction. The seawall can get crowded on summer weekends, but inside the park is a 28-km (17-mile) network of peaceful walking and cycling paths through old- and second-growth forest. The wheelchair-accessible Beaver Lake Interpretive Trail is a good choice if you're interested in park ecology. Take a map—they're available at the park-information booth and many of the concession stands—and don't go into the woods alone or after dusk. ⊠ *Stanley Park, Vancouver.*

Totem poles. Totem poles are an important art form among native peoples along British Columbia's coast. These nine poles—eight carved in the latter half of the 20th century, and one created in 2009—include replicas of poles originally brought to the park from the north coast in the 1920s, as well as poles carved specifically for the park by First Nations artists. The several styles of poles represent a cross section of BC native groups, including the Kwakwaka'wakw, Haida, and Nisga'a. The combination of carved animals, fish, birds, and mythological creatures represents clan history. An information center near the site has a snack bar, a gift shop, and information about BC's First Nations. ⊠ *Brockton Point, Stanley Park, Vancouver.*

Fodor's Choice

★

FAMILY

Vancouver Aquarium Marine Science Centre. Massive floor-to-ceiling windows let you get face-to-face with beluga whales, sea otters, sea lions, dolphins, and harbor seals at this award-winning research and educational facility. In the Amazon Gallery you walk through a rain-forest jungle populated with piranhas, caimans, and tropical birds; in summer, hundreds of free-flying butterflies add to the mix. The Tropic Zone is home to exotic freshwater and saltwater life, including clown fish, moray eels, and black-tip reef sharks. Other displays, many with hands-on features for kids, show the underwater life of coastal British Columbia and the Canadian Arctic. Beluga whale, sea lion, and dolphin shows, as well as dive shows (where divers swim with aquatic life, including sharks) are held daily. Be sure to check out the "4-D" film experience; it's a multisensory show that puts mist, smell, and wind into the 3-D equation. For an extra fee, you can help the trainers feed and train otters, belugas, and sea lions. There's also a café and a gift shop. Be prepared for lines on weekends and school holidays. In summer, the quietest time to visit is before 11 am or after 4 pm; in other seasons, the crowds are smaller before noon or after 2 pm. ⊠ *845 Avison Way, Stanley Park, Vancouver* ☎ *604/659–3474* ⊕ *www.vanaqua.org* ☜ *C$30* ☼ *July–Labor Day, daily 9:30–6; Labor Day–June, daily 10–5.*

GASTOWN AND CHINATOWN

19

Historic Gastown and adjacent Chinatown are full of character. They're favorite destinations for visitors and residents alike, and easily explored together. Both neighborhoods are experiencing gentrifcation as historic buildings get a new lease on life.

GASTOWN

TOP ATTRACTIONS

Coastal Peoples Fine Arts Gallery. The collection of First Nations jewelry, ceremonial masks, prints, and carvings at this gallery is impressive. Check out the gorgeous books and postcards if you're looking for more affordable souvenirs. The gallery has a second location at 1024 Mainland Street in Yaletown. ⊠ *312 Water St., Gastown, Vancouver* ☎ *604/684–9222* ⊕ *www.coastalpeoples.com.*

WORTH NOTING

Byrnes Block. After the 1886 Great Fire, which wiped out most of the fledgling settlement of Vancouver, George Byrnes built what is now Vancouver's oldest brick building. It now houses shops and offices, but for a while this two-story building was Vancouver's top luxury hotel, the Alhambra Hotel, charging a dollar a night. The site of Deighton's original saloon, east of the Byrnes Block where his statue now stands, is the starting point from which all Vancouver street addresses begin. ✉ *2 Water St., Gastown, Vancouver.*

Gaoler's Mews. Once the site of the city's first civic buildings—the constable's cabin and customs house, and a two-cell log jail—this atmospheric brick-paved courtyard is now home to cafés and offices. ✉ *Behind 12 Water St., Gastown, Vancouver.*

CHINATOWN

TOP ATTRACTIONS

Fodor's Choice ★ **Dr. Sun Yat-Sen Chinese Garden.** The first authentic Ming Dynasty–style garden outside China, this small garden was built in 1986 by 52 Chinese artisans from Suzhou. No power tools, screws, or nails were used in the construction. It incorporates design elements and traditional materials from several of Suzhou's centuries-old private gardens. Guided tours (45 minutes long), included in the ticket price, are conducted on the hour between mid-June and the end of August (call ahead or check the website for off-season tour times); these are valuable for understanding the philosophy and symbolism that are central to the garden's design. Covered walkways make this a good rainy-day choice. A concert series, including classical, Asian, world, jazz, and sacred music, plays on Friday evenings in July and August. The free public park next door is also designed as a traditional Chinese garden, though it's smaller and less elaborate—it's a pleasant place to sit but lacks the context that you get with a tour of the Sun Yat-Sen garden. ✉ *578 Carrall St., Chinatown, Vancouver* ☎ *604/662–3207* ⊕ *www.vancouverchinesegarden. com* ✉ *C$14* ⊗ *May–mid-June and Sept., daily 10–6; mid-June–Aug., daily 9:30–7; Oct., daily 10–4:30; Nov.–Apr., Tues.–Sun. 10–4:30.*

YALETOWN

Yaletown is one of Vancouver's most fashionable areas and one of the most impressive urban-redevelopment projects in North America. The brick warehouses were turned into apartment buildings and offices, and the old loading docks are now terraces for cappuccino bars and trendy restaurants. There are brewpubs, day spas, retail and wholesale fashion outlets, and shops selling upscale home decor.

GRANVILLE ISLAND

An indoor food market and a thriving diversity of artist studios as well as performing arts spaces, specialty shops (there's not a chain store or designer label in sight), and a busy marina make Granville Island one of Vancouver's top attractions. Explore at your leisure but try to plan your expedition over a meal, since the market is an excellent place for breakfast, lunch, snacks, and shopping. The buildings behind the market are as diverse as the island's main attractions and house all sorts of crafts shops.

The mini Aquabus ferries are a favorite (and the most adorable) way to get to Granville Island (it's about a two-minute ride). They depart from the south end of Hornby Street (about a 15-minute walk from

Downtown Vancouver) and take passengers across False Creek to the Granville Island Public Market. The larger False Creek ferries leave every five minutes for Granville Island from a dock behind the Vancouver Aquatic Centre, on Beach Avenue. Still another option is to take a 10-minute ride on a TransLink bus: from Waterfront Station or stops on Granville Street, take Bus 50 to the edge of the island.

TOP ATTRACTIONS

Fodor's Choice ★ **Granville Island Public Market.** The dozens of stalls in this 50,000-square-foot building sell locally grown fruits and vegetables direct from the farm and farther afield; other stalls stock crafts, chocolates, artisanal cheeses and pastas, fish, meat, flowers, and exotic foods. On Thursday in summer, farmers sell fruit and vegetables from trucks outside. At the north end of the market, you can pick up a snack, lunch, or coffee from one of the many prepared-food vendors. The Market Courtyard, on the waterside, has great views of the city and is also a good place to catch street entertainers—be prepared to get roped into the action, if only to check the padlocks of an escape artist's gear. Weekends can get madly busy. ⊠ *1689 Johnston St., Granville Island, Vancouver* ☎ *604/666–6655* ⊕ *www.granvilleisland.com* ⊗ *Daily 9–7.*

WORTH NOTING

Granville Island Brewing. Tours of Canada's first modern microbrewery last about 45 minutes and include a four-ounce taste of three brews. You must be 19 years old and wearing close-toed shoes to take a tour. ⊠ *1441 Cartwright St., Granville Island, Vancouver* ☎ *604/687–2739* ⊕ *www.gib.ca* ☎ *C$9.75* ⊗ *Store open daily mid-May–early Sept. 10–9, early Sept.–mid-May 10–8. Tours mid-May-early Sept. daily at noon, 1:30 pm, 3 pm, 4:30 pm, and 5:30 pm; early Sept.–mid-May daily at noon, 2 pm, and 4 pm.*

THE WEST SIDE

19

The West Side, the set of diverse neighborhoods just south of Downtown, has some of Vancouver's best gardens and natural sights as well as some chic shopping. "Kits," as the locals refer to Kitsilano, though, is really where all the action is: the once-hippie neighborhood has evolved into an upscale district of shops, restaurants, museums, and one of the city's best people-watching beaches.

KITSILANO
WORTH NOTING

FAMILY **H.R. MacMillan Space Centre.** The interactive exhibits and high-tech learning systems at this museum include a Virtual Voyages ride, where visitors can take a simulated space journey (definitely not for those afraid of flying); GroundStation Canada, showcasing Canada's achievements in space; and the Cosmic Courtyard, full of hands-on space-oriented exhibits including a moon rock and a computer program that shows what you would look like as an alien. You can catch daytime astronomy shows or evening music-and-laser shows at the **H.R. MacMillan Planetarium.** ⊠ *Vanier Park, 1100 Chestnut St., Kitsilano, Vancouver* ☎ *604/738–7827* ⊕ *www.spacecentre.ca* ☎ *C$18* ⊗ *July and Aug., daily 10–5; Sept.–June, weekdays 10–3, Sat. 10–5, Sun. noon–5.*

Museum of Vancouver. Vancouver's short-but-funky history comes to life at this seaside museum. The 1930s gallery remembers some poignant episodes involving the Japanese internment during WWII, as well as local stories of the war effort. The 1950s Gallery has a 1955 Ford Fairlane Victoria and a Seeburg select-o-matic jukebox. The 1960s-theme Revolution Gallery revisits the city's days as the hippie capital of Canada: visitors can hear local bands from the '60s and poke around a re-created communal house. The museum regularly mounts intriguing temporary exhibits and hosts lectures and other public events. ⊠ *Vanier Park, 1100 Chestnut St., Kitsilano, Vancouver* ☎ *604/736–4431* ⊕ *www.museumofvancouver. com* ⊠ *C$14* ☉ *July and Aug., Fri.–Wed. 10–5, Thurs. 10–8; Sept.–June, Tues., Wed., and Fri.–Sun. 10–5, Thurs. 10–8.*

FAMILY **Vancouver Maritime Museum.** Sharing the seafaring history of the Pacific Northwest and Arctic regions, this family-friendly museum houses the *RCMP Arctic St. Roch,* the first ship to sail in both directions through the treacherous Northwest Passage and the first to circumnavigate North America. You can scramble around the decks and into the St. Roch's cabins, imagining yourself as a sea captain attempting to navigate the Arctic. About a third of this museum has been turned over to kids, with touchable displays offering a chance to drive a tug, maneuver an underwater robot, or dress up as a seafarer. Toddlers and school-age children can work the hands-on displays in Pirates' Cove and the Children's Maritime Discovery Centre. The museum also has an extensive collection of model ships. While you're here, take a moment to look at the 100-foot-tall replica Kwakiutl totem pole in front of the museum. The massive white-and-yellow contraption behind the Vancouver Maritime Museum is the *Ben Franklin* submersible. It looks like something a Jules Verne character would put to sea but was actually built in 1968 as a marine research tool to, among other things, chart the Gulf Stream. A more fascinating claim to fame is that it was once the largest of its kind in America and was instructional for NASA: the information about how people lived in such close quarters for extended periods of time provided preliminary research data on the dynamics of living aboard a space station. ⊠ *Vanier Park, 1905 Ogden Ave., north end of Cypress St., Kitsilano, Vancouver* ☎ *604/257–8300* ⊕ *www.vancouvermaritimemuseum.com* ⊠ *C$11* ☉ *Mid-May–Labor Day, daily 10–5; Labor Day–mid-May, Tues.–Sat. 10–5, Sun. noon–5.*

POINT GREY

TOP ATTRACTIONS

Fodor's Choice **Museum of Anthropology.** Part of the University of British Columbia, the ★ MOA has one of the world's leading collections of Northwest Coast First Nations art. The Great Hall has dramatic cedar poles, bentwood boxes, and canoes adorned with traditional Northwest Coast–painted designs. On clear days, the gallery's 50-foot-tall windows reveal a striking backdrop of mountains and sea. Another highlight is the work of the late Bill Reid, one of Canada's most respected Haida artists. In *The Raven and the First Men* (1980), carved in yellow cedar, he tells a Haida story of creation. Reid's gold-and-silver jewelry work is also on display, as are exquisite carvings of gold, silver, and argillite (a black shale found on Haida Gwaii, also known as the Queen Charlotte

Islands) by other First Nations artists. The museum's visible storage section displays, in drawers and cases, contain thousands of examples of tools, textiles, masks, and other artifacts from around the world. The Koerner Ceramics Gallery contains 600 pieces from 15th- to 19th-century Europe. Behind the museum are two Haida houses, set on the cliff over the water. Free guided tours—given several times daily (call or check the website for times)—are immensely informative. For an extra C$5 you can rent a VUEguide—an electronic device that senses where you are in the museum and shows relevant artist interviews, archival footage, and photographs of the artifacts in their original contexts, on a hand-held screen. The MOA also has an excellent book and fine-art shop, as well as a café. To reach the museum by transit, take any UBC-bound bus from Granville Street Downtown to the university bus loop, a 15-minute walk (or 10-minute ride on shuttle bus C18 or C20) from the museum. Pay parking is available in the Rose Garden parking lot, across Marine Drive from the museum. A UBC Museums and Gardens Pass will save you money if you're planning to visit several attractions at UBC. ⊠ *University of British Columbia, 6393 N.W. Marine Dr., Point Grey, Vancouver* ☎ *604/822–5087* ⊕ *www.moa.ubc.ca* ☐ *C$16.75, Tues. 5–9 C$9;* ⊘ *Late May–mid-Oct., Tues. 10–9, Wed.–Mon. 10–5; mid-Oct.–late May, Tues. 10–9, Wed.–Sun. 10–5.*

Nitobe Memorial Garden. Opened in 1960 in memory of Japanese scholar and diplomat Dr. Inazo Nitobe (1862–1933), this 2½-acre walled garden, which includes a pond, a stream with a small waterfall, and a ceremonial teahouse, is considered one of the most authentic Japanese tea and strolling gardens outside Japan. Designed by Professor Kannosuke Mori of Japan's Chiba University, the garden incorporates many native British Columbia trees and shrubs, pruned and trained Japanese style, and interplanted with Japanese maples and flowering shrubs. The circular path around the park symbolizes the cycle of life and provides a tranquil view from every direction. Cherry blossoms are the highlight in April and May, and in June the irises are magnificent. Because the garden is so exotic, it's worth renting an audio guide. Japanese tea ceremonies are held the last Saturday of every month, May through September; call 604/939–7749 for reservations. A UBC Museums and Gardens Pass will save you money if you're planning to visit several attractions at UBC. ⊠ *University of British Columbia, 1895 Lower Mall, Point Grey, Vancouver* ☎ *604/822–6038* ⊕ *www.botanicalgarden.ubc.ca/nitobe* ☐ *C$7 Apr.–Oct.; C$13 includes admission to the UBC Botanical Garden; by donation Nov.–Mar.* ⊘ *Apr.–Oct., daily 9:30–5; Nov.–Mar., weekdays 10–2.*

FAMILY **University of British Columbia Botanical Garden.** Ten thousand trees, shrubs, and rare plants from around the world thrive on this 70-acre research site on the university campus, which edges on Pacific Spirit Park. The complex feels as far away from the city as you can get, with forested walkways through an Asian garden, a garden of medicinal plants, and an alpine garden with some of the world's rarest plants. A Walk in the Woods is a 20-minute loop that takes you through more than 1,000 species of coastal plant life. The garden gift store is one of the best of its kind. One-hour guided tours, free with garden admission, are offered

19

The exhibits outside the museum, on the cliffs overlooking the water, are part of the attraction of the Museum of Anthropology.

on certain days; call or check the website for schedule. A UBC Museums and Gardens Pass will save you money if you're planning to visit several attractions at UBC. The 308-meter-long (1,010-foot-long) **Greenheart Canopy Walkway**, a swaying network of suspended bridges weaving a trail between gargantuan cedars and hemlocks, is a thrilling way to explore the garden. Along the way, you stop off on eight platforms in the trees, each more than 15 meters (49 feet) high, while an additional two-story viewing platform tops a free-standing tower more than 22 meters (72 feet) in the air. Visits to the walkway are by 45-minute guided tour, where you learn about the forest, local wildlife, environmental issues, and First Nations traditions; call or check the website for seasonal tour schedules. The walkway is a great adventure for kids; just note that small children must either be able to walk on their own or be carried in a child backpack or other carrier (strollers aren't permitted). ⊠ *6804 S.W. Marine Dr., Point Grey, Vancouver* ☎ *604/822–4208* ⊕ *www.botanicalgarden.ubc.ca* ✉ *C$9; C$13 includes admission to Nitobe Memorial Garden; C$20 includes Greenheart Canopy Walkway; C$24 includes Nitobe Memorial Garden and Greenheart Canopy Walkway* ☉ *Daily 9:30–5.*

SOUTH GRANVILLE
TOP ATTRACTIONS
Douglas Reynolds Gallery. In this collection of Northwest Coast First Nations art, which is particularly strong in woodwork and jewelry, some pieces date back to the 1800s, while others are strikingly contemporary. ⊠ *2335 Granville St., South Granville, Vancouver* ☎ *604/731–9292* ⊕ *www.douglasreynoldsgallery.com.*

CAMBIE CORRIDOR
TOP ATTRACTIONS

FAMILY **Queen Elizabeth Park.** Lavish sunken gardens (in a former stone quarry), a rose garden, and an abundance of grassy picnicking spots are just a few of the highlights at this 52-hectare (130-acre) park. Poised at the highest point in the city, there are 360-degree views of Downtown. Other park facilities include 18 tennis courts, pitch and putt (an 18-hole putting green), and a restaurant. On summer evenings there's free outdoor dancing on the Plaza—everything from Scottish country dance to salsa, for all ages and levels. In the **Bloedel Conservatory** you can see tropical and desert plants and 100 species of free-flying tropical birds in a glass geodesic dome—the perfect place to be on a rainy day. To reach the park by public transportation, take the Canada Line to King Edward station; from there, it's a six-block walk to the edge of the park (and a hike up the hill to appreciate the views). Cambie Bus 15, which runs south along Cambie Street from the Olympic Village SkyTrain station, will drop you a little closer, at the corner of 33rd and Cambie. Park activities make for a great family excursion, and unlike Stanley Park with its acres of rain forest, Queen Elizabeth Park is all about the flowers. ⊠ *Cambie St. and 33rd Ave., Cambie Corridor, Vancouver* ☎ *604/257–8584* ⊕ *www.vancouver.ca/parks* ⊡ *Conservatory C$6.50* ☉ *Park daily year-round; Bloedel Conservatory May–early Sept., weekdays 9–8, weekends 10–8; early Sept.–Apr., daily 10–5.*

FAMILY **VanDusen Botanical Garden.** An Elizabethan maze, a formal rose garden, a meditation garden, and a collection of Canadian heritage plants are among the many displays at this 55-acre site. The collections include flora from every continent and many rare and endangered species. The Phyllis Bentall Garden area features hybrid water lilies and carnivorous plants (a hit with kids). From mid-May to early June the Laburnum Walk forms a canopy of gold; in August and September the wildflower meadow is in bloom. The garden is also home to five lakes, a garden shop, a library, and the Truffles Fine Foods Café (serving breakfast, lunch, and afternoon tea). Special events throughout the year include a spectacular Christmas-theme Festival of Lights every December (daily 4:30–9 pm). From Downtown, catch the Oak Bus 17 directly to the garden entrance; alternatively, ride the Canada Line to Oakridge/41st, then take the UBC Bus 41 to Oak Street, and walk four blocks north to the garden. Queen Elizabeth Park is a 1-km (½-mile) walk away, along West 37th Avenue. Because this was once a golf course, pathways make this garden extremely wheelchair accessible. ⊠ *5251 Oak St., at W. 37th Ave., Cambie Corridor, Vancouver* ☎ *604/257–8335 garden, 604/267–4966 restaurant* ⊕ *www.vandusengarden.org* ⊡ *C$10.75 Apr.–Sept.; C$7.75 Oct.–Mar.* ☉ *June–Aug., daily 9 am–9 pm; Apr.–May and Sept.–Oct, daily from 9 am, Nov.–Mar. daily from 10 am (call for seasonal closing times).*

19

THE EAST SIDE

Vancouver's East Side, which spans the area from Ontario Street east to the suburb of Burnaby, was originally a working-class district. These days, as real estate prices across the city have continued to climb, many artists, young families, and professional people have moved east, and this half of the metropolitan area now mixes multicultural residential communities, art galleries, theaters, and an eclectic assortment of restaurants.

MAIN STREET

TOP ATTRACTIONS

FAMILY **Science World.** In a gigantic shiny dome on the False Creek waterfront, this hands-on science center encourages children to participate in interactive exhibits and demonstrations about the natural world, the human body, and other science topics. Exhibits change throughout the year, so there's always something new to see; there's an Omnimax theater, too. Adjacent to the museum, the Ken Spencer Science Park is an outdoor exhibit area focusing on environmental issues. Science World is an easy walk (or mini-ferry ride) from Yaletown; the Main Street/Science World SkyTrain station is on its doorstep, and there's plenty of parking. ⊠ *1455 Quebec St., Main St./Mt. Pleasant, Vancouver* ☎ *604/443–7440* ⊕ *www.scienceworld.ca* ☑ *C$23.50 Science World, C$29 Science World and Omnimax theater* ☉ *July–Labor Day, daily 10–6; Labor Day–June, weekdays 10–5, weekends 10–6.*

NORTH SHORE

The North Shore and its star attractions—the Capilano Suspension Bridge, Grouse Mountain, Lonsdale Quay, and, farther east, the lovely hamlet of Deep Cove—are just a short trip from Downtown Vancouver. The North Shore is where people come to kayak up fjords, and hike, ski, and explore the forest and mountainous terrain. The two main communities on the North Shore are North Vancouver and West Vancouver.

NORTH VANCOUVER

TOP ATTRACTIONS

Fodor'sChoice **Capilano Suspension Bridge.** At Vancouver's oldest tourist attraction (the
★ original bridge was built in 1889), you can get a taste of rain-forest
FAMILY scenery and test your mettle on the swaying, 450-foot cedar-plank suspension bridge that hangs 230 feet above the rushing Capilano River. Across the bridge is the Treetops Adventure, where you can walk along 650 feet of cable bridges suspended among the trees. If you're even braver, you can follow the **Cliffwalk**, a series of narrow cantilevered bridges and walkways hanging out over the edge of the canyon. Without crossing the bridge, you can enjoy the site's viewing decks, nature trails, totem park, and carving center (where you can watch First Nations carvers at work), as well as history and forestry exhibits. There's also a massive gift shop in the original 1911 teahouse, and a restaurant. May through October, guides in 19th-century costumes conduct free tours on themes related to history, nature, or ecology, while fiddle bands, First Nations dancers, and other entertainers keep things lively. In December,

more than 250,000 lights illuminate the canyon during the Canyon Lights winter celebration. Catch the attraction's free shuttle service from Canada Place; it also stops along Burrard and Robson streets. ✉ *3735 Capilano Rd., North Vancouver* ☎ *604/985–7474* ⊕ *www.capbridge. com* ✉ *C$34.95* ◷ *Mid-May–Labor Day, daily 8:30–8; Labor Day–mid-Oct. and mid-Mar.–mid-Apr. daily 9–6; mid-Oct.–Nov. and Jan–mid-Mar., daily 9–5; Dec. daily 11–9; mid-Apr.–mid-May daily 9–7.*

Fodors Choice
★
FAMILY
Grouse Mountain. North America's largest aerial tramway, the **Skyride** is a great way to take in the city, sea, and mountain vistas (be sure to pick a clear day or evening). The Skyride makes the 2-km (1-mile) climb to the peak of Grouse Mountain every 15 minutes. Once at the top you can watch a half-hour video presentation at the Theatre in the Sky (it's included with your Skyride ticket). Other mountaintop activities include, in summer, lumberjack shows, chairlift rides, walking tours, hiking, falconry demonstrations, and a chance to visit the grizzly bears and gray wolves in the mountain's wildlife refuge. For an extra fee you can also try zip-lining and tandem paragliding, tour the wind turbine that tops the mountain, or take a helicopter flight. In winter you can ski, snowshoe, snowboard, ice-skate on a mountaintop pond, or take Sno-Cat-drawn sleigh rides. A stone-and-cedar lodge is home to snack shops, a pub-style bistro, and a high-end restaurant, all with expansive city views. The Grouse Grind—a hiking trail up the face of the mountain—is one of the best workouts on the North Shore. Depending on your fitness level, allow between 40 minutes and two hours to complete it (90 minutes is an average time). Then you can take the Skyride down. The BCMC Trail is a less crowded, slightly longer alternative. From late May through September, you can catch a free shuttle to Grouse Mountain from Canada Place. ✉ *6400 Nancy Greene Way, North Vancouver* ☎ *604/980–9311* ⊕ *www.grousemountain.com* ✉ *Skyride and many activities C$39.95* ◷ *Daily 9 am–10 pm.*

WORTH NOTING

OFF THE
BEATEN
PATH
Lynn Canyon Park. With a steep canyon landscape, a temperate rain forest complete with waterfalls, and a suspension bridge (circa 1912) 166½ feet above raging Lynn Creek, this 616-acre park provides thrills to go with its scenic views. There are many hiking trails, including a popular one that ends at a waterfall where you can swim. Lynn Canyon Park's on-site Ecology Centre distributes maps of area hiking trails, waterfalls, and pools as well as information about the local flora and fauna. There's also a gift shop and a café here. To get to the park, take the Lions Gate Bridge and Capilano Road, go east on Highway 1, take the Lynn Valley Road exit, and turn right on Peters Road. From Downtown Vancouver, you can take the SeaBus to Lonsdale Quay, then Bus 228 or 229 from the quay; both stop near the park. ■ TIP➔ **The suspension bridge here is shorter than the Capilano Suspension Bridge (130 feet versus 450 feet at Capilano) so the experience is less thrilling, but also less touristy.** ✉ *3663 Park Rd., at end of Peters Rd., North Vancouver* ☎ *604/990–3755 Ecology Centre, 604/984–9311 café* ⊕ *www.dnv.org/ ecology* ✉ *Ecology Centre by donation, suspension bridge free* ◷ *Park daily, dawn–dusk; Ecology Centre June–Sept., daily 10–5; Oct.–May, weekdays 10–5, weekends noon–4.*

19

WHERE TO EAT

Listed alphabetically within neighborhoods.

Use the coordinate at the end of each listing (✛ B2) to locate a property on the Where to Eat in Vancouver map.

From inventive neighborhood bistros to glamorous Downtown dining rooms to ethnic restaurants that rival those in the world capitals, Vancouver has a diverse array of gastronomic options. Many cutting-edge establishments are perfecting what we call Modern Canadian fare, which—at the western end of the country—incorporates regional seafood (notably salmon, halibut, and spot prawns) and locally grown produce. Vancouver is all about "localism," with many restaurants emphasizing the provenance of their ingredients and embracing products that hail from within a 100-mile-or-so radius of the city, or at least from within BC.

With at least 40 percent of the region's population of Asian heritage, it's no surprise that Asian eateries abound in Vancouver. From mom-and-pop noodle shops, curry houses, and corner sushi bars to elegant and upscale dining rooms, cuisine from China, Taiwan, Hong Kong, Japan, and India (and to a lesser extent, from Korea, Thailand, Vietnam, and Malaysia) can be found all over town.

WHAT IT COSTS IN CANADIAN DOLLARS				
	$	**$$**	**$$$**	**$$$$**
AT DINNER	Under C$13	C$13–C$20	C$21–C$30	Over C$30

Prices in the restaurant reviews are for an average main course or equivalent combination of smaller dishes at dinner, or if dinner is not served, at lunch..

DOWNTOWN AND THE WEST END

DOWNTOWN

$
CAFÉ

✕ **Caffè Artigiano.** Some of Vancouver's best coffee is served at the several locations of Caffè Artigiano, where the baristas have won prizes for their latte art—making patterns in the froth. Come for the java, although you can assuage your hunger with a pastry or sandwich, too. There are other locations Downtown at 574 Granville Street, 740 West Hastings Street, 763 Hornby Street, and in Yaletown at 302 Davie Street (adjacent to the Opus Hotel). ⑤ *Average main: C$6* ✉ *1101 W. Pender, Downtown, Vancouver* ☎ *604/685–5333* ⊕ *www.caffeartigiano.com* ⊟ *No credit cards* ✛ *E2.*

$$
MEDITERRANEAN

✕ **Café Medina.** For Mediterranean-inspired breakfast and lunch fare, from skillets piled high with eggs, roasted potatoes, and caramelized onions to Moroccan *tagine* stews, try this casually chic (and always busy) Downtown café just off Robson Street. Look for interesting innovations like the *poisson curé* —a salad of wild salmon, crunchy sprouted farro, pistachios, and parsley—but don't leave without sampling their specialty: Belgian waffles, with toppings like dark chocolate or salted caramel. As of this writing, dinner service is planned for the future so check if you're in the neighborhood. ⑤ *Average main: C$14*

✉ *780 Richards St., Downtown, Vancouver* ☎ *604/879–3114* ⊕ *www. medinacafe.com* ⊗ *No dinner* ✛ *F3.*

$$$$ ✕**Hawksworth Restaurant.** With sleek white tables and sparkling chan-
MODERN deliers, chef David Hawksworth's stylish restaurant welcomes locals
CANADIAN toasting new clients or celebrating a romantic anniversary. The food
Fodor's Choice (and the crowd) is suave and swanky, too. You might start with hamachi
★ sashimi dressed with passion fruit, jalapeño, and coconut, or a simpler
roasted carrot salad with avocado, crème fraîche, and dill. Although
the menu changes frequently, mains might include slow-cooked wild
salmon with salt-roasted beets, roasted elk sauced with a gin-barberry
jus and served with savoy cabbage, or the Parmesan-crusted chicken
with potato gnocchi. Look out, yoga-pants-wearing Vancouver—fine
dining is back. ⑤ *Average main: C$40* ✉ *Rosewood Hotel Georgia,
801 W. Georgia St., Downtown, Vancouver* ☎ *604/673–7000* ⊕ *www.
hawksworthrestaurant.com* ✛ *E3.*

$ ✕**Japadog.** There might be other places in the world that sell Japanese-
ECLECTIC style hot dogs but the phenomenon is so very multi-culti Vancouver and
this storefront is the sit-down spin-off of a wildly successful food cart
with a loyal following. Bratwurst and wieners are topped with teriyaki
sauce, nori, and other Asian condiments. You can still find the carts
at two Burrard Street locations—between Robson Street and Smithe
Street and at the corner of West Pender Street—and another one near
Waterfront Station on West Cordova Street at Granville. ⑤ *Average
main: C$6* ✉ *530 Robson St., Downtown, Vancouver* ☎ *604/569–1158*
⊕ *www.japadog.com* ▭ *No credit cards* ✛ *E4.*

$ ✕**Sciué.** Inspired by the street foods of Rome, this cafeteria-style Ital-
CAFÉ ian bakery–café (Sciué is pronounced "Shoe-eh") starts the day serving
espresso and pastries, then moves to panini, soups, and pastas. One spe-
cialty is the *pane romano*, essentially a thick-crust pizza, sold by weight.
There can be lines out the door at lunch, so try to visit early or late.
(Not *too* late, though, as it's only open until 6 pm on weekdays, 4 pm
on Saturday, and 3 pm Sunday.) There are two additional Downtown
branches open weekdays only till 5 pm (*1115 Melville* and *885 West
Georgia*), and if you're in Yaletown, look for the location at 126 Davie
Street. ⑤ *Average main: C$10* ✉ *110–800 W. Pender St., Downtown,
Vancouver* ☎ *604/602–7263* ⊕ *www.sciue.ca* ⊗ *No dinner* ⌱ *Reserva-
tions not accepted* ✛ *F3.*

WEST END

$$ ✕**Kingyo.** Behind its ornate wooden door, this *izakaya* occupies the
JAPANESE stylish end of the spectrum, with a carved wood bar, lots of greenery,
and sexy mood lighting, though the vibe is still casual. The intriguing
Japanese small plates, from salmon carpaccio to grilled miso-marinated
pork cheeks to the spicy *tako-wasabi* (octopus), are delicious, and the
vibe is bustling and fun. To drink, choose from several varieties of *sho-
chu* (Japanese vodka) or sake. ⑤ *Average main: C$13* ✉ *871 Denman
St., West End, Vancouver* ☎ *604/608–1677* ⊕ *www.kingyo-izakaya.ca*
▭ *No credit cards* ✛ *B2.*

19

Burrard Inlet

Coal Harbor Rd.

W. Hastings St.

W. Pender St.

Caffè Artigiano

Thurlow St.

Burrard St.

CANADA PLACE

Canada Place Way

Pan-Pacific Hotel

Fairmont Waterfront

SINCLAIR CENTRE

Waterfront

W. Cordova St.

WATERFRONT STATION

Coal Harbour Rd.

Portside Park

GASTOWN

Water St.

Alexander St.

E. Powell St.

W. Pender St.

Sciué

Burrard

Hornby St.

Fairmont Hotel Vancouver

Hawksworth Restaurant
Rosewood Hotel Georgia

Granville

W. Hastings St.

Richards St.

Homer St.

Cordova St.

Nuba

Cambie St.

Meat & Bread

Abbott St.

Hastings St.

Pidgin

Columbia St.

Main St.

Gore Ave.

Wedgewood Hotel and Spa

Vancouver City Centre

Dunsmuir St.

Pender St.

Carrall St.

CHINATOWN

Howe St.

Café Medina

Granville St.

Seymour St.

Japadog

L'Hermitage Hotel

W. Georgia St.

Stadium

Bao Bei

Keefer St.

Nelson St.

Smithe St.

Hamilton St.

Robson St.

Cambie St.

Hotel Blu

Union St.

Columbia St.

Main St.

YALETOWN

Beatty St.

Georgia St.

Blue Water Cafe & Raw Bar

Expo Blvd.

Pacific Blvd. South

Hamilton St.

Opus Vacouver Hotel

Yaletown-Roundhouse

Marinaside Ct.

Cambie St. Bridge

False Creek

Creek

Main Street

The Acorn
Tojo's

Olympic Village

STANLEY PARK

$$$
CANADIAN

✕ **The Teahouse in Stanley Park.** The former officers' mess at Ferguson Point in Stanley Park is a prime location for water views by day, and for watching sunsets at dusk. The Pacific Northwest menu is not especially innovative but its broad appeal will please those looking for Haida Gwaii halibut, rack of lamb, steaks, and a host of other options, including gluten-free pasta. Lunch menus include burgers, pizzas, and salads. Various tasting boards—charcuterie, cheese, seafood, and vegetarian options—make for good grazing in the afternoon. In summer you can dine on the patio. ⑤ *Average main: C$25* ✉ *7501 Stanley Park Dr., Stanley Park, Vancouver* ☎ *604/669–3281* ⊕ *www.vancouverdine.com* ✦ *A1.*

GASTOWN AND CHINATOWN

GASTOWN

$
DELI

✕ **Meat & Bread.** Like the name, the concept at this trendy sandwich shop is simple. You wait in line (there's nearly always a queue) and choose from the short daily menu of sandwiches. The rich and crispy house-made porcetta (Italian-style roast pork) with salsa verde on a freshly baked ciabatta bun is a must-try. Add a cup of soup, if you want, and a drink, then find a spot at the counter or the long communal table. Who knew simplicity could taste so good? A second weekday-only location at 1033 West Pender Street satiates sandwich enthusiasts Downtown. Neither location is open for dinner. ⑤ *Average main: C$8* ✉ *370 Cambie St., Gastown, Vancouver* ☎ *604/566–9003* ☾ *Closed Sun. No dinner* ⌕ *Reservations not accepted* ✦ *G3.*

$
MIDDLE EASTERN

✕ **Nuba.** You can make a meal of *meze* —appetizers like falafel, tabbouleh, or crispy cauliflower served with tahini—at this subterranean Lebanese restaurant. But if you're looking for something heartier, try a plate of *mjadra*, a spicy mix of lentils and rice. The kitchen serves roast chicken glazed with honey and red pepper, lamb kebabs, and other meat dishes but much of the menu is vegetarian friendly. The Kitsilano branch (*3116 West Broadway*) is a full-service restaurant, while other locations—1206 Seymour Street Downtown and 146 East 3rd Avenue in the Main Street neighborhood—just have a smaller, quick-serve menu. ⑤ *Average main: C$11* ✉ *207B W. Hastings St., Gastown, Vancouver* ☎ *604/668–1655* ⊕ *www.nuba.ca* ☾ *No lunch Sun.* ⌕ *Reservations not accepted* ✦ *G3.*

$$
ASIAN FUSION
Fodor's Choice
★

✕ **Pidgin.** Enter this glossy white space with an appetite for adventure. Chef Makoto Ono draws inspiration from Asia for his inventive sharing plates that are some of Vancouver's most exciting eating options. From the ever-changing menu, you might choose spicy shishito peppers topped with Parmesan and pine nuts, raw scallops, and daikon radish sauced with pomegranate red curry oil, or a Chinese-style "dan dan" noodle salad with shaved rutabega or turnip standing in for the pasta. Sake or one of the house-made cocktails—perhaps the Idle Hands, which blends pisco, lime juice, vanilla sugar, and kaffir lime leaf, or the De Capo Negroni (gin, vermouth, and campari, with a coffee ice ball)—stand up well to the bold food flavors. ⑤ *Average main:*

15 ✉ 350 Carrall St., Gastown, Vancouver ☎ 604/620–9400 ⊕ www. pidginvancouver.com ⊗ No lunch ✛ H3.

CHINATOWN

$$ ✕ **Bao Bei.** Start with an eclectic Chinatown storefront, stir in funky Asian-
CHINESE flavored cocktails, then add a creative take on traditional Chinese dishes, and the result is this hip and happening hangout. Start with a drink—perhaps a Guizhou Donkey (lemongrass-infused shochu, almond syrup, lime, and ginger beer) or a Cheung Po the Kid (rum, Dubonnet, pomegranate molasses, and housemade Chinese plum bitters). Then load up your table with nibbles like Chinese pickles and truffled pork dumplings or tapas-size dishes like *shao bing* (sesame flatbread with cumin-scented lamb, pickled red onion, cilantro, and chilis), *mantou* (steamed buns stuffed with pork belly and preserved turnip), or a salad of wok-charred octopus, mustard root gnocchi, greens, and pickled butternut squash. Old Chinatown may have been tasty, but it never cooked up anything this fun. ⑤ *Average main: C$15* ✉ *163 Keefer St., Chinatown, Vancouver* ☎ *604/688–0876* ⊕ *www.bao-bei.ca* ▭ *No credit cards* ⊗ *Closed Mon. No lunch* ⌙ *Reservations not accepted* ✛ *H4.*

YALETOWN

$$$$ ✕ **Blue Water Cafe & Raw Bar.** Executive chef Frank Pabst focuses his
SEAFOOD menu on both popular and lesser-known local seafood (including frequently overlooked varieties like mackerel or herring) at his fashionable fish restaurant. You might start with Gulf Island swimming scallops in a tomato and caper relish; Dungeness crab salad with baby shrimps, mango, and jicama; or a seafood tower, ideal for sharing. Main dishes are seafood-centric, too—perhaps sturgeon with a cauliflower purée and golden beets, or Arctic char with trout caviar and pearl couscous. Ask the staff to recommend wine pairings from the BC–focused list. You can dine in the warmly lit interior or outside on the former loading dock that's now a lovely terrace. The sushi chef turns out both classic and new creations—they're pricey but among the city's best. ⑤ *Average main: C$35* ✉ *1095 Hamilton St., Yaletown, Vancouver* ☎ *604/688–8078* ⊕ *www.bluewatercafe.net* ⊗ *No lunch* ✛ *E5.*

19

GRANVILLE ISLAND

$$$ ✕ **Edible Canada Bistro.** Looking for a sit-down meal while exploring
MODERN Granville Island? At this contemporary bistro with a patio for people-
CANADIAN watching, you can sample foods from BC and across Canada. Smaller appetites might gravitate toward the kale salad with lentils and summer vegetables, or the heirloom tomato gazpacho served with halibut ceviche. Hungrier travelers can sup on pea and ricotta ravioli with wild greens, Haida Gwaii salmon with fried artichoke, or steak with duck-fat fries. The adjacent retail store sells regional jams, chocolates, and other treats to take home. ⑤ *Average main: C$24* ✉ *1596 Johnston St., Granville Island, Vancouver* ☎ *604/682–6681* ✛ *C6.*

THE WEST SIDE

KITSILANO

$
CAFÉ

✕ **Bean Around the World.** This local minichain, of the "Fuelled by Caffeine" slogan, runs a number of comfortable coffeehouses around town. If you like your cappuccino with no pretension (and perhaps with a muffin or slice of banana bread), head for "The Bean." In addition to this branch near Kitsilano Beach, their many Vancouver locations include 175 West Hastings Street (at Cambie) in Gastown, 1002 Mainland Street in Yaletown, 2977 Granville Street in South Granville, and on Main Street at No. 2528 and No. 3598. ⑤ *Average main: C$4* ✉ *1945 Cornwall Ave., Kitsilano, Vancouver* ☎ *604/739–1069* ⊕ *www. batw.ca* 🖃 *No credit cards* ✛ *A6.*

$$$$
MODERN
CANADIAN
Fodor'sChoice
★

✕ **Bishop's.** Before "local" and "seasonal" were all the rage, this highly regarded restaurant was serving West Coast cuisine with an emphasis on organic regional produce. Menu highlights include starters like smoked salmon with chickpea blini and horseradish crème fraîche, while BC lingcod with bacon, kale, and black truffle sabayon, and locally raised rack of lamb are among the tasty main dishes. All are expertly presented and impeccably served with suggestions from Bishop's extensive local wine list. The split-level room displays elaborate flower arrangements and selections from owner John Bishop's art collection. ⑤ *Average main: C$38* ✉ *2183 W. 4th Ave., Kitsilano, Vancouver* ☎ *604/738–2025* ⊕ *www.bishopsonline.com* ⊘ *Closed Mon. No lunch* ✛ *A6.*

$$$
MODERN
CANADIAN

✕ **Fable.** The name doesn't have to do with fairy tales: it's about "farm to table," which encapsulates the philosophy of this bustling Kitsilano bistro. The idea is creative comfort food, and while the menu looks straightforward—steelhead trout, roast chicken, steak frites—it's full of surprising plot twists. The "Spaghetti and Meat Balls" turns out to be tagliatelle topped with a single oversized duck meatball that spills out the sauce when you cut into it, while pork loin might come with cracklings and a black pudding sauce. The moral? Don't judge this always-entertaining book by its cover (and order dessert when the lemon meringue parfait is on offer). ⑤ *Average main: C$24* ✉ *1944 W. 4th St., Kitsilano, Vancouver* ☎ *604/732–1322* ⊕ *www.fablekitchen. ca* ✛ *A6.*

$
SEAFOOD

✕ **Go Fish.** If the weather's fine, head for this seafood stand on the seawall overlooking the docks beside Granville Island. The menu is short—highlights include fish-and-chips, grilled salmon or tuna sandwiches, and fish tacos—but the quality is first-rate. It's hugely popular, and on sunny summer days the waits can be maddening, so try to avoid the busiest times: noon to 2 pm and 5 pm to closing (which is at dusk). Since there are just a few outdoor tables, be prepared to take your food to go. ⑤ *Average main: C$10* ✉ *Fisherman's Wharf, 1505 W. 1st Ave., Kitsilano, Vancouver* ☎ *604/730–5040* ⊕ *www.bin941.com* ⊘ *Closed Mon. No dinner* ✛ *A6.*

$$
THAI
Fodor'sChoice
★

✕ **Maenam.** Chef Angus An's modern Thai menu brings this Asian cuisine to a new level. Although some of his dishes may sound familiar—green papaya salad, pad thai, curries—they're amped up with local ingredients, fresh herbs, and vibrant seasonings. Look for delicious innovations, too: perhaps crispy BC oysters, a duck confit salad with fried shallots and lychees, or the "eight-spice fish" that balances sweet, salty, and sour flavors. The bar sends out equally exotic cocktails, such as the Rumgari Geng (dark rum infused with coriander seed and mace, tamarind, Thai tea and Drambuie). The sleek dining room is stylish enough that you could dress up a bit, but you wouldn't be out of place in jeans. $\boxed{\$}$ *Average main: C$18 $\boxtimes$ 1938 W. 4th Ave., Kitsilano, Vancouver* ☎ *604/730–5579* ⊕ *www.maenam.ca* ⊗ *No lunch Sun. and Mon.* ✛ *A6.*

SOUTH GRANVILLE

$$$
MODERN
CANADIAN
Fodor'sChoice
★

✕ **Farmer's Apprentice.** Book ahead to nab one of the 30 or so seats in this cozy bistro, where chef-owner David Gunawan and his team in the open kitchen craft wildly creative "vegetable forward" small plates. It's not a vegetarian restaurant, but fresh local produce plays starring roles in such dishes as heirloom tomatoes paired with shiso, shinjuku flower, and pistachios, or zucchini with blackberries, ricotta, and granola. Seafood stars, too; look for creations like smoked octopus with cherries and puffed quinoa, or a Dungeness crab, kohlrabi, and tomatillo gazpacho. Once these exotic sharing plates hit your table, you'll forget all about the cramped seating. If you don't fancy a glass of wine or a cocktail like the Smoked Martinez (smoked gin, vermouth, maraschino, and orange bitters), opt for a glass of their house-brewed kombucha. Reservations aren't accepted for lunch or brunch, but they're essential for dinner. $\boxed{\$}$ *Average main: C$22 $\boxtimes$ 1535 W. 6th Ave., South Granville, Vancouver* ☎ *604/620–2070* ⊕ *www.farmersapprentice.ca* ⊗ *Closed Mon.* ✛ *A6.*

$$$
INDIAN

✕ **Vij's.** Long lauded as Vancouver's most innovative Indian restaurant, this South Granville dining destination, run by genial proprietor Vikram Vij and his wife Meeru Dhalwala, uses local ingredients to create exciting takes on South Asian cuisine. Dishes such as lamb "popsicles" in a creamy curry, BC ruby trout served with a wheat berry pilaf, or vegetables sautéed with *kalonji* (nigella seeds, also known as black cumin) and black chickpeas are far from traditional but are beautifully executed. Mr. Vij frequently circulates through the room, which is decorated with Indian antiques and whimsical elephant-pattern lanterns, greeting guests and suggesting dishes or cocktail pairings. Expect to cool your heels at the bar sipping chai or a cold beer while you wait an hour or more for a table, but if you like creative Indian fare, it's worth it. At this writing, the restaurant is expected to move to a new location at 3128 Cambie St., keeping the same general concept and menu. Check before you go. $\boxed{\$}$ *Average main: C$27 $\boxtimes$ 1480 W. 11th Ave., South Granville, Vancouver* ☎ *604/736–6664* ⊕ *www.vijs.ca* ⊗ *No lunch* ⌁ *Reservations not accepted* ✛ *B6.*

19

$$$$
MODERN
CANADIAN
Fodor'sChoice
★

✕ **West.** Contemporary regional cuisine is the theme at this chic restaurant, one of the city's most splurge-worthy dining rooms. Among executive chef Quang Dang's creations are butter-poached lobster and potato gnocchi in a thyme emulsion, Haida Gwaii sablefish in a three-vinegar glaze, and venison roasted in brown butter and served with an arugula bread salad. If you can't decide, opt for one of the elaborate multicourse tasting menus (C$68–C$95), which include vegetarian, seafood, and meat options. The decadent desserts might include a chocolate-caramel ice-cream cake with salty-sweet almonds or a blueberry crepe filled with lemon pound cake and topped with apricot-elderflower sorbet. Marble floors, high ceilings, and a wall of wine make the space feel simultaneously energetic and cozy. Ⓢ *Average main: C$36* ✉ *2881 Granville St., South Granville, Vancouver* ☎ *604/738–8938* ⊕ *www. westrestaurant.com* ⊹ *B6.*

CAMBIE CORRIDOR

$$$$
JAPANESE
Fodor'sChoice
★

✕ **Tojo's.** Hidekazu Tojo is a sushi-making legend in Vancouver, with thousands of special preparations stored in his creative mind. In this bright modern, high-ceilinged space, complete with a separate sake lounge, the prime perch is at the sushi bar, a convivial ringside seat for watching the creation of edible art. The best way to experience Tojo's creativity is to order *omakase* (chef's choice); the chef will keep offering you wildly adventurous fare, both raw and cooked, until you cry uncle. Budget a minimum of C$80 per person (before drinks) for five courses; tabs topping C$120 per person for six courses or more are routine. Ⓢ *Average main: C$35* ✉ *1133 W. Broadway, Cambie Corridor, Vancouver* ☎ *604/872–8050* ⊕ *www.tojos.com* ⊙ *Closed Sun. No lunch* ⌲ *Reservations essential* ⊹ *F6.*

THE EAST SIDE

MAIN STREET

$$
VEGETARIAN

✕ **The Acorn.** Vancouver's first upscale vegetarian dining room, this barely-bigger-than-an-acorn restaurant serves imaginative plant-based fare that does its vegetables proud. Look for dishes like "linguini" made from raw zucchini and dressed with a mint-walnut pesto; kale Caesar salad with tempeh, olives, and smoked paprika croutons; and pickled beech mushrooms with a cashew herb mousse. Many menu items are vegan, raw, or gluten-free. If you have to wait for a table, pass the time with one of their signature cocktails; the Anniversaire blends gin and cava with a lemon verbena and lavender syrup, while the Old Norse combines Akvavit (from Vancouver's Long Table Distillery) with elderflower liqueur, a house-made tonic syrup, lime juice, and salt bitters. Ⓢ *Average main: C$16* ✉ *3995 Main St., Main St./Mt. Pleasant, Vancouver* ☎ *604/566–9001* ⊕ *www.theacornrestaurant.ca* ⊙ *Closed Mon. No lunch* ⌲ *Reservations not accepted* ⊹ *F6.*

WHERE TO STAY

Vancouver is a pretty compact city, but each neighborhood has a distinct character and its own style of accommodations options. From hip boutique hotels to historic bed-and-breakfasts to sharp-angled glass-and-mirror towers, there are lodging choices for every style and budget. You can choose to be in the center of the shopping action on Robson Street, among the gracious tree-lined boulevards near Stanley Park, or in close proximity to the pulsing heart of the city's core.

WHAT DOES IT COST?

Most hotels let children under 18 stay free in their parents' room, though you may be charged extra for more than two adults. Parking runs about C$25 to C$40 per day at Downtown hotels, and can be free outside the Downtown core. Watch out for phone and Internet charges, which can add up. You'll also be charged a 1.5% accommodations tax, a 10% Provincial Sales Tax (PST), and a 5% Goods and Services Tax (GST) for a total levy of 16.5%.

WHAT IT COSTS IN CANADIAN DOLLARS			
$	$$	$$$	$$$$
Hotels Under C$125	C$125–C$195	C$196–C$300	Over C$300

Prices in the reviews are the lowest cost of a standard double room in high season.

HOTEL REVIEWS

Hotels are listed alphabetically within neighborhoods. Use the coordinate at the end of each listing (✛ B2) to locate a property on the Where to Stay in Vancouver map.

Hotel reviews have been shortened. For full information, visit Fodors.com.

DOWNTOWN AND THE WEST END
DOWNTOWN

$$$$
HOTEL
Fairmont Hotel Vancouver. The copper roof of this 1939 château-style hotel dominates Vancouver's skyline, and the elegantly restored hotel is considered the city's gracious grande dame. **Pros:** full-service spa; great location for shopping; stunning architecture. **Cons:** "standard" room sizes vary greatly; pricey parking. ⑤ *Rooms from: C$365* ✉ *900 W. Georgia St., Downtown, Vancouver* ☎ *604/684–3131* ⊕ *www.fairmont.com/hotelvancouver* ⌁ *556 rooms, 37 suites* ⦿*No meals* ✛ *E3.*

$$$$
HOTEL
Fodor's Choice
★
Fairmont Waterfront. Stunning views of the harbor, mountains, and Stanley Park from the floor-to-ceiling windows of the guest rooms are one of the highlights of this luxuriously modern 23-story hotel across the street from Vancouver's cruise-ship terminal. **Pros:** harbor views; proximity to the waterfront; inviting pool terrace. **Cons:** long elevator queues; busy lobby lounge. ⑤ *Rooms from: C$499* ✉ *900 Canada Pl. Way, Downtown, Vancouver* ☎ *604/540–4509* ⊕ *www.fairmont.com/waterfront* ⌁ *489 rooms, 29 suites* ⦿*No meals* ✛ *F2.*

$$$
HOTEL
L'Hermitage Hotel. Get beyond the marble floors, silk and velvet walls, and gold-cushion benches in the lobby and you'll discover a warm residential character at this boutique hotel. **Pros:** uptown hotel with a refreshingly residential vibe; excellent concierge; valet parking. **Cons:** in the heart of Downtown bustle; one-way streets can make driving to the hotel frustrating. ⑤ *Rooms from: C$255* ✉ *788 Richards St., Downtown, Vancouver* ☎ *778/327–4100, 888/855–1050* ⊕ *www.lhermitagevancouver.com* ⌁ *40 rooms, 20 suites* ⦿*No meals* ✛ *F4.*

19

$$$$ **HOTEL**   **Pan Pacific Vancouver.** Located in the waterfront Canada Place complex, the sophisticated Pan Pacific has easy access to the city's convention center and the main cruise-ship terminal. **Pros:** lovely harbor views; staff has a "go the extra mile" attitude. **Cons:** atrium is open to the convention center, so it's often full of business executives talking shop; lobby ambience not very welcoming. $ *Rooms from: C$369* ✉ *999 Canada Pl., Downtown, Vancouver* ☎ *604/662–8111, 800/663–1515 in Canada, 800/937–1515 in U.S.* ⊕ *www.panpacificvancouver.com* ➘ *465 rooms, 39 suites* ¶○¶ *No meals* ✛ *F2.*

Fodor'sChoice
★

$$$$ **HOTEL**   **Rosewood Hotel Georgia.** One of Vancouver's newest hotels, the classy Rosewood is also one of the city's most historic properties: the 1927 Georgian Revival building once welcomed such prestigious guests as Elvis Presley and Katharine Hepburn. **Pros:** at the center of the city's action; top-rated spa; iconic restaurant. **Cons:** expensive valet parking; restaurant can get very busy. $ *Rooms from: C$425* ✉ *801 W. Georgia St., Downtown, Vancouver* ☎ *604/682–5566* ⊕ *www.rosewoodhotels. com/en/hotelgeorgia* ➘ *156 rooms* ¶○¶ *No meals* ✛ *E3.*

Fodor'sChoice
★

$$$$ **HOTEL**   **Shangri-La Hotel.** On the first 15 floors of the tallest building in Vancouver—a 61-story tower of angled glass studded with gold squares that glint in the sunshine—is this upscale Asian chain's first hotel in North America (the second is in Toronto). **Pros:** first-rate concierge service; not as expensive as you might think; central location. **Cons:** public areas could be more inviting; on the city's busiest thoroughfare. $ *Rooms from: C$395* ✉ *1128 W. Georgia St., Downtown, Vancouver* ☎ *604/689–1120* ⊕ *www.shangri-la.com* ➘ *81 rooms, 38 suites* ¶○¶ *No meals* ✛ *D2.*

Fodor'sChoice
★

$$$$ **HOTEL**   **Wedgewood Hotel and Spa.** A member of the exclusive Relais & Châteaux Group, the lavish, family-owned Wedgewood is all about pampering. **Pros:** personalized service; great location close to shops; Bacchus lounge is a destination in its own right. **Cons:** small size means it books up quickly. $ *Rooms from: C$365* ✉ *845 Hornby St., Downtown, Vancouver* ☎ *604/689–7777, 800/663–0666* ⊕ *www.wedgewoodhotel. com* ➘ *41 rooms, 43 suites* ¶○¶ *No meals* ✛ *E3.*

Fodor'sChoice
★

WEST END

$$$ **HOTEL**   **Sylvia Hotel.** This Virginia-creeper-covered 1912 heritage building is continually popular because of its affordable rates and near-perfect location: a stone's throw from the beach on scenic English Bay, two blocks from Stanley Park, and a 20-minute walk from Robson Street. **Pros:** beachfront location; close to restaurants; a good place to mingle with the locals. **Cons:** older building; parking can be difficult; walk to Downtown is slightly uphill. $ *Rooms from: C$199* ✉ *1154 Gilford St., West End, Vancouver* ☎ *604/681–9321* ⊕ *www.sylviahotel.com* ➘ *97 rooms, 22 suites* ¶○¶ *No meals* ✛ *B2.*

Fodor'sChoice
★

$$$ **HOTEL**   **Times Square Suites Hotel.** You can't get much closer to Stanley Park than this chic but understated all-suites hotel near plenty of restaurants. **Pros:** next to Stanley Park; good location for restaurants; roof deck for guest use. **Cons:** no concierge; on a very busy intersection. $ *Rooms from: C$279* ✉ *1821 Robson St., West End, Vancouver* ☎ *604/684–2223, 877/684–2223* ⊕ *www.timessquaresuites.com* ➘ *42 rooms* ¶○¶ *No meals* ✛ *C1.*

Fodor'sChoice
★

YALETOWN

$$$ **Hotel Blu.** A designer blend of comfort, high-tech, and, especially,
HOTEL   eco-friendly features, Hotel Blu could almost be called "Hotel Green"
because of the focus on sustainability. **Pros:** close to theaters and sports
arenas; free guest laundry; indoor pool and sauna. **Cons:** only suites and
lofts have bathtubs; sports crowds swarm the neighborhood on event
days. Ⓢ *Rooms from: C$275* ✉ *177 Robson St., Yaletown, Vancouver*
☎ *604/620-6200* ⊕ *www.hotelbluvancouver.com* ⤢ *75 rooms* ❘◎❘ *No
meals* ✛ *F4.*

$$$$ **Opus Vancouver Hotel.** Groundbreakingly trendy when it opened in
HOTEL   2002, the Opus continues to reinvent itself and live up to the motto of
Fodor'sChoice   being a "place to be not just a place to stay." The design team created
★   a set of online fictitious characters, then decorated the rooms to suit
each "persona." Guests are matched with room styles using the Life-
style Concierge. **Pros:** great Yaletown location, right by rapid transit;
funky and hip vibe; the lobby bar is a fashionable meeting spot. **Cons:**
trendy nightspots nearby can be noisy at night; expensive and limited
parking. Ⓢ *Rooms from: C$359* ✉ *322 Davie St., Yaletown, Vancouver*
☎ *604/642–6787, 866/642–6787* ⊕ *www.opushotel.com* ⤢ *85 rooms,
11 suites* ❘◎❘ *No meals* ✛ *E5.*

WEST SIDE
KITSILANO

$$ **Corkscrew Inn.** This restored 1912 Craftsman-style house near the
B&B/INN   beach in Kitsilano combines the comforts of a B&B with a quirky trib-
Fodor'sChoice   ute to the humble corkscrew: guests are encouraged to explore the small
★   wine paraphernalia museum. **Pros:** great local neighborhood; delicious
breakfast. **Cons:** not Downtown; a 15-minute bus ride to the Canada
Line airport connection. Ⓢ *Rooms from: C$180* ✉ *2735 West 2nd
Ave., Kitsilano, Vancouver* ☎ *604/733–7276, 877/737–7276* ⊕ *www.
corkscrewinn.com* ⤢ *5 rooms* ❘◎❘ *Breakfast* ✛ *A6.*

NIGHTLIFE

19

Vancouver might be best-known for its outdoors activities but this hip
city delivers plenty of entertainment once the sun goes down. Look for
modern craft breweries, wine bars showcasing wines from the nearby
Okanagan Valley, and some excellent music venues.

NIGHTLIFE

DOWNTOWN AND THE WEST END
DOWNTOWN

Bacchus. Always an elegant choice, the lounge at Bacchus, in the Wedgewood Hotel, is a gathering place for Vancouver's movers and shakers.
There's music every evening, as well as classic cocktails. ✉ *Wedgewood Hotel, 845 Hornby St., Downtown, Vancouver* ☎ *604/608–5319*
⊕ *www.wedgewoodhotel.com.*

Fodor'sChoice   **Tap & Barrel.** The 360-degree views from this convention center patio
★   take in Stanley Park, the seaplane terminal, and the North Shore Mountains. You can sit inside, amid the wooden casks of wine, but waiting

for a seat on the deck is worth it if the weather even hints at sunshine. There's another location—and similarly large patio—on False Creek (*1 Athlete's Way*). ⊠ *1055 Canada Place, Downtown, Vancouver* ☎ *604/235–9827* ⊕ *www.tapandbarrel.com.*

Uva Wine Bar. At street level in the century-old Moda Hotel, Uva puts a modern spin on the Italian wine bar concept, with bold decor and sleek furnishings. The well-dressed crowd comes for the not-too-wild atmosphere, often for a drink before heading to one of nearby Granville Street's performance venues. ⊠ *Moda Hotel, 900 Seymour St., Downtown, Vancouver* ☎ *604/632–9560* ⊕ *www.uvavancouver.com.*

Commodore Ballroom. This 1929 dance hall has been restored to its art deco glory, complete with massive dance floor and state-of-the-art sound system. Indie rock bands and renowned DJs play here most nights. ⊠ *868 Granville St., Downtown, Vancouver* ☎ *604/739–4550, 855/985–5000 Tickets* ⊕ *www.commodoreballroom.com.*

GASTOWN AND CHINATOWN

GASTOWN

BARS

Alibi Room. If beer is your thing, head to Alibi, which specializes in pairing beer with your meal. Kegs of microbrews from around BC and beyond are the pride and joy here and it's known for having one of the best selections of craft beers in Vancouver. There are are also organic wines and a few fun cocktails if you're not feeling beer-inclined. ⊠ *157 Alexander St., Gastown, Vancouver* ☎ *604/623–3383* ⊕ *www.alibi.ca.*

Fodor'sChoice ★ **The Portside Pub.** Nautical kitsch and a friendly maritimer bent woo many a land lover to the Portside Pub. Live bands, weekend DJs, and whiskey on tap handily turn the two-level bar into a packed venue. Pub eats are above par, but lineups start early. ⊠ *7 Alexander St., Gastown, Vancouver* ☎ *604/559–6333* ⊕ *www.theportsidepub.com.*

CHINATOWN

BARS

Fodor'sChoice ★ **The Keefer Bar.** The Keefer Bar has fully capitalized on its Chinatown connection, using ingredients sourced from local herbalists (seahorse tincture anyone?), kombucha, oolong tea syrup, or lychee, for example. Small plates of Asian dishes make good nibbling. The decor is dark and red, with hanging cylindrical neon lights. There's usually a well-attended, weekly burlesque night. ⊠ *135 Keefer St., Chinatown, Vancouver* ☎ *604/688–1961* ⊕ *www.thekeeferbar.com.*

YALETOWN

BARS

Opus Bar. Traveling executives in suits and film industry creatives sip martinis (or perhaps a cocktail made with bourbon and blood oranges) while scoping out the room, on the ground floor of the Opus Hotel. ⊠ *Opus Hotel, 350 Davie St., Yaletown, Vancouver* ☎ *604/642–0557* ⊕ *www.opusbar.ca.*

Yaletown Brewing Company. In a renovated warehouse with a glassed-in brewery turning out several tasty beers, this always-crowded gastropub and patio has a lively singles scene. Even though it's super popular it still feels like a neighborhood place. ✉ *1111 Mainland St., Yaletown, Vancouver* ☎ *604/681–2739* ⊕ *www.mjg.ca/yaletown*.

GRANVILLE ISLAND

BARS

Dockside Restaurant. Overlooking False Creek, Yaletown, and the North Shore Mountains, the Dockside's patio is the big draw, especially for owners of chic yachts moored alongside. Because it faces east, sunsets are behind the building and cool shadows come early, so grab a table beneath a heater. Floor-to-ceiling windows make the inside feel like the outside with decor that exudes a modern vibe and includes a 50-foot aquarium. House-brewed ales and lagers are served from the adjoining casual brewpub. ✉ *Granville Island Hotel, 1253 Johnston St., Granville Island, Vancouver* ☎ *604/685–7070* ⊕ *www.docksidevancouver.com*.

THE WEST SIDE

KITSILANO

BARS

Kits Beach Boathouse. A summer visit to Vancouver isn't complete without an afternoon enjoying cocktails on this rooftop patio overlooking sand-court volleyball matches at Kits Beach. At other times of the year, the views of the vivid sunsets and dramatic winter storms are exceptional, though you may want to retreat behind the floor-to-ceiling windows to sip in comfort. ✉ *1305 Arbutus St., Kitsilano, Vancouver* ☎ *604/738–5487* ⊕ *www.boathouserestaurants.ca/locations/#kitsilano*.

EAST SIDE

MAIN STREET

BARS

Cascade Room. Named after the signature beer the Vancouver Brewery once produced on this very spot, the Cascade Room is a usually busy Main Street lounge. The cocktail menu is lengthy, with a focus on classics. ✉ *2616 Main St., at Broadway, Main St./Mt. Pleasant, Vancouver* ☎ *604/709–8650* ⊕ *www.thecascade.ca*.

Craft Beer Market. The stats at this beer hall in the historic Salt Building are impressive: 140 draft beer taps, more than 10,000 feet of beer lines, 3500 BTUs of chilling power, and space for 450 kegs in the keg room (that's up to 26,000 litres or 6,900 gallons). And the food is good, too. It's now the flagship of Vancouver's new waterfront neighborhood that's risen from infrastructure built for the 2010 Winter Olympics. ✉ *85 West 1st Ave., Main St./Mt. Pleasant, Vancouver* ☎ *604/709–2337* ⊕ *vancouver.craftbeermarket.ca*.

19

SPORTS AND THE OUTDOORS

Blessed with a mild climate, fabulous natural setting, and excellent public-use facilities, Vancouverites, unsurprisingly, are an outdoorsy lot. The Downtown peninsula of Vancouver is entirely encircled by a seawall along which you can walk, in-line skate (which is still quite popular in Vancouver), cycle, or otherwise propel yourself for more than 22 km (13½ miles), with plenty of picturesque jumping on and off points.

You'll find rental equipment and tour operators in Vancouver for every imaginable outdoor activity, from tandem bikes for Stanley Park trails to stand-up paddleboards on Granville Island. Yoga studios seem to be around every corner and hiking trails materialize just at the end of the road. Hotel concierges can recommend the best wilderness trails just as easily as they can top sushi spots. To buy or rent gear, head to the Mountain Equipment Co-op, a local institution (⇨ *see Shopping*).

BEACHES

Greater Vancouver is well endowed with beaches but the waters are decidedly cool, with summer water temperatures ranging from 12 to 18°C (54 to 64°F). Aside from kids and the intrepid, most stick to quick dips, sunbathing, or wearing a wet suit for water activities.

English Bay Beach. The city's best-known beach, English Bay, lies just to the east of Stanley Park's southern entrance. A long stretch of golden sand, a waterslide, volleyball courts, kayak rentals, and food trucks keep things interesting all summer. Known locally for being gay-friendly, it draws a diverse crowd. **Amenities:** lifeguards; water sports; food and drink; toilets; parking (fee). **Best for:** fireworks; partiers; kayaking; swimming; walking; sunset. ⊠ *1700 Beach Ave., between Gilford and Bidwell Sts., West End, Vancouver* ☏ *604/665–3424* ⊕ *www. vancouver.ca/parks-recreation-culture/english-bay-beach.aspx.*

Fodor's Choice
★   **Kitsilano Beach.** West of the southern end of the Burrard Bridge, Kits Beach is the city's busiest beach—Frisbee tossers, beach volleyball players, and sleek young people are ever present. Facilities include a playground, restaurant, concession stand, and tennis courts. **Kitsilano Pool** is here: at 137.5 meters (451 feet), it's the longest pool in Canada and one of the few heated saltwater pools in the world (open May to September). Just steps from the sand, the Boathouse on Kits Beach serves lunch, dinner, and weekend brunch inside and on its big ocean-view deck. There's also a take-out concession at the same site. Inland from the pool, the Kitsilano Showboat, an outdoor amphitheater hosts music and dance performances during the summer. **Amenities:** food and drink; lifeguards; parking (fee); toilets. **Best for:** sunrise; sunset; swimming; walking. ⊠ *2305 Cornwall Ave., Kitsilano, Vancouver* ☏ *604/731–0011* ⊕ *www.vancouver.ca/parks-recreation-culture/kitsilano-beach.aspx.*

Spanish Banks Beaches. The **Spanish Banks** and **Locarno** beaches form a sandy chain, and have huge expanses of sunbathing sand backed by wide lawns full of picnic tables. There are also volleyball courts. The shallow water, warmed slightly by sun and sand, is good for swimming. Farther west along the coastline, toward the Spanish Banks Extension, the scene becomes less crowded. Spanish Banks West and Locarno beaches are designated "quiet beaches," which means that amplified music is prohibited. **Amenities:** water sports; food and drink; toilets; lifeguards; parking (free). **Best for:** swimming; walking; windsurfing. ⊠ *Northwest Marine Drive, at Tolmie Street, Point Grey, Vancouver* ⊕ *www.vancouver.ca/parks-recreation-culture/spanish-bank-beach.aspx.*

Fodor'sChoice ★ **Stanley Park Beaches.** There are two fine beaches accessed from Stanley Park, with other unnamed sandy spots dotted along the seawall. The most popular with families is **Second Beach,** which has a playground and large heated pool with slides. **Third Beach** is a little more removed than the other central beaches. It has a larger stretch of sand, fairly warm water, and unbeatable sunset views. It's a popular evening picnic spot. **Amenities:** lifeguards; toilets; food and drink; parking (fee). **Best for:** sunset; swimming; walking. ⊠ *7495 Stanley Park Dr., Stanley Park, Vancouver* ⊕ *www.vancouver.ca/parks-recreation-culture/third-beach.aspx.*

BIKING

Vancouver's most popular bike path is the 9-km (5½-mile) **Stanley Park Seawall,** which follows the park's perimeter, hugging the harbor along the way. The views of Lions Gate Bridge and the mountains to the north are breathtaking. The path connects at both ends with the city's longer seawall path, if you feel like making a day of it. Rent your bike near the entrance to Stanley Park, in the West End, as there are no rentals once you're inside the park.

For biking on city streets, Downtown Vancouver's "separated bike lanes" have made biking even easier—most bike lanes have a barrier between them and the traffic. Especially useful ones are along Hornby and Dunsmuir streets. These lanes are in addition to the city's many bikeways, identified by green bicycle signs. There are detailed maps and other information on the website operated by the City of Vancouver (⊕ *www.vancouver.ca/streets-transportation/biking-and-cyclists.aspx*). Cycling maps are also available from most bike shops and bike-rental outlets. Helmets are required by law, and a sturdy lock is essential.

Fodor'sChoice ★ **Seawall.** The paved bike paths of Vancouver's 22-km (13½-mile) seawall start Downtown at Canada Place, go around Stanley Park, and follow False Creek to Kitsilano. ⊠ *Downtown, Vancouver* ⊕ *www.vancouver.ca/parks-recreation-culture/seawall.aspx.*

BIKE RENTALS

Bayshore Bike Rentals. If you're starting your ride near Stanley Park, try this friendly store. It has a wide range of bikes as well as bike trailers for kids, and in-line skates. ⊠ *745 Denman St., West End, Vancouver* ☎ *604/688–2453* ⊕ *www.bayshorebikerentals.ca.*

Spokes Bicycle Rentals. Near Stanley Park, Spokes has a wide selection of mountain bikes, tandem bikes, and children's bikes. Everything from hourly to weekly rentals are available. Helmets, locks, and route maps are complimentary. ⊠ *1798 W. Georgia St., West End, Vancouver* ☎ *604/688–5141* ⊕ *www.spokesbicyclerentals.com.*

19

ECOTOURS AND WILDLIFE VIEWING

Given a temperate climate and forest, mountain, and marine environments teeming with life, it's no surprise that wildlife-watching is an important pastime and growing business in and around Vancouver.

Fodor'sChoice
★

Sewell's Marina. This marina near the protected waters of Howe Sound runs year-round, two-hour ecotours of the surrounding marine and coastal mountain habitat. Sightings range from swimming seals to soaring eagles. High-speed rigid inflatable hulls are used. They also offer guided and self-driven salmon-fishing charters in Howe Sound and to the mouths of the Capilano and Fraser rivers. ✉ *6409 Bay St., West Vancouver, Vancouver* ☎ *604/921–3474* ⊕ *www.sewellsmarina.com.*

Steveston Seabreeze Adventures. In April and early May thousands of male California sea lions settle on rocks near the mouth of the Fraser River to feed on the eulachon, a member of the smelt family. Seabreeze's sightseeing boats make the short trip into the estuary from Steveston, in Richmond—south of Vancouver. During the autumn bird migratory season, Seabreeze also ventures to the George C. Reifel Bird Sanctuary on Westham Island; summer means orca and occasional humpback whale sightings. They also operate fishing charters as far west as the Gulf Islands: the seven-passenger boats, with guides, cost C$1,000 on weekends, C$900 on weekdays. ✉ *12551 No. 1 Rd., Richmond* ☎ *604/272–7200* ⊕ *www.seabreezeadventures.ca.*

WHALE-WATCHING

Between April and October pods of orca whales migrate through the Strait of Georgia, near Vancouver. The area is also home to year-round pods of harbor seals, elephant seals, minke whales, porpoises, and a wealth of birdlife, inlcuding bald eagles. Other migrating whales include humpbacks and grays.

Prince of Whales. This established operator runs four-hour trips from Vancouver's Coal Harbour waterfront across the Strait of Georgia to Victoria, in season. ✉ *The Westin Bayshore, 1601 Bayshore Dr., West End, Vancouver* ☎ *888/383–4884* ⊕ *www.princeofwhales.com.*

Wild Whales Vancouver. Boats leave Granville Island in search of orca pods in the Strait of Georgia, often traveling as far as Victoria. Rates are C$135 for a three- to seven-hour trip in either an open or glass-domed boat (trip lengths depend on where the whales are hanging out on a particular day). Each boat leaves once daily, April through October, conditions permitting. ✉ *1806 Mast Tower Rd., Granville Island, Vancouver* ☎ *604/699–2011* ⊕ *www.whalesvancouver.ca.*

HIKING

With its expansive landscape of mountains, inlets, alpine lakes, and approachable glaciers, as well as low-lying rivers, hills, dikes, and meadows, southwestern British Columbia is a hiker's paradise. For easy walking and hiking, you can't beat Stanley Park in Downtown Vancouver but for more strenuous hiking, there are fabulous parks not far away. With their photo-worthy profile, the North Shore Mountains may appear benign, but this is a vast and rugged territory filled with natural pitfalls and occasionally hostile wildlife.

HIKING TRAILS

Fodor's Choice
★
FAMILY

Capilano River Trails. About 26 km (16 miles) of hiking trails explore in and around Capilano Canyon—where the Capilano River is flanked by old-growth forest. There is also a salmon hatchery that's open to the public. Trailheads are off Capilano Road in North Vancouver (near Capilano Suspension Bridge) and near Ambleside Beach. ⊠ *4500 Capilano Park Rd., North Vancouver, Vancouver* ☎ *604/224–5739.*

FAMILY **Grouse Grind.** Vancouver's most famous, or infamous, hiking route, the Grind, is a 2.9-km (1.8-mile) climb straight up 853 meters (2,799 feet) to the top of Grouse Mountain. Thousands do it annually, but climbers are advised to be very experienced and in excellent physical condition. The route is open daily during daylight hours, from spring through autumn (conditions permitting). Or you can take the Grouse Mountain Skyride to the top 365 days a year; a round-trip ticket is C$41.95. Hiking trails in the adjacent Lynn Headwaters Regional Park are accessible from the gondola, including **Goat Mountain Trail.** ⊠ *Grouse Mountain, 6400 Nancy Greene Way, North Vancouver, Vancouver* ☎ *604/980–9311* ⊕ *www.grousemountain.com.*

GUIDED HIKING TOURS

Novice hikers and serious walkers can join guided trips or do self-guided walks of varying approach and difficulty. **Grouse Mountain** hosts several daily "eco-walks" along easy, meandering paths, including a discussion of flora and fauna and a visit to the Refuge for Endangered Wildlife. They're free with admission to Grouse Mountain Skyride.

FAMILY **Stanley Park Ecology Centre.** A calendar of guided nature walks and discovery sessions is filled with fun, kid-friendly options. Despite its urban access, Stanley Park offers incredible wildlife diversity—from the namesake rodents in Beaver Lake to a rookery of great blue herons near the tennis courts. The organizaiton also operates the Stanley Park Nature House on the shores of Lost Lagoon. ⊠ *Alberni and Chilco Sts., Stanley Park, Vancouver* ✛ *Southeast corner of Lost Lagoon* ☎ *604/257–8544, 604/718–6522* ⊕ *www.stanleyparkecology.ca* 🖾 *Free.*

WINTER SPORTS

SKIING, SNOWBOARDING, SNOWSHOEING, AND SNOW-TUBING

Fodor's Choice
★

Cypress Mountain ski resort. Just 30 minutes from Downtown, the ski facilities at Cypress Mountain include six quad or double chairs, 53 downhill runs, and a vertical drop of 610 meters (2,001 feet). The resort has a snow-tubing area and snowshoe tours. This is also a major cross-country skiing area. Summer activities at Cypress Mountain include hiking, geocaching, wildlife viewing, and mountain biking. ⊠ *Cypress Provincial Park, Cypress Bowl Rd., West Vancouver, Vancouver* ☎ *604/926–5612* ⊕ *www.cypressmountain.com.*

FAMILY **Grouse Mountain ski resort.** A 15-minute excursion from Downtown Vancouver, the Skyride gondola takes skiers up to the ski resort on a slope

The hike up Grouse Mountain is no easy feat, but the views from the top, and from Goat Mountain, slightly farther up, are breathtaking. Or you can always take the Skyride gondola.

overlooking the city. The views are fine on a clear day, but at night they're spectacular, and the area is known for its night skiing. Facilities include two quad chairs, 26 skiing and snowboarding runs, and several all-level freestyle-terrain parks. There's a choice of upscale and casual dining in a handsome stone-and-timber lodge. Summer activities at Grouse Mountain include hiking, disc golf, zip-lining (in winter, too), and wildlife viewing. ⊠ *6400 Nancy Greene Way, North Vancouver, Vancouver* ☎ *604/980–9311, 604/986–6262 snow report* ⊕ *www. grousemountain.com.*

SKATING RINKS

FAMILY **Robson Square Ice Rink.** Rent skates and lace them up tight to enjoy this free ice-skating rink in the city center. It's the best of indoor and outdoor skating combined—with a triodesic glass dome covering the open-air rink. The season runs mid-November through February. ⊠ *800 Robson St., Downtown, Vancouver* ☎ *604/822–3333* ⊕ *www.robsonsquare.com* 💲 *Free.*

SHOPPING

Art galleries, ethnic markets, gourmet-food shops, and high-fashion boutiques abound in Vancouver. Shopping here is more unique than in many other North American cities because of the prevalence of Asian and First Nations influences in crafts, home furnishings, and foods. In the art scene, look for First Nations and other aboriginal art, from souvenir trinkets to stellar contemporary art; many galleries showcasing First Nations artists are in Gastown. Area artisans also create a variety of fine crafts, exhibiting and selling their wares at Granville Island galleries.

DOWNTOWN AND THE WEST END

DOWNTOWN

BOOKS

MacLeod's Books. One of the city's best antiquarian and used-book stores, this jam-packed shop is a treasure trove of titles from mainstream to wildly eclectic. ⊠ *455 W. Pender St., Downtown, Vancouver* ☎ *604/681–7654.*

CLOTHING: MEN'S AND WOMEN'S

Fodor'sChoice **Lululemon Athletica.** Power-yoga devotees, soccer moms, and anyone who
★ likes casual, comfy clothes covets the fashionable, well-constructed workout wear with the stylized "A" insignia from this Vancouver-based company. The stores also provide free drop-in yoga classes. In addition to this flagship location, there are several branches around town, including one at 2113 West 4th Avenue in Kitsilano. ⊠ *970 Robson St., Downtown, Vancouver* ☎ *604/681–3118* ⊕ *www.lululemon.com.*

DEPARTMENT STORES

Fodor'sChoice **Holt Renfrew.** This is Canada's ritziest department store name, a
★ swanky showcase for international high fashion and accessories for men and women. Think Prada, Dolce & Gabbana, and other designer labels. ⊠ *Pacific Centre, 737 Dunsmuir St., Downtown, Vancouver* ☎ *604/681–3121* ⊕ *www.holtrenfrew.com.*

Hudson's Bay. A Canadian institution (though it's now American-owned), the Bay was founded as part of the fur trade in the 17th century. There's a whole department selling the signature tri-color blankets and other Canadiana. On the lower level, the Topshop and Topman boutiques carry imports from the trendy British retailer. ⊠ *674 Granville St., at Georgia St., Downtown, Vancouver* ☎ *604/681–6211* ⊕ *www.thebay.com.*

OUTDOOR EQUIPMENT

Atmosphere. You can count on finding high-performance (and high-fashion) gear for hiking, camping, or just battling the rain at this chain of sporting goods stores. ⊠ *Pacific Centre, 777 Dunsmuir St., Downtown, Vancouver* ☎ *604/687–7668* ⊕ *www.atmosphere.ca.*

WEST END

CLOTHING: CHILDREN'S

FAMILY **Roots Kids.** Synonymous with outdoorsy Canadian style, this Canadian company's signature casual wear is also available in children's sizes. The kids store is just down the street from the Roots flagship store on Robson Street. ⊠ *1153 Robson St., West End, Vancouver* ☎ *604/684–8801* ⊕ *canada.roots.com.*

CLOTHING: MEN'S AND WOMEN'S

Fodor'sChoice **Roots.** For outdoorsy clothes that double as souvenirs (many sport
★ maple-leaf logos), check out these Canadian-made sweatshirts, leather jackets, and other comfy casuals. In addition to this Downtown flagship store, there are branches on South Granville Street and on West

19

4th Avenue in Kitsilano. ⊠ *1001 Robson St., West End, Vancouver* ☎ *604/683–4305* ⊕ *canada.roots.com.*

GASTOWN AND CHINATOWN

GASTOWN

ART AND ANTIQUES

Fodor'sChoice **Hill's Native Art.** This highly respected store has Vancouver's largest selec-
★ tion of First Nations art. The main floor is crammed with souvenirs, keepsakes, and high-quality pieces, including carvings, masks, and drums. If you think that's impressive, head upstairs for one-of-a-kind collector pieces and limited editions. ⊠ *165 Water St., Gastown, Vancouver* ☎ *604/685–4249* ⊕ *www.hills.ca.*

CLOTHING: MEN'S AND WOMEN'S

One of a Few. The clothing here, from local and international makers, may not be one of a kind, but as the name of this funky little shop attests, you won't see the designs at mass-market retailers either. ⊠ *354 Water St., Gastown, Vancouver* ☎ *604/605–0685* ⊕ *www.oneofafew.com.*

Fodor'sChoice **John Fluevog.** You might have seen John Fluevog shops in New York and
★ Los Angeles, but did you know that these funky shoes were created by a Vancouverite? The Gastown location is worth a look for the store itself, with its striking glass facade and soaring ceilings. There's another branch Downtown at 837 Granville Street. ⊠ *65 Water St., Gastown, Vancouver* ☎ *604/688–6228* ⊕ *www.fluevog.com.*

YALETOWN

CLOTHING: MEN'S AND WOMEN'S

Fine Finds Boutique. It's hard to predict what you'll find in this pretty little shop—it's a fun spot to browse for cute women's clothing, jewelry, and accessories. ⊠ *1014 Mainland St., Yaletown, Vancouver* ☎ *604/669–8325* ⊕ *www.finefindsboutique.com.*

GRANVILLE ISLAND

ART AND ANTIQUES

Circle Craft. This artist co-op sells finely crafted textiles, wood pieces, jewelry, ceramics, and glass works. Chosen by juried selection, the artists are all local to British Columbia and all their work must be made by hand. ⊠ *Net Loft, 1–1666 Johnston St., Granville Island, Vancouver* ☎ *604/669–8021* ⊕ *www.circlecraft.net.*

FOOD AND WINE

Artisan Sake Maker. You can learn all about sake (Japanese rice wine), and sample the locally made product, at Vancouver's own sake brewery. ⊠ *1339 Railspur Alley, Granville Island, Vancouver* ☎ *604/685–7253* ⊕ *www.artisansakemaker.com.*

Edible Canada. Opposite the Granville Island Public Market, this shop sells jams, sauces, chocolates, and hundreds of other edible items from around the province. It's a great place to find gifts for foodie friends.

✉ 1596 Johnston St., Granville Island, Vancouver ☎ 604/682–6675 ⊕ www.ediblecanada.com.

MARKETS

Fodor'sChoice
★
Granville Island Public Market. Locals and visitors alike crowd this indoor market that's part farm stand, part gourmet grocery, and part upscale food court. The stalls are packed with locally made sausages, exotic cheeses, just-caught fish, fresh produce, baked goods, and prepared foods from handmade fudge to frothy cappuccinos. This is definitely the place to come for lunch. If the sun is out, you can dine on your purchases out on the waterfront decks. The crowds can get crazy, though, so avoid weekends if possible (or come early). *✉ 1689 Johnston St., Granville Island, Vancouver ☎ 604/666–5784 ⊕ www.granvilleisland. com/public-market.*

THE WEST SIDE

KITSILANO

BOOKS

Fodor'sChoice
★
Barbara-Jo's Books to Cooks. Local-chef-turned-entrepreneur Barbara-Jo McIntosh spreads the good-food word with scores of cookbooks, including many by Vancouver- and BC–based chefs, as well as wine books, memoirs, and magazines. The store also hosts special events, recipe demos, and drop-in classes in its sparkling demonstration kitchen—they're a tasty way to explore local cuisine. *✉ 1740 W. 2nd Ave., Kitsilano, Vancouver ☎ 604/688–6755 ⊕ www.bookstocooks.com.*

Fodor'sChoice
★
FAMILY
Kidsbooks. The helpful staff at this cheery shop is happy to make recommendations about books appropriate for young people ranging from toddlers to teens. Choose from the many titles by Canadian authors—excellent for take-home gifts or on-the-road reading. *✉ 3083 W. Broadway, Kitsilano, Vancouver ☎ 604/738–5335 ⊕ www.kidsbooks.ca.*

Wanderlust. Travelers and armchair travelers love this shop, which feeds everyone's wanderlust. There are thousands of travel books and maps, as well as luggage, gear, and accessories. *✉ 1929 W. 4th Ave., Kitsilano, Vancouver ☎ 604/739–2182 ⊕ www.wanderlustore.com.*

FOOD

Chocolate Arts. Looking for a present for a chocolate lover? Check out the chocolates in First Nations motifs, specially designed by Robert Davidson, one of Canada's premier artists. This delicious shop and café, where you can refuel with a hot chocolate, some bonbons, or a handmade ice-cream bar, is a short walk from Granville Island. *✉ 1620 W. 3rd Ave., Kitsilano, Vancouver ☎ 604/739–0475, 877/739–0475 ⊕ www.chocolatearts.com.*

Fodor'sChoice
★
Les Amis du Fromage. If you love cheese, don't miss the mind-boggling array of selections from BC, the rest of Canada, and elsewhere at this shop of delicacies. The extremely knowledgeable mother-and-daughter owners, Alice and Allison Spurrell, and their staff encourage you to taste before you buy. Yum. The fromagerie is located between Granville Island and Kitsilano Beach—useful to keep in mind if you're assembling

19

a seaside picnic. ⊠ *1752 W. 2nd Ave., Kitsilano, Vancouver* ☎ *604/732–4218* ⊕ *www.buycheese.com.*

POINT GREY

Museum of Anthropology Gift Shop. This museum store carries an excellent selection of Northwest Coast jewelry, carvings, and prints, as well as books on First Nations history and culture. ⊠ *University of British Columbia, 6393 N.W. Marine Dr., Point Grey, Vancouver* ☎ *604/827–4810* ⊕ *www.moa.ubc.ca.*

THE EAST SIDE

MAIN ST./MOUNT PLEASANT

OUTDOOR EQUIPMENT

Fodor'sChoice **MEC (Mountain Equipment Co-op).** This warehouse-style store stocks a
★ good selection of high-performance clothing and equipment for hiking, cycling, climbing, and kayaking, and for just looking good while hanging around outdoors. You can rent sports gear here, too. A onetime C$5 membership is required for purchases or rentals. ⊠ *130 W. Broadway, Main St./Mt. Pleasant, Vancouver* ☎ *604/872–7858* ⊕ *www.mec.ca.*

COMMERCIAL DRIVE AND AROUND

CLOTHING: MEN'S AND WOMEN'S

Roots 73 Outlet. You can pay top dollar Downtown or head to this factory outlet, which stocks good quality off-season and closeout items at bargain prices. ⊠ *3695 Grandview Hwy., at Boundary Rd., East Side, Vancouver* ☎ *604/433–4337* ⊕ *www.canada.roots.com.*

VICTORIA

Despite its role as the provincial capital, Victoria was largely eclipsed, economically, by Vancouver throughout the 20th century. This, as it turns out, was all to the good, helping to preserve Victoria's historic Downtown and keeping the city largely free of skyscrapers and highways. For much of the 20th century, Victoria was marketed to tourists as "The Most British City in Canada," and it still has more than its share of Anglo-themed pubs, tea shops, and double-decker buses, but these days, Victorians prefer to celebrate their combined indigenous, Asian, and European heritage, and the city's stunning wilderness backdrop. Locals do often venture out for afternoon tea, but they're just as likely to nosh on dim sum or tapas. Decades-old shops sell imported linens and tweeds, but newer upstarts offer local designs in hemp and organic cotton. And let's not forget that fabric prevalent among locals: Gore-Tex. The outdoors is ever present here. You can hike, bike, kayak, sail, or whale-watch straight from the city center, and forests, beaches, offshore islands, and wilderness parklands lie just minutes away.

At the southern tip of Vancouver Island, Victoria dips slightly below the 49th parallel. That puts it farther south than most of Canada, giving it the mildest climate in the country, with virtually no snow and less than half the rain of Vancouver.

The city's geography, or at least its place names, can cause confusion. Just to clarify: the city of Victoria is on Vancouver Island (not Victoria Island). The city of Vancouver is on the British Columbia mainland, not on Vancouver Island. At any rate, the city of Vancouver didn't even exist in 1843 when Victoria, then called Fort Victoria, was founded as the westernmost trading post of the British-owned Hudson's Bay Company.

PLANNING

WHEN TO GO

Victoria has the warmest, mildest climate in Canada: snow is rare and flowers bloom in February. Summers are mild, too, rarely topping 75°F. If you're here for dining, shopping, and museums, winter is a perfectly nice time for a visit: it's gray and wet, and some minor attractions are closed, but hotel deals abound. If your focus is the outdoors—biking, hiking, gardens, and whale-watching—you need to come with everyone else, between May and October. That's when the streets come to life with crafts stalls, street entertainers, blooming gardens, and the inevitable tour buses. It's fun and busy but Victoria never gets unbearably crowded.

MAKING THE MOST OF YOUR TIME

You can see most of the sights in Downtown Victoria's compact core in a day, although there's enough to see at the main museums to easily fill two days. You can save time by pre-booking tea at the Empress Hotel and buying tickets online for the Royal British Columbia Museum. You should also save at least half a day or a full evening to visit Butchart Gardens.

An extra day allows for some time on the water, either on a whale-watching trip—it's fairly easy to spot orcas in the area during summer—or on a Harbour Ferries tour, with stops for tea at Point Ellice House, a microbrew at Spinnakers Brewpub, or fish-and-chips at Fisherman's Wharf. You can also explore the shoreline on foot, following all, or part, of the 7-mile waterfront walkway.

GETTING HERE AND AROUND

It's easy to visit Victoria without a car. Most sights, restaurants, and hotels are in the compact walkable core, with bikes, ferries, horse-drawn carriages, double-decker buses, step-on tour buses, taxis, and pedicabs on hand to fill the gaps. For sights outside the core—Butchart Gardens, Hatley Castle, Scenic Marine Drive—tour buses are your best bet if you don't have your own vehicle. Bike paths lace Downtown and run along much of Victoria's waterfront, and long-haul car-free paths run to the ferry terminals and as far west as Sooke. Most buses and ferries carry bikes.

AIR TRAVEL

Air Canada, Pacific Coastal Airlines, and WestJet fly to Victoria from Vancouver International Airport. Alaska Airlines (under its Horizon Air division) flies between Seattle and Victoria. Victoria International Airport is 25 km (15 miles) north of Downtown Victoria. The flight from Vancouver to Victoria takes about 25 minutes. There is floatplane service to Victoria's Inner Harbour in Downtown Victoria with Harbour

19

Air Seaplanes. Harbour Air also flies from Whistler to Downtown Victoria, May–September. Kenmore Air has daily floatplane service from Seattle to Victoria's Inner Harbour. Helijet has helicopter service from Downtown Vancouver and Vancouver International Airport to Downtown Victoria.

BC Ferries has daily service between Tsawwassen, about an hour south of Vancouver, and Swartz Bay, at the end of Highway 17 (the Patricia Bay Highway), about 30 minutes north of Victoria. Sailing time is about 1½ hours. An excellent option combines four hours of whale-watching with travel between Vancouver and Victoria, offered by the Prince of Whales. The 74-passenger boat leaves the Westin Bayshore Hotel in Downtown Vancouver daily at 9 am (June–mid-September), arriving in Victoria at 1 pm; there are also departures from Victoria's Inner Harbour at 1:45 pm (one-way C$200)

The Victoria Harbour Ferry serves the Inner Harbour; stops include the Fairmont Empress, Chinatown, Point Ellice House, the Delta Victoria Ocean Pointe Resort, and Fisherman's Wharf. Fares start at C$5. Boats make the rounds every 15 to 20 minutes. They run 10 to 9 from mid-May through mid-September and 11 to 5 from March through mid-May and mid-September to late October. The ferries don't run from November through February. The 45-minute harbor tours cost C$22, and gorge cruises cost C$26. At 10:45 am on summer Sundays, the little ferries perform a water ballet set to classical music in the Inner Harbour.

Contacts Victoria Harbour Ferry. ☎ 250/708–0201 ⊕ www. victoriaharbourferry.com.

EXPLORING

Victoria is small and easily explored. A walk around Downtown, starting with the museums and architectural sights of the Inner Harbour, followed by a stroll up Government Street to the historic areas of Chinatown and Old Town, covers most of the key attractions, though seeing every little interesting thing along the way could easily take two days. Most visitors also make time for the Butchart Gardens, a stunning exhibition garden 20 minutes by car north on the Saanich Peninsula.

DOWNTOWN

TOP ATTRACTIONS

Fairmont Empress. Opened in 1908 by the Canadian Pacific Railway, the Empress is one of the grand château-style railroad hotels that grace many Canadian cities. Designed by Francis Rattenbury, who also designed the Parliament Buildings across the way, the solid Edwardian grandeur of the Empress has made it a symbol of the city. The elements that made the hotel an attraction for travelers in the past—old-world architecture, ornate decor, and a commanding view of the Inner Harbour—are still here. Nonguests can reserve ahead for afternoon tea (the dress code is smart casual) in the chandelier-draped Tea Lobby, meet for a curry under the tiger skin in the Bengal Lounge, enjoy a treatment at the hotel's

Willow Stream spa, or sample the superb Pacific Northwest cuisine in the Empress Room. In summer, lunch, snacks, and cocktails are served on the Verandah overlooking the Inner Harbour. ✉ *721 Government St., Downtown, Victoria* ☏ *250/384–8111, 250/389–2727 tea reservations* ⊕ *www.fairmont.com/empress* ✆ *Free; afternoon tea C$59.95.*

Parliament Buildings. Officially the British Columbia Provincial Legislative Assembly Buildings, these massive stone structures are more popularly referred to as the Parliament Buildings. Designed by Francis Rattenbury (who also designed the Fairmont Empress Hotel) when he was just 25 years old, and completed in 1897, they dominate the Inner Harbour. Atop the central dome is a gilded statue of Captain George Vancouver (1757–98), the first European to sail around Vancouver Island. A statue of Queen Victoria (1819–1901) reigns over the front of the complex. More than 3,300 lights outline the buildings at night. The interior is lavishly done with stained-glass windows, gilt moldings, and historic photographs, and in summer actors play historic figures from British Columbia's past. When the legislature is in session, you can sit in the public gallery and watch British Columbia's democracy at work (custom has the opposing parties sitting 2½ sword lengths apart). Free, informative, 30- to 45-minute tours run every 20 to 30 minutes in summer and several times a day in the off-season (less frequently if school groups or private tours are coming through). Tours are obligatory on summer weekends (mid-May until Labor Day) and optional the rest of the time. ✉ *501 Belleville St., James Bay, Downtown, Victoria* ☏ *250/387–3046* ⊕ *www.leg.bc.ca* ✆ *Free* ☾ *Mid-May–early Sept., daily 9–5; early Sept.–mid-May, weekdays 9–5.*

Fodor'sChoice
★
FAMILY
Royal British Columbia Museum. This excellent museum, one of Victoria's leading attractions, traces several thousand years of British Columbian history. Especially strong is its First Peoples Gallery, home to a genuine Kwakwaka'wakw big house and a dramatically displayed collection of masks and other artifacts. A new exhibit about First Nations languages opened in 2014. The Natural History Gallery traces British Columbia's landscapes, from prehistory to modern-day climate change, in realistic dioramas. An *Ocean Station* exhibit gets kids involved in running a Jules Verne–style submarine. In the History Gallery, a replica of Captain Vancouver's HMS *Discovery* creaks convincingly, and a re-created frontier town comes to life with cobbled streets, silent movies, and the rumble of an arriving train. An IMAX theater presents films on a six-story-tall screen. Optional one-hour tours, included in the admission price, run roughly twice a day in summer and less frequently in winter. Most focus on a particular gallery, though the 90-minute Highlights Tour touches on all galleries. Special exhibits, usually held between mid-May and mid-November, attract crowds despite the higher admission prices. You can skip (sometimes very long) ticket lines by booking online. The museum complex has several more interesting sights, beyond the expected gift shop and café. In front of the museum, at Government and Belleville Streets, is the **Netherlands Centennial Carillon.** With 62 bells, it's the largest bell tower in Canada; the Westminster chimes ring out every hour, and free recitals are occasionally held on Sunday afternoons. Behind the main building, bordering Douglas

19

Downtown Victoria

Galloping Goose Regional Trail

Upper Harbour

Pembroke St.

Discovery St.

Chatham St.

Herald St.

Tree Rd.

Harbour Rd.

Esquimalt Rd.

Sitkum Rd.

Saghalie Rd.

Kimta Rd.

VIA Rail Station

Jonson St. Bridge (Blue Bridge)

Gate of Harmonius Interest

McPherson Playhouse

Centennial Square

Pandora Ave.

Johnson St.

Songhees Rd.

Inner Harbour Pedestrian Path

Harbour Walkway

Floatplane Docks

Bastion Square

Government St.

Broad St.

View St.

Bay Centre

Douglas St.

Fort St.

Inner Harbour

Broughton St.

← TO PORT ANGELES, BILLINGHAM, SEATTLE

Victoria Harbour

Laurel Point Park

Japanese Gardens

Harbour Walkway

Seattle Ferry

Black Ball Ferries

Victoria Marine Adventure Centre

Gordon St.

Humboldt St.

4 Fairmont Empress

Fishermans Wharf Park

Dallas Rd.

Erie St.

Lawrence St.

Montreal St.

Pendray St.

Oswego St.

Belleville St.

Quebec St.

Kingston St.

Superior St.

Michigan St.

Menzies St.

1 Parliament

3 St. Ann's Schoolhouse

Helmcken House

Elliot St.

Onterio St.

Ladysmith St.

Simcoe St.

National Geographic Theatre

Macdonald Park

Niagara St.

James St.

Beckley Ave.

Irving Park

Michigan St.

Parry St.

Powell St.

Heather St.

Government St.

Young St.

Toronto St.

Dock St.

Priot St.

Dallas Rd.

Oswego St.

San Jose Ave.

Boyd St.

Lewis St.

Menzies St.

Medana St.

Clarneece St.

Rithet St.

South Turner St.

Government St.

Niagara St.

Marifield Ave.

St. Andrews St.

2

Douglas St.

Circle Dr.

Federal Marine Ecological Reserve

0   300 yards

0   300 meters

Holland Point Park

KEY

🛈 *Tourist information*

⛴ *Ferry*

---- *Pedestrian trail*

More than 3,300 lights outline Victoria's Parliament Buildings; like the Fairmont Empress hotel, the buildings have a prominent position in the Inner Harbor, and were designed by the same architect: Francis Rattenbury

Street, are the grassy lawns of **Thunderbird Park,** home to 10 totem poles (carved replicas of originals that are preserved in the museum). One of the oldest houses in BC, **Helmcken House** (*Open late May–early Sept., daily noon–4*) was built in 1852 for pioneer doctor and statesman John Sebastian Helmcken. Inside are displays of the family's belongings, including the doctor's medical tools. Behind it is **St. Ann's School House,** built in 1858. One of British Columbia's oldest schools, it is thought to be Victoria's oldest building still standing. Both buildings are part of the Royal British Columbia Museum. ⊠ *675 Belleville St., Downtown, Victoria* ☏ *250/356–7226, 888/447–7977 museum, 877/480–4887 IMAX theater* ⊕ *www.royalbcmuseum.bc.ca* ✉ *C$21.60, IMAX theater C$11.80; combination ticket C$31.40* ☉ *Daily 9–5.*

WORTH NOTING

Emily Carr House. One of Canada's most celebrated artists and a respected writer, Emily Carr (1871–1945) lived in this extremely proper, wooden Victorian house before she abandoned her middle-class life to live in the wilds of British Columbia. Carr's own descriptions, from her autobiography *Book of Small*, were used to restore the house. Art on display includes reproductions of Carr's work—visit the Art Gallery of Greater Victoria or the Vancouver Art Gallery to see the originals. ⊠ *207 Government St., James Bay, Downtown, Victoria* ☏ *250/383–5843* ⊕ *www.emilycarr.com* ✉ *C$6.75* ☉ *May–Sept., Tues.–Sat. 11–4.*

ROCKLAND

TOP ATTRACTIONS

Craigdarroch Castle. This resplendent mansion complete with turrets and Gothic rooflines was built as the home of one of British Columbia's wealthiest men, coal baron Robert Dunsmuir, who died in 1889, just a few months before the castle's completion. It's now a museum depicting life in the late 1800s. The castle's 39 rooms have ornate Victorian furnishings, stained-glass windows, carved woodwork, and a beautifully restored painted ceiling in the drawing room. A winding staircase climbs four floors to a tower overlooking Victoria. Castles run in the family: son James went on to build the more lavish Hatley Castle west of Victoria. The castle is not wheelchair accessible and has no elevators. ✉ *1050 Joan Crescent, Rockland, Victoria* ☎ *250/592–5323* ⊕ *www. thecastle.ca* ✍ *C$13.95* ✆ *Mid-June–early Sept., daily 9–7; early Sept.– mid-June, daily 10–4:30.*

FAIRFIELD

TOP ATTRACTIONS

Abkhazi Garden and Teahouse. Called "the garden that love built," this once-private garden is as fascinating for its history as for its innovative design. The seeds were planted, figuratively, in Paris in the 1920s, when Englishwoman Peggy Pemberton-Carter met exiled Georgian Prince Nicholas Abkhazi. World War II internment camps (his in Germany, hers near Shanghai) interrupted their romance, but they reunited and married in Victoria in 1946. They spent the next 40 years together cultivating their garden. Rescued from developers and now operated by the Land Conservancy of British Columbia, the 1-acre site is recognized as a leading example of West Coast horticultural design, resplendent with native Garry Oak trees, Japanese maples, and mature rhododendrons. The teahouse (*www.abkhaziteahouse.com*), in the parlor of the modernist home, serves lunch and afternoon tea until 4 pm. ✉ *1964 Fairfield Rd., Fairfield, Victoria* ☎ *778/265–6466* ⊕ *www.conservancy. bc.ca* ✍ *C$10* ✆ *May–Sept., daily 11–5; Oct.–Apr., Wed.–Sun., 11–5.*

19

BRENTWOOD BAY

TOP ATTRACTIONS

Fodor's Choice **Butchart Gardens.** This stunning 55-acre garden and National Historic ★ Site has been drawing visitors since it was started in a limestone quarry in 1904. Highlights include the dramatic 70-foot Ross Fountain, the formal Japanese garden, and the intricate Italian garden complete with a gelato stand. Kids will love the old-fashioned carousel and will likely enjoy the 45-minute mini-boat tours around Tod Inlet. From mid-June to mid-September the gardens are illuminated at night with hundreds of hidden lights. In July and August, jazz, blues, and classical musicians play at an outdoor stage each evening and fireworks draw crowds every Saturday night. The wheelchair- and stroller-accessible site is also home to a seed-and-gift shop, a plant identification center, two restaurants (one offering traditional afternoon tea), and a coffee shop; you can even call

Butchart Gardens

ahead for a picnic basket on fireworks nights. To avoid crowds, come at opening time, in the late afternoon or evening (except ultrabusy fireworks Saturday evenings), or between September and June, when the gardens are still stunning and admission rates are reduced. The grounds are especially magical at Christmas, with themed lighting and an ice rink. The gardens are a 20-minute drive north of Downtown; parking is free but fills up on fireworks Saturdays. You can get here by city Bus 75 from Douglas Street in Downtown Victoria, but service is slow and infrequent. CVS Cruise Victoria (⊕ *www.cvscruisevictoria.com; 877/578–5552*) runs shuttles from Downtown Victoria. ✉ *800 Benvenuto Ave., Brentwood Bay* ☎ *250/652–5256, 866/652–4422* ⊕ *www.butchartgardens. com* ✉ *C$30.80* ☺ *Mid-June–Aug., daily 9 am–10 pm; Sept.–mid-June, daily 9 am–dusk* ☞ *Rates are lower between Sept. and mid-June.*

SIDNEY

23 km (14 miles) north of Victoria on Hwy. 17.

Sidney, short for Sidney-by-the-Sea, is an inviting seaside town just 30 minutes north of Victoria. Home to the Washington State Ferry terminal and just five minutes south of the BC Ferries terminal, it's worth a stop or even a weekend visit. The streets are lined with independent shops, including a wealth of bookstores—so many, in fact, that Sidney has earned a place as Canada's only official Booktown (⊕ *www. sidneybooktown.ca*). Sidney's parklike waterfront, which houses a marine ecology center as well as cafés, restaurants, and a wheelchair-accessible waterfront path, is a launching point for kayakers, whale-watchers, and ecotour boats heading out to explore the Gulf Islands National Park Reserve offshore.

TOP ATTRACTIONS

FAMILY **Shaw Ocean Discovery Centre.** A simulated ride underwater in a deep-sea elevator is just the beginning of a visit to this fun and educational marine interpretive center. Devoted entirely to the aquatic life and conservation needs of the Salish Sea—the waters south and east of Vancouver Island—the small but modern center displays local sea life, including luminous jellyfish, bright purple starfish, wolf eels, rockfish, and octopi. Hands-on activities and touch tanks delight kids, who also love the high-tech effects, including a floor projection that ripples when stepped on and a pop-up tank you can poke your head into. ⊠ 9811 Seaport Pl., Sidney, Victoria ☎ 250/665–7511 ⊕ www.oceandiscovery. ca ⊠ C$15 ☉ July–Aug., daily 10–5; Sept.–June daily 10–4.

WHERE TO EAT

Victoria has a tremendous number and variety of restaurants for such a small city; this fact, and the glorious pantry that is Vancouver Island—think local fish, seafood, cheese, and organic fruits and veggies—keeps prices down (at least compared to Vancouver) and standards up. Restaurants in the region are generally casual. Smoking is banned in all public places, including restaurant patios, in Greater Victoria and on the Southern Gulf Islands. Victorians tend to dine early—restaurants get busy at 6 and many kitchens close by 9. Pubs, lounges, and the few open-late places mentioned here are your best options for an after-hours nosh.

Afternoon tea is a Victoria tradition, as is good coffee—despite the Starbucks invasion, there are plenty of fun and funky local caffeine purveyors around town.

19

WHAT IT COSTS IN CANADIAN DOLLARS			
$	$$	$$$	$$$$
Restaurants	Under C$13	C$13–C$20	C$21–C$30	Over C$30

Prices in the restaurants reviews are the average cost of a main course or equivalent combination of small dishes at dinner or, if dinner is not served, at lunch.

DOWNTOWN

Use the coordinate (✛ B2) at the end of each listing to locate a site on the corresponding map.

$$$ ✕ **Aura.** When an award-winning chef names "imagination" as his most
PACIFIC treasured possession, you know the food here is likely to be creative,
NORTHWEST if not exquisite. The seasonal menu uses primarily local ingredients,
Fodor's Choice revealing Asian influences. Think poached BC salmon paired with bar-
★ becued eel and a Japanese rice-cabbage roll; or free-range chicken with a wasabi-pea crust. The wine cellar is full of hard-to-find Vancouver Island wines and Okanagan labels. Sleek lines, warm colors, and water-view windows create a room that's both stylish and cozy. Plus, Aura has

the city's best waterfront patio when the weather is cooperative. ⑤ *Average main: C$26* ✉ *Inn at Laurel Point, 680 Montreal St., James Bay, Downtown, Victoria* ☎ *250/414–6739* ⊕ *www.aurarestaurant.ca* ✦ *C4.*

$$ ✕ **Barb's Fish & Chips.** Funky Barb's, a tin-roofed takeout shack, floats
SEAFOOD on the quay at Fisherman's Wharf, west of the Inner Harbour off St.
FAMILY Lawrence Street. Halibut, salmon, oysters, mussels, crab, burgers, and
chowder are all prepared fresh. The picnic tables on the wharf provide
a front-row view of the brightly colored houseboats moored here, or
you can carry your food to the grassy park nearby. Ferries sail to Fish-
erman's Wharf from the Inner Harbour, or you can work up an appe-
tite with a leisurely stroll along the waterfront. ⑤ *Average main: C$13*
✉ *Fisherman's Wharf, St. Lawrence St., James Bay, Downtown, Victoria*
☎ *250/384–6515* ⊕ *www.barbsplace.ca* ☉ *Closed Nov.–early Mar.* ✦ *B4.*

$$$ ✕ **Brasserie L'École.** French-country cooking shines at this informal Chi-
FRENCH natown bistro, and the historic room—once a schoolhouse for the
Fodor'sChoice Chinese community—evokes a timeless brasserie, from the patina-rich
★ fir floors to the chalkboards above the slate bar listing the day's oyster, mussel, and steak options. Sean Brennan, one of the city's better-
known chefs, works with local farmers and fishermen to source the best
seasonal, local, and organic ingredients. The menu changes daily but
lists such contemporary spins on classic bistro fare as duck confit with
house-made sausage, steak frites, or spring salmon with beets, shallots,
and *pommes rissolées*. Be prepared for lines, as this petite spot does
not take reservations. ⑤ *Average main: C$24* ✉ *1715 Government St.,
Downtown, Victoria* ☎ *250/475–6260* ⊕ *www.lecole.ca* ☉ *Closed Sun.
and Mon. No lunch* ⌂ *Reservations not accepted* ✦ *F2.*

$$$ ✕ **Café Brio.** This intimate yet bustling Italian villa–style room has
MODERN long been a Victoria favorite, mainly because of its Mediterranean-
CANADIAN influence atmosphere and cuisine, which is prepared primarily with
Fodor'sChoice locally raised ingredients. The menu changes almost daily, but you
★ might find local rockfish pan-roasted and paired with heirloom beans
and grilled scallions, or roast duck breast with semolina polenta. Most
dishes come in full or half sizes, which are ideal for smaller appetites
or for those who want to sample the menu more widely. However, the
Family Meal (priced per person) is the choice for sharing, comprising
six chef's choice-of-the-day dishes. Virtually everything, including the
bread, most pastas, charcuterie, and desserts, is made in-house. The
400-label wine list has a top selection of BC choices. ⑤ *Average main:
C$27* ✉ *944 Fort St., Downtown, Victoria* ☎ *250/383–0009, 866/270–
5461* ⊕ *www.cafe-brio.com* ☉ *No lunch* ✦ *H4.*

$$$ ✕ **Camille's.** Working closely with independent farmers, the chef at this
MODERN long-established favorite concentrates on such locally sourced products
CANADIAN as lamb, duck, and seafood; quail and venison often make an appearance, too. The menu is based on what's fresh but might include seafood bisque with lemon and ginger; Hecate Strait lingcod; or organic
beef striploin. The wine cellar–like backdrop, on the lower floor of a
historic building on Bastion Square, is candlelit and romantic, with
exposed brick, soft jazz and blues, and lots of intimate nooks and cran-
nies hung with local art. The wine list is well selected. ⑤ *Average main:*

C$28 ⊠ 45 Bastion Sq., Downtown, Victoria ☎ *250/381–3433* ⊕ *www. camillesrestaurant.com* ⊘ *Closed Sun. and Mon. No lunch* ✛ *E3.*

$$$
ITALIAN
✕ **Il Terrazzo.** A cute redbrick terrace edged with potted greenery and warmed by fireplaces and overhead heaters makes Il Terrazzo—tucked away off Waddington Alley near Market Square and not visible from the street—the locals' choice for romantic alfresco dining. Starters might include steamed mussels with sundried tomatoes and spicy banana peppers, while mains range from such traditional Northern Italian favorites as breaded scaloppini of pork tenderloin to a more local-leaning halibut with blackberries. Thin-crust pizzas come piping hot from the restaurant's open-flame stone oven. ⑤ *Average main: C$24* ⊠ *555 Johnson St., off Waddington Alley, Downtown, Victoria* ☎ *250/361–0028* ⊕ *www. ilterrazzo.com* ⊘ *No lunch weekends* ✛ *E3.*

$$
CANADIAN
FAMILY
✕ **Mo:Lé.** A good choice for vegans, this brick-lined Chinatown café has plenty of wholesome, organic, local fare for meat eaters, too. All-day breakfasts of free-range eggs, locally made sausages, and organic spelt griddle cakes fuel a post-party, pre-yoga crowd. At lunch, locals might pop in for an avocado, seaweed, and sprout sandwich, a yam wrap, or an organic beef burger. The place is popular, so expect to wait on weekends. ⑤ *Average main: C$13* ⊠ *554 Pandora St., Downtown, Victoria* ☎ *250/385–6653* ⊕ *www.molerestaurant.ca* ⊘ *No dinner* ⌲ *Reservations not accepted* ✛ *F2.*

$
ASIAN
✕ **The Noodle Box.** Noodles, whether Indonesian style with peanut sauce, thick hokkien in teriyaki, or Thai-style chow mein, are scooped straight from the open kitchen's steaming woks into bowls or cardboard takeout boxes. Malaysian-, Singapore-, and Thai-style curries tempt those who like it hot. Gluten-free, vegan, and kid-friendly options are all available. There are half a dozen "boxes" around town. The Douglas Street outlet is a loud and busy spot near the Inner Harbour; the branch at 626 Fisgard Street is a tiny hole-in-the-wall near Chinatown. ⑤ *Average main: C$12* ⊠ *818 Douglas St., Downtown, Victoria* ☎ *250/384– 1314* ⊕ *www.thenoodlebox.net* ⌲ *Reservations not accepted* ✛ *F4.*

$
SEAFOOD
✕ **Red Fish Blue Fish.** If you like your fish both yummy *and* ecologically friendly, look no further than this former shipping container on the pier at the foot of Broughton Street. From the soil-topped roof and biodegradable packaging to the sustainably harvested local seafood, this waterfront takeout shop minimizes its ecological footprint. The chef offers a choice of local wild salmon, tuna, and oysters from the barbecue. Portuguese buns are baked daily for the seafood sandwiches, fish tacos come in grilled tortilla cones, and even plain old fish-and-chips are taken up a notch with a choice of wild salmon, halibut, or cod in tempura batter with hand-cut fries. Be prepared for queues on sunny days and for variable closures during the winter months. ⑤ *Average main: C$12* ⊠ *1006 Wharf St., Downtown, Victoria* ☎ *250/298–6877* ⊕ *www.redfish-bluefish.com* ⊘ *No dinner. Call for winter closures* ⌲ *Reservations not accepted* ✛ *E4.*

19

$$$
MODERN
CANADIAN
Fodor'sChoice
★

✕ **Ulla Restaurant.** Victoria's foodies are buzzing about this Chinatown restaurant that's serving up some of the city's most innovative fare. From the frequently changing, locally sourced menu, you could choose starters like grass-fed beef carpaccio, giant Pacific octopus, or perhaps pea soup with cauliflower and an "egg" made from cheddar and carrot. Mains might include chicken with cheddar pierogies, butter radish and cabbage shoots, short-rib steak from a local organic farm, or coho salmon with birch syrup. The high-arched windows, solid fir tables, and art-filled walls make the room feel both airy and relaxed. $ *Average main: C$27* ✉ *509 Fisgard St., Downtown, Victoria* ☎ *250/590–8795* ⊕ *www.ulla.ca* ⊘ *Closed Sun. and Mon. No lunch* ✛ *E2.*

$$$
ITALIAN

✕ **Zambri's.** This lively trattoria, in a glam space with floor-to-ceiling windows and eclectic chandeliers, has a setting to match the top-notch Italian food. The kitchen uses local and organic ingredients to turn out contemporary versions of traditional dishes. During the always-busy lunch service, choose from pizzas, pastas, and hot sandwiches, or in the evening, opt for tagliatelle with gorgonzola cream, leeks, and candied walnuts, or crispy pork shoulder served on a bed of greens, potatoes, and grapes. The mostly Italian wine list includes lesser-known labels, with many available by the glass. $ *Average main: C$22* ✉ *820 Yates St., Downtown, Victoria* ☎ *250/360–1171* ⊕ *www.zambris.ca* ✛ *G3.*

WHERE TO STAY

Victoria has a vast range of accommodations, with what seems like whole neighborhoods dedicated to hotels. Options range from city resorts and full-service business hotels to midpriced tour-group haunts and family-friendly motels, but the city is especially known for its lavish B&Bs in beautifully restored Victorian and Edwardian mansions. Outlying areas, such as Sooke and Saanich, pride themselves on destination spa resorts and luxurious country inns, though affordable lodgings can be found there, too.

WHAT IT COSTS IN CANADIAN DOLLARS			
$	$$	$$$	$$$$
Hotels	Under C$126	C$126–C$195	C$196–C$300	Over C$300

Prices in the hotel reviews are the lowest cost of a standard double room in high season.

Use the coordinate (✛ B2) at the end of each listing to locate a site on the corresponding map.

Hotel reviews have been shortened. For full information, visit Fodors. com.

DOWNTOWN

$$
B&B/INN

⊞ **Beaconsfield Inn.** This 1905 building four blocks from the Inner Harbour is one of Victoria's most faithfully restored, antiques-filled mansions. **Pros:** luxurious; opportunities to mingle over breakfast or sherry. **Cons:** romantic ambience is not suited for kids; several blocks from shopping and dining. $ *Rooms from: C$159* ✉ *998 Humboldt St., Downtown, Victoria* ☎ *250/384–4044, 888/884–4044* ⊕ *www. beaconsfieldinn.com* ⇨ *9 rooms* ❖❉ *Breakfast* ✛ *H6.*

$$$$ 🏨 **Fairmont Empress.** Opened in 1908, this ivy-draped harborside châ-
HOTEL teau and city landmark has aged gracefully, with top-notch service and
Fodor's Choice sympathetically restored Edwardian furnishings. **Pros:** central location;
★ professional service; great spa and restaurant. **Cons:** small- to average-
size rooms and bathrooms; pricey. $ *Rooms from: C$349* ✉ *721 Gov-
ernment St., Downtown, Victoria* ☎ *250/384–8111, 866/540–4429
Central reservations* ⊕ *www.fairmont.com/empress* ⇨ *436 rooms, 41
suites* ❖❉ *No meals* ✛ *E5.*

$$$ 🏨 **Hotel Grand Pacific.** The city's biggest and best health club (with
HOTEL an indoor lap pool, yoga classes, squash courts, and state-of-the-art
equipment), a great spa, and a prime Inner Harbour location appeal
to savvy regulars, including Seattleites stepping off the ferry across the
street. **Pros:** great health club and spa; concierge; complimentary Wi-Fi.
Cons: standard hotel decor in some rooms. $ *Rooms from: C$229*
✉ *463 Belleville St., James Bay, Downtown, Victoria* ☎ *250/386–0450,
800/663–7550* ⊕ *www.hotelgrandpacific.com* ⇨ *258 rooms, 46 suites*
❖❉ *No meals* ✛ *D5.*

$$$ 🏨 **Inn at Laurel Point.** A seaside Japanese garden, a museum-quality art
HOTEL collection, and water views from every room make this Asian-inspired
independent hotel on the Inner Harbour's quiet south shore a favorite
among Victoria regulars. **Pros:** views; quiet, parklike setting. **Cons:**
10-minute walk from Downtown. $ *Rooms from: C$199* ✉ *680 Mon-
treal St., James Bay, Downtown, Victoria* ☎ *250/386–8721, 800/663–
7667* ⊕ *www.laurelpoint.com* ⇨ *135 rooms, 65 suites* ❖❉ *No meals*
✛ *C4.*

$$$ 🏨 **Magnolia Hotel & Spa.** From the on-site spa to the soaker tubs, sauna,
HOTEL and herb tea, this locally owned boutique hotel, without actually saying
so, caters beautifully to the female traveler—though the attention to
detail, hop-to-it staff, and central location won't be lost on men either.
Pros: great location; friendly and helpful service; welcoming lobby with
fireplace, tea, and coffee. **Cons:** no on-site pool or hot tub. $ *Rooms
from: C$249* ✉ *623 Courtney St., Downtown, Victoria* ☎ *250/381–
0999, 877/624–6654* ⊕ *www.magnoliahotel.com* ⇨ *64 rooms* ❖❉ *No
meals* ✛ *F4.*

VIC WEST

$$$ 🏨 **Delta Victoria Ocean Pointe Resort and Spa.** Across the Johnson Street
HOTEL Bridge from Downtown Victoria, this waterfront resort has all sorts of
amenities, from tennis and squash courts to an indoor pool, popular
spa, around-the-clock gym, and a waterfront walking path. **Pros:** water
views; free Wi-Fi; Downtown shuttle and harbor ferry service. **Cons:** not
right in Downtown; gets busy with conferences. $ *Rooms from: C$229*
✉ *45 Songhees Rd., Vic West, Victoria* ☎ *250/360–2999, 800/667–4677*
⊕ *www.deltavictoria.com* ⇨ *229 rooms, 11 suites* ❖❉ *No meals* ✛ *D3.*

19

Where to Eat and Stay in Downtown Victoria

A **B** **C** **D**

1

Upper Harbour

GALLOPING GOOSE REGIONAL TRAIL

Bay St.

Catherine St.

VIC WEST

Tyee Rd.

Harbour Rd.

2

Sitkum Rd.

Esquimalt Rd.

Saghalie Rd.

Johnson St. Bridge (Blue Bridge)

Spinnakers Brewpub

Kimta Rd.

← **WEST BAY MARINA**

Delta Ocean Pointe Resort

← ▲ **Westbay Landing**

Songhees Rd.

Delta Victoria □

3

Outer Harbour

WESTSONG WAY

Inner Harbour

← TO PORT ANGELES, BILLINGHAM, SEATTLE

Laurel Point Park

4

HARBOUR WALKWAY

Aura ▣
Inn at Laurel Point

◆ **CLIPPER TERMINAL**

Fisherman's Wharf

Barb's Fish & Chips ▪

Fishermans Wharf Park

Quebec St.

Belleville St.

Pendray St.

Oswego St.

Dallas Rd.

Erie St.

Hotel □
Grand Pacific

Superior St.

Kingston St.

5

Lawrence St.

Montreal St.

Michigan St.

KEY

□ *Hotels*

▪ *Restaurants*

▣ *Restaurants in Hotels*

⟷ *following reviews indicates a map-grid coordinate*

🛈 *Tourist information*

⛴ *Ferry*

- - - *Pedestrian trail*

▲ *Harbour Ferries*

Ontario St.

Simcoe St.

6

Macdonald Park

Niagara St.

Irving Park

A **B** **C** **D**

ROCKLAND

$$$

B&B/INN

Fodor'sChoice

★

Abbeymoore Manor. This 1912 mansion has the wide verandas, dark wainscoting, and high ceilings of its era, but the attitude is informal and welcoming, from the super-helpful hosts to the free snacks to the coffee on tap all day. **Pros:** good value; friendly hosts; excellent service. **Cons:** a mile from the Inner Harbour; often booked in advance. $ *Rooms from: C$219 ⊠ 1470 Rockland Ave., Rockland, Victoria ☎ 250/370–1470, 888/801–1811 ⊕ www.abbeymoore.com ⇨ 5 rooms, 2 suites ⎸◎⎸ Breakfast ⊹ H5.*

BRENTWOOD BAY

$$$

RESORT

Fodor'sChoice

★

Brentwood Bay Resort & Spa. Every room has a private ocean-view patio or balcony at this adult-oriented boutique resort in a tiny seaside village. **Pros:** magnificent setting; close to Butchart Gardens; free Wi-Fi. **Cons:** pricey rates; 30-minute drive from Downtown. $ *Rooms from: C$289 ⊠ 849 Verdier Ave., Brentwood Bay ☎ 250/544–2079, 888/544–2079 ⊕ www.brentwoodbayresort.com ⇨ 30 rooms, 3 suites, 2 villas ⎸◎⎸ No meals ⊹ F1.*

SIDNEY

$$

HOTEL

Sidney Pier Hotel & Spa. Stylish and ecologically friendly, this glass-and-stone boutique hotel on the parklike waterfront has helped introduce Sidney to more travelers. **Pros:** lovely views; eco-friendly vibe; free airport and ferry shuttle in summer. **Cons:** 30 minutes from Downtown; no pool. $ *Rooms from: C$179 ⊠ 9805 Seaport Pl., Sidney ☎ 250/655–9445, 866/659–9445 ⊕ www.sidneypier.com ⇨ 46 rooms, 9 suites ⎸◎⎸ No meals ⊹ H1.*

NIGHTLIFE AND PERFORMING ARTS

Victoria isn't the busiest destination after dark. But there are two important local sources to help visitors keep on top of the happenings, whether they're looking for a quiet pint, a music festival, or a night on the town. One is a monthly digest of arts and nightlife; the other is the local tourist office, which also sells tickets.

NIGHTLIFE

DOWNTOWN

BARS

The Bard and Banker Pub. This sumptuously decorated Scottish pub, which occupies a historic bank building on Victoria's main shopping street, has bangers-and-mash and shepherd's pie on the menu, plus a great selection of ales and live music every night. ⊠ *1022 Government St., Downtown, Victoria ☎ 250/953–9993 ⊕ www.bardandbanker.com.*

Bengal Lounge. Deep leather sofas and a tiger skin help to re-create the days of the British Raj at this iconic lounge in the Fairmont Empress Hotel. Martinis and a curry buffet are the draws through the week. On

Friday and Saturday nights a jazz combo takes the stage. ⊠ *Fairmont Empress Hotel, 721 Government St., Downtown, Victoria* ☎ *250/384–8111* ⊕ *www.fairmont.com/empress.*

Canoe Brewpub. One of Victoria's biggest and best pub patios overlooks the Gorge, the waterway just north of the Inner Harbour. The interior of the former power station has been stylishly redone with high ceilings, exposed bricks, and wood beams. There's a wide range of in-house brews, top-notch bar snacks, and an all-ages restaurant. ⊠ *450 Swift St., Downtown, Victoria* ☎ *250/361–1940* ⊕ *www.canoebrewpub.com.*

Swans Brewpub. A stunning array of First Nations masks and other artworks hangs from the open rafters in this popular Downtown brewpub, where jazz, blues, and swing bands play nightly. ⊠ *506 Pandora Ave., Downtown, Victoria* ☎ *250/361–3310* ⊕ *www.swanshotel.com.*

MUSIC CLUBS

Hermann's Jazz Club. Dinner, dancing, and live jazz are on the menu at this venerable Downtown restaurant and jazz club. ⊠ *753 View St., Downtown, Victoria* ☎ *250/388–9166* ⊕ *www.hermannsjazz.com.*

PERFORMING ARTS

MUSIC

Summer in the Square. Free jazz, classical, and folk concerts; cultural events; and more run all summer at Centennial Square, which is next to City Hall. Free lunchtime concerts are offered Tuesday to Thursday from noon to 1, from July through September. ⊠ *Centennial Square, Pandora Ave. and Douglas St., Downtown, Victoria* ☎ *250/361–0388* ⊕ *www.victoria.ca/cityvibe.*

Victoria Jazz Society. Watch for music events hosted by this group, which also organizes the annual TD Victoria International JazzFest in late June and the Vancouver Island Blues Bash in early September. ⊠ *Victoria* ☎ *250/388–4423* ⊕ *www.jazzvictoria.ca.*

19

SPORTS AND THE OUTDOORS

BIKING

Victoria is a bike-friendly town with more bicycle commuters than any other city in Canada. Bike racks on city buses, bike lanes on Downtown streets, and tolerant drivers all help, as do the city's three long-distance cycling routes, which mix car-free paths and low-traffic scenic routes.

BIKE ROUTES

Galloping Goose Regional Trail. Following an old rail bed, this 55-km (35-mile) route officially starts at the Vic West end of Johnson Street Bridge, which connects Downtown Victoria to Vic West. The multi-use trail runs across old rail trestles and through forests west to the town of Sooke, finishing just past Sooke Potholes Provincial Park. Just north of Downtown it links with the Lochside Regional Trail to the BC Ferries terminal at Swartz Bay, creating a nearly continuous 55-mile car-free route.

✉ *Johnson St. Bridge, Vic West, Victoria* ☎ *250/478–3344* ⊕ *www.crd. bc.ca/parks.*

Lochside Regional Trail. This fairly level, mostly car-free route follows an old rail bed for 29 km (18 miles) past farmland, wineries, and beaches from the ferry terminals at Swartz Bay and Sidney to Downtown Victoria. It joins the Seaside Touring Route at Cordova Bay and meets the Galloping Goose Trail just north of Downtown Victoria. ✉ *Sidney, Victoria* ☎ *250/478–3344* ⊕ *www.crd.bc.ca/parks.*

Victoria Seaside Touring Route. Starting at the corner of Government and Belleville streets on the Inner Harbour, this 29-km (18-mile) route along city streets and coastal roads, marked with bright yellow signs, leads past Fisherman's Wharf and along the Dallas Road waterfront to Beacon Hill Park. It then follows the seashore to Cordova Bay, where it connects with Victoria's other two long-distance routes: the Lochside and Galloping Goose regional trails. ✉ *Government and Belleville Sts., Inner Harbour, Downtown, Victoria* ⊕ *www.trailsbc.ca/loops-journeys/ vancouver-island/loop-victoria-seaside-touring-39-km.*

BIKE RENTALS AND TOURS

Cycle BC Rentals. This centrally located shop rents bikes for adults and children, as well as bike trailers, motorcycles, and scooters. ✉ *685 Humboldt St., Downtown, Victoria* ☎ *250/380–2453, 866/380–2453* ⊕ *www.cyclebc.ca.*

Cycletreks. Besides renting bikes, this company runs bike tours of Victoria, multiday trips to the Gulf Islands, and vineyard tours of the Saanich Peninsula and the Cowichan Valley. Their self-guided trips include bikes, maps, and a ride to Butchart Gardens or the end of the Galloping Goose or Lochside trail so that you can pedal back. ✉ *1000 Wharf St., Downtown, Victoria* ☎ *250/386–3147* ⊕ *www.cycletreks. com* ☺ *May–Sept. only.*

HIKING AND WALKING

Victoria is one of the most pedestrian-friendly cities in North America. Waterfront pathways make it possible to stroll virtually all around Victoria's waterfront. For some interesting self-guided walks around the city's historic areas, check out ⊕ *www.victoria.ca/tours* or pick up a free walking-tour map at the city's visitor information center. Though popular with cyclists, the area's long-distance paths are also great for long walks. For views and elevation, check out the trail networks in the area's many provincial and regional parks.

Mount Douglas Park. Trails through the forest to the 260-meter (853-foot) summit of Mt. Douglas reward hikers with a 360-degree view of Victoria, the Saanich Peninsula, and the mountains of Washington State. ✉ *Off Cedar Hill Rd., Saanich, Victoria* ☎ *250/475–5522* ⊕ *www.saanich.ca.*

WHALE-WATCHING

The following companies provide whale-watching excursions from Victoria.

FAMILY **Great Pacific Adventures.** This company offers year-round tours with both Zodiacs and covered vessels. Boats are equipped with hydrophones and all guides are marine biologists. In summer a three-hour tour starts at C$105. ⊠ *950 Wharf St., Victoria* ☎ *250/386–2277, 877/733–6722* ⊕ *www.greatpacificadventures.com.*

FAMILY **Prince of Whales.** Victoria's biggest whale-watching company offers a whole range of marine excursions, from three-hour boat or Zodiac tours from Victoria, to five-hour trips that include a stop at Butchart Gardens, to one-way or round-trip crossings between Vancouver and Victoria; all sailings have naturalists on board. Zodiac trips cost C$115 and leave year-round; covered boat sailings on the *Ocean Magic II* are C$110 and run from April to October; and Victoria to Butchart Garden trips run from late May to late September (the C$145 fare includes admission to the gardens). The company's Vancouver to Victoria crossings, running from late May to late September on the 74-passenger *Ocean Magic,* are a great time-saver, combining a sailing to or from Victoria with a whale-watching trip. A stop at the Butchart Gardens or return flights by floatplane or helicopter are options, too. The most popular trip, billed as The Ultimate Day Trip, includes a whale-watching trip from Vancouver to Victoria, a stop in Downtown Victoria, a bus transfer to Butchart Gardens, and a sunset sailing back to Vancouver. This C$300 trip runs daily from late May to late September. The company's Victoria office is on the Inner Harbour Causeway, below the Visitor Info Centre. ⊠ *812 Wharf St., Lower Causeway Level, Downtown, Victoria* ☎ *250/383–4884, 888/383–4884* ⊕ *www.princeofwhales.com.*

SHOPPING

19

VICTORIA SHOPPING

In Victoria, as in the rest of British Columbia, the most popular souvenirs are First Nations arts and crafts, which you can pick up at shops, galleries, street markets, and—in some cases—directly from artists' studios. Look for silver jewelry and cedar boxes carved with traditional images and, especially around Duncan (in the Cowichan Valley), the thick hand-knit sweaters made by the Cowichan people. BC wines, from shops in Victoria or directly from the wineries, make good souvenirs, as most are unavailable outside the province. Shopping in Victoria is easy: virtually everything is in the Downtown area on or near Government Street stretching north from the Fairmont Empress hotel.

DOWNTOWN

AREAS AND MALLS

Chinatown. Exotic fruits and vegetables, children's toys, wicker fans, fabric slippers, and other Chinese imports fill the shops along Fisgard Street. Fan Tan Alley, a narrow lane off Fisgard Street, has more nouveau-hippie goods, with a record store and yoga studio tucked in among its tiny storefronts. ⊠ *Downtown, Victoria.*

Design District. The area where Wharf Street runs into Store Street contains a cluster of Victoria's home decor shops. ⊠ *Downtown, Victoria* ⊕ *www.victoriadesigndistrict.com.*

Fodor'sChoice   **Lower Johnson Street.** This row of candy-color Victorian-era shopfronts
★   in LoJo (Lower Johnson) is Victoria's hub for independent fashion boutiques. Storefronts—some closet size—are filled with local designers' wares, funky boutiques, and shops selling ecologically friendly clothes of hemp and organic cotton. ⊠ *Johnson St., between Government and Store Sts., Downtown, Victoria.*

SPECIALTY STORES

Artina's. Canadian-made jewelry—all handmade, one-of-a-kind pieces— fills the display cases at this unique jewelry shop. ⊠ *1002 Government St., Downtown, Victoria* ☎ *250/386–7000* ⊕ *www.artinas.com.*

Cowichan Trading. First Nations jewelry, art, moccasins, and Cowichan sweaters are the focus at this long-established outlet. ⊠ *1328 Government St., Downtown, Victoria* ☎ *250/383–0321* ⊕ *www.cowichantrading. com.*

Hill's Native Art. Of the many First Nations stores you'll come across, Hill's is one of the best, offering everything from affordable souvenirs to original First Nations totems, masks, and jewelry as well as Inuit sculptures. ⊠ *1008 Government St., Downtown, Victoria* ☎ *250/385–3911* ⊕ *www.hills.ca.*

Irish Linen Stores. In business since 1917, this tiny shop has kept Victorians in fine linen, lace, and hand-embroidered items for generations. ⊠ *1019 Government St., Downtown, Victoria* ☎ *250/383–6812* ⊕ *www.irishlinenvictoria.com.*

Munro's Books. Move over, Chapters: this beautifully restored 1909 former bank now houses one of Canada's best-stocked independent bookstores. Deals abound in the remainders' bin. ⊠ *1108 Government St., Downtown, Victoria* ☎ *250/382–2464* ⊕ *www.munrobooks.com.*

Fodor'sChoice   **Silk Road.** Tea aspires to new heights in this chic emporium. Shelves are
★   stacked with more than 300 intriguing varieties; some you can enjoy in flights at an impressive tasting bar, and others have been restyled into aromatherapy remedies and spa treatments, including a green tea facial, which you can try out in the tiny spa downstairs. ⊠ *1624 Government St., Downtown, Victoria* ☎ *250/704–2688* ⊕ *www.silkroadtea.com.*

TRAVEL SMART
PACIFIC
NORTHWEST

GETTING HERE AND AROUND

■ AIR TRAVEL

It takes about 5 hours to fly nonstop to Seattle or Portland from New York, 4 hours from Chicago, and 2½ hours from Los Angeles. Flights from New York to Vancouver take about 6 hours nonstop; from Chicago, 4½ hours nonstop; and from Los Angeles, 3 hours nonstop. Flying from Seattle to Portland takes just under an hour; flying from Portland to Vancouver takes an hour and 15 minutes; and from Seattle to Vancouver about 45 minutes.

Airlines and Airports AirlineandAirport-Links.com. Here you'll find links to many of the world's airlines and airports. ⊕ *www.airlineandairportlinks.com.*

Airline Security Issues Transportation Security Administration. The agency has answers for almost every question that might come up. It is the most direct resource for confirming what can and cannot be carried on to a plane. ☎ *866/289–9673* ⊕ *www.tsa.gov.*

AIRPORTS

The main gateways to the Pacific Northwest are Portland International Airport (PDX), Sea-Tac International Airport (SEA), and Vancouver International Airport (YVR).

Airport Information Portland International Airport (PDX) ☎ *503/460–4234, 877/739–4636* ⊕ *www.flypdx.com.* **Sea-Tac International Airport (SEA)** ☎ *206/787–5388, 800/544–1965* ⊕ *www.portseattle.org/seatac.* **Vancouver International Airport (YVR)** ☎ *604/207–7077* ⊕ *www.yvr.ca.*

■TIP➔ Long layovers don't have to be only about sitting around or shopping. These days they can be about burning off vacation calories. Check out ⊕ *www.airportgyms.com* for lists of health clubs that are in or near many U.S. and Canadian airports.

AIRLINE TICKETS

The least expensive airfares to the Pacific Northwest are often priced for round-trip travel and usually must be purchased in advance. Airlines generally allow you to change your flights for a fee; most low-fare tickets, however, are nonrefundable.

You can often save money on your car rental (a must for most Pacific Northwest itineraries) by booking a fly-drive package through your airline. Many airlines offer deals on rental cars if you book through them.

FLIGHTS

Many international carriers serve the Pacific Northwest with direct flights. These include Air France, All Nippon Airways, British Airways, Cathay Pacific, Emirates, Japan Airlines, and Lufthansa. Vancouver has the most connections with international cities, but Seattle's a close second. U.S. carriers serving the area include Alaska Airlines, American, Delta, and United. JetBlue has daily direct flights from New York's JFK Airport, Logan International in Boston, and Los Angeles's Long Beach Airport to both Seattle and Portland. Virgin America has daily direct flights to Seattle from San Francisco and Los Angeles (LAX). USAirways flies from Portland and Seattle to Phoenix, Charlotte, and Philadelphia, and from Vancouver to Los Angeles and Phoenix. Frontier Airlines, Horizon Air, and United Express provide frequent service between cities in Washington, Oregon, Idaho, Montana, and California. Southwest Airlines has frequent service to Seattle and Portland from cities in California, Nevada, Idaho, and Utah, as well as some other parts of the country. The major regional carrier in western Canada is Air Canada (and its subsidiary, Air Canada Express), which has flights from Seattle and Portland to Vancouver and Victoria, along with many direct flights between Vancouver and major U.S. cities outside the Northwest.

Airline Contacts Air Canada/Air Canada Express ☎ *888/247–2262* ⊕ *www. aircanada.com.* **Alaska Airlines/Horizon Air** ☎ *800/252–7522* ⊕ *www.alaskaair. com.* **American Airlines** ☎ *800/433–7300* ⊕ *www.aa.com.* **Delta Airlines** ☎ *800/221– 1212* ⊕ *www.delta.com.* **Frontier Airlines** ☎ *800/432–1359* ⊕ *www.frontierairlines.com.* **Japan Airlines** ☎ *800/525–3663* ⊕ *www. jal.com.* **jetBlue** ☎ *800/538–2583* ⊕ *www. jetblue.com.* **Southwest Airlines** ☎ *800/435– 9792* ⊕ *www.southwest.com.* **United Airlines** ☎ *800/864–8331* ⊕ *www.united.com.* **USAirways** ☎ *800/428–4322* ⊕ *www.usairways.com.* **Virgin America** ☎ *877/359–8474* ⊕ *www. virginamerica.com.*

▮ BOAT AND FERRY TRAVEL

Ferries play an important part in the transportation network of the Pacific Northwest. Some are the sole connection to islands in Puget Sound and to small towns and islands along the West Coast of British Columbia. Each day ferries transport thousands of commuters to and from work in the coastal cities. Always comfortable, convenient, and providing spectacular views, ferries are also one of the best ways for you to get a feel for the region and its ties to the sea.

Generally, the best times for travel are 9–3 and after 7 pm on weekdays. In July and August you may have to wait hours to take a car aboard one of the popular ferries, such as those to the San Juan Islands. Walk-on space is almost always available; if possible, leave your car behind. Reservations aren't taken for most domestic routes in Washington.

WASHINGTON AND OREGON

Washington State Ferries carries millions of passengers and vehicles each year on 10 routes between 20 points on Puget Sound, the San Juan Islands, and Sidney, British Columbia. Onboard services vary depending on the size of the ferry, but many ships have a cafeteria, vending machines, newspaper and tourist-information kiosks, arcade games, and restrooms with family

facilities. There are discounted fares in off-peak months.

Black Ball Transport's MV *Coho* makes daily crossings year-round from Port Angeles, WA, to Victoria. The *Coho* can carry 800 passengers and 100 cars across the Strait of Juan de Fuca in 1½ hours. Clipper Vacations operates the passenger-only *Victoria Clipper* jet catamaran service between Seattle and Victoria year-round and between Seattle and the San Juan Islands May through September. ▮TIP→ **Victoria Clipper fares are less expensive if booked at least one day in advance, tickets for children under 12 are discounted, and some great package deals are often available online (be sure to ask about any other promotions or deals, too).**

Contacts Black Ball Transport ☎ *250/386– 2202 in Victoria, 360/457–4491 in Port Angeles, 888/993–3779* ⊕ *www.cohoferry. com.* **Clipper Vacations** ☎ *206/448–5000 in Seattle, 250/382–8100 in Victoria, 800/888– 2535* ⊕ *www.clippervacations.com.* **King County Water Taxi** ☎ *206/477–3979* ⊕ *kingcounty.gov/transportation/kcdot/WaterTaxi.* **Washington State Ferries** ☎ *800/843–3779 automated line in WA and BC, 888/808–7977 WA and BC reservations, 206/464–6400* ⊕ *www.wsdot.wa.gov/ferries.*

BRITISH COLUMBIA

British Columbia Ferries operates passenger and vehicle service between the mainland and Victoria and elsewhere. Most ferries take reservations.

Information British Columbia Ferries ☎ *250/386–3431 in Victoria, 888/223–3779* ⊕ *www.bcferries.com.*

SIGHTSEEING

Argosy cruising vessels make sightseeing, dinner, weekend brunch, and special-event cruises around Elliott Bay, Lake Union, Lake Washington, the Ballard Locks, and other Seattle waterways.

From Portland, the *Portland Spirit, Willamette Star,* and *Crystal Dolphin* make sightseeing and dinner cruises on the

Willamette and Columbia Rivers. Departing from Cascade Locks, Oregon (45 minutes east of Portland), the stern-wheeler *Columbia Gorge* cruises the Columbia Gorge and the Willamette River (December only).

Information Argosy Cruises ☎ *206/622–8687, 888/623–1445* ⊕ *www.argosycruises. com.* **Portland Spirit River Cruises** ☎ *503/224–3900* ⊕ *www.portlandspirit.com.*

▌BUS TRAVEL

Greyhound services the Washington–Oregon region. BoltBus service runs between Vancouver, Bellingham, Seattle, and Portland and features sleek new buses with Wi-Fi, extra legroom, reserved seating, and power outlets. Experience Oregon in Eugene operates charter bus services and scheduled sightseeing tours that last from a few hours to several days. People Mover travels on Highway 26 in Oregon between Bend and John Day. Greyhound serves most towns in British Columbia, and provides frequent service on popular runs. Quick Shuttle runs buses from Sea-Tac Airport, Downtown Seattle, and Bellingham to various Vancouver spots and hotels.

Pacific Coach Lines runs multiple daily buses between Vancouver and Victoria, including a ferry ride across the Strait of Georgia, and between Vancouver and Whistler Village. The company also has connections from Vancouver International Airport, Downtown Vancouver, and the cruise ship terminal, and operates numerous package tours around British Columbia.

Bus Information BoltBus ☎ *877/265–8287* ⊕ *www.boltbus.com.* **Experience Oregon** ☎ *541/342–2662, 888/342–2662* ⊕ *www. experienceoregon.com.* **Greyhound Lines** ☎ *800/231–2222* ⊕ *www.greyhound.com.* **Pacific Coach Lines** ☎ *800/661–1725, 604/662–7575 in Vancouver* ⊕ *www. pacificcoach.com.* **People Mover** ☎ *541/575–2370* ⊕ *www.grantcountypeoplemover. com.* **Quick Shuttle** ☎ *800/665–2122,*

TRAVEL TIMES FROM SEATTLE BY CAR	
Portland	3–3½ hours
Vancouver	2½–3 hours
Victoria	2½–3 hour drive to Vancouver; 1½-hour ferry ride from Vancouver
Mount Rainier National Park (Paradise or Longmire entrances)	2½ hours
North Cascades National Park	3–3½ hours
Olympic National Park	2½ hours to Port Angeles; 1 hour from Port Angeles to Hurricane Ridge
Mt. St. Helens	3–3½ hours
Spokane	4½–5 hours
Yakima Valley	2–2½ hours

TRAVEL TIMES FROM PORTLAND BY CAR	
Bend	3½–4 hours
Crater Lake National Park	4½–5 hours
Columbia River Gorge/ Mt. Hood	1½ hours
Willamette Valley	1½–2 hours

604/940–4428 in Vancouver ⊕ *www. quickcoach.com.*

SIGHTSEEING

Gray Line operates a few day trips from Portland, Seattle, and Vancouver, including tours to Mt. Rainier, the San Juan Islands, Multnomah Falls and the Columbia River Gorge, Vancouver, and Victoria, and schedules a variety of popular bus tours and overnight packages around the Pacific Northwest.

▮ CAR TRAVEL

Driver's licenses from other countries are valid in the United States and Canada. International driving permits (IDPs)—available from the American and Canadian automobile associations and Canada's National Auto Club, and, in the United Kingdom, from the Automobile Association and Royal Automobile Club—are a good idea. Valid only in conjunction with your regular driver's license, these permits are universally recognized; having one may spare you having difficulties with local authorities.

Bookstores, gas stations, convenience stores, and rest stops sell maps (about $5) and multiregion road atlases (about $14). Along larger highways, roadside stops with restrooms, fast-food restaurants, and sundries stores are well spaced. Police and tow trucks patrol major highways and lend assistance.

BORDER CROSSING

⇨ *See also Passports in Essentials below.*

You will need a valid passport to cross the border; passport cards and enhanced driver's licenses are also accepted for land and sea crossings only. In addition, drivers must carry owner registration and proof of insurance coverage, which is compulsory in Canada. The Canadian Non-Resident Inter-Provincial Motor Vehicle Liability Insurance Card, available from any U.S. insurance company, is accepted as evidence of financial responsibility in Canada. If you are driving a car that is not registered in your name, carry a letter from the owner that authorizes your use of the vehicle.

The main entry point into British Columbia from the United States by car is on Interstate 5 at Blaine, Washington, 48 km (30 miles) south of Vancouver. Three highways enter British Columbia from the east: Highway 1, or the Trans-Canada Highway; Highway 3, or the Crowsnest Highway, which crosses southern British Columbia; and Highway 16, the Yellowhead Highway, which runs through northern British Columbia from the Rocky Mountains to Prince Rupert. From Alaska and the Yukon, take the Alaska Highway (from Fairbanks) or the Klondike Highway (from Skagway or Dawson City).

Border-crossing procedures are usually quick and simple. Every British Columbia border crossing is open 24 hours (except the one at Aldergrove, which is open from 8 am to midnight). The Interstate 5 border crossing at Blaine, Washington (also known as the Douglas, or Peace Arch, border crossing), is one of the busiest border crossings between the United States and Canada. An alternate route, the Pacific Highway border crossing (also known as the "truck crossing"), is just east of the Peace Arch crossing and serves all vehicles, not just trucks. Listen to local radio traffic reports for information about border wait times.

CAR RENTALS

▮TIP→ Make sure that a confirmed reservation guarantees you a car. Agencies sometimes overbook, particularly for busy weekends and holiday periods.

Unless you only visit Seattle, Portland, and Vancouver, you will need to rent a car for at least part of your trip. It's possible to get around the big cities by public transportation and taxis, but once you go outside city limits, your options are limited. National lines like Greyhound do provide service between major towns, and Amtrak has limited service between points in Washington, Oregon, and British Columbia (allowing you to get from, say, Seattle to Portland, by train), but it is nearly impossible to get to and around the major recreation areas and national parks of each state without your own wheels. For example, there is no public transportation from Seattle to Mount Rainier National Park.

Rates in Seattle begin at $29 a day ($206 per week) for an economy car. This does not include the 17.2% tax. The tax on rentals at Sea-Tac Airport, which includes an airport concession fee, is more than 30%, so try to rent from a Downtown branch, where base rental rates are often lower, too. Rates in Portland begin at $31 a day and $218 a week, not including the 17% tax. Rates in Vancouver begin at about C$13 a day or C$100 a week, usually including unlimited mileage. Note that summer rates in all cities can be absurd (up to $65 per day for a compact); book as far in advance as possible, and if you find a good deal, grab it. Car rentals in British Columbia also incur a 12% sales tax. An additional 17% Concession Recovery Fee, charged by the airport authority for retail space in the terminal, is levied at airport locations.

All the major agencies are represented in the region. If you're planning to cross the U.S.–Canadian border with your rental car, discuss it with the agency to see what's involved.

In the Pacific Northwest you must be 21 to rent a car. Car seats are compulsory for infants and toddlers; older children are required to sit in booster seats until they are eight years old *or* 4 feet, 9 inches tall. (In British Columbia, children up to 40 pounds or 18 kilos in weight must use a child seat; booster seats are required for children up to nine years old or 145 cm tall.) In the United States nonresidents need a reservation voucher, passport, driver's license, and insurance for each driver.

ROAD CONDITIONS

Winter driving can present challenges. In coastal areas the mild, damp climate contributes to frequently wet roadways. Snowfalls generally occur in low-lying Portland, Seattle, and Vancouver only once or twice a year, but when snow does fall, traffic grinds to a halt and roadways become treacherous and stay that way until the snow melts.

Tire chains, studs, or snow tires are essential equipment for winter travel in mountain areas. If you're planning to drive into high elevations, be sure to check the weather forecast beforehand. Even the main-highway mountain passes can close because of snow conditions. In winter state and provincial highway departments operate snow-advisory telephone lines that give pass conditions.

ROADSIDE EMERGENCIES

Contacts For **police, ambulance,** or **other emergencies,** dial 911. **Oregon State Police** ☎ *503/378-3720, 800/452-7888* ⊕ *www. oregon.gov/oprd/parks.*

▮ TRAIN TRAVEL

Amtrak, the U.S. passenger rail system, has daily service to the Pacific Northwest from the Midwest and California. The Empire Builder takes a northern route through Minnesota and Montana from Chicago to Spokane, from which separate legs continue to Seattle and Portland. The Coast Starlight begins in Los Angeles; makes stops throughout California, western Oregon, and Washington; and terminates in Seattle.

Amtrak's Cascades trains travel between Seattle and Vancouver and between Seattle, Portland, and Eugene. The trip from Seattle to Portland takes roughly 3½ hours and costs $26–$62 for a coach seat; this is a pleasant alternative to a mind-numbing drive down Interstate 5. The trip from Seattle to Vancouver takes roughly four hours and costs $31–$75. The Empire Builder travels between Portland and Spokane (7½ hours, $54–$120), with part of the route running through the Columbia River Gorge. From Portland to Eugene, the trip is just under three hours; the cost is $27–$49.

▮TIP➔ Book Amtrak tickets at least a few days in advance, especially if you're traveling between Seattle and Portland on summer weekends.

Contact Amtrak ☎ *800/872-7245* ⊕ *www. amtrak.com.*

ESSENTIALS

▌ ACCOMMODATIONS

The lodgings we list are the cream of the crop in each price category. Prices are for a standard double room in high season, based on the European Plan and excluding tax and service charges. Seattle room tax is 15.6%. Elsewhere in Washington it ranges from 10% to 16%. Portland room tax is 11.5% (13.5% at hotels with 50 or more rooms) while elsewhere in Oregon it ranges from 7% to 10%. Vancouver room tax is 15% with elsewhere in British Columbia ranging from 12% to 14%. Most hotels and other lodgings require you to give your credit-card details before they will confirm your reservation. Though secure online payment is commonly used for hotel reservations, if you don't feel comfortable providing information this way, ask if you can fax it or provide by phone. However you book, get confirmation in writing, and have a copy of it handy when you check in.

▄TIP➔ **Assume that hotels operate on the European Plan (no meals) unless we specify that they serve breakfast or, in rare cases, other meals are included as well.**

BED-AND-BREAKFASTS

The Pacific Northwest is known for its vast range of bed-and-breakfasts, which are found everywhere from busy urban areas to casual country farms and coastal retreats. Many B&Bs here provide full gourmet breakfasts, and some have kitchens that guests can use. Other popular amenities to ask about are fireplaces, jetted bathtubs, outdoor hot tubs, and area activities.

The regional B&B organizations listed here can provide information on reputable establishments.

Reservation Services American Bed & Breakfast Association ⊕ *www.abba. com.* **BBCanada.com** ⊕ *www.bbcanada. com.* **British Columbia Bed and Breakfasts** ⊕ *www.bcbbonly.com.* **British Columbia Bed and Breakfast Innkeepers Guild** ⊕ *www. bcsbestbnbs.com.* **The Canadian Bed and Breakfast Guide** ☎ *905/641–8484* ⊕ *www. canadianbandbguide.ca.* **Oregon Bed and Breakfast Guild** ☎ *800/944–6196* ⊕ *www. obbg.org.* **Washington Bed and Breakfast Guild** ☎ *253/987–6619* ⊕ *www.wbbg.com.*

CAMPING

Oregon, Washington, and British Columbia have excellent government-run campgrounds. Some accept advance camping reservations. National park campsites—even backcountry sites—fill up quickly and should be reserved in advance. Note that federal forests allow free camping almost anywhere along trails—a good fail-safe if you're unable to secure last-minute arrangements at designated sites, and don't mind hauling your gear.

Privately operated campgrounds sometimes have extra amenities such as laundry rooms and swimming pools. For more information, contact the state or provincial tourism department.

Campground Reservations British Columbia Lodgings and Campground Association ☎ *778/383–1037* ⊕ *www.travel-british-columbia.com.* **Discover Camping (British Columbia)** ☎ *800/689–9025, 519/826–6850 overseas calls* ⊕ *www.discovercamping.ca.* **Oregon Parks and Recreation Department.** ☎ *800/452–5687 reservations* ⊕ *www.oregon. gov/oprd/parks.* **Washington State Parks** ☎ *888/226–7688 reservations, 360/902–8844 information* ⊕ *www.parks.wa.gov.*

HOTELS

When booking a room, always call the hotel's direct number (if one is available) rather than the central reservations number—you'll often get a better price. Deals can often be found at hotel websites. Always ask about special packages or corporate rates. Many properties offer special weekend rates, sometimes up to 50% off regular prices. However, these deals are usually not extended during peak summer months, when hotels are normally full. All hotels listed have private bath unless otherwise noted.

CRUISE LINES

Carnival Cruise Line ☎ 888/227–6482 ⊕ www.carnival.com. **Celebrity Cruises** ☎ 800/647–2251 ⊕ www.celebritycruises. com. **Holland America Line** ☎ 877/932–4259 ⊕ www.hollandamerica.com. **Norwegian Cruise Line** ☎ 866/234–7350 ⊕ www.ncl.com. **Princess Cruises** ☎ 800/774–6237 ⊕ www. princess.com.

▮ CUSTOMS AND DUTIES

You're always allowed to bring goods of a certain value back home without having to pay any duty or import tax. But there's a limit on the amount of tobacco and liquor you can bring back duty-free, and some countries have separate limits for perfumes; for exact figures, check with your customs department. The values of so-called "duty-free" goods are included in these amounts. When you shop abroad, save all your receipts, as customs inspectors may ask to see them as well as the items you purchased. If the total value of your goods is more than the duty-free limit, you'll have to pay a tax (most often a flat percentage) on the value of everything beyond that limit.

U.S. Information U.S. Customs and Border Protection ☎ 877/227–5511 ⊕ www.cbp.gov.

Information in Canada Canada Border Services Agency ☎ 204/983–3500, 800/461–9999 toll-free within Canada ⊕ www.cbsa-asfc. gc.ca.

▮ EATING OUT

Pacific Northwest cuisine highlights regional seafood and locally grown, organic produce, often prepared in styles that reflect an Asian influence (Seattle, Victoria, and Vancouver have large Asian populations) or incorporate European (often French or Italian) influences. See

our *Flavors of the Pacific Northwest* feature at the beginning of this book.

The restaurants we list are the cream of the crop in each price category. Please note that restaurant prices listed as "Average Cost" indicate the price of a main course at dinner; or if dinner is not served, at lunch.

MEALS AND MEALTIMES

Unless otherwise noted, the restaurants listed here are open daily for lunch and dinner.

PAYING

Credit cards—Visa and MasterCard, in particular—are widely accepted in most restaurants, especially in Seattle, Portland, and Vancouver. Debit cards are widely accepted in coffeehouses, delis, and grocery stores.

WINES, BEER, AND SPIRITS

Oregon, Washington, and British Columbia all have thriving wineries, and many restaurants in major cities and many small towns, and even in wilderness areas, take their wine lists very seriously. Most of Washington's wineries are east of the Cascades in the south-central part of the state, but you'll find a few close to Seattle as well. Oregon's wineries mostly lie in the valleys between the southern Cascades and the coast. British Columbia wine-making has become increasingly prominent, with many wineries opening in the Okanagan Valley. The Washington State Wine Commission (⊕ *www. washingtonwine.org*) and the Oregon Wine Board (⊕ *www.oregonwine.org*) both maintain websites with facts, history, and information on local wineries. The

British Columbia Wine Institute's website (⊕ *www.winebc.com*) has facts and information on individual wineries.

Oregon has more than 150 microbreweries, and Washington has no shortage of excellent local microbrews. Both states have festivals and events celebrating their brews—Seattle's Fremont neighborhood has its own Oktoberfest. The website for the Washington Brewers Guild (⊕ *www. washingtonbeer.com*) has info on breweries in the state and events throughout the Pacific Northwest. The Oregon Brewers Guild (⊕ *www.oregonbeer.org*) also has links to breweries and information on events.

You must be 21 to buy alcohol in Washington and Oregon. The legal drinking age in British Columbia is 19.

▮ MONEY

Prices listed for sights and attractions are for adults. Substantially reduced fees are almost always available for children, students, and senior citizens.

CURRENCY AND EXCHANGE

The units of currency in Canada are the Canadian dollar (C$) and the cent, in almost the same denominations as U.S. currency ($5, $10, $20, 5¢, 10¢, 25¢, etc.). Canada stopped distributing pennies in 2013. C$1 and C$2 coins (known as a "loonie," because of the loon that appears on the coin, and a "toonie," respectively) are used in lieu of bills. Check with a bank or other financial institution for the current exchange rate. A good way to be sure you're getting the best exchange rate is by using your credit card or ATM/debit card. The issuing bank will convert your bill at the current rate, though foreign transaction fees may still be added.

▮TIP➜ Even if a currency-exchange booth has a sign promising "no commission," rest assured that there's some kind of huge, hidden fee. (Oh . . . that's right. The sign didn't say no fee.) And as for rates, you're almost always better off getting foreign currency at an ATM or exchanging money at a bank.

▮ PASSPORTS

All people traveling by air between the United States and Canada are required to present a passport to enter or reenter the United States. To enter Canada (or more precisely, to reenter the United States from Canada) by land or sea you need to present either a valid passport or a U.S. Passport Card—sort of a "passport lite" that is only valid for land or sea crossings from Canada, Mexico, the Caribbean, or Bermuda. Enhanced drivers licenses, issued by Washington and other border states, can also be used for land or sea crossings.

For more information on border crossings, see Car Travel above.

U.S. passports are valid for 10 years. You must apply in person if you're getting a passport for the first time; if your previous passport was lost, stolen, or damaged; or if your previous passport has expired and was issued more than 15 years ago or when you were under 16. All children under 18 must appear in person to apply for or renew a passport. Both parents must accompany any child under 14 (or send a notarized statement with their permission) and provide proof of their relationship to the child.

The cost to apply for a new passport is $135 for adults, $105 for children under 16; renewals are $110. Allow up to six weeks for processing, both for first-time passports and renewals. For an expediting fee of $60, you can reduce this time to about three weeks. If your trip is less than two weeks away, you can get a passport even more rapidly by going to a passport office with the necessary documentation. Private expediters can get things done in as little as 48 hours, but charge hefty fees for their services.

U.S. Passport Information **U.S. Department of State** ☎ *877/487–2778* ⊕ *passports.state. gov.*

Canadian Passports Passport Canada ✉ *Passport Canada Program, Gatineau, Québec, Canada* ☎ *819/997–8338, 800/567–6868 toll-free Canada and U.S.* ⊕ *www.ppt. gc.ca.*

U.S. Passport & Visa Expediters American Passport ☎ *800/455–5166* ⊕ *www. americanpassport.com.* Passport Express ☎ *800/362–8196* ⊕ *www.passportexpress.com.* Travel Document Systems ☎ *202/638–3800, 800/874–5100* ⊕ *www.traveldocs.com.* Travel the World Visas ☎ *202/223–8822, 866/886–8472* ⊕ *www.world-visa.com.*

▌ SAFETY

The most dangerous element of the Northwest is the great outdoors. Don't hike alone, and make sure you bring enough water plus basic first-aid items. If you're not an experienced hiker, stick to tourist-friendly spots like the more accessible parts of the national parks; if you have to drive 30 miles down a Forest Service road to reach a trail, it's possible you might be the only one hiking on it.

▌ TAXES

Oregon has no sales tax, although many cities and counties levy a tax on lodging and services. Room taxes, for example, vary from 7% to 13.5%. The state retail sales tax in Washington is 6.5%, but there are also local taxes that can raise the total tax to almost 10%, depending on the goods or service and the municipality; Seattle's retail sales tax is 9.5%. A Goods and Services Tax (GST) of 5% applies on virtually every transaction in Canada except for the purchase of basic groceries.

In British Columbia an additional Provincial Sales Tax (PST) of 7% applies to most goods and services.

▌ VISITOR INFORMATION

British Columbia Tourism Vancouver Island ✉ *65 Front St., Suite 501, Nanaimo, British Columbia, Canada* ☎ *250/754–3500* ⊕ *www. seevancouverisland.com.* Tourism Vancouver Visitor Centre ✉ *Plaza Level, 200 Burrard St., Vancouver, British Columbia, Canada* ☎ *604/683–2000* ⊕ *www.tourismvancouver. com.* Tourism Victoria ✉ *Visitors Centre, 812 Wharf St., Victoria, British Columbia, Canada* ☎ *250/953–2033, 800/663–3883* ⊕ *www. tourismvictoria.com.*

Oregon Travel Oregon ☎ *800/547–7842* ⊕ *www.traveloregon.com.* Travel Portland ✉ *Visitor Info Center, 701 S.W. 6th, Portland, Oregon, United States* ☎ *503/275–8355, 877/678–5263* ⊕ *www.travelportland.com.*

Washington Seattle Convention and Visitors Bureau ☎ *866/732–2695 visitor information, 206/461–5840 main office* ⊕ *www.visitseattle.org.* Washington Tourism Alliance ☎ *800/544–1800* ⊕ *www. experiencewa.com.*

INDEX

PHOTO CREDITS

Front cover: Galyna Andrushko / Shutterstock [Description: Diablo Lake,Washington]. Back cover: Natalia Bratslavsky/Shutterstock; Rachell Coe/Shutterstock; San Juan Safaris. Spine: Jo Ann Snover/ Shutterstock. 1, Arthit Kaeoratanapattama / Shutterstock. 2-3, Jeanne Hatch/iStockphoto. 5, Liem Bahneman/Shutterstock. Chapter 1: Experience the Pacific Northwest. 8-9, Martin Bydalek Photography. 10, Rebecca Kennison/wikipedia.org. 11 (left), Lijuan Guo/iStockphoto. 11 (right), Ashok Rodrigues/iStockphoto. 12, Steve Whiston/Burke Museum. 13 (left), Stacey Lynn Payne/iStockphoto. 13 (right), Washington Wine Commission. 16 (left), Christopher Boswell/Shutterstock, 16 (top right), moohaha/Flickr. 16 (bottom center), Elena Korenbaum/iStockphoto. 16 (bottom right), Brian Holsclaw/ Flickr. 17 (top left), The High Desert Museum. 17 (top center), James Hornung/Shutterstock. 17 (bottom left), Neta Delgany/iStockphoto. 17 (bottom center), Chuck Pefley/Alamy. 17 (right), Norman Eder/iStockphoto. 18 (left), neelsky/Shutterstock. 18 (top right), moohaha/Flickr. 18 (bottom center), Rimasz/Dreamstime.com. 18 (bottom right), thinair/iStockphoto. 19 (top left), Jdanne I Dreamstime. com. 19 (bottom left), Pike Place Market. 19 (bottom center), Tim Thompson. 19 (right), Victor Maschek / Shutterstock. 20 (left), Kenji Nogai21. 20 (top right), Lissandra Melo/Shutterstock. 20 (bottom center), Natalia Bratslavsky/Shutterstock. 20 (bottom right), WordRidden/Flickr. 21 (top left), Steve Rossett/Shutterstock. 21 (top center) Natalia Braslavsky/Shutterstock. 21 (right), fotofriends/Shutterstock. 21 (bottom left), Michel Teiten/Wikipedia.com. 21 (bottom center) Royal BC Museum. 22, Kirk Hirota. 23, (left), Victoria Coffee/Kent Colony. 23 (right), ABC pics/Shutterstock. 25 (left), Rachel Coe/ Shutterstock. 25 (right), Geoffrey Smith. 26, Matt McGee/Flickr. 27 Pacific Science Center. 36, Martin Bydalek Photography. 37 (right), Ben Tobin. 37 (left), Campbell Gordon. 39, Stuart Westmorland/age fotostock. 41, Thomas Kitchin & Vict/age fotostock. 42, San Juan Safaris. 43, Sylvain Grandadam/age fotostock. 44, Andy Simonds. Chapter 2: Portland: 45, Brian A. Ridder/Flickr. 46, -b-/Flickr. 47 (left), David Owen/Flickr. 47 (right), Michael Hashizume/Flickr. 48, Karen Massier/Stockphoto. 55, Greg Vaughan. 59, Greg Vaughan. 69, Rigucci/Shutterstock. 115, Jason Vandewhey/Shutterstock. 119, Realitytimes I Dreamstime.com. Chapter 3: The Oregon Coast. 125, Greg Vaughn. 126, scaredy_kat/Flickr. 127 (top), Oksana Perkins/iStockphoto.127 (bottom), CVA/Flickr. 128, Tom Wald/iStockphoto. 129 (bottom), John Norris/Flickr. 129 (top), Scott Catron/wikipedia.org. 130, Pacific Northwest USCG/ Flickr. 155, Greg Vaughn. 158, Oregon Coast Aquarium. 165, Greg Vaughan. Chapter 4: Willamette Valley and Wine Country: 179, Dennis Frates / Alamy. 180 (top), Don Hankins/Flickr. 180 (bottom), Gathering Together Farms. 181, Doreen L. Wynja. 182, Craig Sherod. 190, Greg Vaughn. 198, Jason Tomczak. 198-99, Greg Vaughn. 200, Fox Hill Vineyards. 202 (left), Jason Tomczak. 202 (right), REX HILL, Newberg, OR. 203, Doreen L. Wynja. 204 (top), Ponzi Vineyards. 204 (bottom), Vercingetorix Vineyards. 205 (left), Adelsheim Vineyard. 205 (center), Box Hill. 205 (right), Norman Eder/iStockphoto. 207 (left), Pennar-Ash Wine Cellars. 207 (center), Polara Studio. 207 (right), Dundee Bistro. 218, Greg Vaughn. 226, Greg Vaughn. Chapter 5: The Columbia River Gorge and Mt. Hood: 231, William Blacke/iStockphoto. 232, Timberline Lodge. 233 (top), Robert Crum/iStockphoto. 233 (bottom), Christian Sawicki/iStockphoto. 234, Rigucci/Shutterstock. 242, zschnepf/Shutterstock. 244 and 247, GregVaughn. 257, Melissa & Bryan Ripka/Flickr. Chapter 6: Central Oregon: 263, Mike Houska. 264 (top), Robert O. Brown Photography/iStockphoto. 264 (bottom), Black Butte Ranch. 265, JonDissed/ Flickr. 266, Sunriver Resort. 273, USGS photo by Lyn Topinka/wikimedia. 277, Sunriver Resort. 286, mariachily/Flickr. Chapter 7: Crater Lake National Park: 291, William A. McConnell. 292 (bottom), Aimin Tang/iStockphoto. 292 (center), Steve Terrill. 292 (top), Ashok Rodrigues/iStockphoto. 293, Michael Rubin/iStockphoto. 294, Vivian Fung/Shutterstock. Chapter 8: Southern Oregon. 303, Greg Vaughn. 304, Michael Dunn-I/Flickr. 305 (top), Michael (a.k.a maik) McCullough/Wikimedia. 305 (bottom), Ellen C. Campbell/Chanticleer Inn. 306, Paula C. Caudill. 311, Larry Turner. 313, nwrafting/ Flickr. 323, Greg Vaughn. Chapter 9: Seattle. 331 José Fuste Raga / age fotostock. 333, Stephen Finn/ Shutterstock. 334, Gregory Olsen/iStockphoto. 335, Mariusz S. Jurgielewicz/Shutterstock. 343, jeffwilcox/Flickr. 346 (top), Mark B. Bauschke/Shutterstock. 346 (bottom), Charles Amundson/Shutterstock. 348 (top), The Tasting Room. 348 (bottom center), piroshky bakery. 348 (bottom right), Beecher's Handmade Cheese. 349 (left), Phillie Casablanca/Flickr. 349 (center), Nick Jurich of flashpd.com. 349 (right), eng1ne/Flickr. 350 (top left), Liem Bahneman/Shutterstock. 350 (bottom left), Pike Place Market PDA. 350 (right), World Pictures/Phot / age fotostock. 351 (left), Stephen Power / Alamy. 351 (right), Rootology/wikipedia.org. 353, Mark B. Bauschke/Shutterstock. 356, Laura Komada. 391, ebis50/Flickr. 393, Agua Verde Paddle Club. 406, LegalAdmin/Flickr. 411, Richard Cummins / age fotostock. 413, Joe Becker / age fotostock. Chapter 10: Washington Cascade Mountains and Valleys: 417, Carlos Arguelles/ Shutterstock. 418 (bottom), Adrian Baras/Shutterstock. 418 (top), Northwest Trek Wildlife Park. 419, Rodefeld/Flickr. 420, Mrs. Flinger/Flickr. 426, John Carlson. 430, Rodefield/Flickr. 443, Richard Cummins / age fotostock. 451, amanderson2/Flickr. 463, tusharkoley/Shutterstock. 464, neelsky/Shutter-

NOTES

ABOUT OUR WRITERS

Shelley Arenas grew up in Spokane and has lived in the Seattle area all of her adult life. She has contributed to Fodor's books for more than a decade, coauthored a guidebook to Seattle for families, and written for regional publications, including *Seattle Woman* magazine. She updated Olympic National Park, North Cascades National Park, Mount Rainier National Park, Eastern Washington, and Travel Smart this edition.

Kimberly Bowker grew up hiking and kayaking in the high desert landscape of Central Oregon. She wrote for Bend's daily newspaper before pursuing a freelance writing career, focusing on the topics of travel, craft beer, and love. For more information, visit ⊕ *www.kimberlybowker.com*. She updated the Central Oregon chapter.

Andrew Collins, a former Fodor's editor, updated Experience the Pacific Northwest, Portland, Oregon Coast, Columbia River Gorge and Mt. Hood, Southern Oregon, Washington Cascade Mountains and Valleys, and the San Juan Islands chapters this edition. A resident of Oregon who travels frequently throughout the region, he has authored more than a dozen guidebooks, is editor in chief of *The Pearl* (about Portland's hip Pearl District), and produces the website ⊕ *GayTravel.About.com*. He also writes a syndicated monthly travel column; writes about restaurants, art, and design or *Four Seasons Magazine* and travel or *New Mexico Magazine*; teaches food riting and travel writing for Gotham /riters' Workshop; and has contributed *Travel & Leisure*, *Sunset*, and dozens other periodicals.

travel writer since 2006, **Chloë Ernst** ten explores her British Columbia backyard writing for Fodor's, Zagat, and Travelandleisure.com. While she loves Vancouver's hiking trails and breweries, Chloë has a special affinity for long ferry journeys and out-of-the-way excursions, and her adventures have taken her to abandoned Alaskan gold mines and along jungle roads in Bolivia. More of her writing can be found at ⊕ *www.chloeernst.com*.

Carolyn B. Heller has been enthusiastically exploring—and eating—her way across her adopted city of Vancouver since she relocated here in 2003. She's a regular contributor to the Forbes Travel Guide and Hotel-Scoop.com, and her travel and food articles have appeared in publications ranging from the *Boston Globe* and the *Los Angeles Times*, to *FamilyFun*, *Real Weddings*, and *Perceptive Travel* magazines. She's the author of two travel books, *Moon Ontario* and *Living Abroad in Canada*, and she's contributed to more than 25 Fodor's guides for destinations from New England to New Zealand.

A newspaper internship first lured Seattle native **Adriana Janovich** to Port Townsend, Washington nearly 20 years ago. Now a food, travel, and lifestyles writer and editor in the Inland Northwest, she loved revisiting her old haunts—and discovering some new ones—for the Olympic Peninsula and North Central Washington chapters this edition. She also teaches journalism at Whitworth University in Spokane.

Freelance writer **Sue Kernaghan** has written about British Columbia for dozens of publications and websites around a world, including several editions of *Fodor's Vancouver and British Columbia*. A fourth-generation British Columbian, she now lives and writes on Salt Spring Island.

Award-winning freelance travel writer Chris McBeath's more than 25 years in the tourism industry have given her an insider's eye about what makes a great vacation. British Columbia is her home, so whether routing through backcountry or discovering a hidden-away inn, Chris has combined history, insight, and anecdotes into her contribution to this book. Many of Chris's articles can be found at ⊕ *www.greatestgetaways.com*; her destination videos are available on YouTube.

Freelance writer Rob Phillips has lived in Central Washington for nearly 50 years. He has written for dozens of publications, mostly on outdoor subjects. His award-winning "Northwest Outdoors" column appears every Tuesday in the *Yakima Herald-Republic*. He updated the Washington Wine Country chapter this edition.

Dave Sandage is a software engineer living in the heart of Willamette Valley wine country. In his spare time he enjoys cooking, wine tasting, and making his own beer and wine. Dave wrote the Willamette Valley wine feature and updated the Willamette Valley and Wine Country chapter.

A native Southern Californian, AnnaMaria Stephens didn't even own a raincoat when she moved to Seattle six years ago. Now she's a proud resident who looks forward to drizzle and loves everything about the Pacific Northwest, from the strong coffee and vibrant culture to the astonishingly beautiful mountains, where she hikes and skis whenever she can. She of course updated the Seattle chapter this edition.

Freelance writer Christine Vovakes updated the Crater Lake chapter and has also written for *Fodor's California*, *Fodor's Complete Guide to the National Parks of the West*, and *Fodor's Essential USA*. Her travel articles and photographs have appeared in many publications, including the *Washington Post*, the *Christian Science Monitor*, the *Sacramento Bee*, and the *San Francisco Chronicle*.